◇◇◇◇◇◇◇◇◇

STANDARD HANDBOOK FOR SECRETARIES

EIGHTH EDITION

STANDARD

HANDBOOK FOR

SECRETARIES

1979

Lois Irene Hutchinson

McGRAW-HILL BOOK COMPANY

Eighth Edition~

TWELFTH PRINTING 1979, Revised.

Copyright © 1969 by McGraw-Hill, Inc.

Copyright renewed 1964, 1967, 1969, 1972, 1975, 1978
by Lois Irene Hutchinson

The Library of Congress cataloged the original printing of the
8th Edition of this title as follows:

Hutchinson, Lois Irene
    Standard Handbook for Secretaries by Lois Irene
      Hutchinson. 8th ed.   New York: McGraw-Hill, 1969.

        x. 638 p.   map.   23 cm.

        Includes bibliographies.

    1. Office practice.   2. English language—Rhetoric.
      3. English language—Grammar—1950   I.   Title.

      HF5547.H77 1969   650   69–19201
                                       MARC

        Library of Congress   15–2

ISBN 07-031537-X

15 16 17 18 19 20 HDHD 898765432

Published by McGraw-Hill Book Company
                             New York, N.Y. 10020

The Eighth Edition

This edition represents a thorough and extensive revision of the text.

Twelve new pages have been added, giving more information on *Reports*—the parts, setup, and terminology—and more information on *Minutes of Meetings*—note-taking and writing, with examples of modern, streamlined Minutes and Agenda.

Additional information has been included on *Formal Invitations* and how to reply to them.

A useful *Interest* table has been added for assistance with monthly installment payments.

Data and tables have been renewed throughout the book, as in

- **Letter Writing**—with an up-to-date list of old-fashioned terms
- **Forms of Address**—with less formal salutations, and Zip Codes
- **Airmail Time Between Cities**—with hours reflecting the jet age
- **Mail Days to Other Countries**—with names of new nations
- **Punctuation**—with a greatly enlarged list of transitional words that may be set off with commas
- **Telephone**—with new services, instruments, and devices
- **Telegraph**—with new services and rates
- **Cables**—with methods of requesting available services
- **Business Organizations**—with enterprises in the news, such as condominiums and consortia
- **Government Offices**—with new departments, agencies, and Zip Codes
- **Foreign Exchange**—with new nations, currencies, and values
- **Metric System**—with new units and abbreviations
- **Weights and Measures**—with an updated miscellaneous list
- **Standard Time Around the World**—with new countries
- **Reference Books**—with new or changed titles and contents

In addition, this Eighth Edition contains hundreds of new items of up-to-date, interesting, and useful information.

The 1979 printing—the twelfth, extensively revised—contains the highlights of the new Copyright Law; new Government offices, including the Energy Department; new and enlarged listing of Government publications; latest rates and regulations of the postal, telegraph, and express services; advance dates for Easter; chief Jewish holidays; an explanation of generic gender; additional information for the office telephone list; and methods of making corrections in typewritten work.

Authorities Consulted

DICTIONARIES

Merriam-Webster's New International Dictionary, 2nd and 3rd Eds. (and *Webster's Collegiate Dictionary,* 8th Ed.), G. & C. Merriam Co., Springfield, Mass.

(Excerpts from *Webster's Collegiate,* 4th Ed., reprinted by permission from the Publishers.)

The Random House Dictionary (unabridged; and College Ed.), Random House, N.Y.
The American Heritage Dictionary, Houghton Mifflin Co., Boston.
Funk & Wagnalls Standard College Dictionary, Funk & Wagnalls, New York.
Webster's New World Dictionary, College Ed., World Publishing Co., Cleveland.
The Oxford English Dictionary (history of words), The Clarendon Press, Oxford.
The Concise Oxford Dictionary (British usage), The Clarendon Press, Oxford.

ENGLISH HANDBOOKS

Bernstein: *The Careful Writer,* Atheneum, New York.
Bryant: *Current American Usage,* Funk & Wagnalls, New York.
Copperud: *A Dictionary of Usage and Style,* Hawthorn Books, New York.
Curme: *Syntax,* and *Parts of Speech and Accidence,* D. C. Heath, Boston.
Evans: *A Dictionary of Contemporary American Usage,* Random House, New York.
Fowler: *Modern English Usage,* 1st and 2nd Eds. (Americanized version: *American-English Usage*), and *The King's English,* Oxford University Press, Oxford.

(Excerpts from *Modern English Usage,* 1st Ed., reprinted by permission from the Publishers.)

Greever and Jones: *The Century Collegiate Handbook,* Appleton-Century-Crofts, New York.
Hall: *English Usage,* Scott, Foresman, Chicago.
House and Harman: *Descriptive English Grammar,* Prentice-Hall, New York.
Jespersen: *Essentials of English Grammar,* Allen & Unwin, Ltd., London.
Kennedy: *Current English,* Ginn and Company, Boston.
Kittredge and Farley: *An Advanced English Grammar,* Ginn and Company, Boston.
Leonard: *Current English Usage,* prepared for The National Council of Teachers of English, Chicago.

(Excerpt reprinted by permission from the Publishers.)

Myers: *Guide to American English,* Prentice-Hall, Englewood Cliffs, N.J.
Pence and Emery: *A Grammar of Present-Day English,* Macmillan, New York.
Perrin: *Writer's Guide and Index to English,* Scott, Foresman, Chicago.
Roberts: *Understanding Grammar,* Harper & Row, New York.
Woolley, Scott, and Bracher: *College Handbook of Composition,* D. C. Heath, Boston.

STYLEBOOKS

Publishers' Stylebooks: The Associated Press; Houghton Mifflin; R. D. Irwin; McGraw-Hill; Prentice-Hall; and John Wiley & Sons.
Skillin, Gay, et al: *Words Into Type,* Appleton-Century-Crofts, New York.

(Excerpt reprinted by permission from the Publishers.)

Reisman: *A Style Manual for Technical Writers & Editors*, Macmillan, New York.
Summey: *American Punctuation*, The Ronald Press Company, New York.
The New York Times: Manual of Style and Usage, New York.
The University of Chicago Press: *A Manual of Style*, Chicago.
Turabian: *A Manual for Writers of Term Papers, Theses, and Dissertations*, The University of Chicago Press, Chicago.
United States Government Printing Office Style Manual, Washington, D.C.
(Excerpts reprinted by permission from the Public Printer.)

BANKING AND FINANCE

American Institute of Banking: *Principles of Bank Operations*, New York.
Clark and Gottfried: *Dictionary of Business and Finance*, Crowell, New York.
Encyclopedic Dictionary of Business Finance, Prentice-Hall, Englewood Cliffs, N.J.
Munn and Garcia: *Encyclopedia of Banking and Finance*, The Bankers Publishing Company, Boston.
Pick's Currency Yearbook, and *Pick's World Currency Reports*, Pick Publishing Corporation, New York.

LAW

Ballentine: *Law Dictionary With Pronunciations*, The Lawyers Co-Operative Publishing Company, Rochester, New York.
Black's Law Dictionary, West Publishing Co., St. Paul, Minnesota.
Bouvier's Law Dictionary and Concise Encyclopedia of Law, Rawle's 3rd Rev., West Publishing Co., St. Paul, Minnesota.
(Excerpts reprinted by permission from the Publishers.)

Corpus Juris Secundum: A Complete Restatement of the Entire American Law As Developed by All Reported Cases, The American Law Book Co., New York.
Martindale-Hubbell Law Directory, Martindale-Hubbell, Inc., Summit, New Jersey.
Words and Phrases, West Publishing Co., St. Paul, Minnesota.

ACCOUNTING

Accountants' Handbook, Wixon (Editor), The Ronald Press Company, New York.
Accounting Research and Terminology Bulletins, American Institute of Certified Public Accountants, New York.
Finney and Miller: *Principles of Accounting*, Prentice-Hall, Englewood Cliffs, N.J.
Holmes, et al: *Elementary Accounting*, R. D. Irwin, Inc., Homewood, Illinois.
Kennedy and McMullen: *Financial Statements*, R. D. Irwin, Inc., Homewood, Ill.

PRINTING AND ADVERTISING

Melcher and Larrick: *Printing and Promotion Handbook*, McGraw-Hill, New York.

INSURANCE

Mehr and Cammack: *Principles of Insurance*, R. D. Irwin, Inc., Homewood, Ill.
Magee: *General Insurance*, Richard D. Irwin, Inc., Homewood, Illinois.

GOVERNMENT PUBLICATIONS

Congressional Directory, Government Printing Office, Washington, D.C.
Domestic Mail Manual, United States Postal Service, Washington, D.C.
United States Government Manual, Federal Register, National Archives and Records Service, Washington, D.C.

AUTHORITIES CONSULTED

United States Government booklets and pamphlets on different subjects, as referred to in the text.

MISCELLANEOUS PUBLICATIONS

BusinessWeek, McGraw-Hill, Inc., New York.
Fortune magazine, Time Inc., New York.
The New York Times, The New York Times Company, New York.
The Wall Street Journal, Dow Jones & Company, Inc., New York.
The Washington Star, Washington, D.C.
Whitaker's Almanack, J. Whitaker and Sons, Ltd., London.
The World Almanac, Newspaper Enterprise Association, Inc., New York.

UNITED STATES GOVERNMENT OFFICES
(Washington, D.C.)

Civil Service Commission.
Copyright Office.
Defense Department.
Department of State.
Federal Reserve System.
Government Printing Office.
International Commerce, Bur. of.
Interstate Commerce Commission.

Library of Congress.
National Archives and Records Service.
National Bureau of Standards.
Naval Oceanographic Office.
Patent and Trademark Office.
Treasury Department.
U.S. Air Force, Project RAND.
U.S. Postal Service.

United Nations Office
International Monetary Fund, Washington. D.C.

BUSINESS ORGANIZATIONS

American Institute of Banking, New York.
Bank of America, San Diego, California.
Crocker National Bank, San Francisco.
The Riggs National Bank, Washington, D.C.
Union Bank of Switzerland, New York.

•

The New York Stock Exchange, New York.
Pacific Coast Stock Exchange, San Francisco.
Merrill Lynch, Pierce, Fenner & Smith, Inc., Washington, D.C.
United Business Service, Boston.

•

Emery Air Freight, Alexandria, Virginia.
Pan American World Airways, Washington, D.C.
Santa Fe Railway Lines, Chicago
Southern Railway Company, Washington, D.C.
United Parcel Service, Landover, Maryland.

•

The Chesapeake and Potomac Telephone Company, Washington, D.C.
The Pacific Telephone and Telegraph Company, San Francisco.

•

ITT World Communications, Inc., Washington, D.C.
The Western Union Telegraph Company, Washington, D.C.

viii

Contents

CONTENTS

on English ————————————————————————

To make your meaning clear—that is the secret of good punctuation, good usage, good speech, and good writing!

> —Ruth Mary Weeks, in the Foreword to *Current English Usage*, by S. A. Leonard, for The National Council of Teachers of English, Chicago.

My point of view is that, in everyday life, good English follows clear thinking rather than that system of rules called Grammar which youth loathes and maturity forgets.

> —John O'London (Wilfred Whitten), *Is It Good English?*

Terms Used in Classification of Words

archaic	antiquated.
colloquial	informal, or conversational.
commercial	used in business.
dialectal	used in certain dialects or local forms of the language.
idiomatic	following no definite rule, as certain expressions characteristic of the language, which usually cannot be translated literally.
illiterate	used in uneducated speech.
obsolete	no longer used.
provincial	used in certain districts or provinces; hence not general.
slang	coarse or grotesque.

ITALICS, throughout this book, signify words that are incorrect or incorrectly used (except in the section on Copy for the Press, where italics are shown as they would appear in print).

GENERIC GENDER (referring to either male or female) is represented in this text as **masculine**, which usage is conventional in grammar. Hence, wherever **he, his, him,** or **himself** occurs in a general sense, it refers equally to the feminine **she, hers, her,** or **herself.**

English

To determine what is right:

Analyze the sentence structure.

By elimination or substitution of words, or completion of unfinished sentences, test the correctness of the whole.

In a single sentence everything should agree—should be in accord. In testing sentences remember that there is a reason—not necessarily a rule, but a reason—for grammatical construction.

The Fifteen Most Common Errors

1. Pronouns incorrectly used.
2. Singular verbs with plural subjects, and vice versa.
3. Tenses of verbs mixed.
4. Collective nouns confused.
5. Possessives, especially of plural nouns, incorrectly formed.
6. Double negatives formed.
7. Foreign plurals unrecognized.
   The misuse of:
8. *Don't* for **doesn't**.
9. *Like* for **as** or **as if.**
10. *Set* for **sit.**
11. *Lay* for **lie.**
12. *Raise* for **rise.**
13. *Affect* for **effect.**
14. **Only** (placement of).
15. *Can* for **may.**

WORD USAGE

a used before all consonant sounds, including h when sounded.
an used before all vowel sounds, except long u.

Consonant Sounds
(Notice the sounded **h.** See Note, p. 4.)

a historical novel	a historic battle	a hysterical action
a hilarious parade	a hereditary right	a habitual thing
a humorous tale	a hallucination	a heroic effort
a Hawaiian	a Hungarian	a hotel
a humble opinion	a hundred tons	a 160-acre farm
a one-day period	a oneness (in the word "one" **o** has a **w** sound)	

Long U Sound

a unit	a uniform	a eulogy	a eucalyptus	a unanimous
a union	a U-turn	a European	a unique method	decision

3

Vowel Sounds
(Notice the silent **h.** See Note, below.)

an hour	an heir	an herb	an onion	an oil burner
an honest opinion		an honorary degree		an unknown fact

an H-bomb ("an aitch bomb")   (BUT: "a hydrogen bomb")
an SOS   an M.C.   an S.R.O. sign   an ROTC call   an FBI case
an LCL shipment   an NLRB rule   an X-ray   an 11-year term
an 8-hour day ("an eight") an 1800-foot canvas (BUT: a 180-foot fall)

NOTE: Some publishers and writers use "an" before a sounded h if the first syllable of the word is not accented, which accounts for **"an historical novel,"** **"an hotel," "an Herculean task,"** etc. British writers sometimes use "an" before a long u sound, as **"an union," "an eulogy."** But these uses are not general, and authorities favor the clear-cut distinction first above given.

Before an abbreviation, usage favors the word that agrees with the **pronunciation of the abbreviation itself,** not with its spelled-out form, as "an H.R. bill," "an L/C form" (not *a* H.R. nor *a* L/C); similarly **an** FHA loan, an A.B., an S&L, an M.I.T. graduate, an NBC station—but a NASA project, a MAC plane, a UFO sighting, a SAC system.

above
above-mentioned } In legal and commercial phrases these words are often
above-named   used as nouns and adjectives.

> ...in accordance with the above. } as nouns
> ...any of the above-mentioned may be signed. }
> ...the above facts. } as adjectives
> ...the above-mentioned data. }

all is commonly used without "of," as in

> ...all the time that we were there.   We counted all the people.
> Practically all the judges are...

all of them is commonly used instead of "they all" or "them all."
all of us is commonly used instead of "we all" or "us all."
     In fact, the "all of" phrases sometimes convey a meaning different from the other phrases.

> Send it to all of them. (OR: them all)
> All of them are involved. (OR: They all)
> All of us are needed for that job. (OR: We all)
> They meant all of us. (OR: us all)

alone means "by itself" or "solitary." Do not use it in the "not only" phrase.

> They not *alone* sold the property but took... (USE: only)

The placement of "alone" affects the meaning of a sentence.

> Alone, he solved the problem. (without company)
> He alone solved the problem. (no one else)
> He solved the problem *alone.*
>   ("Alone" is ambiguous here. Better to move it, or use "only.")
> The plates specified cost, alone, 11¢ a pound. (by themselves)
> The building alone cost $100,000. (NOT: cost $100,000 *alone*)

4

...for that, they alone are responsible.   (no one else)
...for that alone they are responsible.   (nothing else)

Commas should occasionally be used to clarify the meaning.

...and the rambling adobe where he lived in Monterey alone remains.
(CLEARER: ...where he lived in Monterey, alone remains.)

amid   amidst
among   amongst   } Since there is no difference in meaning between
while   whilst   these word forms, the shorter and more
unbeknown unbeknownst modern form is to be preferred.

and   is frequently omitted before the last word in a series, being replaced
by a comma.   This device, implying "etc.," is not approved by
some good authorities; still it is seen in many publications.

They are interested in no past, no present, no future, but only in...
If our aim had been numbers, size, riches, then whatever...

and   should not be used when "but" is intended in an idea of "on the
contrary," "on the other hand," etc.
but   expresses contrast or opposition, either faintly or emphatically,
whereas "and" does not.

They said they were mailing the check, *and* we have heard nothing
since.   (USE: but)
Some people do that *and* they should not be imitated.   (USE: but)

and/or   is a commercialism, used especially in the law of the land.

...transmitting and/or receiving radio communications.—Radio Act.
...secured by warehouse receipts, and/or shipping documents...
mortgages, and/or such other collateral...—Federal Reserve Act.

A subject composed of singular nouns connected by "and/or" may be
considered singular or plural, according to the meaning of the sentence.

Robert B. Logan and/or James T. Hanna **are** hereby appointed my
executors.   (meaning that both are to act; or either one is to act if the
other is not living or is incapacitated)
All loss and/or damage is to be paid for by the carrier.
(one or the other, and possibly both)

any   is used colloquially for "any other" in some comparisons.   In formal
writings, "other" should be used.   (See also p. 43.)

COLLOQUIAL: Their workmanship is better than **any** we have seen.
(FOR THE CORRECT:...than **any other** we have seen.)
NOTE: When a person or thing is being compared with another **in the same
class,** "other" or "else" is used so as to exclude the one compared.

NOT: It is better than anything in its field.   (USE: anything else)
NOT: New York is larger than any city in America.   ("Any city in
America" includes New York, which cannot be larger than itself.)
BUT: New York is larger **than any other** city in America.
New York is larger **than any** city in Europe.   (It is not in Europe.)
New York is the **largest of all** the cities in America.   (largest one)

5

any   may represent an indefinite quantity (large or small).
all   represents a definite quantity (the whole).

> Send us any [letters] that you receive.
> Send us all [the letters] you have received.

"Best of All" and "Best of Any."   When the whole quantity is available for comparison, "all" should be used. When only an indefinite or unknown quantity is available, "any" may be used.

> He is the **best** pilot of **all** on our lines.
> Our planes are held to be the **fastest of all.**
> Pick the **best** of any suggestions that are submitted.
> He is the **most** promising of any of the candidates who are likely to be proposed.

COMMON USAGE:
> Last month was the **best** for any February since 1950.
> The total is the **largest** for any comparable period.
> Naturally the advertiser wants the **strongest** market offered by any newspaper.

CONFUSED:
> He is the **youngest** of any college *president.* (FOR: of all college presidents OR: of any of the college presidents OR: younger than any other college president)
> It was the **best** of all *year's earning* since 1952. (FOR: best of all years' earnings [poor construction] BETTER: of all yearly earnings OR: best year's earning of all since 1952)

anything like } are usual, though homely, phrases. But do not inter-
nothing like } change them; nor use *"nothing like"* for "not nearly."

> They won't receive **anything like** its value. (NOT: *nothing* like)
> It was **nothing like** that. ...**nothing like** what we ordered.
> NOT: They are *nothing like* so well equipped as... (USE: not nearly)

appreciate   is often completed unidiomatically. It takes an object, but idiom resists certain noun constructions as its objects.

> UNIDIOMATIC: We'll appreciate ∧ if you will do that. ("it" omitted)
> (One would not write "We'll enjoy if you will...")
> UNIDIOMATIC: He always appreciates ∧ when they write. ("it" omitted)
> INFINITIVE: I would appreciate *to know if...* (USE: **knowing whether**)
> **THAT** CLAUSE: We fully appreciate **that it is hard.** (This noun clause is correct, but some writers prefer a single noun.)

apt   suggests a habitual or natural tendency—an aptitude.
likely   suggests a probable tendency—a likelihood.
liable   suggests an unfavorable tendency—a liability.

> They are apt to do it. (it is their habit)
> They are likely to succeed. (it is probable)
> They are liable to fail. (an unfavorable possibility)

around }
round } "Round," without an apostrophe, is interchangeable with "around" in American usage; but "round" is preferred in British usage.

> the year round   a round-the-world flight
> the wheels turn round   all round the town

"All-round" is generally preferred to "all-around," although the latter may be used.

an all-round scholar
an all-round machine
a square deal all around (colloquial)

gives economy all round
guesswork all round

as...as usually used with positive statements.
so...as usually used with negative or emphatic statements.

As far as we know, they are reliable. (positive)
They are not so reliable as we thought. (negative)

EMPHATIC:
{
They even went so far as to ridicule the idea.
It will be agreeable so long as the final terms...
...and stimulate so far as possible the new trade.
}

as far as...
so far as...
{
These expressions, to be grammatically correct, should not be left unfinished in sentences. But in commercial writings, the complementary words, "is concerned," "concerns," "goes," etc., are often omitted and supposedly understood.
}

UNFINISHED: So far as reducing the payments, we would not consider...
BETTER: So far as reducing the payments **is concerned**, we would...
UNFINISHED: The project is at a standstill as far as obtaining permission to rebuild.
BETTER: ...at a standstill **as far as concerns** obtaining...
UNFINISHED: Conditions will be changed as far as working overtime with no extra pay.
BETTER: Conditions will be changed **as far as they concern** working overtime with no extra pay.
OR: ...**as far as** working overtime with no extra pay **is concerned.**

as per is a commercialism for "in accordance with," as in the phrase "as per shipping instructions." But it should be kept in its place among abbreviations.

as regards is a commonplace expression meaning "concerning."

as to Do not overwork this phrase. It is properly used to introduce an inverted clause or phrase; or to introduce something that is **especially indefinite.**

As to that, we cannot say.

To avoid the constant use of "as to" substitute "regarding," "concerning," "about," "of," etc. Sometimes "as to" may even be omitted, to the sentence's advantage.

The question is *as to* the employment or nonemployment... (BETTER: The question concerns...)
We cannot plan so long as we are uncertain *as to* what will be done. (USE: about)
Contracts should not be so phrased as to permit a moment's doubt *as to* the correct meaning. (USE: about)
(The first "as" belongs to "so" and not to "to permit.")

7

A controversy arose *as to* whom the money should be **paid**.
(Another "to" is needed at the end to complete the sentence.
BETTER: A controversy arose regarding the one to whom...)
This is usually the test *as to* whether or not a venture is... (USE: of)

"As to" is commonly used before "whether," although it is **not** always necessary.

USUAL: Opinion is divided as to whether both cities are...
UNNECESSARY: We are undecided *as to* whether to increase or decrease
our selling organization.
UNNECESSARY: They give little consideration *as to* whether or not a law
is just. ("As" may be omitted.)

"As to" is often superfluous in other constructions.

UNNECESSARY: *As to* who would file suit was the question.
UNNECESSARY: We have no means of judging *as to* the wisdom of that.

at least is like "alone" and "only" in that its placement in a sentence can affect the meaning.

One should be sent at least. (ambiguous)
One should at least be sent. (if nothing else is done)
At least one should be sent. (if no more)

between should be followed by words that represent two or more things.

between times (NOT: between *time*)
NOT: between the *organization*
BUT: between the members of the organization

If two things are clearly indicated by modifying words (as with "the" before each), a singular word may follow "between"—although plurals are often used in such constructions.

There is a difference between the European and the American **system**.
(OFTEN: ...between the European and American **systems**.)
...the struggle between the Democratic and the Republican **Party**.
(OFTEN: ...between the Democratic and Republican **Parties**.)
...the interval between the red and the green **light**.

If possessives are used, which tend to join rather than separate the ideas, a plural word is used.

...an agreement between his and my attorneys. (NOT: *attorney*)
...the street between Morrow's and our buildings was not paved.
(NOT: between Morrow's and our *building*)
...agreement between Hildreth's and Newell's clients. (NOT: *client*)
NOTE: A better arrangement in many such sentences is to move the noun
forward, as "between the European **system** and the American," "between
Morrow's **building** and ours."
Or repeat the noun, as "between the Korean **War** and the Civil **War**."

between...and is the correct combination, not "between...*or*," "between...*to*," nor "between...*with*."

between right **and** wrong (NOT: between right *or* wrong)
between three **and** four hours (NOT: *to* NOR: *or*)

The decision is between a feast **and** a famine.   (NOT: between *either* a feast *or* a famine)

NOT: ...between 11 p.m. *to* midnight (USE: and)

NOT: It is the difference between performing the analysis in four steps *or* in eight steps.   (USE: and)

between each
between every

> Phrases such as "between each item" and "between every building" are regarded by some as incorrect, because "each" and "every" can refer to only one thing. However, authority now sanctions similar phrases; and such phrases have been used by the best writers for hundreds of years: Shakespeare, Goldsmith, Coleridge, Scott, Dickens, etc.

If it is necessary to be wholly correct, one might use "and the next," as "between each item and the next."

both   introduces two things; and if two things are clearly indicated by modifying adjectives (as with "the" before each), a singular word may follow "both"; but more often a plural is used to agree with the rest of the sentence, especially if possessives are involved, which tend to join rather than separate the ideas.

...in both the common and the civil **law.**
Both the Panama and the Suez **Canal** are built...
   (OFTEN: Both the Panama and Suez **Canals** are built...)
Our consul appealed to both the **Ministers** of Army and of Navy.
Both Washington's and Lincoln's **birthdays** occur in...   (NOT: *birthday*)

NOTE: For rearrangement of such sentences, see note under "between," p. 8.

both   refers to two things collectively (sometimes to two groups).
each   refers to two or more things individually.
either   refers to two things selectively—one or the other.

INCORRECT: There is a road on *both sides* of the river.
      (One road could not be on both sides.)
CORRECT: There are **roads** on **both sides** of the river.
      There is a **road** on **each side** of the river.
      There is a **road** on **either side** of the river.   ("Either" in
      this sense is not commonly used; "each" is preferable.)

both...and   is the correct combination, not "both...*or*," nor "both... *as well as.*"

It will profit both the giver and the receiver.
(NOT: both the giver *as well as* the receiver)

Theoretically, the small words following "both," such as "the," "to," and "for," should be repeated after "and"; but practically, this is not always done.

      ...both **for** the one and **for** the other.
OR: ...**for** both the one and the other.
      ...both **in** theory and **in** practice.
OR: ...**in** both theory and practice.
      ...both **the** incoming and **the** outgoing.

9

both of... The "of" is often dropped before nouns, but is used before pronouns (although not always before pronouns acting as modifiers). The "of" adds a degree of emphasis.

BEFORE NOUNS	BEFORE PRONOUNS AS MODIFIERS	BEFORE PRONOUNS
both men, or	both these men, or	both of these
both the men, or	both of these men	both of us
both of the men	both his partners	both of you

due to... ⎱ "Due to" is now considered a "compound preposition," like
owing to... ⎰ "owing to"—used adverbially as well as adjectivally.

"Owing to" is becoming rare—being overrun by "due to." "Because [of]" is often used in place of either adverbial phrase, especially the wordy "due to the fact that." A few examples of current use:

> The change was **due to** (NOT: *because of*) a reorganization. ("Due" adjectivally modifies "change.")
> It is a common error **due to** ignorance. ("Due" modifies "error.")
> **Owing to** (OR: Because of) a reorganization, the change was made. ("Owing to..." adverbially modifies "was made.")
> **Due to** an oversight, the insurance on the building lapsed. ("Due to..." adverbially modifies "lapsed.")

each other is used with regard to two.
one another is used with regard to more than two.
This is a general distinction and may be varied.

> If two stations interfere with each other... (RARELY: one another)
> ...the waves of radiation cancel one another.

either...........**or** ⎫
neither.........**nor** ⎪
not.......**or** (or **nor**) ⎪
no.......**or** (or **nor**) ⎬ Correct combinations.
never.....**or** (or **nor**) ⎪ (See also Subjects, p. 73.)
nothing...**or** (or **nor**) ⎪
none......**or** (or **nor**) ⎭

Either... **or.** Attempt to make the phrases balance after "either" and "or." (Note the singular nouns in the last two examples.)

> NOT: These loans must either come from the Government or banks.
> BUT: These loans must come **either from the Government or from banks.** ("Must come" belongs to both parts, and therefore should stand before the "either.")
> NOT: ...if they should make some move either toward helping or hindering us.
> BUT: ...if they should make some move toward **either helping us or hindering us.** ("Toward" belongs to both parts.)
> NOT: He will fail either to rise higher there or will seek other work.
> BUT: He **either will fail**...**or will seek**...
> NOT: The rules are either being deliberately disregarded or the people have overlooked...
> BUT: **Either the rules are**...**or the people have**...

NOT: ...cannot be found either in the Republican or Democratic *Parties*.
BUT: ...be found in **either the Republican or the Democratic Party**.
NOT: Southern California has little rainfall and either must draw *their* future water supply from the Columbia or Colorado *Rivers*.
BUT: ...**has** little rainfall and must draw **its** future water supply **either from the Columbia or the Colorado River**.

Neither...nor. "Neither" always takes "nor," never "*or*."

NOT: ...neither to the north, *or* the south, *or* the west.
BUT: ...**neither** to the north, **nor** the south, **nor** the west.

Either...*nor* (incorrect combination). "Either" never takes "nor" even when a negative occurs before the combination.

NOT: It depends upon the man—not **either** the reputation of the firm *nor* the general prospects.
(Use "or" to agree with "either" which introduced it.)
NOT: They are not to be used **either** for this *nor* for that. (USE: or)

Not, No, Never, Nothing, None...or (or **nor**). Where the negative force of the first word carries over, use "or"; that is, where the sentence construction remains the same, and the same negative could be applied to each part.

They need **never** trade, **or** correspond, **or** even exchange courtesies with us. (never trade, never correspond, never exchange)
He did **nothing** that was good **or** that was particularly bad. (nothing that was good, nothing that was bad)
It occurred to **nobody** to obtain a sketch of the proceedings **or** even a summary. (to nobody to obtain a sketch or a summary)

Where the negative force is cut off and needs renewal, use "nor"; that is, where the sentence construction changes, and the same negative could not be applied to each part.

He thinks **nothing** of his misfortunes, **nor** does he talk about them.
It came about with **no** fanfare; **nor** was it received with any rejoicing.

"Nor" is sometimes used after these negatives for particular emphasis —even when the negative force carries over.

...a very great technician—**nothing** more **nor** less.
We will **not** argue **nor** plead with them.
It will **not** be worthwhile to pursue the matter further, **nor** to explain it.

even The placement of this word in a sentence has much to do with the meaning.

Even he could solve this problem. (as dull as he was)
He could even solve this problem. (as well as do other things)
He could solve even this problem. (as well as other problems)
They were ordered even to burn the documents. (if necessary)
They were ordered to burn even the documents. (among other things)
They were even ordered to burn the documents. (as well as being ordered to do other things)

Avoid placing "even" at the end of a sentence, if in that position it could be misinterpreted.

11

NOT CLEAR: They were ordered to burn the documents even.
(This sentence would have to depend on other sentences to clarify its meaning.)

ever so often   means very often.
every so often   means at different times.   (Regarded as idiomatic.)
every now and then ⎫
every once in a while ⎬ Colloquialisms for "occasionally."
every now and again ⎭
more often than not   is a common expression.

first two ⎰ These expressions are preferable to "the *two first* pages," etc.,
last two ⎱ or "the *three last* pages," etc. There could scarcely be two first pages or rows—just one first page or row.

NOT: . . .as regards the *two last* items.   BUT: . . .the last two items.

former ⎰ These words should be used only when two things are referred
latter ⎱ to.   When three or more things are involved, the references should be "first" and "last."

NOT: France, England, and America will sign if the *former* will agree. . .
USE: . . .if France will agree. . . OR: . . .if the first country will agree. . .

good deal ⎱ These are good, idiomatic phrases, used by many authorities,
great deal ⎰ and listed as "colloquial" by only a few.

A great deal of time is lost. . .   . . .contain a great deal of information.
We have tested it a good deal.

hardly. . .when
scarcely. . .when ⎱ These are the correct combinations, not "hardly [or
barely. . .when ⎰ scarcely, or barely]. . .*than* [or *until*, or *till*]"; nor
no sooner. . .than "no sooner. . .*when* [or *until*, or *till*]."

Hardly had the turning point come **when** (NOT: *than* NOR: *until*) a new issue arose.
OR: **No sooner** had the turning point come **than** (NOT: *when*) a new. . .

hence ⎛ These words imply "from" and do not need it as an intro-
thence ⎨ duction.   It is no longer used before "hence" and "thence,"
whence ⎝ but is still common before "whence."   ("Whence" may also imply "to," as "returned whence he came.")

how ever   "How ever did you get here?" ⎫
what ever   "What ever can it mean?" ⎬ Provincialisms, "ever" mean-
who ever   "Who ever can it be?" ⎬ ing "in the world."
where ever   "Where ever shall we end?" ⎭

Note that in the above constructions "how ever," etc., are separate words.   The closed forms, "however," etc., have different meanings, and are of course in good use.   Also, "ever" may follow "what" or "who" in sentences like:

No one knows what ever came of it.   Who ever heard of such a thing?

-ic   **alphabetic**   Although these and similar adjectives may end in
-ical   **parenthetic**   either -ic or -ical, the tendency is to use the shorter
         periodic   form. Yet the two forms of some such words have
         analytic   grown to have distinct meanings:

economic pertaining to man's living, as "economic future."
economical pertaining to thrift, as "an economical budget."
historic pertaining to history-making things, as "a historic spot."
historical pertaining to history, as "a historical tale."
identic pertaining to diplomacy wherein two governments take precisely the same action. ("Identic action" is not "joint action.")
identical pertaining to things exactly alike or equal.
periodic pertaining to a period of time.
periodical pertaining to a publication issued at intervals.

Some words are seen more often in the -ic form; others, in the -ical form:

dramatic, rarely dramatical   BUT: grammatical,* rarely grammatic
fantastic, rarely fantastical   theoretical, rarely theoretic
energetic, rarely energetical   mathematical, rarely mathematic
poetic, rarely poetical   technical, rarely technic

geographic and **geographical** are both widely used, as "U.S. Board on Geographic Names," "The National Geographic Magazine," "National Geographic Society," "Webster's Geographical Dictionary". (The U.S. Government Printing Office uses "**geographic.**")

* The term "grammatical error" has been questioned by some, thinking it means that the error itself is grammatical. But "grammatical" may mean either "of or pertaining to grammar" or "according to the rules of grammar." A "grammatical error," therefore, is an error pertaining to grammar. Similar terms are "grammatical rules," "grammatical analysis," "mathematical error," etc.

if   These words are interchangeable; but when followed by "or,"
whether   or "or not," "whether" is preferable to "if."

They asked **whether** their order would be delayed or shipped at once.
We do not know **whether** we can meet their price [or not].
Check to see **if** (OR: whether) the address is correct.
He asked **if** the telegram had been sent.   I wonder **if** that is true.

After "Doubt." "Whether" or "that" is usual after the word "doubt," although "if" is not incorrect and is frequently used. (See also p. 108.)

We **doubt whether** they really appear in business.
We do not **doubt that** they can do it.
It is to be **doubted,** however, if that will suffice.

is where   Avoid these expressions when giving definitions.
is when

NOT: A "pool" *is where* several groups agree to...
BUT: A "pool" is an agreement between several groups...
NOT: A "low ceiling" *is when* the atmospheric conditions...
BUT: A "low ceiling" means that the atmospheric...

A different and permissible use, with words understood:

Two o'clock is (the time) when the meeting is to be held.
Mexico is (the place) where they have pyramids older...

13

kindly primarily means "in a kind manner"; but it can also mean "obligingly," "helpfully," "graciously," and "with good will." It is in these senses that it is so often used in business letters.

> Kindly send us a receipt for this.
> (MEANING: "Please," which in turn means "to have the kindness.")
> Would you be so **kind** as to do this for us. (obliging, or helpful)

kind of }
sort of } These expressions are used colloquially to mean "somewhat" or "rather." "Kind a" and "sort a" are corruptions.

> It sounds kind of strange.   It seems sort of true.

kind of *a*   The "*a*" is superfluous.

> that kind of thing (NOT: that kind of *a* thing)
> that sort of person (NOT: that sort of *a* person)
> in this kind of country...the same kind of transaction
> COLLOQUIAL: { ...written in kind of *a* dictionary style. }
> { ...written in a kind of dictionary style. } (omit "kind of")
> COMMON: What kind of *an* administration is coming?
> FOR: What kind of administration is coming?

kind of   **style of** }
sort of   **form of** } These words, and the words combined with them,
brand of **type of** } may be singular or plural, according to the sense
make of   **class of** } of the sentence, as

> make of engine (one make of one engine)
> makes of engine (several makes of a similar engine)
> make of engines (one make of similar engines)
> makes of engines (several makes of different engines)
> the kind of man   the kinds of man   the kind of men   the kinds of men
> type of letter   types of letter   type of letters   types of letters
> That **sort of question** is hard to answer.
> ...in the **sort of questions** that occur in print.
> ...used in all three **sorts of question.**
> ...and were asked all **sorts of questions.**

NOTE: When "these" and "those" are used, plurals such as "kinds" and "sorts" **must be used.** To say "*those* kind of people," or "*these* sort of things," is like saying "*those* style of paper," or "*these* make of engines."

> USE: those kinds of people   OR: that kind of people
> these sorts of things   this sort of thing
> these kinds of paper   this kind of paper
> those sorts of lights   that sort of lights
> NOT: It is better than those *kind*. (USE: those kinds OR: that kind)

like   takes an object. It should not introduce a subject and verb.
as or as if   may introduce a subject and verb.

NOTE: The above distinction is not always adhered to by good writers. A possible reason for their deviation from the rule is given on the next page —but first a few examples of the correct forms.

TEST: Substitute "similar to" or "similarly to" for "like."

> It looks **like** rain. (similar to rain or the condition of rain)
> It looks **as if** it might rain. ("as if" introduces a subject and verb)

14

...like the man who sees blindly. It sounded like a Spaniard singing. It was like coming in out of a storm. ... a distinction like being a survivor of... He behaved like a prisoner sentenced to die. This works like that. He fought like a tiger. We mean, like the natives, to live in peace.	"Similar to" or "similarly to" can be substituted in all these constructions.

"As" or "as if" introduces a clause, with a subject and verb.

It looks **as if** it were worn out.
   (NOT: *like* it was worn out)
It is not **as if** we hadn't played fair.
   (NOT: *like* we hadn't)
Do **as** we do. (NOT: *like* we do)
	These sentences will not take the substitution.

BUT: Do **like** us. ("similarly to us" may be substituted)

Commas are used to set off **removable** (nonrestrictive) "like" phrases; but are not used around **irremovable** (restrictive) phrases.

Natural talk, **like ploughing,** should turn up a surface...
They plead that better men **like Johnson and Scott** have set the precedent. (Do not attempt to construe that "like" here introduces a subject and verb. "Like Johnson and Scott" modifies "men.")

REASON FOR DEVIATION FROM THE RULE. The flaw in the above scheme is that understood words are not taken into account when they seemingly should be. For instance:

Send us some like you sent before.
  (Perfectly in order if "those" is understood after "like." **Substituting:** Send us some similar to those you sent before.)
It is better than a homemade one like they usually use.
  (UNDERSTOOD: like that which they usually use)
...fogs like they have in London. (like the ones they have)

Because some writers do not, and because some readers will not, supply the understood words, a misunderstanding exists.

But it would seem that wherever the small word "like" can take the place of the longer phrase "like those," or "like that which," etc., its use is to be preferred.

like in
like at } Under the general rule for "like," these constructions are disapproved, because "like" should introduce a noun or pronoun; but here again usage is more lenient in supplying understood words than grammar is, and so the prepositional phrases are often used.

USAGE: ...certain blues like in deep seas.
RULE: ...blues like those in deep seas. (OR: blues as in deep seas)
USAGE: And now, like in 1945, we have to face another situation...
  (like the situation we had to face in 1945)
RULE: And now, as in 1945, we have to face another... (as we had to face in 1945)
USAGE: Here, like at Washington, we have the facilities... (like the facilities they have at Washington)
RULE· Here, as at Washington, we have the facilities...

15

like if   is an expression of the uneducated.

> CRUDE: Some unforeseen condition *like if* they failed to...
> CORRECT: Some unforeseen condition like their failure to...

like me, like him, like them (See Pronouns, p. 53.)

majority   more than one-half of the total votes cast.   Also the number by which a majority exceeds one-half.

relative majority   the excess of the majority number over the total of the remaining numbers.

plurality   the largest number of votes cast for one person.   Or the excess of the largest number over the next largest number. (A plurality may exist without a majority.)

quorum   an agreed-upon number of members necessary to transact legal business for a group or body.   (Usually a majority, but not necessarily so.)

Example of votes received:

Candidate A	Candidate B	Candidate C	Total Votes
25	10	5	40

Candidate A has a majority of 5 votes.   (5 more than $\frac{1}{2}$ the total)
He has a relative majority of 10 votes.   (10 more than the sum of the other two)
He has a plurality of 15 votes.   (15 more than the nearest candidate)
A quorum of 35 persons was necessary in order to vote.
Forty were present and voted.

mutual   implies a like exchange, or sharing, of feeling or action.
reciprocal   implies that one thing is to be given in return for another.
common   means shared by two or more.

mutual regard	a reciprocal treaty	common sorrow
mutual promises	reciprocal gains	common claims

"**Mutual friend**" is derived from "mutual friendship," and is an expression largely used in preference to "common friend," which has an inferior implication.

never   refers to a period of time.
not   refers to one time.

> NOT: I *never* got the message.   I *never* saw it.
> BUT: I did not get the message.   I did not see it.
> NOT: He never *saw* a koala before.
> BUT: He had never seen a koala before.
>   It will never come again.   (not ever)
>   It will not come again.   (at no one time)

nice   a handy little word with many meanings, which has led to its being noticeably overworked.   It should be restricted in use; but there is no other reason to avoid it.   Primarily, it conveys the idea of discrimination, which may be either tasteful, delicate, or exact.

a nice distinction	a nice choice of words
a nice treatment of a subject	nice judgment
a nice page	a nice gesture

not only is completed by "but" or "but also." The parts of the sentence introduced by "not only" and "but" should be of like construction—should balance. (See also Subjects, p. 75.)

NOT: Their prices not only change with the seasons, but with each new customer.
BUT: Their prices change **not only with the seasons but with each new customer.** ("Change" is a part of both phrases and should therefore be before the "not only.")
NOT: They are not only unreliable, but they are dishonest.
BUT: **Not only are they** unreliable, **but they are** dishonest.
NOT: He does not succeed only in interesting them, but he gains their confidence.
BUT: He **not only succeeds** in interesting them **but gains** their confidence.
NOT: To add not only to the equipment but to provide...
BUT: **Not only to add** to the equipment **but to provide**...

NOTE: A **comma** is used to separate the parts when they are clauses; but it is unnecessary when they are just words or short phrases. A **semicolon** is used between "not only" clauses when "but" is omitted. A **period** breaks the continuity, but is sometimes used for emphasis or between long clauses.

Not only must there be banks; it is essential that there be businesses.
(RATHER THAN: Not only must there be banks. It is essential...)
He not only has blunt and decisive answers to questions. Like any teacher, he also has the knack of asking questions. (long clauses)

no use in ⎱ These are the correct phrases; but they are sometimes
of no use to ⎰ idiomatically reduced to "no use."

There's no use insinuating... (FOR: no use in insinuating)
It is no use arguing... (FOR: is of no use to argue)
It's no use to continue. (FOR: It's of no use to continue.
  OR: It's useless to continue.)

of Never use "of" for "have," as "should *of.*" (See p. 85.)

only The placement of this word has much to do with the meaning of a sentence. It should, if possible, be placed immediately before the word or phrase it modifies.

Only he could work the puzzle. (no one else)
He could only work the puzzle. (not explain it)
He could work only the puzzle. (nothing else)

Avoid the use of "only" before a verb, unless it is expressly meant to modify the verb.

I only heard about the accident. (I didn't see it)
I heard only about the accident. (nothing else)
They only guarantee bank loans. (they do not make them)
They guarantee only bank loans. (nothing else)
...which only added to the confusion. (merely)
We can only consider that unfair treatment. (no less than)

Misplaced "only":
The campaign only commenced with the upturn.
  (USE: commenced only with the upturn)
People will only buy the paper they like. (USE: will buy only)

Colloquial uses—so common that no misunderstanding of the meaning can exist:

It only costs a dollar.	FOR:	It **costs only** a dollar.
I only have a few minutes.		I **have only** a few minutes.
They only sell for cash.		They **sell only** for cash.
It only applies to one part.		It **applies only** to one part.
We only expect what is right.		We **expect only** what is right.

If "only" is out of its logical position, **commas** may be placed around it for clarity or emphasis.

The president, only, was authorized to sign.
Papers could be signed by the president only. (no comma necessary)

Similar words that require care in their placement are:

almost	also	even	just	not
alone	at least	hardly	merely	scarcely

only may be used as a conjunction in the sense of "except that." Yet if "but" is more applicable than "except that," "but" instead of "only" should be used.

They sounded convincing, only they seemed hesitant.
It sounds plausible only it won't work. ("But" would be better.)

"Only" should not be used with the prepositional force of "but" or "except." (See also Double Negatives, p. 110.)

Nobody could decipher it *only* the inventor. (USE: but)

other is primarily an adjective meaning "different."
otherwise is primarily an adverb meaning "in a different manner."

Enter your income, earned and **other** [income], in... (adjective)
Enter your income, earned and **otherwise** [described], in... (adverb)
The circumstances are **other** than reported. (NOT: *otherwise*)
We could not view it **otherwise** than with misgiving. (NOT: *other* than)

others is the plural of "other." "*Other*" as a plural is obsolete.

There **are others** than those to be sent. (NOT: *other* than)
NOT: No *other* than those **are** known. (USE: No others)
BUT: Many **other** (or others) of their products are... (before "of")

other...than "Other" takes "than," not "*but*" or "*except.*"
another...than "Another" takes "than," rarely "from."
nothing...but "Nothing" takes "but" or "except," rarely "other than."

There is no **other** choice **than** to accept. (NOT: *but*)
There is no **other** way to do it **than** carefully. (NOT: *except*)
It is quite **another** matter **than** we thought. (RARELY: from what)
There is **nothing** to do **but** carry on. (OR: except NOT: *other than*)

over may be used to mean "because of" or "more than."

If feelings are injured over that... (because of that)
Over 6 percent of the judges voted for... (More than)

per properly belongs in Latin phrases, as "per annum," "per diem," and "per capita." However, it is widely used in commercial phrases to mean "by the," as

per yard   per day rate   miles per hour   dollars per hundred

But wherever the meaning of "by the" is not foremost, the use of the simpler "a" or "an" is to be preferred.

50¢ an hour   RATHER THAN: 50¢ per hour
$5 a day $5 per day

persons used when the individuality of each person is considered, as "alike to all persons," "the persons in that company."
people used when the individuality of each person is not considered.

The room was full of people.   Three people spoke.

party a person or a group participating in a contract or action. (A legal and commercial term, useful because it can represent either a person or a company, as "the party to the contract," "the party receiving the goods.") Colloquial, when used to refer to an ordinary person.

individual a person. (This word has been discountenanced because of overuse; nevertheless it may properly be used to represent one person as contrasted with a body or class of people, as in referring to "the conduct of some individual.")

reason is because This combination has been condemned, first, because of incorrect grammatical construction and, secondly, because of overlapping meanings—"because" means "for the reason that," and one would not say "the reason is for the reason that." However, "the reason why" is approved, and it may be similarly analyzed in such sentences as "He didn't know the reason why."

Modern usage has decided that "the reason is because" is "good everyday English." (The National Council of Teachers of English.)

But do not use "the reason why...is *because*," as there are here three words implying cause.

NOT: The reason why that location is unsuitable is *because* it is...
BUT: The **reason** that location is unsuitable **is that** it is...

Do not invert a "reason is because" construction:

NOT: *Because* it is inexpensive is no **reason why** they can afford it.
BUT: Its being inexpensive is no reason why they can afford it.

Now that "the reason is because" may be used, it is in order to say that it is preferable to "the reason is due to" or "the reason is on account of," which were poor attempts to circumvent "the reason is because."

But of course the correct form, **"the reason is that,"** may always be used in preference to any of the other combinations.

19

said   meaning "afore-mentioned" is commonly used as an adjective in legal and commercial phrases, as "comply with said terms."

same   meaning "the aforesaid thing" is commonly used as a pronoun in legal and commercial phrases, as "terms covering same."

the same as   is often used as a commercial shortening for "in the same way [or manner] as," or "just as."

> They draw interest the same as the other bonds. (FOR: in the same manner as the other bonds do)

But "the same" should not be used if it is superfluous.

> NOT: . . . if they will work *the same* as he does.
> BUT: . . . if they will work as he does.

In many phrases "the same" represents a noun.

> This is the same as that.   It is considered the same as money.
> The increase is the same as shown here.

seldom if ever   means in few if any instances.
seldom or never   means in few or no instances.
seldom *or ever*   has no meaning.

   "Seldom ever" and "rarely ever" are colloquial contractions of "seldom if ever" and "rarely if ever." In these phrases "ever" can usually be dropped as superfluous.
"Scarcely ever" and "hardly ever" are modifications of "never."

> "What, never?" "Well! hardly ever. . ."—Pinafore.

so   is widely used for "therefore"—often beginning sentences.

> There was yet a judicial principle to be established. So there was ordained a Supreme Court. . .

so that   may be followed by "may," "can," "will," "might," "could," etc.
in order that   should be followed only by "may" or "might."

> . . .**so that** we **can** see the difference. (OR: may)
> . . .**in order that** we **may** see the difference. (NOT: *can*)

some say   **they say**   These and similar phrases may be used to refer
people say   **by many**   indefinitely to people.

> Some approve of that method.   It is felt **by many** to be desirable.
> They have seasons in the tropics.   **People say** it is valuable.
> (The objection to such phrases is that they are often carelessly used.)

somehow or other
sometime or other   These are idiomatic forms in good use. "Or
somewhere or other   other" emphasizes the first word.

such   is often used as a pronoun in legal and commercial phrasings.

> The law provides a redress; but **such** cannot be had.

such a is used to indicate a singular, particularized thing (the "a" being used when it would be used if "such" were not there). "Such" alone is used before plural words, and words that express abstract or general ideas.

GENERAL	PARTICULARIZED
Use such paper as this.	Use such a paper as this.
(Use paper such as this.)	(Use a paper such as this.)
Buy such food as is recommended.	Buy such a food as wheat.
(Buy food such as is...)	(Buy a food such as wheat.)
if they accept such payment	accept such a payment
(a general method of payment)	(one payment)
put it to such use	put it to such a use
(a general use)	(a particular use)
enjoy such liberty	enjoy such a liberty
(general freedom)	(one privilege)
receive such honor	receive such an honor
until such time as	until such a time as
in such manner	in such a manner
to such degree	to such a degree

"Such" alone may be used to indicate a thing previously mentioned, as in legal phraseology.

> A notice should be sent to each nonresident officer, if **such officer** has...

Also "such" alone is used if a modifier such as "any," "one," "no," or "another" occurs before it.

in **one such** place	**any such** thing
no such excuse	**another such** situation

such...as is the correct combination, not "such...*who*," "such...*where*," "such...*which*," nor "such...*when*."

> NOT: ...for such men *who* contemplate that.
> BUT: ...for such men **as** contemplate that.
> NOT: ...from such conditions *which* exist in the cities.
> BUT: ...from **such** conditions **as** exist in the cities.

Understood words can often be supplied to make the sentence clear.

> FAULTY: ...to such territories in which irrigation is impossible.
> BETTER: ...to **such** territories **as** those in which irrigation...
> FAULTY: ...covering such acreage where crops are not grown.
> BETTER: ...covering **such** acreage **as** that where crops are...

Do not use "such as" for "as" before a prepositional phrase.

> NOT: ...*such* **as** in magazines.   (USE: **as** in magazines)
> NOT: ...*such* **as** for traveling.   (USE: **as** for traveling)
> NOT: ...*such* **as** by methods of distillation.   (USE: **as** by methods)

Conversely, do not use "as" for "such as."

> NOT: Under conditions as we have been accustomed to...
>   (USE: conditions **such as** we have)

And lastly, do not overwork "such as." Substitute "that," "those," "which," or "like."

such that   is used in two ways:

> CORRECT: Conditions are **such that** it is impossible. ("That" is
> a connective here **introducing a subject and verb**.)
> Such is the temper of the day **that** men are wary.
> (Note no comma between "such" and "that.")
> COLLOQUIAL: ...from **such** *that* can afford it.   (USE: **such as can**)

that   may be omitted in certain sentences and smoothness gained
thereby.   But it should not be omitted if it is needed to retain the
meaning of the sentence.

> OMITTED: Suppose they question the terms.
> We will sign provided they agree to that.
> We grant it is a common occurrence.
> NECESSARY: We understand **that** the man might be wrong.
> The President emphasized **that** the Government will act.
> They should know **that** inflated credit could not in itself
> bring prosperity.
> NOT: The message pointed out no one country can handle the
> situation.   (INSERT: that)

that that   is a correct combination.   "Which" may sometimes be
used with "that" to avoid repetition, but it is not always
appropriate.

> ...for those who here gave their lives **that that** nation might live.
> ...and enjoy **that which** is the gauge of life.

that...that   The repetition of "that" in introducing a clause is a very
common and noticeable error.

> "It often happens to a writer to embark upon a...'that-
> clause', to find that it is carrying him further than he reck-
> oned, and to feel that the reader and he will be lost in a
> chartless sea unless they can get back to port and make a
> fresh start.   His way of effecting this is to repeat his initial
> 'that'.   This relieves his own feeling of being lost; whether it
> helps the inattentive reader is doubtful; but it is not doubtful
> that it exasperates the attentive reader, who from the moment
> he saw 'that' has been on the watch for the verb that it tells
> him to expect, and realizes suddenly, when another 'that'
> appears, that his chart is incorrect."
> —Fowler, *A Dictionary of Modern English Usage*, p. 633.

One "that" unnecessary:

> They now say **that** if we will agree to their terms *that* they will...
> We hope **that** when you look over the papers *that* you will find...

> TEST: Arrange the clauses in their natural order, as "We hope that you will
> find everything in order when you look over the papers."

The use of more than one "that" in a sentence to introduce separate
clauses is, of course, correct.   No "that" should be omitted unless it
can be legitimately spared.   Both "thats" necessary:

There is no doubt of the fact **that** it is true **that** only because he did not
begin his campaign...
...but if they realize **that** at the same time **that** payment is stopped
they are jeopardizing...

too   or **too much** ⎰ "Much" is employed before past participles used as
very   or **very much** ⎱ verbs, but often omitted before them as adjectives.

    VERB: very [or too] **much** involved   ADJECTIVE: very pleased

NOTE: "Very," as an **intensive**, has been virtually banned from newswritings,
because it **weakens a normally strong word** (by suggesting a degree or limita-
tion). For instance, *"very* delighted" might mean **"more than"** or **"not
quite"** delighted; similarly, *very* elated, stunned, beautiful, marvelous,
wonderful, excellent, outstanding, ridiculous, gracious, lovely, clever, etc.

un-
in- ⎱ The selection of these prefixes for the formation of negative words
il- ⎰ has departed so often from any definite rule that usage has
im- ⎰ arbitrarily established many of the forms.
ir-

    **"The choice of the fitting negative prefix...is largely
governed by established usage..."**
            —Vizetelly, *How to Use English*, p. 436.

Note some of the varieties:

unable	but	inability
unadvised	but	inadvisable
unexpressive	and	inexpressive (both used)
unlawful	but	illegal
unlimited	but	illimitable
unmoved	but	immovable
unpracticed	but	impractical (unpractical is also used)
unresponsive	and	irresponsive (both used)
inartistic	and	unartistic (both used)
incomplete	but	uncompleted
inexperienced	and	unexperienced (both used)
insanitary	and	unsanitary (both used)
irremovable	and	unremovable (rare)
irreparable	and	unrepairable (rare)

unless   introduces a subject and verb.
without   takes an object.
    Do not use "without" where "unless" could be substituted.
"Without" in the sense of "unless" is dialectal.

    They cannot sell unless (NOT: *without*) they consult the authorities.
    They cannot sell without consulting the authorities.
      ("Consulting" here stands as a noun—the object of "without.")

Note that "without," not "unless," is usual **before an -ing word.**

    NOT: No one can get a seat *unless* making reservations.
      (USE: without making a reservation)

23

If "unless" is used before an -ing word, it signifies that some words are missing.

> They never use that form unless quoting prices.
> (UNDERSTOOD: unless they are quoting prices)

Other constructions are often used after "unless" with words understood.

> That is not ordinarily done unless in connection with educational work. (UNDERSTOOD: unless it is in connection)
> There is no occasion to use it unless as a sample.
> (UNDERSTOOD: unless it is used as a sample)

unlike follows the same general rules as "like": it should not introduce a subject and verb, nor should it be followed by a prepositional phrase. A noun or pronoun should follow it.

> NOT: And now, unlike *it was* in 1945, we are forced...
> NOR: And now, unlike *in* 1945, we are forced to...

To remedy such a situation, a few words may be moved up –

> THUS: And now we are forced, as we were not in 1945, to...

Usage often overrides the above rules, depending on understood words to give the proper meaning.

> USAGE: ...but here, unlike *at* Washington, we have not the facilities for... (unlike conditions at Washington)
> RULE: ...but here we have not, as at Washington, the facilities for...
> (as they have at Washington)
> OR: ...but here, in contrast with Washington, we have not...

-ward

afterward	inward	skyward	All written without the final -s,
backward	landward	southward	which is the preferred form in
downward	northward	toward	American usage. This not
eastward	onward	upward	only shortens the words but
forward	outward	westward	in many instances makes them
homeward	sideward		more euphonious.

-ways
-wise

anywise	lengthwise	The generally preferred ending for these words
crosswise	nowise	is -wise, rather than -ways, with the excep-
edgewise	sidewise, or	tion of "sideways," which is considered
endwise	sideways	established.

-where

anywhere	All written without the final -s. To add -s is termed
everywhere	"illiterate." To substitute "any place," "every
nowhere	place," "no place," and "some place" is termed
somewhere	"careless."

> NOT: We couldn't find them ∧ *any place*. ("in" omitted)
> (One would not write: "We couldn't find them *any town*."
> THEREFORE USE: anywhere, which means "in any place.")

who refers to persons (rarely to animals).
which refers to animals and things (and to persons, in questions).
that refers to persons, animals, and things.
whose is the possessive for all the above words. It may refer to either animate or inanimate things.

The choice between "who" and "that" when referring to persons:

who signifies the individual, or the individuality of each member of a group.
that signifies type, class, species, or an impersonal number of people.

> The man **who** is in charge... (a certain individual)
> Anyone **that** believes in the future... (a type or class of men)
> The man that stands by himself... (the type of man)
> Is he the person that he appears to be? (the type)
> People who do such things... (the individuals)
> The people that live in northern climates... (the species)

Special uses of "who": "Who" may refer to personified things.

> A tree...**who** intimately lives with rain...—Kilmer.

"Who" is sometimes used to refer to an animal, if later in the sentence the animal is designated by a pronoun such as "he" or "she."

> Fleeting, **who** was the most brilliant horse of **his** time, won...

But wherever "that" can be used in such sentences, it is to be preferred.

> The dog **that** led **his** teammates in the hazardous trek...

The choice between "which" and "that" when referring to animals and things: These words are interchangeable (except in "nonrestrictive clauses," which see below). Their use is a matter of personal preference. A writer usually selects the word that for him gives the better effect or is the more euphonious or forceful.

"Which" is the more noticeable word, and writers are no doubt often influenced toward its use as a means of emphasis.

Emerson used "which" and "that" interchangeably:

> The power **which** resides in him is new in nature...
> The other terror **that** scares us from self-trust is our consistency...

Ruskin used them interchangeably:

> The best image **which** the world can give of Paradise...
> ...the only supreme flowers **that** the lowlands can show...

Some writers believe that "that" has enough work to do in the language without being substituted for "which"; and so on occasions that call for a choice between these two words, they use "which." Huxley might have followed this method in his writings:

> We live in a world **which** is full of misery and ignorance...

25

Some writers follow a certain distinction between "that" and "which" and assign each word a special job to do. They use

which to introduce a clause that is **"nonrestrictive"** (that is, a clause that does not restrict the meaning and which could be lifted out of the sentence—therefore it is set off with commas).

that to introduce a **"restrictive"** clause (that is, a clause that restricts the meaning and which could not be removed without impairing the sentence—therefore no commas are around it).

> The protests, **which always follow,** are again with us. (removable)
> Should we forgo all **that is valuable in our lot?** (irremovable)

> NOTE: The "which" nonrestrictive (parenthetic) clause may be removed; but the "that" restrictive clause must stay if its sentence is to have its real meaning. ("That" is never used in a nonrestrictive clause—with commas around it.)

"Which" is often used to avoid a repetition of "that."

> ...and enjoy **that** friendly association **which** is the life of business.

If the reference is to both persons and things, use "that," because it is applicable to both.

> Men and machines **that** turn out that work... (NOT: *which*)
> The forty men and eight horses **that** could be transported in one car...
>   (NOT: *which* NOR: *who*)

The choice between "who," "which," and "that," when referring to collective nouns:

who should be used when referring to a noun that signifies a collection of persons, wherein personalities exist (especially if "they" or "their" is used later in the sentence).

> That firm, **who have** (NOT: *which has*) given us **their** business for years,
>   **are** worthy of special consideration.
> The part of the audience **who** (NOT: *which*) demanded **their** money...
> ...of the number of passengers **who** (NOT: *which*) **were** saved.

which or
that } should be used when the collective noun exists as a single thing (especially if "it" or "its" is used later in the sentence).

> That firm, **which has** given us **its** business for years, is worthy of special consideration.
> That group, **which is** in Wall Street, **has** had to retrench in **its** buying.
> Any company **that deals** fairly with us **is** entitled to **its** profits.

Do not mix "who" and "which" in the same sentence when referring to a collective noun.

> NOT: That company, **which is** composed of ten men, **is** one company in *whom* (USE: which) we have the greatest confidence.

which
what } Either word may refer to a particular thing or to several things.

Which team won?   What crews will row this year?
Decide which you want.   (the individual things)
Decide what you want.   (the quantity or kind of thing)
They are brokers or bankers, but we are not sure which.
   (they are one or the other)
They may be brokers or bankers, but we are not sure what.
   (they may be any one of a number of things)

what   may mean "that which" or "those which."

It fairly teems with what are false issues.   (MEANING: those which)

which   usually refers to the word that immediately precedes it; but it may refer to the phrase or entire clause that precedes it.

It soon becomes a badge of gentility which is adopted generally.
   ("Which" here refers to "badge of gentility.")
It soon becomes a badge of gentility, after which it is adopted generally.   ("Which" here refers to the becoming a badge.)

"Which" may of course skip several words, if its reference is clear or made clear by its verb (singular or plural).

Here are five pictures of the building which show the remodeling.
   (The plural verb "show" carries "which" back to "pictures.")
Here are five pictures of the building which shows much improvement.
   (The singular verb "shows" attaches "which" to "building.")
It is part of a pattern of restrictions which has hindered progress.
   ("Has" reflects "pattern"; "have" would focus on "restrictions.")

"Which" is sometimes used before a word to fix definitely the reference.   The phrase **"in which case"** is also used by authorities.

They suggested an alternative, which suggestion was not welcome.

whichever   indicates one or another of a number and may refer to persons as well as things.

...sent to the buyer or the seller, whichever is to pay the insurance.

◇◇◇◇◇◇◇◇

FASHIONS IN WORDS

There are styles in words as in other things.

"New terms are being introduced constantly, and every season brings a fresh crop which it is not advisable to place on record because the lives of such terms are short—the lexicographer cannot be charmed by the vagaries and varieties of fashion as represented by words of but ephemeral character."

—Vizetelly, *How to Use English.*

Passing Fancies

aunt	gladiolus	kilometer	The pronunciation of these words
Copenhagen	Hawaii	leisure	has returned to normal. (See the
depot	humble	pianist	Pronunciation section, pp. 159 ff.
envelope	humor	programme	For "kilometer" see the following
err	interesting	vase	note.)

But "kilometer" is still widely mispronounced because of a confusion with the measuring instruments, thermometer, etc. A kilometer is a unit of length, like a centimeter or a decimeter, and should therefore be pronounced kĭl′ō-mē′ter to agree with its companion words. It should not be accented on the second syllable like the registering devices, as barom′eter, thermom′eter, and speedom′eter.

all right—has withstood the onslaught of "*alright*" and "*allright*."
an historical—is gradually giving way to "a historical." (See note, p. 4.)
authoress—is losing out to "author"; used only to make the gender clear.
aviatrix and **poetess**—are having a hard time to stay.
concern—although condemned by some when used to mean "a business organization," is so given in the dictionaries, and so used by business authorities.
depot—has been largely replaced by "station," when meaning a passenger station. But it is used to mean a storehouse or supply base.
kiddies—has been displaced by "children."
master of ceremonies—is correct for a woman; also "mistress of ceremonies."
Pleased to meet you—has been investigated and found to be correct English, if somewhat abbreviated and old-fashioned.
I am very glad to have met you—is quite all right.
render a bill—has been returned to favor.
saleslady—appears to be holding its own with "saleswoman" and "salesperson."
someone's else—has given way to the more common "someone else's."

Discountenanced Words

ain't USE:	isn't, or aren't	*Hindu* (for a USE:	East Indian, or
boat (for	ship	non-Hindu)	Moslem, etc.
large vessel)		*Jap*	Japanese
Chinaman	Chinese	*nigger*	Negro
complected	complexioned	*Portugee*	Portuguese
consumption	tuberculosis (TB)	Rio Grande *River*	(Rio means "river")
davenport	sofa (Arabic)	Sahara *desert*	Sahara (which
Frisco	San Francisco		means "desert")
Harvard *campus*	Harvard Yard	*Scotch*	Scottish
High *Sierras*	High Sierra	*Xmas*	Christmas

Words and Phrases Being Countenanced

ad—is widely used in commercial phrases for "advertisement." Note that it is written without a period.
anxious—used for "eager."
awfully—used for "very," as "awfully bad."
Britisher—formerly classed with "Irisher," but it is now very generally used instead of "Briton."
burglarize—used for "commit burglary upon."
don't think so—very generally used for "think not."
drive slow—widely used for "drive slowly."
enthuse—used for "become enthusiastic."
have got and **have gotten**—both used.
healthy climate and **healthful climate**—both used.
I wish I was rich—used for "I wish I were rich."
If it was not for that—used for "If it were not for that."
individual—used for "person" when contrasted with a group or class of people.
It's me—used for "It is I."
peruse—used for "look over." (The correct meaning is "to read carefully.")
phone—for "telephone." It needs no apostrophe now.
quite—used for "rather" or "very." ("Quite" means "wholly" or "actually.")

reason is because—used for "reason is that."
shall and will—used interchangeably now in many instances.
that—used for "so," as "They're not that busy," for "They're not so busy as that." "It isn't that bad," for "so bad as that."
this—used for "thus" or "so," as "They're never this late," for "They're never so late as this"; or "about this high" for "about so high"; or "after working this far" for "after working thus far."
transpired—for "happened." (Strictly, "transpired" means "leaked out.")
Who do you mean?—used in conversation for "Whom do you mean?"

Many shortcuts are favored in commercial phrases, as

write him	FOR:	write to him
phone us		telephone to us
sent us		sent to us
work nights		work at night
promoted to captain		promoted to the rank of captain
plays piano, or trumpet		plays the piano, or trumpet
at table (British)		at the table
if they want out		if they want to get out

The announcement will be Wednesday. (FOR: will be **made on**)
He was in town the first three days of last week. (FOR: in town **during**)
He reserved seats for himself and friends. (FOR: and **his** friends)
If it works out that way... (FOR: **in** that way)
Summers they go to Maine. (FOR: **Each** summer)
...gaining what is hoped will be an advantage. (FOR: what, **it is hoped**,)
...landed on top the building. (FOR: on top **of** the building.)
It should help reduce the traffic hazard. (FOR: help **to** reduce)
I will write it when I am home. (FOR: when I am **at** home)

But words should not be omitted if an ambiguous sentence might result.

NOT: ...when he was home sick. (FOR: was **at** home, sick)

COLLOQUIALISMS

A "colloquial" expression does not necessarily mean a condemned expression —although some of them are—but rather an expression heard chiefly in conversation or used in informal writing. Discountenanced colloquialisms are italicized below.

a—for "of." Do not say "what time *a* day" or "that sort *a* thing."
ahold—for "hold," as "take *ahold* of the proposition." (FOR: take hold)
  But "take a hold on the ladder" is right.
all kinds of—for "many" or "much," as "all kinds of money," "all kinds of mistakes."
all the further or **farther**—for "as far as."

COLLOQUIAL: { "Is that all the further [or farther] you got?"
{ "Is that all the faster it can go?"

FOR: { Is that as far as you got?
{ Is that as fast as it can go?

There is an approved use of "all the farther," "all the faster," etc., when "all" means "so much."

It will go all the faster with the new tires.
We can see all the better from here.

29

anywhere near—for "nearly," as "...couldn't fill anywhere near all the orders."

  nowhere near—for "not nearly," as "There is nowhere near enough time." However, these expressions are quite correct wherever "near" alone could be used, as "hit anywhere [in any place] near the mark," "comes nowhere [to no place] near our price."

around—for "about" or "near," as "around the holidays," "around ten o'clock."

as—for "that." NOT: "I don't know *as* I do." "We can't see *as* it will."

as like as not—for "likely." "As like as not it will break."

balance—for "rest" or "remainder," as "the balance of the week," "the balance of the supplies." When actually referring to a financial balance, it is correct, as "the balance of the account."

bank on—for "rely on." "You can bank on that."

because—for "the fact that," as "*Because* it is cheap may influence some."

blame it on—"We can't blame it on anything in particular."
  FOR: We can't blame anything in particular for it.

broke—for "without money" or "bankrupt." "He went broke."

can't seem—for "seem unable." "They can't seem to see it."

Chinaman—a whimsical and often belittling term for a Chinese.

climb down—to withdraw from a high stand, as to "climb down meekly."

considerable—for "much," as "nothing to lose, but considerable to gain."

contact—for "get in touch with," as "if we can contact him."

don't ever—for "never." "Don't ever do that." (FOR: Never do that.) "If we don't ever see it again..." (FOR: If we never see)

every bit—for "quite" or "in every way," as "every bit as good."

expect—for "suppose." "I expect so."

fine—for "well" or "very much." "It grew fine." "We like it fine."

first off—for "in the first place," as "First off, they wanted to know..."

folks—for "relatives," or "family members."

funny—for "strange," "puzzling," "odd," or "queer."

game—for "business," as "the newspaper game." (resented by some)

going on—for "approaching" or "about." "He is going on fifty."

got—for "was," as "got married," "got promoted," "got hurt," "got discharged."

guess—for "think," without uncertainty. "I guess I'll go to work."

hear—for "have heard." "We hear they are doing well."

hear of—for "listen with consent." "We won't hear of his doing that."

in our midst—for "here," "with us," "among us," or "in our city."

inside of—for "within," as "inside of a month."

Jap—a derogatory or resentful term for a Japanese.

learn—for "have learned." "I learn from them that..."

leave—for "let." NOT: "*leave* go," "*leave* it be," "*leave* us face it."

leave off—for "quit" or "stop" is approved, as "Where did we leave off?"

line—for "business" or "occupation," as "not in his line."

locate—for "settle" or "become established." "They located in Kansas."

lose out—for "fail to succeed" or "be left out." "We might lose out."

lot—for "much" or "a great deal." "It helps a lot." "It's a lot better."

mighty—for "very," as "It was mighty kind of them."

most—for "almost," as "most any day," "most always," "on most every page." While "most all the time" (meaning "almost all of") is colloquial, "most of the time" (meaning "the largest part of") is naturally correct. TEST: Try "almost" first to see whether it sounds right.

mostly all—for "almost all" or "nearly all." "It has *mostly* all evaporated."

on the side—for "besides" or "in addition," as "a dividend and a bonus on the side"; "selling insurance on the side."

operate—for "operate on"—used in medical parlance, as "The patient was operated at noon." This usage is not, however, considered correct.

outside of that—for "other than that," "besides that," or "except that."

overly—for "too much" or "excessively," as "not overly pleased."

photo—for "photograph."

plenty good enough—for "sufficient" or "good enough."

posted—for "informed," as "Keep us well posted."

price—for "ask the price of," as to "price articles."

proposition—for "business venture" or "project."

put in—for "spent" or "worked." "The men each put in ten hours."

read where—for "read that." "I read where they are selling..."

real—for "very." "That's real nice." "It works real well." "Really" may be substituted, but it implies "actually" rather than "very." "That's really nice." "It works really well," or "It works very well."

right—for "very." "It is progressing right well."

right along—for "repeatedly," as "They renew it right along."

run—for "manage," as to "run a business."

see—for "have seen." "I see by the papers..." (FOR: I have seen in...)

see where—for "see that." "I see where the market went up..."

shape—for "condition." "It is in good shape."

show—for "chance." "It doesn't stand a show."

some—for "somewhat" or "a little." "That helped some." "They talked some of doing that."

sooner—for "rather" or "just as soon." "He'd sooner work than eat."

such a—for "so great a." "It is such a drain on our economy."

sure—for "yes." "Will it work? Sure, it will." This use may be derived from the older phrase "to be sure."

"Sure" may properly be used for the adverb "surely."

> They are going forward today, sure.
> And sure enough it stopped.
> It will return as sure as we live.

But "sure" should not be used in a typically slang manner to mean "certainly" or "indeed," as

> "We were *sure* glad to get it." "It *sure* works well."
> "I *sure* would appreciate it." (USE: surely)

suspicion—for "suspect." "We didn't *suspicion* the conniving."

take in—for "see." "We took in the exhibition."

take sick—for "become sick." "He took sick last week."

through—for "finished," as "When will it be through?"

upwards of—for "more than," as "upwards of fifty men."

wait on—for "wait for." "We can't wait on them."

way—for "away," "considerably," or "far." "They are way off." "They went way around the subject." "...looking way ahead."

ways—for "way," as "a long ways off" for "a long way off."

win out—for "succeed." "Who will win out?"

wire—meaning a telegram, or to telegraph, is listed by some British authorities as correct, and by American authorities as "a colloquialism." It is a very practical, concise, and widely used "commercialism."

worst way—for "very much." "They seem to want it in the *worst way*."

write-up—for "article" or "press report," as "...got a good write-up."

◇◇◇◇◇◇◇◇

SUPERFLUOUS WORDS

Do not burden a sentence with unnecessary words. Superfluous words are italicized in the following expressions.

again **regain**—could be used only if once before something had been regained—but not the first time it is regained.

ago **since**—NOT: "It is ten years *ago* since we have seen..."

alone...*only*—One word or the other is superfluous in such sentences as "That alone is the *only* reason."

also...*too*—NOT: "They also want that *too*." Use one or the other.

and **etc.**—would mean "*and* and so forth." (See "etc., etc.," below.)

assemble *together*—"Assemble" means to bring or come together.

at **about**—NOT: "It happened *at* about one o'clock." (BUT: about one o'clock.)

attached *herewith*—"Herewith" is not only superfluous but wrong. "Hereto" would be more nearly right, but it is also unnecessary.

bars *out*—NOT: "This bars *out* the possibility that..."

both *alike*—"Both" is unnecessary if it is obvious that two are meant; otherwise "both" may be used.

> The terms are both alike. (the two terms)
> The terms are alike. (many terms)
> NOT: "There is no question that *both* employer and worker alike will profit." ("both" unnecessary)

both...*also*—One word is unnecessary in such expressions as "for the purpose both of improving the product and *also* of reducing the cost."

both...**as well as**—NOT: "...adequate *both* for the present population as well as future generations." (Omit "both.")

both *equally*—If it is obvious that two are meant, "both" is superfluous; otherwise "both equally" may be used, as "The methods were both equally good," or "The two methods were equally good."

both *together*—"Both" is often superfluous in this combination, as "Were the two messengers *both* together?" But "both together" is necessary at times, as "Use one word or the other, but not both together." (meaning one following the other)

but...*however*—One or the other is unnecessary. "We did not expect it, but it came, *however*." Most connectives should be used singly, though "but yet [still]," "although...yet [still]," "if...then," and "and yet [still or so]" are occasionally seen together.

cancel *out*—"Cancel" implies "out"; therefore "out" is usually unnecessary.

consensus—means, in itself, "general agreement or collective opinion." But if the implication "of opinion" is doubtful, it may be added; for there may be a consensus of ideas, or suggestions, evidence, testimony, editorial opinion, masculine opinion, informed opinion, nationwide surveys, ratings, etc.

(The Funk & Wagnalls Standard College Dictionary says: "The phrase 'consensus of opinion,' although redundant, is now widely used.")

contemplate *on*, or *over*—NOT: "They contemplated *on* raising prices."

continue *on*—NOT: "Let them continue *on* with the work."

continue to **remain**—NOT: "If they *continue to* remain as they are..."

converted *over*—NOT: "It was to be converted *over* into a new loan."

cooperate *together*—NOT: "Can they not cooperate *together*?"

customary **practice**—"Practice" means a customary action. "It is our practice."

depreciate *in value*—"Depreciate" usually means "to decrease in value," but some things may depreciate in size or quality also.

each in its respective way—used for emphasis instead of "each in its way."

either...or *else*—NOT: "They either start a new business or *else* retire."

else **but**—NOT: "No one *else* but him..." (FOR: No one but him...)

enclosed *herewith*—is used, although the second word is superfluous.

encore *again*—could be used only if once before someone had been encored.

endorse on the back—"Endorse" usually means "to inscribe on the back of," but not always. Certain papers may be endorsed "on the face"; hence "on the back" may be used for definiteness.

equally as good as—used for emphasis for "as good as," or "equally good."

etc., etc.—sometimes used for emphasis; but one "etc." is usually sufficient.

ever...*yet*—NOT: "No one has ever lived there *yet*." Use one or the other.

far *more* **worse**—NOT: "Times are far *more* worse now." (BUT: far, or much, worse)

finish off—"Off" is unnecessary but in good use, as "finish off the design."

first before—used for emphasis, as "Investigate first before buying."

first begin—used for exactness, as "When they first begin to see..."

follows after—"Follows" implies "after," yet this is a usual phrase.

free **gratis**—"Gratis" means free. (pronounced grā′tis, or grăt′is)

help *from*—NOT: "They couldn't help *from* doing it that way."

in among
in around
in back of } These are usually simply careless constructions. Sometimes, but rarely, they are justifiable, as
in between
in under
   ...like dancers weaving in around the Maypole.
   ...it was slipped in among the papers.

inside of—"Inside the city limits," rather than "inside of." "Within an hour," or colloquially "inside of an hour."

joint partnership—"Partnership" often implies "joint ownership," but not always. There are several kinds of partnership; hence "joint partnership" may be used to designate a certain kind.

like *for*—for "like," as "We should like *for* them to see it."

mental **telepathy**—"Telepathy" means "thought or mind [mental] communication."

near *to*—NOT: "near *to* a school" or "near *to* town."

new **beginner**—One person alone could not be a "*new* beginner"; but if there were several beginners and a new one arrived, he then might be.

not *a* **one**—Use "not one."

off *of,* or **off** *from*—NOT: "...fell off *of* the pedestal." "...jumped off *from* it."

often **accustomed to** } NOT: "He was *often* in the habit of going..."
often **in the habit of** } NOR: "He was *often* accustomed to going..."
   BUT: People are often accustomed to hardships.

old adage—a combination so welded together that even good authorities use it.

outside of—"Outside the jurisdiction," rather than "outside of." "Other than that," "besides that," "beyond that," or "except that," is better than the colloquial "outside of that."

over *with*—NOT: "We're glad that's over *with*."

pair of twins—This phrase is explained by the fact that "a twin" may be one of two persons known as "twins." Thus in a group there may be "three twins," none of whom are related. Therefore, two that are related may be referred to as "a pair of twins," which seems as defensible as to say, correctly, "a pair of glasses."

pretend *like*—NOT: "They pretend *like* they haven't heard it."
   BUT: They pretend they haven't heard it.

remember *of*—NOT: "We don't remember *of* it." "Not that I remember *of*."
   But "know of" is used to mean "know about."

repeat *again*—Only if a thing has been repeated before, can it be repeated again.
revert *back*—"Revert" means "to go back" or "to return."
same identical—"Identical" means "the very same."
such as (as or like)...etc.—A widely used combination, even in dictionaries.
such as, *for example*⎱ Use one or the other.   NOT: "In small states, such as,
   as, *for instance* ⎰ *for example*, Rhode Island and Delaware,..."
think *for*—for "think," as "more than you think *for*."
those *ones*—NOT: "It refers to those *ones* that are crossed out."
          BUT: ...to those... OR: ...to the ones...
up above—for "above."   "It is *up* above the headwaters."
up until—"Until" itself means "up to the time of," as "until today."
   ...up

burn up	finish up	scratch up
buy up	fix up	settle up
call up	follow up	shape up
climb up	hurry up	show up
connect up	lift up	sign up
count up	mar up	size up
cripple up	mix up	start up
divide up	open up	strike up
double up	pay up	talk up
drink up	polish up	tear up
eat up	rest up	turn up
end up	run up	wake up
even up	scar up	write up

The "up's." Some termed "commercial," some "colloquial," some "idiomatic," some "correct." All used, although many are superfluous.

"Legal" Duplication.   For particular emphasis, a duplication of words is often indulged in by commercial writers.   (In some of the following well-known phrases, the words are not duplications but of different meaning, which adds to definiteness.)

if, as, and when	over and above	one and the same thing
due and payable	save and except	good and sufficient reasons
unless and until	each and every	right, title, or interest

FAMILIAR PHRASES

Familiar phrases often vary slightly in wording, spelling, or meaning from preconceived ideas of them.   (Familiar phrases are usually to be found in the dictionary under the principal word in each phrase.)   The following are examples of phrases that are sometimes misconstrued.

anchors aweigh—not "anchors *away*."   (Compare "under way," below.)
All is not gold that glisters—is the old proverb.   "All that glisters is not gold"
          is the way Shakespeare wrote it; but it is now commonly seen as "All that glitters is not gold," or
          "All is not gold that glitters."
at first blush—means "at first glance."   Also written "at the first blush."
at swords' points—not "at *sword* points."
balled up—spelled differently from "bawled out."

beyond the pale—also "outside the pale," or "without the pale" ("pale" meaning an enclosed territory or a protective realm).

brand-new—not "*bran*-new."

by and by—not "by and *bye*."

by the bye—has been written "by the by" and "by*é* the by"; but the first is considered correct.

chock-full—or "choke-full," or "chuck-full"; but the first is preferred.

derring-do—not "*daring*-do," although the meaning is literally "daring to do."

devil's advocate—one who champions a bad cause for the sake of argument.

Eat, drink, and be merry, for tomorrow we may die—from two Biblical lines:

"Take thine ease, eat, drink, and be merry."—Luke 12:19.
"Let us eat and drink; for tomorrow we shall die."—Isaiah 22:13

egg on—to urge (derived from the older "edge on").

gave way—is the phrase in the following uses, not "gave *away*": "The bridge gave way." "The mob gave way." "They gave way to grief."

gentleman's agreement—or "gentlemen's"—an unwritten agreement of honor.

God rest ye merry, gentlemen—note the comma, "rest" meaning "keep," and "merry" meaning "in good spirits."

had as lief or **would as lief**—not "*leave*."

hail-fellow-well-met—not "*hale*." Used chiefly as an adjective, hence hyphened.

hand in glove—or "hand and glove." The latter is older.

hem'd and haw'd
hum'd and ha'd   }in fact any combination desired may be used.
hum'd and haw'd

hotchapotch }Although "hotchpot," which exists in legal use, is nearest to the
hodgepodge   original French "hochepot."

I fear the Greeks, even when bringing gifts—Vergil. Often "Beware the..."

if worse comes to worst—more logical than "if worst comes to worst."

make assurance double sure—is the Shakespearian quotation, which is now often written "doubly sure."

{**Music hath charms to soothe a savage breast**—is the original form (1697).
{**Music hath charms to soothe the savage beast**—is an adaptation (1729).

new lease on life—sprang from the older phrase "new lease of life."

not by any manner of means—rather than "not by any manner or means."

Nothing venture, nothing have—from the old English proverb "Nought venter, nought have." It has been variously interpreted as "Nothing venture, nothing win," and "Nothing ventured, nothing gained."

on the wrong tack—is the seafarer's expression that the landsman has changed into "on the wrong track."

plane sailing—is the nautical term, from which "plain sailing" has been derived. Both are used.

rack and ruin—now common instead of "wrack and ruin."

read the riot act—not "*right*" or "*Wright*" act. (An act in England for the suppression of mobs.)

round robin—(not capitalized). Signatures written in a circle to avoid making any name stand first.

rule of thumb—means measurement by the thumb; hence a practical rather than a scientific method.

run the gamut—to run the whole scale of anything.

run the gantlet—to experience hazards. (Formerly a punishment between rows of men with clubs.)

stormy petrel ⎰ One fond of storm and strife. (A bird said to portend storms)
storm petrel ⎱ (pron. pĕt′rĕl)

straight and narrow path—is an interpretation of the Biblical quotation:

> "Strait is the gate, and narrow is the way, which leadeth unto life; and few there be that find it."—Matthew 7:14.

swan song—is a writer's or composer's last work before death. (From the fabled song of a dying swan.)

the three R's—"reading, 'riting, and 'rithmetic."

three sheets in the wind—not "*from* the wind." A sailors' term.

To err is human; to forgive, divine—Pope. NOT: "To err is human; *forgiveness is divine.*" (pron. ĕr or ûr)

to the manner born—is sometimes written "to the manor born." Shakespeare used the former, and it is regarded as correct.

under way—rather than "under weigh." Originally from a ship's gaining motion or starting on its way. The deduction "under weigh" is presumably from a ship's weighing anchor before it starts.

Vanity of vanities; all is vanity—a Biblical quotation (implying futility). NOT: "*Vanity, vanity, all is for vanity.*"

walk the plank—to be expelled or forced out. (A pirates' method of putting prisoners to death at sea.)

walk Spanish—to be forced along on tiptoe through being seized by the collar and the seat of the trousers; to walk gingerly; to be thrown out.

weighed in the balances, and found wanting—is from the Bible. NOT: "*weighed and the balance found wanting.*"

COLLECTIVE WORDS

A collective word is a word that represents the grouping of two or more things. It may be treated as a singular or as a plural, according to the sense of the sentence.

Plural, when the persons or parts are considered separately:

The **company have** agreed upon a course of action.

Singular, when considered as one unit:

The **company is** financially strong.

BUT: After establishing a collective word as a singular in a sentence, **keep it singular;** or after establishing it as a plural, **keep it plural.**

NOT: That **firm** never *employs* (sing.) a man unless he has been recommended by someone **they** (pl.) know. (USE: employ)

NOT: The **company announces** *their* new policy of... (USE: its new policy OR: announce)

NOT: The **Board** of Directors *has* a code of **their** own. (USE: have)

NOT: The **customer** [a corporation] **has** complied with our terms and **has** indicated *their* willingness to carry out... (USE: its)

NOT: The **family** *is* all grown now and **have** scattered. (USE: are)

NOT: The **jury** *was* out but twenty minutes when **they** returned a verdict. (USE: were out OR: when it)

NOTE: "**Who**" when used to refer to a collective word represents the individuals that comprise the group, and therefore makes the collective plural.

NOT: There **was** an **element** in that district *who were* . . .
    (USE: district that was)
NOT: It is not the small-town **audience who** still *believes* . . .
    (USE: who still believe OR: that still believes)
NOT: In that little province there *exists* a **people who are** unknown.
    (USE: exist OR: that is unknown)

The following long sentence establishes "humanity" as a singular, and then changes it to a plural:

Has not **humanity** always ignored the advice of philosophers, and gone on leaning farther and farther to one side, until even the **majority** could not help seeing that in another instant all would be lost, and then with a feeling of panic, righted **themselves** and **begun** to lean as much too far the other way?
    (At first reading we might suppose that "themselves" refers to "majority," and puzzle about "begun." But upon second consideration we see that "begun" goes back to "humanity" and takes "themselves" with it. The simplified construction is: **Has** not humanity always ignored . . . and gone on leaning . . . and . . . righted **themselves** and begun . . . "Have" should have been used instead of "Has" if the rest of the sentence is to stand.)

Company names may be regarded as singular or plural. In publications a company is considered an impersonal being; therefore singular verbs and the impersonal pronouns **"it"** and **"which"** are used with each company name (yet in advertisements **"we"** is used by the company itself). When a name is treated as a plural, **"they"** and **"who"** refer to it.

Hill Bros. **is** the **distributor** for . . . (OR: agent, importer, etc.)
Day & Sons, **who are** our **agents, say** . . . (OR: which is . . . agent, says)
The King Company, **which has** issued **its** . . . (OR: who have . . . their)
Mills, Lee & Kent, Inc., through **which** . . . (OR: through **whom**)

Common Collectives. The number of collective words is unlimited, and has grown to include almost any word that represents the grouping of two or more things.
The following is a list of the common collectives:

army	company	flock	pair
assembly	congregation	generation	party
association	corporation	government[1]	people (populace)
audience	council	group	press
band	counsel	herd	public
board	couple	jury	race (a people)
bulk	crew	majority	royalty
cabinet	crowd	mankind	society
class	department	mass	staff
clergy	element	minority	troop
clientele	enemy	mob	union
club	family	nation	United States
committee	firm	number	United Nations
community	fleet	pack	youth

[1] "Government" is usually singular in the United States; plural, in Great Britain.

For example:

committee   The **committee are** debating... (among themselves)
            The **committee is** considering... (acting as one)
counsel   While the **counsel are** attempting to agree...
          Counsel for the company closed **their** arguments...
          His **counsel objects** to that.
couple   A* **couple have** been issued since then.
         ...to help the **couple** insure **their** home.
         Records reveal that the **couple was** last seen...
majority   The **majority come** from the lowlands.
           The **majority was** strong in its position.
           A* **majority** of people **are** against it.
number   A* **number** of improvements **are** to be made.
         The **number** of **alterations is** small. (the number by count)
pair   This* **pair match** well.
       That **pair looks** new.
press   Never **has** the **Press** been so royally received. (newspapermen)
        The **Press were** accorded places of honor. (newspapermen)
        The **press has** sufficient power to... (publications)
        The **press are** in accord on the issue. (publications)

* Notice that "a" or "this" may stand before a plural collective word.

Small Collectives. The following small words may be singular or plural, according to their reference.

all	more	none	that	who
any	most	some	what	which

BUT: "Much" is always singular, as "**Much** of their calculations **is** useless." (NOT: *are*)

For example:

all   **All has** been used. (a quantity)
      All have been used. (separate things)
any   **Any** of the motors **responds** instantly. (any one)
      Are there **any** left? (any separate things)
      Is there **any** left? (any portion)
none   **None** of these things **find their** way into print. (not any)
       Of all the predictions, **none is** to be fulfilled. (not one)
       ("None" in the plural is the commoner construction.)
that   The crowd **that was** cheering was in the bleachers.
       The group **that were** objecting were questioned.
which   **Which are** to be insured? (which ones)
        Which is to be registered? (which one)
who   **Who is** to sign it? (what person)
      Who are to sign it? (what persons)

Fractions or Parts. Fractions or parts may be singular or plural, according to the sense of the sentences.

first, last	part	portion	rest
fraction	percent	proportion	three-quarters
half	percentage	remainder	whole

For example:

first   The **first** of the shipments **have** arrived. (the first ones)
        The **first** of the shipments **was** damaged. (the first one)

half Half of the pages **are** proofread.
  Half **is** proofread.   (half of the book)
part Part of the crowd **was** held back.   (a portion)
  A **part** of the crowd **were** unable to see.   (the individuals)
percent Eighty **percent** of us despise the conditions...
  Explain why this 13 **percent was** released.
  NOT: Ten percent *was* chosen, but **they** were...   (USE: were)
percentage A large **percentage are** sold by subscription.   (items)
  A large **percentage has** been sold.   (quantity)
proportion A large **proportion** of the extracts **are** from newspapers.
  A larger **proportion** of the trade **is** expected to subscribe.
three-quarters Three-quarters of the year **has** passed.
  Three-quarters of the committee **were** against it.
rest The **rest were** little more than mediocre.   (separate things)
  The **rest is** in good condition.   (quantity)

◇◇◇◇◇◇◇◇◇

Singulars and Plurals

Some seemingly plural words may be used as singulars, and some seemingly singular words may be used as plurals.

-ics Words. Almost all the -ics words may be construed as either singular or plural, although the -s is the old plural form (compare "music," "logic," and "arithmetic," which have retained the singular form).

They are regarded as singular if they refer to one thing, as to a science or a course of study; plural if they refer to several things that make up a whole, as qualities or activities.

Acoustics is the science of sound.   (one thing)
The **acoustics are** good in that building.   (the several qualities of sound)
Athletics is a required subject.   (one study)
Athletics are too important to dismiss.   (the several sports included)

aeronautics[1]	gymnastics[2]	mechanics[1]
civics[1]	heroics[4]	physics[1]
dramatics[2]	hysterics[4]	politics[3]
economics[1]	italics[4] (italic, sing.)	statistics[2]
ethics[3]	mathematics[1]	tactics[2]

[1] Usually singular.   [2] Usually plural.   [3] Either singular or plural.   [4] Always plural.

Often a modifier, like "the," "such," or "his," will induce the choice of a plural verb.

The mathematics of it **are** complicated.
Such ethics **are** not practiced.
His politics **are** interfering with his judgment.

Or a singular complement (representing the subject under discussion) will induce the choice of a singular verb.

Dramatics **is a diversion** with some...
Economics **is** also the **study** of wealth.

-s Words. Some words end in -s and yet are singular.

apparatus plural may be "apparatus" or "apparatuses," but **is rare.**
gallows plural is "gallowses."
lens plural is "lenses."

39

news always singular. In such sentences as "Last week the following were news:", the word "following" is plural, with "items" understood, and "news" is still singular. ("News" was once used as a plural.)

summons plural is "summonses," as "Send out summonses."

taps as "Taps was sounded."

whereabouts as "His whereabouts is unknown." (now often plural)

Some words ending in -s may be either singular or plural.

alms	goods	measles†	shambles
amends	gross	molasses	species
chassis*	headquarters	mumps†	straits
corps*	means (way	rendezvous	sweepstakes
falls	to an end)	series	works (a factory)

* "Chassis" and "corps," although spelled the same in the singular and plural, are differentiated by pronunciation.

Singular: shăs'ē   kŏr   Plural: shăs'ēz   kŏrz

† "Mumps" and "measles" although listed as singular in the dictionaries are frequently referred to as plural, as "Have you had the mumps?" "Yes, I've had them." (RARELY: it)

The **goods were** marked. (any sort of goods)
The **goods was** faded. (dress goods)
No other **means was** in sight. (one thing)
What other **means are** offered. (several things)

Some -s words, plural in form and used with plural verbs, are singular, or collective, in meaning.

archives	means (income)	proceeds	thanks
assets	nuptials	quarters	trumps
belongings	oats	remains	wages
earnings	odds	riches	winnings
grounds	pains (care)	savings	woods
links (golf)	premises	scales	works (mechanism)

The names of two-part tools and appliances, ending in -s, are considered as plurals although designating but single things.

bellows	pincers	scissors
forceps	pliers	shears
glasses	scales	tongs

When the word "pair" is used before certain of these words, it may induce the choice of a singular verb.

A plural name, title, or term that refers to one thing is singular.

Twentynine Palms **is** on the desert about fifty miles... (a town)
"Adventures in Europe" **was** first published... (a book)

A definition or explanation of a plural term is singular.

TEST: Insert "the term" or "the name" before the word or phrase.

"State rights" **means** all the rights vested in the separate states.
"Thousand Islands" **covers** the island group between Canada and...

An -ing phrase standing as a subject takes a singular verb.

Overcoming obstacles **seems** to be his forte.

Unchanging Words. Some words singular in form are unchanged in the plural, commonly in the names of **races, tribes, and wildlife.**

aircraft	elk	moose	salmon
Chinese	grouse	Norse	sheep
cod	Iroquois	Portuguese	Sioux
deer	Japanese	quail	trout

NOTE: Plurals in -s may be conceived for some of these; for instance, if several kinds of trout are meant, "trouts" may be used, as "Trouts flourish in northern waters."

Some collectives with no plural are used as plurals –

cattle	gentry	police

and some are used as singulars (or occasionally as plurals):

livestock	offspring	wildlife	mankind

Idiomatic Plurals.   Some words idiomatically take their singulars as plurals in certain constructions.

cannon   After the cannon die down...
brick   a ton of brick
dozen   several dozen of them
duck   When the duck fly south they foretell winter.
fish   All the fish in the stream were trout.   (as a whole)
          All the fishes in the stream were silver.   (each fish separately)
head   Some six million head of cattle were...
heathen   ...take advantage of what the heathen make possible.
pair   two pair of gloves   or   two pairs of gloves
          several pairs of gloves   many pairs of gloves
prisoner   Several were taken prisoner [captive].   (as prisoners)
score   three score and ten
shot   Four shot were embedded in the wood. } (lead pellets)
          Shot was falling fast.
          Ten shots were fired.   (firearm discharges)
ton   ten ton of lead
yoke   six yoke of oxen

Abstract Collectives.   There is another kind of word ("abstract" or general noun) whose singular often has a plural application, that is, when the word represents a common feeling, emotion, or action, etc.

But if a common or general idea is not foremost, the regular plural should be used.

Where the singular alone is applicable:

consent   Several gave **their consent** to the proposition.   (NOT: *consents*)
attention   People will buy if we can attract **their attention.**
sense   ...according to the **sense of the different phrases.**
force   These and others have shown **their force.**
interest   **Their interest** was not in buying.
          BUT: **Their interests** were elsewhere.
leaving   We cannot prevent **their leaving** once in a while.
          BUT: We cannot govern **their comings and goings.**
work   It will not interfere with **their work.**
          BUT: It will not interfere with **their careers.**
failure   The **contractors' failure** to fulfill their contracts will be...
          BUT: What accounts for **their failures?**

41

Where singular or plural is applicable:

meaning ...according to **their meaning.** (OR: meanings)
measure If we can take **their measure** first... (OR: measures)
opinion Others expressed **their opinion** on the subject. (OR: opinions)
business We know men better if we know **their business.**
    (OR: businesses)
amount ...will issue bank drafts for any amount. (OR: amounts)
use What **use** can be made of such devices? (OR: uses)
tendency People have **a tendency** to do things that...
    (OR: tendencies)
time The only **time** those rules are in order **is** when persons...
    OR: The only **times** those rules are in order **are** when...
payment ...if they fail to make **payment** on their notes.
    (would indicate final payment)
    OR: ...if they fail to make **payments** on their notes.
    (would indicate installments)

◇◆◇◆◇◆◇◆

COMPARISON

-er indicates comparison between two, as "the better of two things."
-est indicates comparison between three or more, as "the best of all."

Which way is farther? (of two)
Which way is the farthest? (of three or more)
NOT: He was *more* famous than **all** the writers of the '40s.
    (USE: than **any other** writer OR: was the **most** famous of all)

The following comparisons stand as opposites:

much, more, most   little, less or lesser, least
  (referring to quantities or degrees)
many, more, most   few, fewer, fewest
  (referring to numbers)
good } better, best   bad } worse, worst
well }   ill }
great, greater, greatest little, less or lesser, least
large, larger, largest   small, smaller, smallest
big, bigger, biggest   little, smaller, smallest (littler, littlest [colloq.])
high, higher, highest   low, lower, lowest

fewer refers to number of—by actual count. Wherever "a smaller number of" could be mentally supplied, "fewer" should be used. (Consequently, **before plurals.**)
less refers to amount, degree, or quantity of. (Chiefly used **before singulars.**)

They have fewer (NOT: *less*) delays than before. (a smaller number of)
They have less delay than before. (a smaller amount of)
    fewer men or animals   less time
    fewer words   less work
    fewer advantages   less opportunity
    fewer troubles   less trouble
less than ten minutes (means less time)
fewer than ten minutes (means a smaller number of minutes)

less of two.
least of three or more.

> Which is the less commercial? (of the two)
> Which is the least commercial? (of all)

lesser means "smaller" or "in a less degree."

> ...no lesser fate than India.   Fog prevailed to a lesser extent.
> **"Less"** is commonly used instead of "lesser."
> > This lamp gives **less** light.   UNUSUAL: ...gives the lesser light.
> > ...papers of **less** importance   UNUSUAL: ...of lesser importance.
> > ...to a greater or **lesser** degree   make the margin **less** not greater.
> > NOTE: **"Much** [or still] **less"** is often used where **"much** [or still] **more"** is meant.
> > TEST: Weigh the meaning and supply understood words.
> > Foreign claims on our gold are now in excess of our total holdings, **much** *less* our free supply. (FOR: **much more** [in excess of our free supply])
> > ...amazing that such bills could even be proposed, **much** *less* passed.
> > (FOR: **much more** [amazing that they could be passed])
> > People do not want war, *least* of all nuclear war.
> > (FOR: **most** of all [they do not want nuclear war])

had best   **is best** ⎱ idiomatic combinations, used apparently without
had better   **is better** ⎰ regard for comparison, but for forcefulness.

> Such literature **had best** be destroyed.
> Such literature **had better have been** destroyed.
> It **is best** to be consistent and use this method rather than that.
> That **is better** avoided.   OR: That **is best** avoided.

to get the worst of it   is used of two or more.
to get the *worse* **of it**   is not used.
to get the better of ⎱
to get the best of   ⎰ are both used of two or more.

best of all ⎱ rather than "best of any," "most of any," etc. (See
most of all ⎰   "any" and "all," p. 6.)

> We like that the best of any.   FOR: We like that the best of all.

Excluding the Thing Compared.   When a person or thing is being
compared with another **in the same class,** "other," "else," "before,"
etc., should be used so as to exclude the one being compared.

> NOT: Ours is better than *any* leading filter. ("Any leading filter"
>   includes our product, which is in the "leading filter" class
>   and could not be better than itself. USE: than any other)
> BUT: It is better than **any** ordinary soap. (It is not in the "ordinary
>   soap" class. *"Other"* would not apply.)
> AND: You will say our sauce is as good as **any** homemade sauce. (Our
>   sauce is not homemade; hence *"other"* would not apply.)
> NOT: Of all the air conditioners, *none* is so well proportioned as...
>   (USE: **no other one is**... OR: **no others are**...)
> NOT: We make them better than *anyone*. (USE: anyone **else**)
>   No car is finer [than ours]. (Here, some writers would use
>   "other," but others would omit it on the theory that "No car"
>   may include our car, which cannot be finer than itself.)

43

NOT: *Nothing* does as much for you as a new car. (USE: Nothing **else**)
NOT: You will find that it outwears *any* flooring you have ever tried.
    (USE: any **other** OR: have tried **before** OR: have **yet** tried)

Omissions in Comparisons. Understood words must often be taken into consideration in comparisons—especially in advertising.

More people buy our product than ∧ any other brand. (they buy)
Twice as many people fly 747s as ∧ all other planes combined. (fly)

CAUTION: Guard against making illogical comparisons, or asking the reader to supply too many missing words.

NOT: Our dealers sell more cars per dealer than competition.
BUT: Each of our dealers sells more cars than any competitive dealer.
NOT: ...gives you the cleanest teeth of all leading toothpastes.
BUT: Among leading toothpastes, ours gives the cleanest teeth of all.

Remember, too, that **"more," "better,"** etc., take **"than,"** not *"as"* or *"not."*

NOT: It is at least three times **more** common among city dwellers *as* among farmers, and possibly nine times *as high.*
BUT: ...**more** common among...**than** among..., possibly nine times **higher.**
NOT: It is **better** to win confidence *rather* than votes. (omit "rather")
NOT: We are more interested in *them* supplying necessities, *not* novelties.
BUT: ...more interested in **their** supplying necessities **than** novelties.

Words Representing the Highest Degrees. Some words are supposed not to admit of comparison, representing in themselves the ultimate degrees, as

accurate	flawless	inseparable	sufficient
complete	fundamental	perfect	supreme
correct	genuine	preferable	unanswerable
dead	ideal	real	unique
decisive	impossible	right	universal
eternal	incessant	round	unprecedented
exact	incurable	square	vertical
faultless	indelible	stationary	wrong

However, since perfection in anything is rare, there must be degrees of approaching perfection or of appearing perfect, accurate, round, ideal, universal, etc. It is in this sense of "more nearly" or "most nearly" that comparisons are often made.

...in order to form a **more perfect** Union...—The Constitution.
If we know the meaning of a word, how much **more accurately** we can...
For **more complete** information, write to...
...a **very complete** and interesting work.
They seem **more dead** than alive.
What could be **more eternal**?
That is **absolutely right!**
...something that is **less indelible.**
Which is **more correct**? ...**more or less exact.**
...a delusion that was **extremely real.**
...under the **most ideal** conditions possible.
This is **far preferable** to that.
The ground plan looks **too square.**
The **rounder** the circle, the better.

The idea is **most unique.**   (most unusual)

...a **rather unique** arrangement.

Make it **so unique** that it can't be copied.

If it is **unique enough** to be considered new...

...one of the **most universally** known facts.

Is this **as unanswerable as** that?

The dictionaries give:

blind, blinder, blindest	pure, purer, purest
choice, choicer, choicest	ripe, riper, ripest
extreme, extremer, extremest	straight, straighter, straightest
full, fuller, fullest	sure, surer, surest
divine, diviner, divinest	true, truer, truest

From all of the above, it is to be assumed that practically any adjective or adverb may be compared, if the comparison makes sense.

ADVERBS AND ADJECTIVES

When adverbs and adjectives overlap, these guides may be applied.

Use an adjective when describing the subject:

TEST: Substitute "is," "are," "was," or "were" for the verb.

The **movement grew rapid.**   (TEST: The movement was rapid.)

He arrived **safe.**   (He was safe.)

Stocks closed **irregular** today.   (Stocks were irregular.)

They desire that their **records** be kept **secret.**   (are secret)

She acts **natural** always.   (She is natural [true to her nature] always.)

Use an adverb when describing the verb:

TEST: Substitute "in a...manner" for the -ly word.

The movement **grew rapidly.**   (TEST: ...grew in a rapid **manner.**)

The plane **landed safely.**   (in a safe manner)

Stocks **sold irregularly.**   (Stocks sold in an irregular manner.)

Their records were **kept secretly.**   (kept in a secret manner)

She **acts naturally.**   (acts in a natural manner)

"In some cases either the adjectival or adverbial form would be correct, and the choice between them is a matter of force, emphasis, or individual taste."

—Vizetelly, *How to Use English,* p. 40.

Many Words Have Two Adverbial Forms.   When a word has two adverbial forms, the choice between them is a matter of usage. (The two forms give rise to two comparison forms, as "walk slower" and "more slowly," or "think quicker or quickest" and "more or most quickly.")

cheap	cheaply	AS:	sell cheap	travel cheaply
clean	cleanly		sweep clean	cut cleanly
close	closely		knit close	bind closely
deep	deeply		drink deep	think deeply
direct	directly		ship direct	talk directly to

fair	fairly	AS:	play fair	treat fairly
free	freely		sail free	move freely
full	fully		full-grown	fully known
heavy	heavily		rests heavy	suffer heavily
high	highly		price high	praise highly
light	lightly		weigh light	step lightly
loud	loudly		speak loud	call loudly
quick	quickly		think quick	act quickly
right	rightly		guess right	understand rightly
sharp	sharply		turn sharp	watch sharply
short	shortly		stop short	answer shortly
slow	slowly		drive slow	move slowly
soft	softly		speak soft	touch softly
straight	straightly		think straight	remember straightly
wide	widely		open wide	space widely
wrong	wrongly		figure wrong	accuse wrongly

Often the two forms convey different meanings, as

sent free	rest heavy	ship direct	stop short	play fair
given freely	lose heavily	directly opposed	go shortly	fairly well

After Verbs of the Senses. The verbs "look," "smell," "sound," "taste," and "feel" may denote action as well as reaction of the senses.

REACTION OF SENSES	ACTION
The sea **looks calm.** (is calm)	He **looked calmly** about.
The rose **smells fragrant.**	The deer **smelled timidly** along.
The signal **sounds clear.**	**Sound** the signals **clearly.**
It **tasted dreadful.**	He **tasted** it **suspiciously.**
The air **feels marvelous.**	...must **feel** our way **cautiously.**
We **felt curious** about them.	The child **felt** the toy **curiously.**
That star **appears bright.**	...**appears brightly** above the...
(It looks or seems bright.)	(comes into view brightly)

Adverbs Before Prepositions. When a preposition immediately follows an adverb, the adverbial (-ly) form is usually used; but occasionally the adjectival form is idiomatically preferred. The following are examples of common phrases:

according to ...done according to directions. (NEVER: *accordingly* to)
agreeably to or with ...performed agreeably to the terms thereof.
agreeable to or with is also used adverbially.
conformably to or with ...prepared conformably to their wishes.
conformable to is also used. ...done in accordance with or conformable to the law.
consistently with It works consistently with our plan.
contrary to ...signed contrary to their orders.
differently from ...operates differently from that.
exclusively of ...judged exclusively of the testimony.
independently of ...financed independently of the bank.
irrespective of ...bought irrespective of conditions.
previous to ...was granted previous to that.
preparatory to ...was arranged preparatory to leaving.
pursuant to ...was made pursuant to their request.
regardless of ...was spent regardless of the consequences.
separately from ...was sold separately from the others.
similarly to ...handled similarly to the other order.
subsequently to ...dated subsequently to the contract.

46

The summary of this might be: Theoretically, the adverbial form (-ly) in the above and similar uses is always grammatically correct. But usage has sometimes rejected the adverbial and preferred the adjectival form. Therefore, if in doubt about the proper word to use in any of these adverbial constructions, choose the adverb, unless the adjectival form is so common as to sound correct.

according as   is an idiomatic expression which means "just as" or "precisely as." "Accordingly" is not used here.

> ...done one way or the other, **according as** the performer wishes.

as near as ⎱ Adverbs between "as...as" often take the shorter adverbial
as late as ⎰ form.

> ...as **near** as I can remember them. (RATHER THAN: as nearly as)
> ...occurred as **late** as 1950. (RATHER THAN: as lately as)
> We can buy as **cheap** as anyone.

bad   The adjective "bad" is used where "offensive," "defective," "disagreeable," "wicked," "sorry," or "ill" is meant.

TEST: Substitute a similar adjective: "sad," "glad," or "mad." (One would not say or write "I feel *sadly*," etc.)

He looks bad. (ill)	It tastes bad. (offensive)
He feels bad. (ill)	It sounds bad. (disagreeable)
We feel bad about it. (sorry)	That looks bad. (defective)

badly   The adverb "badly" is used where "in a bad manner" is meant.

He behaved badly.	He was injured badly.
He acts badly on all occasions...	It stains badly.
They look badly upon it. (disagreeably)	

"Badly" is colloquial when used for "very much."

COLLOQUIAL: They wanted to close the deal badly. (very much)
COLLOQUIAL: He needed the money badly. (very much)

clean ⎱ These words, when used as adverbs, may mean "wholly," or
clear ⎰ "quite." Sometimes, however, they have a colloquial sound.

> Such methods are **clean** against established practice.
> ...swept the audience **clear** off its feet.
> Shut it **clear** off.   ...threw it **clear** across the room.

comparative(ly) few   "Comparative" is used idiomatically after "a."

> ...shown in only a **comparative few** key cities. (note use of "a")
> **Comparatively few** people have seen it. (-ly form is usual)
> The **comparative few** who buy on margin... ("few" is a noun here)

different and differently   These words are widely misused.

TEST: Use "different" where "is different" would apply. Use "differently" where "in a different manner" or "to a different degree" would apply.

> ...if we think (know, wish, or are taught) **differently.**
> NOT: They look at it *different.* (USE: differently)
> NOT: That's why I say it *different.* (USE: differently)

47

NOT: Don't let anyone tell you ∧ different. ("anything" omitted)
NOT: She drinks coffee here because the tea tastes so *differently*.
(Use "different" after verbs denoting reaction of senses.)
RIGHT: ...until I am compelled to believe differently.
(to believe in a different manner or to a different degree)
It looks **different** now. (It is different [changed] now.)
He feels **differently** about it. (considers it in a different way)
Does he feel **different** from the others? (unlike them)
It appears (or sounds) **different** to some. (It is different.)
By spring, we may be hearing **differently**.
(in a different manner or to a different degree)

-ed modifiers   The -ed is sometimes dropped; sometimes retained.

Dropped: { skim milk   wax paper   going barehead   a barefoot boy
{ secondhand stores   underhand dealings   a left-hand turn
Retained: { whipped cream   iced tea   waxed paper   a bareheaded girl
{ barefaced lie   barehanded fight   left-handed compliment

-sized, -faced, etc., are used as adjective forms, but "-size," "-face," etc., are coming into use.   The -ed words convey the idea of actual action. For instance, "a low-priced car" conveys the idea of the actual pricing of the car; whereas "the low-price field" conveys the idea of a field where the prices are low.   "Letter-sized paper" conveys the idea of the actual sizing of the paper; while "letter-size paper" represents a size usually used for letters.   Other examples are:

medium-sized loans AND:	medium-size loans	a life-size portrait
desk-sized computers	executive-size desk	("Size" may often
solid-fueled rockets	solid-fuel rocket	be omitted after
gilt-edged cards	gilt-edge securities	"large" or "small.")
old-fashioned house	old-style building	medium-weight packs
middle-aged employees	a teen-age girl	ten-letter words
rear-engined car	twin-engine plane	ordinary-type goods

NOTE: When **both parts** of a compound adjective may take -ed, drop one -ed.

thatched-roof huts NOT:	thatched-*roofed*	jagged-edge fins NOT:	-*edged*
freckle-faced lad	*freckled*-faced	pear-shape-toned NOT:	-*shaped*-
square-toed shoes AND:	pointed-toe shoes	BUT: an armed-guarded room	

"Of" is often understood after **"size"** in commercial phrases –

what size unit   any size machine   that size paper

which compare with the common terms:

what type (of) unit   what make (of) machine   what color (of) paper

electric } Both are adjectives, but the shorter "electric" is widely
electrical } used in preference to "electrical," except in a few phrases
such as "electrical work" and "electrical engineer."
electrically   is the adverb.

There is to be electric lighting. (adjective)
The plant is to be electrically lighted. (adverb)
(NOT: *electric* lighted)
There is to be electric welding throughout. (adjective)
The tower is to be electrically welded throughout. (adverb)
(NOT: *electric* welded)

48

fast   is the adverbial form.   "Fastly" is archaic.

> It was fast locked.   ...seeping fast toward the bridge.

first, second, third   and   **first, secondly, thirdly** (See p. 414.)

good   is an adjective, sometimes used colloquially as an adverb.
well   may be either an adjective or an adverb.

> It works (or runs, wears, goes) **well**.   (COLLOQUIAL: good)
> NOT: He speaks (or writes, sings, drives) *good*.   (USE: well)
> BUT: It tastes (or smells, sounds, looks, feels) **good**.   (It is good.)

NOTE: In speaking of health, "feel good" and "looks good" although grammatically correct—the opposites of "feel bad" and "looks bad"—are avoided by some writers, who prefer "feel well" and "looks well."

hard } are both adverbs; but "hardly" is reserved for use when
hardly } "scarcely" is meant; and "hard" is used in all other instances.

hard-hit, hard-put	RATHER THAN:	hardly hit, hardly put
hard-fought		hardly fought
our hard-won liberties		our hardly won liberties
took it hard		took it hardly

ill } are both adverbs, but "ill" is usually preferred.   "Illy" has not
illy }   yet become "established" by usage.

> He was ill advised.   ...was neither well nor ill received.
> ...an ill-balanced sentence.   They took the news illy.

low } are both adverbs; but "lowly" is usually reserved for use when
lowly }   "meekly" is meant; and "low" is used at other times.

> swing low   threw low   talked low
> They lowly submitted to the laws.

more important   is short for "what is more important." } Each is
more importantly   means "in a more important way." }   often used.

most   as an adverb, means "in or to the greatest degree."
mostly   means "chiefly," or "for the most part."

> They were most concerned over the strike.   (in the greatest degree)
> They were mostly concerned about wages.   (chiefly concerned)

muchly   no longer exists.   "Much" is the adverb.

> It was much overdone.   (NOT: *muchly*)

rather a... } These combinations are perhaps as much used as "a rather
quite a... }   ..." and "a quite..."

> It is rather a difficult process.   It was quite a satisfactory reward.
> ...in rather a quiet manner.   ...at quite a late hour.

thusly   is colloquial.   "Thus" is the usual adverb.

> It is significant when considered thus.   (NOT: *thusly*)

◇◇◇◇◇◇◇◇

PRONOUNS

A pronoun's form depends always upon the grammatical construction of the sentence, and not upon the pronoun's position in the sentence. For instance, a pronoun used as a subject may be found far after its verb, or a pronoun used as an object may and often does stand somewhere before its verb.

One of the chief confusions concerns the forms to be used when pronouns occur in combinations.

for him and me
to her and them } The simple test to determine the form of these pronouns
by us and him } is to make each pronoun stand alone.

NOT: This is for you and *I* to learn.
("I" could not stand alone in this construction. NOT: This is for *I* to learn. Therefore "me" must be used.)
THUS: This is **for you** and me to learn.
NOT: To you and *he* belongs the credit.
("He" could not stand alone; therefore, "him.")
THUS: **To you** and him belongs the credit.
It is now ready **for him** and his **committee** to sign. (NOT: *he*)

Let's you and me ("You and me" is often superfluous, but not always.)

NOT: Let's you and *I* be the first.
(The simple sentence is: Let us be the first. "You and I" then is only an explanation of "us" and must be in the same form as "us"; therefore "me" must be used because "I" could not stand alone, as "Let *I* be the first.")
THUS: Let's **you** and **me** be the first. (Let us—you and me—be...)
OR: Let's be the first—you and me.
Let **him** and **them** figure it out. (NOT: *he* and *they*)

called him and me
told him and me

NOT: They called him and *I* to report for work.
(Again "I" cannot stand alone; therefore, "me.")
THUS: They **called him** and me to report for work.
NOT: They told both *he* and *I* that the deal was closed.
(They told him, and they told me...)
THUS: They **told** both **him** and **me** that the deal was closed.

for us workers
We workers

NOT: It is a good rule for *we* **workers** to follow.
(The simple construction is: It is a good rule for us to follow. "Workers" merely explains "us.")
THUS: It is a good rule for us workers to follow.
BUT: **We workers** should follow that rule.
(The simple sentence is: We should follow...)
NOT: Strange ways *us* journeyers have to take.
(The simple sentence is: Strange ways we have to take. "Journeyers" explains "we.")
THUS: Strange ways **we** journeyers have to take.

50

between you and me }
between him and them } "Between" is a preposition. To test the pro-
between us three } nouns, substitute another preposition.

NOT: This is just between you and *I*.
(Substitute "for" as a test preposition, and the sentence would
incorrectly read: This is just for you and *I*. Since "I" could
not stand alone here, the word is therefore "me.")
THUS: This is just **between you** and **me.**
NOT: Between *he* and *they*, we see no peace.
(Substitute "for" for "between," and "*he* and *they*" must
become "him and them." AS: For him and them, we see...)
THUS: **Between him** and **them**, we see no peace.
NOT: ...an agreement between *we* three.
(Simplified it is: an agreement between us. "Three" simply
explains "us.")
THUS: ...an agreement **between us** three.
NOT: The difference between the man who reads and *he* who listens is...
(The simple construction should be: The difference between
the man and him is... "Who reads" modifies "man,"
and "who listens" modifies "him.")
THUS: The difference **between** the **man** who reads and **him** who...

After Forms of the Verb "Be"

It is I	I am he	It should be I	It could be they
It is we	He is I	It will be I	It may be I, he, we, they
It is he	We are they	It was we	It might have been I, he, we, they
It is they	They are we	They were we	It has always been I, he, we, they

The simple rule is that these pronouns should be capable of replacing
the words to which they refer. Test them by substitution.

It is me   is favored by the British in conversation, and is generally
used in America. (It is accepted as a "good colloquialism.")

BUT: If **I were he**... (NOT: *him*) (SUBSTITUTING: If he were I...)
It was I, not he, who wrote. (I was it [the person], he was not.)
No matter what comes, **he will** always **be he.** (NOT: *him*)
Still **I am I,** and you are you.
Among those named **were he and we.** (NOT: *him* and *us*)
(An inverted sentence: He and we were among...)
If any man is right, **it should be he.** (NOT: *him*)
They imagined **it was we,** and we thought **it was they.**
(NOT: *us* NOR: *them*)
How can **they be we?** (NOT: *us*)
The **defendants are he, they,** and **we.** (NOT: *him, them,* and *us*)
Is it he that they refer to? (NOT: *him*)
They thought that the **applicant was I.** (NOT: *me*)
If it had been I, I should have done differently.
("If it had been me" is colloquial.)
These are they. (NOT: *them*)

If these uses sound unnatural or pedantic, repeat them often enough
to become accustomed to them, and the stilted sound will disappear.

51

being he
he being

> They were concerned over **its being we.**   (NOT: *us*) , (over our being it)
> No one thought of **its being he.**   (NOT: *him*)   (his being it)
> The **person in charge being he,** there can be no change in policy.
>   (NOT: *him*)   (He being the person in charge...)
> There being a definite place for him, and **he** (NOT: *him*   NOR: *his*)
>   **being** the logical man, we decided...

let it be him } Here also the pronoun must be capable of changing
let us be them } places with the word to which it refers.

> If anyone profits, **let it be him.**   (NOT: *he*)   (let him be it.)
> **Let us be them** that give.   (OR: Let us be **those who** give.)

to be he
to be him } Again the rule holds: A pronoun after "to be" should be
to be I } capable of replacing the word to which it refers.
to be me

> The **fugitive** was thought **to be he.**
> REPLACING: **He** was thought **to** the fugitive.
> They thought the **fugitive to be him.**
> REPLACING: They thought **him** to be the fugitive.
> They knew **it to be him.**
> It seems **to be he.**
> I am often taken **to be he.**   (He is often taken **to be I.**)
> Some take **him to be me.**   (Some take **me to be him.**)
> We are sure **it** was **to have been they.**
> **Whom** did they suppose **him** to be?   (NOT: *who*)
>   (Straightening: Did they suppose **him to be whom?**)
> There was a man standing by the door **whom** the officers
>   unfortunately took **to be him**   (NOT: *he*) whom they
>   intended to arrest.
>   ("Him" refers to "whom" rather than to "man."   The
>   clause is: the officers unfortunately took **whom to be him.**)

as being
as (when it means "to be") } When "as being" or "as" (meaning "to be") is used, the pronoun that follows should be capable of replacing the word to which it refers.

> **You** were disguised **as he.**   (to be he)
> They disguised **you as him.**   (to be him)
> That **man** was remembered **as being he** who blocked...
>   (**He** was remembered **as being that man**...)
> They remembered the **man as him** who blocked...
>   (They remembered the **man to be him**...)

him me   Sometimes "to be" is understood, as "They thought him me." Similarly used pronouns should be capable of replacing the words to which they refer.

> They thought (called, or considered) the **slacker him.**   (NOT: *he*)
>   (They thought the **slacker to be him.**)

They adjudged the **winner me.** (NOT: *I*)
 (They adjudged **me to be** the **winner.**)
That made the only **signers her and him.** (NOT: *she* and *he*)
He thought **us them** whom he was supposed to meet. (OR: **those**)
 (He thought **them to be us**—he was supposed to meet whom.)

Governing Words. Often the form of a pronoun is determined by a remote or missing word. (As a test, insert the governing word.)

That would let him carry the burden and **them** ride free. (let them)
Picture the pastoral scene—**him** plowing and **her** raking. (picture...)
He deserves thanks, not **I.** (I do not)   OR: Thank **him,** not **me.**
They've had several managers since **him.** ("Since" is a preposition
  here. But it may be a conjunction if completed: since **he** left.)
Whatever prompted **them** to call **him,** and [prompted] **him** to accept?
Someone—we are not saying **who** [it is], understand—is trying to...
If they'll vote for him, why not [for] **me?**   If he runs, why not **I?**

as good as I
as much as he }Pronouns following "as" take the forms they would
as well as they } take if the sentences were complete.

They are as good **as we.** (NOT: *us*)
  (They are as good as we are.)
We like him as much **as them.**
  (We like him as much as we like them.)
We like him as much **as they.** (as they like him)
We can fight as well **as they.** (as they can)
He will have to fight us as well **as them.** (as well as fight them)
You will be notified as soon **as I.** (as I am)
They will notify you as soon **as me.** (as soon as they notify me)
It should be up to them as well **as us** to get results.
  (NOT: as well as *we*) (as well as to us)
We were informed as well **as they.** (NOT: *them*) (as well as they were)

so...as he }"As" here still takes the form of pronoun necessary
such...as he } to complete the phrase.

They are not **so** dependable **as he.** (NOT: *him*) (as he is)
They are not **so** much interested **as you and I.** (NOT: *me*)
There are always **such as they.** (NOT: *them*)
 NOT: ...if such **as** *him* should win. (USE: such as he [is])
A DEVIATION: It is for **him** and **such** offenders **as him** that these laws...
  (This "him" is permitted to match the preceding
  "him.")

like him)Since "like" means "similar to" or "similarly to" and
like them } takes an object, "as" should be used wherever a subject
like me   ) and verb are introduced. (See also p. 14.)

He is **like me.** (similar to me)
 (NOT: He is like *I am.* It could not read: He is similar to *I am.*)
He writes **as I do.** (in the manner that I do)
 (Note that "as" introduces a subject and verb.)
He writes **like me.** (similarly to me)

Men **like him and you** should not be involved.   (NOT: *he*)
("Like him and you" means "similar to him and you" and does not introduce a verb, but explains "men."   The simple sentence is: Men should not be involved.)
Artists **like her and him** are interested in...   (NOT: like *she* and *he*)
Those who, **like them,** have spent a fortune...   (NOT: like *they*)
People **like them** can't tell the difference.   (NOT: like *they are*)

but me) When these introductory words have the meaning of "except"
but him } or "besides," they may logically be considered prepositions
save me) and followed by "me," "us," "him," "her," and "them."

Everyone signed **but him.**   (except him)
Everyone **but him** was notified.
(The simple sentence is: Everyone was notified.   "But him," meaning "except him," modifies "everyone.")
No one **but you and me** is to receive a check.
(NOT: No one but you and I *are* to...)
All **save him** were drowned.   (except him)

When "but" stands as a conjunction and does not have the meaning of "except," it takes the pronoun necessary to complete its clause.

We, **but not he,** expect to join.
(We expect to join—but he does not.)   ) Here "except"
They are interested, **but not I.**   (NOT: *me*)   } could not be
(They are interested—but I am not.)   } substituted
It is not they who are right, **but he.**   (but it is he)) for "but."
It benefited not them, **but him.**   (but it benefited him))

than I)
than he } Pronouns following "than" take the forms they would take
than me { if the sentences were complete.
than him)

It is a test of him more **than me.**   (than it is of me)
He is being tested more **than I.**   (than I am)
Several were older **than she** [OR: **they**].   (NOT: *her*)
They need you more **than him.**   (than they need him)
None have worked for it more **than we.**   (NOT: *us*)
Financially you rate higher **than he.**   (than he rates)
The Credit Bureau rates you higher **than him.**   (than it rates him)
He is no better **than you or I.**   (NOT: *me*)
(He is no better than you are or I am.)
If any nation that is stronger **than we**...   (NOT: *us*)
The man who plans is more valuable **than he** (NOT: *him*) who only plods.   (than he is who only plods)
Praise is given more often to the man who asks for it **than him** who deserves it.   (than to him who deserves it)
The peasants are voiceless and no more **than we** (NOT: *us*) to be censured.   (no more to be censured than we are)
We disliked both of them—but **him more than her.**   (but we disliked him more than we disliked her)
Both were experienced—but **he more than she.**   (but he was more experienced than she was)
A DEVIATION: It defeated not only **him,** but men much stronger **than him.**
(This "him" is permitted to match the preceding "him.")

other than*

It was none **other than he** who sent the message.   (than he is)
It is someone **other than I** that they mean.   (than I am)
They spoke to someone **other than me.**   (than to me)
No one, **other than they,** knows about it.   (NOT: other than *them know*)
Other than he and I (OR: we two) nobody knows.

rather than*

They should be responsible, **rather than we.**   (than that we should)
The firm is involved **rather than he.**
. . .look to the firm **rather than him.**   (than to him)
We, **rather than they,** are entitled to consideration.

* "Than" phrases such as this are, by some writers, regarded as having the prepositional force of "except," "besides," "instead of," etc., and are therefore followed by the pronouns "me," "us," "him," "her," and "them."

than whom   is an idiomatic combination, with "than" having the prepositional meaning of "in comparison with."

Midas **than whom** no man was richer. . .
The working people, **than whom** no more trusting souls exist, voted. . .

---

who and whom   can be either singular or plural, or first person, second person, or third person, according to the words to which they refer.

. . .for **you who have** worked.   (NOT: *has*)   (for you, you have worked)
. . .for **him who has** worked.   (for him, he has worked)
. . .for **those who have** worked.   (usage for "for them who")
. . .for **us who have** worked.   (for us, we have worked)
. . .for **me who have** worked.   (for me, I have worked)
It is **I who am** interested.   (NOT: who *is*)   (It is I, I am interested.)
He **who** never **wastes** anything. . .
You **who** never **waste** time. . .(NOT: *wastes*)   (You, you never waste)

The fundamental guides in choosing "who" or "whom":

Use "who" wherever "he" or a similar pronoun could be substituted.
Use "whom" wherever "him" or a similar pronoun could be used.

They couldn't tell **whom** the cable was **from.**   (NOT: *who*)
   (They couldn't tell—the cable was from whom [him].)
Guess **whom** we saw today!   (NOT: *who*)
   (Guess—we saw whom [him] today!)
Who does he think he is?   (NOT: *whom*)
   (Does he think—he is who?)
Whom does he think he's hurting?   (NOT: *who*)
   (Does he think—he's hurting whom?)
Who could it have been?   (NOT: *whom*)
   (Could it **have been who** [he]?)
Don't you know **who** it was?   (NOT: *whom*)
   (Don't you know—it was who [he]?)
Here is a man **whom** no one can accuse of being selfish.
   (Here is a man—no one can accuse whom [him] of being. . .)

Remember that **entire clauses or phrases may be subjects or objects** and "who" may be just a part of such a clause or phrase.

Now you know **who should be given preference.** (NOT: *whom*)
  (Now you know—who should be given preference. The entire
  clause "who should be given preference" is the object of "know.")
You have observed **who is always first.** (NOT: *whom*)
  (You have observed—who is always first.)
The matter of **who should pay was** not determined. (NOT: *whom*)
  (The matter of—who should pay—was not determined.)
But there are people **whom to admire** is difficult.
  (There are people—to admire whom [them] is difficult. The entire
  phrase "to admire whom" is the subject of "is difficult.")
There was no question about **who the winner would be.**
  (There was no question about—who would be the winner.)
It depends on **who is meant.** (NOT: *whom*)
  (It depends on—who is meant.)
It depends on **whom they mean.** (NOT: *who*)
  (It depends on—they mean whom. "Whom" is the object of
  "mean," and the entire clause "they mean whom" is the object
  of "on.")

In speech, "who" is sometimes used for "whom."

**Established
colloquialisms:**
  Who are you looking for? (whom)
  Who do you mean? (whom)
  I don't remember who with. (with whom)

The verb form "to be" often affects the construction of "who"
or "whom." (See also "to be he," "to be him," etc., p. 52.)

Whom did they take **it** to be?
  (Did they take **it** to be **whom** [him]?)
Is he **who** he pretends to be?
  (Is he—**who** pretends to be **he?**)

he who OR: **him who**
they who*   **them who**   To test these pronouns break the sentences
we who   **us who**   into their separate clauses.
I who   **me who**

Everything comes to **him who** waits. (NOT: *he*)
  (Everything comes to him—who waits. "Him" is the object **of**
  "to," and "who" the subject of "waits." "Who waits" modifies
  "him." To use "*he* who" would give two subjects to "waits.")
He who waits will find that everything comes.
  (He—who waits—will find that everything comes.)
Him who is loyal, repay. (Repay him—who is loyal.)
It was **he whom** they summoned. (NOT: *him who*)
  (It was he—they summoned whom [him].)
Give **him who** runs a chance to read. (Give him—who runs—a...)
He who runs has no time to read. (He—who runs—has no time...)
It was **they who** told. (NOT: *them*) (It was they—who told.)
It was **they whom** you told. (It was they—you told whom [them].)
...but **they who*** cannot yet read English, can read this.—Emerson.
. .traders might ask whether **they, who** have the excuse of having to
  contend with...competition, are alone to be blamed.—Spencer.
...returned with his prisoner to **them that** sent him...—Emerson.
  (Usually "to those that" or "to those who")
They wonder why security is not for **them, who** have always worked.

* "They who" and "them who" have been almost entirely displaced by "those who."

He told **them who** was to be the next chairman. ⎫ different meaning
He told **them whom** we had elected chairman. ⎭
The results of this will be important only to **those whom** it concerns.
We who have had that experience do not doubt it.
What is in line for **us who** have that training?
It was **I who** was called upon.   OR: It was **I whom** they called upon.
They called upon **me whom** no one knew.
  (They called upon me—no one knew whom [me].)
It was like willing a ranch in Texas to **me who** live in Wales.
  (NOT: *lives*)   (. . .to me—who [I] live in Wales.)

whoever   means "anybody who."
whomever   means "anybody whom."

  The "anybody" belongs to what goes before the word, and the
"who" or "whom" to what follows.

A political trap was set for **whoever** would fall into it.
  (. . .was set for anybody—who would fall. . .)
They set a political trap for **whomever** they could catch.
  (. . .for anybody—whom they could catch.)
This applies to him or **whoever** is given the job.   (NOT: *whomever*)
  (. . .to him or anybody—who is given. . .)
Whoever is successful they dislike.   (NOT: *whomever*)
  (They dislike anybody—who is successful.)
Whomever he envies he dislikes.   (NOT: *whoever*)
  (He dislikes anybody—whom he envies.)
Whomever they want, will be the next chairman.   (NOT: *whoever*)
  (Anybody—whom they want—will be the next chairman.)
To **whoever** writes in, we will send a sample.   (NOT: *whomever*)
  (To anybody—who writes in. . .)
To **whomever** they designate, we will send samples.   (NOT: *whoever*)
  (To anybody—whom they designate. . .)
Appoint **whoever** is suited for the position.   (NOT: *whomever*)
  (Appoint anybody—who is suited. . .)
Appoint **whomever** you wish.   (NOT: *whoever*)
  (Appoint anybody—whom you wish.)

whosever   is the possessive, rather than "whoever's."   (See p. 151.)

whosoever ⎫
whomsoever ⎬ are the more formal and precise forms.
whosesoever ⎭

as to who   means "regarding who [is]."
as to whom   means "regarding whom."

A debate **as to who** should be appointed took up most of the afternoon.
  (NOT: *whom*)   (A debate regarding—who should be appointed—took
  up. . .   The entire clause "who should be appointed" is the object
  of "as to" [regarding].)
A question might arise **as to who** is responsible.   (NOT: *whom*)
  (A question might arise regarding—who is responsible.)
. . .an investigation **as to whom** the Court is shielding.   (NOT: *who*)
  (. . .an investigation regarding—the Court is shielding whom [him].)

  If another "to" is necessary after "as to" to complete the "whom,"
it is better to rewrite the sentence.

57

INCOMPLETE: No decision was made as to whom the contract should be
awarded.
(Another "to" is necessary if the sentence is to be complete: **as to whom** the contract should be awarded **to.**)
BETTER: No decision was made **as to who** should be awarded...

Intervening Statements After "Who" and "Whom." Explanations,
suppositions, asides, etc., are often inserted immediately after "who"
and "whom," and tend to cloud the construction. If such intervening
statements can be temporarily removed without destroying the basic
meaning of the sentences, they are not considered in determining upon
"who" or "whom."

Who **did they say** is leaving tomorrow?
("Did they say" is the intervening statement. "Who is leaving
tomorrow?" is the simple question.)
Whom **did they say** the speaker meant?
(The speaker meant whom?)
...a man who **we thought** needed the work. (NOT: *whom*)
(...a man who needed the work.)
...a man whom **you would think** they could interest.
(...a man whom they could interest.)
...someone who **they specified** could live at home.
Send it to anyone who **you think** will be interested.
Send it to anyone whom **you think** they would care to interest.
...a representative who **the interpreter said** could act for us
...a mechanic who **they well knew** could not do the work.
...an investor whom **the owners state** they did not want.
He appoints those who **he believes** are the proper persons.
Who **do you suppose** is the donor?
Whom **do you suppose** this is from?
They paid those who **they felt** might bring suit.
...an agent who **I think they imagine** was not playing fair.
NOT: The playwright *whom*, the critics say, is recounting his life...
("The critics say" is parenthetic.)

When similar statements cannot be even temporarily removed without
destroying the sense of the sentences, they govern the form of "who" or
"whom."

A man **whom I knew** was made president. (irremovable)
(A man—whom I knew—was made president.)
He was the man **whom I believed** to be our pilot.
(To remove "I believed" would destroy the sentence. SO: He was
the man—I believed whom [him] to be our pilot.)
The man **whom we thought** to be our client deserted us.
(The man—we thought whom [him] to be our client—deserted us.)
We do not trust even those **whom we think** our friends.
("We think" here means "we consider." SO: ...we consider whom
[them] our friends.)

If such statements could be temporarily removed, but if their removal
would destroy the true sense of the sentences, they must be considered
in determining upon "who" or "whom."

There were but a few natives left, **whom we found** engaged in
gambling. (...we found whom [them] engaged in gambling.)

BUT: There were but a few natives left who, **we found**, engaged in gambling. (Here "we found" may be removed, giving the sentence a different meaning.)

---

one The indefinite "one" refers to "anyone" or "everyone."
one's is the possessive, written with the apostrophe.
oneself is now written solid. It was formerly "one's self."
  In formal American usage "one" is followed in a sentence by "one," etc. In informal writings "he," "his," etc., is often used.

> One must work out **one's** own salvation. (OR: his NOT: *your, their*)
> One should not take **oneself** seriously. (OR: himself NOT: *themselves*)

one Definite. This "one" refers to one person, and is followed by "he," "his," "her," or a corresponding pronoun. (See p. 2.)

> One [man] improves **his** mind to grow rich; another to grow wise.
> **No one** [person] likes to think that **his** fortune is founded on sand.
> (NOT: *their*)
> As **one** [person] who knows a bargain when **he** sees it, I believe...
> (NOT: when *I see* it)

you Indefinite. This "you" means "anyone." Do not mix it with "one" in the same sentence. Keep one point of view.

> If **you** are responsible for a debt, **you** (NOT: *one*) should pay it.

we Indefinite. This "we" may mean the writer and the **reader**, or people in general. It should not be mixed indiscriminately with other indefinite pronouns.

> **We** now come to a theory which **we** (NOT: *one* NOR: *you*) cannot prove.

* * *

A jumbled viewpoint:

> If **one** is inclined to doubt the truth of this **you** should investigate it, because **we** cannot always tell from the surface what the situation is.

From one viewpoint:

> If **you** are inclined to doubt the truth of this, **you** should investigate it, because **you** cannot always tell from the surface what the situation is.

* * *

Editorial "we" The "editorial we" should be used only when "we" actually implies the opinion of the editors, or of a corresponding group; it should not be used to state the opinion of one writer, one speaker, or one thinker.

National "we" The "national we" may be used by anyone, to mean a nation; but it should not be mixed with the "editorial we" in the same sentence.

> NOT: **We** [editorial] are not attempting to dictate to Washington, but **we** [editorial] believe that **we** [national] should now take **our** [national] first fearless or fearful step.
> BUT: ...**we** believe that **this Nation** should now take **its** first fearless ...

Sovereign "we" The "sovereign we" or "royal we" is used instead of "I" by royalty and governing officials, who consider themselves a part of, and spokesmen for, their people. **"Ourself"** instead of "ourselves" is used with this "we."

Personification Pronouns. Do not break off into personification after establishing a word as a neuter thing.

> NOT: If the **world** should somehow find peace within **itself**, so that all **her** people would stop fighting everlastingly... ("Itself" establishes "world" as a neuter, but "her" personifies it.)
> USE: ...world...itself...its people   OR: ...herself...her people

myself
ourselves
yourself
yourselves These pronouns should be used to reflect or intensify nouns
himself   or pronouns that have been expressed. In the absence
herself   of such introductory words, regular pronouns should be
itself   used.
themselves

Reflecting:

> He laughed at **himself.** ("Himself" reflects "he.")
> The **man** saw **himself** in that situation.
> **People** appoint **themselves** to such positions.

Intensifying:

> I **myself** will attend to it. ("Myself" intensifies "I.")
> He **himself** has said so.

> NOTE: Commas are usually unnecessary but may occasionally be used around the appositional "myself," "himself," etc., for emphasis or clarity.
>
> ...a bitter medicine for the **doctor, himself,** to take.
> ...just a little too early for **them, themselves,** to rise. (NOT: *they*)
> **Coexistence** is, itself, a compelling reason for...

The -self pronouns may be used in combination with other pronouns.

> He saved a place for **himself** and **me.** (NOT: *myself*)
> I saved a place for **him** and **myself.** (NOT: *himself*)
> They saved places for **him** and **me.** (NOT: *himself* and *myself*)

Occasionally these pronouns stand alone in sentences, when the words they reflect or intensify are implied but not expressed.

> There is no one to blame but **himself.** (He has no one...)
> Keep it for **yourself,** alone. (You keep it...)
> But as for **themselves**—nothing is too good. (But they think...)
> So many people, including **myself,** have started on that course.
>   (including me myself)

The following constructions are commonly seen; but most of them could be improved if the shorter pronouns were used as indicated.

> My associates and *myself* are interested in... (USE: I)
> *Yourself* and directors are requested to consider...
>   (USE: You and your directors)

There must be other persons like *myself*... (USE: me)
Nobody knows how to operate it but *myself*. (USE: me)
They insinuated that it was Barton and **ourselves** who...
   ("We" [it was Barton and we] might sound a bit strained in this
   everyday sentence, but should be used on all formal occasions.)
Send it to *myself* at the above address. (USE: me)
Both Mr. Hale and *myself* are writing him direct. (USE: I)
We do not think that any American manufacturer other than **ourselves**
   is quoting. ("We," while correct here, would not appear to bridge
   the gap so well as "ourselves." Some writers would treat "other
   than" as a preposition meaning "besides," and use "us." Others
   would avoid the pronoun and use "our Company.")

"Yourself" is commonly used in the following phrases:

Regards to **yourself** (OR: you) and Mrs. Hale.
Regards to **yourself** (OR: you) and your associates...

NOTE: "Yourself" or "you" is placed first in these combinations as a courtesy to the reader.

"Yourselves" is often used in such sentences as the following, because
it expresses the plural; whereas "you," in itself, does not.

I was pleased to find letters from both **yourselves** and the Sun Company.
...in all the patents that have been issued to **yourselves**.
("You" might be ambiguous here, in that it might seemingly refer
to but one person—the reader of the letter.)

Possessive Pronouns in Combination.

your and our ⎞ When using two or more possessive pronouns, check
yours and ours ⎪ each one separately to make sure that its form is
her and their ⎪ correct for its position in the sentence.
hers and theirs ⎠

NOT: This is **his,** *yours,* and **my** problem. (USE: your)
   (his problem—your problem—my problem)
BUT: This problem is **his, yours,** and **mine.** (NOT: *your*)
   (is his—is yours—is mine)
NOT: *Theirs* instead of **his** instructions will be followed.
   (their instructions—his instructions)
BETTER: **Their** instructions instead of **his** will be followed.
NOT: *Theirs* and **our** offices adjoin. (USE: Their)
   (their offices—our offices)
NOT: It is for *hers* as well as **his** benefit. (for her benefit—as well as
   his benefit)
BETTER: It is for **her** benefit, as well as **his.**
NOT: It must have been *mine* and not **their** car. (my car—their car)
BETTER: It must have been **my** car and not **theirs.**
OR: The car must have been **mine** and not **theirs.**

Possessive Pronouns Before -ing Words and Phrases.

your going   ⎞ An -ing word may serve as a noun; and a phrase containing
my being   ⎪ a word ending in -ing may express one thought (as if
his asking   ⎪ it were one word). A possessive pronoun should be
their writing ⎠ used before an -ing word or phrase standing as a noun.

61

Their having finished the work proves that it can be done.
(The entire -ing phrase, "Their having finished the work," is the subject of "proves.")
They, having finished the work, **now desire compensation.**
(Here the -ing phrase simply modifies "They.")
His having read the speech caused much comment. (NOT: *He*)
(Again the entire -ing phrase is the subject.)
He having read the speech, **the committee adjourned.**
(Here the -ing phrase is again a modifying [absolute] phrase.)
It is hard to conceive of **their not doing good work.** (NOT: *them*)
(The entire -ing phrase is the object of "of.")

If the one-thought -ing phrase is broken into by another phrase or clause, the possessive cannot of course be used.

It isn't pleasant to contemplate him **who really wants to work** being forced to accept charity. (The simple sentence is: It isn't pleasant to contemplate **his being forced to accept charity.** But "who really wants to work" breaks in, and "his" cannot be used. Therefore, the next best pronoun is "him.")

Guard against the splitting of these one-thought -ing phrases. Not only does it make a phrase very difficult to follow, but a sentence can be made wholly meaningless thereby. The best rule is to rearrange the sentence.

The debate had been personal, and a question arose regarding it, **which should not have been a part of the minutes anyway,** being stricken from the record. (The simple clause is: ...a question arose regarding **its being stricken from the record.** But another long clause intrudes, ruining the grammatical construction of "its" and making the whole sentence a puzzle.)

(See also Possessives, p. 151.)

Pronouns Used Parenthetically or in Apposition. Pronouns used parenthetically or in apposition should be of the same form as the nouns or pronouns which they explain, or which they could replace.

They sent **us, him and me,** on the mission. (NOT: *he* and *I*)
("Him and me" explains "us." SUBSTITUTING: They sent him and me, us, on the mission.)
We should be cautious, **we** Americans, that we do not...
("We Americans" explains "we" and could be substituted for it.)
Let **us** be cautious, **us** Americans, that we do not...
("Us Americans" here explains "us.")
We can take a lesson from them, **we** Americans, and begin again.
(NOT: *us* Americans) (Again "we Americans" is of the same construction as "we" and should not be influenced by "them.")
Who won—**you or I?** (NOT: *me*)
(Who—you or I—won?)
Let's start the wheels turning—**you and me**—and before...
("You and me" explains the "us" of "Let us" or "Let's." **Let** you and let me, us, start the wheels turning...)
They wanted **us** both, **me as well as him.** (NOT: *I* as well as *he*)
("Me as well as him" simply explains "us both." They wanted **me as well as they wanted him—us both.**)

All were interested—**he, they,** and **we.** (NOT: *him, them,* and *us*)
It was interesting to all—**him, them,** and **us.**
To treat a **man** so despicably, **him** (NOT: *he*) who is bigger than they...
("Him" explains "a man." To treat him so despicably, a man...)
The **man** was treated despicably, **he** (NOT: *him*) to whom they owed
everything. (He was treated despicably, the man to whom...)
It encourages the **planter,** even **him** who is skeptical. (NOT: *he*)
("Him" may replace "the planter." It encourages him, even the
planter who is skeptical.)
The **planter** is encouraged, even **he** who is skeptical. (NOT: *him*)
(He is encouraged, even the planter who is skeptical.)

Misleading Pronouns. If a pronoun is liable to be misleading in its
reference, it should not be used. Either the word in question should
be repeated, or the sentence should be rearranged.

The solution to this problem is still a matter of guesswork, but it **looks**
as if it could be brought about by analyzing its fundamental causes.
(The first "it" is general; the second "it" refers to the solution;
and the third "its" refers to the problem. Better to discard the last
"its" and use "the": ...but it looks as if it could be brought about
by analyzing the fundamental causes.)
The secretary admitted that it was **his** own fault that the president
had been asked to resign. (Whose fault?)
("His" presumably refers to "president," but the reader does not
know that until late. Better to rearrange: It was the president's
own fault that he had been asked to resign, the secretary admitted.
Or if a different meaning applies, and a rearrangement is not desirable,
parentheses may be used: The secretary admitted that it was his (the
secretary's) fault that the president had been...)
Without explanation **he** informed **him** that **he** must leave.
(Who must leave—the speaker or the listener? BETTER: Without
explanation he informed him that he found it necessary to leave.
Or for another meaning: Without explanation he asked him to leave.)
Men giving charity to men less fortunate than they, **who** desire that
their names be kept secret, seek such obscurity because...
(Which men desire that their names be kept secret?—the reader
does not immediately know. BETTER: Men who desire that their
names be kept secret when giving charity to men less fortunate than
they, seek such obscurity... OR: Men who, in giving charity...,
desire...)

Clear Reference. Pronouns should agree in person and number
with the words to which they refer.
After establishing a word as a singular, keep it singular.

NOT: This Nation should be able to protect **its** (sing.) resources if **we** (pl.)
are called upon to do so.
(Use "it is," instead of "*we are,*" to agree with the first "its.")
If a worker **is** justified in tendering **his** (NOT: *their*) resignation, **he**
(NOT: *they*) should receive...

The masculine pronouns ("he," "his," "him") are used to refer to
words of indefinite gender, as "everyone," and "a person," and to refer
also to antecedents of mixed gender, as "every man and woman." (See
p. 2; also Subjects, pp. 71 and 72.)

63

Everybody told **his** side of the story.   (NOT: *their* side)
Everyone wants **his** outlook to be bright.   (NOT: *their*)
Each desires a place for **himself** in the sun.   (NOT: *themselves*)
Which of us is to have **his** way?   (NOT: *our* way)
If **a man or a woman meets his** equal...   (NOT: *their* equal)
Every girl and boy looks to his future.   (NOT: *their* future)

"His or her" is sometimes used for exactness.

If **a man or a woman changes his or her** mode of dress...(NOT: *their*)
If **a man or a woman wants** to obscure **himself or herself**...
(NOT: *him* or herself)

The feminine pronoun "she" or "her" may of course be used if the reference is clearly to women.

Everyone should include this in **her** wardrobe.   (NOT: *their*)
Each of the teachers subscribed **her** share.   (NOT: *their* share)

"He or it" or "his or its" is not usually used in an attempt to avoid "they" or "their." Either "they" or "their" is used (in the absence of a fitting singular pronoun), or the sentence is rearranged.

UNUSUAL: If **a person or an event** is mentioned in the text, **he or it** should be clearly identified.   (OR: they)
REARRANGED: If mentioned in the text, a person or an event should...
OR: If persons or events are mentioned in the text, they should be clearly identified.

PREPOSITIONS

Prepositions overlap each other in meaning; but an attempt should always be made to select the best word for the sentence in hand.

after } used interchangeably in such phrases as "30 days after date,"
from }   "ten days from today."

among   used when three or more things are referred to.
between   used when two things are referred to. If used with more than two things, it brings each into individual relationship with the others.

An agreement between France, England, Germany, and Italy.

It sometimes groups them in twos, as

...between the pages of a book.   ...between the garden rows.

at   implies geographical location, and can mean either **in** or **near** a city, as "the airport **at** New York," "the races **at** Palm Beach," "a plant **at** Toledo."
in   usually means actually **within** the boundaries of a city, as "The Olympic Games were once held **in** Los Angeles."
on   implies geographical location **on** a wide or long area, as "**on** the Coast," "**on** an Indian reservation," "**on** a street."

He is **on** the Coast, **in** San Francisco, **at** the Lakeside Hotel.
A person lives **on** a street **in** a city.

"In the street" is a commercial phrase meaning in the financial district of a city, as "in Wall Street."
"In...street" is common in British usage, instead of "on...street," as "living in Waverley Street."

in implies within.
into implies entrance; or change of form.
in to two separate words.

> He walked **in** the office. (within the office)
> He walked **into** the office. (he entered)
> ...divided **into** three parts. (a change of form)
> Send the telegrams **in to** them immediately.

next may be used as a preposition meaning "nearest to."

> Place this one **next** the other.
> ("To" is unnecessary after "next" in this construction.)

on indicates position.
onto indicates movement toward.
on to two separate words.

> The cadets marched **on** the field.
> The cadets marched **onto** the field.
> They marched **on to** the next encampment.

on
upon } are interchangeable. Their use is a matter of choice.
up on two separate words.

> On further consideration...   That depends **upon** the man.
> He has climbed **up on** the ladder since then.

within...of is often loosely used to mean "within...from," "within...after," "within...before," "within...above," or "within...below."

> ...within two hours **of** its receipt. (after)
> ...within ten degrees **of** the boiling point. (below)
> ...within ten days **from** the date hereof. (NOT: *of*)
> ...within an hour's ride **from** here. (OR: of)

"Within" can be confusing if not carefully used, as

> All bids must be deposited **within** ten days of the meeting of
> the Board. (ten days before or after?)
> DEFINITE: All bids must be deposited within the ten days immediately
> preceding the meeting of the Board.

ENGLISH

Prepositions Combined With Other Words

There is no definite rule for the combining of prepositions with other words. Some combinations are established idioms, and are therefore used because they "sound right." Other combinations are deduced by analogy; that is, meanings are applied as tests. The following is a list of the ordinary combinations:

abounds in—means "is rich in." "Abounds with" means "teems with."
absolve from—means "to free from," as "absolved from blame." "Absolve of" is older.
accompanied by—is usual, although "accompanied with" is also used.
acquiesce in—is usual. "Acquiesce to" and "acquiesce with" are older forms.
acquit of—is correct, not "acquit *from*," as "acquitted of a crime."
adapted to—means "adjusted to." "Adapted for" means "made [over] for." "An adaptation of a novel," "an adaptation from a play."
adept at—or "in," as "adept at designing," "adept in art."
admit of—used in the sense of "permit" or "allow," as "too numerous to admit of classification." Ordinarily, the "of" does not apply, as "He will not admit defeat."
agreeable to—is usual, although "agreeable with" is also used.
alien to—is preferred to "alien from."
all of—(See p. 4.)
allow of—is similar to "admit of." (See above.)
alongside—"of" is unnecessary and now rarely used, as "alongside the plane."
analogous to—means "correspondent to." "Analogous with" is sometimes used.
angry at—or "with" a person. "Angry at" or "about" an action.
apposition with—Some grammarians favor "with"; others use "apposition to."
approve of—is a common combination, although just "approve" is almost always better.
apropos of—is the usual combination, rather than "apropos to."
at hand—or "to hand" refers to something "within reach."
  in hand—refers to something "in preparation," or "being dealt with."
at issue—a point affirmed by one side and denied by the other is "at issue" (the issue is joined).
  in issue—A point involved in or drawn into a controversy, and which will be affected by the judgment, is "in issue."
attest—"to" is often superfluous, as to "attest the truth of a statement."
aversion to—is usual. "Aversion toward," "for," or "from" is rare.
beneficial to—not "*for*"—meaning "useful, helpful, or advantageous to."
bill for \
bill of / are both used in referring to amounts, as "a bill of $85" (in the amount of), or "a bill for $85" (a statement for).
both of—(See p. 10.)
buy from—rather than "buy of." By analogy: "to purchase from" rather than "of."
cause for—means the reason for, as "a cause for action."
cause of—means that which produces the result of, as "the cause of action."
center in—or "on" is technically correct. "Center around" or "about" is colloquial.
clear of—as "to clear of guilt" is used more often than "clear from."
compare to—used when things are only likened, as "an electric light compared to the sun."
compare with—used when things are, or may be, compared in detail, as "one man compared with another."
compatible with—is the usual combination, although "compatible to" is used, probably by deduction from "agreeable to."
complementary to—not "*with*," as "research complementary to our own."
compliance with—is usual, not "compliance *to*."
conceive of—is a common combination, although often "of" is unnecessary.
concur in—an opinion, an action, a belief, a decision, or a decree.
concur with—a person, or a thing.
conducive to—is usual, not "conducive *of*."
confide in—means "to tell confidentially." "Confide to" means "to entrust [to]."
conform to \
conform with / both used. "Conform to" and "in conformity with" are usual.
consequent to—is usual, rather than "consequent upon."
consist in—means "lies in," or "dwells in."
consist of—means "is made up of."

> Life **consists of** little things. (is made up of)
> Enjoyment **consists in** work as well as pleasure. (dwells in)
> The error **consists in** writing only what we hear. (lies in)

contemporary with—not *"to,"* as "contemporaneous with our times."

contrast to ⎫
contrast with ⎰ interchangeable when "contrast" is a noun.

> What is that in contrast with?
> ...a candle in contrast to the sun.

When "contrast" is a verb form, "with" follows it.

> ...the eye contrasted with a camera.
> That is like contrasting night with day.

correspond to—means "to be analogous to"; also "to match."
correspond with—means "agree with"; also "to communicate with."
credit for—is usual, not "credit of," as to "get the credit for."
cure of—is usual, rather than "cure from."
danger in—means the danger that lies in.
danger of—means the full danger of, or the possibility of. "The **danger in** introducing
    this is the **danger of** establishing that."
die by—to die by the process of, as by violence, by suffocation, by drowning.
    NOT: He died *from* drowning. (drowning is dying)
    BUT: ...narrowly escaped death by drowning.
die from—to die from the effects of some outward agent, as from exposure, from suffocation,
    from wounds, from want.
die of—to die from the effects of some inward agent, as of a disease, of fever, of old age, of
    grief, of thirst.
die with—to die with (or by) the sword, or with (or of) humiliation.
differ from—means "to be distinguishable from," as "light differs from air."
differ with—means "to disagree with," as "Men differ with each other."
different from—is the preferred combination.
different than—is used, although mildly condemned by some.
different to—is used colloquially in England.

> It was **different from** that.   is no doubt better than
> It was **different than** that.   but
> It was **different than** I thought.   because of its smoothness is
>   no doubt better than "It was **different from what** I thought."

"Than" permits many shortcuts:

> They have **different** methods today **than** in 1940.
> (Is surely more practical than: They have **different** methods
> today **from those which they had** in 1940.)
> We are considering it from a **different** angle **than** they. (Is much better
> than:...from a **different** angle **from that from which** they are.)

disappointed in—is the usual combination. "Disappointed with" is also used.
discrepancy in—a thing. "Discrepancy between" two things.
discretion—"At the discretion of" and "in the discretion of" are both used.
dispense with—not "dispense *of*."
dissent from—is usual, not "dissent *with*," nor "dissent *of*."
dissociate (or disassociate) from—not "*with*," as "dissociated ourselves from the conference."
enamored of—is usual. "Enamored with" may refer to inanimate things.
foreign to—is usual. "Foreign from" is also used.
free from—is usual. "Free of" is also used, as "free of (OR: from) foreign entanglements."
half of—The "of" is used before pronouns, as "half of these"; and before nouns when the
    fractional part is thought of, as "half of the boxes." But it may be dropped when
    a quantity is meant, as "Half the sales were final."
identical with—means "uniform with." "Identical to" means "equal to."
ill with—a disease, rather than "ill of."
immune to—resistant to, as a disease. "Immune from" means "free from," as taxation.
incompatible with—is usual, meaning "incapable of association with."
incongruous with—is usual. "Incongruous to" is also used.
incorporate in—is usual. "Incorporate into" and "with" are also used.
independent of—not "*from*," as "done independently of us." "We are independent of
    them."
indifferent to—not "*of*," as "indifferent to debt."
in distinction from—is usual. "In distinction to" is rare.
in regard to—Note "regard" and not "*regards*." (See "with respect to," below.)
insensible of—means "not aware of," as "insensible of danger."
insensible to—means "indifferent to," as "insensible to pain" or "fear," etc.
insert in—is usual. "Into," "between," and "among" are also used.

instill into—is the idiomatic combination, but "instill in" is also used.

martyr—A sufferer is a "martyr for" a cause, but "to" pain or a disease.

monopoly of—means "control of"; yet "monopoly on" is widely used.

motive for—is usual, as "the motive for being honest"; rather than "motive in."

necessity for—means the urgent occasion for.

necessity of—means the unavoidable obligation of.

need for—means the urgent occasion for, as "the need for financing."

need of—means the lack or want of something, as "the need of money."

oblivious of—means "unaware of," "unmindful of," "forgetful of." "Oblivious to" is now commonly used to mean "indifferent to," or "aloof toward."

occasion for—means "call or reason for," as "There was no occasion for that."

occasion of—means "cause of," as "Such things are the occasion of much suffering."

of record—means "recorded," as in the legal phrase "to the owner of record."

on record—as to "place it on record." "He is on record as saying. . ."

omit in—is usual, although "omit from" is also used.

on behalf of—means "on the side or part of," as "pleading on behalf of the farmers."

  in behalf of—means "in the interest of," as "acting in behalf of peace."

opposite of—is used when "opposite" is a noun, as "This is the opposite of that."

opposite to—"To" is usually dropped after "opposite," as "Place this opposite that." But either "to" or "from" may be used if necessary, as "This testimony is opposite to that of. . ."; "done oppositely to (OR: from) their way"; "took the opposite side from him."

parallel to—is usual. "Parallel with" is used when comparison with is meant.

part from—means "to separate," as persons and things are "parted from" each other.

part with—means "to give up," as "He parted with his possessions, ideals, and hopes."

payment for—one makes "payment for" an article, a garment, a house, goods, etc.

payment of—one makes "payment of" a fee, a price, an invoice, a bill.

permission from—as "by permission from the publishers" (by authorization from).

permission of—as "with the permission of the author" (with the consent of).

permit of—The "of" is often superfluous. (See "admit of," above.)

precedence of—is considered correct; but "precedence over" is widely used.

prevent from—is a usual combination. (See also Possessives, p. 153.)

prohibit from—is usual.

purpose in—means the intention in, as "his purpose in doing that."

purpose of—means the object or idea of, as "the purpose of doing that."

recommend above ⎫ should be used if one thing is recommended more than or rather
recommend more than ⎬ than another thing, as "We recommend this rather than that."
recommend rather than⎭ (NOT: *to* that)

recommend to—A person or thing is recommended to someone for consideration.

reconcile to—means to bring to quiet submission to, as "reconciled to poverty."

reconcile with—means to make consistent with, or to harmonize with, as to "reconcile one thing with another," or "reconcile one person with another."

recover from—not "*of*" a disease, as "recovered from tuberculosis."

resentment toward—or "against" a person; "at" or "for" an action or wrong.

rests in—means "lies in," as "The significance of the term rests in the idea of obligation."

rests on—means "is based on," as "The essential difficulty rests on the charge that. . ."

rests with—means "remains with," as "that duty rests with the President."

retroactive to—means "active backward to." "A wage increase, retroactive to June 10," not "retroactive *from* June 10."

right of—takes a noun, as "the right of organization, of veto, of search, of protest, of trading, of self-determination, of recovery, of appeal, of voting."

right to—takes a verb, as "the right to organize, to protest, to trade, to vote."

search—"In search of" is usual. "In search for" is less common.

sick with—a disease, rather than "sick from."

speak to or talk to ⎧ largely interchangeable. The former may be particularly
speak with or talk with ⎨ applied to the addressing of words to a person whether he
  ⎩ replies or not. The latter may be applied to conversation.

  ⎧ Strictly speaking, one subscribes one's name to a document **for** a periodical,
subscribe for ⎬ or stock, etc. The New York Times uses "subscribe for," "a subscrip-
subscribe to ⎨ tion for," etc.; but some other publishers use "subscribe to," "a sub-
  ⎩ scriber to," etc.

suitable to—or "for," as "suitable to the occasion," "suitable for the purpose."

superior to—not "*than*." "They are superior in every way to the old ones."

surround by—as "surrounded by water." "With," as "Surround it with troops."

under the circumstances—indicates action under given conditions.

  in the circumstances—indicates situation in given conditions.

68

vary from—means "differ from," as "one thing varies from another."
with regard to } are both used. Note that "regard" and not "*regards*" is used in the
with respect to } first phrase.
with the view of—means "with the purpose of."
with a view to—means "with an outlook toward."
    Note that "the" is used with "of," and "a" is used with "to"; not "with a view *of*," nor "with the view *to*."
    Note also that an -ing word usually follows "with a view to," as "with a view to **curtailing** production," rather than "with a view to **curtail** production."
withheld from—is usual, not "*in*" nor "*on*," as "withheld from your payment of our invoice."

SUBJECTS

    The **true subject** of a verb is often obscured by an intervening phrase, or an inverted construction.

> "Some writers are as easily drawn off the scent as young hounds. They start with a singular subject; before they reach the verb, a plural noun attached to an 'of' or the like happens to cross, and off they go in the plural; or vice versa."
> —Fowler, *A Dictionary of Modern English Usage*, p. **389**.

To determine the true subject:

Break down the sentence structure and test it.

Intervening Phrases.

NOT: The **total** of the bills which were charged to "campaign expenses" *were* high. (The simple sentence is: The total was high.)
NOT: The **shape** of the heads *show* that... (USE: shows)
    (The shape shows...)
NOT: A large **amount** of information and news *are* to be found there.
    (USE: is) (A large amount is to be found there.)
NOT: The arrangement of wires that *connects* with the central office *are* something like a tree. (USE: connect...is)
NOT: The only times the gentlemen are photographed *is* when...
    (The only times are when...)
NOT: **Reports** that the long **battle** between the two shipping interests over intercoastal service *were* settled in New York **were** denied. (Reports were denied that the long battle was settled.)
NOT: A new set of rules and regulations *have* been adopted.
    (A new set has been adopted.)
NOT: His association with big industries and foreign governments *make* him the most sought-after... (USE: makes)

Inverted Constructions.
Many writers have a tendency, when a subject follows its verb, to allow what precedes to govern the verb. But a plural verb should be used wherever necessary to prepare the reader for a plural subject; and a singular verb, for a singular subject.

NOT: ...in which *was* stored the books. (USE: were)
    (in which the books were stored)
NOT: But from these extracts *are* gleaned one single thought...
    (One thought is gleaned from...)
NOT: Clearly visible against the sky *was* the *peak* of Mount Rainier and Mount Adams. (USE: were the peaks)

NOT: ...a forecast in which *is* seen two bright spots.   (USE: are)

NOT: To him *falls* the duties of...   (USE: fall)

NOT: Among the spectators *was* the Queen and members of...   (USE: were)

NOT: From that source *has* frequently come to us many enlightening facts.   (USE: have come)

Awaiting the outcome was a new government and an old. (To use "was" might mean that the new government and the old were one.   Use "were" if two distinct governments are meant.)

On the success of this conference hang the future happiness and prosperity of the world.   (If "hangs" had been used, "happiness and prosperity" would have been considered a single thought. See One-Thought Subjects, p. 78.)

"One of."   When "one of" occurs in a sentence, it is often misleading. To test it, determine upon the simple sentence first, and then decide whether a singular or plural verb should follow the object of "of."

It is one of the **things that are** worth doing.   (NOT: *is* worth)
(It is one—of the things—that are worth doing.   "It is one" is the simple sentence; "of the things" modifies "one"; and "that are worth doing" modifies "things"—telling what things.)

The following sentences will bear the same analysis.   The simple sentences are set off by straight lines.

He is one | of those **people who are** (NOT: *is*) cautious.

Now we come to one | of the very few **men who have** (NOT: *has*) ever served their (NOT: *his*) country in such a capacity.

That is just one | of the exclusive **features that make** (NOT: *makes*) our product the finest.

A planet is one | of the opaque **bodies** of the solar system **that revolve** (NOT: *revolves*) around the sun.

One | of the **things which have** (NOT: *has*) interested us most | is the perfection of a new accelerator.
(The simple sentence is: One is the perfection.)

One | of the first signs of spring | **is** the breaking sod and the warm...

One | of the sources of Florida's wealth | **is** deposits of phosphate...

On that date one | of the most spectacular sky **disturbances that have** (NOT: *has*) taken place in our generation | will occur about midnight.

He is one | of those **hosts who entertain** by lecturing.   (NOT: *entertains*)

Not **one** | of you who **hear** me | will remember this.   (NOT: *hears*)

He is one of *these* men who *sits* down to read and *falls* asleep.
(FOR: He is **one** | of **those** men who **sit** down to read and **fall** asleep.)

It was one | of those **days that carry** us back...   (NOT: *carries*)

Note the difference in meaning in the following sentences:

He is one | of our **customers who do not pay** promptly.
(There are a number who do not pay promptly.)

Here is one of our customers | **who doesn't pay** promptly.
(Here is perhaps the only one who doesn't pay promptly.)

It was considered one | of the **finest** of its kind **that have** (NOT: *has*) ever been grown.   (It was one—of the finest that have been grown.)

It was considered the **finest** of its kind **that has** (NOT: *have*) ever been grown.   (It was the finest—that has ever been grown.)

It is the **only one** | of that group of stars | that **shines**.   (one shines)

It is **one** | of a group of stars that **shine**.   (all shine)

Singular Subjects. The following words are singular and should be followed by singular verbs and singular pronouns. (See Gender, p. 2.)

anybody	everything
anyone (meaning anybody)	neither* (singular when alone.
any one (meaning any one thing,	See also p. 73.)
or any one of a group)	nobody
anything	no one (For none, see p. 38.)
each	nothing
either* (singular when used alone.	one
See also p. 73.)	a person
every	somebody
everybody	someone (meaning somebody)
everyone (meaning everybody)	some one (meaning some one
every one (meaning every one	thing or person)
of a number)	something

Does **anyone** ever **consider** that **his** (NOT: *their*) lot is fair?
Has **any one** of them **stopped** to consider **his** (NOT: *their*) own fate?
Each resident **is** allowed $500 of **his** (NOT: *their*) purchases...
Each of us **is** what circumstances make **him**. (NOT: *us*)
Each of them **has** to answer that question **himself**. (NOT: *themselves*)
But **each has** chosen to go **his** separate **way**. (NOT: *their...ways*)
Has **each** of you **decided** upon **his** course? (NOT: *Have* each of you
  decided upon *your courses?*)
The tricks that **each is** in the habit of playing... (NOT: *are*)
Every American will have to pay **his** part. (NOT: *their*)
Everybody wants enough money to satisfy **his** needs. (NOT: *their*)
Everyone—from schoolboy to President—**knows** that **his** chances...
Every one of them **was** asked to prepare **his** story. (NOT: *their* story)
If **either** of these terms **is** (NOT: *are*) accepted...
  (SIMPLIFIED: If either [one] is accepted...)
Either of the men **is** (NOT: *are*) influential enough to control the situation.
  (Either one is...)
Does **either** of you care to join? (NOT: *Do*)
Is **either** of you going to investigate it? (NOT: *Are*)
There are two reasons, **neither** of which **is** (NOT: *are*) important.
  (SIMPLIFIED: ...neither [one] is important.)
Neither of them **knows**. (SIMPLIFIED: Neither knows.)
Neither of the solutions **is** (NOT: *are*) right.
Nobody knows what is in store for **himself**. (NOT: *themselves*)
Not one of them **has** (NOT: *have*) given **his** (NOT: *their*) consent.
No one thinks it is **himself** (NOT: *themselves*) who **is** (NOT: *are*) meant.
Only **one** man in a hundred **has** the ability to... (NOT: *have*)
A person presumes **his** (NOT: *their*) luck will not desert **him** (NOT: *them*).
Someone who **is** not always trying to prove **his** (NOT: *their*) theories..
Some one of the group will be rewarded for **his** (NOT: *their*) perseverance.

* Note that "**either of**" and "**neither of**" refer to one of two persons or things, **not to three or more.** Therefore, "**two**" is superfluous in such as "either of the *two* men." Similarly, do not use such expressions as "*either* [or *neither*] of the three men"; use "**one** [or **none**] of the three men."

Even when two of the above subjects are joined by "and" they take a singular verb.

  Anything and **everything is** to be sold.
  Anybody and **everybody was** invited.

Something and somebody is to be considered in each case.
There is something to be criticized and something to be praised in...

Grouped subjects, preceded by "each," "every," "no one," etc., also remain singular. (See Generic Gender, p. 2.)

Every man ahd [every] woman in America is interested in his tax bill.
(NOT: *are* interested in *their* tax *bills*)
As an experiment, each city, county, and state is to elect its own representative. (NOT: *are* to elect *their* own *representatives*)
No one country and no one ruler has a right to be so honored.
Some one man and some one organization is sure to profit.

no This word, like "none," can mean "not one" or "not any." Hence, it can modify either singular or plural nouns.

No man and no woman was exempt. (no one)
No time and money was spared. (not any)
No group of people are so secure that they can afford to ignore the future. (not any of the individuals of the group)
No data are to be submitted.

everybody⎫ These words are sometimes regarded as collectives, and
everyone ⎬ followed by "they," "their," or "themselves"—if not
etc. ⎭ restricted by singular verbs.

Everybody could have more profit if they would work together...
Everyone voted but they could not agree.
Should every nation go off the gold standard they would find no difficulty in adjusting themselves.
Every one of them would fight for what they believe is their just due.

each (when in apposition with a plural subject)

In ordinary sentences, a parenthetic or explanatory "each" may be inserted before a plural verb (or its complement); the plural form is undisturbed and should be continued throughout.

The stockholders each hope to receive their dividends. (NOT: *dividend*)
Washington, London, and Paris, each hope to succeed in turning their trade concessions into gold.
The directors each want their own way.
(For the use of the singular "way," see p. 41.)
The governors, each for his own sake, want their candidates elected.
The president, the vice president, and the secretary, each wrote their own speeches. (NOT: *speech*)
There are three directors who, each in turn, plan to carry on their private campaigns. (NOT: *campaign*)
They each have fortunes in their own right.
(For the use of the singular "right," see p. 41.)

In formal writings, the parenthetic or explanatory "each" should be set after the plural verb (or its complement). In this position, the words that follow "each" are governed by it and are singular (see p. 2).

The stockholders expect each to receive his dividend.
The president and the vice president wrote each his own speech.
There are several kinds of bills, each of which serves (NOT: *serve*) a special purpose.
They have fortunes, each in his own right.

more than one This phrase, although plural in implication, is used as a singular, undoubtedly because of the necessity of joining a singular noun to "one."

> **More than one tear** was shed.
> BUT: More tears than one **were** shed. (NOT: *was*)
> **More than one person** in the employ of the Commissioners **was** needed to keep the peace. (NOT: *were*)

many a This phrase also conveys a singular idea, and the verb should be singular.

> **Many an hour and day was** spent in contemplation.
> Although there has (NOT: *have*) been many a trying day...

"many's the time" is the shortening of the colloquial phrase, "**many** is the time." Do not write "many's *a* time."

When Alternative Subjects Are Introduced by "Or," or by

either...or
neither...nor } "Or" and "nor" do not blend words into one subject; they simply join alternative subjects.

If the subjects are singular, the verb must be singular:

> A feast or a famine **is** (NOT: *are*) always to be expected.
> If **this, that,** or **the other thing is** (NOT: *are*) to be used...
> **One** or **the other** of those men **is** (NOT: *are*) responsible.
> **Either one method** or **the other is** (NOT: *are*) to be tested.
> **Neither imagination nor industry is** (NOT: *are*) to be found in...
> **Neither page nor paragraph nor line** is given.

If one subject is singular and the other plural:

NOTE: There is a difference of opinion regarding this. The rule most commonly followed is that the verb should agree with the subject nearer it—if no later complications arise. Another rule is that a plural verb should be used regardless of the position of the subjects. A third rule is to evade the problem by reconstructing the sentence.

1. Using a verb to agree with the subject nearer it:

> One or more **men are** needed.
> Neither the men nor the **machine accomplishes** the work.
> Neither the machine nor the **men accomplish** the work.
> **Do** real **hazards** or only a slight risk **present themselves?**

But this method can lead into difficulties, as

> Neither the men nor the **machine accomplishes its?** (their?) work.
> **Does** only a slight **risk** or real hazards **present itself?** (themselves?)

2. Using plural verb regardless of position of subjects:

> Neither the men nor the machine **accomplish their** work.
> **Do** only a slight risk or real hazards **present themselves?**

3. Reconstructing:

> Neither do the men accomplish their work, nor does the machine.
> Does only a slight risk present itself, or real hazards?

73

If the subjects are of different person:

> Either you or he is (are?) to be the judge of that.
> Neither he nor I am (is?) the one to decide.
> Is he or I to be responsible?

This awkwardness should be overcome by reconstruction.

> Either you are to be the judge of that, or he is.
> Neither is he the one to decide, nor am I.
> Is he to be responsible, or am I?
> OR: Is he, or am I, to be responsible?

Words or Phrases That Do Not Affect Subjects. An explanatory, modifying, or parenthetic phrase, introduced by or containing a word similar to those listed below, and inserted immediately after a subject, does not combine with the subject or influence the verb.

The verb agrees with the true subject. Commas or dashes may be used to set off the intervening phrase if a definite separation is deemed necessary. However, if the intervening phrase causes the construction to be awkward, the sentence should be rearranged; or a verb to agree with the phrase should be used.

after Snow **after the rains** delays the coming crops.
along with This document, **along with other papers,** completes the...
also But certainly the first, **and the second also,** is to be considered.
as much as Fog, **as much as the winds,** makes landing difficult.
as well as A day, **as well as years,** changes a life.
before Sometimes the merchant, **before the customers,** is considered.
besides Who **besides them** is to sign the contract?
but No one **but you and him** is aware of it. (See "but him," p. 54.)
   No one **but the officers** is allowed on the 32nd floor.
but not ...in so far as its form **but not its contents** is concerned.
certainly This dealer—**and certainly those you mentioned**—is fair.
else It gives the distinction that he **and everybody else** wants.
   He **and who else** is to report?
especially South America, **especially Venezuela and Brazil,** has products that we cannot produce.
etc. Lumber, **etc.,** was to be shipped by rail.
even America, **and even England,** has become interested.
every other He **and every other buyer** knows the difference.
except The book, **except two certain parts,** is finished.
for that matter This account, **and for that matter many others,** is...
in addition to That fact, **in addition to the testimony,** is enough...
including The mortgage, **including the notes,** is to be signed...
in fact That company—**and in fact all its subsidiaries**—is to be...
instead of The product, **instead of the prices,** is to be changed.
like Our workmanship, **like our prices,** is right.
much less No European country, **much less any of the Asiatic countries,** has reason to...
much more England, **and much more France,** is looking toward...
no less than The depositor, **no less than the directors,** is interested...
no more than The banker, **no more than the depositors,** is to be...
not Great wealth, **and not meager savings,** is what causes...
   Not great wealth, but meager savings are what build...
not even Nobody, **not even presidents,** is immune.
often A grownup, **and often a child,** is inclined to...

other   That job **and other work** is to be done.
       AWKWARD: France, **and other European countries,** is...
       BETTER: France and other European countries are...
other than   No equitable offer, **other than those,** has been made.
particularly   Reckless driving, **particularly cutting-in,** tends to...
perhaps   One, **and perhaps two,** seems to be necessary.
plus   That amount, **plus interest,** gives a net...
therefore   Every delegate, **and therefore his country,** has but one vote.
together with   This, **together with those,** is to be transmitted...
too   It appears that this, **and that too,** is incorrect.
       AWKWARD: It appears that he, **and they too,** is to benefit.
       BETTER: It appears that he and they too are to benefit.
usually   The first copy, **and usually the second,** is clear.
with   This **with that** is sufficient.
       The sight draft **with documents attached** is to be...
without   One **without the others** is incomplete.

not only...but { When these introductory words are used, the subject nearer the verb governs it.

Not only **are those** to be sent, but this also.
Not only those but **this** also **is** to be sent.
It is true that not only the health, growth, and prosperity, but also the mental **development** of a nation **depends** (NOT: *depend*) on...
Behind the remarkable progress *is* (USE: **are**) seen not only persistent **ideals** but a vast knowledge...

Participles Modifying a Subject, such as

accompanied by...
followed...
following... } These and similar verb forms do not join words into plural subjects. The phrase introduced by the participle simply modifies the true subject.
considered...
considering...

The jet plane **pursued by the red bomber** was (NOT: *were*) plainly seen.
   ("Pursued by the red bomber" modifies "plane.")
The jet plane **pursuing the red bomber** was next seen.
That letter, **followed by these,** is (NOT: *are*) quite enough proof.
That, **considered in the light of these,** is not surprising.
The code message, **accompanied by a translation,** was delivered.

There is...
There are...
Here is... } "There," "here," or "where" may stand in the place of either a singular or a plural subject.   To determine the correct verb form, substitute the true subject.
Here are... CAUTION: Do not use *"There's"* or *"Here's"* (meaning "There is" or "Here is") before a plural subject.
Where is...
Where are...

There are (NOT: *is*) to be two **discounts.**
   (Two discounts are to be...)
There are (NOT: *is*) approximately **twenty** in the company.
There were (NOT: *was*) the **six** of them—sitting in silence.
There appear (NOT: *appears*) to be **conditions** which govern...
There **stand** (NOT: *stands*) the **monuments** to our prosperity.
Where **go** (NOT: *goes*) the American **dollars...**
Here **begin** (NOT: *begins*) the **histories** of two nations.

When a compound subject follows and clearly indicates two or more distinct things, a plural verb is used.

> There **were** an **industry** and several **arts** to be considered.
> (several distinct things)
> There **were** a **judge** and two **consuls** to be appointed.   (three people)
> Here **are quality and quantity** at last.   (two distinct things)
> Where **are man and woman** so equal?
> There **have been** a large **number** of plays that have been censored.
> (The collective "number" is here regarded as a plural.   See p. 38.)

But when the compound subject indicates one thought or idea, a singular verb may be used.

> There **is distinction and truth** in that slogan.   (a combination)
> There **was neatness and dispatch** in that order.   (a combination)
> There **was** a **beach and palm trees** in the foreground.   (one scene)
> Here, before us, **is the problem and its solution.**   (one thing)
> Where **is the power and the glory** that was ours?   (one greatness)

Or when the parts of the compound subject are separated by several words, or are listed, the verb may be considered to be understood before each subject after the first.

> There **is** a lake **camp** in that vicinity and several **resorts.**
> (There is a camp...and [there are] resorts.)
> There **was** a report **charge,** a filing **fee,** a time **fee,** and a copying **cost.**

What is . . .
What are . . . { "What" may be singular or plural. It may mean "that which" or "the thing which" and be considered a singular; or it may represent "those which" or "the things which" and be considered a plural.

> **What** they require is five or six good salesmen.
> (The thing which they require is...)
> Material advantages **are what** make people strive...
> (...are the things which)
> Here **are what** appear to be the reasons.
> (...are the things which)

What is . . . is
What are . . . are { After "what" has been established as a singular, it should logically be kept singular. But often it is changed to a plural to agree with a plural complement.

Singular:
> **What is** needed **is** laws to govern...   (OFTEN: What is...are...)
> (The thing which is needed is laws...)
> **What seems** to be the cause of the trouble **is** (OFTEN: are) the promises
> on the part of the sellers...
> (The thing which seems to be the cause is...)
> **What delays** the deliveries **is** (OFTEN: are) the transfers.
> (The thing which delays...is...)

Plural:
> But **what were** fairly good points **were** overlooked.
> (The things which were good points were...)
> **What appear** to be nuisances sometimes **turn** out to be advantages.
> (The things which appear...turn...)

all some ⎫
any that ⎪ These words may stand as singular or plural subjects,
more who ⎬ according to the sense of their sentences. (See Small
most which ⎪ Collectives, p. 38.)
none ⎭

SINGULAR: **Who thinks he** can outwit **his** own shadow? (NOT: *they . . . their*)

PLURAL: He is among the few authors **who do** not experience difficulty with. . . (NOT: who *does* not)

SINGULAR: I hope if **any** reader **has** this problem, **he** will. . . (NOT: *they*)

PLURAL: . . .if **any** of your readers **have** this problem, **they** will. . .

Collective Words as Subjects. (See pp. 36–42.)

"Is" or "Are." The true subject of a sentence is the subject that is being discussed. It may occur after the verb or before it.

In questions, the true subject follows the verb.

What guarantee are these promises of your ability to pay?
("These promises" becomes the true subject by the rearrangement of the question.)

But in straight sentences –

". . .when. . .subject and complement can change places without alteration of sense, so that it may be doubted which is which, the verb must agree with what precedes, and not with what follows . . ."

—Fowler, *A Dictionary of Modern English Usage,* **p. 29.**

An ever-present **threat was** price **reductions.**
Price **reductions were** an ever-present **threat.**
Possibly **taxes are** a tender **spot** in that issue.
Possibly a tender **spot** in that issue **is taxes.**
Dr. Jekyll and Mr. Hyde are the same **person.**
The same **person is** at different times **Dr. Jekyll and Mr. Hyde.**
His **wages are** his only **income.** OR: His only **income is** his **wages.**
("Wages" was formerly regarded as singular, as in the Biblical phrase, "The wages of sin is death.")
"State rights" is a term. . . (Definitions take the singular. See p. 40.)

"Is" After Numbers. When a number and a plural noun represent a singular idea, they are followed by a singular verb.

Twenty years is long enough.
(The period of twenty years is long enough.)
Fifty dollars is not too much.
(The sum of $50 is not too much.)
Seventy inches is usually figured for that pipe.
(The length of 70 inches is. . .)
Nine-tenths of it **was** salvaged.
A million dollars is a lot of money.
One hundred men is the quota for each field.
There **is just $100** involved.

But when the individual parts are thought of, a plural verb is used.

Twenty **years have** now passed since...
One hundred **men are** needed to fill that quota.
There **are hundreds** of dollars wasted.
There **are ten** in the organization.
Nine-tenths of the public **are** in favor of...

"Is" or "equals" is now generally used in arithmetical calculations.

Two times three is six.
One hundred plus fifty is one hundred and fifty.

However, when **"and"** is used, **"are"** usually follows:

Five thousand and four hundred are five thousand four hundred.

"And" Joining Two Subjects. When "and" joins two true subjects, whether they are both singular, one singular and one plural, or both plural, they form a compound subject and take a plural verb. (Unless but one thought is conveyed by the two subjects—see below.)

NOT: We shall assume no new obligation until times and our own future
looks (USE: look) more promising.
("Times" and "future" are the subject of "look.")
NOT: The services rendered by these people and their share in making the
work a success *is* (USE: are) to be commended.
("Services" and "share" are the subject.)
NOT: Trees and lakes and even a mountain *was* (USE: were) on the place.
("Trees" and "lakes" are the subject.)

"And" Introducing Explanatory Phrases After a Subject.

and also   **and often**
and certainly **and other**
and even   **and particularly**
and especially **and perhaps**
and every other **and usually**

"And" often introduces an explanatory or parenthetic phrase which does not compound the subject. (See also p. 74.)

Commas or dashes may be used to set off such explanatory or parenthetic phrases if a definite separation is deemed necessary.

Every idle telephone in this city—and millions of other telephones—
stands ready to obey.

One-Thought Subjects. When the parts of a compound subject blend into one idea, they may be treated as a singular subject.

"If two or more nouns can fairly be considered as together expressing a single idea, a singular verb may be used with them."

—**Ives,** *Text, Type, and Style: A Compendium of Atlantic*
Usage, **p. 244.**

"Two nouns of closely allied meaning are often felt to make no more than a single notion..."

—**Fowler,** *A Dictionary of Modern English Usage,* **p. 641.**

The **tumult and the shouting dies**...—Kipling.   (the excitement **dies**)
The **beginning and end lies** somewhere in that.   (the entirety)
The **wear and tear is** to be considered.   (the depreciation)
The **rise and fall** of the tide **has been** measured...   (the movement)
The **organization and commencement** of business **is** announced.
   (the beginning)
To see clearly and **to act wisely is** sometimes difficult.   (one course)
Prosperity on the one hand **and poverty** on the other **is** not a pretty
   picture.   (one vision)
Mexico and the Southwest is the fairest and finest of lands.   (one land)

Singular Subject Made Plural by Modifiers.
If a singular subject is so modified as to suggest two different things, a plural verb may be used.

...but American and East Indian **culture** in many respects **are** not alike.
   (two different kinds of culture)
Modern and ancient **architecture are** sometimes similar.   (two styles)

When a Second Verb Is Understood, in Inverted Constructions.
"And" does not compound two subjects if a second verb can be reasonably understood from the first.

...wallowing in the channel **was** (NOT: *were*) a freighter, and farther
   along a whaler.   (and farther along was a whaler)

VERBS

Many verbs are misused because the meanings are not thoroughly understood. The definitions of troublesome verbs should be applied as tests when doubt arises regarding correctness.

affect   to act upon; to alter; to assume; to adopt.
effect   to bring about. (As a noun it means: that which is brought about, as a result or an impression; [plural] belongings.)

Remember that "affect," which begins with "a," means four things that begin with "a"—act upon—alter—assume—adopt.

The one test meaning of "effect"—bring about—can be applied wherever "effect" is a verb.

TEST: Substitute meanings.

Would that **affect** their decision?   (act upon or alter)
That might **affect** our school system.   (alter or act upon)
He just **affects** that manner.   (assumes)
They always **affect** the trend in styles.   (adopt)
Can they **effect** the compromise?   (bring about)
...if unable to **effect** delivery.   (bring about)
They **effected** a solution.   (brought about)
What was the **effect** of it?   (the result of, or impression made by)

Sometimes either word might suit; in that event the exact meaning must decide the matter.

One act may **effect** both things.   (bring about)
One act may **affect** both things.   (act upon or alter)
...to **effect** a law.   (bring it about)
...to **affect** a law.   (act upon or alter)

A few further aids toward determining the difference:

"**Affect**" is not used as a noun, except in rare medical phrases. Therefore, if a noun is necessary, "**effect**" is the word, meaning a result or an impression.

a far-reaching **effect** (NOT: *affect*)	personal **effects**
as soon as it takes **effect** (NOT: *affect*)	a studied **effect**

"**Affect**" meaning "to assume" may be remembered by association with "affectation." "**Affecting**" means "moving the affections."

English grandees **affect** to be farmers.—Emerson.
It is a deeply **affecting** story.   ...an **affecting** scene.

Study the following sentences which illustrate the different uses:

That law cannot **affect** us, although it may **effect** great changes as soon as it goes into **effect.**
It **affected** some but had no **effect** on others.

Wrong choices:

Its advance is apparently having an *affect* on the price of gold.
("Effect" was meant—having a result or making an impression.)
A drop in the price would not *effect* it seriously.
("Affect" was meant—act upon or alter it.)
...if we are able to *affect* the transfers.
("Effect" should have been used—to bring about.)
...unless it *affects* radical reform. (Again, "effects"—brings about.)
It may have a telling *affect* on such cases.
("Effect" is the noun—a result or impression.)

as follows
as follow ⎰ "As follow" might seem correct for the introduction of plurals, as "The items are as *follow:*". But "as follows" has come to be generally used for both singular and plural.

The items are as follows:

From this it should not be deduced that "follows" should always be used for the plural.

NOT: ...in the forms of advertising that *follows*.   (USE: follow)

bring   to carry toward.
take   to convey away from.
Never carelessly use "bring" when "take" is intended.

NOT: May I *bring* that book home tonight?   (USE: take)
You may **take** it home if you will **bring** it back tomorrow.

can   signifies ability to do: is able, is competent, has a right, or is empowered to do.
may   signifies permission.   Also it may signify a possibility.   Wherever **permission** is involved, use "may."

Can he read the chart?   (Has he the ability?)
May he read the chart?   (asks permission)
Can he draw up the agreement?   (Is he able to?)
May he draw up the agreement?   (asks permission)

We **can** expect no more.   (have no right **to)**
He **cannot** sign checks.   (is not empowered **to)**
I think we **can** count on that.   (are able or have a right to)
I think we **may** count on that.   (a possibility)

(See also "so that," p. 20; and "may," p. 84.)

come
go

These words are often confused by letter writers when writing to persons about proposed trips.   The writer should take into consideration the reader's geographical position.   For instance, when writing to a person in New York, do not say:

I expect to *go* to New York this fall.
(Use "come," which will sound correct from the reader's viewpoint.)

But when writing to a person at any point other than the destination, use "go."

do have   FOR: **have**
does have   **has**
did have   **had**

As a general rule (which has exceptions) when possession is implied, "have" alone is used; "do," "does," or "did" is considered unnecessary before it.

IDIOMATIC USAGE	GRAMMATICAL USAGE
Does he **have** time to do it?	**Has** he time to do it?
Do they **have** a cable address?	**Have** they a cable address?
Did he **have** recommendations?	**Had** he recommendations?
Does he **have** the papers?	**Has** he the papers?

They **have** quite a collection.
Have they?   (RATHER THAN: **Do** they?)
He **has** an appointment to Germany.
Has he?   (RATHER THAN: **Does** he?)

But when possession is not implied, "do," "does," and "did" are used with "have" to avoid very great formality or awkwardness.

Did you **have** a pleasant vacation?   (NOT: Had you a...)
(Did you experience a pleasant vacation?)
We **don't have** to do it their way.
(We are not compelled to do it their way.)
Does he **have** to go back next year?
(Will he be obliged to go?)
Did they **have** an X-ray made?
(Did they obtain an X-ray?)
Did they **have** an accident?
(Did they experience or suffer an accident?)
Do they **have** benefit performances every year?
(Do they hold benefit performances every year?)

At times, even though possession is implied, "do," "does," or "did" is used before "have" as a mark of special emphasis—particularly in negative sentences.

He **did** not **have** the courage to say so.   (did not possess)
He **did have** the courage to say so.
When the letters **do** not **have** that significance...
ORDINARY: They **don't** all **have** incomes.
FOR: They all **haven't** incomes.

did
have
has
"Have" should be used instead of "did" in questions where it is desired to cover all points of time up to the moment of asking the question, as

Have they come yet?   NOT: *Did* they come yet?

"Did" represents past or closed action; whereas "have" continues the action up to the present moment.

Did you hear from them yesterday? (past action)
Have you heard from them this morning? (OR: Did you hear...)
Did they agree to that? (OR: Have they agreed to that?)
Have they agreed yet? (NOT: *Did* they agree yet?)
Have they finished it already? (NOT: *Did* they...)

don't is a contraction of **"do not."**
doesn't is a contraction of **"does not."**
To say "he *don't*," "she *don't*," "it *don't*, "that *don't*," etc., is like saying "he *do* not," "she *do* not," "it *do* not," "that *do* not," etc.
"Doesn't" should always be used with "he," "she," "it," and "that," and with any other word that requires "does not."
To use "don't" with these words is as conspicuous an error as to say illiterately, "I *seen*," and "I *done*."
A headline from a paper published in 1876 reads:

What General Kidder Knows and *Don't* Know.

"Let's *don't*" means "let us *do* not," which is obviously wrong.

NOT: Let's *don't* forget that we too... (Let us *do* not forget?)
BUT: Let's not forget that we too... (Let us not forget...)

graduate Strictly speaking, a school graduates a student.
The student is graduated from the school.

He **was graduated** (OR: is to be graduated) from Stanford in June.
But common usage also favors:
He **graduated** (OR: will graduate) in June.

had better have been
had rather have been
would rather have been
In these idiomatic phrases the word "have" must always be used before "been."

He had better be careful. (He should be careful.)
BUT NOT: He had better been careful. (He should been careful?)
CORRECT: He **had better have** careful. (He should have been...)
NOT: He would rather said nothing at all. (He would said...?)
BUT: He **would rather have** said nothing at all.

had I *have* known it
had we *have* done that
if I had *have* seen it
"Have" is totally unnecessary in these phrases, and is termed "illiterate."

Had I known it, I could have called.
Had we done that, we should have profited.
If I had seen it, I should have told you. (OR: **Had I seen it**)

had *of*   Never use "had *of*" for the almost equally bad "had *have*"

CRUDE: Had we *of* heard it...   (FOR: Had we heard it...)
If we had *of* known it sooner...   (FOR: If we had known it...
OR: Had we known it...)

has got } These are usual verb forms, but are colloquial when used where
have got } "has" or "have" alone will suffice.   (See "got," p. 99.)

That's all we **have** to say.   (COLLOQUIAL: have got to say)
COLLOQUIAL: **Has** he **got** the money?   (FOR: Has he the money?)
COLLOQUIAL: We **have got** to go.   (FOR: We have to   OR: We must...)
BUT: He did not seek recognition, but he **has**, indeed, **got** it.
(meaning "has obtained" or "has been awarded")

learn   to acquire knowledge. } NOT: "It will *learn* them a lesson."
teach   to impart knowledge. } BUT: "It will **teach** them a lesson."
It would seem unnecessary to mention the distinction between these
two words, except to say that once they were interchangeable.   To
use one for the other now is, by the dictionaries, termed "a vulgarism."

lend   is the usual verb, meaning the opposite of borrow.
loan   is also used as a verb, especially in financial writings, as to "loan
money on goods of value."
Possibly the tendency to use "loaned" for all purposes is caused by a
desire to avoid "lent," which is a perfectly good word.

They **lent** us their drawings.

lay   to put.   } "Lay" represents the actual putting down
lie   to rest or stay, or   } of something; and "lie" represents the
take a position of rest. } resting or reposing there.
lay, laid, laid, laying   take an object.
Something must always be laid (put) down by someone.
lie, lay, lain, lying   do not take an object.
Someone or something lies (rests or stays) somewhere.

Now I **lay** me down to sleep.   (put myself down)
He maketh me to **lie** down in green pastures.   (take a position of rest)
Lie down and rest.   (take a position of rest)
Had you **lain** down before?   (rested)
Lay it over there.   (put it)
Let it **lie** there.   (stay there)
The soldiers **lay** in the mud.   (stayed or rested)
They **laid** their guns in a row.   (put)
The papers **lay** on the desk unsigned.   (stayed)
The papers were **laid** on the desk.   (put)
The fields **lie** unploughed.   (stay)
The fields **lay** unploughed for years.   (stayed)
It has **lain** there all these years.   (stayed)
It seems to have **lain** dormant for many years.   (stayed)
The years have **laid** wisdom at his feet.   (put)
Time is **lying** heavy upon his hands.   (resting)
Time is **laying** heavy hand upon him.   (putting)
The blame **lies** with them.   (rests)
Lay the blame on them.   (put)

The ship is **lying** in the harbor.   (staying)
Land **lying** to the north...   (staying)
The story is **laid** in England.   (set)

Common uses, in which it will be noted that "lay" takes its object; but in the nautical phrases the object is unexpressed:

to lay stress on...to lay out a plan...to lay in supplies
to lay [cars] over (stop over)...to lie over (be deferred)
to lay goods down (deliver), as "goods laid down in Chicago"

NAUTICAL: { to lay forward (to lay oneself forward)
{ to lay to the oars (to lay hand to the oar)

lie in wait, as "He lay in wait."   (NOT: *laid*)
lie low (NOT: *lay* low)
a ship **lies** to the wind (stays toward the wind)
land **lies** (stays or rests)

NOTE. The one phrase, **"the lie of the land,"** is more frequently written **"the lay of the land"**; but "lie" would seem preferable, to conform to other uses, as "see how the land lies."

may   expresses a **strong** possibility.
might   expresses a **weak** or **remote** possibility.

These words are practically interchangeable.   Still there remain distinctions that are observed.

It **may** be true.   (present—a strong possibility)
It **might** be true.   (present or future—a remote possibility)
It **may** (OR: **might**) have been true.
   (a past possibility, which may be strong or weak)
We **may** (OR: **might**) donate something.
   (a present possibility, which may be strong or weak)
The same question **may** (OR: **might**) arise years hence.
   (a future possibility, which may be strong or weak)
This **may** prove to have been an aid.   (a present, strong possibility)
They **might** have seen him.   (a past, weak possibility)
That **may** have encouraged him.   (a past, strong possibility)
It **may** have turned out all right.   (a past, strong possibility)

Wherever a possibility is contrary to fact or is a mere supposition, **might** should be used.

Had they telephoned, they **might** have got the order.
   (contrary to fact—they didn't get the order)
They **might** have subscribed, but they were not asked.
   (contrary to fact—they didn't subscribe)
Even some Roman pagan **might** have realized the plight of ancient
   Rome.   (a supposition)
I think of it as it **might** have been...   (a supposition)
The reader **may** have observed how the story **might** have been written.
   (The first is a strong possibility; the second, a supposition.)
It was something that he himself **might** have said.
   (a supposition—he did not say it)
It looks as if it **might** work out.   (a supposition)

May should be used when **present permission** is implied.   **Might** may be used when **past permission** is implied.

May I do that?   (RATHER THAN: Might I do that?   [subjunctive])
May I have the honor...   (RATHER THAN: Might I have the honor...)

They do not know whether they **may** venture to print that.
(whether they would be permitted to)
Might he stay? he inquired with mild politeness. (a past asking)
He **asked** if he **might** be permitted to use our name. (a past request)

The sequence of tenses should be preserved if there is no other indication for a choice between the words.

They **think** that it **may** be to our advantage.
They **thought** that it **might** be to our advantage.

may *of*
might *of*   **should** *of* ⎞ To use "*of*" for "have" in these verb forms is
must *of*   **would** *of* ⎬ termed "illiterate." Use "may have," "might
could *of*   **ought** to *of* ⎠ have," "should have," etc.

need ⎞ "To" may be omitted after these forms in an idiomatic use,
dare ⎬ usually in **questions** and in **negative** sentences. But if the "to"
     ⎠ is used, the regular verb forms should be used.

Need

IDIOMATIC: No one **need** hesitate about doing that.
REGULAR: No one **needs** to hesitate about doing that.
BUT NOT: No one need *to* hesitate... NOR: No one *needs* hesitate...
IDIOMATIC: A journalist **need not be** told that... OR: does not need **to**
     be... (NOT: *needs* not be NOR: need not *to* be)
     ...unless it is assumed that the layman **need** be warned.
     ...though no notion of time **need** be introduced.
     Need it be mentioned that...? (Does it need to be...?)
     One **need** only glance through the pages...
     It was done sooner than it **need** have been.
OR: It was done sooner than it **needed** to be.
     (BUT NOT: than it need *to* have been)

Dare

IDIOMATIC: He **dare** not sign it.   AND: **Dare** he sign it?
SOMETIMES: He **dares** not sign it.   Does he **dare** sign it?
REGULAR: He **does** not **dare** to sign.   Does he **dare** to sign?
BUT NOT: He **dare** not *to* sign it.   Dare he *to* sign it?
IDIOMATIC: No one **dare** criticize them.   ...if one **dare** do it.
SOMETIMES: No one **dares** criticize them.   ...if one **dares** do it.
REGULAR: No one **dares** to criticize them.   ...if one **dares** to do it.
BUT NOT: No one **dare** *to* criticize them.   ...if one **dare** *to* do it.

needs meaning "of necessity," is an adverb, and its form is invariable.

We must needs inform him...   They needs must have...

ought to should never be preceded by "*had*" or "*hadn't*."
"Ought to" in itself can represent present, past, or future time—it needs no introductory word.

It **ought to** be finished now. (present)
(NOT: It *had* ought to be finished now.)
It **ought to** have been finished yesterday. (past)
(NOT: It *had* ought to have been...
NOR: It ought to' been finished... NOR: ought to *of* been)

85

It **ought to** be finished next week. (future)
  (NOT: It *had* ought to be...)
It **ought** not to be told. (OR: ought not be)
  (NOT: It *hadn't* ought to be told.)
Nothing **ought to** be said about that, ought it? (OR: should it?)
  (NOT: *had* it?—which would mean *"had* it ought?")

"To" should always be used after "ought"—unless "to" is supplied in another verb form; or unless it is understood, as in negative sentences.

NOT: Many people ought and do give generously.
BUT: Many people **ought to** and do give generously.
    They ought and are to have the privilege. (Here "to" is supplied in another verb form.)
    They seem disinclined to do that, but we think they **ought**. ("To" has already been supplied.)

Negative sentences without "to":

Perhaps they ought not be sent.
This use ought not, however, be confused with that.

ought not   is formal.
oughtn't   is colloquial.

He ought to pay for that, ought he not?   (formal)
He ought to pay for that, oughtn't he?   (colloquial)
BUT NOT: He ought to pay for that, *hadn't* he?
    ("Hadn't" should not be used before an implied "ought to," which would make *"hadn't* he ought to?")

prefer...to   is a correct combination.
prefer...rather than   is a correct combination.
prefer...than   is a colloquial shortening of "prefer...rather than."

REGULAR: { We should **prefer** standing pat **to** trying to win.
         { We should **prefer** to stand pat **rather than** to try to win.
COLLOQUIAL: { We should **prefer** standing pat **than** trying to win.
            { We should **prefer** to stand pat **than** try to win.
REGULAR: We should **prefer** dealing with them **rather than** (dealing) with anyone else.
COLLOQUIAL: We should **prefer** dealing with them **than** anyone else.

The expressions after "prefer" and "to" or "rather than" should balance as nearly as possible; that is, if an -ing word has been used after "prefer," an -ing word should follow "to," etc.

NOT: We prefer **to sell** than *buying*.
BUT: We prefer **selling** to buying.
OR: We prefer **to sell** rather than [to] **buy**.

raise   to lift something.
rise   to move upward by itself.
raise, raised, raised, raising   take an object.
  Something must be raised (lifted) by someone or something.
rise, rose, risen, rising   do not take an object.
  Something rises (moves upward) of its own accord.

Uses of "Raise"		Uses of "Rise"	
(Note the Object)		(No Object)	
to raise a voice	to raise money	a voice rises	funds rise
to raise a price	to raise a question	a price rises	a question **arises**

They **raised** the price.   (they lifted or boosted it)
Prices are **raised**.   (by someone)
Prices are **rising**.   (moving upward themselves)
Prices seem to **raise** themselves.   (to lift themselves)
They are going to **raise** wages.   (to lift wages)
Wages will soon **rise**.   (move upward themselves)
The sun **rises**.   (moves upward itself)
The river **rose** several feet.   (moved upward itself)
The temperature **rose** ten degrees.   (moved upward itself)
The sun **raised** the temperature.   (lifted the temperature)
The temperature was **raised** ten degrees.   (lifted by outside force)
Raised bread is baked from dough made to **rise** by leavening.
The mist is **rising** rapidly.   (moving upward itself)

Rise is the noun meaning a self-increase.

a rise in salary	a rise in temperature
a rise of two points in the market	a rise in price

Raise may be used as a noun if it represents that which has been **raised** by some outside force and which did not rise by itself.

price raises (liftings or boostings)   a salary raise
the raise of wages   a raise of an inch (a lifting)
     We expected a rise in salary.   (a self-increase)
     The Government effected a salary raise.   (a lifting or boosting)

Rising and **raising** are both used as nouns.

"Raising" is used to denote the act of something's being raised by some outside force.
"Rising" is used to denote the act of something's moving upward itself.
     We watched the **raising** of the tower.   (raised by someone)
     We watched the **rising** of the sun.   (The sun rose by itself.)
     We witnessed the **rising** of the floods.
     the raising of wages
     the price-raising campaign ⎫raised by people
     the raising of the question ⎭

rise ⎱ These verbs are interchangeable; but "arise," probably because of
arise ⎰ its poetic flavor, has given way to "rise" in most instances.

men rise to the occasion (RATHER THAN: arise)
farmers rise early (RATHER THAN: arise)

Arise is used when "comes up" or "springs up" can be substituted.

a question arises   a debate arose   occasions arise

Arisen is the past participle, not "*arose*."

It is declared to have suddenly arisen.   (NOT: *arose*)

raised ⎰ practically interchangeable as applied to persons.   "Reared" is
reared ⎱ favored in some sections of the United States; "raised" in
others.   "Brought up" may be used to avoid either.

set   to place. } "Set" represents the actual placing down of something;
sit   to rest.   } and "sit" represents the resting or reposing there.

set, set, set, setting   usually take an object.
  Someone must set something.   (place it)
sit, sat, sat, sitting   do not take an object.
  Someone or something sits.   (rests or reposes)
  To remember the forms of the two verbs, associate them with these ideas:
  People themselves sit—sat—have sat—are sitting.   (rest or repose)
  People set things—set things—have set things—are setting things.
    (place things)
  When inanimate objects are said to "sit" or be "sitting," they are really personified.

> The President **sat** there once.   (rested)
> The President **set** the statue there.   (placed)
> Responsibilities **sit** heavy upon him.   (rest)
> He **sets** his responsibilities before his opportunities.   (places)
> ...having a **sitting** for a portrait.   (resting or posing)
> ...the court **sits** tomorrow.   (sits down or convenes)
> ...in a **sitting** room.   (resting room)
> The cowboy **sits** his horse well.   (sits on)
> ...inclined to **sit** (NOT: *set*) out a dance.   (rest)
> The committee expects to finish the business at one **sitting.**   (a session)
> The suggestion did not **sit** well with them.   (rest well)
> **Sit** down and tell me about it.   (rest)
> When I had **sat** (NOT: *set*) down to think...   (rested)
> **Set** a price on it.   (place)
> The sun **sets.**   (places itself below the horizon)
> ...in a rural stage **setting.**   (placement)
> ...goods **set** down in Chicago.   (placed down)
> The men **set** to work on it.   (placed themselves at work)
> **setting-up** exercises...cement **sets** (hardens)...gelatin **sets** (congeals)

Overlapping uses:

> Sit the guest there.   (cause to sit) } OR BETTER: **Seat** the guest there.
> Set the guest there.   (place)   }
> "A **sitting** hen" was supposed to be the proper term, but
> "A **setting** hen" (the farmers' term) is now recognized as correct.

  When inanimate objects are referred to, often some other word than "sit" is more appropriate, although "sit" is not incorrect.

> The building **sits** (USE: stands) on government land.
> BUT: The house **sits** back from the road.
>   (A house may appear to "sit" in its surroundings.)
> That landmark has **sat** (OR: has been) there for years.
> The machinery was **sitting** (OR: resting) on the ground.
> Let the mixture **sit** for an hour.   (OR: stand)
> The table is **set,** but the dishes **sit** (OR: remain) untouched.
> The coat **sits** (OR: fits) well across the shoulders.
>   (The "set" of a coat is colloquial.)

  Likewise, another word is sometimes more appropriate than "set."

> The house was **set** (USE: placed, built, or erected) on government land.

shall
will } The formal rule:

Use **shall** in the first person, **will** in the second and third, to { I shall / we shall / you will / he will / they will } denote simple futurity.

Use **will** in the first person, **shall** in the second and third, { I will / we will / you shall / he shall / they shall } to denote determination or command—or willingness, promise, consent, or choice.

In commands, "will" is often used instead of "shall" to soften the tone, or by way of courtesy, as

> You will then report to the New York Office.
> You will then proceed with the work.

The above general distinctions between "shall" and "will" are still followed. But the finer shades of usage have led to so much confusion that even these broad differences are disappearing.

> **"Unfortunately the distinction in meaning of 'shall' and 'will' is being effaced . . ."**
>
> —Vizetelly, *How to Use English,* p. 539.

NOTE: "Shall" is still widely used to indicate the simple future (first person)—in speeches, letters, newspapers, magazines, and books. But "will" is gaining in this use. "Shall" is still regularly used in legal papers to denote obligation or compulsion (often in all persons), as "It shall be done." In questions, "shall" is now usually confined to queries seeking permission or consent (where "should" could be substituted), as "Shall we sign it?"

should
would } These words follow mainly the simple rule that applies to "shall" and "will." ("Should" is of course used to mean "ought to.")
Some verbs, such as the following, already signify willingness, promise, or choice; therefore only simple futurity need be expressed before them.

I should like to see them.	I should be content to work alone.
I should not care to read it.	I should not mind it, I'm sure.
We should be glad to do it.	We should be willing to sign it.
I should be pleased to comply.	I should prefer not to talk.

"Would" is accordingly used with the second and third persons:

You would like it, I'm sure.	You would not find it difficult.
. . . easier than one would think.	They would be willing to sign.

stay means to remain for a time.
stop means to pause or halt. } "Stop" for "stay" is colloquial.
One "stays" at a hotel, rather than "stops."
One may "stop" in a town on a journey.

> We **stopped** in St. Louis and **stayed** at the Parkland Hotel.
> At what hotel are you **staying**? (COLLOQUIAL: stopping)

89

suffice it to say
OR:
suffice to say
} is a form of the subjunctive, meaning "let it suffice **to** say." Often the "it" is dropped, as

Suffice to say that the matter has been settled.
FOR: Suffice it to say that the matter has been settled.

than comply INSTEAD OF: **than to comply**
but ask **but to ask**
except listen **except to listen**
besides tell **besides to tell**
than complying
than complied

In such sentences as the following, "to" is often not used with verbs after "than," "but," "except," and "besides" —usually when these words are introduced by "do," "did," or "done."

After "than":

USUAL: {
They **do** little more than **comply** with the rules.
They **did** little more than **comply** with the rules.
They **have done** little more than **comply** with the rules.
}

UNUSUAL: {
They **do** little more than **to comply** with the rules.
They **did** little more than **to comply** with the rules.
They **have done** little more than **to comply** with the rules.
}

NOT: {
They **did** little more than *complied* with the rules.
They **have done** little more than *complied* with the rules.
}

BUT: They **have** more than **complied** with the rules.
(Here "have complied" is a single verb form.)

USUAL: They **will do** more than **comply** with the rules.

USUAL: They are **doing** more than **complying** with the rules.
(Here, they are actually "complying," but below they are not.)

IDIOMATIC: ...**doing** that rather than **comply** with the rules.
(Here, they are not "complying"; hence "[to] comply" is used.)

USUAL: It **has done** more than **demonstrate** the value of study and **prove** the value of work.

UNUSUAL: It **has done** more than **to demonstrate** the value of study and **to prove** the value of work.

NOT: It **has done** more than *demonstrated*...and *proved*...

BUT: It **has** more than **demonstrated**...and **proved**...
(Here "has demonstrated and proved" is the full verb form.)

USUAL: Most persons **know** better than **to try** to stop progress.
(NOT: *than try*)

USUAL: ...like one who **perishes** rather than **submit**.
(UNUSUAL: to submit   NOT: *submits*)

After "but," "except," and "besides":

USUAL: They **have done** everything but **ask** advice.
(INSTEAD OF: to ask   NOT: *asked*)

USUAL: He **has done** little except **listen** attentively.
(INSTEAD OF: to listen   NOT: *listened*)

USUAL: It **does** nothing besides **tell** the direction of the current.
(INSTEAD OF: to tell   NOT: *tells*)

to do	OR: **to doing**
to give	**to giving**
to use	**to using**
to work	**to working**
to call	**of calling**

Whether to use an -ing verb form or a plain verb is often a question. Idiomatic usage influences some combinations; therefore, if in doubt about the proper form, test both to see which "sounds right." The idiomatic use should be distinguishable by its familiar sound; if it is not, and one phrase seems to fit as well as the other, choose the -ing form—it is almost always right.

Some idiomatic combinations are:

They had no **hope of succeeding.** (NOT: *to succeed*)
BUT: They had no **desire to succeed.**
They are not **equal to meeting** the demands. (NOT: *to meet*)
BUT: They are not **able to meet** the demands.
They **set** themselves **to performing** the task. (NOT: *to perform*)
BUT: They **set to work** on it.
...every **opportunity of becoming** acquainted. (OR: to become)
AND: ...every **chance to become** acquainted.
...with an **aim to help** rather than **(to) hinder** progress.
OR: ...with an **aim at helping** rather than **hindering** progress.
...**intention to appeal, to wed, to build, to resign,** etc.
...no **intention of going,** allowing, retiring. (OR: to retire)
...has declared his **intention to withdraw** as a delegate.
(NOT: to *withdrawing*)
...**interested in knowing.** (OR: to know)
...take that **way of calling** their attention. (OR: to call)
They should reserve the **right of deciding** in each case.
(OR: to decide)
They should be credited with the **ability to make** their **way.**
(RATHER THAN: for making   NOT: *of making*)
Things that we **remember** long ago **to have** taken delight in.
(OR: having   BUT NOT: *of having*)
...terms that they have been **accustomed to use**   (OR: to using)
We have become so **accustomed to seeing** that in print...
They have not been **accustomed to doing** it in that manner.
...are **used to doing.** (RATHER THAN: are used to do)
...if they will **consent to give** (OR: to giving) aid (or credit, etc.).

see your way clear (Colloquial) { to handle this / to assist us / to do this }   RATHER THAN: { to handling / to assisting / to doing }

try and come	The use of "and" instead of "to" with these verbs is termed "colloquial." Yet some of the combinations are widely used, the word "and" appearing to strengthen the verbs by implying result.
come and see	
look and see	
be sure and tell	

Try and come to some conclusion.
(Means more than "try to come." It means first to try and then actually to come to some conclusion.)
Look and see for yourself if it is...
(Means more than "look to see." It means first to look and then to see or be convinced.)

91

But phrases which really imply but one thought had better be written with "to."

Come to see us. Be sure to tell them.

used to   is the form that means "was accustomed to" (pron. ūzd to; Br. ūst to)
use **to**   is obsolete.

> That firm **used to** pay promptly.   (NOT: *use* to)
> CLUMSY: Didn't they use to pay promptly?
>   FOR: They used to pay promptly, didn't they?
> CLUMSY: We didn't use to do it that way.
>   FOR: We used not to do it that way.   (COLLOQ.: usen't OR: usedn't)
> CLUMSY: We used to *could* see it from here.   (FOR: used to be able to)

would have   Never use this combination for "had," after "if."

> NOT: If they *would have* done that they might have succeeded.
> BUT: If they had done that...   OR: Had they done that...
> NOT: If they *would have* asked, we could have told them.
> BUT: If they had asked...   OR: Had they asked...

TIME EXPRESSED

To bring out the meanings of sentences, select the verb forms that best express the time elements involved.

is   represents an existing fact or condition.
was   represents a past or closed fact or condition. } See note below.

> The message said that thousands **are** starving.
>   (The condition still exists.)
> The message said that thousands **were** starving.
>   (The condition may have been remedied.)
> The lecturer said that Fuji **is** an extinct volcano.
>   ("Is" represents an existing fact—Fuji is still an extinct volcano.)
> It was demonstrated that air **is** composed chiefly of oxygen and nitrogen.
>   (An existing fact—air is always composed of these elements.)
> In the argument they maintained that America **was** less democratic than Europe.   (In the argument they probably said "America is...," but since they did not prove it, it is now a past statement.)

> NOTE: Some writers prefer to maintain the sequence of tenses, and use verbs in the past tense to express existing facts.

> How did you guess that I **was** an American?
>   (RATHER THAN: that I am an American)
> He said his name **was** Stanfield.   (RATHER THAN: is)
> ...but for that ancient sailor who knew that the earth **was** round.

will be   represents a future fact or condition.
is   may also represent a future fact or condition.

> The train is to be sent on a trial run.   (OR: will be)
> The Olympic Games are next year.   (FOR: will be held)
> Tomorrow is Wednesday.   (FOR: will be)
> Next year is presidential election year.   (FOR: will be)
> Christmas is on a Sunday this year.   (FOR: will be)

Although expressions such as the last four and the following are by some considered "colloquial English," they are widely used.

This year he is in Japan, and next year he **goes** to Spain.   (FOR: will go)

has }represent an action which still exists, or the result of which still
have } exists; that is, they carry the action up to the present time.
had   represents a past or closed action.

He **said** that he **had** taken it up with them.   (a past action)
He **says** that he **has** taken it up with them.   (an existing action)
They **returned** last week from Florida, where they **had been**
   spending the winter.
   ("Returned" closes the fact that they were in Florida; therefore
   "had been" is used rather than "have been." Their vacation
   should not continue past their returning.)
They **have been** spending the winter in Florida.
   (The vacation still exists.)
At least he **had** the courage to say what he **thought**.   (past action)
At least he **has** the courage to say what he **thinks**.   (existing
   action)
One who **has** a real claim to fame **would have done** otherwise.
   ("Has" indicates an existing claim to fame.)
At the trial they **swore** that they **had** always given away the
   tickets.   (They swore to what had happened previously.)
NOT: At the trial they **swore** that they *have* always given away the
   tickets.   (They could swear only to what had gone before, not to
   what is still their practice.)

has been   represents an action which still exists, or the result of which
      still exists.

was   represents a past or closed action.

The manager **was** forced to resign.   (past action)
The manager **has been** forced to resign.   (existing action)

to be }
to do } imply the same time as the main verbs or future time.
to have }
to have been }
to have done } imply time before the main verbs.
to have had }

The flyers **were thought to be** near Berlin at six o'clock.
   ("To be" indicates the same time as "were thought.")
The flyers **were thought to have been** near London at noon.
   ("To have been" indicates time prior to "were thought.")
It **would have been** simple **to do** that.
NOT: It **would have been** simple *to have done* that.
   ("To have done" places the action further into the past than
   "would have been.")
NOR: It *would be simple to have done* that.
   ("To have done" places the action before the being simple, which
   is not the meaning.)
NOT: It **has been** pleasant *to have met* you.   (USE: to meet you)
   ("To have met" places the meeting before the being pleasant.)
NOT: We **hoped** *to have completed* the job before the new year.
   (USE: to complete—which places the action after the hoping)

93

NOT: They **would have been** the last *to have admitted* defeat.
(USE: to admit)
NOT: It **would have been** enough *to have told* them that.   (USE: to tell)
NOT: We **intended** *to have shipped* the goods sooner.   (USE: to ship)
NOT: He **said** that he~~had hoped~~ **had hoped** *to have seen* them before that.
("To have seen" places the seeing into the distant past, beyond "had hoped," which is still beyond "said," which is itself in the past.)
USE: He **said** that he **had hoped to see** them before that.

FOUR WAYS OF EXPRESSING TIME:

These changes **seem** to us **to be** for the better.
(all present)
These changes **seemed** to us **to be** for the better.
(all past)
These changes **seem** to us **to have been** for the better.
(The changes that were made in the past now seem or still seem to be for the better.)
These changes **seemed** to us **to have been** for the better.
("To have been" places the time into the distant past, before "seemed" which is itself in the past.)

should have liked
would have liked
These expressions should be followed by the present instead of the past of verbs with "to." (See "to be" and "to have been," above.)

NOT: I **should have liked** *to have seen* it.
BUT: I **should have liked to see** it.
("To have seen" in the first sentence places the seeing in the far past, before the liking, which is itself in the past.)
I **should like to have seen** it.   (has a different meaning)
(This means that the desire or the liking exists now, after the sight or the seeing is past.)
I **should like** very much **to have gone.**
OR: I **should have liked** very much **to go.**
NOT: I know I **would have liked** very much **to have had** a similar guide.
BUT: I know I **should have liked** very much **to have** a similar guide.
NOT: We **should have disliked** *to have been forced* to do that.
BUT: We **should have disliked being forced** to do that.
JUMBLED: I **would have liked to see** you and *talked* about this.
CORRECTED: I **should have liked to see** you and [to] **talk** about this.

being
doing
imply the same time as the main verbs or future time.

having been
having done
imply time before the main verbs.

Even when used as nouns or adjectives, -ing verbs can be governed by time.

There **was** no question of his not **doing** his work.
("Doing" implies that the work was going on at the time the question might have arisen.)
There **was** no question of his not **having done** his work.
("Having done" implies that the work was finished at the time the question might have arisen.)
The writer **was quoted** as **saying** in his article...
("Saying" implies the same time as the quoting.)

The writer **was quoted as having said** in his article...
("Having said" implies time prior to the quoting.)
He, **being told** to report, **refused** to go. (or: having been—if the
refusing occurred after the being told)
NOT: It is true, *being* announced yesterday. (USE: having been)

after having is an idiomatic expression that is commonly used—even
by authorities. Some writers condemn it on the ground
that "after" definitely places the action before the main
verb, and the word "having" is superfluous.

After having talked we decided the issue. (BETTER: After talking)
He was instructed to see the President, **after having had** his company's
views made clear to him. (or: after having his company's views)
He wandered to safety out of the deep woods here today **after having
been** lost for two days. (BETTER: after being lost)

would be
should be } imply the same time as the main verbs or time after the main
could be verbs.

would have been
should have been } imply time before the main verbs.
could have been

It **was** not **thought** that funds **could** so easily **have been obtained.**
(or: could be) ("Could have been" places the obtaining before the
thinking; whereas "could be obtained" would imply the same time as
the thinking, or time after the thinking.)
They **decided** that it **would have been** unwise to do that.
("Would have been" indicates a possible action before the deciding.
"Would be" would indicate action after the deciding.)
We should not have sent the statement if we **had known** that it *would
have embarrassed* them. (USE: would embarrass)
("Would have embarrassed" puts the embarrassing before the
knowing, which is not what is meant.)

shall have been
will have been } indicate action performed before some future time.
They may also indicate action performed before the
present time. But should not be used to indicate
action performed before some past time.

We **shall have received** instructions before then. (future time)
The news **will have been dispatched** by now. (before the present time)
It **will have occurred** to the reader that... (before this time)
The check **would have been paid** before they received our letter.
(NOT: *will* have been)
The check **will have been paid** before they **receive** our letter.
(before a present or future time)

◇◇◇◇◇◇◇◇◇

PROPER RELATION OF TENSES

The verbs in one sentence should be in agreement; that is, they
should present a smooth and logical continuity of time and thought.

The tense (time) of the verb in the main clause **governs the tense** of
other verb forms in the same sentence—unless, occasionally, a dependent
clause is expressing an existing fact.

NOT: Four days after his release from the Navy, he **enlisted** in the Army, joining comrades with whom he *went* to war.
("Went" places the time of going to war with the time of enlisting. USE: had gone to war)

NOT: We saw the wing of the plane **break** and later *dropped* (USE: drop) into the sea. (MEANING: and later we saw it drop)

NOT: It was thought that she might **have fainted** and *fell* from...

BUT: It was thought that she might **have fainted** and **fallen** from...

When nothing is to be gained by shifting from one tense to another, keep the tenses the same.

NOT: The Mayor **said** that as soon as he *learns* the provisions of the bill he **would cooperate** with...

BUT: The Mayor **said** that as soon as he **learned**...he **would**...

OR: The Mayor **says** that as soon as he **learns**...he **will**...

NOT: As one thing **becomes** necessary, another thing *has become* useless.
(USE: becomes...becomes)

NOT: He **thought** he *can* meet his payments tomorrow.

BUT: He **thinks** he **can**...

OR: He **thought** he **could**...

can expresses present or future ability.

could expresses past or future ability.

These verbs should agree with the other verbs in a sentence.

NOT: He **could** do the work if he *will*.

BUT: He **can** do the work if he **will**.

OR: He **could** do it if he **would**.

NOT: He **said** he *can* do it.

BUT: He **says** he **can** do it.

OR: He **said** he **could** do it.

NOT: If I **thought** that he *can* do the work...

BUT: If I **thought** that he **could** do the work...

can have ⎫ The proper one of these verbs should be selected to preserve
could have ⎭ the logical relationship of time in a sentence.

It **can** not **have been** received if they **say** it **has** not. (all present)

It **could** not **have been received** if they **said** it **had** not. (all past)

No one who **has observed** them **can have failed** to note...

No one who **had observed** them **could have failed** to note...

That is an instance in which the display **can have been prompted** only by pride.

...**was** an instance in which the display **could have been prompted**...

should...would ⎫ A past-tense clause usually follows a "should,"
should...will ⎭ "would," or "could" clause, to maintain the sequence of tenses.

But the present tense is sometimes employed in the second clause to give force or reality to the second verb (called **"vivid sequence"**).

We **should** appreciate it if he **would** do that. ⎫
We **shall** appreciate it if he **will** do that. ⎭ (regular sequence of tenses)

We **should** appreciate it if he **will** do that. (vivid sequence)
("Will" brings out the last verb—makes it real or positive of accomplishment.)

96

I **should** not be surprised if he **succeeded.**   (regular sequence)
I **should** not be surprised if he **succeeds.**   (vivid sequence)
If we **could** guess what they **would** do...   (regular sequence)
If we **could** guess what they **will** do...   (vivid sequence)
I **should** be glad to do it provided I **returned** in time. ⎰ (regular
I **shall** be glad to do it provided I **return** in time.   ⎱ sequence)
I **should** be glad to do it provided I **return**...   (vivid sequence)
If there are any further questions you **would** like to take up with me, I
shall be glad to answer them.

❖❖❖❖❖❖❖❖

Principal Parts

Verbs seem constantly to undergo change.   Usage makes one form popular and discards another.   Some quaint old forms show how far we have progressed, or digressed –

snown	*catched*	*awoken*	*washen*	*teached*
ruinate	*foughten*	*growed*	*sitten*	*stang*

The following forms are set down to point out the fluctuations or idiosyncrasies of verbs and to point up the advice:

When in doubt, consult the dictionary.

bankrupt—bankrupted—bankrupted
They have bankrupted the county.   (NOT: have *bankrupt*)
He was bankrupt.   (Here "bankrupt" is an adjective.)
He was bankrupted by the crash.   (Here "was bankrupted" is the verb.)

bear—bore—born or borne
"Born" is used when "given birth to" is the meaning.   ⎱ (See also
"Borne" is used when "carried" or "endured" is meant. ⎰   p. 191.)

beat—beat—beaten or (colloquial) beat
COLLOQUIAL: It can't be beat.   FOR: It can't be beaten.

begin—began—begun
It began to look promising.   (NOT: *begun*, which is archaic)
It has begun...   (NOT: has *began*)   Begun in 1954, it represents...

bet—bet or betted—bet or betted
They bet on the race and lost.   ...even time can be betted away.

bid—bade—bidden or bid   (to command; to address)
They were bidden to come.   The general bade them stay.
We try to do as we are bid.   ...guests were bid farewell.
"Bade" is pronounced băd, not băde.

bid—bid—bid   (to make an offer)
But they bid above us last week.   Twenty dollars was bid.
We might as well have bid six spades.

bite—bit—bitten or (colloquial) bit
It was bitten by the frost.   COLLOQUIAL: He has bit the dust.

bless—blessed or blest—blessed or blest
"Blessed" (the verb) is pronounced blĕst.
"Blessed" (the adjective) is pronounced blĕs′ĕd, as "the blessed day."

97

blow—blew—blown
"Blowed" is considered "dialectal."
The storm has blown several buildings down. (NOT: *has blowed*)

break—broke—broken
"It was broke" is obsolete or archaic.
  USE: It was broken... It got broken..., etc.

broadcast—broadcast (or -ed)—broadcast (or -ed)
"Broadcast" is more commonly used for the past than "broadcasted"—although either is correct—as "The news was broadcast yesterday."

build—built—built
"Builded" is archaic or poetic.

burst—burst—burst
"Bursted" is dialectal, as "The keg had bursted." (FOR: had burst)
"Bust" or *"busted"* is considered "inelegant," or slang.

buy—bought—bought
"Boughten" is archaic as the past participle of "buy," as "I have *boughten* a suit." But it is still used colloquially as an adjective, as "boughten cake."

choose—chose—chosen
Guard against interchanging "choose" and "chose." (chōōz; chōz)
Buy whichever you choose. We chose three. It was chosen by all.

climb—climbed—climbed
Never, of course, say *"clum,"* as "had *clum.*"

cling—clung—clung
They clung (OR: have clung) to their beliefs.

copyright—copyrighted—copyrighted
In the copyright notices, as "Copyright, 1956, by...," the owner is simply declaring his claim of copyright—the right to produce copies, etc.—which claim he may subsequently have registered in the Copyright Office ("copyrighted").

dig—dug—dug
"Digged" is colloquial.

dive—dived or dove—dived
"Dove" is colloquial in the United States, especially in sports.
Use "dived into the water"; or if informal "dove in."

drag—dragged—dragged
Never use *"drug"* for the past of "drag," as "The play *drug.*"
"Drug" is a verb in its own right, meaning to stupefy with drugs.

drink—drank—drunk
Do not attempt to avoid "has drunk," "have drunk," and "had drunk"; they are the only correct forms. "Has *drank,*" "have *drank,*" and "had *drank,*" are incorrect.
  NOT: He had not *drank* any of it. BUT: He had not drunk any of it.
"Drunken" is used as an adjective, as "a drunken stupor."

drown—drowned—drowned
Note that "drowned" is pronounced "dround," not *"drown-ded."*

fit—fitted or fit—fitted
It fitted well. (OR: fit)

flee—fled—fled
Many fled (NOT: *flew*) before the oncoming armies.

flow—flowed—flowed
NOT: The mud had *flown* down and covered the fields.
BUT: The mud had flowed down...
"Flown" is the past participle of "fly"—**fly, flew, flown.**

forbid—forbade—forbidden
"Have forbid" is archaic; use "have forbidden."
"Forbade" is pronounced fôr-bǎd´, not *-bāde*.

forecast—forecast—forecast
"Forecasted" is considered awkward, although it is not incorrect.

forget—forgot—forgotten or forgot
"Have forgot" may be used; many prefer the better sounding "have forgotten."

forsake—forsook—forsaken
He forsook (OR: has forsaken) his benefactors.

get—got—got or gotten
"Gotten" appears to be gaining favor in the United States, though it is scarcely used in England, except in such phrases as "ill-gotten," or "the rate per ton gotten."
A British sentence: That invention should be got rid of.
"Gotten" is sometimes used as a modifier, as
The amount of money gotten back was small.
Performances gotten up by amateurs are usually...
"Gotten" is often superfluous, as
The oil (gotten) from that field tests high.
The leases (gotten) on that timberland are not...

hang—hung—hung and **hang—hanged—hanged**
"Hanged" is used in referring to death by hanging, as
The prisoner is to be hanged.
"Hung" is used in all other instances.

hide—hid—hidden or hid
"Have hid" is commonly used.

hyphen, hyphenate, or **hyphenize** may be used as the verb; but
hyphen—hyphened—hyphened—is to be preferred because it is shorter.

lead—led—led
Note that the past forms are spelled "led" and not "*lead*," as is sometimes seen, the writers evidently thinking of "read."

light—lighted or lit—lighted or lit
For "started a light," "lighted" is usually preferred to "lit."

mow—mowed—mowed or mown
They were mowed (OR mown) down.
"Mown" is used as the adjective, not "*mowed*," as "mown weeds."

oversee—oversaw—overseen
He oversaw the entire job. He has overseen many like projects.

plead—pleaded—pleaded
"Plead" and "pled" as the past forms are colloquial, as "All pled guilty."

prove—proved—proved or proven
"Proven" is rapidly coming into use again, especially in legal phrases, as "not proven." It is also used as an adjective, as "proven land," "proven facts." And as an adverb, as "a provenly successful policy." (NOT: *provedly*)
CORRECT: It has sometimes proven true that... (OR: proved true)

99

ring—rang—rung
"Rang" is preferable to "rung" for the past tense.
He rang the bell.   He has rung the bell.   (NEVER: has *rang*)

run—ran—run
We ran into a thick fog.   (DIALECTAL: run into)
"Had run" is correct, though some avoid it and waver along with "had *ran*."

saw—sawed—sawed or sawn
The board has been sawed in two.   (RATHER THAN: has been sawn)
Both "sawn" and "sawed" are adjectives, as "the sawn strip," "sawed lumber."

shake—shook—shaken
"Shaked" is dialectal, as "Houses shaked in the tremor."
It shook like a leaf.   They were shaken up.   (NOT: *shook up*)

shape—shaped—shaped
"*Shapen*" is archaic, except in "well-shapen," "ill-shapen," etc.

shine—shone—shone
"Shined" is archaic in any sense but "to polish," as shoes or a car.

show—showed—shown or (less commonly) showed
They had shown that they understood it.   (RATHER THAN: had showed)

shrink—shrank or (colloquial) shrunk—shrunk
"It shrank" and "It has shrunk" are usual.
COLLOQUIAL: It shrunk.   AND: It has shrunken.
"Shrunken" is used as an adjective, as "shrunken goods."

sing—sang—sung
"Sang" is preferable to "sung" for the past tense.
They sang his praises.   (RATHER THAN: sung)
They have sung their swan song.

sink—sank—sunk
"Sank" is preferable to "sunk" for the past tense.
It sank into the sand.   It has sunk down.   (NOT: has *sunken*)
"Sunken" is used as an adjective, as "a sunken grave."

slay—slew—slain
NOT: They could have *slayed* him.   BUT: They could have slain him.
NOT: He *slayed* the thought.   BUT: He slew the thought.

slide—slid—slid or slidden
It had slid past.   (RATHER THAN: had slidden)

sneak—sneaked—sneaked
"Snuck" is dialectal.

sow—sowed—sown or sowed
They have sown the crops.   (RATHER THAN: have sowed)

speak—spoke—spoken
He has spoken about that.   (NOT: has *spoke*, which is archaic)

spin—spun—spun
"*Span*" is an older form.   "*Spinned*" is not a recognized form.

spring—sprang—sprung
"Sprang" is preferable to "sprung" for the past tense.
They sprang a surprise.   (RATHER THAN: sprung)

100

sting—stung—stung
"*Stang*" is archaic.   USE: It stung.   It has stung.

stride—strode—stridden
"*Strid*" is, of course, obsolete.
After they, like soldiers, had stridden past.

strike—struck—struck or stricken
"Stricken" is used in court phrases, and when meaning "struck by misfortune."
"Struck" is used elsewhere.
    LEGAL: It shall be stricken from the record.
    SPECIAL: They were stricken with calamity.
    COMMON: That has been struck out.

string—strung—strung
"Stringed" is rare and used only as an adjective, as "stringed instruments."

strive—strove or strived—striven or strived
He strove for recognition.   Many have striven for that goal.

swell—swelled—swollen or swelled
The funds have swollen.   (OR: have swelled   NEVER: *swole*)

swim—swam—swum
Things swam by us.   (DIALECTAL: swum)
Never use "had *swam*" for "had swum" as in the following line from a newspaper
story: "He had *swam* out to save his ten-year-old brother."

swing—swung—swung
"*Swang*" is archaic and dialectal.
It swung past them.   (NOT: *swang*)   It has swung into a new cycle.

thrive—thrived or throve—thrived or thriven
They thrived on it.   (OR: throve)
They have thrived on it.   (OR: have thriven)

throw—threw—thrown (never "*throwed*")
He threw a curve.   It was thrown from a plane.

tread—trod—trodden or trod
The past tense "trod" should not be used for the present "tread."
    Today sandaled friars tread the streets.   ...where padres have trodden.
    He is now in New York treading the boards.   (acting on the stage)

wake—woke or waked—waked or (dialectal) woken
waken—wakened—wakened
awake—awoke or awaked—awaked or (rarely) awoke
awaken—awakened—awakened
"Wake" and "waken" usually apply to physical rousing from slumber.
"Awake" and "awaken" usually apply to mental awakening.
"Awake" is the adjective, as "They are awake to the possibilities."

weave—wove or (rarely) weaved—woven
They wove cloth.   It was woven.   The car weaved through traffic.
...proud of having woven enough wool to make a blanket.   (NOT:
weaved)

worsen—worsened—worsened
A useful verb, as "The storm worsened."   "Conditions are worsening."

wring—wrung—wrung
"Wringed" is very rare; and "*wrang*" is obsolete.
Things are wrung dry.

101

Wrong Forms Used as Modifiers. A common mistake in the use of verbs is the selection of the wrong form as the modifier of a noun.

TEST: Substitute a full clause as a modifier.

...like a race run (NOT: *ran*) against time.
(like a race **that is run** against time)
...followed by a song sung (NOT: *sang*) by the audience.
(a song **that was sung** by the audience)
They were poisoned by water drunk from a well.   (NOT: *drank*)
(by water **that was drunk** from a well)
The new study, begun last year, is to be continued.   (NOT: *began*)
(study, **which was begun** last year)

SUBJUNCTIVES

It is admitted that the subjunctive mood is dying. Its last stand is in the use of the two verbs "be" and "were."

"Subjunctives are nearly dead..."
—Fowler, *A Dictionary of Modern English Usage*, p. 67.

The reason for the survival of a few forms of the subjunctive is that they allow the writer or speaker to imply that what he is saying is not a fact, or that he does not believe it is a fact. Ordinary verb forms refer to facts or assumed facts.

be   indicates uncertainty.
were   indicates unreality.
is
was }indicate reality.

The subjunctive "be" is properly used to express uncertainty or doubt, although many writers prefer "may be," "might be," "should be," etc. (See also Subjunctives in "That" Clauses, p. 104.)

UNCERTAINTY:
If this **be** treason, make the most of it!
(If this might be considered treason..., but the speaker does not believe that it is.)
Though its meaning **be** beyond us, we can still...   (the meaning may be beyond us)
...unless they **be** known to live. (may be known)

Modern usage is rapidly discarding the subjunctive "be" where it does not imply doubt or uncertainty but really means "is" or "are."

If that **be** the case, most of our efforts are useless. (BETTER: is)
...whether the methods used **be** direct or indirect.
Though there **be** no reason, still it is done. (BETTER: is)

**"...there is no question that the 'prim and pompous be' is
rapidly passing out of use, together with all similar forms."**
—Ives, *Text, Type, and Style: A Compendium of Atlantic
Usage*, p. 268.

The subjunctive "were"—the most used of surviving subjunctives— is properly employed to express an imaginary state (present or future) that is contrary to fact, as in a supposition or wish. "Were" should be complemented by other past forms, such as "should" and "would."

UNREALITY:
> If that **were** true, we might..
> (The "were" indicates plainly that it is not true.)
> If I **were** rich, nothing could...
> ("Were" indicates that I am not rich.)
> If I **were** he, I should...
> (Purely imaginary, I cannot be he.)
> If it **were** not for the fact that it is overdue, we should...
> (an imaginary condition outside the fact)
> If that **were** the end of the matter, it would...
> (Imaginary—it is not the end.)
> I wish it **were** possible.
> It would be impossible, even **were** it desirable, to...
> ...just **suppose** this city **were** to be destroyed.
> **Though** that **were** so, it would not help.
> **Were** it not for that, we should be glad to comply.
> **Were** such a prize offered me, I confess I would think...
> **Unless I were** destitute, I believe I would turn it down.
> No person would use those methods **unless** he **were** dealing with experts.

The subjunctive "were" is not often used in referring to **past time** (it usually refers to present or future time). **"Was"** or **"had been"** may be used to express unreality in the past.

> It seemed as if it **was** winter.
> If it **had been** (NOT: *were*) raining when they took off, they would have had a hard time of it. (an imaginary condition in the past)
> If it **was** raining when they took off, they must have had a hard time. (The writer assumes a past fact.)
> If it **were** raining today, they could... (a present imaginary condition)

Assumed Facts. When a writer assumes a fact, "is" or "was" should be used to express it. In such suppositions "if" is sometimes almost equal to "when." (Note that a writer may treat a supposition as a fact and base his conclusions thereon without knowing the actual truth or untruth of the situation.)

REALITY:
> If that **is** true, why do we ponder it? (NOT: *be*)
> (The writer assumes or has been told it is true.)
> If he **is** rich, why did he not contribute? (NOT: *were*)
> (The writer assumes or knows that he is rich.)
> If it **was** as you say, he should have been told.
> (Assuming it was true, he ought to have been told.)
> If it **was** not for the reason you mention, what was the reason?
> If the company **was** solvent, why did it fail?
> They were still necessary if the business **was** to maintain...
> So they compromised, believing if that **was** done the thing would die of itself.
> The occasion on which it was done (if it really **was** done)...
> He did not know of any cause, unless it **was** human folly.
> He threatened to leave if this request **was** not granted.
> They asked him if he **was** aware of the offense.
> The mistake looks almost as if it **was** due to avoidance of an imagined danger.

103

Subjunctives in "That" Clauses. In the expression of commands, orders, demands, etc., often verbs are used without an introductory "should" or "shall"—and are considered subjunctive.

> REGULAR: It is important that he should go.
> SUBJUNCTIVE: It is important that he go.

This kind of subjunctive occurs usually in "that" clauses introduced by such expressions as

ask that	rule that	demand that	is necessary that
require that	move that	insist that	is essential that

TEST: Simply insert "should" or "shall" before the verb in the "that" clause.

It is necessary that **one of us remain.** (should remain)
We must ask that **he attend** to business. (should attend)
To be accurate requires that **one make** use of... (should make)
...on the condition that **someone** with experience **draft** the bill. (should draft)
They demand that **industry increase** the number of... (shall increase)
It is essential that **he do** this. (should do)
We move that **he be** nominated. (shall be)
The Court rules that **he be** awarded... (shall be)
It is necessary that exact **figures be** used. (should be)
We have repeatedly urged that **this be** done. (should be)
They were afraid to announce it, lest **it fail.** (lest it should fail)
Lest tomorrow's emergency **cancel** today's and we **be** caught...

Note that "remains," "attends," "makes," etc., would not be appropriate in these sentences.

as if
as though ⟩ Since these interchangeable introductory words always imply condition, past conditional verb forms are used after them rather than verbs in the present tense.

It looks **as if** it **would** (OR: might) rain. (COLLOQ.: will, or may, rain)
It seems **as if** a new courage **had been born** (COLLOQ.: has been) that **would** (COLLOQ.: will) save the race.
It looks **as if** he **were** going to win. (COLLOQ.: is)
It looked **as if** he **was** going to lose. (OR: were)
It appears **as if** he **knew** it. (COLLOQ.: knows)
They feel as **though** the barrier **were** (COLLOQ.: is) about to lift.
As though they **didn't** care. (COLLOQ.: don't)

Mixed Constructions. Do not mix a subjunctive and a regular verb in a combined construction. Two verbs with the same subject must both be subjunctive or both regular.

> MIXED: If that **be done** and *turns* out badly, we shall see...
> ALL SUBJUNCTIVE: If that **be done** and **turn** out badly...
> ALL REGULAR: If that **is** done and **turns** out badly...

NOTE: The **past subjunctive "were,"** although referring to present or future time, should be complemented by other **past forms,** such as "should" and "would."

> NOT: If that **were** done, it is highly probable that further cancellations *will* take place, so that we *may* be...
> BUT: If that **were** done, it **is** (OR: **would be**) highly probable that further cancellations **would** take place, so that we **might** be...

NOT: Suppose the customer **were** a corporation, then your first diagram *looks* like this.   (USE: would look)
NOT: If this cushioning **were** not installed, whenever the lever *returns*, it *will* pound...   (USE: returned...would pound)

General Guide for Subjunctives. As a closing remark on subjunctives: Whenever a sentence offers a puzzle regarding the use of the subjunctive "were" or "be," or the regular verb "was" or "is," choose the regular verb and dismiss the subjunctive.

They swore that they would not deviate from their policy in the event that any agreement reached at Geneva **were** thereafter broken.
(OR: was   OR: should be)
There were implied threats that their delegates would walk out unless action **were** (OR: was) taken at once.
He said that any president should be impeached if he failed to act instantly after his country *were* attacked.   (USE: was)
If it **were** spring and I *was* young again, I should start...   (USE: were)
Assuming one of us **were** (OR: was) to tackle the job and it proved too much...   (OR: Assuming one of us tackled the job...)
No trader would defy the law if he knew he **were** (OR: was) liable to...
I wish I **were** experienced in that work.   (COLLOQUIAL: was)
("Was" after "I wish" is considered "established usage.")
If this **be** (USE: is) true, the balancing of the books will be facilitated.
Unless that **were** (OR: is   OR: was   OR: has been) done on all jobs, they should not expect it here.
(Here, four different meanings can be expressed; and the **exact** meaning must decide the choice of the verb.)

SPLIT INFINITIVES

"Splitting an infinitive" is simply placing a word, or several words, between "to" and its verb.   This is considered awkward.

SPLIT INFINITIVES	SIMPLE INFINITIVES
to harshly criticize	to criticize
to steadily maintain	to maintain
to further hope	to hope
to quickly comprehend	to comprehend
to painstakingly prepare	to prepare
to never tell	to tell
to sometimes hear	to hear
to often see	to see
to never even think	to think
to thus permit	to permit
to so desire	to desire

Although there is much prejudice against the split infinitive, it is not wholly incorrect and has been used by good writers of all times.

> **"The 'split' infinitive has taken such hold upon the consciences of journalists that, instead of warning the novice against splitting his infinitives, we must warn him against the curious superstition that the splitting or not splitting makes the difference between a good and a bad writer."**
> **—Fowler, *The King's English*, 3d Ed., p. 329.**

105

The commonly suggested remedy is to remove the intervening word and place it before "to" or after the verb, as

| so to arrange the work | TO AVOID: | to so arrange |
| to prepare carefully | | to carefully prepare |

It is impossible **fully to satisfy** everyone.
OR: It is impossible **to satisfy** everyone **fully.**

However, some split infinitives are to be preferred to any rearrangements that suggest stiffness, or permit vagueness or ambiguity.

They intend **to partially do away** with ceremonies.
BETTER THAN: They intend partially to do away with ceremonies.
OR: They intend to do away with ceremonies partially.
He agreed **to personally supervise** the group employed.
BETTER THAN: He agreed personally to supervise the group employed.
OR: He agreed to supervise personally the group employed.
...if they want **to so regulate** activities.
BETTER THAN: ...if they want so to regulate activities.
Even now measures **to severely restrict** racing are...
BETTER THAN: Even now measures severely to restrict racing are...
They are planning **to vigorously protest** hasty action.
BETTER THAN: They are planning vigorously to protest hasty action.
OR: They are planning to protest hasty action vigorously.

Note this distinction:

" 'To really understand' is a split infinitive;
'to really be understood' is a split infinitive;
'to be really understood' is not one;
the havoc that is played with much well-intentioned writing by
failure to grasp that distinction is incredible."
—Fowler, *A Dictionary of Modern English Usage*, p. 558.

to readily observe ⎫
to readily be observed ⎪
to readily have observed ⎬ are split infinitives.
to readily have been observed ⎭

to be readily observed ⎫
to have readily observed ⎪
to have readily been observed ⎬ are not split infinitives.
to have been readily observed ⎭

The simple infinitives above are:

| to observe | to be | to have |

The completed infinitives are:

| to be observed | to have observed | to have been observed |

But the splitting takes place in the simple infinitive, not in any combination of the verbs that complete the simple infinitive.

Two sentences used by authorities:

It is still **to be so classed** as to...
They are liable **to be carelessly combined.**

Observe, too, that an -ing word following "to" is a noun form; and no splitting of an infinitive is involved in such constructions as

> They came nearest to really solving the problem by admitting that it did not matter.

❧❧❧❧❧❧❧❧

DOUBLE NEGATIVES

Double negatives are often incurred when the negative implication of certain words is overlooked. When one negative intentionally cancels another, a subdued affirmative is the result —as "not uncommon."

but that   means "that...not" in some questions and negative sentences. (Ordinarily it means "except that.")

but what   is colloquial when used for "but that." (Ordinarily it means "but that which.")

Common uses:
> There is no question **but that** he will sign.   (OFTEN: no question that)
>   (MEANING: There is no question **that** he will **not** sign.)
> We have no fear **but that** they will pay.   (that they will not pay)
> There is no thought **but that** he will accept.
> We don't know **but that** that's right.
> We have had no word **but that** they are coming.
>   (MEANING: except that OR: **that** they are **not** coming)
> We don't know **but what** we can arrange it.   (colloquial)
>   (MEANING: We don't know **that** we cannot arrange it.)
> They do nothing **but what** they care to.   (but that which)

Double negative:
> Who can tell **but that** this might *not* prove a boomerang?
>   (MEANING: **that** this might not *not* prove)
> RIGHT: Who can tell **but that** this might prove a boomerang?
>   (MEANING: **that** this might **not** prove)

not but what   is colloquial and should be avoided in favor of "not but that." A double negative is often formed with this construction.

> DOUBLE NEGATIVE: Not but what we can *not* do it if we tried.
>   RIGHT: Not **but that** we could do it if we tried.
>   (MEANING: Not **that** we could **not** do it...)

but   doubles the negative in some sentences because of its meaning of "only" (in the sense of "no more than").

> NOT: There *weren't* but four left.
> FOR: There were but four left.
> NOT: They *hadn't* but two orders last week.
> FOR: They had but two orders last week.
> NOT: It *won't* take but a second.
> FOR: It will take but a second.   OR: It won't take a second.
> NOT: We *couldn't* see but a few feet ahead of us.
> FOR: We could see but a few feet ahead of us.
> NOT: One *doesn't* have to take but half a glance at it to see...
> FOR: One has to take but half a glance at it to see...

107

NOT: I *never* saw him but once.   (OMIT: never)
NOT: ...but we *can't* live but once.   (USE: can live only once)

"But," with its meaning of "except," may of course be used **after** negatives, as

Nobody but him went.   (except him)
We have none but that.   (except that)

but only   In some sentences, "but" is a duplication of "only."

NOT: We have *but* only two left.
FOR: We have only two left.   OR: We have but two left.

"But only" is sometimes necessary—when "but" is a connective.

They will sometimes applaud, **but only** when extremely pleased.
...not alike in their entirety, **but only** in certain particulars.

can but ask   means "can only..."
cannot but ask   means "can do nothing except..."
cannot help asking   means "cannot avoid..."
cannot help but ask   is colloquial or idiomatic, but is giving way to the shorter and better "cannot help asking."

Ordinary uses:
We **can but** ask them.   (MEANS: We can only ask them.)
We **cannot but** ask them.   (MEANS: We can do nothing except ask...)
We **cannot help** asking them.   (MEANS: We cannot avoid asking...)

Colloquial or idiomatic (and practically a double negative):
We cannot help but ask them.
(MEANS: We cannot avoid not asking them.)
BETTER: We **cannot help asking** them.

Mixed:
No one can help *believe* the next two years will...
(FOR: No one **can help believing**...)
We cannot help *make* the suggestion that...   (FOR: **cannot help making**)
Governments of the great powers **cannot** *but* **fail** to heed the voices of the people.   (OMIT: but)

doubt that   is usually used with negative statements, or questions.
doubt whether or **if**   is usually used with affirmative statements.
doubt but   }is a passing idiom, meaning "doubt that...not"—
doubt but that}   wherein "doubt" has the meaning of "question."
doubt *but what*   is colloquial for "doubt that."

I **doubt whether** (OR: if) it is true.   (affirmative statement)
Who can **doubt that** it is true?   (question)
I do **not doubt that** it is true.   (negative statement)
There is **no doubt that** it is true.   (negative statement)
There is little **doubt but that** it is true.   (waning idiom)
There is little **doubt that** it is true.   (approved usage)
We don't think there's a **doubt** in the world **that** you'll like it.

The reason for the growing avoidance of "but that" (meaning "that...not") after "doubt" is that "doubt" itself conveys a negative impression of uncertainty or indecision. The statement "I **doubt** | that you will like it" means "I am uncertain whether you will like it." Consequently, "I do **not doubt** | that you will like it" means "I am certain that you will like it."

hardly) These words contrive to form double negatives because of
scarcely) their negative implication of "not quite."
The simple double negatives are:

> We *haven't* hardly enough time.
> (WOULD MEAN: We haven't not quite enough...)
> RIGHT: We have hardly enough **time.**
> I *can't* hardly believe it. (MEANS: I can't not quite...)
> RIGHT: I can hardly believe it.
> That *doesn't* seem scarcely enough.
> RIGHT: That seems scarcely enough.

The more concealed forms are:

> *Nothing* in the world scarcely is ever found without search.
> FOR: Scarcely anything in the world is ever found...
> *No one* in our organization hardly would agree to that.
> FOR: Hardly anyone in our organization...
> After twenty years scarcely *nothing* remains.
> FOR: After twenty years scarcely anything remains.
> They seem to succeed without *hardly* trying.
> FOR: They seem to succeed almost without trying.
> It was unnecessary to say *scarcely* anything about it.
> FOR: It was unnecessary to say anything much... (OR: much at all)
> OR: It was necessary to say scarcely anything about it.

not is used in simple questions, with the suggestion of a positive rather than a negative answer.

> That is right, is it not?   May we not hear from you?
> **Is it not true** that they have failed?
> ("Is it not true?" is the simple question.)

But if "not" appears in a clause attached to the simple question, it retains its negative force.

> Is it true **that they have not failed?**

Disregard of this distinction causes many double negatives.

> Is it **untrue** that they have *not* failed?
> (MEANS: Is it untrue that they have succeeded?)
> RIGHT: **Is it not untrue** that they have failed?
> Who can **deny** that they have *not* tried?
> (MEANS: Who can deny that they have shirked?)
> RIGHT: Who can deny that they have tried?
> How can they **refuse to admit** that aviation has *not* succeeded?
> (that aviation has failed?)
> RIGHT: How can they refuse to admit that aviation has succeeded?

Superfluous "nots":

> We wouldn't be surprised if they *didn't* bring it along.
> (MEANS: We shouldn't be surprised if they left it.)

109

RIGHT: We shouldn't be surprised if they brought it along.

It wouldn't surprise us if they *hadn't* made a fortune.

RIGHT: It wouldn't surprise us if they had made a fortune.

It depends upon whether *or not* they can or cannot see it.

RIGHT: It depends upon whether they can or cannot see it.

OR: It depends upon whether or not they can see it.

At present we are trying to figure how much may *not* be charged to overhead.

RIGHT: ...how much may be charged to overhead. (which is the intended meaning, not how much is not chargeable)

We must look to our future, lest we be *not* enslaved.

RIGHT: We must look to our future, lest we be enslaved.

Nothing is too trivial *not* to be included.

RIGHT: Nothing is too trivial to be included.

...if they are too inhuman *not* to care. (OMIT: *not*)

They will be unwilling to compromise, we *don't* believe.

RIGHT: They will be unwilling to compromise, we believe.

Let us *not* end this unpleasant controversy.

(perhaps intended as a question)

RIGHT: Let us end this unpleasant controversy.

OR: Should we not end this unpleasant controversy?

only conflicts with the negative in some sentences.

They will *not* work only when they are forced to.

RIGHT: They will work only when they are forced to.

They do *not* want to sell, only a part of it.

RIGHT: They want to sell only a part of it.

That can*not* be understood only by scientists.

RIGHT: That can be understood only by scientists.

In some sentences "only" may be used in a second clause, after a negative, if certain words carry over to give it support.

They cannot realize that they have grown old, only that time has passed. (they can realize only that time has passed)

Miscellaneous double negatives:

No American city is less *un*blurred by hurry.

(USE: is more unblurred   OR: is less blurred)

The Western World would sorely *miss* the loss of the oil.

(USE: feel the loss   OR: miss the oil)

...must not try to conceal faults by concealing evidence that they *never* existed. (USE: ever)

(Headline) Teen-Agers' *Lack of* Ethics Conspicuous by Absence.

(OMIT: *Lack of*)

The Army *nor* any other Government agency should **never** be called upon to... (USE: The Army or any other...   OR BETTER: Neither the Army nor any other Government agency should ever...)

Irregardless of that, let us proceed. (USE: Regardless)

Such a course would give nothing to *no one*. (USE: nothing to anyone)

There *aren't* no more. (FOR: are no more   OR: aren't any more)

Stocks couldn't then move *neither* up or down. (USE: either)

She is not, in a word, brittle; and this is an engaging thing for a successful actress *not* to be. (Omit the last "*not*")

Not only shall we never *not* invoke war, but we shall try...

(Omit the second "*not*")

...for which we make—*nor* need to make—no apology. (USE: or)

Several "nots" may appear in close formation, if the writer knows his way about when using them.

> The distinction is not only not useless, but not even arbitrary.
> —From a Fowler sentence.

And seeming double negatives appear in literature:

> If this be error and upon me proved,
> I never writ, **nor no** man ever loved.—Shakespeare.

SENTENCES

Logical ideas are the first step toward clear writing.

Simple words are the next.

Clean sentence construction is the next.

Singulars and Plurals Mixed. Singulars and plurals may be logically used in the same sentence; but often there is an indiscriminate mixing of singulars and plurals that leads to ambiguity.

Therefore, the best practice is to make all singulars conform to singulars and all plurals to plurals where nothing is to be gained by writing them otherwise.

ILLOGICAL: Write the names (pl.) on the backs (pl.) of each receipt (sing.).
("Each receipt" could not have "backs.")

BETTER: Write the **name** on the **back** of **each receipt.** (specific)

OR: Write the **names** on the **backs** of **all receipts.** (general)

ILLOGICAL: When meeting **a person,** shake hands if **they** extend **their hand.**

BETTER: When meeting **a person,** shake hands if **he extends his hand.**

OR: When meeting **people,** shake hands if **they extend their hands.**

ILLOGICAL: I was pleased to find **a letter** from both you and him.

BETTER: I was pleased to find letters...

ILLOGICAL: Above the skyline rose the **top** of the Flagler and Southern buildings. (Until the reader reaches "buildings" he believes it one building.)

BETTER: Above the skyline rose the tops...

ILLOGICAL: All of them had their heads buried in **a book.**

BETTER: All of them had their heads buried in books.

ILLOGICAL: Both men and women must be 18 years of age before they can become a registered **voter.** (BETTER: registered voters)

ILLOGICAL: Both of them will receive **a silver dollar.**

BETTER: Both of them will receive silver dollars.

OR: Each of them will receive a silver dollar.

ILLOGICAL: Those **officers** wear **a rating badge** on **their arm.**

BETTER: Those officers wear rating badges on their arms.

OR: Those officers wear a rating badge on their arms. (if it is the same kind of badge)

ILLOGICAL: Today men send their **boy** to college that he may become "**a gentleman.**"

BETTER: Today men send their boys to college that they may become "gentlemen."

OR: Today a man sends his boy to college that he may become "a gentleman."

111

Singulars and plurals are sometimes idiomatically mixed, when the singular represents a class of things. (See Abstract Collectives, p. 41.)

IDIOMATIC: If they are treated as if they were **beginners,** it is only because their writings are available and those of the **beginner** are not.
REGULAR: . . .and those of the beginners are not.

Omitted Words. Omitted words and supposedly understood words are the cause of much controversy regarding grammatical construction.

Commercial usage countenances certain omissions, for the sake of brevity, if the omitted words can be readily understood. But in formal writings most missing words should be supplied.

NOT: They are as good, if not better, than these.
BUT: They are as good as, if not better than, these.
OR: They are as good as these, if not better.
NOT: They had no knowledge or faith in the proposition.
BUT: They had no knowledge of, or faith in, the proposition.
NOT: The conference is being watched by shipping men with as much interest, or possibly more, than that of any other group.
BUT: . . .with as much interest as, or possibly more than, that of. . .
NOT: They arrange prices for the benefit of the industry and the detriment of the consumer.
BUT: . . .for the benefit of the industry and to the detriment of. . .

Small words, such as "the," "a," "an," "our," and "some," should be repeated wherever necessary for definiteness.

The vice president and secretary signed for the firm.
(This could mean one officer.)
The vice president and the secretary signed for the firm. (two officers)
. . .a blue and black car (one car). . .a blue and a black car (two cars)

Carry-Over Constructions. When a construction carries over in a sentence and depends on a later word for completion, it should agree with the form of the word expressed. A word should be mentioned before any reconstruction of it is assumed.

FAULTY: It was in one of the late, if not the latest, **editions.**
(Testing each phrase to see if it carries over: . . .one of the late editions. . .if not the latest editions?)
REARRANGEMENT: It was in one of the late editions, if not the latest.
(Here "edition" can be understood after "latest," because "editions" has been mentioned before.)
FAULTY: They always have and still **pay** all their own expenses.
(Testing each verb to see if it carries over: . . . always have pay?. . .and still pay)
BETTER: They always have paid and still pay all their. . .
FAULTY: No one has or ever will **paint** such a living thing. (No one has paint. . .?)
BETTER: No one has painted, or ever will paint, such a. . .

The following are examples of sentences in which the constructions carry over.

He was one of the best, if not the best, **of scholars.**
(Testing each phrase: ...one of the best of scholars...if not the best of scholars)
They can and will **pay** all their own expenses. (...can pay...will pay)

Often a clause appears before the word on which it depends; but if **the** sentence were in its natural order, the clause would follow the word, as

They, just as we would, **took no notice of it.**
(Straightening the sentence: They took no notice of it, just as we would [take].)

But more often such a clause should stand after the word on which it depends.

FAULTY: ...at the old hotel where Washington, as did Lafayette, **lived** during...
BETTER: ...at the old hotel where Washington lived, as did Lafayette, during...

Balanced Construction. To acquire clean sentence construction, make similar parts of a sentence balance as nearly as possible.

DEFECTIVE: They neither spare man nor beast.
BALANCED: They spare **neither man nor beast.**
("Spare" applies to both words, hence should stand before "neither.")
DEFECTIVE: We are not only interested in that but also in this.
BALANCED: We are interested **not only in that but also in this.**
("Interested" applies to both parts, hence should stand before the "not only.")
DEFECTIVE: They have started buying and to look for new bargains.
BALANCED: They have started **buying** and **looking** for new bargains.
OR: They have started **to buy** and **to look** for new bargains.
DEFECTIVE: They expect to go to Chicago, as well as going to St. Louis.
BALANCED: They expect to go to **Chicago as well as St. Louis.**
DEFECTIVE: They are now more interested in buying than was the case prior to 1954.
BALANCED: **They are now more interested in buying than they were** prior to 1954.
DEFECTIVE: The best way to do that is by doing this.
BALANCED: The best way **to do that** is **to do this.**
DEFECTIVE: It foretells a good future as well as giving warning.
BALANCED: It **foretells** a good future **as well as gives** warning.
DEFECTIVE: It checked buying rather than causing sales.
BALANCED: It **checked** buying **rather than caused** sales.

Clear Reference. Definite word reference is necessary to good construction.

The reference of the words "which" and "that" is often vague. They will pick up and reflect whatever is immediately before them. (See also "which," p. 27.)

CONFUSING: They have a pamphlet covering the item, which is to be sold by the separate copy.
(The reader first believes that "which" refers to "item," but later finds that it refers to "pamphlet.")

113

BETTER: They have a pamphlet which covers the item and which is to be sold by the separate copy.

CONFUSING: This is the list showing the names of the dealers that we spoke to you about yesterday.

PUNCTUATED: This is the list, showing the names of the dealers, that we spoke to you about yesterday.

OR BETTER: This is the list that we spoke to you about yesterday, which shows the names of the dealers.

Other pronouns may also be confusing in their reference. (See p. 63.)

"Dangling" or "Hanging" Words. There has been much talk about the status of the -ing word (adjective) that is suspended in a sentence with no definite word upon which to lean. The -ing words that are nouns can of course stand alone—unsupported. But an -ing word that is an adjective should supposedly have a definite word to modify.

Seeing is believing. (both nouns)
Seeing it there, we could hardly believe...
(Here "seeing" modifies "we," as "We, seeing it there, could...")
Seeing it there, it appeared much larger...
(Here "seeing" cannot modify "it," so must call upon understood words for support, as "Upon our seeing it there...," which makes "seeing" a noun.)

Thus, because a pronoun, or a pronoun with a preposition, can so easily be understood before an -ing word, the objection to the simple unsupported -ing word may be overcome.

Sentences such as the following are in general commercial usage:

Being a retired officer, his pension was assured.
("He being a retired officer" is understood.)
Investigating the situation, several new angles were uncovered.
("By our" is understood before "investigating.")

The real objection to the "dangling participle" is aimed at downright awkward constructions, and at constructions that can readily be changed for a marked improvement.

MEANINGLESS: Being in the bank, we were not concerned over our bonds being stolen.
("Being" immediately attaches itself to "we"; but it was not "we" who were in the bank, but the bonds.)

IMPROVED: Being in the bank, our bonds were in no danger of...

Arrangement. The ill arrangement of words in a sentence may cause a reader to reread in order to puzzle out the meaning. Keep one point of view and write in a straight line, so to speak.

INVOLVED: The notice was sent to all those whose payments for the quarter our treasurer had not received.

CLEARER: The notice was sent to all those whose payments for the quarter had not been received by our treasurer.

INVOLVED: The marks indicate that all coupons were with the original bonds and must have been detached if not there now.

CLEARER: The marks indicate that all coupons were with the original bonds and, if they are not there now, they must have been detached.

114

INVERTED: And so the changes have gone on until only very recently has been felt the influence of the papers.

CLEARER: And so the changes have gone on until—only very recently—the influence of the papers has been felt.

JUMBLED: His actions revived the insinuations before he was elected by many newspapers.

CLEARER: His actions revived the insinuations made by many newspapers before he was elected.

MISLEADING: To be meaningful, the writer should rewrite the sentence.

CLEAR: To be meaningful, the sentence should be rewritten.

Every inverted or introductory phrase should have a definite connection with the rest of the sentence.

TEST: Place the inverted phrase in its regular position in the sentence.

NOT: In reply to your inquiry relative to the issuance of licenses, such licenses are issued by the district offices.
(Rearrangement shows improper connection: Such licenses are issued by the district offices, in reply to your inquiry relative to the issuance of licenses.)

BETTER OPENING: The licenses that you asked about in your letter of April 6 are issued by the district offices.
(By beginning with the subject, the writer avoids the use of the unnecessary and old-fashioned "we wish to say that," which is required if the original phrasing is to be properly connected.)

Forceful Beginnings and Endings. The attention-catching part of a sentence is at the beginning; the climax is at the end.

Notice the difference in emphasis in the following sentences:

WEAK: The decision should be final to be fair.
FORCEFUL: To be fair, the decision should be final.

Sentences Beginning With "And," "But," "For," etc. A sentence may correctly begin with "and," "but," "for," "or," etc. It is usually started thus for emphasis, or as a continuation or a summing up. The only restriction is that the device should not be overused.

And information is to be found in the 24 volumes of the Britannica of such unquestionable authority...

And now at last the highest truth on this subject remains unsaid... —Emerson.

And it is perhaps already time to mark what advantage and mischief... —Ruskin.

But it is only by deliberate effort that I recall the long morning hours of toil, as regular as sunrise...—Ruskin.

But the sense of joint discovery is none the less giddy and inspiriting. And in the life of the talker...—Stevenson.

But call it worship, call it what you will...—Carlyle.

For, in fact, I say the degree of vision that dwells in a man is a correct measure of the man.—Carlyle.

And the evening and the morning were the first day.—The Bible.

Various sentence beginnings are shown in these successive sentences:

Nor is this all. If digestion were a thing to be trifled with... **And** were I to return to... **Or,** if nothing better were to be had... **Hence** it appears to be a matter of no great moment...—Huxley.

115

Prepositions at End of Sentences. A sentence may end with a preposition. Often the final preposition is superfluous, which has undoubtedly led to the prejudice against its use. Sometimes it is rather awkward; but more often it is a very effective ending.

Effective endings:
> The world we live in.
> But dost thou love life? Then do not squander time, for that's the stuff life is made of.—Franklin.

Common endings:
> It is difficult to account for. Those are things to get rid of.
> Not that I know of. See that the matter is attended to.
> Where are they from? Give us money to buy things with.
> What is it for? That's what I'm talking about.

Superfluous endings:
> It means more than we think *for*. Where am I *at?*

Awkward endings:
> What are they going there for?
> BETTER: Why are they going there?
> A preposition is not a good word to end a sentence with. (awkward but effective)

Rearrangement:
> Send the machines our men are accustomed to work with.
> Send the machines with which our men are accustomed to work.
> (Some writers prefer the first method, others the second.)

Long Sentences. A sentence may be long if it is perfectly clear. Long sentences create a slow tempo; short sentences, a fast tempo.

Short sentences can become as monotonous as long ones. Do not overwork either style.

Sentences Without Subjects or Verbs. A phrase may stand as a sentence—and often does.

> Now to get down to business. And the next?
> Hence the grief over wars. Not many; very few.
> So much for that. On the other hand, freedom!

on Capitalization

It is impossible to give rules that will cover every conceivable problem in capitalization. But by considering the purpose to be served and the underlying principles, it is possible to attain a considerable degree of uniformity.

*—United States Government
Printing Office Style Manual.*

Cap or lower case? That is a question that constantly arises to plague the writer and the editor.

In a capitalization perplexity, the best advice is:

*Look up the correct form, if possible; if not,
follow a similar form; if still in doubt,
don't capitalize.*

Other Instances of Capitalization

ᗡ

See the following pages for capitalization –

❖❖❖❖❖❖❖❖

Capitalization

One of the primary purposes of capitalization is to designate the **actual name or title of a specific person or thing.** But capitalization opinion varies.

Two styles of capitalization have evolved: the **up-style,** in which capitals are used freely, as in books, magazines, and business writings; and the **down-style,** in which capitals are used sparingly, as in newspapers, "to avoid the excessive use of caps."

UP-STYLE: { Federal Government; Senate and House; Republican Party; Mississippi River; State Street; Stanford University; Chrysler Building; The First National Bank; National Security Council; Chairman of the Board; President of . . .

DOWN-STYLE: { federal government; senate and house; Republican party; Mississippi river; State street; Stanford university; Chrysler building; the First National bank; national security council; chairman of the board; president of . . .

Style sheets or **stylebooks** have been compiled by most publications and many business houses for their own use, in which are shown the approved forms for using capitals and lower-case (small) letters in each particular publication or organization. Therefore, a very important factor to be considered in capitalization is the **nature of the publication or the group of readers** for which the writing is being prepared.

Business forms of capitalization that are commonly used are shown in the following list:

CAPITALS (Specific Names)	SMALL LETTERS (General Designations)
ARMED FORCES, CHIEFS OF STAFF, CAMP, FORT, ACADEMY, MEDAL	
the **Armed Forces** (of the U.S.)	in the **armed services**
the Joint **Chiefs of Staff**	the chiefs of staff of the . . .
the **Army,** the **Navy,** the **Air Force**	has no army, navy, or air force
the **Marines, Coast Guard, Seabees**	a marine, a soldier, and a sailor
the **Eighth Army** (8th* in newspapers)	the army of occupation
the **508th*** Fighter Escort **Wing**	a wing of the Air Force
at **Camp** Pendleton on the oceanfront	at a Marine camp
to **Fort** Sam Houston	the fort named in honor of . . .
the United States **Military Academy**	attended a military academy
the Congressional **Medal of Honor**	received a medal of honor
the **Distinguished Flying Cross**	a cross for distinguished flying
the **Croix** de guerre (or Guerre)	a war cross for gallant action
ASSOCIATION, INSTITUTE, INSTITUTION, ORGANIZATION	
American Automobile **Association**	an association for owners of . . .
Mutual Building & Loan **Association**	ten building and loan associations
American **Institute** of Architects	an institute for architects
the Smithsonian **Institution**	an institution for collecting . . .
the **Organization** of American States	an organization of Pan-American . . .

* For the use of figures or words in ordinal numbers, see p. 287.

CAPITALIZATION

CAPITALS (Specific Names)	SMALL LETTERS (General Designations)

BOARD, COUNCIL, COMMISSION, CHAMBER OF COMMERCE

the Board of Trade	set up a board of trade
the City Council	served on the city council
State Highway Commission	a ruling of the highway commission
the local Chamber of Commerce	any chamber of commerce

BUILDING, HOTEL, TOWER, HALL, HOUSE, CAPITOL, MONUMENT, STATUE

the Empire State Building	tallest building in the land
the Mayflower Hotel	is a corporation-owned hotel
the Terminal Tower (Cleveland)	a tower at the terminal
Independence Hall; the City Hall	the old hall in Philadelphia
the White House	a white courthouse
the Capitol (in Washington)	a state capitol (statehouse)
the Washington Monument	a monument in memory of Washington
the Statue of Liberty	the statue was a gift from France

CHURCH, CATHEDRAL, TEMPLE, CONGREGATION, CHAPEL, RELIGION
(See also p. 129)

services at Holy Trinity Church	a Roman Catholic church
the Reims Cathedral (or Rheims)	in the cathedral of Reims
B'nai Israel Congregation	a Hebrew congregation
the Navy Chapel	a chapel for military personnel
a Protestant, a Catholic, a Jew	a catholic mind (broad, liberal)
a Gentile, a Christian, a Moslem or Mohammedan, a Quaker, a Mormon	by clergymen of the various denominations (or faiths)
Father Lee; Rev. Mr. Day; Rabbi Marx	a priest, a minister, and a rabbi

CITY, CAPITAL, PORT, HARBOR, PARK, AIRFIELD, BOROUGH, DISTRICT, PRECINCT, WARD

NOTE: When "City" is used to refer to a corporate body, it is capitalized.

New York City; Washington City	in the city of Washington
the City of Chicago (incorporated)	a Federal Reserve city
the National Capital (D.C.)	in any state capital
the Port of New Orleans (a title)	New Orleans has a fine port
in Golden Gate Park	a ride through the park
landed at La Guardia Field	the large airfield at New York
the Borough of Manhattan	New York is divided into boroughs
the Adams School District	in that school district
Precinct 11, or 11th* Precinct	for all the precincts
Ward 5, or Fifth* Ward	results from any ward

CLUB, SOCIETY, GUILD, ORCHESTRA, FRATERNAL ORDER

the Cosmopolitan Club; a 4-H Club	a club member; the clubhouse
the American Chemical Society	a technical society
Radio and Television Directors Guild	a directors' guild
the Independent Order of Odd Fellows	an old fraternal order
the Boston Symphony Orchestra	a symphony orchestra

COMPANY, CORPORATION, BANK, RAILROAD

Standard Oil Company	is the largest oil company
our Company is (See also p. 125)	more than any other company
the First National Bank	it is a national bank
the Pennsylvania Railroad	that railroad system

Company Department or Division (See also p. 124)

our Research Department	in any research department

CONFERENCE, CONVENTION, MEETING

the Governors' Conference	told a news conference
the Democratic National Convention	hold an annual convention
the Annual Meeting of Stockholders	those present at the meeting

CONGRESS, CONGRESSMEN, CONGRESSIONAL DISTRICT, COMMITTEE

the Eighty-fourth (or 84th*) Congress	in the national legislature
when Congress convenes	elect a congress
the Senate and the House	having a senate and a house
the Senator or Congressman from...	a senator and a representative
Fifth* Congressional District	in that congressional district
the Ways and Means Committee	the chairman of each committee

* For the use of figures or words in ordinal numbers, see p. 287.

CAPITALS (Specific Names)	SMALL LETTERS (General Designations)

COURTS
(See also p. 484)

the Court of Appeals	a court of appeals
in the Probate Court of...	in a court action
the Court ruled (See also p. 128)	haled into court

DOCUMENTS
Act, Law, Bill, Code, Report, Treaty, Constitution, Amendment, Bond

the Social Security Act	an act to provide benefits
amends Public Law 729	a law to further national defense
the Economic Controls Bill	a bill authorizing controls
the Bill of Rights	a veterans' bill of rights
the Code of Federal Regulations	the civil code; building code
the Annual Report of the...	issues an annual report
the Versailles Treaty	the treaty of peace
the Constitution (of the U.S.)	each state adopted a constitution
the Nineteenth Amendment	a constitutional amendment
the Declaration of Independence	a declaration of independence
a Victory bond; an E-bond	a (war) savings bond; a defense bond

GAMES AND SPORTS
NOTE: Games are not capitalized unless unusual or trademarked.

the Tournament of Roses (a title)	playing in a golf tournament
singing "The Farmer in the Dell"	playing hide-and-seek with us
dancing the Virginia reel	play bridge, or tick-tack-toe
playing Monopoly (See also p. 125)	in canasta; blindman's buff

GEOGRAPHIC NAMES
Bay, Beach, Canal, Canyon, Channel, Coast, Continent, Creek, Desert, Equator, Gulf, Harbor, Hemisphere, Hill, Island, Lake, Mountain, Ocean, Peninsula, Plain, Pole, Reservation, River, Sea, Strait, Tropics, Valley

NOTE: Some publications do not capitalize the above words after geographic names. But other publications regard these words as part of the titles, and therefore capitalize them. Such capitalization is usual in typewritten work.

the Gulf Coast climate	on the Texas coast
on the Continent of Asia	Asia is a large continent
on the Equator (scientific, equator)	in the equatorial belt
the San Francisco Harbor	in the harbor of San Francisco
in the Northern Hemisphere	in that hemisphere
from the Canary Islands	the island of Cuba
crossing Lake Pontchartrain	between the river and the lake
across the Rocky Mountains	the mountains of California
the Atlantic Ocean; in mid-Atlantic	transatlantic* airways; in mid-ocean
out on the Alaska Peninsula	the upper peninsula in Michigan
the Great Plains; a Plains Indian	grass on the plains
at the North Pole	a magnetic pole
by the Rio Grande†	on the river Rhine
on the Hudson River	up the river from New York
in the High Sierra‡ (Nevada)	over a low sierra‡
Trans-Siberian Railroad	transpacific* shipping lanes
trans-Andean flights; trans-Canadian	transalpine* peoples; subarctic*
in the Tropics (or tropics)	tropical storms; subtropical lands
from the Mississippi Valley	the valley of the Nile

* After long use in certain constructions, some geographic words are not capitalized.
† "River" is sometimes added but is unnecessary, as "Rio" means "River."
‡ "Mountains" or "Sierras" is unnecessary, as "sierra" means "a chain of saw-toothed mountains."

GOVERNMENT (FEDERAL), UNION, NATION (NATIONAL), REPUBLIC, EMPIRE, COMMONWEALTH

NOTE: "National" is capitalized only when preceding a capitalized word.

The Government (of the United States)	a government by the people
the Federal (or National) Government	a federally administered program
the National Treasury	a national park; national income
the British Government	the labor government
the French and German Governments	the two local governments
this Nation; this Republic	any nation; nationwide; a republic
the state of the Union	a labor union
the Holy Roman Empire	the rich empire of Indonesia
the Commonwealth of Nations	in that commonwealth
the United Nations	all the nations represented

121

CAPITALIZATION

CAPITALS (Specific Names)	SMALL LETTERS (General Designations)

GOVERNMENT DEPARTMENT, BUREAU, OFFICE, AGENCY, COMMISSION, AUTHORITY
SERVICE, SYSTEM
(See also pp. 502–7.)

the **Department** of Justice	is one **department** that will...
Bureau of the Census; Weather **Bureau**	in a Government **bureau**
the **Office** of Naval Research	the Admiral's **office** said only...
the San Francisco **Post Office**	in any branch **post office**
the British **Foreign Office**	the **foreign offices** of countries
the Housing and Home Finance **Agency**	an insurance **agency**
the Atomic Energy **Commission**	a **commission** to control atomic energy
the Tennessee Valley **Authority**	a water-power **authority**
the Federal Reserve **System**	a **system** of reserve banks

HISTORIC EVENTS AND TIMES: WAR, ARMISTICE, AGE, ERA

the **Battle** of Bunker Hill	a **battle** for freedom
the Revolutionary **War**	after the **war** (**prewar, postwar**)
in World **War** II	the last **war**; no third world **war**
the Korean **Armistice**	the post-**armistice** talks
the **Stone Age**	the coming **electronic** or **atomic age**
the **Christian Era**	the new Elizabethan **age**, or **era**
the **Renaissance**	a **renaissance** of learning
in early **Colonial** times	from British **colonial** possessions
the Nineteen **Thirties** (See p. 280)	in his late **thirties**

HOLIDAYS AND OBSERVANCES
(See also pp. 595–98.)

the **Fourth** of July; the **Fourth**	the **fourth** holiday this year
New Year's Day (or Eve)	on the **eve** of the **new year**
Fire Prevention Week	a **week** devoted to **fire prevention**

IMAGINATIVE NAMES, EPITHETS, COMMON APPELLATIONS
(See also pp. 253 and 254.)

NOTE: No quotes are used around these names unless they are unfamiliar, or are
being defined or supposedly spoken, as: It came to be called "The Dust Bowl."

the **Old World**; the **New World**	in a **new world**
the **Big Three** (countries)	the **"big three"** (auto makers)
the **Allies**; the **Allied** armies	France and Britain were our **allies**
behind the **Iron Curtain**	silenced by an **iron curtain**
the **Wheat** State; the **Keystone** State	a **wheat**-growing state
the **Corn Belt**; the **Dust Bowl**	the **rain belt** where corn grows
from **Down Under** (Australia)	it is **"down underneath"** the globe
Frederick the **Great**	a **great king** of Prussia
the **First Lady**	the **first lady** at social functions
the **Big Board**; the **Big Top**	a **big** electric **board**; a **big tent**
two **Super Sabres**; a **Thunderjet**	a **saber** thrust; a **jet fighter**
the **Stars and Stripes**; **Old Glory**	the **stars** in the American **flag**
the **Liberty Bell**	the **bell** cracked as it tolled

LEGISLATURE, GENERAL ASSEMBLY, LEGISLATIVE ASSEMBLY

NOTE: In some states the legislative body (**legislature**) is called "the Legis-
lature"; in others "the General Assembly"; in still others "the Legislative
Assembly"; and in Massachusetts and New Hampshire "the General Court."
(See also p. 599.)

the Nebraska **Legislature**	a state **legislature**
the **General Assembly** of Indiana	a **general assembly**
the Oregon **Legislative** Assembly	a **legislative** body

PARTY

NOTE: Some publications capitalize "**Party**" and others do not.

the **Republican Party**; a **Republican**	a **republican** form of government
the **Democratic*** **Party**; a **Democrat**	a **democratic** way of life
the **Labor Party** in Great Britain	an important **party** victory

---

* A recent tendency (among Republicans) is to use "**Democrat**" as an adjective, as "the **Democrat**
Party," on the theory that both parties are "democratic." But this adjectival use of "**Democrat**"
is rare except where "**Democratic**" would be misleading, as in the headline, "**Democrat** Aide to Speak."

CAPITALS	**SMALL LETTERS**
(Specific Names)	(General Designations)

SCHOOLS, COLLEGES, UNIVERSITIES, CLASSES, COURSES OF STUDY, ACADEMIC DEGREES

from Franklin **High School**	attended **high school**
at Vassar **College**	**college** requirements
the **University** of Virginia	the **university** founded by Jefferson
the **Senior Class**; for **Grade 7**	a **senior** in college; **seventh*** **grade**
taking **Ancient History** and Latin	studied **electrical engineering**
Robert T. **Brown, Doctor of Laws**	awarded a **doctor of laws** degree
member of **Phi Beta Kappa Fraternity**	an honorary **fraternity**

STATE, PROVINCE, COUNTY, PARISH, NATIONAL PARK

NOTE: **"State"** (when part of a name or when referring to a certain state or states) is now very generally capitalized to fix definitely the reference. The United States Government Printing Office capitalizes "State" except when used in a general sense, as

foreign states	statehood	statehouse	stateside
statewide	upstate	welfare state	state's evidence

Washington **State**	before Washington became a **state**
in the **State** of Wyoming	in any **state**
this **State** (Ohio) has given	for **state** rights, or **states'** rights
the Kentucky-Tennessee **State** line	results of **out-of-state** voting
in the **State-owned** projects of Iowa	a **state** bank, university, or **prison**
the Thirteen Original **States**	from their home **states**
the Gulf **States**; New England **States**	the **states** north of New York
the **Province** of Ontario	a **province** in Canada
in Grant **County**	at the **county** seat
the **Parish** of Orleans	a Louisiana **parish** is a **county**
in Yellowstone **National Park**	in a **national park**

STREET, AVENUE, ROAD, BRIDGE, HIGHWAY, TURNPIKE, FREEWAY, EXPRESSWAY, SPEEDWAY

NOTE: Some publications, especially newspapers, do not capitalize the above words even when parts of names; but other publications, and most business writers, do capitalize them in all actual names.

Thirty-sixth***** **Street**; Willow **Road**	it is the main **street**
Grand **Avenue**; Sunset **Boulevard**	shops on that **avenue** or **boulevard**
the Golden Gate **Bridge**	the **bridge** across the Golden Gate
the Coast **Highway**; Memorial **Parkway**	the **highway** along the coast
the Pennsylvania **Turnpike**	the new pay-as-you-go **turnpike**
the Hollywood **Freeway**	the **freeway** system
the Washington–Annapolis **Expressway**	the heavily traveled **expressway**
the Indianapolis **Speedway**	a record on the **speedway**
the New York **Thruway**	the **throughway** of the future

TITLES—CIVIL, MILITARY, RELIGIOUS

(See p. 124 for explanation of variations. For other civil and military titles, see pp. 268 and 324 ff. For "The Honorable...", see p. 318. For other religious titles, see pp. 332–35. For "The Reverend...", see p. 317.)

the **President** (of the United States)	elect a **president**
the **Presidency**; **Presidential** edicts	a **presidential** candidate
the **Chief Executive** (the President)	the **chief executive** of a city
signed by **President** Monroe	when Monroe was **president**
the (**President's**) **Cabinet**	reshuffling the French **cabinet**
the **Secretary of State**	any **secretary of state**
the **Under Secretary** of Commerce	the **first Secretary** under the
Assistant to the Attorney General	appointed as an **assistant** to
the **Acting Governor**; **Acting Mayor**	the **acting** British minister
the **Governor** of South Carolina	if the **governor** of a state
General Lee and **Captain** Hale	a **general** and a **captain**
Chairman Fred O'Neill; Mr. **Chairman**	the Dallas banker was **chairman**
the coronation of **Queen** Elizabeth II	crowning a beauty **queen**
the late **King** of England	a dethroned **king** and **queen**
to **Her Majesty**; **His Royal Highness**	to her majesty, the Apple **Queen**
by **His Holiness** the Pope	by his **Holiness**... (less formal)
from **Your Grace**; **His Grace** (formal)	a gift from her **grace**, the Duchess
His Excellency; **Their Excellencies**	"Yes, your **Excellency**, we shall..."
Madam Ambassador (See also p. 323)	"But, **madam**, we cannot..."
Sir Winston Churchill	"Please step aside, **sir.**"

***** For the use of figures or words in ordinal numbers, see p. 287.

Personal Titles. Publications usually follow the "before-and-after style" of capitalizing personal titles; that is, they capitalize a title immediately preceding a personal name, but lower-case it if after, removed from, or in apposition with a personal name. EXCEPTION: Titles of very prominent or distinguished persons are always capitalized.

BEFORE	AFTER	REMOVED FROM
President Ralph Lee	Ralph Lee, **president** of	the **president** of
Chairman Hudson	Mr. Hudson, **chairman** of	the **chairman** of
Professor Morgan	Ray Morgan, **professor** of	the **professor** of

IN APPOSITION: ...their **district manager,** John Steel, was...

BUSINESS STYLE: In business writings, personal titles are usually capitalized wherever they occur—if they refer to specific persons.

R. C. Blake, **President** of...   Dr. Christie, **Head** of...
Vice President Len Barr of...   ...their **Treasurer,** Tom Hoyle.
He is **Secretary** of Gale Bros.   ...was **Chairman** of the Board.
...by **Attorney** John Thorne.   ...from Commission **Counsel** Hart.

NOTE: Designations not used as titles are not capitalized, as lawyer...banker ...publisher...hotelman...clerk...bookkeeper.

Business Offices and Departments. A company or organization usually capitalizes the names of its own departments, divisions, or offices, but does not capitalize such names in other companies.

Our **Sales Department**...   ...their **sales department.**
Call your Telephone **Business Office** for...
Call the **business office** of a utility for...

Plurals of Proper Names. These plurals are usually capitalized in business writings; and often in publications. (The U.S. Government Printing Office prefers capitalization, but some publications do not.)

UP-STYLE	DOWN-STYLE
Atlantic and Pacific **Oceans**	Atlantic and Pacific **oceans**
35th and R **Streets**	35th and R **streets**
Republican and Democratic **Parties**	Republican and Democratic **parties**

Similar **capitalizations are:** Hudson and Potomac **Rivers, Lakes** Huron and Erie, British and French **Governments,** State and Commerce **Departments,** Unitarian and Lutheran **Churches,** Vassar and Bryn Mawr **Colleges,** Santa Fe and Southern **Railroads,** World **Wars** I and II, the **Foreign Ministers'** meeting.

Plural titles before proper names are generally capitalized. But plural titles **after** proper names follow the style used in the singular.

Presidents Wilson and Roosevelt   **Governors** (or **Govs.**) Hill and Ward
Senators (or **Sens.**) Miles and Day   **Generals** (or **Gens.**) Lee and Grant

Family Titles. The words "father," "mother," "aunt," etc., are capitalized when used as proper names; that is, when **no modifiers,** such as possessive pronouns, are used before them.

124

Tell **Father** (or **Dad**) and **Aunt** Mary to sign, but not **Mother.**
Ask **Brother** Jack to call us after he sees **Cousin** John.

They are not capitalized when **modified** and mere reference is made to the persons.   (Note the carry-over of the possessive pronoun.)

a generous **father**   the **mother** of the bride   a maiden **aunt**
It is necessary for **my father** and **aunt** to sign, but **not mother.**
Our **brother** Jack will call us after he has seen our **cousin** John.

Shortened Names.   Well-known shortened forms of proper names are capitalized both in printing and in typewritten work.

the Continent (of Europe)   the Channel (English)   the Street (Wall)
the Dominion (of Canada)   the Canal (Panama)   Treasury notes (U.S.)
the District (of Columbia)   the Stream (Gulf)   the Bay (Chesapeake)

Likewise, capitalized **titles of important persons** are often used instead of personal names.

the President...the Prime Minister...the Governor...the Senator...
the Secretary (of Defense)...the Attorney General...the Mayor...

BUSINESS METHOD.   Other shortened forms, although not often capitalized in publications, are very generally capitalized in business writings, after the full name or designation has been introduced in the text.

...the General Electric Company...   ...the **Company** has...
...the National Research Council...   ...the **Council** is...
...the City of Detroit...   ...the **City** will issue...
...adopt a Salary Adjustment Plan.   Under the **Plan** all salaries...
...in our Annual Report.   ...the **Report** dealt with...

Legal usage: ...and Philip Brown (hereinafter designated the "Tenant").
          The **Landlord** does hereby let unto the **Tenant** the premises...
     (Often in caps, as MORTGAGOR and MORTGAGEE. See p. 480.)
In minutes of meetings: The **Treasurer** reported that the Corporation has...
     (In minutes, "Company," "Corporation," etc., should always be capitalized; and usually the titles of officeholders.)

Trade Names and Commercial Products.   A trademarked name is capitalized unless the name has become so common as to represent a class or type.   (Yet some trademark owners insist upon capitalization.)

NOTE: Only the trademarked name is capitalized and not the following word unless the expression is used as a trade term, as "Du Pont House Paint."

Technicolor   a Mirado pencil   Sky Chief gasoline
Coca-Cola   an Anacin tablet   Sealtest ice cream
Life Savers   in Pyrex glass   Crisco shortening

Trade names used as common nouns or adjectives:

nylon   cellophane   mimeograph   photostat
aspirin   sanforized   multigraph   polaroid

Personal names used as common adjectives and nouns:

the braille system   a curie unit   diesel engines
a bunsen burner   a half nelson   monel metal
under klieg lights   a pullman car   a mason jar

125

Trade names set in full caps for advertising value:

ANSCO Film   BAND-AID   the MAGIC MONITOR
MAINLINER Stratocruiser

Market names indicating special variety, grade, or brand:

buy Delicious apples...Prime beef...Early Rose potatoes...the
Peace rose
BUT: winter wheat...summer squash...snap beans...freestone
peaches (and similar general designations)

In advertising, capitals are used freely—to designate new services, special features of products, catchwords, and the like.

the Safety-Tested seal   latest High Fidelity television
guaranteed DuraPower Mainspring   these De Luxe Super-Cushions

Sometimes quoted: ...called "Phonorama" ...finest "Golden Throat" sound
Advertising derivative: ...the "Model T" atomic bomb that...

Industries. Within an industry, occasionally the name of that industry is capitalized, but otherwise no capitalization is used.

the textile industry... chemical industry... automotive industry

Intra-industry: The outlook for the **Tire and Rubber Industry** depends...
In newspapers: The normally uncompromising **tire industry** has...

Taxes. The names of taxes are not capitalized, unless a proper name is involved—and sometimes not then.

the excess profits tax...social security tax...Federal income **tax**
a withholding tax...personal property tax...excise tax...sales **tax**
...known as "Federal Old-Age and Survivors Insurance taxes."

Numbered Items. A common noun **before** a serial or code number, **or** letter, is usually capitalized in business writings, but not in printing. Small, common words, such as "car," "page," and "line," are not capitalized. Nouns **after** such numbers or letters are capitalized only in advertising.

NOTE: "No." is usually unnecessary, as "Order 892." See also pp. 286–87.

Reorganization Plan (No.) 16   Policy 996743   U.S. Route 240
the Point IV (or 4) program   Bulletin R   Flight 324
Stock Certificate W19366   Catalogue T-36   Account 202
...on customer's Purchase Order (No.) 6325, and our Job 828
BUT: car C&O 51067   page 2   line 14   vitamin C

Catalogue names of commercial products are capitalized in this manner:

Type H Air Conditioners   Triple-Tempered 3-T Nylon Cord

Plurals of numbered items are either capitalized or lower-cased, according to their form in the singular. (For singulars, see p. 287.)

in Chapters I and IV... revised Forms 110 and 116... from **pages** 1 to 8
Fill out three Forms 1859-B, and mail two **forms** to...
...canceling **Policies Nos.** 567934 and 856882 (two words capitalized)
...granted **Patents Nos.** 2,674,813–36 ...in **Orders Nos.** 819 and 823
Informal: All **Form 1040s** are to be... (pluralizing the number)
Singular in apposition: These **applications, Form Ar-11,** are to be sent...

Directions. "North," "South," "East," and "West" are capitalized when used as the names of certain sections of the country.

out West	the East Side	Middle West; Midwest
the Far West	living Down East	the Pacific Northwest
back East	the Deep South	Southern California
in the East	the Solid South	Northern Ireland
going West	the Old South	Western Australia
coming East	in the Far East	Eastern Shore (Md.)
from the South	the Western World	in the North Atlantic
from the North	on the West Coast	at the South Pole

When used as nouns or adjectives to designate natives or residents of certain sections, they are capitalized.

a Westerner	BUT: a western (motion picture)	Southerners
Western buyers	an Eastern visitor	a Southern drawl

They are not capitalized when used as simple directions or to refer to parts of the country—or to describe things in general.

east of Chicago	looking north	in the north of Ireland
traveling west	in northern Italy	in the south of France
toward the south	in western Canada	the east coast of Africa
a northern winter	eastern mountains	a western settlement
the southern states	the eastern part	middle western towns

Nations, Nationalities, Races, Languages, Peoples (and Derivative Words). These names should always be capitalized—as shown in dictionaries. However, certain names have, after long use, lost association with their countries and are no longer capitalized.

American, -ism, -ization		Canadian	part-Hawaiian	Pan-Asiatic
Caucasian	Semitic	Negro	Indian Malayan	Latin

Japanese	BUT: japan (varnish)	from Manila	BUT: manila paper
an Oriental	oriental rugs	Roman art	roman candle
Moroccan	morocco leather	Jersey cow	jersey cloth
Turkish	turkish towels	Chinatown	chinaware
a Venetian	venetian blinds	the Swiss	dotted swiss
Bohemians	bohemian life	in Panama	panama hats

General terms: the white, or brown, race; red men; redskins; a U.S. citizen; a Korean national; a bushman (Australian); a head-hunter

Natives or residents of certain states may be designated by the endings -n, -an, -ian, -er, and -ite.

Coloradan	Indianian	Kansan	Connecticuter	Wyomingite
Idahoan	Delawarean	Texan	Mainer	Wisconsinite

Personification. The name of a personified thing may be either capitalized or lower-cased, according to the distinction or emphasis to be accorded it. (Note that if capitalization is used, only the thing personified is capitalized, not what it is, or what it possesses.)

the wheel of **Fortune**	OR:	the wheel of fortune
When **Necessity** is the **mother** of invention...		...as **logic** dictates.
But **Reason** was the staying hand.		Came a voice of **reason**:
After life's fitful fever, he sleeps well.—Shakespeare.		

127

"Vivid personifications" are capitalized in business writings.

The **Chair** recognized the speaker... ...appointed to the **bench**.
If **Headquarters** issues the order... ...at company **headquarters**.
The **Administration** is considering... ...the previous **administration**.
The **Court** (Judge) has so ordered. This **court** is not subject to...
...lands belonging to the **Crown**. ...the group around the **throne**.
...concurrence of **Church** and **State**. The field of the **church**...
If **Labor** and **Capital** will sit down.... ...a **labor-management** dispute.

Seasons. These names are not capitalized unless personified.

spring   summer   autumn or fall   winter   midwinter

Personified: ...came **Autumn** with her robe of brown.

Sun, Moon, Stars. The common names of heavenly bodies are not capitalized unless used in connection with the names of other planets or stars that are always capitalized.

sun   earth   moon   stars   polestar   lodestar
...studying Mercury, Arcturus, the Sun, Mars, and the Earth.

Imaginative names are capitalized, as

the Milky Way   the Great Bear   Southern Cross   North Star

Poetry. The first word of every line of poetry is usually capitalized.

> There are gains for all our losses,
>   There are balms for all our pain;
> But when youth, the dream, departs,
> It takes something from our hearts,
>   And it never comes again.—Richard Henry Stoddard.
>
> (Reprinted by permission from Charles Scribner's Sons, New York.)

There is no definite rule for the indention of lines of poetry. Each poem is a law unto itself; and the lines may be indented or not, in any style that best suits the meaning.

Modern poetry often dispenses with capitalization, to achieve a certain effect.

> if I had the lake
> in my own front yard
> I never would work at all
> just smoke my pipe
> and dream
>   by the waves
>   from April
>   to frosty fall
>   and in winter
> I'd skate
>   from early to late
>   wrapped up
>   in a Paisley
>   shawl

—Riq. (Pen name of Richard Atwater)—As quoted in the
11th Ed. of *A Manual of Style*, The University of Chicago Press.

Biblical Terms. All words denoting the Deity are capitalized.

our Saviour	the Supreme Being	God
All-Wise	our Creator, or Maker	Godforsaken land
Heavenly Father	Ruler of the universe	God-given right
the Almighty mercy	the Son of Man	an act of God
in the year of our Lord	divine Providence	a Christian

BUT: a savior of men...a heathen god...a Greek god...sun-god...
goddess...godsend...godless...godlike...godchild...godmother

Pronouns referring to the Deity should be capitalized if they stand for His name.

He   His   Him (BUT: himself)   Thee   Thou   "Come unto Me."
Other pronouns referring to the Deity are not capitalized:
who   whom   whose   thy   thine
Pronouns immediately after the Deity's name need not be capitalized:
And on the seventh day God ended his work which he had made...
—The Bible.

Biblical references and terms are capitalized (in text, lc. "biblical").

the Ten Commandments	Heaven (meaning God), but not
Bible, but "office bible"	as in "a heaven on earth"
Scriptures, but scriptural	Satan and Hades, but not hell

Principal Words in Headings or Titles. The important words in headings or titles are capitalized, such as nouns, pronouns, verbs, adverbs, and adjectives—and the first word (in each line), and the last word.

Small or unimportant words are not capitalized, such as short prepositions ("of," "in," "to," "by," etc.); conjunctions ("and," "but," "or," etc.); articles ("a," "an," and "the"); and abbreviations like "etc." and "et al."

The Battle of the Coral Sea
Markets or Exchanges, etc. } Note that the last word is always
How to Write a Short Story } capitalized unless it is an abbre-
Whence Are We So Lately Come? } viation like "etc." or "et al."

However, prepositions and other small words may be capitalized in headings if they are stressed, or if four or more letters.

Decide Before Not After Doing	Lincoln: The Lawyer
Standards In Business and Out	Ages—A Study of Man

A preposition that is an **indispensable part of a verb form** is often capitalized. (**Infinitives** are an exception—in most newspapers.)

Costs **to** Be Pointed **Out** in Survey   Finances **to** Be Held **Up** by Court

The main words in all actual proper names should be capitalized. Occasionally, quotes or hyphens are also necessary for clarity.

Webster's New Collegiate Dictionary
BUT: a Merriam-Webster dictionary
...join the Write-a-Letter-to-Your-Congressman-Now! drive.
...the 3-cent "Women in the Armed Services" commemorative stamp.
...for the display of Christmas "Shop and Mail Early" posters.

129

Hyphened Words. Both parts of a hyphened word are capitalized if each part is ordinarily capitalized.

Spanish-American War   the East-West game   a President-Congress debate

In a heading or title, both parts may be capitalized to conform to the general style of capitalization in headings. (That is, capitalize the words that would be capitalized if the hyphens were not there.)

Out-of-Town Exchanges	Air-Conditioned Theaters
Strong Mid-April Buying	A Down-and-Outer's View
New Runner-up in Golf	The Ever-Present Threat
Forty-Second-Street Signs	Our Listeners-In
The Wage-Earning Masses	Tourists Re-Enter Paris
Ten Ex-Governors Meet	Postal Rate on 16-mm Films

NOTE: Some publications, following rules of style, capitalize in headings only nouns used as the second parts of hyphened words; others capitalize no second parts unless they are proper names; however, the above method is the newspaper style, and is largely used by good authorities.

In the text, the first part only, or the last part only, may be capitalized, according to the manner in which the single words are ordinarily written.

...mid-April...Forty-second Street...ex-Governor Hayward (but, an ex-governor)...non-Christian...pro-British...the President-elect (but, a president-elect)...un-American...inter-American...English-speaking people

The. The word "The" should be capitalized when part of a title; but often this is not done in running text, especially in newspapers.

The Hague	BUT:	the Netherlands
The Riggs National Bank		the Bank of America
The New York Times, or The Times	TEXT:	in the Times (or The Times)
The Washington Post		in the Post (or The Post)
The Associated Press		the Associated Press story

(See also "The Honorable," p. 318; and "The Reverend," p. 317.)

Emphasis. A word is sometimes capitalized for emphasis, or to give a deeper meaning.

Its lifeblood for generations has been **Research.**
Then the **American Road** came into being.
Signs everywhere said PRIVATE PROPERTY.   (quotes unnecessary)
...put it with your outgoing mail RIGHT NOW!

Caps Without Quotes. Topics, subjects, and parts of compositions or books are often distinguished by capital letters without quotes.

This volume discusses such subjects as Planning for the Future, The Coming Electronic Age, and A World at Peace.
...in the Weights and Measures section of that book.
...a panel discussion of What We Can Offer the World.

Parts of a specific book: ...in the Preface...a complete Index...
Table of Contents...Appendix...Bibliography, etc.
BUT: In the third edition, a preface and appendix were added.

Quotes Without Caps.   Remember that many quoted common-noun names are not capitalized.   (See also pp. 252–54.)

> ...publishes its own "house organ"   ...called it "a sword of Damocles"

Sentences Within Sentences.   If a complete sentence is introduced within another sentence, it may or may not begin with a capital according to the emphasis desired.   (If the inner sentence is quoted, it should begin with a capital, unless it is indirectly introduced as by **"that."**

> The debated question was, Is there room for all?
> ...with these words above his desk: This, too, shall pass away.
> There are two stands: one is questionable, the other commendable.
> Their reply was, "Conditions will not warrant it."
> BUT: They replied that "conditions will not warrant it."

Partially quoted sentences should not begin with capital letters:

> They talked about "price cutting and price fixing."

If several sentences are introduced into one sentence, but are joined by "and," or "or," etc., they are often not begun with capitals.

> There are three good reasons: we are experienced in the work; we are equipped to do it; and our prices are undoubtedly right.   (For further examples, see the Punctuation section, pp. 249 and 258.)

Foreign Names.   Small words in foreign names (as van, von, du, de, di, da, d', de la, della, ter, and ten—meaning "from," "of," etc.) are not capitalized, unless such foreign names begin sentences, or stand alone within sentences, that is, are not preceded by forenames or titles.

> The writer Guy de Maupassant...   (with forename)
> De Maupassant, the writer...   (beginning sentence)
> The writer De Maupassant...   (standing alone)

Many foreign names have become Americanized and are written with capital letters.   The preference of the owners of the names usually governs in this.

> De Laval   OR: de Laval   Van Dyke   OR: van Dyke
> Du Pont   BUT: the firm name is still carried as E. I. du Pont de
>   Nemours & Co.
> Van Rensselaer (still written "van Rensselaer" also)

Foreign Languages.   In many foreign languages, capitals are not used so freely as in English—or are used differently.   Therefore, if numerous foreign phrases occur, it is best to consult a foreign language dictionary or a stylebook showing foreign capitalization.

> French: l'Académie française   (the French Academy)
>   la Conférence de la paix   (the Peace Conference)
>   le moyen âge   (the Middle Ages)
> Italian: aprile; la lingua italiana   (April; the Italian language)
> Swedish: juli; måndag   (July; Monday)
> German: Juli; Deutschland   (July; Germany)
>   das deutsche Volk   (the German people)

131

Prefixed Names in Caps. When prefixed names are being set in caps, the prefixes, if disjoined, are set in caps.

DES MOINES   LA SALLE   VON GRISWOLD

But if the prefixes are joined, they are made clearer if only the first letter is capitalized.

McDONALD   RATHER THAN: MCDONALD
MacDOWELL   MACDOWELL

NOTE: The prefixes "Mc" and "O'" are always followed by a capital letter, but "Mac" may not be, as "Macmillan" and "MacMillan."

Possessive Names in Caps.   (See p. 154.)

◇◇◇◇◇◇◇◇◇

Attempt to be uniform in capitalization.   Do not capitalize a word at one time and not another, when using it in the same construction.

Spelling

The business rule:

Constantly consult the dictionary.

It is the exceptions that prove this rule.
Question the spelling of every unusual or infrequent word.

Words Frequently Misspelled

(Notice how "right" most of the "wrong" words appear at first glance.)

absorbent	NOT:	*absorbant*	existence	NOT:	*existance*
absorption		*absorbtion*	extension		*extention*
accommodate		*accomodate*	February		*Febuary*
acquiesce		*aquiese*	fiery		*firey*
analyze		*analize*	Filipinos		*Philipinoes*
antarctic		*antartic*	flammable*		*flamable*
asinine		*assinine*	forthright		*fortright*
assistance		*assistence*	forty		*fourty*
auxiliary		*auxillary*	fulfill		*fullfil*
banana		*bananna*	gnawing		*knawing*
bankruptcy		*bankrupcy*	government		*goverment*
brethren		*bretheren*	grammar		*grammer*
Britain		*Britian*	heart-rending		*heartrendering*
buoyancy		*bouyancy*	hemorrhage		*hemorrage*
category		*catagorey*	hindrance		*hinderence*
chauffeur		*chauffuer*	hygiene		*hygeine*
chimneys		*chimnies*	idiosyncrasy		*idiocyncracy*
		chimleys	incense		*insense*
coliseum		*colosium*	incidentally		*incidently*
colossal		*collosal*	infallible		*infalable*
commitment		*committment*	inoculate		*innoculate*
committee		*commitee*	insistence		*insistance*
concede		*consede*	intercede		*intersede*
conscientious		*conscientous*	interfered		*interferred*
consensus		*concensus*	jeopardize		*jeprodise*
controversy		*controvercy*	kimono		*kimona*
corrugated		*corrigated*	license		*lisence*
cynical		*synical*	liquefy		*liquify*
deuce		*duece*	maintenance		*maintainance*
develop		*devellope*	management		*managment*
dignitary		*dignatary*	maneuver		*manuveur*
disappoint		*dissapoint*	mortgaged		*mortgauged*
drastically		*drasticly*	nickel		*nickle*
ecstasy		*ecstacy*	ninety-ninth		*ninty-nineth*
embarrass		*embarass*	nowadays		*nowdays*
exaggerate		*exagerate*	occasionally		*ocassionaly*

* Note that **"flammable"** is now being used instead of **"inflammable,"** because "inflammable" may be construed to mean "*not flammable.*"

occurrence	NOT:	*occurence*	repel	NOT:	*repell*
pamphlet		*phamplet*	rhapsody		*raphsody*
permissible		*permissable*	rhododendron		*rhododrendon*
perseverance		*perseverence*	rhubarb		*ruhbarb*
persuade		*pursuade*	rhythm		*rythm*
Philippines		*Phillipines*	sacrilegious		*sacreligious*
Pittsburgh, Pa.		*Pittsburg*	safety		*safty*
plagiarism		*plaigarism*	scissors		*sissers*
playwright		*playwrite*	seize		*sieze*
prairie		*prarie*	separate		*seperate*
preceding		*preceeding*	shepherd		*sheperd*
precipice		*presipice*	similar		*similiar*
preferable		*preferrable*	sincerity		*sincerety*
presumptuous		*presumptous*	souvenir		*souviner*
privilege		*privelege*	specimen		*speciment*
propeller		*propellor*	suing		*sueing*
psychological		*psycological*	surreptitious		*sureptitous*
publicly		*publically*	transferable		*transferrable*
pursuer		*persuer*	unparalleled		*unparalelled*
questionnaire		*questionaire*	usage		*useage*
recipient		*resipient*	vegetable		*vegatable*
relevant		*revelent*	Wednesday		*Wedensday*
renown		*renoun*	weird		*wierd*

Simplified or Modern Spelling.   Simplified or modern spelling should be used only in **informal work,** such as interoffice communications.

Regular Spelling.   Regular academic spelling should be used in all **formal** letters, documents, and legal papers, and in all copy for publication.

Adding -ed or -ing.   When -ed or -ing is to be added, and it is permissible to use either a single or a doubled consonant, American and especially business usage prefers the simpler form.

> labeled, signaling, etc.   **PREFERRED TO:**   labelled, signalling, etc.

The "rule of accent" may be used as a guide.   The rule is: When the accent falls on the **last syllable** of a word ending in a **single** consonant (except h or x) preceded by a **single** vowel, the final letter is doubled in adding -ed or -ing (or another suffix beginning with a vowel):

> committed   controlling   occurred   referring   equipped (u equals w)

This of course includes all such words of one syllable, as without the doubled letter there would be danger of confusion with similar words:

> barring   fatted   pinning   planned   ragged   stripped   tubbing

The continuation of this rule is that if such a word is not accented on the last syllable, the final letter is not doubled:

> ben′efited   can′celing   e′qualed   fo′cusing   to′taling   trav′eled

(Many writers carry the rule out even in such words as "kidnaped" and "worshiped"; but they except "handicapped," "humbugged," "outfitted," "wigwagged," "zigzagged," and "chagrined.")

When forming an **unusual -ed or -ing** ending do not drop or change a final letter.   If the form is not given in the dictionary at hand, leave the word intact.   It is more easily recognized.

radioed ballyhooed moneyed taxied taxiing relayed NOT: *relaid*

Unusual Endings. A hyphen or an apostrophe may be used to set off an unusual ending—to preserve the appearance of the root word.

chic-est city-fied maple-y ah-ed to'ings, fro'ings OK'd

Endings -cede, -ceed, and -sede. It will repay a writer to take a few minutes to memorize the following:

> "Only one word ends in *sede* (supersede); only three end in *ceed* (exceed, proceed, succeed); all other words of this class end in *cede* (precede, secede, etc.)."
> —*United States Government Printing Office Style Manual.*

Remember that the three words ending in -ceed ("exceed," "proceed," and "succeed") change form when taking different endings—as "procedure," "procession," "excess," and "successive."

Endings -ize and -ise. American preference is for the -ize ending, and British preference is largely becoming so.

characterize humanize economize criticize

Consequently, when forming new words, use the -ize form, as

finalize accessorize definitize BUT: televise (from television)

Many established American words, however, retain the -ise form.

advertise merchandise enterprise surprise

Endings -able and -ible. The more usual suffix, and the living form, is -able. It is generally employed in forming new words.

incorporable connectable findable typable publishable do-able

The -ible form is retained on many established words.

convertible deductible forcible reversible susceptible

Words Ending in -ic. If -ed, -er, -ing, or -y is added to a word ending in -c, the letter **k** is inserted for clarity, to prevent the **c** from being sounded as **s**.

frolicking mimicked panicky picnicker (NOT: *picknicker*)

But the **k** is not used in forming plurals (or other forms) of such words, because here the **c's** sound of **k** is undisturbed.

antics panics picnics frolics almanacs critics hecticness publicly

Endings -us and -ous. Some words differ in noun and adjective form.

NOUNS:	callus	fungus	mucus	phosphorus	viscose
ADJECTIVES:	callous	fungous	mucous	phosphorous	viscous

135

SPELLING

Words Ending in Silent -e. The general rule for adding suffixes is:
Drop the e before a vowel; keep it before a consonant. But some e's
are retained to preserve the sound of a preceding letter, or to differentiate
words.

Dropped before vowels:

arguing	forcing	raging	excitable	movable	desirous
bluing	judging	suing	likable	salable	grievous
dining	managing	using	livable	usable	truism

Retained to preserve sounds (as of a soft c or g):

advantageous	courageous	gaugeable	noticeable	pronounceable
changeable	enforceable	manageable	peaceable	serviceable
ageing	canoeing	eyeing hoeing meteing	shoeing	tiptoeing mileage

Retained to differentiate words:

singeing from singing   dyeing from dying   tingeing from tinging

Retained before consonants:

awesome	careful	likeness	lonely	management	ninety
gruesome	hopeful	politeness	homely	involvement	safety

EXCEPTIONS: acknowledgment argument duly judgment ninth truly

æ and œ. The ligatures ("diphthongs") æ and œ are not commonly
used in business spellings. Not only is it difficult to write them on the
typewriter, but the dictionaries now very generally drop the silent letter.

maneuver	encyclopedia	RATHER THAN:	manœuvre	encyclopædia
medieval	anesthetic		mediæval	anæsthetic

In some words, especially in trade names, both letters are retained
but the ligature is dismissed.

Phoenix   Aeolian   subpoena   amoeba   aesthetic   aeon   aegis

British and American Variations. British and American spelling
often differs in minor particulars. The following are examples:

AMERICAN	BRITISH	AMERICAN	BRITISH
airplane	aeroplane	-er: caliber	-re: calibre
aluminum	aluminium	center	centre (makes centring)
ax	axe		
check (bank)	cheque	kilometer	kilometre
connection	connexion	saber	sabre
cozy	cosy	theater	theatre
curb (edge)	kerb		
goodby	goodbye	-l: counselor	-ll: counsellor
gray	grey	labeled	labelled
gypsy	gipsy	medalist	medallist
jail	gaol	quarreled	quarrelled
mold	mould	traveling	travelling
mustache	moustache	woolen	woollen
pajamas	pyjamas		
peddler	pedlar	-ll: dullness	-l: dulness
plow	plough	enrollment	enrolment
practice (v.)	practise (v.)	fulfill	fulfil
skeptical	sceptical	installment	instalment
specialty	speciality	skillful	skilful
veranda	verandah		
-ed: learned	-t: learnt	-m: kilogram	-mme: kilogramme
spelled	spelt	program	programme

AMERICAN	BRITISH	AMERICAN	BRITISH
-or: color	-our: colour	-se: defense	-ce: defence (but
endeavor	endeavour		defensible)
favorite	favourite	offense	offence
honorable	honourable	pretense	pretence
humor	humour (yet	-ze: analyze	-se: analyse
	humorous)	civilize	civilise
labor	labour (yet	criticize	criticise
	laborious)	organization	organisation
neighbor	neighbour	realize	realise

Foreign Spellings. Foreign and American spellings sometimes differ in the names of cities and countries.

AMERICAN	FOREIGN	
Antwerp, Belgium	Anvers, Belgique	(French)
Athens, Greece	Athenai, Ellas	(Greek)
Brussels	Bruxelles	(French)
Chile	Chili	(Sp., Fr., It.)
Cologne	Köln	(German)
Copenhagen	Köbenhavn	(Danish)
Cordova, Spain	Córdoba, España	(Spanish)
Florence, Italy	Firenze, Italia	(Italian)
Geneva	Genève	(French)
	Genf	(German)
Gothenburg	Göteborg	(Swedish)
The Hague	's Gravenhage	(Dutch)
Havana	La Habana	(Spanish)
Lisbon	Lisboa	(Portuguese)
Moscow	Moskva	(Russian)
Munich	München	(German)
Prague	Praha	(Czech)
	Prag	(German)
Rome	Roma	(Italian)
Rumania	România	(Rumanian)
Venice	Venezia	(Italian)
Vienna	Wien	(German)
Warsaw	Warszawa	(Polish)

The names of several foreign cities have been permanently changed.

FORMERLY	Now	
Batavia, Java	(D)Jakarta, R.I.	(jä-kär′tä)
Christiania, Norway	Oslo	(ŏz′lō)
Constantinople, Turkey	Istanbul	(is′täm-bo͞ol′)
Peiping, China	Peking	(pē′king′)
Pernambuco, Brazil	Recife	(rä-sē′fĕ)
Queenstown, Irish Free State	Cóbh, Ireland (Eire)	(kōv)
St. Petersburg, Russia	Leningrad, U.S.S.R.	(lĕn′ĭn-grăd)
Stalingrad, U.S.S.R.	Volgograd	(vŏl′go-grăd′)

Russian words are seen spelled in different ways.

Czar OR: Tsar   Romanof OR: -off, -ov, -ow   Grozny OR: -sny
Dostoyevsky   Dostoyefsky   Dostoïeffsky   Dostoevski   Dostoevskii
Dostoevsky   and   Dostoievsky

137

Standardize on Spellings. If two or more forms for spelling a word exist, adopt the preferable form and use it consistently.

For instance, "employee" is usually preferred to the French form "employé" so that it will be uniform with "payee," "lessee," etc.

Remember spellings by association of ideas, or by photographing words on the mind, with the troublesome parts magnified, as

aCCoMModate   ecStaSy   coMMiTTee   sepArate   oCCuRRence

Also, learn to **spell by syllables,** carefully pronouncing each one so that certain letters may be remembered by sound, as

absorption arctic authoritative government prescription tempestuous

An understanding of the construction of a word will often be of assistance. For instance, the **prefixes dis- and mis-** have but one s; and two s's occur only when the joining word begins with **s.**

disappear	dissatisfied	misapply	missent
disapprove	dissimilar	misguided	misspell
disprove	dissolve	mismanage	misstate

In the **ending -ful,** the l is single unless an -ly is added.

careful	restful	tearful	wishful
cheerful	skillful	thoughtful	wistful
cupful	spoonful	useful	woeful
hopeful	successful	willful	youthful
carefulness	restfulness	skillfulness	thoughtfulness	willfulness
carefully	hopefully	restfully	skillfully	thoughtfully	willfully

Also, **-ful,** indicating a measurement, is joined, and not written *"full."*

Note the difference between:

enough for a **cityful** of people	AND:	a **city full** of quiet people
pour a **glassful** of refreshment		a crystal **glass full** of water
entertain a **houseful** of guests		found his **house full** of guests
before a **roomful** of people		entered a **room full** of people
brought an **oceanful** of joy		in an **ocean full** of ice
ate several **platefuls** of food	NOT:	*plate fulls, plates full*
booked ten **carfuls** of students	NOT:	*car fulls, cars full*

(For other plurals, see p. 141.)

With the **ending -ness,** two n's occur if the original word ends in **n.**

barrenness	greenness	meanness	suddenness
commonness	leanness	plainness	thinness

Technical and unusual words often present a spelling problem unless they can be quickly verified. Such words should be entered—when first encountered or first looked up—in a small indexed notebook, or compiled into a list and kept in the front of a small dictionary. In a large office, new words to be added to the list should be posted on a bulletin board.

This notebook or list can be made to act as a "stylebook" or "style sheet," such as is used by printers and publishers, to keep the spelling, capitalization, division, hyphenation, and abbreviation of words uniform throughout a writer's or a company's work.

PLURALS

If the plural form of an unusual noun (as one ending in -a, -e, -i, -o, -u, -f, or -y) is not given in the dictionary at hand, form the plural as simply as possible, by adding -s only.

mesas	visas	taxis	avocados	menus	hoofs	moneys
lavas	coupés	Hopis	hairdos	luaus	scarfs	standbys

Sibilant Sounds. To form the plural of a common noun ending in a sibilant sound (-s, -ss, -sh, -ch soft, -x, or -z), add -es.

buses	businesses	churches	dishes	boxes	quartzes
gases	actresses	lunches	lashes	taxes	blitzes
citruses	classes	scratches	relishes	axes	buzzes

Words ending in **silent -s** do not change form in the plural. In pronunciation the plural may be indicated by sounding the -s.

two corps	several faux pas	many Mardi Gras
ten chassis	two early Degas	all the King Louis

Names Ending in Sibilant Sounds. To form the plural of proper names ending in -s, -ch, -x, -z, or another such sound, add -es.

the Harrises	the Frenches	the Essexes	the Lentzes

Names Ending in -y. Simply add -s to proper names ending in **-y.** Do not change any letters, or strange-looking words will result.

the Macys and Gregorys	six Marys	three Cicelys	ten Henrys
in both Kansas Citys	BUT:	the Alleghenies and Rockies	
Januarys, Februarys, Julys	OR:	Januaries, Februaries, Julies	

Names Followed by Jr., 2nd, or III. The plurals of names followed by "Jr.," "2nd" or "III," etc., may be formed in two ways:

FORMAL: ...the John B. Blaines, Jr.
...the Jason Lloyds III (or 3rd, or 3d)
INFORMAL: ...the John B. Blaine, Jrs.
...the Jason Lloyd IIIs (or 3rds, or 3ds)

A Common Title Before a Common Name. If two persons of the same name bear the same title, they may be referred to in the following manner. ("The" is capitalized only in addresses, not in running text.)

FORMAL	INFORMAL
The Doctors (or Drs.) Mayo	The Dr. Mayos
The Attorneys McLeod	The Attorney McLeods
The Captains Linden	The Captain Lindens
The Superintendents Lewis	The Superintendent Lewises
The Presidents Markham	The President Markhams
The Messrs. Lee	The Mr. Lees

139

The Mesdames Harland	The Mrs. Harlands
The Misses Stewart	The Miss Stewarts

If an indefinite number of people is meant, the informal form is used.

> They would defy all the Governor Harrises in the states.
> . . .found more than fifty Sgt. John Smiths stationed over there.
> All the Mrs. Browns were to be honor guests.

Words as Words. When words are referred to as words, the plurals may be indicated by the simple addition of -s, if the words are common, and such plurals are clear. (See also Quotation Marks, p. 253.)

> pros and cons   ifs and ands   ins and outs   whys and wherefores

If the words are uncommon, or may be misread, the plurals should be indicated by an 's.

> or's and nor's   thank-you's   which's and that's

If the words are liable to be read into the text incorrectly, or if special emphasis is desired, they may be quoted (in printing, italicized).

> All of their "whereases" are indefinite.
> There are numerous "ifs" and "buts" in their language.
> . . .made out a list of "musts," "don'ts," and "nevers."

If the word to be pluralized already contains an apostrophe, the -s alone is added.

> don'ts and doesn'ts   RATHER THAN: don't's and doesn't's
> BUT NOT: *dont's* and *doesnt's*
> do's and don'ts   'tis's (both apostrophes necessary)

The following established plurals should be used rather than the 's.

> ayes (or yeses) and noes   RATHER THAN: yes's and no's
> yeas and nays   yea's and nay's

When plural and possessive coincide, rearrange the sentence.

> We do not understand his ifs' implication.   (NOT: *if's'*)
> BETTER: We do not understand the implication of his "ifs."

Compound Words. These plurals are formed on the main words.

TEST: Ask of each title, "What actually are these persons or things?"

attorneys general	(they are attorneys, not *generals*)
governors general	(they are governors, not *generals*)
("General" here means "overall"—like "General Manager"—and not a military general.)	
major generals	(they are generals, not *majors*)
adjutants general	(they are administrators, not necessarily generals)
judge advocates	(they are military prosecutors, not *judges*)
courts-martial	(they are military courts)
brides-elect	(they are brides-to-be)
notaries public	(they are notaries, not *publics*)
mother superiors	(they are superiors; "mother" modifies)
ambassadors-designate	(they are designated ambassadors)
assistant postmasters general	("assistant". . ."general" are adjectives)
associate general counsels	("general counsel" is a title of office)

Prepositional phrases, as "in chief," "de [of] camp," are descriptive of the main words. Hence plurals are formed on the main words.

commanders in chief	rights of way*	chiefs of staff
chambers of commerce	bills of lading	mothers-in-law
attorneys at law	letters of credit	chargés d'affaires
powers of attorney	leaves of absence	aides-de-camp†
points of view	grants-in-aid	coups d'état†

* United States Government usage is "rights-of-way." Dictionaries show both the open and the hyphened form. And some give a second plural, "right-of-ways."

† Note that in French, as in English, plurals are not formed on modifying prepositional phrases, as coups de grâce, tables d'hôte; but that in French, **adjectives are pluralized** because they must agree in number and gender with the nouns they modify, as bêtes noires, bons mots, faits accomplis, grandes maisons, petits fours.

A few plurals of phrases are idiomatically formed on the last word.

Johnny-on-the-spots	jack-in-the-boxes	trick or treats
Johnny-come-latelies	BUT: hail-fellows-well-met	

When a preposition is hyphened to a noun, the noun is pluralized.

lookers-on	listeners-in	backers-up	helpers-out
hangers-on	fillers-in	runners-up	triers-out
goings-on	droppers-in	callers-up	time-outs*

* The solid "timeouts" is shown in dictionaries, and used by the Government Printing Office.

Where neither word is a noun, the plural is formed on the last word.

also-rans	go-betweens	lean-tos	slip-ups
come-ons	hand-me-downs	make-dos	trade-ins
go-aheads	higher-ups	on-and-offs	write-ins

Both parts are pluralized in some compounds—where the words are of almost equal importance.

men cooks, or drivers	Heads of Departments OR: Department Heads
BUT: man-hours	Boards of Directors
women pilots, etc.	Courts of Appeals (sing., Court of Appeals)

IN SOME PUBLICATIONS: woman Marines, woman officers, etc.
(For plurals in such phrases as "types of radios," see p. 14.)

Solid Compounds. The plural is usually formed at the end of a solid compound, but may be on the root noun within the compound.

armfuls or armsful	handfuls or handsful	pocketfuls or pocketsful
cupfuls or cupsful	spoonfuls or spoonsful	BUT: glassfuls, only

If the word is broken into and the plural formed on the first part, the meaning is changed (**-ful** denotes a measure). (See also p. 138.)

two arms full of wood	(MEANS: two arms filled at one time)
two armfuls of wood	(MEANS: two armloads—one amount)
four bucketfuls of earth	(one bucket filled four times)
four buckets full of earth	(four separate buckets)
about two shelffuls of books	(enough books to fill two shelves)
two shelves full of books	(two shelves filled with books)

A word denoting a class of people may be pluralized in the regular way, or by adding -ers.

tenderfeet or -footers	webfeet or -footers	greenhorns or -horners

141

Other Plurals.   Collective Words, p. 36.
　　　　　　　　　　 Company Names, p. 37.
Plurals of Capitalized Words.   (See pp. 124, 126, and 253.)
Plurals of Quoted Words. (See p. 253.)
Plurals of Abbreviations and Letters.   (See p. 555.)
Plurals of Figures, Weights and Measures.   (See pp. 280 ff.)

FOREIGN PLURALS

Many words adopted from foreign languages have both original and English plurals.   Some have only their original foreign plurals.

If the plural of a foreign word is not given in the dictionary at hand, form a simple English plural.

Regarding the use of Latin or English plurals:

> "All that can safely be said is that there is a tendency to abandon the Latin plurals, and that when one is really in doubt which to use the English form should be given the preference."
>
> —Fowler, *A Dictionary of Modern English Usage,* p. 316.

Observe the pronunciation of vowel sounds in foreign words, especially the long vowels in modernized Latin.   They are marked in some words below.

SINGULAR	ENGLISH PLURAL	FOREIGN PLURAL
addendum		addenda
agendum (or agenda, sing., with pl. agendas)		agenda (à-jĕn′dȧ)
alumna (fem.)		alumnaē (fem.)
alumnus (mas.)		alumnī (mas., or **mas.** and fem.)
analysis		analysēs
antenna	antennas (radio)	antennaē
āpex	apexes	ăpicēs
apparātus	apparātuses	apparātus (NOT: -tī)
appendix	appendixes	appendicēs
aquarium	aquariums	aquaria
automaton	automatons	autŏmȧtȧ
axis		axēs
bacterium		bactēria
bandit (It. bandito)	bandits	banditti (It. -tē)
basis		basēs
beau	beaus	beaux (bōz; Fr. bō)
bureau	bureaus	bureaux (-rōz; Fr. -rō′)
cactus	cactuses	cactī
campus	campuses	campī
candelabrum	candelabrums	candelabra
("Candelābra" is used as a singular, with "candelābras" as plural.)		
cello	cellos	'celli (It. chĕl′ē)
census	censuses	
château		châteaux (-tōz′; Fr. -tō′)
cherub	cherubs	cherūbim (Hebrew)
colossus	colossuses	colŏssī
crisis		crisēs
criterion	criterions	critēria
crocus	crocuses	croci (-sī, not -kī)

Singular	English Plural	Foreign Plural
curriculum	curriculums	curricula
datum		dāta
dēsiderātum (a thing desired		dēsiderāta
diagnōsis		diagnōsēs
dilettante	dilettantes	dilettanti (It. -tē)
discus	discuses	disci (dĭs'ī)
dogma	dogmas	dogmáta
ellipsis		ellipsēs
emphasis		emphasēs
errātum (an error)		errāta
eucalyptus	eucalyptuses	eucalyptī (New Latin)
Fascista		Fascisti (It. fä-shē'stē)
focus	focuses	foci (fō'sī)
formula	formulas	formulaē
fungus	funguses	fungi (-jī)
genius (a spirit)		genii (jē'nē-ī)
genius	geniuses	
genus (jē'nŭs)	genuses	genera (jĕn'ēr-á)
gladiolus	gladioluses	gladīolī (scientific)

("Gladiolas" is now commonly used instead of "gladioluses.")

gymnasium	gymnasiums	gymnāsia
hīātus	hiatuses	hīātūs
hippopotamus	hippopotamuses	hippopotamī
hypothesis		hypothesēs
ignorāmus	ignorāmuses	(NOT: ignorami)
impediment (-um)	impediments	impedimenta
index	indexes (common)	indicēs (scientific)
indicium (rare)		indicia (ĭn-dĭsh'ē-á)
insignē		insignia
larva		larvaē
larynx	larynxes	larynges (-jēz)
libretto	librettos	libretti (It. -tē)
literātus (a scholar)		literātī (men of letters)
loggia	loggias	loggie (It. lŏd'jĕ)
Magus		Magi (mā'jī) ("wise men")
mātrix	matrixes	mătricēs
maximum	maximums	maxima
medium	mediums	mēdia
memorabile (rare)		memorabilia (-rá-bĭl'ē-á)
memorandum	memorandums	memoranda
metropolis	metropolises	metropoleīs (Greek)
minimum	minimums	minima
minutia		minutiae (mĭ-nū'shĭ-ē) (small details)
narcissus	narcissuses	narcissī
nebula	nebulas	nebulaē
nemesis		nemēsēs
nucleus	nucleuses	nucleī (nū'klē-ī)
oasis		oasēs
octopus	octopuses	octopī, or octopodes (-pō-dēz)
opera (It.)	operas (musical compositions)	
opus (a literary or musical composition)		opera (Latin)

SINGULAR	ENGLISH PLURAL	FOREIGN PLURAL
paralysis		paralysēs
(no singular)		paraphernalia
parenthesis		parenthesēs

(The singular "parenthesis" may mean one or both curves, or the expression enclosed, as "a parenthesis.")

SINGULAR	ENGLISH PLURAL	FOREIGN PLURAL
phenomenon	phenomenons	phenomena
planetārium	planetariums	planetāria
prospectus	prospectuses	
radius	radiuses	radĭī
referendum	referendums	referenda
residuum	residuums	residua
rostrum	rostrums	rostrá
sanatōrium	sanatoriums	sanatōria
sanitārium	sanitariums	sanitāria
sērum	serums	sērá
sinus	sinuses	
solo	solos	soli (It. -lē)
spectrum	spectrums	spectra
sphinx	sphinxes	sphinges (sfĭn'jēz)
stadium	stadiums	stādia
status	statuses	(NOT: *stati*)
stigma	stigmas	stigmáta
stimulus		stimulī
strātum	stratums	strāta
streptococcus		streptococci (-kŏk'sī)
stylus (pointed tool)		stylī
synopsis		synopsēs
tableau	tableaus	tableaux (-lōz; Fr. -blō')
tempo	tempos	tempi (It. -pē)
terminus	terminuses	terminī
thesis		thēsēs
trousseau	trousseaus	trousseaux (Fr. -sō')
ultimātum	ultimatums	ultimāta
vacuum	vacuums	vacūa
vertebra	vertebras	vertebraē
virtuoso	virtuosos	virtuosi (It. -sē)
vortex	vortexes	vorticēs

Note that the familiar form of some words is the foreign plural; therefore, a plural verb is required.

> Data* are... Bacteria are... Insignia are... Addenda are...
> Advertising media are... Paraphernalia* are... Phenomena are...
> One of the vertebrae... (NOT: one of the *vertebra* NOR: *vertebraes*)

Also note that the foreign plural forms require plural modifiers and plural pronouns.

this memorandum	BUT:	these memoranda
this medium		these media
that phenomenon		those phenomena
that datum		those data*
that analysis		those analyses
this insigne		these insignia

* "Data" and "paraphernalia" are now often used as singulars, as "This data is catalogued with its ultimate use in mind." "Too much paraphernalia weighs a boy down."

And a few seemingly **plural** foreign and Latin words are **singular.**

apologia (an apology in defense)   (Note pronunciation: ăp'o-lō'jĭ-a)
fantasia (a fanciful composition)   (pron. făn-tā'zhē-a, or făn-tá-zē'á)

Remember, too, that the foreign **singular** is required wherever a similar English word would be singular.

NOT: *gladioli* bulbs, *cacti* plants   BUT: gladiolus bulbs, cactus plants
   (One would not write "*tulips* bulbs" or "*roses* bushes.")
NOT: In spite of some erratic changes of *tempi*, the violinist played...
   (USE: "changes of tempo," which corresponds to "changes of speed")
NOT: Television is a serious and powerful new *media* of communication.
   (USE: "new medium," which corresponds to "new channel.")

◇◇◇◇◇◇◇◇

POSSESSIVES

Possessives of Singular Words Ending in -s and -z. There are two ways to form these possessives: (1) by adding an apostrophe and s, to indicate pronunciation; and (2) by adding just an apostrophe (as frequently seen in newspapers and magazines).

Adams's election	Arkansas's history	OR: Adams'	Arkansas'
Paris's fame	Dumas's works	Paris'	Dumas'
Strauss's waltzes	Mardi Gras's legend	Strauss'	Gras'
Ross's trade	Cortez's journey	Ross'	Cortez'
The Times's story	Díaz's leadership	Times'	Díaz'
Louis's reign	a princess's life	Louis'	princess'

If **several s's occur together**, the apostrophe alone is almost always used:

Confucius' sayings   Jesus' words   Des Moines' streets

Words ending in -x usually take the apostrophe and s:

Knox's products   St. Croix's course   a fox's cunning
(pl.) the Sioux' claim to lands   (pl.) her beaux' flowers

CAUTION: Do not cut into a word and place the apostrophe before the final -s.

NOT: { *Keat's*   BUT: { Keats's or Keats'
     { The *Time's*   { The Times's or The Times'

Descriptive Words. Some words are considered to be more descriptive than possessive; hence the possessive is not used.

United States laws   state rights*
Massachusetts roads   the Hastings ranch
Federal Waterways Bill   a merchants exchange
the Bureau of Standards circular   the company name
                        the shipping and mails section

* Possessive not used in singular, but used in plural—states' rights.

Possessives of Plurals. It is easy to misplace the apostrophe when forming plural possessives.

Form the plural of the word first; then add the possessive. If the plural ends in -s, all that is needed is an apostrophe. If the plural does not end in -s, an 's is needed.

NOT: *childrens'* games   *womens'* votes   *boy's* and *mens'* interests
BUT: children's games   women's votes   boys' and men's interests

145

SINGULAR	SINGULAR POSSESSIVE	PLURAL	PLURAL POSSESSIVE
boy	boy's	boys	boys'
man	man's	men	men's
woman	woman's	women	women's
workman	workman's	workmen	workmen's
child	child's	children	children's
lady	lady's	ladies	ladies'
witness	witness's, or -ness'	witnesses	witnesses'
company	company's	companies	companies'
church	church's	churches	churches'
deer	deer's	deer	deer's
Mr. Essex	Mr. Essex's	The Essexes	The Essexes'
Mr. Burns	Mr. Burns's	The Burnses	The Burnses'
Mr. Montgomery	Mr. Montgomery's	The Montgomerys	The Montgomerys'

Note that the word following a plural possessive is plural, unless a combined possession is intended.

> those authors' **styles** (NOT: *style*) (not one style, but several)
> the rich men's **fortunes** (not one fortune, but many)
> BUT: those men's consent (their combined consent)
> those buyers' business (a common or combined business)
> those speakers' use of the word (a common use)
> those speakers' uses of the word (means they used it differently)
> (See also Collective Words, p. 41.)

Possessive When a Common Title Precedes a Common Name. If the possessive is to be used when a common title precedes a common name, it may be added in the following manner:

FORMAL	INFORMAL
The Messrs. Blake's theory	The Mr. Blakes' office
The Mesdames Hill's reception	The Mrs. Hills' tearoom
The Misses Davis's School	The Miss Davises' shop
(OR: The Misses Davis' School)	
The Attorneys McLeod's suit	The Attorney McLeods' case

Double Possessives. When a possessive follows an **"of phrase"** (which, as well as an 's, signifies possession), an idiomatic "double possessive" is formed. This double possessive is used only to denote **one** (or a certain number) **of several like possessions.**

TEST: Substitute "among" for "of" and complete the phrase.

> a friend of Mr. Gale's   (FOR: a friend among Mr. Gale's friends)
> those friends of mine   (FOR: those friends among my friends)
> a friend of Whittier's and mine   (NOT: of *Whittier* and mine)
> a book of theirs, or his   a rule of Ralph's   a painting of Whistler's

Where "among" cannot be substituted for "of," do not use the possessive:

> the works **of Dickens**   ...in the footsteps **of his father**
> ...remembered clearly those warning words **of his companion.**
> ...although the voice cannot be that **of Wagner.** (NOT: of *Wagner's*)
> We have the word **of the President**...   (FOR: the President's word)

EXCEPTION: When "this" or "that" is used before the thing possessed —

> **that** fine voice of Jack's   **this** land of ours
> **those** boys of Brown's   **these** hands of mine

Do not tack a possessive on a pronoun that is already possessive.

NOT: a client of *ours'* building   BUT: the building of a client of ours
NOT: a friend of *mine's* car   BUT: the car of a friend of mine
NOT: at a *neighbor's* of *his* house (NOR: at a *neighbor*)
  BUT: at the house of a neighbor of his

Phrases such as the following should be avoided in writing. But they occur in conversation and, if started, should be finished correctly.

in one of the men's desks (NOT: men's *desk*)
  (The simple phrase is "in one of the desks.")
from one of our relatives' vineyards (NOT: *vineyard*)
at one of the girls' homes (NOT: *girl's home*)
BETTER: {
in the desk of one of the men
from the vineyard of one of our relatives
at the home of one of the girls
}

With Names Consisting of Several Words.
The possessive may be placed at the end of a name composed of several words if the construction remains clear.

the Standard Oil Company of California's offer
the American Relief Association's report
the Attorney General's office
Columbus, Ohio's most famous citizen   (no comma after possessive)
Bard Winton, Jr.'s account   The Bard Winton, Jrs.' cards
Philipp Whitney III's plane   The Philipp Whitney IIIs' home
Stanfield, Inc.'s order
   (See also Possessives of Abbreviations, p. 555.)

If the construction is awkward, an "of phrase" should be used.

AWKWARD: the delegates from Way Down East's vote
  BETTER: the vote of the delegates from Way Down East
AWKWARD: the Manager of Construction and Repair's report
  BETTER: the report of the Manager of Construction and Repair
AWKWARD: the Society for the Prevention of Cruelty to Animals' action
  BETTER: the action of the Society for the Prevention...

With Explanatory Words.
Explanatory words or phrases usually carry the possessive. But if they are distinctly set off, as by commas, the possessive may be formed on the main words as well.

Dumas the elder's writings
...to get the man in the street's opinion.
That was John the handy man's idea.
That idea was John the handy man's.
NOT: He wants to have a role in his *friend*, James Hopewell's, play.
BUT: He wants to have a role in his friend's, James Hopewell's, play.
  (OR: [without commas] in his friend James Hopewell's play)
  (BETTER: ...in the play of his friend, James Hopewell.)
NOT: It is the same at his local *broker*, George Lane's.
BUT: It is the same at his local broker's, George Lane's.   (OR: Lane)
  ...from his mother's (Maude Mason's) estate.

147

Compound Possessives. The possessive of compound words is formed by adding an 's to the last word.

sister-in-law's	commander in chief's	listener-in's
brother-in-law's	ambassador at large's	passer-by's

With names that already contain a possessive, an "of phrase" should be used.

NOT: after Villon's-at-the-Beach's style
BUT: after the style of Villon's-at-the-Beach
NOT: Benson's-by-the-Sea's orchestra
BUT: the orchestra of Benson's-by-the-Sea

When a plural and a possessive are both involved, use an "of phrase" to show possession.

the governors general's decisions
BETTER: the decisions of the governors general
his brothers-in-law's estate
BETTER: the estate of his brothers-in-law
the listeners-in's viewpoint
BETTER: the viewpoint of the listeners-in

Joint Possession. When joint possession is intended, the possessive may be formed on the last of two or more nouns—if there is no possibility of a misreading.

James, Robert, and Charles's venture	the Soldiers and Sailors' Club
Coolidge and Dawes's administration	Randall & Ives's "Chronicles"
Drs. Wright and Helton's discovery	Blake and Hayward's note

But if the possibility of an error in reading exists, each noun should be made possessive.

NOT: They held John *Blake* and Don Hayward's note.
BUT: They held John Blake's and Don Hayward's note.
    ("Note" indicates that it was one note.)
OR: They held the note of John Blake and Don Hayward.
NOT: George *Davis* and Ralph Clayton's truck was damaged.
BUT: George Davis's and Ralph Clayton's truck was damaged.
NOT: Is this a *farmer* and a merchants' bank?
BUT: Is this a farmers' and a merchants' bank?

Or if a pronoun is involved, each word is possessive.

James's, Robert's, and his word	Ryan's and your patent
Bankwell's and my refusal	Rand's and our agreement

Separate Possession. If separate possession is intended, each noun should be possessive.

Note that the thing possessed is plural, unless it is something that can be commonly possessed, as "attention," "consent," "handbook."

Those are the owner's, lessee's, and mortgagee's rights.
...in soldiers' and sailors' language.

Lincoln's and Roosevelt's administrations can be compared.
James Bryson's and Daniel Mack's fathers were childhood friends.
(NOT: James *Bryson* and Daniel Mack's fathers...)
...the lot between Harmon's and Hazelton's homes. (NOT: *home*)
It is desirable that the sender's and addressee's names and addresses
appear on both portions...
...working to earn their master's and doctor's degrees.
That is apparently Gray's (and other authors') use of the word.
("Use" here represents a common use.)

NOTE: For clarity, the noun is often moved forward, as "from both the
reader's **standpoint** and the writer's."   Or the noun is repeated, as "the
Artists' **Club** and the Florists' **Club**."

Alternative Possession.   If alternative possession is indicated, each
noun should be possessive.

Note that the thing possessed may be either singular or plural, to
conform to the rest of the sentence.

a boy's or a girl's effort   an author's or an editor's opinion
men's or women's interests   the authors' or editors' opinions
a man's or a period's style   in a senator's or a member's office

Parallel Possession.   Do not forget the possessive when a word stands
parallel with another possessive.

NOT: A child's food requirements differ from the *adult* in that...
BUT: A child's food requirements differ from an adult's in that...
NOT: ...a navy to equal *Britain* or the *United States*.
BUT: ...a navy to equal Britain's or the United States'.
NOT: ...whose faults were no worse than their *neighbors*.
BUT: ...whose faults were no worse than their neighbors'.
NOT: Like a *watchmaker*, his work is exacting.
BUT: Like a watchmaker's, his work is exacting.

Words Understood After Possessives.   Often the thing possessed
is understood.

Send it to Blackmore's [shop] for repair. (NOT: *Blackmores*)
It can be bought at Clarendon's. (NOT: *Clarendons*)
NOT: At your *druggist*.   At your *dealer*.   At your *grocer*.
BUT: At your druggist's...your dealer's...your grocer's. [store]
OR: From your druggist.   At your drugstore.   At your grocery.

Piled-up Possessives.   Avoid the piling of one possessive on another.

It was sent at *his partner's brother's* request.
BETTER: It was sent at the request of his partner's brother.
...caused by that company's representative's being absent.
BETTER: ...caused by the absence of that company's representative.
The Authors' League's report...
BETTER: The report of the Authors' League...
The firm's New York manager's signature was necessary.
BETTER: The signature of the firm's New York manager was...
That corporation's attorney's decision...
BETTER: The decision of that corporation's attorney...
ALLOWABLE: ...depend on one's hearers' readiness to... (which is
comparable to "his hearers' ")

149

Names and Titles Containing Possessives. In some names and titles the apostrophe is omitted.

Citizens National Bank	American Bankers Association
Pikes Peak; Farmers Valley	Teachers College
Governors Island	Funk & Wagnalls dictionaries

In other names and titles it is retained.

McCall's	The Ladies' Home Journal
Reader's Digest	State Teachers' College
Boys' Clubs of America	Webster's New Collegiate Dictionary

Abbreviated Possessives. (See Abbreviations, p. 555.)
Quoted Possessives. (See Quotation Marks, p. 253.)
Periods of Time. Expressed by hyphen or possessive. (See p. 281.)

Inanimate Possessives. Some grammarians state that possession should not be given to inanimate things (it personifies them); but this has been done throughout good literature for hundreds of years, and has grown in present usage to such an extent that it can hardly be put aside now. Some such idiomatic possessives are:

a moment's* notice	a month's interest	six dollars'* worth
a few minutes'* study	6 months' coverage	a dollar's* worth
an hour's* time	in one year's time	ten cents' worth
ten hours'* delay	twenty years' growth	at arm's length
a day's work	this morning's mail	a stone's throw
a week's stay	the ship's papers	a hair's breadth
two weeks' vacation	New Year's Day	at swords' points

* Note the use of the singular and plural possessives. (See also Numbers, p. 281.)

...that 1930's cost of living was but a percentage of 1954's.
...and April's level showed a similar gain over March's.

The final -s is omitted in the following idiomatic possessives; that is, with words that end in an s sound. (Note "sake," not "*sakes.*")

for acquaintance' sake	for convenience' sake	for neatness' sake
for appearance' sake	for goodness' sake	for peace' sake
for conscience' sake	for justice' sake	righteousness' sake

But the **'s or s'** is used with other words:

for art's sake	for heaven's sake	for old times' sake
for mercy's sake	for pity's sake	for the boys' sake

General Possessives. These possessives may be written as singulars or as plurals. The idiomatic use is singular; but logic favors the plural.

SINGULAR: {	writer's cramp	fool's gold	a poet's poet, BUT
{	printer's ink	fuller's earth	the artists' artist

Some possessives are used both ways:
a man's or men's club... a child's or children's disease... a gentleman's or -men's agreement... employer's, employers', or employers liability

Some singular possessives idiomatically remain singular when their phrases are pluralized; others conform and become plural possessives:

SINGULAR: {	traveler's checks	collector's items	attorneys general's
{	cashier's checks	sons-in-law's cars	opinions
PLURAL: {	drivers' licenses	proofreaders' marks	apothecaries'
{	officers' checks	writers' magazines	measures

Some possessives remain singular because they imply no grouping:
master's degrees   world's fairs   Mother's Days   New Year's Days

150

Anybody Else's.   The vogue for saying "anybody's else" has passed, and the "else's" have been restored.

anybody else's	nobody else's
anyone else's	no one else's
everybody else's	somebody else's
everyone else's	someone else's

"Who else's" is supplanting the older form, **"whose else."**

whosever   is usually preferred to "whoever's," but the latter may yet become the accepted form to agree with similar possessives.

whosesoever   is the possessive of "whosoever"—used in formal writings.

anybody's
everybody's Since these words are singular, the possessives are singular.
another's   Do not write: *anybodys'*, each *others'*, etc.
each other's

anybody's	nobody's	one's	each one's
anyone's	no one's	another's	either's
everybody's	somebody's	one another's	neither's
everyone's	someone's	each other's	both's (pl.)

each other's and **one another's**   are usually followed by plural nouns.

We saw each other's **faces.**—Merriam-Webster dictionaries.
. . .cutting one another's **throats** without hatred.—Macaulay.

But if the plural noun would convey an unintended meaning, the singular is used.   (Note the use of "other's" not "*others'*.")

Artists are not inclined to admire each other's talent.
("Talents" would give a different meaning.)
They did not ask each other's opinion.
Men take each other's measure. . .   . . .and waste each other's time.
("Measures" would give a different meaning.)
. . .an appraisal of each other's power.

others'   is plural.

. . .others' troubles.   (NOT: other's, unless referring to only one)

Possessive Personal Pronouns.   No apostrophe is used in these.

NOTE: "Its" is the possessive of "it."   "It's" means "it is" or "it has."

ours   mine   yours   its   hers   theirs   (EXCEPTION: one's)

NOT: *Our's* is the first. . .   . . .until it met *her's* and my approval.
BUT: Ours is the first. . .   . . .until it met her and my. . . (See p. 61.)

Possessive Pronouns in Combination.   (See p. 61.)

Possessives Before -ing Words and Phrases.   The possessive form should be used before an -ing word or phrase when the -ing word or phrase stands as a noun representing the focal idea.

NOT: We did not object to *them* selling.
(It is the selling that is under discussion, not the people themselves.)
THEREFORE: We did not object to **their selling.**

151

Some writers disregard this form of possessive, believing that a sentence is clear without it; but a perusal of the sentences below should convince the reader that the possessive makes the -ing word clearer and more meaningful in most instances.

TEST: Substitute a possessive pronoun, such as "his" or "their," before the -ing word.

NOT: Can we depend on *you* doing that?
BUT: Can we depend on **your** doing that?
NOT: They insisted upon *me* writing the letter.
BUT: They insisted upon **my** writing the letter.
NOT: It would result in *him* losing his job.
BUT: It would result in **his** losing his job.
NOT: ...if it comes to *us* being called.
BUT: ...if it comes to **our** being called.
NOT: ...that leads to *it* being misinterpreted.
BUT: ...that leads to **its** being misinterpreted.
NOT: It depends on the *President* accepting the compromise.
BUT: It depends on the **President's** accepting the compromise.
NOT: There is no reason for the *people* waiting there.
BUT: ...for the **people's** waiting there.
NOT: The *president*, the *secretary*, and the *manager* having to resign caused a sensation.
BUT: The **president's**, the **secretary's**, and the **manager's** having...
NOT: The First National Bank of the *North* closing made...
BUT: **The First National Bank of the North's** closing made...
COMMON: ...considered the possibility of anything destroying the crops.
FOR: ...of **anything's** destroying the crops.
COMMON: We can't imagine anybody caring to do that.
FOR: ...**anybody's** caring...
COMMON: It resulted in the hotel operating at a loss.
FOR: ...in the **hotel's** operating...
COMMON: They are responsible for New York being so street-conscious.
FOR: ...for **New York's** being so street-conscious.
COMMON: ...the possibility of the event never happening.
FOR: ...of the **event's** never happening.
COMMON: That should be left to those who can rely on their words not being misunderstood.
FOR: ...on their **words'** not being misunderstood.
COMMON: If you don't like that prophecy coming true...
FOR: If you don't like that **prophecy's** coming true...
COMMON: No danger of the rule being broken...
FOR: ...of the **rule's** being broken...
COMMON: It was caused by a night watchman falling asleep.
FOR: ...by a night **watchman's** falling asleep.
COMMON: We must insist on all employees being punctual.
FOR: ...on all **employees'** being punctual.
COMMON: You can rely on our goods arriving on time.
FOR: ...on our **goods'** arriving on time.
COMMON: It was caused by the printer or the editor mistaking...
FOR: ...by the **printer's or the editor's** mistaking...
COMMON: ...with neither buyer nor seller being advised of it.
FOR: ...with neither **buyer's nor seller's** being advised of it.
COMMON: Instead of labor and capital working together...
FOR: Instead of **labor and capital's** working together...
COMMON: That is like an hors d'oeuvre being served after dinner.
FOR: That is like an **hors d'oeuvre's** being served after dinner.

152

If a singular verb follows an -ing phrase, check to see whether or not a possessive is needed before the -ing phrase to make it a singular thought.

NOT: The small banks extending credit **violates** the law.
BUT: The **small banks' extending credit violates** the law.
OR: The small **banks** [that are] extending credit **violate** the law.

"This," "that," "any," "all," "each," "few," "several," and **"some,"** and naturally **"these"** and **"those,"** do not take the possessive.

We had not heard of **that** being done.   (NOT: *that's*)
There is no likelihood of **any** being sold.   (NOT: *any's*)
There is a chance of **this** going on indefinitely.

After "prevent"—the possessive is used if an -ing word immediately follows; but it is not used if "from" is employed.

NOT: A guard was called to prevent *them* carrying away souvenirs.
BUT: ...to prevent **their** carrying away souvenirs.
OR: ...to **prevent them from** carrying away souvenirs.
NOT: We could not prevent the *men* going ahead with it.
BUT: ...prevent the **men's** going ahead with it.
OR: ...**prevent the men from** going ahead with it.

When Possessives Are Not Used Before -ing Words and Phrases. Not all -ing words and phrases require the possessive.   The sense of the sentence must be considered first.   When in doubt, analyze meanings.

TEST: Insert **"who is"** or **"that is"** before the -ing word.

It depends upon the man reporting the proceedings whether or not we get the whole story.
(This means that it depends on **the man** [who is] reporting.)
It depends upon the man's reporting the proceedings whether or not we get the whole story.
(This means that it depends on **the reporting.**)
A man [who is] spending everything he earns is like an improvident beaver [that is] tossing away everything it gathers.
(This means that **the man** is like **the beaver.**)
A man's spending everything he earns is like an improvident beaver's tossing away everything it gathers.
(This means that **the spending** is like **the tossing.**)
We watch the newcomer struggling for a foothold...
(We watch **the newcomer** himself [who is struggling].)
We watch the newcomer's struggling for a foothold...
(We watch **the struggling.**)

Three ways of using -ing words:
The **convention** being held in Chicago will bring many on to New York.
(This means that the convention [that is being held] will bring...)
The **convention's being held** in Chicago will bring many on to New York.
(This signifies that the "being held in Chicago" is the primary idea.)
The convention being held in Chicago, travel-time will be divided.
(This is a detached or "absolute" phrase, in a parenthetical use.)

— — — —

In view of the **consideration** [that is] being given their petition...
With no **consideration's being given** their petition, they are now...
("That is" could not be inserted after "consideration" here.)
No consideration being given them, they are forced...   (absolute phrase)

153

If the one-thought -ing phrase is broken into by another phrase or clause, the possessive, to avoid awkwardness, is not used.

> We appreciated the difficulty of any man with so slight an education accomplishing the task.
> (The simple sentence is: We appreciated the difficulty of any man's accomplishing the task. But "with so slight an education" intervenes.)

Also, in other sentences where the possessive would be awkward, it is not used.

> The possibility of his **absence** being considered as evidence...
> We object to its **truth** being assumed without...
> They insist on **none** being left out.
> There was no necessity for **all the rest** declining.

Possessive Names in Caps. In running text, as in legal papers, the possessive 's following a name set in full caps may be lower-cased, as "Mr. **NELSON's** testimony." But in a headline or title set in full caps, the possessive is also capitalized, as

GOVERNOR NELSON'S TAX PLAN

Yet, the plural or singular possessive of an **abbreviation** in an all-cap heading may, for clarity, be lower-cased as usual:

MPs' JURISDICTION   SDRs' GOLD BACKING   FDR's WAY

～

on Pronunciation

WORDS

Emerson says that reading lists of words may inflame the imagination.

* * *

Conrad once wrote: . . . "Give me the right word and the right accent, and I will move the world."

—Ellsworth, *Creative Writing*,
Funk & Wagnalls Company,
New York

Pronunciation undergoes change. Know first, however, that which is correct, then gradually adopt the change.

Abbreviations Used in This Section

abbr.	abbreviation	L.	Latin
adj.	adjective	mas.	masculine
adv.	adverb	mil.	military
Am.	American	n.	noun
Ar.	Arabic	naut.	nautical
Aus.	Austrian	Nor.	Norwegian
Boh.	Bohemian	pert.	pertaining
Br.	British	Pg.	Portuguese
colloq.	colloquial	pl.	plural
dial.	dialectal	Pol.	Polish
Du.	Dutch	prep.	preposition
Eng.	English	pron.	pronounced, or pronunciation
fem.	feminine	Prus.	Prussian
Fin.	Finnish	Rus.	Russian
Fr.	French	sing.	singular
Ger.	German	Sp.	Spanish
Gk.	Greek	Sw.	Swedish
Hung.	Hungarian	syl.	syllables
It.	Italian	U.S.	United States
Jap.	Japanese	v.	verb

PRONUNCIATION SYMBOLS

Marking	Sound	As in
ā	long a............................	āle
ă	short a...........................	ădd
â	the ă(r) sound....................	câre
ä	the Italian a.....................	ärt
á̇	between ä and ă...................	fȧst
a̤	the aw sound......................	a̤ll
a	(unmarked) a soft uh sound.........	about
ch	soft ch...........................	chin
ē	long e............................	ēve
ĕ	short e...........................	lĕt
ẽ	the uh sound......................	fẽrn
e	(unmarked) a soft eh sound.........	moment
g	hard g............................	go
ī	long i............................	īce
ĭ	short i...........................	ĭll
i	(unmarked) a soft ih sound.........	habit
j	soft..............................	jet
k	hard..............................	park
K	German fricative ch sound..........	ich, ach
ṅ	French nasal tone.................	embonpoint (äṅ′bôṅ′pwăṅ′)
ō	long o............................	ōld
ŏ	short o...........................	ŏdd
ô	the aw sound......................	nôrth
o	(unmarked) a soft uh sound.........	won
ōō	long double o.....................	mōōn
ŏŏ	short double o....................	fŏŏt
ou	the ow sound......................	out
oi	the oy sound......................	oil
ū	long u............................	ūse
ŭ	short u...........................	ŭp
û	the ŭ(r) sound....................	bûrn
ṳ	same as short double o — ŏŏ........	fṳll
u	(unmarked) a soft uh sound.........	submit
ü	a muted e sound, as in a German umlaut (as if one started to say ōō and said ē)	München (mün′Kĕn)

′	primary accent	¯	macron (mā′kron)	(for names of other
′	secondary accent	˘	breve (brēv)	marks, see p. 228)

◇◇◇◇◇◇◇◇◇

Foreign Pronunciations. In the lists of foreign words, the pronunciations given are those commonly used in English, whether they are the foreign pronunciations or English versions thereof. If the foreign and English pronunciations differ widely, both are given.

∾

Pronunciation

To speak correctly signifies accuracy.

COMMON WORDS

A

abdomen ăb-dō′men, or ăb′do-men
ablution ăb-lū′shŭn
abnormality ăb′nôr-măl′i-ty
abstemious ăb-stē′mi-us
accent (n.) ăk′sent; (v.) ăk-sĕnt′
accessory ăk-sĕs′o-ry, not *assess-*
accidentally ăk-si-dĕn′tal-ly, or
   -dĕnt′ly
acclimate a-klī′mat, or ăk′li-māt
accompaniment a-kŭm′pa-nĭ-ment, or
   a-kŭmp′nē-
accompanist a-kŭm′pa-nĭst, or
   a-kŭmp′nist, not *-nē-ist*
accurate ăk′ū-rat, not *ak-rit*
acrimony ăk′rĭ-mō-ny
acumen a-kū′men, not *ăk′*
addict (n.) ăd′ikt; (v.) ă-dĭkt′
address ă-drĕs′ (note accent)
adept (adj.) ă-dĕpt′; (n.) ăd′ĕpt
admirable ăd′mĭ-ra-bl, not *ad-mīr′*
adult á-dŭlt′ (note accent)
advertisement ăd-vĕr′tĭz-ment, or
   ăd′vĕr-tīz′ment
aeon ē′ŏn, not *ā′on*
aerate ā′ĕr-āt, or âr′āt, not *air′ee-ate*
aerial ā-ē′ri-al, or âr′
aesthetic ĕs-thĕt′ik (Br. ēs-)
affluent ăf′lū-ent, not *a-flu′*
agape á-gāp′, or á-găp′
aged ā′jed, as "an aged person"
   ājd, as "aged 47"
aggrandizement ă-grăn′dĭz-ment, or
   ăg′grăn-dĭz′ment
albeit ạl′bē′it, not *ăl-*
albino ăl-bī′nō (Br. ăl-bē′nō)
albumen ăl-bū′mĕn
alchemist ăl′ke-mĭst
a'ias ā′lē-as, not *a-lye′us*
alienate āl′yĕn-āt

align a-līn′
alleged a-lĕjd′, not *a-lej′ed*, but
allegedly ă-lĕj′ed-ly
alloy (n.) ăl′oi; (v.) ă-loi′
almanac ạl′ma-năk, not *ăl-*, nor *ŏl-*
altercation ạl′ter-kā′shun, or ăl′
alternate (n. & adj.) ạl′tĕr-nĭt, or ăl′
alternate (v.) ạl′tĕr-nāt, or ăl′
altimeter ăl-tĭm′e-ter, or ăl′tĭ-mē′ter
altruism ăl′trōō-izm, not *awl-*
aluminum a-lū′mĭ-num, not *-mē-um*
ambergris ăm′ber-grēs
ambiguity ăm′bĭ-gū′i-ty
amen ā′men′, or ä′men′ in singing
amenable a-mē′na-bl, but
amenity a-mĕn′i-ty
Amish ä′mĭsh, or ăm′ish (a sect)
analogous a-năl′ō-gŭs, not *-ajus*
analytical ăn′a-lĭt′i-kal, not *-lĕtt*
anathema a-năth′e-ma (a curse)
   ăn′a-thē′ma (an offering)
antarctic ănt-ärk′tĭk, not *ăn-är′tik*
antipathy ăn-tĭp′a-thy
antipodes ăn-tĭp′o-dēz, not *antĭ-pōds*
apparatus ăp′a-rā′tus, or -răt′us
appellate a-pĕl′ĭt (note accent)
applicable ăp′li-ka-bl (note accent)
appreciate a-prē′shĭ-āt, not *-see-ate*
aquamarine ăk′wá-má-rēn′, or äk′
aquaplane ăk′wá-plān′, or äk′
aqueduct ăk′we-dŭkt
arbiter är′bĭ-ter, not *-bīte′*
archangel ärk′ān′jĕl
archipelago är′ki-pĕl′a-gō, not *arch-*
archives är′kīvz
aristocrat a-rĭs′tō-krăt, or ăr′ĭs-
artistically är-tĭs′ti-kal-ly
artistry är′tis-try
asinine ăs′i-nīn
asphalt ăs′fạlt, or -fălt

āle, ădd, câre, ärt, fȧst, ạll, about | ēve, lĕt, fērn, moment | īce, Ĭll, habit | ōld, ŏdd, nôrth, won | mōōn, fŏŏt
158

aspirant ă-spīr′ant, or ăs′pi-rant
associate (v.) a-sō′shē-āt; (n., adj.) -it
asterisk ăs′ter-ĭsk, not-*rich*
athletic ăth-lĕt′ik, not *atha-*
atrophy ăt′rō-fĭ, not -*fī*
attacked a-tăkt′, not *a-tak-ted*
attar ăt′ar
attorney ă-tûr′ny, not *a-tawr-*
audacious ạ-dā′shus, not -*dăsh*
aunt ănt, or ȧnt
aura ạ′rȧ, not ō-*ra*
austere ạs-tēr′, not -*tĕr*
authoritatively ạ-thôr′i-tā′tiv-ly, not
    a-thor′a-tively
autocracy ạ-tŏk′ra-sy
automation ạ-tō-mā′shun
automaton ạ-tŏm′a-tŏn
autopsy ạ′tŏp-sy, not *autop′sy*
auxiliary ạg-zĭl′ya-ry, not *awk-zil′ree*
aviation ā′vĭ-ā′shun, or ăv′
avoirdupois ăv′ōr-dụ-poiz′, not *adver-*
avuncular ȧ-vŭng′kū-ler (of an uncle)
awry a-rī′, not *aw′ry*

B

baccalaureate băk′a-lạr′ē-et
bacchanalian băk′a-nā′li-ăn, not -*năl*
bagatelle băg′a-tĕl′, not -*teel*
bailiwick bāl′i-wĭk, not *băl-*
bakelite bā′kĕ-līt
balderdash bạl′der-dăsh, not *băl-*
balsam bạl′sam
baptize băp-tīz′, not *bab-*
barbecue bär′be-kū, not *barber-*
beleaguer bē-lē′ger, not -*lĕgūar*
benignant bē-nĭg′nănt
bequeath bē-kwēthe′ (like "breathe")
bestial bĕs′chal
betrothed bē-trōthe′d, or -trôtht′
Biblical bĭb′lĭ-kal, not *bib-i-kal*
binocular bĭn-ŏk′ū-lar, or bī-nŏk′
biography bĭ-ŏg′ra-fy, not *bee-*
bituminous bĭ-tū′mĭ-nus, not *bī-*
blackguard blăg′ärd
blaspheme blăs-fēm′, not -*fĕm*
blatant blā′tant, not *blăt-*
blouse blouss, or blouz
brethren brĕthe′rĕn, not -*ern*
brigand brĭg′and (note accent)
brogan brō′gan, or brō-găn′
buncombe bŭn′kum

bureaucracy bū-rŏk′rȧ-sy
burglar bûr′glar, not *berg-u-ler*

C

cachinnation kăk′ĭ-nā′shun
cacophony kă-kŏf′o-ny, not *kăck′a-fōny*
calumny kăl′ŭm-ny, not *calum′*
candidate kăn′dĭ-dāt, or -dĭt
cantonment kăn-tōn′ment, or -tŏn′
caramel kăr′a-mĕl (dial. kärm′el)
cartridge kär′trĭj, not *cat-*
catch kăch (colloq. kĕch)
cater-cornered kăt′er-
cavil kăv′il
Cayenne pepper kī-ĕn′, or kā-ĕn′
centaur sĕn′tôr
centrifugal sĕn-trĭf′ū-gal, not -*trifical*
chaos kā′ŏs, not *ka-ōss′*
chasm kăz′m
chastisement chăs′tĭz-ment, or -tĭz′
cherubic che-rōō′bĭk (note accent)
chimera kī-mē′ra, or kĭ-
chimney chĭm′ny, not *chim-ley*
choleric kŏl′ĕr-ĭk, not *kō-lĕr′ek*
circuitous sēr-kū′i-tus, not *serkit-*
clandestine klăn-dĕs′tin (note accent)
claret klăr′ĕt, not *klary-et*
cleanly (adj.) klĕn′ly; (adv.) klēn′ly
cognomen kŏg-nō′men (note accent)
coleslaw kōl′slaw, not *cold-*
collegiate kŏ-lē′jĭt, or -jĭ-at
column kŏl′ŭm, not -*yŭm*, nor -*yūme*
columnist kŏl′ŭm-ist, or kŏl′ŭm-nist
comatose kō′ma-tōs, or kŏm′a-tōs
combatant kom-băt′ant, or kŏm′
comely kŭm′lē, not *kōam′lee*
commandant kŏm′an-dănt′, or -dänt′
communal kŏm′ū-nal, or ko-mū′nal
comparable kŏm′par-a-bl (note accent)
condolence kŏn-dō′lens
conduit kŏn′dwit, or kŏn′dōō-it
confiscate kŏn′fis-kāt, not -*fisti-*
conjugal kŏn′jụ-gal (note accent)
connubial kŏ-nū′bi-al, not -*nŭb*
constable kŭn′sta-bl, or kŏn′
construe kŏn-strōō′ (Br. kŏn′strōō)
contemplate kŏn′tem-plāt, or -tĕm′
contiguous kŏn-tĭg′ū-us
contrast (n.) kŏn′trăst; (v.) kon-trăst′
controversial kŏn′trō-vēr′shal
conversant kŏn′ver-sant, or -vērs′

---

oil, out | ūse, ŭp, bûrn, fụll, submit; ü—a muted e | chin; go; jet; park; K—Ger. ch; Fr. n̂—a nasal tone

Cordovan kôr′dō-van
corroborate ko-rŏb′ō-rāt, not *cor-rŏb′*
counterfeit koun′ter-fĭt (Br. -fēt)
covert kŭv′ert, or kō′vert
crayon krā′on, not *krĕn*
credence krē′dĕns, not *krĕd-*
crematory krē′ma-tō′ry, or krĕm′
cretonne krē-tŏn′ (Br. krĕt′ŏn)
crucial krōō′shal
culinary kū′lĭ-nĕr′y, not *kŭl-*
curator kū-rā′tor (law kūr′a-tor)

D

daguerreotype da-gĕr′ō-tīp
dais dā′is, not *dī-*
damask dăm′ask, not *da-mask′*
daub dąb, not *dŏb*
dawdle dą′dl, not *dwä-*
decadence dē-kā′dĕns, or dĕk′à-
decibel dĕs′i-bĕl (note accent)
decorous dē-kō′rus, or dĕk′o-rus
decoy (n.) dē′koy; (v.) dē-koy′
decrepit dē-krĕp′it, not *-id*
deficit dĕf′i-sĭt (Br. dĭ-fĭs′it)
degradation dĕg′ra-dā′shun
delete dē-lēt′, not *dā-*
demoniacal dē′mō-nī′a-kal
depot dē′pō (Br. and mil. dĕp′ō)
deprivation dĕp′rĭ-vā′shun
derelict dĕr′ĕ-lĭkt, not *deer-*
derisive dē-rī′sĭv, not *-rĭz*
despicable dĕs′pĭ-ka-bl, or dĕs-pĭk′
desultory dĕs′ŭl-tō-ry (note accent)
detail (n.) dē-tāl′, or dē′; (v.) de-tāl′
deteriorate dē-tēr′ē-ō-rāt (5 syl.)
deterrent dē-tûr′ĕnt, or -tĕr′
detestation dē′tĕs-tā′shun
detonation dĕt′ō-nā′shun, or dē′to-
diagnosis dī′ăg-nō′sis, not *-nŏs*
diffident dĭf′i-dĕnt, not *div-*
digest (n.) dī′jĕst; (v.) dĭ-jĕst′
diminution dĭm′i-nū′shun, not *-uāshun*
diocese dī′ō-sĕss (Br. dī′ŭ-sĭss)
dirigible dĭr′i-jĭ-bl
discharge dĭs-chärj′, or dĭs′
disconcerting dĭs′kŏn-sĕrt′ing
discretion dĭs-krĕsh′un, not *-krē*
disheveled dĭ-shĕv′eld, not *dis-hē′veld*
dissoluble dĭ-sŏl′ū-bl
distillate dĭs′tĭ-lāt, or dis-tĭl′āt
docile dŏs′ĭl (Br. dō′sīl)

doldrums dŏl′drŭmz, or dōl′
dolor dō′lor, but
dolorous dŏl′ĕr-us, or dō′, not *do-lōr′*
domicile dŏm′i-sĭl (Br. -sīl)
donor dō′nor, not *dŏnner*
dotage dōt′ĭj, not *dŏt-*
dour dour (Br. dōōr)
drama drä′ma, or drăm′à
dramatize drăm′a-tīz
dross drôs, not *drŏss*
drowned dround, not *drown-ded*
duchy dŭch′y, not *duke-y*
dynamite dī′na-mīt, not *dăn-*
dynamo dī′na-mō, not *dăn-*
dynasty dī′nas-ty (Br. dĭn′)

E

eclipse ē-klĭps′ (note accent)
economical ē′kō-nŏm′i-kal, or ĕk′ō-
edict ē′dĭkt
eerie ēr′ee, not *ĕrr′y*
effervesce ĕf′ĕr-vĕs′, not *ep′er-fess*
efficacious ĕf′ĭ-kā′shŭs, not *-kăsh*
ego ē′gō, or ĕg′ō
electrolysis ē-lĕk′trŏl′i-sis, not *-trōl*
embroider ĕm-broi′der, not *-ry*
embryo ĕm′brē-ō
emeritus ē-mĕr′i-tus, not *-ī′tus*
emolument ē-mŏl′ū-ment
ensconced ĕn-skŏnst′, not *ĕss-konst′*
ensign ĕn′sīn (Navy ĕn′sĭn)
envelope ĕn′vĕ-lōp (Fr. äṅ′v′lup′)
environment ĕn-vī′run-ment, not *-vĭrm*
epaulet ĕp′ŏ-lĕt
ephemeral ĕ-fĕm′er-al
episodic ĕp′i-sŏd′ik, not *-sōd′*
epitome ē-pĭt′ō-mē (4 syl.)
equanimity ē′kwa-nĭm′i-ty, or ĕk′
era ē′ra, or ĭr′a, not *ĕrr′a*
err ĕr (Br. ûr)
erudite ĕr′yōō-dīt, or ĕr′ōō-
escalator ĕs′ka-lā′tor, not *escū-*
exigency ĕk′sĭ-jĕn-sy, or ĕg-zĭj′
exit ĕk′sit, or ĕg′zit
experiment ĕks-pĕr′i-ment, or -pĕr′
exquisite ĕks′kwi-zit, or ĕks-kwĭz′it
extol ĕks-tōl′, or -tŏl′
extraneous ĕks-trā′nē-us
extraordinary ĕks-trôr′di-ner′y
extreme unction ĕks′trŭm-ŭngk′shŭn

ăle, ădd, câre, ärt, fàst, ạll, about | ēve, lĕt, fẽrn, moment | īce, ĭll, habit | ōld, ŏdd, nôrth, won | mōōn, fŏŏt

F

February fĕb'rų-er'y, commonly fĕb'ū-
finagle fĭ-nā'gl
finance fĭ-năns', or fī'
flaccid flăk'sĭd, not *flăss-*
flagrant flā'grant, not *flăg-*
flammable flăm'à-bl (preferred to "inflammable" [See p. 133.])
forehead fôr'ĕd, or fôr'hĕd
formidable fôr'mĭ-da-bl, not *for-mid'*
fossil fŏs'il, not *faws-*
fracas frā'kas (Br. frăk'ä) (Fr. frȧ'kä')
fragile frăj'il (Br. -īl)
fraternize frăt'er-nīz, not *fratra-*
funereal fū-nē'rē-al

G

gala gā'la, or găl'a (Br. gä'la)
garrulous găr'ŭ-lus, or găr'ū-
genealogy jĕn'ē- or jē'nē-ăl'ō-jy, or -ăl'
generic je-nĕr'ĭk (opp. of "specific")
genuine jĕn'ū-in, not *-u-wine*
giblets jĭb'lĕts (note j sound)
gigantic jī-găn'tik, not *jĭ-*
government gŭv'ẽrn-ment, not *guvver-*
granary grăn'a-ry, or grăn'a-ry
grievous grēv'us, not *-i-ous*
grimace grĭ-mās'
grimy grīm'y, not *grĭmy*
grovel grŏv'l
guarantee găr'an-tē', not *gär-*
gubernatorial gū'bĕr-na-tō'rĭ-al, not
gŭb- (pert. to a governor)
guillotine gĭl'ō-tēn (Fr. ghē-yȧ-tēn')
gums gŭmz, not *gōōmz*
gyroscope jī'rō-skōp, not *guy-*

H

halo hā'lō, not *hăl-o*
harass hăr'as, or hȧ-răs'
hearth härth (dial. hẽrth)
heathen hē'then, not *-ern*
hegira hē-jī'ra, or hĕj'ĭ-ra
height hīt, not *hīthe*, nor *hydth*
heinous hā'nŭs, not *hee'nee-*
helicopter hĕl'ĭ-kŏp'ter, or hē'li-
Herculean hẽr-kū'lē-an, not *hurk-ya-lăn*
hiatus hī-ā'tŭs
hierarchy hī'er-är'ky
hirsute hûr'sōōt, or -sūt (hairy)

holocaust hŏl'o-kôst, or hō'lo-
homage hŏm'ĭj, not *hōm-*
homicide hŏm'ĭ-sīd, or hō'mi-
honorary ŏn'ẽr-ĕr'y, not *oner-ry*
hoof hōōf, or hoof, not *hŭf*
horizon hō-rī'zun
hosiery hō'zhẽr-ē (colloq. hōz'rē)
hospitable hŏs'pi-ta-bl (Br. hŏs-pĭt')
hostage hŏs'tĭj, not *hōst-*
hostile hŏs'tĭl (Br. -tīl)
hovel hŭv'l, or hŏv'el
hover hŭv'er, not *hō-*
humble hŭm'bl, rarely ŭm'bl
humor hū'mor, rarely ū'mor
hundred hŭn'drĕd, not *-derd*
hurricane hûr'i-kān, not *hẽr-*
hysteria hĭs-tēr'ĭ-a, or -tẽr'

I

identify ĭ-dĕn'ti-fī, not *ĭden-*
identity ĭ-dĕn'ti-ty, not *ĭd-ĕn'ŭ-tee*
ignominious ĭg'nō-mĭn'ē-us, not *ig-nŏm'*
ignominy ĭg'nō-mĭn-y (note accent)
ignoramus ĭg'nō-rā'mus, not *-răm*
illustrate ĭl'us-trāt, or il-lŭs'
imbecile ĭm'be-sĭl (Br. -sēl, or -sĭl)
impious ĭm'pĭ-us (note accent)
implacable im-plā'ka-bl, or -plăk'
impotent ĭm'pō-tent (note accent)
improvisation im'prŏv-i-zā'shun
inaugurate in-a̤'gū-rāt (colloq. -a̤g'ẽr-)
incidentally in'sĭ-dĕn'tal-ly
incognito in-kŏg'nĭ-tō, not *-nee'to*
incongruous in-kŏng'grų-us
indefatigable in'dē-făt'ĭ-ga-bl
indigenous in-dĭj'e-nus
indomitable in-dŏm'ĭ-ta-bl, not *-nit-*
inebriety in'ē-brī'e-ty
inexplicable in-ĕks'plĭ-ka-bl (Br. splĭk')
infamous ĭn'fȧ-mus (note accent)
infantile ĭn'fan-tĭl, or -tĭl
inherent in-hĭr'ent, or -hẽr'
initiative ĭ-nĭsh'e-a-tĭv, not *-ŭ-ā-tiv*
inquiry in-kwīr'y, or ĭn'kwĭ-ry
interesting ĭn'tẽr-est-ing (Br. -trĭs-ting)
introduce ĭn'trō-dūs', not *inter-*
inveigle in-vē'gl, or -vā'
irate ī'rāt', not *ĭr-*
ironical ī-rŏn'i-kal, not *ĭr-*
irradiate ĭ-rā'di-āt
irrelevant ĭr-rĕl'e-vant, not *irrev'e-lent*

---

oil, out | ūse, ŭp, bûrn, fųll, submit; ŭ—a muted e | chin; go; jet; park; K—Ger. ch; Fr. ñ—a nasal tone

irremediable ĭr'rē-mē'di-a-bl
irreparable ĭ-rĕp'a-ra-bl
irrevocable ĭ-rĕv'ō-ka-bl
isolate ī'sō-lāt, or ĭs'ō-
itinerary ī-tĭn'ĕr-er'y, not -tin-e-ry

J

jewelry jōō'ĕl-ry, not jū'luh-ree
jocose jō-kōs'
jocund jŏk'und
just jŭst, not jest
juvenile jōō've-nĭl (Br. -nīl)

K

kerosene kĕr'ō-sēn', not kăr-a-
kilometer kĭl'ō-mē'ter, not ki-lŏm'
Ku Klux Klan kū'klŭks'klăn, not klōō-

L

lambaste lăm-bāst'
lamentable lăm'en-ta-bl, or la-mĕnt'
laser lā'zer (focused light)
latent lā'tĕnt, not lăt-
Latter Day Saint lăt'er, not lāte-
laundered lạn'dĕrd, not -drēd
learned (adj.) lûr'ned (erudite)
legerdemain lĕj'er-de-mān'
leisure lē'zhur (Br. lĕzh')
length lĕngkth, not lĕnth
lethal lē'thal
lethargy -ic lĕth'ar-jē, but le-thär'jĭk
lever lĕv'er, or lē'ver
limning lĭm'ing, or lĭm'ning
lissome lĭs'um, not lī-
literary lĭt'ĕr-er'y, not lit-re-ry
literature lĭt'er-a-chur, or lĭt'ra-chụr
longevity lŏn-jĕv'i-ty, not long-gev'
long-lived -līvd (Br. -lĭvd)
lowering lou'er-ing, not lō' (glowering)
lugubrious lŭ-gōō'brē-us, not -gŭb'

M

macabre mȧ-kä'ber, or -brŭh, not -bray
macadamized măk-ăd'am-īzd
machination măk'i-nā'shun, not mash-
magneto măg-nē'tō
maintenance mān'te-nans, not -tān'
malefactor măl'ē-făk'tor, not māl-
malevolent ma-lĕv'ō-lent
marcasite mär'ka-sīt, not -zĭt
marshmallow märsh'măl'ō (colloq.
　　　-mĕl-)

mausoleum mạ'sō-lē'um, not mō-
medieval mē'dĭ-ē'val (Br. mĕd')
melancholia mel'ăn-kō'lĭ-a, not -kŏl
melodic mē-lŏd'ik, not -lōd
memento mē-mĕn'tō, or mĭ-, not mō-
menace mĕn'as, not men-ance
mercantile mĕr'kăn-tĭl, or -tīl
mercury mĕr'kū-ry, not murk-ry
metallurgy mĕt'a-lûr'jy
metamorphosis mĕt'a-môr'fō-sis
microscopic mī'krō-skŏp'ik, not -skōp
mineralogy min'er-ăl'ō-jy or -räl'
miniature mĭn'ĭ-a-chụr
minority mĭ-nŏr'i-ty, or mī-
minute mĭ-nūt', or mī-nūt' (tiny)
mischievous mĭs'chĭ-vŭs, not -chee'vē-
misled mĭs-lĕd', not mizzeled
misnomer mis-nō'mer, not -nŏm
modicum mŏd'ĭ-kŭm, not mōd-
momentous mō-mĕn'tus, not -tu-ous
monetary mŏn'e-ter'y, or mŭn'
mongrel mŭng'grĕl, or mŏng'
monologist mō-nŏl'ō-jĭst, or
　　　mŏn'ō-lôg'ist
morganatic môr'ga-năt'ik (4 syl.)
moron mō'rŏn (note accent)
motorcycle mō'ter-sī'kl (note long ī)
mountebank moun'tē-bangk (3 syl.)
municipal mū-nĭs'i-pal, not muni-sip'ul

N

nape nāp (colloq. năp)
napery nā'pēr-y, not năp-
naphtha năp'tha, or năf'
narrator nă-rā'ter (note accent)
noisome noi'sŭm (offensive)
nomad nō'măd (Br. nŏm'ad)
nomenclature nō'men-klā'tūr, not nŏm'
nuptial nŭp'shal, not -shōō-al

O

oaf ōf, not ōōf
obdurate ŏb'dū-rāt
obese ō-bēs'
obesity ō-bēs'i-ty, or ō-bĕs'
obituary ō-bĭt'ū-er'y
obsequious ŏb-sē'kwē-ús
occult ŏ-kŭlt', or ŏk'ult
octogenarian ŏk'tō-je-nâr'i-an
often ôf'n, or ôft'n
ogle ō'gl, not ŏg'l

ogre ō′ger, not ôrg
olfactory ŏl-făk′tō-ry not ōle-
omen ō′men, not ah-men, but
ominous ŏm′i-nus
omnipotent ŏm-nĭp′ō-tent, not
        omni-potent, but
omnipresent ŏm′nĭ-prĕz′ent
once wŭnss, not wunst
onerous ŏn′er-us, not ōn-, but
onus ō′nus
onyx ŏn′iks, or ō′niks
operative ŏp′ēr-ā′tĭv (Br. ŏp′rȧ-tĭv)
orgy ôr′jy, not org′y
overalls ō′ver-ạlz, not -halls

P

pageant păj′ent, not pā′jent
pandemonium păn′dĕ-mō′nē-um, not
        -mōm′
panorama păn′ō-rä′ma, or -răm′
pantomime păn′tō-mīm, not -mine
papal pā′pal, not păp-l
paradisiacal păr′a-dĭ-sī′a-kăl, not -dizy-
paraffin păr′a-fĭn
paraphernalia păr′a-fēr-nā′li-a
parasitic păr′a-sĭt′ik, not -sīt
parboil pär′boil′, not păre-
parliament pär′la-ment, not -li-a-
parochial pa-rō′kĭ-al
partition pär-tĭsh′un, not păh-tish′n
partner pärt′ner, not pard′
pastoral pás′tōr-al, not pastōr′al
patronize pā′trŭ-nīz′, or păt′rŭn-īz
pecuniary pe-kū′ni-er′y
pedagogy pĕd′a-gō′jy
pedantry pĕd′ănt-ry
penalize pē′nal-īz, or pĕn′al-īz
peninsula pĕn-ĭn′su-la (colloq. pŭn-)
penury pĕn′ū-ry (note accent)
percale pēr-kāl′, or -kăl′
percolate pēr′kō-lāt, not per′kew-
perform pēr-fôrm′, not prē-
perfume (n.) pēr′fūm; (v.) pēr-fūm′
peroration pĕr′ō-rā′shun, not prē-
perspiration pēr′spī-rā′shun, not prēs
pessimistic pĕs′ĭ-mĭs′tik, not pesta-
philanthropy fĭ-lăn′thrō-py, not -fy
philatelic fĭl′a-tĕl′ĭk (note accent)
philatelist fĭ-lăt′e-list (stamp collector)
phosphorus (n.) fŏs′fō-rus, not fŏss-for′
picture pĭk′chûr, not -tūr, nor pitch′er

piteous pĭt′ē-us, not pit-yus
placard plăk′ard
placate plā′kāt, or plăk′ăt
placer plăs′er, not plā- (mining)
plebeian plē-bē′an, not pleeb′yun
poem pō′ĕm, not pōme
poignant poin′yănt, or -ănt
portrait pōr′trāt, or -trit
posthumous pŏs′tū-mus, not pōst
precedence prē-sēd′enss, or prĕs′e-
precedent (n.) prĕs′e-dent; (adj.)
        prē-sēd′ent
predecessor prĕd′ē-sĕs′er (Br. prē′)
predicament prē-dĭk′ȧ-ment, not pûr-
prediction prē-dĭk′shun, not pûr-
preferable prĕf′er-a-bl
premature prē′ma-tūr′ (Br. prĕm′a-)
premonition prē′mō-nĭsh′un, not prĕm-
prerogative prē-rŏg′a-tiv, not pûr-og-
presage (v.) prē-sāj′; (n.) prĕs′ĭj
prescience prē′shĭ-ĕns, or prĕsh′
prescription prē-skrĭp′shun, not pûr-
presentation prĕz′en-tā′shun, or prē′
pretend prē-tĕnd′, not pûr-
pretty prĭt′y, not pŭrty, nor prĕty
preventive prē-vĕn′tiv, not -ta-tiv
processes prŏs′ĕs-ĭz (Br. prō′sĕs-ĭz)
prodigal prŏd′i-gal, not proj-i-gŭl
produce (n.) prŏd′ūs, or prō′dūs
profile prō′fĭl (Br. prō′fēl)
program prō′grăm, not -grŭm
progress (n.) prŏg′rĕs (Br. prō′grĕs)
promulgate prō-mŭl′gāt (Br. prŏm′ŭl-)
pronunciation prō-nŭn′sē-ā′shun, not
        pro-nown-
propaganda prŏp′a-găn′da (Br. prō′)
protocol prō′to-kŏl, not -koal
puerile pū′er-ĭl (note accent)
pulpit pụl′pit, not pŭlp′it
pyramidal pĭ-răm′i-dal

Q

qualitative kwŏl′i-tā′tĭv, not kwol-i-tive
quantitative kwŏn′ti-tā′tiv, not -ti-tive
quintuplets kwĭn′tū′plĕts, or -tŭp′

R

raillery rāl′er-y
rancor răng′kĕr, not ran-ser
rapier rā′pĭ-er, not ră-peer
ration rā′shun, or răsh′un
really rē′a-ly, or rē′ly, not rĭlly

oil, out | ūse, ŭp, bûrn, fụll, submit; ü—a muted e | chin; go; jet; park; K—Ger. ch; Fr. ṅ—a nasal tone

recluse (n.) rē-kloōs', or rĕk'loōs
recognize rĕk'ŭg-nīz, not rĕka-nize
reconnoiter rĕk'ŏ-noi'ter, or rē'kŏ-
recuperate rē-kū'per-āt
regatta rē-găt'a
renege rē-nēg', not -nāg
repast rē-pàst', not ree'past
repatriate rē-pā'trē-āt (Br. rē-păt')
repercussion rē'pĕr-kŭsh'un, not rĕp-er
reputable rĕp'ū-ta-bl (note accent)
research rē-sĕrch', or rē'
reservoir rĕz'er-vwôr, not rĕz'uh-voy
respite rĕs'pĭt, not ree'spīte
revocable rĕv'ō-ka-bl, not re-vōk'
rhapsodical răp-sŏd'i-kal, not raf-sō'
ribald rĭb'ald, not rye-bawld
rigmarole rĭg'ma-rōl, not riga-
rinse rĭnss, not rench
risibility rĭz'i-bĭl'i-ty, not rīse-
robot rō'bŏt, or rŏb'ŏt, not rō-bŏt
robust rō-bŭst', or rō'bŭst
romance rō-mǎns', or rō'mǎns
rotund rō-tŭnd' (note accent)

S

saccharine săk'a-rĭn, or -rīn, or -rēn
sacrifice (n.) săk'ri-fīs, not -fĭs, nor -fŭs
sacrilegious săk'ri-lē'jus, or -lĭj', not
    săk'
sagacious sà-gā'shŭs, not -găsh'us
salve săv, or säv
sandwich sănd'wich, or săn' (Br. -wĭj)
sapient sā'pĭ-ent, not săp-
satiety sà-tī'ĕ-ty
satirical să-tĭr'ĭ-kal, not -tīr
scenic sē'nik, or sĕn'ik
schism sĭz'm, not skism
scintillate sĭn'ti-lāt, not sink-, nor skĭn-
scion sī'un
scourge skûrj, not skōrj
secondhand -hand, not -handed
secretive sē-krē'tiv, or sē'krĭ-tiv
seismograph sīz'mō-graf, not sīs-a-mo-
senile sē'nīl, or -nĭl
sepulchral se-pŭl'kral
sergeant sär'jent
servile sûr'vĭl (Br. sûr'vīl)
short-lived -līvd (Br. -lĭvd)
significant sĭg-nĭf'i-kănt, not -gant
similar sĭm'ĭ-ler, not sim'you-ler
simultaneous sī'mŭl-tā'nē-us, or sĭm'

since sĭnss, not sense
skillet skĭl'et, not skĕl'
sobriety sō-brī'e-ty
solace sŏl'as, not sōl-
solder sŏd'ér (Br. sô'der)
solemnize sŏl'em-nīz (note accent)
somersault sŭm'er-sôlt ⎱ (inter-
somerset sŭm'er-sĕt ⎰ changeable)
sonorous sō-nō'rus (Br. sŏn'ō-rus)
soot sŏŏt, or soōt
sophomore sŏf'o-mōr (3 syl.)
spa spä
specimen spĕs'i-men, not -ment
spontaneity spŏn'ta-nē'i-ty, not -nā'
spurious spū'rē-us
squalor skwŏl'or, not skwä'lor
stabilize stā'bi-līz, rarely stăb'
stereotype stĕr'ē-ō-tīp', or stĕr'ē-
stipend stī'pĕnd, not stĭp-
stodgy stŏj'ē, not stō'gē
strategic stră-tē'jik
stupendous stū-pĕn'dus, not -jus
subsidiary sub-sĭd'ē-er'y (5 syl.)
succinct sŭk-sĭńkt'
superb sū-pĕrb', not su-berb
superfluous sū-pĕr'flŭ-us (note accent)
supple sŭp'ŭl, not soup'el
surprise sûr-prīz'
surreptitious sûr'ĕp-tĭsh'us, not sū-
sword sōrd, not s'ward
sycophant sĭk'ō-fant, not sin-ko-
syrup sĭr'up (colloq. sûr'up) (2 syl.)

T

tapestry tăp'ĕs-try, not tāpe-
tassel tăs'el, not tôss-
tedious tē'dĭ-us, or tē'jŭs
telescopic tĕl'e-skŏp'ik, not -skōpik
temperament tĕm'pĕr-à-ment (4 syl.)
temporal tĕm'po-ral, not tempō'ral
tensile tĕn'sĭl, or -sīl
tepid tĕp'id, not tee-pid
terrestrial tĕ-rĕs'trĭ-al
textile tĕks'tĭl, or -tīl
the thŭ, before a consonant sound, as
    "the temple," "the proceeds"
    thĭ, before a vowel sound, as "the
    end," "the act"
    thē, for emphasis, before either a
    vowel or a consonant sound, as
    "The End," "He is just the man."

āle, ădd, câre, ärt, fàst, ąll, about | ēve, lĕt, fĕrn, moment | īce, ĭll, habit | ōld, ŏdd, nôrth, won | moōn, fŏŏt |

theater thē'ȧ-ter, not *the-ā'ter*
thermometer thẽr-mŏm'e-ter, not *thŭh-*
tiara tī-âr'ȧ, or tē-ä'rȧ
titanium tī-tā'nē-ŭm (a metal)
toupee tōō-pā', or -pē'
tournament tŏŏr'nȧ-ment, or tûr'
toward tōrd, or to-wạrd'
transistor trăn-zĭs'tẽr, not *trăn'sĭter*
translate trăns-lāt', not *tran-si-*
trek trĕk, not *treek*
tremendous trē-mĕn'dŭs, not *-jus*
trenchant trĕnch'ănt
trespass trĕs'pȧs (note accent)
tribunal trī-bū'nal, or trĭ-
triumph trī'ŭmf, not *-umpth*
truculent trŭk'ū-lent (Br. trōō'kū-)
tryst trĭst, or trīst
tumultuous tū-mŭl'tū-us, not *-mul-tus*
tune tūn, or tōōn
turgid tûr'jid
tyro tī'rō

U

ultimatum ŭl'tĭ-mā'tum, not *-măt*
umbrella ŭm-brĕl'ȧ, not *umber-ella*
unrequited ŭn-rē-kwī'ted, not *-kwĭt'*
usurp ū-zûrp'
utensil ū-tĕn'sil, not *-tĭn*

V

vagary vȧ-gâr'ry, or -gā' (Br. vā'gȧ-ry)
vagrant vā'grant, not *văg'*
vague vāg, not *văg*
valiant văl'yant
vapid văp'id, not *vāp-*
vase vās (Br. väz)
vehement vē'e-ment, not *ve-heem'*
vehicle vē'ĭ-kl, not *ve-hĭk'l*

vehicular vē-hĭk'ū-lar
veld(t) vĕlt, or fĕlt, not *vĕld*
verbose vẽr-bōs', but
verbosity vẽr-bŏs'i-ty
versatile vẽr'sȧ-tĭl, or -tĭl
viand vī'ănd, not *vee-*
vicarious vī-kâr'ĭ-us, or vĭ-
viceroy vīs'roy, not *vīs-e-roy*
victuals vĭt'lz
viscid vĭs'ĭd, not *vis-kid*
viscount vī'kount', not *vĭs-*
visor vī'zer, rarely vĭz'er
vivacious vī-vā'shus, or vĭ-

W

waistcoat wĕs'kŭt, or wāst'kōt'
⎰ wharves (U.S.) hwôrvz
⎱ wharfs (Br.) hwôrfs
width wĭdth, not *with*
winebibber wīn'bĭb'er, not *-bībe'er*
wrestle rĕs'l, not *răssel*

X

(Note that x at the beginning of a
word has a z sound.)
xylography zī-lŏg'ra-fy

Y

⎰ yolk yōk, or yōlk
⎱ yelk (dial.) yĕlk

Z

zealot zĕl'ut, not *zeel-*
zenith zē'nith (Br. zĕn'ith)
zircon zûr'kŏn (note accent)
zodiacal zō-dī'a-kal
zoology zō-ŏl'ō-jy, not *zōō-*

ANIMALS—BIRDS, FISH, ETC.

abalone ăb'a-lō'nē, not *-a-loan*
aigrette ā-grĕt', or ā'grĕt
anchovy ăn-chō'vy, or an'chō-vy
bovine bō'vīn, not *-veen*
canine kā'nīn (Br. kăn'īn)
capon kā'pŏn
caterpillar kăt'er-pĭl'ar, not *catta-*
chameleon kȧ-mē'lē-on, not *sha-*
chimpanzee chĭm'păn'zē', not *shim-*

cobra kō'bra, not *kor-*
dinosaur dī'nō-sôr
elephantine ĕl'e-făn'tĭn, or -tīn, or -tēn
equine ē'kwīn
falcon fa'kn, or fal'kun
feline fē'līn
Gila monster hē'la, not *gee-la*
jaguar jăg'wär, not *jag-u-ar*
leonine lē'ō-nīn, or -nĭn

PRONUNCIATION

muskrat mŭsk'răt', not *mush-*
orangoutang ō-răng'ōō-tăng'
reptile rĕp'tĭl (Br. -tīl)

salmon săm'un, not *săm-*, nor *săl-*
serpentine sĕr'pĕn-tēn, or -tīn
tarantula ta-răn'chŭh'la, not *-ular*

ARCHITECTURE

acoustics a-kōōs'tĭks (Br. a-kous')
archîtect är'kĭ-tĕkt, not *ärch'*
atrium ā'trē-um, not *ăt-* (pl. ātria)
bas-relief bä'rē-lēf'
Byzantine bĭz'ăn-tēn, or bĭ-zăn'tĭn
clapboard klăb'erd, or klăp'bōrd
coping kōp'ing, not *kŏp'*
cupola kū'pō-la, not *-lō*
Della Robbia dĕl'lä rōb'byä (It.)
façade få-säd', or få-
figurine fĭg'ū-rēn'
foyer foi'er (Fr. fwå-yā')
gargoyle gär'goil
Gothic gŏth'ik, not *gō-*
Ionic ī-ŏn'ik, not *-ōn*
jalousie zhăl'ōō-zē', not *ja-louse'ee*
loge lōzh

loggia lŏj'å (It. lôd'jä)
metope mĕt'ō-pē
mezzanine mĕz'a-nēn, or -nĭn
Moorish mōōr'ish, or mōr'
pediment pĕd'ĭ-ment
pergola pĕr'gō-la, not *pergōh'la*
piazza pē-ăz'a, not *pĭ-* (It. pyät'sä)
porte-cochere pôrt'kō'shâr'
promenade prŏm'e-nād', or -näd'
proscenium prō-sē'nĭ-um, not *-sĕn*
roof rōōf, not *ruf*
rotunda rō-tŭn'da
terrazzo tĕr-rät'sō (flooring)
Tuscan tŭs'kăn
veranda ve-răn'da, not *-rähn*
wainscot wān'skŭt, not *-kōt*

ARTISTS

Bellini (It.) bĕl-lē'nē
Bonheur, Rosa (Fr.) bō'nûr'
Botticelli (It.) bŏt'tē-chĕl'lē
Cellini, Benvenuto (It.) chĕl-lē'nē,
     bĕn'vä-nōō'tō
Corot (Fr.) kō'rō'
Correggio (It.) kōr-rĕd'jō
da Vinci, Leonardo (It.) dä vēn'chē,
     lā'ō-när'dō
Degas (Fr.) dē-gä'
Dürer, Albrecht (Ger.) dü'rĕr, äl'brĕKt
El Greco ĕl grä'kō (Sp., The Greek)
Gainsborough (Eng.) gānz'bŭ-rŭ, or
     -brō
Goya (Sp.) gō'yä
Hals, Frans (Du.) häls, fräns
Holbein, Hans (Ger.) hōl'bīn, häns

Michelangelo (It.) mī'kĕl-ăn'jĕ-lō
     (It. mē'kĕl-än'jä-lō)
Millais (Eng.) mĭ-lā'
Millet (Fr.) mē'lĕ', or mĭ-lā'
Monet (Fr.) mō'nĕ'
Murillo (Sp.) mū-rĭl'ō (Sp. mōō-rēl'yō)
⎰Raphael răf'ā-ĕl, or rä'fā-ĕl
⎱Raffaello (It.) räf'fä-ĕl'lō
Rembrandt (Du.) rĕm'bränt
Renoir (Fr.) rē-nwár'
Rodin (Fr.) rō'dăň'
Titian (It.) tĭsh'an
Van Gogh (Du.) văn gō', or gôK'
     (Du. vän KôK')
Velásquez (Sp.) vä-läs'käth
Watteau (Fr.) vå'tō', or wä'tō'
Zuloaga (Sp.) thōō'lō-ä'gä

BRITISH

again a-gān'
ate ĕt (in England and Ireland)
Avon (Stratford on) ā'von
Axminster ăks'mĭn-ster, not *-minister*
Beauchamp bē'chŭm
been bēn
Berkeley bärk'ly

Berkshire bärk'shĭr
Buckingham bŭk'ing-am, not *-ham*
Cheltenham chĕlt'nam
Chisholm chĭz'ŭm
Cholmondeley chŭm'ly
cinema sĭn'e-ma, not *kĭn-*
clerk klärk

āle, ădd, cåre, ärt, fåst, ạll, about | ēve, lĕt, fẽrn, moment | īce, ĭll, habit | ōld, ŏdd, nôrth, won | mōōn, fŏŏt |

Covent Garden kŭv'ent, not kō'

Derby där'by

dictionary dĭk'shŭn-ree

Edinburgh ĕd'in-bŭ-rŭ

either, and neither ī'ther, and nī'ther

epoch ē'pŏk

Eton ē'tn, not e-tän'

evolution ĕ'vŏ-lū'shun

Gladstone glăd'stŭn

Glasgow glás'gŏ, or -kŏ

Gloucestershire glŏs'tĕr-shĭr, or glŏs'

immediately ĭ-mē'jĭt-ly

laboratory lá-bŏr'á-tree (note accent)

Leicester lĕs'tĕr

lieutenant lĕf-tĕn'ănt

Michaelmas mĭk'ĕl-más, not mīke-

Midwick mĭd'ik, not -wick

Pall Mall pĕl'mĕl', or păl'măl'

patent pă'tĕnt

petrol pĕt'rŏl (gasoline)

plaid plăd (Scotch)

quieten dialectal English

Salisbury sąlz'bur-y

schedule shĕd'ūl

scone skŏn (Scotch), or skŏn

Sealyham sē'lĭ-ăm, or -hăm

Shrewsbury shrōz'bûr-y

Shropshire shrŏp'shĭr

Southampton sou-thăm'tŭn

St. George sĕnt jŏrj', or sĭn'jŏrj'

St. John sĭn'jen

Taliaferro tŏl'i-ver

Thames tĕmz

Trafalgar trá-făl'gĕr

Warwick wŏr'ik, not -wick

Westminster wĕst'mĭn'ster, not--minister

Worcestershire wŏŏs'tĕr-shĭr, not -shĭre

worsted wŏŏs'ted, not wŭr'sted

Yorkshire yŏrk'shĭr

When speaking of England, Great Britain, etc., note the following distinctions:

England is the southern division of the island of Great Britain.

Great Britain is the island of England, Scotland, and Wales.

United Kingdom is Great Britain and Northern Ireland.

British Empire is the United Kingdom and former colonies and dependencies.

The Commonwealth is an association of independent nations: United Kingdom, Canada, Australia, New Zealand, India, Bangladesh, Sri Lanka, Malaysia, Cyprus, Nigeria, Ghana, Kenya, Malawi, Tanzania, Uganda, Zambia, Jamaica, etc.

COMMON FIRST NAMES—MEN

Abraham ā'bra-hăm (note accent)

Adolph á-dŏlf', or ăd'ŏlf

Anthony ăn'tŏ-ny, or ăn'thŏ-

Aubrey ą'brĭ (fem. Audrey)

Basil băz'ĭl, or bā'zĭl

Bernard bĕrn'ard (note accent)

Cecil sĕs'ĭl, or sē'sil

Cedric sĕd'rĭk, or sē'drĭk

Clive klĭv

Cyril sĭr'ĭl

Eli ē'lī

Emil ē'mĭl, or ā'mĭl
Émile (Fr.) ā'mēl'

Eric ĕr'ik

Ernst ĕrnst, not ûrnst

Evan ĕv'ăn

Evelyn ĕv'lĭn (fem. ĕv'ĕ-lĭn)

Francis frăn'sĭs (fem. Frances)

Giles jīlz, rarely gīlz

Gouverneur gōō'vĕr-nĕr' (Fr.)

Grosvenor grŏv'nĕr (Br.)

Gustavus gŭs-tā'vŭs, or -tä'

Hans häns, not hănz (Ger., John)

Henri äṅ'rē' (Fr.)

Hilary hĭl'á-ry

Isaac ī'zák (ē'zäk', foreign)

Ivan ī'van (ĕ-vän'; Rus., John)

Jacques zhák (Fr., James or Jacob)

Juan hwän (Sp., John)

Laurence, or Lawrence lą'rĕns

Leslie lĕz'lĭ, or lĕs'lĭ

Louis lōō'ĭs (Fr. lōō'ē')

Maurice mą'rĭs (Fr. mō'rēs')

Miguel mĕ-gĕl' (Sp., Michael)

Nigel nī'jĕl

Pedro pā'drŏ (Sp., Peter)

Philippe fē'lēp' (Fr.)

Pierre pyâr (Fr., Peter)

Quentin kwĕn'tin (means "the fifth")

Ralph rălf (Br. rāf)

Sean shôn, or shăn, not sĕn (Ir., John)

Ulysses ū-lĭs'ēz, not -lĭss'us

Vincent vĭn'sĕnt (Du. vĭn-sĕnt')

Wilhelm vĭl'hĕlm (Ger., William)

COMMON FIRST NAMES—WOMEN

Adela ăd′e-la (note accent)
Agatha ăg′a-tha (note accent)
⎰ Alicia (It.) ä-lē′chä
⎱ Alícia (Sp.) ä-lē′thē-ä
Andrea ăn′drē-a, or -drä′ (It. än-drĕ′ä)
Antoinette ăn′tŏ-nĕt′ (Fr. än′twȧ′nĕt′)
Athalie ăt′ȧ-lē (Fr. ȧ′tȧ′lē′)
Audrey a̤′drĭ (mas. Aubrey)
Beatrice bē′a-trĭs (note accent)
Bernice bûr′nis, or bûr-nēs′
Candace kăn′dȧ-sē, or kăn-dā′sē
Caroline kăr′ō-lĭn, or -lĭn
⎰ Cécile (Fr.) sā′sēl′
⎱ Cecily sĕs′i-ly
Charlotte shär′lŏt (Fr. shȧr′lôt′)
⎰ Clarice klăr′ĭs
⎱ Clarisse (Fr.) klȧ′rēs′
Corinne kō′rĭn′, or -rēn′
Deborah dĕb′ō-ra
Deirdre dēr′drē (Irish dâr′drä)
⎰ Diana dī-ăn′a
⎱ Diane (Fr.) dē′än′
Dolores dō-lō′rĕs
Enid ē′nĭd
Evangeline ē-văn′je-lĭn, -lĭn, or lēn
Evelyn ĕv′ĕ-lĭn (mas. ēv′lĭn)
Frances frȧn′sĕz (mas. Francis)
Greta grĕt′a, or grē′ta (Ger. grä′tä)

Helena hĕl′e-nȧ, or hĕ-lē′na
Jacqueline jăk′wĕ-lĭn (Fr. zhȧk′lēn′)
Janet jăn′ĕt, or ja-nĕt′
Jeanne (Fr.) zhȧn (Eng. jēn)
Joan jōn, jō′ăn, or jō-ănn′
Lois lō′iss, not loyce
Margot mär′gō, or mär′gŏt
Marguerite mär-gē-rēt′, not mär-gyōō-
Maria mä-rē′a, or mȧ-rī′a
Olivia ō-lĭv′ĭ-a
Pamela păm′ĕ-la, or pȧ-mē′la
Paulina pa̤-lī′na (Sp. pou-lē′nä)
Penelope pe-nĕl′ō-pē (note syl.)
Philippa fĭ-lĭp′a (note accent)
Rosalie rŏz′ȧ-lē, or rōz′
Rosalind rŏz′ȧ-lĭnd
Rosamond rŏz′ȧ-mŭnd
Rowena rō-ē′na
Sarah sâr′a, or sā′ (Fr. sȧ′rȧ′)
Sheila shē′la
Stéphanie stä′fȧ′nē′ (Fr.)
⎰ Theresa tĕ-rē′sa
⎱ Teresa (Sp.) tä-rā′sä
Ursula ûr′sū-la
Vivienne vē′vē-ĕn′ (Fr.)
Wilhelmina vĭl′hĕl-mē′nä
Yvonne ē-vŏn′ (Fr. ē′vôn′)
Zoe zō′ē

COMPOSERS

Bach (Ger.) bäK
Beethoven (Prus.) bā′tō-vĕn (note accent on first syl.)
Berlioz (Fr.) bĕr′lē-ōs′
Bizet (Fr.) bē-zĕ′ (Eng. bē-zā′)
Brahms (Ger.) bräms
Chopin (Pol.-Fr.) shō′păṅ′
Dvořák (Boh.) dvŏr′zhäk
Flotow (Ger.) flō′tō
Handel (Ger.) hăn′dl (Ger. hĕn′dĕl)
Lehár (Hung.) lĕ′här (Eng. lä′här)
Liszt (Hung.) lĭst
Mendelssohn (Ger.) mĕn′dĕls-zōn

Offenbach (Jewish-French) ŏf′ĕn-bäK (Fr. ŏ′fĕn′bȧk′)
Paderewski (Pol.) pȧ′dĕ-rĕf′skē
Rachmaninof (Rus.) räK-mä′nē-nŏf
Ravel (Fr.) rȧ-vĕl′ (note accent)
Respighi (It.) rĕs-pē′gē
Schubert (Aus.) shōō′bĕrt
Schumann (Ger.) shōō′män
Sibelius (Fin.) sĭ-bā′lĭ-ŏŏs
Smetana (Czech) smĕ′tä-nä
Tchaikovsky (Rus.) chĭ-kôf′skē
Weber, von (Ger.) vä′bĕr, fôn

(For other composers, see Operas, p. 182.)

EAST INDIAN

amah ä′ma (a servant)
Benares bĕ-nä′rĕz
Brahma brä′ma (Supreme Being)

Buddha bụd′a, not boo-da
copra kŏp′rȧ (Am. kō′prȧ)
Delhi dĕl′ē, not -hĭ

āle, ădd, câre, ärt, fȧst, a̤ll, about | ēve, lĕt, fērn, moment | īce, ĭll, habit | ōld, ŏdd, nôrth, won | mōōn, fŏŏt |

gymkhana jĭm-kä′na (athletic meet)	**mahatma** má-hät′má (Eng. -hăt′)
Himalaya hĭ-mä′lä-yá (note accent)	(a great soul)
jodhpurs jŏd′pûrz (Am. jŏd′)	**pajamas** pá-jä′maz (Am. pa-jăm′az)
⎰ **ketchup** kĕch′up	**Pakistan** pä′kĭ-stän′ (Am. păk′ĭ-stän)
⎱ **catchup** kăch′up	**pekoe** pē′kō (Br. pĕk′ō) (a tea)
⎱ **catsup** kăt′sup	**sahib** sä′ĭb (Sir or Mr.)
khaki kä′kĭ (Am. kăk′ē)	**sari** sä′rē (a draped gown)
maharaja má-hä′rä′já (a ruler)	**Taj Mahal** täj má-häl′
maharani má-hä′rä′nē (a queen)	**yogi** yō′gē, not *yo-jē*

EGYPTIAN AND ARABIC

Aladdin á-lăd′ĭn	**houri** hōō′rĭ, or hou′rĭ
Ali Baba ä′lē bä′bä, not *ă-lī*	**khedive** kĕ-dēv′
Allah ăl′a (Ar. ál-lä′)	**minaret** mĭn′a-rĕt′
Arab ăr′ab, not *ā′rab*	⎰ **Mohammed** mō-hăm′ĕd
Bedouin bĕd′u̯-ĭn, or -ēn	⎱ **Mahomet** má-hŏm′ĕt (Br. mā′ŏm-ĕt)
burnoose bûr-nōōs′	**mosque** mŏsk, not *môs′kā*
Cairo kī′rō, not *kā-*	**muezzin** mū-ĕz′ĭn
caliph kā′lĭf, or kăl′ĭf	**Port Said** sä-ēd′, or säd, not *sĕd*
⎰ **caravansary** kăr′á-văn′sá-ry	**Ramses** răm′sēz
⎱ **caravanserai** kăr′á-văn′sĕ-rī	**safari** sá-fär′ē
Cheops kē′ŏps	**Sahara** sá-hä′rá, or -hâr′
dromedary drŏm′e-der′y (Br. drŭm′)	**salaam** sá-läm′, not *-lăm*
Fatima făt′ĭ-ma (Am. fá-tēm′a)	**Scheherazade** shĕ-hä′rá-zä′dĕ
harem hā′rĕm, or hâr′ĕm	**sheik** shēk, or shāk

FRENCH

Note that in French words the main accent is usually at the end. An initial **h** is always silent; **ç** denotes an **s** sound; **ch** usually an **sh** sound, but **k** before consonants; **au** and **eau** are ō; **er** and **ez** (endings) are ā; **oi** is wá; and **j** is **zh**.

(See also note on Foreign Pronunciations, p. 157.)

aide-de-camp äd′dĕ-käṅ′ (Am. -kämp′)	**Autres temps,** ō′trĕ täṅ′,
à la mode á′lá-mōd′	**autres mœurs.** ō′trĕ mûrs′ (Other
amateur ăm′á-tûr′ (Eng. ăm′á-tūr)	times, other customs.)
apache á-pásh′, not *a-pătch′ee* (a dance)	**avant-garde** á-väṅ′gärd′ (vanguard)
apéritif á′pä′rē′tēf′ (Eng. á-pĕ′rĭ-tēf)	**baguette** bă-gĕt′ (rectangular gem cut)
aplomb á′plôṅ′	**baton** bá′tôṅ′ (Eng. bă-tŏn′)
artiste är′tēst′ (mas. or fem.)	**beau monde** bō′ môṅd′
atelier á′tĕ-lyä′ (a studio)	**beaux-arts** bō-zär′ (the fine arts)
attaché á′tá′shä′ (Am. ăt′a-shā′)	**belles-lettres** bĕl′lĕt′r
au courant ō′kōō′räṅ′ (up-to-date)	**bête noire** bât′ nwär′ (Eng. bāt′ nwär′)
au gratin ō′ grá-täṅ′	**billet-doux** bē-yĕ-dōō′ (Eng. bĭl-ā-)
au jus ō′ zhü′ (in the meat juice)	**blasé** blä-zā′
au naturel ō′ ná′tü′rĕl′	**bon ami** bôṅ′ná′mē′ (good friend)
au revoir ō′rĕ-vwár′, not *rĕ-voi*	**bon mot** bôṅ′ mō′ (pl. bons mots—
	bôṅ′ mōz′)

oil, out | ūse, ŭp, bûrn, fu̯ll, submit; ü—a muted e | chin; go; jet; park; K—Ger. ch; Fr. ṅ—a nasal tone

169

bon vivant bôṅ' vē'väṅ'

bon voyage bôṅ' vwå'yȧzh'

bouquet bo͞o-kā' (Am. bō-kā')

bourgeois bo͝or-zhwä' (middle class)

boutonnière bo͞o'tŏ-nyȧr'

Braille brä'ĭ (Eng. brāl) (printing)

brouhaha bro͞o'ȧ-ȧ' (uproar)

buffet bu̯-fā' (Br. bǔf'ĭt)

cabaret kăb'ȧ-rā'

camaraderie kȧ'mȧ-rä'dĕ-rē

Camembert kȧ'mäṅ'bȧr'

canaille kȧ'nä'ĭ (Eng. kȧ-nāl')

canapés kȧ-nȧ-pāz' (Eng. kăn'a-pēz)

carte blanche kȧrt' bläṅsh'

cause célèbre kōz' sā'lĕb'r (celebrated case, not cause [law])

chaise longue shâz' lôṅg' (Eng. shāz)

chanteuse shäṅ-tûz' (a woman singer)

chargé d'affaires shär'zhā' dȧ'fâre'

charivari shä'rē-vä'rē (Am. shĭv'ȧ-rē)

cherchez la femme shĕr'shä' lȧ fȧm' (Find the woman.)

chic shēk

clientele klē'äṅ-tĕl' (Eng. klī'ĕn-tĕl')

cloisonné klwȧ'zô'nā' (Eng. kloi'zŏ-nā')

Coeur de Lion kûr' dē lē'ôṅ'

coiffure kwȧ-für' (Am. kwä-fūr')

communiqué kŏ-mū'nĭ-kā', not -neek'

compagnie kôṅ'pȧn-yē' (abbr. Cⁱᵉ)

comte kôṅt (a count)

comtesse kôṅ'tĕs' (a countess)

concierge kôṅ'syĕrzh' (mas. or fem.)

confrère kôṅ'frâr'

congé kôṅ'zhā' (leave-taking)

connoisseur kŏn'ĭ-sûr'

contretemps kôṅ'tr-täṅ'

cortège kôr'tĕzh'

coterie kō't-rē'

coup d'état ko͞o' dā'tȧ'

coup de grâce ko͞o' dē gräs'

coupon ko͞o'pŏn (Am. kū')

couturier (mas.) ko͞o-tü-ryā' (a modiste)

couturière (fem.) ko͞o-tü-ryȧr'

crème de la crème krȧm' dlȧ krȧm'

crêpes suzette krĕp' sü-zĕt' (Am. krăp')

Croix de guerre krwä' dē gâr', not kroy

cuisine kwē-zēn'

cul-de-sac küd'sȧk' (Eng. kŭl'dē-săk')

danseuse däṅ'sûz'

debacle dā'bä'klē (Am. de-băk'el)

debris dā'brē'

debut dā-bü' (Eng. dĕ-bū')

débutante dā'bü'täṅt' (Eng. dĕb'ū-)

déclassé dā'klȧ'sā'

décolleté dā'kôl-tā', not dĕk'o-lĕt

décor dā-kôr' (home decoration)

de luxe dē lüks' (Eng. dē lŭks')

dénouement dā-no͞o'mäṅ

dernier ressort dĕr'nyā' rē-sôr'

dernier cri dĕr'nyā' krē' (last word)

de trop dē-trō' (too much; unwanted)

diablerie dē'ä'blĕ-rē'

dishabille dĭs'ȧ-bēl', not dĭsh'

distingué dĭs'täṅ'gā'

divorcé (mas.)
divorcée (fem.) dĭ'vôr'sā'

divorcee (Eng.) dĭ-vôr'sē' (any divorced person)

dossier dô-syā' (Eng. dŏs'ē-ā)

double entente do͞o'bl äṅ'täṅt'
double-entendre do͞o'bl-äṅ'täṅ'dr

echelon ĕsh'ĕ-lŏn (like ladder steps)

éclair ā-klâr', not eek'lär

éclaircissement ā'klâr'sēs'mäṅ'

éclat ā-klä'

élan ā'läṅ'

elite ā-lēt', not ē-lēt

émigré ā-mē-grā' (Am. ĕm'a-grā)

en banc äṅ bäṅ' (in full authority)

encore äṅ-kôr', not ĕn-

enfant terrible äṅ'fäṅ' tĕ'rē'bl

en masse äṅ mȧs', not ĕn masee

ennui äṅ'nwē' (weariness)

en passant äṅ pä'säṅ'

en route äṅ ro͞ot', not ĕn rout

ensemble äṅ'säṅ'bl

entente cordiale äṅ'täṅt' kôr'dyȧl'

entourage äṅ'to͞o'räzh'

entr'acte äṅ'träkt'

entrée äṅ'trā'

entre nous äṅ'tr no͞o' (between us)

entrepôt äṅ'trē-pō' (distribution center)

entrepreneur äṅ'trē-prē-nûr' (enterpriser)

epergne ā-pârn' (a centerpiece)

esprit de corps ĕs-prē' dē kôr'

etiquette ĕt'ĭ-kĕt, not -kwĕt

exposé ĕks'pō-zā'

fait accompli fĕ'tȧ'kôṅ'plē' (accomplished fact)

faux pas fō'pä' (a social error)

fiancé (mas.) ⎫ fē'än'sā'
fiancée (fem.) ⎭
filet mignon fē'lĕ' mē'nyôn'
fleur-de-lis flûr'dĕ-lēs', or -lē', not *flūr*
force majeure fôrs' má'zhûr' (major
  force, or act of God)
frère frâr (brother)
garage gà-räzh' (Br. găr'ĭj)
gaucherie gōsh'rē' (awkwardness)
genre zhän'r
grand prix grän' prē'
Gruyère grü'yâr'
habitué à'bē'tü-ā' (Eng. hà-bĭt'ū-ā)
hauteur ō-tûr' (Am. hō-tûr')
hors de combat ôr' dĕ kôn'bà' (out of
  the combat)
hors d'oeuvres ôr' dû'vr (Am. ôr dĕrvz)
impasse ăn'päs' (Eng. ĭm-pàs')
ingénue ăn'zhā'nü'
insouciance ăn'soō'syäns'
je ne sais quoi zhĕ-nĕ-sā-kwà' (I know
  not what.)
jeu d'esprit zhû' dĕs'prē' (a witty sally)
joie de vivre zhwà' dĕ vē'vr (joy of
  living)
julienne zhül-yĕn' (in thin strips)
laissez faire lĕ'sā' fâr' (let do, that is,
  noninterference)
lamé là-mā' (fabric with metallic
  threads)
lapin là-păn' (Am. lăp'ĭn) (rabbit)
légionnaire lā'zhon'nâr' (Eng.
  lē'jŭn-âr')
l'envoi län'vwà'
Le roi est mort, lē rwà' ĕ môr',
  vive le roi! vēv' lē rwà' (The
  king is dead, long
  live the king!)
⎧ lèse-majesté lĕz'mà'zhĕs'tā' (treason)
⎩ lese majesty (Eng.) lēz măj'ĕs-ty
liaison lē'ā'zôn' (Br. lē-ā'zn)
lingerie län'zhē-rē', or län'
lorgnette lôr'nyĕt', not *lorg-*
madame mà'dàm' (Eng. măd'ăm)
mademoiselle màd'mwà'zĕl' (colloq.
  màm'zĕl')
maître d'hôtel mâ'tr dō'tĕl'
mal de mer màl' dĕ mâr' (seasickness)
Mardi Gras mär'dĕ grä' (fat Tuesday)
⎧ marquis (mas.) màr-kē' (Eng.
⎪   mär'kwĭs)
⎩ marquise (fem.) màr-kēz'

Marseillaise màr'sĕ'yâz' (Eng.-lāz')
⎧ masseur (mas.) mă-sûr' (massager)
⎩ masseuse (fem.) mă-sûz'
mauve mōv, not *mawv*
mayonnaise mà'yô'nâz' (Eng.
  mā'ŏ-nāz')
mélange mā'länzh'
mêlée mĕ'lā' (Eng. mā'lā)
memoirs mĕm'wôrz, not *mĕm'orz*
ménage mā'nàzh'
menu mē-nü' (Eng. mĕn'ū)
merci mĕr-sē' (thank you)
mésalliance mā'zà'lē'äns'
mesdames mā'dàm'
messieurs mā'syų' (Eng. mĕs'ĕrs)
métier mā-tyā' (one's calling)
milieu mē'lyų' (environment)
mirage mē-räzh'
mise en scène mē'zän sân' (stage
  setting)
modiste mō-dēst' (a dressmaker)
monsieur mē-syų'
moyen âge mwà'yĕ'näzh' (Middle
  Ages)
naïveté nä-ēv'tā'
née nā, not *nee* (born)
n'est-ce pas? nĕs-pä' (Isn't it true?)
noblesse oblige nō'blĕs' ō'blēzh'
  (nobility is obliged to
  be noble)
nom de plume nôn' dĕ plüm' (Eng.
  nŏm'dĕ plōōm')
nonpareil nŏn'pà-rĕl' (having no equal)
nouveau riche nōō'vō' rēsh' (newly rich)
nuance nü'äns'
objets d'art ôb'zhĕ' dàr'
outré ōō'trā' (bizarre)
papier-mâché pá'pyā'mä'shā' (Eng.
  pā'per-ma-shā')
pari-mutuel pà'rē'mü'twĕl' (Eng.
  păr'ĭ-mū'tū-ĕl, not *Paris
  mu-chel*) (mutual wager; a
  betting machine)
passé pă-sā' (outmoded)
pasteurize păs'tĕr-ize (colloq. -chŭr-)
pâté de foie gras pä-tā' dĕ fwà' grä'
patois pà'twà' (a dialect or jargon)
penchant pän'shän' (Eng. pĕn'chant)
petits fours pĕ-tē' fōōr' (Am. pĕt'ē-fôrz')
pièce de résistance pyĕs' dĕ rā'zēs'täns'
pierrot pyĕ'rō'
pierrette pyĕ'rĕt'

oil, out | ūse, ŭp, bûrn, fųll, submit; ü—a muted e | chin; go; jet; park; K—Ger. ch; Fr. n̄—a nasal tone

pince-nez păns'nā' (nose glasses)
piquant pē'k'nt, not *peek-went*
plaque plȧk, not *plăke*
plissé plē-sā' (crinkled material)
poilu pwȧ'lü' (French soldier)
portière pôr'tyȧr', not *-teer*
poseur pō-zûr'
potpourri pō'pŏō'rē'
praline prä'lēn
précis prā-sē' (a brief summary)
première prē-myȧr' (Am. pre-mēr')
prestige prĕs-tēzh' (Eng. prĕs'tĬj)
purée pū-rā', not *pŏō-ree'*
qui vive kē vēv', not *kwee*
raconteur rȧ'kôn'tûr' (a storyteller)
ragout rȧ-gōō' (a meat dish)
raison d'être rā'zôn' dȧ'tr (reason for existence)
rapprochement rȧ'prŏsh'män'
rendezvous rän'dä-vōō' (Eng. rän'dĕ-)
{ repartee (Eng.) rĕp'ĕr-tē', not *-tā*
{ repartie (Fr.) rĕ-pȧr-tē'
répertoire rā'pĕr'twȧr' (Eng. rĕp'ĕr-)
restaurant rĕs-tō-rän' (Am. rĕs'to-rant, not *rest-urnt*)
résumé rā'zü'mā'
retroussé rĕt'rōō-sā' (turned-up [nose])
reveille rā-vĕ'Ĭ (Am. rĕv'ĕ-lō') (Br. rĬ-vĕl'Ĭ)
riposte rē-pōst' (a quick retort)
risqué rēs'kā'
Roquefort rōk'fôr' (Eng. rōk'fĕrt)
rôtisserie rō'tēs'se-rē' (spindle roasting)
roué rōō-ā' (a rake)
rouge et noir rōōzh' ā nwȧr' (red and black)
sabotage sȧ'bô'täzh' (Eng. săb'o-täzh)

sang-froid sän'frwȧ' (coolheadedness)
sans gêne sän' zhȧn' (free and easy)
sans souci sän' sōō'sē' (without care)
sauté sō-tā' (Am. sạ-) (to fry quickly)
savant sȧ'vän' (Eng. să-vänt')
savoir-faire sȧ'vwȧr-fȧr' (tact; poise)
séance sā'äns'
s'il vous plaît sēl' vōō plĕ' (if you please)
silhouette sĬl'ŏō-ĕt', not *sĬl'you-*
soirée swȧ'rā'
solitaire sŏl'Ĭ-tȧr', not *-tar-ee*
sobriquet sō'brē'kā' (a nickname)
soupçon sōōp'sôn' (a slight trace)
suave swäv (Br. swāv)
surveillance sür'vĕ-yäns' (Eng. sûr-vāl'yäns)
svelte svĕlt (slender; lissome)
table d'hôte tȧ'bl dōt'
tête-à-tête tāt'ȧ-tāt' (head to head)
thé dansant tā' dän'sän'
timbale tän'bȧl' (Eng. tĬm'băl)
touché tōō-shā' (touched, in fencing)
tour de force tōōr' dĕ fôrss' (a feat)
tout ensemble tōō'tän'sän'bl
valet vȧl'ā (Br. văl'Ĭt)
vaudeville vōd'vēl' (Eng. vōd'vĬl)
vers libre vȧr' lē'br (free verse)
vichyssoise vē-shē-swȧz' (a cold soup)
vignette vēn-yĕt' (Eng. vĬn-yĕt')
vis-à-vis vē'zȧ-vē' (face to face)
{ vive la France vēv lȧ fränss
{ viva (It.) vē'vä
voilà vwȧ'lä' (look, or there it is)
vraisemblance vrĕ'sän'bläns' (appearance)
wagon-lit vȧ'gôn'lē' (a sleeping car)

FRENCH CITIES, PLACES OF INTEREST, ETC.

Arc de Triomphe ȧrk' dĕ trē'ônf'
Bastille bȧs-tēl' (Fr. bȧs'tē'y)
Biarritz bē-ȧ'rēts'
{ Bretagne brĕ-tȧn'yē
{ Brittany (Eng.) brĬt'ȧ-ny
Cannes kȧn (Am. kăn, or kȧnz)
Champs Élysées shän'zä'lē'zä' (Elysian Fields)
Chantilly shän-tē-yē' (Am. shăn-tĬl'ē)
Chartres shär'tr (cathedral)
Château-Thierry shä'tō' tyĕ'rē'
Cherbourg shĕr'bōōr'

Côte d'Azur kōt dä-zür' (azure coast)
Eiffel Tower ĕ'fĕl' (Eng. ī'fel)
Fontainebleau fôn'tän'blō'
Île de France ēl' dĕ fränss'
{ Le Havre lĕ ä'vr
{ Havre (Eng.) hä'vĕr, not *harv*
Lille lēl
Limoges lē'mōzh'
Lourdes, Our Lady of lōōrd
Louvre lōō'vr, not *louve*
{ Lyon lē'ôn'
{ Lyons (Eng.) lĬ'unz

Marseille már'sĕ'l
Marseilles (Eng.) mär-sā', or -sālz'
Menton män'tŏn'
Mentone (It.) mĕn-tō'nä
Neufchâtel nû'shä'tĕl'
Nice nēs
Notre Dame nŏ'trĕ dȧm'
Pyrenees pē'rā'nä' (Eng. pĭr'e-nēz)

Reims răns (Eng. rēmz)
Rue de la Paix rü' dē lȧ pĕ' (Street of Peace)
Saint-Cyr săn'sēr'
Saint-Mihiel săn'mē'yĕl'
Versailles vĕr'sä'ĭ (Eng. vĕr-sālz')
Vosges vōzh
Ypres ē'pr (in Belgium)

GEOGRAPHIC NAMES—FOREIGN

Adriatic ā'drĭ-ăt'ĭk, or ăd'
Azores ȧ-zōrz' (note accent)
Bagdad băg'dăd
Baghdad bäg-däd' (note accent)
Bahamas bȧ-hā'maz (Br. -häm')
Banff bămf
Barbados bär-bā'dōz, not -băd'us
Barranquilla bär'än-kēl'yä, not -kwilla
Bering Strait bēr'ing, or bâr'
Bethlehem bĕth'lē-ĕm, not -hăm
Borneo bôr'nē-ō, not barn-
Bosporus bŏs'pō-rŭs (note accent)
Capri kä'prē (note accent)
Caribbean kăr'ĭ-bē'an, or kȧ-rĭb'
Carlsbad (Eng.) (Czech, Kärlôvy Väry)
Karlsbad (Ger.) kärls'bät
Caspian kăs'pē-an, not kăsa-
Copenhagen kō'pen-hā'gen (Ger. -häg')
Costa Rica kŏs'ta rē'ka
Crimea krī-mē'a, or krĭ-
Curaçao kōō'rä-sä'ō, or kū'rȧ-sō'
Edam ē'dăm, or ā'däm'
Etna (L. Aetna) ĕt'nȧ, not eet-
European ū'rō-pē'an, not -peen
Gatun gä-tōōn'
Gobi gō'bē
Gotham (England) gŏt'am
Gotham (N.Y.C.) gō'thăm, or gŏth'am
Haiti hā'tē, not -tī
Hebrides hĕb'rĭ-dēz
Iran ē-rän' (Br. ĭ-rän') (See p. 181)

Iraq ē-räk'
Java jä'va, not jăv-a
Levant lē-vănt' (note accent)
Lima lē'mä (Peru)
Mediterranean mĕd'ĭ-tĕ-rā'nē-an, not -trăn-yan
Newfoundland nū'fŭnd-lănd', or nū'found-lănd'
Nicaragua nĭk'ȧ-rä'gwȧ (Br. -răg'ū-ȧ)
Pago Pago päng'ō päng'ō
Palestine păl'ĕs-tīn, not -teen
Papeete pä'pa-ā'tä, or pȧ-pē'tē
Peiping bā'pĭng'
Prague (Eng.) präg, or prāg
Praha (Czech) prä'hȧ
Prag (Ger.) präK
Puerto Rico pwĕr'tō rē'kō
Rhodesia rō-dē'zhĭ-a, not -dĕss
Rio de Janeiro rē'ō dä zhȧ-nā'rō (Pg., River of January)
Saint Helena sānt hĕ-lē'na, not hĕl'ena
Santiago sän'tē-ä'gō, not sănte-ā'
Singapore sĭng'gȧ-pōr
Sri Lanka shrē län'ka (former Ceylon)
Stromboli strôm'bō-lē (note accent)
Tahiti tä-hē'tē, not ta-hāy'te
Thailand tī'lănd, not thĭ'
Tibet tĭ-bĕt' (note accent)
Transvaal trănz-väl', not -văl, nor -vāl
Valparaiso văl'pȧ-rī'sō (Sp. väl')
Venezuela vĕn'e-zwē'la (Sp. -swä'lä)

GEOGRAPHIC NAMES—UNITED STATES

Abilene, Tex. ăb'ĭ-lēn
Adirondacks ăd'ĭ-rŏn'dăks, not adrē-
Albuquerque, N. Mex. ăl'bū-kûr'kē
Appalachians ăp'ȧ-lăch'ŭnz, or -lā'chē-
Arkansas är'kăn-saw (official)
Eaton Rouge băt'ŭn rōozh'

Boise, Idaho boi'zē
Cincinnati sĭn'sĭ-nă'tĭ
Colorado kŏl'ō-rä'dō, or -răd'ō
Concord, Mass. kŏng'kērd
Des Moines dē moin', or moinz'
Detroit dē-troit' (note accent)

oil, out | ūse, ŭp, bûrn, fu̩ll, submit; ü—a muted e | chin; go; jet; park; K—Ger. ch; Fr. n̄—a nasal tone

173

PRONUNCIATION

Greenwich, Conn. grĕn'wich, or
grĭn'ich, or grĕn'
Greenwich Village, N.Y.C. grĕn'ich
Greenwich, England grĭn'ĭj
Haverhill, Mass. hā'vēr-ĭl
Helena, Mont. hĕl'e-na, not *he-lēn'a*
Hialeah, Fla. hĭ'a-lē'a, not *-lāya*
Hoboken, N.J. hō'bō-kĕn (note accent)
Illinois ĭl'ĭ-noi', or *-noiz'*
Joliet, Ill. jō'lĭ-ĕt' (note accent)
La Jolla, Calif. lä hoi'ä, or hō'yä
Laredo, Tex. la-rā'dō
Lead, S.D. lēd, not *lĕd* (a gold lead)
Lima, Ohio lī'ma, not *lee'ma*
Los Angeles lôs ăn'jĕl-ĕs (Sp.
lōs äng'hā-lās)
Louisiana loo-ē'zē-ăn'a (dial. looz'ē-)
Louisville, Ky. loo'ē-v'l (silent s)
Mackinac Island măk'i-naw, not *-nack*
Miami mĭ-ăm'ĭ, not *mē-äm'ē*
Missouri mĭ-soo'rĭ, not *mi-zur-ree*
Mobile mō-bēl', not *mō'bĭl*
Mojave Desert mō-hä'vä
Nevada nĕ-văd'a, or nĕ-vä'da
New Orleans ôr'lĭnz (dial. ôr-lēnz')
Niagara nī-ăg'a-ra (colloq. nī-ăg'ra)
Norfolk, Va. nôr'f'k, not *-fōlk*

Oregon ôr'ĕ-gon (3 syl.)
Palo Alto, Calif. păl'ō ăl'tō, or
pä'lō äl'tō
Passaic, N.J. pă-sā'ĭk
Peekskill, N.Y. pēks'kĭl, not *pigs-*
Pierre, S.Dak. pēr
Poughkeepsie, N.Y. pō-kĭp'sē,
not *-keep'*
Puget Sound pū'jĕt, not *pug-*
Quincy, Mass. kwĭn'zĭ, not *kwins'ē*
Reading, Pa. rĕd'ĭng, not *read-*
Rio Grande rē'ō grän'dā, or gränd'
San Diego săn dē-ā'gō
San Jose, Calif. săn hō-sā'
Santa Fe săn'ta fā, not *-fee*
Sault Sainte Marie soo' sänt ma-rē'
Shreveport shrēv'pōrt, not *shrĕv'*
Spokane spō-kăn', not *-kain*
St. Louis loo'ĭs, or loo'i
Terre Haute tĕr'ē hōt'
Tucson, Ariz. too-sŏn'
Waco, Tex. wā'kō
Washington wäsh'ing-ton, not
wôrsh'n-dun
Willamette wĭ-lăm'ĕt (note accent)
Worcester, Mass. wus'ter
Yosemite, Calif. yō-sĕm'ĭ-tē

GERMAN AND HUNGARIAN

Note that in the pronunciation of the German combinations **ie** and **ei**, a long sound is given to whichever letter stands last: **ie** is ē, and **ei** is ī. Also, **j** has a y sound; **w** is like **v**; and **z** like **ts**.

(See also note on Foreign Pronunciations, p. 157.)

auf Wiedersehen ouf' vē'dĕr-zā'ĕn
Baden-Baden bä'dĕn-bä'dĕn, not *bä'*
Bremen brä'mĕn (Eng. brĕm'en)
Budapest bu'da-pĕst', or boo'
dachshund däKs'hunt', not *dash-hound*
Deutschland doich'länt'
edelweiss ā'dĕl-vīs, not *ĕd-*
ersatz ĕr-zäts', not *-sāts* (substitute)
frankfurter frănk'fur-ter not *-fritter*
Frau frou
Fräulein froi'lĭn, not *frou-*
Hungary hŭng'ga-ry (note accent)
Ungarn (Ger.) un'gärn
Ich dien ĭK dēn' ("I serve"—motto of
the Prince of Wales)
Junker yoong'kĕr, not *junk'er*

kindergarten kĭn'dĕr-gär'ten,
not *-garden*
Lebensraum lā'bĕns-roum' (room
to live)
Luftwaffe looft'väf'ĕ (air force)
meerschaum mēr'shum, not *mur-*
Munich mū'nĭk
München (Ger.) mün'Kĕn
Nazi nät'zĭ
Oberammergau ō'bĕr-äm'ĕr-gou' (scene
of the Passion Play)
rathskeller räts'kĕl'er (town-hall cellar)
Rhenish (Eng.) rĕn'ish, not *rain-*
Steuben shtoi'bĕn (Am. stū'bĕn)
Tirol tē-rōl' (Eng. tĭr'ōl)
Viennese vē'ĕ-nēz', not *-nāz*

ale, ădd, cāre, ärt, făst, all, about | ēve, lĕt, fērn, moment | Ice, Ill, habit | ōld, ŏdd, nôrth, won | moon, foot |

174

von   fôn, or fŭn (of, or from)
wanderlust   vän'dẽr-lụst'
Weimar   vī'mär, not *wī'mer*
Weltschmerz   vĕlt'shmĕrts' (world
   sorrow)

Wien   vēn (Vienna)
wienerwurst   vē'nẽr-vụrst' (Eng.
   wē'nẽr-wûrst)
Zeitgeist   tsīt'gīst' (spirit of the time)
zwieback   tsvē'bäk (Am. swī'băk)

GREEK

Note the long vowel sounds that predominate in Greek words.

Adonis   à-dō'nĭs
Aeolian, or Eolian   ē-ō'lĭ-ăn, not *ā-o-*
Aesop   ē'sŏp
alpha and omega   ăl'fà and ō-mē'gà (the
   beginning and end)
Androcles   ăn'drō-klēz
Aphrodite   ăf'rō-dī'tē
Archimedes   är'kĭ-mē'dēz
Aristophanes   ăr'ĭs-tŏf'à-nēz
epicurean   ĕp'ĭ-kū-rē'ăn
Eros   ē'rŏs, or ĕr'ŏs (god of love)
Euripides   ū-rĭp'ĭ-dēz
Hippocrates   hĭ-pŏk'rà-tēz
hoi polloi   hoi'pŏ-loi', not *oi-poloi*
Mephistopheles   mĕf'ĭ-stŏf'e-lēz
naiad   nā'yăd, or nī'ăd
nemesis   nĕm'e-sĭs
Olympiad   ō-lĭm'pĭ-ăd

paean, or pean   pē'an
Pegasus   pĕg'à-sŭs (note accent)
Pericles   pĕr'ĭ-klēz
Pierian   pī-ē'rĭ-ăn
Pleiades   plē'yà-dēz, or plī'
pseudo   sōō'dō, not *swāy'dō*
Pygmalion and   pĭg-mā'lĭ-ŏn and
   Galatea   găl'à-tē'à
Scylla and   sĭl'à and
   Charybdis   kà-rĭb'dĭs (two dangers)
sesame   sĕs'à mē (3 syl.) (Open sesame!)
Socrates and   sŏk'rà-tēz and
   Xantippe   zăn-tĭp'ē
Sophocles   sŏf'ō-klēz
Stygian   stĭj'ĭ-an (note accent)
Terpsichore   tẽrp-sĭk'ō-rē, not *-sē-kōr*
{ Venus of Milo   vē'nŭs of mī'lō, or mē'
{ Vénus de Milo   (Fr.) vä'nüs dē mē'lō

HAWAIIAN

The Hawaiian alphabet has only 12 letters: vowels, a,e,i,o,u; and consonants, h,k,l,m,n,p,w.
All words end in vowels; consonants must be separated by vowels; but vowels may follow vowels.

aloha   ä-lō'hä
Hawaii   hä-wī'ē, not *-wī-à*, nor *-vä'ē*
Hilo   hē'lō
Honolulu   hō'nō-lōō'lōō (Eng. hŏn'ō-)
Kamehameha   kä-mā'hä-mā'hä (first
   king of Hawaii)
Kanaka   kà-năk'à (a native)
lanai   lä-nä'ē (a veranda)
lehua   lä-hōō'à (a Hawaiian flower)
lei   lā'ē (a wreath)

Liliuokalani   lē'lē-ụ-ō-kä-lä'nē   (last
   queen of Hawaiian Islands)
luau   lōō'ou (a feast)
Mauna Loa   mou'nä lō'à (a volcano)
Molokai   mō'lō-kä'ē (leper island)
Oahu   ō-ä'hōō
Pele   pā'lä (a goddess)
poi   pō'ē, or poi, not *pwäh* (a native dish)
ukulele   ū'ke-lā'lē, or ōō'kụ-lā'la
Waikiki   wä'ē-kē'kē

HISTORICAL NAMES

Alden, John   ạl'dĕn, not *ăl-*
Antony, Mark   ăn'tō-ny, not *anth'*
Appian Way   ăp'ĭ-ăn (ancient paved
   road from Rome)
Babel   bā'bĕl, not *băb'el* (the tower)
Carnegie   kär-nā'gĭ (note accent)
Cleopatra   klē'ō-pā'tra, or -păt'
Croesus   krē'sŭs

Curie, Madame   kü'rē', not *ku-rā*
Disraeli   dĭz-rā'lĭ, not *-rằl*, nor *-rẽl*
Du Barry   dü bà'rē' (note accent)
Elizabethan   ē-lĭz'à-bē'thăn, or *-bĕth'ăn*
Galileo   găl'i-lā'ō (It. astron.-physicist)
Jeanne d'Arc   zhàn'dàrk' (Joan of Arc)
Lusitania   lū'sĭ-tā'nĭ-à
Magna Charta   măg'na kär'ta, not *char-*

oil, out | ūse, ŭp, bûrn, fụll, submit; ü—a muted e | chin; go; jet; park; K—Ger. ch; Fr. ṅ—a nasal tone

Marconi mär-kō′nē, not -kŏni

Monticello mŏn′ti-sĕl′ō (It. -chĕl′ō)
(little mountain)

Nobel nō-bĕl′ (prizes)

Rockefeller rŏk′e-fĕl′er, not rocka-fella

Roosevelt rō′zĕ-vĕlt, not roōs-

INDIAN (AMERICAN)

{ Algonquian ăl-gŏng′kĭ-ăn, or -kwĭn
{ Algonquin ăl-gŏng′kĭn, or -kwĭn

Apache a-pătch′ē (Fr. à-pásh′)

Arapaho à-răp′à-hō

bayou bī′ōo, or -ō, not bā-ū (Choctaw)

Chinook chĭ-nōōk′, or -nōŏk′

Choctaw chŏk′tạ, not chōk-

Hiawatha hī′à-wä′tha (Mohawk chief)

Hopi hō′pē

Maya mä′yä, not mā-

Navaho, or Navajo năv′à-hō, not năv-

Nez Percé nĕz pûrse (Fr. nä′pĕr′sā′)
(French for "pierced nose")

Osage ō′sāj′

Powhatan pow′hà-tăn′, not powee- (a
chief, father of Pocahontas)

Pueblo pwĕb′lō, not pū-eb-lo

sachem sā′chĕm, not săch-em

Shoshone shō-shō′nē

Ute ūt, or ū′tē

Yakima yăk′ĭ-mạ, not ya-kī′ma

Yaqui yä′kē, not yăk-e

IRISH

colleen kŏl′ēn, or kŏ-lēn′, not kōl-

Dail Eireann dôl âr′ĭn (lower house of
Legislature of Ireland)

Eire âr′ĕ (Gaelic name for Ireland)

Erin go brath!, or bragh! âr′ĭn gŭ brạ′
("Ireland forever!")

shillelagh, or shillalah shĭ-lā′là, or lē

Sinn Fein shĭn fān (a political party)

ITALIAN

Note that in Italian pronunciation, ch before e or i has a k sound; and c before e or i has a ch sound. Z has a ts sound. And doubled letters are separately pronounced.

(See also note on Foreign Pronunciations, p. 157.)

al fresco ăl frĕs′kō, or äl (in open air)

arrivederci är-rē′vĕ-dĕr′chē (goodbye)

Assisi äs-sē′zē (St. Francis of . . .)

benvenuto bĕn′vä-nōō′tō (welcome)

Bologna bô-lōn′yä

bravo brä′vō

campanile kăm′pà-nē′lē (bell tower)

Chianti kē-än′tē, not shī–

cognoscente { kō′nyō-shĕn′tä
conoscente { (a connoisseur)

con amore kŏn ä-mō′rä (with love)

dilettante dē′lĕt-tän′tä (pl. -ti -tē)
(Eng. dĭl′ĕ-tän′tĭ)

dolce far niente dōl′chä fär nyĕn′tä
(sweet do-nothing)

Duce, Il ēl dōō′chä (The Leader)

Fascisti fä-shē′stē (pl.)

Fata Morgana fä′tä môr-gä′nä

Firenze fē-rĕnt′sä (Florence, Italy)

{ Genoa jĕn′ō-à, not je-noh′a
{ Genova (It.) jĕn′ō-vä

ghetto gĕt′ō

gondola gŏn′dō-là (note accent)

imbroglio ĭm-brōl′yō (an embroilment)

intaglio ēn-täl′yō (Eng. ĭn-tăl′yō)

Italian ĭ-tăl′yăn (like Italy), not ī-tăl′

italics ĭ-tăl′ĭks, not ī-tăl′

Lido lē′dō

maestro mä-ĕs′trō (Am. mīs′trō)*

maraschino măr′à-skē′nō, not -shee

Medici mĕd′ē-chē (note accent)

{ Milan mĭ-lăn′
{ Milano (It.) mē-lä′nō

minestrone mē′nĕ-strō′nä (a soup)

Pisa pē′sä (Eng. pē′zà)

pizza pēt′sà, not pēēs′a, nor pē′zà

* When the Italian ä is followed by ĕ (or by the long ē sound), the combined sound is like the English long I.

āle, ădd, câre, ärt, fȧst, ạll, about | ēve, lĕt, fērn, moment | īce, ĭll, habit | ōld, ŏdd, nôrth, won | mōōn, fŏŏt |

Riviera rē-vyä′rä. (Am. rĭ-vē-âr′a)
scenario shā-nä′rĭ-ō (Eng. sē-nâr′ĭ-ō)
sotto voce sŏt′tō vō′chä, or sŏt′ō
Trieste trē-ĕs′tā (Eng. trē-ĕst′)

Venice vĕn′ĭs, not *vi-nees'*
Venezia (It.) vä-nĕt′syä
villa vēl′lä (Eng. vĭl′a)

JAPANESE

banzai bän′zä′ē, or -zī (Forever!)
geisha gā′sha ("girl" unnecessary)
hara-kiri hä′rá-kĭr′ē (suicide)
hibachi hĭ-bä′chē (grill)
jujitsu jōō-jĭt′sōō (or judo—jōō′dō)

kimono kĭm′ō-nō (Am. kŭ-mō′na)
Nippon nĭp′pŏn′ (Land of Rising Sun)
Nisei nē′sā′ (second generation)
sayonara sä′yôn-är′ä (goodbye)
sukiyaki sōō′kē-yä′kē (Jap. skē-yä′kē)

LATIN WORDS AND PHRASES

There are two methods of pronouncing Latin—the **Roman** (taught in schools); and the **English**, with long vowels (used in law, etc.), as shown below.

(See Webster's New International Dictionary, 2nd Ed., p. liv.)

absente reo ăb-sĕn′tē rē′ō (in the absence of the defendant)
a datu ā dā′tū (from the date)
ad finem ăd fī′nĕm (to the end)   ad infinitum ăd ĭn′fi-nī′tum (to infinity)
ad hoc ăd hŏk′ (for this case only; for one special purpose)
ad litem ăd lī′tĕm (for the suit or action)
alma mater äl′ma mä′ter, or ăl′má mä′ter (fostering mother)
alter ego ạl′ter ē′gō, or ăl′ter ĕg′ō (a second self)
anno Domini ăn′ō dŏm′ĭ-nī, or -nē (in the year of our Lord)
ante bellum ăn′tē bĕl′ŭm (before the war)
a priori ā′ prī-ō′rī, or ä′ prē-ôr′ē (deductive; from cause to effect)
aqua pura ăk′wa pū′ra, or äk′wa, or ä′kwa (pure water)
Ars gratia artis ärz grä′shĭ-á är′tĭs, or grä′tē-á är′tēs (Art for art's sake)
Ars longa, vita brevis ärz lông′á vĭ′tá brē′vĭs (Art is long; life is short.)
aurora borealis ạ-rō′rá bō′rē-ā′lĭs, or -ăl′is (the northern lights)
ave ā′vē (It. ä′vā) (hail)
bona fide bō′ná fī′dē (colloq. bŏn′a fīd) (in good faith)
casus belli kā′sŭs bĕl′ī, not *kăshus* (a cause for war)
caveat emptor kā′vē-ăt ĕmp′tôr (let the buyer beware)
Corpus Christi kôr′pŭs krĭs′tĭ, or -tī (the body of Christ)
corpus delicti kôr′pŭs dē-lĭk′tī (the body of the crime, that is, the facts of a crime)
corpus juris kôr′pŭs jōō′rĭs (the body of the law)
Cui bono? kwē′ bō′nō, or kī′ (Who benefits?; Of what good is it?)
cum laude kŭm lạ′dē, or kōōm lou′dĕ (with praise or honor)
data dā′tá, or dä′tá; colloq. dăt′a (plural of "datum"; also used as a singular)
de facto dē făk′tō (actually; in fact)
de jure dē jōō′rē (by lawful right)
de novo dē nō′vō (anew; afresh; from the beginning)
Deo volente dē′ō vō-lĕn′tē (God willing; if God so wills it)
dramatis personae drăm′á-tĭs pēr-sō′nē (the characters in a play)
Ecce Homo ĕk′sē hō′mō (Behold the Man! [Christ])
E Pluribus Unum ē plōō′rĭ-bŭs ū′nŭm (one [made] out of many)
ergo ĕr′gō (therefore)
erratum ĕ-rā′tŭm (an error); pl. **errata** -tá (a list of errors with corrections)

---

oil, out | ūse, ŭp, bûrn, fu̇ll, submit; ü—a muted e | chin; go; jet; park; K—Ger. ch; Fr. n̄—a nasal tone

Et tu, Brute! ĕt tū brōō'tē (Even thou, Brutus!)

ex cathedra ĕks ká-thē'drá (from the chair; with authority)

ex libris ĕks lĭ'brĭs (from the books [of])

ex officio ĕks ŏ-fĭsh'ĭ-ō (from office; by virtue of position)

ex parte ĕks pär'tē (pertaining to only one side)

ex post facto ĕks pōst făk'tō (done afterward but retroacting)

facile princeps făs'ĭ-lē prĭn'sĕps (easily first)

fiat fī'ăt (let it be done; hence, a sanction)

hic jacet hĭk jā'sĕt (Here lies...[on tombstones])

homo sapiens hō'mō sā'pē-ĕnz (the species—mankind)

in absentia ĭn ăb-sĕn'shĭ-á (in the absence [of the person])

in re ĭn rē (in regard to)

in situ ĭn sī'tū (in [the original] place)

in statu quo ĭn stā'tū kwō (in the same state)

ipse dixit ĭp'sē dĭk'sĭt (an assertion made but not proved)

ipso facto ĭp'sō făk'tō (by the fact itself; by that very fact)

lapis lazuli lā'pĭs lăz'ū-lĭ, or lăp'ĭs lăz'ū-lĭ (an azure blue stone)

lapsus linguae lăp'sŭs lĭng'gwē (a slip of the tongue)

lares and penates lär'ēz, or lā'; pe-nā'tēz (household gods; cherished possessions)

lex loci lĕks lō'sī (the law of the place)

lis pendens lĭs pĕn'dĕnz (a pending lawsuit)

literati lĭt'e-rā'tī, or -rä'tē (men of letters; scholarly people)

Magi mā'jī (the "wise men") ("The Adoration of the Magi")

magna cum laude măg'ná kŭm lạ'dē, or kōōm lou'dĕ (with great praise or honor)

magnum opus măg'nŭm ō'pŭs (a great work)

mala fide mā'lá fī'dē (colloq. măl'a fīd) (in bad faith)

modus operandi mō'dŭs ŏp'ĕ-răn'dē, or -dī (mode of operating)

modus vivendi mō'dŭs vĭ-vĕn'dē, or -dī (mode of living)

mutatis mutandis mū-tā'tĭs mū-tăn'dĭs (with the necessary changes)

ne plus ultra nē plŭs ŭl'trá, or nā (the highest point of achievement)

nolle prosequi nŏl'ē prŏs'e-kwī (to be unwilling to prosecute)   (See also p. 490.)

non sequitur nŏn sĕk'wĭ-tûr (it does not follow)

O tempora! O mores! ō tĕm'por-a ō môr'āz, or -ēz (O the times! O the manners!)

paterfamilias pā'tĕr-fá-mĭl'ē-as (male head of a household)

per diem pĕr dē'ĕm, or dī'ĕm (by the day)

per se pĕr sā, or sē (by or in itself)

persona non grata pĕr-sō'ná (or -sŏn'a) nŏn grä'ta, or grä' (an unacceptable person)

prima facie prī'má fā'shĭ-ē, or -shē (on the face of it; apparent, if not contradicted)

pro bono publico prō bō'nō pŭb'lĭ-kō (for the public good)

pro rata prō rā'tá, or rä'ta (colloq. răt'a) (in proportion)

Prosit! prō'sĭt (or **Prost!**, prōst) (May it benefit you!—a drinking toast)

quasi kwā'sī (seeming, or in a way)

quid pro quo kwĭd prō kwō (something [in return] for something)

Quo vadis? kwō vä'dĭs, or vä' (Whither goest thou?)

rara avis rär'a ā'vĭs, or rä'rá (a rare bird)

re rē (in regard to)

requiem rē'kwĭ-ĕm, or rĕk' (rest—a Mass for the dead)

Requiescat in pace rĕk'wĭ-ĕs'kăt in pā'sē (R.I.P.—rest in peace)

res judicata } rēz jōō'dĭ-kā'tá (a thing adjudicated; a matter previously and
res adjudicata } finally decided by law, on which suit cannot be brought again)

sanctum sanctorum sănk'tŭm sănk-tō'rŭm, not -torium (the holy of holies)

āle, ădd, câre, ärt, fást, ạll, about | ēve, lĕt, fẽrn, moment | īce, ĭll, habit | ōld, ŏdd, nôrth, won | mōōn, fŏŏt |

Semper fidelis sĕm′pēr fĭ-dē′lĭs (Always faithful—motto of U.S. Marine Corps)
Semper paratus sĕm′pēr pa-rä′tus (Always ready—motto of U.S. Coast Guard)
Sic semper tyrannis sĭk sĕm′pēr tī-răn̥′ĭs (Thus ever to tyrants—motto of Virginia)
Sic transit gloria mundi sĭk trăn′sĭt glō′rĭ-à mŭn′dī (So passes away the glory of the world)
sine die sī′nē dī′ē (without [fixing a] day [on which to reconvene])
sine qua non sī′nē kwā nŏn′ (an indispensable thing)
status quo stā′tŭs kwō (the existing state)(See "in statu quo," above)
sui generis sū′ī jĕn′ēr-ĭs (of its own kind; in a class by itself)
summa cum laude sŭm′à kŭm la̦′dē, or sōōm′mä kōōm lou′dĕ (with highest honor)
tempus fugit tĕm′pŭs fū′jĭt (time flies)
ultima Thule ŭl′tĭ-mà thōō′lē (farthest or northern limit; unknown region)
ultra vires ŭl′trà vī′rēz (beyond the powers [of a corporation, court, etc.])
vale vā′lē, or väl′ā (farewell)
Veni, vidi, vici vē′nī, vī′dī, vī′sī ("I came, I saw, I conquered." Caesar's terse announcement of a victory) (Roman pron. wā′nē, wē′.lē, wē′kē)
verbatim et literatim vĕr-bā′tĭm ĕt lĭt′ēr-ā′tĭm (word for word and letter for letter)
via vī′à, or vē′a (by way of)
vice versa vī′se vĕr′sà, or vīs′ vĕr′sa (conversely)
viva voce vī′va vō′sē (It. vē′vä vō′chä) (by word of mouth; orally, as in voting)
vox populi vŏks′ pŏp′ū-lī (the voice of the people) (abbr. vox pop)

LITERATURE

Admirable Crichton, The ăd′mĭ-ra-bl krī′ton
Alcott, Louisa May a̦l′kŭt, not ăl-
Americana à-mĕr′ĭ-kä′nà, -kä′, or -kăn′
ana ā′nà, or ä′ (scraps of literature)
Ananias ăn′à-nī′ăs
Apocalypse à-pŏk′a-lĭps
Ballad of Reading Gaol, The rĕd′ing jāl
Balzac (Fr.) bàl′zàk′ (Eng. bŏl′zăk)
Baudelaire (Fr.) bōd′lâr′
Blasco Ibáñez (Sp.) bläs′kō ē-bän′yäth
Boccaccio (It.) bōk-kä′chō
Brontë—Jane Eyre brŏn′tē; âr, not īre
Candide käṅ′dēd′
Cather, Willa kăth′er (th as in breathe)
Cervantes (Sp.) thĕr-vän′tās (Eng. sēr-văn′tēz)
Chekhov (Rus.) chĕ′Kōf
Coleridge (Eng.) kōl′rĭj, not cōōl-
Cowper kōō′per, or kou′
Cyrano de Bergerac sē′rà′nō′ dē bĕr′zhē-ràk′
Dante (It.) dän′tā (Eng. dăn′tē)
D'Artagnan dàr′tà′nyäṅ′ (Dumas hero)
Daudet (Fr.) dō′dĕ′
Diderot (Fr.) dēd′rō′
Don Juan dŏn hwän′ (Sp.) (Eng. dŏn wän, or jōō′ăn)

Don Quixote dŏn kē-hō′tā (Sp.) (Eng. dŏn kwĭk′sot)
Dostoevski (Rus.) dôs′tŏ-yĕf′skē
Dumas (Fr.) dü′mä′
Endymion ĕn-dĭm′ĭ-ŏn
Flaubert (Fr.) flō′bâr′
Forsyte Saga fôr-sīt′ sä′gà
Galsworthy, John (Eng.) ga̦lz′wûr′thĭ
Gautier (Fr.) gō′tyä′
Goethe (Ger.) gú′tĕ
Heine (Ger.) hī′nĕ
Hugo (Fr.) ü′gō′ (Eng. hū′gō)
Jekyll jē′kĭl (Dr. Jekyll and Mr. Hyde)
Lagerlöf, Selma (Sw.) lä′gĕr-lŭf
La Rochefoucauld (Fr.) là rôsh′fōō′kō′
Les Misérables lā mē′zä′rà′bl
Machiavelli (It.) mä′kyä-vĕl′lē, or măk′
Maeterlinck (Belgian) (Du. mä′tĕr-lĭngk) (Eng. mä′)
Maupassant, Guy de (Fr.) mō′pà′säṅ′, gē dē
Molière (Fr.) mōl′yâr′
Montaigne (Fr.) môṅ′tàn′yē (Eng. mŏn-tān′)
My Ántonia än′tōn-ē-äh, or än′tō-nē′à
Nietzsche (Ger.) nē′chĕ
Omar Khayyám (Persian) ō′màr kī-yäm′ (note accent)

oil, out | ūse, ŭp, bûrn, fu̦ll, submit; ü—a muted e | chin; go; jet; park; K—Ger. ch; Fr. ṅ—a nasal tone

PRONUNCIATION

Ouida (Eng.) wē′då (a pen name)
Pepys (Eng.) pēps, or pĕps
Perrault (Fr.) pĕ′rō′
Prévost (Fr.) prȧ′vō′
Pulitzer Prizes pū′lĭt-sēr, or pŏŏl′
Rabelais (Fr.) rȧ′bĕ-lĕ′ (Eng. răb′e-lā)
Renan (Fr.) rē-näṅ′
Rousseau (Fr.) rōō′sō′
Rubáiyát rōō-bī′yät′, or -bē-
Shavian shā′vĭ-an (pertaining to Shaw)

Southey (Eng.) south′y, or sŭth′y (th as in breathe)
Stendahl (Fr.) stäṅ′dȧl′
Sue (Fr.) sü, not sōō-ā (Eng. sōō)
Tolstoy (Rus.) tŏl-stoi′ (Eng. tŏl′stoi)
Turgenev (Rus.) tŭr-gĕn′yĕf
Villon, François (Fr.) vē′yôṅ′, fräṅ′swä′
Volpone vŏl-pō′nē (It., old fox)
Voltaire (Fr.) vôl′târ′
Zola (Fr.) zō′lȧ′ (Eng. zō′lȧ)

MEDICAL TERMS

allergic a-lēr′jik (note accent)
angina ăn-jī′na, or ăn′jĭ-nȧ
arthritis är-thrī′tĭs, not arthur-
asafetida ăs′ȧ-fĕt′ĭ-dȧ, not -fit-ity
astigmatism ȧ-stĭg′mȧ-tĭzm
bronchial brŏng′kē-al, not brŏn′ick′l
caffeine kăf′ēn, or -ē-ĭn
cerebral se-rē′brăl, or sĕr′ē-brăl
chiropodist kī-rŏp′ō-dist, not shi-
chloroform klō′rō-fôrm, not klera-
cholera kŏl′ēr-ȧ, not kŏl-ry
cocaine kō-kān′, or kō′kȧ-ēn
delirium tremens trē′mĕnz, not -mers
diabetes dī′ȧ-bē′tēz (colloq. -tĭs)
digitalis dĭj′ĭ-tăl′ĭs, or -tā′lĭs
diphtheria dĭf-thē′rĭ-ȧ, not dĭp-
eczema ĕk′zē-mȧ, or ĕg-zē′ma
erysipelas ĕr′ĭ-sĭp′ĕ-lăs, or ĭr′
Eustachian tube ū-stā′kĭ-ăn, or -shŭn
febrile fē′brĭl, or fĕb′rĭl
formaldehyde fôr-măl′de-hīd, not -mala′
glycerin glĭs′er-ĭn
heroin hĕr′ō-ĭn (note accent)
hiccup hĭk′ŭp, not hee′cup
homeopathy hō′mē-ŏp′a-thy (5 syl.)
hypochondria hī′pō-kŏn′drē-a
iodine ī′ō-dīn, or -dĭn

ipecac ĭp′e-kăk, not ĕpp-
jugular jŭg′ū-lēr, or jōō′gū-lar
larynx lăr′ĭnks, not lär′nicks
leprosy lĕp′rō-sy, not leper-sy
meningitis mĕn′ĭn-jī′tĭs
nauseate nô′shē-āt, or -sē, not -zee
neuralgia nū-răl′jȧ, or -jĭ-ȧ not -roul
orthodontist ôr′thō-dŏn′tist, not -den′
pediatrician pē′dē-ȧ-trĭsh′an, or pĕd′
pharmaceutical fär′mȧ-sū′tĭ-kăl
pharmacist fär′mȧ-sĭst, not -tist
pleuropneumonia plōō′rō-nū-mō′nĭ-ȧ
podiatrist pō-dī′ȧ-trist (foot doctor)
psychiatry sī-kī′ȧ-try
psychosomatic sī′kō-sō-măt′ik
pulmonary pŭl′mō-nĕr′y, not pull-
quinine kwī′nīn (Br. kwĭ-nēn′)
rabies rā′bēz, or rā′bĭ-ēz, not răb′
respiratory rē-spīr′a-tō′ry, or rĕs′pĭ-
sarsaparilla sär′sȧ-pȧ-rĭl′ȧ
  (dial. săs-pa-)
sclerosis sklē-rō′sĭs, not slĭ-
syringe sĭr′ĭnj, or sŭ-rĭnj′
tourniquet tûr′nĭ-kĕt, or tōōr′
veterinary vĕt′ĕr-ĭ-nĕr′y, not veta-
virus vī′rŭs

MUSIC

a cappella ä käp-pĕl′lä (unaccompanied)
adagio ȧ-dä′jō
allegro äl-lā′grō
andante än-dän′tä
Ave Maria ä′vä mä-rē′ä (Hail, Mary)
basso profundo bäs′sō prō-fŭn′dō
berceuse bĕr′sûz′, not bŭr-sūs′
calliope kȧ-lī′ō-pē (dial. kăl′ē-ōp)
cantabile kän-tä′bē-lä

cantata kȧn-tä′ta
carillon kăr′ĭ-lŏn (Fr. kȧ′rē-yôṅ′)
cello chĕl′ō
coloratura kŭl′ēr-ȧ-tū′rȧ (It.
  kō′lō-rä-tōō′rä)
concerto kōn-chĕr′tō
diva dē′vȧ
finale fē-nä′lä
fine fē′nä (It., the end)

flautist flô'tist (a flutist)
fugue fūg (note hard g)
impresario ĭm'prā-sä'rĭ-ō
madrigal măd'rĭ-găl
mezzo mĕt'sō (It. mĕd'zô)
Miserere 'mĭz'e-rē'rē, or -rā'rē
oboe ō'bō (a hautboy)
oboist ō'bō-ĭst
orchestral ôr-kĕs'trăl, or ôr'
Peer Gynt Suite pēr' gĭnt' swēt
pianist pē-ăn'ist (Br. pē'a-nĭst)

polka pōl'ka (colloq. pōk'a)
prelude prĕl'ūd, or prē'
prima donna prē'må dŏn'å
roundelay roun'dē-lā
scherzo skĕr'tsō, not *shertso*
soprano sō-prä'nō, or -prăn'
Stradivarius străd'ĭ-vâr'ĭ-ŭs
Träumerei troi'mĕ-rī'
trio trē'ō, or trī'ō
violoncello vē'ō-lŏn-chĕl'ō, not *violin-*
xylophone zī'lo-fōn, or zĭl'

NATIONALITIES AND RACES

Anglo-Saxon ăng'glō-săk'sn (English)
Breton brĕt'un (of Bretagne [Brittany])
Briton brĭt'un (of Great Britain)
Celtic sĕl'tik ⎫
Keltic kĕl'tik ⎭ (usually refers to Irish)
Creole krē'ōl (does not necessarily signify race mixture. The American Creole is a descendant of the Louisiana Settlers, speaking a French or Spanish dialect.)
Czech (n. & adj.) chĕK (a native, or the language, of old Bohemia).
Danish dăn'ish, not *dăn-*
Deutscher doich'er (a German)
Dutchman a Hollander
English ĭng'glish, not *ĕng'*
Filipino fĭl-i-pē'nō (Sp. fē'lē-)
Gaelic găl'ik (Irish, Scottish, etc.)
Gallic găl'ik (French)
Iranian ĭ-rä'nē-an (See Iran, p. 173)
Iraqi ē-rä'kē (rather than "Iraqian")
Israeli ĭz-rā'lē (of Israel)

Latin races French, Italian, Spanish, etc., with Latin languages
Manxman măngks'm'n (of the Isle of Man)
Nipponese nĭp'ŏ-nēz' (Japanese)
Pakistani pä'kĭ-stä'nē (of Pakistan)
Panamanian păn'å-mā'nĭ-an
Portuguese pōr'tū-gēz (colloq. -gē)
Romany rŏm'å-ny, not *rōme-* (pertaining to the gypsies)
Semitic se-mĭt'ĭk (pertaining to the Hebrews and Arabs)
Senegalese sĕn'ē-găl-ēz' (of Senegal)
Singhalese sĭng'gà-lēz' (of Sri Lanka)
Sino- sī'nō, or sĭn'ō (Chinese, as Sino-Russian, Sino-American)
Slavic släv'ĭk, or släv' (pertaining to the Slavs: Russians, Bulgarians, Serbians, Czechs, Slovaks, etc.)
Teuton tū'ton (German)
Thai tī (of Thailand [old Siam])
Welshman wĕltch'm'n (of Wales)
Yugoslav yōō'gō-släv', or -släv'

NAUTICAL TERMS

boatswain bō'sn (from bo's'n)
bow bou, not *bō*
bowsprit bou'sprĭt, or bō'
conning tower kŏn'ing, not *kōn-*
coxswain kŏk'sn, rather than kŏk'swān
flotsam flŏt'sam, not *float-sum*
forecastle fōk's'l, rather than fōr'kås-l
gunwale gŭn'l

larboard lär'bĕrd ("port side"—left)
leeward lū'erd, rather than lē'ward (opposite of windward side)
mainsail mān'sl, rather than mān'sāl
maritime măr'ĭ-tīm (note long ĭ)
sou'wester sou'wĕs'ter
starboard stär'bĕrd (a ship's right side)

NORWEGIAN AND NORSE

fiord, or fjord fyôrd
maelstrom māl'strŏm, not *măl-*
ski shē (Eng. skē)

slalom slä'lōm (zigzag skiing)
Valhalla văl-hăl'a
Valkyrie văl-kĭr'ĭ, or văl'kĭ-rĭ

oil, out | ūse, ŭp, bûrn, fŭll, submit; ü—a muted e | chin; go; jet; park; K—Ger. ch; Fr. ñ—a nasal tone

181

OPERAS

OPERA	COMPOSER
Aïda ä-ē'dä	Verdi (It.) vâr'dē
Cavalleria Rusticana kä'väl-lä-rē'ä roō-stē-kä'nä	Mascagni (It.) mäs-kän'yē
Der Rosenkavalier dĕr rō'zĕn-kä-vä-lēr'	Richard Strauss (Ger.) rĭK'ärt shtrous
Die Fledermaus dē flä'dĕr-mous (The Bat)	Johann Strauss (Aus.) yō'hän shtrous
Die Meistersinger dē mīs'ter-sĭng'er	Wagner (Ger.) väK'nēr (Eng. väg'ner)
Die Walküre dē väl-kü'rĕ (The Valkyrie)	Wagner
Don Giovanni dôn jō-vän'nē (Don Juan)	Mozart (Aus.) mō'tsärt
Faust foust (Fr. fōst)	Gounod (Fr.) goō'nō'
Götterdämmerung gŭt'ēr-dĕm'er-ung	Wagner
Hänsel und Gretel hĕn'sĕl unt grä'tĕl	Humperdinck (Ger.) hum'pēr-dĭngk
Il Trovatore ēl trō'vä-tō'rä	Verdi
Iolanthe ī'ō-lăn'thē	Gilbert and Sullivan (Eng.)
Iris ē'rĭs	Mascagni
La Bohème lä bô'ĕm'	Puccini (It.) poō̄t-chē'nē
L'Africaine lä-frē-kān', or -kĕn'	Meyerbeer (German-Jewish) mī'ēr-bār
La Gioconda lä jō-kōn'dä	Ponchielli (It.) pōn-kyĕl'lē
Lakmé läk'mā'	Delibes (Fr.) dē-lēb'
La Traviata lä trä-vyä'tä	Verdi
Le Coq d'Or lē kōk'dōr (Golden Cockerel)	Rimski-Korsakov (Rus.) rĭm'skē-kôr'sä-kôf
Lohengrin iō'ĕn-grĭn (note accent)	Wagner
Lucia di Lammermoor loō̄-chē'ä dē läm'mĕr-moōr'	Donizetti (It.) dō'nē-dzĕt'tē
Lucrezia Borgia loō̄-krât'sē-ä bôr'jä	Donizetti
Manon Lescaut mä'nôn' lĕs'kō'	Puccini
Mignon mē'nyôn'	Thomas (Fr.) tō'mä'
Pagliacci päl-yä'chē	Leoncavallo (It.) lä'ōn-kä-väl'lō
Parsifal pär'sĭ-fäl	Wagner
Pelléas et Mélisande pĕ'lā'äs' ā mä'lē'zänd'	Debussy (Fr.) dē-bü'sē' (note accent)
⎰ Salome (Eng.) sä-lō'mē ⎱ Salomé (Fr.) sä'lō'mä'	Richard Strauss
⎧ Samson and Delilah (Eng.) săm'sn and dē-lī'lä ⎨ ⎩ Samson et Dalila (Fr.) sän-sôn' nä dä'lē-lä'	Saint-Saëns (Fr.) sän'säns'
Siegfried sēg'frēd (Ger. zēK'frēt)	Wagner
Tannhäuser tän'hoi-zēr	Wagner
Thaïs tä'ēs'	Massenet (Fr.) mä's-nĕ'
⎧ The Barber of Seville (Eng.) sē-vĭl', or sĕv'ĭl ⎪ Il Barbiere di Siviglia (It.) ēl bär-byä'-rä dē sē-vēl'yä ⎨ ⎪ Le Barbier de Séville (Fr.) lē bär-byä' dē sä-vēl'	Rossini (It.) rôs-sē'nē
The Pirates of Penzance pĕn-zäns'	Gilbert and Sullivan

āle, ădd, câre, ärt, făst, ạll. about | ēve, lĕt, fērn, moment | īce, ĭll, habit | ōld, ŏdd, nôrth, won | moōn, fŏŏt ,

OPERA	COMPOSER
Tosca tŏs′kä	Puccini
{ Tristan and Isolde (Eng.) trĭs′tăn and ĭ-sōld′ } Tristan und Isolde (Ger.) trēs-tän′ ụnt ē-zōl′dĕ	Wagner
Turandot { tōōr′än-dō (It.) { tụ′rän-dŏt (Ger.)	Puccini

RUSSIAN

babushka ba-bōōsh′kȧ (head kerchief)	Leningrad lĕn′ĭn-grăd (Rus. -grät′)
Baku bȧ-kōō′	{ Moscow mŏs′kou, or -kō
balalaika băl′a-lī′ka (Russian guitar)	{ Moskva (Rus.) mŏs-kvä′
Bolshevik(i) bŏl′shĕ-vĭk (pl. -vē′kē)	nyet ñ′yĕt (no); da dä (yes)
caviar kăv′ē-är′ (from the Turkish)	Pavlova päv′lŏ-vȧ (note accent)
Cossack kŏs′ăk, not *kōs-*	Pravda präv′dä (Truth)
dosvedanya dōs′vē-dän′yä (goodbye)	Russian rŭsh′an, not *rōōsh′*
droshky drŏsh′ky (a carriage)	soviet sō′vē-ĕt′, or sō′vē-ĕt′
icon ī′kŏn (from the Greek)	Stalin stä′lĭn, or -lēn (Rus. stȧl′yĭn)
intelligentsia ĭn-tĕl′ĭ-jĕnt′sē-ȧ, or -gĕnt′	steppes stĕps, not *steeps*
kulak kōō-läk′ (a rich peasant)	ukase ū-kās′, or ū′ (an official decree)
Lenin lyä′nyĭn (Eng. lĕn′ĭn)	Vladivostok vlȧ′dĭ-vŏs-tôk′, or -vŏs′tŏk

SPANISH, MEXICAN, AND SPANISH AMERICAN

Standard Spanish or pure Spanish is Castilian (kăs-tĭl′yăn) spoken by the citizens of Castile, the old ruling kingdom of castles.

Mexican language is a combination of Castilian and Andalusian Spanish, and some of the best elements of several of the native Indian tongues. It is a very rich and flexible language.

Spanish American is the language spoken in the Spanish American countries. It is largely Castilian, but may be, as the Mexican language is, a combination of Spanish and native tongues.

Note that in Spanish pronunciation, an initial **h** is always silent; **j** has a guttural **h** sound; **ll** an [l]y sound; **ñ** a nasal **ny** sound; and **z** is like **th** in "thank."

(See also note on Foreign Pronunciations, p. 157.)

adios ä′dē-ōs′ (goodbye)	centavo cĕn-tä′vō
adobe ä-dō′bä, not just *do-be*	chaparajos chä′pä-rä′hōs (Short Am. form, chaps—shăps)
alameda ä′lä-mä′dä (Eng. ăl′ȧ-mē′dȧ)	
amigo ä-mē′gō (a friend)	chaparral chăp-a-răl′ (dial. shăp-)
apartado ä′pär-tä′dō (post office box)	chaqueta chä-kä′tä (a jacket)
Armada är-mä′dȧ (Eng. -mä′)	Chihuahua chē-wä′wä, not *shĕ-*
arroyo är-rō′yō (Eng. a-roi′ō)	desperado dĕs′pēr-ä′dō, or -ä′dō
bolero bō-lä′rō, not *-lĕra*	Don dôn (Sir) (Eng. dŏn)
bravado brȧ-vä′dō (Br. -vä′dō)	Doña dō′nyä (Lady)
Buenos Aires bwä′nōs ĭ′räs (Eng. bō′nos âr′ēz)	{ dueña dwä′nyä { duenna (Eng.) dū-ĕn′a
caballero kä′bäl-yä′rō	El Camino Real ĕl kä-mē′nō rä-äl′ (the King's Highway)
cabaña kä-bä′nyä (a cabin)	
cafeteria kä-fä-tä-rē′ä (Eng. kăf′e-tēr′ĭ-a)	embarcadero ĕm-bär′kä-dä′rō (wharf)
	enchilada ĕn′chē-lä′dä
cañon kä-nyōn′ (Eng. canyon)	fiesta fē-ĕs′tä

---

oil, out | ūse, ŭp, bûrn, fụll, submit; ŭ—a muted e | chin; go; jet; park; K—Ger. ch; Fr. ñ—a nasal tone

frijoles frē-hō'lās (beans)
hacienda ä-syĕn'dä (Am. hä'sē-ĕn'dä)
Hasta la vista äs'tä lä vēs'tä (So long)
Hispano- ĕs-pä'nō (prefix, Spanish-)
hombre ôm'brä (man)
huaraches wä-rä'chāz (sandals)
incommunicado in'ko-mū'nĭ-kä'dō
jai alai hī'ä-lī' (a game)
Joaquin wô-kēn'
junta hōŏn'tá (a council)
lasso lä'sō (Am. lăss'ō; dial. lă-sōō')
llama [l]yä'mä (Am. lä'mȧ)
Llano Estacado [l]yä'nō ĕs'tä-kä'dō
⎰Majorca (Eng.) mȧ-jôr'kȧ
⎱Mallorca (Sp.) mä-[l]yôr'kä
mañana mä-nyä'nä (tomorrow)
mantilla măn-tē'[l]yä (Am. măn-tĭl'a)
mesa mā'sä
México (Méjico) mĕ'hē-kō
Montevideo mŏn'te-vĭ-dā'ō
no nô (no); sí sē (yes)
⎰norteamericano nôrt'ȧ-mĕr'ē-kä'nō
⎱sudamericano sōōd'ȧ-mĕr'ē-kä'nō
Olé! ō-lā' (Bravo!)
padre pä'drä
⎰palmetto păl-mĕt'ō (small fan palm)
⎱palmito (Sp.) päl-mē'tō
palomino päl-ō-mē'nō (Am. păl-)

patio pä'tyō (Eng. păt'ē-ō)
peccadillo pĕk'a-dĭl'ō, or -dĕl'yō
peón pā-ōn'
peseta pĕ-sä'tä
peso pā'sō
⎰pimento pĭ-mĕn'tō
⎱pimiento (Sp.) pē-myĕn'tō
plaza plä'thä (Eng. plä'za)
poncho pŏn'chō (a cloaklike blanket)
presidio prä-sē'dyō (Eng. prē-sĭd'ĭ-ō)
pronunciamento prō-nŭn'sĭ-ȧ-mĕn'tō
quién sabe? kyĕn sä'bä (Who knows?)
riata rē-ăt'a, or -ä'ta (a lariat)
rodeo rō-dā'ō (Am. rō'dē-ō)
señor sā-nyôr', not see-nor
señora sā-nyō'rä
señorita sā'nyō-rē'tä
sierra sē-ĕr'rä (saw-toothed mountains)
siesta sē-ĕs'tä
sombrero sŏm-brâr'ō
Tampico täm-pē'kō
tapadera tä-pä-dā'rä (Eng. tăp'ȧ-dĕr'a)
⎰tomato to-mā'tō, or tō-mä'tō
⎱tomate (Sp.) tō-mä'tä
tornado tōr-nä'dō (Eng. tôr-nä'dō)
tortilla tōr-tē'yä (a flat, round cake)
vaquero vä-kā'rō (Am. buckaroo)
vigilante vē-hē-län'tä (Am. vĭj'ĭ-lăn'tē)

SWISS

There is no Swiss language. Languages of surrounding countries are spoken.

Alpine ăl'pĭn, or -pīn
Bern bĕrn, or bûrn
chalet shȧ-lā' (Fr. shȧ'lĕ')
hospice hŏs'pĭs (Fr. ôs'pēs') (an inn)
Jungfrau yu̯ng'frou'
Lausanne lō'zȧn'

Matterhorn mät'ĕr-hôrn, or măt'
Saint Bernard săn̊ bĕr'när' (Eng.
      sänt bĕr-närd')
⎰Saint Moritz sänt mō-rĭts' (Fr.
⎱   săn̊ mō-rēts')
⎱Sankt Moritz (Ger.) zängkt mō'rĭts

UNIVERSITIES, COLLEGES, AND SCHOOLS

College—a small or restricted institution of higher learning, granting degrees in specialized subjects.

University—a large institution of higher learning, comprised of several colleges—as colleges of arts, literature, and science—and professional schools or colleges of law, medicine, etc.

Amherst College—Mass. ăm'ĕrst
Antioch College—Ohio ăn'tĭ-ŏk, not
      -oak
Bowdoin College—Maine bō'dn
Brigham Young University—Utah
      brĭg'am

Bryn Mawr College—Pa. brĭn'mär', not
      more
Canisius College—N.Y. kȧ-nĭsh'ŭs
Colgate University—N.Y. kōl'gāte, not
      kŏl-
Dartmouth College—N.H. därt'mŭth

āle, ădd, câre, ärt, fȧst, ạll, about | ēve, lĕt, fērn, moment | ice, ĭll, habit | ōld, ŏdd, nôrth, won | mōōn, fŏŏt |

DePauw University—Ind. dĕ-pạ'
Duquesne University—Pa. dōō-kān'
Fordham University—N.Y. fōrd'ăm
Gonzaga University—Wash. gŏn-zăg'à
Groton School—Mass. grŏ'ton, not
    grōt-
Juniata College—Pa. jōō'nĭ-ăt'à
Loyola University—Ill. loi-ō'là
Marquette University—Wis. mär-kĕt'

Mount Holyoke College—Mass.
    hŏl'yōk
Notre Dame, University of—Ind.
    nō'tēr dăm'
Rutgers University—N.J. rŭt'gērz
Wellesley College—Mass. wĕlz'ly, not
    wel-es-ly
Wesleyan University—Conn. wĕs'lĭ-ăn
Xavier University—Ohio ză'vē-er

VEGETATION

acacia à-kā'sha, not -*kăsh-ia*
acorn ā'kôrn, or ā'kērn
almond ä'mŭnd
amaryllis ăm'à-rĭl'ĭs
anemone á-nĕm'ō-nē
apricot ā'prĭ-kŏt, or ăp'rĭ-
arbutus är-bū'tŭs
asparagus ăs-păr'a-gŭs, not *a-spar-grass*
avocado ăv'ō-kä'dō
banana bà-năn'à (Br. bà-nä'nà)
bougainvillea bōō'gĭn-vē'lē-a
broccoli brŏk'ō-lē
camellia kà-mĕl'ĭ-a, or'-mĕl'ya
camomile kăm'ō-mīl
catalpa cà-tăl'pa, not -*tawl*
cauliflower kô'lĭ-flou'er, not *cŭl-*
cereus sē'rē-ŭs (night-blooming)
chive chīv
chrysanthemum krĭs-ăn'thē-mŭm, not
    -*thium*
cinchona sĭn-kō'na (quinine bark)
cineraria sĭn'ĕ-rā'rĭ-a
clematis klĕm'a-tĭs (Br. klē-mā'tĭs)
cranberry krăn'bĕr-y, not *cram-*
cyclamen sĭk'la-mĕn, or sīk'
dahlia dăl'ya, or däl' (Br. dāl'ya)
elm ĕlm, not *el-um*
endive ĕn'dīv (Fr. äṅ'dēv')
espalier ĕs-păl'yẽr (to train)
eucalyptus ū'kà-lĭp'tŭs
forsythia fôr-sĭth'ĭ-a, or -sī'thĭ-a
gherkin gûr'kĭn (small cucumber)
{**gladiola** glăd'ē-ō'la, or glà-dī'o-la
{**gladiolus** (plant) glăd'ĭ-ō'lus
{**Gladiolus** (genus) glà-dī'ō-lus
heliotrope hē'lĭ-ō-trōp
herb ûrb (Br. hûrb)
hibiscus hī-bĭs'kŭs

hydrangea hī-drăn'jē-a, or -drān'ja
lichen lī'kĕn, not *litch'en*
licorice lĭk'ō-rĭs (colloq. lĭk'rĭsh)
lignum vitae lĭg'nŭm vī'tē
lilac lī'lăk, not *lī'lŏck*
mesquite mĕz-kēt'
mushroom mŭsh'rōōm, not *musha-roon*
muskmelon mŭsk'mĕl'un, not *mush-*
nasturtium năs-tûr'shŭm
orégano ō-rā'gà-nō (Sp., note accent)
papyrus pa-pī'rŭs (paper plant)
passionflower so named because the
    parts suggest the story
    of Christ's crucifixion
pecan pē-kän', or -kăn'
peony pē'ō-ny (note accent)
pistachio pĭs-tä'shĭ-ō
poinsettia poin-sĕt'ĭ-a, not -*setta*
pollen pŏl'ĕn, not *pōle-*
pomegranate pŏm'grăn'at, or pŭm'
pumpkin pŭmp'kĭn (colloq. pŭng'kĭn)
radish răd'ĭsh, not *red-*
raspberry răz'bĕr-y, or răz'
{**resin** rĕz'ĭn (a gummy substance)
{**rosin** rŏz'ĭn (a hard residue)
rind rīnd, not *rine*
saguaro sà-gwä'rō, or sà-wä'rō (cactus)
shallot shă-lŏt' (variety of onion)
sumac shōō'măk, or sū'măk
turmeric tûr'mẽr-ik, not *tōōm-*
vanilla và-nĭl'a, not -*nĕll*
verbena vẽr-bē'nà, not -*bēen'yuh*
{**Wistaria** (genus) wĭs-tā'rĭ-a
{**wisteria** (plant) wĭs-tēr'ĭ-a
woodbine wŏŏd'bīn', not -*bĭn*
yucca yŭk'à, not *yū-*
zucchini zōō-kē'nē (a summer squash)

◈◈◈◈◈◈◈◈

oil, out | ūse, ŭp, bûrn, fu̬ll, submit; ü—a muted e | chin; go; jet; park; K—Ger. ch; Fr. ṅ—a nasal tone

AFTERWORD ON PRONUNCIATION

Many mispronunciations are the result of a hazy idea of the spelling of, or syllables in, a word.

To mispronounce an unfamiliar word is not so noticeable an error as to mispronounce a familiar one.   Familiar words are bungled because they are taken for granted.

Do not use a word and then wonder about the pronunciation. Question. the pronunciation of every infrequent or unusual word and defer its use until it has been checked with the dictionary.

Memorize the pronunciation by repeating it at least five times when looking up a word.   If the pronunciation of a word stays in the memory a day, it is usually indelibly imprinted there.

When two or more pronunciations are given for the same word, choose the one that is the most generally used, whether this pronunciation is given first or last in the dictionary.

When speaking of dictionaries or reference books, note these pronunciations:

> **Merriam-Webster** dictionaries—mĕr′ĭ-ăm, not *mē-*, nor *mĭr-*
> **Funk & Wagnalls** dictionaries—wăg′nalz, not *wäg-*, nor *väg-*
> **The Roget Dictionary**—rō′zhā′, not *rō′jet*
> (from Roget's Thesaurus)—thē **sŏ′rŭs**
> **Encyclopædia Britannica**—ĕn-sĭ′klō-pē′dĭ-a, not *-săk-la,*
> brĭ-tăn′ik-a, not *-tān′*

"The best kind of education is unquestionably that acquired through individual effort—by experience, practice, and research."
—The late Frank H. Vizetelly, Editor of Funk & Wagnalls Dictionaries.

Similar Words

Many words are so similar in sound or spelling that they are liable to be interchanged if a writer glances too quickly in the dictionary, or does not stop to comprehend the meanings.

NOTE: Words that have two spellings, such as "catalogue" or "catalog," "disk" or "disc," "dispatch" or "despatch," "gauge" or "gage," "skeptical" or "sceptical," are not included in the list. Choice of spelling is a matter of usage.

A

abjure adjure	to renounce or reject solemnly (ăb-jŏŏr′) (noun, abjuration) to command or entreat solemnly (ă-jŏŏr′) (noun, adjuration)
absorption adsorption	a taking up or drinking in; engrossment (verb, absorb) adhesion of gas or liquid to the surface of a solid (verb, adsorb)
ad add	abbreviation of advertisement (no period) to make an addition
adapt adopt adept	to adjust or fit for a new use ("adaptation"—adjustment) to choose or take as one's own ("adoption"—a taking by choice) skilled
adhesion adherence	a sticking together, as of substances or tissue a steady attachment, as of a person to a rule; fidelity
admittance admission	actual entrance; permission or right to enter, as "No admittance," "gain admittance" entrance for a certain purpose, or with certain rights and privileges, as "admission to a theater"; a fact or point admitted
adverse averse to	opposing; unfavorable disinclined toward
advice advise	(noun) recommendation; counsel; notice given (ăd-vīs′) (verb) to counsel; to notify (ăd-vīz′). (These words, though useful, are overworked in letters. They should be limited to instances in which the idea of "recommendation" is involved. "Inform," "tell," "information," etc., should be used at other times.)
agenda addenda	a list of things to be done at a meeting (a-jĕn′da) (pl.) things to be added, as in a supplement or an appendix
aid aide	to help; to facilitate. A helper a confidential assistant, as a military or White House aide (ăd)
ail ale	to affect painfully a beverage
air heir	the atmosphere; a tune; manner ("airs"). To broadcast; to expose one legally entitled to inherit an estate (ĕr or âr)
alinement⎫ alignment⎭	interchangeable, but the English form "alinement" (used in U.S. Government printing) seems preferable to the French "alignment"
all awl	the whole of a tool

allocate	to set apart or assign
locate	to fix or find the place of

allusion	reference by suggestion	
elusion	avoidance or evasion (rare)	
illusion	a visual deception; a romantic idea	
delusion	a false idea	

Similarly:

allude	allusive
elude	elusive
illude (rare)	illusive
delude	delusive

ally	an associate (ă-lī′, or ăl′ī)
alley	a narrow way

aloud	audibly
allowed	permitted

Alpine	pertaining to the Alps (ăl′pīn, or ăl′pĭn)
alpine	of or like the Alps, as "alpine flowers," "alpine heights"
alpen-	(used in compounds) "alpenglow," "alpenhorn," "alpenstock"

already	previously, as "They have already been sent."
all ready	all in readiness, as "packages all ready to mail" (not "already")

altar	a place of worship
alter	to change

alternate	a substitute (a person). Occurring by turns (ăl′tĕr-nĭt, or ăl′)
alternative	a choice between two (or more) courses or things (ăl-tûr′na-tiv)

although } though	interchangeable; but "although" being slightly emphatic is often preferred to introduce facts, and "though," suppositions

altogether	entirely, as "They are altogether too light."
all together	in one group, as "Were they all together?" (not "altogether")

amnesia	loss of memory
aphasia	loss of speech
astasia	inability to stand or walk
asphyxia	suffocation; suspended animation

anachorism	something foreign to a place or condition
anachronism	a chronological error

analyst	one who analyzes
annalist	a writer of annals (records)

angel	a spiritual being; (colloq.) a financial backer, as of a play
angle	a corner

ant	an insect
aunt	a relative

ante-	a prefix meaning "before." (Noun) a cardplayer's stake (ăn′tē)
anti-	a prefix meaning "against" (ăn′tĭ, not ăn′tī). (Colloq. as a noun) a dissenting person (ăn′tī)

antedate	to date back to some past date (before the present date)
postdate	to date forward to some future date (after the present date)

antidote	a remedy
anecdote	an interesting incident or brief story

antiseptic	an agent that destroys bacteria
anesthetic	an agent that produces insensibility
aseptic	free from germs

anyhow } anyway	interchangeable. Sometimes used as connectives, as "He says he doesn't need it; anyway, he will buy it."

anyway	in any event, as "Anyway, we are not interested."
any way	in any one way, as "not interested in any way"

a piece	by the piece, as "a mailing charge of 2¢ a piece"
apiece	each, as "priced at 10¢ apiece"
appertain	to belong—more formal than "pertain"
pertain	to belong—denotes a closer relationship than "appertain" ⎫ Note
appurtenance	that which belongs; accessory ⎬ spellings
pertinent	related; applicable ⎭
appraise	to estimate the value of (noun, appraisal)
apprise	to inform
apprize	to appraise or apprise (not commonly used)
Arabian	pertaining to the country of Arabia
Arabic	pertaining to the language or numerals of the Arabs (ăr′a-bĭk)
area	surface; extent or range (ā′rē-a)
aria	a melody (ä′rĬ-à)
Argentina	(noun) a republic in South America (är′jĕn-tē′na)
Argentine	(adj.) pertaining to the republic of Argentina (är′jĕn-tēn)
ark	a place of refuge
arc	a curved line
arrange	to put in order
arraign	to call into court (a-rān′, not *a-rānj′*)
ascetic	austere and self-denying (ă-sĕt′ik)
acetic	sour, as the acid in vinegar (à-sē′tik)
assay	to analyze or test, as an ore. An analytical evaluation
essay	to attempt. A short composition
assembly	an organized, purposeful gathering of people or things
assemblage	a vast, unorganized gathering of people or things
assent	consent
ascent	a rise
accent	a stress
astray	straying, as "gone astray," "astray freight," "free astray"
estray	a stray, especially a valuable farm animal (formal, legal)
stray	a wanderer. To wander
astrology	the study of the influences of the stars on human destinies
astronomy	the science of the heavenly bodies
ate	did eat
eight	a numeral
auger	a tool
augur	to foretoken, as "It augurs well..."
aught	anything (For a cipher, see "naught," below.)
ought	should
aviary	a place for birds (ā′vĬ-ĕr′y)
apiary	a place for bees (ā′pĬ-ĕr′y)
away	as "away from," or "gone away"
aweigh	(naut.) lifted, as an anchor
way	in the phrase "give way," not "*away*," as "the bridge gave way," "the people gave way," "gave way to grief"
awhile	(adv.) for a while
a while	(noun). Note that "awhile" means "for a while"; therefore, if "for" is used, "a while" should be used, not "*awhile*."

189

B

bad	defective
bade	told or commanded (băd, not *bāde*)
bail	to dip up; to parachute from. Release security; pail handle
bale	a large, compact bundle, as "a bale of hay"
bait	a lure. To torment, as "bear baiting"
bate	to moderate, as "with bated breath"
bald	bare
balled	wound into a ball, as "balled up"
bawled	shouted, as "bawled out"
ball	a round object; a dance
bawl	to cry out
ballet	a graceful, pantomimic dance, telling a story (Fr. bȧ-lā′)
ballot	a printed ticket or sheet used in voting; voting in general
baneful	poisonous, as "baneful drugs"; ruinous, as "a baneful ideology"
baleful	sinister; menacing, as "a baleful glance"
barbaric	gaudy; wild
barbarous	cruel; brutal (bär′ba-rus, not *bär-bair′-ee-us*)
barbarian	uncivilized
bark	the outer part of a tree; the call of a dog or animal
barque	a three-masted sailing ship (a barquentine) (also spelled bark)
baron	a nobleman
barren	unfruitful
base	a foundation. Small; mean; low
bass	a deep tone or voice (bās); a kind of fish (băs)
basis	a figurative foundation; basic principle (L. pl. bases, bā′sēz [rare])
base	a material foundation, as of a structure (pl. bases)
bathos	a descent from the sublime to the ridiculous; absurd pathos (bā′thŏs)
pathos	sadness (pā′thŏs, not *păth-ōs*)
bay	a calm sea inlet; a tree; a compartment; a projecting window arrangement; a reddish brown; a dog's bark. To stand cornered, as "at bay"
Bey	a Turkish title of respect (after the name); the Tunisian ruler (bā)
Bayreuth	a Bavarian city, scene of Wagnerian festivals (bī-roit′, not -*ruth*)
Beirut	the capital of Lebanon (Fr. Beyrouth) (bā-rōōt′)
bazaar	an Oriental market place; a fair for charity
bizarre	fantastic
be	a verb
bee	an insect
beach	the shore
beech	a tree
bear	to wear, carry, or endure; to incline or be directed. An animal
bare	unadorned; naked (barefaced); destitute of ordinary things
beat	to strike; to vanquish
beet	a vegetable
beer	a liquor
bier	a funeral litter

190

Belgium	a country
Belgian	of or pertaining to Belgium. A native of Belgium.
bellow	to make a loud, bawling noise, as to "bellow forth"
billow	a high wave; a surging mass, as "billows of clouds"
benzine	a product of petroleum
benzene	a product of coal tar ("Benzol" is crude benzene.)
berry	a fruit
bury	to cover deeply
berth	a place to sleep; an allotted place for a ship
birth	a coming into life
beside	by the side of, as "beside the roadway"; disjoined from, as "That is beside the point."
besides	moreover; other than; in addition to, as "Besides that, it is new."
biannual	occurring twice a year ("semiannual"—every six months)
biennial	occurring every two years, as "biennial elections"
billed	charged; listed; advertised
build	to construct
blew	moved rapidly
blue	a color
bloc	a combination for political strength, as the "Farm bloc"
block	a piece of wood; a quantity or unit, as "a block of stock"; a pulley; a mold; a city square. To outline; to obstruct; to restrict, as "blocked currency," "blocked bonds," "blocked credits"
boar	a swine
bore	to drill; did bear. A wearisome thing or person; a high, rushing tide
boor	a peasant; a rude or clownish person (boor)
Boer	a South African colonist (Boer War) (bōr; Du. boor)
board	a piece of wood; meals; an organized group
bored	pierced; penetrated; wearied
boarder	one who pays for meals
border	edge
bolder	more bold
boulder	a large rock (old spelling, bowlder)
bomb	an explosive device (bŏm, not *bum*)
balm	something that soothes (bäm, not *bäl-um*)
born	brought into life ("a son born **of** [or **to**] his first wife")
borne	held; endured; carried ("a son borne by her"; "had borne a son")
bourn	a brook; a realm; a goal (bōrn) (also spelled bourne)
bow	(bō) a tie; a weapon; a violin bow. To bend
bow	(bou) the forward part of a ship; an inclination of the head
bough	a branch of a tree
beau	a dandy
boy	a youth
buoy	a floating signal (boo′y, or boi)
braze	to solder, join, or cover with metal
braise	to brown and then cook slowly in an oven or braising kettle
breach	a break; a gap, as "stepping into the breach"
breech	the rear or lower part ("breech-loading")
bread	a food
bred	produced; brought up

191

break	an opening or fracture
brake	a device for retarding motion; a thicket
breath	a slight stirring of air
breathe	to respire
breadth	width (brĕdth, not *brĕth*)
bridal	pertaining to a wedding
bridle	a horse's headgear; anything that restrains
Britain	Great Britain—England, Wales, and Scotland
Briton	a native British subject, particularly an Englishman
Breton	a native of Bretagne (Brittany, in France) (brĕt'un)
Britisher	a British subject. Although the word "Britisher" is objected to by some—on the ground that it is no better than "Irisher"—it is noted by American authorities as correct.
Englishman	pertains only to England. An Irishman or a Scotsman should **not** be called an "Englishman."
broach	to open; to introduce
brooch	an ornamental pin (brōch, rather than brōōch)
bullion	gold or silver metal
bouillon	a broth (bōō'yôn')
burrow	a hole for shelter. To dig under
burro	a little donkey
borough	a division of New York City; a village
by	a preposition ("by and by"; "by the way")
buy	to purchase
bye	secondary; in passing, as "by the bye"

C

cagey	sly; shrewd (kā'jy) (also spelled cagy)
cadging	begging or sponging (kăj'ing)
calendar	a schedule of time; a list
calender	a press for cloth, paper, etc. To glaze
colander	a sieve or strainer
callous	(adj.) hardened
callus	(noun) a hardened surface (pl. calluses)
Calvary	where Christ was crucified
cavalry	mounted military forces
cane	a walking stick; a bamboolike stem, as sugar cane; rattan for chairs
Cain	the brother of Abel—a murderer. (Colloq. "raising cain")
cannon	an immense gun
canon	a law or rule; "canon law," religious or moral law; a list; a church dignitary
canyon	a ravine or narrow valley (Sp. cañon)
cannot	the common form of "can not"
can not	slightly more emphatic than "cannot"
canvas	strong tent cloth
canvass	to solicit. An inspection or survey
capital	chief; vital; first-rate. The head; a capital city; money or assets
Capitol	(capitalized) the official building of Congress in Washington, D.C.; (not capitalized) a statehouse

carousal	a boisterous revel of drinking
carrousel	a military tournament on horseback; a merry-go-round (kăr′ụ-zĕl′)
carton	a pasteboard box; a target
cartoon	a large sketch or caricature
cash	money
cache	a hiding place (kăsh)
cachet	a seal or stamp; hence a distinctive mark, trait, or character; a design stamped on philatelic mail (postal cachet) (kă-shā′)
cast	a group of actors; a mold or pattern; a tinge. To throw off
caste	a class of society (kȧst)
caster	a small wheel or roller; a cruet
castor	a beaver or its fur; a drab color (castor oil)
casual	incidental; unimportant ("casualty"—accident; injury)
causal	pertaining to a cause ("causality"—relation of cause and effect)
censor	an examiner or critic. To suppress objectionable parts (sĕn′sẽr)
censure	condemnation; blame. To criticize rebukingly (sĕn′shụr)
censer	a vessel for burning incense
ceremonious	formal; done with ceremony
ceremonial	pertaining to a ceremony
chafe	to anger; fret; irritate (chāf)
chaff	that which is light or worthless. To banter (chȧf)
champaign	level expanse or open country
champagne	a sparkling white wine
chased	pursued; ornamented, as "chased gold"
chaste	virtuous; pure in design or style; not ornate
chassé	a dance step (Fr. shȧ′sā′). (Colloq. sashay [sȧ-shā′])
chassis	the framework of an automobile or airplane (shăs′ē; pl. -ēz)
cheap	not expensive
cheep	to chirp or peep
childish	pettish; small; weak
childlike	innocent; trustful
choose	to select
chews	masticates; meditates
chose	did choose (chōz). (Law) a piece of personal property (shōz)
clamor	noise; outcry
clamber	to climb or scramble [up]
clause	a group of words
claws	an animal's nails
click	a light, sharp sound. (Colloq.) to register
cliché	a stereotyped or trite phrase; a printing plate (klē′shā′)
clique	a small social set (klēk)
claque	paid applauders (klăk)
climatic	pertaining to climate, as "climatic conditions"
climactic	pertaining to a climax, as "a climactic scene"
climacteric	indicating a crisis. A crucial year or period of time
clinch	to grapple; to clamp, as a nail; to conclude, as a deal
clench	to grip tensely, as the fist; to close tightly, as the teeth

193

clothes	garments (klōz)
close	to shut; to end (klōz). Near; dense; tight (klōs)
cloths	fabrics (tablecloths) (klôths)
coal	a mineral
cole	a vegetable ("coleslaw"—a cabbage salad)
kohl	a beauty powder used by Arabian women to darken the eyelids
coarse	unrefined; rough; common
course	a passage; a way; part of a meal; prescribed series; natural order
cocoa	a powdered chocolate; a beverage
cacao	seeds of cacao tree, ground for chocolate (kà-kā′ō; Sp. kä-kä′ō)
coconut	the fruit of the coconut palm (has no connection with cocoa)
coin	money. To invent, as "coin a phrase"
quoin	a wedge; a corner block of stone or brick (koin, or kwoin)
coign	a corner position, as "a coign of vantage" (koin)
collie	a Scotch shepherd dog (kŏl′ĭ)
coolie	an Oriental laborer (kōō′lĭ)
collision	a clash
collusion	a secret scheme to defraud
coma	a state of deep unconsciousness; a blur of light (kō′mà)
comma	a punctuation mark
comic	of comedy, as "a comic actor"; humorous, as "comic books [or strips]"
comical	funny; laugh-provoking (often unintentionally), as "a comical gait"
complacent	self-satisfied (kŏm-plā′sent) (noun, complacency)
complaisant	obliging; affable (kŏm-plā′zànt) (noun, complaisance)
complement	that which completes (adj., complementary[to])
compliment	praise; a greeting with a gift, as "With the compliments of. . ."
compose	to make up; to settle or calm, as to "compose a quarrel"
comprise	to embrace or cover [all the parts]; to consist or be made up of
comprehensible	intelligible; understandable
comprehensive	extensive; of wide range or scope
compute	to calculate
commute	to substitute or exchange for a lesser burden; to travel daily
condemn	to pronounce opinion or sentence against
contemn	to despise or view with contempt
confidant	one to whom secrets are entrusted (fem. -e) (kŏn′fĭ-dănt′)
confident	possessed of firm belief or self-assurance
confidently	with confidence or self-assurance
confidentially	secretly; privately; in trust
congenial	kindred in tastes or interests; satisfyingly suited
genial	hearty; cheering; cordial, as "a genial host"; enhancing life
congenital	existing at birth, as "a congenital disease"
conjurer	a magician or juggler (kŭn′jûr-er)
conjuror	a confederate; an entreater (kŏn-jōŏr′er)
contagious	spreading by contact with diseased persons
infectious	spreading by germs or parasites which may be carried in the air or water (not necessarily by contact with diseased persons)
contemptible	deserving of contempt; despicable
contemptuous	expressing contempt; disdainful

continual	endless; of broken occurrence, but frequently or constantly repeated
continuous	ending, but of unbroken occurrence while it continues
continuation	pertains to length—the prolongation, or extension, of something
continuance	pertains to time—the duration of, lasting of, or succession of things
controller } **comptroller** }	an officer, private or public, who controls accounting and auditing ("Comptroller" is from Fr. compte [account]; pron. kŏn-trōl′er.)
coo	to murmur softly, as a dove, as to "bill and coo"
coup	a brilliant, unexpected stroke or successful maneuver (kōō)
coop	a poultry cage. To confine, as to be "cooped up" (kōōp)
coral	a small sea animal, or its skeleton (kôr′al)
corral	an enclosure or pen for animals (kō-răl′)
choral	pertaining to a chorus (kō′ral) (Carol, a song, is kăr′ŭl.)
chorale	a sacred song, sung in chorus (kō-räl′)
cord	a string; tendon; wood measure
chord	musical tones in harmony; a straight line; part of a bridge truss
core	the central part
corps	a body of persons, especially a military division (kōr; pl. kōrz)
corporal	bodily, as "corporal punishment." ("Capital punishment" is death.)
corporeal	having a material body (not spiritual); tangible (kôr-pō′rē-al)
correspondent	one who communicates by letter
corespondent	a joint respondent in a divorce suit (kō′rē-spŏn′dent)
corrosion	an eating away, as by chemical action
erosion	a wearing away, as of land by the action of water
cost	whatever is paid to produce or obtain something, as "a high cost"
price	what the seller asks for something, as "a low price"
costume	dress; ensemble
custom	practice
council	an assembly for legislative or administrative purposes (councilor)
counsel	advice; one who is consulted for advice; an attorney or group of attorneys conducting a case, as "legal counsel" (a camp counselor)
consul	a commercial representative of a foreign country (kŏn′sŭl)
courtesy	a favor; politeness
curtsy	a genuflection or bending of the knee
curtesy	a widower's life interest in his wife's real property
creak	a squeaking sound
creek	a stream (krēk; colloq. krĭk)
crick	a muscular cramp, as in the neck
credible	believable, as "a credible explanation"
credulous	prone to believe on slight evidence; overtrustful; easily deceived
creditable	deserving esteem; praiseworthy
credit	to give credit for or to
accredit	to attribute; to furnish with credentials, as "an accredited representative"; to certify as maintaining prescribed standards, as "accredited schools"
crevice	a narrow split or crack
crevasse	a large, deep fissure; a breach in an embankment (krĕ-văs′)
critic	one who judges and expresses a considered opinion
critique	a critical estimate or discussion of some work (Fr. krĭ-tēk′)

195

crumble	to break into fragments; to fall apart gradually
crumple	to crush and wrinkle; (colloq.) to collapse or give way
cue	a catchword; a signal; a billiard rod
queue	a pigtail; a waiting line. To form a line, as to "queue up"
currant	a berry, used for jelly
current	a swift flowing, as in a stream or of electricity; the general course. Of the present, passing time, as "current events"

D

dam	a barrier
damn	a curse
Dane	a native of Denmark
deign	to condescend
days	plural of "day"
daze	to stun. A stupefied condition
dear	valued highly
deer	an animal
decant	to pour gently
descant	to discourse; to sing or play (dĕs-kănt′)
decease	death
disease	illness
demise	death, as of royalty (dē-mīz′) (See also "device," below.)
decent	respectable; proper; fitting
descent	downward progress
dissent	disagreement
decree	a decision or order in the nature of a law
degree	a step or point in a series; an academic title conferred
decry	to censure or discredit
descry	to espy something distant or obscure (dē-skrī′)
definite	clear; fixed; well-defined
definitive	final; conclusive
demean	to conduct [oneself]; to degrade, as to "demean his reputation"
demesne	lands or estate held by ownership (dē-mān′, or -mēn′)
depository	the place where something is deposited
depositary	the person or trustee with whom something is deposited
deprecate	to express earnest disapproval of, often regretfully
depreciate	to decrease in value; to belittle
desecrate	to profane; to put to an unholy use
descendant	(noun) an offspring; a part of the heavens; "in the descendant," on the decline
descendent	(adj.) descending; coming down from an ancestor or source
desert	to abandon. Reward, or punishment, as "just deserts" (dē-zĕrt′)
desert	barren land (dĕz′ert)
dessert	the last course of a meal (dĕ-zĕrt′)
deserve	to be worthy of
disserve	to treat or serve badly; to do an ill turn to (noun, disservice)
desirable	worth desiring
desirous	entertaining desire. ("Desirous" for "desirable" is obsolete.)

196

detract	to reduce or take from
distract	to divert the attention of; harass
device	(noun) a contrivance (dē-vīs′)
devise	(verb) to contrive; to convey real estate by will (dē-vīz′)
demise	to lease; to convey a life estate (dē-mīz′) (See "decease," above.)
remise	to surrender title to, as to "remise, release, and forever quitclaim" (rē-mīz′)
diary	a daily record
dairy	a place where milk products are made
dictograph	a detective device; an interoffice telephone
dictaphone	a dictation device
die	to cease living (dying). A tool; a machine; a perforated metal block; one of a pair of dice, as "the die is cast"
dye	material for staining or coloring. To color (dyeing)
disassemble	to take apart
dissemble	to disguise, or feign
disburse	to pay out
disperse	to scatter
discomfit	to baffle; to overwhelm or defeat (noun, discomfiture)
discomfort	to make uneasy (noun, discomfort)
discreet	prudent (dĭs-krēt′)
discrete	distinct or separate (an opposite of "concrete") (dĭs′krēt)
disinterested	impartial; acting without self-interest
uninterested	not interested; indifferent; unconcerned
dispense	to distribute; administer
dispense with	to forgo or do without
disprove	to prove to be false, as to "disprove their theories"
disapprove	not to approve of, as to "disapprove his methods"
disseminate	to spread widely or broadcast
dissimulate	to conceal by pretending
dissociate } **disassociate }**	interchangeable, both meaning "to disunite" or "separate from"; but there is a tendency to use the shorter form
dissoluble } **dissolvable }**	interchangeable, both meaning "capable of being dissolved"
distinct	clear; individual; separate (noun, distinctness)
distinctive	distinguishing; characteristic (noun, distinction)
distrait	absent-minded (dĭs′trā′; Fr. dēs′trĕ′)
distraught	distracted (dĭs-trôt′)
divers	various or sundry (dī′verz)
diverse	different (dĭ-vērs′)
do	to perform
due	owing; proper, as "in due course"; directly, as "due west" (dū)
dew	condensed moisture, as "the dew point" (dū, not dōō)
doe	a deer
dough	a paste
done	performed
dun	a demand for payment; a tannish color

dose	a measured quantity
doze	a light sleep
draft	a sketch; an air current; a pulling; an order; conscription
draught	a damper; a drawn drink; a vessel's depth in water (dräft)
drought	(drout)
drouth	(drouth) } a parching dryness from want of rain
dual	twofold
duel	a combat between two persons
dungeon	a dark prison
dudgeon	sullen anger; resentment (dŭj'on)
Dutch	pertaining to the Netherlands ("Pennsylvania Dutch" are German.)
Deutsch	the German language (doich)
dying	being overcome by death
dyeing	coloring
dieing	cutting or stamping with a die

E

earn	to acquire by effort
urn	a vessel or vase
earnest	serious; sincere; binding, as "earnest money"
Ernest	a man's name
earthy	like earth or soil
earthly	worldly or material (opposed to "heavenly")
East, the	the oriental countries east of the Mediterranean. The East in the United States is regarded as the states east of the Mississippi River; or particularly, the states east of the Allegheny Mountains.
West, the	the Americas (the Western Hemisphere or the New World) and Europe. The West in the United States is regarded as the states west of the Mississippi River; or particularly, the states west of the Rocky Mountains.
East, Far	China, Japan, and neighboring countries—so called because they are the countries farthest east of Europe
East, Near	the Balkan States (Yugoslavia, Rumania, Albania, Bulgaria, Greece, and Turkey in Europe)
East, Middle	the Levant (the countries washed by the eastern Mediterranean: Egypt, Turkey in Asia, Syria, Lebanon, Israel, and Jordan), and also Arabia, Iraq [Mesopotamia], and Iran [Persia]
effete	worn out; barren (ĕ-fēt')
au fait	skilled; expert (Fr. ō'fĕ')
egoism	excessive thought of self; self-interest
egotism	excessive talk of self; self-conceit
eldest	pertains to the age of persons in one family
oldest	pertains to the age of other persons and things
elemental	of or like the elements: primal, natural, powerful, or phenomenal
elementary	basic; rudimentary, as "elementary education"
eligible	qualified to be chosen, elected, or appointed
legible	plain; easy to read or decipher, as "legible writing"
illegible	impossible or hard to read or decipher
emerge	(See "immerge," p. 205.)

emigrate	to go from one country (or part of a country) to another to live
immigrate	to come into a country, from another country, to live. (People emigrate out of one country, but they immigrate into another.)
migrate	to move slowly, or periodically, from a place, country, or climate
eminent	(See "imminent," p. 205.)
emollient	a soothing application
emolument	remuneration; salary
empire	an imperial organization
umpire	a judge or arbiter
referee	one to whom things, or points of a game, are referred for decision
ended	indicates past time, as "for the week ended May 1"
ending	indicates present or future time, as "for the week ending Saturday" (this coming Saturday), or "for the quarter ending today"
endorse	is the form generally used in business papers
indorse	is sometimes used in legal papers
enervate	to weaken or lessen the vigor of
innervate	to stimulate [through the nerves]; to invigorate
energize	to give energy to
enormousness	vastness of size
enormity	greatness of horror or depravity
entomology	insect zoology
etymology	the history of words
envelop	(verb) to wrap around (ĕn-vĕl′up)
envelope	(noun) a cover or wrapper (ĕn′vĕ-lōp; Fr. äṅ′v′lup′)
epic	a poem of action in heroic style
epoch	a period of time characterized by a memorable event or events
epitaph	an inscription for the dead
epithet	an appropriate descriptive word or phrase
epigram	a clever, compact saying
equable	even; uniform, as "an equable climate" (ĕk′wȧ-bl)
equitable	fair; just
erasable	capable of being erased (ē-rās′a-bl)
irascible	quick-tempered (ĭ-răs′ĭ-bl, or ĭ-răs′)
err	to commit an error (ĕr or ûr) (For "heir," see "air")
ere	before (no apostrophe before this word)
e'er	a contraction of "ever"
errant	wandering
arrant	notoriously bad; downright
eruption	a bursting out
irruption	a bursting in
euphemism	a softened statement; substitution of an agreeable expression for a disagreeable one (ū′fe-mĭz′m)
euphuism	high-flown style in language (ū′fū-iz′m)
exalt	to lift up; to glorify, as "exalted deeds"
exult	to rejoice; to glory, as to "exult in victory"
exceed	to surpass; to go beyond, as to "exceed the speed limit"
accede	to assent or yield [to]; to attain, as to "accede to the throne"
except	to leave out, as to "except them from consideration"
accept	to receive with approval, as to "accept a gift"

199

exceptional	uncommon; extraordinary; superior (negative, unexceptional)
exceptionable	open to exception or objection (negative, unexceptionable)
excess	beyond the usual or specified amount, as "taxes on excess profits"
excessive	beyond what is reasonable, just, or endurable, as "Government contractors must return excessive profits."
exercise	to put into action or practice; to train; to be worried or vexed
exorcise	to drive out, as an evil spirit
exhibit	to display. Something shown, as in an exhibition or in court
exhibition	a public display, as of art, manufactures, or feats of skill
exposition	exposure; explanation, hence a public display with explanation
exit	a going out; a leaving
exodus	a going away, as a migration
exotic	of foreign origin; colorful, as "an exotic dance" (ĕg-zŏt′ĭk)
exoteric	popular; understandable by the general public (ĕk′sō-tĕr′ĭk)
esoteric	private; understandable by only a select few (ĕs′ō-tĕr′ĭk)
expatiate	to enlarge [upon], as to "expatiate upon a theme" (ĕks-pā′shĭ-āt)
expiate	to atone for, as to "expiate a wrong" (ĕks′pē-āt)
expeditious	quick or prompt dispatch; speedy, as "expeditious action"
expedient	personally advantageous, as "expedient moves." A means to an end
extant	still existing or living, not destroyed
extinct	no longer existing or having a living representative; extinguished
extent	measure; length; degree
extract	a selected literary passage (usually large)
excerpt	a carefully selected literary passage (usually small)
eye	the organ of sight ("eyebeam"—a glance; "eyebolt"—a looped-head bolt) ("Eye Street" or "I Street")
I	personal pronoun; a shape, as "I-beam," "I-rail"
aye	yes (ĭ) (opposite of "no"); (poetic) always (ā)

F

facet	one of several small flat surfaces; a certain aspect (făs′et)
faucet	a tap
facetious	causing frivolous laughter (fà-sē′shus)
factitious	artificial; made-up, as "a factitious value" (făk-tĭsh′us)
fictitious	not real; like fiction (fĭk-tĭsh′us)
factious	caused by a faction or party strife (făk′shus)
fain	gladly; reluctantly willing
feign	to pretend
faint	weak. To lose consciousness
feint	a deceptive movement; a trick
fair	just; light; moderately good; favorable ("bid fair") An exhibition
fare	food; cost of transportation. To go [forth]; to get on
faker	one who fakes; a peddler
fakir	(or fakeer) a wandering religious wonder-worker (fà-kēr′ or fā′)
farther	pertaining to actual distance; more remote
further	additional; to a greater extent. To help forward
fatal	like fate; causing death or destruction, as "a fatal accident"
fateful	fraught with grave or dangerous possibilities, as "fateful days"

200

fate	destiny
fete	a festival. To honor (fāt; Fr. fête, pron. fât)
faun	a woodland deity—half-human, with pointed ears and goat's feet
fawn	a young deer; a yellowish brown color. To court favor
faze	(colloq.) to worry or disturb (also spelled feeze and feaze)
phase	a stage in development; an appearance or angle of a subject
feaze	(dialectal) to unravel (fēz)
feet	plural of "foot"
feat	an act of skill or strength
fellow	an associate; one holding a fellowship; an equal
fellah	a laborer or peasant in Egypt, Syria, etc.
ferment	to change, as with yeast; to be agitated from within
foment	to stir up; instigate, as to "foment revolt" (fō-mĕnt´)
file	a steel tool; a case for papers; a line, as "single file"; a body of soldiers, as in "rank [abreast] and file [one behind another]"
phial	a small bottle (fī'al) (See "vial," p. 225.)
faille	a ribbed silk or rayon fabric (fĭl; Fr. fà'yĕ)
fission	a breaking up; a splitting of an atomic nucleus to release energy
fusion	a melting together; a fusing of atomic nuclei to release energy
flare	a spreading or blazing out; a torch
flair	instinctive discernment; aptitude; scent
flaunt	to brandish, display, parade, or show off
flout	to insult, mock, scoff at, or treat with contempt
flea	an insect
flee	to speed away from (fled, not *flew*)
flew	did fly
flue	a chimney
flu	(colloq.) influenza
flounder	to struggle clumsily as if miring in quicksand. A flatfish
founder	to fill with water and sink, as a ship; to go lame from overeating
flow	to move smoothly, as in a stream
floe	a flat mass of floating ice
flower	a blossom; a plant that blooms
flour	ground meal
foggy	beclouded; misty
fogy	one behind the times, as "an old fogy" (fō'gy)
follow	to come after
fallow	to plow and harrow land but leave it unseeded for a season, as to "summer-fallow." A pale yellowish color
font	a receptacle for holy water, as "a baptismal font"
fount	a spring or fountain; a source or origin
for	a preposition
fore	first; preceding. The front; a shouted signal in golf
four	a numeral
forbear	to refrain from; to bear with; to be patient
forebear	an ancestor
forceful	effective; full of [mental] force, as "a forceful speech"
forcible	powerful; accomplished by [physical] force, as "a forcible entry"

201

forgo	to go without; to relinquish, as "forgoing all pleasures"
forego	to go before, as "the foregoing parts," "foregone conclusions"
formerly	heretofore; previously
formally	in a formal, dignified, or conventional manner
fort	a fortified place
forte	a special talent
forth	forward; outward
fourth	next after the third
forward	eager; bold; advanced
froward	obstinately willful
foul	unfavorable; unfair; unclean. Entangled, as "a foul anchor"
fowl	a bird or chicken
frays	skirmishes. Wears out
phrase	a group of words
freeze	to chill, congeal, or become ice
frieze	an ornamental strip; a coarse cloth
full	abundant; brimming; not vacant; complete; maximum
fulsome	coarse; offensive by being excessive, as "fulsome praise"
funeral	burial
funereal	sad or solemn (fū-nēr′ē-al)
fur	the hairy coat of an animal
fir	a tree

G

Gaelic	pertaining to certain branches of the Celts, such as the Irish and Scottish Highlanders (gāl′ik)
Gallic	pertaining to ancient Gaul or modern France (găl′ik)
gamble	to hazard; to wager; to play at a game of chance
gambol	to frolic or frisk about
gantlet	a punishment, as to "run the gantlet" (See also p. 35.)
gauntlet	a glove ("throw down the gauntlet"—a challenge)
gamut	the scale or range, as to "run the gamut" (găm′ŭt)
gap	an opening
gape	to yawn (găp); to stare stupidly with open mouth (gāp, or gäp)
gate	the closure for a passageway; an opening
gait	manner of walking or moving
genius	inspired talent; extraordinary creative power; a guardian spirit
genus	a classification of species (jē′nŭs)
gentle	mild; of or pertaining to good birth
gentile	one of a different religious belief; one not a Jew (jĕn′tĭl)
genteel	well-bred
German	of Germany. (Not cap.) a dance; a cotillion, as "a Monday german"
germane	closely related; pertinent, as "not germane to the issue"
gild	to embellish with gold
guild	a group of persons, or plants
gilt	gold-surfacing material. Gilded
guilt	liability for blame or wrongdoing

202

glazier	a glassworker
glacier	an ice formation
goal	an end or aim
ghoul	a demon (gōōl, or goul)
gored	cut in triangular or tapering form; pierced as with horns
gourd	the dried shell of a squashlike melon ("gourde"—Haitian money)
gorilla	an African ape
guerrilla	one who wages irregular or predatory warfare (gĕ-rĭl′a)
gourmet	an epicure; a connoisseur of fine food (gōōr′mā; Fr. gōōr-mĕ′)
gourmand	a hearty eater; one overfond of good food (gōōr′mänd; Fr. gōōr-män′)
grease	fat
Greece	a country
great	large
grate	a frame of bars. To scrape; to irritate
grill	a gridiron. To broil
grille	a wrought-iron framework, grating, fence, or barrier
grisly	ghastly (grĭz′ly)
grizzly	somewhat gray (grizzly bear)
grove	a group of trees
groove	a hollowed-out space; a rut
guarantee	to promise the performance of; to secure. A short-term (sometimes long-term) backing of quality or performance
guaranty	a pledge or written responsibility for performance of a contract or payment of a debt. (Some writers use "guarantee" for "guaranty" as the noun. "Guarantee" is the verb always.)
warranty	an absolute, legal assurance of title, stated facts, or conditions
guest	an invited visitor; a patron of a hotel. To appear by invitation
guessed	did guess
Guinea	a gulf and country on the west coast of Africa (gĭn′ē) (guinea hen, guinea pig). New Guinea is a large island north of Australia
guinea	a coin first made of Guinea gold; formerly a British monetary term for one pound one shilling
Guiana	a region in South America (gē-ä′na) (now Guyana; French Guiana; and Surinam [Du. Suriname])

H

hail	frozen rain. To come [from]; to call to ("hail-fellow-well-met")
hale	robust ("hale and hearty"). To pull or haul, as "haled into court"
hair	a filament that grows from the skin ("hair-triggered")
hare	a rabbitlike animal ("harebrained")
hall	a room
haul	to pull or drag
hardy	able to withstand hardship or exposure, as "hardy trees"
hearty	vigorous; abundant; heartfelt, as "a hearty welcome"
hay	cut and dried grass; an old country dance
hey	an exclamation (hā) ("heyday"—period of highest vigor)
heal	to restore or cure
heel	a part of the foot

203

healthful	producing good health, as "a healthful climate"
healthy	enjoying good health, as "a healthy person." ("Healthful" and "healthy" are interchangeable to a certain extent, and such phrases as "a healthy climate" and "a healthy recreation" are used and sanctioned. But in other than these few phrases, the distinction between the words is rather well observed.)
hear	to perceive by the ear
here	in this place
heard	did hear
herd	a drove
hearsay	rumor
heresy	an opinion opposed to the commonly accepted doctrine (hĕr'ĕ-sy)
heart	a part of the body
hart	a stag
hew	to cut or chop. (For "Hugh," see "huge," below)
hue	color; tint. A shout of alarm, as in "hue and cry"
high	lofty
hie	to hasten
him	a masculine pronoun
hymn	a sacred song
historic	history-making; famous in history, as "a historic speech"
historical	pertaining to history, as "a historical pageant"
histrionic	pertaining to theatricals, as "histrionic ability"
hoard	a supply stored and hidden away
horde	a roaming tribe or pack
hoes	garden tools
hose	stockings; rubber tubing
hole	an opening
whole	entire
holy	sacred; hallowed
holey	full of holes
wholly	entirely
holly	a tree or shrub
homey	homelike; warm and informal; intimate
homely	plain; not pretty; unpretentious, as "homely fare"
homogenous	alike in structure because of a common origin (hō-mŏj'e-nŭs)
homogeneous	composed of like parts (opposite of "heterogeneous") (hō'mō-jē'nē-ŭs)
hoop	a stiff circular strip; a large ring or band (hōōp) ("hoopla")
whoop	a shout or hoot (hwōōp) ("whoopee") ("whooping cough" [hōōp'ing])
whop	(colloq.) to plump down. A thud ("whopping"—thumping [hwŏp'ing])
horse	an animal
hoarse	rough or harsh of sound
huge	immense
Hugh	a man's name
human	pertaining to man
humane	compassionate; merciful; refining ("humanitarian"—benevolent)
hypercritical	overcritical (hī'per-)
hypocritical	deceitful; smug with pretense (hĭp'ō-)

204

I

idle	inactive; groundless, as "an idle rumor"
ideal	perfect
idol	an object of worship
idyl	a scene of rustic life
illicit	unlawful
elicit	to draw out
imaginary	nonexistent, that is, existing only in the imagination, as "imaginary fears," "imaginary people" (not real)
imaginative	existing, but created from or characterized by imagination, as "an imaginative drawing," "an imaginative person"
imbue	to saturate; to impress deeply; to tinge deeply or dye
imbrue	to stain or drench [with blood]
endue	to clothe; to invest with some quality
endow	to enrich; to benefit with a gift
immerge	to plunge under; to sink in; to immerse (noun, immersion)
emerge	to rise out of; to come into view (noun, emersion)
immersed	sunk in (especially in a liquid)
emersed	standing out of
imminent	threatening to happen at once; impending
immanent	inherent; indwelling, as "an immanent kindness"
eminent	distinguished; outstanding; evident
emanate	to originate, or start [from]
immoral	contrary to moral law; wicked; sinful
unmoral	without morals; knowing nothing of moral law, as savages
amoral	not governed by moral law; neither moral nor immoral (ā-môr′al)
impassable	not passable, as a roadblock. ("Unpassable" refers to speed.)
impassible	capable of unflinching suffering or of not feeling pain
impassive	unemotional; unfeeling; calm; serene
imperial	sovereign; pertaining to an empire, or an emperor
empirical	based on experience and not theory, as rule-of-thumb methods
empyreal	celestial, as "empyreal blue" (ĕm-pĭ-rē′al)
imply	to suggest indirectly, as to "imply by a remark"
infer	to gather or deduce from, as to "infer from a remark"
impostor	a pretender
imposture	act or conduct of a pretender; fraud
incarnation	embodiment in a living form
incarceration	imprisonment
incidents	occurrences
incidence	a falling upon; range of occurrence, as "the incidence of a disease"
incredible	unbelievable, as "incredible happenings"
incredulous	unbelieving; skeptical, as "incredulous listeners"
indention	the setting in of a line in typewriting or printing
indentation	a dent or depression; a notch in a border
indigent	poor; destitute [of]; in need, as "indigent migrants" (in′dĭ-jent)
indigenous	native [to]; originating in a certain region, as plants (in-dĭj′e-nus)
indiscreet	imprudent
indiscrete	compact; made up of similar elements

205

indite	to put into words or writing (in-dīt′)
indict	to accuse; to charge with an offense (in-dīt′)
inept	awkward; inappropriate; absurd; foolish, as "an inept remark"
inapt	unfitted; not ready; unsuited; unqualified (also spelled unapt)
infect	to implant with germs, as of a disease, courage, or corruption
infest	to overrun or beset, as "cares that infest the day"
ingenious	clever; inventive; resourceful (in-jēn′yŭs) (noun, ingenuity)
ingenuous	artlessly frank; naïve (in-jĕn′ū-ŭs) (noun, ingenuousness)
insensate	incapable of sensation; senseless; brutal
insentient	inanimate
insensible	unable to feel; unconscious
insensitive	not sensitive; unimpressionable
insight	mental vision
incite	to instigate; to arouse to action; to spur on
insipient	unwise; foolish, as "an insipient idea"
incipient	coming into being; commencing, as "incipient fears"
insoluble	incapable of being dissolved (indissoluble)
insolvable	not solvable or explainable (often "unsolvable")
insolvent	pertaining to a debtor who is unable to pay his debts
instance	example; solicitation; occasion, as "in the last instance"
instant	a moment. Urgent; current; immediate
insulate	to protect so as to prevent the transfer of heat, electricity, etc.
insolate	to expose to the sun, as for drying, curing, or bleaching
insure	to guarantee against financial loss, as to "insure a building"
ensure	to make sure or certain (assure: to make confident of fulfillment)
intelligent	possessed of intelligence or understanding
intelligible	understandable, as "an intelligible contract"
interpolate	to insert new (often unauthorized) words; to insert computed values
interpellate	to ask formally for an explanation of an action (ĭn-tĕr-pĕl′āt)
extrapolate	to deduce unknown values from known values (ĕks-trăp′ō-lāt)
interstate	between two or more states (also interdepartmental, interparty, etc.)
intrastate	within one state (also intradepartmental, intraparty, etc.)
inure	to toughen, as "inured to cold"; to take effect [to the benefit of]
immure	to surround with walls; to confine; to imprison; to entomb
isle	a small island
aisle	a passageway
its	possessive of "it" (no apostrophe)
it's	contraction of "it is" or "it has"

J

jam	to crowd; to cause to become wedged, as to "jam a lock"; to thrust with force, as to "jam on the brakes." A food
jamb	the side part of a doorway, window, or fireplace
jest	to banter. A joke
gist	the main idea involved, as "the gist of the matter" (jĭst)
jibe	to shift a sail; (colloq.) to agree, as "their stories don't jibe"
gibe	to taunt. A sarcastic remark, as "a mean gibe" (jīb)

judicial	pertaining to a judge or the administration of justice; judging, as "a judicial mind"
judicious	showing sound judgment; wise, as "a judicious decision"
junction	a joining of things, as roads, railroad lines, and rivers
juncture	a joining of times or events; a crisis; a joint or connection

K

karat	a measure for gold
carat	a measure for precious stones
caret	a correction mark
carrot	a vegetable
kernel	a seed; the central part
colonel	a military officer
key	that which controls or unlocks; a low island or reef
quay	a paved landing place or wharf (kē, or kwā)
kill	to put an end to
kiln	a furnace (kĭl, or kĭln)

L

laboratory	a workshop for conducting scientific experiments
lavatory	a place for washing
lain	rested; reposed
lane	a narrow way; an ocean route
last	final; after all others; most recent ⎫ largely interchangeable
latest	last up to the present time ⎭
later	at a subsequent time; more recent
latter	the second of two; near the end, as "the latter part of the **year**"
lath	a strip of wood (lȧth)
lathe	a machine for shaping material (lāthe)
leach	to filter through something, as ashes (lēch)
leech	a blood-sucking worm; the edge of a sail (lēch)
leash	a thong or strap for a dog; three, as hounds (lēsh)
leaf	a part of a plant; a page. To bear leaves, as to "leaf out"
lief	willingly, as "would [or had] as lief" (lēf)
leave	to go from; to let be; to bequeath. Permission; vacation
lean	to incline. Thin
lien	a legal claim (lē′ĕn, or lēn)
least	smallest; slightest degree, as "not in the least"
leased	rented under a lease
led	did lead; guided; followed; began, as a game
lead	a heavy metallic element. To fit with lead (lĕd)
legend	a tradition; an explanation or inscription (lĕj′ĕnd)
legion	a multitude
lesson	a teaching
lessen	to diminish
levy	to assess or collect; (law) to attach property
levee	an embankment; a wharf; a court reception

liable	responsible; having an unfavorable tendency toward (lī'a-bl)
libel	written, published defamation (lī'bĕl); (adm. law) a complaint
liar	a falsifier
lyre	a musical instrument (līr)
lie	to rest or recline; to deceive (lying) (For "lay," see p. 83.)
lye	a caustic alkaline solution or powder
lifelong	lasting throughout life
livelong	seemingly long in passing
lightening	making lighter; flashing, as lightning
lightning	a sudden flash of light in the sky
limb	a branch
limn	to draw (lĭm)
linear	pertains to lines or measurement, as "linear feet" (noun, linage)
lineal	pertains to ancestral lines (noun, lineage [lĭn'ē-ĭj])
liniment	an ointment
lineaments	the outline, or contour, as of a face (lĭn'ē-a-mentz)
links	connections
lynx	an animal
liquor	a liquid, usually alcoholic
liqueur	an alcoholic cordial (lē-kûr')
literal	according to the letter or exact facts
littoral	pertaining to a shore; a coastal region (lĭt'ō-răl)
livid	discolored, as black and blue; lead-colored; ashy pale, as "livid with rage." A certain reddish tone, as "livid violet."
lurid	ghastly; weirdly glaring, as flame through smoke (loor'ĭd, not lûr-)
load	a burden or cargo ("loadstone," a magnet, not a "millstone")
lode	an ore deposit ("lodestar," a guiding star; "lodestone," a magnet)
loan	a lending (For "lend," see p. 83.)
lone	solitary
loath	reluctant; averse; unwilling (lōth)
loathe	to detest (lōthe [-the as in clothe])
local	relating to a limited space, or to one city, as "local delivery"
locale	locality; a spot with unusual features (lō-kăl')
lose	to part with unintentionally; to fail to obtain; to wander (looz)
loose	not restrained; unfastened; free; not compact (loos)
luxuriant	abundant; rich in growth, design, or display, as "luxuriant foliage"
luxurious	promoting luxury or ease, as "luxurious living"

M

madding	raging, as "far from the madding crowd"
maddening	enraging
made	did make
maid	a young girl; a servant ("the Maid"—Joan of Arc)
magnet	that which has magnetic attraction
magnate	an influential, rich, or powerful person (măg'nāt)
magnificent	having splendor or grandeur
munificent	unusually generous or lavish

mail	that which is posted; flexible armor, as "a coat of mail"
male	masculine
main	chief. A principal pipeline; utmost, as "with might and main"
mane	long hair on the neck of certain animals, as "a lion's mane"
manner	a mode; a way ("to the manner born"); sort ("any manner of means")
manor	a mansion or estate
mantel	the structure around a fireplace
mantle	a cloak; a net cap for a burner; a covering wall
marine	of, in, or on the ocean, as "marine life," "marine insurance"
maritime	bordering on or connected with the ocean, as the "Maritime Provinces of Canada," "maritime law"
marshal	an officer. To arrange in order; to lead
martial	military, as "court-martial," "martial law," "martial music" (mär′shăl)
marital	pertaining to marriage (măr′ĭ-tal)
martin	a bird
marten	a fur-bearing animal
mast	a tall pole or spar; forest nuts used as food for animals
massed	formed into a mass
Mass	a Catholic service. (A Mass is "celebrated" or "sung"— not "held" or "conducted." "High Mass" is celebrated with full rites, music, and incense. "Low Mass" is said without music.)
masterful	filled with mastery—having power or command
masterly	like a master—having superior skill, ability, or knowledge
material	substance, or parts, of which anything is made
matériel	equipment (opposite of "personnel") (mȧ-tĭr′ē-ĕl; Fr. mȧ′tā′rē-ĕl′)
mean	to intend. Low; unkind; ignoble; average, as "mean distance"
mien	appearance; demeanor (mēn)
mesne	(law) middle; coming between, as "a mesne encumbrance" (mēn)
meantime ⎰ meanwhile ⎱	used interchangeably; but "meanwhile" usually stands alone, and "meantime" is used in the phrase "in the meantime"
meat	food; the flesh of animals; the edible portion of anything
meet	to join. (Law) just, as "whatever may be meet in the premises"
mete	to measure, as to "mete out justice [or supplies]." Measurement, as in the legal phrase "metes and bounds"
medal	a metal decoration of reward
meddle	to interfere
meritorious	deserving of praise
meretricious	tawdry, as "meretricious dress" (měr′e-trĭsh′us)
meticulous	careful, as "meticulous dress"
metal	a hard, heavy substance
mettle	spirit; courage
meter	a measure
métier	a calling or profession (Fr. mā-tyā′)
millinery	hats
millenary	a 1000th anniversary
miner	one who mines
minor	smaller. A person under age

209

missive	a letter; a message
missile	an object that is thrown or hurled, as "guided missiles"
mist	vapor; haze
missed	failed to do; noted the absence of
mite	a tiny particle; an insect; a small sum, as "a widow's mite"
might	force; strength, as "with might and main." Past of "may"
mitigate	to make less severe, as to "mitigate grief [or wrath]"
militate	to operate [against, or for], as "age militates against him"
modal	pertaining to a mode (mōd′al)
model	a pattern; an example; a fashion; a mannequin, as "a fashion model"
mood	disposition; feeling; a grammatical term (mōōd)
mode	fashion; method; grammatical mood (mōd)
moral	pertaining to right conduct. A lesson
morale	state of mind; spirit or feeling, as of a body of people (mō-răl′)
morality	virtue; ethics
mortality	occurrence of death; death rate
mores	ethical customs or unwritten laws (L. môr′āz, or mōr′ēz)
Moors	natives of Morocco (mōōrz)
moors	heaths (mōōrz; Br. mōrz) ("moor"—to anchor a ship [mōōr])
morning	early day
mourning	sorrowing ("mourning dove," not "morning dove")
motive	the moving power or idea; the theme
motif	(Fr.) the theme; the recurring unit of a pattern (mō-tēf′)
leitmotif	(Ger.) an identifying phrase in a musical composition (līt′mō-tēf′)
muscle	a part of the body
mussel	a shellfish (mŭs′el)
muzzle	the mouth of a thing. To bind the mouth

N

nap	a doze; a rough surface on fabrics
nape	the back of the neck (nāp)
knap	a mound; a blow. To chip off ("knapsack" —a case for clothing)
naught	zero; a cipher
nought	nothing
naval	pertaining to the navy
navel	the central part; a part of the body. Pitted, as "navel orange"
nave	the center part of a church (nāv)
knave	a rogue
nay	no
née	born (used to designate a married woman's maiden name) (Fr. nā)
neigh	the call of a horse
necessities	things that are urgently needed, as "the necessities of life"
necessaries	things that are usually needed, as "necessaries supplied to a minor"
need	to require
knead	to work into a mass
needed	wanted
needful	necessary
needy	in need

neglect	the act of neglecting
negligence	the habit of neglecting
new	recent; fresh
knew	did know
gnu	an African antelope (n$\overline{oo}$, or nū)
night	darkness
knight	one who has been knighted
no	a negative
know	to have knowledge of
none	not one
nun	a woman member of a religious order
not	a word expressing negation or denial
knot	a tie; a node in lumber; a unit of speed—one nautical mile an hour

O

O and Oh	(See Exclamation Point, p. 259.)
oar	a rowing implement
ore	a natural deposit
o'er	over
obelisk	a tapering column, as "Cleopatra's Needle" (ŏb'ĕ-lisk)
odalisque	a slave in a harem (ō'dȧ-lisk) (also spelled odalisk)
observance	act of attending to, complying with, or commemorating, as the "observance of a rule," "observance of a holiday"
observation	act of seeing, watching, noticing, fixing the gaze or mind upon, as "clear observation," "learning by observation"
oculist	one who treats diseases of the eyes; an ophthalmologist
occultist	a believer in supernatural powers (ŏ-kŭlt'ist)
optician	one who makes optical glasses according to prescriptions
optometrist	one who measures the range or powers of vision (ŏp-tŏm'e-trĭst)
of and off	These small words are often mixed, simply because of hasty spelling.
official	one holding public office with executive powers. Authorized
officer	one holding an office of rank, as in the Armed Forces. To command
officious	unauthorized; meddlesome; forward in giving advice or services
one	a single thing
won	did win
oral	spoken. ("Oral" suggests the act of speaking.)
verbal	by word of mouth; word for word. ("Verbal," when applied to spoken words, suggests words that are lasting or binding, as "a verbal agreement." "Verbal," when applied to written words, calls attention to the words themselves and means literal, as "a verbal translation.")
ordinance	a law, as "a city ordinance"
ordnance	military ammunition and supplies
ordonnance	an arrangement in order
Orient	the Far East
Occident	Europe and the Western Hemisphere
orient	to cause to face the east, hence to get the bearings of; to adjust
orientate	(transitive verb) to orient; (intransitive verb) to face the east

211

osculate	to kiss
oscillate	to swing back and forth
vacillate	to waver or stagger
our	a pronoun
hour	a measure of time
overdo	to do to excess
overdue	past due

P

pact	an agreement
packed	did pack; crowded; filled compactly
pail	a bucket
pale	wan; faint. A stake; an enclosure, or protective realm, as "outside the pale"
pain	a hurt; suffering; care, as to "take pains"
pane	a window glass; a panel; a division
pair	a couple
pare	to cut or peel
pear	a fruit
palate	a part of the mouth
palette	an artist's color board
pallet	a shabby bed, as of straw; a wooden implement; a board; a tool
pall	gloom; a dark covering. To become insipid, as "pleasures pall"
Paul	a man's name
partake	to take a portion of, as to "partake of food [or hospitality]"
participate	to take part in, as in games or debates; to share in, as profits
partly	in part, as "wholly or partly destroyed"
partially	to some degree, as "completely or partially established"
past	pertaining to time gone by
passed	gone beyond; transferred; passed an examination, as "a passed master." (A "past master" is one who has been master.)
patience	endurance; calm or quiet waiting; forbearance
patients	persons being treated medically
peace	calm; content; harmony
piece	to put together. A portion; a short composition
peak	a point; the top. To become thin, as to "peak and pine"
peek	to peep
pique	to provoke; to stir up; to pride [oneself]. Resentment (pēk)
piqué	a ribbed cotton fabric. To stitch through edges (pē-kā′)
pearl	a gem. Formed into pellets, as pearl barley or tapioca
purl	to flow in swirls or make a murmuring sound. A knitting stitch
pedal	a foot lever. Pertaining to the feet
peddle	to sell from house to house
peel	to remove the rind or skin of
peal	to resound, as a bell
peer	to look intently. An equal; a nobleman
pier	a pillar for support; a landing place
pendant	(noun) that which hangs
pendent	(adj.) suspended; hanging; pending

percent	number of parts to 100. ("Percent" is usually used after a number, but may stand alone as a noun if referring to a definite number, as "What percent were turned back?" Note that "percent" is now written as one word, and without a period—U.S. Government Printing Office usage.)
percentage	relationship of a part to the whole of 100 parts. ("Percentage" is often used when the word does not refer to a definite number, as "A small percentage had to be replaced." "Percentage" is used in commerce to mean a rate per hundred, as in commissions, allowances, duties, and discounts.)
peremptory	absolute; decisive; dictatorial, as "a peremptory command"
preemptive	having the right of preference; shutting out (also "preemptory")
perfect	faultless; complete. To make perfect
prefect	an official
perpetrate	to carry through; to be guilty of
perpetuate	to make lasting or perpetual
perquisite	an extra profit or privilege
prerequisite	something required as a preliminary
persecute	to torment; oppress
prosecute	to pursue in order to accomplish; (law) to sue
personality	distinctive personal qualities; total characteristics
personalty	(law) personal property (opposite of "realty") (pûr′son-ăl-ty)
personnel	the persons engaged in a certain service; the staff
personal	individual; private
perspective	mental or physical view in correct proportion
prospective	expected; anticipated
perspicacious	mentally sharp (pûr′spĭ-kā′shus) (noun, perspicacity)
perspicuous	clear; understandable (pûr-spĭk′ū-us) (noun, perspicuity)
physic	a medicine ("physical"—material)
psychic	pertaining to the soul, mind, or spirit ("psychical"—mental)
physique	the structure of the body
picaresque	pertaining to rogues or vagabonds
picturesque	having the rugged, quaint, or charming qualities of a picture
pigeon	a dove; (slang) a dupe
pidgin	a Chinese corruption of "business," as "pidgin English" (pĭj′ĭn)
pipe	a tube
piping	a system of pipes
plain	flat; simple; clear. Level prairie land, as the "Great Plains"
plane	a flat surface; a level or grade; a tool; an airplane. To make level. ("Plain sailing" and "plane sailing" are both used.)
plaintiff	(law) the one who brings suit; the accuser
plaintive	mournful
plate	a flat piece. To overlay with metal
plait	to braid (plāt, or plăt)
pleat	to fold cloth (plēt) (sometimes spelled plait)
plat	(not generally used) to braid; to plot [a piece of land]
plum	a fruit
plumb	a weight. To sound or test, as to "plumb the depths"
pole	a long wooden rod; end of a magnet; polar region, as "North Pole"
poll	a voting; the head or top ("poll tax"—a tax per head)

politicly	discreetly; with tact on the surface and shrewdness underneath
politically	with regard to politics
poor	meager; unfortunate; not good (pŏŏr)
pour	to stream
pore	to ponder intently [over]. A small opening
poplar	a tree
popular	pertaining to people; regarded with general favor
populace	the common people
populous	thickly populated
portion	a part. To divide into portions ("apportion"—to allot)
potion	a drink or dose, as of poison or magic medicine (pō'shun)
proportion	relationship or ratio of parts. To adjust in relationship
post card postal card }	The Post Office Department makes the distinction that a "post card" is a "private mailing card," while a "postal card" is one printed by the Government with the stamp impressed thereon.
power	strength; force
prowess	strength and courage combined; skill and daring
practical	efficient, yet sensibly governed by actual, everyday conditions, not theories or ideals, as "practical ways," "a practical man"
practicable	capable of being efficiently accomplished or used [in the future]
pray	to beseech
prey	a victim of capture. To plunder; trouble, as "prey on the mind"
precede	to go before
proceed	to advance (noun, procedure)
precedence	priority (prē-sēd'enss or prĕs'e-denss)
precedents	established rules (prĕs'e-dents)
precipitous	as steep as a precipice, as "precipitous cliffs"
precipitate	falling headlong; sudden; premature. To hasten; to condense, as dew
precipitant	rushing heedlessly; rash. A cause of condensation
predicate	to assert; affirm; (U.S.) to base [on] or establish
predict	to foretell
premier	first; chief (prē'mĭ-er). A prime minister (prĭ-mēr')
première	the opening performance of a play; a leading lady (Fr. prē-myâr')
prescribe	to designate; dictate
proscribe	to outlaw; prohibit
presentiment	a foreboding
presentment	a presentation [of papers for payment]; a report by a grand jury
presentation	a presenting; a showing (prĕz'en-tā'shun, or prē')
presents	gifts; (law) present writings, as "have signed these presents"
presence	attendance; bearing; alertness, as "presence of mind"
pretend	to make believe; to lay claim [to]
portend	to foreshow; to indicate by an advance sign
preview	a view in advance of public showing, as of a motion picture
purview	the range, scope, or fixed limits of, as an authority or order
principal	(adj.) chief; main. (Noun) the head or leader; the most important one; the employer of an agent; invested capital bearing interest
principle	(noun only) a rule of conduct; integrity; ethics; a basic truth, law, or element; method of operation; basics, as "agreed in principle"

214

proceeding	moving forward. A course of action, as "legal proceedings"
preceding	going before, as "the preceding page"
prodigy	a marvel, as "a child prodigy"
protégé	(mas.) one cared for by another (fem., protégée) (prō'tā'zhā')
progeny	offspring
profit	gain
prophet	one who foretells
program	a plan; a list
pogrom	devastation; massacre (pō-grŏm')
prone	lying face downward. Inclined to, as "prone to doubt"
supine	lying face upward; sluggish; inactive (soo-pīn')
prophecy	(noun) an inspired prediction (prŏf'e-sē)
prophesy	(verb) to foretell (prŏf'e-sī)
proportional	determined by proportion, as "proportional representation"
proportionate	in proportion to, as "proportionate to his means"
proposal	an offer submitted for consideration, as "a proposal to buy"
proposition	a project for adoption, with terms, good points, etc., outlined
protagonist	the chief actor or advocate; the leader
antagonist	an opponent; foe
provided	on condition that (introducing a definite stipulation)
providing	just in case that (introducing a supposition; often "if" is better)
provisional	based on temporary conditions
provincial	pertaining to a province or small region; narrow
Provençal	pertaining to Provence, a region in France (Fr. prô'vän'säl')
purpose	(verb) to have as a purpose; to intend. (Noun) intention; object
propose	to offer for consideration, as a plan, a topic, or a candidate

Q

quarts	measures
quartz	a mineral
questionnaire }	interchangeable; meaning a set of questions submitted to a number
questionary }	of people in order to obtain data or statistics
quiet	still; calm
quite	wholly; considerably
quit	to stop; leave
quire	a paper measure; a set of pages
choir	a company of singers; any trained group, as "a string choir"

R

rabbit	an animal; "Welsh rabbit," a cheese dish, now "Welsh rarebit"
rabbet	a groove; a joint
rack	a frame; a gait; a gear; thin clouds. To torment, as "nerve racking'
wrack	debris cast ashore by the sea; wreck ("rack" as "rack and ruin")
rail	a bar. To scold
railing	a continuous bar, composed of several rails
railroad }	interchangeable in American usage. "Railway" is preferred in
railway }	British usage.

SIMILAR WORDS

rain	falling waterdrops
rein	a part of a bridle; a curb; restraint ("reindeer"—**an animal**)
reign	to rule. Time or term of power, as "a king's reign"
raise	to lift something; to produce something. A lifting
raze	to destroy; demolish
rays	beams
rise	to lift itself or oneself. A self-increase (See also Verbs, p. 86.)
ranger	a horseman who roves over a wide area, as "a forest ranger"
wrangler	a horseman who rounds up, brands, tends, or herds horses
rap	to strike a quick blow
wrap	to enfold. A cloak
rapt	engrossed
rapped	struck with quick blows
wrapped	enfolded (also spelled wrapt)
read	to interpret by reading (past tense, "read" [rĕd])
reed	a bamboolike plant; a musical instrument; a molding
red	a color; a revolutionary; red ink showing a deficit, as "in the red"
real	true; existing; actual
reel	a winding device; a spool; a dance. To whirl
realty	real estate (opposite of "personalty")
reality	that which is real
rebound	to bounce back from impact with another object
redound	to return or flow back; to accrue, as to "redound to one's credit"
receipt	a written acknowledgment of things received; a receiving
recipe	a formula for ingredients, as for cooking or medicine
recognizance	(law) a recorded promise (rē-kŏn′ĭ-zăns, or rē-kŏg′nĭ-zăns)
reconnaissance	a survey tour; act of reconnoitering (rē-kŏn′ĭ-săns)
recourse	a resorting to for assistance; resort
resource	that supply to which one turns for support
reek	to fume or smell
wreak	to inflict, as vengeance
refectory	a dining hall, as in a school or convent ("refectory table")
refractory	unmanageable; obstinate; difficult to fuse, as ore; firebrick
reference	a directing of the attention; the person or thing referred to
referral	the act of referring something to someone ("a referral notice")
regimen	a regulated course of procedure, or diet, etc. (rĕj′ĭ-mĕn)
régime	a term or form of government, as "during a régime" (Fr. rā-zhēm′)
register	a record; a list; the one who records
registrar	an official keeper of records
registry	the place where a register is kept
remediable	capable of being remedied (rē-mē′dĭ-a-bl)
remedial	providing a remedy (rē-mē′dĭ-al)
Renaissance	the revival of art and literature from the 14th to the 16th centuries; hence (not capitalized) any similar period of revived and active interest, especially in things old (rĕn′ĕ-săns′, or rē-nā′sȧns)
renascence	a general revival; awakening or being reborn (rē-năs′ĕns)
repulsive	driving back or repelling; causing dislike or disgust
revulsive	causing or caused by a desire to draw back or turn away from

residence	a dwelling
residents	those who reside in a place
respectfully	with respect
respectively	each to each in the order designated
rest	to repose
wrest	to twist or pull away
restive	balky; fretting under restraint, as "a restive audience"
restless	fidgety; constantly moving; unable to rest, as "a restless nature"
restful	giving rest; free from care; quiet; peaceful
restrict	to confine; to limit; to keep within bounds, as to "restrict trade"
restrain	to hold back; to curb; to keep down, as to "restrain trade"
reverend	worthy of reverence. "The Reverend" is a title of respect.
reverent	expressing reverence
reverence	profound respect. To revere
riffraff	rubbish. The rabble
riprap	a broken-stone foundation, retaining wall, or wearing bed, in water
rifle	a firearm. To rob
riffle	a shallow in a river. To shuffle [through], as a book (rĭf′l)
raffle	a lottery. To give or sell by lottery, as to "raffle off"
right	correct; conservative. A just claim or privilege
rite	a ceremony; a prescribed procedure
write	to set down in writing
wright	a craftsman, as a shipwright or playwright (not *playwrite*)
rime	hoarfrost
rhyme	a verse (sometimes spelled rime)
ring	to sound, as a bell; to encircle
wring	to twist
risky	hazardous; fraught with risk
risqué	daringly close to being improper, as "a risqué story" (Fr. rēs′kā′)
road	a highway
rode	did ride
rowed	did row
roll	to move with a revolving or undulating motion; to trill. A prolonged sound; a rounded mass; a bread; a list, as "roll call"
role	a part in a play
roomer	a lodger
rumor	an unverified report
root	the underground part of a plant (rōot, not rŏot); a mathematical quantity. To dig up; to implant deeply; (colloq.) to cheer for
route	a way (rōot). To send over a certain course (usually pronounced "rout" in military and shipping parlance)
rout	to put to flight; to drag forth; to rummage about. An uproar
roster	a list of names (rŏs′ter; Br. rō′ster)
roaster	for roasting
rooster	a chanticleer
rote	repetition, as "by rote"; the noise of the surf on the shore
wrote	did write
row	(rō) a line of things; (rou) (colloq.) a quarrel. To propel a boat
roe	fish eggs; a kind of deer

royalty	descendants of kings; the house of kings
nobility	titled persons, as duke, marquis, earl, viscount, and baron
ruff	a ruffled collar; neck feathers; a fish. To trump
rough	not smooth or even; not calm; coarse; crude; unfinished; shaggy
ruffle	to gather or fluff; to turn [pages] rapidly; to vex. A frill; a curling wavelet; a low beat on a drum, as "ruffles and flourishes"
ripple	to form tiny undulations, as on water or wheat by the wind; to remove seeds from flax. A wavy surface; a sound as of running water
rung	sounded. A crossbar, as on a ladder or chair
wrung	twisted
rye	a grain
wry	distorted, as "a wry grin"

S

sac	a pouch containing fluid; (capitalized) a tribe of Indians
sack	a bag. To pillage; (Br. slang) to dismiss ("sack coat"—a man's coat)
sacque	a woman's short, loose-fitting housecoat
safe deposit } safety deposit }	both used, but the first is preferable because it is shorter, as "safe deposit box." (Commercially, it is not hyphened.)
sail	to move or glide rapidly, as a ship. A ship's wind-catching canvas
sale	the process of selling
salary	a fixed compensation paid regularly for office-type work
wages	daily or weekly pay for manual or mechanical labor
salon	a luxurious drawing room; a fashionable reception (sȧ-lŏn'; Fr. -lôṅ')
saloon	a spacious room, as "a dining saloon"; (U.S.) a barroom
solon	a lawmaker, hence a congressman (sō'lŏn)
sanatorium	a health resort, primarily where natural remedies, such as climate and altitude, are employed as curatives—usually for tuberculosis
sanitarium	a place where conditions are sanitary and therefore conducive to health, and where medical treatment is given
sane	having a sound mind
seine	a fishing net
Seine	a river in France, running through Paris. On the "left bank" is the educational center or "Latin Quarter" of the city. On the "right bank" is the more modernized section.
sanguine	hopeful; cheerful; ruddy; blood-red (săng'gwĭn)
sanguinary	attended with bloodshed
Scots	the Scottish people or their language; Scottish, as "Scots law"
Scotsman	a native of Scotland; a Scot (formerly, Scotchman)
Scottish	of or pertaining to Scotland or the Scots
Scotch	now used only in common phrases, as "Scotch plaid"
scrip	a certificate entitling the holder to receive a dividend, stock, or land, etc. (Colloq.) old U.S. fractional paper currency
script	style of handwriting; the working scenario of a motion picture, or radio or television program; (law) an original document
sculptor	one who carves, or models designs to be carved or cast
sculpture	the art of carving statues, etc.; carved work

sealing	fastening, as with a seal or glue
ceiling	overhead covering
see	to perceive. A Catholic province center, as "the Holy See"
sea	a body of water
C	a shape, as "C-spring" (preferred to "cee spring")
seed	a part of a plant
cede	to give over
seem	to appear
seam	a meeting line; a thin layer of rock
seen	past participle of "see"
scene	a view; a setting; a division of a play
seer	one who foresees; a prophet
sear	to burn; to deaden. Dried up; withered (also spelled sere)
cere	to wrap in cerecloth ("cerement"—a waxed cloth)
seize	to lay hold of
cease	to stop
sell	to transfer for a price
cell	a small place of confinement
seller	one who sells
cellar	an underground storeroom ("saltcellar")
senses	faculties
census	statistics of population
sensible	intelligent; impressible through the senses, as "sensible to pain"
sensitive	quickly affected; easily offended
sensuous	appealing to the finer senses, as "sensuous poetry"; charming
sensual	of the baser senses, implying gross or worldly pleasure; voluptuous
sent	dispatched
scent	an odor. To smell
cent	a coin
sense	intelligence; meaning. To perceive by the senses; to feel
serial	in a series or installments. A periodical, as "serial rights"
cereal	grain used for food
session	assembly; a sitting together; the time of being convened
cession	a giving over; a ceding
secession	a withdrawal or separation from
cessation	a stopping or ceasing
sewage	refuse or matter carried in sewers
sewerage	a system of sewers; the removal of waste matter through sewers
shear	to cut, clip, or trim. A sliding displacement ("shearing stress")
sheer	fine or thin; unadulterated; utter; perpendicular. To swerve
shone	emitted light; excelled
shown	displayed; indicated; explained; guided
shoot	to fire; to sprout; to pass over rapidly, as to "shoot the chutes"
chute	a steep watercourse; a slide; a narrow passage; a parachute
sight	vision
site	location
cite	to quote; to name or summon ("citation"—act of citing)
sinecure	a position with few duties (sī′ne-kūr, or sĭn′)
cynosure	the North Star, hence center of attraction (sī′no-shụr, or sĭn′o-)

single	one. To select one from others, as to "single out"
signal	to inform by sign. Outstanding, as "a signal triumph"
Sinicism	that which is peculiar to the Chinese
cynicism	cynical quality; a disbelief in human goodness
slack	relaxed; inactive
slake	to allay; to mix lime with water (slāk, not *slăk*)
slay	to kill
sleigh	a winter vehicle
slew	killed. (Colloq.) a large number, as "a slew of sightseers"
slue	to twist; to slide or swing around, as "The car slued round."
slough	(slou) a mudhole; a quagmire; a state of moral despair
slough	(slo͞o) slowly flowing water in a marsh (also spelled slew, or slue)
slough	(slŭf) to cast off, as old tissue (also spelled sluff)
slick	slippery
sleek	glossy
slight	small; slender; trifling. To neglect
sleight	skill; a trick; a quick, deceptive movement, as "sleight of hand"
slow	not rapid
sloe	a plumlike fruit ("sloe-eyed"—dark-eyed)
sluff	(See "slough," above.)
so	in such a manner, or to such a degree; thus; therefore; in order that
sew	to stitch
sow	to scatter, as seed (sō). A swine (sou)
sough	the sighing or murmuring of the wind (sou, or sŭf)
soared	did soar
sword	a weapon (sōrd)
sward	turf; greensward (swạrd)
soluble	capable of being dissolved
solvable	capable of being solved
some	a portion
sum	an amount; the total
sometime	at an indefinite time. Former, as "sometime Judge of the Court"
some time	a period of time, as "some time ago," "some time elapsed"
sometimes	now and then
son	a male descendant
sun	a heavenly body
sore	painful
soar	to rise aloft
soul	spiritual nature
sole	the under part of the foot; a fish. Single, as "for the sole purpose"
spacious	large; occupying much space, as "spacious rooms"
specious	apparently, but deceptively, right or fair, as "specious arguments"
special	not general; specific; pertaining to a single thing, as "a special job," "a special occasion," "a special friend," "special delivery" "a special performance," "requires special training"
especial	extraordinary; particular, as "take especial care" "no especial need"
spatial	pertaining to space (spā'shal) (also spelled spacial)

specially	in a special manner, as "books bound specially" (a special job) "He was specially trained for the work." (special training)
especially	particularly, as "books especially for children" "He was especially fitted for the work." (particularly)
specialty	a distinctive thing; a particular line or product (common in American usage). (Law) a sealed contract (spĕsh'al-ty)
speciality	a distinctive quality; a special characteristic or product (common in British usage) (spĕsh'ē-ăl'ĭ-ty)
specie	coin; "in specie," in U.S. currency (spē'shē)
species	a sort; kind; variety; class (both singular and plural) (spē'shēz)
specter	a ghost; phantom (spĕk'ter)
scepter	a staff carried by a sovereign as a symbol of power (sĕp'ter)
spiritual	pertaining to the spirit. A religious song
spirituel	(mas.) spirited; witty; ethereal (fem., -le) (Fr. spē'rē'tü'ĕl')
spy	to discover by careful or secret examination
espy	to catch sight of
stable	steady; firm, as "stable prices." A barn
staple	chief; regular. A principal commercial article; a fastener
stair	a step or a series of steps
stare	a fixed gaze
stamp	to tramp about heavily ("stamp out") ("stamping ground")
stomp	to bring the foot down forcibly, as in applause or anger
stationary	in a fixed condition or position; not moving; unchanging
stationery	writing materials
statue	a carved or modeled likeness
statute	an enacted law
stature	the height of man; elevation attained
staunch	firm; steadfast, as "a staunch friend"; sound, as a ship (stônch)
stanch	to check the flow of blood from a wound (stănch)
stayed	remained; held back; supported; pacified; (law) postponed, as "stayed judgment"
staid	sedate
steak	a slice of beef or fish
stake	a pointed stick; a hazard; a prize; a property; grubstake
steel	a metal alloy
steal	to take wrongfully; to go secretly
sticker	one who adheres; a gummed label; a bur; (colloq.) a puzzler
stickler	one who insists unyieldingly, as "a stickler for details"; a baffler
stimulant	an excitant, as coffee
stimulus	an incentive; a driving force, as "the stimulus of ambition"
stimulation	the effect produced by either a stimulant or a stimulus
stop	to cease
estop	(law) to bar ("estoppel"— a bar because of a previous action)
strait	narrow; tight, as "strait-laced," "strait and narrow path," "strait jacket," "in straitened circumstances." (Pl.) distress; a waterway
straight	not curved; unbroken; direct; unaltered; upright
stray	(See "astray," p. 189.)

style   mode; fashion; an etching needle. To name
stile   a set of steps; turnstile; a piece of a paneled door

subjugation   a conquering and controlling, as of a people
subjection   an exposing to some force or agent, as to pressure or heat

subtile   delicate; ethereal; finely drawn, as a spider's web (sŭb′tĭl or -tĭl)
subtle   sly; clever; deep; fine, as "a subtle distinction" (sŭt′l)

subtitle   a secondary title, as in the title of a book or play
subhead   a subdivision heading, centered; a secondary newspaper heading
sidehead   a subdivision heading placed at the side of the page

sucker   a fish; a part of a plant; a √alve; (slang) a dupe
succor   relief. To give aid

sue   to prosecute (suing)
sou   a French coin (sōō)
Sioux   an Indian tribe (pl. Sioux [sōō or sōōz])

suit   a set, as of garments or cards; a court action; a wooing. To fit
suite   a retinue; a connected series, as "a suite of rooms" or "a music
suite"; a set of matched furniture, as "a bedroom suite" (swēt)
sweet   saccharine; pleasing

summon   to call or command to appear
summons   a call or command to appear. To take out a summons

surge   a rising and falling roll; a swelling wave
serge   a fabric (sŭrj); (cap.) a man's name (Fr. sĕrzh)

suspect   to imagine; surmise; mistrust
expect   to count upon; look forward to
suppose   to think; believe; conclude

sustenance   that which sustains life; nourishment
subsistence   maintenance; livelihood; living expenses (in contracts)

swathe   to wrap or bandage (swāthe)
swath   the sweep of the blade in mowing (swôth)

symbol   an emblem; a sign
cymbal   a platelike musical instrument

T

tail   the end. (Law) restricted [inheritance], as "an estate [or fee] tail"
tale   a story; total, as "tale of years"; count, as "payment by tale"

talisman   a charm (tăl′ĭs-man)
talesman   (law) one of the persons added to a jury (tā′lēz-man, or tālz′)

tantamount   equivalent
paramount   the highest; chief

taper   to diminish. A candle
tapir   an animal

tare   allowance for the weight of a container, wrapping, and packing
tear   to rip or rend; to move fast. Depreciation, as "wear and tear"

tasty   (of food) pleasing in flavor; savory, as "a tasty morsel"
tasteful   (of persons or things) conforming to good taste, as "tasteful rooms"

taught   instructed
taut   tense; tight

tax	an assessment
tacks	small nails (For "tack," see "track," below.)
tea	a beverage
tee	a mark in games; a small support for the ball in golf
T	a shape, as "T-iron," "T-square" (preferred to "tee iron," etc.)
team	two or more that work together
teem	to abound or swarm [with]
tear	a teardrop (See also "tare," above.)
tier	a layer; a row in a series, one above another (tĭr)
temblor	an earthquake (from Sp., to tremble) (tĕm-blōr')
trembler	(elec.) a vibrating hammer
tremor	a vibration; a trembling; a slight earth disturbance (trĕm'or)
temerity	rashness; reckless boldness (tĕ-mĕr'i-ty)
timidity	shyness
tenant	a lessee; an occupant in temporary possession, paying rent
tenet	a principle or belief held to be true, as "a basic tenet"
tenor	trend; intent; nature; a part in music; (law) an exact copy
tenure	a holding; a holding term
terminal	the end; especially the end of a railroad line
terminus	the boundary or goal; especially a city at the end of a railroad line
their	a pronoun ⎫ As common as these words are, it is not uncommon to
there	in that place ⎬ see them confused. And the possessive "theirs"
they're	they are ⎭ is confused with "there's" (there is, or has).
therefore	consequently
therefor	for that thing or that purpose
thrash	to flog; to toss about; (naut.) to sail a ship against the wind
thresh	to beat out grain; to argue, as to "thresh the matter out"
through ⎫	from beginning to end; by means of; because of. ("Thru" is less
thru ⎭	formal than "through.")
threw	did throw
thorough	fully or completely done; through and through ("thoroughgoing")
	("Thoroughbred"—a racehorse. "Standardbred"—a harness
	horse. "Purebred" is used of cattle; "pedigreed" of dogs, etc.)
throw	to fling or hurl
throe	agonized pain or effort, as "in the throes of creation"
thrown	hurled
throne	a royal chair; sovereign power
tick	a faint beat; a dot; mattress cover; insect; (colloq.) credit; score
tic	a twitching; a spasmodic muscular contraction, as in the face
tide	the rise and fall of the ocean. To carry through, as "tide over"
tied	fastened; bound; equaled in a contest
timber	building wood; tall growing trees
timbre	a quality of tone (tĭm'ber; Fr. tăṅ'br)
time	duration, or a measure of duration
thyme	a plant used as a food seasoning (tīm)
to	a preposition indicating direction, attachment, or connection
too	also, as "that too"; to an excessive degree, as "too tired"
two	a couple ("cut in two")

223

toe	a part of the foot ("toe the mark"); a part of a machine, or rod
tow	to pull along, as to "take in tow"
tortuous	twisting or winding, as "a tortuous path"; not forthright
torturous	inflicting pain or torture; cruelly distorting
track	a footprint or trace; a path or way; a racecourse; a railway
tract	a piece of land; a system ("digestive tract"); a treatise; sacred verses
tack	a tiny nail. To attach loosely; (naut.) to sail a zigzag course into the wind, hence to shift abruptly, as to "take another tack"
transcribing	copying, as "transcribing notes"; reproducing, as radio skits
transcription	a copy or reproduction
transmission	the transmitting of something without substance, as news, messages by telegraph, light, heat, power, and radio waves.
transmittal	the transmitting of something with substance, as papers, goods. A "letter of transmittal" often accompanies transmitted papers.
transmittance	(physics) transmission of radiant energy
travel	journeying
travail	painful toil; anguish suffered for achievement (trăv′āl)
triumphant	victorious; exulting over success
triumphal	pertaining to the celebration of a victory, as "a triumphal return"
troop	a body of soldiers. To march
troupe	a theatrical company. To travel as a troupe; to play any part well
troublesome	worrisome; bothersome; burdensome; vexatious
troublous	turbulent; widely troubled, as "these troublous times"
trustee	one who holds property in trust
trusty	reliable. A prisoner with special privileges
tuberculous	pertaining to, or having, tuberculosis
tubercular	pertaining to tubercles
turban	a headdress
turbine	a rotary motor (tûr′bĭn)
typical	conforming to the type; symbolic; characteristic
atypical	not the typical kind; irregular, as "atypical schools" (ā-tĭp′i-kal)
typography	the arrangement of type; art of printing
topography	the geographical or surface features of a region

U

unabridged	entire; in full, as "an unabridged dictionary"
abridged	shortened
expurgated	cleared of objectionable things
undo	to unfasten; unravel; annul; reverse; ruin, as "his undoing"
undue	not due; excessive or improper, as "undue haste," "undue influence"
undoubtedly	without a doubt
indubitably	with too much evidence to doubt (ĭn-dū′bĭ-ta-bly)
unquestioned	has not been questioned, as "unquestioned loyalty"
unquestionable	cannot fairly be questioned, as "unquestionable statements"
unconscionable	without conscience; unjust; unreasonable
urban	pertaining to cities or towns (opposite of "rural")
urbane	courteous; suave (ûr-bān′)
usable	workable; capable of being put to use
useful	helpful; full of use

use	act of employing or putting into service, as to "put to good use," "after several years' use" (not *usage*)
usage	customary way of doing; long-continued and adopted practice

V

vain	futile; conceited ("vainglorious")
vane	a blade turned by the wind or water; a feather; a compass sight
vein	a blood vessel; a strain or streak; a lode
vale	a valley (vāl); farewell (L. vā′lē)
veil	a thin covering that conceals or protects ("take the veil")
valued	highly esteemed or regarded; prized, as "a valued friend"
valuable	having monetary or intrinsic worth or usefulness, as "a valuable man"
invaluable	priceless; of inestimable worth, as "invaluable assistance"
venal	mercenary; capable of being bribed (vē′năl)
venial	forgivable; pardonable, as "a venial sin" (vē′nĭ-al)
vender	one who vends or sells in the streets; a vending machine
vendor	(law) the seller (opposite of "vendee")
veneer	to coat or overlay, as with fine wood. A superficial appearance
venire	a writ to summon jurors (vē-nĭ′rē)
venerable	worthy of respect (because of age)
vulnerable	capable of being hurt or wounded
veracious	truthful (noun, veracity)
voracious	greedy (noun, voracity)
verses	divisions of poetry
versus	against
vice	depravity; a defect; a bad habit; a prefix in a title of office
vise	a clamp for holding materials securely
visa	an endorsement on a passport (vē′zȧ) (Fr. visé [vē-zā′])
vicegerent	an officer appointed to act for a ruler (vīs′jē′rĕnt)
vice-regent	a person who acts for a regent. (A regent is a type of vicegerent.)
vile	despicable; loathsome; worthless
vial	a small bottle or vessel for liquids (also spelled phial)
viol	a stringed instrument
vindictive	revengeful (vĭn-dĭk′tiv, not *-dĭk′a-tiv*)
vindicative	tending to justify or clear of suspicion (vĭn′dĭ-kā′tĭv)
viscous	(adj.) sticky or adhesive (vĭs′kŭs)
viscose	(noun) a viscous solution (vĭs′kōs)
viscosity	stickiness or resistance to flowing (vĭs-kŏs′ĭ-ty)
vocation	a regular occupation
avocation	an occupation for diversion or amusement, as a hobby

W

waist	a narrow central part; a garment
waste	worthless; barren [land]; debris; loss. To expend idly; to lose size
wait	to stay
weight	a measure of heaviness. (For "weighted," see p. 226.)

225

want	desire; lack
wont	habit (wŭnt; Br. wŏnt)
won't	will not
wave	to motion with the hand, as to "wave aside," not "*waive* aside"
waive	to relinquish [a right to], as to "waive preliminary examination"
waver	to fluctuate, or hesitate; to falter; to sway
waiver	(law) a relinquishment
way	a distance; a course; manner; (naut.) progress, as "under way"
weigh	to find the weight of; to be a burden; (naut.) to lift [anchor]
ways	the plural of "way." A structure for shipbuilding
weak	not strong
week	a period of seven days
wear	to have on; to bear; to last; to waste; to consume by use or friction. Depreciation, as "wear and tear"
ware	a class of merchandise; pottery
weir	a dam; a water-measuring plate (wēr)
weighing	measuring the heaviness of; considering the worth of
weighting	loading, or adding weight to
weighted	made heavy; calculated or evaluated from statistics, as "a weighted average," "a weighted wholesale price index," "a weighted opinion" (but "weighed down" rather than "weighted down")
whose	a possessive pronoun, as "someone whose word is reliable"
who's	who is, or has, as "someone who's reliable"
winch	a windlass for hoisting or pulling
wench	a rustic servant; a peasant girl
wrangle	to argue or dispute angrily and noisily; to round up horses
wangle	to bring about by contrivance or scheming
wreck	to damage or ruin; devastate. Destruction
wrack	to torture, as "wracked by unrest." Fragment (See "rack")
wreak	to inflict, as vengeance ("wreak havoc")

Y

yoke	a working frame for oxen
yolk	the yellow of an egg (yōk, or yōlk)
you	a pronoun
ewe	a sheep
U	a shape, as "U-bolt," "U-tube," "U-turn"
yew	a tree
your	belonging to you
you're	you are (ū′er, or yŏŏr, not *yŏre*)
yore	time gone by, as "of yore"

on *Punctuation* ~~~~~~~~~~~~~~~~~~~~~~~~~~~~

Punctuation should be as uniform as possible. Unfortunately not only is there often a difference of opinion in regard to what is the best or the correct punctuation, but also it is difficult for even the same writer to be always consistent in this matter.

—From *Webster's Collegiate Dictionary,* Fourth Edition. Copyright, 1916, 1925, 1931, by G. & C. Merriam Co., Springfield, Mass.

I have never yet come across a book on the subject which did not leave me more puzzled than it found me.

—The late Barrett Wendell of Harvard University.

Marks of Punctuation

Punctuation

Authorities are agreed that:

Punctuation is a matter of judgment, and not of definite rule.

It adds expression and meaning to written words.

Open or Close Punctuation. "Open punctuation," or rather the absence of punctuation, is not recommended for use in other than routine work, form letters, etc., where the saving of time is an important factor. Many persons are confused by the absence of punctuation. Others think it eccentric.

The regular or "close" (or "closed") style of punctuation should be used in all dignified correspondence, formal documents, and legal papers. It is always clear and businesslike.

Regarding open punctuation:

> "This style of punctuation is best suited to the more simple, direct forms of writing, such as plain narrative; but if carried to extremes it results in ambiguity and an appearance of slovenliness. The primary aim of punctuation is to convey to the reader the exact meaning intended, and any text should be punctuated more or less 'closely,' according as clearness demands."
>
> —From *Webster's Collegiate Dictionary,* Fourth Edition, p. 1213. Copyright, 1916, 1925, 1931, by G. & C. Merriam Co., Springfield, Mass.

The law recognizes the importance of punctuation:

> "Punctuation may be considered in determining the meaning of a contract, when it is doubtful. 138 U.S. 1."
> —*Bouvier's Law Dictionary* (Baldwin's Revision), p. 1004.

COMMA

Commas give pause and clarity to sentences. Do not attempt to omit them altogether, or to use them indiscriminately. A wide difference in meaning may be indicated by commas.

Ambiguous:
The seller says the buyer is profiteering.
Unfortunately neglected opportunities cannot be recaptured.
In daylight streets in the Eighties are deserted.
Shortly before this testimony was given by a student who had witnessed the strike.

Clear:
The seller, says the buyer, is profiteering.
Unfortunately, neglected opportunities cannot...
In daylight, streets in the Eighties are deserted.
Shortly before this, testimony was given by a...

Commas have six chief uses:

1. Around parenthetic words
2. Around explanatory expressions
3. Between listed words or phrases
4. In place of omitted words
5. After inverted constructions
6. Between clauses.

Parenthetic and Transitional Words. If pauses are clearly indicated by any of the following words, they may be set off with commas.

But if no real interruptions are caused by such words, they need **not** be set off with commas.

above all	by contrast	in any case	meanwhile	say
accordingly	by the bye	in any event	mind you	second -ly
actually	by the same token	in brief	more important -ly	similarly
after all	by the way	in conclusion	more or less	simply
afterward	certainly	in due course	moreover	so [or so far]
again	consequently	in effect	namely (viz)*	so it seems
alas	conversely	in essence	naturally	so to speak
all in all	do you think	in fact	needless to say	still
also	doubtless	in general	nevertheless	strictly
among other	even now [or then]	in large measure	next	[speaking]
[things]	even so	in many ways	no	surely
and rightly so	eventually	in my opinion	no doubt	thank goodness
and so on	finally	in other words	notwithstanding	that is (i.e.)*
anyway	first	in part -icular	now [and then]	that is to say
apparently	for example (e.g.)*	in passing	nowadays	the fact is
as a matter of	for instance	in reality	obviously	the fact remains
fact	for one [thing]	in short	occasionally	then
as a result	for that matter	in sum -mary	oddly enough	theoretically
as a rule	for the most part	in the circum-	of course	therefore
as I see it	for the time being	stances	of necessity	they say
as if happens	fortunately	in the final	oftener than not	third -ly
as it were	frankly	analysis	on balance	though
as of now	further -more	in the first place	on occasion	thus
as time goes on	generally	[or long run, main,	on the contrary	to a degree
as usual	[speaking]	meantime]	on the other hand	to a great extent
as well	God willing	in time [or theory]	on the whole	to be sure
as yet	hence	in turn [or truth]	or the like	to begin [with]
as you know	however	incidentally	ordinarily	to say the least
at any rate	I believe [or	inclusive	originally	to tell the truth
at best	think, imagine,	indeed	otherwise	to this end
at first [or last]	wonder]	inevitably	particularly	too ("moreover,"
at least	I feel sure	instead	perforce	or "also")
at the same time	I take it	it goes without	perhaps	true [enough]
basically	ideally	saying	personally	ultimately
be that as it may	if all goes well	it is said	possibly	unfortunately
believe it or not	if any [or ever]	it is true	presumably	usually
besides	if necessary	it would seem	primarily	well
better yet	if need be	just the same	probably	what is more
briefly	if possible	knowingly	rather	whereas
by all means	in a sense [or way]	later on	really	without doubt
by and large	in addition	likewise	respectively	yes
by [any] chance	in all	literally	rest assured	yet

* Do not use the abbreviations "e.g.," "viz," and "i.e.," unless in abbreviated work, or in texts where such abbreviations will be perfectly understood.

Indicated pauses:

That is, **in short**, the story.

In other words, it has got into a snarl.

Send us samples of, **say**, three varieties.

The truth, **of course**, is that it does not, **as a rule**, go anywhere and, **therefore**, nobody has it.

It is true, **yes**, but can they prove it?

It was illegible, **that is**, blurred.

Substantially, **indeed**, the depositor is...

A rule, **by the way**, is not necessarily a practice.

Here, **meanwhile**, are some of the characteristics.

Many things, **however**, are neither emphatic nor...

By eliminating, **for the time being at least**, certain...

It may be true, or, **again**, it may be only a rumor.

(The commas around "again" give it the meaning of "on the other hand." Without the commas it could mean "once again.")

Uninterrupted sentences:

It is very necessary **indeed.**

...which **of course** is nonsense.

...but **at any rate** we have tried.

...on Friday and Saturday **respectively.**

...owing **perhaps** to the increased costs.

We **theoretically** sold for that amount.

Commercial activity will **of necessity** find...

It **therefore** involves no prejudices.

Short examples, or **namings:**

Native birds, **for example**, the ptarmigan and partridge, are found...

...for two apparent reasons, **namely**, that it was due and that it represented an honest debt.

To get what is worth getting, **namely**, an education, one must strive...

(For long enumerations, see Semicolon, Colon, and Dash pp. 239–45)

One comma: Only one comma (or a semicolon) may be used if the parenthetic expression acts as a connective, or blends more naturally with one part of the sentence than with another.

He was going to Europe, **in fact** leaving the next day.

They have asked for immediate shipment; **therefore** we must comply.

Two elements, **for instance** mercury and gold, cannot be...

Intervening Phrases or Clauses. If an explanatory phrase or clause breaks into a sentence at any point, it may be set off by commas to give it distinction or to preserve the clear continuity of the sentence.

Note that **two commas** are necessary to set off completely an explanatory phrase or clause within a sentence.

Men, **like animals,** live in herds. (BUT: Men like him live long.)

They often said, **and I believe they were right,** that...

It seems strange, **the circumstances being as you say,** that...

That, **so far as we are concerned,** is the situation.

Remember that, **from the buyer's point of view,** the discount...

Some customers are, **as is sometimes apparent,** not willing...

More snow, **along with rain and a warmer temperature,** is...

These men, **together with Colonel James,** make up the Cabinet.

All the items, **except those listed in the supplement,** are to be...

There is nothing smaller, **in the laboratory or out,** than...

In the mountains, **where rain fell heavily,** fear was...

And we say to you, **advisedly and unqualifiedly,** that...

A ship, **sunk during the war,** has been located...

When we offer them this, **the best of opportunities,** they refuse.

231

If two phrases have the same continuation, the intervening phrase may be set off by commas to give it definiteness.

> It is as good as, **if not better than,** the rest.
> The difficulty is due to, **and arises with,** a lack of...
> ...bought as reasonably as, **if not more reasonably than,** land in...
> ...shall not be used for, **nor in connection with,** advertising.

Always enclose within commas the full intervening expression, not just a part of it. Test a sentence to determine what constitutes a full phrase or clause and what does not.

> NOT: It is as large as, if not larger, than their holdings.
> BUT: It is as large as, **if not larger than,** their holdings.
>   (The complete intervening phrase is "if not larger than." The
>   simple sentence is "It is as large as their holdings.")
> NOT: On, but not exactly of the waterfront...
> BUT: On, **but not exactly of,** the waterfront...
> NOT: No one can equal or even approximate, their work.
> BUT: No one can equal, **or even approximate,** their work.
> OR: No one can equal or even approximate their work.

As shown in the last example, if it is considered that the intervening phrase or clause does not noticeably break the continuity of a sentence, no commas are used around it.

> If **and when** reductions are made...
> ...owner of a large **and at present none too profitable** realty company.
> ...on **or near** the seaboard.
> ...characteristic of **or peculiar to** the native.
> Sounder policies must **and will** emerge.
> ...first to come into **and first to go out of** the land.

Closing Explanatory Expressions. An explanatory remark at the end of a sentence may be set off with a comma to give it emphasis.

> Some asked for more than they wanted, **to make sure of getting enough.**
> It is a medium of trade, **ever changing.**

Contrasts. Emphatic contrasting phrases or clauses may be set off by commas. (For "not only...but," see p. 17.)

> It is work we want, **not charity.**
> A situation that no one likes, **not even the politician.**
> We pay for being protected, **rather than for being saved.**
> Machines, **not men,** should do the work.
> We ordered the goods, **not because we liked them,** but because our
>   customers called for them.
> It is nonetheless highly important, **not only because it puts extra weight
>   on the Atlantic alliance,** but also because it brings...
> Unexpected, **not unforeseen,** is this move.
> ...for these are not man's gifts, **but God's.**

Unemphatic contrasting phrases are not set off by commas:

> They are poor **but honest.**
> He is satisfied **though skeptical.**
> It comes **not from skill** but from patience.
> They are bound **not from** but to the Orient.

232

Emphatic Words. Single words may be set off by commas if emphasis is desired.

> They must remain invisible, **forever.**
> ...for the time specified, **only.**
> Some, **foolishly,** imagine that it is good business.

-ing Phrases. A common mistake in punctuation is the cutting into an -ing phrase with a comma and setting some words adrift.

> NOT: The Governor, having finished his investigation, steps are now being taken toward legal action.
> (To set off "having finished his investigation" with commas leaves "The Governor" to bump into "steps" without reason. The full first phrase (called an "absolute phrase") is "The Governor having finished his investigation.")
> THUS: **The Governor having finished his investigation,** steps are now being taken toward legal action.

If, of course, the -ing phrase acts as a simple modifier of a word which has another construction, the phrase may be set off with commas; that is, if it could be **temporarily removed** without impairing the meaning of the sentence.

> The Governor, **having finished his investigation,** now intends to...
> ("Governor" is the subject of "intends," and "having finished his investigation" is a modifying phrase which could be removed.)
> Such decisions, **wavering as they do,** offer no solution.
> The stock, **having now earned its dividend,** is worth...
> We can suggest, **knowing they will understand.**
> They are again together, **continuing a long association.**

But commas should not be used around an -ing phrase if it **could not be removed** without impairing the meaning of the sentence.

> A statement **modifying his previous views** may be expected.
> The men **working on that project** are to be paid by the day.
> **Running such a risk** is not good business.

"That" and Commas. Keep the word "that" outside the commas which often enclose an inserted explanatory clause or phrase. Guard against repeating "that" in such constructions.

> TEST: Place the intervening clause or phrase at the end of the sentence.
> NOT: He maintained, that if prices are lowered, costs must be cut.
> NOR: He maintained, that if prices are lowered, *that* costs must be...
> BUT: He maintained that, **if prices are lowered,** costs...   (emphatic)
> OR: He maintained that **if prices are lowered,** costs...   (usual)
> The act states that, **before securities can be sold,** they must...
> It proves that, **while we cannot win alone,** we can join...
> He said that, **so long as they believe in freedom,** they will...
> ...recognize that, **although the ways are many,** there is one...
> ...declared that, **because of his contributions,** it is fitting...
> ...suggested that, **where needed,** channels should be opened.

"Or" Phrases. If appositional, "or" phrases are set off with commas.

> APPOSITIONAL: They will table, **or shelve,** the bill.   (in other words)
> ALTERNATIVE: We must await his decision to retire **or** not to retire.

Between Two or More Adjectives. A comma is used between listed adjectives when the word "and" has seemingly been omitted.

> ...a quiet, efficient man. (a quiet and efficient man)
> ...a good, reliable old American firm. (a good and reliable old...)
> ...for specific, detailed instructions.
> His words were simple, direct, and forceful.

No commas should be used when the adjectives contribute to one complete thought.

> ...tell the plain honest truth. ...of the few remaining good old
> ...a tall brown church spire.   tried-and-true methods.

Specific designations may be made by using "and" with the commas.

> ...red, and white, and blue flags. (flags of three different colors)
> ...red, white, and blue flags. (three-colored flags)

Modifying Clauses. These clauses should be set off with commas if they **could be removed** from sentences without impairing the meanings.

REMOVABLE: {
...that company, **which was started in 1841,** leads the field.
The new president, **who is soon to take office,** will be...
}

But if a modifying clause **could not be removed** without impairing the meaning of the sentence, it should not be set off with commas.

IRREMOVABLE: {
All persons **who are old enough to vote** should register.
The nation **that looks to its industries** will be the...
The barrier **which it represents** cannot be abolished.
}

Direct Address. Words used in direct address should be set off with commas.

> **Father,** forgive them; for they know not what they do.
> Et tu, **Brute!** (Even thou, Brutus!)
> At last, **Paul,** you are right.   Yes, **sir,** we agree.
> Don't think, **my son,** that you can't do it.
> Is that, **Mr. Ellson,** what you think of the proposition?
> I appreciate the honor, **gentlemen,** but I shall be detained.

Identification. Identifying words or phrases are usually set off with commas, although some publications omit commas around "of" phrases.

> Our representative, **Mr. Scott,** will call upon you.
> ...as J. R. Darton, **one of the drafters of the bill,** testified.
> ...to be held on Wednesday, **the 24th,** at 10 a.m.
> President James **of Garfield University** was...
> They were sent to Denver, **the state capital,** for...
> ...an agreement with one nation, **Cuba.**
> ...to reach the summit of Mount Everest, **the world's loftiest peak.**
> Lee, **my brother,** is here.
> My brother, **Will,** is in the East. (indicates there is but one brother)
> My brother Will is in the East. (indicates there are other brothers)

No commas are used if the identification could not be removed:

> the poet Gray   the song "America"   the year 1960   the ship "Maine"

Himself, Itself, Myself, etc. These words are not usually set off with commas, but may be for emphasis or clarity. (See also p. 60.)

> They **themselves** must study it.   Life **itself** has been changed.
> ...none other than the Señor, **himself.**   ...it was the man **himself.**

Inc., Jr., State Names, Years. These are considered explanatory and are set off with commas. But no comma follows the possessive form.

> NOTE: Some publications omit commas around "Inc.," "Jr.," and years after months alone (see p. 281). (For "III" after names, see p. 311.)

> Mason, Miller & Wood, **Inc.,** have announced... (See also p. 37.)
> John Maynard, **Jr.,** is now...   (BUT: Lee Scott, **Jr.'s** home is...)
> Seattle, **Washington,** had an earthquake on October 27, **1940,** at ..
>   OR: Seattle, **Washington** had an earthquake on October 27, **1940** at ...

Inverted Constructions. If a word, phrase, or clause is out of its natural order in a sentence, it may be set off with a comma—unless such a word or phrase **immediately precedes a verb.**

> **Simultaneously,** an extensive program was started.
> **Elsewhere,** bitter cold was endured.   (BUT: Elsewhere **was endured...**)
> **After his speech in the Senate,** he returned to Canada.
> **In view of that situation,** the Secretary of State said...
> **Like them,** we are not interested.
> **Thanks to your insistence,** they have been taken care of.
> **Admitting that an estimate is impossible,** he declared that...
> **If by any chance you agree,** you might write...
> **That it is not always easy,** we are well aware.
> **For us,** it amounts to a considerable profit.
> **These,** they at any rate know how to sell.
> **To save time,** we are sending you...
> **Although it might not function smoothly at the start,** it should...
> **Whether it lasts only a few days or is prolonged,** its effects will...
> **Because the book was written thoughtfully,** it is a rich piece of work.
> **By the time we reach a conclusion,** we have traveled the hard road...

Immediately before a verb (See also p. 69):

> On the floor of the deep sea lie the sediments of centuries.
> Among the chorus of voices that were heard **were** only three...
> EXCEPTIONS: { With the left hand, **turn** the dial to...   (imperative)
>   { If they request aid, **can** we assist them?   (question)

No comma is necessary if there is no pause after a simple phrase:

> **Even then** we should consider the circumstances.
> **Throughout the night** they worked on it.

But a comma may be necessary for clarity:

> **Ever since,** it has been considered lucky.   **Just why,** we do not know.
> **When the reviewers say that,** we object.   **In printing,** books are...

Omitted Words. A comma is used to signify the omission of a word or phrase. Although no comma is necessary if the meaning is clear.

> This method is easy; that, difficult.   This, to prove a point.
> So it seems—the more of the one, the less of the other.
> The sooner that is done, the better.   (BUT: the sooner the better)
> Analogy always wins, is forever successful.
> Must we give up, leave the job undone?
> One man longs for wealth; another, fame; another, peace and security.
> One man's ambition is wealth, another's fame, another's security.

Between Listed Words. A comma is placed before the concluding "and," "or," or "nor," in listed words, so that the last two items will not be erroneously grouped. (Publications often omit this final comma.)

> ...assign delivery dates for cotton, tobacco, corn, and wheat.
> (The comma before "and" implies definitely that corn and wheat are not to be grouped in one shipment.)
> ...invested in banks, insurance companies, mortgages and home-building loans. (The last two items are here grouped.)
> Is it for display, distinction, or advertising?
> Ocean, clouds, and hills will still be there.
> ...deliverable when, as, and if issued.
> That will not bring down freight rates, interest, or rents.
> ...sealed, insured, loaded on trucks, and shipped away.
> ...questions of what, who, how, when, and where.
> ...an outgrowth of social, scientific, and cultural life.
> ...someone whose judgment will be practical, firm, and fair.

After Listed Words. No comma is necessary after the concluding word in a list if a verb or phrase unmistakably applicable to the entire group follows.

> Ten, twenty, forty, and sixty are the percentages.
> Large shipments of wheat and grains, butter and cheese, wool and flax, sugar and foodstuffs will come out of that country.

But if there is danger of connecting only the last listed item with what follows, a comma should be used after the concluding item.

> The revenue collected by the State from tobacco, candy, and theaters, alone amounts to a large sum.
> Several subjects were discussed—taxes, deterioration, and overhead, in particular.
> They were more balanced, more reserved, than we expected.

If an explanatory or parenthetic phrase or clause applying to the entire group immediately follows listed words, it is set off with commas.

> The promising of notes, certificates, or bonds, which cannot possibly be delivered, violates...

But if a phrase or clause follows the list and applies only to the last item, it should be bound to the item it modifies and separated from the following part of the sentence by a comma.

> Bankers, professional men, and farmers as well as laborers, are expected to... (Here "as well as laborers" is joined to "farmers.")
> Bankers, professional men, and farmers, as well as laborers, are... (Here "as well as laborers" applies to the entire group.)

Before and After "Etc." Commas are usually placed before and after "etc.," "and so on," or "and the like," in a sentence, because such expressions are regarded as parenthetic statements.

> Logs, lumber, tools, etc., are to be shipped...
> Printer's copy, etc., is to be prepared accordingly.
> ...buy materials (lumber, tools, etc.) now. (OR: —..., etc.—now.)

When Connecting Words Are Repeated in Lists. No commas are necessary between listed words if the connecting "and," "or," or "nor" is repeated. But if emphasis is desired, commas may be used.

> He had faith in the future and in business and in men.
> If we can have faith in the future, and in business, and in men.

"Such as" or "Like" Introducing Illustrations. When "such as" introduces an illustration, it should not be followed by a comma, although it is preceded by one if the writer is pausing to give examples. But if no pause is indicated, and the "such as" or "like" phrase is a vital part of the sentence, which could not be removed, no comma should break its connection with the other words.

> Many famous men, such as Edison, Burbank, and Bell, contributed...
> Men such as Edison, Burbank, and Bell contributed... (irremovable)

Phrases or Clauses in Series. Commas may be used to separate simple phrases or clauses in series. Long or inter-punctuated phrases or clauses should be separated by semicolons. (See p. 240.)

> The first is established, the second under way, and the third being...
> One man profits by it, another is impoverished, another is untouched.
> ...a message from across the road, across the country, across the sea.

Between Clauses. A comma is usually placed before a common connective, such as **"and," "as," "but," "for," "or," "nor," "since,"** or **"although,"** when it introduces a separate subject and verb conveying an additional idea. The comma prepares the reader for the second clause.

> That is exactly what it is, **and** it can be nothing more.
> The process is slow, **but** it protects the rights of...
> We shall never see them, **for** they are infinitely small.
> The situation is more serious now, **since** (OR: **as**) it finds workers...
> The shortage is less acute here, **though** of course all parts...
> Certain things cannot be done, **while** certain others can be.

No comma is used if the clauses are short and the relationship is close—or if the second clause is irremovable (restrictive).

> Responsibility will increase **and** few measures will survive.
> They wrote to us **because** they knew us. We will agree **if** they accept...
> That must be done **before** we can proceed.
> Not only was the time ripe **but** it proved golden. (See also p. 17.)
> Do not expect too much **or** you may be disappointed.
> It should be analyzed **so that** we can weigh its value.
> Articles are subject to customs duty **unless** they are bona fide gifts.
> The mercury stays at the same reading **until** the instrument is reset.
> People migrate to places **where** they can find work.
> They sang **while** (OR: **as**) they marched. It's been years **since** I have...

For emphasis, clarity, or when the second clause is removable (nonrestrictive):

> The President has declined to state his choice, **if** he has made one.
> Long-range planning is essential, **because** (OR: **as**) raw materials are...
> It produced a rippled surface, **so that** we could tell at a glance...
> We will stay there until October, **unless** it becomes clear that...
> The same rhythm occurs in lakes, **where** there are no tides.

(For the use of a semicolon between clauses, see p. 239.)

Around a Connective.   When an interpolation follows a connective, commas may be used in four ways to indicate desired pauses.

Omitted before connective: [Rare]
It was nicknamed **and,** as usual, the name made it distinctive.
It is highly recommended **and,** if it is as good as they say it is, we shall certainly be interested.
It is perishable **and,** therefore, nobody can afford it.

Used before connective and omitted after it: [Most favored method]
This course was followed, **and as a result,** we found...
Has it been canceled, **and if so,** has the record been...
They made a holiday of it, **and by noon,** supplies were...
They belittled that account, **and therefore,** they lost it.

Used both before and after connective: [Infrequently used]
That is unlikely, **or,** as they put it, the prospects are...
Things will eventually change, **for,** very rapidly, we are...
That had not occurred to him, **but,** on being called to his attention, was received...

Omitted around the parenthetic expression: [Frequently used]
They may put up a fight, but **on the other hand** they may not.
We had no recent data, and **therefore** no prices were quoted.

Between Parts of a Subject.   If a subject is long or involved, or if the second part is to be emphasized, it may be punctuated with commas. Ordinarily no commas are used, as this is not a compound sentence.

The spelling, **and usage** in regard to separating the two parts, are variable.
FOR EMPHASIS: Its fine **detail, and rich quality** of reproduction, give many striking effects.
USUAL: **That cost and the present market price** do not agree.

Between Parts of a Verb.   If a verb is long or involved, or if the second part is to be emphasized, it may be punctuated with commas. Ordinarily no commas are used, as this is not a compound sentence.

Here we find the word **traced** back to its earliest appearance, **and analyzed** into its elements.
FOR EMPHASIS: We **secured** the volume, **and presented** it to the library.
It **may check** the trend, **or may not.**
USUAL: They **changed** their tactics **and voted** for the bill.
The tenants **must buy** the land **or release** it promptly.

Between Subject and Verb.   Ordinarily a single comma should not be placed between a subject and its verb.   But there are times when a single comma is so used to hold the subject together, as it were, for clearness or for emphasis.

For clarity:
Whatever is, is right.—Pope.
And what they decide, shall be the law.
The people who fled before the onrushing waters, returned to find...
To know the student, is to recognize that he is wise beyond his years.
Everyone not watching the Prime Minister studying the speaker, was watching the President contemplating the proceedings.
Something went wrong.   What, was not exactly known.

For emphasis:

> Two senators were rewarded; but the one spurring the debate, was not.
> A man convinced against his will, is of the same opinion still.
> Whoever thinks that job is easy, is wrong.
> To have something to say and to want to say it, are the main things.

Usual:

> What happened to them is as yet unknown.
> To say that the coastal states had no claim is to challenge the...
> The subject with which that article deals has no bearing on the case.
> Whether any new rules are necessary depends on the nature of the...
> The best thing to do would be to agree.

Between Verb and Object. Ordinarily a single comma should not appear between a verb and its object or complement. However, there are times when a single comma is so used to make the meaning clear.

> NECESSARY: Congress will submit to all the states that have not yet ratified the amendment, a resolution designed to...
> UNNECESSARY: Congress will submit to the states a resolution...

Before a capital: { Their thought seems to be, Live and let live.
{ The question is, Who will survive?

SEMICOLON

Semicolons are used to separate phrases, clauses, or enumerations, of almost equal importance, especially when such phrases or clauses contain commas within themselves.

When Connective Is Omitted. If the connecting word between clauses is omitted, a semicolon is used.

> That is old-fashioned; it suggests senility.
> Don't let them get the better of you; change your viewpoint.
> We are not telling you anything new; we are repeating something old.
> Not only are they not interested; they feel a resentment toward...
> We thought greatness was infallible; we know better now.

When Connective Is Used. If a connective introduces a clause, or clauses, that could **stand alone as a sentence,** or if the connective could be **"embedded"** in its own clause, a semicolon is used before it. Connectives often preceded by semicolons are:

accordingly	hence	moreover	still
also	however	nevertheless	that is
at least	if	notwithstanding	then
besides	indeed	on the contrary	therefore
consequently	in fact	otherwise	thus
for	in short	similarly	whereas
furthermore	likewise	so	yet

> This will be mentioned again; **for** it is a bit of hard-earned information.
> We live in an interesting age; **at least** we know that.
> The manual shall be our guide; **if** there is room for doubt we...
> All numbers should be indicated; **likewise** all queries should...
> It is true the method is difficult; **but** it is believed to be the better way.
> It can be done; **and** we venture to say that it will be done; **but** there are right and wrong ways of doing it.

If the connecting word itself is to be emphasized, a comma is placed after it.

> They argued the question at length; **however,** we were right.
> This reduces the difficulty; **nevertheless,** care must be...
> It is important that we find a substitute; **moreover,** we should not...

Before Enumerations and Explanations. A semicolon is used before a word introducing a **listing** or a **complete clause**—at the **end** of a sentence. A comma follows the word. (See also pp. 230–31 and 241.) Words and abbreviations usually thus set off are:

for instance	that is (or i.e.)	to wit
for example (or e.g.)	namely (or viz)	as

> ...a number of exceptions; **namely,** furs, hides, jute, and copra.
> ...many bright prospects; **for example,** new materials, new methods.
> It should be brief; **that is,** it should tell its purpose succinctly.

> NOTE: If **"namely,"** etc., is **omitted,** a colon or dash replaces the semicolon. But if **"namely,"** etc., is **retained,** a dash may replace the semicolon.

In a Series. Semicolons are used between phrases or clauses in a series, usually when such phrases or clauses themselves contain commas.

> Stocks had reached the following levels: steel, 21; coal, 15; tin, 30; radio, 3; nickel, 4.
> The orders are: Lieutenant John Lee, transferred from the Mission to the Presidio; Corporal Joseph Moore, from the Southern to...
> Miscellaneous freight loaded, 198,000 cars; forest products, 20,024; ore, 6,724; coal, 81,046; livestock, 17,441.
> ...a fast-moving story—of rerouting ships; of sending planes; of...
> Time and space are not considered: where it is, is day; where it was, is night; and history is being made.
> He is forever working; studying curves; measuring distances; figuring...
> He sat down slowly; dialed the number; then waited tensely.
> ...resolve **that** these dead shall not have died in vain; **that** this Nation, under God, shall have a new birth of freedom; and **that** government...
> **If** a company has made every effort to lower its debt; **if** it has reduced its overhead to a minimum; **if** it has undertaken no new obligations, [then] it may seek... (Either comma or dash may end this series.)

Before Phrases. A semicolon may be used to set off a phrase **when words are missing but understood.** (Often a comma is preferred.)

> To some observers, it resembled a glowing candle; to others, a bonfire.
> Perhaps he persuaded them they were being unduly cautious; perhaps not.
> There's nothing more we can do; that is, not just now.
> We often received communications from them; sometimes of a critical nature; sometimes merely seeking information.
> Some men are at their best when mingling with people; shaking hands and talking with them face to face.
> There he remained the rest of his life; unifying, not dividing; building, not destroying.
> Our scientists are bold enough to chart for us the routes we must travel; to tell us how big our ships must be.
> It is interesting because it tends to confirm our first impression; reassuring because it may lead to a better world.

Between Parts of a Subject, and Between Subject and Verb. Semicolons should not ordinarily be used to divide the parts of a compound subject; nor should they otherwise appear between a subject and verb. However, if a strong separation is desired, they are sometimes so used.

UNUSUAL: Valuable papers of which only one copy exists; or original, signed documents; or papers that could not be replaced, should be registered.

USUAL: Valuable papers of which only one copy exists, or original, signed documents, or papers that could not be replaced, should be registered.

FAULTY: This information; namely, that we are reducing prices, is not to be released.

CORRECT: This information, namely, that we are reducing prices, is...

In some sentences, semicolons seem the only logical punctuation to use in dividing the parts of a subject.

All financiers; probably 95 percent of the business men, including publishers; a large part of the women voters; and even a number of school children, know that bank credit was unobtainable...

COLON

The colon may introduce a summing up, an illustration, quotation, or enumeration, for which the previous words in the sentence have prepared the reader. A dash is unnecessary after a colon. The colon itself indicates a definite break in the sentence.

As an Introduction. A colon usually stands for the word **"namely."** It may also replace **"in other words"** or **"the reason"** before a second clause that explains, repeats, or summarizes the first.

The purpose of the organization is told in its name: to further better business relations.

Another thing: they are colorful.

He could offer but one excuse: they were delayed.

...a man once the center of attention: Wilson.

...two things you seldom find together: democracy and capital.

The current thought is:* Let down the tariff bars.

It's hard to say who is the more frustrated: those who know the truth about what's going on here or those who don't know.

Emerson was right: The sky is the daily bread of the eyes—and of the mind.

...for two reasons: first,...; and second,...

It has two uses: it can be..., and it is...

Introducing Quotations. Long quotations are usually introduced by colons; and short quotations may be if emphasis is desired.

Their motto was: "First come, first served."

(OR: ...was "First...")

We might say to them: "Now it's your move."

(OR: ...them, "Now...")

* Some writers avoid the use of a colon **between a verb and its complement or object**, except (1) to introduce a quotation, or an implied quotation; (2) to introduce a tabulation. However, many publications use colons after verbs in order to avoid extra words when introducing lists.

Introducing Tabulations.   Colons usually introduce tabulated items.

Note that a colon, **when introducing a tabulation,** may follow a **verb, preposition, or conjunction.** But in **running text** (untabulated), no colon is used after most such introductory words.

A few were listed, namely:	Note the trends in:
Ship the following f.o.b.:	It may be used for:
. . .complete data. For example:	Please mail it to:
. . .various subjects, such as:	. . .for the purpose of:
. . .were registered thus:	. . .will be suitable if:
Among those present were:	What is the price of each
In any event, it would:	item? (no colon)

A parenthesis just before the listing is placed before the colon, not after it.

NOT: The following are recommended: (because of price)
BUT: The following are recommended (because of price):

If an enumeration is indirectly introduced, a colon is not used.

The goods will be shipped in the following order, and an invoice will be mailed for each shipment. . . . .

After an Introductory Phrase.   A colon is often used after an introductory phrase in a letter, to enable the writer to begin his main statement with a paragraph.

Re (or Regarding, Answering, or Referring to) your letter of the 18th:
(Note: Such an opening is not recommended, but is often dictated.)

Good openings : { Looking ahead, as it were:
Just a few words of explanation:
Some afterthoughts on our conference:

Between Subject and Verb.   A colon should never break into a sentence between a subject and its verb.   The matter introduced by the colon should conclude the sentence.

FAULTY: The old familiar saying: All's well that ends well, is proved again.
CORRECT: The old familiar saying "All's well that ends well" is. . .
FAULTY: To say: "It can't be done," is just an evasion.
CORRECT: To say "It can't be done" is just an evasion.

Capital Letters After Colons.   If a complete sentence follows a colon, it may or may not begin with a capital letter, according as emphasis is desired.   (A **quoted** sentence after a colon always begins with a capital.)

The question naturally arises: Why should it cost so much?
First of all: what is "normal" business?
There is but one thing wrong: it costs too much.
The decision rests with the writer: what looks right usually is right.
The inscription read: "Time goes, you say? Ah, no, time stays; we go."

Other Uses of Colon.   (After salutations, see p. 292; in clock time, see p. 586; in literary references, see p. 435; in enumerations, p. 414.)

❖❖❖❖❖❖❖

DASH

A pair of dashes are necessary to segregate material completely. If but one dash is used, it is in effect to the end of the sentence, or to the end of a parenthesis. A comma, semicolon, or colon does not conclude the authority of a dash.

> "All that follows a dash is to be taken as under its influence until either a second dash terminates it, or a full stop is reached."
> —Fowler, *The King's English*, 3d Ed., p. 281.

Punctuation With Dashes. The dash is a definite mark of punctuation and needs no other punctuation to support it. To use commas to set off dashes is double punctuation. (Sentence commas, semicolons, and colons were formerly used with dashes, but the combination has gone out of use. The dash alone is now considered sufficient punctuation.)

It is not because we have played our last card—we have not done that—but because we... (FORMERLY: —...—,)
It sometimes implies encouragement—we will succeed. It sometimes implies assurance—we shall succeed. (FORMERLY: —...—; it...)
The following terms are correct—and acceptable: (FORMERLY: ...—:)

Some writers believe that a semicolon or colon terminates the influence of a dash. But it does not always; and often the reader must decide whether or not the effect of the dash is ended by a semicolon or colon.

Sentences in which the dash carries through to the period:
Today that organization is fifty years old—an age at which it should attain a balance; at which it should lean upon experience.
The waves make a confused pattern—overtaking and engulfing one another; each differing from the other; some never to reach a shore.
The national eagle is often seen—except in one place: the American sky.

Sentences in which the dash ends at the semicolon:
That trouble is easily overcome—by shifting from one hand to another; but when a new difficulty arises, they cannot cope with it.
(BETTER: ...—by shifting from one hand to another—but when...)
The treatment is not even thorough—it is exceedingly sketchy and vague; yet somehow he has painted a picture—a scene that is real.
(BETTER: ...sketchy and vague. Yet somehow he has painted...)

Punctuation Within Dashes. This pertains to the segregated matter only. Commas, abbreviation periods, question marks, exclamation points, and quotes may be used. The words within the dashes may or may not be grammatically independent of the rest of the sentence.

NOTE: Capitals are used only for proper names and to begin quoted sentences.

They are always—naturally, considering their position—the first...
...sent one of their—not colorless, but—"most accomplished" speakers.
In the capital city—Washington, D.C.—the cherry blossoms...
He handles the material—or should we say the lack of it?—very well.
The second question—"Is it worthwhile?"—raised so many doubts...
They might have recovered—think of it!—their long-lost freedom.
He said they would select a man—"We have several in mind"—who...
The guiding theme—"Westward the course of empire"—was depicted...

Dashes Following Dashes. Dashes may follow dashes without extra punctuation. They sometimes denote hesitation, faltering, or suspense.

> People everywhere—men and women—young and old—are interested.
> A faint signal came through—faded—was detected again—and then died.
> "I—well—er—I—"} (Note no period, but a question mark or exclama-
> "Well, I'll—be—!" } tion point may be used after the last dash.)

Explanations or Repetitions. Dashes may set off a repetition, explanation, variation, or summary of what has been said.

> **Repetition:**
> Buy now—today—if you can.
> June 19—next Monday—is the date set for...
>
> **Explanation:**
> That firm—an old customer of ours—has never failed to...
> We feel that we—that is, the average person—could not...
> Do we really want to be governed—told what to do and when to do it?
>
> **Variation:**
> They feel badly treated—betrayed—and the feeling is...
> It has been known for days—for weeks, in fact—that...
> Business is convalescing—or, to put it another way, it is improving.
> They have given notice of acceptance—in other words, approved it.
> Their future is certain if they elect the right kind of leader—or better
> yet, the right kind of man.
>
> **Summary:**
> Farmer, laborer, merchant prince—they are all included.
> Drifting government, planless government—that's what they have
> today.
> So it goes—trials within trials, all to the same end.
> To believe that what is true for you is true for all—that is genius.

Side Thoughts and Comments. Dashes are used to segregate a quick change of thought or of sentence construction; or to set off an afterthought, comment, or contemplation, provoked by the text but not necessarily a part of it.

> If it is good reading—and it is—the style of the book...
> It, too—with its many sidelights—impressed me.
> By a stroke of good fortune—or so it seemed to me—I was sent...
> He hardly deserved credit, but he has—anonymously, indeed—got it.
> We think it the finest—but let it speak for itself.
> We, the people—if we are not enlightened, how can we judge?

For Emphasis. A dash may be used to set off a single word or expression for emphasis.

> It seems that they lack only—starch.
> They pretended to want the contract and then—they refused it.
> ...a strange situation—and yet, harmonious.
> ...and, then, solemnly vowing they would never give in—gave in.
> Turn from this—to what?
> If you don't know the meaning of a word—look it up.

Instead of Parentheses. Dashes may be used instead of parentheses. They are a slightly less noticeable mark of punctuation than parentheses, and do not so definitely segregate the parenthetic material.

The conditions are ripe—except money circulation—to begin...
The technical terms—"rays," "streams," "jets"—were confusing.
...ruled that a 6% return—the fixed rate—could not be considered.
...an early winter—this was in October, 1958—added to the suffering.

Instead of a Colon. A dash is sometimes used instead of a colon where the word "namely" has seemingly been omitted.

...added these names to the list—Jasper, Lynn, and Martin.
It ended with a query—Will this land remain undeveloped, forever?
Two things are needed—to get started again, and to keep going.
...turned to the only alternative—the ballot box.

Instead of a Semicolon. A dash is sometimes used instead of a semicolon before the words "namely," "for instance," and the like.

There were three questions to be discussed—namely, the deeding of lands to the homesteaders, townsites, and the mapping of roads.
...a new use for plastics—for example, in trains, aircraft, and ships.

A dash may be used instead of a semicolon when a connective has been omitted.

The expense is ours—the saving is theirs.

Broken Sentences. A dash may be used to indicate that a sentence is broken by spacing. Yet, often no punctuation is used.

He suggested –
1. That we buy...
2. That we install...
3. That we sell...

It should be carried in
1. All newspaper advertising, and
2. The annual catalogue.

Let us now consider
The Summary

Regarding the Use of Dashes. Do not employ dashes for any and every purpose. They are an outstanding mark of punctuation, and their value is increased by a restriction of their use. Still, do not overrestrict the use of dashes and omit them where they seem necessary.

CONFUSING: It is singular that Edison, Burroughs, and Coolidge, man of science, naturalist, and president, all belonged...
CLEARER: It is singular that Edison, Burroughs, and Coolidge—man of science, naturalist, and president—all belonged...

Do not omit the last dash necessary to complete an earlier dash.

NOT: Such leadership sends confidence—even restores courage, to us.
BUT: Such leadership sends confidence—even restores courage—to us.

Typewriting Dash. Three styles of typewritten dash are used: (1) a single mark with a space on each side (a usual form, especially in tabulations); (2) two marks with a space on each side (gaining in favor); (3) two marks with no space on each side (printers' style).

A line of writing should be divided **after** a dash, not before one.

.... – .... – ....   or   .... –– .... –– ....   or   ....––....––....

PARENTHESES

Parentheses are a noticeable, and therefore very strong, mark of punctuation, holding the matter enclosed within them entirely to itself. They are used when it is desired to segregate material very definitely.

Punctuation With Parentheses. Parentheses are a punctuation in themselves, and need no additional commas or dashes to set them off.

Use ( )   not ,( ),   nor —( )—

Another mark of punctuation is used **after**—not before—a parenthesis when such other mark is punctuating the entire sentence. Only in enumerations, etc., is punctuation used **before** parentheses (see. p. 414).

Sentence Marks With Parentheses.

( ),
( );
( ):
( )—

Comma, semicolon, colon, and dash are **always** outside the parentheses (unless, in rare instances, they are **part** of quoted parenthetic material).

> Thus the matter, so far as we know (and we have no right to speculate), breaks up into...
> It is in many of our contracts (but not in all); nevertheless, we will agree to...

( ).
( )!
( )?
(.)
(!)
(?)

A period, exclamation point, or question mark, when **punctuating** the entire sentence, is outside the parentheses.

These marks are inside the parentheses when punctuating **only** the parenthetic material. (For parentheses with quotes, see pp. 247 and 249.)

> It was held in Washington (D.C.).
> (It was held in Washington, D.C.)
> But was the year as late as that (1953)?
> ...to make such a deal (and call it honest!).
> ...a closed hearing.   (The testimony was not released.)

Continuous parenthetic paragraphs have an opening parenthesis mark before each paragraph, but a closing one only after the last paragraph.

Confirming Figures.   (For prices, see p. 279; legal work, p. 476.)

Enumerations.   (For figures or letters in parentheses, see p. 414.)

Punctuation Within Parentheses.   This is the same as in ordinary sentences, except that no periods are used, unless after abbreviations, or after parenthetic sentences standing alone.

> ...on the south lay the valley of the Oro (doubtless shortened from Copa de Oro, meaning the "Cup of Gold" lake; recently, I regret to say, bridged over for the convenience of Mr. Laidlaw, engineer, and others); while on the north...
> Our purpose in using the "reinforced filling" (or "reinforced covering", the terms are practically interchangeable) was to secure...
> Years ago someone (I haven't forgotten his name, my friend!) said...
> An eminent physician (his name does not matter—any one of a dozen men might have done as well) was called upon...

Parentheses may be placed within parentheses, if the two sets are not confusing.   However, dashes or brackets are usually used as inner parentheses, or around parentheses.

(( ))	...according to the locality. (See West (former Dutch) New Guinea, p. 1156.)
([ ])	...the books bore "ex libris" (Latin, from the library [of]).
[( )]	"It was penned by the French philosopher [Voltaire (see below)] and succinctly disposes..."
(— —)	We are not sure of the date (we thought it was 1952—some said 1953—and that it was in the spring).
— ( ) —	It was late for them to be starting on a venture—really gambling on a scheme (a "plan" they called it) of doubtful character—that might yield them nothing.

Capitalization Within Parentheses. The first word of parenthetic material within a sentence is not capitalized, unless it is a proper name or part of a proper name, or begins a **quoted** expression.

NOTE: Only **independent** parenthetic sentences take periods—not inner parenthetic sentences, although question marks and exclamation points may be used after inner parenthetic statements.

USUAL: The prevalent method is there indicated (the newspaper excerpts are exact).   (Note only one period.)

QUOTATION: It is intriguing ("See what's coming!"), and we...

QUESTION: ...read by the midnight sun (have you ever seen it?); for this was June in Norway.   OR: ...by the midnight sun. (Have you ever seen it?) For this was June ..

EXCLAMATION: After a year of victories (what victories!), he was...

PROPER NAME: They advertised as "The Western Company (Successors to Oregon Traders)."

Grammatical Construction Within Parentheses. The construction of words within parentheses may or may not be grammatically independent of the rest of the sentence.

He does not know a bargain when he sees (or even when he makes) one.

But always, the sentence should be grammatically independent of the parenthesis. Enclose within the parentheses only what could be removed without impairing the sentence. If the parenthetic matter could not be removed, parentheses should not be used.

NOT: They operate (like the savages of old upon the western movement), and man fights...

BUT: They operate like the savages of old upon the western movement, and man fights...

NOT: It is (not the first) but the last straw that counts.

BUT: It is not the first but the last straw that counts.

NOT: This is an exception (that instead of destroying) proves the rule.

BUT: This is an exception that (instead of destroying) proves the rule.

Explanations and Identifications. Parentheses are used around explanatory phrases or comments, or phrases of identification or reference, which are not a part of the continuous thought, and which it is desired to set off completely or noticeably from the rest of the sentence.

The old rate (that is, the legalized rate) was not...

As the gentlemen (Mr. Hanna and Mr. Mills) observed...

In the example given (No. 3) the total is correct.

A sinking fund was authorized (see Minutes of Meeting, May 2) for...

To Clarify Sentences. If the meaning of a sentence is obscure with ordinary punctuation, parentheses may help to clarify it.

> OBSCURE: Our Company will furnish all specified items, with the exception of foundations, all brickwork, and insulating material.
>
> CLEAR: Our Company will furnish all specified items (with the exception of foundations), all brickwork, and insulating material.

◇◇◇◇◇◇◇◇◇

QUOTATION MARKS

There are two methods of using **periods and commas** with "quotes":

1. The "inside" method—established and preferred in printing—places the period and comma always inside the final quotation mark, no matter what the sentence construction. This facilitates typesetting.

> " ." Each country has "rights," and each wants "justice."
>
> " ," "Progress," he reminded us, "means scientific work."

2. The "outside" method*—adopted for exactness by such authorities as those listed below—places the comma always outside the quotes, because it punctuates the entire sentence. Likewise, the period is placed outside the quotes when it punctuates the entire sentence; and inside the quotes when it punctuates the quoted matter.

> " ". Each country has "rights", and each wants "justice".
>
> " ", "Progress", he reminded us, "means scientific work."
>
> " ." They drove home this truth: "We are not independent."

NOTE: The logical "outside" method is used in exacting work, such as technical and legal writings. The U.S. Government Printing Office employs it for all congressional legislative work, as bills and acts of Congress. It is the European method, often seen in United Nations publications. It is also employed in many authoritative British publications, such as the great *Oxford English Dictionary,* and the *Dictionary of Modern English Usage* by H. W. Fowler (foremost authority on English).

There is **only one method** (employed by all) **for the use of all other marks of punctuation** with quotation marks.

> **Semicolon, colon, and dash** are always outside the quotes (unless, in a rare instance, one such mark is an inseparable part of the quotation).

> " "; We are told "Might does not make right"; yet,....
>
> " ": ...found a "collector's item": a four-pointed star.
>
> . " "— It is "standard equipment"—in fact, indispensable.

> **Question mark and exclamation point** are outside the quotes when punctuating the entire sentence; and inside the quotes when punctuating only the quoted matter. (If in a quotation that ends the sentence, these marks may suffice for punctuation for the entire sentence.)

> " "? Why talk about "photoelectric cells"?
>
> " "! ...forged ahead as if nothing were "impossible"!
>
> " ?" The natural question arose, "Is it legal?"
>
> " !" ...until they cry "Enough!"

---

* If preparing material for a publication, use the "inside" method for all commas and periods. It is suggested that students be taught the "inside" method first; later, with a knowledge of both methods, they can adopt the "outside" method when working in offices that prefer it.

Choice of Two Marks. When either of two punctuation marks (or doubled marks) may end the sentence, the stronger mark only is used.

But did anybody say, "Good work!"   All were marked "O.P."
Why ask, "What next?" (NOT: ?"?)   BUT: Were all "O.P."?

Parentheses With Quotes. (See also pp. 246–47.)

"   (   )."   Parentheses should be inside the quotes if more than the parenthetic matter is quoted.

("   .")   Parentheses should be around the quotes if the entire quotation is parenthetic.

" . "(   )"   ."   Quotes should be broken and renewed when parentheses are inserted containing unquoted matter.

...("   ?")?   Sentence punctuation marks are added after parenthetic
...("   ").   quotations.

> What does it mean ("Wie geht's?")?
> ...live by their motto ("Always ready").
> They all bore the same label ("N.Y.").

Inner Quotes.

"   '   '   ."   Single quotes are used for inner quotations. (British practice favors the use of single quotes for regular quotations, and double quotes for inner quotations. Some American publishers have adopted this form. '   "   "   .')

"   '   .'"   Punctuation marks are used with inner quotes in the same
"   '   ','"   manner as with regular quotes. But many publications now put the **period between the single quote and the double quote.**

"   '   ?'"   Extra sentence punctuation is not now used after a punc-
"   '   !'"   tuated final inner quotation; the inner quotation's punctuation is considered sufficient.

> He asked quietly, "What do you suppose they meant by saying, 'Haven't you heard?'" (not ?'?")
> He testified: "I heard them say 'It's hopeless!'"

"   '   "   "   ,'   ."   A second inner quotation takes the double quotes. Quotations should not go further.

"   :'   ';'   ';'   .'"   Example of punctuation with inner quotes:

> He reported, "Their excuses were: 'We don't have the time'; 'We don't have the money'; and an implied 'We don't have the courage.'"

Other Marks.

"   – – –"   Three dashes inside quotes indicate broken-off speech.

"   "– – –   Three dashes outside quotes indicate that the sentence breaks off after the quotation is finished.

"   ..."   Three dots inside quotes indicate that part of the quotation has been deleted.

"   ***   "   Three stars indicate an omission or unprintable words.

—"   "—   Plain dashes may be used around a quoted passage to set it
—"   !"—   off from the rest of the sentence. (See also p. 243.)

"Etc." Not Quoted. "Etc." should not be within the quotes unless it is actually a part of the quoted matter.

> On the order was marked "Inserts," etc.
>   (Meaning that something besides "Inserts" was marked on the order.)
> On the order was marked "Inserts, etc."
>   (Here "etc." is a part of what was actually marked on the order.)

249

Setting Off Direct Quotations. A long quotation (of more than three lines) is usually separated, indented, and introduced by a colon.

> That statement was made by the Secretary, but he added:
> "We are going ahead with the order as if the debt had been canceled, and will put the billings on the books for next year. Our Company can see no improvement in the situation until..."

A short quotation may be set off if it closes the sentence, and is important enough to be so emphasized. Ordinarily it is not separated.

> He strode from the room saying:
> "That's ridiculous!"

Conversation. When a conversation is being recorded, the speeches of each speaker are given separate paragraphs, unless the conversation is very short.

> "Their action is no mystery," replied the visitor knowingly.
> "Ah, but they may make a false move!" cried Holman.
> "If they do, they will lose," said the other, smiling.
> "No," Holman replied; and with a careless gesture, "whatever they do, they will win. It is their nature."

Plays and Court Testimony. It is unnecessary to use quotation marks when recording a dialogue if each speech is prefaced by the name of the person speaking. (See also pp. 276 and 486.)

Broken Quotations. When a quotation is interrupted by non-spoken words, various punctuation is used—although commas are usual.

> "Now I must tell you"—he smiled slyly—"a really curious thing."
> (Dashes set off interruptions that do not indicate speaking.)
> "If you make a bad bargain," he said, "stick to it." (usual commas)
> "You wouldn't mind," he said; "you would go right on." (semicolon)
> "Why, it's only a trifle," she murmured, "—a mere trifle." (inner dash)
> "How interesting!" he cried—"how very interesting." (outer dash)
> "Tell me —I insist—" for he had to know—"what do you think of it?"
> "What would I do?" he repeated slowly. "Why, I would—"
> "Yes," she mused, "years have passed and now———" She looked away.
> "I did say 'parachute,'" he fumed. "Now look here..."
> "You mean that I—?" He weighed it carefully. "Then it's true!"

> NOTE: For an unfinished speech, some publications use an ordinary dash; others, a long dash; still others, three dots. No period follows such a dash, although a question mark or exclamation point may.

Capitalization in Quotations. The first word in a quotation is capitalized only when it is a proper name, or when it begins a sentence.

A **comma** is usual before a quotation; but it may be omitted if the quotation is woven into the sentence (as when preceded by "that").

> ...with the legend "We shall see" scrawled upon it.
> ...in the passage beginning "Canst thou not minister..."
> The maxim that says "People who live in glass houses" is not followed.
> He asked, "What does that indicate?"
> He asked them to help, and they said "No."
> The Vice President emerged with "nothing to say."
> He said that "we have no right to interfere." (no comma, no capital)
> BUT: He said, "We have no right to interfere." (without "that")

250

Fragmentary Quotations. Pick up a fragmentary quotation with the exact words uttered. Do not include any introductory remarks, or any reconstruction of the spoken words.

> He admitted the goods were "not up to standard."
> (What was probably said was, "I'll admit that the goods **are** not up to standard," which gives the privilege of quoting only "not up to standard"; and which would not permit quoting something like this: He admitted "that the goods *were* not up to standard.")
> NOT: They said he "*had* the most analytic mind..."
> BUT: They said he had "the most analytic mind..."
> (What they probably said was, "He **has** the most...")

The same caution applies when quoting the exact words from another text: Quote the actual words, not a rearrangement of them.

> The clipping said that prices were being "forced down because of the general unrest."
> NOT: The clipping said "*that* prices *were* being forced down..."

Also, when quoting a familiar saying or phrase, do not quote words that are not an actual part of the saying or phrase.

> NOT: There is a saying "that if you make a better mousetrap..."
> BUT: There is a saying that if you "make a better mousetrap..."
> NOT: And "your gentle reader" will not long tolerate...
> BUT: And your "gentle reader" will not long tolerate...

Quoted Words Listed. When quoted words, phrases, or sentences are listed, each has its separate set of quotation marks.

> They would refer to each other as "my honorable opponent," "my rival," and "the gentleman of the opposition."
> Answer "Yes" or "No."
> ...the three compositions, "Serenade," "Prelude," and "Venetienne."

Indirect Quotations. Do not use quotation marks around indirect quotations (that is, when the actual words spoken are not given).

> He said the order had been checked. (NOT: said "*that* the order had...")
> He said very well, he would comply. We say no; they, yes.

Common Expressions Not Quoted. Common expressions borrowed from certain vernaculars (and not considered slang), or familiar quotations and figures of speech, need not be quoted.

set off a chain reaction	jump the gun	right on the beam
take a rain check on it	cause a bottleneck	get off the ground
experience growing pains	try it on for size	backing and filling
shed crocodile tears	come a cropper	just double talk
method in our madness	met his Waterloo	go to the wall

take the wind out of their sails	make him the underdog
pulled the rug from under him	gave us a long song-and-dance
scheme was nipped in the bud	another job is in the bag
killing two birds with one stone	means passing the buck
more sinned against than sinning	can't make head or tail of it
the game is not worth the candle	call a spade a spade
learn that silence is golden	that all's well that ends well
an old saying: Haste makes waste	the slogan: The life you save...

However, such phrases **may be quoted** for clarity, or because of the tone of the writing. But quote **all** the usual phrase, not just a part of it.

> Big changes usually "telegraph their punches."
> They want "cash on the barrelhead." (NOT: ...cash "on the...")
> ...just "doubling in brass." (having one man play two horns)
> "All's well that ends well" was the comforting thought.

Colloquial Words. In everyday writings—as in newspapers—words accepted as "colloquial" are not usually quoted.

the production know-how	speaking off the cuff
he's a big wheel there	by the military brass
picked up the tab	give it the once-over
played it deadpan	work the bugs out of it
did a double-take	take a look-see at it

Slang or Coined Words. In semiformal writings, quote slang or coined words, or any phrases which might cheapen the text if it is not known that the writer is aware of them.

But it "ain't so" any more.	We "was robbed"...
...submit a big "swindle sheet."	...a "souped-up" job.

Humorous Words, Misnomers, and Clichés. If a word or phrase is intended to be awkward, whimsical, or humorous, it may be quoted.

> Then, indeed, there might be "trouble in paradise."

It is supposed not to be good form to label one's own humor, but it is worse form, in a serious text, to expose one's writing or mentality to criticism by having a light or slang remark taken seriously.

> **"Most of us would rather be taken for knaves than for**
> **fools; and so the quotation marks are usually there."**
> **—Fowler,** *The King's English,* **3d Ed., p. 58.**

Foreign Words. Foreign words need not be quoted if they are common enough to have been embraced by the English language. But if they are likely to be unfamiliar to the reader, they should be quoted.

In printing, foreign words are often italicized; but that does not necessarily mean they should be underlined or quoted when typewritten.

résumé	junta	incommunicado	aficionados
BUT: "Autres temps, autres mœurs"		"nyet"	"mañana"

Technical or Trade Terms. If technical or trade terms are likely to be unfamiliar to the reader, quote them. If they are familiar, do not quote them.

If a technical or trade word occurs repeatedly throughout a text, it may be quoted on first appearance, and written without quotes thereafter. (Trade names and trademarks are often written in caps instead of being quoted. See also p. 125.)

> We will make a "cut" of the photograph for reproduction.
> ...and send the cut direct to the printer.
> They will "spud in" the well on your property next week.

They are spudding in Well 660 on adjoining property today.
A "melon" of $5,000,000 was available.   . . .divided the melon equally.
. . .and in selling SUNGLOW we are offering. . .   (trade name)

Nicknames. Do not quote familiar nicknames. (See p. 311.)

Words as Words. Words referred to as words—especially if defined or explained—are quoted in typewriting, and italicized in printing.

> The word "pretty" should be reserved to mean "attractive" or "pleasing" and not be used where "quite" or "very" is appropriate.

But in some texts, words are distinctive enough not to need quotes:

> Many similar words are interchanged (for example, affect and effect, cite and site, block and bloc, and observance and observation).

And if the actual words are not meant, no quotes are necessary:

the ups and downs of life   know the ins and outs
no ifs, ands, or buts about it   an iffy question   (or "iffy")

Although some words having extended meanings are usually quoted:

a "must"   the "haves" and "have nots"   a few "for instances"

Letters as Letters. Letters referred to as letters need not be quoted, unless they are liable to be misread. Street names are not quoted.

the letter M   mind your p's and q's   a store on F Street
a U-turn   the road makes an S   a V-shaped insertion
a small y   a ball with "8" on it   cutting figure 8s
If A rents to B, and B subleases to C. . .   it begins with "a"

Letters representing a common appellation may be quoted:

a "Y" hut in war   study at the "U"   BUT: a G-man

Possessives or Plurals of Quoted Words. If the possessive or plural of a quoted word becomes necessary, it is less awkward to include the 's or -s within the quotes than to add it after the quotes.

Possessive:

The SS. "United States'" record	NOT:	SS. "United *States*"'s
The "Y's" advantages		The "Y"'s
"Oklahoma's!" earnings		"*Oklahoma!*"'s

Plural:

too many "That's rights"	NOT:	"That's *right*"s
successive "Oklahomas!"		"*Oklahoma!*"s
said their "I do's"		their "I *do*"'s

Quoting "a," "an," "the." When the articles are an actual part of a title, saying, or expression, include them within the quotes.

called him "a blithering idiot"   BUT: held a "Monday german"
for "the right of self-determination"   buy only the "blue chips"

"So-Called" Expressions. A word or phrase is quoted if the expression "so-called" or "what is termed" can be mentally supplied before it.

> An "off the record" news conference. . .
> . . .by persons other than "authorities."
> "Panhandling" is street-begging.
> It is just "a horseback guess."
> Public opinion "freezes," and no one can tell. . .

In Peking, "the Forbidden City" is enclosed in...
Universes that lie "fifty million light years" away...

When the actual terms "so-called," "called," "termed," "known as," "supposed," etc., are used, the following words may or may not be quoted, according to the writer's preference:

a so-called "Liberal"   termed "generosity"   the much-talked-of "life"
OR: so-called Liberal   termed generosity   the much-talked-of life

But when the very definite terms "entitled," "named," "marked," "signed," and "endorsed" are used, the following words are quoted:

entitled "Roads"; named "Mary"; marked "6X"; signed "J. M. Hill"

Titles of Books, Stories, Plays, Poems, Paintings, Music.

In typewritten work—and in newspapers—titles of compositions are set in small letters and quoted (with only the main words capitalized).

...the book was "The Virginian" by Owen Wister.
...in the short story "The Apple-Tree," by Galsworthy.
Dr. Thomas's article was entitled "Does Tomorrow Come?"
...in Rosa Bonheur's painting "The Horse Fair," several...
...will be a guest on the "Meet the Press" TV program.

In the publishing trade, titles of books and compositions are often set in caps, and not quoted; or sometimes underlined to indicate that they would be set in **italics** if in print. (See also p. 436.)

...an order for THE VIRGINIAN by Owen Wister.
...the style of the Oxford English Dictionary.

Magazines, Newspapers, Periodicals, and Reference Books.

Titles that are constantly seen are not quoted, unless liable to be misread. "The" beginning a name is capitalized, though often not in running text.

The New York Times   in the Evening Star (OR: The Star)
The Random House Dictionary   in The World Almanac (OR: the)
in Fortune magazine   BUT: in "Time"

Credit Lines.

In credit lines, the name of the work or book is quoted, unless it is an everyday name. (In printing, it is often **italicized.**)

—Irving, "Life of Washington," Vol. II, p. 210.
BUT: —Webster's New Collegiate Dictionary, p. 1201.
(See also Copy for the Press, pp. 435–36.)

Ships, Trains, Aircraft.

These names are usually quoted when typewritten. (In printing, they are often **italicized.**)

the SS. "Transatlantic"   the "Super Chief"   the "Independence"

In the shipping trade, the names of ships are often set in caps and not quoted. (And no periods are used after the abbreviations SS, MS [motorship], MV [motor vessel], and NS [nuclear ship].)

the SS ATLANTICLAND   the MS MONARCH OF THE SEAS

Words Set in Caps.

When words are set in full caps for distinction, it is not necessary also to quote them. (See also pp. 126 and 253.)

...hereinafter called the SELLER [or "Seller"].   The Seller agrees...

◇◇◇◇◇◇◇◇◇

QUOTED MATTER

Paragraphs Quoted.   Quotation marks are placed at the beginning of each paragraph of continuous quoted material, but not at the end of each paragraph—at the end of the entire quotation only.   This indicates that the quotation is still in effect at the beginning of each new paragraph, and that it does not end until the final quotation mark is reached.

      " ....
....
....
    " ....
....?
    " ....
....
...."

If the material quoted is not continuous, but is extracted from various parts of a text, each extract should be closed with a quotation mark, and stars run between the quotations to indicate intervening space.

    " ....
...."

            * * *

    " ....
...."

Sentences Quoted.   Single sentences are often quoted in block style, with the first quotation mark set one space to the left of the block margin.

        " ....
...."

Indenting Quoted Excerpts.   Quotations of three or more lines should, as a rule, be set apart and indented from the body of the text. They are usually introduced by colons.

Quotation marks are often used as well as indention.   Mere indention in typewritten work does not signify that the material is also quoted.

Elimination of Quotation Marks When Credit Line Is Given.   If the quoted excerpt is indented and followed by the author's name or a credit line:

In printing, quotation marks are often omitted **when a smaller type is used.**   But they may be retained for definiteness.

In typewriting, quotation marks are sometimes omitted, but more often retained for exactness.

In legal papers, they are always used.

Quoting Poetry.   An excerpt of poetry should be set in the original form, and quoted, unless the author's name is given before or after it. Place a quotation mark before each stanza, and one at the end of the poem.

Punctuation Copied in Quoted Matter. When quoting material, copy the punctuation exactly, unless it is obviously or strikingly incorrect. For instance, if the copy has "to-day" (the British form), retain the hyphen instead of writing "today."

In legal papers, copy the punctuation exactly, right or wrong—underlining any mark that is obviously incorrect. Changing the punctuation may change the meaning.

Remember, however, to change the double quotation marks in the text to single marks in the copy (if quotation marks are being used around the material being copied), as any matter quoted in the original becomes an inner quotation in the copy.

Italicized Words in Quoted Matter. If a word has been italicized for emphasis in the original text, it should be underlined in the quoted typewritten copy. In the following excerpt from Frederic Harrison, the word "must" was originally italicized:

> "For in the wilderness of books most men, certainly all busy men, must strictly choose."

If a word has been italicized instead of quoted in the original text, it should be single-quoted in the typewritten copy. In the following excerpt from Charles Lamb, the words "for" and "against" were originally italicized:

> "When we coveted a cheap luxury...we were used to have a debate..., and to weigh the 'for' and 'against'..."

Quoting Letters or Telegrams. When quoting letters or telegrams, always include the date, with a quotation mark before it; so there can be no possible question about that most important part of the instrument.

The address need not be copied unless some later question might arise regarding the actual addressee. In legal papers the address should always be copied, with a quotation mark before the first word, but not after the last word in the address.

If a letter or telegram is short enough to be copied on one page, only three quotation marks are necessary: one before the date, one before the address or salutation, and one after the last word in the signature.

"April 12, 1971

"Gentlemen:

....

....

....

....

Sincerely,

/S/ Thomas V. Law
President"

TVL:mb

If the letter or telegram to be copied is long and will carry over to another page, a quotation mark should be placed before each paragraph to indicate the continuation of the quotation.

◇◇◇◇◇◇◇◇◇

QUESTION MARK

The peculiarity of the question mark is that it may occur within a sentence without ending the sentence.

Direct Questions. If an answer to a direct question is expected, a question mark should be used (note abbreviation period is retained).

> Can we achieve that?　　...in the U.S.A.?　　What, for instance?

If an answer is not expected, and the question is intended as a suggestion or request, no question mark is necessary.

> May we ask for a settlement.　Would it not be well to do it that way.
> May we hear from you soon.　Will you please send it to this address.
> (A question mark would make these sentences more emphatic.)

If no answer is expected, but if the question is a supposition or statement intended to make the reader think, a question mark is used.

> Why cannot nations come to terms?
> But who indulges in the belief that such a thing may yet be realized?
> Why not help others to help themselves?
> People often ask, Is time working for us or against us?
> We sometimes wonder: What would we have done?

Indirect Questions. If a question is not directly put, that is, if it is changed from its original form, it does not take a question mark.

> They asked how we would make shipment.
> It was a question of where and when to talk.
> ...but they wondered what difference it made.
> A frequent question is why the bridge curves toward the shore.
> Whether or not they should have so much authority is another question.
> With whom they hope to win is the puzzle.
> The question was how to go about it.

Questions Not in Question Form. The question mark alone may make a question of an ordinary expression.

> They said that?　Really?　　And so they were going to abandon it?
> They intend to do no more advertising?　　Never?

Unpunctuated Questions. Some questions ending within sentences are left "open," that is, without question marks, because the question mark would unduly stress them.　(Only actual quotations take quotes.)

> Relief has been promised, yet what of it, they ask.
> How can we exist, is the question in every mind.

Quoted Questions. A quoted question is begun with a capital; but if only part of a question is quoted, no capital is used.　A comma, colon, or dash (or no punctuation) may introduce the question.

> Their only question was, "Is it too late?"
> Someone inquired: "What will that cost us?" and everyone smiled.
> Ask "Why do you believe that?" and silence is the answer.
> One question involves "from whom?"—the other "to whom?"
> "Oh, yes?" say the others, "but what about us?"
> "Just what do you mean by 'free speech'?" they inquired politely.

257

Doubt or Irony. If the accuracy or truth of a statement is questionable, a question mark in parentheses may follow it.

They were discovered in 1886 (?) and were...

Irony, doubt, or humor is sometimes expressed by the question mark in parentheses. Some authorities do not sanction this; but still it is used, and is often a quick and effective means of giving the writer's conclusions regarding his subject when otherwise his statements might be misunderstood. Of course, if the text clearly indicates the irony or doubt of the expression, the question mark is superfluous.

They also conducted a business (?) in Boston.

Court Testimony Questions. (See Court Papers, p. 486.)

Placement of Question Mark. A question mark should immediately follow a question, whether the question ends within a sentence or not. A question mark placed within a sentence does not conclude the thought nor break the continuity of the sentence. No capital letter is necessary after it, and no punctuation other than sometimes a dash.

Commas, semicolons, and colons are not usually used after interior question marks, although in rare instances they may be.

Would it be wise to undertake that? is the puzzling question.
Can such things happen? he thought. Well, we know they do.
Will they accept? and if they do, how long before we are notified?
How can they be superior?—unprincipled and unethical as they are!
They were fined (but could you call it "fined"?) sixty cents.
What is it they say?..."Ars longa, vita brevis." (question answered)
...the same question "What's new?" and the same answer "Nothing."
The article "Science—Where Away?", appearing in the last issue, ...
...three subjects: War; Is There a Road to Peace?; and, Prosperity.
Are they old enough to drive a car? sail a ship? fly a plane?
  BUT: What are (a) assets, (b) liabilities, (c) book value?
What did you see? Did you spot a camel, a dragon, or a castle door?

CAUTION: Do not insert a question mark before the end of the question.

TEST: Read the question part alone to see whether it is complete.

NOT: Did you see the press notice? that we wrote about.
BUT: Did you see the press notice that we wrote about?

Beginning a Question Within a Sentence. A question may originate at any point in a sentence. It may be introduced by a comma, a semicolon, a colon, or a dash.

It may begin with a capital or small letter, according to the emphasis desired; and it is not quoted unless it is an actual quotation.

One naturally asks: Why hunt up all those things?
They debated it from several angles—Was it businesslike? Was it ethical? or, even further, Was it honest?
In all doubtful cases our first questions will be, what was the author's purpose in choosing such a theme? is it his own, or a borrowed idea? if the latter, did he use it consciously or unconsciously?
The distinction is far from clear; who can say what would be fair?
That is right, isn't it?   It is true, isn't it, that they have come?

EXCLAMATION POINT

An exclamation point should be used to point up or enliven words used forcefully, but which in themselves might convey only a mild impression.

It may be inserted at any point in a sentence; and it is followed by no mark of punctuation other than sometimes a dash.

Expressing Emotion. An exclamation point is used to punctuate expressions of intense feeling or great emotion.

The King is dead—long live the King!   In other words, war!

Ejaculations or Commands. An exclamation point is used to set off impulsive or emphatic remarks, such as ejaculations or commands.

Impossible!   Splendid!   Very good!   What grace!
That's absolutely untrue!   I can't believe it!
That sounds strange indeed!   Make the most of it!
Something must be done about it, now!   Watch your words!

For emphasis:
Of all things!   ...but, after all, we did it!
Just see what happened!   ...and that goes for them, too!

Exclamation in Question Form. An exclamation point, instead of a question mark, is used after an exclamation in question form.

It might end well, who knows!   What!
How could it be misunderstood!   Haven't they had enough!
What difference does it make!   Why not!

Polite or Satirical Emphasis. An exclamation point may be used to express contempt, irony, doubt, or amusement.

Quite!   Just so!   Not really!   How clever!
They referred the scholar to a tabloid! for information.

Sarcasm, disbelief, or surprise is sometimes expressed by an exclamation point enclosed in parentheses immediately after a word in the text.

The favored position (!) was the first in line.

Mild Exclamations. A comma or period, instead of an exclamation point, is often used after an expression of mild force or pleasant surprise.

Well, well, so that is what you thought.   Truly, we can't believe it.
But, alas, it can never be.   As if it mattered.

Other Exclamations. (Parenthetic, see pp. 246–47; quoted, p. 248.)

"O" and "Oh." "O" is used when persons or personified things are directly addressed.

O my friends!   O mighty land!   O Pioneers!

"O" is also used in expressions of plaintive hope or despair.

O the times!   O the manners!   O for a house by the sea!

259

"Oh" is the more common word and is used in practically all other instances.   It may be followed by a comma, exclamation point, or no mark.

Oh, my!   Oh what a life!   Oh, yes, we can!   Oh! Let it pass!

In mild expressions containing "oh," the exclamation point is not used.

Oh, we do not question their statement...
You think you can't afford a vacation; but, oh, why not?
Oh, what's the use?

Note that "O" has no apostrophe after it; is always capitalized; is never used alone; and is not separated from the following words by any mark of punctuation.

Note that "oh" is not capitalized unless it begins a sentence; and that it is usually followed by a comma.

Placement of Exclamation Point.   An exclamation point is placed immediately after the words that it describes or dramatizes—in the body of a sentence or at the end.

If in the body of a sentence, it needs no other punctuation mark to support it, except sometimes a dash; nor does it break the sentence sufficiently to require a capital letter after it.

Commas, semicolons, and colons are not usually used after inner exclamation points, although in rare instances they may be.

Imagine that! the only times they have been civil have been...
Absolutely incredible!—but what can we do?
When you hear "Forward, march!" chances are you will...
He was greeted with approving shouts of "Arriba! arriba!", a sort of "hurrah," when he quoted...
...gained fame for a novel, "Behold This Dreamer!", issued in 1924.

If the entire sentence is an exclamation, or if a series of words are exclamatory, the exclamation point is usually reserved for the final word.

My, how they laughed!   Ah, that mysterious wall!
Why, so it was, to be sure!   Thank goodness, they are safe!
It was the old, old story of "Going; going; gone!"

If the first words alone are exclamatory, the exclamation point is used immediately after them, and a period or question mark at the end of the sentence.

Too bad! too bad! we thought, but we could not remedy it.
Ah! then they haven't told?
Ho, ho, ho! That's funny, indeed.

Several exclamation points may appear in the same sentence.

If they cry "Wolf! Wolf!" once more, we'll annihilate them, so help us!
What a piece of work is man! how noble in reason! how infinite in faculty!... —Shakespeare, "Hamlet."

◇◇◇◇◇◇◇◇◇

APOSTROPHE

The apostrophe has four uses. It is used in forming
    Contractions of words and figures,
    Possessives,
    Plurals of letters, figures, and words used as words, and
    Verb forms of letters and unusual words.

Contractions. The omission of letters in words and word combinations is indicated by apostrophes. Make sure that the apostrophe is in the exact place of the omitted letters.

> isn't, 'tis, 'twasn't, where'er   NOT: *is'nt, t'is, 'twas'nt, wher'ere*

> **"Can't," "won't," and "shan't"** present the problem of having two places for the apostrophe. But only one apostrophe is used—between the **n** and the **t,** as in similar contractions.

Note that **a contraction is not an abbreviation.** It does not require a period. To use both an apostrophe and a period is double punctuation.

> NOTE: Abbreviations are preferred to contractions. See also p. 552.

NOT: *cont'd.*	*Corp'n.*	*Dep't.*	*Gov't.*	*Int'l.*	*Sec'y.*
BUT: cont'd	Corp'n	Dep't	Gov't	Int'l	Sec'y
BETTER: contd.	Corp.	Dept.	Govt.	Intl.	Secy.

Common Contractions—now widely used in business letters.

I'll, we'll, you'll, he'll
they'll, it'll, who'll
{ Colloquial shortenings of "will" and "shall"; but "I'll" and "we'll" are so common as no longer to be considered colloquial.

I'd, we'd, you'd, it'd,
they'd, he'd, who'd
{ Colloquial shortenings of "had," "would," and "should."

I've, we've, you've, it's, that's,
he's, who's, they've, who've
{ Shortenings of "have" and "has."

would've, could've, should've—are distinctly colloquial.

I'm, we're, you're, he's, it's, they're,
who's, that's, there's, here's, where's
{ Shortenings of "am," "is," and "are."

haven't, hasn't, needn't, can't, shan't
wouldn't, shouldn't, won't, don't
isn't, aren't, wasn't, weren't, doesn't
} Shortenings of "not."

Ain't is "illiterate."   **"Aren't I?"** is a Briticism—rare in America.

o'clock	is a contraction of "of the clock"
a 'copter	a helicopter
'tween decks	between decks
sou'wester	southwester
Let's	means "let us" (NOT: Let's *don't*...[see p. 82])
O'Neil	originally meant "of Neil"
M'Donald, M'Call	used for "MacDonald," "McCall," etc.

> "Sure an' 'tis a happy endin' now 'cause all's forgiven." (for dialect)

"Till," "O," and "round" are not contractions, but single words. No apostrophe should be used with them, as "till Christmas," "O Romeo!", "year-round," "round-the-clock."

cello, teens, phone,
plane, possum, ricksha,
varsity, Halloween
} are written now without an apostrophe. They have become known as words and have been forgotten as contractions.

Other Uses of Apostrophe. The apostrophe is also used to indicate

Omission of figures:	'49er	'30s	(See Numbers, p. 280)
Plurals of figures:	10's	20's	(See Numbers, p. 285)
Plurals of letters:	ABC's	t's	(See Abbreviations, p. 555)
Plurals of words:	if's and and's		(See Plurals, p. 140)
Addition of -ed or -ing:	comma'd off		(See Spelling, p. 135)
	X'd out, OK'ing		(See Abbreviations, p. 556)
Possessives:	Keats's	men's	(See Possessives, p. 145)

HYPHEN

No two authorities agree on the use of hyphens. Therefore, a writer must be guided by rules of usage in the matter of hyphening or eliminating hyphens and writing solid or separate words.

One-Thought Expressions. When two or more words have the force of one word, that is, convey a single thought, they are hyphened.

a ne'er-do-well	the know-how	stick-to-itiveness
in make-believe	Mr. So-and-So	go-it-aloneisms
will-o'-the-wisp	the four-o'clock	wait-and-see-itis
a drive-in	a lawyer-banker	up-to-dately made
a follow-up	the well-to-do	well-in-handish
by year-end	a free-for-all	cat-and-canary-like

One-Thought Modifiers Before Nouns. When two or more words have the force of a single modifier before a noun, they are hyphened.

a straight-from-the-shoulder talk	at such-and-such a time
a run-of-the-mill American	U.S.-owned ships
new, up-to-the-minute styles	an 8-to-5 choice
catch-as-catch-can methods	a gray-blue uniform*
a three-minute conversation	a would-be statesman
a frivolous-sensible manner	of Irish-French descent
an economy-within-reason law	the free-and-easy, first-
the old horse-and-buggy days	come, first-served type

* Two-color combinations are hyphened: red-yellow; a blue-green silk. But a color need not be hyphened when one part thereof modifies another: an orange red; a yellowish red; a bluish green sea; a bright red car; dark gray sky; navy blue suit. (BUT: an off-white satin)

Modifiers Before and After Nouns. Often when a one-thought modifier is transposed and placed **after a noun,** the construction is changed, giving the words their separate force, and no hyphen is needed.

BEFORE A NOUN	AFTER A NOUN
a well-known name*	a name well known
a two-hour-long debate	a debate two hours long
a so-called law	a law, so called because
the above-mentioned item	the item above mentioned
an ill-designed plan	a plan, ill designed but worthy
out-of-town shopping	shopping out of town

* In "a very well known name," "very" qualifies "well," thus destroying the unity between "well" and "known." Similarly: "large-sized envelopes" and "extra large sized envelopes," etc.

Also, when such an expression follows the noun and other words are added to connect the parts, no hyphen is needed.

BEFORE A NOUN	AFTER A NOUN
an up-to-date record	a record brought up to date
a first-class proposition	a proposition of the first class
a right-hand drive	the drive on the right hand
a rule-of-thumb calculation	a calculation by rule of thumb
the 800-meter race	a race of 800 meters
a coast-to-coast broadcast	a broadcast from coast to coast
their take-home pay	the amount they take home

But when such an expression follows the noun and still retains its force as a one-thought modifier, the hyphen is used.

BEFORE A NOUN	AFTER A NOUN
a hand-to-mouth existence	an existence that became hand-to-mouth
a first-class proposition	the proposition is not first-class
the dust-covered street	the street was dust-covered
a never-ending task	a task that seems never-ending
a tax-exempt bond	a dividend declared tax-exempt
an air-cooled engine	an engine that is air-cooled
a rust-gold color	a color almost rust-gold (OR: red-gold)

Compound Names as Modifiers. Proper compound names and, in business usage, many ordinary compound names retain their original forms when used as modifiers: if hyphened they retain the hyphen; if not hyphened no hyphen is added, they being naturally joined in the reader's mind.

Civil Service Commission	The Anglo-French pact
Post Office Department	Supreme Court decisions
Far Eastern customs	Postal Union mails

Compound ordinary names as modifiers:

income tax statements	high school students
civil service examinations	foreign exchange values
motion picture screens	night letter rates
real estate values	rural route deliveries
daylight saving time	safe deposit boxes
direct mail advertising	long distance calls

NOTE: Many printing establishments, following definite rules of style, hyphen these compound names when used as modifiers; but business usage very generally omits such hyphens so as to avoid getting too deep in the matter of hyphening.

Names of three or more words are usually hyphened as modifiers.

bill-of-lading forms	right-of-way grants	change-of-address cards
collect-on-delivery service	a public-utility-control setup	

Occasionally a proper name is hyphened, if joined in a three- or four-word modifier before a noun, to prevent misreading.

the White House-ruled Senate	OR:	the White-House-ruled Senate
Foreign Legion-Bent Soldiers		Foreign-Legion-Bent Soldiers
a Mardi Gras-like carnival		a Mardi-Gras-like carnival

Although more often the hyphens are unnecessary, as

the Federal Reserve banking methods

Adverb Ending in -ly Not Hyphened. An adverb ending in -ly is not hyphened to the word that follows, even though the two form a single idea. The -ly itself shows the relationship between the words, by indicating that the first modifies the second; therefore the hyphen seems superfluous. (But an **adjective ending in -ly** is hyphened.)

TEST: To determine -ly adjectives, try them alone before nouns.

Adverbs:	a publicly owned company	highly valued packages
NOT:	a *publicly-owned* company	*highly-valued* packages
Adjectives:	worldly-minded scholarly-sounding	homely-phrased

Verbs and Verb Forms Hyphened. Verbs composed of two or more words forming a single thought should be hyphened.

blue-pencil the drawing   double-spacing the copy
question-mark the points   if it is cross-referenced

But verbs are not hyphened to prepositions that follow them as adverbs, unless such combinations stand as nouns or adjectives.

As verbs:
set off such words (NOT: *set-off*) is marking up the price
turn down the page   has crossed off the names

As nouns:
a send-off a step-down a cross-out a tie-in
But not when only the first part is a noun (unless the combination has a special meaning—different from the ordinary sense).
the writing down of names the crossing off of figures
the writing-down of assets reckless cutting-in (driving)
the opening up of new fields the holding over of a play
the bringing-up of children the rounding out of the year

As adjectives:
built-in fixtures the hoped-for chance a crossed-out figure
start-up time a cooling-off period a marked-up price

When a noun is followed by an **-ing** word (a verbal noun), no hyphen is necessary, unless the combination is used as an adjective.

As nouns: a profit taking **As adjectives:** a profit-taking period
a price cutting   a price-cutting war
in map making   a map-making company
in letter writing   a letter-writing contest

Most **-ing, -ed, -d, -en, -n** words in compound modifiers are hyphened.

-ing: far-reaching	**-ed:** old-fashioned	**-en:** soft-spoken
ever-changing	following-described	weather-beaten
odd-looking	quick-witted, -ly	panic-stricken
long-suffering	left-handed, -ly	power-driven
fact-finding	air-minded	**-n:** full-blown
interest-bearing	Government-owned	half-grown

But if the preceding word ends in a **comparative -er or -est**, which in itself indicates the connection between the words, no hyphen is necessary (unless two meanings could apply).

a small-sized book	a smaller sized book
a high-priced car	the highest priced car
a slow-burning candle	a slower burning candle
a deep-toned voice	a deeper toned voice
a well-established firm	a better established firm
a well-informed man	the best informed people
a much-needed rest	the more convincing way (or most)

NOTE: Often an adverb is added that qualifies only the first word of a usually hyphened modifier, thus destroying the unity. No hyphen is then used, as "a **very slow** burning candle," "a **not too high** priced car," "an **unusually deep** toned voice," "the much-heralded (**too much** heralded, some said) event," "the often-heard [yes, **quite often** heard] lament." Occasionally the entire modifier is hyphened, as "a **none-too-even-tempered** man."

A hyphen to distinguish two meanings:

a better **burnished copper**	(a burnished copper that is better)
a better-burnished copper	(a copper that is better burnished)
the best **accepted usage**	(the accepted usage that is best)
NOT: the *best-accepted* usage	(meaning usage that is accepted best)
larger **stamped envelopes**	(stamped envelopes that are larger)
NOT: *larger-stamped* envelopes	(envelopes with larger stamps)

Words Grow Together or Apart. After long use the hyphen is often discarded. Words grow together or they grow apart.

"...the conversion of a hyphened word into an unhyphened single one is desirable as soon as the novelty of the combination has worn off, if there are no obstacles in the way of awkward spelling, obscurity, or the like."
—Fowler, *A Dictionary of Modern English Usage,* p. 244.

GROWN TOGETHER		GROWING TOGETHER		REMAINING APART	
airline	northwest	airmail	passbook	air conditioner	no one
airport, airfield	nowadays	briefcase	passersby	air travel	oil well
bookstore	offhand	bylaws	payroll	all right	plate glass
businessman	outtalk	bypass	percent	book end	post card
checkbook	postwar	byproduct	pipeline	box office	post office
checkup	proofread	Christmastime	prizefight	can opener	price list
counterclockwise	radioactive	fingertips	pushbutton	common sense	question mark
crosscut	seaboard	goodbye	secondhand	cross reference	real estate
deadline	semicircle	goodwill	shortcut	day labor	red tape
downtown	showdown	lineup	sidelights	dead weight	right of way*
fireproof	streamlined	looseleaf	sideline	dining room	safe deposit
groundwork	supermarket	loudspeaker	sidestep	drug store	sea level
headquarters	taxpayer	mailbox	sightseer	dry goods	side show
highlights	textbook	manpower	standby	fountain pen	so far as
homemade	timesaver	midafternoon	takeoff	good night	tank car
inasmuch as	timetable	midair	tieup	half past	tax rate
insofar as	transship	nationwide	trademark*	high school	time limit
interrelated	turnover	nearby	underway	ice cream	title page
layout	update	nonetheless	waterfront	ill will	trade name
letterhead	waterproof	nonnuclear	weekend	income tax	vice president
nevertheless	widespread	officeholder	westbound	mail order	water power
nonnegotiable	wildlife	overall	worldwide	motion picture	wave length
nonstop	yearbook	paperwork	worthwhile	night club	wrist watch

*"Trademark" is now solid, and "right-of-way" is hyphened, in all Government publications.

Some words have difficulty in settling down to a permanent form. The word "cooperate" is still seen in its three stages of evolution:

co-operate   coöperate   cooperate

but **co-operate** (indicating pronunciation) is now favored by many.

265

Three Stages of Transition. Similar words (or the same word) may be seen in any one of three forms: as two words; hyphened; or as a single word.

ONE WORD	HYPHENED	TWO WORDS
blueprint	blue-blood	blue book
courthouse	boarding-house	clearing house
crossroad	cross-examination	cross section
handwork	metal-work	road work
horsepower	horse-hour	horse race
midwinter	mid-August	mid air
postmark	post-box	post office
schoolhouse	road-house	bond house
steppingstone	stepping-stone	stepping stone
tinware	tin-plate	tin can, tin foil
windshield	wind-drift	wind force

"Suspending" Hyphens. Suspending hyphens should be used in a series of hyphened words having a common ending, or beginning.

long- and short-term notes   one-, two-, and three-year stays
...expects a four- to five-million-barrel-a-day output.
a grooved ring in circular-, pear-, or heart-shaped form
on a 120- or 130-inch wheelbase   BUT: wheelbase of 120 or 130 inches
for 8- and 10-cu.ft. models   in 1st-, 2nd-, and 3rd-class
French- and Spanish-speaking provinces   a chart- or map-maker
between a well- and an ill-sounding verse
twenty-six or -seven   a family-owned and -managed business

Some writers drop suspending hyphens in common expressions, such as "five and ten-dollar bills"; still, it seems better to use them consistently to avoid misreadings.

Words should be repeated if a part does not naturally carry over.

NOT: Was it "tax-exempt" or "*-deductible*"?   (USE: tax-deductible)
NOT: . . . building a high-rise and *-rate* hotel.   (USE: high-rate)

Solid words are not often separated, although they may be.

eastbound or westbound   OR: east- or westbound
intrastate and interstate rates   intra- and interstate rates

Spelling, Stammering, or Repeating. Hyphens may indicate these.

d-e-u-c-e   X-E-R-O-X   S-r-i L-a-n-k-a   (2 spaces between words)
S-s-s-surprise!   Wha-wha-what?   No-no-no!

Hyphening Prefixes and Suffixes. A different meaning may be conveyed by setting a prefix or suffix off with a hyphen.

recover the loss   BUT: re-cover the furniture
recount a tale   re-count the votes
reform a youth   re-form the bylaws
city sewers   home sew-ers
a fruitless search   a fruit-less diet
prayers   pray-ers

To avoid the doubling or tripling of letters, prefixes and suffixes may be set off with hyphens.

re-employ   pre-establish   shell-like   heel-less

Unusual Words Formed With Prefixes. Prefixes are hyphened to **unusual** words, and to words beginning with **capitals** or **numbers**.

anti-open-shop	intra-industry	pre-1970	semi-invalid
co-worker	non-euphonious	pro-inflation	sub-Asia
inter-American	post-prosperity	pseudo-pious	un-actorish

Familiar words with prefixes (except **ex-, self-,** and **quasi-**) are written solid.

anticlimax	noncommissioned	prehistoric	pseudoclassic
coauthor	postgraduate	preschool-age	semiannual

Ex- ("former") is hyphened (p. 268): ex-U.S. judge ex-serviceman

Quasi- (meaning "seemingly but not wholly") is hyphened: quasi-official
quasi-judicial quasi-legal quasi-comic quasi-corporation

Self- is hyphened: self-explanatory self-evident non-self-governing
self-conscious (EXCEPTIONS: unselfconscious, selfhood, selfless, selfsame)

NOTE: "Self-addressed" is a correct form, and is so given in dictionaries. The term "self-addressed envelope" has been disputed by some (thinking it means an envelope that has addressed itself); but "self" here means "to or for oneself." (Often just **"addressed"** or **"return"** is sufficient.)

If a prefix is added to a two-or-more-word expression, **the entire** combination may be hyphened to preclude a misreading.

anti-Red-Rule	a semi-American-citizen
(RATHER THAN: anti-Red Rule)	(NOT: a *semi-American* citizen)
pre-Flag-Day ceremonies	a semi-well-wisher
pre-World-War II commerce	the mid-Twentieth-Century **fair**
a pro-National-Republic man	the ex-Air-Force chief
a pseudo-East-Indian art	non-civil-service examinations

MISLEADING: The style goes back to pre-Henry the Eighth days...
CLEARER: The style goes back to pre-Henry-the-Eighth days...

Or if such a combination would be confusing, the prefix may **stand** one space away from the first word.

a pro- ex-Mayor candidate   an ex- G.O.P.
Note the difference between: anti- war demonstrations, anti-war demonstrations, and anti-war-demonstrations (the last form being ambiguous).

Hyphening Long Double Names. Two familiar long names, each of two words or more, are often joined with a single hyphen (or "en dash").

San Francisco–New York flight	public works–industries control bill
Great Britain–South Africa affair	G.K.T.–Union Corporation stock

Two unfamiliar long names should not be hyphened. Rather, **the** construction should be changed.

OBSCURE: A Republic of Cuba–Isle of Pines agreement...
IMPROVED: An agreement between the Republic of Cuba and the Isle...

Capitalization in Hyphened Words. (See p. 130.)
Numbers Hyphened.   (See pp. 277–86.)
Abbreviations Hyphened.   (See p. 556.)

Civil and Military Titles.

"Do not hyphen a civil or military title denoting a single office..."

—United States Government Printing Office Style Manual.

CIVIL TITLES

Ambassador at Large	Consul General	President General
Assistant Secretary	Deputy Commissioner	Purchasing Agent
Attorney at Law	Director in Charge	Secretary General
Attorney General	Editor in Chief	Secretary of State
Chief Clerk	General Manager	Sergeant at Arms
Chief Engineer	Governor General	Under Secretary
Chief Justice	Lieutenant Governor	Vice Chairman
Chief of Police	Managing Editor	Vice Consul
Congressman at Large	Postmaster General	Vice President

MILITARY AND NAVAL TITLES

Adjutant General	Lieutenant Colonel
Brigadier General	Lieutenant Commander
Chief of Staff	Lieutenant General
Commander in Chief	Major General
Fleet Admiral	Quartermaster General
General of the Army (or Air Force)	Rear Admiral
Inspector General	Surgeon General
Judge Advocate General	Vice Admiral

If a title represents two offices, it is hyphened.

Secretary-Treasurer   Auditor-Treasurer

Ex- and -elect are hyphened to titles; and titles of two or more words are hyphened in these combinations.

ex-President, ex-Vice-President   President-elect
ex-Editor-in-Chief   Vice-President-elect
ex-Governor-General   Lieutenant-Governor-elect

Designations of offices are hyphened.

the vice-presidency   vice-presidential duties   the chief-clerkship

Foreign Phrases.

It is unnecessary to hyphen a foreign or Latin phrase, even when it is used as a modifier before a noun. Such a phrase is distinct and will be interpreted as one expression without hyphening.

prima facie evidence   per diem employees
bona fide agreements   ex officio member
a bon voyage gift   an ex parte hearing

Letters.

Letters used to designate shapes or abbreviations are usually hyphened to words to form nouns—and always to form adjectives. Do not quote the letters, as *"I"* beam; nor spell them out, as *el, eye, ess, tee, wye*—because the letter itself may represent the **actual shape.**

NOUNS			ADJECTIVES
an A-bomb	an H-bomb	a T-square	E-shaped
an A-frame	an I-beam	a U-turn	S-curved
a C-spring	an L-desk	the V-sign	V-necked
a G-man	a T-bone	an X-ray	Y-connected

268

Regarding the Use of Hyphens. Misplacement or omission of a hyphen can completely change a meaning.

NOT: lighter than *air-craft*	BUT: lighter-than-air craft
tenement *house-act*	tenement-house act
a forest *fire-lighter*	a forest-fire lighter
check-and-double check service	check-and-double-check service
slow *motion-pictures*	slow-motion pictures
ten dollar bills	ten-dollar bills
a lot of *little used* cars	a lot of little-used cars
saw *no parking* signs	saw no-parking signs
the rich *girl-barber's* romance	the rich-girl-barber's romance
for her *father* and mother-in-law	for her father- and mother-in-law
poor *mud and thatched* villages	poor mud-and-thatched villages
in *wheat and cattle-raising* states	in wheat-and-cattle-raising states
	OR: in wheat- and cattle-raising

Do not drop a necessary hyphen at the end of a line. Such omitted hyphens often make the reader read twice to get the meaning.

NOT: ...they will score good sized gains.	BUT: ...they will score good-sized gains.
It means a long drawn out process.	It means a long-drawn-out process.
...will buy 30 or 60 day paper.	...will buy 30- or 60-day paper.

◇◇◇◇◇◇◇◇◇

DIVISION OF WORDS

Words are divided only between syllables. In the dictionary, follow the **boldface-entry syllabications,** not the parenthetic.

Division According to Syllables. The following words illustrate the method of division between syllables:

	NOT:			NOT:
anx- ious	*an- xious*	knowl- edge		*know- ledge*
di- shevel	*dis- hevel*	mon- eyed		*money- ed*
dis- organize	*disorg- anize*	morn- ing		*mor- ning*
di- vided	*divi- ded*	occa- sion		*occas- ion*
eight- een	*eigh- teen*	privi- lege		*privil- ege*
eve- ning	*even- ing*	prob- ably		*pro- bably*
for- tune	*fort- une*	repu- table		*reput- able*
fur- nished	*furn- ished*	sci- ence		*scien- ce*
han- dled	*hand- led*	trav- eled		*tra- veled*
hin- drance	*hind- rance*	un- equaled		*uneq- ualed*
illus- trate	*illust- rate*	wrin- kling		*wrink- ling*

Note the difference in the division of noun and verb forms, as (n.) prod- uce, and (v.) pro- duce.

Dictionaries sometimes differ.

ONE GIVES: assist- ance	ANOTHER: assis- tance
attend- ance	atten- dance
preced- ence	prece- dence
stand- ard	stan- dard

AMERICAN USAGE		BRITISH USAGE	
foun- tain	pos- sible	fount- ain	poss- ible
impor- tant	prog- ress	import- ant	pro- gress
pas- sage	tes- timony	pass- age	test- imony

Doubled Letters. Words are usually divided between doubled consonants.

clas- sic	mes- sage	cor- rect	neces- sary	accom- modate
mas- sive	mil- lion	war- rant	puz- zled	recom- mend

When the final letter is doubled because of an added -ing, -ed, -er, -est, -ence, -able, etc., the division is between the doubled letters, to preserve the appearance of the original word.

stop- ping	NOT:	*stopp- ing*	omit- ted	NOT:	*omitt- ed*
begin- ning		*beginn- ing*	hid- den		*hidd- en*
occur- rence		*occurr- ence*	thin- nest		*thinn- est*
regret- table		*regrett- able*	bid- der		*bidd- er*

But if the word itself ends in a doubled letter, the original form is preserved (with a few exceptions, as instal- lation).

pass- ing	full- er	refill- able	forestall- ing	buzz- ing
NOT: *pas- sing*	*ful- ler*	*refil- lable*	*forestal- ling*	*buz- zing*

Vowels. Divide on a single vowel forming a syllable within a word. And divide between two vowels separately pronounced.

sepa- rate	tele- vision	criti- cism	pano- ramic	particu- lar
cre- ation	deteri- orate	situ- ation	radi- ator	insinu- ate

One-Syllable Words. These words cannot, of course, be divided.

freight	thought	width	strength	friend	chasm
height	church	breathe	through	scheme	tongue

Note that many words remain but one syllable after taking -ed:

billed	named	shipped	trumped	occurred (2 syl.)
asked	drowned	stopped	weighed	preferred (2 syl.)

Prefixes and Suffixes. Divide, if possible, on a prefix or suffix.

anti-, dis-, inter-, mis-, non-, over-, per-, pro-, semi-, sub-, trans-
-cally, -ceous, -cial, -cient, -cion, -cious, -geous, -gion, -gious, -ment, -ness, -scious, -sial, -sion, -tial, -tion, -tious, -tive, -ture

NOTE: -able and -ible are usually carried over; but occasionally the a or i forms a syllable with a preceding letter, as

capa- ble	dura- ble	comprehensi- ble	permissi- ble

Dividing One or Two Letters. Do not divide on a single letter; and in most instances, do not divide on two letters. Two-letter prefixes are sometimes divided, but usually not two-letter endings.

ad- bi- by- co- de- en- ex- im- in- ir- re- un- up-
BUT NOT: -al -cy -ed -ee -en -er -es -fy -ic -ly -ry -ty

Short words should not be divided, as

mon- ey	*ev- ery*	*aft- er*	*up- on*	*on- ly*	*wa- ter*

Hyphened Words. Divide hyphened words only at the hyphens.

...in the above- mentioned book.	NOT:	...in the *above-men- tioned* book.

Contractions.   Do not divide contractions, such as

haven't	doesn't	wasn't	shouldn't

Proper Names.   Although proper names are divided in printing, they should not be divided in typewriting if it can be avoided.

WRITE:	NOT:
. . . . Theodore	. . . . Theodore Wil-
Wilson.	son. . . . .
. . . . Billings,	. . . . Bill-
Montana. . .ˑ. . . .	ings, Montana. . . . . . .
. . . . to	. . . . :. to St.
St. Louis.	Louis. . . . .
. . . . on Wednesday	. . . . on Wednes-
morning.	day morning.
. . . . R. B. Hill,	. . . . R. B. Hill, Pres-
President.	ident. . . . .

Initials should not be separated from each other, and preferably not from the surname.

Degree or other letters after a name should not be separated from each other, and preferably not from the surname; yet if they are long, there is often no other choice than to separate them from the name.

"Mr.," "Dr.," "Rev.," "Sr.," "Jr.," "Esq.," etc., should preferably not be separated from surnames, but occasionally this is necessary.

WRITE:	NOT:
. . . . Superintendent	. . . . Superintendent J.
J. B. Martin.	B. Martin.
. . . . . Baldwin M. Blaine,	. . . . Baldwin M. Blaine, Ph.
Ph.D., LL.D.,.	D., LL.D.,. . . . .
. . . . . . Wm. Mansford, Jr.	. . . . Wm. Mansford,
. . . .	Jr. . . . .
. . . . for	. . . . for Mr.
Mr. Leland.	Leland.

Figures, Abbreviations, and Dates.   Never divide figures or abbreviations; nor separate signs, letters, or short abbreviations from that to which they apply. (Publications sometimes make such divisions to "justify" [even] the lines.)

WRITE:	NOT:
. . . . $500,126	. . . . $500,-
. . . .	126. . . . .
. . . . 4:20 p.m.	. . . . 4:20
. . . .	p.m. . . . .
. . . . 36 deg. F.	. . . . 36 deg.
. . . .	F. . . . .
(a).	. . . . (a) . ᵗ . . . . (b)
(b). . . . . (c).	. . . . (c)
Divide after a dash --	Newspapers often divide
not before one.	—before a dash.

Divide dates between day and year, not between month and day.

. . . . February 14,	NOT: . . . . February
1965.	14, 1965. . . . . .

Foreign Words. Do not divide foreign words unless they are familiar enough to have become a part of the English language. Then divide according to pronunciation.

Last Word in a Paragraph, and Last Word on a Page. Do not divide the last word in a paragraph. To do so leaves but a portion of a word for the last line, which is not an effective ending.

Do not divide the last word on a page and carry a portion over to the next page. This is sometimes done in printing to fill out lines; but in typewriting it is unnecessary and should not be practiced.

Consecutive Divided Endings. Do not allow more than two consecutive lines to end in word divisions. Divided words are hard to follow; and too many divided words on a page produce a choppy effect.

◇◆◇◆◇◆◇◆◇

DIACRITICAL MARKS

Diacritical marks are carried on some foreign words. But before using any unfamiliar mark, consult the dictionary.

Put all accent marks in by hand, with pencil or ink. The pencil mark blends naturally with the typewritten letter, but ink is more lasting.

Accents and Markings.

French :   **As in :**

Acute	é	Champs Élysées, résumé, visé
Grave	à è ù	mise en scène, vis-à-vis
Circumflex	â ê î ô û	tête-à-tête, maître d'hôtel
Dieresis	ë ï ü	naïveté, Noël
Cedilla	ç (a comma on c)	garçon (ç denotes an s sound)
Apostrophe	(denotes omission of letters)	chargé d'affaires, entr'acte

Spanish :

Acute	á é í ó ú	Sí, compañía

(indicates a stress of the syllable, not a change in vowel sound)

Crema	ü	

(indicates that u is to be pronounced)

Tilde	ñ	Señor, cañon, doña

(indicates a special pronunciation of n, similar to ny in English)

Italian :

Grave	à è ì ò ù	capacità, abilità

(indicates a stress of the syllable, not a change in vowel sound)

German :

Umlaut	ä ö ü	Götterdämmerung, Walküre (ö is often expressed by oe, as in Goethe, Roentgen, etc.)

English :

Dieresis ·· over a second vowel indicates that the vowels are to be pronounced separately.

coördination   reënter   preëmpt   zoölogical

    In printing, it often replaces a hyphen. In typewriting, the hyphen is usually used; or if the word is familiar, it is written solid, without markings.

Grave ` indicates that the syllable is to be pronounced separately.

belovèd   learnèd   agèd   blessèd   wingèd

◇◆◇◆◇◆◇◆◇

ASTERISK

Footnote Indicators. A reference mark in a text is placed **after a word,** not before it (but not after a possessive word). In printing, reference marks are, for symmetry, placed after any and all immediate marks of punctuation except the dash or a closing parenthesis or bracket if the mark applies only to matter within the parentheses or brackets.

They cited a quotation from the "Official Bulletin,"* and it was...
It is a sort of office daily—house organ*—which all are expected to read.
...adopted by France, England, and Germany (the "key countries"*).

In printing, these signs are used in this sequence:

* (asterisk or star)   † (dagger)   ‡ (double dagger)   § (section mark)
‖ (parallels)   ¶ (paragraph sign)   ° (degree sign)   √ (radical sign)
     If more marks are needed, these may be doubled in the same sequence:
**, ††, ‡‡, §§, although other single symbols are clearer.

In typewriting, not more than three asterisks should be used to indicate footnotes (*, **, ***); some other mark should then be used. Several other footnote reference marks may be made on the typewriter:

dagger (a slant with a hyphen struck over it)	⁄
double dagger (a slant with two hyphens struck over it)	≠
section mark (two small s's, one slightly above other)	§
parallels (depress space bar, strike slant; backspace, strike slant)	∥
paragraph sign (depress space bar and strike small l; release bar; backspace and strike capital P)	¶
Greek phi and theta (depress space bar to superimpose)	∅ θ
star (a small v with a capital A struck over)	⋀
cross (a single raised x or a double x)	✖
flower (depress space bar, strike asterisk over capital Q)	✿
tree (depress space bar, strike asterisk over capital I)	✦

CAUTION: Do not use as indicators signs that have other meanings, as #, %, and @, unless in a text where they could not be misconstrued.

Superior (raised) figures or letters may be used if they are not likely to be confusing. The Government writes them on a "shelf": 1/ or a/.

France,[1]...England;[2]...   Or letters with figures: 1342,[a]...2978[b]
Government usage: Gold 1/   Fund 2/   or   1950 a/   1960 b/
     In the footnotes: 1/ Gold certificates.   or   a/ Revised list.

In tabulations the indicator is placed **after** that to which it refers. But if two sets of indicators are used, one set may be **before** the words.

April*   Silver[1,2,3]   Gold 2/
Spain*†   or   *Spain†   1960[a]   a/ 1965*

Footnotes. In footnotes, symbols should be set (alined on the right) one space before the first words. (See also pp. 420k and 436.)

          * Formerly the capital   ** "Parish" (county)

A footnote should be on the same page as its indicator, not one or two pages later (except in tables). (See also Copy for the Press, p. 436.)

Headnote Indicators. A "headnote indicator" may be an asterisk or other mark which refers the reader to a headnote instead of a footnote.

NATIONALITIES
(Nations not using a Latin alphabet are marked *)
Chilean   *Korean
*Chinese   Colombian[1]

◇◇◇◇◇◇◇◇◇

SLANT LINE (VIRGULE)

In tabulation headings and in abbreviations, a diagonal line, often called a "slant" or a "**shilling mark,**" may indicate an omission of words.

barrels/day   for   barrels per day   an L/C   for   letter of credit

Interchangeable words may be indicated by a slant. Slants may also separate "**run-in**" **lines** (those not set apart) of poetry, titles, etc.:

and/or......shipper/seller   And envy him/ His calm repose.

◇◇◇◇◇◇◇◇◇

OMISSIONS

Omission of Words or Sentences (Ellipsis). Three dots ("points") are usually used to denote the omission of words in a quoted sentence. A fourth period, or a question mark or exclamation point, may be added to indicate the end of a sentence, if this is deemed necessary.

The pact specifically stated: "...and we will refrain from action...."
"Prints..., mailed by publishers or news dealers, ...must be..."
The spice of life is battle...—Stevenson.

Three spaced dots or asterisks may indicate the omission of entire sentences. In poetry, several spaced dots indicate a missing line.

"There is a time when no thing seems worthwhile.
. . .   And that is the key to the situation."

Suspension Dots or Points. Three dots are sometimes used—especially in advertising copy—to replace other marks of punctuation, particularly the dash. They tend to retard the sentence and hold the reader's attention on the context.

This is a particular series...particular in that it is directed toward a special market...a market that is on the march.
The machines are used for proofing...for imprinting...for duplicating...for addressing...for filling in...for listing.

Unfinished Sentences. Three dashes are used to denote an unfinished sentence, or one in which the thought or speech falters and breaks off, or turns sharply. (In printing, only one long dash is used.)

That cannot happen unless- - -but of course it might.

Unprintable Words. Three asterisks are used to indicate unprintable words in a quotation or a text.

He said ***—what he thought.
...wrote: "Paid, if the *** thing sticks."

Omission of Paragraphs. Three or four spaced asterisks may be used to indicate the omission of paragraphs in copied work.

* * *

Change of Subject Matter. A row of four hyphens may be used to indicate a break between two subjects. (In printing, often an ornament, a swung dash, or three large dots ["bullets"] are used.)

– – – –   or   ● ● ●   or   ⌒   or   ✄

End of Manuscript. The end of a manuscript may be indicated by

– – –oOo– – –   or   *.*.*   or   # # # (printers' mark)

◇◇◇◇◇◇◇◇◇

UNDERSCORE

Underline headings with an unbroken line.

Underline parts of the text with an unbroken line, unless some words or parts are to be emphasized separately, in which case break the line at the spaces. Do not underline **beginning** or **ending** punctuation.

Delivery will be made soon ("not later than Monday, June 20").
Temperature at the airport registered 95°F. or 35°C.

◇◇◇◇◇◇◇◇◇

TYPEWRITER SPACINGS

The following typewriter spacings are used in connection with **the** various marks of punctuation:

period	two spaces* (three, with elite type) after each.
question mark exclamation point }	two spaces* (three, with elite type) after each; one space after each within a sentence.
comma, semicolon abbreviation period }	one space after each.
colon	two spaces after each.
dash	one space on each side. (See also p. 245.)
parentheses	one space before the first parenthesis and one after the last, but no spaces between parentheses and the words enclosed.
quotation marks	spacings are governed by the accompanying marks of punctuation. No spaces between quotes and the words they enclose, nor between final quotes and other punctuation marks—except dashes.

* Two spaces are usually specified in schools to promote speed; but three spaces are often used by experienced secretaries to make each sentence more distinct, more readable—especially with elite type where spaces are small. Three spaces are, in a way, a luxury to the eye, just as fine paper is to the touch.

In printing, various spaces (thin and thick) are used after periods. But printers are sometimes warned against too little space between sentences, as in an authoritative text on printing:

"While there may be some esthetic advantage to be gained from this close spacing, it leaves little chance for the reader to group words that belong together. Educators voice the objection that this practice is helping to break down students' notion of the integrity of the sentence. A little more open spacing between sentences in textbooks and books of reference is generally to be preferred."
—*Words Into Type*, by Skillin, Gay, et al; p. 110.
Copyright, 1948, Appleton-Century-Crofts, Inc.

◇◇◇◇◇◇◇◇◇

BRACKETS

Brackets are used around remarks inserted by a writer when quoting another writer or text, or reporting a procedure. The words so enclosed are entirely separate from the rest of the sentence in the matter of punctuation and construction.

The first word in the insertion is not capitalized unless it begins a separate sentence or is a proper name. No break in the quotes is necessary for the insertion of a bracketed statement.

Typewritten brackets are made with "slants" and underscores: [ ]

"Since that time [1859] the right of agents to use..."
...said that it was "characterized [by solemn "critics"] in the press as 'stupendous'."

Q. You said the document was a poem? [Laughter.]
A. Yes, it seems to be. [Reads:]
Q. You call that poetry [laughter]; then explain it.

If the year or name of a city has been omitted in a date line and is inserted by the one copying the manuscript, brackets should be used around the insertion.

[New Orleans] May 5 [1971]

"Sic" in Brackets. (See p. 432.)
Brackets With Parentheses. (See p. 247.)

◇◇◇◇◇◇◇◇◇

BRACE

Braces may be used before, after, above, or below items that are grouped—hence may be vertical or horizontal. The point is turned toward the fewer number of lines or the smaller group. If the lines are equal in number, a vertical brace points toward the right.

curved
("old style") $\left\{ \begin{array}{l} \text{May be} \\ \text{drawn in} \\ \text{or typed.} \end{array} \right\}$ OR: $\overbrace{\underbrace{\hspace{3cm}}}$ straight ("modern")

◇◇◇◇◇◇◇◇◇

PERIOD

Abbreviation Periods. An abbreviation period at the end of a sentence also serves as the sentence period. (See also p. 552.)

Period After Sentences. No sentence should be left "open," that is, with no punctuation, unless it is segregated as a title, heading, or part of a tabulation.

An expression does not necessarily need a subject or verb in order to be followed by a period, question mark, or exclamation point.

Important, if true.   More of that later.
Bare facts, nothing more.   Not to mention other things
Some good; some bad.   After that—what?
Not in the past, not in the future, and not now!

Numbers

When to Use Figures, and When to Use Words. In modern business practice very few numbers are written out. Almost every number that is used is inserted for quick reference or calculation; hence it is in a form to catch the eye.

All definite numbers above ten should be in figures—and below ten, if given for quick reference. (For ordinal numbers, see p. 287.)

It is in 24 volumes.	...27¢ each...at 6%...weighing 8 lbs.
We will ship 7 cases.	...for 2 years 5 months and 19 days.
...in 20 to 30 days.	...charged $1 for 5 months.

NOTE: Always use figures with abbreviations, as 6 in., 8 cu.ft., Fig. 3; not *six* in., *eight* cu.ft., Fig. *Three*.

Indefinite or approximate numbers are often written out; but if a ready calculation of them is necessary, they may be in figures.

	OR:	
about sixteen hundred tons		about 1600 tons
sold more than sixty houses		about 60 lots
some twenty-odd years ago		250-odd pages
a fifty-fifty proposition		will split 50–50
ten or twenty years ago		10 or 20 pieces
lost nearly a thousand dollars		almost $1000

At the beginning of a sentence, numbers are usually spelled out if they are short; but if long, they may be written in numerals to avoid a cumbersome lot of words. (Many examples in expensive advertising.)

Seventy crates, 12 bundles, and 42 cartons were...
Twenty-five to thirty barrels will be sent.
1926 saw...—Prof. W. E. Atkins, "Gold and Your Money," p. 126.
33,612 miles in 5 months is...—Ford Motor Company advertisement.

If two sets of figures occur in a sentence, one set may be spelled out to differentiate it from the other.

Only three wells were producing 2000 barrels each; twenty-five were producing 1000 each; and sixty were pumping about 100 barrels each.

When two numbers occur together, a comma or dash is used to separate them. Or one of the numbers may be spelled out.

In 1968, 25 million barrels were...	We ordered 350 – 50 of
Instead of 5, 25 were necessary.	which are to be bound.

Note that "million," "billion," and occasionally "thousand" (or "K" [for kilo])—but not "hundred"—may be used after a **round number** to avoid many ciphers and afford a quick interpretation of the number.

5 million	$3.6 billion	8⅗ millions	a $50 million fortune
76 billion pieces of mail	$½ billion		a 35-million-acre tract

$35 to $50 thousand	USUAL:	$35,000 to $50,000
NOT: 5 to 8 *hundred* pounds	BUT:	500 to 800 pounds

Numbers in legal papers are now commonly written only in figures. (See Legal Papers, p. 476.)

If two numbers form one item, one number, usually the first, is spelled· out.

four 6-inch frames	ten 5¢ stamps	eight 5-gallon cans
six ⅜-inch boards	two $1 bills	five 3-way switches

But if the second number is the shorter, it may be spelled out instead:

85 five-cent stamps	20 one-dollar bills	269 five-gallon tins

In tabulations two spaces or a spaced dash separates such numbers.

12 5″ pipes	160 4-in. slots	6 – ⅜″ boards
	(See also p. 413.)	

Commas Separating Thousands From Hundreds. Do not run figures together in a long number without the necessary dividing commas. Long undivided numbers are very hard to read.

Write all numbers above 10,000 with commas, as 1,324,576 instead of 1324576—even in tabulations, unless spaces are left to indicate commas.

The even hundred numbers below 10,000 may be written with or without commas, as 9500, 4200; but when used with other numbers below 10,000, all usually have commas, as 9,500, 9,568, 4,200, 4,234— unless they are in tabulations. If written in succession as the foregoing are, two spaces instead of one should be left between the numbers.

Serial numbers, such as insurance numbers and motor numbers, are printed without commas; but good authorities use commas or **spaces** when rewriting these numbers.

Patent numbers are printed with commas, as "Patent No. 2,674,813."

Numbers having no commas are: year, page, form, style, list, room, house or street, post office box, Zip Code, and telephone.

Decimals and most **large fractions** have no commas (see pp. 284–85). A comma is not necessary between the thousands and hundreds when a number is written out.

> Nine hundred and eighty-five thousand seven hundred and thirty-two.
> ("And" may be used or omitted. It is used by many authorities.)
> ...sixteen hundred twenty-five items.

Hyphening Written-Out Numbers. Note that numbers below one hundred are hyphened when written out, but that the hundreds and thousands are not hyphened, unless in a modifier before a noun.

twenty-five	forty-three	seventy-six
fifty-five hundred	eight hundred	three thousand
five hundred thousand	one hundred million	sixty-two million
NOT: *four-hundred*	*seven-hundred-thousand*	*six-hundred* feet below
BUT: a six-hundred-foot drop		20-million-year-old mosses

> ...in the year of..., and of the independence of the United States of America the one hundred and seventy-ninth.
> BUT: our one-hundred-and-thirty-second report; the 50-millionth phone

Dollars. When an even amount of money is written in the text, the decimal point and ciphers are usually omitted.

$7 $35 $750 $35,955   FOR EXACTNESS: $7.00 $76,875.00
...a $0.00 balance   (meaning a zero-zero balance)

The dollar sign is used before definite numbers, rather than the word "dollar" or "dollars" after the numbers.

a $20 bill   RATHER THAN: a 20-dollar bill, or a twenty-dollar bill
an $85-a-week fee   NOT: an eighty-five-dollar-a-week fee
a $100,000 project   a $6 million outlay   OR: a six-million-dollar...
$20½ million   OR: twenty and one-half million dollars (indefinite)
a million-dollar profit   about ten thousand dollars' worth (indefinite)

The dollar sign should be repeated before numbers in succession.

at $75, $154, $196, and $200   NOT: at $75, 154, 196, and 200
$10–$20   NOT: 10–$20   NOR: $10–20
between $15 and $20
$10 to $20   OR: ten to twenty dollars (indefinite)
a $10 or $20 fine   OR: a ten- or twenty-dollar fine (indefinite)

(For $ and ¢ in columns of **tabulations,** see pp. 288 and 417.)

Cents. In ordinary business papers and in advertising, the **cent sign** is used after amounts less than one dollar. "Cts." is seldom used because it is almost as long as "cents." In printing, **"cents" is spelled out;** but in financial writings, often just "c" is used.

BUSINESS USAGE: 35¢   2¢   10¢
PRINTING USAGE: 35 cents   two cents   ten cents

The dollar sign is not ordinarily used with cents alone, as $0.65, unless it is in statistical work or tabulations, or unless the cents are in three or four figures, as $0.4567.

Never write ".75¢" or ".75 cents" unless it is intended. This would mean $^{75}/_{100}$ of a cent. Write "75¢" or "75 cents."

Some ways of writing cents are:

at 75¢ a pound   @ 75¢/lb   a price of 95¢
$0.7535 an ounce
50¢ to 60¢   50 to 60 cents
a 6¢ tax   a 6-cent tax   a six-cent tax
a 5¢-a-pound increase   a five-cent-a-pound increase
an 18¢-an-hour raise   an 18-cent-an-hour raise
(Note the use of the **singular "cent"** in the modifying forms.)

Prices Written Out. Prices are usually written in words as well as figures in legal documents; also in some quotations in which the prices are firm. A series or list of prices is written in figures only.

Approximate prices are written in figures only.

The parenthesis containing the figures should be written after the word "Dollars," because a parenthesis can sum up only what has been written before it begins. Capitalization follows legal usage in prices.

The price is Fourteen Hundred and Sixty-five Dollars ($1465.00).
...price is Four Thousand Five Hundred and One Dollars ($4,501.00).

The word "and" is usually written before the numbers below one hundred in prices; but on checks, notes, etc., it is generally omitted. Therefore, if a writer desires not to use this "and," he may omit it.

> The price is Five Hundred Fifty-six and $^{75}\!/_{100}$ Dollars ($556.75) each, f.o.b. Chicago, Illinois.

Prices in texts are often set apart and indented in order to be quickly seen.

Double-check every written-out price to make sure that the words and figures agree. Many discrepancies occur between these two sets of numbers. Type carefully so that no erasures will be necessary in the figures of a price or in the written-out form.

Terms of Payment. Terms of payment are now usually written in figures only. And for definiteness, the percent sign is repeated down the column.

> 10% – 10 days after date of order
> 25% – 30 days   "   "   "   "
> 30% – 2 months "   "   "   "
> 35% – upon completion of contract.

Street Numbers. (See p. 339.)

Dates. It is unnecessary to use -st, -nd, -rd, -d, or -th in dates unless the day is written before, or is separated from, the month.

> On January 20, 1973, the...   In the May 28 issue...
> BUT: On the 20th of January 1973, the...   ...from June 2 to 23.
> ...by the 1st or 10th of July.   May 5 to July 15, 1972
>
> Note the distinction between:
>
> the first of the month (corresponding to the last of the month)
> the 1st of the month (meaning the first day of the month)

Do not abbreviate a date in a text, as 1/7/74, 1–7–74, or 01–07–74, unless it is in tabulated or statistical work.

Armed Forces and Foreign Dates. (See p. 291.)

Dates Written Out. Dates are written out only in the most formal legal documents, such as wills. Note that A.D. (meaning "in the year of our Lord") is placed before the year, not after it, and is not followed by a comma. And the numbers in the year are not capitalized. (See also "A.D." and "B.C.," pp. 558 and 559.)

> ...this twentieth day of May, A.D. nineteen hundred and seventy-two.
> ULTRA FORMAL: ...in the year of our Lord one thousand nine hundred and seventy-two.   (or nineteen hundred and seventy-two)

Years may be abbreviated, as

> in the winter of '54   in the '40s and mid-'50s
> Spirit of '76   in the 1920s and '30s
> Class of '59   Government '55s
> a '49er
> (Note that -er or -s may be joined without a second apostrophe.)

When written in words, these contractions do not take an apostrophe, but may be capitalized for distinction.

in the twenties (or Twenties)		a Forty-niner	back in Forty-five
in the midsixties	NOT:	*mid-'Sixties*	*'twenties* *'Forty-five*

It is also unnecessary to use the apostrophe when a "slant" or a hyphen is used before an abbreviated year.

1/8/70 or 1-8-70 (exact, 01-08-70)   1965-75   NOT: *1/08/'70*   *1965-'75*
(For consecutive years indicated by a hyphen, see p. 286.)

"**Of**" may be omitted in year phrases, as "the year 1972." Note that the word "year" is not capitalized.

Month and year when written together need not be separated by a comma. But some authorities still use this comma to conform to the usual punctuation in dates. Another comma now often dropped is that which follows the year, unless the sentence structure requires it.

In April 1968 and May 1970 OLDER:	In April, 1968, and May, 1970
the November 1972 elections	the November, 1972, elections
In our May 1, 1970 issue	in our May 1, 1970, issue

Periods of Time. A figure may be hyphened to a **singular word** to express a single term of minutes, hours, days, weeks, months, or years. Note that when the description is placed **after** the noun the figure is not hyphened to the word, and a **plural** word is used (unless of course the figure one or a fraction is used before it).

a 20-minute wait	BUT:	a wait of 20 minutes
24-hour-a-day driving		driving for 24 hours a day
60-day options		options for 60 days
a 5-day-long holdout		a holdout for 5 days
an 11-week term		a term of 11 weeks
a 6-month, 8% note		a note for 6 months at 8%
a 2-month extension		an extension of 2 months
a 5-year guarantee		a guarantee for 5 years
in the 40–50-year age group		ages from 40 to 50 years
a four-and-one-half-hour meeting (Do not omit the last hyphen.)		
a two-hour, five-day-a-week program SPECIAL: a months-long trial		

Periods of time may also be expressed by the **possessive,** if the idea of a single term is not foremost. The hyphen is not then used.

after six weeks' sailing	give them one month's extension
take six months' leave of absence	within five to ten minutes' time

CAUTION: **Do not use both the hyphen and the possessive here.**

NOT: after *six-weeks' sailing*   *one-month's* trial   *24-hours'* service

(For use of "suspending hyphens," such as the following, see p. 266.)

a small 30- or 60-day loan

A term of years, months, and days is considered a single unit and needs no commas within it.

interest for 3 years 5 months and 17 days

Ages.   Ages may be written in figures, or spelled out.   The general rule applies: Use figures if the ages are definite and given for quick reference or calculation; write out if the ages are indefinite, or if the writing is formal.

> He was 31 years old when first elected.   (definite)
> A boy about ten years old came...   (indefinite)

In the following age combinations, note that the singulars, and not the plurals, of "month" and "week" are now used to conform to "day" and "year."   CAUTION: Do not omit the last hyphen—before "old."

a 2-year-old animal	a two-year-old plan
a 3-year-old	a three-year-old
a 10½-year-old map	a ten-and-one-half-year-old map
an 8-month-old child	an eight-month-old debt
an 11-week-old infant	an eleven-week-old paper
the 20-day-old news	the twenty-day-old news
a 2000-year-old engraving	the sixty-odd-year-old actress
the 150-year-old, elm-shaded campus	an eight-year-old, worn-out car

In the following combination of years, months, and days, no commas are used because the age is considered one unit.

> His age was 21 years 6 months and 15 days.

Write "aged" instead of "age" in such phrases as

> In 1918 he died, aged 21, and his work...
> A man aged 45 was chosen...   ...a middle-aged man

Time.   (See Clock Time, p. 586.)

Dimensions.   Dimensions are written in figures; and abbreviations are often used in ordinary business papers.   In technical work, ′ is used for feet, ″ for inches, and x for "by."

> USUAL: 6 by 12 inches   6 x 12 in.   ten 6-by-12-inch mats
> TECHNICAL: 18′ x 9″ x 3′6″   18 x 5 x 6″ indicates that all dimensions
>   are inches.   But to avoid possible misinterpretation,
>   the designation is usually written after each number:
>   18″ x 5″ x 6″   5′ x 3′ x 2′

To indicate exact measurement, dimensions are often written **with** ciphers for inches or feet.

> 10′0″ x 0′8″   gauge height 15.0 feet
> Fractional dimensions are written: 1/16″   5/8′
>
>   Fractions are disjoined: 7 5/16″ x 16 3/8″ x 9 5/8″
>   Or joined: 7-5/16″ x 16-3/8″ x 9-5/8″
> (The second method is preferred by some because the fractional part
> is more definitely bound to the unit.)

If a dimension is written **before** a noun, the figure is idiomatically hyphened to a **singular** word.   But if the dimension is written **after** the noun, the figure is not hyphened to the word, and the word is **plural** (unless of course the figure one or a fraction is used before it).

a 50-foot mast; a one-foot hedge	BUT: a mast 50 feet high; a hedge of one foot
two-foot-deep clay; a 40-acre farm	clay two feet deep; a farm of 40 acres
a 24-foot-diameter tower	a tower 24 feet in diameter
a 37° 35-foot slope	a slope of 35 feet at 37 degrees
on 16-mm film	on film of 16 mm
a 281-foot, four-masted yacht	a yacht 281 feet long with four masts
a .38-caliber revolver	a revolver of .38 caliber
a 12-gauge shotgun	shotguns of ten or twelve gauge
an 800-mile-an-hour goal	a goal of 800 miles an hour
an 8-mile-long, 6-inch pipeline	a pipeline 8 miles long and...
a 10-inch-wide strip (or 10″-wide)	a strip 10 inches wide
a ⅓-inch pipe (or ⅓″, or ⅓-in.)	a pipe measuring ⅓ inch
3x5-inch cards (or 3″ x 5″ cards)	cards 3 x 5 inches in size
a 5-by-9-foot top (or 5′ by 9′ top)	a top 5 by 9 feet overall
a 15-in.-by-2-ft. shaft	a shaft 15 inches by 2 feet
a 6-foot-4-inch, 180-pound man (a 6-footer)	a man 6 feet 4 inches tall, weighing 180 pounds

Dimensions are abbreviated in everyday work—and not capitalized. In more formal work they are written out, but not capitalized.

5 ft. 8 in. or 5′8″	10 yds.	6 mi.
231 sq.ft. or ft²	27 cu.yds. or yd³	16 sq.mi. or mi²
MORE FORMAL: 5 feet 8 inches	27 cubic yards	16 square miles

Note that no comma is used between feet and inches, because a dimension is considered one unit.

Weights and Capacities. In everyday work, weights and capacities are abbreviated. In the more formal papers they are written out. They are not capitalized.

8 lbs. 2 oz. (or lb.)	26,625 lbs. of steel	2000 bbls.
MORE FORMAL: 8 pounds 2 ounces	26,625 pounds	2000 barrels

Note that no comma is used between pounds and ounces, because a quantity is considered one unit.

If a weight or capacity is written **before** a noun, the figure is idiomatically hyphened to a **singular** word. But if the weight or capacity is written **after** the noun, the figure is not hyphened to the word, which is **plural** (unless of course the figure one or a fraction is used before it).

5000-barrel-a-day rate (or bbl.) BUT:	rate of 5000 barrels a day
a 10-pound weight (or lb.)	a weight of 10 pounds
a 75-horsepower engine	an engine of 75 horsepower
a 3¼-ton truck	a truck weighing 3¼ tons
an 8-cylinder engine	an engine with 8 cylinders

Some weights and capacities may be expressed by the **possessive,** if the idea of a single unit is not foremost. No hyphen is then used.

...build a plant of about 5000 barrels' capacity.
...applied about 10 pounds' pressure. (10 separate pounds)
("A 10-pound pressure" would mean a single unit of pressure.)

Fractions. When writing fractions in figures, use the diagonal line, as 5/8, not a hyphen, as 5-8, which can be read "5 to 8."

A fraction may be joined to a unit number with a hyphen to show that the two definitely belong together. (-nds, -rds, -ths are not used.)

4 3/8 miles 3 9/32 acres OR:	4-3/8 miles	a 3-9/32 -acre farm
BUT NOT: 4 3/8ths miles	NOR	a 3-9/32nd acre farm

Isolated fractions are often written out. Some authorities hyphen written-out fractions; others do not, unless the fractions are used as modifiers. In business usage all fractions are very generally hyphened, which appears to be good practice, inasmuch as it affords a quick interpretation of the fraction. (For singular or plural use, see also p. 38.)

two-thirds	...the remaining two-thirds.
one-fourth	...weigh one-fourth as much.
three-fourths	About three-fourths of it was saved.
one-half	Almost one-half of the delegates were in favor of...
one half	One half was good, the other bad. (a special use)
cut in half	is colloquial for "cut into halves."
another half dozen	the first half-dozen notations (modifier)
half-a-dozen books (modifier)	
half a yard half an hour half a hundred	OR: a half yard, etc.
one-half yard one-half foot	
half-and-half (used as one word)	
a quarter of a yard	
three-quarters of a mile	OR: three-fourths of a mile
three-quarter length a three-quarter turn	OR: three-quarters turn

Do not write one part of a **small fraction** as a figure and the other as a word. If using **figures,** do not add "th," "ths," "of a," or "of an." (This may, however, be done with very large fractions.)

seven-eighths inch pipe
7/8-inch pipe or 7/8" pipe } NOT: *7-eighths*-inch   NOR: *7/8ths*-inch
three-fourths of a yard
3/4 yard   5/16 mile } NOT: *3-fourths of a* yard   NOR: *3/4ths*
BUT: 5/10,000ths of an inch   less than 5-millionths of a second

NOTE: Common expressions often carry "th," etc., as "at the 5/16ths pole"; "a loan on 15/16ths staple cotton"; "amounts to 7/100ths of 1 percent"; "the 47 and 7/8ths other states"; "Government bonds are traded in 1/32nds."

When either part of a spelled-out fraction contains a hyphen, omit the usual connecting hyphen. It is often better, however, to use numerals than to write out such ponderous fractions.

nine thirty-seconds of an inch (not *secondths*)   9/32
ninety-nine one-hundred-sixteenths   99/116

A hyphen can change the meaning of a fraction.

forty-two hundredths (42/100)   forty two-hundredths (40/200)

When a fraction is joined to the number "one," the following noun is plural, and the verb singular.

1³⁄₁₆ inches   NOT: *inch*
1¼ yards   1½ miles   NOT: *yard* or *mile*
One and seven-eighths **inches is** required...
One and one-fourth **feet is**...   OR: A foot and a quarter **is**...
A yard and a half **is** sufficient.

Write all fractions alike in one composition. (See also p. 283.)

NOT: ...**page** or form size, 16½" wide by 22-3/8" deep.
BUT: ...**page** or form size, 16-1/2" wide by 22-3/8" deep.

Decimals. If a decimal occurs in the text with no unit before it, a cipher is usually supplied to point up the decimal.

a 0.65-inch difference   specific gravity 0.3857

But if the decimal itself begins with a cipher, no other cipher is necessary.

an .08-inch difference

In technical work, the extra cipher is often used to express exactness:

0.0144 sq.ft   0.353 ounce   0.0010 gram

Commas are not used in decimals, but spaces are: 6.451 6   0.111 111 12

Percentages. "Percent" may be written as one word or as two words, and now without a period. The United States Government Printing Office writes it as one word, "percent"; and that form, being largely used in business papers, is followed in this book.

Definite percentages in commercial work are written in figures with the percent sign.

at 10% $33\frac{1}{3}\%$ 112%

Our price is $62.50; 5% discount for cash; 2% 10 days; net 30 days.

In more formal work, the word "percent" is used instead of the sign "%," but the numeral is retained before it.

a 20-percent profit   a reduction of 20 percent
one-half of 1 percent (commonly $\frac{1}{2}$ of 1%)
Nearly 20 percent of the bonds were forfeited.
About 60 percent of the crop was lost.

Note that percentages may be singular or plural, according to their meaning or reference. (See Collective Words, p. 38.)

Do not use both the decimal point and the word or sign "percent" unless it is intended.

0.5% is one-half of 1 percent, or 5/1000
For instance, if 65% is intended, do not write: *.65%* nor *.65 percent,*
which would be 65/10,000

For definiteness, the percent sign is usually used after each of several percentages in succession.

40% to 50%   10% or 20%   5%, 10%, and 15% discount
SOMETIMES: 40 to 50%   10 or 20%

But if "percent" is used, it is written only after the last number.

40 to 50 percent   about 10 or 20 percent

Plurals of Figures and Characters. These plurals may be formed by adding s or **'s.** Written-out numbers take regular plurals, not 's.

6s and 7s   OR: 6's and 7's   OR: at sixes and sevens (NOT: *six's*)
2 x 4s; 2x4s   2 x 4's; 2x4's   two-by-fours (NOT: *four's*)
B52s; DC10s   B-52's; DC-10's   all the fifty-twos (NOT: *two's*)
the 1970s   the 1970's   in the Forties   OR: the '40s*
Treasury 6¼s   Treasury 6¼'s   in his fifties...in the 120s
&s, +s, %s   &'s, +'s, %'s   ampersands, pluses, percent signs

* A simple s is usually added to a contracted year, to avoid two apostrophes. (See also p. 280.)

Omission ("Elision") of Figures. Consecutive numberings may be shortened, and "to" replaced by a hyphen (in printing, by an "en dash"). But if the first number ends in "00," a full number must follow.

YEARS: 1970–80   1880–1925   1900–1908   1906–9   180–144 B.C.
MONTHS: July–October 1976   April 15, 1974—June 30, 1977
PAGES: pp. 11–15   45–9   116–18   135–216   200–210   203–9
LETTERS: A–H   R–Z   BUT: . . .names **from A to** H (NOT: *A–H*)

Parts of two years may be indicated by a hyphen, a slant, or an en dash.

the 1975-76 (or '75-76) budget   winter 1974/75   fiscal 1975-6

If **"from"** is used before the first number or word, **"to"** should follow it instead of the hyphen.   Likewise, **"and"** should follow **"between."**

from 1975 to 1976   *from 1975–76*
from May 2 to July 16, 1974   NOT: *from May 2–July 16, 1974*
between 1965 and 1975   *between 1965–1975*

If a **continuous numbering** is not intended, a comma should be used instead of a hyphen, or an en dash.

the years 1945, 1952, and 1956   OR: the years 1945, '52, and '56
BUT NOT: the years *1945–52–56*

If **symbols** are involved, one should be placed after each number, to prevent the numbers from being read as a fraction. If **abbreviations or words** are used after the last numbers only, the word "to" should be used instead of the hyphen, or en dash.

5°–16° F   OR: 5 to 16 deg. F.
$75–$100   5¢–10¢   5 to 10 cents
10%–25%   3#–8#   10 to 25 percent   3 to 8 lbs.

When consecutive items are indicated by a hyphen, or en dash, it is loosely understood that the last item is "inclusive." But if definiteness is desired, "inclusive" should be written in.

January–June 1972, inclusive,   P–Z, both inclusive,
pp. 5–29, inclusive,   Nos. 66–168, both inclusive,

Page Numbering. (See Typewritten Work, p. 415.)

Capitalization Before Numbers. In business papers, common nouns standing **before serial or code numbers** are usually capitalized. In printing, such nouns are often lower-cased. (See also p. 126.)

BUSINESS USAGE: . . .Model No. 16325. . .Order (No.) 611. . .Invoice 74
          . . .Policy (No.) D491334. . .Patent (No.) 2,674,813
PRINTING USAGE: . . .model No. 163965. . .order No. 655. . .invoice 774
          . . .in policy No. D491334. . .by patent No. 2,674,813

NOTE: **No comma** is used before "No." The **plural** is formed on both words, as "Orders Nos. 456 and 634." And no capitals are used if an **actual number** is not mentioned, as "Their invoice number was not given."

No. and #. Avoid the use of "No." or "#" before a number, unless the number is standing alone and it is necessary to identify it as a number.

Room 15   Grade 10   Order 36   Invoice 867   page 286
   CLEARER THAN: Room *No.* 15   Order *No.* 36   OR: Room #15, etc.

"No." or **"Nos."** is used in ordinary work; **"#"** in tabulations, etc.

No. 45...Nos. 456–598...Nos. 18, 45, and 84   #45...#456–598...#18, 84

Numbered References. In typewritten work, references to numbered parts of compositions are usually capitalized, with the exception of the small or common divisions "page," "line," "note," and "verse." In printing, such designations are often all lower-cased.

	ABBREVIATION		ABBREVIATION
Appendix II	App.	Paragraph 16	Par. (Pars. or ¶¶)
Article 245	Art.	Part II	Pt.
Book I	Bk.	Plate X	Pl.
Chapter 14	Chap., Ch., or C.	Question 8	Qu. or Q. (pl. QQ.)
Chart 5	Cht.	Reference 18	Ref.
Class 5	Cl.	Rule 204	R.
Column 7	Col.	Schedule 3	Sch. or Sched.
Diagram 3	Diag.	Section 3	Sec. or s. (ss.; §§)
Division III	Div.	Series 10	Ser.
Example 12	Ex. (pl. Exx.)	Table V or 5	Tab.
Experiment 16	Exp. or Expt.	Volume I	Vol.
Figure 9	Fig.	page 230	p. (pl. pp.)
Graph 4	Gr.	folio (page)	fol. or f. (pl. ff.)
Illustration 10	Ill.	note 6	n. (pl. nn.)
Lesson XIV	Les.	line 19	l. (pl. ll.)
Number 4	No. (L. numero)	stanza 7	st.
Numbers 5 & 8	Nos. or No.	verse 3	v. (pl. vv.)

Commas: "in Article V, Section 8, of"   "in line 5, page 2, of"
Caps: Whether these references are capitalized or lower-cased, they should be kept uniform. Do not use a capital in one place and a small letter in another, as

...pursuant to Section 4 of the Act and subject to sections 7 and 10, and any other sections that... (WRITE: to Sections 7 and 10)
(The last "sections" may stand because no specific sections are named.)

First, Second, Third. These are called **ordinal numbers** because they show the order. The shortened forms are regarded as contractions rather than abbreviations; therefore, no periods are used after them.

1st   2nd or 2d   3rd or 3d   4th   5th   6th

NOTE: The shorter "2d" is, by some authorities, preferred to "2nd," and "3d" to "3rd." (For further uses, see Typewritten Work, p. 414.)

Ordinals Spelled Out. In **formal** writings, ordinals are spelled out up to "one hundredth." In **informal** writings, ordinals are often written entirely in figures. Or they are spelled out up to "tenth"— except (1) in dates (when the day precedes the month), and (2) when used in connection with higher ordinals that are in figures.

the sixth floor   between the 6th and 15th floors
our ninth milestone   our 35th anniversary
on Fifth Street   from 5th to 45th Street
a first edition   in the 1st, 8th, and 12th editions
INFORMAL: the 84th Congress   the 14th Amendment
FORMAL: the Eighty-fourth Congress   the Fourteenth Amendment

Numbered Headings and Items in Outlines. (See p. 412.)

Alinement of Numbers. Aline columns of whole numbers on the right; decimals on the decimal point; Roman and ordinal numbers on the right; dates and words, left; mixed items, left, or each centered.

9.	Wheat	$ 100	8.25	$+ 55\frac{1}{4}$	(115)	Art. VIII	8th Ave.
10.	Corn	50	25.675	$-$ 8	64	Art. IX	42d St.
100.	Cotton	1000	.027	$+110\frac{1}{2}$	(5328)	Art. X	125th St.

Superior and Inferior Figures. Superior figures are raised figures that indicate a footnote or reference, or show that a number is to be squared or cubed, etc. (Also called **"exponents"** or **"superscripts."**)

reference[1]   footnote[3] 25^2 10^3 5^5

Inferior figures are lowered figures, used in scientific work to indicate chemical formulas, etc., as H_2SO_4, CO_2. (Such figures are also called **"subscripts"** or **"subindices."**) (See also Chemical Symbols, p. 552.)

By the Dozen, By the Hundred, etc. Note that in "by" phrases the singular form of the words "dozen," "pair," "hundred," "thousand," "million," etc., is used **if "the" precedes the words.** The analogy is that a unit is meant, as "by the (unit of one) hundred."

But if "the" does not precede the word, the plural is used.

by the dozen	AND: by dozens	INSTEAD OF: by the dozens
by the pair	by pairs	by the pairs
by the hundred	by hundreds	by the hundreds
by the thousand	by thousands	by the thousands
by the million	by millions	by the millions
by the ten dozen	by tens of dozens	by the tens of dozens
by the hundred dozen	by hundreds of dozens	by the hundreds of dozens
by the hundred pair	by hundreds of pairs	by the hundreds of pairs
by the hundred thousand	by hundreds of thousands	by the hundreds of thousands

Hundred, Thousand, Million. "Hundred," "thousand," and "million" are idiomatically singular if a figure or the word "several" is used before them. But if "many" is used before them, they are usually plural.

five hundred books
several hundred books
many hundreds of books   RATHER THAN: many hundred books
ten thousand   OR: tens of thousands
several thousand
many thousands of   RATHER THAN: many thousand of
four million people   four millions of people
several million people
many millions of people   many million people
population of about two million   NOT: two *millions*
ten or twenty billion dollars' worth
        RATHER THAN: ten or twenty billions of dollars' worth
        BUT NOT: ten or twenty *billions dollars* worth

◆◇◆◇◆◇◆◇◆

Roman Numerals

ARABIC	ROMAN	ARABIC	ROMAN
1	I	100	C
2	II	150	CL (ancient Y)
3	III	200	CC
4	IV or IIII	300	CCC
5	V	400	CD or CCCC
6	VI	500	D
7	VII	600	DC
8	VIII	700	DCC
9	IX or VIIII	800	DCCC
10	X	900	CM or DCCCC
11	XI	1000	M
12	XII	1500	MD
13	XIII	2000	MM
14	XIV or XIIII	3000	MMM
15	XV	4000	MMMM or $M\overline{V}$
16	XVI	5000	$\overline{V}$
17	XVII	1,000,000	$\overline{M}$
18	XVIII		DATES
19	XIX or XVIIII	1800	MDCCC
20	XX	1900	MCM or MDCCCC
30	XXX	1920	MCMXX
40	XL or XXXX	1930	MCMXXX
50	L	1940	MCMXL
60	LX	1950	MCML
70	LXX	1960	MCMLX
80	LXXX or XXC	1970	MCMLXX
90	XC or LXXXX	1980	MCMXXC
		1990	MCMXC

RULES FOR READING ROMAN NUMERALS

A repeated letter repeats the value.

III 3 XX 20 CCC 300

A letter occurring after one of greater value is added thereto.

VI 6 LX 60 MC 1100

A letter occurring before one of greater value is subtracted therefrom.

IV 4 XL 40 CM 900

A dash over a numeral multiplies it by 1000.

$\overline{V}$ 5,000 $\overline{VIII}$ 8,000 $\overline{L}$ 50,000

$\overline{C}$ 100,000 $\overline{DLVI}$ 556,000 $\overline{M}$ 1,000,000

The old form for 500 was a disjoined D—IƆ; but it is no longer used. The old form for 1000 was CIƆ. In medieval Roman numerals, Y was 150.

The old form for 4 (IIII) is still seen on clocks; but otherwise it is not used.

USE OF ROMAN NUMERALS

Capitalized Roman numerals should be used to designate only the most important divisions of a paper. Small (lower-case) Roman numerals may be used for subdivisions.

No period is necessary after a Roman numeral (although it was formerly used). The numeral is not an abbreviation.

Henry VIII Denis J. Polk III Mark (Model) IV
Louis XIV World War II Chapter XI

But if used in headings or enumerations, Roman numerals may be followed by periods in accordance with the general punctuation.

When writing consecutive Roman numerals, leave an extra space after each numeral to facilitate reading.

Chapters IX, XIV, XL, CL

Small Roman numerals are uniformly used to number introductory pages in a book.

iii v viii x xix xxiv

Letters

Preferred positions in the business letter:

LETTERHEAD

Date

File No.
Order No.
Your letter (date)

Address

Attention

Salutation: (or Subject replacing Salutation)

Subject

   Paragraphs blocked, or indented 5 to 10 spaces—**to** aid the eye in distinguishing paragraphs.

   Body single-spaced unless the letter is very short.

   Paragraph Heads.   A letter may and should have underlined paragraph heads if the main subject has subdivisions.   Or if the letter refers to more than one subject, each subject should have a sidehead.

Complimentary close,

COMPANY NAME

(Writer's signature)

Writer's typed name, and
Title if used

Initials

Enc.
Mailing notation
c.c. or cc –

. . . . Postscript . . . .
. . . .

Date. Place the date where it is naturally looked for—and where it will not be hidden in the files—that is, toward the upper right corner, rather than in the center or at the left margin. If in the center it is apt to blend with the letterhead and be lost to the casual glance.

Write the date so that the end of the date line will be approximately even with the right margin of the letter below it.

The date is not abbreviated on the first page of a letter.

To make the date instantly clear, write it professionally: that is, write it all on one line; spell out the month in full; write the figures for the day of the month without -st, -nd, -rd, -d, or -th; and write the year in full without a period after it. Any other form for the date detracts from its quick readability.

February 24, 1980

Date letters the day they were dictated, and not the day they were transcribed (unless otherwise instructed), so that words referring to the dictation day, such as "this morning," or "today," may stand and not be changed to "yesterday," etc. The transcription day may be shown after the initials, if this is thought necessary, as SLH:dm–2/21.

Armed Forces Dates. The military offices have adopted the inverted (foreign) method of writing dates—using no commas or periods.

5 June 1980   abbreviated as: 5 Jun 80   (never *5/6/80*)*
(Abbreviation of the month is always the first 3 letters.)

* But in other countries, it would be 5-6-80 or 5.6.80; or in some postmarks, 5 VI '80.

Addresses. (On letters, see p. 309; on envelopes, p. 338.)

File References. For convenience and quick reference in filing, set numerical references—file numbers, order numbers, etc.—about four spaces below the date. They should be completely separated from the subject of the letter.

Avoid placing numerical references too near the date, as the two sets of figures tend to run together and lose distinctness. For clearness give each item a separate line. Do not underline or set in caps; file references should not obtrude. The receiver's reference should be placed first for his convenience in locating files when the letter is received.

| Your letter 2/12/80   or | OR: | Order 3458 |
| Your File C-SW82 | | Our Job 921 |

The word "References" is unnecessary. From the placement and context it is known immediately that they are references.

As a matter of courtesy—if the sender's file reference has been given in an incoming letter, indicate it in the reply, whether instructed to do so or not. It is a valuable aid in the office of the receiver of the reply.

Attention. The word "of" after "Attention" is superfluous. A colon has been used instead of "of," but now that is being omitted. In ordinary work, even the word "Attention" is unnecessary. The placement of a name below the company's name and address indicates "Attention of." (Sometimes just "Mr. ......, please" is used.)

291

The Attention line should be placed **below the main address, not** above it. It is less important than the company's name and address, especially in filing, and yet it is a part of the address. Do not place it below the salutation, nor in the center of the page as if it were a subject. It should not be written in caps; and now it is not indented or underlined. Always use the word "Mr." or a similar title in the Attention line.

The salutation after an Attention line—on impersonal business letters—agrees with the name in the main address, as "Gentlemen:" or "Dear Mr. ...:". But often in informal, friendly correspondence the salutation agrees with the Attention line, as "Dear Mr. [Mrs., Ms., or Miss] ...:". This may properly be done—since the Attention line is a part of the address—and thus the letter is given a personal tone.

> Attention Mr. F. C. Gordon, Advertising Director
> Gentlemen: or   Dear Mr. ......:   (name of main addressee)

Do not neglect the Attention line. It is of very definite meaning. It signifies that the letter contains company business and should be opened and attended to in the absence of the Attention addressee.

Notations Under "Attention." If a copy of a letter is being sent to a second person in the same company as the addressee, and if the letter is of almost as much importance to the second person as it is to the addressee, the "Copy to" notation may be written immediately beneath the Attention line. Ordinarily the copy notation is **at the end of the letter.**

> Attention Mr. F. C. Gordon
> Copy to Mr. George Talbot

Salutations. A colon is usual after a salutation. A comma is used only in social letters. (But it is common in British practice.)

Do not use abbreviations in salutations, other than "Mr.," "Mrs.," "Ms.," "Mss.," "Messrs.," "Dr.," and "Drs."

Capitalize, besides the first word, all titles and salutatory words, such as "Sir," "Friend," "Reader," "Editor," "Subscriber," "Stockholder," "Manager," "Customer," "People." (See also Addresses, pp. 313 ff.)

Salutations to men and women (by substituting feminine titles):

Gentlemen:	used for companies; but if women are also officers, then "Ladies [or Lady] and Gentlemen:"—or personal names. (See p. 293.)
Dear Sir:	used with a title of office, as "City Clerk."
Sir: or Sirs:	is the formal, diplomatic salutation.
My dear Mr. ...:	was the formal form, but has given way to
Dear Mr. ...:	the less formal, widely used form.

(In British usage these formal and informal forms are reversed.)

Dear Mr. and Mrs. ...:	to a man and wife.
Dear Jim:	to a friend called by his first name.
Dear Thompson:	to a business associate.
Dear Messrs. Scott and Lee: or Dear Mr. Scott and Mr. Lee:	
Dear Messrs. Page:	to two men of the same name.

("*Messrs.:*" is never used **alone,** although "Messieurs:" alone is the French salutation.)

If a company is to sign the letter, do not use only a last name or a nickname in the salutation. Use "Dear Mr. . . . . :" or "Dear Sir:".

Salutations to Women. Avoid the use of "Dear Madam:" except on impersonal or routine letters; and especially avoid it when addressing an unmarried woman—it is an unpleasant approach. Use instead:

Dear Mrs. (or Ms.) ..: }
Dear Miss (or Ms.) ..: } the informal form, generally favored.

My dear Mrs. (or Ms.) ..: }
My dear Miss (or Ms.) ..: } formerly formal; now quite personal.

(In British usage these formal and informal forms are reversed.)

Dear Ms. . . . . for either "Mrs." or "Miss" (See p. 310.)
("Dear *Miss*:", without a surname, is not used.)
Madam: is the formal, diplomatic form. (See p. 324.)
Madam President [or Chairwoman]: or Dear Madam President:

To an organization of women use:

Mesdames: the French form, or the American
Ladies: which corresponds to "Gentlemen:".
Dear Mesdames (or Mss.) Page and Lee: or Dear Ms. Page and Mrs. Lee:
Dear Misses (or Mss.) Brent and Ray: or Dear Miss Brent and Ms. Ray:
Dear Mesdames (or Mss.) Rogers: }
Dear Misses (or Mss.) Duncan: } to two women of the same name.

To an organization of men and women:

Ladies [or Lady] and Gentlemen: or Dear Sirs and Mesdames:
Dear Mrs. [or Ms.] Grant and Mr. Lee: or Dear Sir and Madam:
(**To a professional group:** Dear Doctors [or Teachers, etc.]:)

Salutations to Charitable Organizations and Churches.

Gentlemen: or Ladies: or Ladies and Gentlemen:
Dear Friends: or Dear Friend:

Subject. The word "Subject," "In re," or "Re:" is unnecessary before the subject on a letter. The placement shows that it is a subject. One would not write "Title" before the title of a story or article; and similarly no such introduction is needed before a letter subject. (Though "Subject" is used on military letters, and is printed on some interoffice memorandums; and "Re:" is used in legal work.)

Center the letter subject **below** the salutation, not above it (or let it replace the salutation). The subject is an introduction to the body of the letter and not a part of the address.

It is unnecessary to set a subject in caps. All capitals are hard to read. Capitalize only the most important words and underline the last line only.

Gentlemen:

Venezuela Land Option, and
Texas Leases Expiring in April

Every letter should bear a subject. This practice is becoming more important every day. It facilitates the handling of letters in both the senders' and the receivers' offices. Especially is it valuable in subject filing and for the distribution of letters to the various departments of an organization.

"One subject in one letter" should be the rule, unless the letter is about matters in general. In that event it may carry headings down the side.

If two or more subjects are included in a letter and the subjects change abruptly, a short dividing line of four dashes may be drawn between the paragraphs to indicate the changes, unless sideheadings are used.

If two or more subjects are discussed in a letter, make enough copies so that each subject file will receive a copy of the entire letter.

Subjects Replacing Salutations. Letter writers now often replace the salutation with a subject, or, in advertising, a catchline, as

Valuable New Book on Market Methods...	The Business Outlook —	CANADIAN OIL LANDS Proposed Pipelines

In the "simplified," full-block-style letter sponsored by the Administrative Management Society, neither a salutation nor a complimentary close is used. (A subject replaces the salutation.)

Sideheads. These are often used in letters—placed at the left margin and underlined. The subject matter may or may not be indented. (Or, to save space, **paragraph headings** may be used, as in this book.)

Body of Letter. The professional setup of a letter is:

Single-spaced, unless unusually short
Double-spaced between paragraphs
Paragraphs blocked or indented 5 to 10 spaces.

Arrange the letter so that the points to be emphasized, calculated, or answered will stand out. For instance, set out lists, quoted matter, addresses, etc., by indenting them in block style, as

Please reply to Mr. H. F. Hale, whose address is
200 Fifth Avenue, Suite 608
New York, NY 10010

Paragraphing. (See Typewritten Work, p. 414.)

Complimentary Close. This may be written in block alinement with the signature, or begun five or ten spaces to the left of the signature. The latter arrangement is preferred by some because it assists the eye by keeping the complimentary close from entangling with the signature.

Capitalize only the first word in a complimentary close—it is a simple phrase, not a title. A comma always follows it.

Two spaces— sometimes three— are left above it.

BLOCK: Sincerely,	INDENTED: Very truly yours,
Vice President – Finance	Chairman

Always write the complimentary close that is dictated. The dictator may have some reason for saying "Cordially," for instance, rather than "Sincerely."

If the complimentary close is not dictated, use a closing that corresponds to the tone of the letter. When in doubt use "Very truly yours."

Modern complimentary closings—with **"yours"** eliminated—are:

Sincerely,	the most generally used.
Cordially,	a friendly closing.
Very sincerely, } Most sincerely, }	informal, intensive.
Respectfully, Very respectfully, Respectfully submitted,	formal—used in diplomatic correspondence; and often to government officials and church dignitaries.
Faithfully,	used to high officials—and to the clergy.
Fraternally,	used in brotherhoods.
Gratefully,	used when acknowledging a favor.
Appreciatively, Hurriedly, Regretfully,	appropriate for certain letters.
Thanks, or Thank you,	informal, yet businesslike, closing.
Best wishes, } Regards, }	informal and rather personal.
Very truly yours,	the impersonal, business form.

"I am," "we remain," etc., are old-fashioned and no longer used before complimentary closes.   The comma is considered sufficient.

With kindest regards,
    Sincerely,
With all good wishes,
    Cordially,
With the compliments of the Season,
We wish you a merry Christmas
    and a happy New Year,
With best wishes to you and Mrs. . . . ,
    ("You" is first out of courtesy to
    the receiver of the letter.)

Often informal phrases replace the complimentary closings:
    Kindest [OR Warmest] regards,
    Kindest personal regards,
    With warm regard,
    Best of luck, OR Good luck!
    As ever, OR As always,
    Truly thankful [OR grateful],
    Thank you very much,

Signatures in General. A signature should be in the lower right corner of the letter and not in the center, nor past the halfway mark toward the left. If a signature is thus misplaced it loses its identity as a signature.

A name should be signed in the form that is expected in the reply; or at least the typed signature should indicate that form.

"Doctor," "Professor," "Colonel," etc., while not used in the pen-and-ink signature, may be indicated in the typed signature in the form of a title after the name.

L. M. Lansdowne, M.D. President	Benj. B. Scott Major General, U.S.A. Chief of Engineers
Edwin T. Masters Professor of Economics	David Ward Blythe, D.D. Chairman, Program Committee

It is better to type the name beneath the signature than to write it in the initials' space. Some readers do not reconcile one name with the other, if the signature is poor.

If a name is printed on the letterhead, it is unnecessary to type it beneath the signature, unless the signature is known to be illegible; then the reader may not connect the signature with the printed name.

Signing Company Name. Company names are being increasingly omitted from signatures, in order to save time and effort—and to produce a less formal effect. But on formal or contractual letters, in which the writer acts as a representative of his company, the company's name should always be typed in caps (two spaces below the complimentary close) **exactly as it is printed on the letterhead.** A discrepancy between these names may cause the answerer to debate which is correct.

Four spaces below the company's name, type in small letters the name of the person signing for the company. "By" or "Per" is unnecessary.

THORNWALL & SONS, INC.   SCOTT & GRANT COMPANY

R. K. Laidlaw   V. O. R. Scott, Vice President
Vice President - Sales

Certified public accountants and firms of attorneys, when giving professional opinions or advice, often sign the company name in longhand, with no individual's name appearing.

Occasionally a business writer places the company name beneath his own.

Milbrand, Price & Co.   *James Whitman*

Certified Public Accountants   The Business Review

Some **titles of officers** are used constantly in typed signatures, and others are not. Individual preference governs in this. But if a letter is of a legal nature and the writer is signing in an official capacity, his title should always be typed after or below his typed name.

Always leave enough space for the signature, so that the name will not be signed over the typed name, which makes both names illegible.

Signing Personal Name. On informal letters, it is unnecessary to sign the company name—the letterhead is sufficient identification.

The writer's name alone may be signed; or the writer's name, title and/or department, if customarily used.

Hugh Langdon   R. M. Lowe
Travel Editor   Marketing

NOTE: The names (or just the titles) of two or more signers of one letter may be typed **one beneath the other**, if not, **side by side** across the page:

Spencer W. Harrison   Eric J. Hill
Chairman of the Board   President

Value of the Typewritten Signature. Even though the writer is well known to his correspondent, his typed name is of definite value.

It is an indelible record of correct initials and spelling. If the pen-and-ink signature is difficult to decipher, the typewritten signature will aid members of the receiver's staff in transcribing the name.

The typed name also leaves a record on the carbon copies, thus providing a later reference regarding the signer of the letter. Further, it allows the signer the privilege of simply initialing the line above the typewritten signature if he so desires.

Women's Signatures. On an incoming letter—if "Miss" or "Mrs." is not enclosed in parentheses before a woman's signature, or indicated in the typed signature, it is to be assumed that the title is "Miss."

(In the reply, "Miss" may be used; or the abbreviation **"Ms.,"** meaning either "Miss" or "Mrs."—in both the address and the salutation.)

An unmarried woman may use "Miss" or "Ms." in parentheses before her signature, or include it, without parentheses, in her typed name.

> (*Miss* [or *Ms.*]) *Frances Linton*   or   *Frances Linton*
> Miss (or Ms.) Frances Linton

A married woman may use "Mrs." or "Ms." in parentheses before her signature, or include it, without parentheses, in her typed name.

> (*Mrs.* [or *Ms.*]) *Janet Meade*   or   *Janet Meade*
> Mrs. (or Ms.) Janet Meade

If a married woman wishes to be addressed by her husband's first name or initials, she may so indicate in her typed signature. (In social usage she is preferably addressed by her husband's full name.)

> *Eleanor Martin*
> Mrs. Rex L. Martin, Jr.

A widow may use her own first name in business, even though she retains her husband's full name in social usage.

> Mrs. Leland K. Fair   or   Ruth Ryan Fair   or   Mrs. (or Ms.) Ruth Fair

A divorced woman uses her first name, maiden name, and ex-husband's last name, unless she has regained her maiden name. Socially, she combines her maiden name and her divorced surname.

> *Jeanne Brown Benton*   or   *Jeanne Benton*
> Mrs. (or Ms.) Jeanne Brown Benton   Mrs. (or Ms.) Jeanne Benton
> or just
> Mrs. Brown Benton (social usage)

Signing for Another. When signing another's name, it is not usually necessary to use "Per" or "By." (See p. 477.) Simply sign the name and initial it with small but clear initials, to indicate responsibility.

Deputy signers should be careful to sign the right names. They have a tendency to sign their own names; or if they have prepared the letters, they have a greater tendency to forget to sign them altogether.

"By" is sometimes used when one person signs for another in an official capacity.

> In reply, one addresses the first⎫   Ralph V. James, President
> signer (Mr. James), attention of ⎬   By *Howard Gray*
> the second (Mr. Gray); with the ⎪   Howard Gray
> salutation "Dear Mr. James:" ⎭   Assistant Manager

"Secretary to" should be used only by actual secretaries.

> *Katherine Miller*
> Secretary to Mr. Stewart

If not officially a secretary, the signer may use "For."

> *Claire McKay*   or   *Claire McKay*
> For Mr. Kent   For John M. Martin
>   Manager, Marketing

After signing and sending dictated letters, always put copies of them on the dictator's desk, in a folder marked "Signed and Sent."

Initials. Put initials on all but legal papers. Initials are important, especially on telegrams. They indicate responsibility. (See also p. 301.)

Initials may be set in caps or small letters (often the dictator's are capitalized and the transcriber's lower-cased). In large offices, sometimes a transcriber's number is used instead of initials.

Dividers may be a colon, a slant, a hyphen, a period, or a space. (A colon is usual because it is unnoticeable and easy to type.)

> JTL:RT JTL:rt JTL/rt JTL-rt JTL.T jtl rt JL:8 L:T
>
> NOTE: For Mc..., Mac..., O'..., and like names, only the first letter need be employed.

Some offices prefer to have only the transcriber's initials shown when the dictator's name is typed beneath his signature.

> RT or rmt or just T   James T. Lamont

Typing the entire name of the dictator in the initials' space is uncommon. It is considered better practice to type the dictator's name beneath his signature so that the eye will not have to travel across the page to compare the signature and the typewritten name.

But there is an instance in routine letters where it is good practice to write the dictator's name in full in the initials' position—that is, when the letter is dictated, and often signed, by one person for another.

> *H. M. Granville*
> *W. B.*
> W. Benson:jm   Director of Purchases

If the letter is to be signed by someone other than the dictator, the signer's initials should be first, the dictator's second (joined with, say, a hyphen), and the transcriber's third (joined with a colon).

> JTL-KF:rt   or to signify dictator, transcriber, typist: JTL/rt.m

If the letter or wire is composed by the one who types it (for another's signature), that fact may be indicated by single initials in parentheses.

> (VT) or (vt)

"Jr." and "Sr." need not be carried with the initials unless the Junior and Senior are in the same organization. In that event the initials may be written:

> JVTJr:hm

Enclosures. Write "Enc." **below** the initials, and not in caps.

The number of enclosures may be indicated, as "Enc. 3," to guard against the omission of one—especially if a third person is to mail the letter—and to aid the receiver in checking the enclosures. (An attached paper is counted as an enclosure.)

If the papers to be enclosed are of unusual importance, they should be listed and identified in short lines.

Enc.: Deed - Jason to Hill, June 8, 1970
Contract – Martin and Lane, April 14, 1970

If they are to be returned, or are being sent separately, write:

Enc. 2 (to be returned)   OR   Sep. cov. 2 - p.p.i.   OR   Air express 4

Mailing Notations. Type these (in small letters with initial caps) below the "Enc." notation, on all letters dispatched otherwise than by regular mail. Such notations are valuable in tracing letters or in computing delivery dates—and are often of legal significance.

Certified - ret.rec.   By messenger   Special delivery

NOTE: In merchandising, Government, and military correspondence, these notations are usually set in caps and placed at the top of the letter, above the address or below the date, so as to be noticeable and conveniently close to the address when the envelopes are being prepared.

In ordinary correspondence, these notations are preferably set inconspicuously at the end of the letter, to avoid too many notations at the beginning. (Or they may be typed on the carbon copies only.)

Carbon Copy Notations. The carbon copy notation, "cc," should be the last one. If it appears before the mailing and enclosure notations, the reader might think that these phrases pertain also to the copies. If they do pertain to the copies, that fact may be definitely indicated.

cc: Mr. Hall	Att.: News release	cc: Mr. J. T. Dare, Tulsa
J. C. Coe	cc: Public Relations	cc + enc, certified: JTL
cc + enc: Lee Day	cc & att.: R&D (2)	— KW
Dan Reed	--- Ray Hill	— N.Y.

NOTES: "Mr.," etc., is used before surnames standing alone, and before outsiders' names.
An address may be added, or just the city—if not to the usual address.
Names are listed **alphabetically** or in the **order of importance**, with outsiders first.
Either "**+**" or "**&**" may be used before "enc." or "att." (attachment).
A long dash may indicate, as in printing, a **repetition** or ditto in subentries.
Three other abbreviations are sometimes used:
  "**ic**" for "**internal copy**"—that is, within the organization;
  "**xc**" for "**extra copy to addressee**" (to cc recipients, just the number, as "(2)");
  "**bc**" or "**bcc**" for "**blind copy**" (see below).
Carbon copy notations may appear **only on the copies**—not on the original—if they will be of no interest to the addressee.
Carbon copies are **not usually signed**—but may be. The signature is sometimes typed or stamped on with "/S/" or "(s)" or "(Sgd.)" before it.

"Blind Copy" Notation (bc or bcc). If a copy is to be sent to a second person, and the addressee is not to be made aware of it, type the notation at the top left corner of the carbon copies, not at the bottom. This shows definitely that it did not appear on the original letter.

Notations in General. Before removing a letter from the machine, pause to make sure that some notation is not needed, such as "Enc.," "cc," "In duplicate," or "Registered"—to save the effort of reinsertion.

Drop the notations at least two spaces below the initials. The "cc" notation especially should be spaced so that it will stand out.

Postscripts. A postscript is usually important; therefore it should stand out. Indent its margin about five spaces from the margin of the letter. If it bears a date different from that on the letter, put the date above it. The abbreviation "PS." or "P.S." may be used or omitted. (If a handwritten postscript or note is added, type it on all copies.)

PS. – Samples of the different materials have just arrived, and we will proceed at once with the analyses.

J. B. K. [or unsigned]

In ordinary letters, postscripts may be initialed (by hand or in type) or left unsigned. In sales letters, postscripts are not signed.

A postscript is the last notation on a letter (see p. 290).

Post-Postscripts. If a second postscript is added, it may bear the abbreviation "P-PS." or "P.P.S." meaning post-postscript. It is set in the same form as the first postscript, and two spaces below it.

Second Pages. Never carry only the signature over to the second page of a letter. There must always be two or three lines of writing on the second page to connect the signature definitely with the letter.

Attempt to carry the entire last paragraph over if it is very short. This gives good balance and a nice finish to a letter.

NOTE: The "right side" of bond paper is the side from which the watermark can be read.

Second-Page Notations. In the second-page headings use "Mr." or another title before the addressee's name. In formal correspondence the company's name is carried above the individual's name.

(For letters to Government officials, see p. 324.)

It is unnecessary to write "Page 2." Use just the figure. Put the page number in the center of the page, and not under the name, where it is not easily seen.

Mr. Kingston   –2–   Feb. 20, 1980

Note that the date is usually written as shown, and not abbreviated to 2/20/80. It is considered of more trouble to code and decode the latter form, with a chance of error, than to write simply the date with only the month abbreviated.

It is unnecessary to draw a line or put dots beneath the second-page notation to separate it from the letter. But leave at least four spaces, if possible, between the heading and the body of the letter. Particularly, set the second-page notations well down on the page if there is very little writing to follow. Too often a letter is seen crowded to the top of the second page with most of the page below it blank.

"Personal" Business Letters. Business letters that are marked "Personal" are written in regular business letter style on business letterheads, with the word "Personal" above the receiver's name and address, which is at the top of the letter. The sender's name may be typed beneath his signature as usual. (For initials, see p. 301.)

Business Letters on Plain Paper. If a business letter is written on plain paper, the sender's address may be typed either above the date line or below the typewritten name in the signature. The latter arrangement is preferable from the reader's viewpoint, in that it puts the writer's address conveniently close to his name.

Robert V. Pierce
5426 University Dr.
Omaha, Nebraska   68166

Diplomatic and Personal Letters. In diplomatic correspondence, and in personal business letters, such as letters of thanks, appreciation, congratulation, and condolence—often written on executive-size letterheads—the address may be placed at the end of the letter, two to five spaces below the last line of the signature.

The **date** is usually at the top, but may be placed beneath the address. **Initials and "cc's"** are omitted (but may be shown on the carbons). An **"Enc."** occasionally appears two to four spaces below the address.

September 14, 19..

Dear Mr. Harkness:

....

....

Sincerely,

Mr. James F. Harkness
428 Coronado Terrace
Cleveland, Ohio   44152

The writer's name is not typed beneath his signature if he is well known to his correspondent. If he is not well known to the addressee, his name and title may be typed beneath his signature. His address— if it does not appear on the letterhead—should be typed above the date.

Initials on Social and Personal Letters. The writer's and transcriber's initials are not used on social letters. They are used on personal business letters, unless a letter is confidential, in which instance they are omitted so that it will not appear that a third person has knowledge of a strictly private matter. (But they can be shown on the carbons.)

Letter Conveying a Message for Another. The writer should never insinuate himself into a letter written to convey a message for another. The other person's name should always appear first and foremost.

NOT: { I am glad to inform you that Mr. Scott...
{ This is to inform you that Mr. Scott is unable...
{ I should like to know the amount of Mr. Scott's dividend...

BUT: { Mr. Scott has asked me to say that...
{ Mr. Scott regrets that...
{ In Mr. Scott's absence, I have been asked to obtain...

Letters of Introduction. Letters of introduction are written in the regular form, and are usually begun:

I should like to introduce Mr. ...., who is...   or   May I introduce...
I want you to meet a friend ...   or   May I present...

A letter of introduction should be left unsealed, as a courtesy to the bearer. He may seal it if he cares to.

The receiver's address should be in the ordinary place on the envelope, and above it to the right may be typed if desired: Introducing Mr. ...

NOTE: Often an introduction is made on the introducer's business card, by his writing on the face of the card: "Introducing Mr. ... to Mr. ... And on the back of the card, a little note giving the reason for the introduction.

301

Letters of Acknowledgment. If an incoming letter cannot be answered reasonably soon, an acknowledgment of its receipt should be sent to the writer of the letter.

In everyday letters, the formal words "This will acknowledge receipt" are unnecessary (they are understood); nor should the acknowledgment always start with "Thank you for..." (the incoming letter may not merit that); nor should an immediate answer upon the addressee's return always be promised (he may be too busy). All that is necessary is something like this:

> Your letter of April 16 came (or was received, arrived, or reached us) during Mr. Lee's absence (on a short business trip, or because of illness, etc. [if the reason can be told]).
> He will return next Thursday, and your letter is being (or will be) held for his attention (or will be on his desk for his consideration).

Or with the personal name first:

> Mr. Lee has been away for a short time, but plans to return next week.
> Your letter of June 3 about the advertising schedule will be (or is being) held for his attention.

Clip the carbon copy of the acknowledgment to the incoming letter.

Letters of Confirmation. If an important agreement has been made by telephone or in a conversation, send a letter confirming it, as

> To confirm our telephone conversation of this morning – my understanding is: (tabulate the points of agreement)

Letters of Recommendation. A letter of recommendation replying to an inquiry is written in **regular** letter form. But often a **general** letter of recommendation is given when a position is terminated.

The general letter requires no heading except the date, which is important. It may bear the simple title **"Recommendation"** (the legal "To Whom It May Concern:" is rarely used now). No salutation is necessary on a general letter, nor is any complimentary close.

Another type of recommendation letter is that which is addressed to the **person** himself. It mentions the position he has held, length of service, his qualifications, **and** satisfactory work.

Letters Making Reservations. Reservations are usually made by telephone or wire, but may be made by letter if time permits. They are begun:

> Please make the following reservation for Mr. ....(full name)...: or
> Please reserve for me a...   (Ending) Thank you,
> (For a hotel reservation give the exact accommodation desired, and the price range, if necessary; the date and time of arrival, and departure; and request a confirmation giving the check-out time, if desired.)

Letters of Transmittal. Always write a letter of transmittal when mailing papers of any value, if no other letter accompanies them. Describe briefly the papers, enumerating or identifying what is being sent so that a permanent record may be had in the carbon copy of the

302

letter, and further so that the receiver will not be confused by receiving just a bunch of papers. (Beware of sending only a note, and having no copy thereof for the files.) A letter is always looked for with papers; even though the receiver knows they are coming he wants to be told again, if in no other words than simply

> Here are the papers we mentioned: (list them)
> **Other openings may be:**
>> Mr. ... has asked me to send you the following papers: **or**
>> With this letter I am returning...   **or**   Enclosed are...   **or**
>> Three copies of the remodeling contract are enclosed.   Please sign...

Register letters containing original papers which could not be replaced if lost, or of which there exist no other copies.

Letter Writing. Begin a business letter with the **subject**, if possible, and state what **action** is to be taken regarding it.

> The...(subject)...that you ordered (or asked about, enclosed, etc.) in your letter of...has been (or is, will be, etc.)...

Write as you would speak. Natural expressions make good openings.

> Thank you for...   You are right...   Yes, we issue...   Here are...
> Please send...   Do you publish...?   There are...   It has been...
> We are sending...   I know...   Of course...   Evidently...   Since...

Do not waste time reviewing the incoming letter—merely mention it.

It is permissible to begin a letter with "I," "We," or the name of a person or company, if no other opening presents itself.

Avoid stilted or old-fashioned phrases at the beginning and end.

Avoid the repetition of any certain word in a sentence or throughout a letter. Check the meaning and spelling of all unusual words.

Do not use big or "elegant" words, or foreign or Latin phrases, simply to impress the reader. And do not "write down" to anyone.

Use contractions, as "I'll," "that's," for ease and friendliness.

Use "Mr." or a proper title when introducing a surname in a letter; do not introduce the name alone. Thereafter the person may be referred to by his last name only, if he is familiarly known to both writer and reader, or if his name occurs repeatedly in an impersonal manner.

Do not be too enthusiastic or ingratiating in a letter. Be very dignified yet courteous, definite, and sincere.

Consider the reader's time and make all letters clear and concise.

Vary the sentence lengths. Short sentences increase the pace; long sentences retard it. Either form constantly used becomes monotonous.

Keep the paragraphs short—ten lines or fewer. Opening and ending paragraphs especially should be short—four lines or fewer.

Use sideheads or paragraph heads (underlined) to clarify items.

Answer, and check off, every question asked in the incoming letter.

If a letter is to contain a disappointment to the reader, state the reason for the disappointment first, as a preliminary to the final unfavorable news. And, wherever possible, offer a helpful alternative solution.

Never write a letter in anger—wait a day.

303

Old-Fashioned Phrases. Many stereotyped phrases are being discarded from letters in favor of the "direct approach" and businesslike end. Among expressions considered worn-out, stiff, or cumbersome are:

This will acknowledge receipt of...
We are in receipt of your inquiry...
In reply [or Replying] to your letter...
In response to your request of...
Reference is made [or Referring] to...
As per instructions in your letter of...
Re [or In re] your letter... (*legal use*)
I have before me your letter dated...
We have your recent letter in which...

Feature the subject.
Mere mention of a letter tells that it has been received. A better opening would be:
The [subject] that you asked about [or requested] in your letter of... is...

Most -ing beginnings (as Replying [but not Thinking, etc.]) are condemned.
All -ing endings (Hoping, Trusting, Awaiting, Thanking, etc.) are outmoded.
The telegraphic style is also censured, as "Received check for $100."

Trite or mechanical phrases to be guarded against in letters are:

take this opportunity...take the liberty of...take pleasure in (Don't take; just thank, commend, etc.)
at your earliest convenience (FOR: promptly)...*valued order...went forward* (was shipped or sent)
Please *feel free to contact us* (Please call upon us)...Please *do not hesitate to get in touch with us* (Please let us know)...Please *give this matter your attention* (Please consider this)...Please *be good enough to forward* (Please send)...Please *accept our thanks* (Thank you)
May I *offer the suggestion...Permit me to say* (omit)...May we *beg your kind indulgence...*
We trust this will *meet with your approval...*We shall be happy *to oblige* (We'll be pleased...)
advise—This is to *advise...*regret to *advise...*Please be *advised...*We would [or wish to] *advise...* You are *advised* (Unless it is real advice, just tell the reader what you have in mind.)
date—at an early date (soon)...recent date (recent)...as of this date (today)...present date (at present)...under date of (on)...at a later date (later)...letter dated (of)...
find—*Enclosed please find...*Attached [or With this letter] you will *find* (We are enclosing...Here is...A check for $8 is enclosed—the reader will "find" it if enclosed)
hand—We *hand you herewith* (Here are...We are enclosing)...It should *be in your hands* (reach you) ...*has just *come to hand* (just arrived or been received)...We have *at hand* (omit "at hand")
herewith or **hereto**—*Enclosed herewith...Attached hereto* (Enclosed is...Attached is...)
inform—This is to *inform* you...wish to *inform...*would like to *inform...*regret to *inform...for your information* (Just give the information without sounding formidable.)
state—*wish to state...would state...*pleased to *state* (omit)...recently *stated* (said)
wish to or would [like to]—*wish to* call your attention...*wish to* say, state, inform, advise, notify, thank you for *same* (Don't "wish," just do.)
writing—at the present *writing* (at present)...up to this *writing* (up to now, or since then)

"Wordy" old phrases take time to write and to read. Omit or shorten such as

along these lines (like this)	*by means of* (by)	*in the amount of* $5 (for $5)
until such time as (until)	*in the event that* (if)	in *the month of* June (in June)
during the course of (during)	*in order to get* (to get)	in *the city of* Flint (in Flint)
in connection with (concerning)	*for the purpose of* (to)	for *a period of* 6 months (omit)
due to the fact that (because)	*subsequent to* (after)	blue *in color* (blue)
not in a position to (cannot)	*previous to* (before)	large *in size* (large)
with the result that (so that)	*are in possession* (have)	round *in shape* (round)

Some "tried and true" phrases are still widely used by good writers:

in the near future (soon)...in due course...as a matter of fact (in fact)...at the present time (now)
as the case may be; in that, which, this, each, such, any case; in case (if); in some cases; this being the case; than was the case in 1965 (than it was in 1965)
In accordance with your request (As requested)...In compliance with...Pursuant to...in lieu of according to our records...our records show...for your records (Such phrases can often be omitted.) under separate cover (separately)...by return mail (Please send; promptly, or by [date])
our Mr. Lee (our representative, Mr. Lee; or Mr. Lee)...It is suggested (passive for We suggest)
"The writer" or "the undersigned" (approved by some, frowned on by others) is an appellation often used by letter and report writers, writing in the third person, who wish to remain impersonal. Similar terms are constantly seen in newspaper columns: this reporter, this reviewer, your columnist, and this writer. But such a designation should not be used interchangeably with "I."

Negative Expressions. Avoid the making of negative suggestions or the calling up of unpleasant thoughts in letters, business papers, advertisements, etc. Never suggest failure, inaptitude, or possible trouble. Acknowledge difficulties, but acknowledge them in a positive way, as if something would immediately be done to rectify them.

304

Words and phrases that create a bad impression are:

complaint	damage	inability	unfortunately
trouble	delay	mistake	failure, etc.

(For "disapproved" may be substituted "not favorably considered," etc.)

"If this information is not sufficient, kindly call upon us for more."
(Why suggest that it is insufficient? Why not say "If any further information is desired, please call upon us.")

"We regret our inability to comply with your request."
(Do not admit any inability. Better to rest the inability on the request—"We regret that your request cannot be complied with.")

"This industry's soundness can best be gauged by the number of failures recorded within it—only 4 in 60 years."
(Why not say "by the few failures" or "by the almost complete absence of failures" instead of "by the number of failures" which immediately sounds large.)

"Unfortunately, your letter was misplaced, and we cannot..."
(The unfortunate part should be subdued, not emphasized—"Your letter was misplaced, unfortunately, and we...")

"Purchaser shall withhold payment until guarantees are met or not met."
(Omit the "or not met." It puts the idea in the purchaser's mind that perhaps the guarantees will not be met. Also, how long should the purchaser withhold payment if "guarantees are not met"?)

"All conflicts and controversies shall be settled in accordance with the California State Code."
(This sounds like trouble. Wouldn't it give a better feeling to say "The California State Code shall govern in all questions to be settled between the parties hereto.")

"The Contractor shall be responsible for any and all liens filed during the course of construction."
(This actually predicts the filing of many liens, which would give the owner an uncomfortable feeling. Would not this be easier to contemplate: "If any lien whatsoever is filed during the course of construction, the Contractor shall be responsible therefor.")

Instead of saying "Thanks for all your trouble..." why not say "Thanks for the assistance..." And so on.

Spacing. Setup is very important in a business letter. It is a noticeable feature of a letter and can interest or prejudice a reader at a glance.

Lopsided letters, top-heavy letters, letters running off the bottoms of pages, all bespeak of inefficiency and reflect on the merits of the senders. If an ill-balanced letter is received, it suggests that all other products of the sending company might be as carelessly constructed.

No matter how busy you are, take a moment to contemplate each letter before writing it. Change the margins on the typewriter for **every letter,** if necessary, to get the proper spacing. A uniform style of work will be the reward. Employers are not usually in as much of a hurry for letters as they are concerned over the finished product.

Pattern of a Top-Heavy Letter | Pattern of a Letter Set Too Low

These unbalanced arrangements are caused by an inability to judge the length of letters.

Patterns of Lopsided Letters

These misarrangements result from failure to change the left marginal stop for each letter.

Frame every letter, with the left margin always slightly wider than the right margin. And keep the right margin as even as possible. Long letters should have a left margin of about an inch and a quarter, and a right margin of at least an inch. Longer lines in single-spaced letters are difficult to follow. Short letters may have still wider margins, and be double- or triple-spaced; or written on smaller stationery.

To lengthen a letter, add spaces between signature lines; to shorten, reduce spaces. But if a letter turns out noticeably off-balance, rewrite it. This is good self-discipline in the matter of space judging.

Critics that a writer is not aware of notice and comment upon the merits of typewritten work: the staff at the receiving end of the line. Their conclusions, good or bad, may influence their employer in doing business with a company. They are harsh judges of what they consider inefficiency, or ignorance, or both.

Efficient Method of Preparing Letters, and of Handing Them In. Proofread each letter as it is finished. If this is done, all typed letters will be ready at any time they might be called for. Do not write several letters and then proofread them.

Proofread slowly so that no typographical errors will be overlooked. No defense can be offered for these. Check carefully all initials, addresses, reference numbers, and the spelling of infrequent words.

Every page must be immaculately clean: **no struck-over letters,** no half erasures, and no finger marks or smudges.

Clip the pages of each letter together **in the upper left corner,** not in the center, nor on the right.

Clip pencil notations to letters that require special handling. These notations can remind the dictator of things to be done, as "Check to accompany this," "Date necessary," "Enclosures necessary," or "To be held."

If there is a question about a certain letter, write it on a note and clip it to the letter; the dictator can then answer when he returns the letters and at his convenience.

In special instances when another than the dictator is to sign the letter, clip a note to that effect **over the place for signature.** This will prevent the dictator from absent-mindedly signing the letter.

Manila File Folder for Letters to Be Signed. When handing in letters, put them in a manila file folder on which is marked "For Signature." The manila folder not only keeps the letters all together so that they can be considered at one time, but keeps them clean, and keeps them private.

Arrange the letters in the folder in the order of their importance; the most important always on top.

It is not necessary to clip the envelopes or enclosures to the letters (unless the dictator prefers that this be done). This extra bulk makes the letters awkward to handle when they are being signed.

307

LETTERS

When to Address Envelopes. Address them from the carbon copies, while the letters are being read and signed. **This saves time.** Assume responsibility for correct addresses, the manner of dispatch of letters, and enclosures. If an address is changed on a signed letter, **correct the envelope first,** then the letter.

Carbon Copies to Be Mailed Out. (See Carbon Copies, p. 428.)

Postal Cards. On the address side, no return address is necessary. On the message side, no receiver's name and address is necessary; nor, if the message is long, is any salutation or complimentary close. ("Thanks" is often used as an ending when appropriate.) The **date** is always required. The **sender's name and address** should be typed beneath the space for his signature, if room (in one long line, if necessary, divided by slants); otherwise as a return address on the front of the card. A good margin is ½ inch all round; but ¼ inch may be used. There are 16 single-spaced writing lines (**lengthwise**) on a postal card.

Invitations, Announcements, Programs, and Business and Social Cards.

Modern and correct forms for these may be obtained from any reliable stationer.

INVITATIONS—examples of wording. Line-spacing is wide; and **type faces** vary.

FORMAL, social—engraved (or partially), or handwritten (**prompt reply obligatory**):

> Mr. [and Mrs.] . . . (full name) . . .
> request(s) the pleasure of your company
> at a dinner
> in honor of
> . . . (name of honoree, with title) . . .
> Thursday, the twenty-fifth of April
> at half after seven o'clock
> The Mayfair Hotel
> R.s.v.p. [OR The favor of
> a reply is requested]
> **2488** Shasta Drive   **Black Tie**

BUSINESS, printed invitation (no reply necessary, although if unable to attend it is courteous to write or telephone a congratulatory response):

> The . . . (organization or official) . . .
> cordially invites you to attend the
> Dedication
> of the
> . . . (name of building, etc.) . . .
> on Friday morning, the sixth of June
> at ten-thirty o'clock
> **2725** Montlake Boulevard East
> Seattle, Washington

Style of handwritten ACCEPTANCE:

> *Mr. [and Mrs., OR Miss] . . . (full name;*
> *no initials unless always used) . . .*
> *accept(s) with pleasure*
> *the kind invitation of*
> *Mr. [and Mrs.] . . . (last name) . . .*
> *to a dinner [in honor of]*
> *on Thursday, April the twenty-fifth*
> *at half past seven o'clock*

Style of handwritten REGRET:

> *Mr. . . . (name as in acceptance) . . .*
> *regrets [exceedingly] that*
> *[because of a previous engagement*
> *OR absence from the city]*
> *he is unable to accept*
> *the kind invitation of*
> *Mr. [and Mrs.] . . . (last name) . . .*
> *for the twenty-fifth of April*

RULES for replying—always **promptly**—to **formal** invitations from individuals:

Stationery—use only fine, white or cream, double-fold paper; and write on the first page—not on the inside. (A card, personal stationery, telegram, or phone call may be employed for an **informal** or urgent reply.)

Writing—reply in handwriting, never on the typewriter (unless it is to a business invitation issued by an official or an organization).

Wording—always use the third person when replying to a formal, third-person invitation. (**Informal** invitations, only, are answered in the first person.)

Form—follow the same form and spacing of lines as in the invitation.

Note that the **date** (spelled out) is repeated in both the acceptance and the regret; the **hour** and **event** only in the acceptance; and the **year** does not appear at all. The **place** may or may not be included in the acceptance, but is unnecessary in the regret. **No excuse** is needed, but is courteous, in a regret. The **envelope** is addressed by hand to the host(s), or to a designated person.

Wedding Invitations—A formal invitation to a **church wedding** need not be acknowledged unless it includes also the reception. Then a formal reply **must** be sent to the parents of the bride (or the one issuing the invitation). No mention is necessary of the wedding, the participants, or the reception. The acceptance or declination is **for the day,** as "for Wednesday, the fifth of June [at four o'clock]."

A **gift,** if sent before the wedding, is addressed to the bride alone, in her maiden name. If sent after the wedding, it is addressed to the couple, Mr. and Mrs.

A **wedding announcement** requires no reply; but a congratulation is appreciated.

Note of Appreciation—after a dinner party, a little informal thank-you note is gracious—in handwriting on a card or personal stationery.

Business Invitations—if formal, should be answered formally (third person), and may be typewritten on executive letterheads. If informal, they are answered informally.

Style of Address.   The block style is the form now universally used on letters; and on envelopes to accommodate "scanners."   (See p. 338.)

"Open punctuation" (that is, no punctuation at line ends) is standard in addresses, the separation into lines being sufficient punctuation. "Close punctuation" is time-consuming and no longer used.

Lines.   An address may be written in two lines if it is very short: the name on one line, the city, state, and **Zip Code** on the next.   Or it may be set in four or five lines if long.   It is much better to give all of an address and make it clear than to leave out some part and allow it to be vague.   (On letters themselves, all addresses should be single-spaced.)

Street Numbers, Names of Buildings, Hotel Names.   (See p. 338 ff.)

The U.S. Postal Service requests that **every address**—even if to a small town—**bear a street name and house or building number;** or a **post office box number;** or "General Delivery"; and a **Zip Code.**   Incomplete addresses often cause delay in delivery and extra postal handling.

Post Office Box.   If a box number is in an address, use "Box..." and not the street address.   If both appear on the envelope or wrapper, the piece will be delivered to whichever is on the line next above the city-state-Zip line (Zip must be that of **actual delivery**).   The street address is for special deliveries, telegrams, express shipments, etc.

Care of.   Do not use "In care of" before a company's name if the person addressed is employed by or is a member of the company named If he is not immediately connected with the company, use "In-care of."

Or if a letter is being sent in care of a third person, use "In care of" (usually expressed by "c/o"; or "%" in routine work such as billing).

Cities and States.   City names should not be abbreviated unless space is limited, as on address plates.   State names **should be** abbreviated (see p. 338) when the Zip Code is used; otherwise spelled out.

"New York City" (which is the actual corporate name) is often used for "New York, N.Y.," although the latter is considered formally correct.

Never abbreviate the name of a city in a letter, as "N.Y." for New York City, "Phila." **for Philadelphia,** "L.A." for Los Angeles, or "Balto." for Baltimore.

Personal or Confidential.   Write "Personal" or "Confidential" (whichever has been dictated) about three spaces above the address on the letter.   It is not necessary to set it in caps; but it may be underlined for distinction.

"Confidential" should not be used on the envelope; it applies only to the contents of the letter, and is not considered a part of the address. Use "Personal" on the envelope if "Confidential" is used on the letter.

309

Titles. Always use **"Mr.," "Mrs.," "Miss,"** or **"Ms."** before a personal name, unless another title is applicable, as "Dr." or "Hon."

If unable to tell whether the addressee is a man or woman, use "Mr." or no title before the full name and just "M." in the salutation.

If in doubt about "Miss" or "Mrs.," use the alternative "Ms."

Messrs. This title is used before the names of two or more men associated in business when their association is more of a personal combination or partnership than a company.

"Messrs." is usually used before the names of firms of attorneys.

    Messrs. Logan, Spencer & Raeburn

It is not used before company or corporate names (except in Britain):

    Lord & Lyons (a company)   Ryan & Bro., Ltd. (a corporation)

Two men of the same name may be addressed as

    Messrs. R. W. and S. J. Hale (formal)   or   The Messrs. Hale
        or   The Mr. Hales (informal)

Never use "Messrs.:" **alone** as a salutation; use "Gentlemen:".

"Messrs." is the English abbreviation of the French "Messieurs," which is pronounced měs′ērs, or French mā′syụ′, but not *mě-sū′ers*. "MM." is the French abbreviation. (See also Salutations, p. 292.)

Esquire. This title is used in the United States only after the names of distinguished professional men, such as attorneys and architects. In England, however, it is quite generally used after the names of persons prominent in the social, diplomatic, and business world.

If "Dr.," "Mr.," "Hon.," or a similar title is used before a name, "Esq." is of course not used after it—and never in salutations. It is pronounced ěs′kwīr or ě-skwīr′; and it may be combined with titles as follows:

    K. V. T. Stuart, Esq., President   John Morgan Welford, Esq., M.P.
    J. Leslie Snowden, Jr., Esq.   Stuart and Atkins, Esqs.

NOTE: When "Esq." is used, "Attorney" is not added unless in an informative line: "Attorney(s) for..." or "Counsel for...." (Some bar associations address women lawyers too as "Esq." [Esquiress].) But usual addresses are: **Mr., Mrs., Ms.,** or **Miss** (or **Messrs.,** etc.) ... (full name) ... , **Attorney(s)** [or on the next line] **Attorney(s) at Law** (unabbreviated).

Junior and Senior. As a matter of courtesy to the bearer of the name, capitalize the abbreviation for "Junior" or "Senior" when it is part of a personal name. A comma may or may not be used to separate "Jr." or "Sr." from the name. The comma is commonly used, however, to conform to the general method of making additions after names.

    Mr. Lewis Hamilton, Jr.   or   Mr. Lewis Hamilton Jr.

"Jr." or **"Sr." may be used in combination with any title:**

    Mr. Max Hildreth, Jr., President   Paul Thomas, Jr., M.D.

The possessive is formed as follows (note no comma after it):

    John J. Rogers, Jr.'s office   The John J. Rogers, Jrs.' home

The plural is:

    The John J. Rogerses, Jr. (formal)   The John J. Rogers, Jrs. (informal)

310

Note: "Sr." is not usually used unless the two identical names are closely associated. "Jr." and "Sr." are usually dropped after the death of father or son, although they may be retained for identification.

"II, III," or "IV" is used after the name of a grandson, nephew, or cousin. A son is always "Jr." unless his father is "Jr." or "II"; then he is "III."

Second and Third. These designations after names may be written in Roman numerals, "II, III, IV," or in ordinal numbers, "2nd (or 2d), 3rd (or 3d), 4th." Either form is correct; and commas may or may not be used around the numeral. Often the separating comma is omitted before the distinctive Roman numeral (as in royal names), but is used with the ordinal number to conform to the general method of making additions after names. No period is necessary after either form.

Mr. Jason Lloyd III has...	or	Mr. Jason Lloyd, 3rd, has...
PLURAL: The Jason Lloyds III	(or 3rd or 3d)	(formal)
The Jason Lloyd IIIs	(or 3rds or 3ds)	(informal)
POSSESSIVE, SINGULAR: III's or 3rd's		PLURAL: IIIs' or 3rds'

Personal Names. A personal name should be written exactly as the bearer writes it. If he uses initials, or abbreviates his first name, it is permissible to follow that form. The common abbreviations are:

Benj.	Benjamin	Geo.	George	Robt.	Robert
Chas.	Charles	Jas.	James	Sam'l	Samuel
Dan'l	Daniel	Jno.	John	Thos.	Thomas
Edw.	Edward	Jos.	Joseph	Wm.	William

Check surnames to make sure that they are spelled exactly as the bearers spell them. There is nothing a person is so particular about as his own name. Many common names are spelled in different ways, as

Dickson	Dixon		Stewart	Stuart
Frederick	Fredericks		Stevens	Stephens
Louis	Lewis		Thompson	Thomson

Nicknames. Nicknames or shortened forms of names should not be used in addresses, unless a shortened form is the actual name.

They may be used in salutations and need not be quoted. No periods are required after them; they are not considered abbreviations, but shortened forms, or substitute names.

Dear Tom: Dear Hap: Dear D.B.:   Dear Doc: Dear Syd:

When used in the body of a letter, a nickname need not be quoted if it is as commonly known as a true name.

Bill Gibson   Hap West   J.B.   BUT: T. J. "Tim" O'Connor

Company Names. Write a company's name exactly as it appears on that company's letterhead; or in the absence of a letterhead as the company writes its name in an advertisement; or as the name is listed in the telephone book.

Do not abbreviate or hyphen a company name, or use "&" in it, unless the company itself does so. If a company name has "The" before it, use "The" in the address.

311

If there is a slight discrepancy between the way a company name is signed and the way it appears on the letterhead, take the letterhead as a guide—it should be authentic.

Note whether or not an organization is a "company" or a "corporation." A "corporation" usually dislikes being called a "company," and vice versa. Many large concerns are companies, as

Ford Motor Company   The Boeing Company   Union Oil Company

Sometimes there are a company and a corporation with related names:

McGraw-Hill, Inc.   and   McGraw-Hill Book **Company**
Carrier **Corporation**   Carrier Transicold **Company**

Check to make sure that each name is **right,** not almost right. There are various ways to confuse names.

The Johns Hopkins University   NOT: *John* Hopkins University
                                NOR: *John's* Hopkins Univ.
Holland-America Line   Holland-*American* Line
American Telephone and   American *Telegraph* and
  Telephone Company   *Telephone* Company
Johns-Manville Corporation   *John Mansville* Corp.

Divisions and Departments.   When addressing a division or department of a company or an organization, put the company's or organization's name first, because it is more important than the division's or department's, and because this form will be useful later for reference and filing.   (See also Government addresses, p. 502.)

The name of a division or department may also be written in the Attention line.

Hanover & Sons, Inc.   OR: Hanover & Sons, Inc.
Accounting Department   230 Park Ave. - 20th Floor
230 Park Avenue, 20th Floor   New York, NY   10017
New York, NY   10017   Attention Accounting Dept.

NOTE: Sometimes a large company has subdivisions of its departments. In that case, the department name should be in the main address as shown, and the subdivision name in the attention line.

On the envelope the name of the division or department may be in the address proper or in the Attention space in the lower left corner.

Personal Names With Company Names.   If a letter is intended for the consideration of but one person, the personal name may be placed above the company name.   This placement signifies that the letter is of a semi-personal nature.

But if the letter pertains to company business and should be opened and handled in the absence of the person addressed, the personal name should be written below the address, in the Attention line.   (See p. 291.)

Do not neglect to write the company name when addressing a person connected with a company.   The company's name may seem superfluous, but it is of value for later reference, and is of definite value on the envelope

312

in assisting the postman to locate the person if the address has been changed or is wrong, or if a large building is involved.

WRITE: Mr. Thornton J. Mills   NOT: *Thornton J. Mills*
        Harrison Wells Company   *160 State*
        160 State Street   *Boston, Mass.*
        Boston, MA   02109

Attention.   (For Attention line and salutation, see pp. 291–92.)

Personal Names Used as Company Names.   It is unnecessary to use "Mr." or "Messrs." before personal names used as company names (unless the concerns are law firms or similar organizations—for which see "Messrs.," p. 310).   The salutation should be "Gentlemen:".

Lord & Lyons   John Harper
1701 K St., NW.   50 W. 50th St.
Washington, DC   20005   New York City   10020

Gentlemen: Gentlemen:

Women's Names.   (See Women's Signatures, p. 296.)

Madam or Madame.   "Madame" is the original French form and is used only in connection with foreign names.   (pron. mȧ′dȧm′)   The abbreviation is "Mme" (with no period).

The English form, "Madam," should be used only in salutations on impersonal or routine letters.   (pron. măd′ăm)

(See also Salutations to Women, pp. 293, 323, and 324.)

Mesdames or Mss.   This title is used before the names of two or more married women (or married and unmarried) associated in business.

("Mesdames" is pronounced mā-däm′; abbreviated "Mmes"—no period.)

Mesdames (or Mss.) Kent and Reed   or   Mrs. Kent and Ms. Reed

Two married women of the same name may be addressed as

Mss. (or Mmes) J. V. and T. L. Ellis (formal)   or   The Mesdames Ellis
or The Mrs. (or Ms.) Ellises (informal)
(See also Salutations to Women, p. 293.)

Misses or Mss.   This title may be used before the names of unmarried women associated in business.

Misses (or Mss.) Hart and Mills   or   Miss Hart and Miss Mills

Two unmarried women of the same name may be addressed as

Misses (or Mss.) Joan and Ellen Day (formal)   or   The Misses Day
or The Miss (or Ms.) Days (informal)
(See also Salutations to Women, p. 293.)

Master.   This is the proper designation for a small boy.   The plural is "Masters."

Masters Weldon and Blaine Cartwright

Two boys of the same name may be addressed as

The Masters Turner (formal)   or   The Master Turners (informal)

Business Titles in Addresses. The modern tendency is to omit business titles in addresses, unless the title is needed for identification, or unless the letter is of a legal nature and it is desired to address the person in his official capacity.

A business title, if used, may be written on the line with the personal name, or on the line with the company name, or on a line by itself, whichever arrangement gives the best balance.

Mr. J. G. Barnes, President
Merchants Association of Brentwood

Mr. Hamilton W. Pennington, Jr.
Secretary, Maitland Bros., Inc.

Mr. Nathaniel W. Burke
Vice President and General Manager
The Stone and Marshall Company
720 N. Michigan Ave.
Chicago, IL 60611

NOTE: An extra-long title may be broken and carried over to the second line—indented two spaces:

Mr. ..., President and Chairman of the Board

(The last example is one of the reasons why titles are being discontinued. They can make addresses needlessly heavy and long.)

A business title may be used after a name even though a professional title or "Mr." has been used before it. ("**Mr.**" is always correct before any man's name if the proper title is not known.)

Prof. Blake Taylor, Treasurer   Dr. Emerson F. Lowell, President
Capt. J. O. Helm, Chairman   The Rev. David Blythe, Secretary

Titles Unhyphened. Titles need not be hyphened unless they represent two titles. (See Titles, p. 268.)

Vice President   BUT: Secretary-Treasurer (two titles)

Abbreviating Titles. A title may be abbreviated if it stands before a full name; but if a title stands immediately before a last name it is not abbreviated, unless it is "Mr.," "Messrs.," "Mrs.," "Ms.," or "Dr."

Prof. John C. Reade   BUT: Professor Reade
Lieut. William Rogers   Lieutenant Rogers

Hence in salutations titles are usually written out.

Dear Professor Reade: Dear Lieutenant Rogers:

Doctor. Other titles may be used in connection with "Dr.," except "M.D." or other degree letters that mean "Doctor."

Dr. J. Mason Blake   Dr. James C. Hartwell
Superintendent of Education   President, Southwestern Institution

Dr. Stephen E. Lee   Dr. Joseph B. Blair, Chairman
Professor of Economics

In the salutation, "Doctor" may be written out, to conform to the rule of writing out titles before surnames; or it may be abbreviated.

My dear Doctor Blake: (formal)   Dr. and Mrs. L. V. Merriville
Dear Dr. Blake: (informal)   Dear Dr. and Mrs. Merriville:

If the addressee is the holder of a doctor's degree, and is referred to in the address by a title other than "Doctor," he may be referred to as "Doctor" in the salutation.

ADDRESS: President Lawrence Merrill
SALUTATION: My dear Doctor Merrill: or   Dear Dr. Merrill:

Do not use "Doctor" without a surname in the salutation, unless it is in personal correspondence.

PERSONAL: My dear Doctor: or   Dear Doctor:

If a married woman is a doctor, her title is sometimes—in social correspondence—abandoned in addressing her and her husband.

Mr. and Mrs. James O. Madison

But in professional writings, a woman doctor is accorded her title and own name. (Many professional women retain their maiden names.)

Dr. Mary C. Hartwell, and
Mr. James O. Madison

Dear Dr. Hartwell and Mr. Madison:

Or if both are doctors, and she uses her married name:

Dr. Mary H. Madison, and
Dr. James O. Madison   or   The Doctors (or Drs.) Madison

My dear Doctors Madison: or   Dear Drs. Madison:

Many doctors of medicine prefer the degree letters "M.D." after the name to the title of "Dr." before it, because of the large number of persons now using the title "Dr."

Mary C. Hartwell, M.D.   James O. Madison, M.D.

When two doctors are being addressed, the abbreviation "Drs." is customary.

Drs. S. G. Blake and V. M. Mason
Dear Drs. Blake and Mason:

Two doctors of the same name may be addressed as

The Doctors (or Drs.) Jones (formal)   or   The Dr. Joneses (informal)

Degree and Professional Letters. Letters signifying college or honorary degrees are used chiefly in publications and in formal writings where it seems desirable to apprise the reader of a person's academic standing. Degree letters (with the exception of "M.D." and "D.D.") are not commonly used in addresses on business letters and envelopes.

If degree letters (or certain **earned** professional letters) are used in the address, neither "Mr.," "Dr.," nor "Hon." precedes the name.

James Blake, M.D.   John Trevor, CPA
President of...   Accounting Manager
Ellen M. Lowden, Ph.D.   BUT: Miss (or Mrs.) Ruth Day, R.N.
Dean of the College of...   Sister Teresa, CSC, FHFMA

315

A title (other than "Dr.") is sometimes used before a name when degree letters follow it—in writings other than addresses.

Professor Jason Stanfield, Ph.D.
President Edward L. Masters, LL.D.
The Reverend David A. Merrill, S.T.D.
Rev. John Wayne, D.D.   (Note that "Rev." does not signify "D.D.")
...the Honorable W. Park Wills, Sc.D.
Dean Hugh C. Reade, A.M., Ph.D.
Captain Leland F. Scott, M.A.
Miss Jessica Harland, Litt.D.
Sir Sidney Graystone, LL.D., D.Litt.

Occasionally "Dr." is used before a name in a text with the explanatory degree letters shown in parentheses after the name.

Dr. Paul T. Nelson (Ed.D.)

Degrees and orders are arranged after a name in the following sequence: "Orders, religious first; theological degrees; academic degrees earned in course; and honorary degrees in order of bestowal."—Government Printing Office Style Manual.

Keith M. Taylor, B.S., M.A., LL.D.
Leslie A. Ryan, M.D., Ph.D., Medical Director
John F. Franklin, Ph.D., Litt.D., Editor
James E. Russell, M.D., Dr.P.H., Instructor in Hygiene
Rev. Daniel Stuart Blythe, D.S.O., D.D., Litt.D., LL.D., Chaplain

Professor.   The title "Professor" should be used only for instructors of the highest rank, or persons upon whom the title has been conferred by academic authority.   It should not be used indiscriminately for all teachers.   Since the title "Professor" signifies rank, it is usually preferred to "Doctor" by those who also hold doctor's degrees.

"Professor" should be written in full if used alone with a surname; but it may be abbreviated if used before a first name or initial.   Accordingly, it is usually abbreviated in an address, but written in full in the salutation.   (See also p. 331.)

Prof. Samuel J. Linden   Dear Professor Linden:

"Professor" is not generally used without a surname in the salutation, unless it is in personal correspondence.

PERSONAL: My dear Professor: or   Dear Professor:

In an address to a professor and his wife, "Professor" is commonly written in full, but it may be abbreviated if the name is long.

Professor and Mrs. E. B. Masters
Prof. and Mrs. Alexander B. Hawthorne   Dear Professor and Mrs. ...:

If the wife is the professor, her title is abandoned in the combination of names.

Mr. and Mrs. R. B. McGregor   Dear Mr. and Mrs. McGregor:

316

But if the names represent official capacities, they may be separated.

Dr. E. B. Trainor, President, and
Prof. Caroline V. Trainor, Secretary
The Wilkes School of Fine Arts

My dear Doctor and Professor Trainor:

When addressing two professors, write "Professors," not "*Profs.*"

Professors S. J. Linden and E. B. Trainor

Two professors of the same name may be addressed as

The Professors Linden (formal)   or   The Professor Lindens (informal)

Reverend

In all formal writings, "The" should always precede "Reverend"; but the long "The Reverend" is usually abbreviated to "The Rev." or just "Rev." in addresses on business letters and envelopes, in advertisements, and in church notices.

Rev. John J. Polk

The title of "The Reverend" is used in the following manners:

The Reverend   before the names of most clergymen.
The Very Reverend ⎫ before the names of the higher dignitaries in
The Right Reverend ⎬ various churches. (See Forms of Address,
The Most Reverend ⎭ pp. 333 ff.)

"The Reverend" should not be used with a surname only, as "*The Reverend Clarkson.*" "The Reverend" is a title of respect, not one of rank or office. To say "*The Reverend Clarkson*" is like saying "*The Respected Clarkson,*" which of course immediately suggests a correction to "The Respected Mr. Clarkson" or "The Respected Benjamin C. Clarkson." Hence there must always be an intervening Christian name or initial, or a title such as "Dr.," "Mr.," or "Professor," between "The Reverend" and the surname.

The Reverend Mr. Clarkson
The Rev. Dr. John Phillips
The Reverend Professor Meredith
The Reverend R. M. Alden, Chaplain
The Very Reverend President Blythe
The Very Reverend Father Wayne

"The Reverend" does not necessarily signify "Doctor of Divinity" (D.D.). "Doctor of Divinity" is an honorary degree conferred upon clergymen. Hence "The Reverend" is often used in texts in connection with "D.D.," or other degree letters signifying "Doctor."

The Reverend Paul Kenworth, D.D., Litt.D.
The Reverend John Lane, S.T.D.
BUT NOT: *The Reverend Dr. Parsons, D.D.*   (two "Doctors")

A clergyman is addressed as "Mr." in conversation unless he has a doctor's degree; then he is addressed as "Doctor."

Use in Salutations. "Reverend" should not be used in a salutation before a surname. Use "Mr.," "Dr.," or another appropriate title.

Dear Mr. Clarkson:	My dear Professor Meredith:
Dear Dr. Phillips:	My dear President Blythe:
BUT: Reverend dear Father: and	Reverend Sir:

To a Clergyman and His Wife. When a clergyman and his wife are being addressed, "The Reverend" is usually abbreviated to shorten the address, since the full name must be used, not the last name alone.

The Rev. and Mrs. Benjamin C. Clarkson
(NOT: *Rev. and Mrs. Clarkson*)

My dear Mr. and Mrs. Clarkson: or   Dear Dr. and Mrs. Clarkson:

If the full name is not known, the address may be:

The Reverend Mr. Clarkson and Mrs. Clarkson

Plurals. Two clergymen of the same name should not be addressed as "The *Reverends*..." They may be addressed as "The Reverend Messrs. ..." or "The Reverend Drs. ...". Or "The Reverend" or "Rev." may be used before each man's full name.

The Rev. Messrs. S. J. and D. V. Parke ⎱ or   Rev. S. J. Parke, and
The Reverend Drs. Parke ⎰   Rev. Daniel Parke

In Texts. "The" is not capitalized when the title occurs in the body of a letter or in a text, but "Reverend" is always capitalized.

...by the Reverend Dr. John Phillips. Then Dr. Phillips said...

In Lists. In formal writings, "The *Reverends*" or "*Revs.*" is not used as a plural title before a list of names. "The Reverend Messrs." or "the Reverend Doctors (Drs.)" may be used; or "the Reverend" or "Rev." may be repeated before each name. Or if the word "clergymen" or "clergy" is mentioned in the introduction to the list, the first "the Reverend" will serve for all the names. ("Revs." is sometimes seen in newspapers, catalogues, and directories, but it rarely appears in formal texts.)

...present were the Reverend Messrs. Clarkson, Blythe, and Parke.
...among the clergy were the Reverend J. Polk, Mr. Clarkson, David Blythe, and Dr. Page.
...addresses will be delivered by the Rev. J. Polk, Rev. Mr. Clarkson, Rev. David Blythe, and Rev. Dr. Page.

Honorable

There is a tradition that "Honorable" should not be used without "The" before it; but "The Honorable" is now very generally abbreviated to "Hon." in all addresses to government officials.

Hon. Stephen Sanderson

Use of "Honorable." Regarding the use of "The Honorable" or "Hon." remember that:

In the United States it is a title of distinction accorded any **elected or appointed** government official (but not a **career** officer).

And it is **never** used by the person rating it—in his signature, on his letterheads, visiting cards, or invitations.

"Right Honourable" and "Most Honourable" are used in Britain.

Not With Surname Only. "The Honorable" should never be used before a surname only, as *"The Honorable Gray."* "The Honorable" is a title of respect, not one of rank or office. To say *"The Honorable Gray"* is like saying *"The Respected Gray,"* which of course immediately suggests a correction to "The Respected Mr. Gray" or "The Respected Frank J. Gray." Hence there must always be an intervening first name or initial, or a title such as "Dr.," "Mr.," or "Judge," between "The Honorable" and the surname.

The Honorable Mr. Fulton	The Honorable Judge Nelson
The Honorable Paul Fulton	The Honorable Dr. Starr

Alike for Men and Women. "The Honorable" or "Hon." may be used alike for men and women; and no other title is necessary with the full name.

Hon. Josephine Lande	NOT:	Hon. *Mrs.* Josephine Lande
Hon. Douglas Mills		Hon. *Mr.* Douglas Mills

But if the first name or initial is not known, another title must be used with "The Honorable," as

The Honorable Mrs. Lande	The Honorable Dr. Stanfield
The Honorable Miss Merrick	The Honorable Mr. Mills

Never in Salutations. "Honorable" is never used in a salutation. "Mr." or a similar title may be used, or the title of the office.

Dear Mr. Fulton:	Dear Governor Clayton:
Dear Mrs. Lande:	Dear Mr. Secretary:

To an Official and His Wife. When an official and his wife are being addressed, the full name should be given, not the last name alone.

The Honorable and Mrs. Benjamin J. Clark
(NOT: *Hon. and Mrs. Clark*)

Dear Mr. and Mrs. Clark:

If the full name is not known, the address may be:

The Honorable Mr. Clark and Mrs. Clark

If the wife is "The Honorable," her name comes first; or, socially, her title may be abandoned in the combination of names.

OFFICIAL: The Honorable Mary M. Downs and Mr. Downs
SOCIAL: Mr. and Mrs. J. Evan Downs

In Texts. "The" is not capitalized when the title occurs in the body of a letter or in a text, but "Honorable" is always capitalized.

...by the Honorable Theodore Adams. Later Mr. Adams said...

319

In Lists. In informal texts, "The Honorables" or "Hons." is used as a plural title before a list of names. More formal is "The Honorable Messrs."; or "the Honorable" or "Hon." repeated before each name.

> INFORMAL: . . .meeting the Hons. Oscar Adams, Margaret Hamilton, Seth Blackmore, and Joseph Anderson.
>
> FORMAL: . . .was supported by the Honorable Mss. Heath and Barnhart, and Messrs. Clarke, Goodfellow, Thomas, Carlton, and Reade.

Permanency of Title. "Honorable" may be conferred on former government officials—addressing them as they were addressed in office (unless another title is preferred by the ex-official, or is more appropriate, as "Dr.," "General," "Professor," or even "Mr.").

Card Index of Addresses. When numerous addresses are being dealt with, it is efficient to keep a card file of them on or in the desk. Each person's or company's name, address, and telephone number is typed on a 3-by-5-inch card, with pertinent information added, such as a company's business, branch offices, and officers' names, titles, and the manner in which each person should be addressed.

Address Book. When addresses are not numerous, it is convenient to keep them in a 5-by-7-inch book. Larger books are unwieldy, and smaller ones haven't space enough for long addresses. A looseleaf book is unnecessary: it is easier to make entries by hand than to type them.

Make all entries in ink, and either print or write them in **clear, round letters.** Pencil notations become illegible with constant handling. Enter the names according to companies, with personnel listed:

		TELEPHONE
Washington Corporation 383 Madison Ave. New York, N.Y. 10017	Thomas R. Hill, Pres. J. J. Moore, V.Pres. Ray Evans, Sales Mgr.	(212) 759-7743

Make it a rule to verify each name after it is written, to be sure it is correct—so that the address book will be a final authority on names.

Adopt the further rule of entering, when first encountered, every name that will undoubtedly be needed again, even if this necessitates several pauses in the course of a busy day. If this is not done, addresses will be overlooked, and the efficiency of the address book impaired. Time seems much more valuable when wasted in an attempt to look up an address in the files than when used simply to write down a name.

Addresses of Personnel. The correct name, home address, and telephone number of every person in the organization should be written in the address book or kept in a convenient place in the files. These addresses and telephone numbers are often of vital importance when an endeavor is being made to reach someone connected with the organization.

Temporary Addresses. Temporary addresses (traveling addresses, etc.) should be written on slips of paper and clipped into the address book at the proper places. These can be removed when no longer useful; then the address book will not contain a number of scratched-out names.

Traveling Addresses. (For addresses to trains, etc., see p. 381.)

Foreign Addresses

English Lettering. All foreign addresses on envelopes should be **typewritten or written in ink** (never in lead pencil) and should be in English or in English (roman) lettering, if possible. An address in a foreign language, as Greek, is permissible if the names of the post office, province, and country are in English, or at least in roman characters.

The foreign titles corresponding to "Mr.," "Mrs.," and "Miss" may be used if desired, even if the rest is in English. But "Mr.," "Mrs.," and "Miss" may always be used and will be changed to the proper titles in translation.

Capitalization of Foreign Names. (See p. 131.)

Postal Codes or Districts. These should be placed **before** the city name or **between** the city and country—never **after** the country.

Name of Country. Every foreign address should be complete, with the country as well as the city. The country name (in **caps** and **never abbreviated**) should **stand alone on the last line.** Canadian addresses must carry **CANADA,** even though the name of the province is given:

Victoria, BC
K1A 0N4
CANADA

{ Two-letter abbreviations for Canadian Provinces are:
Alberta, AB; British Columbia, BC; Manitoba, MB; New Brunswick, NB; Newfoundland, NF; Northwest Territory, NT; Nova Scotia, NS; Ontario, ON; Quebec, PQ; Saskatchewan, SK; Yukon Territory, YT }

In many foreign addresses, postal districts are given, as

London SW1P 3EB	00100 Rome	Paris 75020
1 Berlin 42	Tokyo 100	Athens 208

Mexico City is a Federal District, similar to the District of Columbia in the United States. Letters are addressed with a postal zone as

Mexico 1, D.F.—which means "México, Distrito Federal"

Foreign Addresses From Telephone Books. (See p. 404.)

Translation Bureaus. Translation bureaus are listed in the classified sections of telephone books, under T. Large public libraries usually have foreign departments that will assist in short translations.

FOREIGN TITLES CORRESPONDING TO "MR.," "MRS.," AND "MISS"

American	French		German		Spanish		Italian	
	Title	Abbr.	Title	Abbr.	Title	Abbr.	Title	Abbr.
Mr.	Monsieur	M.*	Herrn†	‡	Señor	Sr.	Signor	Sig.
Messrs.	Messieurs	MM.*	Herren	‡	Señores	Sres.	Signori	Sigg.
Mrs.	Madame	Mme*	Frau	Fr.*	Señora	Sra.	Signora	Sig.ra*
Miss	Mademoiselle	Mlle*	Fräulein	Frl.*	Señorita	Srta.	Signorina	Sig.na*
Mesdames	Mesdames	Mmes*			Señoras	Sras.*	Signore	Sig.re*
Misses	Mesdemoiselles	Mlles*	Fräulein	Frl.*	Señoritas	Srtas.*	Signorine	Sig.ne*

* Abbreviation not often used in addresses. The title is written out.
† Form used in addresses because it implies "to."
‡ Abbreviation not used.

Don—is a Spanish title of respect, corresponding to the English "Esquire." It is used only before Christian names or initials, as

Don Juan	Señor Don Francisco Diaz	Señor Dr. Don José Diaz
Don Alfonso	Don L. Diaz	BUT NOT: *Don* Diaz

Doña—is the corresponding feminine Spanish title of respect.

Señora Doña Dolores Montez   Doña Dolores   NOT: *Doña* Montez

Sir—The British title "Sir" is never followed by a last name only. It must be followed by a forename, initial, or title as "sir knight."

NEVER: *Sir* Lindon   ALWAYS: Sir George Lindon   or   Sir George
The Honourable Sir Evan Lang, K.B.E.   Lt.Gen. Sir Roger Reid

◇◇◇◇◇◇◇◇◇

ADDRESSES TO GOVERNMENT OFFICIALS

"No title of nobility shall be granted by the United States."
—The Constitution of the United States, Art. I, Sec. 9.

From the above, it follows logically enough that any official of the government may and should be addressed with simplicity.

Flowery wordings are outmoded—charming when sometimes used by the older generation, but not in keeping with the new.

Use of Personal Name. In ordinary correspondence with government offices, titles of offices rather than personal names should be used, as

The Commissioner of Patents	The Attorney General
The Register of Copyrights	The American Consul

In special correspondence, the personal name may be used in the address.

Names of Government Officials. Names of the United States Government officials may be found in the Congressional Directory in any public library; or in the current American almanacs. (See also Reference Books, p. 605, and Government Departments, p. 503.)

Names of state officials may be found in the state directory or roster in the public libraries in each state. The names of the governors of the different states are given in the current American almanacs. (See also Reference Books, p. 609.)

Names of city officials may be obtained from the city hall, or from the public library, in each city.

Addressing "The Office of." In seeking general information from any office, it is well to address simply "The Office of...," as

The Office of the Secretary of State
The Office of the Attorney General

The salutation to an office is "Gentlemen:".

Women Officials. Women holding official positions are accorded the same titles and forms of address as men. "Madam" is substituted

322

for "Mr." in the diplomatic salutation, as "Dear Madam Secretary:" or "Dear Madam Mayor:" (alike for "Mrs.," "Ms.," and "Miss").

"Madam Secretary" (the American form) is preferred, in Government usage, to "Madame Secretary" (the French form). The latter is sometimes seen in texts in publications.

Some women officials prefer to retain their own titles, "Mrs.," "Ms.," or "Miss" (as **"Mrs. Secretary"**), and dispense with "Madam."

Retired Officials. Titles of office may be retained after retirement—usually used in letter salutations, with "Honorable" in the addresses. Career military, religious, and judicial titles are always retained.

Capitol and Capital. Note that "capitol" means a building (a statehouse); while "capital" means a city. "The Capitol" in Washington, D.C., is the building where Congress convenes; whereas Washington, D.C., is the capital of the United States.

Wives of Officials. In American usage, wives do not share their husbands' titles. Their title is always "Mrs."

> The President and Mrs. Hanover
> The Secretary of State and Mrs. Danvers
> The British Ambassador and Lady Manton
> The American Ambassador and Mr. James   (if Ambassador is a woman)
> The Chief Justice and Mrs. Helm
> Mr. Justice and Mrs. Marshall   (to an Associate Justice and wife)
> Senator and Mrs. Rogers   or   Senator and Mrs. Thomas Rogers
> The Honorable and Mrs. Stephen Scott   (to a Representative and wife)
> The Honorable Mary Lee and Mr. Lee   or   Mr. and Mrs. Max Lee
> The Governor and Mrs. Kellogg   or   Governor and Mrs. John Kellogg
> The Mayor and Mrs. Lane   or   Mayor and Mrs. William Lane
> General and Mrs. Norwell   or   General and Mrs. Carl Norwell

State Department Forms. The Department of State in Washington, D.C., by reason of its traditional dignity and because of its large diplomatic correspondence, employs certain ceremonious forms that are not used by other Departments of the Government, or by the general public.

Yet the State Department has recently simplified some parts of its forms of address. For instance, "The" is now generally dropped before "Honorable"; "My" is omitted from most salutations; "Sincerely yours" is the usual complimentary close; and most addresses are placed, as in business, at the beginning of letters, not at the end.

Official Complimentary Closings. The ordinary complimentary closings may be used in all forms of official correspondence. Common official closings are:

Sincerely [yours], (the most used)	Respectfully [yours],
Very truly yours, (more formal)	Very respectfully,
Sincerely, OR Cordially, (informal)	Faithfully [yours],

The **diplomatic closing** is more ceremonious:

> With respectful regard,   OR   Accept, Excellency [or Sir],
> the [renewed] assurances
> of my high[est] consideration.

❖❖❖❖❖❖❖❖

FORMS OF ADDRESS

(All forms given herein have been checked by, or furnished by, representative offices.)

To make the **forms of address applicable to women** as well as men, it is to be assumed that feminine titles may be used wherever masculine titles are shown.

Mrs., Miss, or Ms.	may be substituted for	Mr.
Madam: or Dear Madam:	for	Sir: or Dear Sir:
Dear Madam (or Mrs., Miss, or Ms.) Secretary:		Dear Mr. Secretary:

NOTE: In salutations, **"My"** is now infrequent—being largely reserved for letters of dignity, as to diplomats and the judiciary; and letters with a personal import, as to the clergy.

Second-Page Headings. If "Honorable" has been used in an address, the second-page heading may be "Hon. ...(full name)...," or "Mr. ...(last name)..." Or the title may be used, as "Senator Hall," "Governor James."

TO FEDERAL GOVERNMENT OFFICIALS

(Names of Government officials may be found in the reference books listed on pp. 604 ff. Names of Government Departments are given on pp. 503 ff. [Note that each U.S. Government office in Washington, D.C., now has its own Zip Code number.])

If personal name is not used: If personal name is used:

THE PRESIDENT

The President or
The President of the United States
The White House
Washington, D.C. **20500**
Mr. President: (formal) or
Dear Mr. President:

The Honorable...(full name)... or
President...(full [or last] name)...
The White House
Washington, D.C. **20500**
My dear Mr. President: or
Dear President........:

THE VICE PRESIDENT

The Vice President or
The President of the Senate
United States Senate
Washington, D.C. **20510**
Sir: (formal) or
Dear Mr. [Vice] President:

The Honorable...(full name)...
The Vice President
of the United States
Washington, D.C. **20510**
Dear Mr. Vice President: or
Dear Mr.........:

THE SPEAKER OF THE HOUSE

The Speaker of the House
of Representatives
Washington, D.C. **20515**
Sir: (formal) or
Dear Mr. Speaker:

The Honorable...(full name)...
Speaker of the House
of Representatives
Washington, D.C. **20515**
Dear Mr. Speaker: or
Dear Mr..........:

THE CABINET

Formal, diplomatic form:
The Honorable
The Secretary of ....
Washington, D.C. (Zip Code)
Sir:
     or similarly
The Honorable
The Attorney General
Washington, D.C. **20530**
Sir:
Business form:
The Secretary of ....
Washington, D.C. (Zip Code)
Dear Mr. Secretary:

The Honorable ...(full name)...
Secretary of ....
Washington, D.C. (Zip Code)
Dear Mr. Secretary: or
Dear Mr. ....:
     or similarly
The Honorable ...(full name) ...
The Attorney General
Washington, D.C. **20530**
Dear Mr. Attorney General: or
Dear Mr. ....:
     or to an Administrator
Dear Mr. Administrator:

If personal name is not used: If personal name is used:

COMMISSIONER, CHAIRMAN, DIRECTOR, OR CHIEF OF A GOVERNMENT OFFICE

The Commissioner of ....
Department of .... (or agency)
Washington, D.C. (Zip Code)
Sir:

Hon. ... (full name)... (if appointed) or
Mr. (or Dr.) ... (full name)... (if career)
Commissioner of ..... (or other title)
Department of ..... (or agency)
Washington, D.C. (Zip Code)

Dear Mr. Commissioner: or
Dear Mr. (or Dr.) ......:

Similarly addressed may be: The Director or Chief of an office;*
The Chairman of a Board or Committee;* The Librarian of Congress;
The Comptroller General of the United States; and The Public Printer.

THE CONGRESS

SENATOR

Hon. ... (full name)... or
Senator ... (full name)...
United States Senate
Washington, D.C. 20510
  or to a home-state address
Hon. ... (full name)...
United States Senator
(Local address, and Zip Code)
Dear Senator ....: (man or woman) or
Sir: (formal)

REPRESENTATIVE

Hon. ... (full name)... or
Representative (or Congressman) ......
House of Representatives
Washington, D.C. 20515
  or to a home-state address
Hon. ... (full name)...
Representative, U.S. Congress
(Local address, and Zip Code)
Dear Congressman ....:† or
Dear Representative (or Mr.) ......: or
Sir: (formal)

COMMITTEEMEN

Congressional Committee chairmen are similarly addressed:

Hon. ... (full name)...
Chairman, Committee on ......
          or just
The Chairman
Committee on ....
United States Senate or
House of Representatives
  or for a Joint Committee
Chairman, Joint Committee on ...
Congress of the United States
Dear Mr. Chairman:

CONGRESSMEN-ELECT

Congressmen elected but not yet
seated are addressed with the
title below the name:

Hon. ... (full name)...
Senator-elect or
Representative-elect
Dear Mr. ....:

TO DIPLOMATIC REPRESENTATIVES

The diplomatic representatives are ambassadors, ministers, and occasionally chargés d'affaires. (The **heads** of all U.S. missions are now ambassadors.)

It is customary to address a foreign ambassador as "His Excellency," followed on the next line by his personal title, if any, as "Sir," "Baron," or "Dr.," before his full name. (The names and titles of diplomatic represer.tatives may be found in the Congressional Directory in any public library; or in the current American almanacs listed on p. 607.)

Note that the headquarters (and home) of an ambassador is called an **"embassy"**; and the business office of each country is a **"chancery."** (The headquarters of a minister was, formerly, a **"legation."**)

Ordinary communications should be addressed to the Secretary of the Embassy, and not to individual members of the staff.

* Although "Dear Mr. Commissioner:" and "Dear Mr. Chairman [or Ms. Chairwoman]:" are used as salutations, "Dear Mr. Director:" is rarely used, and "Dear Mr. Chief:" is not considered possible.

† The term "Congresswoman" is now coming into general use with the changing status and individualism of women. However, "Representative" or "Senator" is usually to be preferred when addressing or referring to a woman in the Congress.

ADDRESSES

If personal name is not used: If personal name is used:

AMBASSADOR

(Note "His Excellency [H.E.]" for foreign ambassadors, but "The Honorable" for American.)

His Excellency
The Ambassador of . . . .
Washington, D.C. (Zip Code)

The Honorable
The American* Ambassador
(Foreign Capital, and Country)
Sir: (formal) or
Dear Mr. Ambassador:

> NOTE: United Nations delegates are similarly
> addressed, with appropriate changes. For
> instance, for "The American Ambassador,"
> substitute: United States* Representative
> To the United Nations
> New York, NY 10017

His Excellency
. . . . ([personal title] full name) . . . .
Ambassador of . . . .
Washington, D.C. (Zip Code)
Excellency: (formal)
Dear Mr. Ambassador: (informal)

The Honorable
. . . . (full name) . . . .
The American* Ambassador
(Foreign Capital, and Country)
Sir: (ultraformal)
Dear Mr. Ambassador: (formal)
Dear Mr. . . . (surname) . . . : (informal)

MINISTER

The Honorable
The Minister of . . . .
Washington, D.C. (Zip Code)

The Honorable
The American* Minister
(Foreign Capital, and Country)
Sir: (formal) or
Dear Mr. Minister:

The Honorable
. . . . ([personal title] full name) . . . .
Minister of . . . .
Washington, D.C. (Zip Code)

The Honorable
. . . . (full name) . . . .
The American* Minister
(Foreign Capital, and Country)
Dear Mr. Minister: (formal)
Dear Mr. (or Dr.) . . . . : (informal)

CHARGÉ D'AFFAIRES

The Chargé d'Affaires
of (Country)
Washington, D.C. (Zip Code)
Sir: (formal) or
Dear Mr. Chargé d'Affaires:

Mr. (or personal title) . . . . or
. . . . (full name) . . . . , Esq.
Chargé d'Affaires of (Country)
Washington, D.C. (Zip Code)
Dear Mr. (or Dr.) . . . . : (informal)

DIPLOMATIC OFFICERS

The diplomatic officers are:

Ambassador. A diplomatic representative of the highest rank. The full title is "Ambassador Extraordinary and Plenipotentiary," meaning an ambassador vested with special and full power to transact business.

Minister. A diplomatic representative of high rank. The full title is "Envoy Extraordinary and Minister Plenipotentiary." (pron. ĕn'voi, or ăn'voi)

Chargé d'Affaires. The officer in charge during the absence of, or instead of, an ambassador or minister. (pron. shär'zhā' dá'fâre')

Counselor of Embassy or Legation. The adviser of the embassy or legation; one versed in matters pertaining to the certain country.

Secretary of Embassy or Legation. One who handles the official papers.

Attaché. A subordinate officer attached to a diplomatic corps. There are military, naval, and commercial attachés. (pron. ăt'a-shā')

Aide-de-Camp. A confidential assistant to a general, or a sovereign—as a naval or military aide. (pron. ād'dĕ-kän'; Am. ād'da-kămp')

* "American" is properly used (as by the State Department) to refer to the United States. But where exact reference is necessary, "United States" may be used adjectively.

TO COMMERCIAL REPRESENTATIVES

The commercial representatives are:

Consul General. The officer in charge of all or several of the commercial representatives of a country.
Consul. A commercial representative of a country.
Vice Consul. A substitute or subordinate consul.
Consular Agent. A representative of a principal consular officer.

American consular officers are located in all of the principal commercial cities of the world. The office of a consul is a **"consulate."**

Foreign consular officers are located in all American cities where the certain countries have interests—usually in seaport cities.

The names of the cities where foreign and American consular offices are located may be found in the Congressional Directory in any public library.

NOTE: The Office of the **United States High Commissioner**, for a trust territory, performs certain consular duties as well as diplomatic functions. It is best to address the office, although the High Commissioner may be personally addressed as "Hon.... (full name)..., United States High Commissioner for... My dear Mr. Commissioner:"

If personal name is not used: | If personal name is used:

AMERICAN CONSUL

The American Consul
(Foreign City, and Country)
Sir:

.............., Esq.
American Consul
(Foreign City, and Country)
Sir: (formal)
Dear Mr. ....: (informal)

FOREIGN CONSUL

The French Consul
(American City, and State)
Sir:

Hon. ... (full name)...
French Consul
(American City, and State)
Sir:

(Because consular officers are transferred frequently, and their duties call them away from their posts, it is better to address the office than the individual. Hence the form in the left column is the preferable form of address, alike for consuls general, consuls, vice consuls, and consular agents.)

TO STATE OFFICIALS

GOVERNOR

The Governor of........
    or the diplomatic form:
The Honorable
The Governor of........
(State Capital)
Sir:

Hon. ... (full name)...
Governor of....... or
Governor... (full name)...
(State Capital, and State)
My dear Governor: or
Dear Governor........:

LIEUTENANT GOVERNOR

The Lieutenant Governor
State of ....
(State Capital, and State)
Sir: (formal) or
My dear Governor:

Hon. ... (full name)...
Lieutenant Governor of ... (state)
(State Capital, and State)
Dear Governor ....: or
Dear Mr. ....:

327

ADDRESSES

If personal name is not used:	If personal name is used:

HEADS OF STATE DEPARTMENTS

* (Secretary of State, Treasurer, Auditor, Attorney General, Commissioners, etc.)

The Secretary of State or The State Treasurer or The Attorney General State of . . . . (State Capital, and State) Dear Sir:	Hon. . . . (full name) . . . Secretary of State or Hon. . . . (full name) . . . Attorney General (State Capital, and State) Dear Mr. Secretary: or Dear Mr. Attorney General:

TO MEMBERS OF THE STATE LEGISLATURE

STATE SENATOR

Senator from . . . . (District) . . . . The State Senate (State Capital, and State) Dear Sir: or My dear Senator:	Hon. . . . (full name) . . . or Senator . . . (full name) . . . The State Senate (State Capital, and State) My dear Senator: or Dear Senator . . . . : or Dear Mr. . . . . :

STATE ASSEMBLYMAN, REPRESENTATIVE, OR DELEGATE

(In some states the lower branch of the legislature is called the "Assembly"; in others, the "House of Representatives"; in still others, the "House of Delegates." See p. 599. [Nebraska's "unicameral" (one-house) members are all "Senators."])

Assemblyman from . . . . (District) . . . . The State Assembly or Representative from . . . . (District) . . . . House of Representatives or Delegate from . . . . (District) . . . . House of Delegates (State Capital, and State) Dear Sir:	Hon. . . . (full name) . . . The State Assembly (State Capital, and State) Dear Sir: or Dear Mr. . . . . : and similarly to a member of a House of Representatives or House of Delegates

TO COUNTY OFFICIALS

SUPERVISOR OR COMMISSIONER

The Board of Supervisors (or Commissioners) . . . . County (County Seat, and State) Gentlemen:	Hon. (or Mr.) . . . (full name) . . . Supervisor, ... County (County Seat, and State) Dear Sir: or Dear Mr. . . . . : and similarly to a Commissioner of a County

HEADS OF COUNTY OFFICES

(County Clerk, Sheriff, Treasurer, Recorder, Auditor, Engineer, etc.)

County Clerk (or Clerk of the Superior or Circuit Court) or Sheriff of . . . . County or County Treasurer or County Recorder (County Seat, and State) Dear Sir:	Mr. . . . (full name) . . . (or Esq.) County Clerk (County Seat, and State) Dear Sir: or Dear Mr. . . . . : Hon. (or Mr.) . . . (full name) . . . Sheriff, ... County (County Seat, and State) Dear Sir: or Dear Sheriff . . . . :

* Four of the older states, Kentucky, Massachusetts, Pennsylvania, and Virginia, are known as "commonwealths" rather than "states." Their officers are accordingly addressed as "The Secretary of the Commonwealth," "The Auditor of the Commonwealth," etc.

If personal name is not used:	If personal name is used:

PROSECUTING ATTORNEY, COUNTY ATTORNEY, STATE'S ATTORNEY, OR DISTRICT ATTORNEY

The Prosecuting Attorney or The State's Attorney .... County (County Seat, and State) Dear Sir:	Hon. ... (full name) ... Prosecuting Attorney or State's Attorney (County Seat, and State) Dear Sir: or Dear Mr. .... :

TO CITY OFFICIALS

MAYOR

The Mayor of the City of .... (City, and State) Sir: (formal) or Dear Sir: or Dear Mr. Mayor:	Hon. ... (full name) ... Mayor of the City of .... or Mayor ... (full name) ... (City, and State) My dear Mr. Mayor: or Dear Mayor .... :

CITY COUNCILMAN, ALDERMAN, OR SELECTMAN

The City Council or The Board of Aldermen or The Board of Selectmen City Hall (City, and State) Gentlemen:	Hon. (or Mr.) ... (full name) ... Councilman, City of .... (or Alderman, or Selectman) City Hall (City, and State) Dear Sir: or Dear Mr. .... :

HEADS OF CITY OFFICES
(City Clerk, Treasurer, Chief of Police, etc.)

City Clerk or City Treasurer City Hall (City, and State) The Chief of Police (City, and State) Dear Sir:	Hon. (or Mr.) ... (full name) ... City Clerk (or City Treasurer, or Chief of Police) (City, and State) Dear Sir: or Dear Mr. .... :

TO THE JUDICIARY

CHIEF JUSTICE OF THE UNITED STATES

The Chief Justice of the United States Washington, D.C. 20543 or The Chief Justice The Supreme Court Washington, D.C. 20543 Sir: (formal) or Dear Mr. Chief Justice:	The Honorable The Chief Justice of the United States Washington, D.C. 20543 or Mr. Chief Justice ... (last name) ... Supreme Court of the United States Washington, D.C. 20543 (My) dear Mr. Chief Justice:

ASSOCIATE JUSTICE OF THE SUPREME COURT OF THE UNITED STATES

The Supreme Court of the United States Washington, D.C. 20543 Sirs:	The Honorable ... (full name) ... Justice, Supreme Court of the United States Washington, D.C. 20543 or Mr. Justice ... (last name) ... The Supreme Court Washington, D.C. 20543 (My) dear Mr. Justice: or Dear Justice .... :

ADDRESSES

If personal name is not used: If personal name is used:

CHIEF JUSTICE, CHIEF JUDGE, PRESIDING JUSTICE, OR PRESIDING JUDGE
STATE SUPREME COURT OR COURT OF APPEALS

The Chief Justice
Supreme Court of the State of ....
(State Capital, and State)
Dear Sir:
    and similarly to
The Chief Judge   or
The Presiding Judge   or
The Presiding Justice

Hon. ... (full name) ...
Chief Justice of the Supreme Court
(State Capital, and State)
Dear Mr. Chief Justice: or
Dear Mr. Justice:
    and similarly to a
Chief Judge or Presiding Judge
Dear Judge .... :

ASSOCIATE JUSTICE OR ASSOCIATE JUDGE
STATE SUPREME COURT OR COURT OF APPEALS

The Supreme Court
(State Capital, and State)
Sirs:

Hon. ... (full name) ....
Associate Justice of the Supreme Court
(State Capital, and State)
Dear Justice .... :   or
Dear Sir:
    and similarly to an
Associate Judge
Dear Judge .... :

JUDGE

The Judge
.... Court
(City, and State)
Sir:

Hon. ... (full name) ...
Judge of the .... Court
(City, and State)
Dear Judge .... :   or
Dear Sir:

JUSTICE OF THE PEACE

The Justice of the Peace
.... District
(City, and State)
Dear Sir:

... (full name) ..., Esq.   or
Hon. (or Mr.) ... (full name) ...
Justice of the Peace
(City, and State)
Dear Sir: or
Dear Mr. .... :   or
Dear Judge. .... :

CONSTABLE

The Constable of ... (District) ...
(City, and State)
Dear Sir:

Mr. ... (full name) ..., Constable
(Street Address)
(City, and State)
Dear Sir: or
Dear Mr. .... :

TO SCHOOL OFFICIALS

(The names and addresses of educational officials may be found in the "Education Directory" issued by the U.S. Office of Education, or in "Patterson's American Educational Directory," in public libraries. The names of the governing officials of American colleges and universities may be found in the current American almanacs, listed on p. 607.)

FORMS OF ADDRESS

If personal name is not used: **If personal name is used:**

PRESIDENT OF A SCHOOL

The President of ....
(City, and State)
My dear Sir: (formal) or
Dear Sir:

*Dr. ...(full name)...
President of ....
(City, and State) or
President ...(full name)...
University of ....
(City, and State)

My dear President ....: or
Dear Dr. ....:

CHANCELLOR OF A SCHOOL

The Chancellor of ....
(City, and State)
My dear Sir: (formal) or
Dear Sir:

*Dr. ...(full name)...
Chancellor of ....
(City, and State) or
Chancellor ...(full name)...
University of ....
(City, and State)

My dear Chancellor ....: or
Dear Dr. ....:

PRESIDENT OF A RELIGIOUS SCHOOL (PROTESTANT)

The President of ....
(City, and State)
My dear Sir: (formal) or
Dear Sir:

†The Reverend ...(full name)...
President of ....
(City, and State)

My dear President ....: or
Dear Dr. ....:

DEAN

Dean of the College of ....
.... University
(City, and State)
My dear Sir: (formal) or
Dear Sir:

Prof. (or Dr., or Mr.) ...(full name)...
Dean of ....
.... University
(City, and State) or
Dean ...(full name)...
School of ....
University of ....
(City, and State)

My dear Dean ....: or
Dear Professor ....: or
Dear Dr. ....:

PROFESSOR

Professor of ....
.... University
(City, and State)
My dear Sir: (formal) or
Dear Sir:

Prof. ...(full name)...
Department of ....
.... University
(City, and State) or
Dr. (or Mr.) ...(full name)...
Professor of ....
University of ....
(City, and State)

My dear Professor ....: or
Dear Dr. ....: or
Dear Mr. ....:

* "Dr." is the usual title for the president or chancellor of a school, since most of such officials are the holders of doctor's degrees. "Dr." is used in preference to degree letters in such addresses.
† "The Reverend" is used unless the president of a school is entitled to a higher ecclesiastical title, such as "The Very Reverend." (For Catholic Schools, see p. 334.)

331

ADDRESSES

If personal name is not used: If personal name is used:

STATE SUPERINTENDENT OF PUBLIC INSTRUCTION, OR SCHOOLS, OR
STATE COMMISSIONER OF EDUCATION

The Superintendent of Public Instruction or   Mr. (or Dr.) ...(full name)...
The Commissioner of Education   Superintendent of Public Instruction or
(State Capital, and State)   Commissioner of Education
Dear Sir: (State Capital, and State)

                                              Dear Mr. ....: or
                                              Dear Dr. ....: or
                                              Dear Sir:

SUPERINTENDENT OF SCHOOLS

The Superintendent of ....   Mr. (or Dr.) ...(full name)...
(City, and State)   Superintendent of .... Schools or
Dear Sir: Supt. ...(full name)...
                                              .... Schools
                                              (City, and State)

                                              Dear Mr. ....: or
                                              Dear Dr. ....: or
                                              Dear Sir:

PRINCIPAL OF A SCHOOL

The Principal of .... School   Mr. ...(full name)...
(City, and State)   Principal of .... School
Dear Sir: (City, and State)

                                              Dear Mr. ....: or
                                              Dear Sir:

TEACHER

                                              Mr. ...(full name)...
                                              .... (School) ....
                                              (City, and State)

                                              Dear Mr. ....: or
                                              Dear Sir:

MEMBER OF SCHOOL BOARD OR BOARD OF EDUCATION

The .... School Board or   Mr. ...(full name)...
The Board of Education   Member, ... School Board
(City, and State)   (City, and State)
Gentlemen: Dear Mr. ....: or
                                              Dear Sir:
                                                    and similarly to a
                                              Clerk, Chairman, Director, etc., of a
                                              School Board or Board of Education

TO CHURCH DIGNITARIES AND OFFICIALS

Roman Catholic Church

(The name and correct title of any official or dignitary of the Catholic Church
may be obtained from "The Official Catholic Directory" to be found in any
large public library, or in the offices of any large Catholic Church. The
names of cardinals, archbishops, and bishops may be found in the current
American almanacs, listed on p. 607.)

THE POPE

His Holiness the Pope   His Holiness
Vatican City   Pope ....
Italy   Vatican City
Your Holiness: (formal)   Italy
Most Holy Father: (usual)   Most Holy Father:

332

FORMS OF ADDRESS

If personal name is not used: If personal name is used:

CARDINAL

His Eminence (first name) Cardinal (last name)
  (as "His Eminence James Cardinal Vincent")   or just
His Eminence Cardinal...(last name)...
Archbishop of ....
Your Eminence: (formal)
Dear Cardinal .....:   (informal)

APOSTOLIC DELEGATE (FROM "APOSTLE")

(The representative of the Holy See when diplomatic relations are not established; but when established, a "Papal Nuncio" is sent.)

The Apostolic Delegation   His Excellency
Washington, D.C. 20008   The Most Reverend ...(full name)...
Sirs: (formal) or   The Apostolic Delegate
Gentlemen: **Your Excellency:**

ARCHBISHOP OR BISHOP

The Archbishop of .... or   The Most Reverend ...(full name)...
The Bishop of ....   Archbishop (or Bishop) of...........
Your Excellency: (formal) or   **Your Excellency:** (formal) or
Most Reverend Sir: **Dear Archbishop (or Bishop) ....:**

*MONSIGNOR

The Right Reverend Monsignor...(full name)...
      or abbreviated as
   The Rt. Rev. Msgr. ....
My dear Monsignor: or
My dear Monsignor ....:

PRIEST

The Pastor of ....   The Rev. ...(full name)... or
Dear Father: The Rev. Father ...(last name)...
                                         Reverend dear Father: or
                                         Dear Father..........:

MOTHER SUPERIOR

The Reverend Mother Superior   The Reverend Mother ...(full name)...
Reverend Mother: or   **Reverend Mother:**   or
Dear Reverend Mother: **Dear Reverend Mother:** or
                                         Dear Reverend Mother ....:

SISTER

NOTE: "Sister" is the title of address   Sister...(full name)...
for all nuns, whether cloistered or not.   **My dear Sister:** or
"Nun" is never used in an address.   **Dear Sister ....:**

SUPERIOR OR DIRECTOR OF A BROTHERHOOD

Brother Superior or   Brother...(full name)...
Brother Director   **Dear Brother ....:**
Dear Brother:

MEMBER OF A BROTHERHOOD

                                         Brother...(full name)...
                                         My dear Brother: or
                                         Dear Brother..........:

* There are two classes of Monsignori: one (Domestic Prelates) are addressed as "The Right Reverend"; the other (Papal Chamberlains) are addressed as "The Very Reverend." The Official Catholic Directory will give the correct designations. In the absence of definite information it is always courteous to address any Monsignor as "The Right Reverend."

ADDRESSES

If personal name is not used:	If personal name is used:

Abbot

The Abbot of .... Abbey Dear Father Abbot:	*The Rt. Rev. ....(full name)... Abbot of .... or The Rt. Rev. Abbot...(last name)... Reverend dear Father ....:

Vicar General, Superior, Prior, Chancellor, Rector, Dean, Canon, Provincial, etc.

(These are titles of offices or appointments, and are used in much the same manner as "President" or "Director" would be. By courtesy, the holders of these offices are accorded the title "The Very Reverend," unless, of course, they are entitled to a higher designation, as "The Right Reverend" or "The Most Reverend.")

The Vicar General or The Chancellor of........ or The Dean of .... Dear Father:	The Very Rev. ...(full name)..., V.G. (for a Vicar General) or The Very Rev. ...(full name)... Chancellor of.......... or The Very Rev. ...(full name)... Dean of .... Very Reverend dear Father:

Heads of Catholic Colleges, Universities, and Seminaries

(By courtesy are addressed as "The Very Reverend," unless by their ecclesiastical standing they are entitled to a higher designation, as "The Right Reverend" or "The Most Reverend.")

The President of .... or The Chancellor of .... or The Rector of .... Dear Father:	The Very Rev. ...(full name)... President, ... University Very Reverend dear Father: and similarly to a Chancellor or Rector

Episcopal Church

(The names of the clergy of the Episcopal Church may be found in "The Episcopal Church Annual," in most public libraries. The names and addresses of Episcopal bishops may be found in the current American almanacs listed on p. 607.)

Bishop

The Bishop of .... My dear Bishop: or Dear Sir: or Right Reverend Sir: (ultra formal)	The Right Reverend ...(full name)... Bishop of .... My dear Bishop: or My dear Bishop ....:

Archdeacon

The Archdeacon of .... My dear Mr. Archdeacon: or Venerable Sir: (ultra formal)	The Venerable ...(full name)... Archdeacon of .... My dear Mr. Archdeacon: or Dear Archdeacon ....:

Dean

The Dean of .... My dear Mr. Dean: or Very Reverend Sir: (ultra formal)	The Very Reverend ...(full name)... Dean of .... My dear Mr. Dean: or Dear Dean ....:

* "The Right Reverend" is used unless the Abbot is of higher ecclesiastical standing and entitled to be addressed as "The Most Reverend."

334

If personal name is not used: If personal name is used:

CANON

The Rev. Canon ...(full name)...
.... **Cathedral**
Reverend Sir: (ultra formal)
My dear Canon ....:

RECTOR (PRIEST), VICAR, CURATE, OR DEACON

The Rector (or Vicar) of.........
My dear Sir (or Madam): or
Reverend Sir (or Madam): (ultra formal)

The Reverend...(full name).......
Dear Dr. (or Mr., Mrs., Ms.).....: or
Dear Father (but not *Mother*).....:

Other Churches

UNITED METHODIST BISHOP

(The names and addresses of the bishops of The United Methodist Church may be found in the current American almanacs listed on p. 607.)

The Bishop of .... **Area**
The United Methodist Church
(City, State, and Zip Code)
My dear Bishop: or
Reverend Sir: (ultra formal)

Bishop .... (full name)....
My dear Bishop: or
Dear Bishop ....:

PRESBYTERIAN MODERATOR

The Moderator of ....
My dear Sir: or
My dear Mr. Moderator: or
Reverend Sir: (ultra formal)

The Reverend ...(full name) ... or
Dr. (or Mr.) ...(full name)...
Moderator of ....
My dear Dr. (or Mr.).........:

RABBI (HEBREW OR JEWISH FAITH)

The Rabbi of ......
My dear Rabbi: or
Sir: (formal)

"The Reverend Dr......" is used in Britain, but is rare in America. "Congregation," "Temple," or "Synagogue" is used instead of "Church."

Rabbi (or Dr.) ...(full name)..
My dear Rabbi: or
Dear Rabbi (or Dr.) ....:

*MORMON PRESIDENT, BISHOP, AND ELDER

The President
Church of Jesus Christ
  of Latter Day Saints
My dear President: or
My dear Brother:

President (or Brother)...(full name)... or
Bishop (or Brother)...(full name)... or
Elder (or Brother)...(full name)...
My dear Mr. (or Brother)..........: or
Dear President (or Bishop, or Elder)...:

*SEVENTH-DAY ADVENTIST PRESIDENT, AND ELDER

The President
General Conference of
  Seventh-day Adventists
My dear (Mr.) President:

President (or Mr.)...(full name)... or
Dr. ....(full name)... or
Elder ....(full name)....
Dear President (or Dr., or Elder)....:

CLERGYMEN OF VARIOUS DENOMINATIONS

(The names and addresses of prominent clergymen in the United States may be found in the "Yearbook of American Churches," in public libraries.)

The Pastor of ....
My dear Sir: or
Reverend Sir: (ultra formal)

The Rev. (or Dr.) ....(full name)....
My dear Mr. (or Dr.)..........:
    If the first name or initial is not known, use
The Rev. Mr. (or Dr.) ...(last name)...

* The title "Reverend" is not used in either the Mormon Church or the Seventh-day Adventist. "Mr." may be used for any of their ecclesiastical ranks; or preferably, "Elder" for their pastors.

TO ARMED FORCES OFFICERS AND ENLISTED MEN

Officers and enlisted men in the Army, Air Force, Navy, and Marine Corps should be addressed by their titles, not by "Mr."

> "...every officer in the Navy shall be designated and addressed by the title of his rank without any discrimination whatever."–Navy Department.

Titles Abbreviated in Addresses. Titles of rank or rating are usually abbreviated in addresses—before full names. ("Ret." means "retired.")
Relative rank is:

ARMY, AIR FORCE, AND MARINE CORPS	NAVY AND COAST GUARD
General of the Army (or Air Force)	Fleet Admiral ...(full name)..........
General (Gen.) ...(full name)..........	Admiral (Adm.) ....
Lieutenant General (Lt. Gen.)	Vice Admiral (Vice Adm., VAdm) ......
Major General (Maj. Gen.)	Rear Admiral (Rear Adm., RAdm) ....
Brigadier General (Brig. Gen.)	Commodore (Como.) ....
Colonel (Col.)	Captain (Capt.) ....
Lieutenant Colonel (Lt. Col.)	Commander (Comdr., Cmdr., Cdr) .....
Major (Maj.)	Lieutenant Commander (Lt. Cmdr., LCdr)
Captain (Capt.)	Lieutenant (Lieut., Lt.) ....
First Lieutenant (1st Lt., 1 Lt)	Lieutenant (junior grade) (Lt. (jg)) ....
Second Lieutenant (2d Lt., 2 Lt)	Ensign (Ens.) ....
[Chief] Warrant Officer (CWO or WO) ...	Midshipman (Midn.) ....
Cadet (or Air Cadet—AC)	For petty officers and seamen, the title
Sgt. (SMaj, [C]MSgt, TSgt, SSgt)	is now also written before the name, as
Cpl. (or Airman 1st class—A1C)	Gunner's Mate (GM)...... (No.), USN
Pfc. (or Pvt.) (or A2C or A3C)	Seaman (Sn.) .... (No.), USN

USA, AUS, USAF, USN, etc. (See footnote, p. 337.) "USA" (United States Army), "USAF" (United States Air Force), "USN" (United States Navy), "USMC" (United States Marine Corps), or "USCG" (United States Coast Guard), may be added after the personal name, or after the branch of the service in the address.

Capt. ...., USA	Lt. (jg) ....CEC, USN or
Company G, Seventh Infantry	Rear Adm. ....USN (Ret.)

Salutations to Military and Naval Officers. The business salutation for all ranks, grades, and ratings, is

Sir: (formal)	or	Dear Sir:

In informal letters, the titles (unabbreviated) may be used in the salutations.

ARMY, AIR FORCE, AND MARINE CORPS	NAVY AND COAST GUARD
Dear General ....:	**Dear Admiral** ....:
(Alike for General, Lt. Gen., Maj. Gen., and Brig. Gen.)	(Alike for Admiral, Vice Admiral, and Rear Admiral)
Dear Colonel ....:	**Dear Captain** ....:
(Alike for Colonel and Lt. Col.)	**Dear Commander** ....:
Dear Major ....:	**Dear Lt. Commander** ....:
Dear Lieutenant ....:	**Dear Lieutenant (jg)** ....:
(Alike for First and Second Lieutenant)	**Dear Midshipman** ....:

Army, Air Force, and Marine Grades. All are addressed by their military titles:

Dear Sergeant (or Corporal, Specialist, Private, Airman).................:

Navy and Coast Guard Ratings. All may be addressed in salutations by their titles:

Dear Petty Officer..............:   **Dear Seaman**..................:

Warrant Officers. All are addressed in salutations as "Mr.," "Mrs.," "Ms.," or "Miss."

Doctor. In the Army Medical Corps, officers of the grade of Captain and above are orally addressed by their military titles—"Captain," "Major," "Colonel," and "General." Lieutenants may be orally addressed as "Doctor."
In the Naval Medical Corps, officers below the rank of Commander may be orally addressed as "Doctor." In fact, "Doctor" is used for all doctors of whatever rank.

If personal name is not used: If personal name is used:

CHAPLAIN IN ARMED FORCES

The Chaplain of . . . .   Chaplain . . . (full name) . . .
                                       Major, USA   (or other rank)
My dear Chaplain: or
Reverend Sir: (ultra formal)   My dear Chaplain: (formal)
                                       Dear Chaplain . . . . : (informal)

TO MILITARY OFFICIALS

Adjutant General, Commandant, Surgeon General, Judge Advocate General, Provost Marshal General, and Inspector General are titles of office, not rank. The heads of these offices are usually addressed by office.

The Adjutant General   Maj. Gen. . . . .
Department of the Army   The Adjutant General
Washington, D.C. **20310**   Department of the Army
Sir: Washington, D.C. **20310**
                              Dear Sir: or
                              Dear General . . . . :

State Adjutant General. An Adjutant General is the military administrative officer in each state. "The Adjutant General" may be addressed as

Official: Informal:
  The Adjutant General   *Brig. Gen. . . . .
  State of . . . .   The Adjutant General
  (State Capital, State, and Zip Code)   State of . . . .
  Sir: (State Capital, State, and Zip Code)
                                   Dear General . . . . :

* Adjutants General may be of different military rank. They are not always Brigadier Generals.

To an Officer and His Wife. Since all officers and noncommissioned officers of the Armed Forces are addressed by the titles of their rank (usually abbreviated) in official written communications, so are they being addressed in social correspondence (with titles unabbreviated). Examples of this "accepted usage" may be found in newspapers and magazines reporting social events.

Major General and Mrs. . . . (full name) . . .   Lieutenant Commander and Mrs. . . . .
Lieutenant and Mrs. . . . .   Chief Warrant Officer and Mrs. . . .
  (Alike for 1st and 2d Lieutenant)   Lieutenant (jg) and Mrs. . . . .
Staff Sergeant and Mrs. . . . .   Ensign and Mrs. . . . .

The salutations follow the forms for salutations given on p. 336.

◊◊◊◊◊◊◊◊◊

The **United States Army (USA)** is the Regular Army—the permanent, professional military force. **USAR**—United States Army Reserve. **ORC**—Officers Reserve Corps.

The **Army of the United States (AUS)** is the wartime army, composed of the Regular Army, the National Guard (NG), the Organized Reserves, and the Selective Servicemen of the National Army.

The **United States Navy (USN)** is the Regular Navy—the permanent, professional naval force. (Note that "naval" is the usual adjective, not "navy.")

The **United States Naval Reserve (USNR)** is the trained, inactive peacetime naval force, which becomes a part of the wartime navy.

The **United States Air Force (USAF)** is the "active duty" Air Force, comprising: the Regular Air Force, Air Force Reserve, and Air National Guard of the United States.

The **Air Force Reserve (AFRes)** is the trained, inactive Air Force, which, when called into the service of the United States, becomes a part of the USAF.

ᔒ

337

Envelopes

In the swift handling of mails, postal sorters look to the **right side of envelopes** for guidance—and read or scan addresses from the bottom up. **Preferred positions** on the business envelope are therefore:

Return Address[1]		Stamps
	Class of mail and service as	
Material Enclosed (if necessary, as PHOTOGRAPH)	Certified Mail sticker Return Receipt (on back)	FIRST CLASS, and/or SPECIAL DELIVERY INSURED[2] REGISTERED[2] THIRD CLASS SPECIAL 4th CL.— (item enclosed)
	PERSONAL	
Attention or Division or Department Holding or Forwarding Directions	Name, and Business Title (if used)[3] Company (or other organization) Room, Suite, or Apt. No. with Building Name (If no bldg., after Street on line below)	
NOTE: Write nothing beside or under last two lines of address (scanners reject).	Street Address (or Box No.[4]), or Rural Route City, State[5] and Zip Code[6]	

NOTE: **Mechanical scanners require blocked addresses, single- or double-spaced. Printed or stamped addresses should be set in full caps with no punctuation.**

[1] **Sender's last name** may be typed above a company's return address—with his room, department, or division number, as "Evans, Sales, 20".
[2] **No valuation** should be shown on the envelope of registered or insured mail.
[3] See also p. 314. (An "**In care of [c/o]**" line should be below the addressee's name.)
[4] **Street address** is unnecessary with P.O. box number, which **precedes** a station. See p. 309.
[5] State's name may be abbreviated (in 2 letters as shown below if a Zip Code follows; or in the "traditional" or "official" style); or spelled out. (For unknown Zips, call P.O. Information.)
[6] **Zip Code must be typed** (with no comma before it) **2 spaces** after the state name or its abbreviation. It should not be set **singly** on the line below—scanners reject.

Two-letter abbreviations of state names are authorized for use with Zip Codes **only**—all caps; no periods or inner spaces necessary:

Alabama....	AL	Hawaii...	HI	Massachusetts..	MA	New Mexico...	NM	South Dakota.	SD
Alaska.....	AK	Idaho.....	ID	Michigan.......	MI	New York......	NY	Tennessee....	TN
Arizona.....	AZ	Illinois....	IL	Minnesota......	MN	North Carolina.	NC	Texas........	TX
Arkansas...	AR	Indiana...	IN	Mississippi.....	MS	North Dakota..	ND	Utah.........	UT
California..	CA	Iowa....	IA	Missouri.......	MO	Ohio..........	OH	Vermont......	VT
Colorado....	CO	Kansas...	KS	Montana.......	MT	Oklahoma.....	OK	Virginia......	VA
Connecticut.	CT	Kentucky.	KY	Nebraska.......	NE	Oregon.......	OR	Washington...	WA
Delaware...	DE	Louisiana.	LA	Nevada........	NV	Pennsylvania...	PA	West Virginia.	WV
Florida.....	FL	Maine....	ME	New Hampshire.	NH	Rhode Island...	RI	Wisconsin....	WI
Georgia....	GA	Maryland.	MD	New Jersey.....	NJ	South Carolina.	SC	Wyoming.....	WY

Building Names. On letters not mailed for local distribution, a street address is preferable to a building name, unless the building is very well known. The reason for the preference of the street address

338

is that mail sorters arrange each city's mail according to street numbers, and if the street number of a building is unknown to them, they must group that building's mail in a separate package for re-sorting in the city of destination.

If a building is named, the **suite** or **room number,** or the **company name,** should also be given. Before a building name, it is not necessary to write "Room," "Suite," or "No."—**just the number, as**

820 Commerce Bldg.   but after: Tower Bldg., Suite 1620

Hotel Names. What has been said above regarding building names applies also to hotel names: if the hotel is large or well known, the street address is not necessary, but if the hotel is small or not well known, the street address should also be given.

Do not address a traveler or resident **"In care of"** a hotel. Instead, after the addressee's name, write **"Guest."**

"Hotel" is usually written **after** the name of a large hotel.

Mr. James R. Wilson, Guest   Highland Hotel

"No." or "#". Do not use this abbreviation before a number unless "Room," "Suite," or "Apt." is omitted, and the number stands alone.

Street Numbers. In formal correspondence, if the avenue or street name is a number below ten, it is spelled out. But now in informal work —in everyday business addresses—all street names that are numbers are usually in figures, with –st, –nd, –rd, or –th after them.

A dash, not a comma, should be used between a house number and a street number. A dash separates numbers and makes each distinct.

formal: 500 Fifth Avenue, Apt. 914   usual: 500 – 5th Ave. #914
245 East Second Street   245 E. 2nd St.
5022 – 27th Avenue, NW.   5022 – 27th Ave., NW.

Note: The post office prefers -st, -nd (or -d), -rd (or -d), or -th after numerical street names in figures, to differentiate them instantly from street numbers.

"Avenue," "Street," and "Building" are usually abbreviated "Ave.," "St.," and "Bldg." in addresses on ordinary letters and envelopes. In formal correspondence they are written out.

Local Delivery. Local letters should bear the name of the state as well as the name of the city—and the Zip Code.

"City" or "Local." Never use this word in an address unless it is on routine mail such as billing. On that type of mail, give also the house or building number, street name, and Zip Code (as "City 13411").

Room, Apartment, or Box Number. A room, apartment, or box number should be written in the address itself, and not in the lower left corner of an envelope.

Postal sorters and carriers look for all numbers that pertain to their handling of the mail in the address proper, not down at the side.

Any notation or instruction that pertains to the mail after it is delivered, such as "Attention Mr. . . . ," or "Hold for Arrival," may be placed on the **mid-left side,** slightly below the addressee's name.

339

Full Addresses. Give a complete address on an envelope always; for instance, do not omit the company name when addressing a person connected with a company. Should the street address or room number be incorrect, the post office will endeavor to effect delivery. However, letters with insufficient addresses will not be given "directory service," but will be returned.

Do not omit **street addresses** on mail to towns of any considerable size, even though the persons or companies addressed are well known. There may be several persons or companies of similar or like name in one city. "Letters without street addresses or box numbers are subject to delay."—United States Postal Service.

The **ZIP Code must** be given. (If unknown, ask Postal Information.)

County names are not required in addresses; but if one seems necessary, as "Julian/San Diego County/California," it should be typed on a separate line in the main address, between the city and the state name.

Return Addresses. "A return address should be on everything deposited in the mails."—U. S. Postal Service. The return address should be in the upper left corner on the address side of every piece of mail, **not on the back,** nor on the bottom of an address tag or label.

It is unnecessary to specify the number of days that a piece of mail is to be held before it is returned; post office regulations govern this.

"Mr." and **"Miss"** are not used in return addresses. Other titles are.

When using **hotel or club envelopes,** write a personal return address beneath the hotel or club name, together with a request for return. Mail is not returned to hotels, clubs, schools, and other public institutions whose names appear on the envelopes as advertisements.

Returned Letters. If a letter is returned to the sender, after a proper effort has been made to deliver it, it may not be remailed without new postage; and it should be placed in a new envelope—never remailed in the old one—to avoid confusion and secure prompt service.

Dispatch Method. If a letter is to be dispatched by a special postal service, this information should be noted in capital letters **immediately below the stamps, but never on them.** Such a notation not only serves as a reminder to the one stamping the mail in an office, but aids postal clerks when sorting the mails, as the eye or optical scanner sees the stamp and the notation at one glance.

SPECIAL DELIVERY	should be below all special delivery stamps.
CERTIFIED	sticker should be placed on face of article.
REGISTERED	should be written on mail to be registered.
Return Receipt	should appear if such a receipt is desired.
FIRST CLASS	should be on all unobvious first-class mail, i.e., **large** or odd-sized first-class pieces.
PRIORITY	(or Airmail sticker) should be on all sides.
THIRD CLASS	**must** be legibly marked below the postage on all **sealed,** single-piece, third-class mail.
SPECIAL 4th-CL. -	followed by item enclosed, as **"Manuscript."**

If a letter is marked REGISTERED, or SPECIAL DELIVERY, etc., and it is finally not to be sent by that method, obliterate the words, or

340

confusion in the post óffice handling will result. Also, the use of green-diamond-bordered envelopes for other than First Class is not permissible.

Foreign Mail Markings. (See pp. 321 ánd 364 ff. **For the method** of addressing mail via certain ships, see p. 370.)

When addressing an international mail article on which foreign-rate postagè will be required, pencil the amount in the stamp position, as a reminder to place sufficient postage on that article.

Delivery Method. If the delivery method is to be by hand, a notation to that effect should be written in the upper right corner, as

    By Messenger, or
    Courtesy of Mr. (or Ms.) . . . .   or   Kindness of Mr. (or Ms.) . . . .

Without one of these notations, a question might later arise in the receiving office regarding the method of delivery. Someone will ask, "How did this come?" or "Who left this?"

Personal. PERSONAL, when used, should be written in capital letters above the address.

"Confidential" should not appear on an envelope. It applies only to the contents, not to the delivery, and should be written only on the letter. Use the word PERSONAL on the envelopes of such letters as are marked "Confidential." The word "Private" is not generally used.

Attention. The "Attention" line should appear on the mid-left side. It is unnecessary to write "of" after "Attention"; and on letters between companies well known to each other, even the word "Attention" may be omitted. A personal name, or division or department, set to the left of—and slightly below—the company name signifies "Attention."

Holding or Forwarding Directions. "Hold for Arrival" should appear on the mid-left side of every piece of mail that is likely to be received before the arrival of the addressee.

"Please Forward" should be written on the mid-left side of every piece of mail that is likely to arrive after the departure of the addressee.

Hotel addresses especially should carry these notations. Many misunderstandings arise because it is believed that these instructions will be naturally assumed. They are not always.

Chain-Feeding Envelopes. To address a large number of envelopes with the least effort, feed them into the typewriter in a continuous line; that is, with the left hand keep feeding a new envelope next the roller and beneath the disappearing edge of the envelope that is in the machine. This saves turns of the roller by bringing a new envelope into position as each envelope is removed with the right hand.

Envelope Flaps. To guide an envelope squarely into the typewriter and to give a smoother writing surface for the address, open the envelope flap before insertion in the machine. When addressing a large number of envelopes, opening can be done swiftly by first shuffling the envelopes together so that each one slips under the flap of the one next it, and finally all the flaps can be opened at once.

341

Preparing Letters for Envelopes. Before any letter is placed in an envelope, check it for **signature, corrections,** and **enclosures.** And lastly, check to make sure that the right letter is being placed in the right envelope. Serious mistakes have occurred because of interchanges.

When stapling the pages of a letter together, place the staple **slant-wise** (diagonally) in the upper **left corner.** This provides the proper angle for turning pages without tearing the paper at the staple.

If the enclosures accompanying a letter are to be a permanent part of the letter, staple them to the letter in the manner above.

The use of pins in letters is not approved by postal authorities.

A metal clip, if used, should be placed on the upper left corner, and the letter folded so that the clip will be within the folds and not next the envelope. The letter should be placed in the envelope so that the clip is at the left end of the envelope. If it is at the right end—under the stamp—it will interfere with the stamp-canceling machine and make the postmark blur.

Enclosing Stamps. Stamps for reply are not usually enclosed to any but charitable organizations.

It is courteous, however, to enclose stamps for reply to an inquiry if the information desired will benefit only the inquirer.

It is unnecessary to send stamps to the Federal Government offices, unless a special postal service is desired (then postage should be enclosed). Government ordinary mail is "franked"—sent postage free.

Folding Letters. Letters should be folded carefully, not haphazardly. The fold of a letter adds to or detracts from its appearance when received. Because so many letters are folded into unshapely forms, the following well-known advice is here repeated:

To make a straight fold, match the edges before creasing the paper.

For a **legal-size envelope,** fold a letter twice in almost equal distances, first from the bottom and then from the top, being very careful not to catch the bottom of the letter in the top fold and thereby cause an annoying crease at the foot of the letter when it is opened.

For a **letter-size envelope,** fold it in half from the bottom to the top, and then fold each side in, an equal distance—making three folds in all.

Folding "Quantity Mail." To fold a very large number of circular letters—in the absence of a folding machine—fold a pile of six or ten at one time, pressing the folds down with a ruler if necessary. The creases will not be deep, but the letters can be slipped apart sidewise so as not to disturb the folds. Then the creases can be pressed into each letter as the letters are stacked or stuffed into envelopes.

Sealing. Do not seal letters until they are ready to be sent out. If anything is forgotten or to be added, it can be put in without the necessity of making a new envelope and destroying the one that has been sealed.

Use a wet sponge or device for sealing envelopes. Never "lick" them. Not only is it unsanitary, but the sharp edges of the paper may cut the mouth.

Do not moisten the envelopes too much in sealing; too much water may dampen the letters enclosed and cause them to be crinkly; or the glue may run, and if several letters are piled together one may stick to the back of another and go astray. This has happened many times.

Conversely, do not attempt to seal the envelopes with too little moisture. They will dry and crack open before being received.

To seal a number of envelopes, spread them (address side down) so that the gummed edges of the opened flaps will fall one beneath the other in a row. Run a moistener over the gummed edges and seal the letters one at a time.

A clean blotter is an aid in sealing envelopes. It not only absorbs all extra moisture and glue, but keeps the envelopes and hands clean.

Stamping. Use a moistener for stamps. Never "lick" them.

Do not affix stamps carelessly, upside down or out of place, or at a crooked angle. This not only reflects on the merits of the company mailing such letters, but causes postal clerks extra work when reading and canceling the stamps. (The **excess edge** on border stamps may be removed for appearance' sake; otherwise its removal is immaterial.)

If one stamp overlaps another—according to postal rules—the one that is partly covered is not counted.

Make sure that every stamp is thoroughly stuck to the envelope. Many important letters have been returned because of lost stamps. Postal clerks are not required to affix stamps to mail.

To stamp a number of envelopes rapidly: pile them in a stack; tear the stamps in rows; moisten a row of five or six stamps, and pull them apart as each is affixed, pushing each envelope down as it is stamped to make room for the next stamp.

Mutilated or defaced stamps cannot be used as postage. Therefore, care should be taken in tearing stamps apart to see that no portions are torn away. The post office has the right to refuse torn stamps, but often accepts such stamps if neatly pasted (**but not taped**) together.

Weighing. Weigh every piece of mail about which there can exist the slightest doubt regarding postage. It will be weighed in the post office and "postage due" charged the addressee if insufficient postage is affixed. Not only is it annoying to receive postage-due mail, but if it occurs repeatedly from any one correspondent, it is unforgivable.

Keep the postal scales accurate by balancing them through an adjustment of the screw at the top or side. In weighing a piece of mail, if the scales balance on an ounce line, that ounce may be figured; but if they balance on the slightest fraction of an inch above an ounce line, the ounce next above must be figured. The sender is not given the benefit of this shade of weight difference.

Do not estimate weights. Mail too heavy to be weighed on the office scales should be taken to the post office.

An office postal scale of sufficient size to weigh moderately heavy mail is a good investment. It saves frequent trips to the post office, or the much disliked "postage due" on heavy mail.

The postal pound is the standard or avoirdupois pound of 16 ounces.

343

Mailing. The United States Postal Service urges that mail be posted throughout the day:

> "Avoid delay by depositing mail early and continuously throughout the day, thus insuring prompt dispatch. Much mail is deposited just at the close of the business day, and frequently such congestion follows that all of it can not be distributed in time to be given the first dispatch."
>
> * * *
>
> "You will often gain a day's time in delivery by depositing mail as soon as it is ready."

Before mailing make three final checks: (1) see that each letter is sealed; (2) that the proper postage is on; and (3) that the address is correct.

Letters have been sent out unsealed, infrequently of course; but more frequently without proper postage; and altogether too frequently with incorrect addresses.

Do not put heavy mail down a chute—it may break open from the long fall.

And also, do not leave mail outside a box on the street. It may be blown away, or if it is of any value it is liable to be stolen.

Collection Times. Keep—in the stamp box, or in the office phone list under Postal Information—the collection times at the **nearest mailbox** (in the building or on the street); and **post mail well before those times.**

If the last collection is missed, take **important mail** to a post office that will dispatch it the soonest.

Postal Information

(Compiled from Postal publications, and by consultation with the U.S. Postal Service.)

The general divisions of mail matter are:

First Class   handwritten or typewritten matter, and all matter **sealed against postal inspection.** Post cards and postal cards are included in first-class matter.

Second Class   newspapers, magazines, and periodicals, containing notice of second-class entry.

Third Class   all mail matter not in the first and second classes which weighs **up to but not including 16 ounces.**

Fourth Class   parcel post—all mail matter not in the first, second, and third classes.

NOTE: The difference between third- and fourth-class mail is just a matter of weight.

The postal pound is the standard or avoirdupois pound of 16 ounces.

Domestic Mail.   This term includes mail transmitted within and between the United States, its territories, and its military and naval post offices.

The term **"Territories and Possessions of the United States"** includes: Commonwealths of Puerto Rico and Marianas, U.S. Virgin Islands, Canal Zone, Guam, Wake Island, American Samoa, Caroline Isls., and Marshall Isls.

A **Domestic Mail Manual** is issued by the United States Postal Service. This revisable manual contains complete **domestic** postal information. It, and other postal publications, may be purchased from the Superintendent of Documents, Government Printing Office, Washington, D.C. 20402.

Domestic Mail Manual; looseleaf, with occasional supplements (est. ...	$38.00)
Postal Bulletin; current mail changes (weekly); 1-yr. subscription......	$35.00
National ZIP Code and Post Office Directory (issued yearly in January);	
contains the Zip Code for all U.S. addresses......................	7.50
International Mail Manual; looseleaf, with occasional amendments.....	9.00

The **Directory of Post Offices** contains an alphabetic list of all domestic post offices; also such a list by states; by Zip Codes; and by counties, with county seats, delivery services, number of rural mailboxes, drop-letter boxes, etc. The directory also gives abbreviations; parcel post sectional centers; Army, Navy, and Air Force post offices; and discontinued offices.

International Mail gives postage rates, services available, prohibitions, import restrictions, etc., for each country—listed alphabetically.

Postal publications may be consulted at any post office.

FIRST-CLASS MAIL (Includes Airmail)

Rate*

Letters; bills; handwritten or typewritten matter, and carbons or } 15¢ first oz. &
duplicates thereof; and all matter sealed against postal inspection. } 13¢ ea. addl. oz.

* Rate for pieces **weighing 12 oz. or less;** above that weight, **Priority** rates apply.   (See p. 354.)
Presort rate, for mailings of 500 or more pieces: 2¢ discount per piece.   Annual fee: $30.

345

First-class **"written matter"** covers **printed** pieces that contain occasional handwritten or typewritten entries, and thereby convey "live and current" information to the addressees. Included are filled-in forms, requisitions, orders, checks, receipts, autograph albums, notebooks, revised price lists, cards or letters with a date entered in the text, and identical letters signed by different persons but to the same addressee. Also included are all bills or statements of account, no matter how prepared or in what quantity mailed.

Manuscripts for books, periodical articles, and music are an exception and may be sent third class or at the "Special Rate" (see p. 350).

For **mimeographed or multilithed** copies of letters, etc., see p. 348.

Size Limit: 100 inches length and girth combined. Envelopes, cards, and self-mailers must be rectangular: minimum, 3½″ x 5″. **Weight Limit:** 70 pounds.

Sealing. Pieces should be sealed or secured on all four edges.

Marking. When sending a large envelope or any package first class, mark below the stamps FIRST CLASS in large letters (with a **green** pencil or felt-tip marker, or a rubber stamp). Or preferably use a **green-diamond-bordered envelope** (or **mailing label**), marked FIRST CLASS. This ensures against any oversight that might cause the article to be sent with mail of a lower class.

Post Cards—and Postal Cards (sold at post offices)

10¢ each   Presort rate: 9¢ each

(**No attachments** to postal and post cards are permitted—except **adhesive address labels**.)

Included under **"post cards"** are picture cards, and in fact any regulation-sized cards. Cards **unmailable** as post cards are odd-sized cards and those bearing substances that might rub off; also those bearing statements of past due accounts, or anything of a dunning or defamatory nature.

Size limits for post cards are: maximum, 4¼″ x 6″; minimum, 3½″ x 5″; all must be rectangular. Cards larger than post card sizes must not bear the words "Post Card" or "Double Post Card," and are subject to the letter rate or third-class, regardless of whether they are printed or otherwise written upon.

Double or Reply Post Cards. 10¢ each portion; 20¢ both portions.

The reply portion of a double post card does not have to bear postage when originally mailed. The reply half may be a "business reply card."

Double or reply cards must be folded before mailing so that the return address is on the inside. And the two edges should be closed with plain stickers, seals, or a single wire staple, but not a metal clip. **Enclosures** are prohibited.

The specified use of double or reply cards is the obtaining of orders or specific information. If used for messages or statements of account, letter rates apply.

Business Reply Mail (Domestic Only)

Business reply mail may be cards, envelopes (including window but not open panel), cartons, or labels (cards and envelopes cannot serve as address labels).

A **permit** for the issuance of business reply mail is necessary and may be obtained by application at the post office. Annual permit fee: $30.

An **advance deposit** must cover the **lower surcharge.** Annual fee: $75.

Mail may be returned to a **company's branches** or **dealers** in other cities.

A return-mailer may **register** a piece by paying postage and registry fee.

Rates (first-class, plus a collection fee):
Post cards.......................... 22¢ each.
Envelopes, large cards, and parcels...... 15¢ 1st oz. and 13¢ ea. addl. oz.
(thru 12 oz.; then Priority rates) plus a collection fee or "surcharge" of
12¢ per piece   or   3.5¢ per piece under advance deposit.

The heavy **parallel bars** printed on business reply mail **are** the **flag** that prompts a collection of return postage.

All printing on the address side of such cards and envelopes must be done at the expense of the sender and must be in strict accordance with forms prescribed by the post office. The Government prints no business reply mail.

Reply mail may be distributed in any quantity desired **in the United States** or its **territories**—including **military post offices** overseas—but **not in the Canal Zone.** It should not be sent into other countries, such as Canada and Mexico, because it cannot be returned from any foreign country without prepayment of postage.

A **deposit** may be made when the cards or envelopes are sent out, to pay the postage on all that are returned.

SECOND-CLASS MAIL

	Rate
Newspapers, magazines, and other periodicals (bearing notice of second-class entry). These rates and conditions are for the general public. Publishers and registered news agents have other rates.	10¢ for first 2 ounces, & 6¢ each addl. oz., or fourth-class rate, whichever is lower

No Weight or Distance Limit—to domestic destinations.

Stenciled or Mimeographed Publications. Alleged periodical publications produced by the stencil, mimeograph, or hectograph process, or in imitation of typewriting, are not admissible as second-class matter. (See Third-Class Mail.)

Wrapping. Sealed or unsealed—and no writing permissible; except on the wrapper may be written, if desired, "Marked Copy" or "Sample Copy," or both, as the case may be. (No advertisement may appear on the wrapper.)

"On the matter itself the sender may place all that is permitted on the wrapper; correct typographical errors in the text; and designate by marks, not by words, a word or passage in the text to which it is desired to call attention. Other writing will subject the package to the first-class rate."

A wrapper for such mail may be made by slitting the ends of an envelope and rolling the newspaper or magazine into it.

Address. Write SECOND CLASS above the address.

If the addresses are close together on the wrapper, write "From" before the return address, and "To" before the receiver's address. Addresses are often so placed on this type of mail as to be indistinguishable.

Communications. Letters may be enclosed in second-class matter in the same manner as described under Parcel Post, p. 351.

Mailing. Second-class mail may be posted in ordinary mailboxes. But if a package is large enough to become parcel post, it should be taken to the post office to determine whether the second- or the fourth-class rate applies.

THIRD-CLASS MAIL

	Rates
Circulars, books, catalogues, cards, and other printed matter, including printed letters (identical except date, address, and signature); photographs; drawings; manuscripts and proof sheets; merchandise; seeds, cuttings, bulbs, roots, scions, and plants. (Bills or statements of account must now be sent first class—no matter how produced or mailed.)	20¢ 1st 2 oz.; 20¢ next 2 oz.; 13¢ ea. addl. 2 oz. (up to 16 oz.)*

* Keys and identification items, sent loose in mails: 32¢ 1st 2 oz; 18¢ ea. addl. 2 oz.

347

Weight Limit: up to but **not including** 16 ounces. At exactly 16 ounces (1 pound) the classification becomes "parcel post."

Size Limit: same as for first-class mail, p. 346.

Postage on Single-Piece Mailings. Any method of paying postage may be used on non-bulk third-class mail, and any number of pieces mailed at one time, except when permit imprints are involved. With permit imprints, minimum quantities required to be mailed at one time are 300 pieces of identical matter (or 50 pounds or 200 pieces of identical bulk mail).

Mimeographed or Multilithed Copies. Single copies of reproductions of handwriting or typewriting may be mailed as third- or fourth-class matter.

Contest Mail. Envelopes containing such harmful articles as plastic or metal lids or bottle tops are nonmailable. Such articles must be packed in cartons with adequate protective material.

No Writing Permitted—in or on any third-class mail, except as follows: On the wrapper, besides the necessary addresses, may be a designation, as PROOFS, or "Please do not open until Christmas"; but no special directions can be inscribed, as "Please send out" or "Post up." (Yet handstamped directions may appear on **identical** copies mailed in lots of 20 or more.)

On the matter itself may be marks citing passages, and a correction of **typographical errors** (proofs may be corrected or altered in text). **Form letters** may bear these written, typewritten, or handstamped additions: date (at the top, not in the body); name and address of receiver and sender; and a salutation. On a gift or photograph may be written a simple **dedication or inscription,** unlike personal correspondence, as "With best wishes." And on or with an article, such as a **medicine,** may be written **instructions** for the use thereof.

Enclosures. With books and catalogues, these **printed** forms are permissible: an invoice; order form; reply envelope or card; and circular or price list.

Letter Enclosed. A communication may be enclosed in third-class matter, in the manner described under Parcel Post, p. 351.

Christmas Cards. Greeting cards weighing **one ounce or less** may be sent as cheaply by first-class mail as by third-class. Heavier cards are cheaper by third-class, but may bear only simple written inscriptions, like "Best Wishes," and the names of senders. (For sealing, see p. 349.) It is better to send all such cards first-class—for fast service, forwarding, and return privileges.

Birth-Announcement Cards. These cards filled out in **writing** cannot be sent at the third-class rate. They are subject to the letter rate.

Breakable Mail. When mailing photographs, drawings, charts, etc., enclose a cardboard protection, or use a heavy-duty mailing folder, and mark on the address side the nature of the contents, as PHOTOGRAPH—DO NOT BEND.

Local Advertising Matter. Advertising matter for delivery to **post office boxholders** at offices not having city letter carrier service, and **on rural or star routes,** may have a uniform address (on each piece), in a number of styles, as

Postal Customer or	OR: Box (Number)
Rural (or Star) Route Boxholder	Rural Route (Number)
(Town and State, or Local) (optional)	Local (or Town and State)

Designations such as *Farmer, Food Buyer,* and *Voter* are not permitted.

Not International. Articles mailed in this country for delivery in Canada or any other country must bear complete names and addresses, not form addresses.

All pieces for the same post office must be put up by the mailer, so far as practicable, in packages of 50; each package must be securely tied and labeled with a facing slip showing the distribution desired, as

All Rural or Star Route (or Post Office) Boxholders
(Town and State)

Delivery may be restricted to selected rural or star routes if desired.

Postage at the appropriate rate (or at bulk rates) must be fully prepaid by a method that does not require cancellation: by use of permit imprints, meter stamps, precanceled stamps, or precanceled stamped envelopes or postal cards.

"Occupant" mail for delivery on letter carrier routes and to certain post office boxes must bear specific street or box numbers, in the following style:

> Resident (or Postal Customer, or Postal Patron)   or
> (Full name) or Current or Present Resident (for catalogs, samples, etc.)
> (Street and Number; Apartment Number, if any—or
> Post Office Box Number and Station, if any)
> (City, State, and Zip Code)

Sealing. All third-class mail should be sealed or secured so that it can be handled by machines; yet it must be prepared so that it may be easily examined. (Postal inspection is automatically granted on all third-class mail.)

All **sealed** pieces must be marked THIRD CLASS, **below the postage.**

Parcels not to be opened for inspection must be sent as **first-class mail.**

Mailing. Third-class mail may be deposited, in small quantities, in ordinary large mailboxes, unless of course it is to be registered or insured.

Bulk Mail (Domestic Only—Must Be Presorted by ZIP Code)

What May Be Mailed in Bulk. Identical pieces of third-class matter may be mailed in bulk lots of not less than either **50 pounds or 200 pieces.**

Each piece may weigh up to but **not including 16 oz.;** and the separately addressed pieces must be identical in size and weight (with exceptions), but not in number of enclosures or text. Cannot be insured, certified, or sent COD.

Each piece must be marked (beside the stamp or within the meter stamp or permit imprint) BULK RATE (or Blk.Rt.), or NONPROFIT ORG.* if applicable.

Permit. A permit to use one of three methods of paying postage (described below) must first be obtained. (Two of these permits are free, but the third ["imprints"] costs **$30.** See also p. 360.) Under such a permit, a **bulk-mailing fee of $40** is charged for each calendar year, for any number of mailings.

Rates per pound (16 ounces):

> Circulars, miscellaneous printed matter, and merchandise (no bills) ...... 41¢ a pound
> Catalogues (no attachments) and booklets (of 24 or more bound pages,⎰
>   including covers†); seeds, cuttings, bulbs, roots, scions, plants.⎱ 36¢ a pound
> **Minimum charge per piece:** 8.4¢ (when a piece weighs not more than 3.278 or 3.733 oz.)

* **Nonprofit rates:** circulars, etc., 19¢ a pound; catalogs, etc., 16¢ lb. Minimum, 3.1¢ a piece.
"Controlled circulation" advertising publications (not "house organs") may weigh more than one pound each. Rate: 13.8¢ a pound, plus 4.9¢ a piece.
† Booklets of fewer than 24 bound pages, or with fewer than 22 printed pages, are not considered "books," and must be sent at the 41¢-a-pound rate.

Methods of Paying Postage. The postage may be paid under a mailing permit in any one of three ways (see also p. 360):

1. **Meter Stamps.** A meter is used to imprint the postage on each piece.
2. **Precanceled Stamps** (including precanceled stamped envelopes). Precanceled stamps (sold at post offices) afford such mail fast handling. (Uncanceled stamps cannot be used.)
3. **Permit Imprints.** The permit is printed on the matter, and the postage is paid in cash; thus no time or labor is required to affix stamps.

349

PARCEL POST

Fourth-class mail is parcel post. It includes all mailable matter weighing 16 ounces or more, and not in the first and second classes.

Size Limit:* 100 inches in length and girth combined. Parcels weighing less than 15 pounds but measuring over 84 inches in length and girth combined, are subject to the 15-pound rate.

Weight Limit:* 70 pounds for all zones. (A pound is 16 ounces.)

* For parcels (except special-rate & library articles and raw agricultural products) mailed **at any first-class post office** for delivery **at the same or any other first-class post office** (in contiguous U.S. only—rural routes excepted), the size limit is 84 inches in length and girth combined; and the weight limit 40 lbs. for all zones.

Special Rate—on **books, music, recordings, manuscripts, tests, 16-mm films** and **film catalogues** (except to commercial theaters), **charts;** and **looseleaf medical information** to doctors, hospitals, etc. (See also Books, p. 351.) Mark parcel: SPECIAL 4th-CL. —(and exact item, as BOOK).

Rate, all zones: 59¢ 1st lb.; 22¢ ea. addl. lb thru 7 lbs.; then 13¢. (May be insured.) Presort discounts on 500 & 2000 mailings.

Library Rate—on loans or exchanges of **books, bound volumes, sound recordings, printed music,** etc., between **nonprofit** libraries, schools, and organizations. Also **16-mm films, sound recordings, scientific devices,** and **related catalogues** to or from such agencies. Mark parcel: LIBRARY RATE— (and exact item, as BOOK).

Rate, all zones: 17¢ 1st lb.; 6¢ ea. addl. lb. thru 7 lbs.; then 5¢ lb. (May be insured.)

PARCEL POST RATES

POUNDS	Local	1 & 2 Up to 150 miles	3 150 to 300 miles	4 300 to 600 miles	5 600 to 1,000 miles	6 1,000 to 1,400 miles	7 1,400 to 1,800 miles	8* Over 1,800 miles
1, 2	$1.15	$1.35	$1.39	$1.56	$1.72	$1.84	$1.98	$2.22
3	1.23	1.45	1.53	1.73	1.86	2.04	2.24	2.61
4	1.29	1.56	1.65	1.82	2.00	2.23	2.50	3.00
5	1.36	1.66	1.77	1.92	2.14	2.43	2.77	3.39
6	1.42	1.71	1.84	2.01	2.28	2.62	3.03	3.78
7	1.47	1.76	1.90	2.11	2.41	2.82	3.29	4.17
8	1.51	1.80	1.97	2.20	2.55	3.02	3.56	4.56
9	1.54	1.85	2.03	2.29	2.69	3.21	3.82	4.95
10	1.57	1.89	2.10	2.39	2.83	3.41	4.08	5.34
11	1.60	1.94	2.17	2.50	3.00	3.65	4.42	5.73
12	1.64	1.98	2.22	2.56	3.09	3.77	4.57	6.12
13	1.67	2.02	2.27	2.63	3.17	3.89	4.72	6.41
14	1.70	2.05	2.32	2.69	3.25	3.99	4.86	6.62
15	1.73	2.09	2.36	2.74	3.33	4.09	4.99	6.80
16	1.76	2.13	2.41	2.80	3.40	4.19	5.11	6.98
17	1.79	2.16	2.45	2.85	3.47	4.28	5.23	7.15
18	1.82	2.20	2.49	2.91	3.54	4.37	5.34	7.31
19	1.86	2.23	2.53	2.96	3.61	4.46	5.45	7.47
20	1.89	2.27	2.58	3.01	3.67	4.54	5.55	7.62
21	1.92	2.30	2.62	3.06	3.74	4.62	5.66	7.76
22	1.95	2.34	2.66	3.14	3.85	4.78	5.80	7.90
23	1.98	2.37	2.72	3.25	3.99	4.96	6.02	8.03
24	2.01	2.44	2.80	3.35	4.12	5.13	6.24	8.16
25	2.04	2.51	2.89	3.46	4.26	5.31	6.46	8.28
26	2.07	2.58	2.97	3.56	4.39	5.48	6.68	8.40
27	2.11	2.65	3.06	3.67	4.53	5.66	6.90	8.52
28	2.14	2.72	3.14	3.77	4.66	5.83	7.12	8.63
29	2.17	2.79	3.23	3.88	4.80	6.01	7.34	8.75
30	2.20	2.86	3.31	3.98	4.93	6.18	7.56	8.85
31	2.68	3.09	3.46	4.09	5.07	6.36	7.78	9.41
32	2.71	3.12	3.49	4.19	5.20	6.53	8.00	9.51
33	2.74	3.16	3.57	4.30	5.34	6.71	8.22	9.61
34	2.77	3.19	3.65	4.40	5.47	6.88	8.44	9.80
35	2.80	3.22	3.74	4.51	5.61	7.06	8.66	10.06
36	2.83	3.28	3.82	4.61	5.74	7.23	8.89	10.32
37	2.86	3.35	3.91	4.72	5.88	7.41	9.10	10.58
38	2.89	3.42	3.99	4.82	6.01	7.58	9.32	10.84
39	2.93	3.49	4.08	4.93	6.15	7.76	9.54	11.10
40	2.96	3.56	4.16	5.03	6.28	7.93	9.76	11.36
41	2.99	3.63	4.25	5.14	6.42	8.11	9.98	11.62
42	3.02	3.70	4.33	5.24	6.55	8.28	10.20	11.88
43	3.05	3.77	4.42	5.35	6.69	8.46	10.42	12.14
44	3.08	3.84	4.50	5.45	6.82	8.63	10.64	12.40
45	3.11	3.91	4.59	5.56	6.96	8.81	10.86	12.66
50	3.27	4.26	5.01	6.08	7.63	9.68	11.96	13.96
55	3.42	4.61	5.44	6.61	8.31	10.56	13.06	15.26
60	3.57	4.96	5.86	7.13	8.98	11.43	14.16	16.56
65	3.73	5.31	6.29	7.66	9.66	12.31	15.26	17.86
70	3.88	5.66	6.71	8.18	10.33	13.18	16.36	19.16

Zones (For mileage, see table of distances, p. 583.)

* 8th zone covers Hawaii and U.S. distant territories; but Alaska, Puerto Rico, and U.S. Virgin Islands are zoned from U.S.

Bulk Rate. Fifty or more parcels (each **8 oz.** or over) of identical or nonidentical weight, size, or content—with postage paid by meter stamps and permit imprint—sorted by postal zones, take a **piece-pound** rate based on average weight per piece, per zone. Bulk mailings may be insured, or sent special delivery, special handling, or COD.

Special-Rate Bulk Presort. Mailings of 500 (or 2000) or more identical pieces presorted by Zip Codes, receiving identical service, are given discounts. Annual fee: $30.

Bound Printed Matter. Pieces, such as advertising and catalogs, each 90% printed, bearing permit indicia, and weighing from 1 lb. to 10 lbs., may be mailed in two ways:

Bulk: Each mailing must contain 300 or more separately addressed, identical pieces, presorted by postal zones, with charges totaled from a piece-and-pound rate.

Single Piece: Pieces (no mailing permit required) take graduated-weight rates, from 1.5 lbs. to 10 lbs., for each parcel post zone.

Books. A special rate, irrespective of domestic destination, applies to **bound or unbound** books (of 24 or more pages, at least 22 of which are printed) that are wholly reading matter or textbooks (or largely music, pictures, or maps) and contain **no advertisements** except book announcements. This rate **does not apply** to second-class matter, periodicals, house organs, promotional publications, directories, annual reports, rate books, and looseleaf **or blank books.** (**Manuscripts,** typed or handwritten, may be sent at the "Special Rate.")

Permissible enclosures are: an invoice; a reply envelope or post card; one order form; printed incidental book announcements, and book-ordering methods.

Mark such a parcel SPECIAL 4th-CL.—BOOK. No permit is necessary.

No Communications Enclosed. Typewritten or handwritten matter cannot be enclosed in surface parcel post packages, except as follows:

Invoices and customers' orders may be enclosed with the merchandise to which they relate, provided all references to articles not enclosed are obliterated.

No checks or money orders are permissible, and **no messages regarding merchandise** (as "Please exchange for size 7") when articles are sent for replacement, repair, or credit, or when films are being sent for development, etc.

Inscriptions, such as "Merry Christmas" or "With best wishes," may be written on or enclosed in parcel post packages. Books may bear simple written dedications or inscriptions not in the nature of personal correspondence.

Letter Enclosed in Parcel. A letter may now be enclosed in a parcel if LETTER ENC. or 1st-CLASS ENC. is written immediately below the place for postage on the package, and separate postage paid for the letter.

Similarly, a letter may be enclosed in second- or third-class matter; and third-class mail may be placed in parcel post. Provided, always, that disclosure thereof is made, and postage paid for **each article** at its own rate.

If special delivery is desired, only one special delivery fee is necessary on the parcel, at the fourth-class special delivery rate.

Packaging
(The U.S. Postal Service issues a free pamphlet, "**Packaging Pointers.**")

Packing and Wrapping. Articles dentable, crushable, or breakable require: individual wrapping; cushioning on all sides and between articles; and packing in solid or corrugated fiberboard boxes, closed with 2″-wide **filament reinforced tape (not cellophane or masking tape).** The box must be large enough to hold the items and still have sufficient space for cushioning. If the box is too large and articles not blocked-in and cushioned, they will shift and might break; if the box is too small and bulging, adequate closure cannot be made, and the parcel might split open in the mails.

Fragile articles may also be sent in wooden, metal, or plastic containers.

Addresses of sender and receiver should be enclosed in each package.

Discontinuance of Wrappers. The Postal Service prefers "that paper wrappers be omitted if the box itself constitutes an adequate shipping container." But if a box needs reinforcement, it may be tightly wrapped in heavy manila paper (not dark-colored or red, whereon stamps and addresses are obscured), and sealed with reinforced plastic, or Kraft-paper 2″-wide, tape. If such tape is not at hand, a parcel may be tied with strong twine, fishline cord, or rope, wrapped twice around the package in each direction, pulled tight, and all crossings looped or securely tied. However, the Postal Service prefers that twine and cord not be used for closure—unless needed for reinforcing—because string tends to become entangled in mechanical equipment.

Fragile and Perishable. Mark parcels with easily broken articles FRAGILE or GLASS. Mark spoilable things PERISHABLE, and send **special delivery.** **No extra charge** is made for parcels so marked, but they should be **insured.**

351

POSTAL INFORMATION

Mailable liquids* in glass or earthenware containers cannot be mailed **unless** specially packed. The bottle must be of strong material, sealed against leakage, wrapped in sufficient absorbent (but not excelsior) to insulate it against shocks and to absorb completely the contents if broken. And all must be packed in a sealed, **waterproof** metal or plastic container, marked FRAGILE—LIQUID when in quantities of 16 fluid ounces (1 pint) or less; and FRAGILE—LIQUID—THIS SIDE UP when in quantities of more than 16 fluid ounces.

Mailable liquids* in one-gallon or more, extra-strong metal containers with handles, and with friction tops soldered on in six different places, or with locking rings or screw-cap closures, may be mailed without boxing or crating.

Iced or moistened items require special packing. Consult the post office.

Markings. Words like **"Rush"** may be used only on packages being sent by special delivery or as "special handling" mail.

Obsolete markings or labels must be covered or obliterated.

Parcels **improperly labeled** as to nature of contents are not acceptable.

Addresses. All addresses should be written **boldly** with a **felt-tip,** or **ink, pen,** or be typed on a label. **Pencil addresses** rub off and become illegible.

The **return address** of the sender **must be on the face of every parcel post package,** or the package may be rejected for mailing.

If the two addresses are close together on a small package, write "From" before the return address, and "To" before the receiver's address, the latter being below and to the right of the former address.

Do not put any addresses on the back of the package.

Tags should not be used unless there is insufficient room on the packages for the addresses. If a tag is used, the addresses of the sender and receiver must be written on a **card in the package,** for identification if the tag is lost.

Seals or stickers should not be placed on the address side of mail.

Mailer's Numbers. Private numberings must not be placed **near Zip Codes.**

Sealing. Parcel post packages may now be **sealed or unsealed** but, in either case, should be so wrapped that the contents can be easily examined.

Sealed parcel post packages (as well as those of second- and third-class mail) are now deemed to carry the consent of the senders to postal inspection. Therefore, no label or endorsement giving such permission is necessary.

Packages **not to be opened** for inspection must be sent as **first-class mail.**

Mailing. Parcel post packages should be mailed at post offices, and not deposited in mailboxes. They cannot be posted in train mails.

Special Handling (Fast Dispatch)

This service accords third-class mail and parcel post the fastest handling, transportation, and delivery practicable (but not special delivery).

"Special handling" applies **only** to these **two classes.** It means "fast dispatch and special attention" (as for baby chicks), but **does not insure a** package.

Write or stamp SPECIAL HANDLING immediately below the stamps.

Such parcels may also be **insured** or sent **C.O.D.**

Fees. Are according to weight (in addition to regular postage):

Up to 10 lbs.......... 70¢   Over 10 lbs.......... $1.25
(For "Special Handling with Special Delivery," see Special Delivery, p. 354.)

* Nonmailable liquids are intoxicating liquors (above 3.2% alcohol); poisons (except those for scientific use, and those sent to licensed dealers); and explosive, flammable, corrosive, or toxic fluids.

INSURANCE

Third-class mail and parcel post (including special-rate) may be insured.

Insuring a package provides for careful handling and indemnity **against loss,** rifling, or damage. No indemnity is payable on ordinary (uninsured) parcels.

Write on each insurance receipt the name of the person or company to whom the package was sent. Identify the contents in a few words.

Fees. Are according to valuation (in addition to regular postage):

| Up to $15*. .50¢ | to $50. .85¢ | to $100. .$1.10 | to $150. .$1.40 |
| to $200. .$1.75 | to $300. .$2.25 | to $400 (limit). .$2.75 | |

* No return receipt or restricted delivery services available with these low-value parcels.

Return Receipts. These may be had on insured, registered, certified, and C.O.D. mail. Write Return Receipt below the space for stamps. Fees are:

45¢ if requested at time of mailing $2.10 if requested after mailing
55¢ if requested at mailing, to show to whom, date, and address where delivered
(Insurance claim may be filed at **any post office,** not necessarily at that of mailing or address.)

Small Valuable Articles. Small articles of value, such as precious stones, jewelry, and money, should be sent as sealed, first-class registered mail.

Indemnity up to $25,000 is paid on registered mail.

Restrictions in Delivery. (Same as for Registered Mail, p. 356.)

AIRMAIL (Merged With First-Class Mail)

Rate

Anything mailable, **sealed or unsealed,** except unconfined magnets⎫ Same as
and **unprotected** articles that may be damaged by low temperatures ⎬1st Class *
or high altitudes, or made harmful by changing air pressures. ⎭See p. 345

* Now, on 1st-cl. mail of 12 oz. or less, it is unnecessary to use airmail stamps, labels, etc.

Foreign Airmail. (See pp. 369–70.)

Express Mail

This **high-speed service** guarantees **next-day delivery** of articles brought, before 5 p.m., to an Express Mail post office. A shipment may be **picked up** at the destination post office by 10 a.m. the next **business day.** "Door" delivery will be by 3 p.m. the next day (including weekends and holidays).

A still **faster, 24-hour-a-day, service** guarantees **same-day airport-to-airport transit,** with the sender delivering the shipment to an airport mail facility; the receiver picking it up at the destination airport. No restricted delivery.

Special **Express Mail address labels** are furnished at the post office.

A **receipt** is given the sender, and a **record of delivery** kept at destination.

Anything **mailable,** up to **70 pounds,** may be sent: letters, reports, magnetic tapes, merchandise, etc., combined in one package—at no extra cost.

A **weight-and-distance charge** for the entire carton applies.

Insurance up to $500 (with exceptions) is free; mailer must **declare value.**

Custom Designed Service

Express Mail may be sent on a **regularly scheduled basis**—daily, weekly, monthly —for shipments one-way, round-trip, or in any combination . . . with a **money-back guarantee of delivery within 24 hours.**

Anything mailable, up to 50 pounds, may be combined in the same pouch—letters, merchandise, documents, proofs, data, artwork, etc.

Four pickup and delivery options are offered: (1) door-to-door; (2) door to destination airport; (3) originating airport to addressee's door; (4) airport-to-airport—shipper bringing package to local airport, and receiver picking it up at destination airport.

International Programmed Express Mail may be sent to some countries (p. 370).

POSTAL INFORMATION

Air Parcel Post (Priority Mail)

Parcels of **any class of mail,** sealed or unsealed, may be sent by airmail. "Rush" parcels should also be sent **special delivery.**

The sender's **return address must** be on the address side of each parcel.

Write **PRIORITY** boldly, or place **Airmail stickers,** on each side.

Air parcels **must** be mailed at **post offices,** or through **rural carriers.**

Registered and C.O.D. first-class packages must be **securely sealed.**

Insurance may be had on third- and fourth-class matter (letter enclosed).

Write also on an insured parcel **"Contains 3rd-Class [or 4th-] Mail."**

Weight Limits: Over 12 ounces and up to 70 pounds.

Size Limit: 100 inches, length and girth combined.

> Less-than-15-pound parcels over 84 inches in length + girth, take 15-pound rate.

To U.S. military addresses overseas: the above limits generally apply, but to some places, weight limit is 50 lbs., and size limits vary from 63″ to 72″ in length-plus-girth (max. length 48″). Such parcels take the zone rate from the mailing post office to the U.S. gateway post office addressed.

AIR PARCEL POST ZONE RATES

Zone*	Weighing over 12 ounces and not exceeding (in pounds):									Each addl. lb. or frac. (approx.)
	1	1½	2	2½	3	3½	4	4½	5	
1, 2 & 3	$1.71	$1.86	$1.99	$2.11	$2.23	$2.35	$2.47	$2.59	$2.72	24¢
4	1.81	1.96	2.12	2.27	2.42	2.58	2.73	2.89	3.04	30
5	1.88	2.07	2.27	2.46	2.65	2.84	3.03	3.22	3.42	38
6	1.97	2.21	2.44	2.68	2.91	3.15	3.38	3.62	3.85	47
7	2.06	2.34	2.61	2.89	3.17	3.45	3.73	4.01	4.29	55
8†	2.25	2.50	2.83	3.16	3.50	3.83	4.16	4.50	4.83	67

* For mileage, see table of distances, p. 585. (Same zones as for surface parcel post, p. 350.)
† 8th zone covers Hawaii and U.S. distant territories. But Alaska, Puerto Rico, and U.S. Virgin Islands are now zoned from United States points. (For Armed Forces overseas, see note above.)

◇◇◇◇◇◇◇◇◇

SPECIAL DELIVERY

All domestic mail (except 3rd-class bulk-rate), sealed or unsealed, may be sent special delivery. Registered, certified, insured, and C.O.D. mail, also air parcels and parcel post, may be sent special delivery.

Special delivery does not guarantee safety, nor a personal delivery to the addressee. When valuables are so sent they should also be registered or insured.

Fees. Are according to weight (in addition to regular postage):

First Class and Air Parcel Post (Priority Mail)

Up to 2 pounds	$2.00
Over 2 and up to 10 pounds	2.25
Over 10 pounds	2.85

Other than First Class (includes also Special Handling [fast dispatch])

Up to 2 pounds	$2.25
Over 2 and up to 10 pounds	2.85
Over 10 pounds	3.25

Special delivery postage on second-, third-, and fourth-class mail entitles it to preferential handling, expeditious dispatch and transportation, and also to special delivery at destination.

Hours of Delivery:

At city delivery offices—from 7 a.m. to 11 p.m.
At all other post offices—from 7 a.m. until the closing hour, but not later than 9 p.m.
Later delivery hours may be fixed in particular cases.
Sundays and holidays from all post offices.

354

Service Limits:

In large towns, special delivery mail is delivered within city delivery limits; or within one mile of the main post office or delivery station or branch thereof.

In small towns with no fixed delivery limits, special delivery mail will be delivered within one mile of any post office.

On rural routes, delivery is by rural carriers on their regular trips, and then only to persons residing within one-half mile of the rural routes.

Stamps. Ordinary and meter stamps (and airmail on air parcels) may be used if such mail is marked or labeled conspicuously: **SPECIAL DELIVERY.**

Even if special delivery stamps are used, which might be overlooked, **SPECIAL DELIVERY** should be marked on all such mail (by a [free] double-sticker over the edge, or written boldly in red below the stamps). Special delivery stamps are good only for the special delivery fee—not for postage.

"Shortpaid." All special delivery mail should be fully prepaid. But if inadvertently mailed with **insufficient** postage (but not **without** postage) it will be dispatched promptly as intended, and "postage due" collected from the addressee. If he refuses payment, such mail will be returned to the sender with postage due.

REGISTERED MAIL

All classes of domestic mail may be registered—first, second, third, and fourth (parcel post). All articles must be **thoroughly sealed** (see p. 356); and postage paid thereon at the **first-class or priority** (air parcel) **rate.**

Fragile items must be declared. Mail **liable to damage from freezing** cannot be registered. **Special delivery** and **COD** mail may be registered.

Fees. In addition to regular postage:

Note: The sender must declare the full value (he can no longer select the fee he wishes to pay). And he must not write, or disclose, the value on the envelope or wrapper.

Declared Value (Must be full value)*	Fees		Postal Indemnity†
	If mailer has no other insurance	If mailer has other insurance	
Up to $ 100	$3.00	$3.00	The declared value if no other insurance carried. If other insurance, the declared value prorated.
200	3.30	3.30	
400	3.70	3.70	
600	4.10	4.10	
800	4.50	4.50	
1,000	4.90	4.90	
2,000	5.30	$4.90 plus 35¢ per $1,000 or fraction over first $1,000	($1,000 maximum postal liability, through proration.)
3,000	5.70		
4,000	6.10		
5,000	6.50		
6,000	6.90		
7,000	7.30		
8,000	7.70		
9,000	8.10		
10,000	8.50		
On up to 25,000	40¢ ea. addl. $1,000		

Handling charges on $25,000 to $1,000,000: $14.50 plus 35¢ per $1,000 above $25,000. Over $1,000,000: $355.75 plus 30¢ per $1,000 above $1,000,000.

* On matter having no intrinsic value, such as valuable papers—checks, drafts, deeds, wills, legal documents, abstracts, warehouse receipts, non-bearer securities (including stock certificates and "rights"), bank books, insurance policies, passports, birth certificates, drivers' licenses—the known or estimated cost of duplication should be declared, and a registration fee paid accordingly.
On securities payable to "the bearer," the market value on the date of mailing must be declared.
† The maximum postal indemnity payable is $25,000 on any declared value.

Return Receipts. If proof of delivery is desired, a return receipt should be requested at the time of mailing. Articles for which return receipts are desired should be plainly marked: REGISTERED—Return Receipt, or Return Receipt Showing Address Where Delivered.

Return receipt fees: (Same as for insured mail, p. 353.)

What Should Be Registered. Money should always be registered, if not sent, preferably, by money order.

Valuable papers of which only one copy exists, or original, signed documents, or papers that could not be replaced if lost, should be registered.

Valuable articles, such as jewelry and precious stones, should be sent by registered mail instead of by insured parcel post, because of the additional safeguards provided for registered mail.

Sealing. All mail to be registered (note that **padded** and **self-sealing envelopes** are not acceptable) must be securely sealed in every part with mucilage, glue, or plain paper strips—the strips so placed as not to interfere with postmarking. Nothing should suggest that the article has been opened and resealed.

Packages containing **money or securities** may not be sealed with paper strips alone, but must first be sealed securely with mucilage or glue.

Restrictions in Delivery. Registered mail that the sender desires delivered to the receiver **in person** or to his **authorized-in-writing agent** should be boldly marked above the address: **Restricted Delivery.** The fee is 80¢.

(Such mail must bear a **personal name**; not just a title, as "President.")

If the delivery is not so restricted, registered mail will be delivered to any responsible person who customarily receives the ordinary mail. The word PERSONAL does not restrict delivery. **Government executives, congressmen,** etc., do not personally receive mail restricted in delivery.

Marking Registered Mail. Breakable articles should be marked FRAGILE.

Write REGISTERED on the envelope or wrapper beneath the place for stamps. This prompts the one who stamps the article to have it registered. If a return receipt is desired, indicate that as shown above. (If an article is not to be registered after it has been so marked, obliterate the marking.)

Note on each registration receipt the name of the addressee (if not already written on it) and the article sent—for future reference.

Firm registration books are available, without cost, to patrons customarily registering three or more articles at a time. These books save waiting time.

Certified Mail (Domestic Only)

First-class mail, including **mailgrams,** having no intrinsic value, with only **"proof of delivery"** desired, may be sent "Certified." Such mail is handled as ordinary mail—not safeguarded as registered mail—but the receiver's signature is obtained and kept on file at the post office of delivery for 2 years.

To prepare this mail, paste a **certified mail sticker** above the address, and fill out and save the coupon (stickers, coupons, and blank return receipt cards are free). If a return receipt is desired write Return Receipt below the sticker; then fill in your name, address, and the certified number on the card and paste it (by its gummed edges) on the front (if room) or back of the article.

Fee (in addition to first-class postage)............................ 80¢
Return receipt (same as for insured mail, p. 353)
Restricted delivery (same as for registered mail, above).............. 80¢

(Fees and postage may be paid by ordinary and/or meter stamps, or by permit imprints.)

❖❖❖❖❖❖❖

MONEY ORDERS

Do not send money in ordinary mail—tempting theft. Obtain a **money order;** or send currency by **registered mail.** (A **travelers check** will be accepted in payment if the money order is at least 50% of the value of the check.)

Fill in a money order **immediately in handwriting,** to establish ownership if lost. (Typewriting is less safe.) If paying, say, an insurance premium, add your policy number in parentheses after your name for identification.

Never make an **erasure or alteration** of any significance on a money order.

Money orders are issued for sums from **1¢ to $400.** More than $400 may be sent by purchasing additional money orders.

Fees. Are according to the amount sent (foreign fees are on p. 369):

Up to $10...55¢ $10.01 to $50...80¢ $50.01 to $400...$1.10

American Express money order fees vary with different sellers—some charging 60¢ for any amount up to $200 (limit). Telegraph money order fees are on p. 389.

Bank money orders up to $500 (domestic), $1000 (international), and cashier's checks or foreign drafts for any amounts, may be obtained at banks. (See p. 523.)

Payment. A money order will be paid to the payee named therein, or his endorsee, or to his agent or "attorney in fact" upon his written order.

Only **one endorsement** on a postal money order is permissible; but a bank money order may be endorsed any number of times—like a check.

Titles, such as "Dr." and "Rev.," are not required in an endorsement.

Postal money orders may be cashed at any post office or bank (or deposited in any bank) in the United States. A rural carrier will cash a money order for a patron on his route if the order is endorsed in his presence.

Identification. Proof of identity is required in cashing a money order at a post office. A driver's license or military identification card is helpful.

Signatures known to the post office officials may be affixed for the purpose of identifying the payee or endorsee, or of guaranteeing his signature.

Lost Money Orders. These will be replaced without charge.

When a money order is believed lost, the patron must wait 60 days after its date of issue before filing an inquiry.

◇◇◇◇◇◇◇◇◇

COLLECT-ON-DELIVERY (Domestic Only)

Third- and fourth-class mail, and sealed domestic mail of any class bearing first-class postage, may be sent C.O.D. (but not APO, N[F]PO, and C.Z. mail).

C.O.D. mail sealed against postal inspection and bearing postage at the first-class rate may also be **registered.**

Amount of C.O.D. Collections: From 1¢ to $400, limit.

Purpose of C.O.D. When articles are ordered but not paid for, they may be mailed C.O.D.—the amount due to be collected and returned by money order.

Registered C.O.D. service is used for valuable articles and papers.

C.O.D. shipments **must be based on bona fide orders or understandings.**

C.O.D. service cannot be used for the collection of debts.

Firm Mailing Books. These are free to regular C.O.D. patrons.

Inspection. No examination of the contents of a C.O.D. article is permitted until the article has been receipted for and all charges paid.

Insurance. C.O.D. fees automatically insure articles against loss, rifling, damage, and nonreceipt of returns. (A **return receipt** may be obtained.)

Restrictions in Delivery. (Same as for Registered Mail, p. 356.)

Fees (in addition to regular postage).   For collection or insurance:

Up to $10... $1.10	to $25... $1.35	to $50... $1.65	to $100...$1.95
to $200... $2.30	to $300... $2.75		to $400 (limit)...$3.25

Registered C.O.D. collections and indemnity up to:

$100.... $4.40	$200.... $4.70	$400 (limit)....$5.10

Registered C.O.D. collections not exceeding $400, but indemnity up to $25,000:
$1.40 (for C.O.D. collection) in addition to registry fee on p. 355.

For changing terms or **addressee**.... $1   **For notice of nondelivery**.... $1

C.O.D. collection fees and postage **must be prepaid by the sender.**   But they may be included in the amount of the C.O.D. collection if the sender so desires. The receiver must also pay for the money order remitting the collection.

◇◇◇◇◇◇◇◇◇

FORWARDING MAIL

Only first-class mail (weighing 12 ounces or less), including postal and post cards, may be forwarded from one city to another without a new payment of postage.   Such mail may be reforwarded.

Second- and third-class mail (of obvious value) **and parcel post** may be forwarded locally (in same post office's delivery range) without a new payment of postage.   But such mail must have new postage if forwarded to another city (unless forwarding postage has been guaranteed, or it is third- or fourth-class mail of "obvious value"; then it will be forwarded and rated with postage due). If the forwarded articles are small and the changed addresses are liable to be confusing, the articles should be rewrapped and new postage paid thereon.

"Resident," "Occupant," or **"Postal Customer"** mail will **not** be forwarded.

Perishable articles of obvious value may be forwarded with postage due.

"Special handling" parcels when forwarded will receive fast dispatch at no extra fee.   Only the third- or fourth-class rate will be collected on delivery.

Air parcel post may be forwarded by air (unless it bears instructions to forward by surface mail); forwarding postage will be collected on delivery.

Registered mail may be forwarded without charge **if it is not signed for.** But if delivery is accepted, the article must be reregistered before forwarded.

Special delivery mail may be forwarded under the same rules as ordinary mail; but special delivery will not be made at the final address if an attempt was made to deliver the article at the first address, unless new special delivery postage is affixed when the mail is forwarded.

Fan Mail.   Numerous letters received for the same addressee, such as "Advertiser's," "Audience," or "Viewer" mail, may—if **still unopened**—be assembled in one package and remailed to that addressee at the third- or fourth-class rate.   If the letters are opened and then offered for remailing in bulk, or if remailed singly, they are subject to new first-class postage.

Window Envelopes.   A forwarding address **on a window envelope** should be written at the side, not on the window.

Ink.   Changes of address should be made **in ink,** never in pencil.

Insufficient Postage or Incorrect Address.   If mail is returned to the sender because of insufficient postage or for better direction in the address **before dispatch to another post office,** the postage already placed thereon is still good.

Opened by Mistake.   Mail opened by mistake may be sealed with tape, endorsed "Opened by Mistake," and signed by the person who opened it (with his address added if necessary).   It may then be dropped in a mailbox.

Misdelivered Mail. Such articles (unopened) should be marked "Not at this address," "Not for . . .," or "Unknown here," etc., and then remailed.

Personal Notes. No message may be written on a forwarded article.

To U.S. Service Personnel. Mail of all classes may be forwarded without new postage to persons in the United States service (civil and military) whose change of address has been caused by official orders. Such forwarded mail must be marked "Address Changed by Official Orders."

Returned Letters. (For preparation for remailing, see p. 340.)

Forwarding Foreign Mail

Incoming foreign surface mail of all classes (except parcel post) may be forwarded in the United States, or to another country, without new postage.

Surface mail may be forwarded by air if airmail postage is placed thereon.

Incoming airmail (except parcel post) needs new postage only if sent abroad.

Incoming parcel post may be surface-forwarded to any U.S. point, with postage due. Air forwarding must be prepaid. Foreign parcels cannot be forwarded to another country without new postage (except that a parcel may be surface-forwarded to its country of origin with postage due).

Only **domestic letters** (containing no merchandise) **and post or postal cards** may be forwarded to a foreign address, by surface or air, with deficiency postage due. But **any** domestic article may be forwarded if prepaid—by adding new postage to that already thereon to equal the rate to the country addressed.

MAIL, GENERAL

Unpaid Mail. Mail bearing **no postage** will be returned to the senders. Mail with **insufficient postage** will be sent to addressees with "postage due."

Recall of Mail. Mail collectors cannot return mail posted in a mailbox. The sender must make written application at the post office, and present a similarly addressed envelope or wrapper (or registration receipt) for identification.

Mail cannot be recalled by telephone, but it will be held a short time pending the receipt of a written application. Mail may be recalled **by telegraph**—by the postmaster, at the sender's expense—if it is necessary to stop delivery.

Change of Address. A change of address should be reported immediately to the post office, on a change-of-address card; or the information (including both old and new addresses) may be sent in a letter or telegram to the postmaster.

Neglect to notify the post office of a change of address causes annoyance to persons at the old address. The post office is reliable in forwarding mail.

A change-of-address card may be obtained from any postman or from the post office. Convenient **mailing cards** on which to notify business houses—publishers, bank, etc.—of a change of address are also free at post offices.

(If a person has failed to register his change of address, a card should be obtained and mailed to him to be filled out and returned.)

Mail will be forwarded for **one year** on a change-of-address card. General delivery mail will be forwarded for 30 days only, unless the request is renewed; but it will be forwarded for 6 months to a permanent local address.

Sender May Obtain Changes of Address. If the mailer of any class of mail desires to know addressees' new addresses, he may have these three words printed, stamped, or written beneath his return address:

Address Correction Requested

(The sender's name and return address must appear in the upper left corner of the address side.)

Charges for this notification, for all classes of mail .... 25¢

First-class mail is forwarded, and only the notification sent the mailer.
Second- and fourth-class mail is not returned unless it bears also "Return
Postage Guaranteed"; then single-piece "postage due" is collected besides.
Third-class mail (of 4 oz. or less) is returned, for only the notification fee.
Pieces above 4 oz., to be returned, must bear "Return Postage Guaranteed."

Undeliverable Mail. First-class mail is returned to the sender, if known, without charge. Postal and post cards are not returned unless they bear the sender's address and "Return Postage Guaranteed." Other classes, as above.

Refused Mail. An addressee may refuse to accept a piece of mail at the time of delivery; or if delivered, he may return it (except a registered, insured, certified, or COD piece) to the mails **unopened** and marked REFUSED.

Certificates of Mailing. If proof is desired that ordinary mail of any class was mailed—or for additional evidence of the mailing of registered, certified, insured, or COD mail—a sender's receipt may be had if requested at the time of mailing. **Fees:** for each piece of ordinary mail posted, 15¢ (additional copy of certificate or receipt, 15¢ for each piece of mail); for **bulk** 1st and 3rd class, up to 1000 pieces (1 certificate), 75¢ (each additional 1000 pieces, 15¢).

Mailing Lists. Post offices will correct addresses on **business** mailing lists, but cannot compile lists or give information about persons on such lists.

Lists may be **typed or printed in sheet form** (carrier arranged); or may be **computer printouts; or on 3x5", or data-processing, cards**—one name and address to a card—with the owner's name in the upper left corner on each card or sheet.

Charges: 10¢ a name; minimum, $1; Zip Coding, $23.00 per 1000 addresses.

Stamps for Collections. Current regular stamps and many commemoratives are sold at face value, plus a handling charge, by the Philatelic Sales Branch, U.S. Postal Service, Washington, DC 20265. A **price list,** for stamps currently for sale, will be sent upon request. No old or rare stamps are sold.

The U.S. Postal Service does not purchase canceled postage stamps; nor can it furnish information regarding the collection value of rare stamps.

Stamps cannot be canceled in any color of ink but that authorized. If a clear cancellation is desired, write PHILATELIC MAIL near the stamps.

An illustrated (in color) pocketbook, "**U.S. Stamps and Stories** [from 1847]," is sold in **post offices** and by the **Philatelic Sales Branch:** $3.50.

Mailgrams. Night telegrams may be sent by Western Union to a **destination post office** to be delivered with the next day's mail. (See pp. 388, 391.)

Permit Imprints. Permits may be had for mailing any class of mail without stamps affixed but with **printed indicia** thereon, the postage being paid in cash—provided the mailings are presented in accordance with certain regulations. Persons or companies who frequently send out large quantities of mail should take advantage of this method of prepaying postage. A fee of $30 is charged for a permit to mail imprinted matter indefinitely. (Bulk mailings of third-class matter cost an extra $40 a year.)

Precanceled Stamps. Permits may be had for mailing any class of mail with precanceled stamps (that is, stamps canceled before they are sold) — provided the mailings are presented in accordance with certain regulations. Precanceled stamps and precanceled stamped envelopes are sold at post offices.

No charge for these permits (except $40 a year for bulk third-class mailings).

The advantage of precanceled stamps is that they facilitate the handling of "quantity mail" in post offices, thereby affording such mail a quick dispatch.

Meters. A license may be had to use meter stamps on any class of mail.

No charge for the licenses (except $40 a year for bulk third-class mailings).

Metered mail does not mean that the mail is sent at any reduced rates, the meter simply being used to save time and the work of affixing stamps.

Any color of ink that is a strong contrast to the paper may be used for meter indicia on any class of mail—or the color of the like denomination of stamp.

Postage stamps may be affixed in addition to the meter indicia if it is necessary to pay extra postage on a piece of metered mail.

Franked Mail. "Franked" and "penalty" mail (implying a penalty for private use) is sent without postage by the senders, who serve in the Federal Government, or who have been granted the franking privilege by the Government.

Franked mail is handled as **ordinary mail;** but it is entitled to any **special services** for which it may be properly marked.

Stamped Envelopes. Government stamped envelopes may be purchased in different sizes and with different denominations of stamps embossed thereon.

Stamped envelopes may be had in only one color, **white,** and one grade or quality, "standard"—and in only two sizes: $6\frac{3}{4}$ ("small") and **10** ("legal").

Window stamped envelopes may also be had—in lots of 500 or 1000, only.

Precanceled stamped envelopes are sold only to holders of permits therefor.

When stamped envelopes are ordered from the post office in lots of 500 or its multiple, of a single size and denomination, the U.S. Postal Service will, for a small fee, print a **return address** (with a title and two lines of advertising) on the envelopes. (Longest line length: 47 characters and spaces; 7-line limit; last 2 lines reserved for city address.) Printed envelopes should be ordered **six weeks in advance** of the date of contemplated use.

Unmailed **misaddressed or damaged** stamped envelopes may be redeemed.

Envelopes—Size and Shape. All envelopes must be **rectangular,** and no smaller than $3\frac{1}{2}''$ wide or $5''$ long. It is recommended that they be no larger than $9''$ wide or $12''$ long; and the ratio of width to length be not less than 1 to 1.414. On the right end, a **clear space** of $3 \times 4\frac{1}{4}''$ must be left for addresses.

Colored Envelopes, Cards, etc. Dark-colored and highly glazed stationery is objectionable because of the difficulty of reading addresses thereon. White, or **very light tints** of yellow, pink, blue, gray, green, or manila should be used for all envelopes, cards, folders, and wrappers. **Brilliant colors** cannot be used.

Excessive Printing on Address Side. On mail that bears printing, there should be at least $3\frac{1}{2}$ inches of clear space (from top to bottom, on the right end—$2\frac{3}{4}'' \times 4''$ on large pieces) for the address, stamps, postmark, etc.

Nonmailable Matter. This category covers the following things:

Defective address.   **Insufficient postage.**   **Improper size, weight, or permit.**
Game, unlawfully killed, or prohibited from mailing.
Meat and meat-food products, without certificate of inspection.
Plants and plant products not accompanied by required certificate.   Certain plants are prohibited from shipment into certain states by quarantine order.
Narcotics and other dangerous drugs.
Poisons (except those for scientific use, and those sent to licensed dealers).
Explosive, flammable, corrosive, toxic, or radioactive substances.   **Bombs.**
Intoxicating liquors (containing more than 3.2 % of alcohol by weight).
Live animals, except harmless, tiny ones needing no care, as day-old chicks or bees.
Foul-smelling articles.
Harmful articles, as sharp-pointed or sharp-edged tools insufficiently protected.
Firearms capable of being concealed on the person (with exceptions); **loaded guns.**
Matter tending to incite **arson, murder, assassination, insurrection, or treason.**
Obscene or indecent matter, written or otherwise presented.
Libelous, defamatory, dunning, or threatening matter on post cards, or on the outside of any piece of mail.
Lottery, gift or endless-chain enterprises; and **fraudulent or fictitious** schemes.

NOTE: The postal laws provide severe penalties for mailing articles in several of the above classes.

APPROXIMATE TRAIN MAIL TIME BETWEEN PRINCIPAL CITIES OF THE UNITED STATES

Approximate Number of Days or Hours

h = hours
d = days 1 day = 24 hours
Note: The days or hours herein given are estimated traveling times for mails. Additional hours must be allowed for collection and delivery.

From: \ To:	Atlanta, Ga.	Boston, Mass.	Buffalo, N.Y.	Chicago, Ill.	Cincinnati, Ohio	Cleveland, Ohio	Dallas, Tex.	Denver, Colo.	Detroit, Mich.	El Paso, Tex.	Houston, Tex.	Indianapolis, Ind.	Kansas City, Mo.	Los Angeles, Calif.	Memphis, Tenn.	Mexico, D.F.	Miami, Fla.	Minneapolis, Minn.	Montreal, Canada	New Orleans, La.	New York, N.Y.	Oklahoma City, Okla.	Omaha, Nebr.	Pittsburgh, Pa.	Portland, Oreg.	Salt Lake City, Utah	San Francisco, Calif.	Seattle, Wash.	St. Louis, Mo.
Atlanta, Ga.																													
Boston, Mass.	1½d																												
Buffalo, N.Y.	1d	13h																											
Chicago, Ill.	1d	1d	10h																										
Cincinnati, Ohio	12h	1d	14h	8h																									
Cleveland, Ohio	1d	15h	4h	8h	7h																								
Dallas, Tex.	1d	2d	1½d	1d	1d	1½d																							
Denver, Colo.	2½d	2½d	1d	18h	1d	2d	1d																						
Detroit, Mich.	18h	16h	6h	5h	6h	3h	1d	1½d																					
El Paso, Tex.	1½d	2½d	2d	1½d	1½d	2d	15h	1d	1½d																				
Houston, Tex.	1d	2½d	1½d	1d	1½d	2d	7h	1d	1½d	1d																			
Indianapolis, Ind.	16h	20h	8h	4h	2h	5h	1d	1d	6h	1½d	18h																		
Kansas City, Mo.	1d	1½d	18h	9h	14h	16h	11h	11h	14h	1d	18h	10h																	
Los Angeles, Calif.	3d	3½d	3d	2d	2d	2½d	2d	1½d	2d	1½d	2½d	2d	1½d																
Memphis, Tenn.	12h	2d	1½d	12h	18h	1d	13h	1½d	1d	1d	1d	20h	11h	2½d															
Mexico, D.F.	3d	4d	3½d	3d	3d	3½d	2d	3d	3½d	1d	1d	3d	2½d	2½d	2½d														
Miami, Fla.	1d	2d	1½d	2d	1½d	2d	2d	3½d	1½d	3d	2d	1½d	2d	4d	1½d	4d													
Minneapolis, Minn.	1½d	1½d	1d	10h	20h	19h	1½d	1½d	17h	2d	1½d	16h	13h	2d	1d	3½d	2½d												
Montreal, Canada	1½d	12h	12h	1d	1d	15h	2½d	2½d	17h	2½d	2d	18h	1½d	4½d	2d	4d	2d	1½d											
New Orleans, La.	14h	2d	1½d	1d	1d	1½d	14h	1½d	1½d	1½d	10h	1d	1d	2½d	9h	2d	1½d	1½d	2d										
New York, N.Y.	1d	5h	9h	18h	19h	13h	2d	2½d	19h	2½d	2d	18h	1d	3½d	1½d	4d	1½d	1½d	8h	1½d									
Oklahoma City, Okla.	1½d	2d	1d	1d	1d	1d	6h	18h	1d	1d	12h	20h	8h	1½d	1d	2½d	2d	18h	2d	1d	1½d								
Omaha, Nebr.	1½d	1½d	1d	12h	1d	1d	1d	1d	1d	1d	1d	18h	6h	2d	1d	3d	2½d	12h	1½d	1½d	1½d	14h							
Pittsburgh, Pa.	20h	14h	9h	9h	7h	3h	1½d	1d	7h	2d	2d	8h	18h	2½d	1d	3½d	1½d	1d	18h	1½d	9h	1d	1d						
Portland, Oreg.	3½d	3½d	2½d	2½d	3d	2½d	2½d	1½d	2½d	2d	3d	2½d	2d	1½d	3d	3d	4½d	2d	3½d	3d	3½d	2½d	2d	3d					
Salt Lake City, Utah	2½d	2½d	2d	1½d	2d	2d	2d	14h	2d	1½d	2½d	1½d	1d	1d	2d	4d	4d	1½d	2½d	3d	2½d	1½d	1d	3d	1d				
San Francisco, Calif.	3½d	3½d	2½d	2½d	3d	3d	2½d	1½d	3d	2d	3d	2½d	1½d	12h	3d	3d	4½d	2d	3½d	3d	3½d	1½d	2d	3d	1d	1d			
Seattle, Wash.	3½d	3½d	3d	2½d	3d	3d	2½d	1½d	3d	2d	3d	2½d	1½d	2d	3d	4½d	4½d	2d	3½d	4d	3½d	1½d	2d	3d	6h	1d	1½d		
St. Louis, Mo.	1d	1d	14h	7h	8h	11h	1d	2d	10h	1d½	1½d	4h	6h	2½d	8h	3d	1½d	14h	1½d	1d	1d	16h	1d	13h	2½d	2d	3d	3d	
Washington, D.C.	15h	11h	12h	21h	13h	12h	1½d	3d	18h	2½d	1½d	1d	1½d	3½d	1d	3½d	1d	1½d	14h	1d	5h	1½d	1½d	8h	3½d	2½d	3½d	3½d	1d

—Data by courtesy of the United States Postal Service.

APPROXIMATE AIRMAIL TIME BETWEEN PRINCIPAL CITIES OF THE UNITED STATES

Approximate Number of Hours

From: / To:	Atlanta, Ga.	Boston, Mass.	Buffalo, N.Y.	Chicago, Ill.	Cincinnati, Ohio	Cleveland, Ohio	Dallas, Tex.	Denver, Colo.	Des Moines, Iowa	Detroit, Mich.
Atlanta, Ga.										
Boston, Mass.	3½									
Buffalo, N.Y.	3	1⅓								
Chicago, Ill.	3	2	1¼							
Cincinnati, Ohio	2⅓	2¾	3	1						
Cleveland, Ohio	3	1⅓	¾	1	2¼					
Dallas, Tex.	1⅔	4½	3⅔	2	5⅓	3⅔				
Denver, Colo.	4⅔	3⅓	4¼	2¾	4	4	2⅔			
Des Moines, Iowa	5⅓	4⅔	4	1	4¾	3½	6¾	5		
Detroit, Mich.	3½	4	1	1	2¾	⅔	4¼	4	3	
Houston, Tex.	1½	6	8¼	4½	4½	6	¾	3	7	4⅓
Indianapolis, Ind.	3	5½	5⅓	1¾	1½	4½	4½	5⅔	5	2¼
Kansas City, Mo.	3⅓	5¼	5⅔	1½	4¾	6	2¼	1⅓	1	3¼
Los Angeles, Calif.	4⅓	6	5¼	3½	6½	4	2½	2	5½	3¾
Memphis, Tenn.	2⅓	6¼	6½	2	4½	4¾	2	6¼	5⅓	4¾
Miami, Fla.	1⅔	2⅔	5⅓	2⅔	2¼	2⅓	7	6½	7	2½
Milwaukee, Wis.	4⅔	4	3⅓	⅔	4	2⅔	5¼	4⅓	4	2¼
Minneapolis, Minn.	5	5½	7	1¼	3½	4¼	5¼	5	4¼	2¾
New Orleans, La.	1¼	6¼	9	4¼	2¾	5½	3¼	5½	8½	2⅔
New York, N.Y.	2	¾	1¼	2¼	4¼	1½	3¼	6	5	1⅔
Oklahoma City, Okla.	7	7½	6½	3¼	6¾	6¼	¾	2	6	5½
Omaha, Nebr.	6	4	4¼	1¼	4	3	4¼	1¼	⅔	3
Phoenix, Ariz.	6½	6½	6¾	3⅔	5⅔	6¼	3½	5	4¼	5⅔
Pittsburgh, Pa.	1½	3¾	⅔	2	5	3⅔	7	5½	3¾	¾
Portland, Oreg.	8⅓	6¾	5¾	5	6	5½	7½	7⅔	5	6
Salt Lake City, Utah	8	8⅔	7⅔	5½	7½	7½	4¼	1	6	4⅓
San Francisco, Calif.	4	6½	6	3⅔	6¼	5⅔	4	2	5¼	5⅓
Seattle, Wash.	7¾	6½	7	3½	6	5½	7¾	7⅔	5	4
St. Louis, Mo.	1¼	3½	3½	1	1½	3	4⅔	2½	4	3¼
Washington, D.C.	1½	1	1½	1⅔	1⅓	1¼	3	4	5⅓	2

From: / To:	Houston, Tex.	Indianapolis, Ind.	Kansas City, Mo.	Los Angeles, Calif.	Memphis, Tenn.	Miami, Fla.	Milwaukee, Wis.	Minneapolis, Minn.	New Orleans, La.	New York, N.Y.
Indianapolis, Ind.	5½									
Kansas City, Mo.	3	2								
Los Angeles, Calif.	5	4¾	3							
Memphis, Tenn.	2⅓	1	3¼	6						
Miami, Fla.	6¼	5½	5	7⅔	6½					
Milwaukee, Wis.	4	1½	2¾	5½	3½	5¼				
Minneapolis, Minn.	5½	5⅓	4⅓	3¼	4¼	7¾	1½			
New Orleans, La.	¾	2¼	5	4⅓	1½	1½	7	6½		
New York, N.Y.	4¼	3¼	4	5½	4½	2½	3⅓	5	4½	
Oklahoma City, Okla.	2¾	3⅓	¾	2⅓	4	8	5	6⅔	3¾	6¼
Omaha, Nebr.	4	7⅔	1	4⅔	4¼	8½	5⅔	1	6⅓	3½
Phoenix, Ariz.	4¼	6½	6	1	5½	9½	5	5⅔	4½	5
Pittsburgh, Pa.	6	1¼	3⅔	6⅓	3½	2¼	4¼	4	4¾	2⅓
Portland, Oreg.	7½	5	8	1¾	6⅔	9	4¾	5	5½	8
Salt Lake City, Utah	8	6¾	6	2¼	6	8¼	6⅔	2	7⅔	4
San Francisco, Calif.	4	4	3	1	4¾	5¾	5	5¾	6¼	5
Seattle, Wash.	7½	5	5⅔	3	6⅔	8¼	4¾	3⅔	8	4½
St. Louis, Mo.	3¼	1	¾	3½	¾	7¾	4¾	5	4	2
Washington, D.C.	3⅓	1⅙	4⅓	4⅔	2⅔	2	2⅔	2½	3½	1

From: / To:	Oklahoma City, Okla.	Omaha, Nebr.	Phoenix, Ariz.	Pittsburgh, Pa.	Portland, Oreg.	Salt Lake City, Utah	San Francisco, Calif.	Seattle, Wash.	St. Louis, Mo.
Omaha, Nebr.	2¾								
Phoenix, Ariz.	5	4½							
Pittsburgh, Pa.	6½	3½	6						
Portland, Oreg.	5¼	1⅔	6¼	6					
Salt Lake City, Utah	6¼	4	1¼	8	3¼				
San Francisco, Calif.	4½	3¾	3	7	1⅓	3			
Seattle, Wash.	7¼	6¼	7¼	6	⅔	2¼	1½		
St. Louis, Mo.	3¾	3¾	8⅓	4¼	7½	6	5	7	
Washington, D.C.	4⅓	4	4⅔	1	8	5½	5½	6¼	2

Note: The hours given herein are estimated flying and transfer times for **evening mails.** Additional hours must be allowed for collection and delivery.

To calculate special-delivery time: Add a minimum of 1 hour for post office handling. Also, for **eastbound mail,** add the time-zone-difference hours between mailing point and destination.

(For **airmail time to foreign places,** see p. 372.)

ALASKA: Seattle to
- Anchorage 3⅓
- Fairbanks 3½
- Juneau 2¾

HAWAII: to Honolulu
- Los Angeles, San Francisco 5¼
- Seattle 5½

MONTREAL, CANADA: from
- Boston 1½
- Chicago 2
- New York 1⅓

MEXICO, D.F.: from
- Los Angeles 3
- New York 4¾

—Compiled from Airmail Schedules of the U.S. Post Offices named, and the Official Airline Guide.

Matter Mailable Under Special Rules. Certain items ordinarily barred from the mails may be mailed if properly packaged. Consult the post office.

ZIP Code. Each city's **ZIP Code directory** is free at its post offices.

The **National ZIP Code Directory,** enabling the user to determine the ZIP Code for any address in the Nation, is for sale (see p. 345). The booklet **"Abbreviations for Use With ZIP Code"** is free at local post offices.

Presorting. Bulk mail **must** be presorted by ZIP Code, tied, and labeled. Other **volume** mail **should** be presorted into "Local," "In-State," and "Out-of-State" packs, tied and labeled (labels and bands are free at post offices).

Complaints. When it is necessary to complain about the mishandling of mail, submit the envelope or wrapper of the mishandled or damaged mail.

INTERNATIONAL MAIL

Pieces of mail for other countries are classified in general as

Letters	Letter Packages	Printed Matter ("Prints")
Post Cards	Small Packets	International Parcel Post*

* **Often cheaper ways** are as Small Packets, Letter Packages, or Prints (especially Books).

Envelopes must be light colored; "windows" acceptable (but no "open or two panels").

Postage is paid by U.S. stamps or bright red meter stamps (or imprints for quantities).

Export Control Regulations. For export regulations, restrictions, licenses, etc., inquire of the Exporters' Service Section, Bureau of International Commerce, Department of Commerce, Washington, D.C. 20230, or any field office thereof.

Customs Duty. For rates of duty on imported articles, or customs procedures, inquire of customs officers in various U.S. cities, or write the U.S. Customs Service, Treasury Department, Washington, D.C. 20229. Its free pamphlet, **"Customs Hints for Returning U.S. Residents,"** gives a "Tariff List of Most Popular Tourist Items."

No prepayment abroad may be made of duty on mail for the United States; nor can prepayment be made here on mail for other countries (for exception, see p. 371).

No information can be furnished about articles (particularly gifts) that might be duty-free and/or not require import permits in other countries. Intended recipients abroad might obtain such information from their own customs authorities.

Letters and Post Cards to Other Countries by surface mail (airmail, p. 369).

Rates

To all countries except Canada and Mexico	{ Letters—1 oz., 20¢; 2, 36¢; 4, 48¢; 8, 96¢; 1 lb., $1.84; 2 lb., $3.20; 4 lb., $5.20. Post Cards—14¢ each

To Can. & Mex.: same as domestic 1st-cl. rates (over 12 oz., 8th zone priority rates).

Weight limit: 4 pounds (except to Canada, where it is 60 pounds).

Maximum letter dimensions to all foreign destinations:
  Length, breadth, and thickness combined—36 inches. Greatest length, 24 inches.
  Rolls—length (maximum 36 inches) plus twice diameter is limited to 42 inches.
  Indivisible objects must conform to the above dimensions.

Maximum post card dimensions: 4¼″ x 6″. (Larger sizes take letter rate.)

Minimum dimensions for the address side of articles: 3½″ x 5½″; tags, 2¾″ x 4″.
  Rolls—length 4″; or length plus twice the diameter, 6¾″.

Letter Packages. Dutiable merchandise may be sent in letters or sealed packages at the letter rate. (Some countries do not accept letter packages; others require registration of those containing dutiable articles.)

A **green customs label** must be affixed if dutiable articles are enclosed. The nature of the contents must be shown on the label or, if preferred, on a **customs declaration** in the package. Write LETTRE on the wrapper.

Sound-recorded correspondence takes letter rates—except if sent by schools.

Printed Matter ("Prints"). **Unsealed** (stapled padded envelopes sent at sender's risk); or **sealed** (if postage paid by permit imprints, postage meter stamps, precanceled stamps, second-class or controlled circulation indicia). May be **registered,** sealed or unsealed. **No customs label** unless article is **dutiable.** Write on the wrapper: PRINTED MATTER (or **Imprimés**) and BOOKS, if books; or SHEET MUSIC, or DIRECTORIES, or CATALOGS, etc.

The following are accepted as prints:

In general, all impressions or reproductions obtained **upon paper,** or materials similar to paper, parchment, or cardboard, by means of **printing,** engraving, lithography, photography, or any other easily recognizable mechanical process, with the **exception** of reproductions made by stamps with movable or immovable type, and the typewriter.

Included are newspapers; periodicals; books; pamphlets; sheet music (except perforated papers for automatic musical instruments); visiting cards; address cards; greeting cards; printing proofs (corrected or uncorrected and with or without relative manuscripts); unframed photographs; engravings; albums containing photographs; printed pictures; drawings; plans; maps; patterns to be cut out; calendars (except calendar pads with blank pages for memoranda); catalogues; prospectuses; advertisements; notices; cards (including those marked "Post Card") provided they fulfill the general conditions for prints; matrices of material similar to paper or cardboard; scores or sheets of music in manuscript; manuscripts of literary works or for newspapers; original and corrected exercises of students, without any notes not relating directly to the execution of the work; and correspondence between students, sent through heads of schools.

Reproductions of handwriting or typewriting obtained by a mechanical process may be sent as prints if mailed at a post office window in lots of 20 or more identical pieces.

For **permissible additions,** such as invoices, inscriptions, and notations—and for **inadmissible matter,** such as films, stamps, recordings, and writing—consult the post office.

Rate (except Can. & Mex.): 2 oz., 20¢; 4, 40; 8, 66; 1 lb., $1.05; 2, $1.26; 4, $1.68; ea. addl. 2 lb., 84¢. To **Canada** and **Mexico:** 2 oz., 20¢; 4, 40¢; 13¢ ea. addl. 2 oz. up to 1 lb.; 2 lb., $1.26; 4 lb., $1.68; ea. addl. 2 lb., 84¢.

Book and Sheet Music Rate (on bound books of 24 or more pages, with at least 22 printed, and with no advertising except book announcements):

To all countries, incl. Canada: 1 lb., 48¢; 2, 66¢; 4, 84¢; ea. addl. 2 lb., 42¢.

Weight limit to most countries: 4 lbs. (for books, 11 lbs.); but to Mexico, Central and South America, and Spain, 22 lbs. for all printed matter, including books.

Maximum and minimum dimensions: same as for Letters, p. 364.

WRAPPING (**sealed or unsealed**): Prints may be placed either in **transparent plastic film containers,** with address labels; under **wrapper** (in very strong paper—with the wrapper of a periodical extending between the pages to prevent slipping); in **rolls;** between **cardboard;** in **open cases;** or in **strong or padded envelopes.** Make sure that articles are so prepared that other articles cannot slip into them. **Postal inspection** is automatically granted.

Cards need no wrapper or envelope, unless they are folded.

Direct Sacks. Quantity mailings (by surface or air) of **unregistered** Prints, especially books, from one sender to one addressee may be sacked and tagged by the mailer to save costs. Each package then need not conform to normal weight and size limits—but it must be **addressed,** and endorsed "Postage Paid."

Minimum sack weight: 22 lbs.; **maximum,** 66 lbs. (sack and contents).

Enclosures permitted are: an open invoice (if mailed separately, the letter rate applies); an order form with books, and a printed circular about an accompanying book or announcing other books; a reply card, envelope, or wrapper (not "business reply") bearing the sender's printed United States address.

Closings permitted are: steel-band or wire fastenings (but some countries prohibit); staples (1, 2, or 3) on padded envelopes; one or two spots of glue to hold the side flap of an envelope having the main flap sealed.

Insurance is not available for books and other printed matter, unless they are prepared and prepaid as parcel post, with documents attached.

Samples of Merchandise are now mailed as Small Packets, Letter Packages, or Parcel Post.

Merchandise Packages to Canada. This classification has been discontinued. Small articles may now be sent as Small Packets, Letter Packages, or Parcel Post.

Small Packets. Sealed or unsealed—may be registered—green customs label necessary. Write SMALL PACKET (or **Petit Paquet**) on the wrapper.

Mailable to all countries except Cuba and North Korea.

Small packets **may contain**:

> Dutiable merchandise, commercial samples, and/or documents, records, tapes, and data processing cards that do not have the character of correspondence. Invoices may be enclosed; also certain particulars regarding samples.
>
> They **may not contain** current personal correspondence in either written or sound-recorded form; coins; bank notes, paper money, postage stamps, or any values payable to the bearer; manufactured or unmanufactured platinum, gold, or silver; precious stones, jewelry, or other precious articles.
>
> **Rate:** 2 oz., 20¢; 4 oz., 40¢; 8 oz., 66¢; 1 lb., $1.05; 2 lbs., $1.26.
> **Can. & Mex.:** 2 oz., 20¢; 4, 40¢; 13¢ ea. addl. 2 oz. up to 1 lb. **Mex.,** 2 lb., $1.26.
> **Weight limit:** 2 lb.; to some countries, as Canada, Chile, and Australia, 1 lb.
> **Maximum and minimum dimensions:** same as for Letters, p. 364.

WRAPPING (**sealed or unsealed**): Small packets may be in **envelopes, bags, boxes, or plastic wrappers.** The **nature and value** of the contents must be shown on the customs label or, if preferred, on an invoice or a customs declaration in the packet. **Postal inspection** is automatically granted.

Matter for the Blind. Unsealed packages, weighing not more than 15 lbs., within letter dimensions (p. 364), containing books, periodicals, unsealed letters, or other matter impressed in Braille or other special type; plates for embossing blind literature; and (if sent to or from officially recognized institutions) discs, tapes, or wires bearing voice recordings, and special paper, may be sent FREE by surface mail, or at the "AO" (2-oz.) air rates. Weight limit: 15 lb.

Write MATTER FOR THE BLIND in the upper right corner.

Services Not Available. Certain domestic services are not available in the international mails—particularly to Canada and Mexico:

Certified Mail	Business Reply Mail	Reply-paid Cards
C.O.D. Mail	Bulk 3rd-Class Mail	Double Cards

> **Grouping** of printed matter and samples in one package is no longer permitted.
> **"Combination Packages,"** consisting of sealed letters attached to unsealed packages of samples or prints are no longer accepted. But to Canada, a sealed letter, with letter postage thereon (or to Switzerland, a letter or card), may be securely attached to **a parcel post package.** Such parcels are treated as parcel post.

Letters Within Letters, or Packages Within Packages. Separately addressed letters within letters, or packages within packages, are prohibited, unless such enclosed letters or packages are those of the sender or his family for members of the original addressee's household or for persons residing at his address.

Registered Mail—Foreign. Regular mail may be registered to almost all countries. (Parcel post packages may be insured, but no longer registered, to most countries.) International airmail may be registered.

> **Fees,** in addition to postage, for each piece of mail: $3.00. (To Canada, up to $3.30.)
> **Return receipt** (mark article *"Avis de reception"* or *"A.R."*), fee: 45¢. Must be requested at **time of mailing.** Will be returned by **airmail. (International return receipt cards [pink]** are free at post offices. Do not use **green** domestic cards.)
> **Restricted delivery,** in some countries: 80¢ plus charge for return receipt.
> Mark above the address and underline in red, *"À remettre en main propre."*

366

All registered letter mail **must be sealed** and in heavy or padded envelopes (not self-sealing). Registered mail must not bear any trace of having been opened and resealed before mailing. All addresses must be typewritten or in ink.

Letter mail containing the following valuables **must** be registered: coins, bank notes, paper money, or any values payable to bearer; manufactured or unmanufactured platinum, gold, or silver; precious stones, jewelry, and other precious articles. Some countries prohibit the importation of these articles (even in registered mail), and invariably confiscate them without indemnity to the senders.

If the mail is especially valuable, inquiry should be made about indemnity in case of loss. Maximum indemnity is usually $15.76; but to Canada, $200.

Special Delivery—Foreign. A few countries do not have this service; so it is well to inquire at the post office about any questionable destination.

Fees (in addition to regular postage):	Up to 2 lbs.	Over 2 lbs. up to 10 lbs.	Over 10 lbs.
Letters, letter packages, post cards, and airmail except air parcel post............	$2.00......$2.25.....$2.85		
Surface other articles*...................	$2.25......$2.85.....$3.25		

* To Canada, only articles prepaid at the letter rate may be sent special delivery; but to other countries, practically all pieces of mail except parcel post packages may be sent special delivery.

U.S. special delivery stamps may be used (for the special delivery fee only). Also, for both postage and fee, ordinary or meter stamps may be used—and airmail stamps on airmail only. Write boldly in red ink near the name of the country of destination (or obtain a free sticker at the post office):

EXPRES
SPECIAL DELIVERY

"Shortpaid" (insufficiently prepaid) foreign special delivery mail will be dispatched as intended (usually by air), and will receive special delivery in the country of destination. The deficiency in postage will be collected from the sender or the receiver, whichever way is more expeditious and less costly.

General Delivery—Foreign. General delivery for foreign post offices should be marked at the left of the address:

POSTE RESTANTE

This French marking is universally accepted for general delivery, although the English words GENERAL DELIVERY may also be used. The number of days that general delivery mail is held in foreign post offices varies according to the regulations of the different countries.

International Parcel Post

Parcel post packages may be sent to every country in the world. **But before preparing a foreign parcel, consult a postal authority for regulations and prohibitions of the country of destination.** (And send as a **Small Packet** if possible.)

Rates to all countries (except North America): $2.34 for the first 2 pounds, and 59¢ for each additional pound. To Canada, Mexico, Central America, Bermuda, and the West Indies: $2.19 for first 2 pounds, and 52¢ for each additional pound.
Weight limits: **no minimum,** but up to 2 lbs. the **Small Packets** rate is cheaper.
Maximum is 22 pounds to some countries; 44 pounds to others. To Canada, the surface limit is 35 pounds; to Bermuda, 33 pounds; to Panama, 70 pounds.
Maximum dimensions: In general, the greatest length is $3\frac{1}{2}$ feet; and greatest length and girth combined, 6 feet. Variations apply to certain countries.

No communication of the nature of personal correspondence may be enclosed.

Extra-heavy packaging is necessary to withstand the numerous handlings and friction to which foreign parcels are unavoidably subjected. Packages **must** be packed in: canvas or similar material; strong cartons,· wrapped, if need be, in heavy wrapping, or waterproof, paper; double-faced corrugated or solid fiber boxes or cases; or wooden boxes of lumber at least one-half inch thick, or of 3-ply plywood. Ordinary paperboard containers are wholly inadequate. **Strapping tape** may be used for sealing; and extra-strong **cord or rope** for tieing.

A fragile or easily breakable article, as of china, crockery, or glass, should be packed in a strong (preferably wooden) box and cushioned with a liberal supply of excelsior, crushed paper, wood wool, or cotton, etc., between the article and the top, bottom, and sides of the box. Mark FRAGILE, or PERISHABLE, or GLASS, etc., on all such boxes.

Liquids and substances which easily liquefy must be packed in **two receptacles.** Between the first (bottle, flask, etc.) and the second (box of metal, strong wood, strong corrugated cardboard, strong fiberboard, or receptacle of equal strength) there must be left a space to be filled with sawdust, bran, or other absorbent material sufficient to absorb all the liquid in case of breakage.

The **sealing** of parcel post packages (with wax, lead seals, or other material) is compulsory to some countries, while to others it is optional with the sender. However, insured parcels **must** be securely sealed. (See below.)

Christmas seals or stamps must not be affixed to the address side of a foreign parcel. They may, however, be affixed to the back of the article.

All addresses should be typewritten, or written in ink; pencil addresses are not permitted. (See also Foreign Addresses, p. 321.) The receiver's address and the sender's return address should appear on the face of the package; and they should also be written on a slip of paper enclosed in the package. Nothing should be written on the back of the package.

Alternative disposition must be indicated by the sender; that is, if the parcel is undeliverable as originally addressed, it is to be either (1) tendered for delivery **at a second address** in the country of destination, (2) treated as abandoned, or (3) returned to the sender. If returned, it will be at the sender's expense.

International parcel post cannot be addressed **via any certain ship.**

All parcel post must be **mailed at post offices,** not in mailboxes.

Customs declaration tags (listing each kind of article, quantity and value [general descriptions like "Clothing," "Foodstuffs," "Gifts" are not acceptable]) and a yellow parcel post sticker must be on every parcel. In addition, there may be required to some countries one or more of the following documents:

Dispatch Note	Consular Invoice	Certificate of Disinfection
Export License	Commercial Invoice	Shipper's Export Declaration
Import License	Certificate of Origin	(for commercial purposes)

Special Handling—on foreign surface **small packets, prints, and parcel post.** This service accords articles the fastest handling possible within the United States **only**; they are not accorded any preferential dispatch from the United States, and receive no special treatment in the countries of destination.

Write or stamp SPECIAL HANDLING above the address (beneath the stamps) on the wrapper. Fees are the same as domestic fees, p. 352.

Insurance—Foreign. Only parcel post (which **must be sealed**) may be insured to most countries. Book parcels, prints, small packets, and merchandise packages may be registered, but cannot be insured unless prepared, paid for, and sent as parcel post. **Indemnity** varies greatly in the different countries.

A parcel may be insured for a **portion of the value** of the contents.

Parcels containing **coin, bullion, precious jewelry,** etc., must be insured.

Seal the package tightly and remove all traces of wax, mucilage, or other evidence suggesting that the package might have been opened and resealed.

Write INSURED on the address side beside the country of destination.

Insurance fees: from 90¢ to $5.70. (To Canada, same as domestic insurance fees.)
Return receipts: (Same as for Registered Mail, p. 366.)

Money Orders—Foreign. Money orders payable in almost any country in the world are obtainable at all large post offices and at many small ones.

Orders (valid for 1 year) are payable at foreign post offices in foreign currency. About **3 weeks** elapse before payment is effected in a foreign country.

Fees: Up to $10... 90¢ $10.01 to $50... $1.10 $50.01 to $300... $1.40
(Fees to Canada and some W.I. islands are same as domestic fees.)

Certificates of Mailing—Foreign. If proof is desired that certain ordinary mail, airmail, or parcel post was mailed—or for additional evidence of the mailing of registered or insured articles—a sender's receipt may be had if requested at the time of mailing. **Fees:** 15¢ for each piece of ordinary mail (additional copy of certificate or receipt, 15¢ for each piece of mail); for identical pieces, up to 1000 (1 certificate), 75¢ (each additional 1000 pieces, 15¢).

Airmail—Foreign. There are four different rate classes for international airmail: (1) letters and letter packages; (2) post cards; (3) prints, samples, etc.; (4) air parcel post. Each piece of mail should be prepared exactly as it would be for surface transportation. All foreign airmail postage **must be fully prepaid.**

INTERNATIONAL AIRMAIL RATES
(Half-ounce rate for Letters and Letter Packages)*
Weight limit: 4 pounds to most countries.

CENTRAL AMERICA AND ISLANDS per ½ oz.		OTHER COUNTRIES per ½ oz.	
To: Central America.......		To: All of Europe and Azores...	31¢ per
Venezuela & Colombia.	25¢ per ½ oz.	USSR and Middle East.....	½ oz. up
Bermuda..............	up to 2 oz.	Asia, Australia & Philippines	to 2 oz;
Bahamas..............	21¢ ea. addl.	Africa—entire continent....	26¢ ea.
Caribbean Islands.....	½ oz.	South America (except	addl.
St. Pierre & Miquelon..		Venezuela & Colombia) ..	½ oz.

To Canada and Mexico: Same as U.S. domestic 1st-class rates for letter airmail and air post and postal cards, from any point in the United States. (Pieces over 12 oz. take 8th zone priority rates.)

Post cards by air to all countries, except Canada and Mexico: 21¢ each.

Aerogramme (Air Letter)—a single, folding sheet that seals; sold at post offices. Message may be written on all parts except address side (address labels permitted). It may be registered. No enclosures or sealing stickers permitted. Rate to all countries: 22¢.

* Prints, Small Packets, and Matter for the Blind have a special 2-ounce air rate, which is about ⅓ the 4-ounce air parcel post rate. (For examples of air parcel post rates, see next page.)
NOTE: To Canada, all airmail packages take the letter air rate to that country.

Marking Foreign Airmail. It is desirable that all international letter airmail be in distinctive airmail envelopes.

All international airmail should bear a blue PAR AVION sticker **below the return address.** (These stickers are free at post offices.) Or PAR AVION may be printed or stamped boldly in blue ink thereon. (pron. pär ăv'yawn')

Air parcel post must have an AIRMAIL label below the country name, and a PAR AVION sticker on the dispatch note if such a note is required.

369

International Express Mail (to certain countries). This is an ultra-high-speed delivery of **letters and business documents** (and of **samples** to some countries), with pickup or bring-in service, volume discounts, free insurance, etc.

International Air Parcel Post (**daily service to most countries**)

Sealing of air parcels is compulsory to some countries; optional. to others.

Insurance on **sealed** air parcels, only, is available to most countries.

Size limitations, packing, customs declarations, and other regulations governing international surface parcel post, apply, in general. to air parcels.

INTERNATIONAL AIR PARCEL POST RATES—EXAMPLES

NOTE: To Canada, all air parcels take the letter air rate.

Country	1st 4 oz.	Ea. add. 4 oz.	Country	1st 4 oz.	Ea. add. 4 oz.
EUROPE			**MEXICO & ISLANDS**		
France	$2.98	66¢	Bermuda	$1.77	35¢
Germany	2.10	70	Cuba	(no service)	
Great Britain	2.08	66	Haiti	2.25	35
Italy	2.63	79	Jamaica	2.36	33
Netherlands (Holland)	2.36	66	Mexico	1.77	35
U.S.S.R. (Russia)	2.84	95	**CENTRAL AMERICA**		
MIDEAST & AFRICA			Costa Rica	$2.06	43¢
Egypt	$2.32	92¢	Guatemala	2.51	46
Ghana (Gold Coast)	2.92	92	Honduras	2.14	46
Iran	2.67	96	Nicaragua	2.08	43
Israel	2.93	91	**SOUTH AMERICA**		
South Africa	2.66	$1.27	Argentina	$2.46	$1.07
FAR EAST			Brazil	2.94	79¢
Australia	$2.62	$1.21	Chile	2.92	89
India	2.67	1.27	Colombia	2.86	50
Japan	2.19	80¢	Peru	2.88	60
Malaysia	3.23	$1.42	Uruguay	2.93	90
Philippines	3.03	1.17	Venezuela	2.71	43

Addressing Mail via Special Ships. It is the practice of the U.S. Postal Service to dispatch mails on ships of United States and foreign registry.

Senders desiring to have their letter mail (letters, letter packages and post cards) forwarded on certain ships should plainly indicate the name of the ship diagonally across the face of each piece of mail between the address and the return address, as follows:

Per SS. BRITANNIA   via   New York (or port of departure)

Closing Time for Foreign Mails. The closing hours for ships' mails are printed each day in seaport newspapers, under the shipping and mails sections.

The hours in the papers are the closing hours at the post office of dispatch. Branch post offices usually close such mails one hour before the post office of dispatch.   Therefore, mail for a certain ship should be in a branch post office at least **one hour before the closing hour in the paper.**

If such mail is to be deposited in a mail box in the business district, it should be in the box at least **three hours before the closing hour in the paper.**

Registered mail, parcel post, and ordinary printed mail matter is closed from one to two hours earlier than other mail; therefore, such mail must be in branch post offices from **two to four hours** before the closing hour in the paper.

Preparation for Mailing. All regular mail articles for other countries should be securely wrapped in heavy paper or enclosed in heavy envelopes, to withstand the many transfers and handlings and the friction of the mail bags in transit to destination.

370

Sealing wax may now be used in sealing both letters and parcels.

Prohibitions in international mails cover potentially **harmful articles** (which include all kinds of **matches**), etc. In many ways the restrictions are the same as those for domestic mails, p. 361.

Consult a postal authority before preparing any package or questionable piece of mail for delivery in another country.

Addresses to Other Countries. (See Foreign Addresses, p. 321.)

Prepayment of International Mail. Articles to all countries should be fully prepaid. The sender should never guess at the postage on foreign mail.

In most countries, if there is postage due when mail arrives, the addressee is charged **double the amount of the deficient postage.**

Customs Declarations and Duties. Customs tags, labels, and declaration forms are obtainable at post offices. Customs duties cannot be prepaid through the post office; they must be collected from the addressees when the articles are delivered. (An exception is that customs duties may be prepaid on certain advertising to Canada. Information and duty stamps may be obtained from the Department of National Revenue, Customs and Excise, Ottawa, Ont., Canada.)

Gifts. Although an article may be marked GIFT—with other required information, such as the nature of the contents and the actual value—it is liable to customs inspection and possible duty in the country of destination.

Incoming Dutiable Mail. An extra postal charge is made for the work of clearing dutiable articles through customs and effecting delivery:

$1.00 for each article on which duty or a tax is collected.

Recall or Changing Address—Foreign. Posted mail may be recalled by the postmaster, or the address thereon may be ordered changed. (Some countries do not permit this.) The sender must furnish a facsimile of the address side of the article, and the date mailed. **Fee:** $1.00 plus airmail or telegraph charges.

Reply Coupons. As a means of supplying foreign correspondents with reply postage, reply coupons may be purchased (for 42¢ each) and sent to other countries. A reply coupon entitles a correspondent abroad to receive return postage for a one-rate **surface letter** upon presentation of the coupon at his post office. For an **airmail reply,** several coupons will be accepted.

Forwarding of Foreign Mail. (See p. 359.)

Insufficient Foreign Address. An article returned from another country must have new postage affixed before being remailed with a corrected address. (It is best to prepare a new envelope or wrapper, with new postage thereon.)

Returned for Postage. When an article is returned for additional postage, the postage thereon is still good. Only the indicated amount need be affixed, and the article remailed immediately.

CAUTION: Cross out the "Returned for postage" endorsement.

Return of Unclaimed Foreign Mail. A return address **must** be shown in the upper left corner of the address side of every piece of international mail.

Undeliverable regular mail articles which have been fully prepaid to foreign destinations are returned to the senders without charge, except that ordinary printed matter will not be returned unless it bears "Return Requested."

An undeliverable parcel post package will be returned to the sender in the United States with return postage due, and may be assessed with other charges, such as storage, customs clearance, and delivery fees.

Samples and mail without value will not be returned unless a sender, by a notation on an article, requests its return and guarantees return postage.

◇◇◇◇◇◇◇◇◇ **371**

MAIL DAYS TO OTHER COUNTRIES AND U.S. OUTLANDS

The days listed in the following table are approximated data supplied by the U.S. Postal Service, with very little time figured for mail connections at various points. Sailings to some distant countries or isolated islands are "four times a month," "every two weeks," or "irregular." Therefore, several days may elapse in some ports while mail is waiting for a ship.

The days given apply to **letter mails only.** Parcel post mails usually take several days longer; and to some distant or isolated countries, surface parcel post may take several weeks longer.

Christmas foreign surface mail should be dispatched early because of the long sea transit frequently involved, and customs inspection and other formalities which retard delivery in the countries of destination. Christmas mail should be posted in sufficient time to arrive at Atlantic or Pacific seaports at least one day before the approximate dates given in the table below.

APPROXIMATE NUMBER OF LETTER MAIL DAYS
(Data by courtesy of the U.S. Postal Service.)
(Surface mail time in roman type. Airmail time in boldface type in parentheses.)

To:	New York	San Francisco or Los Angeles	Seattle	New Orleans	Miami	Latest Christmas Mailing Dates (approximate)*
Afghanistan....................	30–40 (3)	.....	.....	.....	.....	Oct. 15
Africa (See individual countries)						
Alaska† { Juneau..............	.....	.....	4 (1)	.....	.....	Nov. 30
{ Anchorage............	.....	.....	5 (1)	.....	.....	Nov. 30
Albania......................	10–14 (3)	.....	.....	.....	.....	Nov. 15
Algeria......................	12–17 (2)	.....	.....	.....	.....	Nov. 15
Angola (former Port. W. Africa)..	25–30 (3)	.....	.....	.....	.....	Nov. 1
Arabia (Saudi Arabia)..........	20–30 (3)	.....	.....	.....	.....	Nov. 1
Argentina....................	18–21 (2)	.....	.....	18–20	(2)	Nov. 15
Australia....................	.....	19–25 (3)	.....	.....	.....	Nov. 1
Austria......................	10–15 (2)	.....	.....	.....	.....	Nov. 15
Azores‡......................	10–15 (2)	.....	.....	.....	.....	Nov. 15
Bahamas.....................	.....	.....	.....	.....	1 (1)	Nov. 22
Barbados.....................	10–18 (2)	.....	.....	10–18	(2)	Nov. 22
Belgium.....................	8–10 (2)	.....	.....	.....	.....	Nov. 15
Bermuda.....................	2–3 (1)	.....	.....	.....	.....	Nov. 22
Bolivia......................	19–22	.....	.....	19–22	(2)	Nov. 15
Brazil......................	15–18 (2)	.....	.....	15–18	(2)	Nov. 15
British Honduras (now Belize)....	.....	.....	.....	6 (2)	.....	Nov. 22
Bulgaria.....................	15–20 (3)	.....	.....	.....	.....	Nov. 15
Burma......................	.....	40–45 (4)	.....	.....	.....	Oct. 15
Cameroon....................	25–30 (4)	.....	.....	.....	.....	Nov. 1
Canal Zone..................	6–8	8–10	.....	6–10 (1)	(1)	Nov. 22
Canary Islands..............	15–18 (2)	.....	.....	.....	.....	Nov. 15
Cape Verde Islands..........	18–20 (3)	.....	.....	.....	.....	Nov. 15
Caroline Islands.............	.....	30–35 (4)	.....	.....	.....	Oct. 15
Ceylon‡ (now Sri Lanka)........	35–40 (3)	(3)	.....	.....	.....	Oct. 15
Chile.......................	17–20	.....	.....	17–20	(2)	Nov. 15
China‡ (See Hong Kong & Taiwan)						
Colombia....................	11 (2)	15	.....	11	(2)	Nov. 22
Congo ([Kinshasa] now Zaire)	15–20 (3)	.....	.....	.....	.....	Nov. 1
Costa Rica..................	10–12	15	.....	9 (1)	(1)	Nov. 22
Cuba.......................	15	.....	.....	15	(5)	Nov. 15
Czechoslovakia................	12–15 (2)	.....	.....	.....	.....	Nov. 15
Denmark....................	10–12 (2)	.....	.....	.....	.....	Nov. 15
Dominican Republic...........	6–8 (1)	.....	.....	5	(1)	Nov. 22
Ecuador.....................	10–12 (2)	16	.....	11	(2)	Nov. 22

APPROXIMATE NUMBER OF LETTER MAIL DAYS—contd.

| To: | Mails dispatched from: | | | | | Latest Christmas Mailing Dates (approximate)* |
	New York	San Francisco or Los Angeles	Seattle	New Orleans	Miami	
Egypt (United Arab Republic)....	15–20 (3)	.....	.....	.....	.....	Nov. 1
England.......................	8–10 (2)	.....	.....	.....	.....	Nov. 15
Ethiopia (including Eritrea)......	25 (2)	.....	.....	.....	.....	Nov. 1
Fiji Islands....................	.....	35–40 (3)	.....	.....	.....	Oct. 15
Finland.......................	14–17 (2)	.....	.....	.....	.....	Nov. 15
Formosa‡ (now Taiwan).........	.....	20–25 (3)	20–25 (3)	.....	.....	Nov. 1
France........................	8–10 (2)	.....	.....	.....	.....	Nov. 15
Germany‡......................	10–12 (2)	.....	.....	.....	.....	Nov. 15
Ghana........................	18 (3)	.....	.....	.....	.....	Nov. 1
Great Britain..................	8–10 (2)	.....	.....	.....	.....	Nov. 15
Greece........................	14–21 (2)	.....	.....	.....	.....	Nov. 15
Guam.........................	.....	15–20 (3)	.....	.....	.....	Nov. 1
Guatemala.....................	.....	10	.....	(1)	8–10 (1)	Nov. 22
Guinea........................	15–20 (4)	.....	.....	.....	.....	Nov. 1
Guyana (formerly Br. Guiana)...	14–18 (2)	.....	.....	14–18	(2)	Nov. 15
Haiti.........................	6–8	.....	.....	6–8	(1)	Nov. 22
Hawaii........................	.....	6 (1)	(1)	.....	.....	Nov. 30
Holland (The Netherlands)......	8–10 (2)	.....	.....	.....	.....	Nov. 15
Honduras......................	7–10	.....	.....	6 (1)	(1)	Nov. 22
Hong Kong (incl. Kowloon)‡....	.....	19–22 (4)	20	.....	.....	Nov. 1
Hungary.......................	10–15 (3)	.....	.....	.....	.....	Nov. 15
Iceland.......................	10–15 (2)	.....	.....	.....	.....	Nov. 15
India.........................	30–35 (3)	30 (3)	.....	.....	.....	Oct. 15
Indonesia.....................	(4)	35–40 (4)	.....	.....	.....	Oct. 15
Iran..........................	30–35 (3)	.....	.....	.....	.....	Nov. 1
Iraq..........................	30–35 (3)	.....	.....	.....	.....	Nov. 1
Ireland (Eire).................	9–12 (2)	.....	....‡	.....	.....	Nov. 15
Israel........................	25–30 (3)	.....	.....	.....	.....	Nov. 1
Italy.........................	12–15 (2)	.....	.....	.....	.....	Nov. 15
Ivory Coast...................	15–20 (3)	.....	.....	.....	.....	Nov. 1
Jamaica.......................	8–10	.....	.....	8 (1)	(1)	Nov. 22
Japan.........................	.....	15–18 (3)	15–18 (3)	.....	.....	Nov. 1
Jordan........................	25–30 (3)	.....	.....	.....	.....	Nov. 1
Kenya........................	28–32 (3)	.....	.....	.....	.....	Oct. 25
Korea........................	.....	20 (3)	20 (3)	.....	.....	Nov. 1
Lebanon......................	22–25 (2)	.....	.....	.....	.....	Nov. 1
Leeward Islands...............	10–20 (2)	.....	.....	.....	(2)	Nov. 15
Liberia.......................	18–21 (2)	.....	.....	.....	.....	Nov. 1
Libya (Cyrenaica & Tripolitania).	15–20 (4)	.....	.....	.....	.....	Nov. 1
Malagasy Rep. (Madagascar)....	28 (3)	.....	.....	.....	.....	Oct. 25
Madeira Islands................	15–20 (2)	.....	.....	.....	.....	Nov. 1
Malawi (formerly Nyasaland)....	28–32 (3)	.....	.....	.....	.....	Oct. 25
Malaysia (incl. Sarawak)........	.....	25–30 (4)	.....	.....	.....	Oct. 15
Mexico, D.F...................	4–5 (1)	.....	.....	(1)	(1)	Dec. 5
Morocco.......................	12–15 (2)	.....	.....	.....	.....	Nov. 1
Mozambique (former Port. E. Afr.)	20–25 (4)	.....	.....	.....	.....	Oct. 25
Netherlands, The (Holland)......	8–10 (2)	.....	.....	.....	.....	Nov. 15
Newfoundland, Canada..........	3–4 (1)	.....	.....	.....	.....	Dec. 10
New Guinea...................	.....	30–35 (6)	.....	.....	.....	Oct. 15
New Zealand..................	.....	25–30 (3)	.....	.....	.....	Nov. 1
Nicaragua.....................	.....	8	.....	8 (1)	10 (1)	Nov. 22
Nigeria.......................	20–25 (2)	.....	.....	.....	.....	Nov. 1
Norway.......................	11–15 (2)	.....	.....	.....	.....	Nov. 15
Nova Scotia (port of Halifax)....	2–3 (1)	.....	.....	.....	.....	Dec. 10
Pakistan‡.....................	35–40 (3)	32 (3)	.....	.....	.....	Oct. 15
Palestine (See Israel & Jordan)‡						
Panama.......................	6–8	8–10	.....	6–10 (1)	(1)	Nov. 15
Papua........................	.....	30–35 (6)	.....	.....	.....	Oct. 15
Paraguay......................	22–26 (2)	.....	.....	22–26	(2)	Nov. 1
Peru.........................	12	.....	.....	14	(2)	Nov. 15
Philippines....................	.....	24 (3)	22 (3)	.....	.....	Nov. 1
Poland........................	13–16 (3)	.....	.....	.....	.....	Nov. 15

APPROXIMATE NUMBER OF LETTER MAIL DAYS—contd.

To:	Mails dispatched from:					Latest Christmas Mailing Dates (approximate)*
	New York	San Francisco or Los Angeles	Seattle	New Orleans	Miami	
Portugal	10–13 (2)	....	....	....	....	Nov. 15
Puerto Rico	5 (1)	....	....	6	(1)	Dec. 1
Rhodesia	20–25 (4)	....	....	....	....	Oct. 25
Rumania	15–20 (3)	....	....	....	....	Nov. 1
Russia (U.S.S.R.)	14–17 (2)	....	....	....	....	Nov. 15
Salvador (El Salvador)	....	12	....	(1)	8–10 (1)	Nov. 22
Samoa (port of Pago Pago)	....	20 (3)	....	....	....	Nov. 1
Saudi Arabia	20–30 (3)	....	....	....	....	Nov. 1
Scotland	8–10 (2)	....	....	....	....	Nov. 15
Senegal	15–17 (2)	....	....	....	....	Nov. 1
Singapore	....	25–30 (4)	....	....	....	Oct. 15
Somalia (formerly Somaliland)	25 (3)	....	....	....	....	Oct. 25
South Africa, Republic of	18–22 (3)	....	....	23	....	Nov. 1
Spain	12–14 (2)	....	....	....	....	Nov. 15
Sudan	20–23 (4)	....	....	....	....	Nov. 1
Surinam (formerly Du. Guiana)	14–18 (2)	....	....	....	....	Nov. 15
Sweden	10–12 (2)	....	....	....	....	Nov. 15
Switzerland	10–14 (2)	....	....	....	....	Nov. 15
Syria	22–25 (3)	....	....	....	....	Nov. 1
Tahiti	....	30 (4)	....	....	....	Oct. 15
Taiwan‡ (formerly Formosa)	....	20–25 (3)	20–25 (3)	....	....	Nov. 1
Tanzania (Tanganyika-Zanzibar)	28–32 (3)	....	....	....	....	Oct. 25
Thailand (formerly Siam)	....	35–40 (4)	....	....	....	Oct. 15
Tunisia	12–15 (2)	....	....	....	....	Nov. 1
Turkey	15–20 (3)	....	....	....	....	Nov. 1
Uganda	28–32 (3)	....	....	....	....	Oct. 25
Uruguay	19–22 (2)	....	....	19–22	(2)	Nov. 15
U.S.S.R. (Russia)	14–17 (2)	....	....	....	....	Nov. 15
Vatican City State‡	12–15 (2)	....	....	....	....	Nov. 15
Venezuela	8–10 (2)	....	....	9	(2)	Nov. 22
Vietnam	....	30 (4)	....	....	....	Oct. 15
Virgin Islands	6 (1)	....	....	6	(1)	Dec. 1
Windward Islands	10–20 (2)	....	....	....	(2)	Nov. 15
Yugoslavia	12–15 (2)	....	....	....	....	Nov. 15
Zambia (formerly No. Rhodesia)	20–25 (4)	....	....	....	....	Oct. 25

* For surface packages. (For air packages, the latest Christmas mailing dates are December 15 to the Americas and Europe, and December 10 to the rest of the world.) Christmas letters and greeting cards should be mailed not later than 5 days after surface dates. CAUTION: These dates do not apply to deadlines for mailings to Armed Forces overseas. Consult the post office.

† Winter mails to Alaska are no longer restricted, but bad weather may delay surface mail.

‡ Note separate governments and do not address mail to: Azores, *Portugal;* Sri Lanka, *Ceylon, India;* Pakistan, *India;* Hong Kong, *China;* Vatican City, *Rome;* or *Palestine.* Distinguish between **East and West Germany;** and **Republic of China (Taiwan) and People's Republic of China (mainland).**

INCOMING MAIL

Opening Mail. When a person is new in a position, he should ascertain office preferences regarding the opening of mail or telegrams. Do not open any mail until instructions to do so have been received. This is one of the points that cause misunderstandings in an office.

Some one person in an office should open all mail addressed to the company and "route" it, or see that it is attended to in the absence of the addressees. Do not open mail if the person delegated to open the mail is only temporarily absent. Sort out the individually addressed letters and distribute them.

To Open Envelopes Quickly. First, sort them into sizes; then reverse the stacks and in doing so, jog the contents down so that the letter opener will not cut any papers in two. (For mending torn money or checks, see p. 523.) Now slit all envelopes open before removing the contents of any. Attach small enclosures—by· clip if temporary, by staple if permanent—to the front of letters; large enclosures to the back.

Incoming Envelopes. Save incoming envelopes if they bear addresses that do not appear on the letters, or if they show forwarding or any other marks of delay. Clip such envelopes to their letters; or if just the return address is needed, cut it out and staple it to the letter.

Check every envelope to see that it is empty before it is thrown away. Valuable small enclosures are often thrown into the wastebasket.

Attending to Parts of Letters. If some part of a letter or wire is answered or attended to before it is delivered to the addressee, clip a note to that effect to the incoming paper; or write "Noted" and initial it.

If a letter or wire refers to certain correspondence, hand that correspondence to the addressee with the incoming paper.

Check all enclosures carefully; if any are missing, clip a note to that effect to the incoming letter. Note the omission also on the bottom of the letter opposite "Enc."

Distributing Mail. Distribute letters immediately, either by placing them in individual letter boxes, or by delivering them to the persons to whom they are addressed, unless such persons are in conference; in that case do not disturb them with mail, unless it is with special communications they have been waiting to receive.

Incoming mail that has been opened may be distributed in separate folders marked "Incoming Mail," if the quantity is sufficient to make this advisable.

Opening Magazines and Circulars. Open all magazines, circulars, and advertisements; unfold or unroll them; and clip or staple all papers pertaining to each item together before placing them on the addressee's desk.

Absent Addressees. If a person is to be absent from the office for a period of time, ask his preference regarding the opening, forwarding, answering, or acknowledging of his mail.

If the mail is to be opened and important letters forwarded, determine whether the originals or copies thereof are to be sent. If the originals are to be sent, make copies for the office. Transient mail is sometimes undelivered because of changes in traveling schedules; therefore, copies are recommended for forwarding. Anything of unusual importance should be registered.

A letter of transmittal should accompany all mail so forwarded, in order that a record may be had of the letters sent.

Every letter of importance should be acknowledged in the addressee's absence. The correspondent should be informed that his letter has been received, and that it is being forwarded or will be held awaiting the return of the addressee.

Express

Shipments of any value, and any transportable size or weight, may be made by express.

Pickup and Delivery Service. Express companies have pickup and delivery service for an additional charge, depending upon distance. The drivers can accept prepayment of charges; or shipments may be made "express collect."

Express companies in one city will accept orders for pickups in other cities, and deliver the articles "express collect."

Charges and Insurance. Shipments may be sent prepaid, collect, or C.O.D.

Amtrak Economy Express Rates (by train)*—Examples

All one class.   Rates per pound.   Minimum charge $7.50 per shipment.

Mileage	Up to 30 lbs.	40 lbs.	50 lbs.	60 lbs.	75 lbs.	100 lbs.
225	$7.50 min.	$ 7.50	$ 7.50	$ 7.50	$ 7.50	$ 7.50
454	7.50 "	7.50	7.50	7.50	7.50	7.50
1083	7.50 "	7.50	7.50	7.50	7.50	9.00
2141	7.50 "	7.50	8.50	10.20	12.75	17.00
3049	7.50 "	10.00	12.50	15.00	18.75	25.00

* Amtrak has three different express services for small shipments:

Priority—for "rush" packages weighing up to 25 lbs. per shipment. Maximum size per piece: 90″ in length and girth combined; no dimension more than 48″. Charges, $10 or $12.50.

Economy—for small packages; but larger and/or heavier shipments may be arranged. Between certain cities, the maximum weight per piece is 50 lbs.; 250 lbs. per shipment; and size per piece, 36″ × 36″ × 36″ . . . and between other cities, 100 lbs.; 1000 lbs.; and 48″ × 48″ × 48″, respectively. Dimensional or space charges are 216 cu.in. to the pound (8 lbs. per cubic foot).

Custom—for frequent, regular, heavy, or unusual shipments, on a "reserved space" basis. Rates and services are negotiated with shipper.

Amtrak has no C.O.D. service (a collection of the invoice value), nor "collect" service (a collection of express charges only).

Amtrak gives insurance up to $25 per shipment. Additional insurance costs 40¢ per $100.

Unacceptable articles are those that are dangerous, or valuable, or negotiable (securities).

Grouping. Charges are made on weight; and two or more pieces from one shipper to one receiver are grouped and charged for on the basis of the combined weight (provided the weight is sufficient to give an average of not less than 10 pounds a package). Or two or more packages from one shipper to one receiver may be tied together and will be charged for as if they were one package.

Wrapping, Crating, or Boxing. Heavy wrapping paper, or cardboard or wooden containers, should be used in preparing articles for express shipment, according to the articles' need of protection.

Storage companies may be engaged to crate, box, and·"steel [or plastic] strap" articles at a charge representing the actual cost of the labor and material.

All packages containing jewelry or other valuables **must be sealed.**

The address of both the sender and the receiver should be written on a slip and enclosed in the package, for identification in case the outside addresses become effaced in transit.

Breakable articles should be thoroughly cushioned with packing material, and the packages marked FRAGILE.

Bottles containing liquids must be tightly sealed and surrounded with sufficient packing to absorb the entire contents of the bottles, should they break.

Animals (dogs, pets, etc.—crated) may be sent by Amtrak Express if an owner or other responsible person is on the same train.

C.O.D. Shipments. There is no definite limit to the amount that may be collected. (Amtrak accepts no C.O.D.s; but Greyhound Express does.)

376

Typewritten or Handwritten Matter. This matter when of the nature of correspondence cannot be sent by express; it must be sent by first-class mail.

However, typewritten or handwritten matter that is **not of the nature of correspondence** (such as manuscripts to publishers, drawings, blueprints, specifications and certain data processing materials) and papers having a monetary value (such as securities, checks, drafts, policies, bills of lading, mortgages, deeds, and other legal papers—especially C.O.D.s) may be sent by express.

Refrigeration. Refrigeration is not available for express shipments. But some services will accept articles packed in dry-ice, **non-leakable** containers.

Parcel Service by Ground-Air Express (Domestic)

Small packages may be sent by such as the United Parcel Service (UPS).

Weight limit per package: 50 lbs. Maximum weight of all packages from one shipper at one location to one consignee at one location on any one day is 100 lbs.

Size limit per package: 108 inches in length and girth combined. Parcels of less than 25 lbs., but over 84 inches in length and girth combined take the 25-lb. rate.

Strapping tape must be used to seal; not twine, which catches in the mechanism.

Grouping of packages—by tieing together—is not permitted; but several parcels may be placed in a large box, and sent as one package.

Rates are determined by Zip-Coded zones; for example, 82¢ for 1 lb. to Zone 2, and $15.64 for 50 lbs. to Zone 8. **Pickup charge** is approximately $2. Delivery is free.

All charges must be prepaid. But a shipper may be reimbursed for transport charges by attaching a C.O.D. tag to the package for that amount. Charge: 85¢ for C.O.D.

C.O.D. charge is 85¢; and the limits of collection are $1000 if parcel is sent by air; unlimited if by ground. Checks are accepted in payment of C.O.D.s.

Delivery Receipt, or **Acknowledgment of Delivery (AOD)** costs 20¢ extra.

Unacceptable articles are those that are dangerous, perishable, or of unusual value; also household goods, and commodities in bulk or requiring special equipment.

Valuation limits on a parcel are $1000 if by air transport; unlimited if by ground.

Free insurance: up to $100 a parcel. Additional insurance costs 25¢ per $100.

AIR FREIGHT (AIR EXPRESS)—DOMESTIC

Air freight is handled by "freight forwarders" such as Emery Air Freight (with **pickup and delivery,** for a small extra charge). Emergency packages may receive same- or next-day delivery to all major U.S. airport cities.

Regular express wrapping and packing is acceptable—plastic-strapped or bound with fishline cord or strong twine. Some forwarders offer packing and crating services.

Shipments may be prepaid, collect, or C.O.D. (No C.O.D. on fast **"express"** service.)

All types of merchandise are accepted. **No size or weight limit,** but extra large shipments require advance notice and arrangements. (Weight limit on **"express"** is 70 lb.)

Space charges: 194 cu.in. to the pound, if that figure is greater than weight.

Valuation of packages is not limited; but those over $25,000 require inspection.

Not acceptable are live animals or dangerous materials—except by arrangement.

Free insurance: 50¢ a pound up to 100 pounds. Added insurance: 20¢ per $100.

Air freight rates may be obtained from such air forwarders as Emery Air Freight.

Air Freight Rates—Domestic (Examples from Emery Air Freight)

All one class. Minimum charges: $7.47 to $25.86
("Flyte-Pak" small packages, up to 5 lbs., U.S. overnight delivery; $10 airport to airport)
(For air mileage, see table of distances, p. 585.)

Air Miles	5 lbs.	10 lbs.	15 lbs.	25 lbs.	50 lbs.	75 lbs.	100 lbs.
205	$10.62	$19.23	$24.49	$27.45	$33.57	$37.70	$41.43
306	10.62	19.23	24.58	27.69	34.19	38.75	42.79
404	10.62	19.23	24.70	28.11	35.29	40.54	45.44
543	10.62	19.23	24.74	28.32	35.87	41.41	46.76
765	10.62	18.88	24.65	28.84	38.06	45.48	52.79
1014	10.62	18.88	24.89	29.79	40.85	50.42	59.82
1494	10.62	18.88	25.05	30.36	42.34	52.90	63.37
1848	10.62	18.52	24.76	30.49	43.58	55.37	67.05
2442	10.62	18.52	25.20	32.13	48.65	63.74	78.72

INTERNATIONAL EXPRESS (SURFACE CARRIERS)

International express shipments are handled by "freight forwarders," such as those in the "Yellow Pages" that accept "sea" or "ocean" shipments.

For small shipments, parcel post is cheaper than international express. However, there are certain shipments that cannot be sent by parcel post and must be sent by international express. **Insurance** is available, for an additional charge, on all international express shipments.

Packing. All international express packages should be in wooden containers. The packages may or may not be sealed; valuables are usually sealed, while merchandise is often not sealed. Storage companies will crate or box articles if requested, at a charge representing the actual cost of labor and material.

Documents Necessary. The following papers are required for all shipments:

1. **Commercial invoice** (a dated invoice on a billhead [in multiple copies] giving a description of the articles: markings, packing, valuations, gross weight, etc.)
2. **Shipper's export declaration,** 4 to 9 copies (blanks at express office).
3. **Export and import licenses, and visas** (for certain articles only).

Other papers or documents are required on shipments to certain countries. Before preparing an international shipment, call the express company and ascertain whether **consular documents** and **certificate of origin** will be required.

INTERNATIONAL AIR CARGO

Air cargo is handled by **freight forwarders**—listed in the "Yellow Pages." **"Through" shipments** may be made on domestic and international airlines. **"Surface–air" shipments** may be made to the international gateways:

> Baltimore, Boston, Brownsville, Chicago, Dallas, Detroit, Houston, Los Angeles, Miami, Minneapolis, New Orleans, New York, Philadelphia, Portland, Oreg., San Antonio, San Francisco, Seattle, St. Louis, Washington, D.C.

Check with the local express office for **weight** and **size limitations, valuation, insurance, C.O.D. service, minimum charges,** and **documents** required.

Space charges: 194 cu.in. to the pound, if that figure is greater than weight.

General Air Cargo rates per lb.—examples from **Pan Am** (rates decrease at 100 lbs.):*

> From **New York** to: Amsterdam, $1.73; Athens, $2.28; Bombay, $3.39; Cairo, $2.40; Frankfurt, $1.85; Johannesburg, $3.87; London, $1.63; Madrid, $1.73; Moscow, $2.48; Paris, $1.73; Rome, $1.90; Stockholm, $1.88.
> From **Miami** to: Bogota, 78¢; Buenos Aires, $2.05; Caracas, 53¢; La Paz, $1.51; Lima, $1.22; Montevideo, $2.00; Panama, 59¢; Quito, 90¢; Rio de Janeiro, $1.77; San Jose, C.R., 50¢; Santiago, Chile, $1.82; Sao Paulo, $1.77.
> From **New Orleans** to: Guatemala City, 44¢; Managua, 55¢; Mexico City, 31¢; San Juan, P.R., 35¢; San Salvador, 49¢; Santo Domingo, 36¢.
> From **San Francisco** to: Bangkok, $2.67; Hong Kong, $2.60; Honolulu, 62¢; Jakarta, $2.70; Manila, $2.60; Sydney, $2.98; Tokyo, $2.50.
> From **Seattle** to: Anchorage, 33¢; Fairbanks, 33¢; Juneau, 32¢; Guam, $2.30.

> * **Minimum charges,** in general, are $18 to $29 to North and South America, Bermuda, and Hawaii; $18 to $30 to Europe, Africa, and Asia.

MESSENGER SERVICES

Heavy packages or letters for local delivery can sometimes be sent as cheaply by messenger as by first-class mail. And with greater dispatch.

Messenger services are listed in the classified telephone directory under M. Mark all packages or letters so sent: "By Messenger."

Receipts. If a receipt is desired, write it out and clip it to the letter or package. This not only reminds the messenger to obtain the receipt, but is convenient for the receiver to sign.

Telegraph

Preferred method of writing telegrams:

Telegram ⬚X	Full-Rate Cable (FR)	⬚
Overnight Telegram (NL) ⬚	Cable Letter (LT)	⬚
(Mailgram has a separate blank)	Shore-Ship Radiogram	⬚

CAUTION: The desired service **must be marked**—or the wire will go "full-rate."

AR (Answer Requested)	Paid, Collect, or Charge

Date
Hour and Minute

Full Address

Body—double-spaced—in ordinary lettering,
not caps.

Signature (typed)

Initials
Name, Address, and Telephone Number of Sender (if not
printed elsewhere on the blank)

Note that: The time of day should always be given.
The body of the wire should be double-spaced, and not written in caps.
Initials should be used, as on letters.
The accounting information is placed in the space above the date.
The name, address, and telephone number of the sender should always be added, if it does not appear elsewhere on the blank, unless the sender is well known to the telegraph company.

Date

The time of day is as important as the date on a wire. The two questions most frequently asked concerning telegrams are "When was it sent?" and "When should it be received?"

The city need not be written above the date, unless the wire is uncommon and its point of origin might later be questioned.

April 9, 1970
11:15 a.m.

379

Address

Addresses on telegrams are not charged for—on cables they are. Give a complete address always. Include the **company name** whenever possible; this facilitates location of the addressee if the street or building number happens to be wrong. No charge is made for any number of words in a telegram's address, if they are solely to aid in locating the addressee.

Code addresses cannot be used on domestic messages.

An **"Attention"** line may be used below the company name in an address, and is not charged for. (If "Attention..." is written at the beginning of the message proper, it is charged for.)

    Northern Company, Inc.
    Attention John Baxter
    2631 Woodward Ave.
    Detroit, MI 48202   (Zip Code, if available, should be added)

"Personal" refers to the contents of a wire, not especially to delivery. **"Personal Delivery Only"** insures delivery to addressee in person.

    Ralph James, Personal   Dan Lee, Personal Delivery Only

"Mr." should not be used before names in telegraphic addresses. It is not sent, because it is so often confused with **"Mrs."** by persons receiving messages. (**"Mr."** is sent if no first name or initial is given.)

"Mrs.," "Miss," or **"Ms."** may be used, and will be sent.

"Dr.," "Prof.," "Capt.," "Hon.," "Rev.," etc., may be used.

"Hold for Arrival" may be written after a name. Or a **time for delivery** may be specified. It is not charged for.

    Robert V. Mason, Hold for Arrival   or   Deliver 8 p.m.
    Biltmore Hotel
    New York City

"Will Call" should be written beneath the name in the address if a message is to be called for at the receiving telegraph office in a certain city. The message will be held at a central station and may be delivered at any branch office in that city.

    James T. Scott
    Will Call
    Louisville, Kentucky

"Care of" may be used in a telegraphic address without extra charge.

A **telephone number, or post office box, rural route number, or "General Delivery, Mail"** (with Zip Code), may be given as an address.

"DLR, Don't Phone" may be written after the name-to in address.

"Deliver by Messenger Only" may be written after the name-to.

"Don't DWR" after a name-to means "don't deliver without receipt."

Building names or street numbers may be used in addresses. Both are not necessary if the building is large or well known.

Numerical street names do not need -d, -th, etc., as "4 W. 45 St."

The room number in a building should always be given, if known.

Two addresses may be given for the same name, with the word "or" between them. The second address will be charged for.

Two names may be given for the same address, or for different addresses; the second name and address are charged for.

James Lee or Max Day
Suite 5020
60 Federal St.
Boston, MA   02110

J. P. Mason
61 Wall St.   or
James Scott/80 Wall St.
New York, NY   10005

Two or more names and addresses may be given for a single message, with the following notation above them:

Please send same message to each of the following addresses:

Multiple-Addressed Telegrams. If copies of one wire are to be sent to many addresses, the addresses should be written on special perforated and sectioned sheets, obtainable from the telegraph company. Above the addresses should be written:

Please send attached message to the following addresses:

The message itself should be on a regular telegraph blank, only one copy being necessary for the telegraph company. Extra copies are made in the telegraph offices on a duplicating machine, and the addresses are cut and pasted on the copies.

Address Unknown. In replying to a wire when the street address is unknown, write "Answer Date" (if of the same date as the incoming wire), or "Answer [and the figures for the back-date]" under the name of the addressee. Send the message in care of the originating telegraph office in the city from which the original message came.

James T. McNeil
Answer Date   B MSA092, Care MS*   (OR Answer 14, etc.)
New York, N.Y.

* The identifying message number and originating branch office are indicated on an incoming wire by letters and figures immediately before the place-from in the date line.

Radiotelephone addresses to trucks, buses, trains, boats, etc., require only the radiotelephone number (or the subscriber's name and place of registry), and the delivery city, followed by RADIOFONE.

Train and Bus Addresses. The following information should be given when a wire is addressed to a train or bus:

Name of passenger	AS:	Thomas L. Meade, Passenger
Destination		En route Los Angeles
Train or bus name, number and section, if any		The Southwest Limited No. 3 First Section
Car and berth number		Car 4, Room D†
Station, and arrival time		Due Union Station, April 14, 2:00 a.m.
City, and state		Kansas City, Missouri

† If the car and room or berth numbers are not known, the passenger's name will suffice. Train or bus data may be secured from "Information" at the station in question.

Addresses to Airports. Messages may be dispatched to airports to be delivered to airplane passengers. They are addressed as follows:

Name of passenger	AS:	J. E. Macaulay, Passenger
Name of airline		United Air Lines
Trip or flight number, and direction traveling		Flight 645, Westbound
Airport, and arrival time		Due Stapleton Airfield, June 10, 2:05 p.m.
City, and state		Denver, Colorado

Addresses to Sailing or Arriving Ships. Messages may be dispatched to sailing or arriving ships to be delivered to passengers as they embark or disembark. Such messages are addressed as follows:

Name of passenger	AS:	Robert V. Blair, Passenger
Name of steamship line		The American Line
Name of ship, and stateroom number*		SS. TRANSATLANTIC, Stateroom B 110
Pier, and sailing time		Sailing from Pier D, End West 55 St., August 20, 11 p.m.
Port of departure		New York City

* If the stateroom number is not definitely known, it may be omitted and will be supplied by the steamship officials from the passenger list.

Addresses to Ships at Sea. (See Radio to Ships at Sea, p. 396.)

Addresses to Isolated Places. A message may be addressed to any isolated place that has a telephone. Such an address might read:

William Granger
Mountain Creek Cabins—Telephone
150 miles above
Montpelier, Vermont

Words

The rule for counting words in the body of a wire is: If a word is given as one word in the dictionary, it is counted and charged for as one word. Therefore, if dictionary words are run together, they will be separated in the count, and each word charged for.

An abbreviation representing more than one word may be written solid or with periods, but **without spacing,** and will be counted as one word (if not more than 5 letters), as "fob" or "f.o.b.," "pm" or "p.m." Single words should be written out rather than abbreviated.

Initials, if spaced, are each counted as a word in the text of a wire; a name such as "L. B. Towne" would be three words. If initials are written **without spacing,** or written solid, they are counted as one word, as "J.B.T. (or JBT) Parke" is but two words.

Single letters need not be written out, as "aitch" for H. They will be transmitted as letters and charged for as one word each.

Hyphens are now transmitted, and not charged for. However, words that are hyphened in the dictionary should be run together, and others written apart. Hyphened words are counted according to the number of words they contain. (For written-out numbers, see Figures, below.)

Proper names from any language are now counted (in the texts of domestic messages) according to the number of words they contain: United States (2 words), New Mexico (2), St. Louis (2), New York City (3), van Fleet (2), de la Fontaine (3), DeWitt (1). **Abbreviations** of proper names, if of not more than 5 letters each and written **without spacing,** are counted as one word each: N.Y. or NY, S.C., B&O, LOSA, NBC, U.S.A.

"Mr." and "Mrs." in the text of a wire are transmitted in abbreviated form. Do not spell them out.

Common coined 5-letter words are permissible in any wire.

> **relet** (re your letter); **urlet** (your letter); **arlet** (our); **mylet** (my)
> **retel** (re your telegram); **urtel** (your); **artel** (our); **mytel** (my)
> **refon** (re your phone call); **urfon** (your); **arfon** (our); **myfon** (my)
> **antel** (answer by telegram); **anfon** (by telephone); **anlet** (by letter)

Code words are permissible in any domestic wire. They are counted at the rate of 5 letters to a word. All code words should be set in caps.

Trade names, as SWIFTNING, are counted at 5 letters to the word.

Profane words are prohibited in all dispatches.

Foreign language words are permissible in any domestic wire.

Figures

Figures in the texts of **domestic messages** are now counted at the rate of one word for every 5 characters or fewer.

A period or decimal point, comma, colon, hyphen, or apostrophe, used with a figure group, is now considered **punctuation** and not counted.

The **affixes** -st, -d, -nd, -rd, and -th in ordinal numbers are counted as characters in the figure groups.

These **signs** are counted as one character each: dollar ($), fraction bar (/), number or pounds (#), ampersand (&), feet or minutes ('), inches or seconds ("), and "by" (x). Percent (%) is three characters.*

Note that **each unbroken sequence** of figures, signs, and/or letters, is counted as one word for every 5 characters or fewer.

One Word Each			Two Words Each		Three Words Each	
12,345	500th	$15.45	123456	110-hp. 8	and/or	100 37mm. guns
95–100	1500#	75cts	33LC45	125DEGF	125 deg. F.	18,000-ton C-3
10&20.	10pm	4.5%	B/L196	2/10, n/30	$10 to $15	132-1/4:186-3/4
6-14-56	4327'	PB4Y1	$245.75	12:30 p.m.	6/15/55 60	1/20 14K $25
2-1/2†	5x12"	B-52s	6/14/56	75 cts	18 3/8-5/8	Aug. 29, 1957

* The signs ¢, @, °, and * are not on the teleprinters; hence the corresponding words should be used.
† If written "2½," it will be transmitted as "2 1/2" and counted as two words.

If writing numbers out, observe the following:

Use **"zero"** or **"naught"** instead of "oh" in spelled-out numbers.

Compound numbers, such as "fifty-six," may now be hyphened, but will still be counted as two words. They should not be run together. (However, in cables they may be run together.)

Four-figure numbers may sometimes be grouped in their written-out forms to save words, as "nineteen fifty-seven" rather than "one nine five seven"; "eighty thirteen" instead of "eight naught one three."

Body of Wire

Double-space all wires, regardless of the length.

Do not set them in caps. Use ordinary type and set only the code words in caps. All caps are difficult to write and difficult to read. Telegrams are received in caps because of the telegraph-machine type.

Do not divide a word at the end of a line.

Endeavor to make wires easy to read, both for later reference in the office and for the convenience of the telegraph operators. Do not run words incoherently together, thinking to avoid cost.

Do not eliminate words when transcribing a wire. Suggest words to be eliminated (by pencil check) and let the dictator cross out whatever he wishes. Small words are often necessary to make the meaning clear.

Paragraph if it seems advisable to separate different subjects. Paragraphing is valuable for office reference. If it is desired that paragraphs be transmitted, write SEND IN PARAGRAPHS at the top of the message. They will be sent but not charged for.

Poems or **verse** may be sent in lines if SEND IN LINES is written at the top of the message. There is no extra charge for this.

Punctuation

Punctuation marks are now transmitted without charge in all domestic messages, and in messages to Canada and Mexico. But punctuation marks are still counted and charged for in cables.

The allowable free punctuation marks are the comma, period, colon, semicolon, question mark, dash, hyphen, quotation marks, parentheses, and apostrophe. There is no exclamation point on the teleprinters.

If punctuation marks are spelled out, such as "Stop," or "Comma," they will be counted, charged for, and transmitted as words. However, it is often advisable, around important quoted matter, to use **"Quote"** and **"Unquote"** (and **"Innerquote"** and **"End Innerquote"**) instead of the quotation marks, which might be overlooked.

> Retel Collier wires Quote Will ship 612 partially conditioned XBLMC crates Monday 28th, and 312 W36LM (Carmen's) Thursday Unquote. We will dispatch these immediately. What is meaning "partially conditioned"?
>
> Dayton canceled 210 crates Tallmen's Best Saturday. No reason except wanted late Des Moines–Omaha f.o.b. delivery.

(The count for this message would be 46 words.)

Signatures

Single signatures on telegrams are not charged for. That is, a personal name may be signed; or a company name with "Inc." or "Ltd." as part of the name; or a company name and a department **or** a personal name, considered as one—but if the word "by," "per," or "for" is used, it is charged for.

L. J. Ranger & Sons Co.—J. B. Henderson

A title, as "President," with a name is not charged for; but if it occurs with a compound signature, as above, it is charged for.

If two personal names are used as a signature, one is charged for, unless the two represent a company or firm name.

H. J. Bower and M. C. Lowe

An address immediately beneath a signature is sent and charged for.

"Care of" in a signature is counted and charged for.

A family signature (of two or three given names) is considered one signature, and no extra charge is made.

The Ray Davises   OR   Ann and Ray   OR   Tom, Bill, and Bob

"Mrs." or "Miss" may be used before a woman's signature without extra charge.

Initials may be used as a signature.

Messages may be unsigned, in which case "Unsigned" should be written in the place for signature.

Initials. The initials of both the dictator and the transcriber should appear on every wire. They are as important here as on a letter.

Place the initials in the lower left corner. The telegraph company disregards these notations.

Do not use only the transcriber's initials. This could indicate that the transcriber also composed the wire.

If two persons dictate a wire, use both sets of initials, or ask their preference regarding initials. If both dictators' initials are to be used, they may be written as—HJB-RL:vm.

Paid, Charge, or Collect. If a message is sent prepaid (paid for at the time of sending), write PAID in the space above the date.

If a message is to be charged to an account, and the name of the account appears as the signature or is printed elsewhere on the telegraph blank, write simply CHARGE in the space above the date.

If a message is to be charged, and the name of the account does not appear elsewhere on the wire, write the name and address of the account under the words CHARGE TO THE ACCOUNT OF.

If a message is to be sent collect, write the one word COLLECT in the space above the date.

Address of Sender. The name, address, and telephone number of the sender should appear in the lower left corner **of every wire,** if it is not printed elsewhere on the blank, unless the sender is well known to the telegraph company. This provides a means of identification of the sender if it should be necessary to report an undelivery; and it also provides a check for the telegraph company's accounting department in billing.

Second Pages. Use telegraph blanks for second pages. Plain paper may be used, but the telegraph company prefers its own blanks.

Head these pages as letter second-pages are headed.

James Scott   -2-   Oct. 24, 19..

If using plain paper for a second page, leave at least a two-inch space above the heading for the telegraph company's use. (Some telegraph offices paste the pages of a wire together.)

Staple the pages of a wire together in the extreme upper left corner before sending it out. The telegraph company can clip the corner to separate the pages and paste them. Pins or clips are not so satisfactory as staples for this purpose.

Extra Copies. **Confirmation copies** of wires are often mailed to the addressees. If a confirmation copy is to be mailed, and a confirmation blank is not at hand, use a regular telegraph blank for this copy, and write the word CONFIRMATION across the top.

An extra, "billing," copy of each wire should be made on cheaper paper, and these copies kept in a separate file folder for checking against the monthly telegraph bill. These copies may be destroyed each month after the bill has been checked.

Outgoing Wires. Every wire, no matter how short, should be shown to the dictator before it is sent. There may be some last-minute change necessary in the wording or method of dispatch.

Do not fail to check the **class of service** desired.

Telephoning a Wire. Wires may be telephoned to the telegraph companies and charged to telephone numbers. It is unnecessary to ask for a special department or operator. When the telegraph company answers, simply say "I should like to send a message."

When telephoning confidential messages, **use a private telephone** so that no visitors will interrupt or overhear.

Give the telegraph company the information in the following manner:

1. I wish to send a (paid or collect) (fast telegram, overnight telegram [night letter], or letter cable, etc.) to (addressee).
2. The message reads: ....
               Signed.....................
3. Please read it back (always thus check for error).
4. My telephone number is....... (after the Operator requests it).

If frequently spelling out words to a telegraph operator, memorize and use the following standard telegraph code for identifying letters:

A FOR: Adams		J FOR: John		S FOR: Sugar	
B	Boston	K	King	T	Thomas
C	Chicago	L	Lincoln	U	Union
D	Denver	M	Mary	V	Victor
E	Edward	N	New York	W	William
F	Frank	O	Ocean	X	X-ray
G	George	P	Peter	Y	Young
H	Henry	Q	Queen	Z	Zero
I	Ida	R	Robert		

Time Differences. Senders of wires should consider the time differences in the United States, and abroad, when calculating the delivery of messages. (See Standard Time, p. 588.)

Often savings can be effected by the use of the cheaper service; for instance, if a non-rush message is to be dispatched from San Francisco at 3:30 in the afternoon to New York, where it is 6:30, an overnight telegram would be as effective as a fast wire. The night message would reach the addressee at the beginning of the next business day in New York (3 hours earlier than in San Francisco); and the matter involved could receive attention and be ready for action and/or reply before the western opening hour of business.

Conversely, fast telegrams should be used from the East Coast to the West Coast up to the eastern closing time of business. The 3-hour difference would give time for consideration of the matter and a night message reply that would be delivered before the opening of business in the East the following morning.

TELEGRAPH SERVICES

Only **three classifications** of messages are now available: **telegrams; overnight telegrams;** and **mailgrams** (see p. 388).

Delivery: Messages may, at the option of the telegraph company, be delivered by telephone, by tieline, or by messenger.

Messenger delivery, at an extra charge, is regularly undertaken (unless a sender specifies that it is not required) on the following types of messages: greetings, congratulations, condolences (also messages pertaining to death, casualty, or reburial), and those sender-marked "Don't Phone."

(For rates, see pp. 390–91)

Straight or Fast Telegram*

Fifteen words at full rate. Day and night delivery.
Transmission and delivery time: 15 to 60 minutes.
("Urgent" messages, marked "Rush," are often received, transmitted, and delivered within 7 minutes—across the United States.)

Code or foreign language—straight or mixed with English—may be used without extra charge.

* No abbreviation or indicator is used on straight telegrams. Therefore, the absence of an indicator on an incoming wire means that it is a straight, fast telegram.

Overnight Telegram (OT)   (former Night Letter [NL])

One hundred words or fewer at minimum rates.
Each additional word at reduced rates.

Note that in this single **domestic overnight service** the initial charge is for 100 words. Therefore, long or complicated business reports, proposals, and instructions can be transmitted at low cost.

Accepted until midnight for delivery on the morning, usually after 8 o'clock, of the following business day (in business districts). No deliveries on Sundays or nationwide holidays to business offices, unless specifically requested. Deliveries on any day in residential districts. A night message is not mailed unless addressed for mail delivery; or an addressee resides beyond the telegraph company's delivery limits, and all efforts to reach him by telephone have failed.

Code or foreign language—straight or mixed with English—may be used without extra charge.

387

OTHER SERVICES (For Charges, see pp. 390–91)

Telex Service (domestic and international). Direct-dial teleprinters (on a monthly rental) transmit written messages and data; some provide punched tape for automatic send-receive sets. Telex also connects with Western Union. Rates depend upon time and distance. No domestic minimum time charge.

Private Wire System is a leased **teleprinter network** that connects numerous offices, and automatically distributes messages, or transmits data for processing.

Datacom is a low-cost service for the low- or medium-speed transmission of digital data around-the-clock between 2 or 3 cities, on a multi-mix of channels.

CND Service (Commercial News Department) furnishes reports of market quotations and sports events by ticker, private wire, or telegraph message.

Mailgrams (Mgm's). Letter-telegrams are accepted by Western Union, until 7 p.m. (**destination time),** to be sent during the night to a post office nearest each recipient's address—there to be placed in distinctive Mailgram envelopes and delivered next day with the regular mail.

Quantity mailgrams may be sent by companies as **Business Reply Mailgrams** or as **Certified Mailgrams;** but **individual mailgrams** may not be sent Certified, Registered, Restricted Delivery, or Special Delivery.

Mailgrams may be sent to Alaska, Hawaii, and Canada.

Credit Cards. Domestic and international messages may be charged on **WU** credit cards in the U.S. and Canada.

Gifts—candy and flowers—may be selected at any **WU** office and will be delivered promptly, with a message, in another city.

Discontinued Services:

Intrafax	Wirefax	Hot Line	Broadband Exchange	Singing Telegrams
Time (Clocks)	Collections	Distributions	Operator 25	Wake-up Service
Errand Service	Pickup of Charge Plates and Credit Cards			Dollygrams
Hotel-Motel Reservations	Desk-Fax	Surveys	Inventory and Inspection	

Delivery Hours. Fast telegrams are delivered—within 4 to 6 hours— throughout the day and evening, until midnight. Emergency messages are delivered after midnight. **Overnight telegrams** ("night letters") are delivered by 2 p.m. the next day. (See also Mailgrams, above.)

Delivery Limits are "within the established city or community limits of the destination"—delivery beyond is by any available means, arranged at a charge.

Forwarding. Messages will be forwarded at the sender's or addressee's request and expense; but local forwarding is automatic and without charge.

Recall of Wires. If a telephoned cancellation reaches **WU** before or during the dispatch of a message, it can be "killed"—at no charge. (Written confirmation must follow.) If the message has already been sent, a recall-wire may be flashed to destination—and the sender may ask for a report collect.

Report Delivery. To obtain a report, write after the name-to: REPORT DELIVERY or REPORT DELIVERY AND ADDRESS (chargeable words). The report (returned "collect") will show the time and, if requested, the place of delivery, but not the person to whom delivery was made.

If any message is undeliverable, a free report will be given, whether a report of delivery has been requested or not.

Repeat Back. If it is desired that a message be checked or repeated over the wires, write REPEAT BACK above the message. These two words are charged for. All messages of a legal nature should be repeated.

Charge of ½ the regular rate for repetition.

Telegraphing Money ("Telegraphic Transfer"). Money may be dispatched by telegraph and cable to all parts of the world. Payments in foreign countries are made in foreign currency—subject to fluctuations in exchange.

Night, Sunday, and holiday payment service is available at principal telegraph offices all over the world.

Domestic Money Orders by Telegraph

The following charges do not include tolls for supplementary (individual or personal) messages. (Money orders may be sent by phone—on a **Master Charge card**.)

Amount of Order	Money Order Charge* Day	Overnight
$ 50.00 or less	$ 5.70	$ 4.95
50.01 to $ 100	6.65	5.90
100.01 to 300	8.90	8.15
300.01 to 500	13.25	12.50
500.01 to 1000	17.70	16.95
1000.01 to 1500	22.15	21.40
1500.01 to 2000	26.60	25.85
2000.01 to 2500	31.05	30.30
2500.01 to 3000	35.40	34.75
3000.01 to 3500	39.95	39.20
3500.01 to 4000	44.40	43.65
4000.01 to 4500	48.85	48.10
4500.01 to 5000	53.30	52.55

For higher amounts: the money order charge for the first $5000 is $53.30 (day) and $52.55 (overnight) plus $4.45 for each additional $500 or fraction thereof.

* Fees quoted are for payment at a WU office. Messenger delivery: $3 per money order draft.

International Money Orders by Cable

The charges for foreign orders by cables are:

$3\frac{1}{4}$% of the first $250 (or a minimum charge of $2.50); then $2\frac{1}{4}$% of the next $250; and $\frac{3}{4}$ of 1% of the amount over $500; plus the cost of the full-rate cable transmitting the money order. And if relayed through The Chase Manhattan Bank in New York, there is an extra charge of $10.50 for the first $250 sent; and $11.50 for any amount over $250.

Payment is in foreign currency at the daily exchange rate.

Messages of Greeting. Greeting messages of the senders' own composition may be dispatched as straight telegrams, overnight letters, or mailgrams, and are now delivered on regular telegraph blanks, and in ordinary WU envelopes—for birthdays, weddings, anniversaries, etc. Regular rates are charged.

Personal Opinion Messages. A flat-rate, 15-word, plain English message (prepaid and signed with sender's name and address) conveying an opinion on a general issue, may be sent—from any point in the continental United States—to the President, Vice President, or a congressman, in Washington, D.C. Or it may be sent from any point within a state to that state's Governor, Lieutenant Governor (or Secretary of State), or a state legislator, at the state capital. (For fee, see p. 390.)

Legality of Wires. Telegraphic messages may be considered as legal evidence in court, just as any other written correspondence; therefore, the necessity for correctness. All signatures on telegraphic messages given to authorized operators are valid at law. To disclaim a telegraphic signature, a person must prove that he had no knowledge of the sending of the message.

"A contract may be made and proved in court by telegraphic despatches."
—*Bouvier's Law Dictionary* (Baldwin's Revision), p. 1168.

~~~~~~~~~~~~~~~~~~~~~~~~~~~~~~~WESTERN UNION RATES AND

Rates are subject to change.

FLAT RATES FOR MESSAGES (in Contiguous United States)

	Fast Telegram			Overnight Telegram	
	For 15 Words or Fewer	For Each Additional Word		For 100 Words or Fewer	For Each Addl. Word Over 100 Words
		16 to 50 Words	Over 50 Words		
Intrastate Interstate	$4.95	13¢	10¢	$4.00	3¢

To Alaska: the above rates (plus the Alaska-line rate from Seattle)

To Hawaii: cable rates only { Fast message: 21¢ a word; minimum charge, $1.47
Letter message: 10½¢ a word; minimum charge, $2.31

Personal Opinion Message (flat rate)........$2.00 anywhere in contiguous United States

From Alaska.......... $2.00 (plus Alaska-line rate to Seattle)
From Hawaii.......... (cable rates only; see above)
(For identical messages sent at the same time to all U.S. Senators, $80;
to all U.S. Representatives, $120; to all U.S. Congressmen, $160.)

Service Charges on messages (besides tolls):

Collect message.....................................	50¢
Phoned message (filed by sender)......................	no charge
Messenger pickup (within WU delivery limits)...........	$3.00
Messenger delivery (within WU delivery limits)..........	$3.00
Confirmation copy of message, mailed to sender..........	75¢
Confirmation copy by mailgram.....................	$1.25

Valuation of Messages—the liability of the telegraph company for mistakes in, and delays or non-delivery of, messages is limited to:

$500 for an ordinary, unrepeated message
$5000 for a repeated message

A specially valued, repeated message (above $5000) bears a charge of $\frac{1}{10}$ of 1% of the amount by which the valuation exceeds $5000.

Candygram—a 1 lb. or 2 lb. box of chocolates may be ordered through Western Union, and will be delivered—with a message of greeting—at cost plus telegraph tolls.

Flowers by Wire—Flowers may be ordered through Western Union by sending a telegraphic money order to a "leading florist" in the recipient's city, and in an accompanying telegram asking the florist to deliver the specified flowers.

* * * * *

—Compiled from data furnished by courtesy

FEES FOR MESSAGES AND SERVICES

Mailgrams
Flat, prepaid, rate: $2.95 per 100-word message, anywhere in contiguous U.S. and Hawaii; $1.50 each additional 100 words.

To **Alaska**, $3.10 (to **Canada**, $3.30) for first 100 words; $1.25 for each additional 100 words.

For Telex and Info-Com, $1.05 per message, plus usage charges.

Telex Service (direct-dial teleprinters)—rental of keyboard send-and-receive set equipped with automatic answerback and dial, $66.50 a month, plus a line charge of $30.

If machine is punch-tape equipped, $15 additional per month.

USAGE CHARGES are based on time and distance. No minimum time or usage charge. Example of Telex charges between New York and Los Angeles:

  1 min., 52½¢   2 min., $1.05   3 min., $1.58   addl. min., 52½¢

Tieline (a direct connection with WU)—equipment is furnished at a monthly rental of $12 per facsimile (Desk-Fax) instrument; and $12 per teleprinter.

USAGE GUARANTEE—a minimum "paid" message revenue of $15 a month per tieline; or a charge of $15 a month if minimum usage is not reached. (The monthly machine rental applies even though the usage charge is above $15.)

❖❖❖❖❖❖❖❖

CABLES AND RADIO

Cable Addresses. Cable addresses are counted and charged for.

A code address is preferable, and may be registered with the cable companies for $15 to $25 a year; or $9 to $15 for six months.

A registered code address must be just **one word** of not more than ten letters or fewer than five. It must be a **coined or abbreviated form,** and not a proper name or surname.

Code addresses, set **in caps,** may be used on any class of cable.

> LT   October 25, 1970
> John Harland   10:15 a.m.
> Chez AMEXCO*
> Rome (Italy   Via ITT)†

* If a traveler has no definite foreign address, messages may be sent him in care of telegraph offices or large travel bureaus, such as Thos. Cook & Son and the American Express Company. Code addresses may be obtained from these companies; and "Care" or "Chez" should be written before such code addresses.

† The name of the country and a routing indicator are necessary in a cable address, for the telegraph company's information. They are not charged for; hence, in parentheses.

Reversible Address. A U.S. company and its foreign offices may register an identical, exclusive code address; no signatures then needed.

Routing of Cables. Senders should specify direct routings to avoid relays overseas. The four routings available are:

> Via ITT   Via RCA   Via TRT (Tropical)   Via WUI

Delivery and Handling. A sender may order any of the following services by writing the indicator before the address (1-word charge).

Available on both Full-Rate (FR) and Letter (LT) Messages:

CHEZ – "Care of" (Fr.); or **CARE** (before name)
RP – reply paid by sender (insert amount prepaid)
NUIT – night delivery, or after business hours
TR – "Hold for" in "Will Call" at telegraph office
FS – forward (at sender's request); **REEXPEDIE DE** (at addressee's)
POSTE – mail   **GP** – general delivery at the post office

Available only on Full-Rate Messages:

GPR – general delivery, registered
BOITE POSTALE – post office box (give number)
PAV – airmail   **PAVR** – airmail, registered
PR – mail, registered
MP – personal delivery to addressee   (Fr. mains propres)
REMETTRE (date) – deliver on specified date
TF – telephone (give phone number)
TLX – telex (give telex number)
EXPRES – any delivery faster than mail (addressee pays for)
XP – any delivery faster than mail (sender pays for)
PC – report time and date of delivery, by cable
PCP – confirm delivery, by mail
J (number) – shore-ship, number of calling days

"Collect" messages cannot be sent (except to Canada and Mexico).

Cable Signatures. Cable signatures are counted and charged for.

Cables may be sent **unsigned,** or signed with a **code signature.**

Coding Cables. Numerous codes are in use, such as the A.B.C., Acme, Bentley, and Universal Trade. Many are for special subjects, as for banking (ABA and Peterson's), securities, commodities, shipping (Lombard), and travelers. Some are printed in different languages.

Most countries will accept any type of code, provided the code words do not contain more than 5 letters each. However, some countries do not permit incoming cables to be coded in any but standard codes. If using a private code, check with the telegraph company to determine whether such code will be received in the country for which it is destined.

Double-check every word when coding or decoding a cable. One wrong letter can make the entire cable unintelligible.

If a code message is received in an unknown code, consult the telegraph company for assistance in determining the code if possible.

Numbering Cables. If a series of cables are being sent, they should be numbered consecutively, both for checking delivery and for future reference.

Make up a page of numbers (1 to 99) on ruled paper. As each number is used on an outgoing cable, check it off and write opposite it the date sent, the addressee, and the initials of the sender.

Begin the cable message with the outgoing number followed by the incoming number, if any—in figures. (A plain-language letter message may include a check word or number as the first text word; but such check word or number is limited to 5 characters.)

> STELDOT
> Sydney (Australia)
>   45/26   Compare prices with those cabled...
> (This check number would be counted as one word and would mean "Our cable 45, your cable 26.")

Word Count

In cable texts, in plain or secret language, each word appearing in a standard dictionary of one of the admitted languages, or each word in common use in one of those languages, is counted at the rate of 15 letters to the word.

A proper name, such as the family name of one person, the full or abbreviated name of a place, square, boulevard, street or other public way, the name of a ship, or the designation of an aircraft or railway train, may be run together as one word, as "Vandekamp," "Newyork," "Stjamesstreet," and "Queenmary," and will be counted at the rate of 15 letters to the word.

Hyphened words are counted as separate words, unless they appear in a standard dictionary of one of the admitted languages, in which case they are joined and counted at 15 letters to the word.

Coined words, as "retel" and "relet," are now considered code words and, in full-rate messages, are counted at 5 letters to the word. Such coined words are not permitted in letter messages.

393

Common abbreviations when written solid, as "FOB," are counted at the rate of 5 letters to the word.

Groups composed of letters, figures, signs, or a mixture thereof, where authorized (such as commercial marks and trademarks appearing in a published catalogue, price list, or the like), house numbers and ordinal numbers consisting of figures and letters—when written solid—are counted at the rate of 5 characters to the word. If spaced out, each separate letter or figure is counted as one word.

A whole number, fraction, decimal or fractional number, when written in words, may be run together as one word, as "sixfoursix," and will be counted at the rate of 15 letters to the word. When written in figures, numbers are counted at 5 characters to the word, as "12345."

Punctuation marks not essential to the meaning of a cable, such as hyphens and apostrophes, are not transmitted, except at the request of the sender, in which case they are counted and charged for as one word each. Punctuation marks essential to the meaning of the message, such as quotation marks and parentheses, are transmitted, counted and charged for as one word for each pair.

Dollar and cent signs ($ and ¢) and the pound sterling mark (£) are counted as one word each. The number sign (#) is counted as one word.

In figure groups, decimal points, commas, slants, colons, hyphens, apostrophes, and quotation marks are counted as one character each.

The percent sign (%) is counted as three characters in a figure group.

Examples of Word Count in Cables

Airmail	1 word	**12345** (5 characters)	1 word
Air express	2	**12,345** (6 characters)	2
Parcel post	2	**15/16** (5 characters)	1
Twothreefour (for 234)	1	**15–162** (6 characters)	2
Threetwothirds (for 3 2/3)	1	**15⅔** (5 characters)	1
Twentyfive tons	2	**133rd** (ordinal number)	1
May/July (with slant)	3	**"Life"** (with quotes)	2
CIF (abbreviation)	1	**GHF45** (commercial mark)	1
C&F (transmitted CANDF)	1	**TD14's** (trade term)	2
*RECAB (for re cable)	1	**$50.25** (dollar sign)	2
*RELET (re letter)	1	**£120.15.0** (sterling sign)	3
*RETEL (re telegram)	1	**Fr 10,50** (French francs)	2
*REURTEL (re your telegram)	2	**#80592** (number sign)	2
*RYCAB (re your cable)	1	**12½%** (8 characters)	2
*MFIVE (my five)	1	**15x6** (dimension)	1
*YLTWO (your letter two)	1	**8'9"** (feet and inches)	1
*RYC15 (re your cable 15)	2	**30'45"** (minutes and seconds)	2

* In letter (LT) and press messages, counted at number of words represented.

VARIOUS TYPES OF GLOBAL SERVICE

Telex, International—an extension of domestic Telex. (See p. 388.)

Leased Channel—a private, **direct "hot line"** overseas, under patron's exclusive control, for telex, telephone, facsimile, and data transmission.

Data—voice-controlled high-speed transmission of data for use in computers.

Voice/Data—on a single circuit, fills silent gaps in a conversation with data.

Radiophoto—transmission of photographs, documents, forms, statements, signature specimens, drawings, maps, blueprints, and hand- or typewritten material.

News, Broadcast Programs, TV—transmission by cable, radio, and satellite.

◇◇◇◇◇◇◇◇

CABLE AND RADIO SERVICES

There are now only two classifications of international messages (INTL):

Full-Rate or Ordinary Messages   and   Letter Messages

Full-Rate Messages (FR)

Any number of words at full rate per word (21¢ to 34¢ a word).
Minimum charge is for 7 words, counting address and signature.
Day and night service. Straight, fast dispatch.

Plain language and secret language may both be used, alone or together in the same message, with the plain language words (dictionary or commonly used words) being counted at the rate of 15 letters to the word, and the code words at 5 letters to the word.

Any foreign language that can be expressed in letters of ordinary type may be used—straight or mixed with English.

Cipher words are figure groups used as a code, as "46548." A cipher message may be entirely in figures, or in plain language mixed with cipher.

A combination of figures and letters, figures or letters and signs with a **secret meaning,** within a single group, is not admitted. But **non-secret,** authorized groups of letters and figures, and/or signs, are counted at 5 characters to the word.

Letter Messages (LT)

Any number of words at ½ the full rate (10½¢ to 17¢ a word).
Minimum charge is for 22 words, counting address and signature—or from
$2.31 to $3.74. Therefore, up to 10 words, full-rate cables cost less.

Overnight service for delivery after 8 o'clock local time the next morning. Accepted until midnight. Delivery in the Far East, Australia, and South Africa is delayed because of time differences—delivery in some countries, such as India, being made at 2 p.m. the next day; and in countries like Australia at 9 a.m. on the second morning, or about 36 hours, after filing. Delivery in the Hawaiian Islands (not across the date line) is made after 8 o'clock on the following morning.

Only plain language (English, or any foreign language that can be expressed in letters of ordinary type) may be used—being counted at 15 letters to the word.

Secret language is not admitted in letter messages.

All words and figures must have a connected meaning, that is, each word, figure, or expression must have the meaning normally assigned to it in the language to which it belongs.

Code words cannot be used (with the exception of registered code addresses and signatures). But a check word or number may be used as the first text word.

Coined words, such as "relet," are now considered code words and not permitted in letter messages.

Numbers written in figures (used in their natural sense), **commercial marks, trade terms, and abbreviations** are admitted—provided they present a connected meaning—and are counted at 5 characters to the word.

LT (meaning "letter telegram") **must be written above the address** on every letter message. It is transmitted and charged for as one word.

◇◇◇◇◇◇◇◇◇

RADIO MARINE SERVICE

Radio to Ships at Sea. One class of service.

Rate to ships of United States registry: 33¼¢ a word; to ships of foreign registry, 38¼¢ a word. If a ship cannot be reached from an American radio station, the message will be sent to a foreign station and relayed to the ship, at an additional charge for the radiogram to the foreign station.

Radio messages to passengers on ships at sea will be dispatched by any telegraph company.

Routings should be indicated, the two most used being "Via ITT" and "Via RCA." Addresses should be as follows:

Radio indicator (to foreign ships only)		INTL
Name of passenger	AS:	John McLane
Name of ship		SS BRITANNIA
Radio station and routing		Newyorkradio Via RCA

Note the brevity of the address. It is not necessary to give the ship's destination or the name of the steamship company, unless there are two ships of the same name.

The passenger's **stateroom number** is unnecessary; that can be supplied from the passenger list when the message is received at sea.

The name of the **radio station** is run together as shown.

Addresses and signatures are counted and charged for.

Plain and code language may be used, together or alone.

Minimum charge is for 7 words, counting address and signature.

WIRES, GENERAL

Incoming Wires. An understanding should be had in every office regarding the opening of incoming wires.

All wires should be either opened or delivered immediately to the addressees, whether they are engaged or not. In the addressees' absence, business wires should be opened by some responsible person in the office, to determine whether any immediate action is required.

Personal wires should be held an agreed length of time for absent addressees, and after that time should be opened, or an effort should be made to reach the addressees by telephone.

No wire should lie unopened or unattended to for more than ten minutes, awaiting the return of the addressee. The significance of a wire is "immediate attention."

If responsible for carrying out the orders or attending to the details mentioned in incoming wires, **mark off the sentences by diagonal lines, and check and double-check** to make sure that everything is complied with. It is very easy to overlook an important point because of the continuous and often blind phrasing of a wire.

If code words appear in an incoming wire, write the meaning above each code word. If a large number of the words are in code, write the decoded message on a separate page and attach it to the wire.

Garbled Words. If garbled or unintelligible words appear in an incoming wire, they will be "serviced" by the telegraph company for correction, without charge.

Copying Wires. When making copies of wires, copy in small, ordinary type, and not in capital letters.

Write at the top of all copies, as a means of identification:

(COPY OF WIRE RECEIVED) or (COPY OF WIRE SENT)

Copy the name of the telegraph or cable company always. It is important for future reference.

Copy or indicate the class of message received or sent, as "Fast Telegram," "OT" for "Overnight Telegram," or "LT" for "Cable Letter."

Copy the hour of receipt, as well as the date, and the name of the city of origin.

It is not customary to copy the various indicia—letters and numbers— that appear above the address on an incoming wire, unless the person who is to use the copy is likely to refer to the telegraph company concerning the wire. In that event the figures and letters would be necessary for identification of the wire.

Punctuate a copied wire with periods, quotes, etc., wherever such marks are indicated. Paragraph it if several subjects are mentioned— this for convenience in reading.

Copy numbers, prices, dates, etc., in figures, and double-check to make sure that they correspond with the spelled-out numbers in the wire. But when copying a wire **for legal purposes,** copy it **exactly as it is written,** in the manner of punctuation, caps, spelled-out numbers, etc. (underlining any letter or mark that is obviously wrong).

Always write " (Sgd.) " or " /S/ " before the signature on a copied wire.

Telephone

Listings in the telephone directories are sometimes difficult to find.

Government offices are under U, "United States Government."
Post Office is under "United States Government," if not under P.
State offices are under the name of the state.
County offices are under the name of the county.
City offices are under the name of the city.
Consulates are under C, or the names of countries or nationalities.
Public libraries are under the name of the city, or under P.
Buildings are under "Office Buildings" in the Yellow Pages.
Company names beginning with letters are immediately under the alphabetizing letters (as "RCA Communications" would be among the first names under "R"). (See p. 456 for alphabetizing method.)
Television stations are immediately under the alphabetizing letters, or under "Television [or Radio] Broadcasting" in the Yellow Pages.
Weather forecast is in the front of the directory, or under W.
Time-of-day is in the front of the directory, or under T.
Telegram (to send) is under W—Western Union.
Emergency numbers—fire, police, ambulance, etc.—are in the front of the directory. Or just **911** may be dialed for quick assistance.
Directory Assistance (formerly "Information") is **411**, and there may be a charge. (For obtaining out-of-town numbers, see p. 402.)
Long Distance is just **"0"** (for Operator).
Telephone company's business offices are in the front of the directory.

Telephone List. In every office the numbers most frequently called should be listed—if **few names,** on a single sheet or large card to be taped inside the front cover of the directory, or under plastic on a pull-out "breadboard" shelf; **if many entries,** in a card file or flip-open index.

The telephone list should always include the following numbers:

Bank (& acct. no.)	Post office nearest ⎰ and mail col-
Building superintendent	Post office Information ⎱ lection times.
Express office	Stationer (& acct. no.)
Home telephone number of	Taxicabs
every office employee	Telegraph office (& credit card no.)
Hotels frequently called	Ticket offices of airlines
Insurance agent (& policy nos.)	and railroads used
Lawyer	Time of Day – and Weather
Messenger service	Typewriter repair

Also included should be the employer's personal telephone numbers, as dentist, doctor, broker, druggist, florist, tailor, dry cleaner, garage, stores (and acct. nos.), clubs, family members, and friends.

New Numbers. Whenever an office telephone number is changed, all regular callers should be notified immediately. Especially should those be notified who might call over long distance.

Likewise, new telephone numbers should be noted in all office telephone books, and in the telephone directory itself.

398

Calling Numbers. Be sure that you have the **right number** before calling it. Give the called number time to answer; and **have the caller ready to talk** when the called person answers.

If seemingly the wrong party has answered, verify the number, as "Is this Capital 4–8892?" Never ask bluntly, "Who is this?"

Answering Telephone. The telephone companies spend money to advertise this request: "Please answer promptly." It is discourteous to the caller to permit a telephone to ring and ring.

When answering outside calls, state the business name or number not just say "Hello." On extension calls—for brevity, the secretary's name is not given unless she has an executive position. Examples are:

Direct call:	"National Manufacturing Company" (or shortened)
Extension:	"Mr. Lee's office [desk or secretary] (Miss Hunter)"
Executive:	"(Mr.) Lee (speaking)"; "R. B. Lee";
	"This is Mr. Lee"; or just "Lee here"
Department:	"Research [Department] (Miss Day [or (Mr.) Lee])"
	For brevity, "speaking" is usually omitted.
Private line:	"(Mr.) Lee [or Miss Hunter]"; "Lee here";
	"This is Miss Hunter"; or simply "Hello"
PBX operator:	"Desk"; "Yes?"; or "Operator" (for inside calls)

To soften "Who's calling, please?" preface the inquiry by an honest statement, such as "Mr Lee is engaged [or out] at the moment, may I ask [or tell him] who's calling?" or "May I take a message?"

Do not let an incoming caller wait indefinitely without asking whether he prefers to hold the line, call (or be called) back, or give a message.

Put the receiver down carefully always, especially when another is telephoning on an extension line. The sharp impact of a receiver's being banged down can stop his conversation or hurt his ear.

Transferring Calls. In transferring a call to another department, first tell the caller that you will transfer him and give him the name of the person and/or extension number to call in case the connection is broken. Then signal the operator **slowly** three or four times. (If the signal is too fast, the operator cannot see it.) Stay on the line until the operator answers, and tell her where to transfer the call.

Manner Over Telephone. Do not affect a detached air of speaking away from the mouthpiece, or over it. **Speak directly into it.**

Speak slowly and clearly, in an even, pleasant tone of voice. Do not attempt to speak too low or in a muffled tone. But do not shout.

A telephone conversation should be in a rather deliberate, yet friendly and unhurried manner, which gives the hearer time to understand and the speaker time to think.

Be brief, but courteous. Every caller may be a prospective customer. Telephone insolence is almost always reported to an employer.

Never call a woman "Madam." It is not complimentary.

Taking Messages. On an incoming call—if the person called is not in, always offer to take a message.

Write down every message taken for another, and put it on his desk if he is absent; or keep a separate file of such messages for his immediate

399

attention when he returns. Never attempt to "remember" telephone calls. Be sure to **write down** all of the pertinent and exact information that is given, not just a part of it. Vague messages are only confusing. **Never guess** at what was said or meant.

Date every message and give the hour of the call—without fail. **Telephone numbers and names must be absolutely correct.** Ask the person to repeat them, or spell them, if necessary.

Instead of writing "called" on a telephone message, write "phoned." "Called" could mean that the caller came in person.

Printed slips are often used for telephone messages; but if not used, all telephone memorandums should be written in this approximate form:

1. **Hour and date**	3:45 p.m. May 18
2. **Name and identity**	Mr. Meredith of the Lyons & Walsh Co.
of caller	phoned. He would like to obtain a copy of our
3. **Exact message**	drawings on the Tower job so they can figure
4. **Caller's telephone**	foundations.
number	Ph: 855–7834 X 326 [or Ext. 326]
5. **Your initials**	L. M.

If a message has been difficult to take, repeat it to the caller, so he will know that it will be delivered correctly.

But if taking a difficult message when outsiders are present, do not repeat the information being received. Ask the telephoner to repeat it, and simply write it down.

Giving Messages. When calling a number for someone else, and the person called is not in, **find out when he will be in,** and do not hang up without first relaying this information to the person who is calling. Give the caller the privilege of leaving a message, always.

If telephoning about anything that will be particularly hard to explain, or about which something may be overlooked, make notes beforehand and talk from them; or have a file on the subject at hand. Do not trust to memory.

When telephoning a wire, or giving a message of any importance, use a private telephone if possible, so that visitors cannot overhear.

Getting Information. When seeking information from a large organization, ask for a department or division under the name of the nature of the business in hand.

For instance, if desiring to order carbon paper from a large stationery store, and it is not known whether the order would be handled in the order department or the carbon paper department, phrase the request so as to cover the nature of the call:

"May I have the department that handles carbon paper orders?" Their operator will know immediately which department to call. Similar requests for departments may be phrased:

"May I have the typewriter repair department?"

"May I have the accounting department that handles accounts under the letter M?"

Never phrase an opening request like this: "We want to know something about our April bill." With such a beginning, the caller will probably be shifted from one department to another, telling his name over and over, until he strikes the right department.

Giving Information. Never give any information voluntarily over the telephone unless authorized so to do. Speak rather in a general way.

Such a casual sentence as "He is in Chicago today" may be telling something very important to the listener. Business is a large game, and everything is information.

A friendly explanation, as "He's busy on another wire, talking long distance to Denver," may be to the listener definite information. All that need be said in such an instance is "He is talking on another wire. Will you hold the line, please?"

Note the difference in the following:

Definite information:	Indefinite yet sufficient:
"He hasn't come in yet."	"He isn't here just now."
"He's in Houston today."	"He is out of town today."
"He's playing golf this afternoon."	"He won't return to the office today."
"He's ill."	"He won't be in today."
"He has gone to California for a couple of months."	"He is on a trip and not expected back for several weeks."
"You can reach him at Los Angeles."	"I can get in touch with him and have him wire you." or
	"Is there anything that I can do?"

There are times, of course, when definite information should be given, but such information should be given only with the full knowledge of the person responsible for or affected by it. Transmit to him all incoming queries, and let him be the one to indicate the replies. Or have an understanding with him regarding information to be given out.

If, for example, a caller asks about an unfamiliar order or project, never say "I don't recall it," or "I haven't heard of it." Say rather, "I'll look it up"; and if after looking it up, it is found that a delay in delivery or some such bad news must be given to the inquirer, make sure that the person responsible knows that this information is being given out **before it is given out.**

When Others Are Telephoning. Stop typing when anyone is telephoning near the desk, or ascertain if it is all right to continue.

If the person telephoning appears to be having difficulty in hearing, or if he is talking over long distance, make the room as quiet as possible by closing doors and windows. Refrain from making the slightest unnecessary noise, such as turning papers or pulling out desk drawers.

If it is necessary to give a message to the person telephoning, write it on a slip of paper for him to read. He can read and listen, but he cannot listen to two people at once. If it is necessary to speak to him, let him break his conversation to listen.

If someone enters an adjoining room when an important telephone conversation is being held, close the connecting door.

If the conversation seems to be of a personal nature, find some excuse to leave the room quietly.

◇◇◇◇◇◇◇◇

TELEPHONE SERVICES

Long Distance—Station-to-Station and Person-to-Person Calls. On a "station call," the caller agrees to talk with anyone who answers at the called number; but on a "person call," the caller may specify the particular person, department, room, or extension number that he wishes to reach.

Because station-to-station calls are cheaper than person-to-person, always, when asked to place a long distance call, inquire about the type to be used.

How to Place Long Distance Calls. **Station calls** may be dialed direct by use of area codes—in the front of the directory. (A **one-minute rate** applies.)

All other calls—**person, collect, coin, credit-card, bill-to-third-number,** and **hotel-guest,** also to **Hawaii or Alaska**—may be dialed direct: by first dialing "O" for Operator, then continuing to dial the area code and distant number.

When the Operator comes on the line, give her this information on a . . .

> **Person call:** the name of the person being called.
> **Collect call:** say "Collect," and give her the name of the caller.
> **Credit Card call:** say "Charge. My credit card number is. . . . . "
> **Bill-to-Third-Number call:** the number the call is to be charged to.
> **If time and charges** on completed call are desired, notify the Operator now.

The call is completed automatically while the Operator obtains information.

Local Calling Area. Small towns and suburbs surrounding a city are in the local zone and do not involve long distance. **No area code** is used. Limits of, and inclusions in, local areas are shown in the front of the directory.

Long Distance Numbers. Out-of-town numbers may be obtained (often for a small charge) from "Directory Assistance" in certain cities. Dial the desired area code, then the "Distant City Assistance" number 555–1212 (as 212–555–1212 for New York). For non-coded towns, dial "Operator."

Numbers 5 and 9 Confused. When placing a call, stress the difference between the numbers 5 and 9. An error in the telephone records may often be traced to a misunderstanding of 5 or 9. Notice that telephone operators usually sound these words very distinctly by elongating them into "fī-ĭv" and "nī-yĕn."

List of Calls Placed. Make a memorandum of every long distance call placed. Keep these memorandums in a file or an envelope and check them against the monthly long distance bill. If any errors have been made in the billing, they can be corrected by this checkup.

Charges. Long distance rates, including overseas rates, are given in the front or back of the telephone directory. Study these schedules carefully so as to be able to consult them intelligently and quickly when called upon to do so.

If any question exists regarding possible charges, call the Long Distance Operator for rates before placing the call. When the rate is received, write it in the address book beside the respective telephone number or address.

If the charges on a call are requested when it is being placed, they will be quoted by the Operator soon after the call is completed.

If there has been trouble or dissatisfaction regarding a call, or if a wrong number has been reached (and the city and number noted), that information should be reported immediately to the Operator for adjustment.

Appointment Calls. A definite time for conversation may be specified when a long distance call is being placed, so that the Operator may make arrangements in advance with the called person. Person-to-person rates apply.

Messenger Calls. A call may be placed to a person not having telephone service. A messenger is sent to summon the person to a telephone. A messenger charge, as well as a toll charge, is made for this service.

Night and Weekend Rates. Out-of-state **"station"** rates are reduced daily from 5 p.m. to 8 a.m. ("direct-dial" further reduced at 11 p.m.); all day on weekends (slightly higher after 5 p.m. Sundays), and on these 5 holidays: **New Year's, July 4th, Labor Day, Thanksgiving, and Christmas.** The time at the calling point governs. **"Person"** 3-minute calls are no longer reduced at any time; but the additional-minute rate is reduced at the above times.

Ship-to-Shore Calls—may be made to and from many ships and some small pleasure craft while cruising. No reduced rates apply. Ask for the "Marine Operator," and give the name of the vessel, the person called (and stateroom number); the caller, his phone number, and whether he desires to know the charges on the completed call.

Ships in Harbor. Some large ships (and many small craft) have direct telephone service when docked. Or messages may be delivered to passengers by the steamship lines.

Overseas Service. Overseas calls are placed through regular Long Distance operators, in exactly the same manner as ordinary long distance calls. (Some calls may be dialed direct.) **If the foreign telephone number is available,** it should be given.

    Person, station, collect, and credit-card calls may be made to many countries. **Reduced night-and-Sunday rates** also apply.

    Rates to foreign countries may be found in the front of the telephone directory, or obtained from the Long Distance Operator.

Mobile Service. Calls may be made to and from moving cars, trucks, trains, and aircraft equipped for such service. Some calls may be dialed direct; others through Long Distance and the "Mobile Service Operator." No reduced rates apply.

Trains in Stations. In some large cities, calls may be placed—through railroad stations—to certain trains within half an hour before their departure.

Conferences. Up to 10 telephones in different places may be connected by the "Operator" for discussions. A Speakerphone in an office permits group participation.

Vacation or Suspension Rates. In some cities, if a business telephone is not to be used for 4 weeks (residence, 2 weeks) or longer, a reduced rate may be had.

Wide Area Telecommunications Service (WATS)—unlimited interstate or intrastate calling within selected areas, at a flat monthly rate—full time or part time.

Private Line Service—unlimited calls and data between 2 fixed points, at a monthly rate.

Telpak—a bulk package of communications lines for voice, teletype, photograph (facsimile), data, and other high-speed transmissions, at a low monthly rate.

Federal Telecommunications System (FTS)—a nationwide direct-dialing private network for Federal Government agencies, which provides transmission of regular voice, encrypted (scrambled) voice, teletype, high-speed data, and facsimile.

Data-Phone—transmits data (on punched or magnetic tape), often at night. Transmits digital data, words, figures, drawings, charts, photographs, and mechanical instructions; also voice/teletypewriter. May be used for ordering supplies by coded cards.

Touch-Tone Data Service. The telephone is linked with a computer which may be "consulted" (by special codes) for credit authorizations, ordering, billing, inventory control, bank balances, travel reservations, etc.

Six-Key Desk Phone—enables the user to answer, hold, transfer, and make calls.

Switchboards. There are many types, small and large, of "private branch exchanges" (PBXs), or switching devices, each tailored to office needs.

    Call Director—a desktop, cordless PBX equipped with 12 to 30 keys to provide intercom, conference, holding, multiline pickup, signaling, and transfer service.

    Console PBX—a desktop, cordless, key-type switchboard which may or may not handle **only** incoming calls—outgoing and intracompany calls often bypass it.

    Cord Plug-in PBX—a large board, with many trunks and hundreds of extensions.

Hands-Free Phone—equipped with a "jack" (outlet) into which a headset may be plugged to free the user's hands for other work. A **shoulder rest** may serve the same purpose. Both are available from the telephone company.

    Speakerphone—equipped with a microphone/loudspeaker, permitting the user to talk and listen without lifting the receiver. May be used normally for privacy.

    Spokesman—a small loudspeaker that broadcasts both sides of a conversation, for group listening—the talker using the telephone normally.

Picturephone—permits callers to talk face to face—either "hands free" (with several persons participating), or privately by handset (receiver). By appointment only.

Volume Control (for hearing)—a device to boost an impaired voice or incoming voices.

"Call-Waiting" Service permits handling two calls at once; **"Three-Way,"** permits adding a third party to a two-way call; **"Forwarding,"** permits transferring calls automatically to another phone; and **"Speed,"** permits dialing only one or two digits for certain calls.

{ **Card Dialer**—a compact telephone that automatically dials a local, long distance, or extension number when a pre-coded plastic card is inserted in a slot and a start-bar pressed. Regular dialing is also possible.

Magicall—an automatic dialer that may be connected to any phone. Names (up to 1000) and numbers are indexed, and the numbers recorded on magnetic tape. Names are selected by a "scanner," and the number dialed by a "call" button.

Bell Chime—a soft, melodic ringer for reception areas, executive offices, homes, and wherever noise should not intrude. Can be changed at will to the regular ring.

Exclusion Button—(in the "cradle") cuts off other phones on the same line, for privacy or freedom from interruption. Hanging-up automatically reconnects all phones.

Bell Cutoff. An extension-line bell may be silenced by a cutoff button.

Annoying Calls. Harassing calls can be stopped by the phone company's business office.

Recorded Conversations—may be made with a recorder that gives off a "beep" every 15 seconds. Unwanted recordings may be stopped by a request that the device be disconnected. (Recording without the beep or verbal notification is unlawful.)

Automatic Answerer—can take incoming calls; deliver a recorded message; and, on some sets, record a message from the caller. The accumulated messages may be transmitted to a distant executive by his using a playback "Outerkey."

Message-Taking Service. If an office telephone is to be left unattended for a considerable time, the calls should be transferred to another number; or a telephone-answering service should be engaged (if available) to take all messages.

Calls cannot be transferred for less than 24 hours, except in emergencies.

Bellboy—a pocket radio receiver (with a 40-mile radius) that, by a tone signal, alerts the carrier to call his office or home for a message.

Pageboy, a similar unit, has a choice of tone only or tone-and-voice message.

Telephotos. Photographs may be transmitted by telephone, through a Press Service.

Attachments. Privately owned telephone equipment may be connected to the network if registered—by its manufacturer or supplier—with the Federal Communications Commission.

Out-of-Town Telephone Directories—of domestic and some foreign cities may be consulted at telephone companies' principal business offices, and in large public libraries. (Some books are also available at rail, bus, and air terminals.) Individual books may be secured through the business offices of the telephone companies.

Street Address Telephone Directories—(arranged by addresses of customers) are available in some large cities, and may be rented for a minimum period of 6 months.

Credit Card—permits a traveler to charge long distance calls (from any telephone). Several foreign countries honor credit-card calls to or from their own countries.

Architects and Builders Service. Free consultation is offered by the telephone company for planning modern telephone layouts and communications services in new buildings.

Writing Telephone Numbers. **Area codes** may be in parentheses, or followed by a hyphen, raised dot, slant, or space, as **(311) 936-1212; 311-936-1212; 311·936·1212; 311/936-1212; 311 936-1212,** or **311 WE 6-1212.** In local numbers, a space is left after exchange letters, as **WE 6-1212;** but none after all-digits, **936-1212.**

◇◇◇◇◇◇◇◇

INTERCOMMUNICATION SYSTEMS

(Manufacturers in "Yellow Pages" under Intercommunication, Facsimile, Paging, Radiotelephone)

Intercom—a microphone/loudspeaker enabling persons in different offices to talk as if face to face. (For privacy, a handset may cut off the loudspeaker.)

Business Interphone has an intercom service built into the regular telephone system.

Interoffice Telephone—an independent, private system (leaving outside lines clear), whereby executives may consult and conferences be held without anyone's leaving his desk. Each connection is normally a private line—which may have extensions.

Dictation-Telephone System—connects executives' telephones with removed dictation-recording units—for transcription by typists.

Interoffice Telegraph—a small, independent system that transmits handwritten communications, business forms, etc., exactly as written or filled in on a sending device.

Facsimile—a method of transmitting signatures, charts, formulas, requisitions, photographs, art work, etc., with accuracy.

Closed-Circuit Television (CCTV)—a private TV system for viewing remote objects, persons, or papers, as in banks and factories. It may be coupled with an intercom.

Two-Way Radio—a send and/or receive private radio system (mobile or portable) used for reaching men in the field or on the job, as in traffic or taxi control, and police work. "Private-line" operation and headsets are available.

404

Dictation

The following cautions may seem unimportant to some; but it is surprising how many shorthand writers sidestep these definite aids to efficiency.

Date the notebook every day. Much needless searching through notebooks has been caused by neglect to do this.

Have one place for the notebook on the desk, and keep it there when not in use, so as to be able to find it readily when called for dictation.

Save used notebooks for one year. Then discard the oldest when filing the latest. It is not unusual to be asked to retranscribe notes a year old.

If taking dictation from different persons, put the **initials of each** at the beginning of each block of dictation—or use separate books.

Cross off dictation immediately after transcribing each page. This is an important safeguard against the possible omission of some part of the work.

Keep a rubber band around the notebook to mark the end of the finished notes, in order not to be constantly fluttering pages looking for a place to write when called for dictation.

If dictation, such as a telegram, is taken on a separate piece of paper, date that paper and file it away with the old notebooks. It may be necessary to refer to it again.

Do not be extravagant with notebooks by making large, careless notes. If it is difficult to keep the notes a natural size, use a notebook with unglazed paper. The pencil will not glide so easily over this paper, and the strokes will be retarded, making smaller, neater notes.

Check the notebook at the end of each day to see that nothing important is left undone. Failure to do this has caused trips back to the office at night. Serious consequences might arise if, for instance, a wire is not dispatched as it should be.

Pen and Pencils. Keep a fineline ballpoint pen and two dictation pencils always in readiness in one certain place on the desk. Sharpen pencils **after** taking dictation, not after being called to take dictation.

The best shorthand pencil is the medium soft No. 2. The No. 1 is too soft to hold a point; and the No. 3, while hard and holding its point, tires the hand in pressing down to make the notes clear.

Sit Facing the Dictator. Always sit facing the dictator if possible— across the desk, or at one end of the desk. It is much easier to hear when facing the person who is speaking; and it is also much easier to write on the solidity of a desk than on the insecurity of a shelf or other device.

Taking Notes. In taking very fast dictation, when it is almost impossible to follow the thought, **concentrate on each word.** Pronounce the words mentally as they are written. In transcribing, words will

405

appear of which there is no recollection whatsoever, and the outlines must be depended upon. The memory will assist only if the words were mentally pronounced as written.

Interrupt a dictator, when the dictation is too fast, by repeating the last word written. Repeat any word not clearly understood or that seems incorrect.

Do not omit a single word in taking dictation, or write it indistinctly, thinking to remember it. Guesswork causes a high degree of inaccuracy.

If a sentence is not clear, check it, and read it back to the dictator at the end of the dictation. Do not attempt to "fix it up" in the transcription.

It is more experienced to ask than to be incorrect.

Longhand Notes. Write very little in longhand. Have distinctive outlines for all familiar names and write them in shorthand.

Unfamiliar names, initials, and addresses **should be written in long-hand,** which will later serve to identify them in the notebook.

To Clarify Notes. Use the shorthand mark to indicate a period or a question mark after every sentence. Do not leave sentences open. It is difficult later to tell where one sentence ends and another begins.

If a shorthand character is written too long or too large, put two small marks through it; these will not cancel the character but will indicate that it was intended to be shorter or smaller.

If having difficulty reading the notes, make use of the accent marks to indicate long vowel sounds, etc.—if writing a shorthand that uses such marks. These facilitate transcribing.

Grammatical Errors. Grammatical errors should be corrected in transcribing not in taking dictation. Mention only the noticeable recurrence of a word or phrase, as the dictator might want to correct it.

Insertions. Number insertions by encircled numbers, as ①, ②, ③, and place a corresponding ①, ②, or ③ in the notes at the proper place.

Extra-Copy Notations. When extra copies are to be made of a certain transcription, make this notation at the **beginning** of the notes, not at the end, so that it will act as a prompter at the start of the transcribing and not be discovered only at the finish.

Ask the dictator about making an extra copy of a letter when it seems obvious that a copy should be sent to someone besides the addressee.

Leave a space—of at least two lines—between each letter or item and the next, for making notations and for identification of each item.

Rush Work. When a telegram or other rush item is dictated, mark an encircled Ⓧ beside it, and turn back a corner of the page to serve as a reminder to write the rush item first.

Interruptions. If interruptions occur while taking dictation, read over and correct the outlines of the notes already taken. This always aids in transcribing.

If a caller arrives, leave the room unless asked to remain.

If a telephone call interrupts, it is of course not necessary to leave unless the call is personal, in which case it is thoughtful to find some excuse to leave and close the door.

406

Reading Notes Back. In reading notes back, concentrate on the notes and not on the speed of the reading. Read in a clear, even tone. Do not be embarrassed if it is necessary to pause over a shorthand note. It is better to pause than to read something incorrectly.

Receiving Papers. When papers are received with the dictation, keep them face up on the desk, and make very light shorthand notes (which can be erased later) on those that require special handling; or, if there is time, mark the papers Ⓐ, Ⓑ, Ⓒ, etc., and make notes under corresponding letters in the notebook. It seems easy to remember what is to be done with a paper at the time of receiving it, but later, when many things have intervened, instructions sometimes will have vanished unless they have been written down.

Special Instructions. Make notes of all special instructions. These notes, whether pertaining to the dictation or not, may be written in the notebook, unless an extra pad of paper is handy. If they are written in the notebook, make a distinguishing mark beside them, as Ⓧ, and turn back corners of the pages to serve as reminders to attend to these outside details before beginning the transcribing.

Transcribing. Transcribing is an exacting job. Do not attempt to read notes too fast or indifferently, which invariably results in errors. Learn to follow and not anticipate the shorthand notes. Question things **before** writing them rather than afterward. Check dates, names, etc., against the papers handed with the dictation or that are in the files. Make sure that the dictator has answered all parts of incoming letters. No one is infallible in the matter of detail.

Grammatical Construction. Correct errors in grammar when transcribing. If the dictator questions a correction and desires that the sentence remain as dictated, comply with his wishes—"the dictator is always right."

Rearrange very little, if any, as the original manner of phrasing may mean more than the rearrangement.

If small words, such as "so," "and," "but," "which," "that," and "the," have been noticeably repeated, some of them may be dropped or changed without impairing the meaning. But do not drop a word if without it the meaning will not be clear.

Do not be afraid to use the dictionary. Looking up words is not a sign of stupidity—it is a sign of care.

Mistakes. Never omit an unreadable word in the transcription. If a word is undecipherable, or if one has seemingly been left out of the notes, or if something looks obviously wrong, ask about it; or leave a blank space in the transcription with a pencil question mark after it.

Never hand in anything about which there is a question, thinking that it will "get by." Question-mark it in pencil on the margin, or write a note calling it to the attention of the dictator.

Errors that are discovered after material has been sent out are of much more consequence than those that are admitted and corrected at the start.

◇◇◇◇◇◇◇◇

BUSINESS TERMS

Business terms are often not understood, or but vaguely understood, by those who encounter them in the course of their work.

Attempt to ascertain the exact meaning of all unusual phrasings that occur in business. Look them up, or as a final resort ask about them, rather than work with them for a period of time with only a hazy understanding of their meaning.

The following are given merely to indicate that misconceptions might exist.

Nautical Terms

boxing the compass—not putting it away, but naming its 32 points in order: hence making a complete revolution or turnabout.

charter party—not a person, nor a Magna Carta, but a lease of a ship.

dead reckoning—not guesswork, but navigation without celestial observation— as in dense fog—by readings of the compass, log, and chronometer (time-piece), and a calculation of courses, distance sailed, and drift (current).

flotsam and jetsam—are not the same. Jetsam is a ship's cargo or equipment cast overboard (jettisoned), which sinks or is washed ashore. Flotsam is cargo or wreckage found floating on the sea. (pron. flŏt'sam, not *float-*)

jettison—the casting overboard of a part of the cargo to save the rest, in peril.

lighterage—not ballast thrown overboard, but a charge for conveying goods on a lighter (a barge used for unloading [lightening] or loading ships in harbor).

log—means the speed-measuring and distance-recording instrument towed by a ship; the readings of the log are entered in the "logbook," which contains a complete record of the ship's journey. The logbook is also called "the log."

lying in the harbor—not *"laying,"* but

lay days—the number of days allowed by a charter party for loading or unloading a ship, without extra charge.

naval stores—turpentine, rosin, and pine oil (from use on old wooden ships).

Plimsoll mark—not a watermark on a ship, but a painted line to indicate allowable depth a vessel may sink into the water, through loading.

ship chandler—a dealer who supplies provisions or accessories to ships.

ship's husband—an agent for a ship.

tramp steamer—not a derelict, but a ship legitimately engaged in independent trading.

Oil Terms

cat-cracker—nickname for a "fluid catalytic cracking plant."

cracked gasoline—not undesirable gasoline, but that which is produced by cracking—breaking up petroleum products with intense heat and, usually, pressure.

fractionating—the breaking down of petroleum into its different fractions, such as gasoline, kerosene, lubricating oil, and paraffin.

spud in a well—does not mean clearing a piece of ground, but drilling in the first few hundred feet of hole.

wildcat well—does not imply rank speculation, but means a test well in an unproven area.

Newspaper Terms

banner—a full-page headline in large black type, across the front page.

box—a border (usually a single line) around a printed item or "story."

fourth estate—not a mythical kingdom, but the press with its power, rank, and privileges. Historically, there were three estates or classes in Europe with distinct political powers. The press came to be known as the fourth estate.

408

legman—a reporter who "chases" about gathering news—does "legwork."
masthead—a statement of name, ownership, rates, etc., printed in every issue of a newspaper or magazine (usually on the editorial page).
Sometimes loosely used to mean the name of the paper topping the front page.
potboiler.—a hastily written piece of work, as a book, to keep the pot boiling (provide living expenses).
story—any news article in a newspaper.
The Gridiron Club—not a football association, but a newspapermen's club in Washington, D.C., which holds semiannual dinners, in December and in the spring, and roasts official Washington "on the griddle."
the press—newspapers and periodicals collectively, as "the power of the press."
the Press—the persons working on or representing such publications.
thirty, ㉚ —the end (from old telegraph ending "XXX," like Roman numeral 30).

Railroad Terms

deadhead—to send a car or coach through empty.
reefers—refrigerator cars.
rolling—shipment under way.
rolling stock—the wheeled equipment of a railroad.
shipped knocked down—shipped unassembled.
spot a car—place it at a certain spot on a siding.
spur track—a short sidetrack or branch track.
tariffs—not always import duties, but sometimes schedules of rates or carrying charges made by railroads, steamship lines, etc.

Political Terms

caucus—a meeting (or huddle) of delegates or leaders to decide on policies.
cloture—closure of debate to secure an immediate vote, as to "invoke cloture."
congressman—a member of Congress; may mean either a senator or a representative, but it is more frequently used to mean the latter.
congresswoman—may be used in the same manner as congressman.
filibuster—a blocking of legislation, as by deliberately talking to consume time.
lame duck—an office holder who has been crippled politically; that is, he has not been re-elected to office.
lobby—the persons who frequent the lobbies of Congress, or any legislature, in an attempt to influence votes.
log-rolling—voting for another's project if he will vote for yours.
Old Guard—the older, more conservative members of a political party or group.
omnibus bill—like a public vehicle, it carries many unrelated items.
pocket veto—A chief executive may cause a bill to fail by simply shelving ("pocketing") it until it automatically becomes void.
whip—an influential member of a political party who unofficially manages his fellow members or whips them into line, as "the Democratic Whip" in Congress.

Aeronautical Terms

aircraft—any flying craft (airplane, helicopter, glider, dirigible, or balloon).
blind flying—flying by the use of instruments.
ceiling—the bottom or base of the cloud level. An airplane may fly through a ceiling and fly above it; or it may fly beneath the ceiling.
countdown—a ticking off of time left, down to seconds, before liftoff of a rocket.
fuselage—the entire body of an airplane, including compartments for pilot, passengers, cargo, etc. (pron. fū′zĕ-lǐj; or Fr. füz-läzh′)

Mach 1—the speed of sound (662 mph at cruising altitudes). **Subsonic** (below sound) speeds and **supersonic** (above) are shown decimally. Mach 2 is twice the speed of sound. Named for Ernst Mach, Aus. physicist (pron. mäk).

meteorology—the science of the atmosphere and its variations or changes. Meteorology is not concerned merely with the common meteor or shooting star, but with winds, rain, snow, lightning, rainbows, auroras, etc., all of which are meteors of a sort. (pron. mē'tē-ēr-ŏl'ō-jy)

General Terms

backlog—unfilled orders, which give the security to a manufacturing company that a backlog gives to a fireplace.

bill of materials—not an invoice for materials, but a list of materials or parts that go into the fabricating of a piece of equipment; or a list of all equipment to be furnished on a job. Made up for the purpose of giving specifications or obtaining prices on the materials or equipment necessary.

bonded warehouse—a warehouse under bond to the Government for the storing and processing either of imported merchandise before the payment of duty thereon, or of domestic merchandise (such as liquors) before the payment of taxes thereon. Such a warehouse operates under the supervision of a customs officer or a revenue officer, as the case may be. As the merchandise is removed for domestic consumption, the duty or taxes thereon are collected by the Government. Goods held thus are said to be "in bond."

cost-plus job—a job to be furnished at cost, plus a certain percentage of the cost as compensation to the contractor. (Similarly, a **cost-plus-fixed-fee** job.)

dew point—the temperature at which a vapor begins to deposit dew.

Diesel engine—an engine invented by Dr. Rudolf Diesel of Germany. The engine is economical in that it burns unrefined or crude oil. ("Diesel" is written with or without a capital, as "diesel power"; pronounced dē'zĕl.)

ex dock
ex car
ex elevator
ex store
ex warehouse } "Ex" is a preposition, not a prefix, in these phrases. It means "from" or "out of," as "from the dock," "out of the warehouse." It is not hyphened to the word that follows, unless the two are used as a modifier.

firm price—a price that is unchangeable for a certain time.

forward buying—buying merchandise, or making commitments, for future delivery.

French curve—a stencil-like device for drawing architectural curves.

hallmark—any mark or indication of genuineness, quality, or purity (from the official marking of gold and silver at Goldsmiths' Hall, London).

list price—the catalogue price, or price to consumer, set by the manufacturer.

logistics—the military science of transport and supply of troops (lō-jĭs'tĭks).

logotype ("lôgo")—a distinctive symbol representing a company name or product.

Monel metal—a trademark for a rustproof nickel alloy of high tensile strength. (After Ambrose Monell, Am. mfr.; usually capitalized; pronounced mō-nĕl'.)

nominal price—not necessarily a very low price (although sometimes it is), but often a price in name only—usually an approximate or reasonable figure.

purchase money—money borrowed to purchase property or a business (as money acquired through purchase money bonds, mortgages, or trust deeds).

slide rule—a ruler with a central sliding part for rapid calculations (both parts are marked with graduated logarithmic scales).

turnkey job—a job or contract to be completed in every detail; the owner will have simply to turn a key to start operations.

Typewritten Work

Margins. An inch margin on all sides—slightly wider on the left—is a good standard margin for ordinary typewritten work. The margins on letters vary, of course, to permit good placement.

Headings. **Main titles** should be centered and set in caps. They are not usually underlined, but often the letters are spaced out.

Subheads are centered and underlined, with main words capitalized.

Sideheads are subordinate headings that are placed at the left and underlined, with main words capitalized. These headings stand alone on a line and may be set "flush" with the line of writing or extended two or three spaces beyond it. In the latter case, the typewriter left marginal stop should be set with the line of writing, not with the sideheads.

Paragraph ("run-in") heads, underlined, are used to save space.

To keep headings in line down the page, remember the starting position on the typewriter scale bar for each group of headings. This will save time when attempting to judge alinements.

Centering Headings. First find the exact center of the writing line by adding the scale figures at the left and right **margins** and dividing by two. Then stop the carriage on this number and backspace slowly, spelling out the heading—one backspace for each two letters or spaces in the heading. Drop any odd letter left over.

For **spaced-out headings,** count one backspace for each letter or space.

Punctuation of Headings. No period is necessary after a heading or title that stands alone (although occasionally a period is used after a segregated heading to make it conform to similar headings that are unsegregated). Usually the separating space acts as sufficient punctuation. Question marks and exclamation points, however, are used after headings. (For capitalization of headings, see p. 129.)

Underline headings with an unbroken line, not with a line under each word. Single words may be underlined in the text, but a heading is considered a single unit.

Long Headings. If a heading runs more than one line, do not break into the middle of a phrase when dividing the lines.

NOT: Labor, Materials, and Services to be
Furnished by the Purchaser

BUT: Labor, Materials, and Services
To Be Furnished by the Purchaser

Never divide words at the ends of lines in headings.

Continued Headings. A heading may be carried over to the next page with the abbreviation "contd." after it—joined with a dash. The abbreviation "contd." need not be capitalized, enclosed in parentheses, or underlined. It is an unimportant word and should be unemphasized.

Building Materials – contd.

NOT: "(Cont'd)," which requires three needless shiftings of the carriage.

Division of Headings. The order of importance in the subdivision of compositions is:

MAIN TITLE	Volume	Article
	Book, or	Section
Centered Subheads	Part	Clause, or
	Chapter	Item
Sideheads	Section	Paragraph
	Paragraph	Line
Paragraph Heads. ...	Line	

Outlines—Numbered Headings and Items. The order of importance in numbered headings and items is as follows (see also pp. 420e–420f):

```
  I. Roman Numerals (or Capital Letters) for primary subjects.
     A. Capital Letters for secondary topics.
        1. Arabic numerals (ordinary numerals) for tertiary items.
           a. Small letters               Small letters may be enclosed,
           a-1. Small letters and figures  or half-enclosed, in parentheses
                     or                     (with no periods) if being used
           i) Small Roman numerals          to number paragraphs; or if
           ii) .....................        used for any other numbering
           b. .....................         that might blend with the text.
        2. ...........................
     B. .....................
 II. ...............................
```

If only two divisions are involved, use:

```
  I. ........    OR:  A. ........    OR:  1. ........
     1. .......          1. .......           a. (or 1.1) .......
     2. .......          2. .......           b. (or 1.2) .......
 II. ..........      B. ..........           2. ................
```

The setup under the headings may be indented, block, or hanging style, whichever best suits the text.

```
INDENTED:  1. .........................  }
           ........................... } for numbered paragraphs
           ................
BLOCK:     1. .........................  } for numbered sentences,
           ....................        }   separated by spaces
HANGING: 1. .........................  } for numbered items with
           ................            }   no spaces between
```

Punctuation of Numbered Items. A period is sufficient punctuation to set off a numbering figure or letter ... with two spaces after the period. It is not necessary to put parentheses or dashes around each. Nor is it necessary to use -st, -d, -nd, -rd, or -th after the numbers.

WRITE SIMPLY:	RATHER THAN:
1. Cost of materials	–1– Cost of materials, or
2. Cost of transportation	(1) Cost of materials, or
3. Cost of production	1st. Cost of materials

If the items are short, it is not necessary to use periods after them—the spacing acts as punctuation. Even when such items end a sentence, often no period is used; yet a single period may be used (after the last item) if it is thought necessary.

If items are long, a period may be used to close each one definitely.

If the items occur in a broken sentence, no punctuation is necessary after each one, unless the items run more than one line each and are closely connected; in that case a comma or semicolon may be used after each item, according to the need of separation.

> We have investigated the questions involved in the divisions of
> 1. Shipping and related industries;
> 2. Construction and machinery, including lumber and metals;
> 3. Chemicals, leather, and other manufactures;
> and we find that the points brought up by their attorney...

Capitalize only the first word of each item, unless a proper name occurs in the item.

Quantities are indicated by simple numbers before the items. If the items begin with figures, they are separated from the quantities by two spaces or by single dashes. The first word in each item need not be capitalized, since the number, not the word, begins the item.

The order includes		Necessary parts are:			
4 telescopes		7	6″ frames		7 – 6″ frames
8 microscopes		20	2-5/8″ lids	OR:	20 – 2-5/8″ lids
2 altimeters		8	3-ply sides		8 – 3-ply sides

Simple tabulated subentries need no commas, but may take dashes.

Evans:	or	Evans, Ann L.	or	Re: Evans, Ann L.
Ann L.		— John M.		John M.
John M.		— Mary T.		Mary T.

Unnumbered Headings. Unnumbered subheads should be indicated by underlinings and by unmistakable indention of margins.

Sidehead

¶...
....

First Subhead

¶...
....
¶Paragraph Head. (Captioned paragraphs are set "full measure" when under sideheads with no intervening subheads.)

Column Heading Setup. **Boxheads** are usually all centered. **Open** heads are base-alined, often on an underscore. Short words are centered. Principal words, or first words only, are capitalized.

Year	Percent of Capacity	Total Purchases		Dividend Number	Date Paid	Paid From Earnings (per share)

See also boxheads on pp. 372 and 546–47.

413

Enumerations in Texts. Parentheses are used to set off numberings in a text. Small (lower-case) letters or Arabic (ordinary) numerals are usually used for such numberings. Capital letters are rare; but Roman numerals (lower-case) are sometimes used for subordinate items.

No period or comma is necessary after the numbering in parentheses.

It is not necessary to capitalize unimportant items in an enumeration in the text. But capitalize the first word in each division that is a complete, independent sentence.

> The data required cover (a) weight, (b) dimensions, and (c) capacity.
>
> But if it is assumed that (1) the buyer is interested, and (2) the price is right, an article may be...
>
> It is commonly used (1) to emphasize a point; (2) to separate a phrase; (3) to introduce an enumeration.
>
> It has these important assurances: (1) no adulteration of products; (2) supervision by experts; and (3) constant analysis.
>
> They have three choices: (1) They can retrench. (2) They can consolidate. (3) They can liquidate.
>
> (BUT: It was concluded that (1) they should retrench; (2) they should consolidate; or (3) they should liquidate.)

First, Second, Third, etc.

first, second, third, last or final are adjective forms.

first (or in the first place), secondly, thirdly, lastly (or last) or finally } are adverbial forms.

"Firstly" is not commonly used with the adverbial forms; but it is predicted that it will some day return to favor.

1st, 2nd or 2d, 3rd or 3d, 4th, etc., are used in informal texts, without parentheses or periods.

These spelled-out numberings are usually introduced by a comma, dash, or colon, according to the pause indicated. They may be capitalized if they introduce complete, independent sentences.

> **As adjectives (describing nouns):**
>
> ...for the following **reasons: first,** that we ordered the goods; **second,** that they confirmed the order; **and last,** that shipment was made.
>
> They made three definite **proposals: First,** they will reduce the rent. **Second,** we can pay in quarterly installments. **Third,** the rent payments will apply on the purchase price if we exercise our option.
>
> **As adverbs (describing verbs):**
>
> It represents, **first,** a saving, **secondly,** an improvement, **and last,** a public benefit.
>
> Our discounts **are figured, first,** by the 15's; **secondly,** by the 10's; **thirdly,** by the 5's; and it is our firm intention...
>
> The machines **were classified** carefully—**first,** by the speed, **and secondly,** by the power.

Paragraphing. Paragraph when the thought changes, or when it is necessary to emphasize a specific request or idea so that it will not be overlooked.

A paragraph need not cover an entire subject. One subject may extend over several paragraphs; but each paragraph should contain a

414

certain phase or angle of the subject.

A "long" paragraph should not run more than ten or twelve lines. Paragraph frequently in single-spaced work so that the reader's eye can hold to the copy and his mind can retain the thought of the paragraph.

Avoid the **constant use of short paragraphs** of two or three lines each, unless information is being set down for quick reference. The staccato effect of short paragraphs gives great emphasis, but if the emphasis is not really intended, the value of the short paragraph is soon lost.

Indent the beginning of each main paragraph five or ten spaces, and each subordinate (set-in) paragraph enough spaces to keep the same indention as the main paragraph.

"Block" paragraphs are frequently used in ordinary letters, but "hanging" paragraphs are confined chiefly to advertising and listings.

> This is a sample of block paragraphing. The first line is not indented, and all lines are set out to the same margin.

> This is a sample of a hanging paragraph. The first line is set out to the margin, and all others are indented.

Do not begin a paragraph on the last line at the bottom of a page, unless the paragraph is of only two lines and can be finished on that page. Carry the paragraph over as a good beginning for the new page.

End of Page. **Do not write too near the bottom of a page.** On letters leave at least an inch margin always. Not only do papers slip at the bottom of a page (especially if it is necessary to erase), but some readers are particularly critical of and annoyed by seemingly careless writing too near the end of a page. Especially, **do not crowd the signature almost off a page.** This usually irritates the signer.

Equip the typewriter with a "line gauge" (see p. 423); or measure the page with a sheet of similar paper when nearing the bottom. The space concealed by the roller is often an optical illusion. A carbon paper that has a right marginal guide is useful in determining the bottom margin of a page. Or a pencil dot on each page may be used as a guide.

Page Numbering. A page number may be centered at the extreme bottom of each page (the usual position, as on legal papers); or it may be centered at the top of the page (as on letters); or written in the upper right corner (as on manuscripts and briefs); or in the lower right corner (as on military dispatches and some papers that are bound at the left).

The **first, or title, page** (being distinctive) is often not numbered in legal papers (the next page is 2). _The **last page** is numbered.

To secure uniformity in the position of page numbers—wherever they are placed—select a number on the typewriter scale, and write all page numbers from that scale number. Then when the pages are turned, all numbers will fall in an almost identical position.

Use a simple dash on each side of a page number. Do not surround it with fancy or unusual markings. It is unnecessary to write "Page" each time, or "#". Write simply –2–

NOT: *2*   NOR: =2=   NOR: #2   NOR: Page 2.

Inserted Page Numbers. When a page is inserted after the others are numbered, it should be numbered with a small letter, which is less conspicuous than, and therefore preferable to, a capital or a fraction.

	-18a-		-18b-		-18c-
NOT:	-18A-	NOR:	-18-A-	NOR:	-18½-

Avoid the insertion of extra pages if possible. It is often better to rewrite two pages than to insert a page with very little writing on it.

Canceled Page Numbers. (See Copy for the Press, p. 434.)

Appendix Page Numbers. Carry the regular page numbering straight through a composition, including the appendix, addenda, index, etc.

Prefaces are usually numbered with small Roman numerals.

Dating Papers. Date everything. Dates are one of the most important features on all business papers.

Write the month, the day, **and the year,** on every paper to be kept. Years change rapidly in business.

Date even notations, memorandum slips, and rough drafts.

The time of day is also most important on telegrams, memorandums of telephone calls, messages regarding callers, etc.

Place the date either at the beginning of a manuscript in the upper right corner (if it does not occur in the beginning of the text, as in legal papers), or at the end of the manuscript in the lower left corner (if it does not occur in the ending of the text).

If the date is not to appear on a manuscript—such as an article for publication—place a date on the file copy for future reference.

Charging for Piecework. In charging for occasional piecework, figure the time consumed, at a reasonable salary, and the cost of the material.

What may be considered "a day's work" depends upon the material being typed.

Fifteen to twenty pages of straight material, single-spaced, on letter-size paper, with six or seven carbons, is considered a good day's work.

Thirty to thirty-six pages, double-spaced, on letter-size paper, is a large day's work.

Tabulations

Timesavers. When setting up long tabulations, do not fail to make use of the tabulator bar and stops. This saves time even though it takes time to set the stops.

Make a "practice line" first and set the stops accordingly. Guessing at the stops usually results in having to space twice or backspace once after each stop, which not only causes loss of time but often results in misalinements.

Setup. Put as much information as possible into the headings of a tabulation and avoid the repetition of words or the use of ditto marks down the page. Be concise in wording throughout a table.

416

It is not necessary to type lines of dots or dashes ("leaders") in a tabulation unless the reading lines are hard to follow.

Note in the following illustration how many lost motions there may be in writing a simple tabulation. The second setup takes less time and effort, produces a better result, and is instantly clear.

Instead of this:

		Price
Oct. 19, 1953	Lead.......@	13.5¢ lb.
" " "	Zinc.......@	10.0¢ lb.
" " "	Tin........@	79.0¢ lb.
Dec. 21, "	Copper.....@	29.5¢ lb.
Jan. 14, 1954	Tin........@	84.75¢ lb.
Aug. 2, "	Tin........@	95.875¢ lb.

Use this form:

		Price/lb. in ¢
1953		
Oct. 19	Lead	13.5
	Zinc	10.0
	Tin	79.0
Dec. 21	Copper	29.5
1954		
Jan. 14	Tin	84.75
Aug. 2	"	95.875

NOTE: To aline "spaced" leaders, begin each row of dots on an even scale number.

Dollars and Cents. The dollar sign ($) should appear only at the beginning of each column and before each final total (that is, above a double rule, which marks the end of a column or part). (See p. 539 f.)

In long tabulations, commas and decimal points are sometimes omitted and indicated by spaces. But commas should not be omitted unless spaces are left. Unpunctuated numbers are most difficult to read.

$ 1,873.95	OR:	$ 1 873 95	BUT NOT:	$ 1873 95
248,537.00		248 537 00		248537 00

— (A single, centered dash stands for a nonexistent or zero amount; or an asterisk or other reference mark may be inserted instead.)

Signs and Abbreviations. Signs and abbreviations, such as %, #, @, lb., gals., and bbls., need to be written but once at the beginning of the column (or preferably included in the heading) if the entire column is of the same designation. It is unnecessary to repeat or ditto such designations unless they constantly change.

Ditto. If an entire line is to be dittoed, use "do." (not capitalized) instead of the repeated ditto marks.

Southern Lighting Corporation	8,970 shares
do.	10,260
Pennsylvania & Northern Co.	5,692

If only a few words are to be dittoed, use the ditto marks.

Willow Springs guide meridian
Yellowstone " "
Navajo meridian

Ruling. Horizontal lines are made with the underscore. Verticals are omitted unless column spaces are narrow; then, they are drawn in, or the page turned sideways and the underscore used. Or rulings may be swiftly made with a ball pen held firmly in the card- or ribbon-notch.

◇◇◇◇◇◇◇◇ **417**

MINUTES OF MEETINGS

Forms of minutes of meetings vary with different organizations. However, there is certain general information to be always included:

Title of meeting
{ Name of group, committee, or organization (in caps)
{ Regular or special meeting, or adjourned (of either)
{ Number of meeting, if numbered

Place, date, and hour
Presiding officer – Chairman
Secretary

Attendance (by roll call or observation)—with quorum statement

(For small meetings, the name of every member present is listed; but for large meetings, just the officers' names, with a statement, in either case, that the members present [or shares of stock represented] constitute a quorum.)

Present   Absent

. . . .

Procedure:

Minutes of previous meeting—approved or amended
Reports
Unfinished business
Elections, if any
New business
Next meeting—date, time, and place (if designated)
Adjournment—hour

(Signed)_____
                              Secretary

_____

(Minutes are sometimes countersigned by the President or the Chairman.)

(For an example of Minutes, see p. 420b.)

Corporate minutes follow the form outlined in each corporation's bylaws, or in printed instructions in corporation minute books.

Minutes are not usually recorded verbatim, with the exception of main motions and resolutions, which are recorded exactly as given. Therefore, the secretary should report, not every word said, but the **substance** of what is done, as clearly and in as few words as possible.

Arrangement of Minutes. Arrange the minutes so that important matters, such as main motions, resolutions, votes (how taken), and decisions, can be instantly discerned.

If minutes are long and involved, **margin heads, sideheads,** or **paragraph heads** may be used; and important words underlined for emphasis.

Stock Split | ¶ . . . .
[margin head] | . . . . OR:

New Office Building [sidehead]

¶ . . . .
. . . . OR:

¶ Chemical Plant. [paragraph head] . . . .

An index of all the important subjects acted upon at the different meetings should be kept in the back of the minute book or separately as a card index. An item in the index might read:

418

Louisiana Plant Site	Meeting	Page
Report	6-10-68	116
Survey	10-14-68	125
Firm offer to buy	2-3-69	136

Always make a rough draft of the minutes before copying them into the minute book.   No large erasures should appear in the minute book.

If minutes are amended or corrected at the meeting at which they are read, the corrections should be put in in red ink, or the amendments should be written on a separate page to be attached.   No minutes should be rewritten after they have been read.   They should stand as corrected.

If a certain paper is to be made a part of the minutes, it need not be written into the minutes unless it is very short.   A notation may be made in the minutes saying that the paper is to be incorporated therein, and that it may be found in a certain file or other place of safekeeping.

Preparation for Meeting.   The secretary of the meeting should see:

That a **notice of the meeting** (and, if necessary, a **proxy**) is sent to each member, in accordance with the bylaws of the body that is to meet;

That the **meeting-room** is arranged for and is in readiness on the day of the meeting;

That the **agenda** (list of things to be done) is prepared (see p. 420);

That all **papers** pertaining to the meeting are in a folder; and the **corporate seal** and other necessary incidentals are at hand.

The secretary or recorder of the meeting should sit near the chairman, or in a position to hear every word that is said.   If unable to hear, the recorder should, by a signal, so inform the chairman, who can interrupt the speaker and ask for a repetition of what has been said if he deems it of sufficient importance to do so.

Obtaining Information Beforehand.   It simplifies the taking of minutes if information is obtained beforehand.   Ascertain the purpose of the meeting, and if possible read copies of resolutions, reports, etc., to be presented—so as to understand thoroughly all items on the agenda.

Obtain a list of the persons to be present, and at the meeting simply check the names "p" or "a" (present or absent) on the list.   Note late arrivals and early departures, because an important point may hinge on whether or not a certain person heard a certain discussion.

The more preknowledge that can be had of a meeting, the **easier** it will be to record the minutes.

After the Meeting.   Obtain copies, **immediately,** of all papers read or discussed at the meeting, and write up the minutes as soon as possible.

Resolutions

Formal resolutions follow various forms.   The following is an ordinary outline, with the word WHEREAS set in caps, the first word after it not capitalized unless it is a proper name, and no comma after WHEREAS unless punctuation is necessary for the sense of the sentence. The word RESOLVED is set in caps and followed by a comma and a capital letter.   The "Therefore be it" is set on the line above RESOLVED.

419

WHEREAS it has become necessary......

........................; and

WHEREAS conditions are such as to warrant..............; and

WHEREAS, moreover, on the 18th of May, 1970, ... : Therefore be it

RESOLVED, That.....................

.......................; and be it

RESOLVED further, That..............

NOTE:

In U.S. Government printing, **Whereas** is not set in caps; but in other printing WHEREAS is often set in caps and small caps, followed by a comma, with the next word capitalized.

Resolved is often italicized.

Informal resolutions dispense with WHEREAS and "Therefore be it," and simply state the facts or events leading up to the resolution.

......the following resolution was unanimously adopted:

RESOLVED, That.................

OR:

RESOLVED: First, that........

Secondly, that.....

Agenda

An agenda, or "order of business," is an outline of meeting procedure.

THE CONTINENTAL COMPANY
AGENDA
Board Meeting, July 25, 19.., 10 a.m., EDT, Company Offices, New York

1. Minutes of previous meeting – approve.
   Executive Committee meetings – three.
2. Midyear Financial Report – Mr. Fisk.
3. Quarterly Dividend action – increase.
4. New Chemical Plant – report by
   Mr. Harland, Engineering Consultant.
5. Inspection Committee – for plant sites.
6. Remodeling Warehouse, Bayonne
   a. Approve definitive contract.
   b. Deny renewal of lease.
   c. Direct execution of said contract.
7. Interim Director – elect (Mr. Cordon).
8. Memorial Resolution – Thomas K. Kincaid.
9. Next meeting – reminder: Special 9/1/...
10. Adjourn.

(Agenda items may extend full measure; or space may be left here for the Chairman to make notes opposite each item, either before or during the meeting.

(Note that each item is numbered, and topics are underscored for quick reference.

(Triple-spacing should be used between items for clarity, and to provide writing space in this column.)

(Note that some items, as No. 9, may not appear in the minutes.)

"Agenda," the Latin plural of "agendum," is usually considered singular; with an English plural "agendas."

A **script agenda** is a detailed outline (as for a performance) of involved items.

Preparation of Agenda. Start the agenda several days before the meeting by, first, consulting, **without fail,** every person (officer, committee chairman, and member) who may be readying a report on a topic to be considered, and who may wish it to be placed on the agenda. Then after a conference with the presiding officer, prepare the agenda from the "Recurring Actions" schedule and the reminders accumulated in the "Agenda File" or meeting folder.

Copies of Agenda. Although the agenda is primarily for the chairman's use and guidance, copies may be sent members with the notice of meeting (or the chief topics of business may be mentioned in the notice). More often a copy is handed to, or is in place before, each member at the meeting.

Notice of Meeting. For meetings of organizations such as clubs, just a friendly letter or postal card may be sent, as "This will remind you of the... meeting of... to be held on... in... to consider.... / It is hoped that you can arrange to be present. / Cordially,...."

Or it may be formal, as "A regular meeting of the Board of Directors of ... will be held in... at..., on.... / Please let me know on the enclosed card whether or not you expect to attend. / Respectfully, / Secretary."

Note Taking

Notes are taken "in depth"; but minutes are written in summary.

Remember that what is **done or accomplished**—or **left unfinished**—at a meeting is of the utmost importance, not what is said. Therefore, be alert to recognize and record all definite decisions; all actions to be taken, by whom; and all business left pending.

Number notes, in center page, to correspond with agenda items. Take all notes in one book—not some on the agenda, some on pieces of paper, and some in the notebook—because the notes must be kept permanently, as well as the minutes.

Discussions and Debates. Summarize these, noting highlights, such as the "for" and "against" arguments, and by whom.

Motions. Record every motion, its maker, its seconding (name of seconder not always important), and its final disposition, without detailing its amendments.

Record **only the main motions verbatim.** (For "incidental motions" that were not lost or withdrawn, just say "It was moved and duly seconded that....")

Resolutions. Record **each verbatim** (or obtain a copy), with its proposer, seconder, and disposition.

Reports. Record the presentation, by whom, and the final action on each.

Filed reports and documents from the meeting should bear the endorsement:

In form presented to Board [or other] Meeting of...(date)...

.......(signature)....... / Secretary

Elections or Appointments. Record the names of those elected or appointed, and the voting results in elections.

Voting. Record all voting, how taken, and the count (if countable).

Voting is by these methods in this order of formality:

general (or silent) **assent or consent;**
voice (**viva voce,** "All in favor say 'aye'.") Voice may be recorded as being "by acclamation";
show of hands ("All in favor please raise your right hands");
standing (to be counted); or **rising** (for ceremonial or complimentary motions);
roll call (yeas and nays, or "for" and "against," registered);
secret ballot (if by mail, ballot is in an inner, sealed envelope);
proxy (the usual form for stockholders in a large corporation).

A **seating chart** is often made up by a secretary to identify the speakers:

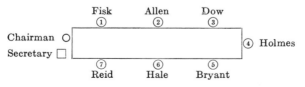

Minutes of[1] Regular Meeting of the Board of Directors
Held, pursuant to due notice,[2] in Board Room, Company Offices
New York, N.Y.
Friday, July 25, 19.., 10 a.m., EDT

Presiding: Mr. James C. Wilson, Chairman[3]
Secretary: Weldon C. Davis

Present (constituting a quorum)		Absent
Messrs.[4] Paul R. Allen	John D. Hale	Roger Malcolm
George Bryant	J. P. Holmes	Jay Stuart Park
R. Alex Dow	(left at 11:30)	(illness)
Thomas L. Fisk	Eric D. Reid	Curtis V. Shaw

In attendance: R. M. Harland, Engineering Consultant (11–11:30 a.m.)

Minutes. The minutes of the Board meeting of May 25, 19.. were approved as read [or as previously circulated; or reading was waived].[5]

The Board further ratified [or confirmed, or approved] each of the actions of the Executive Committee as set forth in its minutes of meetings of May 31, June 8, and July 10, 19...[6]

Midyear Financial Condition. The Vice President–Finance, Mr. Fisk, reviewed the June 30 Earnings Statement. Net income was 25 % above last year's first half, with earnings per share **$2.53** compared with **$2.02** in 19... (Complete report in Finance files.)

Dividend Raise. An increase of 10 cents a share in the quarterly dividend rate was thereupon suggested by the Chairman. After consideration, the following resolution was adopted (with Messrs. Allen and Reid dissenting, each preferring a year-end dividend):

RESOLVED, That a regular quarterly dividend of Sixty-five cents (65¢) per share be and hereby is declared on the common stock of the Company, payable September 15, 19.. to stockholders of record at the close of business August 25, 19...

Thereafter, Mr. Fisk left the room to telephone such dividend action to the Exchange and to release it to the press.

New Chemical Plant Site – Report. The Engineering Consultant, Mr. Harland, was invited in by the Chairman to give a report (with blackboard demonstration) of his firm's findings regarding the suitability of each of the seven sites proposed for the new development–chemicals plant. Three were recommended by his firm. (Complete report in Chemical files.)

Inspection Committee. The Chairman – pursuant to a motion duly seconded – appointed an ad hoc Inspection Committee, composed of the President, Mr. Holmes, as Chairman, and Messrs. Bryant and Hale, to appraise the above-mentioned three favorable sites. It was then moved, seconded, and carried (with Mr. Dow abstaining from the vote because of a possible conflict of interest):

"That the Inspection Committee be and hereby is authorized to obtain, if possible, an option to buy the site found to be the most desirable in the considered opinion of the Committee."[7]

Bayonne Warehouse Remodeling. The Board, on motion duly seconded

— Approved the definitive contract with the Harrison Company, dated July 25, 19..,
    for remodeling the Bayonne, N.J. warehouse;
— Denied the renewal of lease on said warehouse;
— Directed the President and Secretary to execute said contract; and further directed
    the Secretary to notify the lessee of termination of the lease.

Interim Director. On motion duly seconded, Mr. Lamott Cordon was elected a Director of the Company, effective July 30, 19.., to fill the unexpired term of the late Thomas K. Kincaid. The Secretary was directed to notify Mr. Cordon of his election to the Board.[8]

In Memoriam. In memory of Thomas K. Kincaid, the following resolution was unanimously adopted, and a copy thereof ordered sent[9] by the Secretary to the family of the deceased:

RESOLUTION

By this memorial resolution, the Board of Directors of the Continental Company wish to express their sense of sorrow and personal loss in the untimely death of Thomas K. Kincaid, an esteemed and cooperative associate. His quiet humor, patient counsel, and deep understanding in many a trying time will be long remembered – and greatly missed. His contributions to this Company, especially in humanitarian aspects, have become a part of its history. He leaves, indeed, a legacy of far-reaching goodwill.

* * *

The meeting was adjourned at 12:30 p.m.

                                       Secretary[10]

EXAMPLE OF MINUTES OF A BOARD MEETING
(Footnotes on opposite page)

Minute Writing

Minutes are a **brief record** of the proceedings at a meeting. They may be **formal** or **informal,** and set up in **"skeletonized"** form or in **narrative,** whichever best suits the nature of the meeting. But in whatever form—and most important of all—they must record the **action taken: who is to carry it out; who is to make a report; and what is left unfinished or pending.**

The secretary follows up all actions after the meeting:

writing letters, notifying persons, making ticklers, filing papers.

Minutes of small meetings are now usually streamlined (with legal approval) so as to be instantly clear. Whatever is repetitious or obvious is omitted, such as most discussions (they are understood), and the routine making, seconding, and carrying of motions when their net results are entered as resolutions, orders, or other definitive actions. (Such details are of course preserved permanently—for future reference if need be—in the secretary's lengthy notes taken or tape-recorded at the meeting.)

Minutes of large meetings are usually in narrative form, employing familiar phrases such as "The meeting was called to order by...; The Secretary called the roll...; The first item of business to come before the meeting was...; ...moved the acceptance of this report; On motion duly made, seconded, and carried...; Upon being put to a vote, the motion was...; [resolution was] spread upon the minutes; There being no further business...."

"Respectfully submitted" is no longer used before signatures on minutes, but is still used on reports (often just "Submitted" or "Respectfully" on letters of transmittal).

The tone of the minutes should be completely **impersonal,** with no comment whatsoever by the secretary, such as a *"heated"* or *"lengthy"* debate, or a *"moving"* address, or an *"eloquent"* appeal.

Main motions and resolutions are always included, verbatim. But in **unpublished** minutes it is not necessary to give the name of the maker or seconder of a motion, nor the exact vote, unless that information is essential or requested.

Identification of papers by numbers and dates should always be made.

Sums of money in resolutions should be written in words with figures in parentheses.

Capitalization of all proper names is usual: Board, Directors, Company, Corporation, Committee, etc.; and of officers' titles, as President, Chairman, Secretary, Treasurer.

Footnotes for Page 420b

[1] If meetings are numbered, an ordinal, as "165th," may be inserted here or in upper left corner.

[2] If notice is dispensed with, use instead: "(all Directors having waived notice thereof)".

[3] If Chair is temporary: "Mr..., President [or office], Chairman pro tem," or "Vice Chairman."

[4] List alphabetically. Company officers who are also directors are not usually identified by their official titles. "Messrs." may be used or omitted.

[5] If reading is waived: "The reading of the minutes of the Board meeting of April 25, 19.. was waived; and on motion duly seconded such minutes were approved as recorded."

[6] Follow with approval of minutes of any other Board-appointed committee for meetings held since the previous Board meeting (if the bylaws or company practice requires the Board's approval).

[7] This "main motion" might have been a "resolution" or "resolve." In some assemblies, all major actions are taken in the form of resolutions—or orders, as in civic bodies, with the enacting word "Ordered" instead of "Resolved."

[8] This direction is unnecessary if a similar general instruction is in the bylaws.

[9] In a letter of sympathy; or engraved on fine, white, folded paper—with a letter as on p. 301.

[10] If minutes are not read at meetings, but approved by a reading committee, the words "Approved [date] / [Signature of head of approving body]" may appear below the secretary's signature.

420c

The minute book may be any good-quality looseleaf binder, about 10″x12″ with 20 lb. bond paper. But important minutes should be kept in a regular, locking minute book supplied with index dividers and heavy 28 lb. bond paper (so that both sides of a page might be written upon without "show-through"). Such books are obtainable at stationers' for prices from $12 to $15.

Separate minute books are usually kept for the meetings of stockholders ("Stock"), directors ("Board"), and committees. But in some organizations, just one book, sectionalized with index dividers, may suffice.

In the front of each book should be the Constitution or Charter (Certificate of Incorporation) of the body that is meeting; its Bylaws; and its adopted "Policies" and "Plans."

Definitions

Adjourned meeting—a resumed or continued meeting; that is, it follows a first meeting which was adjourned to meet again on a certain date to take up unfinished business.
due or duly—lawful -ly; according to accepted and proper procedure.
Executive Committee—When a large organization meets infrequently, it elects a Board of Directors or Managers to conduct its business between meetings. The Board may, in turn, appoint or elect, from its membership, an "Executive Committee" to manage its affairs between Board meetings.
Main Motion / Resolution—often interchangeable; but the chief difference is that a main motion is framed **orally** and **proposes action**, while a resolution is **written out** and **represents final action.**
Quorum—an agreed-upon number of members (usually a majority) who must be present at a meeting (or voting shares that must be represented at a stockholders' meeting) in order to transact legal business.

References

Am. Society of Corporate Secretaries. Corporate Minutes and Related Subjects. New York, **1964**.
Bridge, Lawrence W. Parliamentary Procedure. Funk & Wagnalls, New York, **1954**.
Davidson, Henry A. Handbook of Parliamentary Procedure. The Ronald Press, New York, **1955**.
Robert, Gen. Henry M. Robert's Rules of Order Revised. Scott, Foresman, Chicago, **1951**.

◇◇◇◇◇◇◇◇◇

REPORTS

Reports may also be called **"Studies," "Surveys,"** and **"Opinions."** They may be long or short; formal or informal; special, routine, periodic, or serial; typewritten, reproduced, or printed. And they may be classified in many ways: research, investigation, technical, statistical, performance, project, progress, final, marketing, financial, annual, etc.

Most reports are made in the following informal form, on letter-size bond paper (but occasionally on legal-size bond paper).

MAIN TITLE

Date*

To* ....
...................:

Introductory statement (mentioning the request or authorization for the project, its purpose, the method of research undertaken—and summarizing [in a short sentence] the findings or recommendations)....

Sidehead

Text is usually double-spaced, with single-space tabulations, quotations, and illustrations. "Short" pages (before tables or graphs) may be filled in with "(contd.)" or "(more)" centered in the space.

420*d*

Sidehead

Reports in letter or memorandum form may be single-spaced; and in these, paragraph heads may be used instead of sideheads.

– – – –

Conclusion and/or Recommendation. . . . .

. . . .

Respectfully,*

Handwritten signature

Typed name and title (if any)

Initials

---

* The date may be placed at the end beneath the initials, if preferred. The "To" line and the complimentary close are often omitted if a "plain" report is being prepared.

Organization of a Report

In the preparation of a report, the three most important things to bear in mind are its **purpose,** its **scope,** and its **readers.** These three considerations govern its **length,** its **depth,** and its **wording.**

Tone—Formal reports should be completely impersonal: third person, dignified, factual. Informal reports may be written in the first person, but are never casual, always businesslike. "Stress the subject, not the author" is the rule.

Brevity—**"Most reports are too long"**—a recurring criticism. They are never fully read by busy executives. Even some "summaries" must themselves be summarized. Therefore, at the outset, try to see, not how long and complicated a report can be made, but how **short and simple—yet complete.**

Guides—A **"Study Schedule"** should first be made for: reading, testing, inspecting, observing, interviewing, and/or surveying (by questionnaire). Then a **"Subject List"** should be set up to provide headings under which to classify information as it is gathered on 3x5" or 4x6" cards, each with a heading in the top left corner, so that the cards may later be sorted to bring all like material together. Also, as the work progresses, a **"Plan of Illustrations and Tables"** should be made.

Outline—After the investigation has been completed and the material assembled, a **"detailed outline"** of the report **must** be made up—to arrange items in logical and balanced order and determine how fully each should be developed.

> **"This task is perhaps the most constructive step in the author's program. . . . The hours or days required to draw up a well-rounded outline are, in the long run, a thoroughly justified invest-ment."**—U.S. Geological Survey.

Divisions. A long report may be divided into Parts and Chapters or Sections, with divisions, subdivisions, and sub-subdivisions.

> **"Excessive subdivision of the text, however, may be confusing rather than enlightening. Three different grades of section head-ings are ample for most technical reports."**—Tennessee Valley Authority.

420*e*

Headings. Divisions may be numbered or, better, unnumbered if possible, to simplify the report. (For numbering sequence, see p. 412; unnumbered headings, p. 413.) Scientists use a complex decimal numbering system, as 1 for chapters or centerheads; 1.1, 1.2 for sideheads thereunder; and 1.1.1, 1.1.2 for subdivisions of sideheads.

Twos. A rule in subdividing outlines is that each set, grade, or order of headings must have at least two parts—never a 1 without a 2, nor an A without a B.

Construction. In each grade or order, all headings should be short and of the same weight or importance (**topic phrases** or **short sentences,** not complete statements). All items alike in thought should be **alike or parallel in grammatical construction**—that is, all noun phrases, or all beginning with a verbal noun, etc.

Parts of a Report

A formal **report, study, or survey,** set up in **"book form,"** may have some or all of the following parts in the order given; or they may be rearranged or consolidated to suit the writer's idea of the reader's needs.

Front Matter
(Prepared after the report has been written and paged)

Cover or Binder—usually carries just the title, author, his company or sponsoring agency, and date. May also have the report, document, or contract number, and classification, if any. (Often the title page serves **as a** cover.)

Frontispiece—a photograph or illustration, usually facing the title page.

Title Page—a repetition of what is on the cover, with a few more credits or descriptive lines. Items may be arranged in any artistic manner, but are usually centered down the page in varying line lengths, with wide spaces between.

The **title** should be **brief,** set in full caps, and usually single-spaced. **"Report"** may or may not be included. The subtitle if short may also be in full caps; but if long, in **"initial caps"** (c & lc). Other directives: **the first word should be an important one; a complete phrase on each line; no divided words; no prepositional line ends** (but a preposition may begin a secondary line or stand alone).

Additions: short informative statements, as "A survey and restudy of..."; and a use line, as "Prepared for...[OR at the request of, on behalf of, OR as part of a program of...], Submitted to..., OR For use of the Committee on...."

By-Lines: name of author or editor, with his title following or below; or name of group, with affiliated company, agency, or institution and address. "By" is usually used, but may not be. No more than four authors should be named; sometimes three with "and Others," or "et al." Other devices may be: "In collaboration with..., Prepared in cooperation with...[OR under the direction of...], With a section on..., by..."; or authorship credit may be given at the beginning of each chapter or part.

Copyright or Notice Page (on, or next after, title page)—copyright notice and other proprietary (ownership) data; may reserve all rights or just some and grant others.

Letter of Authorization, Acceptance, or Approval—from the requester of the report.

Letter of Transmittal or Submittal (sometimes called a **"Covering Letter"**) —a letter, on a regular letterhead, mentioning the request or authorization for the report, its purpose and scope, with sometimes a summary, recommendation, and acknowledgments if few. In printed reports it is usually headed "Letter of Transmittal," but not in unprinted ones. It may bear a subject, that of the report. The complimentary close may be just "Respectfully," or "Sincerely yours," or omitted. On a bound-in letter, no initials and no "Enc." or "Attm." appear. (For signatures, see p. 420*l*.)

Foreword, Preface, and/or Acknowledgments—each on a separate page, or the last two combined. More impersonal than, and usually replaces, a letter of transmittal.

Acknowledgments are presented here or in the end matter. (Financial support is acknowledged, as "This work was supported by....")

Summary or Abstract (sometimes called a **"Covering Brief"**)—a synopsis of the highlights and findings of the report: the problem, the method and scope of the investigation, conclusions, and recommendations if any. **The summary is the most important part of the report**—the most read—the most worked with. Therefore, it should be **"terse but not telegraphic,"** in one or two paragraphs if possible—**"never more than one page,"** although some organizations permit two.

Contents ("Table of" is unnecessary)—a list of important sections, in **outline** form (single- or double-spaced), with beginning, but not inclusive, page numbers. Outline numberings or letterings, if any, are carried only before main items. Column heads (as "Chapter" or "Section" on the left, and "Page" on the right) and leaders may or may not be used. (For alining leaders, see p. 417.) At the beginning, a few parts of the front matter (as letter of transmittal and summary) may or may not be listed. At the end, a list of "Appendixes," etc., may appear, with the heading centered but no dividing line above it. (Varied or long end matter may have its own "Contents," at its inception.)

Setup. All may, preferably, be typed in initial caps with centerheads underlined. Or sections, or chapters, and centerheads if any, may be in full caps, with just the centerheads underlined. **Overrun lines ("turnovers")** are clearer if indented (**"hung"**) 2 spaces, with the page number following the last line of each item, not the first.

Illustrations and Tables ("List of" is unnecessary)—a list of main titles, without subtitles. (All illustrations, **except tables,** are called **"Figures,"** and may include drawings, diagrams, maps, charts or graphs [see below], and photographs [which may be called "plates" if grouped on one page or printed singly on special paper].) Column heads—"Figure" or "Table" on the left and "Page" on the right—are usually used.

Such a list may appear at the foot of the "Contents" or on a separate page in the front or end matter.

Numbering. Illustrations, if many, are numbered consecutively as they are referred to in the text, as **"Figure 1"** (usually **"Fig. 1"**) **below** the illustration and preceding or above its title in initial caps. (See also Citings and Tables, p. 420*j*.)

Charts—a list. Charts, if many, are numbered separately, as **"Chart 1" above** the chart, which always has a caption and sometimes footnotes. (**The terms**

420*g*

"chart" and "graph" are used interchangeably; but a chart is often regarded as the final form of a graph with the "grid" [crosslines] removed, and just the "ticks" [guide marks] remaining.)

Charts that are not graphs are: lineal or directional, sometimes called "flow charts" (diagrams tracing lines of descent, processes, structures, classifications, or organizations); and map charts (showing area differences or distributions).

Graphs, often called "charts," are of several kinds: line (showing trends); bar [horizontal] or column [vertical] (comparisons); pie (proportions); pictograph (with pictorial symbols); and surface (with shaded, or "crosshatched," areas showing cumulative totals).

Notation—a list of symbols (alined vertically on the left) used in a mathematical report.

Text or Body of Report

Introduction—a clear-cut statement of the purpose and scope of the report; method of investigation; findings or results; conclusions, and recommendations. Concise background information, such as a short history of the problem and previous studies, may be given for readers unfamiliar with the subject. The report's title usually appears above the introduction, but may not. The author's name may also be given if it is not placed elsewhere in the front matter.

Discussion—the details and findings of the research conducted for the project.

Conclusions, Recommendations, or Evaluations—the final decisions (often listed; with cost estimates, if any).

Other less definitive but appropriate headings may be:

Closing Remarks...A Concluding Word...The Next Step...Results, or Observations.

Special Sections—In a bid or proposal in report form, there may also be these parts:

Statement of Work (or Task)—specifying the work and equipment the bidder will furnish.
Exceptions—giving valid reasons why certain features of the project should be changed or eliminated.
Program Organization—showing how the bidder will organize the work; and outlining (in chart form) the schedules for completion.
Qualifications—giving the bidder's experience, facilities, and the qualifications (in "résumés") of key technical personnel who will be assigned the project.
Fiscal Statement (submitted separately)—giving bidder's financial standing and capabilities.

References or Literature Cited—a list of books or other authoritative writings that have been cited ("called out") in the text, as "stated by Lee (1968, p. 12)," or "(Ref. 6)," or just "(3)," and which have not been carried in footnotes or listed at the end of each chapter. They may be arranged here alphabetically, or numerically to correspond to their citation numbers in the text. (See also Citings, p. 420*j*.)

End Matter or Back Matter

Supporting data, substantiation of evidence, documentation, and other details referred to in the text (usually by footnotes) may be presented here on separate pages.

Appendixes, Exhibits, or Attachments—supplementary material, titled and identified A, B, C; or 1, 2, 3; or I, II, III if Roman numerals have not been used for chapters.

Additional Statements by Members of Committee or Commission—often dissenting or critical.

Glossary, Vocabulary, Definitions, or Abbreviations—lists, if not in front matter.

Bibliography or Selected Bibliography—pertinent or consulted literature, usually uncited in text. The list may be divided according to subject or type of writing:

Books	Articles	Bulletins	Public Documents	Reports
Unpublished Works		Interviews	Speeches	Lectures

Works are arranged alphabetically—by authors' or editors' surnames, and committee, commission, agency, or corporate authors' full names. (See also pp. 420*l* and 435–36.)

A corporate author is listed from main body to branch, as "...Company, ...Division"; an individual author's name may follow the work's title, after "by." If an organization is both author and publisher, it is named only once, preferably as author.

Titles of books and of **printed company publications** are underscored, as are the names of **magazines and newspapers** (often abbreviated, without "The"). But the titles of sections, chapters, abstracts, patents, articles in newspapers or magazines, and unpublished works are quoted, not underscored.

Numberings (company document or contract number, and classification, if any) may be in parentheses, as may **additional information** about unpublished papers (meetings where presented), and translations.

An "Annotated Bibliography" is one that is supplied with **notes**—a brief comment about or evaluation of each book or paper, run in (without parentheses) after the last line of the entry; or if space permits, blocked below with one space between.

Index—Usually the table of contents suffices; but for long or complicated reports, a well-prepared index (set up like a book index) is very valuable. (See also p. 438.)

Distribution List or Recipients—**complete** list of persons and offices to receive report.

Setup of a Report

Style Sheet. As a guide to placement and uniformity in typing a long report, make up a pattern of headings and indentions, marking in red the typewriter-scale starting number of each. List forms to be used throughout: abbreviations, capitalizations; hyphenations; solid words; and spellings of unusual or technical words.

Paper—usually letter-size bond ($8\frac{1}{2}$x11"). "**Substance**" (weight): 13 or 16 lb. if **typed** on only one side of the sheets; if **typed** on both sides, 24 or 28 lb., to avoid "**show-through.**" If **reproduced** on only one side, 16 lb.; if on both sides, 20 lb.

Margins—one inch all around; 2" above a chapter or section head, which is always on a new right-hand page. If pages are to be bound on the left, leave a $1\frac{1}{2}$" margin on the binding side for the "**gutter.**" In typing pages to be bound on the left, with writing **on both sides** of the paper, remember that the binding margin must alternate from page to page. To accomplish this, without resetting margins and tabs each time, set the left margin ($1\frac{1}{2}''$ indent) for the right-hand (**"odd"** or **"recto"**) pages; then insert the left-hand (**"even"** or **"verso"**) pages 5 scale-spaces to the right of that margin.

Spacing and Indention—double-spaced if fairly short, or if to be printed. Long reports, not to be printed, may be single-spaced or **"half-spaced"** (**"cheat-spaced"** —$1\frac{1}{2}$ line), with double-spacing between paragraphs. Indent paragraphs 5 spaces.

Single-space listings and indent them 10 spaces if unnumbered; or 5 spaces if numbered, with 2 spaces after the numbering period. Space headings thus: **main titles**, 6 above, 4 below; **centerheads**, 4 above, 3 below; **sideheads**, 3 above, 2 below.

Page Numbers (**"Folios"**)—usually centered $\frac{1}{2}''$ from foot of page, to avoid shifting from top to bottom for chapter-head page numbers; yet some are set at top center, and some at margins, top or bottom. Front matter may be unnumbered, or numbered with small Roman numerals as in a book. (Pages that are not numbered but counted are: title, copyright, part or division, and blank pages.) All text pages are numbered in ordinary (Arabic) numerals, consecutively from the first page of text—including illustrations and tables (which may also be separately numbered before their titles)—through the end matter.

New Pages—Each **main division** of front matter, text, and end matter should begin on a new page. **Subdivision** heads should not "break" within two lines of the bottom of a page.

Running Heads—In a printed report, the title may be carried at the top of each page; but in typewritten or reproduced technical reports, just the report number may appear at the top margin, with the page number below it, as

[verso] TR-260   [recto] TR-260   [front matter] TR-260
         16   17   iii

Citings or "Callouts"—These may be woven into the text or placed in parentheses in sentences, without **"see,"** as "(Fig. 7)," "(Ref. 5)," or "(Table 9)." But if the parenthetical citing stands alone as a sentence, **"See"** is used.

Quotations—single-spaced if set off and indented; but may be double-spaced if run in and enclosed in quotation marks. (See also p. 435.) If the report is to be printed, or circulated in reproduced form, written permission from the copyright holder **must be secured** for any quotation of more than 50 words. No permission is required for **short** quotations from **Government publications**, which are not copyrighted. It is courteous, however, to give full credit for every quotation, short or long, from whatever source.

Equations (in technical reports)—Some are run in (**"in-text"**), but most are **"displayed"**—set off and indented 5 or 10 spaces, with the equation number in parentheses (**"parens"**) at right margin, alined with center of, and at least $\frac{1}{2}''$ from, the equation; or alone on the next line, **"flush right."**

Dividing. Long equations are usually **"broken"** before a mathematical sign ($=$, $+$, $-$, etc.), and then alined vertically on equal signs; or if none, the second part is set a few spaces to the right of the equal sign above. Rarely, an equation may be divided **before** an opening parenthesis, brace, or bracket, or an integral ($\int$) or summation (Σ) sign.

Special signs, symbols, and Greek letters may be drawn in, stenciled, transferred, pasted on (by adhesive backing), or typed with interchangeable keys, type heads, or gadgets called **"Typits."**

Tables—may be unnumbered, if close to their references; or numbered (separately from the illustrations) **at top** so as not to interfere with footnotes, as "Table 1," or "VI-1" (showing chapter also), or "C-1" (if in "C" appendix). A concise title, or "caption" (typed in "initial caps" and printed in "caps and small caps"), follows the number, separated by a period and space or just a dash.

The far left column of a table, carrying the **"line heads,"** is called the **"stub."**

Typing. Set tabs and type tables **across** the page, not down each column. For easier reading in long tables, group the lines by fives or eights, with a space between, as on p. 600.

Blank spaces in columns may, for exactness, be filled in by 3 dots or dashes.

Ruling. Tables may be ruled for clarity if long, complicated, or crowded; but they should be left unruled if simple and easy to follow, as on pp. 289 and 572. Often a **horizontal rule** or two will suffice, as on p. 533. **Vertical rules** are time-consuming to insert and therefore expensive—in both typing and printing (especially in printing when they cross horizontal rules). A **double rule** is used to separate **"double-up tables"** (two or more columns), as on pp. 590 and 600.

Continuing. **"Never divide a table unless it is more than one page long"**— stylebook advice. Type it on a new page (single-spaced if necessary to fit), even though that may leave a **"short"** page preceding. A wide table may be split in the center and **"spread"** on facing pages, with careful alinement (often pasted together in typewritten form to be reduced by photography). Or it may be turned sidewise (set **"broadside"**) with heading **always toward the left,** as on pp. 583–85.

A long table may be continued, with title and boxhead repeated on each page, as on pp. 373 and 537; but headings are not repeated if the continued table is set broadside on facing pages.

For further guidance in the setup of tables, acknowledgment of source, footnotes, continuation, etc., see tables in the current almanacs listed on p. 607.

Footnotes—single-spaced below a $1\frac{1}{4}''$ **"cutoff dash"** (underscore) from the left margin, which dash should be 2 spaces below last text line (even on a short page, as a chapter end), and 1 space above the footnotes. (In printing, smaller type is used.)

Long or complicated footnotes should be avoided; rather, a reference should be made to **"Notes"** at the end of the chapter or to an appendix—as, in the text, just "(Note 6)."

Cross-referencing may be done to avoid repetition, as "[12] See footnote 4, p. 9."

Symbols or Numbers—and Sequence. Differentiation and simplification are the keys to choosing indicators. In texts where footnotes are **few,** symbols (in the order shown on p. 273) are favored, especially asterisks (up to 3 [*, **, ***] on a page) as in technical reports. Or numbers (**"superiors"**) may be preferred, and numbering started anew on each page—a method easier for the writer when making revisions.

If footnotes are **many,** superiors are used and numbered consecutively throughout each chapter or section—which method precludes the printer's having to reset numbers in page makeup. Occasionally, in a report having no major divisions, footnotes are numbered straight through the text (in recurring sequences, 1 to 99). (For table footnotes, see p. 420*l*.)

Setup. Indicators may, for clarity, **"bear off"** one space before footnotes.

Long footnotes may be set in paragraph form, **"full measure"** (even below indented matter, as on pp. 355 and 456; but they may be indented if preferred, as on p. 591).

Short footnotes may be blocked on the left, with their indicators alined, one space before them, on the right. **"Turnover lines"** may be blocked; or better, for unspaced footnotes, indented (**"hung"**) 2 spaces under the first word of each footnote, as on p. 537. Numerous short footnotes, as for a table, may be set in columns across the page, with separating spaces. Or, if space is at a premium, footnotes may follow each other across the page, with 4 spaces between each note and the next. (See tables in current almanacs.)

Continued Footnotes. A long footnote may be continued to the foot of the next page, before other footnotes. It should be broken within a sentence to show that it is incomplete. Its number or symbol is not repeated; nor is "continued" necessary, but a guideline may be used, as "Footnotes for Table on Preceding Page—contd."

Footnotes for Illustrations and Tables. Numberings are independent of text footnotes, and begin anew with each table or illustration. (For contrast, symbols or italic superior letters may be used.) Footnotes are placed at the **end** of a table (even if it is continued, as on pp. 372–74), separated by 2 spaces, and a cutoff dash if there is no bottom rule.

In a table, the **order for placement of indicators** is, first, across the boxhead, then across each succeeding line, from left to right. A lone indicator in a column is enclosed in parentheses and centered.

Names in Footnotes. An author's name is **not inverted** in a footnote. (The inversion in bibliographies [as on p. 436] is for alphabetizing only; therefore, the name of a second author need not be inverted, nor the name and address of the publisher.) "The" is omitted from the titles of periodicals. **Italics** in print are indicated by underscores in manuscripts. The page number follows the year, at the end.

Newspaper reference, without authorship, is given in this order: title of article, (quoted), name of paper (underscored), date, part, page.

Space Gauge. To determine where to start footnotes, use side-numbered carbon paper; or make a backing sheet—a colored (Sub. 16) sheet, numbered, single-space, down the right edge (to be inserted ½″ to the right of the pack). Underline in red the page-starting line, page-ending line, and page-number line. In typing, when a footnote indicator appears, subtract the lines in its footnote from the page-end line (with, first, allowance for the separating space and cutoff dash). Check ahead so that an indicator will not appear in the last few lines on a page with no room left for its footnote. Better to carry all over to the next page, even though that leaves a "short page."

Signatures—An informal report is usually signed on the last page, but may be unsigned. In a long or formal report, the signature appears only on the letter of transmittal—handwritten on the original, but in facsimile or printed on the reproductions. An entire committee may sign, but usually only the chairman.

Pocket for Papers—A pocket for holding a folded map, chart, etc., may be made by pasting the front of a proper-sized manila envelope (with the flap cut off) to the inside back cover of the report—the envelope opening to the left.

Foldout—A large, accordion-folded illustration, map, chart, etc., may be bound ("tipped in" on one side) within a report to open out as a "gatefold."

Index Dividers or Tabs—Parts of a long report may be separated by colored index divider sheets (sold at stationers'). Or divisions may be indicated by guide tabs, with major-division tabs of a different color and longer than those for minor divisions. The tabs should be staggered down the pages so that none overlap; with a second set beginning again at the top.

Binding—Short or informal reports may be **stapled (slantwise)** in the upper left corner. Long or formal reports may be bound on the left (with or without a backing), or sometimes across the top like legal papers. CAUTION: Do not bind the report so tightly or so deeply on the left that the pages will not lie flat when open. Tight, curved pages are very hard to read.

References

Reisman, S. J., ed. A Style Manual for Technical Writers and Editors. (Lockheed Missiles and Space Company), Macmillan, New York, 1962.
Tennessee Valley Authority, Office of Engineering Design and Construction. "The Preparation of Engineering Reports for the TVA." Knoxville, Tennessee (being revised, 1970).
U.S. Department of the Interior, Geological Survey. Suggestions to Authors of the Reports of the U.S. Geological Survey, 5th ed. Government Printing Office, Washington, D.C., 1958.
Wellborn, G. P., L. B. Green, and K. A. Nall. Technical Writing. Houghton Mifflin, Boston, 1961.

Various U.S. Government reports and studies may be purchased from the Government Printing Office, Washington, D.C.—such as the following, selected mainly from price lists on p. 500:
Economic Report of the President, 1963; A Study of Mutual Funds, 1962; The Practical Values of Space Exploration, 1961; The Long-Range Demand for Scientific and Technical Personnel, 1961.

◇◇◇◇◇◇◇◇◇

INTEROFFICE CORRESPONDENCE—MEMORANDUMS

Ordinary form for memorandums, or "memos":

Printed informal headings may be: FROM THE DESK OF (printed full name) OR NOTE TO (handwritten name or initials)	Date: .... (Hour if necessary) File: ....

MEMORANDUM [or MEMO] to Mr. ... (last name) ...   OR

To: (full name, without "Mr." but with professional title, as "Dr.")
       Department, room, or full address, if necessary

From: (this line is being eliminated, in favor of the typed signature)

Subject: (on printed forms; but on plain paper, centered, underlined)

      Body single-spaced or double-spaced, so that the writing will not be too high on the page.

Initials Notations cc: (see also p. 299)	Signature or Initials (typed and/or handwritten)

Note that: **The word "Interoffice"** is unnecessary before MEMORANDUM.

              The "From" line may be omitted, unless it is on a printed form.

              No salutation or complimentary close is necessary.

              Initials and notations, such as "Attm." and "Enc.," are typed on.

              The "Copies to" notation may be at the top left, on multi-page memos, or at the bottom as a **"cc:"** if preferred. Each person's name should be checked or underlined in red on his copy. (Names are arranged in order of their importance, or in alphabetic order, without "Mr.")

              Second pages are headed like letter second pages (see p. 300). If there are two addressees, both names may appear; but if several, their names may be replaced by a catch line (an abbreviated subject) and/or the memo number.

              Pages are stapled together, **slantwise,** in the upper left corner.

Paper. Use plain, 16 lb. paper for memorandums unless forms are provided. Memorandums to outsiders should be written on letterheads.

Signatures. Always submit a memorandum to the dictator to read and sign or initial over his typed signature. Some dictators sign memos, and some do not.

Distributing Memorandums. If a memorandum is confidential or personal, enclose it in a sealed envelope with "Personal" above the receiver's name thereon.

      Or if a memorandum has various attachments and will have to travel through different hands, staple the attachments to it and enclose it in an envelope with the recipients' names listed thereon—and the first name checked. This receiver will cross off his name, date it, check the next name, and send it on.

❖❖❖❖❖❖❖

ROUGH DRAFTS

Write ROUGH DRAFT at the top of every draft—on colored, but not thin, paper—to guard against later confusion with the final copy. Also number and date each draft—there may be redrafts.

Double- or triple-space all drafts so that interlineations may be easily made. But single-space quotations, which are unchangeable.

Make only the number of copies to be actually used; otherwise copies may get into the files and be mixed with the final copies.

Staple the pages together to preclude page-interchanging later.

421

Destroying Rough Drafts or Handwritten Copy. Always return rough drafts or handwritten copies to the person responsible for them, for destruction. Clip a note thereto with the question "To be destroyed or filed?" It is his privilege then either to destroy the copies or mark them for the files.

A question often arises whether the final copy is as the original intended it to be; and if the dictator has the original he can compare the two.

❖❖❖❖❖❖❖❖

TYPEWRITING

Touch. To acquire an even touch on a "manual," and produce typing resembling printing—with carbon copies that are very clear—stroke each key with the same force and with the same timing. To perfect this, practice occasionally following each word through mentally letter for letter as the keys are tapped. (On an "electric," with touch control, the ribbon governs clear impressions. It must never become worn or cut.)

Speed. Adopt a steady pace when typing. Never hurry nervously even when working "against time." The time consumed in erasing invariably amounts to more in the long run than the time gained by hurrying.

It is the steady, even, errorless rate of speed that counts.

Learn to follow and not anticipate what is to be written. The practice of following the first few words through mentally, until the mind and the fingers catch the rhythm, will eliminate errors in rush work. Begin slowly, and a practically error-proof speed can be attained.

Concentrate also, word for word, on what is being read. Do not read a line ahead, except in shorthand. The moment the mind leaves the subject and does not follow word for word, the fingers are a little lost.

Do not be disturbed when given a large amount of work. Acquire the habit of arranging the most important work first. One who writes the most important papers or letters first will always seem speedier than another who attempts to do everything in routine order, although the first worker may even be the slower or more conservative typist.

Finger Discipline. When the fingers have a tendency invariably to miswrite or twist the letters of certain words, such as "expecially" for especially, "possible" for possibly, and "enumerate" for enumerate, practice writing such words at least twenty times, or until the fingers get the feel of the combination of the letters. Even experienced fingers slow down on some words such as the above.

Capital Shifts. Capital letters often "jump" or "drop" because the shift is made too quickly. Slow the fingers down a little on capitals, and this difficulty can be overcome. In nine cases out of ten it is the fault of the operator, not of the machine.

Never permit a piece of work to go out with the capitals all awry.

Be sparing in the use of capital letters. Unnecessary capitalization consumes time and effort in typing. To keep raising the carriage with the little fingers all day long is a tiresome job.

Devices. Learn to make use of all the devices on a typewriter, especially the tabulator stops. The use of the stops saves much time in tabulated work, even though it takes a little time to set and reset them.

Learn to use the bell on the typewriter. This is an extra safeguard on margins. Particularly in rush work when the mind has other things to concentrate on besides margins, the bell will save many a line.

Always have the paper holders and paper guide working, and not pushed off to the sides. The holders prevent the paper from slipping when the writing is nearing the end of a page.

Do not attempt to maintain the left margin without the marginal stop. Reset the left marginal stop for every new setup in typing.

Make use of every mechanical device. The value of these mechanical assistants is fully appreciated only by the most efficient workers.

Typewriter Roller (Platen). A hard-rubber roller should be used on a machine **if more than four carbon copies** are usually being made. It is almost impossible to make more than four clear copies with a soft roller; no matter how hard the keys are struck, the fifth and sixth copies blur.

Soft rollers are used for ordinary work—two to four carbon copies— because they make less noise and produce uniform typewritten work.

When using a hard roller, if but one carbon copy is being made, run a piece of heavy paper or a backing sheet behind the copy. This deadens the noise and gives the work an even appearance.

Special rollers may be obtained to hold labels, cards, etc.

Line Gauge. To make a "page-gauge," mark off a half-inch strip on bond paper, and number it vertically up to 30—single space. Cut and wind the strip tightly around either end of the roller and fasten with clear tape. Insert each page when number 1 on the strip has just come into view. End each page at the same number on the strip as the first page ended, and uniform page lengths will result.

Ribbons. Use a black **cotton ribbon** for a manual typewriter; a **nylon** or film ribbon for an electric (cotton holds more ink; nylon wears longer).

Change the ribbon frequently enough so that the work will be clear **and** black. A worker is judged by the appearance of his typewriting.

Never use a ribbon with holes in it, or one that is producing very uneven work. This is not economy of the right sort.

A red ribbon should be used conservatively. (As a substitute for a red ribbon, red carbon paper may be used. See p. 430.) Red may be used to indicate items of great importance, **or to show deficits;** but it should not be used for decorative purposes.

When **changing ribbons,** do this: (1) run in a sheet of paper to protect the roller; (2) set ribbon indicator on red; (3) lock the shift key; (4) strike two center keys and wedge them near the printing point.

Accessories. A sponge rubber or felt pad under the machine deadens the noise and steadies the typewriter; and if a typewriter is fastened down, it adds to the ease of writing. If a typewriter is bolted to a movable stand, the back of the machine should be set-in one inch from the back of the stand—for protection if tipped over.

Typewriter. Oil the carriage way about once a month; otherwise the carriage will become sluggish and "pull hard." Wipe the rails or tracks clean before applying, **sparingly,** new light machine oil.

Keep the machine clean. Dust the typewriter every morning, and clean it thoroughly at least once a month—particularly the type. Clogged letters are a discredit to any typing.

Clean the roller with fine sandpaper and then with denatured alcohol or a special "type cleaner" if it becomes slick and fails to grip the paper. A slick roller causes paper to slip, especially at the bottom of a page.

Cover the machine every night. The dampness of night air injures the delicate mechanism; and dust settling on a machine clogs it. A typewriter is a valuable piece of property.

Ordinary Typewriter Size. A 12-inch-gauge typewriter is the most practical size for ordinary purposes. Letter-size paper may be inserted sidewise in this style of machine; and fairly long envelopes may be addressed on it.

Typewriter Type. The two most popular sizes and styles are:

Elite (small) (pron. ā-lēt′) Pica (large) (pron. pī′kȧ)

Specialized sizes and styles may be had on all standard makes of typewriters, in the following general classifications:

Microtype ⎫ **very small,** for use where space saving is desired, as in
Bank type ⎪ statistical work, and on stencils. A saving of from one-
Miniature ⎬ half to one-fourth of the ordinary amount of space and
Gothic ⎭ paper used may be effected by these small types.

Primer Amplitype ⎱ **very large,** for primary schools; photo-offset;
Bulletin Magnatype ⎰ show cards; tags; labels; and speech writing.

Video or Sight Saver—for use by speakers and script writers.

Medium Roman—for legal documents (a **tall,** compact type)

Boldface ⎰ **very black,** for distance reading, or for photographing.
Book type ⎱

Gothic—**all caps,** resembles printing; large, small, or condensed sizes, for billing, labeling, card systems, etc. Often combined with

Pinpoint—an **indenting** type for check-protection writing.

Check Validation—for **magnetic-ink** sorting.

Policy Print—matches the **chain printer** used by insurance companies.

Multilith—for filling in addresses, etc., on multilithed material.

Italic—resembles *italics.*

Executive Art Gothic Oxford Royal ⎱ distinctive types
Diplomat Artisan Courier Prestige ⎰ for correspondence.

Script Spencerian Corinthian—like handwriting, for personal use.

Old English—for printing on certificates, diplomas, and the like.

Foreign languages—Type can be furnished for almost any language.

Technical—Special keyboards are available for various kinds of work: mathematical, scientific, chemical, engineering, weather, medical, dental, optical, library, educational, radio, legal abstract and title, railroad tariff, shipping, billing, accounting, music, cartoon, and phonetic (for pronunciations).

Fractions—various styles, including "split line," italic, and diagonal.

Numerals—various styles, including rounded, italic, and backhand.

◇◇◇◇◇◇◇◇

CORRECTIONS AND ERASURES

Typographical Errors. Train the mind and hands to avoid these most frequent typographical errors·

Beginning to write without indenting paragraph.
Double-spacing when single-spacing should be used, or vice versa.
Leaving out a line.
Copying a line or paragraph twice.
Repeating a word, or leaving one out.
Repeating a word at the top of the second page.
Misspelling a word or name throughout a composition, because of not having taken the trouble to look it up at first.
Confusing words that sound alike, such as "cite" for "site."
Copying from an old manuscript and not changing names, singulars and plurals, dates, etc., to conform to a new setup.
Writing old month or old year, when date has changed.
Punctuating hurriedly and incorrectly, and having to erase.
Beginning a tabulation too far to the right, and not having enough room to complete the tabulation.
Writing too near the bottom of a page.

And these annoying mistakes that show up only after the copy is out of the machine:

Carbons in backward.
Not enough carbons—one carbon paper having been overlooked.
Carbon corner folded over.
Under pages having gone around roller and printed twice.
Eraser protection slips having been left in, with blank spaces as a result.

Make a **mechanical habit** of guarding against the above errors.

Question constructions **before** writing them, instead of **afterward.**

A few minutes extra time used in **planning and careful typing** on a page will save time and effort wasted in correcting or rewriting.

If the **spelling** of a word is doubtful, look it up **before** typing it.

Decide upon the **punctuation before** putting it in, **not afterward.**

Read **shorthand** notes a line in advance, and be sure of the meaning before writing anything down. Wrong words mean costly time-loss.

Corrections. There are several ways to make corrections ∼

Correcting Originals in the Typewriter. Coated-paper tabs or **opaquing-film tabs** are useful—quick and efficient. They are available in several colors, to match letterheads. CAUTION: Always select a clean, unused spot on a tab for striking a key. If struck too near a used place, some part of the error will not be removed. When **unused portions of a tab** are near the center, trim the edges of the tab so as to make the center accessible.

Liquid "**correction fluid,**" in colors, is also efficient for removing—by dotting not brushing—the outlines of errors; but this process is slightly slower than the tabs . . . it must dry (in a few seconds) before being typed over; and it must be thinned (when it no longer splashes in the bottle) with a chemical thinner or water, according to its base. A **plexiglas "Tilter"** is available to hold the bottle at an angle for easy access.

Correcting Carbon Copies in the Typewriter. Special correction tabs are available for removing errors on **carbon copies**; but the disadvantage is that their chalky residue often comes off on the carbon paper or film carbon.

Correction fluid works efficiently on carbon copies and does not flake off.

If a single letter is misstruck, it is necessary, usually, to correct the original only—unless copies are to be sent to outsiders. But if several letters are twisted, or a whole word struck over, it is necessary to correct every carbon copy; otherwise, letters will be piled on top of each other until the word is illegible.

If a figure is misstruck, it must be corrected on the original and every carbon copy. A struck-over figure cannot be deciphered, and may cause a serious mistake later by being misinterpreted.

Correcting carbon copies near the bottom of a page is difficult, whether the pack is rolled forward or backward—the copies will slip and lose alinement. To avoid this, make a **slight, erasable pencil mark** on the margin of the original, in line with the error, as a reminder to put the correction in the carbon copies after the pack is removed from the machine.

A **pencil eraser** often works well on carbons—followed, if necessary, by the ink eraser. In such erasing in the machine, protect the carbons with a curved metal erasing guard inserted immediately behind the original copy and on top of the carbon paper or film carbon. This prevents smudging and prolongs the life of the carbons. Move the guard along, always immediately behind each copy and on top of the next carbon. Such a guard is handy, and it is clean—and there is no danger of leaving it in the papers and writing over it as there is with bits of paper.

If using a **pencil, ink, glass fiber, or electric eraser,** always move the carriage over and whisk or blow the eraser refuse away, so it will not fall into parts of the machine.

Self-correcting electric typewriters have erasing devices built in.

"Lift-off" tabs are available for use with **correctable film ribbons**.

Erasable bond and onionskin paper—correctable with just a pencil eraser—is useful in some work.

Correcting Originals and Carbons out of the Typewriter. **Correction fluid** is efficient; but this method requires reinsertion in the machine to type corrections.

Another efficient and quicker way is to use **"Tabtype"** transfer letters, figures, and punctuation marks. Simply position the correct "Tabtype" character over the error, rub rather hard with a blunt pencil, and the error is replaced neatly with the correct character, without reinsertion in the machine.

In the absence of either of the above materials, an error may be removed by positioning over the error a small, unused place along the edge of a coated-paper tab, and rubbing with a blunt pencil.

A pencil eraser works well on carbon copies, often leaving enough of a struck-over letter's correct impression (which can be touched up with a sharp-pointed, hard pencil) so that reinsertion in the typewriter is unnecessary.

Pencil-ink erasing is often done on originals out of the machine, with the pencil eraser being used first to absorb as much ink as possible—to avoid smearing—before the ink eraser is employed. A metal eraser shield, with many perforations, should be used to protect other letters or words.

Clean erasers by rubbing them on **cardboard, emery board,** or **fine sandpaper.**

To **reposition a paper in the typewriter** for inserting corrections, switch the ribbon control to white (stencil) and strike over a period. The faint impression will tell if adjustment is necessary.

Soiled margins and **large surfaces** may be cleaned with **"Artgum";** but it should be used with care. Flick off, with a cleansing tissue, all refuse on each page, lest fragments scatter through other pages and be difficult to remove.

Photocopies may be corrected with a special opaquing fluid, without smearing.

Copy to Be Printed. Few erasures are necessary—only misstruck letters and figures. A whole word may be X'd out, and the correct word written after it—or above it if inserted later. And a sentence or paragraph may be rewritten, cut out, and pasted over the original. The printer does not mind interlineations and patching, if the copy is **perfectly clear.** This saves a writer's time and helps to "meet the deadline." (See also p. 438.)

Corrections. Before putting in any corrections, proofread a **carbon copy** of the entire letter or manuscript, noting errors with a light pencil check at the side. A page might require rewriting, and any erasures or corrections made thereon would be useless.

When putting in corrections on originals and carbon copies, do not erase and correct one copy at a time. Erase all copies, and then insert them, with carbons, in the machine and put in the corrections at one time. This can be done easily if the papers were properly alined when first written.

If copy is returned with pencil corrections thereon (they should never be in ink), do not erase the corrections until they have been typed into at least one copy of the manuscript. If they are erased first they may be forgotten.

Never put corrections in haphazardly. No one may see the letter or manuscript again before it is sent out, but the receiver will see and judge it. Then too, a letter may be returned with a notation on it, and the employer can see the condition in which it was sent out.

Repositioning. Aline an "i" or "l" with a typewriter scale mark.

Inserting Letters. To add a letter at the end of a word (on a "manual"), depress the backspacer halfway, hold, and type the letter. On an "electric" without a half-space key, move the carriage by hand.

To insert a **one-letter-longer word** in an erased space, as "which" for "what," stop the carriage where the first letter had been. Space once; then hold the backspacer all the way down and type the first letter. For each succeeding letter, space twice, hold down the backspacer and type the letter.

To insert a **one-letter-shorter word** in an erased space, follow the above method, but space **twice,** instead of once, the first time.

To crowd a **two-letter-longer word** in an erased space (if several letters are "thin," as l), position the carriage as above. Depress the backspacer halfway, hold to strike each letter, and space once between.

To Darken Carbon Corrections. After erasing, set the ribbon control at white (stencil). Type over the correction. Switch the ribbon control to black and retype, which makes both original and carbon the right shade.

Corrections in Bound Copies. Typewritten pages that are bound across the top may be reinserted in the typewriter for corrections. Run a blank piece of paper into the machine as a guide. As soon as it shows about an inch margin in front, insert the **bottom of the typewritten page** behind it, and turn the roller backward, bringing the typewriting to the desired line.

Binding Copies. Bind the carbon copies first so that the original may have the benefit of the experience gained in putting the carbons together. Many things can go wrong in binding, such as holes being punched on the wrong side of the paper, improper spacing of holes, pages omitted, illustrations bound on the wrong side, etc.

Carbon Copies

Various designations of carbon copies are:

Distribution or Information copies (white)—for distribution or sending to interested persons or offices.

Courtesy copy (white)—to accompany the original letter. (Used in intracompany and government work.)

File copy (yellow)—for the files.

Reading copy (blue)—for the "daily" file or folder. (For members of the organization to read, or for quick reference. See p. 452.)

Follow-up copy (pink)—for the follow-up file or folder. (This copy is destroyed after the matter has been attended to. See p. 451.)

Billing copy (green)—for checking telegraph bill; then destroyed.

Conformed copy—corrected, filled in with dates, signatures, etc., to conform with the original.

Number of Carbon Copies. Check the number of carbon copies to be made before starting **each piece of work.** Failure to do this results, time and again, in insufficient copies. If any doubt exists regarding the number of copies, check with the person for whom the work is being done; or in his absence make one or two copies more than the number that seems logically necessary. It is not good practice, however, always to make more copies than are needed, unless it is on long or difficult jobs. Unnecessary copies waste time and material, and fill up the files.

Companies and organizations usually have regulations about the number of copies ordinarily to be made. But the chance for error lies in the special, extra copies of certain papers that are often needed.

Copies for Distribution. When making carbon copies for distribution to a number of persons, list the names, one below the other, at the top of the first page. This list is not only valuable for the files, but also valuable in that each person receiving a copy may know who else received copies.

Check each person's name on his copy.

Notations on Carbon Copies. (For "blind copy," etc., see p. 299.)

Carbon Copies to Be Mailed Out. Ordinary carbon copies being mailed to second and third persons are made on regular copy paper and do not usually bear original signatures. After the original has been signed, the signature is typed on the carbons, and, before it, "/S/" or "/s/"—"(s)" is used in newspapers—meaning "signed."

Special carbon copies (as of legal papers) should be made on paper similar to the original, and should bear original signatures. (See also Legal Papers, p. 476.)

Method of Handing in Contracts, Reports, etc. (Clipping Carbon Copies to Original). When preparing a long manuscript with several carbon copies, clip the original of each page and its carbon copies together upon removal from the machine. When the work is completed the manuscript may be handed in with the pages thus clipped together, in a manila folder bearing the title of the manuscript.

It is comparatively easy to read a manuscript in this form, and it makes the matter of correcting, rewriting, and destroying pages a very simple job.

If a page is to be rewritten, dispose of all the carbons of that page before starting to retype it, so that the old carbon copies will not be on the desk to get mixed with the new.

Assembling Pages ("Collating"). In assembling sets of originals and carbon copies, lay out the last page of the manuscript first—so as to keep the copies face-up and check the page numbers for error. (If page one is laid out first, all pages must be, blindly, face-down.)

To collect a large number of sets—if a mechanical "collator" or desk "gathering rack" is not at hand—place the piles of pages on a table so that by walking around it with a "gathering box" (one end and one side cut out) you may pick up, in order, the sheets for each set.

Carbons and Papers. To make fast progress on a long piece of work that entails a number of carbon copies:

> Clear the desk of all papers but the job on hand. Too many papers about are confusing.
>
> Place the different kinds of paper to be used out on the desk, so there will be no constant pulling out of drawers to get new papers.
>
> Count the number of sheets of carbon paper to be used, and do not have extra carbon paper loose on the desk—it soils other papers.
>
> Count the number of white sheets to be used each time, before inserting the carbons. This will prevent the possibility of two carbon papers' sticking together, and of certain pages' being "one carbon short" in the final assembly.
>
> Keep the carbon paper face up to prevent its smudging the desk, unless the carbon is curling from weather conditions. On these days, keep it face down on a clean sheet of paper or in a folder.

Even Edges. Tap the top and left edges of each pack of pages until absolutely even before insertion into the machine; then after insertion always restraighten the papers by use of the paper release. Pages that have been thus evened may be reinserted later, and corrections will fall in exactly the same place on every sheet.

To guide an assembled pack into the machine evenly—if difficulty is experienced—fit the top into a fold of paper or a large envelope. Drop the fold of paper into the machine first; then fit the edge of the pack down into it; release the paper feed and push the pack until well under the roller; then engage the paper feed.

If the pages are still slightly uneven after removal of the guide, use the paper release to straighten, or pull, them together.

Backing Sheet. To produce clear copies, it is often necessary to use a backing sheet behind the last copy. This sheet is usually a piece of heavy paper, kept solely for this purpose (never typed upon). Commercial backing sheets are useful also for certain kinds of work.

429

CARBON FILM AND CARBON PAPER

For producing carbon copies, there are two types of carbon ∿

Film Carbon. This type "prints" impressions in liquid ink, thus producing permanent carbon copies that are sharp, clear, and even, and can serve as originals for photocopies if necessary.

Film carbon is produced by suspending liquid ink, in thousands of tiny cells, on a film surface. When the typebar strikes the film, cells are squeezed and the ink released. Instantly, as the typebar leaves the paper, ink from other cells flows into the empty cells to replace the used-up ink; and the whole area is again uniformly inked.

Film carbon should be used on **electric typewriters** (to absorb the heavier strokes). And some refined film carbon produces excellent copies on manual machines as well.

Film carbon comes in only **one weight; one finish; and one color, black.** It does not smudge, wrinkle, pinhole, tear, or curl from weather conditions . . . and it wears down uniformly.

Carbon Paper. This type is suitable for use on **manual typewriters,** some of it being coated with the same ink as film carbon, which makes it self-renewing and long-lasting, while costing less.

Carbon paper is available in **one finish, hard; one color, black; and two weights, heavy and medium or light.** (Colored carbon paper must be specially ordered.) Heavy carbon paper should be used for making one to four copies; medium weight, for five to ten copies.

Carbon paper is initially much cheaper than film carbon; but the latter wears longer, thus tending to equalize cost.

Red Carbon (specially ordered). To imprint occasional red figures or letters without changing ribbon or carbons, insert a small piece of red carbon behind the ribbon (if all black), and a piece behind each carbon. After typing the red characters, be sure to remove all red pieces.

If a large part of the page is to be in red, use a red-and-black ribbon (if available); or whole sheets of red carbon paper, and fill in the red parts after the other typing is finished. The pages must be in perfect alinement at insertion in order to have the red parts fall into position.

Pencil Carbon. This type of carbon paper may be used for making pencil copies or tracings. But some film carbons work equally well.

Pencil carbon, usually blue, is sold by the box of 100 sheets.

Care of Carbon Paper. Carbon paper is expensive and deteriorates rapidly. Keep it in its original folders in the desk to prevent waste.

Heat injures carbon. Never put it in sunlight or near a heater.

Do not be reluctant to discard worn-out carbons, especially if typing figures. It is false thrift to produce illegible copies.

Do not permit an unsightly bunch of old carbons to accumulate on or in the desk. Discard them.

∾

430

Copying

Write the word **"(COPY)"** (if it is not printed on the copy paper) at the top of the first page of every manuscript copied. This identifies it immediately as a copy and guards against later confusion with the original.

In making a copy of a copy write **"(COPY OF A COPY)"** as the heading.

In copying a letterhead **always copy the address**; even if the company is well known, the address may not be known to the person using the copy.

Always write "/S/" or "/s/" (meaning "signed") before a signature when copying it, to show beyond question that the original was signed, and that the name was not merely typed on.

Write "(Unsigned)" if no signature appears on the original of a paper that should normally be signed.

Always copy initials—they may give a different meaning to a letter; for instance, if the letter has been dictated by someone other than the signer.

If a number of persons are to receive copies of the copy being made, write the list of names at the top of the first page, and opposite the list write the date the copies are made or are to be distributed. Check each person's name on his copy. It is sometimes necessary to note the disposition of the original, as shown in the following outline:

(Original in N.Y. Office)
July 18, 19..—Copies to R VL   :
                            Lee✓   :
                            Hunt   :
                            Matthews :

- -

(COPY OF A COPY)

LETTERHEAD (including address)

Date

Full address
Salutation:

        (Copy everything just as it is written, unless it is an unmistakable typographical error.)

Complimentary close,
/S/............

Initials
Notations

431

Copying Guide. Always use a copying guide in the form of a ruler or a "line-a-time" device. **This is absolutely essential for accurate work.** It is very easy to leave out a line and cause great delay on urgent work.

Extra Copies. Make an extra copy for the files when copying anything of importance, or note on the original the date the copies were made, and the disposition of each copy.

Questions that recur in a business office are "Who got copies of this, and when were they sent?" or "Whose copy is this, and where is the original?"

Noting Errors and Copying Punctuation. If anything is omitted in the original, such as a figure or letter, make a short line beneath a space or insert a caret to note the omission in the copy.

If a letter or figure is obviously wrong, make a line beneath it. Do not, however, underline an entire word—put a pencil question mark after it.

The Latin word "sic," meaning "thus," is often inserted in brackets to indicate that the copy follows the original exactly.

> ...to determine the new building cite [sic]; although it is...
> In the war of 1821 [sic] our merchantmen were...

Copy punctuation exactly as it is written, unless there is obviously a typographical error. In legal papers, copy punctuation exactly as it is written, right or wrong (underlining any mark that is plainly incorrect); a lawsuit can hinge on the punctuation of a contract.

Page-for-Page Copying. When copying legal papers, or papers of unusual importance, about which there is likely to be a discussion, copy "page for page" with the exact page number on each page. Later reference to a certain page number may be made in a telegram, on the telephone, or in court.

Copying From Thin Paper. If copying from thin paper, place a piece of heavy white paper behind the page to bring out the letters.

Quoting Material. (See Quoted Matter, p. 255.)

Copying Wires. (See p. 397.)

Proofreading Copies. Do not neglect proofreading, nor attempt to escape it. It is a most important part of office work.

Proofread every copy carefully with the original. A wrong figure, for instance, may cost a company money or cause it embarrassment.

When two are proofreading, the one who typed the material should hold his own copy. The original copy should be held by the other reader, who might interpret it differently from the way in which it was copied.

Making a Number of Originals. When making a number of originals from a copy, copy carefully each time from the last copy written. When the copying is completed, compare the last copy made with the original; if it is correct, all the intermediate copies can be assumed to be correct.

Copy for the Press

Copy for the press should be prepared as follows:

Paper. Letter-size ($8\frac{1}{2}$ by 11 inches), white, of good quality (not thin, glazed, or rippled). A **16 or 20 lb. bond** is usual for manuscripts.

Copies. In duplicate, or with as many extra copies as will be needed for the author's work. The publisher or printer usually requires but one copy—the **original** (or sometimes an extra copy on 13 lb. paper).

Nothing should be written **on the backs** of any of the pages.

Ribbon. Black, medium-inked and giving a **very clear** impression.

Margins. One inch on each side, and at the top and bottom; a three-inch "sinkage" above the main title; two above chapter titles. The margins should be uniform throughout the manuscript.

Spacing. Double-space all matter to be printed, to allow room for editors' and printers' interlineations. Never crowd anything. Paper is cheaper than printers' time.

(For the spacing of **quotations,** see p. 435.)

Divisions of Composition. In material intended primarily for study or reference, divisions of the subject matter should be clearly and uniformly indicated; that is, chapters, sections, topics, items, etc., should bear uniform headings. (Begin each chapter on a new page.)

In material intended for lighter reading, subdivisions, beyond chapters, are not often indicated.

Headings. The title of the manuscript and all chapter titles should be centered and set in caps. (Do not underline, unless for italics.)

Other subdivisions may be indicated by centered subheads, or by sideheads, or by paragraph ("run-in") heads.

By-Lines. On magazine articles and stories, two spaces below the title write "By" and the author's name or pen name on the same line.

Author's Address. On magazine articles and stories, the author's (or agent's) name and address should be typed above the title in the left corner. If the author is using a pen name, it should appear in the "by-line," and the author's real name (or the agent's name) should be given in the address. No explanation is necessary regarding the difference between the two names.

Number of Words. Indicate the **rounded** word-count on the title page of a magazine article or story. Estimate the number of words by multiplying the average words in a line by lines on a full page by number of pages—allowing for short pages, short paragraphs, and crowded pages.

It is not necessary to indicate the number of words in a book manuscript; the publisher usually makes his own estimate.

Numbering Pages. Number all pages, except the first or title page, in the upper right corner. Magazine articles and stories usually have lines of information and identification on the first page, as

R. L. Stevens　　　　　　　　　　　　　1st N. Am. Serial Rights
506 Sea Terrace　　　　　　　　　　　　about 5,200 words
Monterey, CA 93940
THE VALUE OF GOLD
By George Lane

. . . .

On succeeding pages—because manuscripts are often separated and reassembled at the printer's—type the author's last name and/or an identifying title word before each page number, as "Lane--Gold--2".

Number every manuscript (even a book) with but one set of numbers from the beginning to the end. Do not start a new sequence of numbers for every chapter or for the appendix, addenda, glossary, bibliography, index, etc. The introductory pages ("front matter") may, however, be numbered separately with small (lower-case) Roman numerals.

Added and Canceled Page Numbers. If extra pages are added, add letters to the number, as 12a, 12b, 12c. Make a note to the printer beneath the preceding page number that an inserted page follows, as "Page 12a follows," or "Next 12a."

If a page is canceled, mark the preceding page with both page numbers, its own and that of the canceled page, as 12 & 13; or if several pages are canceled, the preceding page should be marked to cover all the numbers, as 12–20, the following page number being 21.

Italics. Underline material to be set in italics. A printer's interpretation of an underline is *"italicize."* Italics are used (not with quotes, but often instead of them) for differentiation of

Words: *used as words; emphasized; foreign; Latin.*　　　**Legal:** *citation of cases*
Titles: of *books, art, music, (photo)plays, ships, trains, aircraft, publications*

Underlining. If it is desired that underlinings show as underlinings, mark in red in the margin opposite: "Underscore as shown."

Boldface. If a heavy black type is desired instead of italics or underlining, draw a wavy line close beneath the material to be so set.

Spelling, Capitalization, Punctuation. All must be uniform throughout. Simplified or modernized forms of spelling are not generally used in printing—except in advertisements. Never divide words at line ends lest they be mistaken for hyphened words.

Abbreviations. Do not use "abbrevs" unless they are to be printed as written; in which case, mark the copy: "Follow abbreviations."

Uniformity. To avoid extra charges for "author's corrections" in the proofs, make the final typewritten copy as consistent as possible in the matter of spelling, hyphening, the use of figures or spelled-out numbers, abbreviations, etc. Lastly, proofread it with great care.

Paragraphing. Copy should be paragraphed exactly as desired in the printed form. Paragraphs should be uniformly indented five typewriter spaces only. (Avoid **too many short,** or **long,** paragraphs.)

434

To indicate a new paragraph where none has been shown in the typing, use the sign ¶. If material typed with paragraph indention is to be run in with the preceding paragraph, write "No ¶" on the margin and draw a line to indicate the connection. (See p. 443.)

Each chapter or part should begin on a new page.

Number of Lines on a Page. For estimating, the printer prefers the same number of lines on every page—about 27 typewritten lines.

End of Copy. Indicate the end of all copy, either by the printer's mark (###) or preferably by writing and encircling "---End---".

Quotations. May be indented and single-spaced or double-spaced. If they are double-spaced they may be marked with a distinctive marginal line. Quotation marks may or may not be used if a quotation is to be set apart, indented, and in smaller, "reduced," type. But if the quotation is not to be set thus, quotation marks should always be used.

When making quotations, follow the original copy exactly in the matter of spelling, punctuation, etc. When quoting verse use the exact form, including indention, of the printed copy.

In quoting copyrighted work it is necessary to obtain permission in writing from, and to give a credit line or permission line as approved by, the copyright holder.

Credit Lines. Put only as much information into a credit line as is necessary for the reader's purpose, or as is requested by the copyright holder. The usual forms are:

—Emerson.   OR: --Emerson, "Behavior."
—Emerson, "Behavior," *Masterpieces of American Literature*, p. 289.
    Houghton Mifflin Company, Boston, 1891.
—Matthew 6:5–15   OR: —Matt. vii:14
    (Note colon between chapter and verse.)
—JESPERSEN, *Essentials of English Grammar*, p. 331.

With such a credit line as the last, a permission line might appear either as a footnote on the same page or with another reference to the book in the same publication, as

Excerpt reprinted by permission from Henry Holt and Company, New York.

Bibliographic References. The style of reference to books, and articles in periodicals and books, varies greatly with different publications and among different publishers. Many publishers and scientific and technical societies issue their own recommendations. If a manuscript is intended for a special publication, it is well for the author to ascertain that publication's practice and to secure, if available, a list of recommended abbreviations—if abbreviations are to be used.

One form of complete reference frequently adopted in bibliographies is as follows. (For further arrangements, see p. 420*i*.)

NAME OF AUTHOR. *Title of Book and Subtitle*, edition, volume, chapter, page. Publisher, city, copyright year. [total pages, price.] (In printing, the author's name is often in caps and small caps, or in boldface; the book title is italicized; and subdivisions quoted.)

435

For instance—

> MAETERLINCK. *The Life of the Bee.* Dodd, Mead and Company, New
> York, 1926.
> ROE, FREDERICK WILLIAM, and GEORGE ROY ELLIOTT, eds. "Selections
> From Ruskin," *English Prose*, p. 327. Longmans, Green and
> Co., New York, 1913. (showing manner of indicating a part)
> Urquhart, L. C., and C. E. O'Rourke. *Steel Structures: Stresses in
> Simple Structures*, 2nd ed. McGraw-Hill Book Company, Inc.,
> New York, 1932. (showing manner of indicating a subtitle)
> —— *Design of Concrete Structures*, 4th ed., McGraw-Hill Book
> Company, Inc., New York, 1940. 564 pp., illus. $5.00. (showing
> manner of indicating a second work by the same author or authors)
> University of Chicago Press. *A Manual of Style*, 12th ed. Chicago,
> 1969. (showing manner of listing a book with corporate author)

Publishers' names are usually abbreviated in extensive bibliographies; but in occasional bibliographic references the names are given as in the publications, or as the publishers now write their names.

For a magazine or newspaper article, the information is in this order:

> NAME OF AUTHOR. "Title of Article," *Periodical*, volume, month, year,
> page. (In printing, the author's name is often set in caps and small
> caps; the title of the article is quoted; and the periodical is italicized.)

For instance –

> CRAVEN, THOMAS. "American Men of Art," *Scribner's*, Vol. 92, November 1932, pp. 262–67.
> CHAMBERLAIN, G. C. Intensive Steel Testing, *Am. Jour. Sci.*, 3d ser.,
> Vol. 45 (1893), 171–200.

The volume, page number, and date are often abbreviated thus:

> 92:262-7 N '32   45:171-200 (1893)

In footnotes, a second reference to a cited work is made by abbreviation. (A newer form is: author's surname, [short title], page number.)

> *Ibid.*, p. 529   (L. ibidem, in the same place [in the work just above])
> Scott, *op.cit.*, p. 250   (L. opere citato, in the work cited [not just above])
> *Loc.cit.*   (L. loco citato, in the place cited [the exact passage just cited])
> *Idem* or *Id.*   (L. the same [the author just cited rather than his book])
> *Supra* (above); *Infra* (below); *Circa* (about); *Passim* (here and there)

Page and Illustration References. The page numbers of cross references may be left blank in the manuscript, to be filled in later in the page proofs. But numbers referring to illustrations should be filled in in the manuscript.

Footnotes. Avoid footnotes as much as possible—they are hindrances to smooth reading. Often it is better to place explanatory matter in parentheses in the text than to use footnotes. If footnotes are necessary, they may be typed (double space) in the text immediately after the matter to which they refer. (See also pp. 273 and 420k.)

> ...in a recent book 1/   [in print, this figure will be a superior[1]]

> 1/ (Between two lines, give the footnote. Note that an author's name is **not inverted** in a footnote as it is in an alphabetized bibliography.)

Or footnotes may be typed at the foot of the page (below a $1\frac{1}{4}''$ "cutoff dash"), or written all on one page, with proper reference marks in the text. The printer will place each footnote on the correct page.

If an **added footnote** is too long to be written at the foot of the page, it may be typed on a separate page, with an appropriate note to the printer at the bottom of its page, as "Footnote on p. 12a."

Tables or Tabulations. These should be written on separate pages, unless they are very short, because tabulated matter is usually set in smaller type and is therefore handled separately by the printer. Double-space all but very short tables, and indicate the desired alinement. Never put part of a short table on one page and part on another. A long table, however, may require several pages, or may be on one large sheet folded to letter size. Footnotes should be written below the table.

If the tables do not bear page numbers, they should be numbered in a separate series, and the place for insertion of each table should be indicated both on the table and in the manuscript.

Illustrations. Photographs, drawings, charts, etc., should be submitted with the manuscript, but not inserted in it. They should be separated so that they may be sent to the engraver at the same time that the manuscript is sent to the printer. They should be properly titled on the back (very lightly) or at the bottom (often on a slip pasted to the bottom), and numbered (in separate series) consecutively from the beginning of the manuscript to the end.

The place for each illustration may be indicated in the manuscript, or better, on the galley proofs. A list of the numbers, titles, and manuscript page numbers of all illustrations is necessary (in duplicate).

Drawings, Charts, etc. Should be made with **india ink** on white backgrounds. However, since the size of drawing and lettering suitable for reduction is not easily determined, except by experts, it is often better to submit pencil sketches, from which the engraver may make finished drawings. In case the author is required to make finished drawings, he should consult the publisher for specifications before entering upon the work.

Graphs. In plotting graphs, if the lines are not to show in the reproduction, use **blue** cross-section paper, and specify that the lines are not to show. (Blue ordinarily photographs white, but blue lines can be made to show if necessary.) If the lines are to show, use **green or red** cross-section paper. (These colors photograph black. Light green lines can be taken out, but it is rather a difficult process.)

Glossy Prints of Photographs. Are necessary for clear reproduction. Photostats and dull-finished pictures do not reproduce satisfactorily. Unmounted photographs should not be pasted on sheets of paper; they should be left unmounted. Photographs will not be returned unless a special request is made.

Never use a metal clip on a photograph. It will leave a mark.

Never place numbers, letters, or other marks on the face of photographs or wash drawings. If numbers or letters are necessary, they should be indicated lightly in pencil at the proper point on the backs of

437

unmounted prints. This can be done by holding the print against a window facing a strong light. On mounted photographs, a flyleaf of thin paper pasted on the back of the photograph, at the top, and folded over the face of the photograph can be used for the numbers or letters.

Inserts. To keep the copy uniform, type, tape, or paste (but **do not staple**) all inserts on manuscript paper ($8\frac{1}{2}$x11"). Do not pin or clip an insert as a **flyer** on any page. And do not write or paste **on the back** of any page. Note where the insert is to go: by a caret in the copy; on the margin, as "Insert A on p. 25a"; and above the insert, as "Insert A for p. 25." Encircle both notations in **red** pencil or ink.

If both sides of a printed insert are to be copied, tape the insert along the left edge, and write **"over"** at the bottom of the first page.

Corrections in Manuscript. All corrections must be absolutely clear. No written-over words or struck-over figures are permitted. A short insertion may be interlined (typed or in ink) **above** a caret, or written **horizontally** on the margin. Short typewritten corrections may be cut and pasted or taped **flat** in the manuscript, but the page sizes should not be lengthened thereby; rather, the inserts should be written on separate pages numbered as described above.

If a page bears numerous corrections, making the copy difficult to follow, it should be retyped. (See Patching Copy for Printer, p. 426.)

Verification. All copy sent to a printer should be verified and **final.** Every correction thereafter, even a comma, costs money. Verify all figures, and the spelling, marking, and use of all proper names, foreign words, technical terms, quotations, references, etc. **The printer is not responsible for the authenticity of any part of the copy,** nor is he supposed to correct the spelling or to punctuate the copy.

Instructions to the Printer. Should be written in red ink, or a color different from that used in making corrections; and each instruction should be headed "Ptr:". All numbers, letters, and notes for the printer's guidance should be **encircled in red** to differentiate them.

Style of Printing. If a certain style of printing is desired, attempt to furnish a sample of similar printing as a guide for the printer. If a particular layout is desired, a plan of the arrangement should accompany the manuscript.

If dealing directly with a printer, **always obtain an estimate of the cost of printing.** Prices vary greatly when different specifications are made.

Copyrighting. This is a simple procedure, and an author may—but usually the publisher does—attend to the details of copyrighting.

A printer sometimes does this for a customer, but only upon request.

Indexing. A publisher usually suggests the style of index to be followed; but in the absence of any preferences, select from similar published works the most satisfactory index and use it as a guide in arranging items.

Indexes are made from page proofs, but much preliminary work can be done from the manuscript. To make an index: First underline on one copy of the work all words or titles to be indexed—using a blue line under main headings and a red line under subheads. Then list each subject on a 3x5″ card, in the **upper left corner.** If not working from page proofs, keep the cards in manuscript order until the page numbers can be filled in in ink. Then arrange the cards alphabetically, and copy as a list on regular paper, double-spaced, one column to a page.

Check the completed index against the page proofs.

Index by **key words;** and avoid **prepositions** before subentries. Also avoid **variant forms** of one word (as singular and plural, and the -ing form). Group all such items under one heading if possible.

Do not give **numerous page references** for a single entry.

NOT: Letter writing, 5, 12, 18, 26, 45, 87, 94, 106, 125, 187, 210, 251

Such a reference often forces the reader to look up every page before finding what he wants. There should be some indication of what phase of the subject is treated on every page; or at least the page numbers for each part of the subject should be grouped after a proper subhead.

Printed Office Forms. In making up a blank form to be printed, keep it as simple as possible. Too much information called for in a form is as confusing as too little. Many forms are too complicated; they are never entirely read or filled in.

See that the line spacing corresponds to that on the typewriter, so that spaces may be filled in without adjusting the machine. Leave enough space for the longest possible items under each heading. Cramped space on a form results in illegible entries.

Programs, Announcements, and Invitations. For correct forms for programs, announcements, invitations, etc., consult reliable stationers or printers, who have the latest styles in paper, type, and composition.

Writing a Manuscript. When composing a business manuscript, speech, article, or advertisement, write in a concise, simple, and direct manner—**and state facts.**

A great newspaper office has across its editorial rooms, in large letters, the one word: FACTS.

> "There is no more convincing mark of a cultured speaker or writer than accuracy of statement."
> —House and Harman, *Handbook of Correct English.*

Fiction and Articles. In preparing fiction or articles for submission to publishers, follow the general rules for setup of any copy.

Estimate the number of words and compare with the number of words in similar printed material, so that the manuscript will not be too long. Great length bars consideration in many cases.

Submit the manuscript to a publication that uses similar material. Manuscripts are often returned because the type of material is not suited to the publication. It is well to query the publication by letter beforehand, giving a brief summary of the work.

It is not ethical to send copies of a manuscript to more than one publication at a time. Allow each publisher the privilege of consideration or refusal before submitting the manuscript to another.

439

Prices are fixed by publishers, unless an author is well enough established to set prices on his work. Therefore, do not write "Submitted at the usual rates"—that is understood.

Publication rates and royalties vary with different publications and publishers. An estimate of rates may be found in writers' magazines or magazines that cover the publishing field.

Rights. If an author desires to reserve all rights but the first publication rights to a **story or article,** he may mark in the upper right corner of the title page "First North American Serial Rights," thereby offering only the right of first publication in a **serial** (that is, a **periodical**—magazine or newspaper). All other rights, including **book, condensation, reprint, dramatic, motion picture, radio, television, recording, translation, British** and other **foreign** rights, are then reserved.

If the manuscript of a **book** is being offered, it may be marked "United States Book Rights," and all other rights are then reserved. Details of the various rights sold or retained in connection with a book are included in the contract between the publisher and the author.

Mailing or Sending Copy to Publisher or Printer

1. Send the **original,** not a carbon copy; and send clear, clean copy. Retain, always, a **corrected** carbon copy.
2. Copy may have a **lightweight cover** and be **clipped** together, but **not stapled or bound.** (Printers separate the pages for setting up.)
3. The different **parts or chapters** of a manuscript may be separately fastened with clips or rubber bands for convenience in handling.
4. Send the **complete manuscript,** together with all illustrations, the latter being separated from the manuscript pages. Do not send the manuscript in installments. The index, of course, follows later.
5. Send all manuscripts **flat**—no matter what the number of pages. A flat page is more convenient to read than a page that has been creased in folds; therefore, a flat manuscript has a better psychological effect on the reader. Never send a manuscript rolled. If a large illustration has to be rolled, it should be sent separately in a cardboard tube.
6. Send a **letter of transmittal** (a **"covering letter"**) for each manuscript. The letter should contain a brief summary of material sent, and the name and address of the sender; this for the publisher's or printer's records.
7. Keep a **record** on 3x5″ cards of where and when each manuscript is sent; and if sold, the payment received—for tax purposes.
8. Send large manuscripts in a **cardboard box,** or between **cardboards** bound with twine or rubber bands; write the sender's and receiver's addresses on the cardboard; and wrap in **heavy manila paper** or enclose in a large envelope.
9. Address **unsolicited manuscripts** to the "Editorial Department" of a publisher. Always enclose **return postage** and an **addressed label or envelope.**
10. **Short manuscripts** should be sent as first-class mail (registered if valuable); or as third-class mail, insured.
11. **Large manuscripts** should be sent by parcel post at the "Special Rate," insured. (See p. 350.)
12. **Proofs** being returned to the publisher or printer should be sent by **airmail, special delivery** (if urgent), insured, and marked PROOFS. (Proofs and manuscript may be sent as third-class mail or parcel post.)

PROOFREADING

The proofreading of a printer's work must be done with the utmost care, to catch misplaced letters, missing punctuation marks, etc. Read every punctuation mark and spell out every unfamiliar word.

Recheck one thing at a time, as (1) punctuation, (2) page numbers.

Corrections in Proof. Ink, not pencil, should be used in marking proof. The color of the ink (often **red**) should be different from that used by the printer's proofreader (usually **green**).

All corrections must be **written horizontally on the margins,** first, to attract attention, and secondly, for clearness.

Do not attempt to make a correction by writing over the print or between the lines. Errors marked in this manner are in danger of being overlooked, and are usually illegible.

Before attempting to use proofreaders' marks, study and become familiar with them. If unfamiliar with them, write out the corrections horizontally on the margin and place a caret (∧) in the copy to indicate where each insertion or change is to be made.

All insertions of more than a line should be typed on separate pages, headed with the galley numbers; or, if there is room, inserts may be written or typed at the foot of the galleys. The inserts should be numbered for each galley; and on the margin of the galley proof should be indicated where each item is to be inserted, as "Insert A attached."

Never cut and paste parts of galleys together, nor cut out any part of the material and paste it elsewhere; **leave the galleys intact.** Indicate transpositions of material by drawing lines around the parts to be moved and making marginal notations, as "tr to Gal. 58," and on Galley 58 draw an arrow to where the material is to be inserted and write opposite it "Insert from Gal. 24."

Most printers and publishers make a charge for "author's corrections" in the proof if the changes exceed a certain percentage of the cost of composition. Alterations are made on a time basis and are much more expensive than original composition. A change, if possible, should be confined to a single line; and adjustment in wording should be made wherever possible to avoid resetting a whole paragraph. The insertion of a single word at the beginning of a paragraph often necessitates the resetting of the entire paragraph—unless another word can be removed.

Changes in the page proofs that involve the re-makeup of pages are especially difficult and accordingly expensive.

Do not return blurred or indistinct markings on proof sheets. It is necessary for the printer to see every mark to make corrections.

Always return the original copy, **unchanged,** with the proofs.

Proofs. Two sets of proofs are usually sent to the author:

> **galley proofs**—the first proofs, in long strips, taken from the type on the galleys (long steel trays that hold the set type).
> **page proofs**—the second proofs, after the type has been made up into pages.
> **final or plate proofs**—made after the plates (solid-metal-page impressions) have been cast (not usually submitted to the author).

441

PROOFREADERS' MARKS

Punctuation	Write on Margin (in red ink)	Mark in Copy (in red ink)
Comma	,/ or ⋀	⋀
Semicolon	;/	⋀
Colon	:/ or ⊙	⋀
Period	⊙	⋀
Question mark	(Set) ?/	⋀
Exclamation point	!/	⋀
Hyphen	=/	⋀
Apostrophe	✌	✓
Quotation marks	✌ / ✌	✓ ✓
Parentheses	(/ or (/) or)/	⋀ ⋀
Brackets	[/ or [/] or]/	⋀ ⋀
Brace	*brace*	{ draw brace in position
Underscore	*underscore*	‾‾‾ beneath the words
Dash—long (1-em* or 2-em, etc.)	$\frac{1}{m}$	⋀
Dash—short (en dash)	$\frac{1}{en}$ or $\frac{1}{n}$	⋀
Asterisk	✾	✓
Footnote or other indicators: superior figures or letters (super-scripts), as mathematical indices	✌ or ✎	✓
Chemical indices, inferior figures (sub-scripts) in mathematics, etc.	⋀ or ⋀̸	⋀
Mathematical symbols	*plus* or *minus*, etc.	..... beneath symbols
Fractions: "case" or "nut" (⅓); "spe-cial" or "piece" (½); "slant" or "shil-ling" (1/2); "bar" or "split" (½)	*case, piece,* or *slant*	..... beneath fractions
Leaders (to guide the eye)	*leaders*	..... or ‗‗‗ where needed
Rule (hairline, double, dotted, etc.)	*Rule as shown*	⊤ rule the copy as desired
Delete a rule or brace, etc.	ϑ	–/–/– through rule or brace, etc.
End of copy		### at the end of every piece of copy. (See also p. 435)

NOTE: A diagonal line ("slant"), caret, or circle is used with a punctuation mark on the margin to make the mark stand out. The slant is also used to separate corrections. Two slants indicate that the same correction occurs twice in the same line.

Corrections on the margin should be small but very clear (in round handwriting), made on the nearer margin in the order in which they are to be inserted, and exactly in line with the parts to be corrected.

* "Em" is derived from the letter m, the square of the body of which was used as a unit of measurement. "En" is derived from n, and is half the width of an em.

Wording and Lettering	Write on Margin (in red ink)	Mark in Copy (in red ink)
Let it stand*	*stet*	..... beneath words to be kept
Delete—take out	ϑ	—— or / through stricken material
Discard or strike out (large section)	*kill*	⊠ around and through material
Transpose	*tr*	~ around letters, words, phrases or sentences, to be transposed
		↱ to where paragraph is to be moved
Take out letter, etc., and close space	ϑ͡	/ through deleted letter or word
Ligature (as æ)	*lig*	⌢ over letters run together
Spell out—if in figures or abbreviated	*spell* or *sp*	○ around figures or abbrevs.
Figures—if spelled out	*fig*	○ around words to be in figures
Letterspace, or hair-space between letters	*hr #* or *thin #*	//// between letters to be spaced
Words missing, see copy	*Out, see copy*	⋀ where words are missing
Letter omitted	(Write letter in blue ink)	⋀ where letter belongs
Word omitted	(Write word in blue ink)	⋀ where word belongs
Unusual word, or use, is correct	*OK*	..... beneath questionable word
Reset words in order indicated	*set 1, 2, 3*	①②③Place small ringed numbers above words in order desired
Material on reverse of printed page	*over*	(Written in lower right corner)
Patch (for revision on a page)		☐ (Blue pencil line around size, or edge, of patch)
Note to printer from author	*Ptr:*	(Encircle note in red)
Query from printer to author†	*Au. Qy* or (?)	—or ○under or around matter
Author's approval of proof	*OK* or *OK with 1 change*, etc.	(In lower corner of page—on both galley and page proofs)

* If a correction is to be disregarded, it should not be erased, but a line should be drawn through it and "stet" written beside it on the margin, with dots placed beneath words that are to remain "as is."

† If the copy is right, the author should run a line through the "Qy" or question mark, but not erase it, and write and encircle "OK as set"; or if not right, "OK to change."

PROOFREADERS' MARKS

Spacing	Write on Margin (in red ink)	Mark in Copy (in red ink)
Insert space	#	∧ or >
Less space	*less* # or √ or ‿	√
More space	*more* # or ∧	∧
Equalize spacing	*eq* # or √ ∧	∧ √ ∧ √
Close up space	⌒	⌒
Spread words out	*space out*	∧ ∧ ∧ ∧ ⌐
Aline certain parts	ǀ	ǀ beside parts to be alined
Straighten alinement	= or ‖	= above and below or ‖ at end of lines to be straightened
Paragraph	¶	¶ or ∧
No paragraph	*No* ¶ or *run in*	⸜ line from end of one paragraph to beginning of next
Insert lead (space between lines)	*ld* or #	> where more space is to be between lines
Delete lead (space)	⌢# or ϑ *ld* or ϑ #	> where no space is to be between lines
Lead shows—push it down ("Lead" used for spacing often makes a blotch. Disregard in galley proof)	⊥	(beside the imprint being made by the lead
Move to right or left	[or]	[or] before or after word or part
Move up or down	⌐ or ⌊	⌐ or ⌊ over or under material to be raised or lowered
Set in 2 columns, or 3 columns, etc.	*2 col*	(Indicate positions and ends)
Set full measure of page (do not indent)	*fm* or *full meas*	ǀ before full-measure material
Set at margin indicated	[or]	[or] at place where margin is to be
Line end (indicated by "switchback")		⌐ where line should end
Indent one em (for 2 ems, [2], etc.)	□	∧ where indention is to be
Reset type—so material, through respacing, will run a little longer	*run over*	(around material to be reset
Reset—pulling the syllable, word, or line back to the preceding line or page	*run back*	O⸣ around material to be reset
Overrun or turnover (to next line)	□ (if indented)	□ or [2], etc., before overrun line
No indention, set at margin	*flush*	ǀ beside non-indented material
Move (transpose) word or letters	*tr*	⟲ around material to be moved
Center	*ctr*	→ arrow from material to center

Other changes in spacing, or rearrangements in setup, may be indicated by lines and arrows showing desired positions, with instructions written on margins; but no such lines should cross each other.

Kinds of Type	Write on Margin (in red ink)	Mark in Copy (in red ink)
Ordinary type (roman, not italic)	*rom*	..... beneath words to be in roman
Boldface type (heavy and black)	*bf*	⌇⌇⌇ wavy underscore
Lightface (change from bf to rom)	*lf*	..... under words to be in roman
CAPITALS	*caps*	≡ 3 straight underscores
BOLDFACE CAPITALS	*bf caps*	≡ 3 straight underscores and 1 wavy
SMALL CAPITALS	*sc*	= 2 straight underscores
SMALL CAPITALS, boldface (in only a few styles of type)	*bf sc*	= 2 straight underscores and 1 wavy
CAPITALS AND SMALL CAPITALS	*c & sc*	≡ under letters to be in caps, and = under letters in small capitals
Initial Caps (Upper- and Lower-case)	*c & lc* or *u & lc* or *ulc*	= under caps; ⌒ over lc letters
Italics	*ital*	—— 1 straight underscore
Italics, boldface	*bf ital*	⌇⌇⌇ 1 straight underscore, 1 wavy
ITALIC CAPITALS	*caps ital*	≣ 4 straight underscores
ITALIC BOLDFACE CAPITALS	*bf caps ital*	≣ 4 straight, 1 wavy, underscores
Swash Letters (Ornamental) (𝒩, 𝒬, 𝒯)	*swash*	..... under words or letters
Small type;* or type size	*small type* (or size)	ǀ before material to be smaller
Very small type;* or type size	*very small* (or size)	‖ before very small type part
Type sizes (in points)	*10 pt* or *6/7*, etc.	ǀ before material to be so set
Lower-case (reduce from capital to a small letter)	*lc*	/ through letters to be reduced
Wrong font (letter or character of wrong size or style of type)	*wf*	/ through material of **wrong** type
Turn (type upside down)	9	( ) around upside-down type
Pied (jumbled type)	*pied*	O around disarranged type
Broken letter or bad type	×	— under faulty type
Insets, or boxes, etc.	*Inset* or *Box*	□ around material to be so set

* When two sizes of small type are to be used throughout a manuscript, a single opening note may explain them, as "1st small type marked red on the margin, 2d small type marked blue on the margin."

443

TYPE SIZES AND STYLES

Type sizes are measured by "points" and are designated by the number of points in each type body.

FOR TABULATIONS AND EXAMPLES	ORDINARY BOOK SIZES
This is a sample of 5-point type	This is a sample of 9-point type
This is a sample of 5½-point type	This is a sample of 10-point type
This is a sample of 6-point type	This is a sample of 11-point type
This is a sample of 7-point type	This is a sample of 12-point type
This is a sample of 8-point type	

NOTE: A combined size, as "8 on 9" means an 8-point type on a 9-point body, which, when printed from, provides space between the lines. (Sometimes written 8/9.)

FOR HEADINGS AND ADVERTISEMENTS

This is a sample of 14-point type

This is a sample of 18-point type

There are many designs of type, the following being some of the varieties of type faces:

BOOKMAN	Bookman
BODONI	Bodoni
CASLON	Caslon
CHELTENHAM	Cheltenham
CENTURY EXPANDED*	Century Expanded
KENNERLEY	Kennerley
SCRIPT	Script
TYPEWRITER	Typewriter
FRENCH OLD STYLE	French Old Style
GARAMOND	Garamond
FUTURA (sans-serif)†	Futura (sans-serif)
BERNHARD GOTHIC†	Bernhard Gothic
GOTHIC CONDENSED*	Gothic Condensed
GOUDY BOLD	Goudy Bold
GOUDY OPEN	Goudy Open
SCOTCH FACE	Scotch Face
KENNERLEY ITALIC	Kennerley Italic
CENTURY	Century
Tudor Text	Old English	Goudy Text

* "Expanded" type has a wide, "fat" face. "Condensed" type has a tall, "lean" face.
† "Sans-serif" and "Gothic" types have no serifs—short finishing strokes on letters, as on T⊏.

444

STEPS IN PREPARING ART WORK AND COPY FOR THE PRESS

Two basic methods of printing are **letterpress** (**"relief"**) and **photo-offset.** **Letterpress** **"plates"** require six steps in the preparation of art work and copy, each step being a separate process. **Photo-offset** (**"offset"**) bypasses several of these steps—its plates being made by photography directly on metal.

1. **Art work or photography**—done by artist or photographer.
2. **Zinc etching or copper or zinc halftone**—made by a photoengraver.
3. **Composition** (typesetting)—done by a printer.
4. **Electrotype** ⎫ made by an electrotyper.
5. **Matrix** ⎭
6. **Stereotype**—made by a stereotyper.

A **line drawing**—is made in black and white, by an artist, from which a photoengraver makes a

    line cut—which is known as a

    zinc etching (**"zinc"**)—being the drawing transferred to zinc by a photographic process, and then etched out with acid.

A **wash drawing, painting, photograph,** or any other illustration that contains shading and much fine detail is made into a

    copper halftone or zinc halftone (**"halftone"**)—by a photoengraver. The picture is reproduced on copper or zinc by a photographic process through a screen, the fineness of the screen determining the density of the dots which bring out the lights and shadows or half tones of the illustration. Zinc halftones, made with a coarse screen, are used in newspaper work. They are less expensive than copper halftones, but do not wear so long.

If the zinc or halftone is to be used in an advertisement or printed form, the printer sets type around it, and from the type and the zinc or halftone, an

electrotype (**"electro"**)—is made for the newspaper, magazine, or book. A plastic, **wax,** or lead mold is taken from the original; and copper, nickel, or chrome is then electrically deposited in the mold. The hard metal shell, bearing the impression of the original, is backed with heavy type metal, mounted on a wooden block, and is then ready to be printed from.

If the copy is an advertisement that is to run in many newspapers, the electrotyper makes (**"pulls"**) a

matrix (**"mat"**)—from the electro. The mat is a heavy papier-mâché formation which takes and retains the impression of the electro.

From the mat, the newspaper casts a

stereotype (**"stereo"**)—which is made by pouring molten metal into the mat form. The stereo is printed from, but a new **photocomposition "Cold Type"** process bypasses stereotyping and produces a lightweight metal plate by photography.

PRINTING TERMS

Ben Day or **benday**—a process for shading line drawings and making color plates for photoengraving. (Named after the inventor, Benjamin Day.)

bleed edges—When a picture or advertisement runs to the edges of the paper, with no border (so that the ink "bleeds" over), it is said to "run to bleed."

blow up—enlarge, as a picture or photograph. (opposite of **"reduce"**)

boards—stiff cardboards used as the foundation sides of book covers.

caption—the title above (**"legend,"** the title below) an illustration.
colophon—the trade-emblem device or monogram of a publisher.   (kŏl'o-fŏn)
cropping—trimming off (by masking) an illustration to remove unwanted areas.
cut—(from old "woodcut") an engraved block or plate for printing an illustration.
cut dummy—proofs of illustrations (cuts) sent author to correct, title, and number.
deckle edges—untrimmed ragged edges for a handmade effect.   (deckle-edged)
dingbats—type ornaments used as **"separators"** (also called **"jiggers,"** or **"flowers"**).
dummy—a sketched layout of a proposed publication or advertisement, indicating the final appearance: size, binding, paper, and general printing style.
dust cover—the paper jacket for a book.
end papers—the folds of paper that line the inside covers of a book; one half is pasted down, the other half acts as a **flyleaf** (a blank leaf that flies).
folio—a page number; if at the bottom of a page, a **"drop folio."**
format—the form, size, and style of a book.   (pron. fôr'măt; Fr. fôr'má')
headband—the small cloth band covering the glued ends of bound book pages.
headpiece—an ornament or illustration above printed matter (**"tailpiece,"** below).
intaglio—cut or etched in a plate instead of standing out in **relief.**   (ĭn-tăl'yō)
justify—to space out lines of type so all are equal length.
layout—a rough sketch of the proposed arrangement of an advertisement or page.
leaders—a line of dots or dashes to lead the eye, as in tabular matter.
offset—the transfer of a wet-ink impression from one printed surface to another.
patching or mending—cutting and pasting small revisions on offset copy.
pull a proof—to take (make) a proof.
register—to join perfectly, as to superimpose colors in exact position.
running head—a heading or title repeated at the top of each page of a book.
slip-sheets—porous papers slipped between printed pages to prevent smudging.
tear-sheet—a page torn or cut from a magazine, showing an advertisement, etc.

Book Parts

FRONT MATTER—consists, in the following order, of a **half-title** (book title alone); **announcement** or **book card** (list of books by same author); **frontispiece; title page; copyright page; dedication; foreword** and/or **preface***; **acknowledgments; table of contents; list of illustrations** and/or **tables; introduction***; and **epigraph** (an appropriate quotation).

TEXT—main body of the work, which may consist of **parts,** or **sections,** and **chapters.**

END MATTER—may consist of an **appendix; bibliography** (list of reference books); **glossary** or **vocabulary** (list of technical terms with definitions); various other **addenda, as supplements** or **notes;** and finally an **index.**

> * A preface (by the author) tells the purpose of the book and gives acknowledgments.
> A foreword (by someone other than the author) is a note telling about the author and his work.
> An introduction (by the author or editor) tells how to use the book, how it is arranged, etc.

ADVERTISING PIECES

"Free literature" has many names, such as **"mailing pieces," "stuffers," "circulars," "giveaways,"** and **"throwaways."**   Single sheets to be handed or thrown out are **"handbills," "dodgers,"** or **"flyers."**   **"Posters"** and **"bulletins"** are to be tacked up, although the latter may be mailed.

A **"leaflet"** may be a flat sheet, or folded over once; a **"folder,"** two or more times.

"Booklets" are small, bound, paper-covered books; a **"pamphlet"** is a booklet carrying a timely message; a **"brochure"** is an elaborate, illustrated booklet, describing an enterprise; **"catalogues"** may be booklets or books; a **"manual"** is a small handbook for study or training; a **"treatise"** may be a booklet giving a methodical treatment of a subject; and a **"tract"** is a propaganda booklet.

A **"broadside"** or **"broadsheet"** is a very large printed sheet, often folded; and a **"24-sheet"** is a billboard poster formerly composed of 24 sheets (now only 10 or 12 large ones) pasted together to form one immense sign (8'8" x 19'6").

Filing

There are now five systems of filing:

Alphabetic—the primary or foundation system; the most generally used for all types of filing. Names and subjects are simply filed in alphabetic order, either in the same file drawer or in separate drawers.

Geographic—used where location is important, as in sales work. The files are divided alphabetically, first by states (or territories), then each state by cities, then each city by individual names.

Numeric—used in scientific work. Names and subjects are given consecutive or code numbers and filed numerically. An alphabetic card index is necessary to show the number given each name or subject. (This system is difficult to keep up and has been largely replaced by the alphabetic system.)

Dewey Decimal Classification—used in libraries. Books are numbered first by group, for instance, History is 900; then by class under each group, as 910, 920; then by subclass, 911, 912; finally by subdivision, 911.1, 911.12, 911.2.

Group-Name ("Soundex")—used in voluminous name files, as census records. Surnames that sound alike but have variant spellings, as Berke, Birk, Burke, are grouped according to pronunciation, which insures quick finding. Each name is coded numerically after its initial letter.

No two offices file in quite the same manner, although the fundamental principles may be the same. There are variations to be dealt with and understood, and the filing in each office is a study in itself.

In **starting new files,** first make a study of the papers to be filed to determine how they will be **used and called for**—in what groups, under what names. Begin with a very simple system in a few file drawers. Later, as the files grow, subdivisions and changes will become apparent.

CAUTION: Do not establish a complicated filing system at first and then attempt to find papers to file in it. This simply does not work out. It is even difficult sometimes to remember the system.

File manufacturers issue very helpful free booklets on their methods of filing, and are glad to assist in rearranging and planning files.

The **two general classifications** of filing are **name** and **subject.**

NAME FILING—by the names of persons or companies—is the most widely used and simplest form of filing. The first question to be considered when starting new files or when revising old ones is "How much of this can be filed by name?" Name files may be divided into drawers or cabinets labeled:

Correspondence—in which is filed all general correspondence with customers, clients, and inquirers. Correspondence with salesmen or branch offices may be in separate drawers.

Order, Job, or Case—in which are filed all papers pertaining to each actual order, job, or case, so that the whole story of each—from beginning to end—will be in one folder. In an order folder will be the purchase order, bill of lading, invoice, etc. When a shipment number is assigned, the folder is transferred to the "Shipped Orders" file; thence to the "Unpaid Orders" file, for collection; thence to the "Completed Orders" or dead files.

447

These folders may be filed alphabetically by name of customer, with a numerical index of the order or job numbers. But in some offices it is more convenient to file the folders or papers numerically, by order or job number, and keep an alphabetic index of customers.

SUBJECT FILING is used when papers are called for by subject. In this type of filing it is well to keep in mind that names of actual things are easier to remember and classify than names of abstract things like "Legal," "Financial," "Manufacturing," and "Transportation," which reach out into all transactions of a business. However, when files are extensive and kept in a central filing system, such divisions as those last mentioned may be used to designate the files of different departments of a company; for instance, the Accounting Department files may be called "Finance and Accounts," and the Traffic Department's, "Transportation." But in an ordinary office, names of actual things are used as the main subjects and as subordinate subjects, as

Cement, Copper, White Pine, Wool, Rayon, Cacao Beans, Chemicals
Machinery, Engines, Pumps, Tools, Trucks, etc.
Ships (by name), Books (by author), Motion Pictures (by name), etc.
New Building, Factory, Private Rail Line, Drainage System, etc. (Name of project is main subject, with a folder for each important item, so that the whole story is together.)
Advertising, Insurance, Supplies, Personnel (Applications, Office Staff, Shop Employees).
Drawings, Maps, Charts, Blueprints, Photographs, Clippings, Samples, and Catalogues.

Subdividing Files. If any one folder or any one set of files becomes too large or bulky as one unit, it may be subdivided by date (months, half-year, or year); or by district or location; or by subordinate subjects.

A "Miscellaneous" folder should be kept for each letter of the alphabet and for each main subject, with the papers therein arranged first alphabetically, then chronologically. (The papers for each name should be held together on a yellow backing sheet with a flat spread-tang fastener in the upper left corner.) When six papers have accumulated for any one name—and the matter appears "active"—a separate folder should be made for that name. (The miscellaneous folder should be the last one in its group.)

Changes for the betterment of a filing system often suggest themselves, but they should be made only after their workability has been tested theoretically for a few days, and they have been approved by the person for whom the files are being kept.

Tabs. The type of folder to use—with staggered tabs or one-position tabs—is often a question. But most filing experts recommend "straight-line tabs," either all centered or all in the far right position.

"Folder tabs should be in direct lines, rather than in staggered positions."—(U.S.) National Archives and Records Service, GSA.

NOTE: Staggered tabs are sometimes used in very simple systems—with few guides, where few or no new folders are being added. (Staggered tabs cannot be kept in proper arrangement if new folders are constantly added.)

Various tab positions are: "half cut," with 2 tabs across; "third cut," 3 tabs across; "fifth cut," 5 tabs across; "two-fifths cut," with all tabs centered or at far right; "full [or straight] cut," with tab extending across folder (for very long titles, as in government work).

Colored Tabs. When different sets of files are in use, it has been found an efficient measure to have all the folder tabs in a certain set of one color, with the main guides in the same color or in white. For instance, all the tabs in the "Subject" file may be blue; in the "Correspondence" file, pink; in the "Job" or "Case" file, green; in the "Data" file, yellow. With this color identification, it is instantly apparent to which set of files a certain folder belongs when it is removed.

Labels. Colored gummed labels come in rolls or sheets, to be fed into the typewriter continuously. (CAUTION: **Self-adhesive labels** may become dry and peel off.) For good readability, type the labels thus:

1. Type **immediately below** the top or scoring (folding line), and begin uniformly two spaces from the left edge. Do not underline.
2. Type in **small letters with initial caps**, not in full caps, which are hard to read. (But use full caps for main subject titles.)
3. To save space, use **common abbreviations**, as "Co.," "Mfg.," "&"; and **omit punctuation**. (Although punctuation is optional.)
4. Leave **spaces** between names and numbers (or dates) to make each stand out. And use hanging indention for two or more lines.

Captions on **Subject Tabs**: The labels for the subheads may be typed with the main heading first and the subhead following or below it. But for quick filing and finding, many prefer to see the subhead first (in black), with the main head indented below (in red) in parentheses and in full caps.

Signals. If special meanings attach to certain cards or folders, small colored plastic or metal "signals" may be clipped tightly on such cards or folders. For instance, a red signal may indicate a certain credit rating, and a yellow signal, the current-year folder.

Out Guides. Whenever a file **folder** is to be removed for any length of time, it should be replaced by a colored cardboard "out" guide (or a guide with a colored tab), or by an "out" folder. Regular out guides have pockets for the insertion of small charge-out cards bearing notations identifying the missing papers—as name (and date, if any) of folder, initials of person taking it, and date taken. Some out guides have, instead of pockets, lines on which the pertinent information may be written and later crossed out or erased.

"Out" folders are often used—instead of out guides—to hold accumulating papers. Printed out folders are ruled on the front for notations.

Out Cards or Slips. When **individual papers** are removed from the folders, they should be replaced by "out" cards or slips of the same color as the out guides (or with tabs of that color). Notations are made on the cards.

In some offices, printed "out" slips are filled in by the persons requesting the papers. Thus the slips act first as **requisitions** to the file department, and secondly as **out slips** for the missing papers. They may also act as **ticklers** in the follow-up file if papers are wanted at a future date.

The colored tabs on out cards or slips should show well above the edges of other papers within folders. It is then comparatively easy to check the files from time to time and follow up the charge-outs.

A supply of out guides, out folders, and out cards or slips should be kept handy in the front of each set of files.

> CAUTION: Do not keep on the desk, notations of what is missing from the files, instead of putting out guides, cards, or slips in the files. This "blanks" the files and invariably causes confusion regarding certain papers.

Record of Files Taken Out of Office. If a number of files are to be sent out of the office, make a list of them (besides inserting out guides) so that the files can be checked against the list when they are returned.

"Desk" Filing. If folders or papers are not returned promptly to the files but are kept "filed" in the various desks, it soon disrupts a filing system. If such a condition exists, at some opportune time suggest to the executive in charge that a general memorandum be sent to the staff asking that all files or papers be returned promptly to the files. Usually an authoritative communication will induce more respect for the files than a filing clerk's continual asking for missing papers.

Do not be guilty of "filing" letters in your own desk and forgetting about them. If papers are temporarily placed in the desk, they should be put between the covers of a notebook, or with some article that is constantly used, so they will be automatically brought out when the book or article is removed.

Cross Index. A permanent cross-index card (one side of a folder with tab) should be used for every name likely to be called for in two ways.

Cross Reference. Distinctively colored (and usually printed) cross-reference sheets are placed within folders (chronologically according to reference dates) to direct readers to other folders for certain papers.

Cross-reference sheets are arranged in this manner:

CROSS REFERENCE

(Name of file in which cross-reference sheet permanently belongs)

    Regarding . . . .
    Dated . . . .
    See (or See also) . . . . (Name of file in which material is filed). . . .

While cross references are very necessary, there is such a thing as over-cross-referencing, which can make the files bewildering. Try always to have but one place to look for certain papers—never more than two places.

To avoid too many cross references, make excerpts from various letters to be filed under the appropriate heads. In making an excerpt, head it "Excerpt from..." and put three dots before and after each segregated item to show that it is incomplete. At the bottom of each page state where the entire letter or paper is to be found.

Index of Files. Make an index for each set of subject files, and for each set of mixed subject and correspondence files. The index may be either an alphabetic (triple-spaced) list on very heavy paper, or it may be a card index. Whenever a new folder is made, add its title to the index. And **keep the index up to date.**

Indexes are necessary and valuable aids to the memory in marking papers for filing and in searching for papers, especially by someone new.

Make a **strict alphabetic index** (regardless of grouping in the files) of all headings whether main or subordinate. Type each main head in full caps with its subheads listed below in lower-case and caps; and also type each subhead alone followed by the main head in parentheses and in full caps, as

Acetate Rayon... See Rayon	Gasoline Engines. (ENGINES)
Aluminum........ (METALS)	MATERIALS... See also PLASTICS
Atomic Power... (FUELS)	Canvas Nylon Rayon
Canvas.......... (MATERIALS)	METALS
Coal............ (FUELS)	Aluminum Titanium
Diesel Engines... (ENGINES)	Nylon........... (MATERIALS)
ENGINES	Oil, Fuel........ See Fuel Oil
Diesel Gasoline Steam	PLASTICS...... See also MATERIALS
Fuel Oil........ (FUELS)	Rayon........... (MATERIALS)
FUELS	Steam Engines... (ENGINES)
Atomic Power Coal Fuel Oil	Titanium........ (METALS)

Card Indexes. An **alphabetic card index** of the subject files will serve also as a valuable cross-reference guide. A card should be made for each main subject and each subordinate one (in the above manner), as well as a cross-reference card for every possible name or familiar title of one subject—for instance, the nickname "Cat-Crackers" would be on a card, and below it "See REFINERIES – Cracking Plants – Fluid Catalytic Cracking."

For numeric files, an **alphabetic card index** is a necessity.

A **numeric card index** may be used to advantage with some files, if numbered papers, such as orders, are being received or dealt with. Cards may be filed numerically, as by order number, and the papers themselves filed alphabetically according to name or subject.

Tickler Files. A very compact and reliable form for reminder or follow-up work is the card tickler system in a card box or desk tray. Guides are provided for the 12 months and the 31 days of the month. Small cards, identifying the files or papers and the persons requesting them, are filed chronologically—by dates wanted. When papers are removed from the files for follow-up action, these tickler cards are attached to the large "out" cards, thus identifying the missing files.

A **tickler card** with complete information about a recurring item, as a payment, may be moved along from week to week or month to month, thereby eliminating numerous routine entries on the desk calendar. But a tickler file does not replace the desk calendar. **Both must be consulted each day.**

Follow-up Carbons. For follow-up work, often a distinctively colored (pink) follow-up carbon copy is made of each outgoing letter needing future attention. These copies—prominently marked (in the lower right corner, in colored pencil) with the dates needed and the initials of the persons requesting the papers—are filed chronologically in a special follow-up file (as described below); or if the volume is small, in one follow-up folder, with the earliest wanted carbon on top.

On the follow-up date, these pink carbons are either sent to the persons requesting them, or they are used to replace papers withdrawn from the regular files, and to act as charge-out slips until the original papers are returned. Then the follow-up carbons are destroyed.

Follow-up Files—Chronological. If follow-up work is extensive, one file drawer (or a deep desk drawer) should be used as a follow-up file. Month and day guides may be purchased, but labeled folders will do, as

12 center-tab folders labeled each with the name of a month, and
31 right-tab folders labeled each with just a number, for the days.

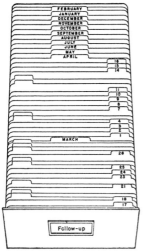

Follow-up

Arrange the day folders, for the current month, in numerical order in the front of the file. After the day folders, arrange the month folders in succeeding order.

In these files place the follow-up carbons described above, and other memorandums or notations concerning awaited information, goods ordered by telephone, and future things to be done or considered.

As the follow-up papers for each day are removed, place that day folder after the next month folder.

Reverse the day folders for Sundays, holidays, and Saturdays (if non-working) so that only blank tabs show, and no papers will be filed in these folders.

The month folders will receive material accumulating for each month until it can be sorted and transferred into the proper day folders for the current month.

CAUTION: **Never place original papers in these follow-up files.** And do not keep originals on or in the desk to act as ticklers or reminders. A futile search may be made for them if they are not in their proper places in the regular files.

Follow-up Files—Alphabetic. Active correspondence needing constant follow-up attention, as in merchandising, may be filed alphabetically in the regular way but in a separate file drawer and in special follow-up folders. These folders each have a calendar scale—numbers from 1 to 31—printed across the full-cut tab (beside the space for a name). Over this scale fits a colored sliding signal (a different color for each month) to indicate the follow-up date.

Pending or Suspense Files. Regular folders or original papers are sometimes held in suspense from day to day awaiting further information. "Pending" papers should be kept where they will be seen **every day,** as in the front of the sorter. Often it is necessary to put "out" cards in the files; or better, to file the pending papers and carry tickler notations along in the follow-up files.

Daily or Reading File. If the correspondence is particularly heavy and on a variety of subjects, it is a good plan to make a thin, blue copy of each outgoing letter, to be placed on a "Daily" or "Reading" file binder on the desk. These bound copies may be filed each month.

As the regular copies are filed each day, their filing disposition should be noted on the corresponding daily copies. Thereafter a missing letter may be traced in the files by reference to its copy in the bound daily files. Letters are **never removed** from this file for any purpose.

Accumulated Filing. Do not permit filing to accumulate on the desk. Sort it and keep it in a sorter or in temporary folders if necessary. This method will facilitate the finding of papers yet unfiled. The temporary folders should bear the five or ten principal classifications of the files; and papers can at least be segregated into these classifications each day.

Preparing Papers for Filing. Before filing anything (other than routine papers) be sure that the person for whom the files are being kept—or a designated superior—has seen or has a knowledge of every paper that is to be filed—in other words, has "released" it for filing. Place all papers about which there can be any question on his desk in a folder marked "For Filing." He can then check them and mark certain ones for certain files if he desires.

The **"release signal"** may be a colored check mark in a certain position; or it may be initials and date—often with a colored line down through the letter to show that all parts have been answered.

Mark each paper for filing, that is, check or write on it the name of the file into which it is to be placed. (And make a cross, or X—on the left margin—beside any name to be cross-referenced.) Use a colored pencil and encircle or underline the filing reference. Thereafter if the paper is removed from the file, it can be returned without question to its proper folder.

Make neat pencil notations on file copies regarding the disposition of other copies of the same material, or any other information which might be helpful later and which should be permanently a part of the file records.

Be very sure that whatever is noted on the papers **is correct,** not just a supposition. Make pencil notations concise, but clear.

If some temporary notation is necessary on a file copy, write it on a slip of paper attached to the copy. The slip can be easily removed when the notation is no longer pertinent. Thus the file papers will remain clean and not be covered with erasures or scratched-over notations.

Make all necessary cross-reference, follow-up, and index entries.

Mend all torn papers with cellophane tape.

Sorting. Sort and arrange all filing before attempting to file it. Sort first into file classifications, if any; then (in alphabetic systems) sort alphabetically, and last chronologically.

Never allow a clip to go into the files; not only are clips too bulky, but they too readily pick up other papers. Staple, with a permanent or temporary stapling machine, all papers that are to be held together.

When stapling a letter and its answer together, **always put the answer on top.** Not only is this chronologically correct, but it immediately tells that the letter has been answered.

If papers are well arranged at the desk, much weary standing at the files will be done away with.

A sorter tray and base, on wheels, is a convenient contrivance for arranging filing. The tray is equipped with file guides, behind which the filing can be segregated as it accumulates.

Several desk types of sorter are also available.

Filing. Arrange the papers chronologically in each file—the **latest paper always on top** (except in the "Miscellaneous"folders. See p. 448.)

Try to attach some meaning to the filing of each paper, so that filing will not become a dull, monotonous task. If it is mechanically done, papers will get into the wrong files.

Much responsibility attaches to filing; but do not be **dismayed if** occasionally it is necessary to search for something in the files. No filing system is infallible, nor is any filer.

Filing Before or Behind Guides. Filing **behind** the guides is the method most widely used, especially in voluminous files that are worked upon and consulted by many people. But in small, individual files of only a few drawers, filing in front of the guides is sometimes practiced and has proved satisfactory. Filing in front of a guide permits its being always in full view; whereas filing behind a guide necessitates its being obscured when folders are being inserted or removed.

Neat Files. Form the habit of pushing the papers down evenly in all files, to give a neat appearance and to avoid frayed or torn edges.

Binder Folders. Use file binders (thin-tang fasteners) in folders, wherever possible, to hold papers neatly together for ready reference and to avoid the misplacement, accidental removal, or loss of any paper.

Sagging or Slumping Files. To eliminate the compressing of files too tightly in an attempt to avoid sagging or slumping, several devices are available: file dividers, side-rod supports, and cloth-pocket holders.

Removing Folders. To remove folders from the file, grasp them across the center—**never pull on or bend the tabs.**

Circulars, Catalogues, Timetables, etc. Some catalogues and circulars are kept in the files under company names; but generally they are too bulky for filing and should be kept in a separate cabinet or file drawer, under the company names. They should be discarded as new issues are received, and not allowed to accumulate and become obsolete and unreliable.

Timetables are often kept in the subject file in one folder under **T.** These especially should be kept up to date. (Everyone in an office should know how, or learn, to read timetables quickly and accurately.)

Filing Stool and Shelf. A small stool on rollers is an available and necessary aid for filing. It eliminates much tiresome stooping. Another aid is a shelf that hooks onto a file drawer, for holding papers.

Inactive Files. Inactive or "dead" files should be kept in the bottom (or most inaccessible) drawers of the filing cases.

Old files should be transferred to storage periodically. Inexpensive, **interlocking steel files** or **wooden** or **pressboard cases,** and cheap guides, are used for stored files. (Often the old alphabetic "Miscellaneous" folders act as guides.) Cross-reference sheets are left in all stored folders.

Retention Periods. The length of time files are to be preserved depends upon the nature of the business and of the records—and the legal aspects involved. The different state **statutes of limitations** govern the retention of some records (such as those pertaining to open accounts, notes, and contracts); **national laws** require the retaining of other records (such as those pertaining to internal revenue, social security, labor relations, and interstate commerce); while still other papers must be kept indefinitely for their reference or historical value. **Vital records** of the company's existence (such as organization papers, minutes of meetings, and accounting records) are never destroyed.

A **Record Retention Schedule** should be made up, listing alphabetically the types of papers in the files. This schedule should be **approved by the company's attorney,** and countersigned by a responsible executive.

RECORD RETENTION SCHEDULE

Type of Paper	Retention Period
Catalogues (other companies')	Until superseded.
Contracts	20 years after fulfillment.
Income tax records	5 years.
Notes	20 years after payment.
Open accounts	7 years, if fully adjusted.
Organization	Permanent.

(etc.)

NOTE: Papers vital to the existence of a company are never sent to storage. (The Government's "Guide to Record Retention" is for sale by Supt. of Documents, Washington, DC 20402—$2.50)

Never destroy a dead file, no matter how old, unless specifically authorized **in writing** so to do.

Microfilm. To save storage space, and/or to have a duplicate set of files stored in a safer place, file records may be photographed on microfilm (strips of very small film). An indexing system makes the films available for reading on a magnifying reader.

Duplication. Important records may be **photocopied** in their natural size for use in cross-referencing; or when needed in branch offices; or when the originals are to be placed in a safe or safe deposit box.

DIARY

A diary should be kept in every office, and in it should be noted the important happenings of each day.

Record should be made of the departure of persons on trips and their return; the signing of important documents or the closing of transactions; the arrival of persons from out of town, or of important callers, etc.

The desk calendar may be used as a diary, although a separate book is better if the notations are likely to be numerous.

SCRAPBOOK

When cutting out pages for a scrapbook, use a sharp knife or a razor blade, and not scissors. Do not attempt to tear the pages out, or the reading matter may be destroyed.

The secret of neat pasting lies in using very little paste, especially on thin paper. Wet pages will wrinkle. In applying paste, start near the center of the page and work outward. Let the extreme edges remain dry until the paper has been pasted; then with the brush apply paste

455

carefully beneath the edges and paste them down. Wipe away all surplus paste immediately so that no pages will stick together; and use a cleansing tissue—not the hand—for smoothing the pasted surface.

There is no excuse for a scrapbook's not being kept clean.

ALPHABETIZING

There are two methods of alphabetizing: the dictionary method and the telephone directory method—the latter generally used in filing.

The **dictionary method** follows strict alphabetic order, down to the last letter if necessary: first, according to surnames or first principal words; and second (if surnames are the same), according to given names, initials, or other words.

Rand, John	Randall Corporation (The)	Rhodes from Paris
Rand, J. P.	RCA Communications, Inc.	Rhodes of London
Rand, J. Ralph	Reade-Taylor Co.	Rockefeller Foundation
Rand, J., & Sons	R.E.M. Corporation	Rock Island Lines

The **telephone directory** method alphabetizes names in three steps:

1. According to the first unit.

L.	E. Q. Corporation*
L &	E Watch Co.*
L	Electrical Co.*
Lea &	Parker, Inc.
Leather	Trades Bureau
Le Baron,	John J.
Lee—	Thurston Co.†
Leeds,	Burton & Hill
Lee's	Apartments
Leland	Stanford Assn.
Long	Island Club‡
Los Angeles	Times‡
New	York Central Syst.‡
Newark	Mercantile Co.
Nine	Forty-Five Broadway§
North	River Company‡
North	West Market‖
Northwest	Airlines‖
Pan	American Airways‖
Panama	Pacific Line
Rock	Island Lines‡
Rockefeller	Foundation
St.	Paul Flour Co.‡
San Juan	Trading Co.‡

2. When first unit is the same, then according to second unit.

Lee,	A.	W.
Lee	Air	Trips
Lee	Aircraft	Co.
Lee,	Art	J.
Lee,	Arthur	B.
Lee,	C.	R., & Co.
Lee &	Company	

3. When first and second units are the same, then according to third unit.

Lee, B.	
Lee, B.	A.
Lee, B.	Albert
Lee, B.	B.
Lee, B.	Co.**
Lee, B.	Leslie
Lee, B.	Novelties**
Lee, B.	Philip
Lee, B.	& Sons, Inc.**

* Company names made up of initials or letters, as are radio stations' names, are alphabetized before all other names beginning with the same letter—each letter being considered a unit.

† Hyphened firm names, and hyphened surnames, are treated as separate units, as "Johns- | Manville | Corp.," "Lincoln- | Mercury | Division," "Lloyd- | Jones."

‡ In geographic names composed of two or more words, each English word is considered a unit, as "New | York," and "Salt | Lake | City." But a non-English semi-prefix is grouped with the following word in one unit, as "Los Angeles |", "San Francisco |", and "El Paso |".

§ Each part of a spelled-out number is treated as a separate unit, as "Six | Fifty- | Four," "Six | Hundred | Ten," and "Sixteen | Fifty- | Four." **Numbers in figures** are sometimes arranged numerically.

‖ A name that may be spelled as one word, hyphened, or as two words, is treated as it is spelled by its bearer. And the word in question is cross-referenced, as "North West, See also Northwest," "Northside, See also North Side," and "Panamerican, See also Pan American, and Pan-American." (In some directories, "Pan American" is one unit.)

** Company names beginning with a personal name (i.e., a given name, or initial, and a surname) are now arranged in strict alphabetic order—with each part of the title being considered in determining the units.

Variations in Alphabetizing. A study of indexes will disclose many variations in alphabetizing. The method used in each index is governed by the number of names being dealt with. The telephone directory method is particularly adaptable to voluminous lists; the dictionary method to shorter or less complicated lists. Good examples of the dictionary method may be found in the Congressional Directory (in the front and back indexes), in lists of advertisers in magazines, and in indexes in books and booklets.

Both methods are often used in the same book; for instance, in a telephone directory one will find all names beginning with "New" grouped before such names as "Newark" and "Newcomb"; but in the front of the same directory, in the shorter lists of out-of-town points, one will find in strict alphabetic order "Newark" before "New Bedford," etc.

The telephone directory method has undergone simplification from time to time. In strict alphabetic order according to surname now are to be found: all "Mc" and "Mac" names; all company names (including those beginning with personal names); all compound or hyphened names (both company and individual, according to the first surname); and all possessive names (no differentiation between singular and plural). And the word "The" within a name, as "John The Florist," is considered in alphabetizing. Also, other small words, such as "of the," "for," and "from," are now being considered as they are in the dictionary method, which method brings together all names beginning alike, as "Association of," "Association for," "Church of the," etc.

Order. The indexing adage **"Nothing precedes something"** means that when names are similar, the shorter name always comes before the longer, as "Ash, Ashe, Asher," "A., Al, Albert," "John, Johns, Johnson."

Company Names. Personal names beginning company names are written with the given names, or initials, immediately after the surnames.

Harper, Geo., & Co.	NOT:	*Harper & Co., Geo.*
Haviland, L. J., & Sons, Inc.	NOT:	*Haviland & Sons, L. J., Inc.*
Hawthorne, W. R., & Co., Ltd.		
Marshall, P. J., Company, The		

Company names, familiar as trade names, are not broken down in telephone directories, even though the first name is a given name.

Marshall Field & Company	Martha Washington Hotel
Johns Hopkins University	Paul Revere Silversmiths

Most company names are, however, more familiarly known by the last name, and are indexed accordingly, as

Wanamaker, John, Philadelphia	Scribner's, Charles, Sons

Always cross-index a name under its familiar title if it is filed under a broken-down title. Telephone directories do this with certain names.

Grace, W. R., & Co.	CROSS-INDEX UNDER: W.
Case, J. I., Co.	CROSS-INDEX UNDER: J.

Small Words. Formerly, small words in names, like **"the," "of," "by," "for," "from,"** and **"on,"** were disregarded in file indexing. But now, since **both the dictionary and telephone directory methods** consider such words in alphabetizing, it seems best that file indexing should conform. (Small words in foreign names have always been considered.)

"The" (but not **"Ye"**) beginning a name is placed after the name.

"And" may or may not be considered. The **sign "&"** is always disregarded.

Club Internationale
Club, The (restaurant)
Dales Market
Dales on the Green

Home Air Conditioning, Inc.
Home for the Aged
Merchants Press, Inc., The
Merchants, The

Titles With Names. Write titles and designations, such as "Dr.," "Capt.," "Jr.," and "Mrs.," after the names and disregard them unless two names are alike. (In book indexing, titles are written thus: Scott, Capt. Robert V., Jr.)

Gray, John R., Jr.
  NOT: *Gray, Jr., John R.*
Gray, John R., III, MD
Henderson, J. W., Dr.
Henderson, J. W., Mrs. – See Henderson, Ruth T. (Mrs. J. W.)

Langford, Paul J., Jr., Col.
Sister Mary [no surname]
Turnquist, David L., Rev.
Wilson, Stuart, Sr., Prof.

But titles that begin trade names, as "Sir Francis Drake Apts.," "Prince Edward Hotel," "Madame [or Mme] Cécile," "Dr. [or Doctor] Day's Shoes," "Mr. [or Mister] John, Inc.," are not inverted and **are considered** in alphabetizing.

Mc and Mac. "Mc" and "Mac" are filed in exact alphabetic order.

Mabury, C. J.
MacArthur, J. H.
MacDonald, D. C.
Mack, Elliot

MacLane, Wm. F.
Matson, M. J.
McAdams, E. W.
McDonald, Robert

Mt., Ft., St., Pt. Treat these abbreviations as if they were spelled out— "Mount," "Fort," "Saint," and "Point"—and cross-index.

Fort Wayne (Indiana)
Mount Shasta Ices
Point Pleasant (W.Va.)
Saint Francis Hospital
Saint Paul Transport Co.

CROSS-INDEX CARDS
Ft. – See Fort
Mt. – See Mount
Pt. – See Point
St. – See Saint

Foreign Names. The "van," "de," "Le," "El," etc., in foreign names are parts of the last names and should begin the names.

1ST UNIT	
D'Antonio,	Francis
De Forest,	J. V.
de la Rue,	O. E.
El Camino	Club

1ST UNIT	
La Fontaine,	Jean
Le Clair,	Dennis J.
van der Zee,	B. T.
von Griswold,	Ernst

Possessive Names. Disregard apostrophes and file in strict alphabetic order, as is done in telephone directories and dictionaries.

Fuller, P. D.
Fullering, Frank
Fuller's Market
Fullers' Rugs

Fullerson Bros.
Fullerton & Son
Fullertons' Inn
Fullerton's Shop

Abbreviations. Treat all abbreviations as if spelled out, except those that begin company names. Disregard the sign "&."

Lee, Chas. V.
Lee Chart Co.

Lee, Colby & Co.
Lee Co., The

Lee Mfg. Co.
Lee & Martin

Numerals as Names. When numerals are used as names, spell out the names, and file under the spelled-out version.

450 Sutter   FILE UNDER: Four Fifty Sutter   CROSS-INDEX: Sutter, 450
308 Formula   FILE UNDER: Three O Eight Formula
The 220 Club   FILE UNDER: Two Twenty Club, The

Identical Names. When names are identical, sub-alphabetize **by address:** if in one city, **by street names or numbers;** if in different cities, **by city names,** and when city names are the same, **by state names.**

Common Phrases in Titles. Titles beginning with phrases common to other titles, such as "Estate of," are inverted and the subjects filed under the principal names.

> Lindon, Emerson S., Estate of

Universities, Schools, Colleges. File under the principal part of the name (and cross-index under the full name, if only a few schools appear in the files).

FILE UNDER: California, University of (Berkeley)
Notre Dame of Maryland, College of (Baltimore)
Notre Dame, University of (Indiana)
Physicians and Surgeons, College of (San Francisco)
Washington, University of (Seattle)
William and Mary, College of (Virginia)
CROSS-INDEX UNDER: University of California
College of Notre Dame of Maryland (Baltimore)
University of Notre Dame (Indiana)
College of Physicians and Surgeons
University of Washington
College of William and Mary

Banks, Churches, Societies, Associations. File under the full straight name; and, if numerous, sub-alphabetize by the names of cities.

Association of Voters	Bank of America – California
Astronomical Society	Laguna Beach, Bank of America
Church of God	La Jolla, Bank of America
Church of the Advent	San Diego, Bank of America
Gardeners' Association	Chase Manhattan Bank, The (New York)
Holy Trinity Church	First National Bank of Chicago, The
Society for Research	Morgan Guaranty Trust Company of New York
Society of Pioneers	Riggs National Bank, The (Washington, D.C.)

Government Departments. Bureaus, boards, and departments of the different governments—Federal, state, county, and city—are filed under the name of the chief governing body.

California, State of	San Francisco, City of
Architecture, Department of	Education, Board of
Highways, Division of	United States Government
Lincoln, County of	Commerce, Department of
Weights and Measures, Bureau of	Census, Bureau of the

NOTE: When government agencies are not numerous in the files—or if the correspondence with one or a few such agencies is large—file under the name of the agency (if distinctive) and disregard the department, as "National Bureau of Standards" under N, and "Bonneville Power Administration" under B.

Diplomacy and Efficiency

(The generic [masculine] gender used herein refers to either male or female. See p. 2.)

Punctuality.   Be on time in the morning—even if working overtime at night.   That is the company's gain.   To make up the overtime, ask occasionally for time off—an afternoon or a day when the work is not heavy—but do not adopt the reasoning that overtime is being made up by being late in the morning.

Nothing signifies an interest in the work more than being on time both in the morning and at noon, and not "watching the clock" to get away in the evening.

If you are continually required to work overtime, ask for a later arrival hour in the morning.   If there is an understanding in such matters no offense is created by arriving late.

Don't be habitually absent from the office for reasons other than illness.   A worker may think his or her absences are not noticed, but usually, and generally suddenly, some action is taken regarding them.

Make very few personal appointments that will consume office time. If it can be seen that something will cause an unusually late arrival at the office, telephone in, explaining the delay; or if an appointment is to be kept at noon which might cause a delay, explain that before leaving the office.   Thus a better feeling is created than if a person simply turns up late and then explains the reason for such tardiness.

It is customary to say "Good morning" when first encountering anyone in the office, even though superiors do not sometimes speak first.

It is also usual to say "Good night," if it is reasonably convenient to do so.   But do not go out of the way to say either.

Office Unattended.   Arrange hours if possible so that the office will not be unattended at any time.   If it is impossible for the office to be attended at the lunch hour, do not leave it open; lock the door and put a card on it giving the approximate time of return.   It is discourteous to let people wait outside expecting someone to return momentarily.

Do not leave an office unattended and take time to shop.   An important caller might be turned away or an important telephone call missed, and someone angered enough to report this to the employer.

Leaving at Night.   When preparing to leave an office at night, do not rush about in a hurry to get away, banging up desks, etc.   Learn to put a desk in order and close things quietly and carefully, and to take a deliberate rather than a hurried leave.   It will consume only a few minutes more, will probably prevent some last minute error or oversight, and will create a much better impression.

If there is a possibility of further work, ask regarding it **before preparing to leave,** not afterward.

Mentally check over the work to see that all is in order before leaving.

460

Interest. Learn to work with a system. Do not be constantly confused. Improve as many conditions as can be improved, and have as many things as possible working mechanically each day, or performed as a habit under a well-thought-out system.

Be consistent in procedure. Do not worry about small things and overlook large ones. Consider them all—**the large ones first.**

Group the work in the **order of its importance**; and arrange to **meet deadlines** by not leaving too much to do at the last minute.

The more **interest** an employee takes in the business, the more she or he becomes an assistant and departs from being a servant. Do not sit back and read books or newspapers, and then feel hurt if asked to do some minor task that should have been done in the first place. If it is unpleasant or embarrassing to be told to do things, think of things to do. A worker can be an **innovator** in a great many ways.

Understand that everything, **and anything,** is to be done willingly. If something gainful can be found in unpleasant tasks, they become easier.

If sometimes the disturbing thought occurs that perhaps someone else could do the job better—or perhaps the company thinks that someone else would be better—attempt to erase all points of doubt by methodically correcting one matter of inefficiency each day.

Cooperation. Attempt to see always from the other's viewpoint. Try once in a while to face the problems an employer is facing in an endeavor to make ends meet. If an executive seems annoyed at times, there might be a chance that he or she has a right to be.

When asking assistance from anyone, ask in the form of a question rather than a command; and do not be constantly disturbing another person by asking small favors. Respect his right to work in peace.

When leaving work for others to do—as when leaving on a vacation—make a list of things to be done, especially if someone unfamiliar with the work is to be assigned to it. Give the new person every assistance.

In explaining work to a new person, or in explaining anything to anyone, give the reasons for doing it in a certain manner, and it will be more easily remembered.

Never criticize one person's work in the presence of another.

Constructive Criticism. If something seems wrong about an office, find a constructive suggestion to offer instead of a criticism of present conditions.

If the suggestion does not meet with favor, try to see also how the other person could be right. If after analyzing the situation, it still seems wrong, wait until it is proved wrong before making a further suggestion for a change.

Recognizing a Superior. Recognize the need for a head of every department—someone who carries the responsibility and knows the work that is being done.

Be tractable when working with a superior. Do not attempt to do things independently or fail to report things done, which really amounts

461

to "going over a superior's head" by keeping him in ignorance of work or arrangements that are supposedly under his supervision.

When given instructions by someone higher in authority than an immediate superior, carry out the instructions, but let the immediate superior know of the arrangements. Then if anything goes wrong, responsibility rests where it should.

Make notes of all important things with which an immediate superior should be acquainted. Leave on his desk carbon copies of all outgoing letters that he has not seen.

If a mistake is made, admit it. Work as accurately and conscientiously as possible, apprising a superior of all things done—praise or blame.

Conferences With a Superior. Make notations of things to be taken up with a superior and choose a time for going over these details when he is not busy. Many things can be disposed of in this way, instead of every day asking something about the office or procedure.

It is necessary, of course, to ask a few questions that need immediate attention. But be very sure that they are urgent before disturbing a busy person. If they can be answered at any time throughout the day, and the person who can answer them is momentarily engaged with other things, simply put notations of the questions on his desk, or in the folder with his letters for signature.

When asking a question, mention the subject first so the person spoken to can grasp the matter and be able to answer immediately. Never preface a remark by saying "I wanted to ask you about..." Begin with the subject, as "The insurance papers that Mr. Barnes wanted—I could find but two..."

When asking for a personal favor or for time off, never say "I want to ask a favor..." or "There's something I'd like to ask you about..." This savors too much of unpleasantness. Simply say something like— "Wednesday, if it's convenient, I'd like to have the morning off..."

Poise. Poise is the manner of doing things in rather a deliberate way, with real thought behind every action. Speed is not nearly so important in a business office as calmness. There is no need for going about work in a constant hurry—entering and leaving rooms too quickly, and saying "Yes" to instructions before hearing half of what is being said.

Listen attentively—not nervously—to all instructions that are given, and act understandingly. Have a surety and firmness about everything that is done.

In a word—to have real poise, be calm, quiet, dignified, and very professional...and always immaculately groomed.

Accent and Speech. Tone down any definite accent and discard all affectations of speech. Many companies will not employ persons with noticeable accents; such voices are difficult to understand over the telephone. Assumed accents expose the speakers at the most awkward moments. Naturalness is in the best taste always.

462

Do not pitch the voice so low that it cannot be understood. If asked to repeat several times, be quick enough to understand that a little louder or clearer speech is necessary. Particularly, speak clearly and distinctly when talking to a superior, whose time is valuable.

Manners. The correct thing in business manners is always the gracious thing. But business deportment should always remain slightly formal, no matter how long persons have been associated or have known each other. Informality generally leads to injured feelings through misunderstandings.

Have consideration for others in an office and do not cause unnecessary disturbances, by humming, whistling, or tapping with a pencil when people are trying to work.

Do not talk or laugh too much, or too loud. Don't be habitually amused. In every office there is an undercurrent of seriousness—have respect for that. If temporarily amused, be able to return immediately to the seriousness of the work. If an amusing incident happens in the presence of a superior, a good rule is not to laugh unless he laughs first. He may not think it funny at all—may even be annoyed to think that someone else is amused.

Callers. Treat every caller as a prospective customer.

If calling, be courteous to the receptionist or secretary. She is really an important person. Do not attempt to ignore her.

When meeting a caller—if he has not been sent in by a receptionist—find out whom he wishes to see, and the purpose of his call, if he is a stranger and has no appointment. Someone other than the person he asks for may be the person for him to see.

If it is not possible for a caller to see the person he is calling upon—because of previous appointments or conferences—ask him if he will not telephone or write for an appointment later. This overcomes much disappointment when people are being turned away.

If it is necessary for a caller to wait, see that he has something to read. Never attempt particularly to entertain him; many callers desire simply to wait and think. If talking to a caller, talk only about things in general—the chief item of commercial news in the paper that day, the weather, etc. If he inquires about anything pertaining to the business, be very courteous in answering, but reply in generalities, giving only such information as has been made public by the company.

Announcing Callers. It is much better to have an understanding with a superior regarding his wishes in the matter of announcing callers, the persons he wishes to see and does not wish to see, etc., than to guess at the proper procedure in each instance.

As a general rule, callers should be announced in the following manner, if the persons they are calling upon are engaged:

An ordinary caller without an appointment should be expected to wait until a conference is finished, or should see someone else in the organization.

463

A person with an appointment should be announced immediately, or if the person he is calling upon is only temporarily engaged, he should be expected to wait a few minutes before being announced.

An important visitor should be announced immediately, whether he has an appointment or not, unless the person he is calling upon is engaged with someone equally as important. In that event, he should be asked to wait a few minutes for the conference to be finished, before he is announced.

When announcing a caller to a person who is occupied with another, simply take the visitor's card in, or write his name on a slip of paper and hand it to the person whom he is calling to see.

If a message is being sent in, write it out on a slip of paper. It may be important that the other caller does not hear the message, or know that someone else is calling. Be extremely careful about presenting information to anyone when another (even someone from the same office) is present.

It is not customary for a secretary or stenographer to knock on a closed door when entering a conference room. It is her privilege to enter when she wills, but she should use that privilege with discretion. She should never enter hurriedly, always quietly and unobtrusively.

When a caller arrives, if it is known that certain papers will be used in connection with his call, obtain those papers from the files and hand them in when admitting the caller.

Introductions. It is not customary for an employer to introduce a caller to an employee, unless the employee is to work for or with the caller. Then they should be introduced.

A secretary often introduces a caller to her employer as she shows the caller in, by saying "Mr. ...[employer], this is Mr. ...[visitor]", although this is not always deemed necessary.

A woman's name should be mentioned first in an introduction, as "Miss Lawrence, Mr. James." When a group are being introduced in an office, the women should be named before the men.

When two men are being introduced to each other (or two women), it is complimentary for the one introducing them to mention the name of the older or more important person first. When the two persons are of almost equal age and importance, it is immaterial which name is mentioned first.

When a woman is being presented to an older person, it is complimentary for her to rise, especially if the older person is a member of the employer's family. In other introductions in business, it is usual for a woman to remain seated. She should always extend her hand if the other person offers his hand in greeting, saying simply "How do you do."

Information. Never give out any office information of any kind, especially financial or credit information, unless specifically authorized to do so. If necessary, obtain first an authorization by telephone or telegraph.

Never give information to anyone, even to someone in the same office, unless it is to be general news.

464

Never voluntarily give out any business information that might be "bad news," such as information about unstarted or unfinished orders, or about anything that does not comply with the customer's wishes. For instance, if a customer telephones about an order, never say "We haven't started on that order yet." Let a superior do the explaining. Every effort should be made to remedy a situation before unpleasant news is given out.

If authorized to give out information, check carefully to see that it is all correct.

Odd Jobs and Dull Times. Dull time is inventory time. Make a list of things to do on dull days, **and do them.** The following are suggestions:

> Rearrange parts of filing system.
> Clean supply cabinet and check for restocking.
> Clean desk and restock it with supplies.
> Clean up the office generally, making it neater by clearing away any papers or other articles that have a tendency to accumulate uselessly.
> Inaugurate newer and more efficient methods where needed.
> Have repairs made to anything in need of them.
> Do cataloguing, listing, or filing to improve later work or perfect office routine.
> Practice shorthand, handwriting, or printing.
> Address envelopes for routine work.

Create an interest in looking for things to improve when there is nothing else to do.

Keep up to date on company policy—new rules and regulations—by studying all directives and instruction memoranda issued.

Practicing Shorthand, Handwriting, etc. Practice is the one way to perfect shorthand. If mistakes occur in shorthand transcriptions, practice in every spare moment to overcome them. Write over and over the words that give trouble in dictation and the words common to the business. Take papers from the files and rewrite them in shorthand, or rewrite articles from technical magazines. Keep a shorthand dictionary handy to verify unusual words.

Also practice handwriting and printing in odd moments. A good handwriting and symmetrical printing show up to advantage in an office.

Reading. Read the newspaper every day—**but not in the office.**

Keep the morning paper throughout the day for reference, but read it only before arriving at work or at lunch time.

Do not read books or magazines unless everything pertaining to the office has been done. If reading becomes a last resort, read the technical magazines or papers of the office. If a better knowledge of the business is needed, read papers from the files. Also **read the dictionary.**

Reading fiction is a dulling distraction in an office. If an important telephone call comes in, it is difficult momentarily to get back to business and know what the caller is talking about. Also, when a reader becomes engrossed in a story, some important office detail is liable to be overlooked, and an employer more annoyed than if the office were busy.

465

Working Habits. Attempt to make a habit of every correct practice. Sooner or later they will all come under the head of "efficiency."

Analyze the reason for every habit, and avoid those that might have a reactive bad result. For instance, the habit of tearing papers in two before putting them in the wastebasket would seem to be efficient. On the other hand, papers are often wanted after being discarded, and if torn in two they are useless, or require time to be mended. Therefore, it would seem a better practice simply to throw papers in the waste-basket, without the added noise of tearing or crumpling them, and decide that once in the wastebasket they are to be considered discarded. (Sometimes, of course, it is necessary to destroy papers thoroughly, such as old or replaced legal documents, so that they cannot be used again.)

These are excellent habits to acquire:

> The habit of being punctual
> The habit of doing first things first
> The habit of meeting deadlines
> The habit of cooperating
> The habit of knowing when to ask questions—and accumulating a list of
> them so as not to annoy another person by frequent interruptions
> The habit of checking continually in order to be correct
> The habit of making notes of things
> The habit of dating everything
> The habit of being consistent, and organizing work
> The habit of being suitably groomed for business **every day**
> The habit of being quiet
> The habit of being clean
> The habit of keeping business information to oneself

Memory Aids. The best method of remembering is by association of ideas. Analyze things and translate them into familiar terms.

Read a meaning into everything—a reason. **Meaningless things cannot be remembered.** Every paper that comes into or originates in an office has some importance. It is written for some purpose; it will bring about some result; it has some reason for existing.

If a real interest is created in the papers that pass through an office— in what they are doing to further or hinder the work—it will be easy to remember them, even though they have to be handled rapidly.

"Infallible Memory." The only way to have an infallible memory is to **write it down.** Make notes of everything: telephone calls, business appointments, supplies to be ordered, things to be done, messages taken—in fact, **everything.** Make a habit of making notes. It is the **only way** to avoid saying "I forgot."

Automatic Memory. To be reminded of something automatically, put the article in question (or a note regarding it) where it will be a reminder in itself. If, for instance, a book is to be returned to the library, or a letter is to be registered, put it with some automatic reminder, such as gloves, hat, or wraps.

If something is to be done at a certain time on a certain day, make a note of it on the desk calendar, and when that day arrives, circle the note in red and place the calendar in a forward position on the desk, to be a constant reminder until that duty is attended to.

Photographic Memory. Certain things may be remembered by "photographing" them on the mind. If, for instance, a mental picture is made of a telephone number the first time it is used, it rarely deserts thereafter. Or the image of the spelling of a word may be imprinted on the mind. Initials may also be remembered in this manner.

Mistakes. Accuracy heads the list of desirable qualifications for an office worker. Speed is secondary.

Standardize on everything to avoid errors. **System is a great aid.** When many of the little error-prevention devices are overlooked, the accuracy average is very low. If they are made use of, the reliability and accuracy average is usually high.

Avoid errors wherever possible by anticipating them. There is much truth in the old advice: think first and act afterward. Do not act first and think and regret it afterward. In deciding how to do anything, **think out the consequences of doing it in several ways.** Then choose the way that has the least possibility for criticism or error, **even though it is the hardest way.**

Never blankly or mechanically follow instructions. Think over the working out of all instructions before executing them.

Don't be uninterested when doing things. Attach some importance to every small task to be done. It is in the small things that the catch lies. They seem unimportant at the time, but if done incorrectly something of great importance may grow out of them.

If tired or ill, double-check the work, and work more slowly. Many errors creep in under these circumstances.

If an error of any consequence is made, never try to "fix it up" and say nothing. Serious outgrowths have come from so doing. Think out a way to remedy the situation if possible, and suggest the remedy along with confessing the error.

Be reasonably sure, but never too sure about anything. It is very easy to be wrong, which always proves embarrassing.

Everyone makes mistakes—and someone tells him about them— but the careful worker need never be told twice about the same thing.

Dismissal or Being "Fired." Carelessness heads the list of reasons for being discharged.

No matter who a person is, unless he is his own employer, there is always the possibility of being "fired."

Therefore the accuracy and interest averages should be kept high. Correct everything that can be corrected. Never depend on another to catch or correct small errors or inefficiencies that are known to exist. Correct them at their inception; there are always enough unavoidable mistakes to count against one.

Reasons for being "fired":
    Being habitually late, leaving early, or taking long lunch hours.
    Inability to cooperate with other people in the organization.
    Long personal telephone calls, tying up the company lines.

467

Talking or laughing too much, or too loud.

Not taking messages correctly, or failing to write them down.

Insubordination (no task should be too small for any person to do if he is unoccupied).

Absence from the office on the slightest provocation.

Disloyalty or dishonesty.

Thoughts on being "fired":

Remember that many of the best people have been "fired";

That instead of being a calamity, it may be a start toward more satisfactory employment;

That something has been learned; and that mistakes in the long run are called "experience."

"Life is a long lesson in humility."—Barrie, *The Little Minister.*

Money Matters

Increases in Salary. When asking for an increase in salary, state simply that it seems necessary and give the reasons. If you are not earning enough to live on, say so. Or if the work is very difficult or trying, perhaps the position warrants a higher salary. These are the main reasons for asking for an increase in salary.

If salaries come under the supervision of an immediate superior, discuss the matter with him first. It may be his position to recommend increases for those in his department.

In large companies, it is often helpful if the one asking for a salary increase submits a written summary of the duties performed in his particular position.

Choose the opportunity for discussing an increase in salary when the person who might grant the request is in an unhurried mood. This discussion can always await an opportune time.

Discussing Money Matters. Money matters are the most private of all matters in a business office. **Never mention a money matter of any kind before a caller,** or before a third person in the same office, or even before members of an employer's family unless the employer mentions it first.

Do not refer to another person's insurance, income tax, your own pay check, or an IOU, except in privacy. If it is necessary to refer to any of these things before others, make a memorandum and hand it to the other person.

Never mention money that a superior owes for office expenses Make an itemized slip and place it on his desk. Instead of writing "You owe..." suggest it in a businesslike way, as "Paid for messenger—$1.45."

Borrowing Money. Do not borrow money from others in the office unless it is absolutely necessary. Much annoyance is caused by trivial borrowing.

Always make a note of money borrowed, even from friends. It is most embarrassing to forget to repay. And **always repay promptly.** Money matters are a very delicate subject—even between the best of friends.

Safeguarding Valuables. Never leave anything of value, money, purse, wraps, etc., in an unguarded place in an office. Many things have been lost or stolen in offices, which are more or less public places. See that all things of value, **especially stamps,** are put away at night in a locked drawer or in some other place of safekeeping.

Personal Matters

Personal Telephone Calls. Do not use the office telephone for long personal conversations. Personal calls at the office, both incoming **and** outgoing, should be very few and far between—and **very brief.**

Using the telephone for social purposes ties up the trunk lines, and a constant "busy" signal is usually reported to an employer. Even a good-natured employer resents the continued use of the office telephone for personal calls.

Personal Letters. Do not **write or read** personal letters in the office, except in privacy.

Do not use company stamps or send personal telegrams without paying for them.

Personal Engagements. Every social engagement should be made contingent upon and subordinate to business. In an office, **business comes first,** and social engagements last.

Ethics. A few of the little "unwritten laws" of business:

Absolute loyalty is expected at all times. Do not say uncomplimentary things about the company that pays your salary—in the office or out. Do not let dissatisfaction be known unless you are ready to resign; the company may request the resignation if rumors of dissension are heard.

Try by cooperation to work out all problems smoothly. If things remain unsatisfactory and irremediable after a thorough trial at betterment, do not resort to a condemnation of the company; simply resign, and attempt to find more congenial work.

Keep out of petty gossip. It is enticing sometimes, to be sure, but those who stay clear of it are always in the advantageous positions in the long run. If asked by a superior about another person under certain circumstances, make whatever is told as kindly as possible, but of course state the truth.

Guard office information carefully. Never tell anything outside the office—even in enthusiasm—that might be giving away valuable secrets. Whatever the company is working on should be kept confidential until it is ready to be released.

Office, General

Desk. Keep the desk clean. It is a workbench, not a catchall.

Never allow a lot of old-fashioned relics to accumulate on a desk. File everything away in its natural place, and dispose of all obsolete things. Keep an efficient and up-to-date follow-up system, if possible; if not, keep current papers in a pending folder or basket, with explanatory notes clipped to them, and look them over **every day,** weeding out the ones that can be disposed of, or that someone else can dispose of. Beware of piling papers in file boxes and forgetting them.

The more papers on a desk, the more to remember.

Keep the telephone book off the desk unless it is in constant use; keep it free from dust in a cabinet or drawer near the telephone.

Keep newspapers and magazines off the desk if they are not in actual use. Save the morning newspaper for one day only, unless a regular file of newspapers is kept.

Do not have anything that might tip over and spill on a desk, such as a vase of flowers, an open soft-drink bottle, or a cup of coffee. Keep such things in safer places.

If near an open window, keep all papers weighted. The wind has often carried valuable papers out the window.

Cover all papers or letters of a confidential nature when leaving the desk. In extremely confidential work, place the papers inside the desk and lock it, thus further protecting responsibility.

Leave the desk clean at night. Especially, put away carbon paper, which deteriorates rapidly. See that the typewriter is covered or closed in a desk. Never put an expensive piece of equipment, such as a "line-a-time," on the floor, where it may be injured by the cleaners.

Much waste comes from improper care of office equipment, and many an employer looks with discouragement upon his carelessly deserted offices at night.

The phrase "taking an interest in the business" means, in fact, "taking care of things."

Chair. An armchair is not a convenient chair for typing. A swivel "posture" chair with a good **back rest** is the most practical and restful.

Chairs are often too high or too low for ease in typing. Adjust the height until the chair seems comfortable.

If the typewriter table or shelf is too low, put a wooden "lift box" or pad under the typewriter to raise the writing level.

Learn to lean back and rest against the chair. If the back of the chair is too far away, fit a small cushion to it for the shoulders to rest against. Pull the chair up close so that the body will be able to sit

470

erect yet braced against the back rest. This eliminates fatigue and the stinging neck and shoulder pains experienced by many who type all day without back support of any kind.

Keeping Supplies. Keep the supply cabinet in perfect order, even if time has to be taken to arrange it one day each week.

Have **only one opened package** of each different supply. Keep all others wrapped, and mark the contents on the outside in red or blue pencil, so there will be no tearing of corners of packages to see the contents, leaving the material to deteriorate. A real loss of money is involved in wasted supplies.

Group everything of one kind in one place. For instance, all the paper should be on one shelf, the envelopes on another, inks and bottled or tube supplies on another, erasers all in one box, and carbon paper in one section. Then if anyone wants a certain supply it is to be found in one place, or it is not in stock.

Keep the most-used supplies in the handiest places on the most convenient shelves, not, for instance, the pencils on the bottom shelf, and the letterheads on the top shelf stacked behind seldom-used papers.

Ordering Supplies. Keep a memorandum order list in the desk, and add a new item whenever a supply is getting low.

Order by number if possible, and state definitely the **size, quality,** and **quantity** desired. Unless this is done, many mistakes will occur.

Check prices and quantities on the invoices for goods, and write "Received by...," instead of "OK," on the bill. "OK" is used by the person passing upon payment.

Printed Supplies. Before reordering any supply of printed matter— letterheads, envelopes, forms, etc.—consult someone in authority about the order. A change in wording, lettering, size, or paper quality may be desired.

Always obtain an estimate from a printer before ordering any printing done. Prices vary greatly, according to the quality of paper used, etc.

When reordering printed forms, give the **printer's number** on the form, and send one form as a sample.

Also allow plenty of time for the printing to be done, by reordering at least **three weeks** before the supply will be actually needed.

Heating, Lighting, and Ventilating. Many discussions arise regarding the temperature of rooms, too much or too little air, and too much or too little light. In these matters attempt to see first from the others' viewpoint; but if their suggestions seem wrong after being given a trial, suggest an improvement of conditions.

Room temperatures should be approximately

> 70 degrees F. in summer, and
> 70 to 78 degrees F. in winter.
> (Air may be warmer in winter because of the cold air currents that
> carry the heat away.)

Windows should not be opened so wide in winter that the air cannot be slightly warmed before it is breathed. Health authorities state

471

that the raw coldness of winter air is a great factor in producing the common cold.

Never place a desk in a draft; and arrange desks so that no one will sit facing a window. Light should come from the side or back. Avoid glares on metal objects or shiny surfaces from the morning or afternoon sun.

When using an electric fan, turn it so it will blow above the heads of workers, and not directly on them.

Dusting. An office should always have the appearance of being thoroughly clean.

Never permit it to become dusty or cluttered up. Such a condition looks old-fashioned. Modern desks are clean, files clean, rooms clean.

Every desk should be dusted every morning. If necessary, desks should be dusted again at noon.

Do not resent dusting—it's a part of the job.

Cabinets. Keep books and magazines or periodicals in a' cabinet or bookcase if possible. Do not permit magazines to pile up and collect dust. The general rule is to save magazines for six months only. Ask the office's preference regarding this.

Arrange books **alphabetically** in the cabinets, first by subject, then by author under each subject, as is done in libraries.

Arrange the issues of each magazine in a separate stack, chronologically, with the latest issue always on top.

Cleaning and Discarding. When cleaning an office, make a list of suggested things to be thrown away. Ask permission, from someone in charge, to dispose of such things. Never discard anything of possible value **without permission.**

Do not let things accumulate anywhere in an office, such as old newspapers or magazines, half-used carbon paper, addressed envelopes, and old files and folders.

Office Details. To keep an office in smooth running order, do not debate about doing small unwanted jobs; simply do them or see that they are done.

Analyze an office and anticipate its needs. If something seems to be necessary or called for a number of times, see if it cannot be procured. If there is a buzzer or bell system that is too loud, have it toned down. Do not permit harsh sounds or disturbing noises to irritate an office, if they are at all remediable.

Ordering Improvements. If contemplating any cleaning, redecorating, additions, or improvements in an office, **get an estimate in writing** of the cost before ordering the work done. (Or if the estimate is received by telephone, send a letter of confirmation.) Submit this estimate to someone in authority for approval. Surprising charges have resulted from ordering without an idea of what the cost would be.

This advice extends even to personal matters; in fact, for any undertaking on which the final charges are unknown—**get an estimate.**

❖❖❖❖❖❖❖

NEW POSITIONS

Letters of Application. If business conditions are such that office workers are in demand, an unsolicited letter of application may bring results. But it is best to attempt to ascertain whether a position exists before applying for it.

In answering an advertisement, comply with all its requirements. If the address given is a newspaper box number, use "Gentlemen:" or "Dear Sir:", whichever seems appropriate, as the salutation.

Begin with a simple statement, such as "I should like to submit my qualifications for the secretarial [or stenographic] position in your office." Then list the information in résumé style, with sideheads such as:

Education; Skills; Experience. Age; Height; Weight; Marital status
Salary expected or now earned (if requested);
References (with permission). (Give complete names and addresses)

Close the letter with a short paragraph, such as "I'll be glad to call for an interview at any time you might wish to see me [or state the hours most convenient]." Beneath "Sincerely," leave sufficient space for your signature, then type your name, address, and telephone number.

If letters of recommendation are thought desirable—in addition to the references—enclose copies, not the originals, of such letters. It is unnecessary to send a stamped, addressed envelope, unless you wish the copies returned.

Use white, bond stationery, and be concise and businesslike in your reply—never artistic or "unusual" in an attempt to catch the interest.

Registering at an Agency. When registering for a position through an agency, state the exact facts about all accomplishments or experience. If these are exaggerated it will be discovered when the applicant is sent to a new position, and both applicant and agency will suffer thereby.

If sent to a position by an agency, keep the agency apprised of all dealings regarding the position. Do not disregard the agency after being sent out by it.

Advertising for a Position. If such advertising is done, it should be very dignified and very conservative.

Interviews. When calling in regard to a position, dress in neat, businesslike clothes. Be courteous to the secretary or girls in the outer office; that impression counts too. It is unnecessary—if you have an appointment—to state the purpose of the call; but in the absence of an appointment, tell the receptionist or secretary why you have called.

Wait to be asked to be seated in an interview. Do not talk too much. Let the other person ask the questions and conduct the interview. Answer fully, of course.

Do not produce letters of recommendation unless asked to do so. Prospective employers usually write to the references given, if they are interested in the applicants.

Speak simply and clearly and use no unfamiliar words. Avoid pronouncing with a noticeable accent; it points toward affectation. Clear speech is immediately indicative of character and judgment.

Salary. Most positions are worth a certain salary. Attempt to arrange a salary commensurate with the position or the work.

A too low salaried person in an important position is not a good thing for the position, the person, or the company; and vice versa, a high-salaried person is misplaced in mediocre work.

A good method is to start at a reasonably satisfactory figure, and if able to fill the position competently and satisfactorily—and the work seems to warrant it—to ask then for an increase in salary.

Tests. Tests are often given in stenographic interviews. Therefore, do not be annoyed at a test. If asked to take dictation, do so graciously, and be careful to hear every word. Ask that a word be repeated if misunderstood; it is not unusual to misunderstand unfamiliar dictation.

In transcribing, do not attempt to hurry. Examine the machine and try it out for a few moments if unfamiliar with the style. Then arrange the setup of the typewriting carefully, and transcribe at an even pace to avoid errors. If corrections are necessary, see that they are especially neat; do not permit a struck-over letter on a sample page.

In anticipation of such a test, the resourceful applicant will have (in a pocket or purse) a large envelope containing a pen and two pencils, a few paper correction (eraser) tabs, a pocket-size dictionary—and a notebook if a special kind is preferred.

New Work. When accepting a new position, anticipate the hardest and heaviest work at first. Positions are usually created when work becomes heavy, or when someone has been absent and things have piled up. Then, too, unfamiliar work is almost always hard or trying.

Ask only necessary questions as a beginner, and have the questions listed so as not to cause constant interruption. See how many things will explain themselves; but of course ask about essential details. Do not attempt to learn everything in one day.

Make notes of the details to be remembered at first. Check the work against these notes to see that everything is being done correctly.

Obtain a list of the names, initials, and addresses of all persons connected with the company.

Make a small list of supplies necessary, if assigned to a new desk, and obtain them from the person in charge of the supply cabinet. Ask for only what is absolutely needed at first. An office regards with disfavor a newcomer who asks for numerous supplies or accessories, such as scissors and a stapling machine, before he knows whether his work is satisfactory and he is going to stay. Borrowed accessories will suffice for a few weeks, and the gradual stocking of a desk will allow time to consider what is definitely needed.

To become familiar with new work, read papers from the files, and use them as guides for typing letters, contracts, reports, minutes of meetings, etc. Read also the technical publications in the office containing articles pertaining to the business. These papers are the most valuable instructors, and give to the beginner an insight into the work that can be gained in no quicker way.

Legal Papers

Some offices other than law offices routinely prepare or handle certain legal papers, under the general supervision of their own legal counsel. For papers such as the following, printed forms to be filled in or to act as guides may be purchased from any large stationery store:

Acknowledgments	Contracts
Affidavits	Deeds (of all kinds)
Agreements	Leases
Articles of Incorporation	Liens
Articles of Partnership	Mortgages (of all kinds)
Assignments	Powers of Attorney
Bills of Sale	Proxies
Builders' Contracts	Releases or Satisfactions of Mortgage
Conditional Sales	Wills
(Agreements for Sale)	

The following points should be observed in preparing legal papers.

Paper. White, legal-size ("legal cap"), or often letter-size; of bond quality, and if thin it must be resistant to tearing.

Margins: top, and left, $1\frac{1}{2}$ inches; right, $\frac{1}{2}$ inch; bottom, 1 inch.

Spacing. Double-spaced. Land descriptions and other descriptions may be single-spaced.

Wording. The primary purpose in the choice of words is to make the document clear—so that it has only one meaning.

The long, formal, ceremonious phrases of a generation ago are being discarded in favor of straightforward wording. For instance, instead of using "party of the first part," etc., many companies are employing "first party" and "second party," or but one word to designate each party, as "Buyer" and "Seller," or "Contractor" and "Purchaser."

Instead of:	Usage is favoring:
made and entered into	made
by and between	between
signed and executed	executed
day and year	date
understood and agreed	agreed
assign, transfer, and set over	assign
the title and ownership of the goods	the title to the goods
personally came and appeared	personally appeared
Know all men by these presents	(is frequently omitted

475

Abbreviations. Should not be used in legal papers unless they are so common as to be understood without question. A personal name should never be abbreviated, as "Jas.," "Chas.," and "Jno.," unless the owner of the name uses the abbreviated form in his legal signature.

Figures. There is a general tendency toward the elimination of the repetition of numbers in legal papers, as "twenty-five (25) percent within thirty (30) days." The figure alone is now commonly used, even in land descriptions—except in papers that transfer title.

> The east fifty (50) feet of Lot Six (6) in Block Ten (10) of...
> East half (E½) of Section Two (2), Township Ten (10) North, Range Six (6) E.W.M.

(For further land descriptions, see Weights and Measures, p. 581.)

Prices in legal papers are still written in words and repeated in figures. But a series or list of prices is written in figures only. (See p. 280.)

Interlineations. Every interlineation in a legal paper must be initialed by all parties to the paper, to make sure that all are aware of, and approve, it. It is better to rewrite a page than to permit an interlineation, if the insertion is noticed before the papers are signed. Nothing can be changed, however, after signatures are affixed.

Inserted Pages. These should be avoided in legal papers. But if extra pages are added they should be numbered a, b, c, etc., and initialed by the signers or by the notary public to show that all parties are aware of the insertions. (See also Inserted Page Numbers, p. 416.)

Date. Every legal paper should bear a date. If the date does not occur in the first or last paragraph, it may be added as a last line before, or be placed on the line with, the signature, simply as

Dated April 20, 1977.

Dates are no longer written in words in legal documents, except sometimes in very formal papers such as wills; but even then it is not necessary that they be written out. (See also Numbers, p. 280.)

The End. Often indicated by this closing mark after the signatures:

– – –oOo– – –

Page Numbers. (See Typewritten Work, p. 415.)

Carbon Copies. Copies that are to be signed should be made on the same quality of paper as the original. Copies that are not to be signed may be made on cheaper paper, and the signatures typed on (after the original has been signed), with "(Sgd.)" or "/S/" before each name.

Copying Legal Papers. (See Copying, p. 432.)

Quotations. (For quotations in legal papers, see p. 255.)

Signatures. Signatures cannot stand alone on the last page of a legal document. There must be at least one line of writing above them to bind them to the rest of the paper.

Names throughout a document should be written exactly as they are to be signed. If there is a difference between the typed names and the signatures, an affidavit will later have to be filed to correct this.

476

Every person should decide upon the form of his legal signature and use it on all legal papers. If a signer uses his initials at one time, his first name and middle initial at another, and his first and middle names at another, he will sooner or later be forced to file an affidavit certifying that the three signatures refer to "one and the same person."

A good legal signature consists of the three full names—first or given name, middle name, and surname—without initials. There can be little question about the identity of a person who signs thus:

James Earle Darmond

The name may be typed beneath the signature, as it is on letters, if the signature is illegible, and if the name does not appear elsewhere in the document.

"By" should be used instead of "Per" when a person is simply signing for a company, or as the representative of another person.

"Per," "Per Pro.," or "P.P.," is used when a lawful agent is signing, under special authorization, for a principal. The full term is "per procurationem" (L., by authorization, or by proxy).

If responsible for the signatures on a document, make sure that all persons sign exactly as their names appear in the document, and that corporation and notarial seals are imprinted beside respective signatures.

Married Woman's Signature. A married woman's legal signature may be written in two ways:

1. The preferable form is a combination of her maiden name and her married name, as
   Elizabeth Lee Snowden
2. Another form is a combination of her first and middle names and her married name, as
   Elizabeth Marion Snowden

The first form more clearly identifies her; and in the text of the legal paper she may be further identified, if necessary, as "(formerly Elizabeth Marion Lee)."

If she signs her legal name in two different ways, as "Elizabeth M. Snowden" and "Elizabeth Lee Snowden," she will sooner or later be obliged to make an affidavit certifying that: "Elizabeth M. Snowden and Elizabeth Lee Snowden are one and the same person."

Seals After Signatures. Seals were once used in English law instead of signatures, and have been continued in present law as a part of the signatures on certain papers ("sealed instruments"). They authenticate the signatures, and in the eyes of the law add a greater dignity to papers. But in some states seals no longer carry any significance.

A "seal" may be written or drawn by the signer after his signature, or it may be printed or typed there. Anything that a signer indicates as his seal will be accepted as a seal.

The letters "L.S." (L. locus sigilli—the place of the seal) are often used as a seal; or the word "Seal" enclosed in a scroll.

Cross for Signature. If a person is unable to write, he may make his "mark" or "hold" (touch) the pen while the mark is being traced for him; or he may make his thumb mark in ink.

Two disinterested witnesses are usually necessary to a mark signature.

Witnesses to mark: [or Attest:]   His
    Daniel Calvin Carter (Address)   Jonathan Henry   X   Booth
    Albert John Maxon (Address)   Mark

Pencil Signatures. Although lead pencil signatures are valid in law, it is not safe to rely upon pencil writing, which not only is easy to erase, but often blurs and becomes illegible with handling. All signatures should be in ink to ensure their lasting qualities.

Papers Signed by Minors. Generally, persons under the age of 21 (or 18) years should not sign legal papers. While in most jurisdictions papers signed by a "minor" are valid if the minor elects, and is able, to carry out his contracts, such papers can be made inoperative if the minor chooses to disregard them. However, contracts and bills for necessaries supplied to a minor are usually not voidable—necessaries being regarded as food, clothing, and other articles necessary to maintain the minor's station in life.

Parts of a Name. The following are the parts of personal names:

Full name   as   Thomas Victor Kirkpatrick
                          Ellen Virginia Lane

Christian name   ⎫
Given name   ⎬ is the first name:
Baptismal name ⎪   Thomas
Forename   ⎭   Ellen
Middle name   is the second given name:
                           Victor
                           Virginia

                 is the last name:
Surname   ⎱
Family name   ⎰   Kirkpatrick
                     Lane
Maiden name   is a woman's surname before marriage: Lane
                 Often a married woman's maiden name is indicated by the French word "née" (born [nā]).
Married name   A woman's married name is written in three ways:
                 Mrs. Thomas Victor Kirkpatrick
                 Mrs. Ellen Virginia Kirkpatrick (née Lane)
                 Mrs. Ellen Lane Kirkpatrick
Legal name   is the full name (without abbreviations):
                 Thomas Victor Kirkpatrick
    Single legal name   Ellen Virginia Lane
    Married legal name   Ellen Lane Kirkpatrick

Legal Age. If an adult does not care to state his true age in a legal paper, he may be referred to as "above the age of 21 [or 18] years," or his age may be listed as "legal."

In many states the legal age, or "age of majority," for both men and women is 21 years. But in some states the age of majority for both sexes has been reduced to 18 years.

In many states women become of age, or are "emancipated from minority," by marriage. For the laws of each state, consult the current Martindale–Hubbell Law Directory, Vol. VI, in any public or law library.

Marriageable Age. The marriageable age in each state is given in the current almanacs, which are listed on p. 607.

Voting Age. The voting age in all states is now 18 years for both men and women (lowered by the 26th Amendment to the Constitution). For "Qualifications for Voting" in each state, see a current almanac, which will give the necessary periods of residence in state, county, and district.

Papers Signed on Sundays or Holidays. Although some papers may be legally signed and acknowledged on Sunday or a holiday in some states (if ratified on a business day), it is better practice to avoid the signing of any legal paper on a Sunday or holiday. The paper should be dated back to the previous business day. **Do not date it ahead,** as it may be made void by the sudden incapacity or death of a signer before the date shown.

Papers Maturing on Sundays or Holidays. If a paper matures on Sunday or a holiday, it is payable on the succeeding business day. This extends to the payment of income taxes, life insurance policies, etc.

Payments on notes, drafts, contracts, etc., must be **in the hands of the payees,** and not "in the mails," on the last day for payment. Payments on certain papers, such as some insurance policies, may be "in the mails" (postmarked) on the last day for payment; but this does not serve as a general rule for all papers.

Recording of Legal Papers. Legal papers, such as deeds, mortgages, chattel mortgages, liens, leases, and bills of sale, may be recorded in the county or city recorder's office upon payment of certain fees.

The papers are indexed, photocopied for the record books, and then returned to the owners or their attorneys. (In some jurisdictions, such papers as chattel mortgages, conditional sales, and liens may remain on file in the recorder's office until they are satisfied or released.)

The recording of papers establishes a prior claim over similar papers that are unrecorded. To be recorded, most papers **must be acknowledged** before notaries public or officers authorized to take acknowledgments.

Notary Public. A notary public originally drew up legal papers (as a "scrivener"), but now only certifies to the authenticity of papers, statements, or signatures; and prepares protests. (See p. 519.)

State laws differ regarding the age, qualifications, etc., for becoming a notary public. Definite information may be obtained from the Secretary of State at the capital in each state.

Officers Who Take Acknowledgments. Acknowledgments may be taken by, and affidavits subscribed to before, notaries public, judges, justices of the peace, clerks of the court, mayors, and certain Government officials, including diplomatic representatives and U.S. consuls.

Laws. (For method of finding or obtaining copies of national or state laws, see Reference Books, p. 606.)

Agreement or Contract. This instrument may be in simple form with simple wording, but it should state fully the understanding and the obligations of each party. The setup of an ordinary contract is:

CONTRACT [or AGREEMENT]

THIS CONTRACT [or AGREEMENT] entered into this .... day of ...., 19...., between .... of ......[address]...... (the "Buyer"* [or other word]) and ......[company]......, a ......[state]...... corporation, with principal office in ......[city and state]...... (the "Seller" [or "Corporation," or other word]),

WITNESSETH:

WHEREAS,† ....[introducing the reasons for, and the intent of, the contract]..; and

WHEREAS, ...[setting forth contributing facts or circumstances]........;

NOW, THEREFORE, the parties hereto mutually agree as follows:

1. [Heading]. ‡ ....
    (a) ....
    (b) ....
2. [Heading]. ....

IN WITNESS WHEREOF, the parties hereto have executed this Agreement as of the day and year first above written.

Witness:§

...............[Individual]...............   ....[Individual]...............

Attest:

                    [Corporate ....[Corporation]...............

.... Seal] By ....
Secretary [of Corporation]   President

[Page number]‖

---

* **A longer identifying phrase** ("herein [or hereinafter] called [or referred to as] the 'Buyer' [or BUYER]") may be used, but the short form shown is now widely employed and understood.

† **The preamble** containing the "Whereases" and "Now, Therefore" may be omitted, and the paragraphs or "articles" of the contract simply numbered 1, 2, 3 or First, Second, Third, etc., under "Witnesseth:"—with, frequently, paragraph ("run-in") heads or titles after the numberings.

‡ **Centerheads, sideheads, margin heads, or paragraph heads** are a convenience—almost a necessity—for guidance through a long contract or agreement.

Often **numberings** are like the following (see also pp. 412–13):

ARTICLE II [or 2]. Time of Completion

Section 1 [or 2.1]. . . . ["Sections" are set "full measure," i.e., margins not indented]. . .
    (a) . . .["Clauses" subnumbered a, b, c; set "short measure," i.e., indented on left]. . .
        (i) . . .["Items" numbered with small Romans may be "run in" the clause or subindented]. . .

§ **Witnesses** are not always necessary; but acknowledgment is, if the paper is to be recorded.

‖ **The number of pages** in a short contract may be shown with the page number, as "Five pages / Page 2" or just "-2 of 5-". Usually the simple page number is used: -2- (See also p. 415.)

Acknowledgment. The short certification at the end of a legal paper proves that it was duly executed and acknowledged. A simple form, according to the latest Uniform Acknowledgment Act, would read:

State of ....⎱ ss.
County of ....⎰

On this the .... day of ...., 19......, before me, ..., the undersigned officer, personally appeared ...., known to me (or satisfactorily proven) to be the person...... whose name...... .... subscribed to the within [or foregoing] instrument, and acknowledged that ....he.... executed the same for the purposes therein contained.

In witness whereof, I hereunto set my hand and official seal.

....
...............[Title of Officer]...............

If one person acts or signs as "attorney in fact" for another, the acknowledgment should read:

State of ....⎱ ss.
County of ....⎰

    On this the .... day of ...., 19......, before me, ..., the undersigned officer, personally appeared ...., known to me (or satisfactorily proven) to be the person whose name is subscribed [to the foregoing instrument] as attorney in fact for ...., and acknowledged that ......he executed the same as the act of h........ principal for the purposes therein contained.

    In witness whereof, I hereunto set my hand and official seal.

....
....
Title of Officer

For a corporation, the following is the form of acknowledgment:

State of ....⎱ ss.
County of ....⎰

    On this the .... day of ...., 19......, before me, ..., the undersigned officer, personally appeared ...., who acknowledged h........self to be the .... of ....,
(title of officer)
a corporation, and that ......he, as such ...., being authorized so to do, executed the foregoing instrument for the purposes therein contained, by signing the name of the corporation by h........self as ....

    In witness whereof, I hereunto set my hand and official seal.

....
....
Title of Officer

Affidavit. An affidavit differs from an acknowledgment in that the affidavit attests the truth or authenticity of the statements made in the paper, or in the affidavit itself; and the "affiant" signs the affidavit. A simple form of affidavit is as follows:

State of ....⎱ ss.
County of ....⎰

    ...., being duly sworn (or affirmed), say ...... that ....is (or are) the .... named in the foregoing instrument, and that every statement or thing contained therein is true *to the best of .... knowledge and belief.

Subscribed and sworn to before me
this .... day of ...., 19.....

      (Notarial
        Seal)

†Notary Public in and for the State of ...., residing in ....
My commission expires ....

---

* This phrase may be added if the affidavit is made upon information and belief.
† Or title of officer before whom affidavit is made.

481

Power of Attorney. Legal written authority to act for another in a certain capacity until the instrument is revoked. The word "attorney" in this sense does not mean an "attorney at law," but rather a "substitute," who can be any adult person empowered to act for another.

Attorney in Fact is the person so empowered.

Proxy. A proxy is a short form of power of attorney, given by a first person to a second person or committee, authorizing the second person or committee to represent the first person in voting at a meeting (usually an Annual Meeting of Stockholders). A sample is as follows:

P R O X Y [Company Name]

........, ..., and ...., or any of them, with full power of substitution, are hereby authorized to vote all stock of the undersigned on all matters, including the election of directors, which may properly come before the [Meeting] of the [Company], to be held in [Place] on [Date], and any adjournment thereof.

Dated........................   [Signature with title if any, as Executor]

Please sign exactly as name appears hereon.

(Notarial certification is not necessary; nor is a witness.)

NOTE: The person appointed to vote as proxy for another need not necessarily be a member of the organization, or a stockholder in the corporation, at whose meeting he is to vote. Some organizations, however, hold closed meetings to which nonmembers are not admitted.

◇◇◇◇◇◇◇◇◇

Deeds

A deed is a written conveyance of real estate (or similar property).

Warranty Deed. A deed in which clear title to the property is guaranteed.

Quitclaim Deed. A deed in which the one giving the deed simply relinquishes his rights in the property, but makes no guarantee of the title to the property.

Grant Deed. The word "grant" implies a special warranty or security.

"Tenancy" Deeds. These signify common ownership, in different ways:

Tenants in Common (Ten Com) implies that two or more parties have each a specified, disposable share in the property without having a separate title to any distinct part. There is no right of survivorship. Each share may be separately sold or willed.

Tenants by the Entirety (Ten Ent) implies undivided and equal ownership of property by husband and wife, which holding cannot be terminated without the consent of both. The survivor becomes the sole owner—without probate, but subject to estate taxes.

Joint Tenants (Jt Ten) implies joint (equal and inseparable) ownership by two or more persons, under which holding the survivor or survivors own the entire property.

Trust Deed. A deed given in trust to secure the payment of a debt; it is a conveyance to a trustee (an individual, bank, or trust company) for the benefit of creditors in case the debt is not paid. It is in reality a form of mortgage.

Tax Deed. A deed issued to one who buys property at a tax sale.

Easement. A conveyance of a perpetual right-of-way across property for a certain purpose, as for a roadway, power line, or pipeline.

Mortgages

A mortgage is a written conveyance of property, intended by the party making it (the "mortgagor") to be a security (to the "mortgagee") for the payment of money, or for the performance of some prescribed act. If the conditions are complied with, the conveyance is voided. Common mortgages are:

Real Estate Mortgage. A mortgage covering a certain piece of real estate and all permanent improvements thereon.

482

Chattel Mortgage. A mortgage covering personal (movable) property.

Crop Mortgage. A form of chattel mortgage, mortgaging a crop.

First Mortgage. A mortgage which represents the first claim on a property.

Second Mortgage. A mortgage that is subordinate to a first mortgage.

Underlying Mortgage. A mortgage representing a prior claim, because it was given before a later "overlying mortgage."

Satisfaction of Mortgage. A discharge of a mortgage that has been paid.

Liens and Assessments

There are many different names for liens, but a lien is primarily a legal right to claim property, or have it sold, for the payment of a debt. (pron. lē′ĕn, or lēn)

"Filing a lien" is recording a legal claim against a property.

Assessment. A levy made on property for improvements, such as water lines and pavements; or for taxes; or on stocks for additional capital.

Wills

There are different names for wills, but the term most generally used is "Last Will and Testament."

Holographic Will. A will "entirely written, dated, and signed" in the handwriting of the maker. Such wills are not valid in certain states. (pron. hŏl′ō-grăf′ik or hō′lō-)

Codicil. A later addition to, or modification of, a will—a supplementary document. (pron. kŏd′ĭ-sĭl, not *kōd*-)

Testator
Testatrix (fem.) (pl. testatrices [tĕs-tā′trĭ-sēz]) } The maker of a valid will.

Intestate. If a person dies without leaving a will (or a valid will), he is said to have died "intestate."

Bequeath. To give personal property by will (to make a bequest).

Devise. To give real property (lands, tenements, and hereditaments) by will; or a gift of real property by will. (pron. dē-vīz′)

Devisor. One who gives real property by will. (pron. dē-vī′zôr)

Devisee. One to whom real property is willed. (pron. dĕv′ĭ-zē′)

Legatee. One who is bequeathed a legacy (money or personal property).

Heirs. Technically, the persons entitled to receive real estate when there is no will. Now very generally used to mean any persons entitled (by will or otherwise) to receive the property of an estate.

Executor
Executrix (fem.) (pl. executrices) } The one named or appointed by the testator to execute his will.

Letters Testamentary. The authority and instructions given by a court to the person named as executor or executrix, to execute a will.

Letters of Administration. The authority and instructions given by a court to a person who has been appointed to administer the estate of one who has died without leaving a will (or a valid will), or if leaving a will, without naming an executor—or naming an executor who is unable to act.

Administrator
Administratrix (fem.) (pl. administratrices) } The one appointed by the court to administer or settle an estate.

Administrator, C.T.A.—with the will annexed (L. cum testamento annexo).

Administrator, D.B.N. Administrator of the goods not [yet administered] (L. de bonis non); appointed when a vacancy occurs in the position of administrator or executor.

Administrator pendente lite. A special administrator appointed to act while a contest or litigation is pending. (pron. pĕn-dĕn′tē lī′tē)

Administrator ad colligendum. Administrator appointed temporarily to preserve an estate, especially to make collections. (pron. ăd kŏl-lĭ-jĕn′dŭm)

Probate. To "probate a will" is to prove it, that is, submit it to a court for approval; or to prove its validity to the court and secure authority to carry out its provisions.

COURT PAPERS

Courts

There are many kinds of courts, but the ones ordinarily referred to are:

Justice Court (a city or district court)
Cases involving small claims are tried, or preliminary hearings are had, before a justice of the peace.

Municipal Court (a city court)
Usually corresponds to a justice court. A municipal judge presides.

Superior Court (a county, circuit, or district court). (In some jurisdictions, called a **County, Circuit, or District Court.**)
Cases involving large claims are tried before a judge or jury.

Supreme Court, or Court of Appeals (a state court)
The highest court in most states—the appellate court.

United States District Court
The trial court in each Federal district.

United States Court of Appeals (a circuit court)
The intermediate Federal appellate court (one in each Federal judicial circuit).

Supreme Court of the United States (in Washington, D.C.)
The highest court in the land.

Besides these, there are courts pertaining to special matters, as the Police Courts, Traffic Courts, Military Courts, Juvenile Courts, Orphans' Courts, Domestic Relations Courts, Probate Courts, Surrogate's Courts, Bankruptcy Courts, Insolvency Courts, Common Pleas Courts, Small Claims Courts, Magistrate's Courts, Chancery Courts, United States Court of Customs and Patent Appeals, United States Court of Claims, United States Customs Court, United States Tax Court, United States Court of Military Appeals.

Juries

There are two kinds of juries:

Petit Jury. An ordinary jury: a body (panel) of, usually, twelve persons selected impartially (impaneled) to hear cases and render decisions (verdicts) under the direction of a judge. (pron. pĕt′ĭ)

Grand Jury. An investigating jury: a body of from twelve to twenty-three persons, called together for the purpose of investigating crimes committed within a certain territory, and bringing the offenders to justice by rendering indictments against them.

Papers in a Lawsuit

Papers in an ordinary lawsuit originate in the following order:

Complaint. Is made by the "plaintiff's" attorney, setting forth the cause of action, or in other words, the plaintiff's grievance. (Also called in some states a "declaration," in others a "petition"; in some actions "narr" [narratio], and in an equity action a "bill.")

Summons. Is attached to the complaint, summoning the "defendant" into court; and the two papers are served on the defendant by a United States marshal, the sheriff or a deputy, or a constable. (Also called a "subpoena" in an equity action.)

Demurrer. May be interposed by the defendant's attorney, asking that the court dismiss the action because of insufficient cause for complaint, or any other reason that would cause the court to dismiss the action. If the demurrer is overruled, the defendant must answer the complaint within a certain number of days. (A demurrer to any of the pleadings may be interposed later.) Instead of a demurrer, in some states a **"motion for judgment"** is interposed, which is in the nature of a general demurrer.

Motion to Quash. May be made to annul the proceedings because of illegality.

Motion to Dismiss. May be made to dismiss the proceedings. The defendant may admit all the facts, yet say that it is not a proper suit because no action lies against him.

Answer. Is made by the defendant through his attorney, setting forth his side of the story. (Sometimes called a "plea.") The defendant may enter a

Cross-Complaint. Seeking affirmative relief against a codefendant.

Also, in an equity action, the defendant may enter a

Disclaimer. Denying any interest in or responsibility for the subject matter.

Reply. Is the plaintiff's refutation of the defendant's answer or defense. (In some states called a "replication.")

The following pleadings may also be entered in some courts of law for the purpose of reducing the charges as much as possible before trial, in order that the points in issue may be clear and distinct:

Rejoinder. The defendant's answer to the plaintiff's reply.

Surrejoinder. The plaintiff's answer to the rejoinder.

Rebutter. The defendant's answer to the surrejoinder.

Surrebutter. The plaintiff's answer to the rebutter.

Bill of Particulars. If the claims of a plaintiff, or defendant, are not understood by the other party, the court may order the plaintiff, or defendant, to deliver a detailed pleading to the other party, which detailed pleading is called a "Bill of Particulars."

The action is then ready to be brought to trial before a judge or jury.

The clerk of the court (with whom the papers have been filed as they were issued) has a complete record of the case, and the court allots it a date for trial on the **"trial docket,"** which is a register of cases to be tried.

Brief. May be prepared by either attorney, setting forth his client's case in brief, and giving the citations of law on which he makes his stand, in an endeavor to prove his case.

485

Subpoenas. Are served on witnesses, summoning them to court. (sŭ-pē′nȧ)

Subpoena Duces Tecum. A subpoena which orders a witness to bring certain papers or documents into court. (pron. sŭ-pē′nȧ dū′sēz tē′kŭm)

Deposition. May be made by a witness who is beyond reach by subpoena, or who is incapacitated. The witness's testimony is reduced to writing, signed, and sworn to before a legal authority. The one making the deposition is called the "deponent." (pron. dĕp′ō-zĭsh′on)

Burden of Proof. Rests on the one making a claim—he must prove it.

If the case is tried before a judge, the court may take the arguments

Under Advisement. Meaning for careful consideration or deliberation. Then an

Opinion, or Findings of Fact and Conclusions of Law. Are handed down by the judge, upon which a

Judgment, or Decree. Is entered in favor of the plaintiff or the defendant.

If the case is tried before a jury –

Instructions. Are given to the jury by the judge, citing the law applicable to the case, and directing a verdict for one party or the other if the jury finds that certain facts are true.

Verdict. The decision of the jury.

Motion in Arrest of Judgment. May be made by the defendant, for the stopping or arresting of judgment on the ground of errors, defects, or omissions apparent on the face of the record.

Judgment. Is the decree, or sentence, of the court based on the verdict.

Motion for New Trial. May be made by reason of newly discovered evidence, irregularity in the proceedings, etc.

Execution. A "writ of execution" may be given to execute the judgment, or enforce it.

Stay of Execution. May be granted to stay or withhold execution of the judgment.

Appeal. To a higher court (an appellate [a-pĕl′ĭt] court) may be made from the judgment, or decree. The one taking the appeal is called the "appĕl′lant"; the other party is called the "appellee [ăp-e-lē′]," or "respondent." The case may then be reviewed by the higher court and the judgment reversed or affirmed; or the case may be sent back for a retrial. (Certain cases cannot be appealed. Decision is final in some actions in the lower courts.)

Certiorari. A "writ of certiorari" may be issued to have the proceedings of a lower court reviewed by a higher court, on the ground that the lower court may have been without its jurisdiction, or that the proceedings may have been irregularly or improperly taken. (pron. sûr′shĭ-ō-rā′rī, or -râr′i)

Bill of Exceptions. Is a list of the exceptions that either party takes to the ruling or decision of the judge.

Transcript of Record. Is the transcription of the record of the papers and proceedings of the trial, including testimony and other evidence offered.

————

Court Testimony Style. The following is the general form for writing testimony. Note that "Q." and "A.", without dashes, are used for "Question" and "Answer," and that a question mark is used after every question. Quotation marks are not used; they are understood.

Q. What is your address?
   A. Westport, Connecticut.
Q. How long have you lived there?
   A. Since I was born. [Laughter.]
Q. Have you ever seen this paper? [Hands paper.]
   A. Not that I remember.
Mr. Martin—That is all.
The Witness—Am I excused?
Mr. Martin—Yes.
Mr. Hanover—May we suspend a few minutes?
The Court—Granted, for five minutes.
              [Recess of five minutes.]

Heading for Court Papers. The form for court papers differs in the different states, but the following is the form generally used for superior court headings:

IN THE SUPERIOR COURT OF THE STATE OF . . . .
    IN AND FOR THE COUNTY OF . . . .
                                    No. . . . .

```
                              )
. . . . . . . . . . . . . . . . . . . . . . . . . . . .)
                   Plaintiff  )
                              )        (Name of Paper, as
        v.                    )            COMPLAINT)
                              )
                              )
. . . . . . . . . . . . . . . . . . . . . . . . . . . .)
                   Defendant  )
```

The fictitious names "John Doe," "Jane Doe," "Richard Roe," and "Jane Roe" (followed by an identification of the persons) are used in court papers if the real names are unknown.

The following phrases are often used after the names of plaintiffs and defendants, to signify the involvement of other persons.

    et al   and others (pron. ĕt awl; from Latin et alii—and others)
    et ux   and wife (pron. ĕt ŭks; from Latin et uxor—and wife)
    et vir   and husband (pron. ĕt vĭr; Latin—and man)

Miscellaneous Court Actions

Attachment. A "writ of attachment" is a court order authorizing a seizure or a taking into custody of property or moneys to satisfy a claim, usually pending a trial to determine the validity of the claim. A bank account may be "attached."

Garnishment. A proceeding wherein a party who owes money to, or holds personal property of, a defendant is ordered to withhold such money or personal property so that it may be applied to the payment of the defendant's debts. Wages may be "garnisheed."

Replevin. A "writ of replevin" is a court order authorizing the repossession of personal property that has been unlawfully taken or is being unlawfully held. To "replevy" property is to recover possession of it. (pron. rē-plĕv′in)

487

Restraining Order.   A court order temporarily restraining a party from committing a certain act until the court can decide whether or not an injunction should be issued.

Injunction.   A court order to a party to enjoin him from doing some particular act that will be detrimental to another.   Occasionally it is an order to do some act that will prevent injury to another, or repay for some injury already done.

Mandamus.   A "writ of mandamus" is a court order to compel a lower court, municipality, corporation, or person, to perform some public duty.   (pron. măn-dā′mŭs, not *man-dăm′us*)

Quiet Title.   A suit to "quiet title," or "quiet title proceedings," may be brought to perfect the title to property.   If the suit is not answered and defended by anyone who may be interested, after due notice has been given, the title to the property is adjudged to be cleared.

Foreclosure Suit.   A suit brought to foreclose a mortgage, that is, to close out a mortgagor's interest if he has defaulted in his payments on the mortgage.

Impeachment.   The trying of a high public official for misconduct in office.

Indictment.   A formal charging with a crime—a "bill of indictment"—is drawn up by the prosecuting authority.   If a grand jury finds the bill to be true—supported by evidence—it is returned endorsed a **"true bill"** for a hearing of the case.   (pron. ĭn-dīt′ment)

Arraignment.   The formal calling of an accused person into court, reading the indictment to him, and asking him whether he is guilty or not guilty.   If he pleads "guilty" he is sentenced.   If he pleads "not guilty" his case is tried. (pron. a-rān′ment)

Habeas Corpus.   Concerns the right to personal liberty.   A "writ of habeas corpus" may be issued by a court, ordering anyone holding or detaining another to bring the detained or imprisoned person into court for a hearing regarding the lawfulness of the detention.   (pron. hā′bē-as kôr′pŭs; L., thou [shalt] have the body [in court])

LEGAL TERMS

abstract of title—a record of the title to a piece of land.   It contains a brief summary of all deeds, mortgages, and other papers that have been recorded pertaining to the property.   It shows how the title has passed from owner to owner, and whether or not the property is free and clear of encumbrances.

accessory before the fact—a person who instigates, or contributes to, but who does not actually take part in, the commission of a crime.
accessory after the fact—a person who knowingly aids or shelters a criminal after the commission of a crime.

appurtenances, tenements, and hereditaments—improvements, rights, and privileges that pertain to the land, and title to which goes with the land. **"Tenements"** are particularly rights and interests, as rents and franchises; **"hereditaments,"** things that may be inherited.   (pron. hĕr′e-dĭt′a-ments)

attest—often used interchangeably with "witness"; but in many states, "attest" means a certification as to the genuineness and correctness of a copy.

barrister (Br.)—a lawyer, admitted to the bar, who may plead in open court.
solicitor (Br.)—a law-agent who prepares cases for trial, but cannot plead in the superior courts.

488

beneficiary—the one who is benefited, as by a gift, the income from a trust estate, the proceeds of an insurance policy, etc.   (pron. bĕn′e-fĭsh′ĭ-er-y, or -fĭsh′er-y)

blanket—covering all in general, rather than one thing in particular, as "a blanket mortgage," "blanket bond," "blanket insurance."

blue sky law—a law to protect the buyers of securities against fraud; so named because it was said that some promoters would "capitalize the blue skies."

capital punishment—death.
corporal punishment—bodily punishment.

certified copy—of an instrument is a copy made from the records in a recorder's (or county clerk's) office, and certified to by the recorder (or county clerk) as being an exact copy of the paper on file or of record.

change of venue—("venue" means "the place"). A "change of venue" is a change in the place of trial, usually for the purpose of securing a fairer trial.

conditional sale—a contract covering goods sold and delivered to a buyer on condition that he make periodic ("installment") payments thereon, and comply with certain stipulations.

covenant—a solemn promise or agreement in a contract or other legal paper.

curtesy—a widower's life interest in his wife's real property.
dower—a widow's lawful right to a portion of her husband's real property.

earnest money—a down payment given to "bind the bargain."

-ee—denotes the recipient of an action, as consignee, employee, grantee, mortgagee, lessee, payee, vendee.
-or—denotes the doer of an action, as consignor, grantor, mortgagor, lessor, vendor. (In some words -er is used, as payer, adviser, employer.)

embezzlement—the fraudulent appropriating "to one's own use" of money or personal property entrusted to one's care, as in a bank.
defalcation—the misappropriating of trust funds by a trustee or fiduciary. (pron. dē′fạl-kā′shun)
larceny—the unlawful taking of personal property without the consent of the owner (stealing or theft).
>   **grand larceny**—theft of a serious nature.
>   **petit** or **petty larceny**—theft of a trivial nature, as shoplifting.

eminent domain—the power of government to take (and pay for) private property.

encumbrance—any claim against property, as a mortgage, lien, unpaid taxes, or assessments.

equity—a system of established rules (not laws) based on equal justice and fairness.   (For financial equity, see pp. 530 and 542.)

escheat—a reverting of property to the state because of the nonexistence, or default, of rightful heirs.

escrow—Papers may be executed and placed "in escrow"—in the hands of a disinterested party, usually a bank—which means that certain conditions are to be fulfilled before these papers can be delivered.

Exhibits A, B, C, etc.—documents attached to court papers as evidence in proof of the statements made in the case.

ex rel.—(L. ex relatione, from or on the relation [of]). Designates the person at whose instance and by whose relation (telling) the state is acting in a lawsuit, as—in a legal citation—"U.S. ex rel. Hayes v. Martin." (pron. ĕks rĕl)

489

fee simple—an absolute title to property, with no limitations or restrictions (Under the old feudal law, a "fee" was a piece of land held by a vassal on condition of service and homage to a superior lord. The word "simple" here means "absolute," indicating that title to the property has no restrictions or limitations regarding the persons who may inherit it as heirs.)

felony—a serious crime punishable by death or a sentence in a penitentiary.
misdemeanor—a minor crime for which the maximum punishment is less than imprisonment in a penitentiary. (pron. mĭs'dē-mēn'or)

fiduciary—held in "faith" or trust; or the one holding something in trust—a trustee. (pron. fĭ-dū'shĭ-er'y, or -shá-ry)

franchise—a special right or privilege granted by a city or a government; for instance, the right to operate a railroad or a public convenience.
enfranchise—to grant a special privilege to, as the privilege to women to vote.

holder in due course—one who has taken or bought a not-overdue negotiable instrument, such as a promissory note, and has acted in good faith in the belief that there are no defects in the instrument and that there has been no previous dishonoring of it.

husbandlike manner—a thrifty or economical manner.

indenture—a written agreement under seal, of which each party thereto holds a copy; so named because originally the paper was indented and cut apart in order that each party might have a copy and that the two parts should match.

interlocutory—intermediate; provisional; not final, as "an interlocutory decree."

leading question—not a main question nor one that "leads a witness on" to tell more than he means to, but a question so worded as to suggest the reply; in other words, a helpful question.

letters patent—may cover rights to an invention; or convey title to public lands.

libel "Libel" is written, and "slander" is spoken, public defamation.
slander (In admiralty law, a "libel" is the plaintiff's complaint.)

licenciado (Sp.)—an attorney. (pron. lē-then-the-ä'dō)

liquidated damages—those damages the amount of which is clear and certain; in contracts often fixed damages agreed upon before, and in case, they occur.

lis pendens—a pending lawsuit, implying that title to the property is in dispute.

litigation—legal action, or a suit at law.

malfeasance—unlawful action; official misconduct. (mal-, evil [doing]) (pron. măl-fē'zans)
nonfeasance—failure to perform a definite duty. (non-, not [doing])
misfeasance—the improper performance of a lawful action, that is, in a manner that infringes upon the rights of others. (mis-, wrongful [doing])

malice aforethought—premeditated malice.

metes and bounds—used in describing the measurements (metes) and boundaries of a piece of property. (Incorrectly written "*meets* and bounds.")

nolle prosequi—(L., [plaintiff] is unwilling to prosecute). When a case is "nol-prossed" it is dropped; but it may be started anew. (pron. nŏl'prŏst')

nolo contendere—a pleading of "no defense," yet not admitting guilt. (L., I do not wish to contend.) (pron. nō'lō kŏn-tĕn'dĕ-rē)

opinion of title—an attorney's opinion or findings regarding the legality of a title to property, after an examination of the abstract of title.

perjury—knowingly and willfully falsifying under oath, or bearing false witness.

490

premises—the matters involved or set forth, as "in the premises." Also **property**—lands or buildings.

prior art (patent law)—prior patents, publications, or public use of a device.

public domain—(patent and copyright law). That which is "in the public domain" is available to the public for free use.

real property—land and whatever is permanently a part of it, as buildings, fences, trees, and minerals.

seised (or **seized**) **and possessed**—lawfully owned and possessed, as lands.

ss.—an abbreviation for the Latin word "scilicet" meaning "to wit"; on legal documents, such as affidavits, it verifies the place of action.

statute—an enacted law as distinguished from an "unwritten law," or the "common law," or "natural law." (pron. stătch′ūt)

statute of limitations—an enacted law (statute) fixing a definite time limit on claims, after which rights cannot be enforced, and lawsuits are forever barred.

surety—one legally bound for the debt, default, or failure of another.

time is the essence hereof—or "time is material and of the essence hereof," meaning that time is important and an essential factor in the contract.

tort—a civil wrong (not a crime) for which damages may be collected; for example, negligence that causes injury to a person or property.

to wit—"namely," or "that is to say." Calls attention or sums up.

trust—an arrangement whereby property is transferred to one party, known as the "trustee," to hold for the benefit of another party, known as the "beneficiary" or "cestui que trust" (meaning "he who trusts"). (pron. sĕs′twē kē)

usury—exorbitant interest rate charged; particularly, in excess of the legal rate. (pron. ū′zhu-rē)

vested rights—rights that are permanent, having become ingrown and undisputed.

waiver—a voluntary relinquishment of a right or privilege.

with covenant of general warranty—with the promise that everything in the contract is warranted or guaranteed to be exactly as stated, or proposed.

without prejudice—without effect upon or detriment to any legal rights that existed prior to this act. **"With prejudice"** ends or precludes such rights.

writ—a court order commanding a person to do, or not do, some act.

BUSINESS ORGANIZATIONS

Company. May be either a partnership, a corporation, an association, or a joint stock company.

Firm. Strictly, a partnership; often loosely refers to any business organization

Partnership. Two or more persons associated in business under a contract to share profits and losses equally, or to prorate them according to the amount of capital invested. Some rules that are generally applicable to partnerships are:
Each partner is liable for the entire debt of the firm.
The business agreements or acts of any one partner bind the entire firm.
No new partner may be admitted, nor may the nature of the business be changed, without the consent of all partners.
The death, incapacity, retirement, or withdrawal of one partner may terminate the partnership.

491

A partnership may exist under a verbal agreement, but this is not a satisfactory arrangement. It is difficult to prove any verbal agreement. Every partnership agreement should be in writing (drawn up by a lawyer), signed and acknowledged by all partners.

A "silent partner" is one who has invested funds in a partnership, but who does not actively take part in the business, nor is he publicly known to be a partner.

Limited Partnership. A partnership in which one or more partners may invest and be liable for only a limited amount. Such partners are known as "limited partners" (or "special partners" in some states) in distinction from the "general partners" who transact the business, share profit and loss, and generally are each liable for the entire debt of the firm.

Limited partners, as a rule, cannot actively engage in the transaction of partnership business, but may have a knowledge of, and give advice regarding, the affairs of the firm.

Corporation. A number of persons combined or "incorporated" into one body under the laws of the state. ("Corporation" comes from the Latin word "corpus" meaning "body.") A corporation acts as a single person; and its powers are limited to those set forth in its Certificate of Incorporation or Charter.

It is a legal being, separate and distinct from the persons who create, govern, or own it. Its members are not individually liable for its debts. Its owners, or stockholders, cannot act individually in making commitments for the corporation. It must act as one body, governed by its officers or board of directors.

When a company is to be incorporated, **Articles of Incorporation** are drawn up, setting forth the terms and conditions or "articles" under which the corporation is to operate. Such articles are sent, usually in triplicate, to a designated public office, such as the office of the Secretary of State, State Corporation Commission, or State Tax Commission, of the state in which the company is to be incorporated. If the articles conform to the state's corporation laws, they are approved by state officials, and a certificate of approval is issued, the articles being recorded and becoming known then as a **Certificate of Incorporation** or **Charter** under which the corporation operates.

Preliminary information regarding incorporation and corporation laws may be obtained from the Secretary of State, State Corporation Commission, or State Tax Commission, at the capital in each state.

A competent attorney should be engaged to handle the incorporation proceedings. The first meeting of the new corporation should be held in the attorney's presence.

Corporation books may be purchased from any reliable stationer. The corporation minute book may be in looseleaf form. It usually bears printed instructions regarding the manner of conducting a corporation meeting.

Certificates of Stock are issued to owners of shares of stock in a corporation (each certificate representing a certain number of shares). If the stock is to be listed on a stock exchange, the stock certificates must be printed in a certain form. These requirements may be ascertained from the stock exchange.

Bylaws are private rules or laws drawn up by a corporation for its self-government.

Delaware Corporation is incorporated in the State of Delaware (to take advantage of the cheap incorporation rates and taxes in Delaware); but may be licensed to do business in other states as well as in Delaware when it has complied with the laws of such other states.

492

Close (or **Closed**) **Corporation** is a corporation whose stock is all privately owned by a few persons—often in a family. As a rule, one stockholder cannot dispose of his stock without the consent of the other stockholders.

Limited, or **"Ltd.,"** after a company name is a British and Canadian term signifying "limited liability company," meaning that the financial responsibility of the shareholders (British term) is limited. (Like a corporation [**"Inc."**] in America—in which the liability of the stockholders is understood to be limited.)

Sole Proprietorship. A business entirely owned and controlled by one person. This type of enterprise is usually small, enjoying low taxation, and being required to submit only a few government reports. But the owner is liable, even unto his personal assets, for all debts of the business.

Mutual Plan, as a mutual savings bank or mutual insurance company. The word **"mutual"** implies a cooperative company, managed by trustees or directors wholly for the benefit of depositors or policyholders, who share in the profits.

Joint Stock Company. In fact, a large partnership, with some of the characteristics of a corporation (although not incorporated). Its members are, as a rule, individually liable for its debts; but the death or retirement of one member does not terminate the company; nor can any one member contract for the company—its acts must be governed by elected directors or governors.

Its stock may be transferred without the consent of its members.

Public Utility. A large, private corporation performing an essential public service and devoting its property thereto, such as a railroad, transportation, water, gas, electric, telegraph, or telephone company. Such companies operate under government franchises, which grant monopolies but subject the companies to rate and service regulation.

Holding Company. A company formed to buy and hold the stocks of other companies—often controlling them through voting power. It derives its income from dividends of such securities. It encounters antitrust action when it buys enough stocks in a certain industry to control that industry.

Operating Company. A company actually engaged in operating a business.

Subsidiary Company. A company wholly or partially owned and controlled by another company—the parent company.

Association. A large number of people united for a common purpose. It is usually governed by bylaws; and it may or may not be incorporated. If unincorporated its members are generally liable for its debts as in a partnership.

Syndicate. A group formed temporarily to finance a project. It usually bids to **"underwrite"** a new securities issue (of stocks or bonds); that is, it guarantees to take the entire block at a certain discount. If awarded, it re-offers such securities to the public. (Or it may buy and sell real estate.)

In journalism, a syndicate is a concern that contracts for and distributes authors' and artists' work to a group of newspapers or other publications.

Cooperative (Co-op). A mutual-benefit enterprise. An apartment co-op sells stock in its building and issues proprietary leases to tenant-stockholders.

Condominium. A joint control (dominion), as by two nations. Or ownership of apartments individually. Unlike a cooperative, each apartment is independent—in financing and selling. (pron. kŏn-do-mĭn′ē-um; pl. -s)

Consortium. A joint participation, usually international and often temporary, of large banking interests or corporations in a venture requiring vast resources.

In education, a reciprocal association, as of universities in a "Graduate Consortium," which pools some courses. (pron. kon-sôr′shē-um; pl. -tia, -shē-a)

Patents and Trademarks

The U.S. **Patent and Trademark Office** issues free **General Information** pamphlets on patents and trademarks. These may be secured by addressing the

Commissioner of Patents and Trademarks
Washington, D.C. 20231

The Superintendent of Documents, Washington, DC 20402, sells: Patent Laws, $2.10; Code of Fed. Regulations, $2.20; Trademark Rules of Practice, $3.50; Guide for Patent Draftsmen, 65¢; Patents and Inventions—An Information Aid, $1.75.

PATENTS

A patent may be obtained by

> "Any person who has invented or discovered any new and useful art, machine, manufacture, or composition of matter, or any new and useful improvements thereof, or who has invented or discovered and asexually reproduced any distinct and new variety of plant, other than a tuber-propagated plant, not known or used by others in this country, before his invention or discovery thereof, and not patented or described in any printed publication in this or any foreign country, before his invention or discovery thereof, or more than one year prior to his application, and not in public use or on sale in this country for more than one year prior to his application, unless the same is proved to have been abandoned..."
>
> —Patent Law, 35 U.S.C. 31; R.S. 4886.

Not patentable are: inoperable or useless things; printed matter; methods of doing business; and mere ideas or suggestions.

Medicines cannot be patented unless they are more distinctive than mere prescriptions. They must be actually "invented." Ordinary medicines may be marketed under trademarks.

A model of the invention is not necessary, unless specifically requested by the Patent Office when examining the application. **A drawing is sufficient** if it shows the complete arrangement. (Drawings must be made in accordance with certain specifications described in the Patent Office pamphlet "General Information Concerning Patents.") Models, if made to be submitted to patent attorneys, need not be elaborate or expensive. They may be made in any size and of any material desired. The **inventor's signature and address** should be on every model, sketch, drawing, or photograph submitted to his attorney.

A detailed description or "specification" of the invention, including the manner of constructing and using it, must accompany the application.

Who May Apply for Patent. Only the actual inventor or joint inventors, or the executor or administrator of the estate of a deceased inventor, or the guardian of an incompetent inventor, may apply for a United States patent.

Patents, when issued, may be sold, licensed, assigned or granted, mortgaged, or bequeathed. Or a patent may be issued direct to an assignee.

"Patent Applied For," or **"Patent Pending,"** may be used on articles only **after the patent application has been filed** in the Patent Office. No definite protection is afforded by law until a patent is actually issued, but "Patent Applied For" or "Patent Pending" is a warning that a patent may be issued which would immediately prohibit any unauthorized use of the patented device.

494

Term of Patent. The life or term of a patent is 17 years. It can be extended only by an act of Congress. After a patent expires the invention is public property—in other words, it is "in the public domain."

Fees. "Basic" filing fee is $65, including 10 claims (one can be "independent"). Each additional claim is $2; each independent claim above one, $10.

The final or "issue" fee is $100, plus $10 for each printed page of the patent, and $2 for each sheet of drawing. No fees are returnable if patent is refused.

Evidence of Date of Invention. To establish the date of conception of an invention, an inventor may write a description of his invention, with a drawing if needed, and file it with the Patent Office as a **"Disclosure Document"** to be kept for 2 years: fee $10. Or he may make an affidavit before a notary, or before two witnesses, which may serve as legal evidence of disclosure.

Record Search. Before an inventor files an application for a patent, he should have a search made of the Patent Office records to determine whether any similar patents exist which would preclude his obtaining a patent.

The Patent Office does not make such searches; but any reliable patent attorney will do so and furnish a report and printed copies of all similar patents, usually for a small fee based upon the time spent in making the search.

Copies of Existing Patents. Printed copies may be ordered from the Commissioner of Patents for 50¢ each; plant patents, 50¢ (in color, $1); design patents, 20¢; photocopies of foreign patents, 30¢ per page. Special handling (fast service) is 50¢ additional for each copy. When ordering, give the patent number or full name of inventor and approximate date of issue. Coupon pads or books may be bought from the Patent Office for the regular ordering of patents.

Patent Attorney. Regarding an attorney, the Patent Office has this to say:

> "An inventor...may prosecute his own case, but he is advised, unless familiar with such matters, to employ a competent registered attorney or registered agent, as the value of a patent depends largely upon the skillful preparation of the specification and claims. The Patent Office cannot aid in the selection of an attorney or agent."

A list of Registered Patent Attorneys and Agents is sold by the Superintendent of Documents—$3.70 a copy. The Roster in the Patent Office is open to public inspection. Also the names of registered patent attorneys may be found in local classified telephone directories, or in any law library.

Foreign Patents. The international **Patent Cooperation Treaty** simplifies the filing of a **patent application** on the same invention in designated signatory countries. But **no international or world patent** can yet be obtained.

Patents may be applied for in various countries, usually within one year after the application has been filed in the United States. Annual taxes are imposed in most countries; and further, in order to maintain a patent in a country, the invention must be manufactured there after 3 years, or be licensed.

Copies of about 8 million foreign patents (and thousands of foreign scientific and technical books and periodicals) are maintained in bound volumes in the Scientific Library of the U.S. Patent Office—and are open to public inspection.

Photocopies of such foreign patents, publications, and records may be obtained at the page-rate quoted above. (Coupons are not accepted in payment for this service.) Foreign patents must be identified by the patent number, date, and country of issue.

The Canadian Patent and Copyright Office is at Ottawa, Canada. Printed copies of patents issued since 1949 (Nos. 445,931 ff.) are available—$1 each. Photocopies of older patents are 25¢ a sheet. The amount of the fee required on any particular document may be obtained on request.

DESIGN PATENTS

A design patent may be obtained by any person who has invented any new, original, and ornamental design for an article of manufacture. Such a patent protects **only the appearance** of an article, not its structure or useful features.

Terms and fees: filing, $20; patent for $3\frac{1}{2}$ years, $10; 7 years, $20; 14 years, $30

TRADEMARKS

Trademarks may be registered in the Patent and Trademark Office.

Ownership rights in a trademark are acquired only by use. Before a trademark can be filed for registration in the Patent Office, it must be in use on, or in connection with, goods sold or shipped in commerce that may lawfully be regulated by Congress, such as interstate or foreign commerce.

A trademark may be a **coined name, sign, symbol, emblem, device, monogram (initials), autograph, picture, or words or names written in a distinctive manner.** Written consent must be had to use a living person's name or portrait.

A **distinguishing package, bottle, or configuration of goods** may be registered. (Medicines, compounds, etc., are often marketed under trademarks.)

No flag or insigne of any state or nation may be used in a trademark.

Other marks now registrable under trademark laws are:

Service mark—a distinctive mark, name, title, symbol, or slogan, etc., used in the sale or advertising of the **services** of one person or one organization.

Certification mark—a mark used by one or more persons to **certify** origin, material, mode of manufacture, quality, accuracy, etc., of goods or services.

Collective mark—a mark used by members of a **collective group** or organization, to indicate membership, etc., as in a union or cooperative association.

A trademark, together with the goodwill connected with it, may be **assigned**.

Term of registration of a trademark is 20 years, with renewal privileges for like periods if the trademark is in use in commerce (as above), and if application for renewal is made within the last six months of each term of registration.

Fees. The cost of filing an application for the registration of a trademark is $35. The cost of renewing a registration is $25. (A renewal application filed within 3 months after registration expires, costs an additional $5.)

Copies Necessary for Registration. Five specimens of the mark as used in commerce, together with a drawing of the mark, must be submitted with the application for registration. After registration, notice should be displayed with the mark, as **Reg. U.S. Pat. and Tm. Off.,** or ® (or ™ if not registered).

Copies of Existing Trademarks. Printed copies of registered trademarks may be procured for 20¢ each from the Commissioner of Patents. The number, registration date, and owner's name should be given, if possible, in the order.

Securing an Attorney. The employment of an authorized attorney or agent in the registration of a trademark is recommended.

"The owner of a trademark may file and prosecute his own application..., or he may be represented by an attorney or other person authorized to practice in trademark cases. The Patent Office cannot aid in the selection of an attorney or agent."

Foreign Trademarks. Trademarks should be registered in foreign countries, if possible, **before goods are sent into such countries.**

Foreign registered trademarks may be registered in the United States if the countries in question grant reciprocal trademark registration rights.

American trademark protection extends to all United States territories.

Copyrights

General information, application forms, and a copy of the new Copyright Law, effective January 1, 1978, may be obtained, free, by addressing the

Register of Copyrights
Library of Congress
Washington, DC 20559

All copyrightable **published** or **unpublished** works may now be registered for statutory protection in the Copyright Office.

Five classes of material have been established; and a copyright claimant should choose the **one class** most appropriate for the work as a whole—or give the Copyright Office a short description of the nature of the work.

Class TX—Nondramatic Literary Works (Application Form TX)

All types of "nondramatic" works, such as fiction, nonfiction, poetry, periodicals, textbooks, reference works, directories, catalogs, advertising copy (but not "commercial prints and labels," which are in Class VA), and compilations of information.

Class PA—Works of the Performing Arts (Application Form PA)

Works to be "performed" directly before an audience or indirectly "by means of any device or process," such as musical or dramatic works with any accompanying words or music; pantomimes; choreographic works; motion pictures; and other audiovisual works.

Class VA—Works of the Visual Arts (Application Form VA)

"Pictorial, graphic, and sculptural works," including two-dimensional and three-dimensional works of fine, graphic, and applied art; photographs; contributions (as drawings or cartoons) to newspapers, periodicals, or collections; prints and art reproductions; maps; globes; charts; technical drawings; diagrams; and models. Within this class are pictorial or graphic labels and advertisements ("commercial prints and labels" that are not trademarks); as well as "works of artistic craftmanship." The "design of a **useful** article" may be registrable it if can be identified separately from, and exist independently of, the utilitarian aspects of the article.

Class SR—Sound Recordings (Application Form SR)

Two situations are covered: (1) a copyright claim for just the sound recording; and (2) a copyright claim for not only the sound recording but also the musical, dramatic, or literary work embodied in the sound recording (but not the right of performance).

The **one exception** covers the audio portions of audiovisual works, such as a motion picture soundtrack or an audio cassette with a filmstrip. These are considered an integral part of the audiovisual work as a whole, and are registrable in Class PA.

Class RE—Renewal Registration (Application Form RE)

All renewal registrations (regardless of classification) for copyrights in their first term on January 1, 1978. Renewal registration can be made **only** during the last calendar year of the first 28-year term; and it will extend copyright protection for an additional 47 years—making 75 years in all.

Three other forms are for use in special cases:

Form CA—Supplementary Registration

To correct errors or amplify facts in a basic registration (not in a copy or phonorecord of the work), such as to name an omitted co-author; to give a change of title; or to clarify inexplicit information. But if the work is changed enough to be considered a "**derivative work**" (such as a dramatization), a new basic registration must be made.

497

Form GR/CP—Group Registration of Contributions to Periodicals

Contributions to periodicals or other composite works may have their copyrights renewed separately (whether first copyrighted independently or as part of a larger work); or they may be renewed as a **group** by a single renewal registration, if all were written or created by the same author, all first published as contributions, and all published in the same calendar year—even in different periodicals. (Group registration is to be used as an adjunct to a basic application on Form TX, PA, or VA.)

Form IS—Request for Issuance of an Import Statement

To be used by the copyright owner of a nondramatic literary work who wishes to import up to 2,000 copies of a foreign edition.

● ● ● ●

Not copyrightable are short expressions, mere ideas, and concepts that do not contain **authorship,** such as names of products, services, businesses, organizations, groups (including performing groups), pseudonyms (including pen names and stage names); titles of works; catchwords; short phrases; mottoes; slogans; coined names; and short advertising expressions.

Brand names, trade names, slogans, and phrases used repeatedly in commerce, may be protected under laws relating to unfair competition; or they may be registered as **trademarks** in the Patent and Trademark Office. (A copyrighted advertisement or label may contain a trademark, but this does not give the trademark protection or eliminate the necessity for its separate registration.)

Phonorecords of nondramatic musical works are subject to "compulsory licensing" for the making and distributing thereof. A license includes the privilege of making a musical arrangement of the work. Under such a license, a copyright owner is entitled to receive royalties on phonorecords.

Jukeboxes are subject to "compulsory licensing" and a payment of an annual royalty fee ordinarily of $8 per jukebox. If an operator fails to comply with the licensing requirements, he or she can be found guilty of copyright infringement. If a **certificate of recordation** should be lost or destroyed, a replacement must be obtained immediately from the Copyright Office.

Cable Television Systems are subject to "compulsory licensing" to retransmit copyrighted works. Statements of account must be filed. And cable systems located outside the 48 contiguous states must **record certain contracts** with the Copyright Office.

Public Broadcasting, noncommercial, of published musical and graphic works is subject to "compulsory licensing." Copyright owners and Public Broadcasting entities may reach voluntary agreement; but if not, terms and rates will be prescribed by the Copyright Royalty Tribunal.

★ ★ ★ ★

Notice of Copyright must be placed on all publicly distributed copies of the work—in a noticeable position—usually on the **title page** or **back** of that page, on the **first page of music,** or on a **masthead;** on the **face, back, base,** or permanently attached **frame** or **label** of other articles; and on the **title frames** of motion pictures. The notice needs no permission to use, and contains:

1. The word "Copyright" or "Copr.", and, or just, the **symbol** © (the latter being required for international copyrighting);
2. The **year** of **first publication;** and
3. The **name** of the **copyright owner** (or a recognizable abbreviation thereof), or a generally known alternative designation.

A full notice would read:

Copyright © 19.. by (name)

On **phonorecords** of sound recordings, the **symbol** ℗ is used, with the **year** of **first publication,** and the **copyright owner's name,** as above.

This notice may be placed on the **surface** of the phonorecord, or on the **label** or **container,** in a conspicuous position, as

℗ 19.. RCA Records

Omission of, or an **error in,** a copyright notice will not immediately result in forfeiture of the copyright; but if such oversight is not corrected within five years, it will result in complete loss of copyright. Innocent infringers will be shielded from liability.

Copy Deposit Requirements are on the application forms. A certain number of copies must be deposited in the Copyright Office with each application for registration. In general, the requirements are:

Two complete copies or **phonorecords** of the best edition of a published work;

One complete copy or **phonorecord** of an **unpublished work**; of a **test**; of a **foreign work**; or if a **contribution to a collective work**, one complete copy of the collective work. Also only **one complete copy** of a **published three-dimensional work** (or of an identifying reproduction); of a **published drawing, photograph, greeting card, or speech**; of a **musical composition** being loaned or rented; and of a **published instructional multimedia kit.**

If **fewer than five copies** of a **pictorial or graphic work** have been published—or a **limited edition** of not over 300 copies—only **one complete copy** (or an identifying photographic print, transparency, drawing, or similar two-dimensional reproduction, in actual colors, showing a full-size image of the work) may be deposited.

NOTE: These copies are not returned; however, "secure test" copies are returned if a sufficient description is provided for the archival record.

Sizes of identifying material must be uniform: at least 35 mm for transparencies (if 3″x3″ or less, must be mounted). For all other types, not less than 3″x3″ or more than 9″x12″—but preferably 8″x10″.

Commercial prints, labels, and other **advertising material** for the sale of merchandise or services, require the deposit of only **one complete copy** of each. If a print or label is published in a newspaper or other periodical, **one copy** of the entire page on which it appeared may be deposited. If such advertising is **physically inseparable** from a three-dimensional object, an **identifying photograph,** etc., as described above, may be deposited instead.

Motion pictures that are **"published"** (reproduced in copies for sale or distribution) may be registered by the deposit of only **one complete copy** of each, accompanied by a separate description of its contents, such as a continuity, pressbook, or synopsis. The Library of Congress may, at its discretion, enter into an agreement with the Depositor for the deposit and retention, or return and recall, of the deposit copy. For **unpublished motion pictures,** including **television transmission programs,** the deposit of identifying material, as described above, or of audio cassettes or soundtracks, will suffice in lieu of actual copies.

Fees. For registering a claim to copyright, for **all works** including foreign, the following fees are charged.

(Remit by check, money order, or bank draft, payable in U.S. currency, to the Register of Copyrights.)

Registration (or for **Supplementary Registration**)	$10.00
Renewal of a copyright in its first term	6.00
Recordation of Statement revealing the identity of, or death of, an author	10.00
Recordation of Document transferring copyright ownership (or for a **Cable Contract**)	10.00
Certification of registration record; or of a search report; or of a photocopy of Copyright Office record, etc.	4.00
Search of official records of Copyright Office, hourly fee	10.00
(Searches are not made, and not necessary, to determine whether a similar work has been copyrighted.)	
Filing Notice of Intention to Make Phonorecords	6.00
Replacement Certificate for coin-operated phonorecord player	4.00
Import Statement (for the issuance thereof)	3.00
Receipt for Deposit (for the issuance thereof)	2.00

* * * *

A **Deposit Account** may be established in the Copyright Office by a frequent user of its services—with at least 12 transactions a year. Initial deposit, and each later deposit, into the account must be at least $250.

Duration of Copyright, for copyrights existing before January 1, 1978, has been extended under the new law to a total term of **75 years**; that is, the second or renewal term of copyright has been lengthened to **47 years.**

Renewal application (for renewal in the author's name or that of a certain "proprietor") must still be made **during the last (28th) year** of the first term. Copyrights already in their **second term** will be automatically extended to a total of 75 years, without a re-renewal.

Duration of Copyright, for works created on or after January 1, 1978, is **"life-plus-fifty"** meaning the work is automatically protected from the moment of its creation, through the author's lifetime and for 50 years after the author's death—without any renewal. For a work created by **two or more authors,** the term lasts for 50 years after the last surviving author's death. For **works made for hire,** such as those ghostwritten or commissioned, and for **anonymous and pseudonymous works** (unless the author is identified in the Copyright Office records), the duration of copyright is 75 years from publication or 100 years from creation, whichever term is shorter.

Works existing, but not published or copyrighted, on January 1, 1978, are automatically given the same copyright protection as new works: the life-plus-fifty or 75/100-year terms. All works in this category are guaranteed at least 25 years protection; and if **published** before December 31, 2002, the term will be extended another 25 years.

All copyright terms will run through the **end of the calendar year** in which they would otherwise expire. All **renewals** must be made in the **last, or 28th, year of copyright protection**—before December 31.

Notice of Renewal of Copyright may be in the same form as the original notice; but a more informative and hence preferable notice should refer to the fact of renewal, as:

Copyright © 19.. by (Publisher)
Copyright renewed 19.. by (Author or Creator)

Copyright Status of a work may be determined by the copyright notice. If the work was copyrighted before 1978, it was protected for either 28 years from the copyright date (if not renewed), or for 75 years if renewed.

If the work was copyrighted after 1978, the fact to be determined is whether the author or creator is living or dead. Published notices—as in newspapers—may be helpful; otherwise a search must be made of the Copyright Office records, either by the concerned person (the Catalog of Copyright Entries is available in some large libraries), or by the Copyright Office itself—which Office will send an estimate of the total search fee. In some cases, a copyright attorney must be consulted to determine rights.

Transfer. Copyrights may be sold, assigned, mortgaged, or bequeathed.

Reclamation of Ownership of Copyright. An author, or specified heirs of an author, of a work copyrighted **on or after January 1, 1978,** may terminate any grant of rights made by the author (as to a publisher), if such termination is effected during a **five-year period after 35 years have elapsed** from the date of execution of the grant, or from the date of publication of the work. Or, on a work copyrighted **before January 1, 1978,** termination may be effected during a **five-year period after 56 years have elapsed** from the date of initial copyright.

499 *a*

The **notice** shall state the **effective date of the termination** (within the five-year period specified); and it shall be served on the grantee not less than **two,** or more than **ten, years** before that date. A copy of the notice must be recorded in the Copyright Office before date of termination.

Change of Ownership in a Copyright may be recorded, for a fee, in the Copyright Office by the filing of the original document transferring title—or a certified copy thereof—with the Register of Copyrights, who will record the document and return it with a certificate of recordation.

Expired Copyrights, and works already "in the public domain" on January 1, 1978, cannot be revived and protected.

"Fair Use" of a copyrighted work, including reproduction in limited copies or phonorecords, for such purposes as criticism, comment, news reporting, teaching, scholarship, or research, is not an infringement. In determining "fair use," these factors are to be considered: (1) the purpose and character of the use; (2) the nature of the work; (3) the amount and substantiality of the portion used; and (4) the effect of the use upon the potential market for, or value of, the copyrighted work.

International Copyright is automatically obtained when a work is copyrighted in any of the countries that have ratified the Universal Copyright Convention, as have most industrial countries, except Russia and mainland China. The UCC requires a participating country to give the same protection to foreign works—that meet Convention requirements—as it gives to its own domestic works.

Authors may collect royalties on their reprinted works in other countries. (The symbol © must appear in the copyright notice.)

British written matter published before 1957 bore no notice of copyright—although often a date of publication—because under British copyright law, copyright exists from the moment of creation of a work and for 50 years after the author's death. "Protection is automatic and no form of registration or notification of copyright is required." But since 1957, British works have carried the international copyright notice, as:

© London Press 19..

The **British term of copyright is 50 years from publication** of artistic, dramatic, musical, and architectural works; photographs; films; sound recordings; motion pictures; and television or radio broadcasts.

U.S. Government publications are not copyrighted if prepared by an employee of the Government as part of that person's official duties. But, the Government "is not precluded from receiving and holding copyrights transferred to it by assignment, bequest, or otherwise." Some U.S. Postal Service works are copyrighted.

Manufacturing of copyrighted **English-language nondramatic literary works** must be done in the United States or Canada (but 2,000 copies may be imported). (Manufacture in Canada equates with manufacture in the United States.) A tentative termination of this requirement has been set for July 1, 1982, but this cutoff date may be extended. **No such manufacturing requirement** has been imposed for dramatic, musical, pictorial, or graphic works; for foreign-language, bilingual, or multilingual works; for public domain material or works not subject to a manufacturing restriction.

United States Copyright Laws have been in effect for almost 200 years, the first statute having been passed in 1790.

∽

Government Information

Government Publications. The Government publishes through the Government Printing Office—the largest printing establishment in the world—a great number of informative and authoritative books and pamphlets, which are sold at nominal prices (50¢, 75¢, $1.50, $5, etc.).

Free price lists describing each available book or pamphlet may be obtained by addressing the

Superintendent of Documents
Government Printing Office
Washington, DC 20402

Ask for the entire price list ("**Subject Bibliography**"); or request the price lists on a **certain subject.** Selected lists, with **list numbers:**

If the publication desired does not appear in the above price lists, ask the Superintendent of Documents for information regarding it. Many pamphlets are distributed free by various Government departments.

How to Order Government Publications. Orders should be sent direct to the Superintendent of Documents, and not to the Government bureaus.

If sending an order and making inquiry about other publications at the same time, write the **inquiry as a separate letter,** giving your full name and address. A different department handles the inquiries.

Order by number if the number of the document is known; the price should also be stated after the title, as

D 101.11:5–760	Electrical Wiring	$0.50
I 27.19/2:P 16	Paint Manual	1.75
(Check [or money order] enclosed)....		$2.25

Orders are filled promptly and usually reach their destinations in the United States within two to three weeks after receipt.

Remittance must accompany the order—payable to the Superintendent of Documents. The **minimum mail order charge** is $1; that is, a 60¢ booklet may be ordered, but the remittance must be $1.

A **check or money order** is the requested form of payment.
An **advance deposit of $50 or more** may be made by regular customers.
Coupons are no longer issued.
No C.O.D. orders are accepted.
Stamps are not accepted. Currency is sent at the sender's risk. (Foreign money and defaced or smooth coins are not acceptable.)

Postage is free to addresses in the United States and its possessions; also to Canada, Mexico, and all of Central and South America, except as hereafter noted. Postage is charged to all other foreign countries, including Argentina, Brazil, Guyana, French Guiana, Surinam, and Belize (formerly British Honduras).

One-fourth of the total amount of the order should be added to the remittance to cover foreign postage. Any excess will be returned. Foreign remittances should be by international money order or draft on an American bank.

Discount. A 25% discount is given to the purchaser of 100 or more copies of a single publication to be mailed to one address.

Addressing United States Government Departments and Divisions. When seeking information from the Government, write to the division or bureau that should logically handle the matter in question.

> "When addressing letters to one of the Executive Departments of the Government, it is to the advantage of the writer to give the name of the department, the bureau therein, and, if possible, the particular division in which the letter will be handled, as this facilitates delivery of the matter and therefore procures a more prompt response."
> —U.S. Postal Service.

For instance, instead of addressing just "The Bureau of Reclamation," write:

Information Division

Bureau of Reclamation
Department of the Interior
Washington, DC   20240

Many departments and bureaus have offices in various cities. Therefore, before writing to Washington, D.C., consult the telephone book under "United States Government" to ascertain whether the office in question has a local branch.

◇◇◇◇◇◇◇◇◇

United Nations (UN). The address is just: New York, NY   10017.

(Headquarters and addresses of affiliated agencies may be found in the Congressional Directory.)

The chief administrative officer is **The Secretary General** (addressed in writing as His Excellency [see Ambassador, p. 326]). Organs and related agencies are:

General Assembly	**Security Council**	**Economic and Social Council**
Secretariat	**Trusteeship Council**	**International Court of Justice**

* * *

Universal Postal Union
World Health Organization
Food and Agriculture Organization
International Labor Organization
UN Industrial Development Org.

World Meteorological Organization
International Telecommunication Union
International Atomic Energy Agency
International Civil Aviation Org.
UN Children's Fund (UNICEF)

United Nations Educational, Scientific and Cultural Organization (UNESCO)
Intergovernmental Maritime Consultative Organization (IMCO)
General Agreement on Tariffs and Trade (GATT)

International Bank for Reconstruction and Development ("The World Bank")
International Finance Corporation   International Development Assn.
International Monetary Fund ("The Fund")   Asian Development Bank

Organization of American States (OAS), Washington, D.C. 20006.

(General Secretariat—**Pan American Union** ["Pan" means "all."])
Inter-American Development Bank   Inter-American Defense Board

THE GOVERNMENT OF THE UNITED STATES
(Compiled from the United States Government Manual.
All addresses; Washington, D.C.—with Zip Code shown)

```
                    ┌─────────────────────┐
                    │  THE CONSTITUTION   │
                    └─────────────────────┘
```

LEGISLATIVE (Law Making)	EXECUTIVE (Administering)	JUDICIAL (Judging)
The Congress	**The President**	**The Supreme Court**
Senate House	The White House	**of the United States**
20510 20515	20500	20543

Under the Executive Branch of the Government and, therefore, the President are the following Departments and Agencies:

Executive Office of the President

The White House Office 20500
Management and Budget, Off. of
Economic Advisers, Council of
Domestic Policy Staff
Trade Negotiations, Off. of

National Security Council
   Central Intelligence Agency (CIA)
Science & Technology, Off. of
Environmental Quality, Council on
Wage & Price Stability, Council on

Department of State   20520   (The Secretary of State)

*Inter-American Affairs
*European Affairs
*East Asian and Pacific Affairs
*Near Eastern and South Asian Affairs
*African Affairs
*Oceans and Intl. Environmental
   and Scientific Affairs
*Consular Affairs
  (incl. Passport and Visa Offices)
Protocol, Office of the Chief of

Foreign Service
  Foreign Service Institute
Agency for Intl. Development (AID)
  Human Rights & Humanitarian Aff.
*International Organization Affairs
*Economic and Business Affairs
*Public Affairs
*Intelligence and Research
*Politico-Military Affairs
  U.S. Mission to United Nations

*Full title: "Bureau of . . . ."

The Treasury Department   20220   (The Secretary of the Treasury)

Mint, Bureau of the
U.S. Customs Service
U.S. Secret Service
Alcohol, Tobacco and
   Firearms, Bu. of

Internal Revenue Service (IRS)
Engraving and Printing, Bu. of
Public Debt, Bureau of the
U.S. Savings Bonds Division
International Affairs

Comptroller of the
   Currency
Treasurer of United
   States, Office of
Monetary Affairs

Department of Justice   20530   (The Attorney General)

Divi-   Antitrust   Tax   Land and Natural   Civil Rights
sions: Criminal   Civil   Resources
Federal Bureau of Investigation (FBI)   Prisons, Bu. of   Community Relations Serv.
Immigration and Naturalization Service   U.S. Marshals   Drug Enforcement A.

Department of Commerce   20230   (The Secretary of Commerce)

Patent and Trademark Office
National Bureau of Standards (NBS)
Census, Bureau of the
Economic Analysis, Bureau of
Natl. Fire Prevention & Control Adm.
National Oceanic and Atmospheric Adm.
  Weather; Ocean Survey; Marine Fisheries
Maritime Administration

Industry and Trade Administration
  Export Development; East-West Trade
  Domestic Business Development
Telecommunications, Office of
Natl. Technical Information Service
Economic Development Administration
Minority Business Enterprise, Off. of
United States Travel Service

503

GOVERNMENT INFORMATION

DEPARTMENT OF DEFENSE (DoD) 20301 (The Secretary of Defense)
Composed of three military departments: Army, Navy, and Air Force.
Overall planning and jurisdiction is maintained in the following fields:

Manpower and Reserve Affairs	Nuclear Agency	National Security
Health and Environment	Communications	Program Analysis
Installations and Logistics	Intelligence	Financial Mgmt.
Research and Engineering	Supply	Mapping Agency
International Security Affairs	Contract Audit	Public Affairs

Joint Chiefs of Staff

Department of the Army 20310 (The Secretary of the Army)

GENERAL STAFF (Chief of Staff)	SPECIAL STAFF
Personnel (including ROTC)	Personnel Operations
Reserve Components	Army Reserve
Manpower and Forces	National Guard Bureau
Forces Development	Civil Functions and Works
Military Operations and Plans	Chief of Engineers
Logistics	Communications–Electronics
Intelligence	Inspector General, Office of
Research, Development, & Acquisition	Judge Advocate General's Corps
ADMINISTRATIVE SERVICES	Military History
The Adjutant General's Office	Information, Public & Command
Provost Marshal General, Off. of	COMPTROLLER OF THE ARMY
The Surgeon General	Financial Mgmt. Audit Agency
Army Medical Service	CIVIL PREPAREDNESS AGENCY
Chaplains Branch	

U.S. Military Academy (West Point, N.Y.)
MAIN ARMY COMMANDS

Army Forces	Training and Doctrine	Materiel Development and Readiness	
Communications	Security	Health	Traffic	Criminal Investigation

Department of the Navy 20350 (The Secretary of the Navy)

THE EXECUTIVE OFFICE OF THE SECRETARY conducts the business management of the Navy Department. Principal offices are:

Chief of Naval Operations	Naval Personnel, Bureau of
Naval Material Command	Civilian Personnel, Office of
Five "Systems Commands":	Medicine and Surgery, Bureau of
Air * Sea * Supply	Naval Telecommunications Comd.
Facilities Engineering *	Military Sealift Command
Electronic	Naval Research, Office of
Naval Oceanographic Office	U.S. Marine Corps, Headquarters

U.S. Naval Academy (Annapolis, Maryland)

Department of the Air Force 20330 (The Secretary of the Air Force)

THE CHIEF OF STAFF, UNITED STATES AIR FORCE (USAF), is head of the Air Staff, and is the senior Air Force officer on active duty. Major commands are:

Air Training Command	Headquarters Command	Military Airlift
Tactical Air Command	Strategic Air Command	Command (MAC)
Aerospace Defense Comd.	AF Logistics Command	AF Communications Serv.
Air University	AF Systems Command	Oversea Commands
USAF Security Service		

U.S. Air Force Academy (Colorado Springs, Colorado)

Department of Energy (DOE) 20545 (The Secretary of Energy)

Energy Research	Energy Technology	Economic Regulatory Adm.
Environment	Resource Applications	Fed. Energy Regulatory Com.
Defense Programs	Energy Information Adm.	Conservation & Solar Appl.

504

GOVERNMENT OFFICES

Department of the Interior 20240 (The Secretary of the Interior)

Land Management, Bureau of
Reclamation, Bureau of
Geological Survey
Mines, Bureau of
Surface Mining Reclamation
 and Enforcement, Off. of
Ocean Mining Administration
Minerals Policy and Research
 Analysis, Office of

Water Research & Technology, Off. of
National Park Service
Heritage Conservation and
 Recreation Service
U.S. Fish and Wildlife Service
 Habitats; Endangered Species
Indian Affairs, Bureau of
Territorial Affairs, Office of
Hearings and Appeals, Office of

Department of Agriculture 20250 (The Secretary of Agriculture)

Animal and Plant Health
 Inspection Service
Federal Grain Inspection Service
Food Safety & Quality Service
Soil Conservation Service
Forest Service
Science and Education Adm.
 Research; Extension Service
Economics, Statistics, and
 Cooperatives Service

Agricultural Marketing Service
Foreign Agricultural Service
Farmers Home Administration
Federal Crop Insurance Corporation
Rural Electrification Adm. (REA)
Commodity Credit Corporation (CCC)
Food and Nutrition Service
 (Food stamps; lunch programs, etc.)
Agr. Stabilization and Conservation Serv.
 (Price support; marketing quotas, etc.)

Department of Labor 20210 (The Secretary of Labor)

Employment Standards Administration
 Wage and Hour Division
 Federal Contract Compliance
 Programs, Office of
Women's Bureau
Labor Statistics, Bureau of
International Labor Affairs, Bu. of
Labor-Management Services Adm.
 Veterans Reemployment Rights

Employment & Training Administration
 U.S. Employment Service (USES)
 Veterans Employment Service
 Employment Development Programs
 Job Corps; Elders; Migrants; Indians
 Apprenticeship & Training, Bu. of
 Unemployment Insurance Service
Occupational Safety & Health Adm.
Mine Safety and Health Adm.

Department of Health, Education, and Welfare (HEW) 20201 (The Secretary of Health
Education, and Welfare)

Public Health Service (PHS)
 Food and Drug Adm. (FDA)
 Disease Control, Center for
 Alcohol, Drug Abuse, and
 Mental Health Adm.
 Health Resources Adm.
 Health Services Adm.
 Natl. Institutes of Health
Health Care Financing Adm.
Civil Rights, Office for

Education, Office of
National Institute of Education
Social Security Administration
Human Development Services, Off. of
 Aging, Administration on
 Rehabilitation Services Adm.
 Native Americans, Adm. for
 Children, Youth, & Families Adm. for
Consumer Affairs, Office of
Child Support Enforcement, Off. of

Department of Housing and Urban Development (HUD) 20410 (The Secretary of
Housing and Urban Development)

Housing Production and
 Mortgage Ins. (FHA)
Housing Management
Federal Insurance Adm.

New Community Development Corporation
Community Planning and Development
Neighborhoods, Voluntary Associations,
 and Consumer Protection, Office of

Government National Mortgage Association (GNMA—"Ginnie Mae")

(Quasi-independent) Federal National Mortgage Association (FNMA—"Fannie Mae")

Department of Transportation (DOT) 20590 (The Secretary of Transportation)

Federal Aviation Adm. (FAA)
Federal Highway Adm.
Federal Railroad Adm.

U.S. Coast
Guard
(USCG)

Natl. Highway Traffic Safety Adm.
Urban Mass Transportation Adm.
St. Lawrence Seaway Dev. Corp.

◇◇◇◇◇◇◇◇◇ **505**

MAJOR INDEPENDENT AGENCIES

(All addresses: Washington, D.C.—with Zip Code shown)

Civil Aeronautics Board (CAB) 20428. Regulates the economics of U.S., air-carrier operation—approves rates, mail transportation, and business relationships between air carriers. Authorizes carriers to engage in interstate and foreign air transport.

Civil Service Commission (CSC) 20415. Under the "merit system," directs Government-wide recruiting and examining for all competitive Federal positions. Establishes job grading standards; directs retirement and insurance; conducts personnel investigations; and enforces political activity restrictions. (See also p. 508.)

Environmental Protection Agency (EPA) 20460. Enforces pollution control laws.

Export-Import Bank of the U.S. (EIB, "Eximbank") 20571. Grants loans, guarantees, and insurance to promote the export-import trade of the United States.

Farm Credit Administration (FCA) 20578. Provides loans to farmers, and supervises and coordinates a cooperative credit system for agriculture.

Federal Communications Commission (FCC) 20554. Regulates broadcast stations and interstate and foreign communication by wire, radio, and television.

Federal Deposit Insurance Corporation (FDIC) 20429. Insures individual deposits (up to $40,000 each) in banks entitled to such insurance benefits. Acts to prevent the development or continuance of unsafe and unsound banking practices.

Federal Home Loan Bank Board 20552. Provides a credit reserve for—and insures (up to $40,000 each) savings in—savings and home-financing institutions.

Federal Maritime Commission (FMC) 20573. Regulates common carriers by water, terminal operators, freight forwarders, and others subject to the shipping statutes. Approves or disapproves tariffs (rates) and agreements of common carriers.

Federal Mediation and Conciliation Service 20427. Acts to prevent, or settle, labor-management disputes that interrupt the free flow of commerce.

Federal Reserve System (FRS, FRB [Board or Bank], "the Fed") 20551. Organized under the Act of December 23, 1913 "to provide for the establishment of Federal Reserve banks, to furnish an elastic currency, to afford means of rediscounting commercial paper, to establish a more effective supervision of banking in the United States..."

Federal Trade Commission (FTC) 20580. Acts to prevent (by cease-and-desist orders) unfair competition and deceptive practices in commerce. Conducts studies of economic problems; prepares manufacturing financial reports.

General Accounting Office (GAO) 20548. Audits Government accounting, and acts as the investigative arm of Congress. Recommends more efficient and effective operations.

General Services Administration (GSA) 20405. Manages Government property, supplies, and records. Services are: **Federal Supply; Public Buildings; Automated Data & Telecommunications; National Archives and Records; Federal Preparedness Agency.**

Geographic Names, Board on 20305. Authorized by law to standardize the **spelling** of **foreign and domestic geographic names** for official United States use.

International Communication Agency (ICA) 20547. Conducts oversea informational, educational, and cultural programs through literature, broadcasting (Voice of America), motion pictures, television, press releases, and publication features.

Interstate Commerce Commission (ICC) 20423. Regulates common carriers and freight forwarders engaged in interstate commerce. Requires all rates and transportation charges to be just and reasonable.

Library of Congress 20540. Established to serve the Congress, the Library of Congress has expanded its range of service to include the entire Government and the public at large, so that it has become, in effect, a national library.
The Copyright Office is a part of the Library.

National Aeronautics and Space Administration (NASA) 20546. Directs the exploration of space; cooperates in international space programs. Conducts research to solve the problems of flight and develop aeronautical and space vehicles.

National Credit Union Administration 20456. Supervises the Federal credit unions.

National Foundation on the Arts and the Humanities 20506. Encourages and supports progress in the humanities (languages, literature, history, philosophy, law, archeology, etc.) and the arts (music, dance, drama, painting, design, photography, etc.).

National Labor Relations Board (NLRB) 20570. Acts to prevent unfair labor practices, and to maintain employees' rights of self-organization and collective bargaining.

National Mediation Board 20572. Prevents interruption of commerce by mediating differences between carriers (railroads, express and Pullman companies, and airlines) and their employees. Also settles disputes among the employees.

National Science Foundation 20550. Promotes basic scientific research and education in the United States through dissemination of information, award of grants and contracts for scientific projects, and award of fellowships and scholarships.

506

Nuclear Regulatory Commission (NRC) 20555. Licenses and regulates nuclear power: enforcing safety, health, environmental quality, national security, and antitrust laws.

Panama Canal Commission 20004. Constituted to manage, operate (including the setting of tolls), and maintain the Panama Canal until the year 2000.

Postal Service, U.S. (USPS) 20260. Processes and delivers the U.S. mail; develops mail-handling systems; and protects the mails from loss and violations. Under the Postmaster General are the following Departments:

Rates and Classification   Customer Services   Delivery Services   Bulk Mail   Research
Employee, and Labor, Relations   Supply   Property   Finance   Inspection   Logistics   Law

Railroad Retirement Board (RRB) 20004 (Chicago 60611). Provides for annuities to aged and disabled railroad employees; unemployment insurance; hospital insurance; sickness benefits; and death benefits to survivors.

Red Cross, The American National (ARC) 20006. Acts as a medium of relief and communication between the American people and their Armed Forces. Conducts disaster relief; nursing services; blood programs; and safety training.

Renegotiation Board (RB) 20446. Reviews financial reports on defense, space, and aviation contracts to determine excessive profits to be refunded by contractors.

Securities and Exchange Commission (SEC) 20549. Protects investors against malpractice in the securities and financial markets. Registers security issues; regulates trading on exchanges and in over-the-counter markets; supervises investment companies and advisers; regulates electric and gas public utility holding companies; and submits to the courts advisory reports on corporate reorganizations.

Selective Service System (SSS) 20435. Conducts the registration and induction (drafting) of men into the Armed Forces for limited training and service.

Small Business Administration (SBA) 20416. Aids, counsels, assists, and protects the interests of, small business concerns; assures them of a fair share of total Government orders; improves and develops management skills; and makes loans to small businesses and to victims of floods and other natural catastrophes.

Smithsonian Institution 20560. "Created by act of Congress in 1846, under the terms of the will of James Smithson, an Englishman, who in 1829 bequeathed his fortune to the United States to found, at Washington, under the name of the 'Smithsonian Institution,' an establishment for the 'increase and diffusion of knowledge among men'." Branches under the direction of the Smithsonian are:

Museum of History and Technology
Museum of Natural History
National Collection of Fine Arts
National Gallery of Art
Freer Gallery of Art
National Portrait Gallery
Kennedy Center for the Performing Arts
Cooper-Hewitt Museum of Decorative
    Arts and Design
Hirshhorn Museum and Sculpture Garden

National Air and Space Museum
Tropical Research Institute
National Zoological Park
Radiation Biology Laboratory
Astrophysical Observatory
Science Information Exchange
International Exchange Service
Woodrow Wilson International
    Center for Scholars
Performing Arts Division

Tennessee Valley Authority (TVA) 20444 (Knoxville, Tenn. 37902). Develops the Tennessee River region by improving the navigability and controlling, through dams, the floodwaters of that river and its tributaries. Generates and sells electric power to assist in the region's economic development. Acts to advance agriculture, forestry, fish and game refuges, watershed protection, and industrial and outdoor recreational opportunities. At Muscle Shoals, Ala., experiments with, produces, sells, and donates to research programs, phosphatic and nitrogenous fertilizers; also produces munitions and other chemical products.

U.S. Arms Control and Disarmament Agency 20451. Conducts research and U.S. participation in international negotiations for arms control and disarmament.

U.S. International Trade Commission 20436. Investigates tariffs and foreign trade, as in the automotive and agricultural industries. Determines injuries from "dumping" and other unfair practices in import trade. Advises regarding the probable effects of **trade agreement** concessions. Examines tariff schedules and the classification of articles. Conducts studies of trade and tariff policy.

Veterans Administration (VA) 20420. Administers laws authorizing benefits for former members, and dependents of deceased former members, of the U.S. Armed Forces. Benefits include: compensation for service-connected (and pension for non-service-connected) disability or death; dependency compensation; vocational rehabilitation; educational assistance; guaranty of loans; life insurance; hospitalization; medical and dental care; and certain special housing.

GOVERNMENT INFORMATION

CIVIL SERVICE

Civil Service examinations are announced through notices posted in post offices, and sent to school and college counselors, Civil Service Regional Offices in several large cities, State Employment Offices, and Veterans' Information Centers.

The announcements give full information on positions: locations; grade levels (duties and salaries); experience, special training, or education necessary; and minimum age limits (no maximum). Other requirements: American citizenship, and good health (even though physically handicapped). The **closing date** for acceptance of applications is stated in each announcement, or publicized later.

Examinations are held only as needed to fill vacancies; seldom regularly on recurring dates. Some tests are for the Federal service generally; others, for specific agencies. Although an applicant may state a preference for employment in one locality or agency, there is no assurance such a position will be available.

Written Examinations. Each applicant for an "open" (announced) written examination, such as a stenographic or clerical test, will receive an Admission Card and a set of sample questions for that particular examination.

Unwritten Examinations. A large number of Civil Service examinations, such as those for statisticians, are not written tests. These are called "unassembled examinations"; and competitors are rated on education, training, and experience.

Congressional Positions. These are filled, not by Civil Service, but through Congressmen's offices or the U.S. Employment Service in the Senate Office Building.

Overseas Positions. Most Federal positions in foreign countries are filled under Civil Service requirements, but some are not. Persons interested in overseas employment should write to the U.S. Civil Service Commission, Washington, D.C. 20415, for a free copy of the pamphlet "Federal Jobs Overseas."

ACTION (including **Peace Corps, VISTA,** etc.)—Inquire at any of the offices mentioned in the first paragraph above, or write ACTION/Office of Public Affairs/Washington, DC 20525.
AID—Write the Agency for Intl. Development/Public Affairs/Washington, DC 20523.

◇◇◇◇◇◇◇◇◇

AMERICAN FOREIGN SERVICE
(Requirements are subject to change.)

Information and application forms for positions in the Foreign Service may be obtained from: Recruitment Branch/Department of State/Washington, DC 20520.

Qualifications for the Foreign Service Staff, which includes **Secretaries,** and **Communications and Records Assistants** (coding, editing, teletypewriting, mailing, filing), are, in general: the candidate must be **at least 21 years of age (no upper age limit,** but, for benefits, applicant should be able to complete 10 years of continuous service before **mandatory retirement at 60)**; must be in **excellent health;** a **high school graduate** or the equivalent; and an **American citizen** (also, if married, spouse must be an American citizen). (Foreigners are employed locally at the posts abroad.) A knowledge of a **foreign language** is desirable, but not essential. **Required experience**—operational not supervisory—is approximately two years. All prospective employees are subject to a **background investigation** as to character and loyalty.

Performance tests (in shorthand, typing, verbal ability, and spelling) are given continuously in Washington, DC, and at local State Employment Service Offices.

A Foreign Service Officer candidate—for appointment in the diplomatic or consular service—must be **at least 21 years of age** (20 if a senior in college)—**no upper age limit,** but mandatory retirement at 60—must be in **excellent health;** an **American citizen** (also, if married, spouse must be an American citizen); and must pass **rigid written and oral examinations.** **Foreign language skills** are not required at first. All prospective employees are subject to a **background investigation.**

Sample questions are contained in an information brochure issued by the Board of Examiners for the Foreign Service/Department of State/Washington, DC 20520.

Candidates **"must be willing to accept initial assignment and subsequent transfer to any foreign post."**—The State Department. An applicant may express a preference for an area of assignment, but there is no assurance he will be sent there.

508 ∽

Business & Banking Papers

The fundamental purpose of business papers is to "keep track of things." They are the written record of what is bought and sold, transported, and paid for.

Every business paper should be dated; and most of them are numbered. Papers usually originate in the following order:

A **Requisition** is made within a company, requesting the purchase of something (often called a "purchase requisition") — When it is approved—

An **Inquiry, Advertisement, Invitation to Bid** (or **For Bids**), or **Request for Proposal** (or **Quotation**) — is issued for prices or bids.

Quotations, Bids, Proposals, or **Presentations** (in report form) — are sent in return.

A **Purchase Order, Firm Order, Letter of Intent** (to negotiate a contract), **Letter Contract** (a preliminary contractual agreement), or formal **Contract** — is sent to or awarded the successful bidder.

A **Confirmation, Acknowledgment, Acceptance,** or signed **Contract** — is returned from the bidder (now called "vendor," "seller," or "contractor").

When the goods are ready for delivery, if they are to be shipped, a **Car-Order Form** may be used to order space for a freight shipment. Some shippers order space or empty cars direct, through their traffic departments, and some order through trucking or transfer companies.

A **Cargo Space Booking** or a **Cargo Commitment** for space may be arranged with a steamship company or airline for an overseas shipment.

When the goods are delivered to the transportation company, a **Bill of Lading** (B/L) is made up and signed by the transportation company (the "carrier"). The bill of lading enumerates the materials being shipped and acts as a receipt and contract for the shipment of the goods loaded (laded) on the carrier. The transportation company may be a railroad, a steamship line, an airline, or a trucking line.

Note: Airlines call a bill of lading an "Airbill" (if domestic), or an "Air Waybill" (if international). All are nonnegotiable. The Government issues its own air bill of lading.

To save time, the bill of lading is often prepared by the shipper on his own forms, or on the transportation company's forms—procured in advance—and simply handed to the carrier or its agent to sign.

Bills of lading are made up **in triplicate.** The first copy is called the **"Original Bill of Lading,"** and is given to the shipper to be sent to the receiver (the "consignee") for presentation when he claims the goods.

The second copy is called the **"Shipping Order,"** and is retained by the transportation company for its records.

The third copy is called the **"[Shipper's] Memorandum," "Memo Copy,"** or **"Shipping Receipt,"** and is given to the shipper for his files.

509

The transportation company may make additional copies for different purposes. For instance, one copy may be given to the freight conductor as a "waybill"; another copy may accompany the shipment as a part of the "manifest" to be delivered to the agent at the receiving end of the line; another copy may be sent to the receiving agent to serve as a "freight bill"; and still another copy to serve as a "delivery receipt" or "delivery order" when the receiver takes delivery of the goods. (See description of these papers on p. 511.)

Bills of lading are of two kinds: "Straight Bills of Lading," and "Order Bills of Lading."

Straight Bill of Lading. This is used when title to the goods passes immediately to the consignee; that is, when the goods are to be delivered to a certain person or company, without any conditions.

A straight bill of lading is not negotiable; that is, it cannot be endorsed and transferred. The goods must and will be delivered to the consignee named in the straight bill of lading (sometimes even without the presentation of the original bill of lading—if the consignee is known to the transportation company). (A straight bill of lading may be transferred only by a written assignment or agreement.)

Order Bill of Lading. This is used when title to the goods is retained by the shipper until certain conditions are fulfilled. Under an order bill of lading, the goods are "Consigned to ORDER of" the shipper (or a bank), which makes this form of bill of lading negotiable; that is, title to the goods may be transferred by the shipper's (or the bank's) endorsing the original order bill of lading. (The original order bill of lading, properly endorsed, **must be presented** to the transportation company before the goods will be delivered.)

Order bills of lading are usually used for the purpose of insuring collections; or they may be used when goods are shipped and sold while "rolling," or en route, because the names of the consignees are not known at the time of shipment; or they may be used when goods are consigned to brokers or agents.

If a collection is to be made, or assured, before the goods are delivered, the shipper endorses the original order bill of lading (if goods are consigned to his order) and through his bank sends it, together with an invoice, insurance papers, and a draft, to a bank in the purchaser's city. This bank will notify the purchaser when the papers have arrived; and the purchaser must then call at the bank and pay, or accept, the draft before the order bill of lading will be delivered to him, and he must present this original order bill of lading to the transportation company before the goods will be released to him.

Different Ways of Collecting on Bills of Lading. Instead of being sent through a bank for collection, an original bill of lading may be mailed C.O.D. to the purchaser, if the amount of the collection does not exceed $400; or an original bill of lading may be sent by express C.O.D. for a larger amount. (See pp. 376–78.)

C.O.D. truck shipments are made on straight bills of lading, the collections being made by the drivers as the goods are delivered.

Through Export Bill of Lading. This is used when a shipment is made from an interior point to a foreign destination, and a transshipment of goods is necessary at the port of exportation. A through bill of lading may be either a straight or an order bill of lading.

Shipping Receipt. A shipping receipt is signed by the transportation company when the goods are delivered to it. It is a detailed list of the goods being shipped, and is usually made up by the shipper on his own short form of bill of lading. This short form is replaced by the transportation company's regular form when the goods are all ready for shipment. On some "short hauls"—and in some coastwise shipping—this short form of bill of lading will suffice and is not replaced by the longer form.

Dock Receipt. A dock receipt is signed by the steamship company when goods are delivered to the docks. This may be on the shipper's short bill-of-lading form, which is later exchanged for the steamship company's regular ocean bill of lading.

Waybill. A waybill is made up by a carrier (as a railroad) for its freight conductor's use, giving shipping instructions for each shipment on his train—description, weight, route, and destination.

A truck driver has a **"script sheet"** covering goods on his truck.

On air cargo, an **air waybill** serves as a bill of lading (see p. 509).

Manifest (or Ship's Manifest). A manifest is made up by the transportation company for its own use—and, internationally, for customs purposes. It is a list and description of all freight or cargo for each destination. The transportation company's agent at each port or receiving station checks all incoming goods against the manifest.

Freight Bill. A freight bill is prepared by the transportation company and presented to either the shipper or the receiver (buyer or consignee)—whichever is to pay the freight. Usually the receiver pays the freight; but on certain shipments the freight must be prepaid.

Expediting and Tracing. These terms are often confused, but—

Expediting is making prearrangements for special handling and quick transport of urgently needed "rush" shipments—and following through to see that they are delivered in the shortest possible time.

Tracing is checking up on delayed, astray, or overdue shipments—not necessarily hastening them. There is no charge for either service.

Arrival Notice. An arrival notice is sent by the transportation company to the consignee when the shipment arrives at destination.

Delivery Order (D.O.). A delivery order is primarily an order for the delivery of certain goods to a certain person. There are several forms of delivery order.

A shipping "delivery order" or **"delivery receipt"** is made up by the transportation company, to be signed by the receiver when he takes delivery of the goods. He may order the goods delivered to himself or to a third party. The delivery order is made up from the incoming manifest, and the items on the order must check with the invoice or the original bill of lading presented by the receiver. **Any shortages** or damage must be noted on the delivery order.

511

Freight Claim. If goods are damaged or lost in transit, or if there is an overcharge in freight, a freight claim is prepared by the transportation company and signed by the shipper or receiver. Such a claim may be called a "Loss and Damage Claim" or an "Overcharge Claim."

If a shipment arrives in bad condition, the receiver—before touching the shipment—should notify the transportation company, so that a transportation inspector can examine the goods; and thus it will be established that a pre-notice was given to the transportation company that the shipment was faulty.

Demurrage. Demurrage is a charge assessed by the transportation company for detention of a carload shipment beyond the "free time" allowance for loading or unloading goods.

On water shipments, demurrage is charged if a vessel is delayed beyond the "lay days" allowed in the charter party for loading or unloading.

Storage. Storage is charged on goods shipped in less-than-carload lots after a certain "free time" for unloading or removing has elapsed.

Warehouse Receipt (W.R.). A warehouse receipt is issued if the goods are stored in a warehouse.

The receipt may be made out for redelivery of the goods to one certain person (nonnegotiable form), or for redelivery of the goods to "bearer" or "to order of" some certain person (negotiable form). Most warehouse receipts are made out in the negotiable form. Banks often lend money on goods in a warehouse—or "on a warehouse receipt."

Pickup Order. A pickup order is a local form of delivery order. It is an order given by an owner to a holder of goods to deliver all or certain parts of the goods to the bearer of the order.

Withdrawal Order. This is another form of delivery order. It is an order given by an owner of goods to a warehouse to deliver certain goods to the holder of the order, or to the person named in the order.

Consignment. When goods are "shipped on consignment" they are consigned by the owner (called the "consignor") to a broker or agent (called the "consignee") to sell or handle for the owner's account.

Order Notify. When goods are shipped "Order Notify" they are shipped on an order bill of lading, and the receiver is notified by the transportation company when the goods arrive.

Store-Door Service. This is a collection of goods from the shipper's door and delivery to the receiver's door, by the transportation company.

Insurance. Insurance should be carried on every shipment. The shipper may insure his shipments separately (the transportation company often arranging or placing the insurance for him); or he may insure his shipments collectively under an "open policy" with an insurance company. If insuring under an open policy, he notifies the insurance company of his shipments periodically—usually each day.

CAUTION: If responsible for the insuring of a shipment, make sure that but one form of insurance is being carried. Through a misunderstanding, separate insurance may be written and charged for when the shipment is already insured under an open policy.

Export Shipping Papers. Various papers are required for export shipments—different papers for different countries—but for all foreign destinations a U.S. Shipper's Export Declaration and some form of invoice must be prepared. Names of the papers are:

Shipper's Export Declaration	Certificate of Origin
Export License	Certificate of Registration
Import License	(for medicines, etc.)
Consular Invoice	Inspection Certificate
Commercial Invoice	Weight Certificate, etc.
Ocean Bill of Lading	Marine Insurance Policy

Information regarding the preparation of a foreign shipment and the papers required may be obtained from any railroad, steamship line, freight airline, or large transportation company. In a seaport city, information and papers may be obtained from the customhouse, or from the consulate of the country to which shipment is to be made; or a **customhouse broker** or **freight forwarder** may be engaged to arrange the entire shipment—packing, documentation, insurance, and shipping.

Invoice. An invoice is an itemized list of goods and prices or valuations. It is usually in the form of a "bill," prepared by the seller and mailed to the buyer, listing the goods sold in a particular transaction and showing the amount due and the terms of payment. The invoice accompanies the original bill of lading.

NOTE: An "invoice" covers one particular transaction or shipment. It is sent when the goods are delivered and is often paid separately. Whereas a "bill" or "statement" covers various services and transactions—purchases and payments—and is rendered monthly to show the balance due.

Paying Invoices. If an invoice reads "Net cash 30 days" it is commonly considered to be payable one month from its date. For instance, if it were dated July 5 it would be payable August 5. Payment, theoretically, should be mailed so as to be in the hands of the payee on the 30th day, but in actual practice payment is often "in the mails" (postmarked) on the 30th day.

Account Sales (A.S.). An "account sales" is an accounting by a broker or commission merchant to the owner of goods shipped on consignment, showing how the goods were sold and for what prices, and what deductions were made for freight, commission, advertising, etc.

Trade Discounts. These are discounts from wholesale price lists. Different discounts are allowed different customers, according to the amount of goods bought, the standing of the customer, etc.

Discounts. Ordinary discounts are allowances for cash or prompt payment. In taking discounts, strictly speaking, payment should be made so that the money, or evidence of money, will be in the hands of the payee within the period allowed for discount. But as ordinarily interpreted, discount can be taken if payment is "in the mails" (postmarked) within the time, or on the last day, allowed for discount.

Some companies are strict about enforcing discount rules. Others will allow the discount to be **taken** several days after the period has

513

elapsed. But it is not well to assume that any concern is of the latter type. Many are of the first type and allow no exceptions to their rules.

Discount days are figured from the **date of the invoice,** not from the date of receipt of the invoice or merchandise, unless a special clause follows the discount rate, as "1% 10 days arrival of merchandise," which means that the discount period may be figured as 10 days from the date of arrival of the merchandise.

Calendar days are figured rather than "business" days. The date of the invoice is not counted. If, for instance, an invoice is dated February 15, and the terms are "2/10, n/30" (2% discount in 10 days, net amount in 30 days), the discount must be taken by February 25.

If the final discount day falls on Sunday or a holiday, the succeeding business day is considered the last day.

Debit and Credit Memoranda. Errors, returns, freight charges, and allowances are adjusted by the issuance of debit and credit memorandums between companies who do a large amount of business.

Commission. A commission is a percentage (of the selling, or purchase, price) paid to a salesman, agent, or broker, for his services.

Rebate. A rebate is a refund of a certain percentage or amount of the original cost of merchandise or services, as "a rebate of insurance," or "a tax rebate."

Credit Reports. (See p. 604.)   **Financial Ratings.** (See p. 605.)

Drafts. A draft is an order drawn by one party (usually a seller) directing a second party (usually a purchaser) to pay a certain sum to a third party (usually a bank), to be credited to the first party.

The purpose of drafts:

> **To obtain assurance of payment of accounts.** When delivering goods, a seller requires assurance that his account will be paid; or he sometimes requires a cash payment. A draft serves this purpose by bringing back the immediate payment (if it is a sight draft), or a promise to pay (if a time draft), thus giving a tangible form of payment. The seller may borrow money on accepted drafts to finance further business transactions; but it is difficult to borrow money on open accounts because of the uncertainty of collection involved.
>
> **To obtain payment of old accounts.** Drafts are sometimes used to obtain payment of old accounts or debts. Such drafts are called "dunning drafts." A purchaser or debtor may be "slow" in sending a check or in signing a note, but if a draft is drawn on him and presented by a bank for collection, he must take some action regarding it. If he refuses or "dishonors" the draft, the bank makes a report, which is written into his credit rating.
>
> **To make collection on papers.** Drafts may be drawn to accompany any papers on which there are to be collections, such as bills of lading, warehouse receipts, stocks, bonds, and deeds. The one upon whom the draft is drawn must, usually, pay the draft before the bank will deliver the papers to him.

Form of Drafts. Drafts are made up in rather an unnatural order; that is, the name of the party upon whom a draft is drawn is placed at the bottom of the draft, instead of at the top. If drafts were arranged in the simplest possible form, they would read, for example, as follows:

No. **892**	Springfield, Illinois	May 11, 19..
To James Thomas & Sons Co.		
San Antonio, Texas		
On June 15, 19..	Pay to the order of ourselves	
Five hundred fifty and no/100 - - -	DOLLARS	(**$550.00**)

ACCEPTED: May 14, 19..
Payable at   Pioneer Bank
                San Antonio, Texas   HAYWARD & RANDOLPH, INC.
        JAMES THOMAS & SONS CO.   By_____
                                              G. C. Hayward
By_____
        James Thomas, Jr.
              President

Instead, drafts may read something like this:

HAYWARD & RANDOLPH, INC.   No. **892**

$550.00   Springfield, Illinois May 11, 19..
                        At thirty days' sight   Pay to the Order of
Pioneer Bank of San Antonio, Texas   for collection
Five hundred fifty and no/100 - - -   _____ DOLLARS
                Value received and charge to the account of
                                    HAYWARD & RANDOLPH, INC.
To James Thomas & Sons Co. }
        San Antonio, Texas   }   By_____
                                            G. C. Hayward

The acceptance on the above draft would be written across the face.

Drafts are drawn payable to banks in order that they may be handed to the banks for collection. Banks in one city send drafts to their representatives in other cities for presentment and collection.

The words "Value received and charge to the account of" make the draft, when it is finally paid, a receipt from the drawer to the payer.

Any certain time may be specified for the payment of a draft. It may be payable "At sight," or "At thirty days' sight," or "Three months after date," or on any definite date, etc.

Drafts may bear interest if it is specified. Such interest is computed as it would be on a promissory note.

Sight Draft. This orders payment "At sight" or "On demand." If honored, a check is given in payment; or the one upon whom it is drawn may write directions to his bank across the face of the draft, asking the bank to pay the draft and charge the amount to his account.

Demand Draft. A sight draft, ordering payment "On demand."

Time Draft. A time draft orders payment at a certain time after receipt or acceptance, or after date. The one upon whom the draft is drawn writes ACCEPTED, the date, the place payable, and his signature on the face of the draft. It is then known as an

Acceptance and is practically the same as a promissory note. Twenty-four hours are usually given the party upon whom the draft is drawn to examine the goods purchased and the papers

515

attached to the draft, and to decide whether or not to accept the draft. If acceptance is refused, the draft is **"dishonored."**

D/A ("documents upon acceptance") means that documents are to be delivered upon acceptance of the draft.

D/P ("documents upon payment") means that documents are to be delivered only upon payment of the draft.

Foreign Bank Draft. A draft drawn by a bank on a foreign bank, and payable to a third party. Banks have deposits, or "carry balances," in other banks much the same as individuals do, and in reality a bank draft is a check drawn by a bank on its own account in another bank.

Bank drafts are regarded as **cash;** and many business men send remittances by bank draft rather than by check, so that the payee may have cash immediately and not have to wait the necessary number of days for a check to be returned to its bank before it is paid. Even a cashier's check must go through a process of "clearing" before it is paid. Charges: $7.50 if obtained by a customer of the issuing bank; $10 if by a non-customer. There is no limit to the amount that can be sent.

Arrival Draft. This is so called because it represents the payment to be made upon the arrival of goods bought.

Clean Draft. A draft with no papers attached is "clean."

Trade Acceptance. A trade acceptance is an accepted time draft, but it differs from an ordinary time draft in that it states definitely that the debt represents merchandise purchased.

An ordinary draft shows no acknowledgment of merchandise received —in fact, it might represent an old debt—and therefore is not so valuable as a trade acceptance, which acknowledges that the acceptor has received goods, with the proceeds from which he should be able to pay the trade acceptance.

A trade acceptance may be sent direct to a customer with the invoice and original bill of lading; or it may be sent to a bank, to be presented to the customer for his acceptance.

An accepted trade acceptance is regarded as a note receivable by the holder thereof. Usually it can be discounted at a bank if the holder is in need of immediate funds.

Banker's (or Bank) Acceptance—often used instead of a trade acceptance. A purchaser establishes credit at his bank in an amount sufficient to pay for certain goods ordered. His bank then notifies a bank in the seller's city (by a letter of credit) that the credit has been established.

When the goods are shipped, the seller draws a draft on the purchaser's bank (or payable through the bank), and sends the draft to the bank together with the original bill of lading, invoice, insurance papers, etc.

When the goods are received, the bank makes an examination of them and, if satisfactory, accepts the draft or guarantees its payment, thus lending the bank's credit instead of money to the purchaser. The purchaser must pay the bank when the draft is due; and the bank charges the purchaser a commission instead of interest for this accommodation of credit.

516

Bill of Exchange. A bill of exchange is a draft; but the term is particularly applied to foreign drafts, that is, drafts drawn in one country and payable in another country. They are the chief means by which settlements are made in international trade. Foreign bills are drawn in duplicate or triplicate—so that a copy may be attached to each set of documents in a transaction. They are always negotiable.

Foreign bills are classified and referred to in different ways, by:

Makers—Government, Bankers', Commercial, Express, or Shippers' bills.
Purpose—bills drawn against: commodities (as cotton or steel bills); services (as freight, insurance, or commissions bills); current balances; or open credits.
Security—documentary bills (documents attached); clean bills (no documents).
Payment Date—at sight; at a time; on demand, arrival, or presentment bills.
Settlement—in foreign currency, dollars, sterling, or European decimal currency.

"With Exchange" written on a draft means that the difference in exchange and all collection charges are to be paid by the one who pays the draft.

Letter of Credit. A letter of credit is a formal document ("letter") from a bank to another bank, or from a business house to its bank or business associates, stating that a certain amount of credit has been established by a certain person or company.

Commercial Letter of Credit. This is largely used by exporting and importing concerns. A purchaser arranges at his bank for a sufficient amount of credit to meet his obligations on a certain purchase of goods. His bank then notifies a bank in the seller's city that the credit has been established. Drafts may then be drawn against, and in conformity with, this letter of credit, and the bank will honor the drafts. The seller is thus assured of receiving his money before he ships the goods. (See Banker's Acceptance, p. 516.)

Traveler's Letter of Credit. This has been discontinued, having been replaced by travelers checks, foreign money orders, and credit cards.

Advice (or Letter of Advice). This is usually a form notice sent by a bank to a customer advising him of something done, as a paper issued or executed, a payment made, or a debit or credit entered in his account.

Another advice may convey shipping information from a consignor to a consignee; or intelligence information from one country to another.

Trust Receipt. This is a receipt for shipping documents delivered upon trust. If a bank holds title to imported goods because of having accepted a draft drawn by the seller of the goods, the bank may permit the importer, or buyer, to take the bill of lading and other documents necessary to obtain possession of the goods, upon his signing a trust receipt. In the trust receipt the importer acknowledges that the title to the goods is vested in the bank, and that the proceeds from the sale of the goods shall be first applied to the payment of the bank's accepted draft.

Days of Grace. On "notes and bills," no grace is now allowed in any state in the United States, and in most foreign countries. But England, Ireland, and Canada still grant three days of grace.

517

Date of Payment. A note or draft must be paid at the place of payment specified and on the due date. Payment cannot be "in the mails" but must be in the hands of the payee on the due date.

To determine the date of payment of a draft or note, count the exact number of days, **excluding the first day.** A draft payable "Sixty days after sight" would be payable 60 calendar days after acceptance (not including the day of acceptance). If accepted September 10, it would be payable November 9.

If a draft is payable "Two months after date," it is payable on the same day of the month, two months later. If dated March 15, it would be payable May 15.

Note that there is sometimes a wide difference between the date of the draft and the date of acceptance, and whichever date is named in the draft should be figured.

Paper Maturing on Sunday or a Holiday. Notes, etc., coming due on a holiday or Sunday are payable on the next business day.

Negotiable Instrument. A "negotiable" instrument is a paper that may be transferred from one person to another, usually by endorsement.

A prime requisite for the negotiability of an instrument is that it be made payable **" to bearer"** or **"to the order of"** the payee. If these words do not appear, a paper is nonnegotiable; that is, it cannot be endorsed or transferred to a third party—the proceeds must be paid to the payee named in the instrument, and to no one else, unless a separate assignment of the paper is made. It is for this reason that so many papers bear the line "Pay to the order of." If they should read simply "Pay to [a named payee]" they would be nonnegotiable.

Promissory Note. A promissory note is a written, unconditional promise to pay a certain sum at a specified time and place.

Unless a definite rate of interest is specified in a note, it will bear interest only after maturity. Some notes do not bear interest even after maturity, if such is the agreement between the maker and the holder of the note.

> **Secured, or Collateral, Note.** A note specifically stating that the maker has pledged certain assets, such as stocks or bonds —or given a mortgage—as security for the loan.

> **Joint and Several Note.** A note signed by several persons who agree to pay it jointly or severally—that is, **separately**—each to be liable for the full amount if the others fail.

Collateral. Collateral is **marketable** security pledged, or "put up" (delivered but redeemable), to ensure payment of a note or obligation.

Hypothecation. Security may be pledged without transferring title to, or possession of, it by "hypothecation." Upon default, the creditor has the right to sell the security to satisfy the claim. Pledged security is often held, as by a broker, under a **"Hypothecation Agreement."**

Future revenues or taxes may be "hypothecated" or pledged by a government as the security for a loan.

518

"Hypothecation" has still another and older meaning, namely, the pledging of an undelivered property for the payment of a debt. The pledged property (as a ship) remains in the possession of the debtor, so that with the earnings therefrom he may pay the debt. If he defaults, the creditor has the right to have the property sold to satisfy the debt.

"Without Recourse." These words, appearing in an endorsement, relieve the endorser of any future liability on the instrument so endorsed. If endorsed **"With Recourse,"** the liability of the endorser continues.

Protest. If payment is not made on a note, draft, or other paper when it becomes due, or if a draft is not accepted when presented, a notary public formally presents the paper again for payment or acceptance. If the instrument is still dishonored, the notary makes up a declaration or "Protest" giving the facts in the case. A copy of this protest is served on all parties whose names appear on the instrument, in order that they may be apprised of their liability.

> **"Protest Waived,"** written above an endorser's signature, means that the protest notice need not be served if the instrument is not paid, and that the endorser will assume his responsibility if simply notified that the maker has defaulted.
>
> **"No Protest,"** written on or attached to a note or draft, signifies that no formal protest is to be made if the instrument is not paid— that is, that no protest fee will be paid thereon.

Commercial Paper. Short-term, unsecured notes made by large companies in good financial standing, and issued to finance industrial products, are called "commercial paper." These notes are sold by "note brokers" to banks that have funds to invest, in different parts of the country. The notes bear no interest; the interest is collected by the banks when they "discount" the notes in buying them.

Accommodation Paper. Negotiable paper that has been endorsed by a disinterested party, simply as a means of lending his credit to the maker of the paper, is called "accommodation paper."

Trade Paper. Notes, trade acceptances, etc., bearing two or more names, given as payment for merchandise in the ordinary transaction of business, are called "trade paper," or **"business paper."**

Two-Name Paper. Paper bearing two names (representing separate interests) as makers, or one as maker and one as. endorser, is called "two-name paper."

An acceptance (accepted draft) is considered two-name paper because both the acceptor and the drawer are liable for the payment if a bank buys or "discounts" the acceptance.

Single-Name Paper. Paper bearing a single name as maker. The maker may be a corporation, and its subsidiary corporation may endorse the note to lend credit, but the note is still regarded as "single-name paper" because of the close connection between the two companies— if one fails the other might fail.

Cattle Paper. Notes secured by chattel mortgages on cattle are called "cattle paper." They are dealt in extensively in cattle-raising regions.

519

Bank Discount.   This is interest, to maturity, deducted in advance.

Rediscount.   Notes or trade acceptances that have been sold to and discounted by a bank, may be resold—usually to a Federal Reserve bank—and rediscounted by the buying bank.

Voucher.   There are many forms of voucher, as "travel voucher," "credit voucher," "salary voucher"; but a voucher is primarily a receipt for, or proof of, money paid.   It vouches for the truth or authenticity of a business expenditure.

Voucher Check.   A check that has a detachable statement (voucher), showing for what the payment is being made.

Warrant.   There are many forms of warrant, but a warrant in banking is primarily a written order to pay money.   (See also p. 529.)

States and counties often make disbursements (pay salaries, etc.) by issuing warrants drawn on their own treasuries.   These warrants may bear interest, if registered, and may be cashed at certain banks at face value, after arrangements have been made for their acceptance.

CHECKS

Making out a check is a simple matter, yet many checks are incorrectly written.

Date.   Never omit the date on a check.   If a check is received without a date, date it the day of receipt, not any earlier or later date.

> **Antedating** is dating a check back to some past date (to a date which has gone **before**).
>
> **Postdating** is dating a check forward to some future date (to a date which is to come **after**).

Money will not be paid on a postdated check, nor can it be deposited, until the day of its date.   If money is inadvertently paid on a postdated check, it may be recovered.   In fact, a postdated check should not be presented to a bank until the day of its date; such a pre-presentment may reflect unfavorably not only upon the maker of the check but also upon the one presenting it for payment.

Checks dated on **Sundays or holidays** are accepted at banks.

Old or "Stale" Checks.   All checks should be presented for payment promptly or within a reasonable time after their dates.   A bank will question any check that may be considered "old"; and if a check bears a date more than six months old, the bank may refuse to honor it on the ground that it is a "stale" check.

Payee.   Attempt always to write the name of the payee correctly and as he writes his name; for he is forced to endorse the check exactly as his name appears on the face.

Leave no space before the name and put three dashes after it.

If the payee is a "Receiver," "Treasurer," or "Secretary" of an organization, use that title after his name on the check.   He then accepts the money in his official capacity when endorsing the check.

520

Pay to the order of <u>Robert May, Treasurer ---</u> $1,503.06

<u>One thousand five hundred three and 06/100 * * *</u> Dollars

Personal titles, like "Dr.," "Capt.," "Judge," "Miss," should, theoretically, not be used before the names of payees on checks, because such titles are not used in endorsements. However, American banks disregard these titles now. But in some foreign countries, personal titles cannot be used; hence are never on travelers checks or letters of credit.

Lead Pencil. Neither a lead pencil nor an indelible pencil should be used in writing a check. Although pencil checks are not prohibited, a bank may refuse a pencil check if it shows any evidence of erasure or alteration. (Mere handling can cause a blurred or erased effect.)

Erasures. Checks should be typed slowly and carefully so that no erasures whatsoever will be necessary. A bank has the right to return a check if "altered" in any manner. Checks are usually printed on a sensitized paper that makes erasures noticeable and sometimes glaring.

Amounts. Leave **no space before** either figures or words. After even amounts of dollars write "and no/100." And put three dashes or stars after every written-out amount. If the amount written in words and the amount in figures differ, the words are considered correct; but the bank may, if convenient, return the check for verification.

Checks may be written for **cents;** but banks do not encourage this practice, because of the cost of handling. If, however, it is occasionally necessary to write a check for cents, put parentheses around the figures and write "Only" before the words. Do not write "$0.65."

Pay to the order of <u>Superintendent of Documents ---</u> $ -(65¢)

<u>Only sixty-five cents * * *</u> Dollars

Changing a Bank's Name. One bank's check should never be changed to direct its payment at another bank. Not only does this make an "altered check," but the magnetic-ink encodings will automatically return it to its original bank, no matter how changed in pen and ink.

Blank checks should be kept in every office; but if one is not at hand, a check may be typed on heavy white paper, and cut to check size. It will be accepted, but delayed in clearing because the bank must apply a magnetic-ink routing symbol, which the Federal Reserve demands.

When filling in the name of a bank on a blank check, **fill in the address** also, and the bank number if it is known. One bank may have several branches in the same city, and the address is important.

Notations on a Check. Any information that the signer desires by way of a receipt may be written in the lower left corner of a check, or on the back above the place for endorsement.

Signatures. A signature should be written in exactly the same manner on every check, and with the same style of pen.

A signer should not use his full name on one check, his abbreviated first name on another, and his initials on a third, as "James F. Scott," "Jas. F. Scott," and "J. F. Scott."

He should sign always as he signed his name when he opened the account. He may add his address below his signature for identification.

521

Endorsements. Endorse a check in ink across the reverse **left** end, never across the right end. And endorse it exactly as the name appears on the face, even though incorrect. If incorrect, write the correct signature immediately below. It is not necessary to write an explanation of the two signatures; they will be understood by the bank. Do not write the correct signature first and the incorrect one below in parentheses. This violates the banking rule that **the last endorser must be the person to whom the money is paid.**

Checks may be endorsed in several ways:

Blank endorsement—with just the payee's signature, which makes the check **payable to bearer.** It should be cashed or deposited immediately.

> *Robert V. Wilson*

Special or full endorsement—with "Pay to the order of..." above the payee's signature. This requires the designated person's endorsement, but is still **negotiable** (transferable).

> *Pay to the order of*
> *Hugh O'Donald*
> *Robert V. Wilson*

Restrictive endorsement—with just "Pay to..." above the payee's signature. The check is then **nonnegotiable**—it must be paid to the designated person and no one else.

> *Pay to James Morgan*
> *Robert V. Wilson*

Qualified endorsement—with "Without recourse" written above the payee's signature. This relieves the endorser of any **future liability** on the check.

> *Without recourse*
> *Robert V. Wilson*

Deposit endorsement—a form of special or restrictive endorsement, which may be typed or stamped on.

> *For deposit only*
> *Robert V. Wilson*

Types of rubber-stamp endorsements

PAY TO THE ORDER OF LA JOLLA BRANCH **Bank of America** THE WESTLAND COMPANY 170–556	For deposit in THE RIGGS NATIONAL BANK to the credit of WILSON PRODUCTS, INC.

Checks for deposit by a business house are, preferably, endorsed with a rubber stamp. A customer's number is often assigned by the bank, as the number 170–556 on the above endorsement. The date is also carried on some rubber stamps.

In the absence of a rubber stamp, type **"For deposit only"** and below it the payee's name (as the check is drawn). If that name is different from the way it appears on the bank account, type the correct form of the name thereunder. No other name or wording needs to appear.

All checks for deposit should be so endorsed to safeguard them in case they are lost while being taken or mailed to the bank.

Identification. If the maker of checks needs identification, he may carry a few of his current canceled checks for this purpose—showing them and writing each new check in the presence of the payee.

If it is the payee who will need identification to cash a check at the maker's bank, he should ask the maker to guarantee his signature. The check should be endorsed by the payee, and the maker should write below, "Signature guaranteed," and sign his name.

Stop Payment. Payment of a check may be stopped upon application of the maker by telegraph or telephone, if confirmed by a written request.

Payment must be stopped before the check reaches the bookkeeper of the bank upon which it is drawn, or it will be paid. The death of a depositor immediately stops payment on all outstanding checks (in most states). Charge for stopping payment: $7 by some banks; $10 by others.

Overdraft fee is $5 to $10. **Uncollectible check** fee: $7 to $10.

Certified Check (often accompanies a bid). It is an ordinary check that has been "certified" or guaranteed across its face by the bank upon which it is drawn. Funds in the amount of the check are immediately set aside from the maker's account to meet the check when returned.

Charges: $3.00, flat rate for all (on "Thrift" checks, $3.00 also).

To stop payment on a certified check, the maker must post a bond.

Never destroy an unused certified check. Endorse it: "Not used for purpose intended," and have the maker sign below. Then deposit it.

Cashier's Check (or Treasurer's, or Manager's, Check) (for payments of any amount). It is a bank's check drawn on its own funds and signed by its cashier or other authorized officer. Its payment is of course guaranteed. It may be obtained by anyone by paying cash therefor or giving a check. Charges: a flat $2.

Bank Money Order (or Register Check), up to $500. Fee: a flat 75¢.

Intl. Money Order (good for 6 months); up to $1000. Fee: a flat $3.

Foreign Draft (cash transfer), fees: $7.50 or $10. (See p. 516.)

Visa letter (financial recommendation) for foreign travel, fee: $7.

Travelers Checks or Cheques. Sold (for $1 per $100) by banks, and large travel agencies—and may be issued in **foreign currencies.**

Unused travelers checks may be countersigned and deposited in banks.

NOTE: The apostrophe has been dropped in commercial usage ("travelers checks"). Dictionaries give "traveler's check." Either way is correct. The spelling "cheques" is British.

Voucher Check. (See Voucher, p. 520.)

Mailing Money. Currency should never be sent in a letter unless such a course is absolutely necessary, and unless the letter is **registered**.

Ways in which money may be transmitted are by

Personal check	Cashier's check	Money order—Postal, Bank,
Certified check	Foreign draft	Telegraph, or Express

Torn Money. Currency that has been torn in two may be pasted and deposited or exchanged for new money at the bank. (If a portion of a bill is missing, but if more than one-half remains, it may be redeemed at a bank.)

Torn checks may also be pasted together and deposited or cashed.

Transparent tape, if available, should be used to mend torn money or checks, so that no writing will be covered.

Deposits. The following may be deposited in banks:

Cash	Warrants
Checks (including travelers checks)	Interest coupons that are due
Money orders	(Tax-free-bond coupons require
Foreign drafts	Ownership Certificates)

Accepted drafts, on or after their due dates, may be deposited in some banks, but generally they are "handled for collection" and credited when paid.

Notes that are due are not deposited, but may be handled through a bank for collection.

Deposit Slips. Checks should be listed on deposit slips **by bank numbers** instead of by bank names.

Banks have adopted a **universal numbering system** to save labor in their clearing and transit departments. Every bank in the United States has been given a number. These numbers are printed immediately after the names of the banks on all checks and on other papers. The number consists of two parts, as 11-8, the first part designating the state or city, and the second part the number of the individual bank. For instance, banks in San Francisco, California, are in city Number 11, and their numbers are 11-1, 11-2, 11-3, etc.; while banks in Los Angeles, California, are in city Number 16, and their numbers are 16-1, 16-2, etc. Banks in the smaller cities of California take the state number, 90, as 90-4, 90-15, 90-621.

A **routing symbol,** containing the Federal Reserve district number, is given below the bank number, as $\frac{1-23}{210}$, which means bank Number 23, in city Number 1 (New York), Federal Reserve District Number 2.

Only the **bank numbers** should appear on a deposit slip, as

11-8	$345.90
16-1	60.80

A **carbon copy** of each deposit slip should be kept until the bank's **deposit receipt** is returned. Then the carbon may be destroyed.

Certificate of Deposit ("CD"). Money may be set aside by a depositor as a special deposit, and the bank will give a receipt (certificate) therefor. Checks cannot be drawn against moneys held under a certificate of deposit, which may be transferable or nontransferable. (Often used as collateral, or as a guaranty of performance of a contract.)

The money held under a certificate of deposit cannot be released unless the certificate is returned to the bank.

If the money is to be held a certain length of time, the certificate of deposit may draw interest; and it may be self-renewing.

To Balance a Checkbook—by the **"all addition"** method (no subtractions):

(1) On the bank statement, pencil-check the canceled-check amounts; then sort the checks by number; (2) on the checkbook stubs, red-pencil-check each returned check, and each deposit, **beside the amount;** (3) list, under a heading "Checkbook," all checks outstanding, by number and amount; also any unentered bank credits; total and **add the checkbook balance.**

(4) List, under "Bank," all deposits not shown on the bank statement; also any bank charges not yet deducted in the checkbook; total and **add the bank-statement balance.** If the two column totals agree, the account is "reconciled."

Make **adjustments** on the stub of the **last check drawn** (to avoid correcting all previous figures); and cross-refer from any incorrect stub or page.

◇◆◇◆◇◆◇◆◇

BANKS AND FINANCIAL HOUSES

There are various kinds of banks and financial houses, organized and operating under different laws. One bank may fall under several classifications; for instance, a "Commercial Bank" may be also a "National Bank," and it may have "Trust" and "Savings" departments. The ordinary classifications are:

National Bank. Organized under the National Bank Act; subject to federal supervision; acts as a commercial bank, often having savings and trust departments. All national banks must have the word "National" in their titles.

State Bank. Organized under state laws; acts as a commercial bank, often having savings and trust departments.

Commercial Bank. Does a general banking business, primarily in financing industries on short-term or seasonal loans. National and state banks are commercial banks, and may have savings departments as well as trust departments, depending on the laws of the various states.

Savings Bank. Primarily for the deposit and investment of savings; but may do a general banking business, depending on laws of the state in which organized.

Trust Company. Acts in a fiduciary capacity, either for individuals or for corporations. It may be a part of a commercial bank, but the trust funds are separate from the banking funds.

Federal Reserve Bank. Organized under the Federal Reserve Act. It acts as agent of the United States in dealing with other banks; in other words, the Federal Reserve banks are the bankers' banks.

Land Bank. Organized under the Federal Farm Loan Act; lends money on first mortgages on farm lands, and issues farm loan bonds secured thereby.

Investment Banker. Buys (underwrites) large blocks of securities (usually new), and later sells them, in small amounts, to the public—thus financing business by supplying it with immediate capital. May act further in an advisory capacity on investment matters.

Private Banker. A type of investment banker, often lending money on a large scale to finance international projects. Some of the few remaining private bankers engage in commercial banking.

Investment Company. Invests in certain authorized high-grade securities and issues and sells its own shares against such investments. There are two types: **open-end** (or **mutual fund**), unlimited in shares; **closed-end,** fixed in size.

Credit Union. A cooperative association that accepts savings from its members, pays dividends, and makes loans to members at low interest rates.

Finance Company. Makes loans to employed persons; or finances industries by loaning money on dealers' and manufacturers' accounts receivable, installment sales contracts, inventories, acceptances (drafts), and/or notes receivable. (Also called a **Credit, Loan, Acceptance, Discount, or Factoring** company.)

Factoring—is buying "receivables" **outright** and assuming all credit risks thereon.

Savings (or Building) and Loan Association. An organization in which the members buy shares (which pay dividends) by depositing their savings. These accumulated savings are loaned by the association to finance the building of homes; they are also loaned on improved real estate.

Clearing House. An establishment where banks each day exchange checks, etc., drawn on one another, and adjust balances. It is maintained and regulated by the association of banks that "clear" through it.

Securities

Stocks and bonds are called **"securities."**

Stocks are shares of ownership in corporations. A stockholder is entitled to vote at company meetings and to share in the assets and profits of the corporation.

Bonds represent money loaned to corporations, municipalities, or governments. **They do not represent ownership.** Bonds are in reality formal, long-term nctes, bearing interest, and issued in series, usually in $1000 denominations.

STOCKS

Stocks are variously designated, according to the manner in which they are issued, or according to the manner in which they share with other stocks in the profits of the corporations.

A **stock certificate** is an engraved instrument evidencing ownership of a specified number of shares of stock. **Dividends** are a proportionate distribution of a company's profits to the shareholders—usually quarterly.

Capital Stock. The total amount of stock (common and preferred) that a corporation is authorized to issue under its certificate of incorporation or charter.

Common Stock. Ordinary stock, with no special preferences, or fixed dividend.

Preferred Stock. Receives preference in the distribution of dividends or assets. Preferred stock may claim a dividend of a specified percentage before the common stock is paid anything. But if the earnings of a corporation are large, the common stock may receive a larger dividend than the preferred.

Prior Preferred Stock. Stock that receives a dividend before any other preferred stock. (Also called "First Preferred," or "Prior Preference.")

Participating Preferred Stock. Stock that is preferred as to certain first dividends, beyond which it participates with the common stock in the division of other dividends—after the common stock has been paid a certain dividend.

Cumulative Preferred Stock. If dividends are passed (not paid), this stock is entitled to receive accumulated dividends (when they are finally paid), before dividends are paid on the common stock.

Convertible Preferred Stock. Can be exchanged for common stock on or after a certain date, and on a specified basis of exchange.

Callable Preferred Stock. Stock that can be recalled and redeemed by the issuing company at a fixed price (the "call price").

Guaranteed Stock. Has its dividends guaranteed by another company.

Floating Stock. The amount of a company's stock that is on the market, or that can be dealt in by the public.

Treasury Stock. A company's own stock (originally issued as full-paid stock) bought back and held in the company's treasury. (Unissued stock is not treasury stock.) Dividends are not paid on treasury stock.

526

Scrip. A certificate showing ownership of a fraction of a share of stock; or showing installment payments on stock; or indicating a promised dividend.

Voting Pool Stock. Capital stock with restricted voting power.

Voting Trust Certificates. Certificates issued instead of stock certificates when the voting privileges of a stock are lodged in voting trustees.

BONDS

Bonds bear many different designations—the variety is large, and the names unlimited.

Bonds are primarily classified according to the corporation, municipality, or government that issues them, as

Corporate bonds   issued by business corporations—distinguished from government.
Government, or Treasury, bonds   issued by the United States Government.
Industrial bonds   issued by companies in various industries.
Irrigation bonds   issued by irrigation districts.
Municipal bonds   issued by local and state governments.   (Interest is **Federal** income-tax-free; also often **State** income-tax-free in issuing state.)
Rail bonds   issued by railroads.
State bonds   issued by states.
Territorial bonds   issued by United States territories.
Utility bonds   issued by public service companies, such as gas, light, power, water, telephone, and street transit or bus companies.
Foreign bonds   issued in foreign countries and sold in the United States.
External bonds   issued in one country and sold externally in other countries; usually payable in the currency of the country in which they are sold.

Bonds may also be designated according to the purpose for which they are issued, as

Bridge bonds   for building bridges.
Construction bonds   for making constructions.
Defense, or Victory, or Liberty bonds   for financing war.
Equipment bonds   for buying equipment.
Improvement bonds   for making improvements.
Purchase Money bonds   for acquiring money with which to purchase property. (Usually secured by a purchase money mortgage.)
Reclamation bonds   for reclaiming land.
Savings bonds   for the small investor's savings.
School bonds   for building schools.
Water bonds   for furnishing water supplies.

Bonds may be named for some particular characteristic, as

Adjustment bonds   issued in a readjustment or reorganization of a company.
Assumed bonds   assumed by a company that purchases or merges with another.
Consolidated bonds   issued for the purpose of consolidating previous bond issues.
Convertible bonds   may be converted into stock under certain conditions and at specified times.   If the earnings of a company are large, a bond-holder may desire to convert his bonds into stock for dividends.
Funding bonds   issued to convert a floating debt into a funded debt (see p. 542).
Refunding bonds   issued to replace ("re-fund") callable bonds on or before maturity; often to obtain lower interest rates.   These are second mortgage bonds until all original mortgages or bonds are paid.
Tax-exempt bonds   municipals, with interest exempt from Federal income taxes.
Unified bonds   issued to replace previous forms of indebtedness, for uniformity.

Bonds may be designated according to the manner of payment, as

Annuity bonds   payable in equal annual installments.
Callable bonds   may be called in for payment before maturity.
Called bonds   called in for payment.   (Interest ceases on the date of call.)
Currency bonds   payable in currency of a certain country rather than in gold.

Extended bonds   on which the maturity date has been extended.

Gold bonds   payable in gold.

Income bonds   interest to be paid out of earnings after all fixed charges are paid.

Participating bonds   besides drawing a stated rate of interest, they participate in the profits of the issuing company.

Perpetual bonds   the principal has no definite maturity date, and the interest is to be paid perpetually.

Revenue bonds   issued by local governments, to be paid from future income.

Serial bonds   maturing at periodic intervals instead of on a fixed date.

Short-Term bonds   issued for short periods of time.

Bonds may be designated according to the manner in which they are secured, as

Collateral Trust bonds   secured by collateral deposited with a trustee.

Debenture bonds   usually unsecured other than by the name and reputation (general credit and assets) of the issuing company.

Equipment Trust bonds   (See Equipment Trust Certificates, p. 529.)

First Mortgage bonds   secured by a first mortgage on property.

General Mortgage bonds   secured by a blanket overlying mortgage on properties.

Guaranteed bonds   payment guaranteed by someone other than the original issuer.

Joint bonds   for the payment of which two or more parties are jointly responsible.

Junior bonds   second-mortgage bonds, or secondary liens on pledged assets.

Prior Lien bonds   represent a prior claim against property—over certain claims.

Real Estate bonds   secured by a mortgage on real estate.

Sinking Fund bonds   any type of bond secured by a sinking fund.

Subordinated Debentures   unsecured; outranked by all other debt of the issuer.

General classifications of bonds are:

Coupon bonds or **Bearer bonds**   those payable to bearer (negotiable merely by delivery), with coupons attached representing the interest payments. As the interest becomes due the coupons are clipped and presented to a bank for deposit or collection.

Registered bonds   are registered on the books of the issuing companies in the names of the bondholders. Interest is paid by check to the registered holders; and the bonds may be transferred only by assignment. Bonds are registered as a protection against loss or theft.

Registered coupon bonds   are registered as to principal, but not as to interest, which is evidenced by coupons payable to bearer.

Bonds Not Securities in the Usual Sense.

Another use of the word "bond" is its application to the form of pledge or surety given by an individual to guarantee his faithful performance of certain duties or his carrying out of a certain trust.   The names of these bonds are self-descriptive:

surety bond	attachment bond	trustee's bond	performance bond
fidelity bond	injunction bond	executor's bond	payment bond
indemnity bond	bail bond	receiver's bond	judicial bond

MISCELLANEOUS SECURITIES

Various general terms applied to securities are:

Assented Securities.   Securities deposited with a trustee for a readjustment of values or some other change.   Such securities are called or stamped "assented" indicating that the owners thereof have agreed or assented to the change.

Certificates of Deposit.   Are given for securities so placed in trust.   These "certificates" are bought and sold on the stock exchanges.

Consols or Annuities   British Government bonds or forms of indebtedness ("consolidated annuities") (pron. kŏn-sŏlz′, note accent).

Equipment Trust Certificates. Bonds issued against an equipment trust mortgage —a chattel mortgage on railroad equipment, held in trust for the repayment of borrowed money. Or bonds issued against a lease of railroad equipment ("Philadelphia Plan"), the railroad leasing the equipment from a trustee that holds absolute title for the benefit of the bondholders, until the railroad pays the last installment of its obligation and takes title to the property.

Deferred Securities. Securities on which the payment of dividends or interest is deferred for a specified length of time.

Definitive Securities. When stocks or bonds are announced and sold but are not actually ready for delivery, receipts, called **"interim certificates,"** are issued therefor by a trustee. These interim certificates are bought and sold as the securities would be, and are later exchanged for the final or complete (definitive) stocks or bonds.

Investment Securities. Securities issued by sound corporations or governments, and purchased by investors who desire safe investments, to provide reliable incomes. (Authorized for purchase by banks, institutions, etc.)

Listed Securities. Securities listed for trading on a stock exchange. Requirements for "listing" involve the furnishing of facts and financial data regarding a corporation, and registration with the Securities and Exchange Commission. **Unlisted securities** are those not listed for trading on a stock exchange (although they are sometimes dealt in on the smaller exchanges, at the request of exchange members). They are usually traded in the "off-board" market.

Mortgage Certificates. Certificates for small amounts issued and sold by mortgage companies against large first mortgages or first mortgage bonds which they hold or own. (Also called "mortgage participation certificates," meaning that the holder participates in the large first mortgage.)

Receipts. American depositary receipts for foreign shares; also receipts for bonds or stocks deposited in trust under a plan of exchange or reorganization.

Rentes. French Government bonds. (pron. ränt; Fr., income)

Rights. Certain rights or privileges are often given to the holders of stocks or bonds, permitting such holders to purchase (usually at reduced rates) new stocks or bonds to be issued by the same company—"when issued." These rights, evidenced by **subscription warrants,** may be sold on the exchanges.

Stamped Securities. Stocks or bonds on which some guarantee, extension, privilege, or changed condition has been stamped.

Tenders. Sealed bids or offers for securities.

Treasury Bills. Short-term Government obligations, which do not bear interest; sold at a discount to provide buyers with interest for the use of their money.

Treasury Certificates. The Government, instead of issuing short-term bonds to finance its current debts, issues **certificates of indebtedness,** which bear interest.

Treasury Notes. Short-term notes (varying from 1 year to 7 years) bearing interest coupons. Sold in "over-the-counter" markets to the general public.

Warrants. Primarily orders to pay money or to deliver goods or papers.

> **Dividend warrants**—issued for the payment of dividends on stocks.
> **Interest warrants**—issued for the payment of interest on bonds or notes.
> **Stock purchase warrants**—issued to give **future** options (or **"subscription warrants,"** to give **immediate** rights) to buy a specified amount of stock at a stated **price** within a certain time. (See also Warrant, p. 520.)

STOCK MARKET TERMS

arbitrage—buying securities, commodities, or moneys in one market, and simultaneously selling them at a higher price in another market to make a profit. "Arbitrage" can also refer to buying one type of security and simultaneously selling another, as rights vs. stock, debentures vs. stock, or one stock vs. another in a proposed merger. (pron. är′bĭ-träzh′)

Big Board—a term for the New York Stock Exchange, derived from its original title of "The New York Stock and Exchange Board." It was once referred to as the "Regular Board" to distinguish it from its competitor the "Open Board." In current usage it is popularly referred to as the "Big Board."

blue chips—high quality, widely held stocks (and high-priced in relation to earning power) of financially strong, well-known companies.

Boerse—the Berlin stock exchange. (Ger. Börse; pron. bûr′zĕ)
Bourse—the Paris stock exchange. (pron. bŏŏrs; Fr., purse)

boiler room—high-pressure telephone peddling of dubious stocks to "suckers."

bucket shop—a sham brokerage where illegal betting against customers is done.

bulls—those who buy on the expectation that the market will advance; and by their transactions tend to, or attempt to, advance the market.
bears—those who sell "short" on the expectation that the market will decline; and by their transactions tend to, or attempt to, depress the market.

call—see "put," on p. 532.

call money—borrowed money that is returnable on call or demand.

cats and dogs—(little stocks) very low priced stocks that are highly speculative.

Change—means "exchange" in the phrase "on Change." (In British usage no apostrophe is placed before "Change"—it is not considered a contraction.)

Chicago Board of Trade—the world's largest grain market. It furnishes also a market for certain other commodities. "Memberships" correspond to "seats" on stock exchanges.

commodities—movable articles of commerce, as grains, feeds, foodstuffs, dairy products, meats, metals, building materials, chemicals, textiles, fuels, oils, lubricants, rubber, leather, hides, paper.

cornering the market—gaining control of enough stock to force those who have sold "short" to pay high prices to "cover."

cover—to buy stocks to cover "short" sales.

cum div.—with, or including, the dividend that has been declared or is due. (L. cum dividendo)

Curb Market—generally refers to the old New York Curb Exchange, which was once a stock market on the curb in Broad Street; later in a building. It has been renamed the **American Stock Exchange.** In the matter of rules and regulations, standards, etc., it does not differ essentially from the New York Stock Exchange.

cutting a melon—distributing surplus earnings to stockholders.

due bill—a form of IOU for undelivered stocks, dividends, or rights. For instance, if certain stocks are not actually available for delivery when sold, a broker may give a due bill for them, listing the stocks and promising delivery.

equity—the value of a property or business in excess of all debts or liabilities against it. A buyer's equity in a stock bought "on margin" is the difference between the market value of the stock and what is still owed on it.

equities—common stocks, so-called because they represent the remaining value or ownership (equity) in a company after everything else is paid.

ex coupon—without or not including the current interest coupon.

ex dividend—without or not including the declared dividend.

ex interest—without or not including the interest due.

ex privileges ⎫ without or not including the right to subscribe for new stock, or
ex rights ⎬ any other granted rights or privileges.

> NOTE: "Ex," meaning "without," is a preposition, not a prefix. Therefore no hyphen is necessary, but it is generally used in the securities world, as "stock selling ex-dividend."

flat—without interest. Bonds traded "flat" bear no accrued interest.

floating a loan—launching or arranging a loan for the financing of a project.

flotation—the marketing or selling of a new issue of securities to the public.

forward buying—trading in commodities for future or deferred delivery.

fractional shares—partial shares resulting from rights to buy, stock split-ups, or a stock dividend, as of one share for each five shares owned. These fractions are often evidenced by **"fractional warrants"** or **"certificates of participation"** (**"scrip"**), which may be bought and sold.

futures—contracts for future deliveries (chiefly a commodity exchange term).

hedge—a buying to offset a sale, or a selling to offset a purchase, as a fortification against loss. Trading in "puts and calls" is often called "hedging."

hypothecation—the pledging and depositing of security for the payment of a loan.

Lombard Street—the financial center of London; the commercial district of London is commonly called "the City."

London Stock Exchange—known in London as "the House."

long—If a trader owns or holds certain stocks, he is "long" of those stocks.
short—If a trader sells stocks that he does not own, hoping to secure them at a lower price on a falling market, he is "short" of those stocks. His broker borrows the stocks to make delivery. If the market rises, the trader must buy at a higher price when he "covers" his short sales.

margin—If stocks are not bought outright, they may be held "on margin"; that is, a trader may deposit a certain amount of money or security with a broker to cover the financing of the transactions, and to act as a "margin of safety" in case the market reverses quickly. "Margin" is generally used to mean the "collateral value that a broker requires a customer to maintain."

melon—surplus earnings distributed in the form of an extra dividend or stock.

odd lots—see "round lots," on p. 532.

option or ⎫ a contract giving one party an option to buy or sell specified securities
privilege ⎬ at a definite price within an agreed time.

Orders:

> **market order**—an order to buy or sell at the market price (for one day only).
>
> **limit(ed) order**—an order to buy at or below a certain price; or to sell at or above a certain price. Or an order limited to a certain period of time.
>
> **day order**—an order good for one day only. If not accomplished on that day, it is automatically canceled.
>
> **open order** ⎱ an order that is to stand until it is withdrawn. Also called a GTC—
> **GTC order** ⎰ "good till canceled" order.
>
> **stop order**—an order to sell and stop the loss (or protect the profit) at a certain figure if a stock is declining; or an order to buy to cover "short" sales and stop the loss at a certain figure if a stock is advancing.

over-the-counter (or off-board) trading—Many securities that are not listed on the exchanges are sold privately by dealers. These tradings are known as "over-the-counter" or "off-board" sales. The "asked" price is what a buyer pays. The "bid" price is what a seller receives.

paper profits—profits indicated by rising prices on securities still held. Paper profits become **"realized profits"** only by actual sale of the securities.

par value—of stocks is the share value assigned in the charter of the issuing company. Stock is carried on the company's books at par (or "no par" stock, at a "stated value"). "Par" has no significance now regarding the **market value** of common stock; but it is the basis of dividend payments on preferred stock.

Par value of bonds is the face value—usually $1000. Bonds may sell below par, "at a discount"; or above par, "at a premium."

passing a dividend—failing to pay a dividend, or not declaring a dividend when one is expected.

pegged—fixed or maintained at a certain price.

pit—(a commodity exchange term) a special section, in the Chicago Board of Trade building, that trades in a certain commodity, as the "Wheat Pit."

point—the unit of price fluctuation. For stocks, one dollar is a "point." For some commodities, as grain, one cent is a "point." Or $\frac{1}{100}$ of a cent may be a "point," as in cotton and coffee trading.

pool—a group of interests combined to control the price of certain securities.

portfolio—a list of all the securities and commercial paper owned by one person or one company. (Originally kept together in a portfolio—a portable case for documents.)

premium—If the market value of a thing exceeds the par value, such thing is said to be selling "at a premium." The premium, or the amount above par, is referred to as a percentage of the par value; for instance, "a premium of 5%" means 5% of the par value. "Premium" is also used to mean the amount paid for an option, or for a loan (as of stocks or money).

pro forma—(L.) for the sake of form only. A financial statement set up as an example or close approximation of the probable results if certain steps are taken, as in a proposed merger. In billing, an abbreviated, advance invoice.

prospectus—a booklet describing a new enterprise or new securities being offered for sale. Information is given about the company's business and its finances.

put—a contract in which a first party agrees **to buy** from a second party certain stock at a fixed price, if the second party chooses to sell (put) it within a specified time. The second party buys this option and may sell it.

call—a contract in which a first party agrees **to sell** to a second party certain stock at a fixed price, if the second party chooses to buy (call for) it within a specified time. The second party buys this option and may sell it.

pyramiding—building on profits, that is, using the profits realized on an advancing or declining market as the "margin" on which to buy or sell more stock.

rehypothecation—repledging stock that is held as security. For instance, a customer pledges stock to a broker as security for payment for the stock, and the broker repledges the stock to a bank to finance the transaction.

rigged market—a manipulated market—one that does not represent true values.

round lots—sales of a round number of shares, as 100—the "unit of trading."

odd lots—sales of fewer than 100 shares. (There are also occasions when sales of fewer than 100 shares are called "round lot" sales.)

532

seat on the stock exchange { a membership in a stock exchange, that is, a share in the assets of the exchange and the privilege of trading on the floor of the exchange.

short—see "long," on p. 531.

spot—on hand for immediate delivery for cash, as spot corn (spot prices).

spread—a combined "put and call," with a difference between the two prices.

squeeze—A "squeeze" is effected when those who have sold "short" are forced to pay high prices to "cover" (usually in the cornering of a stock or commodity).

stock dividend—additional shares of a company's own stock issued instead of, or besides, a cash dividend (as, a 4% stock dividend on 25 shares is 1 share).

stock split—shares divided. High-priced stock is often "split" (divided two or more shares for one) in order to bring it back to a popular market price. A dividend increase often follows.

The Street—Wall Street in New York, or the financial district of any city. In London, the district near the stock exchange.

underwriting—agreeing to buy on a certain date and at a fixed price—usually at a discount—an entire issue of stocks or bonds, with the purpose of handling and selling such issue, in small amounts, to the public. (See also p. 549.)

wash sale—a maneuver in which two traders engage in fictitious trading to make a stock appear active and to establish artificial prices, with no real intention of exchanging money or goods. Or a maneuver in which a trader sells a stock to take a tax-loss, and then buys the same stock back in less than 30 days.

watered stock—stock that is issued, or stock dividends that are declared, against inflated or padded ("watered") fixed assets.

How to Read Reports of Trading on the New York Stock Exchange

Stock and Dividend Rate	Sales in 100s	High	Low	Close	Net Change
Am T&T 2.60	973	41⅞	41⅛	41⅝	− ⅛
Gen Mot 1.70e	276	62	60⅞	61¾	+ ¾
G Mot pf 3.75	z 18	50	49	49	−1¾
Sears R 1.20a	x 322	56⅞	55¼	56½	+1⅛

This means that American Telephone and Telegraph Company stock, paying an annual dividend of $2.60 a share, sold on this day 97,300 shares. The highest price paid for this stock during the day was $41.875, and the lowest $41.125, a share; the closing price was $41.625; and the net change from the day before, 12½¢ less, or − ⅛. (⅛ or 12½¢ is the unit by which stock prices move up and down.)

The "e" after the General Motors dividend rate refers to a footnote ("paid so far this year"). The "pf" after the second General Motors cumulative preferred stock, paying an annual dividend of $3.75 a share. The "z" means "sales in full" on this day.

The "a" after Sears Roebuck's dividend rate refers to a footnote ("also extra or extras") meaning that a cash extra, like a "year-end dividend," is paid. The "x" means that this stock today sold "ex dividend" (the buyer will not receive the latest declared dividend; the seller will).

In the Bond Market reports, the name of the issuing company is followed by the rate of interest on the bonds and the year of maturity. The price of the bonds is expressed in hundreds for convenience (a percentage of the $1000 par value of most bonds).

Am Airlin cv 5½s 91.....74⅝   means that American Airlines **$1000** bonds (convertible into stock), bearing **5½**% interest, maturing in **1991**, today closed at **$746.25** each.

Cities Sv 6⅝s 99 xw.....76½   means that Cities Service **$1000** bonds, bearing **6⅝**% interest, maturing in **1999**, today sold for **$765.00** each, without warrants (xw).

Record of Security Transactions

To keep data on the buying and selling of stocks—and to show profit or loss for income tax purposes—"Investment Record Sheets" may be purchased from stationers. Some brokers furnish their customers with a blank form, "Record of Security Transactions," for a similar purpose.

Foreign Exchange

Foreign exchange rates are figured by the number of each country's currency units that can be bought, on any certain day, for one dollar (as 5 for $1 gives a value of 20¢ each).

The International Monetary Fund, Washington, D.C. 20431, publishes a monthly volume, **"International Financial Statistics,"** which gives **financial information by countries.** Price: $35 a year; $3.50 a copy.

The Department of Commerce, Washington, DC 20230, publishes **"Business America,"** a biweekly magazine, which gives worldwide trade opportunities, by countries and by products. **Licensing and investment proposals** from foreign firms are listed.

> Annual subscription: domestic, by first-class mail, $34; foreign, by surface mail, $42.50. Single copy, $1.40.
> Order from Superintendent of Documents, Washington, DC. 20402 or from any Department of Commerce District Office.

The Federal Reserve Board issues on the 1st of each month the **"Federal Reserve Bulletin,"** which, besides giving U.S. financial and business statistics, gives **international financial statistics,** including gold reserves and foreign exchange rates. The Bulletin may be secured from the Federal Reserve Board, Publications Div., Washington, DC 20551. Annual subscription: domestic (also to Canada and Mexico), $20; single copy, $2—foreign, by surface mail, $24; single copy, $2.50.

Methods of Writing Foreign Moneys. In many foreign countries sums of money are written in much the same manner as they are in the United States; that is, the abbreviation for the monetary unit is written before the figures, or often the dollar sign ($) is used to designate the currency. ("US$" is therefore sometimes used to avoid confusion.)

The principal difference in the manner of writing moneys is that in many countries a point is used instead of a comma to indicate thousands, and a comma instead of a decimal point, as in

> France   Frs 46.859,20 means 46,859 francs and 20 centimes.
> Germany   DM 4.560.348,50 means 4,560,348 Deutsche marks and 50 pfennige.

In some countries the decimal point is raised, as in

> Austria   S 8·—   S 3·90   S—·95   S 1,456.872·50   (Note the use of the period to separate thousands, and the comma, millions.)

In a few countries a space is used instead of a decimal point.

In some countries the symbol $ is placed where ordinarily the decimal point would be placed—between the unit and its fractional part, as in

534

Portugal	46$15 means 46 escudos and 15 centavos.
	$15 means just 15 centavos.
Vietnam	5$25 means 5 piastres and 25 centimes.

The **conto** sign (:) is sometimes used in Portugal to express 1000 escudos. In Uruguay, a colon expresses millions, as

| Portugal | 6.519:218$85 means 6,519 contos 218 escudos and 85 centavos. |
| Uruguay | $2:316,546.15 means 2 million, 316,546 pesos and 15 centesimos. |

In India and Pakistan, commas are used to indicate the number of **lakhs** (lacs) of 100,000 rupees each.; and **crores,** of 10,000,000 rupees each.

Rs 2,56,76,874 means 2 crores 56 lakhs (lacs) and 76,874 rupees.

Several countries have the **pound** as a monetary unit. The countries whose currency is based on the **"pound sterling"** use the symbol £ and the initials of the individual country, as

| £ | British "pound sterling" | £C | Cyprus pound |
| £Ir | Irish pound sterling | £M | Malta pound |

Other countries having the pound—but not based on the British "pound sterling" —now use just **L** (for libra, lira, or livre) with their individual initials, as

| LE | Egyptian pound | LL | Lebanese pound | LS | Syrian pound |
| IL | Israel pound | LSd | Sudanese pound | LT | Turkish pound |

If in doubt about the proper method of writing any item of foreign money, write simply the figures followed by the name, as one might write in American money "89 dollars and 65 cents."

89 pesos and 65 centavos   6,524 francs and 80 centimes

Eurodollars. These are U.S. dollars, spent abroad by investors, travelers, and traders, and held in European banks—and loaned back and forth (at good interest rates) to finance foreign trade and investments.

Special Drawing Rights ("Paper Gold"). "SDRs" are a form of international **reserves.** Participating countries have a right to draw (in proportion to their individual gold and currency subscriptions to the International Monetary Fund) on each other for needed currencies.

British Money. The new decimalized British currency consists of:

A **pound of 100 new pence,** written £1, £1·25, £29·75, etc. (note the raised decimal point). The new abbreviation for pence is a **"p"** rather than the old **"d"** (Latin denarius, "penny"). Amounts less than one pound are written 8p (formal £0·08), 35p, etc.

NOTE: £ represents the Latin "libra" meaning "pound." (£ may be typed by striking a hyphen, or a t or an f, over L, whichever looks best in the typeface being used.)

"Sterling" is standard British money—it may be gold or silver. The "pound sterling" is often called simply "sterling."

The term **"sterling silver"** is derived from the amount of silver in former British standard silver, which had a "fineness" of .925, that is, 925 parts of silver to 75 parts of alloy. British standard silver now has a "fineness" of .500, that is, 500 parts of silver to 500 parts of alloy.

535

Monetary Terms

legal standard—means the standard measure of value, in gold or silver, adopted by the government of a country, by which all forms of its money are rated.

gold standard—means that gold is the measure of value; that paper money has a fixed value in gold; and that exchange is stabilized at a fixed ratio with gold.

silver standard—means that silver is the measure of value; that paper money has a fixed value in silver; and that silver is the principal circulating medium.

legal tender—lawful money that may be tendered in payment of debts.

tolerance—the amount that coins are legally permitted to vary from the exact standard of weight or fineness.

specie—hard money or metal money as distinguished from paper money. "Specie payments" are payments made in coin; but "in specie" payments specified in legal papers are usually understood to mean payments "in United States currency." (pron. spē′ shē)

bullion—uncoined gold or silver in bars, or ingots.

FOREIGN MONEYS

(For values of gold and silver, see p. 579.)

Par values have been suspended by many countries, preferring to have flexible or "floating" currency values. Exchange rates fluctuate from day to day—and some countries have various rates: official, central, free market, commercial, financial, and/or tourist. For variations in value, consult the Foreign Exchange tables in the financial sections of daily newspapers—or ask any large local bank, or the Union Bank of Switzerland, 14 Wall Street, New York, N.Y. **10005.**

Note the difference between "revaluation" (an increase in value) and "devaluation" (a decrease).

Country	Monetary Unit (Plurals are indicated)	Abbreviation or Symbol	Floating Value* in U.S. Dollars	Small Coin (Number in one monetary unit)
Afghanistan	afghani	Af	$0.0222	100 puls
Algeria	Algerian dinar -s	DA	.2398	100 centimes
Argentina	Argentine peso -s	$a	.0009	100 centavos
Australia	Australian dollar -s	$A	1.1297	100 cents
Austria	schilling -s	S	.0793	100 groschen
Bahama Islands	Bahama dollar -s	BI$	1.0000	100 cents
Belgium	Belgian franc -s	BF or fr.	.0346	100 centimes
Bermuda	Bermuda dollar -s	Ber$ or $ber.	1.0000	100 cents
Bolivia	peso-boliviano -s	$b	.0520	100 centavos
Brazil	new cruzeiro -s (A "conto" is 1000 Cr.)	Cr$ as Cr$1.348,50	.0452	100 centavos
Br. Honduras (now Belize)	dollar -s	BH$	.5000	100 cents
Bulgaria	lev -a	Lv	.6060	100 stotinki
Burma	kyat -s	K	.1479	100 pyas
Cameroon	CFA franc -s	CFA	.0040	100 centimes
Canada	Canadian dollar -s	$ or $can	.8582	100 cents
Ceylon (now Sri Lanka)	Ceylon rupee -s	Cey Rs or cR	.0632	100 cents
Chile	Chilean peso -s	Ch$	.0301	100 centesimos
China, People's Rep. of (See Hong Kong & Taiwan)	People's yuan (pl. same)	¥	.5000	100 fen; 10 chou
Colombia	Colombian peso -s	Col$	.0279	100 centavos
Congo (now Zaire)	zaire -s	Z	1.1494	100 makuta
Costa Rica	colón -es	₡ or CR₡	.1166	100 centimos
Cuba	Cuban peso -s	$ or Cub$	.1062	100 centavos
Czechoslovakia	koruna -s	Kčs	.0833	100 heller
Denmark	krone -r	DKr	.2092	100 øre
Dominican Republic	peso -s	RD$	1.0000	100 centavos
Ecuador	sucre -s	S/	.0404	100 centavos
Egypt	Egyptian pound -s (1 tallar = 20 piasters)	LE or egL	1.3500	100 piasters or 1000 millièmes
El Salvador	colón -es	₡ or ES₡	4000	100 centavos
England (See Gt. Britain)				
Ethiopia	Birr (pl. same)	Eth$	.4830	100 cents
Finland	markka -s or -a	Fmk	.2655	100 pennia
France	franc -s	F or fr.	.2515	100 centimes
Germany, Fed. Rep. of	Deutsche mark -s	DM	.5503	100 pfennige
Ghana	cedi -s	₡	.2546	100 pesewas
Great Britain	pound sterling	£	2.1055	100 pence (eff. 2/15/71)

FOREIGN MONEYS—contd.

Country	Monetary Unit (Plurals are indicated)	Abbreviation or Symbol	Floating Value* in U.S. Dollars	Small Coin (Number in one monetary unit)
Greece	drachma -s or -e	Dr	$0.0274	100 lepta
Guatemala	quetzal -es	Q	1.0000	100 centavos
Guinea	syli -s	S	.0487	100 cauris
Haiti	gourde -s	G	.2000	100 centimes
Holland (See Netherlands)				
Honduras	lempira -s	L	.5000	100 centavos
Hong Kong (Colony)	Hong Kong dollar -s	HK$	.2091	100 cents
Hungary	forint (pl. same)	Ft	.0427	100 fillér
Iceland	króna -nur	IKr	.0052	100 aurar
India	Indian rupee -s	Rs or ℞	.1290	100 paise
Indonesia	rupiah (pl. same)	Rp	.0024	100 sen
Iran (old Persia)	rial -s (1 = 20 shahis)	Rls	.0142	100 dinars
Iraq	Iraqi dinar -s	ID	3.4400	1000 fils
Ireland (Eire)	pound sterling	£	2.1055	100 pence (eff. 2/15/71)
Ireland, Northern	(British)			
Israel	Israel pound -s (lira)	IL	.0465	100 agorot
Italy	lira -re	L or Lit	.0012	100 centesimi
Ivory Coast	CFA franc -s	CFA fr	.0040	100 centimes
Jamaica	Jamaican dollar -s	J$	1.1000	100 cents
Japan	yen (pl. same)	¥	.0052	100 sen
Jordan	Jordan dinar -s	JD	3.3990	1000 fils
Kenya	Kenya shilling -s	Sh	.1203	100 cents
Korea, Rep. of (South)	won (pl. same)	₩	.0021	100 chun
Lebanon	Lebanese pound -s	LL	.3355	100 piastres
Liberia	Liberian dollar -s	$ or Lib$	1.0000	100 cents
Libya	Libyan dinar -s	LD	3.3800	100 dirhams
Luxembourg	franc -s	Lux F or fr.	.0346	100 centimes
Madagascar	Malagasy franc -s	FMg	.0045	100 centimes
Malaysia	ringgit (pl. same)	R$	.4310	100 cents
Mexico	Mexican peso -s	Mex$	.0439	100 centavos
Morocco	dirham -s	DH	.2222	100 francs
Netherlands (Holland)	guilder -s (florin)	f. or fl.	.4865	100 cents
New Zealand	New Zealand dollar -s	NZ$	1.0545	100 cents
Nicaragua	córdoba -s	C$	.1422	100 centavos
Nigeria	naira -s	N	1.5400	100 kobos
Norway	krone -r	NKr	.1978	100 øre
Pakistan	Pakistan rupee -s	PRs	.1020	100 paisa
Panama	balboa -s	B	1.0000	100 centesimos
Paraguay	guaraní -es	₲	.0079	100 centimos
Peru	sol -s	S/.	.0054	100 centavos
Philippines	Philippine peso -s	₱	.1358	100 centavos
Poland	zloty -s	Zl	.0301	100 groszy
Portugal	escudo -s	Esc or $	.0216	100 centavos
Puerto Rico	(United States $)			
Rumania	leu (pl. lei)	L or Lei	.0695	100 bani
Russia (See U.S.S.R.)				
Saudi Arabia	riyal -at	SRls	.3005	100 halalat
Singapore	Singapore dollar -s	S$	.4558	100 cents
South Africa, Republic of	rand (pl. same)	R	1.1505	100 cents
Spain	peseta -s	Pts	.0141	100 centimos
Sudan	Sudanese pound -s (livre)	LSd	2.8720	100 piastres
Sweden	krona -nor	SKr	.2290	100 öre
Switzerland	Swiss franc -s	Sw F or fr.	.6013	100 centimes
Syria	Syrian pound -s	LS	.2531	100 piastres
Taiwan (Formosa)	New Taiwan dollar -s	NT$	.0280	100 cents
Tanzania	Tanzania shilling -s	T Sh	.1203	100 cents
Thailand (Siam)	baht (pl. same) (tical)	B	.0500	100 satang
Trinidad and Tobago	TT dollar -s	TT$	.4166	100 cents
Tunisia	Tunisian dinar -s	D or tD	2.3255	1000 millimes
Turkey	lira -s (pound)	LT	.0469	100 kurus
Uganda	Uganda shilling -s	U Sh	.1200	100 cents
Uruguay	Uruguayan peso -s	U$	.1374†	100 centesimos
U.S.S.R. (Russia)	ruble -s	r, R, or Rbl	.8460	100 kopecks
Venezuela	bolívar -es	Bs	.2329	100 centimos
Vietnam	dong (pl. same)	VD	.4818	100 sous (xu)
Yugoslavia	Yugoslav dinar -s	Din	.0549	100 para
Zambia	kwacha (pl. same)	K	1.2500	100 ngwee

* Approximate current "floating" value.

† New Uruguayan peso—financial rate.

537

Financial Statements

No one system of accounting can be applied to every business, because no two businesses are exactly alike. But there are two accounting statements that are generally prepared by all companies. Since these statements are often used in the different departments of organizations they are considered here.

> **Balance Sheet.** A statement of the financial condition—assets and liabilities—of a business on a certain date.
>
> A "balance sheet" is so-called because it balances—that is, the total assets (items owned) equal the total liabilities (items owed) plus the "net worth" (balance of value belonging to owners, or "owners' equity"). It may also be formally designated "Statement of Financial Condition [or Position]," or "Statement of Resources and Liabilities."
>
> The statement of financial condition of a company is often issued or made public for the purpose of giving information to the stockholders and to persons expecting to trade with, invest in, or lend money to the company.
>
> **Profit and Loss Statement.** An operating statement, or summary of income and expense. It is also called an "Income Statement," "Income Account," "Statement [or Record] of Earnings," "Statement of Operations," or "Statement of Income and Retained Earnings." It shows how much was made or lost over a certain period of time—a month or a year.
>
> A **Manufacturing Statement** is sometimes submitted as a supporting schedule to the statement of profit and loss, to show more details with respect to the cost of goods produced. The manufacturing statement contains three main captions: Cost of Raw Materials, Direct Labor, and Manufacturing or Overhead Expense.
>
> (Forms for either of these statements may be purchased at stationery stores.)

The forms for balance sheets vary, as do the forms for profit and loss statements; but the general outlines of all balance sheets and of all profit and loss statements are much the same. The amount of detail to be included in the headings and the grouping of the headings must be governed by individual preference and the purpose for which the statement is being made.

In the preparation of statements, a company should follow the same general form year after year, if possible, not only for uniformity but in order to facilitate the study of trends.

The **American Institute of Certified Public Accountants** publishes a great many pamphlets and books in which is set forth the best modern practice in accounting and auditing, terminology, and the preparation of financial statements. A catalogue of this literature—with description and prices—may be procured from the American Institute of Certified Public Accountants, 666 Fifth Avenue, New York, N.Y. 10019 (See also Financial Records, p. 605.)

FINANCIAL STATEMENTS

Example of a **Profit and Loss Statement** or **"Income Account"**:

THE STEEL-GLASS PRODUCTS COMPANY, INC.
(A Maryland Corporation)
STATEMENT OF INCOME AND RETAINED EARNINGS
For the year ended December 31, 19..

		(Thousands)
Sales		
Gross sales		$315,737
Less: Discounts, returns, and allowances		3,519
Net sales..		$312,218
Cost of Goods Sold		
Inventory at beginning of year (at cost)		30,550
Purchases (net after discounts, returns, and allowances)	$142,860	
Freight, express, storage, and cartage	3,480	146,340
Total		176,890
Less: Inventory at end of year (at cost)		26,970
Cost of goods sold..		149,920
Gross margin...		162,298
Expenses of Operation		
Office expense and salaries		22,100
Selling expense, salaries, and commissions		19,000
Advertising		12,500
Store and workroom expense and wages; and delivery		69,230
Rent, light, heat, power, water, telephone		4,800
Maintenance and repairs		1,250
Depreciation and amortization		4,000
Experiments, research, and patent		3,800
Taxes (miscellaneous) and licenses		1,540
Employee benefits, and social security taxes		2,830
Insurance		810
Uncollectible accounts		1,592
Miscellaneous expenses		380
Total operating expenses................................		143,832
Operating income....................................		18,466
Other Income		
Commissions received, and patent royalties		2,290
Interest and dividends		2,540
Rentals		2,590
Total miscellaneous income...............................		7,420
Total income from operations and other sources..........................		25,886
Deductions From Income		
Interest on mortgage and bank loan		620
Loss on sale of fixed assets		300
Total deductions from income...............................		920
Net income before income taxes..		24,966
Income Taxes—Current Year		
Federal income tax		7,490
State income tax		999
		8,489
NET INCOME after income taxes......................................		16,477
Retained Earnings at beginning of year...		18,279
		34,756
Less: Charges attributable to prior periods		1,350
Cash dividends paid (preferred stock, 80¢ a share; common, 50¢)		7,400
		8,750
RETAINED EARNINGS at end of year.................................		$ 26,006

NOTE: **No cents** are carried (except in some bank reports); rather, "whole-dollar" accounting is used—rounding out figures to the nearest even dollar: An occasional **deduction, decrease, deficit (d),** or **loss** may be indicated by parentheses around the figures. But if such negative or "red-ink" amounts are obvious—from a heading—no "parens" are used. (See also p. 417.)

FINANCIAL STATEMENTS

Example of a Balance Sheet:

THE STEEL-GLASS PRODUCTS COMPANY, INC.
(A Maryland Corporation)
STATEMENT OF FINANCIAL CONDITION—December 31, 19..

ASSETS

		(Thousands)
Current Assets		
Cash and certificates of deposit	$35,268	
Marketable securities (at cost, which approximates market value)	25,000	
Receivables { Accrued interest, dividends, and commissions	1,650	
Notes receivable	5,140	
Accounts receivable (net after allowance of $10,000 for doubtful accounts and cash discounts)	25,783	
Inventory (at last-in, first-out [Lifo] cost—lower than market)	26,970	
Total current assets		$119,811
Prepaid Expenses		
Rent paid in advance and deposit on lease	890	
Taxes, licenses, and insurance prepaid	655	
Advertising contract advances	4,000	
Office supplies on hand	100	
Total prepaid expenses		5,645
Deferred Charges		
Cost of option, plans, and training personnel for new project		1,560
Property, Plant, and Equipment [or Fixed Assets] (at cost)		
Land	15,000	
Buildings and leaseholds	$27,000	
Furniture and fixtures	5,000	
Machinery and equipment	28,060	
Automobiles and trucks	11,847	
	71,907	
Less: Accumulated depreciation and amortization	26,000	45,907
Net property [or fixed assets]		60,907
Intangible Assets		
Patents, trademark, and goodwill (not valued)		
Investments		
In capital stock of affiliated company (at cost, less reserve for losses)	10,000	
In other companies (not readily marketable)	5,900	
Total investments		15,900
TOTAL ASSETS		$203,823

LIABILITIES AND EQUITY [or CAPITAL]

Current Liabilities		
Accounts payable and accrued expenses	$15,900	
Bank loan, notes, and drafts payable	9,460	
Customers' advances on contracts	4,556	
Federal and State income taxes	8,500	
Long-term debt due within one year	2,500	
Total current liabilities		$ 40,916
Long-Term Debt		
Purchase money 5½% mortgage, payable in installments to 1990		25,000
TOTAL LIABILITIES		65,916

Stockholders' Equity* [Net Worth]

Capital Stock			
Preferred stock, 8% cumulative; par value $10; authorized 6,000,000 shares; issued and outstanding 4,000,000 shares		$40,000	
Common stock, par value $5; authorized 20,000,000 shares; issued 10,000,000 shares (including 1,600,000 in treasury)		50,000	
Total capital stock		90,000	
Additional Paid-in Capital (premium on capital stock transactions)	$33,101		
Retained [or Reinvested] earnings	26,006		
	59,107		
Treasury stock, 1,600,000 shares common, at cost	(11,200)	47,907	
Total stockholders' equity			137,907
TOTAL LIABILITIES AND EQUITY [or CAPITAL]			$203,823

* "Shareholder" (the British term) has been adopted by some American corporations following the "Model Business Corporation Act."

- - - -

"Notes" explaining various entries are usually appended to financial statements; for instance, one note may itemize indebtedness; another tell what "Contingent Liabilities" exist, and so on.

ACCOUNTING TERMS

Assets or Resources (What is owned.)

Current Assets. Cash and those assets that will be converted into cash in the ordinary course of operations and in a relatively short time—usually within a year—such as notes and accounts receivable, inventories, and marketable securities.

Liquid ("Quick") Assets. Cash, current receivables, and marketable securities, or any asset that can be quickly converted into cash without loss.

Working Assets. Inventories, or any other assets that must be handled or "worked" before money can be realized on them.

Deferred Assets (or "Deferred Debits"). Assets whose benefit is deferred until a future time. They may be subdivided into:

> **Prepaid Expenses.** Prepayments that have some liquidating (cash-in) value, such as advance payments on contracts, deposits on leases, and office supplies on hand.

> **Deferred Charges.** Development and organization costs incurred in one period but whose benefits extend over succeeding periods; such charges are deferred and prorated over the entire period of benefit.

Fixed Assets (or "Property, Plant, and Equipment"). The assets used in conducting the business which have a relatively long life, such as land, plant, buildings, machinery, furniture and fixtures, and automotive equipment.

Intangible Assets. A term ordinarily applied to such assets as patents, copyrights, trademarks, brands, secret processes, goodwill, subscription lists, leases, licenses, and franchises. Because it is sometimes difficult to determine the real value of these assets, they are often omitted in a financial statement, or are given only a nominal valuation (usually based on unamortized cost).

Contingent Assets. Future, and uncertain, items of possible value, as favorable claims pending. (Not carried in a balance sheet until actually collectible.)

Goodwill. An intangible asset that represents the value of a company's earning power over what it would ordinarily be expected to earn. The extra earning power may be created by advertising, by the manner of doing business, by advantageous location, or by the company's standing or good name in the business world. While of definite value, goodwill is often not valued in a financial statement, or given only a nominal valuation (calculated from excess profits, or based on unamortized cost).

Liabilities (What is owed.)

Current Liabilities. Short-term debts—usually to be paid within one year. Examples: bank loans, accounts payable, short-term notes payable, taxes.

Deferred Liabilities (or "Deferred Credits"). Also are called "deferred income," or "unearned income," and represent income or benefits received and not yet earned, such as rents or interest received in advance.

Fixed Liabilities (or "Long-Term Debt"). Long-term liabilities, such as mortgages, bonds, and contracts, for terms longer than one year. They are usually incurred in the acquisition of fixed assets.

Contingent Liabilities. Future items that may become obligations under certain conditions—such as guarantees given, accommodation paper signed, notes receivable sold (discounted), and adverse litigation or claims pending.

541

Miscellaneous Accounting Terms

Fund. A fund made up of specific assets, usually cash or securities, set aside for a definite purpose.

Reserve. A part of the profits or surplus set aside (or simply designated on the books) for specific purposes, or for general purposes and contingencies.

Funded Reserve. A reserve for which a fund has been established and invested so that it will bring in interest or earnings.

Funded Debt. Long-term indebtedness, for the payment (retirement) of which a fund has been established. (See "sinking fund," below.)

Bonded Debt. Indebtedness represented by bonds.

Floating Debt. Unfunded debt, that is, current debt.

Sinking Fund. Usually a fund that is started when bonds are issued, or other long-term indebtedness is incurred. The sinking fund is increased and invested so that it will completely pay the debt as the bonds or other forms of indebtedness mature.

Amortization. The gradual payment f a debt; or the writing off of intangible assets over a period of time as they e pire. (pron. ăm-ĕr-tĭ-zā'shun)

Capital Accumulations (formerly called **"Surplus"**—the excess of assets over liabilities and capital stock) are now designated:

> **Paid-in Capital**—from the sale of capital stock at a premium ("in excess of par value"), or profits on treasury stock transactions.
>
> **Donated Capital**—from donations of stock, gifts of land, etc.
>
> **Appreciation Capital**—from a revaluation or reappraisal of fixed assets.
>
> **Retained Earnings** (formerly **"Earned Surplus"**). Remaining income—after dividends and other appropriations—for use or reinvestment in the business.

Working Capital. Total current assets minus total current liabilities.

Cash Flow. Ready cash (net income plus set-aside cash, as for depreciation).

Equity. The difference between what is owed on a property and what the property is worth; or the amount by which the assets exceed the liabilities.

Stockholders' [Owners'] Equity (net worth). Total assets minus total liabilities.

"Window Dressing." The manipulation of items on a financial statement to make them appear more favorable than they really are.

Contra. Means "against" or "opposite." A "contra asset" is an opposite or offsetting asset. A "contra credit" is an opposite or offsetting credit.

Book Value. The value at which an asset is carried on the books of a company. A piece of property or equipment may be worth more or less to a "going concern" than it would be worth if sold in the open market. "Book value" may be far above "scrap value." Likewise, the book value of stock may be above or below its market value, because on the books it represents the net assets (excess of assets over liabilities) divided by the shares outstanding.

Bad Debts. Accounts or notes receivable that are uncollectible. They are written off usually by a direct charge to operations. If a "reserve or allowance for doubtful accounts" is carried, it signifies that the company has made a provision for probable losses.

Liquidation. The payment of debts. A business is "in liquidation" when its assets are being sold and its affairs are being closed.

> **Liquidating** may also mean voluntarily turning securities, goods, or properties into cash to take profits or prevent losses.

Insolvency. A company is "insolvent" if it cannot meet its debts as they become due. It may have assets in excess of its liabilities, but if it is unable to convert its assets into ready money with which to meet its current liabilities, it is "insolvent."

Receivership. A receiver may be appointed by the court to conserve the assets of an insolvent company, and to conduct its business in an attempt to pay its debts. If such business operation is successful, the company may be returned to its owners; if unsuccessful, it will be liquidated.

> **Receiver's certificates** (often prior lien) may be sold to provide cash.

Reorganization. Under Chapter X of the Bankruptcy Act, an insolvent company may reorganize with the consent of a majority of its creditors and under court supervision (through an appointed trustee; or, for a bank, a **conservator**).

> Under **Chapter XI,** the **debtor remains in possession,** under court control.

Reorganization is undergone to effect financial compromises on debts, and to avoid receivership expenses or the sale of property as in regular bankruptcy.

Bankruptcy. A company is bankrupt if it is unable to meet its debts, and if its assets do not cover its liabilities.

> **Voluntary Bankruptcy.** A company may voluntarily declare, in writing, its inability to pay its debts and petition the court to be declared a bankrupt.

> **Involuntary Bankruptcy.** The creditors of an insolvent company may "throw it into bankruptcy" by petitioning the court to declare it a bankrupt.

> **A Trustee** is elected or appointed in bankruptcy proceedings to take charge of the assets and wind up the affairs of the bankrupt.

> **Referee in Bankruptcy.** An officer, usually an attorney, appointed by the court to assist in a judicial capacity in investigating and hearing bankruptcy cases.

Defunct. A defunct concern is one that is dead or extinct.

INTEREST

In computing interest:

> 360 days to the year are used in ordinary interest calculations—12 months of 30 days each.
>
> 365 days to the year (366 in leap year) are used in exact interest calculations. The Government uses this figure.

In **ordinary business transactions,** a month's interest (on small amounts) is considered to be 1/12 of a year's interest. On large amounts, the exact number of days is figured.

In **banking,** all interest is figured by the day, whether the amount is large or small, and whether the term is in months or days. For instance, a note dated May 12 and payable 2 months after date would be payable July 12, and the interest would be figured for 61 days.

> **A day's interest** is $\frac{1}{360}$ (approximate) or $\frac{1}{365}$ (exact) of a year's interest.

For sums less than $1500, the basis of a 360-day year will give the interest to within a few cents of the exact figure; and for convenience this basis is ordinarily used.

If the basis of a 360-day year is used, it permits many shortcuts. For instance, 90 days becomes 1/4 of a year; 60 days, 1/6 of a year; 30 days, 1/12 of a year, etc. But if the days are uneven, as 77, the process is, of course, to find the interest for one day and multiply by 77.

To find the interest for an uneven number of days:

Find the interest for one year. Divide by 365 (or 360) to find the interest for one day. (Or use the 6% shortcut method given below.) Multiply the interest for one day by the exact number of days.

Count the exact number of days on the calendar, excluding the first day, which is not counted. (It is reasoned that part of the first day and part of the last day are not covered in the transaction; therefore, one whole day is not counted, and it is usually the first.)

For instance, from the 10th to the 28th of a month would be 18 days, not 19. A note dated April 15, payable 60 days after date, would be due June 14, not June 15.

If a note dated April 15 is payable 3 months after date, 3 calendar months are figured, and the note is payable July 15. But if the same note is payable 90 days after date, the exact number of days is figured (excluding the first), and the note is payable July 14.

To figure 6%, or higher, interest:

A quick method of finding 6% interest for 60 days (2 months) is simply to point off two decimal places. Thus the interest for 60 days at 6% on $1,078 would be $10.78. For 30 days (1 month) at 6%, divide the above result by 2, which gives $5.39. For 90 days (3 months) at 6%, find the amounts for 60 and 30 days and add them, as $10.78 plus $5.39, which gives $16.17. For 1 day at 6%, find the amount for 6 days (by pointing off three decimal places) and divide by 6, as $1.078 divided by 6, which gives 18¢.

To figure 9% interest, find the amount for 6%; divide by 2 (which gives 3% interest); then add the 3% interest.

To figure 8% interest, find the amount for 6%; divide by 3 (which gives 2% interest); then add the 2% interest.

To figure compound interest: add the interest to the principal for each period (year, half-year, or quarter) to form a new principal for the next period—for example:

$100 at 5% compound interest will give a principal of $105 for the second year; $110.25 for the third; and $115.76 for the fourth: a total compound interest of $15.76 for 3 years. (Simple interest would be $15.)

30-DAY INTEREST TABLE—FOR AMORTIZED-MONTHLY LOANS

$	6½%	6.6%	7.2%	7½%	$	6½%	6.6%	7.2%	7½%
1000	5.42	5.50	6.00	6.25	10	.05	.06	.06	.06
2000	10.83	11.00	12.00	12.50	20	.11	.11	.12	.13
3000	16.25	16.50	18.00	18.75	30	.16	.17	.18	.19
4000	21.67	22.00	24.00	25.00	40	.22	.22	.24	.25
5000	27.08	27.50	30.00	31.25	50	.27	.28	.30	.31
6000	32.50	33.00	36.00	37.50	60	.33	.33	.36	.38
7000	37.92	38.50	42.00	43.75	70	.38	.39	.42	.44
8000	43.33	44.00	48.00	50.00	80	.43	.44	.48	.50
9000	48.75	49.50	54.00	56.25	90	.49	.50	.54	.57
100	.54	.55	.60	.63	1	.01	.01	.01	.01
200	1.08	1.10	1.20	1.25	2	.01	.01	.01	.01
300	1.63	1.65	1.80	1.88	3	.02	.02	.02	.02
400	2.17	2.20	2.40	2.50	4	.02	.02	.02	.03
500	2.71	2.75	3.00	3.13	5	.03	.03	.03	.03
600	3.25	3.30	3.60	3.75	6	.03	.03	.03	.04
700	3.79	3.85	4.20	4.38	7	.04	.04	.04	.05
800	4.33	4.40	4.80	5.00	8	.04	.04	.04	.05
900	4.88	4.95	5.40	5.63	9	.05	.05	.05	.06

To figure, say, a principal of **$5,692.16 at 7½%** for 1 month (30 days), first drop the cents (16); then take the figures in the 7½% column, and add:

For $5000, interest =	$31.25
600	3.75
90	.57
2	.01
$5692	$35.58

On a monthly or yearly receipt, record the declining principal, interest, and the monthly payment(s) like this:

$5692.16 remaining principal, May 1, 19. .
+35.58 interest for May 19. .

5727.74
−95.00 paid June 1, 19. .

$5632.74 rem. prin. June 1, 19. . (etc.)

Prime Rate. This is the minimum interest that banks charge top-rated corporations, who are prime credit risks; hence it is a basic rate.

Discount Rate. This is the interest charged by the Federal Reserve on loans to commercial banks. It governs the general level of rates.

"Legal Rate of Interest." This is a rate fixed by law in each state to apply to papers that do not specify interest, but on which it may legally be charged. The legal rate is not, in most states, the maximum contract rate—"the highest rate that can be charged by written agreement."

The legal rates and the highest contract rates in the different states may be found in the current Martindale-Hubbell Law Directory, Vol. VI, in any public or law library; or in the Rand McNally Bankers Directory (The Bankers Blue Book) in any public library or at any bank.

The **statute of limitations** on open accounts, notes, written contracts, sealed instruments, and judgments, in each state may also be found in the above publications.

◇◇◇◇◇◇◇◇

INVENTORIES AND DEPRECIATION

Merchandise is inventoried **"at cost or market, whichever is lower."**

Lifo (last-in, first-out) means the **costs** of the **last** items bought are applied to the **first, or next,** sold; and **fifo, first** bought, to **first** sold.

Depreciation. Depreciation on buildings and such equipment as furniture, tools, and machinery may be calculated in **three ways:**

(IRS "Depreciation Guidelines and Rules" is sold by Supt. of Docs., Washington, D.C. 20402 —$1.20)

> **Straight-Line Method** (if depreciation is about the same each year)— Estimate the life of the equipment and the salvage value; subtract the salvage value from the cost (or from the remaining cost plus improvements); and write off an equal amount of depreciation each year.
>
> **Declining-Balance Method** (if depreciation is heavier in first years)— Write off a uniform percentage (as 10% or 20%) of the remaining cost each year. On new equipment (from 1954) this percentage may equal, but not exceed, twice the straight-line percentage. No salvage value is deducted, as the final unrecovered cost represents salvage.
>
> **Sum-of-the-Years-Digits Method** (if depreciation is heavier in first years)—Subtract the salvage value from the cost, and figure the depreciation on a fractional basis—arrived at by adding the digits in the number of years calculated. For instance, if the life of a piece of machinery is estimated to be 5 years, add the digits 1, 2, 3, 4, and 5, which gives 15. Since the depreciation will be heavier in the first years than in later years, the depreciation for the first year should be figured as the largest fraction, 5/15 of the total depreciation; the second year 4/15; the third year 3/15, etc.
>
> The following is an example:

Cost $2000	Scrap value $200 after 5 years	Depreciation $1800
LIFE OF EQUIPMENT		YEARLY CHARGE-OFF
1 year	5/15 of $1800	$ 600
2	4/15	480
3	3/15	360
4	2/15	240
5	1/15	120
15 fractional basis	15/15	$1800 total depreciation

Petty Cash

A **petty cash account,** or **imprest fund,** may be kept separately from the general books, but it should be so kept that entries may be prepared from it for the general books of account, if necessary. For example:

Petty Cash Book / Optional Account Distribution (Account Numbers are shown.)

Date	Receipt (Voucher) Number	Explanation	Amount Received (Debit)	Amount Paid Out (Credit)	Post- age (7082)	Deliv- ery (6051)	Office Supplies (7011)	Charity (7092)	Sundry Acct.	Sundry Amt.
19.. Mar. 2		Check for cash, #258	$25 00							
3	1	Stationery		$ 4 65			$4 65			
7	2	Stamps		5 00	$5 00					
9	3	Express		11 89		$11 89				
14	4	Messenger		1 50		1 50				
23		Balance (on hand)		1 96	$5 00	$13 39	$4 65			
			$25 00	$25 00						
23		Cash balance	$ 1 96							
23		Revolving check, #412	23 04							
28	5	C.O.D. package		$ 2 35					7090	$2 35
30	6	Donation Boys' Club		5 00				$5 00		

When the petty cash fund is **"revolved"** or renewed, with a check issued on the general bank account for the amount of petty cash expenditures, the petty cash account should be ruled off and the balance of cash actually in the fund brought down as shown in the foregoing illustration.

A **receipt,** often called a **"voucher,"** should be obtained for every disbursement of petty cash. (Printed petty cash voucher forms may be purchased from stationers.) Each voucher will show its number, the date, amount, to whom paid, for what, the account chargeable, and the signature of the person receiving, and of the one approving, payment. Attached should be any bill or paper received pertaining to the matter.

These vouchers should be kept in the petty cash box, and when their total is sufficiently high—as shown from the entries in the petty cash book—they should be sent to the cashier with a request, on a **"revolving voucher,"** for a check to cover their amount.

The **revolving voucher** is in the form of a receipt from the keeper of the petty cash box to the cashier for cash, as

(No.) (Date)   Received from Cash check for $23.04 to reimburse Petty Cash, as per petty cash vouchers Nos. 1–4 attached. (Sgd.)_____

IOU. Whenever cash is borrowed from the petty cash box, an **IOU** for the amount should be placed in the box. Unless this is done, it is difficult to remember what is due the cash box, and the keeper of the box is often obliged to pay for someone else's negligence.

Insurance

The general classifications of insurance are:

Accident and Health (Sickness)
  Hospital Medical Disability
Automobile
  Collision   Property Damage
Aviation (Aircraft, Cargo, etc.)
Boiler and Machinery
Burglary and Robbery (Holdup)
Business Interruption
  (Use and Occupancy)
Casualty
Common Carriers'
Credit
Crop (Hail, etc.)
Earthquake
Explosion
Fidelity Bonds
Fire (with Extended Coverage)
Flood
Forgery and Alteration
Group Life (Group Disability, etc.)
Inland Marine (Transportation)
Jewelry and Furs
Liability
  Business, Professional (Malpractice),
  Personal, and Public Liability

Life
  Annuities   Business Life
  Endowment Double Indemnity
Livestock
Marine (Ocean, and Inland)
Mortgage and Property Improvement
Personal Property [Floater]
Plate Glass (Glass)
Rain (for outdoor events)
Rent
Residence
Retirement (Income, or Annuity)
Riot and Civil Commotion
Social
  Social Security (Old-Age)
  Unemployment
Sprinkler Leakage
Surety Bonds
Theft
Title (to real estate)
Trip Transit (Moving)
Water Damage
Windstorm (Tornado, Cyclone)
Workmen's Compensation (Compensation)
  (Employers' Liability)

Schedule. All insurance policies held by one company or person should be classified and listed on a schedule so that a study of amounts and types may be made, and no policies will lapse because of nonpayment of premiums.

List the policies in the following form, and enter all premium-payment dates on the desk calendar as reminders of the dates on which checks should be mailed. (Also write a tickler card for each policy, giving full information, so that checks may be written therefrom without the bother of looking up policies.)

SCHEDULE OF INSURANCE POLICIES

Company and Agent (Address)	Policy No.	Kind or Plan	Property or Risk Covered	Term		Amount of Policy	Beneficiary	Yearly Premium	Premiums Payable
				Date Issued	Term Expires				

Payment. The time for payment of premiums is specified in each insurance policy. (Life insurance premiums, but not other, may be paid within one month after their due dates.) Payments should be sent early enough to reach the insurance companies well within the prescribed time. Some companies will accept payment, without canceling policies, if checks or money orders are "in the mails" (postmarked) on the last days for payment of the premiums. But it is not wise to mail a check on the last day for a payment of any kind.

Dividends. Some policies pay dividends—deductible from the premiums.

Safeguarding Policies. All insurance policies should be kept in a place of safekeeping, preferably in a safe deposit vault.

❖❖❖❖❖❖❖

INSURANCE TERMS

actuary—the official statistician of an insurance company, who calculates or computes insurance risks, premiums, surrender values, etc.

adjuster—one appointed to determine and make adjustment of loss or damage under insurance policies.

all risk—does not mean any and every possible risk, but only certain common risks; there are certain excluded risks under "all risk" policies.

annuity—provides an annual or periodic income to the annuitant for life or for a specified term.

arson—the malicious burning of the dwelling house of another. Under some state laws, the crime covers the willful and malicious burning of any property.

binder or cover note—a note or memorandum given to the insured before the insurance policy is actually issued. The note certifies that insurance is in effect (provided all conditions are fulfilled) and will be paid if loss or damage is sustained prior to the issuance of the policy.

blanket policy—a policy that covers property collectively, not by specific items.

casualty insurance—This term covers a large field. It is primarily an insurance against accidental injury to persons or property. But it also includes health insurance, burglary insurance, fidelity bonds, etc.

co-insurance (or **average clause**)—a type of insurance wherein the property, for instance, a $100,000 building, is insured for a certain percentage of its cash value in case of loss—usually 80%, or $80,000. If the owner of the property fails to, or does not care to, keep the insurance up to this value, he becomes his own insurer, or "co-insurer," for the difference; and all partial losses are paid in proportion.* If, say, he carries only $60,000 (¾ of $80,000) and suffers a partial loss of $10,000, he can collect only three-fourths, or $7,500.

* Because most losses are partial, an insurance company could not afford to pay full value for them if the owner did not carry at least 80% insurance on his entire property. In the above example, had he been carrying $80,000, he would have received the full $10,000 for his partial loss.

common carriers' insurance—covers transportation companies' liability for loss of, or damage to, cargo or property being transported by them.

credit insurance—insures wholesalers, manufacturers, and jobbers against **excess or abnormal loss** from purchasers' failure to pay for merchandise.

credit life insurance—covers installment buyer's life—thus guarantees payment.

endowment policy—an investment or saving policy—a certain sum or "endowment" is paid to the insured at the end of a specified period of time; or paid to his heirs in case of his death prior to the expiration of the period.

extended coverage—A fire insurance policy may be extended, by an endorsement ("rider"), to cover loss caused by windstorm, hail, explosion (except of steam boilers, steam pipes, etc.), riot, civil commotion, aircraft, vehicles, and smoke. An additional premium is charged for "extended coverage."

fidelity bond—given to insure an employer against loss through dishonesty of an employee in a position of trust.

floater policy—a policy that covers property which is changeable in its quantity, value, and/or location—as a "personal property floater."

general average—in marine insurance, is a general charge made against all parties interested when a certain part of the cargo or ship has been sacrificed for the common safety.

homeowners [or tenants] policy (a package policy)—includes in one policy complete coverage on a home: fire, storm, theft, personal liability, etc.

incendiary—pertains to the willful or malicious burning of property; also one who sets fire to property—a "firebug," or pyromaniac. (pron. in-sĕn′dē-ĕr′y)

Inchmaree clause—covers damage by accident to ship's hull, cargo, or freight.

insured/assured—interchangeable. "Insured" prevails; "assured" is British.

merchandise floater—a floater policy covering merchandise that changes in quantity, value, and/or location. A **"block policy"** covers all stock-in-trade.

moral hazard—signifies the personal hazard in the insured. It concerns dishonesty, carelessness, "rapacity in claims," "willful neglect," "arson," etc.

Mutual insurance company—a cooperative corporation, owned (and managed through directors or trustees) by its policyholders (members), who insure one another against specified losses, and who share in the profits (distributed as dividends or rebates)—above expenses, losses, and reserves. Mutuals issue **"participating policies."**

open policy—a policy in which the value of the property insured is not fixed but left open, and must be proved in case of loss or damage. Periodic reports, as of cargo shipped, are made by the insured to the insurance company.

premium—the amount paid periodically for an insurance policy; it is paid in advance, in one sum or in installments. (See also "premium," p. 532.)

public liability insurance—insures against damages from accidents suffered by members of the general public.

reinsurance—An insurance company, as a protection against possible large or "shock" losses under a policy, may reinsure its own risk (or a part of it) with another insurance company. The first company is called the "direct-writing company," the second the "reinsurer."

reporting form—a policy covering products or merchandise at different locations and of fluctuating volume and value. The insured submits a periodic report to the insurance company (usually monthly), stating the value of the goods covered. The premium is then determined from the report.

riders—separate clauses or agreements (in printed form) attached to policies. Sometimes written endorsements are called "riders," and often printed riders are called "endorsements."

surety bond—given to guarantee the proper performance of certain acts on the part of another, such as the carrying out of a contract, or the execution of an instrument.

title insurance—insures against loss by reason of a defective title to real estate.

transportation insurance—covers loss to shippers by reason of accident to goods in transit. (Includes "ocean marine" and "inland marine" insurance.)

underwriting—means literally "subscribing the name beneath," which in turn means that the underwriter guarantees whatever he "underwrites" or signs his name to. "Underwriting" in insurance involves the whole procedure of the business of making rates and accepting risks. (See also p. 533.)

use and occupancy insurance (now called "business interruption insurance")—covers loss of net profits, and loss by reason of a proprietor's being obliged to pay fixed expenses, such as salaries and taxes, when an establishment is shut down because of fire or other casualty.

valued policy—a policy in which the value of the property insured is fixed, and not left to appraisal and adjustment in case of total loss.

Itinerary

Some travelers, on extended trips, carry itineraries or schedules of their journeys; others, on less complicated trips, do not. Some airlines and travel agents fill out itinerary forms (with maps on the backs) for prospective travelers. Separate appointment schedules are then carried.

When a trip is contemplated—and preferences regarding transportation and hotels are ascertained—a **Trip Folder** should be started, into which are put timetables; tickets; hotel reservation confirmations; letters and memorandums regarding appointments and engagements to be kept, conferences held, topics discussed, material used, speeches made. From this information, a travel-appointment schedule is prepared.

An itinerary should be typed on strong, wear-resistant paper, with one or more copies for the home office, and the traveler's family.

TRAVEL (or ITINERARY)
J. T. Davis, 1910 Smith Tower, Seattle, Wash. 98104
Seattle to Houston — February 23 to March 2, 197. (All times local)

Thursday, February 23 (Seattle to San Francisco)

8:30 a.m. PST	Lv. Seattle, United Air Lines Flight 395 (First Class – Brunch) Driving time from home to airport – 1 hr.
10:10 a.m.	Ar. San Francisco (limousine – 1 hr. to hotel) Reservation, Mark Hopkins Hotel (confirmation attached)
2:30 p.m.	Appointment, James McNair, President, Western Lumber Co. 1456 Monadnock Bldg. Ph: (415) 982–6472
Reminder	Call George Nelson (387–0866) about dinner meeting.

Friday, February 24 (in San Francisco)

10:00 a.m.	Western Woodwork factory tour.
12:00 noon	Commonwealth Club luncheon – Fairmont Hotel
5:30 p.m.	Lumbermen's Reception – San Francisco Hilton

Saturday, February 25 (San Francisco to Los Angeles–Riverside–Laguna)

7:45 a.m.	Lv. San Francisco Intl. Airport, United Flight 503 Commuter. Limousine from hotel – 1 hr. to airport.
8:40 a.m.	Ar. Los Angeles Intl. Airport. Hertz Ford reserved your name – for drive to Riverside yard – Mr. Elkins, Ph: (714) 677–8993; then to Laguna Beach for weekend with the Pattersons, Ph: (714) 499–7287 .

Sunday, February 26 (Los Angeles to Phoenix)

7:45 p.m. PST	Lv. Los Angeles, International Airport, American Airlines Flight 90 (Coach). Leave car with Hertz at airport.
9:47 p.m. MST	Ar. Phoenix (limousine – 35 min. to downtown) Reservation, Ramada Inn (confirmation attached)

(And so on, with similar notations for the entire trip)

All folders containing papers to be used on the trip should be labeled to show the nature of the contents of each. One folder should contain **supplies,** such as expense vouchers, letterheads, second pages, plain paper, carbon paper, envelopes (airmail, plain, manila), stamps, pencils, binders, and clips or fasteners, if such material is likely to be needed.

An understanding should also be had regarding the forwarding of letters or copies thereof, the attending to business matters during the traveler's absence, and the sending of a periodic report of office happenings.

Abbreviations

Use of Abbreviations. The nature of the manuscript governs the use of abbreviations.

Abbreviations are generally reserved for use in technical or scientific work, statistical writings, tabulations, footnotes, and routine work.

Very few abbreviations should be used in letters.

The month of the year should not be abbreviated in a letter, unless it occurs in a tabulation or in a second-page heading.

The name of a state should not be abbreviated when standing alone in a letter. It may be abbreviated in an **address** on a letter, and on the envelope, with a Zip Code. (See Envelopes, p. 338.)

The name of a city should never be abbreviated, unless it occurs in a tabulation or in routine work.

Units of measurement should not be abbreviated unless they are preceded by numerals, or occur in headings.

Manuscripts to be printed should contain no abbreviations unless the abbreviations are to be printed as written, in which case the copy should be marked "Follow abbreviations."

Attempt to be consistent in the use of abbreviations. Do not abbreviate a word in one place in a manuscript and in another place write it out, when it is used similarly. Decide at the beginning of the paper which form is to be employed throughout.

Do not switch back and forth between two forms for the same abbreviation in the text of one manuscript, as between

lb. and #   No. and #   sq. feet, ft², and sq.ft.

Spell out an **unusual abbreviation** the first time it appears in a text, or give an explanation of it in a footnote, heading, or in parentheses.

Capitalization of Abbreviations. Do not capitalize abbreviations unless the word or words represented would ordinarily be capitalized, or unless the abbreviation itself has become established as a capital, as

A. for acre   NE. for northeast

The capitalizing of any and every abbreviation gives too much importance to unimportant words.

Note that "p.m." and "a.m." are now commonly written in small letters.

Periods After Abbreviations. In ordinary writings, a period usually follows each part of an abbreviation that represents a single word. This aids in the quick interpretation of an abbreviation.

f.o.b. RATHER THAN: fob.   i.e. NOT: ie.   a.m. NOT: am.

An abbreviation period is retained in a sentence, even though other marks of punctuation immediately follow it.

...from noon to 2:30 p.m.; from then until midnight.
Was the temperature recorded as 230° F.?

An abbreviation period at the end of a sentence serves also as a final period, unless the abbreviation is enclosed in parentheses.

... explained that "in 20 seconds, it will reach 100° C."
They are shipping fruits, grains, etc.
That is their price to us (f.o.b.).

When Periods Are Not Used

Certain symbols and letters do not take periods.

Metric System. The official National Bureau of Standards abbreviations for the metric system are shown in the list of abbreviations on pp. 558 ff., and also in the tables of weights and measures on pp. 573–582.

The same form is used for both singular and plural.

Periods are not used.

Chemical Symbols. Do not take periods.

H for hydrogen   O for oxygen   Au for gold

The symbols are used in chemical formulas, with inferior figures to show the number of parts (atoms) of each element in each compound, as

H_2O—water—2 parts of hydrogen to 1 part of oxygen
H_2SO_4—sulfuric acid—2 parts hydrogen, 1 part sulfur, 4 parts oxygen
CO_2—carbon dioxide—1 part carbon to 2 parts of oxygen

Two compounds may be combined to form another compound, in which case an ordinary figure may be used to denote the number of parts (molecules) of either compound; and a period may separate the compounds, as

$$ZnSO_4.7H_2O$$

which means that zinc sulfate crystals are composed of zinc sulfate and 7 parts of water. No other periods are used in chemical formulas.

In routine work, the inferior figures are sometimes written as ordinary figures, as H2SO4 and CO2; but this should not be done if there is the slightest danger of misinterpretation.

Contractions. Contractions, such as "Int'l," "Sam'l," and "Ass'n," are not abbreviations, but simply contracted words like "don't" and "doesn't," and need a period no more than these words do. To place a period after a contraction is double punctuation.

Abbreviations, because of their compactness, are generally preferred to contractions; and also because it is considered that the apostrophe has enough work to do without being used promiscuously for contractions. Furthermore, in typewritten work, the ease of writing an abbreviation is to be preferred to the effort of using the shift key to write a contraction. Therefore:

Dept.	mfg. ⎫		⎧Dep't	m'f'g
Corp.	govt. ⎬ ARE PREFERRED TO: ⎨		Corp'n	gov't
Secy.	contd. ⎭		⎩Sec'y	cont'd, etc.

1st, 2nd or **2d, 3rd** or **3d, 4th, etc.** Do not take periods. They are considered shortened forms rather than abbreviations.

Letters. Letters used as letters or as words do not take periods.

> A to Z   IOU   SOS   A-1   an x and a y   a "b"
> (Note that letters need not be quoted unless quotation marks are needed for emphasis or clarity.)

If a letter is used to designate someone or something, it does not require a period.

> Buyer A   the B stock   JB type   C grade   Class A

But if a letter represents an actual name, it takes a period or dash.

> Mr. G. (or Mr. G——) for Mr. Glenn   J.B. for J. B. Towne

Christian Names and Nicknames. (See p. 311.)
Government Offices. (See pp. 502 ff.)
Military Titles. (See p. 336.)
Radio and Television Stations. No periods should follow the letter designations of radio and television stations.

> WABC   WTOP (Ch. 9)   KPO   XEB   CFCF

But if a broadcasting station's letters are the abbreviations of a real name, periods may be used. However, for uniformity with other station designations, the periods are often dispensed with.

> N.B.C. for National Broadcasting Company
> C.B.S. for Columbia Broadcasting System
> USUALLY: NBC   CBS

Slants (Diagonal Lines). These are properly used to signify the omission of words (the word "per" in technical abbreviations); and when so employed, no periods are necessary.

> bbls/day barrels per day   D/A documents upon acceptance
> B/L bill of lading   A/P authority to pay
> (Periods are sometimes retained in three- or four-word combinations, as "lb./sq.in.," although they may be omitted if the writer is dropping all periods, as "oz/sq yd".)

Some writers use the slant to divide any abbreviation of two words; but the line is more useful if reserved to indicate omitted words. Also, in typewriting, less effort is required to write periods than to shift the carriage down from capitals and back again to write the slant; hence the desirability of restricting its use.

Technical Work. If abbreviations occur frequently in technical work, the periods are usually dropped. But in ordinary work, the periods are usually retained.

553

Temperatures	75° F 85° C 295° A 235° K 25° R
Shipping	SS RR fob fas cod cif
Telegraph	DL NL WUX LT INTL
Military	GHQ AWOL USN USA USMC
Engineering	rpm fbm mph bhp kva

Percent. Although "percent" is the abbreviation of "per centum," it is now written as one word with no period. (U.S. Government usage.)

French Abbreviations. No period is used after French abbreviations if the last letter of the abbreviation is the last letter of the word, as

Mme or Mme for Madame   St for Saint   Cie or Cie for Compagnie

But if the last letter of the abbreviation is not the last letter of the word, the period is used.

Fr. for francs   M. for Monsieur

Spacing Abbreviations. Since one of the chief purposes of abbreviating is to save space, no spaces are left in most abbreviations containing periods.

Ph.D.   A.S.T.M.   at.wt.   cu.ft.

Abbreviations of state names may also be written without spaces.

N.H.   N.Y.   Washington, D.C.   N.Mex.   W.Va.

But spaces are usually left between parts of abbreviated titles, unless an abbreviated title appears after a name.

Lt. Comdr. Roger Brooke   Paul Wayland, M.D.
Maj. Gen. Victor Grant   Spencer Winthrop, V.P.
Lt. Gov. Calvin Hughes   The Very Rev. Leo Camden, V.G.

A space is also left between initials, unless there are three initials; then the spaces are commonly omitted.

J. R. Park   J.M.E. Sutherland

Forming New Abbreviations. To form a new abbreviation, use only the first three letters of the word, as "sim." for "similar"; or use the three letters that will best represent the sound of the word, as "mfg." for "manufacturing."

If a word could have several endings, add the last letter to the simple abbreviation, as

rec. for receive   recd. for received
recr. for receiver   recg. for receiving

Attempt to limit all abbreviations to three or four letters. Longer abbreviations defeat the purpose of abbreviating.

If an unfamiliar two-word expression is to be abbreviated, use a three-letter abbreviation for each word, or at least a three-letter abbreviation for the first word, as

whs.stk. for warehouse stock   bal.s. for balance sheet instead of the mere initial of each word; for it is sometimes difficult to remember what unfamiliar initials stand for.

If an abbreviation for a group of three or four words is desired, use the first letter of each important word, as

S.P.C.A. for Society for the Prevention of Cruelty to Animals

Small words are often disregarded in forming abbreviations—or are represented by slants. Rarely are they written in in full.

RARE: OinC   for Officer in Charge
c. to c. (often c-c)   for center-to-center

Plurals of Abbreviations. The plurals of most abbreviations are formed by simply adding -s.

gals.   yds.   bbls.   lbs.   Bs/L   Drs.   Cos.   Secys.

Some are the same in both singular and plural, as

in. for inch or inches   mi. for mile or miles
deg. for degree or degrees   oz. for ounce or ounces

> **"The use of the same abbreviation for both singular and plural is recommended."**
> —**National Bureau of Standards,**
> *Units of Weight and Measure*

Doubled single letters serve as the plurals of some abbreviations.

vv. for verses   JJ. for Justices   LL.D. for Doctor of Laws
pp. for pages   pp. 220 ff. means page 220 and the following pages

Symbols are doubled: §§ 4, 6, 8–11   ("§ 9 ff." and [law] "§ 9 et seq." are plural.)   See ¶¶ 1–7.

Plurals of capitalized abbreviations may be formed by simply adding a small s. (An 's is hardly necessary, since the difference between the caps and the small letter is a sufficient division.)

C.O.D.s   Ph.D.s   CPAs   YMCAs   PTAs   EMFs

Plurals of uncapitalized abbreviations may be formed by adding an 's:

p.m.'s and a.m.'s   Btu's   emf's   f.o.b.'s

Plurals of letters, signs, and symbols are usually formed by adding an 's, although capitalized letters, and some signs and symbols, may be pluralized by the addition of a simple s.

ABC's   IOU's   OK's   p's and q's   three R's   o's   \$'s   ¢'s
or: ABCs   IOUs   OKs   SOSs   three Rs   \$s   ¢s

Possessives of Abbreviations. These are formed in the same manner as other possessives. If the abbreviation is **singular,** an 's is added—now usually outside the final period, in order to retain the original form of the abbreviation, and to keep all such possessives uniform. If the abbreviation is **plural** (ending in -s), only an apostrophe is added.

Since three clear forms are needed, the apostrophe is being largely reserved for possessives, and a simple s used for plurals wherever possible.

Singular Possessive	Plural	Plural Possessive
Jr.'s	Jrs.	Jrs.'
Dr.'s	Drs.	Drs.'
Co.'s	Cos.	Cos.'
Bro.'s	Bros.	Bros.'
RR.'s	RRs.	RRs.'
M.D.'s	M.D.s	M.D.s'
CPA's	CPAs	CPAs'
SOS's	SOSs	SOSs'
B/L's (Bill of Lading's)	Bs/L (Bills of Lading)	Bs/L's (Bills of Lading's)

This method leaves company names undisturbed when possessives are added. Note that no comma follows "Inc." and "Ltd." when the possessive is employed.

Bell & Barnhart Co.'s prices
Barker Bros.' sale
Galt & Bro.'s window display
General Electric Supply Corp.'s report
Hamilton, Inc.'s statement
London Travel, Ltd.'s guide

Hyphens in Abbreviations. Hyphens may be used in abbreviations of hyphened words. If used, they may replace the periods that would otherwise be used.

ft-lb. for foot-pound   h-p.cyl. for high-pressure cylinder

Quoting Abbreviations. Do not quote abbreviations unless they are slang, or unless the words abbreviated would be quoted if spelled out.

That will be OK.
...taped a TVer for them.
...a G.O.P.-led Congress.
He became T.R.'s close friend.
...workmanship looked "n.g."
...sold it on the "q.t."
He always used the title "Dr."
Prices have the "D.T.s" now.

Letters or Abbreviations Used as Verbs. The -s, -d, or -ing is added with an apostrophe. Periods are often dropped.

SOS'd   X'd out   MC'd   OK'd OK'ing OK's (NOT: *O.K.-es*)
...if he "n.g.'s" it.   ...was K.O.'d in the fifth round.
Cross-country P.A.'ing is...   They are c.o.d.'ing the shipment.

Letters as Descriptive Words. When letters are being used as descriptive words, it is not necessary to spell them out. The simple letter is more readily understood, and therefore preferable. (See p. 268.)

T-rail It fits to a T.
S-curve
I-beam
an L
It makes a V in the road.

RATHER THAN:

tee rail   ...to a tee
ess curve
eye beam
an ell
...overhead were Vs of wild geese.

"Tee" is used in derived constructions, as

golf tee   curling tee   wind tee or landing tee

"A" and "An" Before Abbreviations. (See p. 4.)

Compass Points. Since the names of the compass points are practically all single or compound words, the abbreviations require only a final period.

N. north   NE. northeast   NNE. north-northeast
NbE. north by east   NEbE. northeast by east

In technical writings, and on compasses, the periods are not used.

N   NbE   NNE   NEbN   NE   NEbE   ENE   EbN   E

Single Words. An older practice has been to cut into the abbreviations of various single words with a period, as

S.S.   R.R.   H.Q.   S.W.   P.S.

evidently a holdover from the time they were two words.

The newer and more logical practice is to write solid abbreviations of all solid words. This method is followed herein, as

SS.   RR.   Hq.   SW.   PS.

Degree Letters. The three academic degrees, in the order in which they are earned or conferred, are:

B. **Bachelor** or Baccalaureate   AS: B.S. Bachelor of Science
M. **Master**   M.S. Master of Science
D. **Doctor**   D.S. Doctor of Science

Various letters are combined with each of these three degree letters to signify the particular branch of learning in which the degree was earned or awarded. (For **capitalization of degrees**, see p. 123.)

B.S. in Ae.E.   Bachelor of Science in Aeronautical Engineering.
B.A. in Ed.   Bachelor of Arts in Education.
A.B. in B. & B.   Bachelor of Arts in Business Administration and Banking.
M.S. in Arch.E.   Master of Science in Architectural Engineering.
NO CAPS: a bachelor's degree...doctor of science degree...their master's degrees

Since the combinations are unlimited—the number of degrees having increased very rapidly in recent years—only the ordinary degrees are given in the list of abbreviations herein.

Note that the letters are often reversed, as

A.B. for Bachelor of Arts
Sc.D. for Doctor of Science
S.T.P. for Professor of Sacred Theology

Other letters that are often seen in combinations after names are:

A. **Associate**—an associate member of an institution; or a person who has completed a course shorter than the ordinary degree course.
F. **Fellow**—a member of an incorporated academic society or institution; or a graduate elected to a fellowship.
G. **Graduate**—one who has completed a prescribed course of study.
L. { **Licentiate**—one licensed to practice a profession, as S.T.L.
    { **Lector**—a reader, or lecturer, as S.T.Lr.

Letters signifying college degrees, fellowships, etc., are used chiefly in published works and in formal writings. They are not commonly used in letters and other commercial papers. (See Degree Letters, p. 315.)

ABBREVIATIONS
(Compiled from official lists.)

A

a are (metric); ampere (See amp.)
@ at; to (in market reports)
Å, A., A.U. angstrom unit (of light)
A. Army; acre(s); absolute (temperature); answer (in court writings); area
A-1 first-class
A.A. Associate in Arts
Aaa. Alaska (officially spelled out); sometimes **Alas.**
A.A.A. American Automobile Association
A.A.A.S. American Association for the Advancement of Science
a.a.r. against all risks (ins.)
A.A.S. Fellow of the American Academy (Academiae Americanae Socius)
A.A.U. Amateur Athletic Union
ab. about; absent
A.B. Bachelor of Arts (Am.); **B.A.** (Br.)
A.B.A. American Bankers Association; American Bar Association
abbr., abbrev. abbreviation; abbreviated
ABC American Broadcasting Company
ab ex. from without (L. ab extra)
ab init. from the beginning (L. ab initio)
abr. abridged; abridgment
abs. absolute; abstract; absent
Abs., A. absolute (temperature) (See p. 582)
abs.re. the defendant being absent (L. absente reo)
abst. abstract
abt., ab. about
ac author's correction (printing)
a.c., ac alternating current; **a-c.** (adj.)
a/c, ᵃ/c, A/C, acct. account
A.C. Air Corps; account current
accum. accumulative
acre-ft., AF., Ac-ft., A-ft. acre-foot
act. active; actual
Actg. Acting [officer]
ad advertisement (pl. ads) (no period)
a.d. before the day (L. ante diem)
A.D. in the year of our Lord (L. anno Domini) (A.D. is written before the year, with no separating comma, as "A.D. 1960"; or after the year, as "about 1450 A.D.")
A-D-C, ADC Aide-de-Camp
add. addition; **addl.,** additional
ad fin. to the end (L. ad finem)
ad h.l., a.h.l. at this place or on this passage (L. ad hunc locum)
ad inf. to infinity (L. ad infinitum)
ad init. at the beginning (L. ad initium)
ad int., a.i. in the meantime or meanwhile (L. ad interim)
adj. adjective; adjustment (bonds)
Adj. Adjutant
Adj.Gen., A.G. Adjutant General
ad lib. at pleasure (L. ad libitum)
ad loc. at the place (L. ad locum)
Adm. Admiral, -ty; administration, -tive
Admr. Administrator; **Admx.,** -trix
ADRs Am. Depositary Receipts (stocks)
ads. address
ad us. According to custom (L. ad usum)
adv. adverb; advance; against (adversus)
ad val., adv., a/v according to the value (L. ad valorem)

adv.chgs. advance charges
advg., advtg. advertising
advt., ad advertisement
ae., aet. aged; at the age of (L. aetatis)
A.E. Agricultural Engineer
a.f., AF audio frequency; **a-f.** (adj.) (elec.)
Af., Afr. African; Africa
aff. affirmative; **Aff.** Affairs
A1C, A/1c Airman 1st Class; **A2C; A3C**
AFL American Federation of Labor
AFRes Air Force Reserve
AG, Adj.Gen., TAG Adjutant General
agcy., agy. agency
agr., ag., agri. agriculture; agricultural
agt. agent; against; agreement
a-h ampere-hour
A.I.A. American Institute of Architects
A.I.D. Am. Inst. of Interior Designers
A.I.E.E. Am. Inst. of Electrical Engineers
aj., adj. adjustment (bonds)
aka, a.k.a., AKA also known as (law)
Ala. Alabama (official); Zip, **AL**
A.L.A. American Library Association
Alas., Aaa. Alaska (off. spelled); Zip, **AK**
alt. altitude; alternate, -ing; alteration
Alta. Alberta, Canada
a.m. before noon (L. ante meridiem)
Am. American; America
AM, a.m. amplitude modulation (radio)
A.M. Associate Member; Master of Arts (Am.); **M.A.** (Br.)
A.M.A. American Medical Association
Amb. Ambassador
amp., a ampere (elec.)
amp-hr. ampere-hour (elec.)
amt. amount
A.N. arrival notice (shipping)
anal. analysis; analytic; analogy
anon. anonymous
ANPA American Newspaper Publishers Association
ans. answer, -ed; **A.** in court writings
A-OK, A-Okay all perfect (aeronautics)
ap. according to (L. apud); apothecaries'; approximate, -ly; airplane
AP, ₳P Associated Press
A.P. accounts payable
A/P authority to pay, or purchase
API American Petroleum Institute
APO Army Post Office
app. appendix; applied; apparatus
appl. application; appliance
approx., ap. approximate, -ly
appt. appointed; appointment
Apr. April (usually spelled out)
Apt. Apartment (pl. Apts.)
aq. water (L. aqua); aqueous
ar. arrive, -al
Ar. Arabian; Arabic; Arabia
A.R. Army Regulations; accounts receivable; all risk (ins.); return receipt (foreign mail) (Fr. Avis de réception)
ARC American National Red Cross
arch. architect, -ure; archaic
Arch.E. Architectural Engineer
ARI Air Conditioning and Refrigeration Institute (cooling standards)
A.R.I.B.A. Associate of the Royal Institute of British Architects
Ariz. Arizona (official)
Ark. Arkansas (official)

arr. arranged
art. article (pl. arts.); artist
as., asst., ast. assented (securities)
A.S. Academy of Science; Apprentice Seaman; account sales
ASA American Standards Association
A.Sc. Associate in Science (Br.)
ASCAP American Society of Composers, Authors, and Publishers
A.S.C.E. American Society of Civil Engineers
asd. assumed; assented (securities)
asgd. assigned
asgmt. assignment
Asle., A.S. account sales
A.S.M.E. The American Society of Mechanical Engineers
asmt. assortment; assessment
assd. assessed; assigned
Assn. Association (pl. Assns.)
asso., assoc. associate; associated
asst., ast. assented; assessment
Asst. Assistant
AST, AT Atlantic standard time
astd., asstd. assorted; assented
ASTM Am. Society for Testing & Materials
astron., astr. astronomy, -er, -ical
AT Am. terms (grain); assay ton; atomic
athl. athlete, -ic, -ics
Atl. Atlantic
atm. atmosphere(s); atmospheric
att., atch, attm. attach, -ed, -ment
Attn., Att., Atten. Attention
Atty. Attorney (pl. Attys.)
Atty.Gen. Attorney General
at.wt. atomic weight
Au. Author
Aug. August
Aus., Austl. Australian; Australia
AUS Army of the United States (p. 337)
aux. auxiliary
av., avdp. avoirdupois
a/v (See ad val.)
Ave., Av. Avenue (pl. Aves.)
avg., av. average
avn. aviation
A.W.G., AWG American wire gauge
AWOL absent without leave (military)

B

b. base; bay; bond; battery; born
b7d buyer 7 days to take up (securities)
B., Bé., Be. Baumé (hydrometer)
B.A. Bachelor of Arts (Br.); A.B. (Am.); Business Administration; British Academy; British Association
bal. balance
bar. barometer; barometric
bat., b. battery
BBC British Broadcasting Corporation
bbl. barrel (pl. bbl. or bbls.)
bbls/day, b/d barrels per day (See b.p.d.)
B.C. British Columbia, Canada; before Christ (written after the year, with no separating comma, as "80 B.C.")
bch. bunch (pl. bchs.)
bd. board; bond; bound
bd.ft., b.ft. board foot or feet (See f.b.m.)
bdl. bundle (pl. bdls.)
bd.rts. bond rights (securities)
bds. [bound in] boards (bookbinding)
bdy. boundary
Bé., Be., B. Baumé (hydrometer)
Benj. Benjamin

bet. between
b.f. brought (balance) forward; board foot
bg. bag (pl. bgs.); building
Bhn Brinell hardness number (metals)
b.hp., bhp brake horsepower
bk. bank; book (pl. bks.)
bkg. banking
bkt., bsk. basket (pl. bkts.)
bl. bale (pl. bls.); block; black; boulevard
B/L, b/l bill of lading (pl. Bs/L, bs/l)
B/L Att. bill of lading attached
Bldg., Bg. Building
bldr. builder
blk. block (pl. blks.); black; bulk
B.L.S. Bachelor of Library Science
Blvd., Bl., Bv. Boulevard
b.m. board measure (See f.b.m.)
B/M bill of material(s)
b.o. buyer's option; back order
B.O. branch office
Boh. Bohemian
Bor. Borough
bot. bottle (pl. bots.); bottom; bought
B.O.T. Board of Trade
bp., Bp., BP blueprint
b.p., bp boiling point; boiler pressure
B.P., b.p., b.pay. bills payable
b.p.d., bpd, b/d, bbls/day barrels per day
B.Pd. Bachelor of Pedagogy
Br. British; Branch; Brother
B.R., b.r., b.rec. bills receivable
Brig. Gen. Brigadier General
Brit. British; Britain
Bro. brother (pl. Bros.)
brt.fwd., b.f. brought forward
B.S. Bachelor of Science; balance sheet
B/S bill of sale
B&S Brown and Sharpe wire gauge
bsk., bkt. basket
B.S. & W. basic sediment and water [deductions from crude oil]
bt. bought; boat
B.t.u., Btu British thermal unit (pl. B.t.u., Btu, B.t.u.'s, or Btu's)
bu. bushel(s)
bull., bul. bulletin (pl. bulls., bul.)
Bur., Bu. Bureau
bus. business; bushels
b.v. book value
Bv., Blvd., Bl. Boulevard
B.W.G., Bwg Birmingham wire gauge
bx., x box (pl. bxs.)
BX Base Exchange(s) (Air Force)

C

c carat (metric); cycle (elec.); candle
c. coupon; cent; cash; cost; carat; chapter
c., C. cup(s) (measure)
c., ca. about (L. circa)
C 100 (L. centum); gallon, apothecaries' (L. Congius)
C. Centigrade (Celsius); Congress; cup
©, Copr. copyright
ca centare (metric); about (L. circa)
C.A. Chief Accountant; capital, credit, or current account; Central America
CAA Civil Aeronautics Administration
CAB Civil Aeronautics Board
c.a.f., caf, c. & f. cost and freight
cal. small calorie (See g-cal. and kg-cal.); calendar; caliber
Calif. California (official); or Cal.; Zip, CA
Can. Canadian; Canada
canc. canceled; cancellation

559

Cantab. of Cambridge University (L. Cantabrigiensis)
cap. capital; capacity
caps capital letters
Capt. Captain
car., c. carat (metric carat, **c**)
Cash. Cashier
cat. catalogue
CATV community antenna (cable) TV
c.b. currency bond
C.B. Companion of the Bath (Br.)
CBD, c.b.d. cash before delivery
CBS Columbia Broadcasting System
cc, c.c. carbon copy; cubic centimeter (official [NBS] abbreviation is **cm³**)
CCC Commodity Credit Corporation
cd. cord; **cd.ft.** cord foot or feet
CD, C/D certificate of deposit (pl. CDs)
Cdr., Cmdr., Comdr. Commander
c.e. at buyer's risk (L. caveat emptor)
C.E. Civil Engineer; Canada East
Cel. Celsius (Centigrade thermometer)
cem. cement
cen. center; central; century
Cen.Am., C.A. Central America
cert., ct., ctf. certificate, -tion; certified
cf. compare (L. confer); certificate
c. & f., caf cost and freight
C.F.C. Consolidated Freight Classification
cfm (cfs) cubic feet per minute (or second)
CFR Code of Federal Regulations
cg centigram(s) (metric)
c.g. center of gravity
C.G. Consul General; Commanding General; Coast Guard
CGS, cgs centimeter-gram-second [system]
ch. chain (pl. chs.); choice; chests; chief; channel (television); chemical; chart
c.h. candle hours
Ch. Chinese; China; Chaplain; Church
CH. Customhouse; Courthouse
C.H. Clearing House
chap., ch., C. chapter (pl. chaps. or chs.)
Chas. Charles
Ch.Clk. Chief Clerk
Ch.E., Chem.E. Chemical Engineer
chem., ch. chemical; chemistry
chf. chief
chg. charge; change (pl. chgs.)
Chin., Ch. Chinese
Chm., Chmn. Chairman
chron. chronological
cht., ch. chart
Cía. company (Sp. Compañía)
Cie, Cie company (Fr. Compagnie)
c.i.f., cif cost, insurance, and freight
C.I.O., CIO Congress of Industrial Organizations (now with AFL)
cir. circle; circular; circumference
cir. mils, c.m. circular mils (wire measure)
cit. citation; citizen
civ. civil; civilian
ck. cask; check (pl. cks.)
ckt. circuit
cl centiliter (metric)
cl. class, -ification; carload; clause; claim
cl., CL, ₵ center line
cld. colored; cleared; called (securities)
clfd. classified
clk. clerk; clock
clr. color; clear, -ance
C.L.U. Chartered Life Underwriter (ins.)
cm centimeter; **cm²**; **cm³** (See p. 574)
cm. cumulative (interest or dividends)
c.m., cir.mils circular mils (wire measure)

cml. commercial
cm.pf. cumulative preferred (stocks)
cn. consolidated (bonds)
C.N., c.n. cover note (ins.)
c/o, %, c.o. care of; carried over
Co. Company (pl. Cos.); Coast; County
C.O. Commanding Officer; cash order
C/O certificate of origin
c.o.d. certificates of deposit (securities)
C.O.D., c.o.d. collect, or cash, on delivery
coef. coefficient (math.)
C. of C. Chamber of Commerce
C. of S. Chief of Staff
col. column; colony (pl. cols.)
Col. Colonel; College
coll. collection; collateral
colloq. colloquial
coll.tr., clt collateral trust (bonds)
Colo. Colorado (official); often **Col.**
com., comm. commerce; commission, -er; committee; common; communication; commonwealth
comb. combine, -ing, -ation
Comdr., Cmdr., Cdr. Commander
Comdt. Commandant (Navy and Marine)
coml., cml. commercial
Como. Commodore
con., cons., consol. consolidated
Con. Consul; continued
conc. concentrate
cond. conductivity (elec.); condition
Cong., C. Congress; Congressional
Conn. Connecticut (official); often **Ct.**
cons. consolidated; consign, -ed, -ment
const. constant; construction
cont. contract; contents; continent
contd., cont., con. continued
Contl. Continental
conv. convertible (See cv.)
co-op co-operative
Copr., © copyright
cor. corner; correct, -ed
Corp. Corporation; Corporal (now Cpl.)
corr. corrected; corresponding, -ence
Cor.Sec. Corresponding Secretary
cp. compare; coupon; candlepower
cp., corp. corporation
c.p., cp chemically pure; center of pressure
CP Central Press; Canadian Press (news)
CPA, C.P.A. Certified Public Accountant
cpd. compound
CPFF, C.P.F.F., cost-plus-fixed-fee [job]
Cpl. Corporal
cpm (cps) cycles per minute (or second)
cpn., cp. coupon (pl. cps.)
CPO, C.P.O. Chief Petty Officer (Navy)
CPS Certified Professional Secretary
cq sic; that's right (press copy)
cr. credit; creditor (pl. crs.)
C.R., c.r. company's risk (ins.)
crt. crate (pl. crts.)
cs centistere (metric)
cs. cases
C.S. Christian Science
CSC U.S. Civil Service Commission
C.S.T., CST Central standard time
ct. cent; count; certificate (pl. cts.)
Ct. Connecticut (**Conn.**, official); Court
C.T. Central time
C.T.A. with the will annexed (L. cum testamento annexo)
ctf., ct., cf. certificate (pl. ctfs.)
ctg. cartage
ctn. carton
c. to c., c-c center-to-center

ctr.   center; counter
ct.stp.   certificate stamped (securities)
cu.   cubic
cu.ft., ft³   cubic foot or feet
cu.in., in³   cubic inch or inches
cum., cm.   cumulative
cum d., cum div.   with dividend (L. cum dividendo)
cum.pfd., cu.pf.   cumulative preferred (stocks)
cur.   current; currency
cust.   customer
cu.yd.   cubic yard or yards
cv., cvt.   convertible (securities)
cv.db.   convertible debentures (securities)
cv.pf.   convertible preferred (securities)
C.W.   Canada·West
c.w.o.   cash with order
C.W.O.   Chief Warrant Officer (military)
cwt.   hundredweight (c for centum [100] and wt. for weight)
cy.   currency; copy; cycle; capacity; city
cyl.   cylinder, -rical
C.Z.   Canal Zone (official)

D

d   dyne (unit of force); deficit
d.   date; died; dose; distance; penny (L. denarius); pence; daughter
d., da.   day(s)
D.   Democrat; diameter
D.A.   District Attorney
D/A   documents upon acceptance of draft
Dan., Da.   Danish
Dan'l   Daniel
DAR   Daughters of the American Revolution
db   decibel (unit of sound)
d.b.a.   doing business as [company name]
D.B.N.   of the goods not [yet administered] (L. de bonis non)
db.rts.   debenture rights (securities)
d.c., dc   direct current (elec.); d-c. (adj.)
D.C.   District of Columbia
D.C.L.   Doctor of Civil Law
D.Cn.L.   Doctor of Canon Law
dd.   delivered
D.D.   Doctor of Divinity (honorary); delayed delivery
d.d. in d.   from day to day (L. de die in diem)
D.D.S.   Doctor of Dental Surgery
D.D.Sc.   Doctor of Dental Science
D.E., D.Eng.   Doctor of Engineering
deb.   debenture
dec.   decrease; deceased; decimal; declination
Dec.   December
def.   defendant; defense; defined, -ition, -ite; deferred (securities); defective
deg., °   degree or degrees
del.   deliver, -y; he, or she, drew it (L. delineavit)
Del.   Delaware (official); Delegate
Dem., D.   Democrat
Den.   Denmark
dep.   deposit; deputy; depot
dep.ctfs.   deposit certificates (securities)
Dept.   Department (pl. Depts.)
der.   derived, -ation
det.   detached; detachment; detective
dev.   development; deviation
D.F.   Distrito Federal (Mexico City is a Federal District, like D.C.)

dft., Dft.   draft; defendant
dg   decigram (metric)
D.G.   by the grace of God (L. Dei gratia)
DH.   deadhead (freight)
DHQ   Division Headquarters (Army)
dia., diam., D.   diameter
diag.   diagram; diagonal
dict.   dictionary
Dir.   Director
dis.   discount; discharge
disch.   discharge
dist.   district; distance; distribution
distr.   distributed, -tion, -tor
dit   called (Fr., said)
div.   dividend; division (pl. divs.)
DJ   Dow Jones; District Judge; disk (disc) jockey; dust jacket (on book)
dk.   dock; deck; dark
dkg, dag   dekagram or deca- (metric)
dkl, dal   dekaliter or deca- (metric)
dkm, dam   dekameter or deca-; dkm²; dam²
dl   deciliter (metric)
DL   demand loan
D.Lit(t).   Doctor of Literature or Letters
dlr.   dealer; deliver; dlvd., dld., delivered
dlvy., dly., dy.   delivery
dm   decimeter (metric); dm²; dm³
DM   Deutsche mark (German money)
dn.   down
do.   ditto (It., the same)
d.o., DO   delivery order; diesel oil; defense order; Doctor of Osteopathy
DOA   dead on arrival [at hospital]
doc.   document (pl. docs.)
DOD, DoD   Department of Defense
DOE   Department of Energy
dol. dl., $ dollar (pl. dols. or dls.)
dom.   domestic; dominion; domicile
doz.   dozen or dozens
dp, DP   depart; dew point; data processing
DP   displaced person (pl. DPs)
D/P   documents upon payment of draft
DPL, dpl.   diplomat, -ic; diploma
dpt.   department; deponent
D.Q.   direct question
dr.   dram; drum; debtor; debit (pl. drs.)
Dr.   doctor (pl. Drs.); Drive
Dra.   doctora (Sp., doctress)
dram.pers.   characters of a play (L. dramatis personae)
dr.ap., ʒ   dram apothecaries'
dr.av.   dram avoirdupois
D.R.E.   Doctor of Religious Education
ds   decistere (metric)
D.Sc., D.S.   Doctor of Science
D.S.C.   Distinguished Service Cross
D.S.M.   Distinguished Service Medal
D.S.O.   Distinguished Service Order (Br.)
d.s.p.   died without issue (L. decessit sine prole)
D.S.T.   Doctor of Sacred Theology; daylight saving time
dstn.   destination
dtd.   dated
DTs, D.T.s, d.t.'s   delirium tremens
Du.   Dutch
D.V.   God willing (L. Deo volente)
D.V.M.   Doctor of Veterinary Medicine
D.W.   dock warrant
dwg.   drawing
dwt.   pennyweight (d for penny [L. denarius] and wt. for weight); deadweight
d.w.t.f.   daily and weekly till forbidden (advertising)

561

DX [long-]distance (radio transmission)
dy. delivery; day; duty; deputy

E

e erg (unit of work); error(s)
E. East; Engineer, -ing; English; excellent
ea. each
EB eastbound
eccl. ecclesiastic, -al
econ. economy, -ics, -ist
Ed. Editor; Edition (pl. Eds.); Education
Ed.D. Doctor of Education
EDP electronic data processing
E.D.T., EDT., e.d.t. Eastern daylight time
educ. educated; education, -al
Edw. Edward
E.E. Electrical Engineer; errors excepted
eff. efficiency; effect, -ive
e.g. for example (L. exempli gratia)
el., elev. elevation, -ted
elct. electronics
elec., el. electric, -al, -ian, -ity
elem. element(s), -ary
E.Long. east longitude
emf, e.m.f., EMF electromotive force (pl. emf's, e.m.f.'s, EMFs)
e.m.p. end of month payment
enc. enclosure(s); **ency.,** encyclopedia
end. endorsed; endorsement
Eng. English; England; Engineer, -ing
Engr. Engineer; Engraved, -er, -ing
Ens. Ensign
entd. entered
env., ep envelope (pl. envs., eps)
e.o.d. every other day (advertising)
E. & O.E. errors and omissions excepted
e.o.m., EOM end of month
e.p., ep end point (distillation)
eq. equal; equivalent; equalize; equipment; equation; equator
equip., eq., eqt. equipment
equiv. equivalent
erron. erroneous, -ly
esp especially
ESP extrasensory perception
Esq. Esquire (pl. Esqs.) (See p. 310)
est. established, -ment; estimate; estate
E.S.T., EST Eastern standard time
esu electrostatic unit(s)
ET Eastern time; elec. transcription
ETA, e.t.a. estimated time of arrival
et al and others (L. et alii)
etc., &c and so forth (L. et cetera)
etq. etiquette
et seq., seq., sq. and the following (L. et sequens) (pl. et seqq.)
et ux and wife (L. et uxor)
et vir and husband (L., and man)
Eur. Europe; European
ex out of, or from, as: ex dock, ex car, ex elevator, ex warehouse, ex store
ex without, or not including, as: ex coupon, ex dividend, ex interest, ex rights, ex warrant (See p. 531)
ex. example; exchange; exercise; express; exception; extra; executive (pl. exs.)
exam. examined; examination
exc., exch. exchange
Exec., Ex. Executive
ex.fcy. extra fancy
exp. express; expense; export; expiration
expt., exp. experiment, -al
Exr. Executor; **Exrx.,** Executrix
ex rel. by relation (L. ex relatione)

ext. exterior; extended; **extension; extract;** external; extinct
exx. examples

F

f farad; force
f. and the following [page] (pl. ff.); folio (or f°); feminine; female; fathom
F., Fahr. Fahrenheit
f.a.a. free of all average (ins.)
F.A.A.S. Fellow of the American Association for the Advancement of Science
F.A.C.S. Fellow of the American College of Surgeons (...P., Physicians)
F.A.G.S. Fellow of the American Geographical Society
F.A.I.A. Fellow of the American Institute of Architects
f.a.s. free alongside ship
fath., fm., f. fathom
FBI Federal Bureau of Investigation
f.b.m., fbm feet board measure
FCA Farm Credit Administration
FCC Federal Communications Commission
fcp. foolscap
f.c. & s. free of capture and seizure (ins.)
fcy.pks. fancy packs
fd. fund; funding
fdg. funding (bonds)
FDIC Federal Deposit Insurance Corp.
Fdy. foundry
Feb. February
fec. he, or she, made it (art) (L. fecit)
Fed. Federal; Federated; Federation
fem., f. feminine; female
F.E.T., FET Federal excise tax
ff. and the following [pages]; folios
FHA Federal Housing Administration
Fid. Fidelity; Fiduciary
fifo first-in, first-out (merchandise)
fig. figure (pl. figs.)
fin. financial; finance; finish
Fin. Finnish; Finland
Fin.Sec. Financial Secretary
first 1st (no period)
first class A-1, 1 cl., 1C, 1c
fl. fluid; floor
Fla. Florida (official)
fl.dr., f ℥ fluid dram, apothecaries'
fl.oz., f ℥ fluid ounce, apothecaries'
Flt. fleet; flight; filing time
flts., fts. flats
fm. fathom; from; form
FM, f.m. frequency modulation (radio)
fn., ftnt. footnote
fn.p., fnp fusion point
fo., f°, fol., f. folio (pl. ff.)
F.O. Foreign Office
f.o.b. free on board
fol. folio; follow, -ing
for. foreign; forestry
4-H Head, Heart, Hands, and Health
fourth 4th (no period)
f.p., fp freezing point
f.p.a. free of particular average (ins.)
FPC Federal Power Commission
f.pd. full paid
f.p.m., fpm, f/m feet per minute
FPO Fleet Post Office
f.p.s, fps, f/s feet per second
F.P.S., f.p.s., f-p-s., fps foot-pound-second [system]

fr., fm. from
Fr. French; France; francs; Father (Catholic); Frau (Ger., Mrs.)
FR full-rate (cables)
F.R., FR, FRS Federal Reserve System
Fra friar (brother) (no period)
F.R.C.P. Fellow of the Royal College of Physicians (...S., Surgeons)
freq. frequent, -cy, -ly
Fri. Friday; F. or Fr. in tabulations
F.R.I.B.A. Fellow of the Royal Institute of British Architects
Frl. Fräulein (Ger., Miss)
F.R.S. Fellow of the Royal Society
frt. freight
Frwy., Fy. freeway
FS field or foreign service; filmstrip
ft. foot or feet; ft²; ft³ (See sq.ft., etc.)
Ft. Fort
ft-c foot-candle; ft-L, foot-lambert
FTC Federal Trade Commission
ftd. fitted (as sheets)
ft-lb. foot-pound(s)
ft/sec., fs feet per second (See f.p.s.)
ft-tn. foot-ton
fur. furlong
furn. furnished; furniture
fut. futures (exchange)
fwd. forward
FX foreign exchange
FYI, fyi, f.y.i. for your information

G

g gram(s) (metric)
g. gold; gauge; gulf; gravity
g.a. general average (ins.)
Ga. Georgia (official)
GA General Agent; General Assembly
gal. gallon (pl. gals.)
gar. garage
G.B., Gt.Br. Great Britain
g-cal., cal. gram-calorie (small calorie)
GCD, gcd greatest common divisor
GCT, G.C.T., G.c.t. Greenwich civil time
gd(s). good(s)
gen. general; generator; genus or kind
Gen. General (pl. Gens.)
Geo. George
geog. geography, -ic, -ical, -er
geol. geology, -ic, -ical, -ist
Ger. German; Germany
g.gr. great gross (144 dozen)
GHQ General Headquarters (military)
gi. gill or gills
GI Government Issue (Army) (pl. GIs)
Gk. Greek
gloss. glossary (a list of terms)
gm general mortgage (bonds); gram (old)
GM general manager; guided missile
G.m.a.t., GMAT Greenwich mean astronomical time
G.m.b.H. ⎫
GmbH   ⎬ corporation with limited liability (Ger. Gesellschaft mit beschränkter Haftung)
GMBH ⎭
GMT, G.m.t. Greenwich mean time
gn., gen. general
G.N. Graduate Nurse (pl. G.N.s)
G.N.P., GNP gross national product
G.O., GO general orders (military)
G.O.P. Grand Old Party (Republican)
Gov. Governor (pl. Govs.)
govt. government
gp. group
G.P. Graduate in Pharmacy

g.p.m., gpm, g/m gallons per minute, or mile (or...d., day, etc.)
GPO Government Printing Office
gr. gross; grade; grain (spelled out for weight); gravity; graph; great
Gr. Greece; Grecian
grad. graduate, -ed, -tion
grain spelled out (for weight)
gr.wt. gross weight
g.s. ground speed (aviation)
GSA General Services Administration
gt. drop (L. gutta) (pl. gtt.); great
GTC good till canceled (brokerage order)
gtd. guaranteed
gu., guar. guarantee; guaranteed

H

h henry (elec.); hours, as 12ʰ or 12h
ha hectare; in this year (L. hoc anno)
har., h. harbor
Hawaii officially spelled out; often Hi.
hdbk. handbook
hdlg. handling [charge]
hdw. hardware
H.E., HE His Excellency; high explosive
HEW Department of Health, Education, and Welfare
hf. half
h-f., HF high-frequency (sound waves)
hg hectogram (metric)
hhd. hogshead(s)
hist. history, -ical, -ian
hl hectoliter (metric)
hm hectometer (metric); hm²; hm³
H.M.S. His, or Her, Majesty's Ship, or Service
hol. holiday
Hon. Honorable (pl. Hons.)
Hosp. hospital
hp., hp, HP, ℗ horsepower
h.p. high pressure; h-p. (adj.)
hp-hr. horsepower-hour
HQ, Hq. Headquarters
hr. hour (pl. hrs.)
H.R. House of Representatives
H.R.H. His, or Her, Royal Highness
hs., hse. house; hsg., housing
HS hydrofoil ship
HST, HT Hawaiian [standard] time
ht. height; heat
Hts., Hgts. Heights
hund., C hundred; hundredweight, cwt.
Hung. Hungary; Hungarian
hvy., (H) heavy
Hwy., Hy. Highway

I

I. Island(s); Isle(s)
Ia. Iowa (officially spelled out)
ib., ibid. in the same place (L. ibidem)
IBM Intl. Business Machines Corp.
ICBM intercontinental ballistic missile
ICC Interstate Commerce Commission
id. the same (L. idem)
i.d., ID inside diameter; identification
Ida., Id. Idaho (officially spelled out)
i.e. that is (L. id est)
I.E.S. Illuminating Engineering Society
ign. unknown (L. ignotus); ignites, -tion
i.hp., ihp, IHP indicated horsepower
IHS monogram for Greek word for Jesus
ill., illus. illustration; illustrated
Ill. Illinois (official)

imp. improvement; implement; imperial; import, -ing, -ed, -er

in., ″ inch(es); in²; in³ (See sq.in., etc.)

Inc. Incorporated; increase; income, -ing

incl. inclusive; including (See also enc.)

incog. in secret; unknown (It. incognito); unofficially

ind. industry, -ial; independent; induction

Ind. Indiana (official); Indian; India

Ind.E. Industrial Engineer

inf. inferior; below (L. infra)

info information

infra dig undignified (L. infra dignitatem)

init. initial

in-lb. inch-pound

in lim. at the outset (L. in limine)

ins. insurance; inspector; insulated

inst. instant, -aneous; installment

Inst. Institute; Institution, -al

instr. instructor, -tion(s); instrument, -al

int. interest; interior; international; interstate; internal; intermediate

Intl., Int. International

(int.) n.mi. international nautical mile

inv. invoice; investment; inventor, -tion

invt. investment; inventory

IOU I owe you (pl. IOUs) (no periods)

Iowa officially spelled out; often **Ia.**

i.p., ip intermediate pressure; **i-p.** (adj.)

i.p.s., ips inches per second

i.q. the same as (L. idem quod)

IQ, I.Q. intelligence quotient

Ir. Irish

Ire. Ireland

IRS, Int.Rev. Internal Revenue Service

Is., Isl., I. Island (pl. Is. or Isls.)

iss. issue

It. Italian; Italy

Ix. index

J

j joule (elec.)

J. Judge; Justice (pl. JJ.)

J.A. Judge Advocate

Jan. January

Jap. Japanese; Japan

Jas. James

Jc., Jct., Junc. Junction

J.C.D. Doctor of Canon or Civil Law (L. Juris Canonici Doctor, or Juris Civilis Doctor)

J.C.L. Licentiate in Canon Law (L. Juris Canonici Licentiatus)

J.D. Doctor of Laws (L. Jurum Doctor)

JJ. Justices

Jno. John

jnt.stk. joint stock

Jos. Joseph

Jour., J., Jr. Journal

J.P. Justice of the Peace

Jr. Junior (pl. Jrs.); journal

J.S.D. Doctor of Juristic Science (Law)

jt. joint

J.U.D. Doctor of both Canon and Civil Laws (L. Juris Utriusque Doctor)

July spelled out; **Jul.** in tabulations

junc., jct., jc. junction

June spelled out; **Jun.** in tabulations

K

k., kn. knot

K karat (gold meas.); kilo (1000, as $50K)

K. Kelvin (absolute scale of temperature)

Kans. Kansas (official); often **Kan.**

kc kilocycle (radio)

K.C. King's Counsel (Br.); Knights of Columbus

kcal. kilocalorie (See also kg-cal.)

K.C.B. Knight Commander of the Bath

kcps, kc/s kilocycles per second

K.D. knocked down (freight)

kg kilogram (metric)

kg. keg or kegs

K.G. Knight of the Garter (Br.)

kg-cal. kilogram-calorie or kilocalorie (large calorie); sometimes **Cal.**

K.G.F. Knight of the Golden Fleece (Austrian and Spanish)

kgm, kg-m kilogram-meter

kg/m³ kilograms per cubic meter

kgps, kg/s kilograms per second

kip thousand (kilo) pounds (structural)

K.K.K. Ku Klux Klan

kl kiloliter (metric)

K.L.H. Knight of Legion of Honor (Fr.)

km kilometer (metric); km²; km³

kmps, km/s kilometers per second

K.O. keep off (bad risk, ins.); knockout

Kr. krone (a foreign coin)

kt., K karat (gold)

Kt. Knight Bachelor (Br.); karat

kv kilovolt (elec.)

kva, kv-a kilovolt-ampere

kvar kilovar (reactive kilovolt-ampere)

kvarh kilovarhour (reactive kilovolt-ampere-hour)

kw kilowatt(s)

kwh, kw-hr., kwhr kilowatt-hour

Ky. Kentucky (official)

L

l liter (metric); lumen (unit of light)

l. line (pl. ll.); left; league; leaf; length

L listed (securities); lire (Italian money); lambert (unit of brightness); large

L. Latin; law; ledger

£ (British) pound sterling (L. libra)

La. Louisiana (official); Zip, **LA**; Lane

L.A. Local Agent; Los Angeles

lab. laboratory; labor

lang. language

lat., φ latitude

lb. pound (L. libra) (pl. lbs.); **labor**

lb.ap., lb pound, apothecaries'

lb.av. pound, avoirdupois

lb-ft. pound-foot

lb/ft² pounds per square foot

lb-in. pound-inch

lb/in² pounds per square inch (See p.s.i.)

lbr. lumber

lb.t. pound, troy

lc., l.c. lower case (printing); left center

L/C letter of credit (pl. Ls/C); "an L/C"

LCD, lcd least common denominator

LCdr, Lt.Cmdr. Lieutenant Commander

LCL(s), l.c.l.('s) less-than-carload lot(s)

LCM, lcm least common multiple

L.c.t., LCT local civil time

L.D.S. Licentiate in Dental Surgery

lea. league; leather

Leg. Legislature, -tive, -tion; (lc) legal

Les. Lesson

l-f., LF low-frequency (sound waves)

lg, L large; long

l.h., LH left hand

L.H.D. Doctor of the Humanities (L. Litterarum Humaniorum Doctor)

l-hr. lumen-hour
li. link
L.I. Long Island
lib. library; book (L. liber)
Lic. Licenciado (Sp., attorney)
Lieut., Lt. Lieutenant (pl. Lts.)
Lieut. (jg), Lt. (jg) Lieutenant (junior grade) (Navy)
lifo last-in, first-out (merchandise)
lin.ft. linear foot (See "lineal," p. 208)
liq. liquid
lit. literature; literally
liter spelled out (a metric unit); often l
Litt.D. Doctor of Letters or Literature
ll. lines; leaves
LL leased line (securities)
LL.D. Doctor of Laws (often honorary)
ln. lien; loan; (cap) Lane
LNG liquefied natural gas
loc. location; local
loc.cit. in the place cited (L. loco citato)
log logarithm (common); log$_e$, ln, (natural)
long., λ longitude
l.p., lp low pressure; long-playing (records)
LPG liquefied petroleum gas
lpw, l/w lumens per watt
l.s. left side
L.S. place of the seal (L. locus sigilli)
L.S.T., LST, LT local standard time
lt. light; left; ltg. lighting
LT letter message (cables)
Lt., Lieut. Lieutenant (pl. Lts.)
Lt. Col. Lieutenant Colonel
Lt. Cmdr., LCdr Lieutenant Commander
Ltd. limited [liability] (not Lt'd.)
Lt. Gen. Lieutenant General
Lt. Gov. Lieutenant Governor
Lt. (jg) Lieutenant (junior grade) (Navy)
LTL(s), l.t.l.('s) less-than-truckload(s)
ltr. letter; lighter
lub. lubricate, -ing, -cant
lv. leave(s) (or pl. lvs.)

M

m minutes, as 10^m or 10m; meter (metric)
m² square meter; **m³**, cubic meter
m. mass; mile; noon (L. meridies); month; male; masculine; married; mill; model
M 1000 (L. mille) as **2M**; medium [size]
m, m$_e$ minim or drop, apothecaries'
M. Monsieur (Fr., Mr.) (pl. MM. or Messrs.—Messieurs); Master; Monday
ma milliampere (elec.)
M.A. Master of Arts (Br.); A.M. (Am.)
mach. machine; machinery
mag. magazine; magnitude
Maine officially spelled out; often **Me.**
Maj. Major; majority
Maj. Gen. Major General
Man. Manhattan; Manitoba, Canada
mar. market; maritime; married
Mar. March (usually spelled out); Marine
mas., masc., m. masculine
Mass. Massachusetts (official)
mat. maturity (bonds); matinee
math. mathematics, -cian, -ical
MATS Military Air Transport Service
max. maximum
May spelled out
Mbm, M.B.M., MBM thousand [feet] board measure (lumber)
MBS Mutual Broadcasting System
mc megacycle

M.C. Master of Ceremonies (or emcee[s]); Member of Congress; Military Cross
Mcf 1000 cubic feet, gas (**MMcf**, million)
mch., mach. machine
Md. Maryland (official)
M.D. Doctor of Medicine
Mdm. Madam
mdnt., mid. midnight
mdse. merchandise
Me. Maine (officially spelled out)
M.E. Mechanical Engineer; Military Engineer; Mining Engineer (See E.M.); Managing Editor
meas. measure, -ment
mech. mechanic, -ics, -al
med. medium; medicine; medical
memo memorandum
m.e.p., mep mean effective pressure
mer. mercantile; meridian
Messrs., MM. Messieurs (Fr., Misters)
met. metropolitan; meteorological; metal
metal., met. metallurgy
Met.E. Metallurgical Engineer
Mex. Mexican; Mexico
mf millifarad (elec.) (See also mu f)
M/F, M&F, m/f male or female (advtg.)
mfg. manufacturing; **mfd.**, -ed
mfr. manufacture, -r (pl. mfrs.)
mfst. manifest
mg milligram (metric)
m.g.d., mgd million gallons per day
Mgm mailgram (pl. Mgm's)
Mgr. Manager (See also Msgr.)
mgt., mgmt. management
mh millihenry (elec.)
M.H., MH Medal of Honor
mhcp mean horizontal candlepower
mi. mill; mile(s), as **mi²**, sq.mi.
Mich. Michigan (official)
mid., mdnt. midnight
Midn., Mid. Midshipman
mil. military; mileage; million
min. minute(s); minimum; mineral; mining; minim, apothecaries'; minister
Minn. Minnesota (official)
misc. miscellaneous
Miss. Mississippi (official)
M.I.T. Massachusetts Institute of Technology
mk. mark
mks, MKS meter-kilogram-second [system]
mkt., mar. market
ml milliliter (metric)
mL millilambert
Mlle Mademoiselle (Fr., Miss) (pl. Mlles)
mm millimeter (metric); **mm²**; **mm³**
m.m. with the necessary changes (L. mutatis mutandis)
MM. Messieurs (Fr., Misters)
Mme, Mme Madame (Fr., Mrs.)
Mmes Mesdames (Fr.); **Mmes.** (Eng.)
mmf, MMF magnetomotive force
m mu, mμ millimicron
Mn House (Fr. Maison)
M.N.A.S. Member of the National Academy of Sciences
mng. managing
mo. month(s) (pl. mos.)
m.o. money order; mail order
Mo. Missouri (official)
mod. modified (securities); moderate
mol. molecule
mol.wt. molecular weight
Mon. Monday; **M.** or **Mo.** in tabulations

Mont. Montana (official); Zip, **MT**
mot. motor
mp, m.p. melting point
MP Member of Parliament; mounted police; military police (pl. MPs)
M.P.C. Member of Parliament, Canada
m.p.g., mpg, m/g miles per gallon
m.p.h., mph, m/h miles per hour
mphps, m/h/s miles per hour per second
Mr. Mister (pl. Messrs.)
Mrs. Mistress (pl. Mmes.—Mesdames)
ms., MS. manuscript (pl. mss., MSS.)
Ms. Miss or Mrs. (pl. Mss.)
m/s meters per second
MS. motorship; manuscript
M.S., M.Sc. Master of Science
m.s.cp., mscp mean spherical candlepower
msg. message; **msgr.** messenger
Msgr. Monsignor (It., My lord); **Mgr** (Fr. Monseigneur)
M.Sgt., M/Sgt. Master Sergeant
m.s.l. mean sea level
M.S.T., MST Mountain standard time
Mt. mount; mountain (pl. Mts.); material
M.T., MT Mountain time; empty
mt.ct.cp. mortgage certificate coupon (securities)
mtg. mortgage; mounting; meeting
mu, μ micron; μ^2; μ^3
mu a, μa microampere
mu f, μf microfarad
mu mu, $\mu\mu$ micromicron
mun. municipal
mus. music, -al, -ian; museum
Mus.D. Doctor of Music
mu w, μw microwatt
mv millivolt (elec.)
m.v. market value
M.V. motor vessel

N

n. note; net; new; noun; noon; name
n/30 net in 30 days (payments)
N. north; Navy; noon
n.a. no account (bank); not available (data)
NA, N.A. National Assn. (banks); No. Am.
NAM, N.A.M. National Association of Manufacturers
NANA North American Newspaper Alliance, Inc.
NAS National Academy of Sciences
NASA National Aeronautics and Space Administration
Nat., Natl. national
NATO North Atlantic Treaty Org.
naut. nautical
nav. naval; navigation
NAV net asset value
n.b., N.B. note well (L. nota bene)
NB northbound
N.B. New Brunswick, Canada
NBC National Broadcasting Company
NBS National Bureau of Standards
NC, n-c non-callable (bonds)
N.C. North Carolina (official); no charge
n.d. no date; next day's delivery
N.Dak. North Dakota (official); often **N.D.**
NE. northeast
N.E. New England
NEA Newspaper Enterprise Association
N.E.A. National Education Association; National Editorial Association
Nebr. Nebraska (official); often **Neb.**

n.e.c. not elsewhere classified
neg. negative, -ly
nem.con. none contradicting; unanimously (L. nemine contradicente)
n.e.s. not elsewhere specified or stated
Neth., Neld. Netherlands
Nev. Nevada (official)
N.F. no funds (banking); Newfoundland
Nfld. Newfoundland, Canada
n.g. no good, or "out"
N.G., NG National Guard; narrow gauge
N.H. New Hampshire (official)
n.hp., N.HP nominal horsepower
N.J. New Jersey (official)
n.l. it is not permitted (L. non licet); it is not clear (L. non liquet); new line
NL night letter (telegraph)
N.Lat., NL north latitude
NLRB National Labor Relations Board
N.Mex. New Mexico (official); often **N.M.**
nmi, nm nautical mile(s); no middle initial
nn, NN noon; notes
no. number (L. numero) (pl. nos.)
No., N. North; northern
n/o in the name of (finance)
n.o.c. not otherwise classified (ins.)
NOIBN, n.o.i.b.n. not otherwise indexed by name (in freight rates)
nol.pros. be unwilling to prosecute (L. nolle prosequi)
non pros. he does not prosecute (L. non prosequitur)
non seq. it does not follow (L. non sequitur)
noon spelled out; sometimes n., nn, or m.
Nor. Norwegian; Norway
n.o.s., NOS not otherwise specified
Nov. November
np nonparticipating (ins. and stocks)
n.p. no place [of publication]; net proceeds
N.P. Notary Public; no protest (finance)
NPO Navy Post Office
nr. near; **NR,** no ranking or rating
NS, N.S. nuclear ship (pl. NSs, N.S.s)
N.S. Nova Scotia; not specified; new style
N.S.F. not sufficient funds (banking)
nth indefinitely large, as "nth degree"
N.T.O. not taken out (insurance policy)
n.t.p. no title page (cataloguing); normal temperature and pressure
nt.wt., n.wt. net weight
n.u. name unknown
nuc. nuclear
number no. (pl. nos.) (L. numero)
NV no value, -ation; nonvoting
N.V. limited-liability company (Dutch Naamloze Vennootschap)
N.V.D., nvd no value declared (air cargo)
NW. northwest
NW.T. Northwest Territories, Canada
N.Y. New York (official)
N.Y.C. New York City
N.Z. New Zealand

O

o. off; old; only; order; out
O pint, apothecaries' (L. Octarius)
O. Ohio (officially spelled out); Ocean
oa., OA overall
o/a on account; on or about
ob. he, or she, died (L. obiit); obstetrics
obit. obituary (pl. obits.)
O.B/L, ob/l order bill of lading
obs. obsolete; observation, -tory

ob.s.p. died without issue (L. obiit sine prole)
oc. overcharge; ocean
o/c over-the-counter; overcharge
Oct. October
o.d. outside diameter; on demand; overdraft
o.e. omissions excepted
OED Oxford English Dictionary
ofc., off. office; official; officer
Ohio officially spelled out; often **O.**
OK correct (no periods); **OK'd, OK'ing, OK's**—verb forms (pl. OKs or OK's)
Okla. Oklahoma (official)
Ont. Ontario, Canada
op. opera; work (L. opus); overproof
o.p., OP out of print; open policy
op.cit. in the work cited (L. opere citato)
opd. opened (stocks)
opp. opposite
opr. operate, -ing, -tion(s)
opt. optional; optician
o.r. owner's risk (shipping)
Or. Oriental
ord. ordinance; order; ordinary
Oreg. Oregon (official); **Ore.**; or Zip, **OR**
Org., Orgn. Organization
orig. original, -ly
o/s, OS out of stock
OTC over-the-counter (securities)
o.w., OW one way [fare]
Oxon. Oxford University (L. Oxonia)
oz. ounce or ounces (Sp. onza)
oz.ap., ℥ ounce, apothecaries'
oz.av. ounce, avoirdupois
oz-ft. ounce-foot
oz-in. ounce-inch
oz.t. ounce, troy

P

p. page (pl. pp.); per; pressure; population; power; pole; past; pitch
¶ paragraph (or **℗**)
℗ copyrighted sound recording
pa. paper
p.a., per an. per annum (by the year)
Pa. Pennsylvania (official); **Penn.**; Zip, **PA**
P.A. Purchasing Agent; Press Agent; private account; personal appearance; public-address sys. (pl. P.A.s)
P/A power of attorney
Pac. Pacific
P.a.C. put and call (stock market)
p.ae. equal parts (L. partes aequales)
pam. pamphlet
par. paragraph, also **¶** (pl. pars.); parallel
paren., par. parenthesis
part. participating (securities); particular
pat. patent, -ed
Pat.Off. Patent Office
payt. payment
PBX private branch exchange (telephone)
pc. piece (pl. pcs.)
pc., pct., % percent
pcl. parcel
pd. paid
P.E. Professional Engineer
P/E, p/e (ratio) price ÷ earnings per share
P.E.G. prior endorsement guaranteed
Penn. Pennsylvania (**Pa.** is official)
penny d. (L. denarius); **pennyweight, dwt.**
perf. perforated; perfect; performer, -ance
perm. permanent
perp. perpetual (bonds); perpendicular

pet., petr. petroleum
petn. petition
pf., pfd., pref. preferred (securities)
p.f., PF power factor (elec.)
Pfc. Private, first class
Pg. Portuguese; Portugal
ph., PH phase; 3PH; 1PH (single-phase)
Phar.D. Doctor of Pharmacy
Ph.C. Pharmaceutical Chemist
Ph.D. Doctor of Philosophy
Ph.G. Graduate in Pharmacy
P.I. Philippine Islands (official)
pinx., pxt. he, or she, painted it (L. pinxit)
pix pictures; (sing.) **pic, picture**
pk. pack, -ing; park (pl. pks.); peak; peck
pkg. package (pl. pkgs.); parking
Pky., Py., Pkwy. Parkway
pl. (cap) Place; plural; plate (pl. pls.)
P.L. public law; partial loss; price list
Plf., Ptf. plaintiff (pl. Plfs., Ptfs.)
PLS Professional Legal Secretary
Plz. Plaza
pm., prem. premium
p.m. afternoon (L. post meridiem)
pmt., payt. payment
p.n., PN promissory note
P.O. post office; Petty Officer (Navy)
p.o.d. pay on delivery; payable on death
p.o.e., POE port of entry, or embarkation
Pol. Polish; Poland; (lc) politics, -al
pop. population; popular, -ly
p.o.r., P.O.R. pay on return (express)
Port. Portuguese; Portugal
pos. positive; possessive; position
pot. potential
pound lb. (L. libra) (pl. lbs.) (See also £)
pow. power; powder
pp. pages; prepaid; postpaid
p.p. parcel post; privately printed
P.P., Per Pro. by authorization; by proxy (L. per procurationem)
ppd. postpaid; prepaid
p.p.i. parcel post, insured
p.p.m., ppm parts per million
P-PS. post-postscript
P.Q. Province of Quebec, Canada
pr. price; present; pair; prior; province; printed; printing; prime; power
Pr Professeur (Fr., professor)
PR payroll; Public Relations
P.R. Puerto Rico (official); Zip, **PR**
pref., pf. preferred; preference; preface
prem., pm. premium
prep. preposition; preparation
Pres. President
prim. primary
prin. principal
p.r.n. as the occasion arises (L. pro re nata)
prob. problem
prod. product; produce; produced
Prof. Professor (pl. Profs.)
pron. pronunciation; pronounced; pronoun
prop. property; proposition
Prot. Protestant
pro tem. temporarily (L. pro tempore)
prov. province; provision, -al
prox. of the next month (L. proximo)
pr.pf. prior preferred (stocks)
prs. pairs
Ps. Psalm (pl. Pss.)
PS. postscript (pl. PSs.) (See p. 557)
p.s.f., psf pounds per square foot
Psgr., Pass. Passenger
p.s.i., psi pounds per square inch

P.S.T., PST, PT Pacific [standard] time
pstg. postage
pt. part; payment; pint; point; port
PT Pacific time; private terms; pro tempore
P.T.A., PTA Parent-Teacher Association (pl. P.T.A.s, PTAs)
ptc. participating (securities)
ptg. printing
pt.pf. participating preferred (stocks)
Ptr. printer (proofreading)
Pty. proprietary (Austl., privately owned)
PU pickup; **PUD**, pickup and delivery
pub. public, -ation; published, -ing, -er
pur. purchaser; purchasing
Pvt. Private (Army and Marines)
pwr., pow. power
PX Post Exchange (mil.) (pl. PXs)

Q

q quintal (metric)
Q. question; query (pl. QQ.); Quebec
Q.E.D. which was to be proved (L. quod erat demonstrandum)
Q.E.F. which was to be done (L. quod erat faciendum)
qly. quality
QM. Quartermaster
qr. quarter; quarterly; quire (pl. qrs.)
q.s. quarter section; a sufficient quantity
qt. quart (pl. qts.)
q.t., Q.T. [on the] quiet; in secret (slang)
qtr., quar., qu. quarter, -ly
qty. quantity
qu., Q., ques. question
quad. quadrant; quadrangle
Que., Q. Quebec, Canada
q.v. which see (L. quod vide) (pl. qq.v.)
Qy., Q. query

R

r. right; road
R. Range (pl. Rs.); Republic, -an; reports; registered; river; rule; radius; Réaumur (thermometric scale); Regina
® Registered in U.S. Patent Office
R.A. Rear Admiral; Royal Academy
rad. radio; radiant
R.A.F. Royal Air Force
R.A.M. Royal Academy of Music
RB Renegotiation Board
R.C. Red Cross; Roman Catholic
rct. receipt (pl. rcts.); (cap) recruit
rd. (cap) road; rod; round
R&D, Rand Research and Development
rdp., red. redemption (of securities, etc.)
re in regard to
R.E. real estate
REA Rural Electrification Administration
Rear Adm., RAdm Rear Admiral
rec. record, -ed, -er; recipe; receipt; reclamation (bonds)
recd., rcd. received
Rec.Sec. Recording Secretary
ref. reference; referee; refining; refunding
refr. refrigerate, -ed, -ing, -tor
reg. register, -ed; regulation; regular
REITs real estate investment trusts
R.E.O. real estate owned (banking)
rep. repeat; report; repair
Rep. Republic, -an; Representative
rept., rpt., rep. report
req. requisition; required
res. reserve; residence; resort; resolution

ret. retired; return
retd. returned
rev. review; revenue; reverse; **revise,** -ed, -ion; revolve, -ing, -ution
Rev. Reverend (pl. Revs.)
Rev.Stat., R.S. Revised Statutes
rf., rfg. refunding (bonds); refining (oil)
r.f., RF radio frequency; r-f. (adj.) (elec.)
R.F. French Republic
R.F.D. rural free delivery (See R.R.)
rg., reg. registered (bonds)
r.h. right hand; relative humidity
rhp, RHP rated horsepower
R.I. Rhode Island (official); Republik Indonesia
R.I.P. may he, or she, rest in peace (**L.** requiescat in pace)
rm. ream; room (pl. rms.)
r.m.s., rms root mean square
R.N. Registered Nurse; Royal Navy
R.N.R. Royal Naval Reserve
Robt. Robert
Rom. Roman; Romance
r.o.p. run of paper (advertising)
ROTC Reserve Officers' Training Corps
Rp., Rep., R. Republic, -an
RP reply paid (cables); reprint, -ing
R.P.D. Doctor of Political Science (L. Rerum Politicarum Doctor)
r.p.m., rpm, r/m revolutions per minute
r.p.s., rps, r/s revolutions per second
rpt. report
RR railroad (pl. RRs.) (See p. 557)
R.R. rural route
r.s. right side
R.S. Revised Statutes; Recording Secretary
R.S.V.P. Reply, if you please (Fr. Répondez, s'il vous plaît)
rt. right (pl. rts.); round trip
Rte., Rt. Route
Rt. Hon. Right Honourable (Br.)
Rt. Rev. Right Reverend
Rus. Russian; Russia
rva reactive volt-ampere (See **var**)
R/W right of way
Ry. railway (pl. Rys.)

S

s stere (metric); seconds, as 15^s or 15s
s7d seller 7 days to deliver (securities)
s. silver; stock; steamer; shillings; son
S. south; science; Senate; mark a prescription (L. signa); Saint, -e; small
/S/, /s/ signed (before a copied signature)
s/a subject to approval
S.A. South America; South Africa; Salvation Army; an incorporated company (Fr. Société Anonyme); stock company (Sp. Sociedad Anónima)
SAE Society of Automotive Engineers
S.Afr. South Africa, -n
S.A.I. an incorporated company (It. Società Anonima Italiana)
S.Am. South America, -n
Sam'l Samuel
San.D. Doctor of Sanitation
s.ap., sc., ℈ scruple, apothecaries'
Sask. Saskatchewan, Canada
Sat. Saturday; St. or Sa. in tabulations
Sav. Savings
SB southbound
S.B. Bachelor of Science
SBA Small Business Administration

sc., sci.   science
sc., scil., sct.   namely or to wit (See ss.)
sc., sculp.   he, or she, carved or engraved
    it (L. sculpsit); sculptor
S.C.   South Carolina (official)
Sc.D.   Doctor of Science
sch.   school; schooner; schedule
Scot., Sc.   Scottish; Scotch; Scotland
s.cp., scp   spherical candlepower
Script.   Scripture(s); (lc) scriptural
s.d.   without a day [being named] (L. sine
    die); sight draft; special delivery
S.Dak.   South Dakota (official); often S.D.
SDRs   Special Drawing Rights (paper gold)
SE.   southeast
SEATO   SE. Asia Treaty Organization
sec.   section; second(s); security; secured
SEC   Securities and Exchange Commission
second   2nd or 2d (no period)
Secy., Sec.   Secretary (pl. Secys., Secs.)
sel.   select, -ed, -tion
Sen.   Senate; Senator (pl. Sens.); Senior
sep.   separate; sepd.; sepg.; sepn.
Sept.   September; Sep. in tabulations
seq.   the following (L. sequens) (pl. seqq.)
ser.   series; serial; service; sermon
serv., svc., svce.   service
sess.   session
s.f.   sinking fund; near end (L. sub finem)
S1c   Seaman, first class
Sfc   Sergeant first class
Sgd., /S/, (s)   signed (See p. 431)
Sgt.   Sergeant; Sfc, Sergeant first class
sh.   share (pl. shs.); sheet
shp   shaft horsepower; shipping
shpt.   shipment; shpg., -ing; shpd.; shpr.
shtg.   shortage
sh.tn., s.t.   short ton
sic   so written; thus (L.)   (See p. 432)
sig., sg.   signature; write [on medicine]
Sig.   Signor (It., Mr.; p. 321) (pl. Sigg.)
Sig.ra   Signora (It., Mrs.) (pl. Sig.re)
sim.   similar
sing.   singular (For single-phase, see ph.)
S.J.   Society of Jesus (the Jesuits)
S.J.D.   Doctor of Juridical Science (Law)
sk.   sack (pl. sx)
sked   schedule
S&L   Savings and Loan (pl. S&Ls)
S.Lat., SL   south latitude
sld.   sailed; sealed; sold
sltx, SLTX   sales tax
sm   small; statute mile
S.M.   Master of Science
Sn., SN   Seaman
s.o.   seller's option; shipping order
So., S.   South; southern
Soc.   Society; Sociology
sol.   solution; soluble; solicitor
SOR   stockholder of record (pl. SORs)
SOS   distress signal (no periods). These
    letters do not represent words; the
    signal was adopted, because of its
    distinctive character, by the Radio-
    telegraph Conference in London,
    1912.   The SOS signal is . . . — — . . .
    (three dots, three dashes, three dots).
    In radiotelephony the distress signal
    is the spoken expression MAYDAY
    (corresponding to French pronun-
    ciation of "m'aider [Help me!]").
sp.   species; special; spelling; specimen
s.p.   without issue (L. sine prole); single-
    phase (or 1PH) (elec.)
Sp.   Spanish; Spain; Specialist

S.p.A.   a corporation (It. Società per [for]
    Azioni [shares])
spec.   specification (pl. specs); specimen(s)
spg.   spring (pl. spgs.)
sp.gr., s.g., sg   specific gravity
sp.ht.   specific heat
s.p.s.   without surviving issue (L. sine
    prole superstite)
spt.   seaport
sq.   square, as sq.yd., sq.mi.
sq.   the following (L. sequens) (pl. sqq.)
Sq.   square (a block or street); Squadron
sq.ft., ft²   square foot or feet
sq.in., in²   square inch or inches
Sr.   Senior; Sister; Sir; Señor (Sp., Mr.)
S.R.   shipping receipt; star route
Sra.   Señora (Sp., Mrs.) (pl. Sras.)
Sres.   Señores (Sp., Messrs.)
S.R.O., SRO   standing room only (theater)
Srta.   Señorita (Sp., Miss) (pl. Srtas.)
ss.   sections; namely or to wit (See p. 491)
SS.   steamship (pl. SSs.); supersonic
SSA   Social Security Administration
S.Sgt., S/Sgt.   Staff Sergeant
SSR, S.S.R.   Soviet Socialist Republic
SSS   Selective Service System
St.   Street; State; Store; Strait (pl. Sts.);
    Statute(s); Saint (pl. SS.)
Sta.   Station; Santa; stamped; stationary
stat.   statistics; statutes
std.   standard; seated
S.T.D.   Doctor of Sacred Theology
Ste   Sainte (Fr., feminine of Saint)
stg.   storage (or stge.); sterling (or ster.)
stk.   stock
Stk.Ex., St.Ex.   Stock Exchange
Stk.Mkt.   Stock Market
st.mi., sm   statute [legalized] mile(s)
stmt.   statement
stp., st., sta.   stamped (securities)
str.   steamer; store (pl. strs.); strength
stud.   student
S.U.   set up (freight); service unit
sub.   substitute; subway; subscriber, -ption
    substance; submarine; suburb, -an
subj., sub.   subject
subs.   subsidiary; subscription; subsistence
Sun.   Sunday; Su. in tabulations
sup.   superior; supply; above (L. supra)
supp., sup.   supplement, -ary (pl. sup[p]s.)
Supt.   Superintendent
sur.   surface; surplus
surg.   surgeon; surgery; surgical
surv., svy.   survey, -ing, -or; surviving
s.v.   under the word (L. sub verbo)
svc., svce., serv.   service
svgs.   savings
s.v.p.   if you please (Fr. s'il vous plaît)
sw.   switch; swbd., switchboard
Sw., Swed.   Swedish; Sweden
SW.   southwest; seawater; short-wave
S.W.G., SWG   standard wire gauge
sx   sacks
syl.   syllable(s)
sym.   symbol; symmetrical; symphony;
    symptom
synd.   syndicate, -ed
syst., sys.   system

T

t   metric ton (ordinary ton is tn. or T.)
t.   temperature; town; troy; time; teaspoon
T., Tp., Twp.   township (pl. Tps., Twps.)
tab.   table(s)

T.A.G. The Adjutant General
t.a.w. twice a week (advertising)
TB tuberculosis
T.B. trial balance
tbsp., tbs., T. tablespoon(s) (measure)
T.C., TC travelers check
T.D. trust deed (See p. 482)
tech. technical
tel. telephone; telegraph; telegram
temp. temperature; temporary
Tenn. Tennessee (official)
Ter. Territory; territorial; Terrace
Tex. Texas (official)
t.f. till forbidden (advertising)
tg. telegraph; **tgm.,** telegram
third 3rd or **3d** (no period)
Thos. Thomas
thou. thousand; **M** in lumber, etc.
3-D three-dimension, -al (films)
Thurs., Thu. Thursday; **Th.** in tabulations
tkr. tanker
TLC tender, loving care
TLO, t.l.o. total loss only (ins.)
TM, Tmk. trademark (pl. TMs, Tmks.)
tn., T. ton (metric ton is t); town; train
tn.mi. ton-mile (freight) (See p. 576)
tonn. tonnage
tp title page; telephone; (cap.) township
tph tons per hour; **tpm,** tons per minute
tr. trust; trustee; transit; transfer; transpose; translated, -tion, -tor; treasurer
T.R. tons registered (shipping)
trans., tr. translated, -tion, -tor
Treas., Tr. Treasurer; Treasury
t.s., ts tensile strength
T.Sgt., T/Sgt. Technical Sergeant
tsp., t. teaspoon(s) (measure)
TT teletype, -writer
TTS, T.T.s telegraphic transfers (of money)
Tues., Tue. Tuesday; **Tu.** in tabulations
Turk. Turkish; Turkey
TV television; terminal velocity
TVA Tennessee Valley Authority
Twad., Tw. Twaddell (hydrometer)
Twp. township (See T.)
TWX teletypewriter exchange
tx. tax or taxes; text, -book

U

U., Univ. University
UFO unidentified flying object (pl. UFOs)
UGT urgent
UHF ultra-high frequency (broadcasting)
u.i. as below (L. ut infra)
U.K. United Kingdom
UL Underwriters' Laboratories (elec. std.)
ult. last month (L. ultimo); ultimate, -ly
un. unifying or unified (bonds)
Un. Union; United
U.N., UN United Nations (See p. 502)
Univ. University; Universal
unl. unlimited; unlisted (securities)
up., UP underproof (alcohols); upper
UPI United Press International
u.s. as above (L. ut supra)
U.S., US United States
U.S.A., USA United States of America; U.S. Army (See p. 337)
U.S.A.F., USAF United States Air Force
U.S.A.R., USAR U.S. Army Reserve
U.S.C. U.S. Code; under separate cover
U.S.C.G. United States Coast Guard
U.S.D.J. United States District Judge
USIA United States Information Agency

U.S.M.C. United States Marine Corps
U.S.N. United States Navy (See p. 337)
U.S.N.R. United States Naval Reserve
U.S.P. United States Pharmacopoeia
U.S.R.S. U.S. Reclamation Service
U.S.S. United States Senate; United States Ship
U.S.S.R. Union of Soviet Socialist Republics
ut. utilities
U.T., UT, u.t. Universal time
Utah officially spelled out; often **Ut.**
ut dict., u.d. as directed (L. ut dictum)

V

v volt (elec.)
v. verse (pl. vv.); verb; volume; versus
V. valve; velocity
va, v-a volt-ampere (elec.)
Va. Virginia (official)
V.A., VA Veterans' Administration
vac. vacuum
val. value; valuation
var reactive volt-ampere
var. variety; various; variant; variation
V.C. Victoria Cross (Br.); Vice Consul
V.D.M. Minister of the Word of God (L.)
vel. velocity
Ven. Venerable
vert. vertical
v.f., VF video frequency (TV); very fine
V.G. Vicar General; very good
VHF very high frequency (broadcasting)
v.i. see below (L. vide infra)
V.I. Virgin Islands; Vancouver Island
Vice Adm., V.A., VAdm Vice Admiral
Vice Pres., V.P., V.Pres. Vice President
VIP very important person (pl. VIPs)
vis. visibility (aviation); visual; (cap) Vista
visc. viscosity
viz namely (L. videlicet)
V.M.D. Doctor of Veterinary Medicine
vol. volume (pl. vols.); volunteer
vou. voucher
voy. voyage
v.p., vt.pl. voting pool (stocks)
V.P., Vice Pres. Vice President
vs., v. against (L. versus); verse
v.s. see above (L. vide supra); volumetric solution
V.S. Veterinary Surgeon
Vt. Vermont (official)
v.t.c., vtc voting trust certificates (stocks)
vtg., vt. voting (stocks)
vv. verses
v.v. vice versa

W

w watt (elec.); week
W. west
w.a. with average (ins.)
WAC Women's Army Corps (pl. WACs)
war., wt., w. warrant (securities)
Wash., WA Washington (state, not D.C.)
wb. wheelbase (length of car between axles)
WB waybill; westbound
w.d., wd when distributed (securities)
Wed. Wednesday; **W., We.** in tabulations
w.g. wire gauge
wh, w-hr., whr. watt-hour (elec.)
whf. wharf
whge. wharfage

whs.   warehouse
whsle.   wholesale
whs.rec., W.R.   warehouse receipt
w.i., wi   when issued (securities)
W.I.   West Indies
Wis.   Wisconsin (official)
wk.   work: week (pl. wks.)
w.l.   wave length (elec.); water line
W.Long.   west longitude
Wm.   William
w/m   weight and/or measurement (shipping)
Wn., Wa.   Washington (Wash. is official)
W.O., WO   Warrant Officer; wait order
wpc., w/c   watts per candle
wpm   words per minute
w.r., wr   with rights (securities)
W.R., whs.rec.   warehouse receipt
wt.   weight; warrant (pl. wts.)
WUX   Western Union exchange (tele-printer)
W.Va.   West Virginia (official)
w.w., ww   with warrants (securities)
Wyo.   Wyoming (official)

X

x   box(es); by; cross, as X-roads, x-ref.; extension (phone); extra, as x-hvy., XL

xc, xcp.   ex or without coupon (bonds)
Xch., X   exchange
xd, xdiv.   ex or without dividend (stocks)
x in.   ex or without interest (securities)
Xn.   Christian; Xnty., Christianity
XP   monogram for Greek word for Christ
x pr.   ex or without privileges (securities)
xr, x rts.   ex or without rights (securities)
Xtal, xtl   crystal
xw   ex or without warrants (securities)
XQ.   cross-question

Y

yb.   yearbook
yd.   yard (pl. yds.)
yd², sq.yd.   square yard(s)
yd³, cu.yd.   cubic yard(s)
Y.M.C.A.   Young Men's Christian Association
yr., y.   year (pl. yrs.); your; younger
Y.T.   Yukon Territory, Canada
Y.W.C.A.   Young Women's Christian Association

Z

z., Z   zone; zero; zenith distance

SIGNS AND SYMBOLS

+   plus; positive; north, in astronomy
−   minus; negative; south, in astronomy
±   plus or minus;   ∓   minus or plus
×   by, in dimensions, as $3' \times 10''$
:   is to; divided by; ratio of
::   as; equals (in proportion), as $1:3::6:18$
∴   therefore; hence
∵   since; because
...   and so on
∥   is parallel to; | | absolute value of
Π   product; pressure; parity
⊥   is perpendicular to (pl. ⊥s)
≡   identical with;   ≢   not identical with
≐   approaches;   →   approaches limit of
≈ or ≒   is approximately equal to
≠ or ∓   is unequal to
∼   is similar to; difference; cycle
≅   is congruent to
≎   equivalent
∫   integral (sign also called a "fluent")
∞   infinity; indefinitely great
0   infinitesimal; indefinitely small; zero
∝   varies as; is directly proportional to
>   greater than;   ≫   much greater than
≯   is not greater than
≥ or ≧   is greater than or equal to
<   is less than;   ≪   is much less than
≮   is not less than
≤ or ≦   is less than or equal to
! or ⌐   the factorial product, as 5! or |5 is
   $5 \cdot [\text{or} \times] 4 \cdot 3 \cdot 2 \cdot 1 = 120$
✓   double check (√ check)
number, if before a figure; pounds, if after a figure; space, in printing
/   per, as bbls/day; of; by; after; to; upon; shillings; proportion, as $a/b = c/d$
2/10, n/30   means 2% discount in 10 days, net in 30 days
′   feet, as 10′; minutes of arc
″   inches, as 8″; seconds of arc; ditto
□   square; square miles
□′ or □ft   square foot or feet
′□   foot or feet square

□″   square inches
#/□″   pounds per square inch
√‾   root or radical sign; square root
³√‾   cube root
   (To make these signs on the typewriter, use the diagonal line with the underline above it. Draw in only the first short lines.)
′ ″ ‴   accents used to distinguish several things of the same general designation, as A′, A″, A‴—read "A prime, A second, A third," etc.
1 2 3 4 5   superior figures used as footnote indicators; a superior figure (exponent) may indicate the power to which a given number is to be raised, as 12^2 (squared), 10^3 (cubed)
h m s   hours, minutes, seconds, in scientific work, as $4^h\ 30^m\ 10^s$
°   degrees
° ′ ″   degrees, minutes, seconds of an arc, as Longitude $30°\ 08'\ 14''$ W.
°F   degrees Fahrenheit
°C   degrees Centigrade
%   percent; in care of
@   at, as 10¢ each; to, as $10 @ $16
&c   and so forth; etc.
&   ampersand (a corruption of the words "and per se and"; the symbol comes from the Latin Et [&] meaning "and")
§   section
©   copyright
®   registered in U.S. Patent Office
℔   per, as $20 ℔ ton
¶   paragraph (or ℙ)
℄   center line
℞P   horsepower
℣·   the (old printing symbol) (pron. thē)
℞   take (L. Recipe); response (church)
ʒ   dram, apothecaries'
℥   ounce, apothecaries'
Ə   scruple, apothecaries'; Əi, one scruple

571

ABBREVIATIONS

<table>
<tr><td>℔</td><td>pound, apothecaries'</td></tr>
<tr><td>♏</td><td>minim or drop, apothecaries'</td></tr>
<tr><td>f°</td><td>folio</td></tr>
<tr><td>4to, 4°</td><td>quarto (folded in 4—a book size)</td></tr>
<tr><td>8vo, 8°</td><td>octavo (folded in 8—a book size)</td></tr>
<tr><td>12mo, 12°</td><td>duodecimo (folded in 12—a book size)</td></tr>
<tr><td>10d</td><td>tenpenny nails (d means penny)</td></tr>
</table>

1st first
2nd second; 2d is also used
3rd third; 3d is also used
4th fourth
3s, 4s interest rates on bonds
* asterisk; capital cities in geographic work; correct quotations on ticker tape
☞ "fist" or index (pointer)

Greek Letters. The Greek letters are used by different engineers and scientists to mean different things. For instance:

Δ distance, in astronomy; finite difference
Δp pressure drop, or difference in pressure
δ variation; declination, in astronomy
φ phase, in electricity; angle of roll, in aviation; angle of eccentricity, in astronomy
Φ magnetic flux
Σ sum, in algebra
π pi, or 3.14159265 + (generally 3.1416)
ε 2.7182818 + in logarithms; eccentricity; dielectric constant; angle of downwash, in aviation
μ permeability; coefficient of viscosity; mean angular motion in unit of time, in astronomy
μ micron μ^2 square micron μ^3 cubic micron
mμ millimicron (1/1000 of a micron)   μμ micromicron (1/1,000,000 of a micron)
μa microampere   μf microfarad   μw microwatt

◇◇◇◇◇◇◇◇

GREEK ALPHABET

CHARACTER		GREEK NAME	PRONUNCIATION
CAPITAL	SMALL		
A	α α	Alpha	ăl′fȧ
B	β ϐ	Beta	bā′tȧ, or bē′tȧ
Γ	γ	Gamma	găm′ȧ
Δ	δ	Delta	děl′tȧ
E	ε	Epsilon	ĕp′sĭ-lŏn (Br. ĕp-sīl′on)
Z	ζ	Zeta	zā′tȧ, or zē′tȧ
H	η	Eta	ā′tȧ, or ē′tȧ
Θ	θ ϑ	Theta	thā′tȧ, or thē′tȧ
I	ι	Iota	ī-ō′tȧ
K	κ	Kappa	kăp′ȧ
Λ	λ	Lambda	lăm′dȧ
M	μ	Mu	mū, or m̄oo
N	ν	Nu	nū, or n̄oo
Ξ	ξ	Xi	zī, or ksē
O	o	Omicron	ŏm′ĭ-krŏn (Br. ō-mīk′rŭn)
Π	π	Pi	pī
P	ρ	Rho	rō
Σ	σ ς	Sigma	sĭg′mȧ
T	τ	Tau	ta͝u, or tou
Υ	υ	Upsilon	ūp′sĭ-lŏn (Br. ūp-sīl′on)
Φ	φ φ	Phi	fī
X	χ	Chi (Br. Khi)	kī, or kē
Ψ	ψ	Psi	sī, or psē
Ω	ω	Omega	ō-mē′gȧ, or ō-měg′ȧ

Other alphabets—Russian, German, Arabic, and Hebrew—may be found in desk dictionaries, near the entry "alphabet" or in the back pages.
The English alphabet is derived from the **Roman (Latin) alphabet**; therefore, it is expressed in "roman" characters or type.

Weights and Measures

(Checked by the National Bureau of Standards, Office of Weights and Measures, Washington, D.C.)

THE METRIC SYSTEM

The metric system is the basis of the **International System (SI)** of weights and measures. It is used throughout the world, and is accepted as standard in all scientific work. It was originally based upon one ten-millionth of the distance from the Equator to the North Pole.

It was legalized in the United States by Congress in 1866.

The basic units are:

meter	m	for length	Not commonly used:		
gram	g	for mass or weight	**are**	a	for area
liter	liter	for capacity	**stere**	s	for volume

All other metric units are the decimal subdivisions or multiples of these three basic units. The following numerical prefixes are employed:

micro-	μ	1/1,000,000	Higher prefixes are:			
milli-	m	1/1000	giga-	G	one billion
centi-	c	1/100	tera-	T	one trillion
deci-	d	1/10			
Basic unit	**one**				
deka-	da	10			
hecto-	h	100	nano-	n	one billionth
kilo-	k	1000	pico-	p	one trillionth
myria-	my	10,000	femto-	f	one quadrillionth
mega-	M	1,000,000	atto-	a	one quintillionth

The main units are interrelated as follows:

meter	the unit of length—the original, basic unit
kilogram	the unit of mass—equal to the mass (or weight) of the International Prototype Kilogram*
gram	a smaller unit of mass—equal to $1/1000$ of the kilogram
liter	the capacity of 1 cubic decimeter*
are	the area of 100 square meters ⎱ not commonly used
stere	the volume of 1 cubic meter ⎰

* Originally, the basis for determining the **standard kilogram** and the **standard liter** was one cubic decimeter of water. However, an independent standard or "prototype" has since been adopted for the kilogram. And the liter is now defined as "merely a special name for the cubic decimeter."

Metric Abbreviations. The abbreviations given above are those adopted by the National Bureau of Standards.

Note that most metric abbreviations are written in small letters (three being in caps for differentiation); no periods are used; and the same abbreviation serves for both singular and plural.

573

"Square" and "cubic" are indicated by the exponents ^{2} and ^{3}, as

m^2 cm^3 (Some scientists use cc for liquids, and cm^3 for volumes.)

LENGTH
Unit—Meter

Name	Abbreviation	Metric Equivalent	No. of Meters	Common Equivalent
1 millimeter..................	mm	....	1/1000	0.03937 inch
1 centimeter..................	cm	10 millimeters	1/100	0.3937 inch
1 decimeter	dm	10 centimeters	1/10	3.937 inches
1 METER.....................	m	10 decimeters	......	39.37 inches
				3.2808 feet
				1.0936 yards
1 dekameter..................	dam	....	10	393.7 inches
				32.8083 feet
1 hectometer.................	hm	10 dekameters	100	328.083 feet, or
				328 feet 1 inch
1 kilometer..................	km	10 hectometers	1000	0.62137 mile
				3280.83 feet
1 myriameter.................	mym	10 kilometers	10,000	6.2137 miles

Small subdivisions:

Name	Abbreviation	Metric Equivalent	No. of Meters	Common Equivalent
1 micron.....................	μ	1/1000 millimeter	1/1,000,000	0.03937 mil
1 millimicron................	mμ	1/1000 of a micron	....	0.00003937 mil
1 micromillimeter............	μmm	1/1,000,000 millimeter		
1 micromicron................	μμ	1/1,000,000 micron		

To convert meters into feet, and vice versa:

Number of meters = number of feet ÷ 3.28
Number of feet = number of meters × 3.28

Relation to liter:

1 liter = 1 cubic decimeter*
1 milliliter = 1 cubic centimeter

* Formerly, the liter (volume of 1 kg water) differed from a cubic decimeter by about 28 millionths. This was corrected by the Twelfth General Conference on Weights and Measures, Paris, 1964.

WEIGHT OR MASS
Unit—Gram   (in practice, the Kilogram)

Name	Abbreviation	Metric Equivalent	No. of Grams	Avoirdupois Equivalent
1 milligram....................	mg	....	1/1000	0.0154 grain
1 centigram....................	cg	10 milligrams	1/100	0.1543 grain
1 decigram....................	dg	10 centigrams	1/10	1.5432 grains
1 GRAM.......................	g	10 decigrams	....	15.4324 grains
1 dekagram.......	dag	....	10	0.3527 ounce
				0.3215 troy ounce
1 hectogram...................	hg	10 dekagrams	100	3.5274 ounces
				3.2151 troy ounces
1 kilogram.......	kg	10 hectograms	1000	2.2046 pounds
				2.6792 troy pounds
1 myriagram....................	myg	10 kilograms	10,000	22.046 pounds
1 quintal..........	q	10 myriagrams	100,000	220.46 pounds
1 metric ton (millier, or tonneau)........	t	10 quintals	1,000,000	2204.62 pounds

CAPACITY
Unit—Liter

Name	Abbreviation	Metric Equivalent	No. of Liters	Dry Measure	Liquid Measure
1 milliliter..........	ml	1 cm³	1/1000	0.061 cubic inch	0.2705 fluid dram
1 centiliter..........	cl	10 milliliters	1/100	0.6102 cubic inch	0.3381 fluid ounce
1 deciliter..........	dl	10 centiliters	1/10	6.102 cubic inches	0.8454 gill
1 LITER...........	liter (l)	10 dl; 1 dm³	.....	0.9081 quart	1.0567 quarts
1 dekaliter..........	dal	....	10	1.1351 pecks	2.64179 gallons
1 hectoliter..........	hl	10 dekaliters	100	2.8378 bushels	26.4179 gallons
1 kiloliter (or stere)...	kl (s)	10 hl; 1 m³	1000	1.308 cubic yards	264.179 gallons

AREA OR SURFACE
Unit—Square Meter

Name	Abbreviation	Metric Equivalent	Common Equivalent
1 square centimeter.....................	cm²	1/10,000 square meter	0.1550 square inch
1 SQUARE METER (or centare)..........	m² (ca)	1 square meter (m²)	1550 square inches
			1.196 square yards
1 square dekameter (or are).............	dam² (a)	100 square meters	119.6 square yards
1 square hectometer (or hectare)..........	hm² (ha)	10,000 square meters	2.47105 acres
1 square kilometer.....................	km²	1,000,000 square meters	247.105 acres
			0.3861 square mile

VOLUME
Unit—Cubic Meter

Name	Abbreviation	Metric Equivalent	Common Equivalent
1 cubic centimeter.....................	cm³	1000 cubic millimeters	0.06102 cubic inch
1 cubic decimeter.....................	dm³	1000 cubic centimeters	61.0237 cubic inches
1 CUBIC METER (or stere).............	m³ (s)	1000 cubic decimeters	1.30795 cubic yards

❖❖❖❖❖❖❖❖

AMERICAN (OLD ENGLISH) SYSTEM

NOTE: The abbreviations shown below, with periods, are those in general commercial use. The National Bureau of Standards omits periods after all abbreviations of units (and spells some out).

LINEAR OR LONG MEASURE

Name	Abbreviation	Common Equivalent	Metric Equivalent
1 inch..............................	in. or ʺ	1000 mils	2.54 cm
1 foot..............................	ft. or ʹ	12 inches	0.3048 m
			30.48 cm
1 yard..............................	yd.	3 feet; 36 inches	0.9144 m
1 rod..............................	rd. }	5½ yards; 16½ feet; 25 links	5.0292 m
1 pole..............................	p. }		
1 furlong..........................	fur.	40 rods; 220 yards; ⅛ mile	201.168 m
1 mile (statute or land mile)..........	(st.) mi.	8 furlongs; 1760 yards; 5280 feet	1.609 km
1 international nautical mile (see Mariners' Measure, p. 577)			

SQUARE MEASURE

Name	Abbreviation	Common Equivalent	Metric Equivalent
1 square inch........	sq.in.; in²	....	6.4516 cm²
1 square foot........	sq.ft.; ft²	144 square inches	0.0929 m²
1 square yard.......	sq.yd.; yd²	9 square feet	0.8361 m²
1 square rod........	sq.rd.; rd²	30¼ square yards; 272¼ square feet	25.29 m²
1 square chain......	sq.ch.; ch²	16 square rods	404.68 m²
1 acre..............	A. or acre	160 square rods; 43,560 square feet (approximately 69.57 yards or 208 feet 8½ inches on each side)	40.468 a / 0.4047 ha
1 square mile.......	sq.mi.;mi² }	640 acres	258.99 ha
1 section..........	sec. }	640 acres	2.59 km²
1 township.........	T.; T(w)p.	36 square miles (6 miles square)	

CUBIC MEASURE

Name	Abbreviation	Common Equivalent	Metric Equivalent
1 cubic inch............	cu.in.; in³	....	16.387 cm³
1 cubic foot............	cu.ft.; ft³	1728 cubic inches	0.0283 m³
1 cubic yard............	cu.yd.; yd³	27 cubic feet	0.7646 m³

WOOD MEASURE

Name	Abbreviation	Common Equivalent	Metric Equivalent
1 board foot (foot board measure).......	f.b.m.	144 cubic inches (1' × 1' × 1")	0.00236 m³
1 cord foot..........................	cd.ft.	16 cubic feet (4' × 4' × 1')	
1 cord..............................	cd.	128 cubic feet (4' × 4' × 8'); 8 cord feet	3.625 s or m³

SHIPPING MEASURE

Name	Common Equivalent	Metric Equivalent
1 register ton..	100 cubic feet	2.8317 m³
1 displacement ton...................................	35 cubic feet	
1 barrel bulk..	5 cubic feet; ⅛ ton	141.58 l
1 shipping ton, or freight ton (frt.tn.)	40 cubic feet; 2240 pounds	
1 ton mile (air freight) is one ton shipped one mile. (tn.mi.)		

SURVEYORS' MEASURE
(Gunter's Chain)

Name	Abbreviation	Common Equivalent	Metric Equivalent
1 link.............................	li.	7.92 inches	0.2012 m
1 rod..............................	rd.	25 links; 16½ ft.; 5½ yards	5.0292 m
1 chain (See Engineers' chain, p. 577)..	ch.	100 links; 4 rods; 66 feet; 22 yards	20.1168 m
1 furlong..........................	fur.	10 chains; 40 rods	201.168 m
1 mile (statute mile)...............	mi.	80 chains; 5280 feet	1.6093 km

SURVEYORS' AREA MEASURE
(Gunter's Chain)

Name	Abbreviation	Common Equivalent	Metric Equivalent
1 square link	sq.li.	62.7264 square inches	0.0405 m²
1 square rod	sq.rd. ⎫	625 square links	25.29 m²
1 [square] pole	[sq.] p. ⎭		
1 square chain	sq.ch.	16 square rods; 16 [square] poles	404.68 m²
1 acre	A.	10 square chains; 160 square rods	0.4047 ha
1 square mile	sq.mi.	640 acres; 1 section	2.59 km²
1 township	T. or Tp.	36 square miles (6 miles square)	93.24 km²

ENGINEERS' MEASURE

Name	Abbreviation	Common Equivalent	Metric Equivalent
1 link	li.	1 foot; 12 inches	0.3048 m
1 chain (See Gunter's chain, p. 576)	ch.	100 links; 100 feet	30.480 m
1 mile	mi.	52.8 chains	1.6093 km

MARINERS' MEASURE

Name	Abbreviation	Common Equivalent	Metric Equivalent
1 fathom	fath.	6 feet; 8 spans	1.8288 m
1 cable	....	120 fathoms; 720 feet; 240 yards	219.456 m
1 international nautical mile*	nm. or INM	6076.1155 feet; 1.1508 statute miles	1.852 km
1 (marine) league	l.	3 nautical miles (old)	5.5597 km
1 degree (on great circle of earth)	deg.	60 nautical miles (old)	111.19 km
1 knot†	k.	1 nautical mile in 1 hour	

* The international nautical mile has been adopted by the United States Government in lieu of the old U.S. nautical mile (also called the "meridian mile," "geographical mile," and "sea mile"), which was 6080.20 U.S. feet. (The British Admiralty mile was 6080 British feet.)

Conversions: Number of international nautical miles = number of statute miles × 0.86898
Number of statute miles = number of international nautical miles × 1.1508
(roughly 1⅛)

† Note that a knot is a measure of speed, not of distance; therefore it is incorrect to say "33 knots *per hour*" when meaning "a speed of 33 knots."

DRY MEASURE

Name	Abbreviation	Common Equivalent	Metric Equivalent
1 quart	(dry) qt.	2 pints; 67.201 cubic inches	1.1012 l
1 peck	pk.	8 quarts; 537.605 cubic inches	8.809 l
1 bushel	bu.	4 pecks; 2150.42 cubic inches	35.238 l
1 barrel*	bbl.	105 dry quarts; 7056 cubic inches	115.626 l

(British measures differ from the above.)

1 imperial bushel (Br. standard)	imp.bu.	1.032 U.S. bushels; 2219.36 cubic inches	36.367 l

* Sizes of barrels differ for different commodities. "Struck measure" means leveled off, not heaped.

LIQUID MEASURE

Name	Abbreviation	Common Equivalent	Metric Equivalent
1 gill........................	gi.	32 fluid drams; 4 fluid ounces	0.1183 l
1 pint........................	(liq.) pt.	4 gills; 28.875 cubic inches	0.4732 l
1 quart......................	(liq.) qt.	2 pints; 57.75 cubic inches	0.9463 l
1 gallon.....................	gal.	4 quarts; 231 cubic inches; 0.83267 Br. imperial gallon	3.7853 l
1 barrel*....................	bbl.	31½ gallons (32 gallons in some states); 7276.5 cubic inches	119.23 l
1 barrel of oil (petroleum).......	....	42 gallons (U.S.)	
1 hogshead..................	hhd.	2 barrels; 63 gallons; 14,553 cubic inches	238.476 l

(British measures differ from the above.)

1 imperial gallon (Br. standard)	imp.gal.	1.20095 U.S. gallons; 277.42 cubic inches	4.546 l

* Sizes of barrels differ for different commodities.

ORDINARY WEIGHT
(Avoirdupois)

Name	Abbreviation	Common Equivalent	Metric Equivalent
1 grain*...............	(spelled out)	....	0.0648 g
1 dram.................	dr. (avdp.)	27.34375 grains	1.7718 g
1 ounce................	oz. (avdp.)	16 drams; 437.5 grains; 0.911 troy ounce	28.3495 g
1 pound................	lb. (avdp.)	16 ounces; 7000 grains; 1.215 troy pounds	453.5924 g / 0.4536 kg
1 hundredweight........	cwt.	100 pounds (U.S.); 4 quarters	45.3592 kg
		112 pounds† (Br.); 4 quarters of 28 pounds each	50.802 kg
1 ton { short (net) ton....	sh.tn.	2000 pounds (U.S. ton)	0.9072 metric t
{ long (gross) ton†..	gr.tn.	2240 pounds (British ton)	1.0160 metric t
1 metric ton...........	t	2204.62 pounds; 1.1023 short tons	
1 freight ton...........	frt.tn.	40 cubic feet of freight space (See p. 576.)	

* The grain is the same in all weights—avoirdupois, troy, and apothecaries'. It was derived from the weight of a grain of wheat.
† The British "gross ton" and "long hundredweight" are sometimes used in the United States, but their use is limited to certain industries and is decreasing.

TROY WEIGHT
(For Precious Metals and Jewels)

Name	Abbreviation	Common Equivalent	Metric Equivalent
1 grain*.....................	(spelled out)	....	0.0648 g
1 pennyweight...............	dwt.	24 grains	1.5552 g
1 ounce†....................	oz.t.	20 pennyweights; 480 grains	31.1035 g
1 pound†....................	lb.t.	12 ounces; 5760 grains; 0.823 avdp.lb.	0.3732 kg
1 carat grain................	....	¼ carat	
1 metric carat‡..............	c	200 milligrams (standard); 3.0865 grains	0.2 g
1 assay ton.................	AT	29,167 milligrams	29.167 g

* See Ordinary Weight table, above.
† The ounce and the pound are the same in troy and apothecaries' weights.
‡ The carat was originally the weight of a seed or bean from the Mediterranean carob tree.

GOLD MEASURE
(The "fineness" of gold is the purity of it. "Karat" is a measure of the fineness. Standard fineness for gold bullion is 99.9% pure gold; minimum fineness, 99.5%.)

Name	Abbreviation	Common Equivalent
1 troy ounce	....	{ U.S. gold stock official value: $42.22 troy oz. { Floating price above $270 a troy oz.
24 karats fine.............	24K	pure gold
18 karats fine.............	18K	18/24 pure gold—18 parts gold, 6 parts alloy
1 karat....................	K	1/24 pure gold (by weight)

A 14.2-inch cube of gold bullion (0.999 fine) weighs approximately a ton.

SILVER MEASURE
(The "fineness" of silver is the purity of it. "Sterling" is a measure of fineness.)

1 troy ounce.......No official value. Floating price around $8.00. (Standard fineness for silver bars in the commercial market is 99.9% pure silver. Melting of coins can be banned by the Coinage Act of 1965.)

Sterling silver.....has a fineness of .925; that is, 925 parts of silver to 75 parts of alloy. (Silver is commonly alloyed with copper to give it hardness.) (See also British Money, p. 535.)

APOTHECARIES' WEIGHT
(For Compounding Medicines)

Name	Abbreviation	Common Equivalent	Metric Equivalent
1 grain*.............	(spelled out)	....	0.0648 g
1 scruple............	s.ap. (℈)	20 grains	1.296 g
1 dram..............	dr.ap. (ʒ)	3 scruples; 60 grains	3.8879 g
1 ounce†............	oz.ap. (℥)	8 drams; 480 grains	31.1035 g
1 pound†...........	lb.ap. (℔)	12 ounces; 5760 grains	0.3732 kg

* See Ordinary Weight table, p. 578. † See Troy Weight table, p. 578.

APOTHECARIES' FLUID MEASURE
(For Compounding Medicines)

Name	Abbreviation	Common Equivalent	Metric Equivalent
1 minim.............	min. or ℥(♏)	1 drop (approximately)	0.0616 ml
1 fluid dram.........	fl.dr. (f ʒ)	60 minims	3.6966 ml
1 fluid ounce........	fl.oz. (f ℥)	8 fluid drams	2.9573 cl
1 pint*.............	O (L. Octarius)	16 fluid ounces	0.4732 l
1 gallon*...........	C (L. Congius)	8 pints; 231 cubic inches	3.7853 l

(British measures differ from the above.)
* The apothecaries' fluid pint and gallon are the same as the ordinary liquid pint and gallon.

COUNTING MEASURE

Name	Abbreviation	Common Equivalent
1 dozen................	doz.	12 units
1 gross................	gr.	12 dozen; 144 units
1 great gross...........	g.gr.	12 gross; 1728 units
1 score................	....	20 units

WATER VOLUMES

Weight of pure water under specified conditions of temperature and pressure:

Volumes of Water	Weight, Avoirdupois	Metric Equivalent
1 U.S. gallon.............	8.3452 lb. at 4° C (in vacuum)	3.7853 kg
1 U.S. gallon.............	8.3358 " " " (in air)	3.7811 kg
1 U.S. gallon.............	8.3216 " " 20° C (in air)	3.7746 kg
1 imperial gallon.........	10 "	4.5359 kg
1 liter...................	2.2046 " " 4° C (in vacuum)	1 kg
1 cubic inch.............	0.03609 " " " (in air)	0.016 kg
1 cubic foot.............	62.3565 " " " (in air)	28.284 kg

CIRCULAR OR ANGULAR MEASURE

Name	Abbreviation	Common Equivalent
1 minute..............	′	60 seconds (″)
1 degree..............	°	60 minutes
1 sign (zodiac).........	......	30 degrees
1 radian..............	......	57.2958 degrees; $180/\pi$
1 quadrant............	quad.	90 degrees
1 right angle...........	L	
1 straight angle.........	———	180 degrees; 2 right angles
1 circle / 1 circumference	O	360 degrees; 12 signs; 4 quadrants
1 circular mil..........	cir.mil	0.7854 square mil (a circular mil is the area of a circle 1 mil in diameter)

Calculations:

Circumference	= diameter × 3.1416
Diameter	= circumference ÷ 3.1416
Area of circle	= diameter squared × 0.7854
Radius	= circumference × 0.15915
Surface of sphere	= diameter squared × 3.1416
Solidity, or cubic contents, of sphere	= diameter cubed × 0.5236
Surface of cylinder	= (diameter × 3.1416) × length
Cubic contents of cylinder	= (diameter squared × 0.7854) × length
Gallons in cylinder	= cubic contents (in cubic inches) ÷ 231 (number of cubic inches in U.S. gallon)

PAPER MEASURE

Papers are put up in boxes, cartons, bundles, and in cartons lashed on skids.

1 quire (qr.) = **25** sheets (or for some papers, **24** sheets)
1 ream (rm.) = **20** quires; **500** sheets (some papers, **480** sheets); printer's ream, **516** sheets
1 bundle (bdl.) = **2** to **2½** reams; **100** to **125** lbs. (for kraft paper)

Paper is graded by weight (or "substance" [Sub. or S.]). "Basis weight" is that of one ream (500 sheets) in a "basic size," as 17x22" for bond, and 25x38" for book paper.

16 lb. and **20 lb.** (as Sub. 20) bond is usual for letterheads (8½x11"). "Cotton [or rag] content" indicates the amount (25, 50, 75, or 100 percent) of enriching cotton fiber.

9 lb. onionskin (or cheaper manifold) is usual for carbon copies—in smooth, cockle (rippled), or glazed finishes, and in 8 colors. 13 lb. bond or sulfite (pulp) is also used.

Some names of papers are: **pulp** (rough, cheap) and **slick** (glossy, expensive) for magazines; **newsprint** (for newspapers); **book** (for books); **Bible** or **India** (thin, sturdy, for dictionaries); **parchment** (like "sheepskin," for diplomas, etc.); **vellum** (for offset, drafting, drawing); **legal cap** (for legal papers, 8½x13"); **foolscap** [so called from former watermark of a fool's cap and bells] ruled, yellow workpads, 8½x13"); **ledger** (for ledgers and records); [manuscript] **cover** (heavy, often colored, for backing documents, pamphlets, etc.); **manila** (primarily a shade [light brown], but may be a strong, hemplike paper); **kraft paper** (for wrapping and bags); **paperboard** (a general term for "boards"); **cardboard** or **Bristol board** (for cards, signs, etc.); **pasteboard** (for light boxes); **corrugated board** (for cartons); **pressboard** (glazed, strong, heavy, for packing); **millboard** (for book covers); **papier-mâché** ([Fr. chewed paper] for molded cases); and **foodboard** (for foods).

580

LAND MEASURE

Name	Abbreviation	Common Equivalent	
1 lot, or plot	....	a small area of ground (sizes vary)	
1 block	blk.	a city block (sizes vary)	Note the difference between "6 mi.sq." (6 mi. on each side), and "6 sq.mi." (2 mi. x 3 mi.).
1 acre	A.	160 square rods (See p. 576.)	
1 section	sec.	640 acres; 1 square mile	
1 township	T. or Tp.	36 square miles (6 miles square [north border shorter because of convergency of meridians]); 36 sections	
1 range	R.	6-mile strip of land—a row of townships—running north and south, laid out from a principal meridian	

Ranges are numbered east and west of chosen meridians.

Townships are numbered north and south of designated base lines.

County is the largest subdivision in all states in the Union, except in Louisiana, where "**Parish**" (abbr. Par.) is used instead of "county"; and in Alaska, where "**Borough**" (abbr. Bo., Boro.) is used.

Some subdivisions of a section of land, which is one mile square:

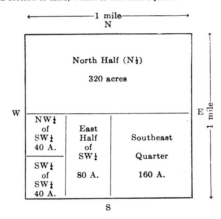

Legal land descriptions are written in abbreviated form:
NE¼ of Sec. 4, T. 6 S., R. 15 EBM
E½ of SE¼ of NE¼ of Sec. 6, T. 8 N., R. 40 EWM

Written out, these land descriptions would read:
The northeast quarter of Section 4, Township 6 south, Range 15 east of the Boise meridian.
The east half of the southeast quarter of the northeast quarter of Section 6, Township 8 north, Range 40 east of the Willamette meridian.

LATITUDE AND LONGITUDE

Latitude lines—the lines of measurement (parallels of latitude) running east and west around the earth, parallel to the equator—north and south of the equator, which is 0°. There are 90° in north latitude, and 90° in south latitude—reaching to each pole.

Longitude lines—the lines of measurement (meridians) running north and south from pole to pole, at right angles to the equator. Longitude is measured east or west of the prime meridian, which is the meridian of Greenwich, England, known as Longitude 0°. There are 180° in east longitude, and 180° in west longitude—360° making the complete globe. The date line approximates the 180° meridian.

Latitude and longitude are figured in degrees, minutes, and seconds (in circular measurement).

Latitude (Lat.) **40° 19′ 12″ N.**
Longitude (Long.) **30° 08′ 14″ W.**

means that this place is located on the line which is 40 degrees 19 minutes and 12 seconds north of the equator, and at a point on that line which is 30 degrees 8 minutes and 14 seconds west of the meridian through Greenwich, England.

Latitude and longitude are also expressed in degrees alone, as

Latitude 10.2 N., longitude 167.43 W.

LONGITUDE IN TIME

1 second of longitude (″)	= 1/15 second of time
1 minute " " (′)	= 4 seconds " "
1 degree " " (°)	= 4 minutes " "
15 degrees " "	= 1 hour " "
360 degrees " "	= 24 hours " "

THERMOMETRIC SCALES

	Centigrade or Celsius (C.)	Fahrenheit (F.)	Kelvin (K. or Abs.)	Réaumur (R.)
Boiling point of pure water at sea level........	100°	212°	373.15°	80°
Freezing point of pure water..................	0°	32°	273.15°	0°
Absolute zero*..........................	−273.15°	−459.6°	0°	−218.52°

Conversions: Centigrade = (F. − 32°) × 5/9 C. = R. × 5/4
Fahrenheit = (C. × 9/5) + 32°

* **"Absolute zero"** is, in theory, the lowest possible temperature—that is, the point at which all molecular motion ceases.

MISCELLANEOUS MEASURES

1 [agate] line (advertising space).... 1 column wide and 1/14 inch deep; ∴ 1″ = 14 agate lines
1 bale (cotton).... 500 pounds
1 bolt (cloth measure).... 15 to 50 yards (varies with materials)
1 Btu (British thermal unit).... the heat required to raise temp. of 1 lb. water 1°F (62°–63°F)
1 button (glove measure).... 1 inch from base of thumb upward (10-button is elbow length)
1 candela (lighting [kăn-dĕl′a; Br. -dē′]).... unit of luminous intensity (candlepower)
(A typical electric light produces between 1 and 2 candelas per watt.)
1 cubit (ancient—now a literary term).... about 18 inches
1 cup (household measure [c. or C.]).... ½ pint; 16 tablespoons; 8 fluid ounces
(¼ cup = 4 tbsp......⅓ cup = 5⅓ tbsp......1 gill = ½ cup)
1 denier (fineness of filaments [dĕn′yẽr; Fr. dẽ-nyā′]).... weight of 1 g per 9000 m of yarn
1 fifth (wine measure).... ⅕ U.S. gallon; ⅘ quart
1 hand (a hand's breadth [for horses' height])... 4 inches
1 horsepower (hp) (mechanical).... the power to lift 550 pounds one foot in one second
1 length (thoroughbred racing).... approximately 7½ feet; or ⅕ second (10 feet)
1 light-year (distance light travels in year in interstellar space).... approx. 6 trillion miles
{1 line (unit of fineness of halftones).... expressed as number of screen lines per linear inch
{1 line or ligne (diameter of buttons).... 1/40 inch
1 magnum (wine measure).... 2 fifths; about 52 fluid ounces
{1 mil (wire measure).... 1/1000 inch; 0.0254 millimeter
{1 mill (monetary unit, as in tax levies).... 1/1000 of a dollar ($.001), or 1/10 cent
{1 pace (length of stride in stepping-off).... 3 feet; 1 yard; sometimes 3.3 feet (⅕ rod)
{1 pace (military).... 30 inches—quick time; 36 inches—double time
{1 perch (linear).... 5½ yards; 1 rod
{1 perch (land).... 1 square rod
{1 perch (stonework).... 24¾ cubic feet (ordinarily)
1 pica (printing).... ⅙ inch; 12 points
1 pipe (wine measure).... 2 hogsheads; 126 gallons
1 point (printing, type size).... 1/12 pica; 0.0138 inch, or about 1/72 inch
1 pole (linear).... 5½ yards; 1 rod *** 1 pole (surface).... 1 square rod
proof (alcoholic content liquors).... twice the percent of alcohol, as "86 proof" = 43% alcohol
1 quarter (of a hundredweight).... 25 pounds (U.S.); 28 pounds (Br.)
1 span (a hand's spread).... 9 inches; ⅛ fathom
[specific] gravity (density measure of gases, liquids, and solids [s.g. or sp.gr.]).... ratio of weight of a liquid or solid to standard weight of pure water (but for gases, standard is air or hydrogen)
1 split (liquors and soft drinks).... 6 ounces, or ½ the usual size bottle
1 square (flooring or roofing).... 100 square feet
1 tablespoon (household measure [tbsp. or T.]).... 3 teaspoons; 4 fl.dr.; ½ fl.oz.
1 teaspoon (household measure [tsp. or t.]).... ⅓ tablespoon; 1⅓ fluid drams
1 tex (fibers).... weight in grams of 1000 meters of yarn
1 therm (heat measure).... 100,000 Btu (see Btu above)
1 ton (unit of air conditioning).... amount of cooling produced by 1 ton of ice melting in 24 hours (rate of 12,000 Btu per hour)
1 ton-mile (shipping measure).... 1 ton freight transported 1 mile (figure tonnage × mileage)
1 tun (wine measure).... 2 pipes; 4 hogsheads; 252 gallons

~~~~~~ RAILROAD MILEAGE ~~~~~~

Distances from the Rand McNally Commercial Atlas and Marketing Guide

Data used by permission.

NOTE: These distances are for the shortest generally traveled routes.

From:	Atlanta, Ga.	Boston, Mass.	Buffalo, N.Y.	Chicago, Ill.	Cincinnati, Ohio	Cleveland, Ohio	Dallas, Tex.	Denver, Colo.	Detroit, Mich.	El Paso, Tex.	Houston, Tex.	Indianapolis, Ind.	Jacksonville, Fla.	Kansas City, Mo.	Los Angeles, Calif.	Memphis, Tenn.	Miami, Fla.	Minneapolis and St. Paul	New Orleans, La.	New York, N.Y.	Oklahoma City, Okla.	Omaha, Nebr.	Pittsburgh, Pa.	Portland, Oreg.	Salt Lake City, Utah	San Francisco, Calif.	Seattle, Wash.	St. Louis, Mo.	Tucson, Ariz.
Atlanta, Ga.																													
Boston, Mass.	1091																												
Buffalo, N.Y.	934	494																											
Chicago, Ill.	734	1018	524																										
Cincinnati, Ohio	490	938	444	281																									
Cleveland, Ohio	750	678	184	340	260																								
Dallas, Tex.	825	1864	1418	968	975	1234																							
Denver, Colo.	1526	2044	1550	1026	1252	1366	835																						
Detroit, Mich.	748	746	252	272	258	164	1200	1298																					
El Paso, Tex.	1471	2414	1920	1396	1561	1736	646	730	1668																				
Houston, Tex.	856	1933	1554	1205	1110	1370	264	1099	1368	827																			
Indianapolis, Ind.	585	962	468	184	109	283	951	1154	303	1500	1107																		
Jacksonville, Fla.	350	1210	1190	1083	840	1100	1096	1811	1098	1764	975	935																	
Kansas City, Mo.	890	1469	975	451	616	791	517	636	723	945	781	518	1175																
Los Angeles, Calif.	2285	3244	2750	2227	2370	2555	1460	1353	2499	814	1641	2272	2578	1776															
Memphis, Tenn.	420	1382	938	527	494	754	481	1120	752	1128	616	491	691	484	1942														
Miami, Fla.	716	1576	1556	1449	1206	1466	1462	2177	1464	2130	1341	1301	366	1541	2944	1057													
Minneapolis–St. Paul	806	1414	920	396	677	736	997	886	668	1425	1261	580	1479	480	2157	879	1845												
New Orleans, La.	493	1569	1280	921	836	1096	506	1341	1094	1152	363	858	612	873	1966	394	978	1273											
New York, N.Y.	862	229	396	908	755	571	1635	1934	648	2310	1703	811	981	1329	3082	1153	1347	1304	1355										
Oklahoma City, Okla.	907	1743	1249	794	880	1065	236	739	1031	718	500	782	1178	343	1490	487	1544	824	742	1592									
Omaha, Nebr.	1025	1506	1012	488	752	828	712	538	760	1140	976	654	1330	195	1809	679	1696	348	1068	1396	538								
Pittsburgh, Pa.	806	668	260	468	316	131	1291	1494	296	1834	1426	371	1052	889	2157	810	1418	865	1152	439	917	1283							
Portland, Oreg.	2798	3217	2723	2199	2470	2539	2227	1372	2505	2002	2491	2427	3184	1968	1188	2496	3514	1803	2732	3107	2131	1773	2668						
Salt Lake City, Utah	2051	2532	2038	1514	1778	1854	1343	570	1786	1238	1607	1680	2344	1206	783	1653	2710	1374	1848	2422	1247	1026	1982	884					
San Francisco, Calif.	2718	3281	2787	2263	2527	2603	1930	1374	2535	1284	2111	2429	2989	1970	470	2298	3355	2123	2436	3171	1811	1775	2731	718	821				
Seattle, Wash.	2824	3159	2665	2141	2422	2481	2394	1554	2413	2184	2656	2325	3129	1954	1370	2438	3495	1745	2900	3049	2293	1799	2610	182	1066	900			
St. Louis, Mo.	612	1202	708	284	338	523	711	914	489	1223	917	240	873	278	1830	305	1205	574	699	1048	542	414	611	2187	1440	2189	2213		
Tucson, Ariz.	1783	2726	2232	1708	1873	2048	958	1042	1980	312	1139	1775	2076	1257	502	1440	2442	1737	1464	2586	1030	1452	2146	1690	1285	972	1872	1572	
Washington, D.C.	638	454	434	764	544	427	1410	1790	592	2056	1478	653	756	1160	2906	929	1122	1161	1115	225	1424	1252	296	3025	2278	3028	2906	882	2368

583

AUTOMOBILE MILEAGE

Distances from the "Transcontinental Mileage Chart."
Data used by permission from The H. M. Goushá Company
San Jose and Chicago.

From: \ To:	Atlanta, Ga.	Boston, Mass.	Buffalo, N.Y.	Chicago, Ill.	Cincinnati, Ohio	Cleveland, Ohio	Dallas, Tex.	Denver, Colo.	Detroit, Mich.	El Paso, Tex.	Houston, Tex.	Indianapolis, Ind.	Jacksonville, Fla.	Kansas City, Mo.	Los Angeles, Calif.	Memphis, Tenn.	Miami, Fla.	Minneapolis, Minn.	Montreal, Canada	New Orleans, La.	New York, N.Y.	Omaha, Nebr.	Pittsburgh, Pa.	Portland, Oreg.	Salt Lake City, Utah	San Francisco, Calif.	Seattle, Wash.	St. Louis, Mo.	Tulsa, Okla.
Atlanta, Ga.																													
Boston, Mass.	1129																												
Buffalo, N.Y.	907	454																											
Chicago, Ill.	724	979	525																										
Cincinnati, Ohio	481	879	430	301																									
Cleveland, Ohio	718	643	189	349	241																								
Dallas, Tex.	826	1868	1414	976	1007	1225																							
Denver, Colo.	1464	2008	1554	1043	1245	1373	805																						
Detroit, Mich.	733	706	252	273	252	166	1194	1302																					
El Paso, Tex.	1471	2428	1974	1519	1590	1785	645	679	1754																				
Houston, Tex.	875	1961	1545	1113	1115	1356	244	1049	1326	762																			
Indianapolis, Ind.	557	948	494	191	110	305	920	1064	273	1480	1052																		
Jacksonville, Fla.	325	1228	1142	1049	806	1028	1101	1789	1058	1722	974	882																	
Kansas City, Mo.	823	1442	988	504	604	799	510	641	752	1015	754	494	1148																
Los Angeles, Calif.	2288	3130	2676	2189	2292	2487	1462	1189	2448	817	1579	2182	2539	1631															
Memphis, Tenn.	419	1389	952	562	492	763	485	1109	751	1130	593	453	672	468	1877														
Miami, Fla.	662	1527	1479	1386	1143	1365	1447	2126	1395	2068	1306	1219	346	1485	2885	1018													
Minneapolis, Minn.	1124	1399	945	420	721	769	988	855	693	1483	1232	611	1449	478	2033	864	1786												
Montreal, Canada	1296	338	389	854	819	578	1775	1883	581	2335	1907	855	1395	1333	3029	1332	1732	1194											
New Orleans, La.	532	1625	1321	977	846	1132	509	1314	1143	1130	389	845	603	887	1947	415	904	1279	1710										
New York, N.Y.	910	219	380	841	660	502	1649	1852	632	2209	1742	729	1009	1223	2911	1170	1346	1261	391	1406									
Omaha, Nebr.	1024	1451	997	486	702	816	693	557	745	1104	937	592	1349	212	1703	680	1686	379	1326	1099	1295								
Pittsburgh, Pa.	727	595	218	465	293	131	1282	1476	294	1842	1396	362	924	856	2544	803	1261	885	607	1172	376	919							
Portland, Oreg.	2776	3229	2775	2250	2495	2599	2145	1365	2523	1745	2368	2385	3101	1953	992	2421	3438	1830	2914	2654	3088	1793	2712						
Salt Lake City, Utah	1959	2431	1977	1466	1682	1796	1285	515	1725	885	1508	1572	2284	1136	744	1600	2621	1310	2306	1794	2275	980	1899	860					
San Francisco, Calif.	2607	3198	2744	2233	2449	2563	1791	1288	2492	1222	1984	2339	2892	1903	405	2188	3238	2077	3073	2300	3042	1747	2666	700	767				
Seattle, Wash.	2807	3163	2709	2184	2485	2533	2222	1442	2457	1822	2445	2375	3132	1984	1183	2452	3469	1764	2848	2731	3025	1824	2649	188	937	888			
St. Louis, Mo.	569	1188	734	295	350	545	665	895	514	1240	817	238	904	254	1942	309	1281	555	1095	724	969	455	602	2207	1390	2157	2238		
Tulsa, Okla.	853	1627	1173	735	789	984	280	736	953	801	529	679	1172	264	1473	434	1514	747	1534	762	1408	408	1041	2085	1225	1814	2162	427	
Washington, D.C.	669	481	379	696	503	362	1414	1707	525	2052	1501	572	764	1066	2754	929	1110	1116	627	1165	241	1150	231	2943	2130	2897	2880	812	1251

AIRWAY MILEAGE

(In statute miles)

Distances compiled from the tables in "Air-Line Distances Between Cities in the United States," issued by the U.S. Department of Commerce, Coast and Geodetic Survey, Washington, D.C. Data used by permission.

Distances of cities outside the United States:

Anchorage, Alaska, to Seattle...	1,438 miles
Fairbanks, Alaska, to Seattle....	1,521
Honolulu to San Francisco......	2,397
Honolulu to Seattle............	2,680
Mexico City to Brownsville.....	457
Mexico City to Los Angeles.....	1,546
Montreal to Boston.............	251
Montreal to Toronto............	314
San Juan, P.R., to Miami.......	1,032
Vancouver, B.C., to Seattle	121

For airline distances between principal cities of world, see current World Almanac.

From:	Atlanta, Ga.	Billings, Mont.	Boston, Mass.	Buffalo, N.Y.	Chicago, Ill.	Cincinnati, Ohio	Cleveland, Ohio	Dallas, Tex.	Denver, Colo.	Detroit, Mich.	El Paso, Tex.	Jacksonville, Fla.	Kansas City, Mo.	Los Angeles, Calif.	Memphis, Tenn.	Miami, Fla.	Minneapolis, Minn.	Nashville, Tenn.	New Orleans, La.	New York, N.Y.	Omaha, Nebr.	Pittsburgh, Pa.	Portland, Oreg.	Salt Lake City, Utah	San Antonio, Tex.	San Francisco, Calif.	Seattle, Wash.	St. Louis, Mo.	Tulsa, Okla.
Atlanta, Ga.																													
Billings, Mont.	1519																												
Boston, Mass.	937	1861																											
Buffalo, N.Y.	697	1473	400																										
Chicago, Ill.	587	1073	851	454																									
Cincinnati, Ohio	369	1304	740	393	252																								
Cleveland, Ohio	554	1369	551	173	308	222																							
Dallas, Tex.	721	1092	1551	1198	803	814	1025																						
Denver, Colo.	1212	453	1769	1370	920	1227	1094	663																					
Detroit, Mich.	596	1283	613	216	238	235	90	999	1156																				
El Paso, Tex.	1291	973	2072	1692	1252	1335	1525	572	557	1479																			
Jacksonville, Fla.	285	1796	1017	879	863	626	770	908	1467	831	1473																		
Kansas City, Mo.	676	846	1251	861	414	541	700	451	558	645	839	950																	
Los Angeles, Calif.	1936	959	2596	2198	1745	1897	2049	1240	831	1983	701	2147	1356																
Memphis, Tenn.	337	1213	1137	803	482	410	630	420	879	623	976	590	369	1603															
Miami, Fla.	604	2085	1255	1181	1188	952	1087	1111	1726	1152	1643	326	1241	2339	872														
Minneapolis, Minn.	907	742	1123	731	355	605	630	862	700	543	1157	1191	413	1524	699	1511													
Nashville, Tenn.	214	1309	943	627	397	238	459	617	1023	470	1169	499	473	1780	197	815	697												
New Orleans, La.	424	1479	1359	1086	833	706	924	443	1082	939	983	838	680	1673	358	669	987	469											
New York, N.Y.	748	1760	188	292	713	570	405	1374	1631	482	1905	838	1097	2451	957	1092	1018	761	1171										
Omaha, Nebr.	817	703	1282	883	432	622	739	586	488	669	878	1098	166	1315	529	1397	290	607	847	1144									
Pittsburgh, Pa.	521	1479	483	178	410	257	115	1070	1320	205	1590	703	781	2136	660	1010	743	472	919	317	836								
Portland, Oreg.	2172	686	2540	2156	1758	1985	2055	1633	982	1969	1286	2439	1497	825	1849	2708	1427	1969	2063	2445	1371	2165							
Salt Lake City, Utah	1583	387	2099	1699	1260	1453	1568	999	371	1492	689	1837	925	579	1250	2089	987	1393	1434	1972	833	1668	636						
San Antonio, Tex.	882	1252	1766	1430	1051	1039	1256	252	802	1238	503	1011	702	1204	631	1148	1110	823	507	1584	828	1291	1720	1087					
San Francisco, Calif.	2139	904	2699	2300	1858	2043	2166	1483	949	2091	995	2374	1506	347	1802	2594	1584	1963	1926	2571	1429	2264	534	600	1490				
Seattle, Wash.	2182	668	2493	2117	1737	1972	2026	1681	1021	1938	1376	2455	1506	959	1867	2734	1395	1975	2101	2408	1369	2138	145	701	1787	678			
St. Louis, Mo.	467	1057	1038	662	262	309	492	547	796	455	1034	751	238	1589	240	1061	466	254	598	875	354	559	1723	1162	792	1744	1724		
Tulsa, Okla.	678	930	1398	1023	598	661	853	236	550	813	674	921	216	1231	352	1176	626	569	548	1231	515	833	1668	917	486	1461	1560	361	
Washington, D.C.	543	1669	393	292	597	404	306	1185	1494	396	1728	647	945	2300	765	923	934	569	966	205	1014	192	1720	1087	1388	2442	2329	712	1058

Time

CLOCK TIME

Writing Clock Time. A colon is used in ordinary work to separate hours and minutes, and minutes and seconds. But a period (or an open space) is sometimes employed for this purpose in tabulations, as timetables, and in statistical work. (Timetables run figures together and use just one letter, without periods, as 730A, 925P, 8.15a, 6.25p .)

> 12:08 p.m. OR: 12.08 p.m. ...the quake began at 2:47:03 a.m., PST.
> ...ran the mile in 3:59.4 (3 minutes 59⅖ seconds) Time: 1:53⅕

Write "a.m." and "p.m." in small letters, with a period after each letter. In telegraphic usage they are written A and P, without periods. In tabulations the periods are omitted.

Use "a.m." and "p.m." with figures, not with words, as

> at 10 a.m. NOT: at *ten a.m.*

Never use "a.m." for "morning," nor "p.m." for "afternoon," in sentences unless figures are used before the abbreviations.

> NOT: ...in our phone conversation of this *a.m.* (USE: morning)
> NOT: They work from nine *a.m.* to five *p.m.* (USE: from nine to **five**
>   OR: from 9 a.m. to 5 p.m.)
> NOT: ...arrives tomorrow *p.m.* at 3. (USE: afternoon OR: at 3 p.m.)

Caution: Do not use "a.m." and "morning" together, nor "p.m." and "afternoon" or "evening"; one is simply a repetition of the other.

> NOT: ...this afternoon at four *p.m.* (OMIT: p.m.)
> NOT: ...at 8 *a.m.* on the morning of April 26. (USE: 8 o'clock)
> NOT: ...broadcast at 8:30 *p.m.* each evening. (OMIT: p.m.)

"O'clock" is preferably not used with "a.m." or "p.m.," because of the rather ungainly construction.

> NOT: at 3 o'clock p.m.
> BUT: at 3 p.m. OR: at 3 o'clock in the afternoon

Even Hours. It is unnecessary to carry the ciphers after even hours, unless it is done for a specific purpose, as in tabulations.

> at 11 a.m. RATHER THAN: at 11:00 a.m.
> at 3 in the afternoon at 3:00 in the...

Figures or Words. Figures should be used if the time of day is inserted for the purpose of ready calculation. Otherwise words or figures may be used, according to the formality of the text.

Manners of writing time are:

586

Figures:

at 4:30 p.m.

at 4:30 in the afternoon

at 4 in the afternoon

at 10 a.m. and 6 p.m.

on the 8-o'clock train

at 4:30 o'clock

this afternoon at 4:30

in the morning at 10

at 10 o'clock in the morning
and 6 in the evening

on the 8:30 train

Words:

at four o'clock

at four-thirty

a quarter to three (or "of" or "past")

on the four-o'clock train

at four in the afternoon

at half past four

three-quarters of an hour

on the four-thirty train

Noon and Midnight. To designate exact noon or exact midnight, write out the words, or use the abbreviations "n." for noon, and "mid." for midnight. Noon is sometimes designated by "m." (L. meridies), but this abbreviation is not recommended because it may be confused with midnight. In airline and railroad timetables, noon is "n".

WRITE: $\begin{cases} \text{at 12 noon or} \\ \text{at 12 n.} \\ \text{at 12 midnight or} \\ \text{at 12 mid. or mdnt.} \end{cases}$ RATHER THAN: $\begin{cases} \text{at 12 m. (for noon)} \\ \text{at 12 p.m. or 0:00 a.m.} \\ \text{(for midnight)} \end{cases}$

European Clock Time. Many foreign countries have the 24-hour system of telling time, and clocks at airports and in railroad and telegraph stations are arranged accordingly. The following tabulation will show the difference between the Continental system and the American.

AMERICAN SYSTEM (12 HOURS)	CONTINENTAL SYSTEM (24 HOURS)
12 midnight	0 hours 0 minutes
1 a.m.	1 o'clock
2	2
3	3
4	4
5	5
6	6
7	7
8	8
9	9
10	10
11	11
12 noon	12
1 p.m.	13
2	14
3	15
4	16
5	17
6	18
7	19
8	20
9	21
10	22
11	23
11:59 p.m.	23^{59}
12 midnight	24 or 0^{00}
12:15 a.m.	0^{15}

ARMED FORCES TIME

The Army, Navy, and Air Force use the 24-hour clock system in official communications, and express time in **four figures always**—from midnight to midnight.

THUS:	12 midnight	IS	**2400**
	12:01 a.m.		0001
	12:30 a.m.		0030
	1:00 a.m.		0100
	6:35 a.m.		0635
	12:00 noon		1200
	12:40 p.m.		**1240**
	1:30 p.m.		**1330**
	5:15 p.m.		**1715**
	11:50 p.m.		**2350**
	12 midnight		**2400**

Seconds may be added in this manner:

2224:30 (meaning 10:24:30 p.m.)

Date. The **day of the current month** is indicated by **two figures** placed before the four showing the time. Thus 3:35 p.m. on the 5th of the current month is expressed as 051535 (seen in newspapers as 05/1535).

Greenwich Mean Time. GMT is used on messages from one time zone to another, and is expressed by Z or the code word "Zulu" (for zero meridian); thus 0915Z is 9:15 a.m. GMT.

Continental timetables are marked accordingly. For instance, a train departing at 14^{45} would be leaving at 2:45 p.m. by a 12-hour watch.

587

Periods of Time. For ready calculation of periods of time, figures instead of words are commonly used. Commas are not necessary between the different parts of one period of time, which is considered a single unit.

5 hours 8 minutes 15 seconds   5 years 10 months 20 days

Ages. (For ages of persons, etc., see p. 282.)

STANDARD TIME

Standard time in the United States is divided into four zones, with one hour's time difference between each zone and the next.

	Comparison With Others *Later (L) or earlier (E) than			
	EST	CST	MST	PST
Eastern standard time (E.S.T.) is............		1 hr. L	2 hr. L	3 hr. L
Central standard time (C.S.T.) is............	1 hr. E		1 hr. L	2 hr. L
Mountain standard time (M.S.T.) is.........	2 hr. E	1 hr. E		1 hr. L
Pacific standard time (P.S.T.) is.............	3 hr. E	2 hr. E	1 hr. E	

* "Later" as used in the tables in this section means later in the day, or having a time that is so many hours faster than the time in question. "Earlier" means earlier in the day, or having a time that is so many hours slower than the time in question.

Daylight [Saving] Time (DT, DST) is observed nationally from the last Sunday in April (when clocks "spring forward" one hour) to the last Sunday in October (when clocks "fall back" one hour). (Often called **"fast time"**; in Europe, **"summer time."**)

World Date Line. The date line in the Pacific Ocean between Hawaii and the Orient marks the ending of one day and the beginning of the next. (The date line approximates the 180° meridian.)

In calculating standard time around the world, consider the path of the sun. When the sun rises on Japan and China a new day is begun. The sun carries that day across Siberia, Russia, Germany, France, England, the Atlantic Ocean, the United States, and on to the Hawaiian Islands. When it sets on the Hawaiian Islands that day is finished, and as it rises again on Japan, China, the Philippines, and Australia, the next day is begun, while the United States is still in the darkness of the night before. Thus it is that a broadcast from the Orient on Friday morning can be received in the United States on Thursday evening.

Greenwich Mean Time (GMT) (also called Greenwich Civil Time or Universal Time). Greenwich time is simply the correct hour time by which other times are set. The prime or zero (Z) meridian passing through Greenwich, England, was adopted as a standard; and other times are reckoned as so many hours earlier or later (slower or faster) than Greenwich. (Am. pron. grĕn′ich) (The "mean" comes from "mean solar [sun] time," which equalizes day-lengths through an average sun-path.)

STANDARD TIME IN THE UNITED STATES

NOTE: Some states on the time border lines have certain counties or cities that use, for economic reasons, the adjoining time zones. Such divergences have been here indicated by naming the principal cities using different times.

———

STATE	STANDARD TIME USED
Alabama.............	Central
Alaska..............	(See p. 590)
Arizona.............	Mountain
Arkansas...........	Central
California...........	Pacific
Colorado............	Mountain
Connecticut.........	Eastern
Delaware...........	Eastern
District of Columbia...	Eastern
Florida.............	Eastern—except part west of Apalachicola River, which uses Central; but Apalachicola, Fla., uses Eastern
Georgia.............	Eastern
Hawaii..............	(See p. 590)
Idaho..............	Mountain—below the Salmon River / Pacific—above the Salmon River
Illinois.............	Central
Indiana.............	Eastern—except in NW and SW corners / Gary and Evansville use Central
Iowa................	Central
Kansas.............	Central—in most of state / Mountain—near Colorado, as in Goodland
Kentucky...........	Central—in western half of state / Eastern—in eastern half of state / Louisville and Lexington use Eastern
Louisiana...........	Central
Maine..............	Eastern
Maryland...........	Eastern
Massachusetts.......	Eastern
Michigan...........	Eastern (Central near Wisconsin border)
Minnesota..........	Central
Mississippi.........	Central
Missouri............	Central
Montana............	Mountain
Nebraska...........	Central—in eastern part / Mountain—in western part / Ainsworth and North Platte use Central
Nevada.............	Pacific
New Hampshire......	Eastern
New Jersey..........	Eastern
New Mexico.........	Mountain
New York...........	Eastern
North Carolina......	Eastern
North Dakota.......	Central—except in SW quarter / Mandan uses Mountain
Ohio................	Eastern
Oklahoma...........	Central
Oregon.............	Pacific (Jordan Valley uses Mountain)
Pennsylvania........	Eastern
Rhode Island........	Eastern
South Carolina......	Eastern
South Dakota.......	Central—in eastern half of state / Mountain—in western half of state / Pierre uses Central time
Tennessee..........	Central—in most of state / Eastern—in eastern tip / Chattanooga and Knoxville use Eastern
Texas..............	Central (El Paso uses Mountain)
Utah...............	Mountain
Vermont............	Eastern
Virginia............	Eastern
Washington.........	Pacific
West Virginia.......	Eastern
Wisconsin..........	Central
Wyoming...........	Mountain

◇◇◇◇◇◇◇◇

STANDARD TIME AROUND THE WORLD

Compiled from the U.S. Naval Oceanographic Office's
"Standard Time Chart of the World," No. 5192

Country	*Hours L or E than EST	Country	*Hours L or E than EST
Aden (port in Southern Yemen)	8 L	Congo } Brazzaville and Kinshasa	6 L
Afghanistan	9½L†	Zaire } Katanga Province: Lubumbashi	7 L
Alaska { Juneau, Ketchikan, Sitka	3 E	Corsica	6 L
Alaska { Central: Anchorage, Fairbanks	5 E	Costa Rica	1 E
Alaska { West coast: Nome; Aleutian Is.	6 E	Crete	7 L
Albania	6 L	Cuba	1 L
Algeria	5 L	Curaçao	1 L
Angola (formerly Portuguese W. Africa)	6 L	Cyprus	7 L
Arabia, Saudi	8 L†	Czechoslovakia	6 L
Argentina	1 L	Dahomey (People's Rep. of Benin)	6 L
Australia { N.S.W.: Canberra, Sydney	15 L	Denmark	6 L
Australia { Queensland: Brisbane	15 L	Dominican Republic	same‡
Australia { Victoria: Melbourne	15 L	Ecuador	same‡
Australia { Northern Territory: Darwin	14½L	Egypt (United Arab Republic)	7 L
Australia { South Australia: Adelaide	14½L	El Salvador	1 E
Australia { Western Australia: Perth	13 L	England	5 L
Austria	6 L	Ethiopia (old Abyssinia; Eritrea)	8 L
Azores	4 L	Falkland Islands	1 L
Bahamas	same‡	Faroe Islands (Faeroes)	5 L
Bangladesh	11 L	Fernando Po (in Equatorial Guinea)	6 L
Barbados	1 L	Fiji Islands	17 L
Belgium	6 L	Finland	7 L
Bermuda	1 L	Formosa (now Taiwan)	13 L
Bolivia	1 L	France	6 L
Borneo (in Malaysia and Indonesia)	13 L	Gabon (formerly in Fr. Eq. Africa)	6 L
Botswana (formerly Bechuanaland)	7 L	Gambia	5 L
Brazil { East coast: Rio de Janeiro, São Paulo, Recife	2 L	Germany	6 L
Brazil { Western regions: Manáos	1 L	Ghana (formerly Gold Coast, et al)	5 L
British Honduras (now Belize)	1 E	Gibraltar	6 L
Brunei	13 L	Gilbert (and Ellice [Tuvalu]) Islands	17 L
Bulgaria	7 L	Great Britain	5 L
Burma	11½L	Greece	7 L
Burundi	7 L	Greenland { Thule, air base	1 L
Cambodia (now Khmer Republic)	12 L	Greenland { Lower western coast	2 L
Cameroon	6 L	Guadeloupe	1 L
Canada { Alberta: Edmonton, Calgary	2 E	Guam	15 L
Canada { British Columbia: Vancouver	3 E	Guatemala	1 E
Canada { Cape Breton; Prince Edward Is.	1 L	Guiana (Fr. [see Guyana and Surinam])	1 L
Canada { Manitoba: Winnipeg	1 E	Guinea	5 L
Canada { New Brunswick: St. John	1 L	Guyana (formerly British Guiana)	1¼L†
Canada { Newfoundland (Labrador 1 L)	1½L	Haiti	same‡
Canada { Nova Scotia: Halifax	1 L	Hawaii	5 E
Canada { Ontario { Ottawa, Toronto	same‡	Holland (The Netherlands)	6 L
Canada { Ontario { W of 90° W	1 E	Honduras	1 E
Canada { Quebec: Montreal, Quebec	same‡	Hong Kong (including Kowloon)	13 L
Canada { Saskatchewan: Regina	1 E	Hungary	6 L
Canada { St. Pierre & Miquelon (Fr.)	2 L	Iceland	5 L
Canada { Yukon: Whitehorse	3 E	India	10½L
Canal Zone	same‡	Indonesia (See also each island)	12 L
Canary Islands	5 L	Iran (old Persia)	8½L
Cape Verde Islands	3 L	Iraq (old Mesopotamia)	8 L
Caroline Islands (those near Truk)	16 L	Ireland (Eire)	5 L
Celebes (in Indonesia)	13 L	Israel	7 L
Central African Republic	6 L	Italy	6 L
Ceylon (now Sri Lanka)	10½L	Ivory Coast	5 L
Chad (formerly in Fr. Eq. Africa)	6 L	Jamaica	same‡
Chile	1 L	Japan	14 L
China: Peking, Shanghai, Chungking	13 L	Java (in Indonesia: [D]Jakarta)	12 L
Colombia	same‡	Jordan	7 L
		Kenya	8 L

STANDARD TIME AROUND THE WORLD—contd.

Country	*Hours L or E than EST	Country	*Hours L or E than EST
Korea	14 L	Rwanda	7 L
Kuwait (on Persian Gulf)	8 L	Salvador, El	1 E
Laos (formerly in Indochina)	12 L	Samoa (islands: Pago Pago)	6 E
Lebanon	7 L	Sarawak (in Malaysia)	13 L
Liberia: Monrovia	4¼L†	Sardinia	6 L
Libya (incl. Tripolitania–Cyrenaica)	7 L	Saudi Arabia (keeps "sun time")	8 L†
Luxembourg	6 L	Scotland	5 L
Madeira Islands	5 L	Senegal	5 L
Malagasy Republic (Madagascar)	8 L	Seychelles	9 L
Malawi (formerly Nyasaland)	7 L	Siberia (See U.S.S.R.)	
Malaysia (Malay States [see Sarawak])	12½L	Sicily	6 L
Maldive Islands	10 L	Sierra Leone	5 L
Mali (formerly French Soudan)	5 L	Singapore	12½L
Malta	6 L	Solomon Islands	16 L
Manchuria (now in China)	13 L	Somalia (formerly Br.–It. Somaliland)	8 L
Marianas, Commonwealth of the	15 L	South Africa (Republic of), and South-West Africa (now Namibia)	7 L
Martinique	1 L		
Mauritania, Islamic Republic of	5 L	Spain (including Balearic Islands)	6 L
Mauritius	9 L	Spanish Sahara	5 L
Mexico {Major part: Mexico, D.F.	1 E	Sudan	7 L
Mexico {Along Gulf of California	2 E	Sumatra (in Indonesia)	12 L
Mexico {Baja California (N of 28° N)	3 E	Surinam (formerly Dutch Guiana)	1½L
Mexico {Baja California (S of 28° N)	2 E	Sweden	6 L
Midway Islands	6 E	Switzerland	6 L
Monaco: Monte Carlo	6 L	Syria	7 L
Mongolia	13 L†	Tahiti	5 E
Morocco	5 L	Taiwan (formerly Formosa)	13 L
Mozambique (formerly Port. E. Afr.)	7 L	Tangier (now in Morocco)	5 L
Nepal	10½L	Tanzania (Tanganyika–Zanzibar)	8 L
Netherlands, The (Holland)	6 L	Tasmania: Hobart	15 L
New Caledonia Island	16 L	Thailand (formerly Siam)	12 L
Newfoundland, Canada: Gander	1½L	Timor (Indonesian and Portuguese)	13 L
New Guinea {Australian: Papua	15 L	Togo	5 L
New Guinea {Indonesian: West Irian	14 L	Tonga (Friendly Islands)	18 L
New Hebrides	16 L	Trinidad and Tobago	1 L
New Zealand	17 L	Tunisia	6 L
Nicaragua	1 E	Turkey	7 L
Niger (in West Africa)	6 L	Uganda	8 L
Nigeria	6 L	Upper Volta (in West Africa)	5 L
Norway	6 L	Uruguay	2 L
Okinawa (in Ryukyu Islands)	14 L	U.S.S.R. (Union of Soviet Socialist Republics) {Russia: Moscow, Leningrad	8 L
Pakistan {West Pakistan: Karachi	10 L	{White Russia: Minsk	8 L
Pakistan {East Pakistan: Dacca	11 L	{Ukraine: Kiev. Moldavia	8 L
Palestine (now in Israel and Jordan)	7 L	{Estonia; Latvia; Lithuania	8 L
Panama, and Canal Zone	same‡	{Georgia: Tiflis. Armenia	9 L
Papua	15 L	{Azerbaijan: Baku	9 L
Paraguay	1 L	{S.S.R., Asia: Vladivostok	15 L
Peru	same‡	(There are 11 time zones across Russia and Siberia.)	
Philippines	13 L		
Poland	6 L	Vatican City State	6 L
Portugal	6 L	Venezuela	1 L
Puerto Rico, Commonwealth of	1 L	Vietnam (formerly in Indochina)	13 L
Réunion Island	9 L	Virgin Islands	1 L
Rhodes, Isle of	7 L	Wake Island	17 L
Rhodesia (now Zimbabwe)	7 L	West Irian (West New Guinea)	14 L
Río de Oro (in Spanish Sahara)	5 L	Yemen	8 L†
Río Muni (in Equatorial Guinea)	6 L	Yugoslavia	6 L
Rumania	7 L	Zambia (formerly Northern Rhodesia)	7 L
Russia (See U.S.S.R.)		Zanzibar (now in Tanzania)	8 L

* Hours later (faster) or earlier (slower) than Eastern standard time.
For CST, MST, or PST, add the time difference between that zone and EST, to all "L" times; subtract the time difference from all "E" times.
† Not on standard time, but an approximate time is indicated.
‡ Same as Eastern standard time.

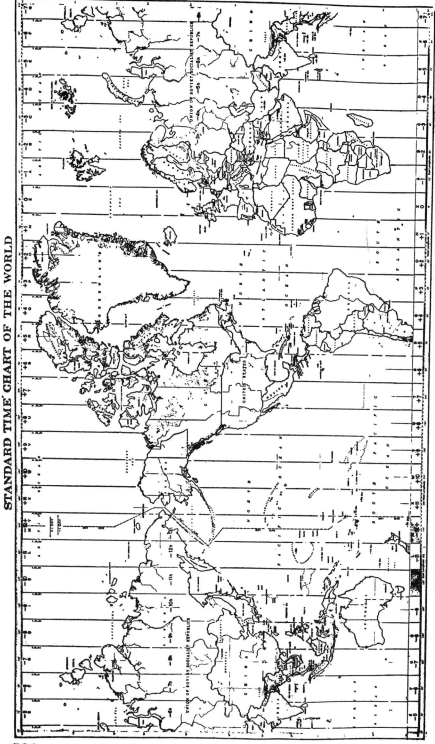

STANDARD TIME CHART OF THE WORLD

Partial reproduction of U. S. Naval Oceanographic Office's large chart, No. 5192. Reprinted by permission.

0 indicates the zero (Z) meridian of Greenwich. − indicates hours later (faster) than Greenwich. + indicates hours earlier (slower) than Greenwich.
The date line in the Pacific Ocean (along the 180° meridian) indicates where one day ends and a new one begins.

DIVISIONS OF TIME

Minute 60 seconds	ABBREVIATIONS:	sec., s., or "
Hour 60 minutes		min., m., or '
Day 24 hours		hr., h. (pl. hrs.)
Week 7 days		da., d. (pl. same)
Fortnight "14 nights"; 2 weeks		wk., w. (pl. wks.)
Month 30 days (for general calculations)		mo., m. (pl. mos.)

(For exact calculations, the exact number of days in the given months must be figured.)

Months with 30 days—April, June, September, November.

Months with 31 days—All the rest, except February, which has 28, and in leap year, 29. The old rhyme (slightly modernized) is still an effective aid in remembering the number of days in each month:

> Thirty days hath September,
> April, June, and November;
> All the rest have thirty-one,
> Save February, which alone
> Hath but twenty-eight in time,
> Till leap year gives it twenty-nine.

Lunar month period of a complete revolution of the moon, approximately 28 days.
Lunar day a day reckoned by the moon
Solar month average time taken by the sun to pass through a sign of the zodiac.
Solar day a day reckoned by the sun
Sidereal month average time of the moon's revolution from any star back to the same star, approximately 27⅓ days
Sidereal day a day reckoned by a star

Year 365 days (360 days for general calculations); 52 weeks; 12 months. (yr. or y.)
 Calendar year the civil or legal year—from January 1 to December 31
 Fiscal year a financial year—an accounting period of 12 months. The end of a fiscal year implies a closing of the books. (Financial statements may be issued without a closing of the books.) The Government fiscal year ends on September 30; but a business fiscal year may end on the last day of any month.

> Under the Income Tax Law, a fiscal year may be "established" as ending on the last day of any month except December (for computation of rates and dates for tax payment). Fiscal years ending on December 31 are already established under the Law—as calendar years.

 Leap year 366 days ... in years divisible by 4, as 1976 and 1980. (Even-century years must be divisible by 400.) Dates in ordinary years move forward **one** day each year. But in leap years they "leap" forward **two** days following February.

Equinox when the sun crosses the equator, and day and night are equal length everywhere. **Vernal equinox**—about March 21, when spring begins. **Autumnal equinox**—about September 22, when autumn begins. (pron. ē'kwĭ-nŏks)
Solstice when the sun is farthest from the equator. About June 21, the **summer solstice** gives the Northern Hemisphere its longest day of the year, and summer begins; and about December 21, the **winter solstice** gives us the shortest day of the year, and winter begins. (pron. sŏl'stĭs)

Decade 10 years (pron. dĕk'ād)	**Fourscore** 80 years
Century 100 years	

 Twentieth Century—The years 1901 to 2000 are called the "Twentieth Century" because nineteen centuries have passed, and it is in fact the twentieth century that is elapsing. The first century covered the years 1 to 100; the second century, the years 101 to 200. Thus the year 114 was in the second century; and the years 19— are in the twentieth century, which will have elapsed when the numbers reach 2001.

Olympiad In ancient Greece, the 4 years between Olympic Games; but in modern times, the celebration of the Olympic Games (1956, 1960. 1964, 1968, etc.).

WORDS RELATING TO PERIODS OF TIME

diurnal	daily; of a day
semidiurnal	occurring twice a day; pertaining to half a day
semiweekly	occurring twice a week
biweekly*	occurring every 2 weeks
triweekly*	occurring every 3 weeks
thrice-weekly	occurring 3 times a week
semimonthly	occurring twice a month
bimonthly*	occurring every 2 months
trimonthly*	occurring every 3 months
thrice-monthly	occurring 3 times a month
semiannual	occurring every 6 months (equally spaced)
biannual	occurring twice a year (unequally spaced)
annual	yearly; pertaining to a period of 1 year
perennial	occurring year after year
biennium	a period of 2 years
biennial	pertaining to a period of 2 years
biyearly	occurring every 2 years
triennium	a period of 3 years
triennial	pertaining to a period of 3 years
quadrennium	a period of 4 years
quadrennial	pertaining to a period of 4 years
quinquennium	a period of 5 years
quinquennial	pertaining to a period of 5 years
sexennium	a period of 6 years
sexennial	pertaining to a period of 6 years
septennium	a period of 7 years
septennial	pertaining to a period of 7 years
octennial	pertaining to a period of 8 years
novennial	pertaining to a period of 9 years
decennium	a period of 10 years
decennial	pertaining to a period of 10 years
decennary	a 10th anniversary
undecennial	pertaining to a period of 11 years
undecennary	an 11th anniversary
duodecennial	pertaining to a period of 12 years
quindecennial	pertaining to a period of 15 years
vicennial	pertaining to a period of 20 years
tricennial	pertaining to a period of 30 years
semicentennial	pertaining to half a century or a period of 50 years
semicentenary	a 50th anniversary
septuagenarian	pertaining to the 70s, in age
octogenarian	pertaining to the 80s, in age
nonagenarian	pertaining to the 90s, in age
centenarian	pertaining to 100 years, in age
centennium	a period of 100 years; a century
centennial	pertaining to a period of 100 years
centenary	a 100th anniversary
sesquicentennial	pertaining to a period of 150 years
bicentennial	pertaining to a period of 200 years
bicentenary	a 200th anniversary
tricentennial	pertaining to a period of 300 years
tercentenary	a 300th anniversary
quadricentennial	pertaining to a period of 400 years
quincentennial	pertaining to a period of 500 years
quincentenary	a 500th anniversary
millennium	a period of 1000 years
millennial	pertaining to a period of 1000 years
millenary	a 1000th anniversary

The Millennium—the thousand years of Christ's kingdom on earth; also an imaginary period of perfection—a Utopia.

NOTE: A useful distinction in the above words is the application of the -ium endings to nouns denoting periods of time; the -ial endings to adjectives; and the -ary endings to anniversaries.

---

* "Biweekly" is used to mean either "twice a week" or "every two weeks." To avoid this ambiguity, use "semiweekly" for "twice a week," and "biweekly" for "every two weeks." "Triweekly" is similarly interchanged. To avoid confusion, use "thrice-weekly" for "three times a week," and "triweekly" for "every three weeks." The same remarks apply to "bimonthly" and "trimonthly."

Holidays

Nationally observed holidays are nine:

New Year's Day.......... January 1
Washington's Birthday.... February 22   (in 1971, 3rd Monday in February)
Memorial Day............ May 30*   (in 1971, last Monday in May)
Independence Day....... July 4
Labor Day.............. 1st Monday in September
Columbus Day.......... October 12   (in 1971, 2nd Monday in October)
Veterans Day........... November 11†   (in 1978, returned to Nov. 11)
Thanksgiving Day....... 4th Thursday in November
Christmas Day.......... December 25

* Memorial Day is observed on different days in the South.   (See table p. 596.)
† Formerly "Armistice Day."   Named "Veterans Day" in bill signed by President on June 1, 1954.

"National" is often used to describe holidays that are legalized in every state in the Union.   The "legalizing" of holidays by Congress pertains only to holidays for the District of Columbia and for Federal Government employees, who are thus authorized to observe the nine nationwide holidays (in some instances they observe also the holidays of the states in which employed).   Thanksgiving Day is proclaimed by the President each year, but it is legalized in each state.

State holidays are the individual holidays observed in each state.

Post office holidays, in all states, are the nine holidays listed above. (Postmasters have discretionary authority to reduce, but not suspend, postal service on state or local holidays.)

Bank holidays are the nine above, and the respective state holidays.

Stock exchange holidays follow the New York Stock Exchange holidays—seven of those named above (exceptions: Columbus Day and Veterans), Good Friday, and Election Day.   All closed on Saturdays.

When a holiday falls on Sunday, the following Monday is observed; **when on Saturday,** the previous Friday (but not by postal employees).

Calendar for 200 Years.   In the current American almanacs, and in telephone directories, may be found a reference calendar for 200 years, from which may be ascertained the day of the week on which any given date fell, or will fall, from approximately the year 1800 to 2000.

Rules for Display of the Flag.   The rules for display and use of the flag, as established by the Congress, and approved by the President, may be found in the current American almanacs listed on p. 607.

Or an illustrated booklet, **"Our Flag,"** may be purchased from the Superintendent of Documents, GPO, Washington, D.C. 20402 −80¢.

◇◇◇◇◇◇◇◇

HOLIDAYS

LEGAL HOLIDAYS IN THE UNITED STATES

Holiday	Date Observed	Range of Observance
New Year's Day	January 1	**Nationwide**
Battle of New Orleans	January 8	Louisiana
Robert E. Lee's Birthday	January 19	Ala., Ark., Fla., Ga., Ky., La., Miss.,
	(In Al, Ms, Va, 3rd Mon. Jan.)	N.C., S.C., Tex., Va.
Inauguration Day	January 20	District of Columbia, every four years
Franklin Roosevelt's Birthday	January 30	Kentucky
Lincoln's Birthday	February 12	General, except in Ala., Ark., D.C.,
	(In De, Il, Or, 1st Mon. Feb.	Fla., Ga., Hi., Id., La., Me., Mass.,
	In several states, 3rd Mon.	Minn., Miss., Nev., N.H., N.C., Oh.,
	with Washington's)	Ok., R.I., S.C., S.D., Tn., Tx., Va.
Admission Day	February 14	Arizona
Mardi Gras	Shrove Tuesday	Ala., Fla. (in some counties), La. (in some parishes)
Washington's Birthday (Feb. 22)	3rd Monday in February	**Nationwide**
Town Meeting Day	1st Tuesday in March	Vermont
Texas Independence Day	March 2	Texas
Andrew Jackson's Birthday	March 15	Tennessee (a memorial day)
Maryland Day	March 25	Maryland
Kuhio Day	March 26	Hawaii
Seward's Day (Mar. 30)	last Monday in March	Alaska
Good Friday	before Easter	Conn., Del., Fla., Hi., Ind., La., Md., N.J., N.D., Pa., Tenn.
Halifax Resolution Day	April 12	North Carolina
Thomas Jefferson's Birthday	April 13	Ala. (in Mo., Ok., & Va. a memorial day)
Patriots' Day (Apr. 19)	3rd Monday in April	Maine, Massachusetts
Battle of San Jacinto	April 21	Texas
Arbor Day	April 22	Nebraska
Oklahoma Day	April 22	Oklahoma (a memorial day)
Confederate Memorial Day	April 26	Fl, Ga (in Al, 4th Mon.; in Ms, last)
Fast Day	4th Monday in April	New Hampshire
Arbor Day	last Friday in April	Utah
Arbor Day	usually 1st Monday in May	Wyoming
R.I. Independence Day	May 4	Rhode Island
Harry Truman's Birthday	May 8	Missouri
Confederate Memorial Day	May 10	North Carolina, South Carolina
Mecklenburg Declaration Day	May 20	North Carolina
Memorial Day (May 30)	last Monday in May	**Nationwide**, except in Al., Miss., S.C.
(Decoration Day)		(A post office holiday in all states.)
Jefferson Davis's Birthday	June 3	Fla., Ga., Ky., La., S.C. (in Ala.,
Confederate Memorial Day	June 3	and Miss., 1st Mon. in June)
Kamehameha Day	June 11	Hawaii
Flag Day	June 14	Pennsylvania
West Virginia Day	June 20	West Virginia
Independence Day	July 4	**Nationwide**
Forrest's Birthday	July 13	Tennessee (a memorial day)
Pioneer Day	July 24	Utah
Colorado Day (Aug. 1)	1st Monday in August	Colorado
Victory Day (Aug. 14)	2nd Monday in August	Rhode Island
Bennington Battle Day	August 16	Vermont
Admission Day (Aug. 21)	3rd Friday in August	Hawaii
Lyndon Johnson's Birthday	August 27	Texas
Huey P. Long's Birthday	August 30	Louisiana
Labor Day	1st Monday in September	**Nationwide**
Admission Day	September 9	California
Defenders' Day	September 12	Maryland
Columbus Day (Oct. 12)	2nd Monday in October	In most states; a memorial day in some
Alaska Day (Oct. 18)	3rd Monday in October	**Alaska**
Nevada (Admission) Day	October 31	Nevada
All Saints' Day	November 1	Louisiana
General Election Day	1st Tues. after 1st Mon. in Nov. in even years	In most states
Veterans Day	November 11	**Nationwide**
Thanksgiving Day	4th Thursday in November	**Nationwide**
Thanksgiving holiday	Friday after Thanksgiving	Oklahoma
Christmas Day	December 25	**Nationwide**
Christmas holiday	December 26	South Carolina

MISCELLANEOUS DAYS

Arbor Day. Observed on different days in different states—usually by proclamation. It is a legal holiday now only in Nebraska, Utah, and Wyoming.

Armed Forces Day. Third Saturday in May. Army, Navy, and Air Force day.

Children's Day. The second Sunday in June.

Father's Day. The third Sunday in June

Flag Day. June 14—by proclamation. Not a legal holiday, but nationally observed.

Groundhog Day. February 2—a weather-forecasting day. The legend is that the groundhog, or woodchuck, comes out for the first time on this day after his winter's sleep. If he sees his shadow he is frightened into his retreat again for another six weeks—which portends bad weather. If the day is cloudy and he does not see his shadow, he stays out unafraid—which means that spring is at hand.

Halloween. The evening of October 31. The legend of Halloween, or "Allhallow-e'en," is that wicked spirits roamed the earth the night before All Saints' Day (Allhallows), November 1. To ward off these evil spirits, various antics were indulged in. Thus the evening has developed into a maskers' revel.

Leap year. Occurs every 4 years. (See Divisions of Time, p. 593.)

Mother's Day. The second Sunday in May. It is nationally observed.

Olympic Games. Held every 4 years, in years divisible by 4—1956, 1960, 1964, etc.

Presidential Election Day. The first Tuesday after the first Monday in November, every 4 years—in years that can be divided by 4, as 1956, 1960, 1964, 1968.

St. Patrick's Day. March 17; named in honor of St. Patrick, patron saint of Ireland.

United Nations Day. October 24—anniversary of founding of United Nations (1945).

Valentine's Day. February 14; named in honor of St. Valentine, a Christian martyr.

Victory Day. August 14—by proclamation. Anniversary of Japan's surrender, 1945.

CANADIAN HOLIDAYS

New Year's Day
Good Friday
Easter Monday
Victoria Day—1st Monday
  before May 25
Civic Holiday—usually 1st
  Monday in August

Dominion Day—July 1
Labour Day—1st Monday in September
Thanksgiving Day—2nd Monday in October
Remembrance Day—November 11
Christmas Day

Anniversary of the birth of the Sovereign (day in June fixed by proclamation) (The birthday of the present Sovereign, Elizabeth II, is April 21 [1926]; the birthday of Prince Charles is November 14 [1948].)

And any other day appointed by proclamation as a holiday.

Names of the Months in Six Languages

English	French	German	Spanish	Italian	Portuguese
January	janvier	Januar	enero	gennaio	janeiro
February	février	Februar	febrero	febbraio	fevereiro
March	mars	März	marzo	marzo	março
April	avril	April	abril	aprile	abril
May	mai	Mai	mayo	maggio	maio
June	juin	Juni	junio	giugno	junho
July	juillet	Juli	julio	luglio	julho
August	août	August	agosto	agosto	agôsto
September	septembre	September	se(p)tiembre	settembre	setembro
October	octobre	Oktober	octubre	ottobre	outubro
November	novembre	November	noviembre	novembre	novembro
December	décembre	Dezember	diciembre	dicembre	dezembro

Compiled from data in the Style Manual of the United States Government Printing Office.
Note that the names of the months are capitalized in English and German, but are not capitalized in French, Spanish, Italian, and Portuguese.

EASTER

Easter Sunday. The commemoration of the resurrection of Christ is fixed as the first Sunday following the Paschal Full Moon, which happens on or next after the 21st of March. The date was so determined in ancient times, it is said, because of the pilgrims' need of moonlight to travel yearly to the great Easter festivals.

Lent. A 40-day period of fasting, beginning on **Ash Wednesday,** which is 40 weekdays before Easter. Sundays are not counted in Lent, because Sunday is always a feast day.

Shrove Tuesday. The day before Ash Wednesday. The Mardi Gras (Fr., "Fat Tuesday") carnival on Shrove Tuesday marks the final festivities before Lent.

Good Friday. The Friday before Easter. Devotions are held on this day in memory of the crucifixion of Christ.

Palm Sunday. The Sunday before Easter, in commemoration of Christ's entry into Jerusalem, when palm branches were strewn in his path.

DATES ON WHICH ASH WEDNESDAY AND EASTER SUNDAY FALL

Year	Ash Wednesday	Easter Sunday	Year	Ash Wednesday	Easter Sunday
1979	February 28	April 15	1990	February 28	April 15
1980	February 20	April 6	1991	February 13	March 31
1981	March 4	April 19	1992	March 4	April 19
1982	February 24	April 11	1993	February 24	April 11
1983	February 16	April 3	1994	February 16	April 3
1984	March 7	April 22	1995	March 1	April 16
1985	February 20	April 7	1996	February 21	April 7
1986	February 12	March 30	1997	February 12	March 30
1987	March 4	April 19	1998	February 25	April 12
1988	February 17	April 3	1999	February 17	April 4
1989	February 8	March 26	2000	March 8	April 23

Excerpt from the World Almanac table which gives the dates of Ash Wednesday and Easter Sunday for 200 years—from 1901 to 2100. Reprinted by permission from The World Almanac.

JEWISH HOLIDAYS—on variable dates (all begin at sunset on the previous day):

Rosh Hashana[h] (Jewish New Year)—in September or October; opening the **Ten Days of Penitence,** closing with **Yom Kippur** (Day of Atonement). (pron. rōsh'hä-shä'nä, and yôm kĭ-pŏŏr')

Hanukkah (the Festival of Lights)—in December; celebrating the rededication and purification of the Temple of Jerusalem. A candle is lighted, on a **menorah,** for each night of the eight-day festival. (pron. hän'u-kä, and mĕ-nō'ra)

Purim (the Feast of Lots)—in March; celebrating deliverance of the Jews in Persia from a massacre—by the intervention of Queen Esther. (pron. pŏŏr'im)

Passover (the Feast of the Passover, or the Feast of Unleavened Bread)—in April; commemorating the escape from slavery (**Exodus**) of the Jews from Egypt. During the flight, they ate **unleavened bread,** now symbolized by **matzos.** (pron. mät'soz)

WEDDING ANNIVERSARIES—Traditional List

(Modern lists reflect new products. See also latest books on "Etiquette," and World Almanac.)

1st	paper	10th	tin	30th	pearl	50th	golden
2nd	cotton	12th	silk	35th	coral or	55th	emerald
3rd	leather	15th	crystal		jade	60th	diamond
4th	linen	20th	china	40th	ruby		or
5th	wooden	25th	silver	45th	sapphire	75th	diamond

BIRTHSTONES: January, garnet; February, amethyst; March, aquamarine (or bloodstone); April, diamond; May, emerald; June, pearl (or alexandrite); July, ruby; August, peridot (or sardonyx); September, sapphire; October, tourmaline (or opal); November, topaz; December, turquoise (or blue zircon).

"Precious stones" are the hardest gems: diamond, sapphire, ruby, and emerald. "Semiprecious stones" are less hard: aquamarine, topaz, tourmaline, amethyst, peridot, garnet, opal, and turquoise

States, Counties, and Cities

THE UNITED STATES

State and Resident (For nicknames, see current almanacs.)	Official Abbr.*	Name of State Legislature†	Capital	State Flower
Alabama -n	Ala.	Legislature	Montgomery	Camellia
Alaska -n	Alaska	Legislature	Juneau, till 1980	Forget-me-not
Arizona -n	Ariz.	Legislature	Phoenix	Saguaro (Giant Cactus)
Arkansas -nsan	Ark.	General Assembly	Little Rock	Apple Blossom
California -n	Calif.	Legislature¹	Sacramento	Golden Poppy
Colorado -dan	Colo.	General Assembly	Denver	Blue Columbine
Connecticut -er	Conn.	General Assembly	Hartford	Mountain Laurel
Delaware -an	Del.	General Assembly	Dover	Peach Blossom
District of Columbia -n	D.C.	(U.S. Congress)	Washington	American Beauty Rose
Florida -n or -dian	Fla.	Legislature	Tallahassee	Orange Blossom
Georgia -n	Ga.	General Assembly	Atlanta	Cherokee Rose
Hawaii -an	Hawaii	Legislature	Honolulu	Hibiscus
Idaho -an	Idaho	Legislature	Boise	Syringa (Mock Orange)
Illinois -an	Ill.	General Assembly	Springfield	Native Violet
Indiana -n or -nian	Ind.	General Assembly	Indianapolis	Peony
Iowa -n	Iowa	General Assembly	Des Moines	Wild Rose
Kansas -nsan	Kans.	Legislature	Topeka	Sunflower
Kentucky‡ -kian	Ky.	General Assembly	Frankfort	Goldenrod
Louisiana -n	La.	Legislature	Baton Rouge	Magnolia
Maine -r	Maine	Legislature	Augusta	Pine Cone and Tassel
Maryland -er	Md.	General Assembly²	Annapolis	Black-eyed Susan
Massachusetts‡ -an	Mass.	General Court	Boston	Mayflower (Arbutus)
Michigan -der	Mich.	Legislature	Lansing	Apple Blossom
Minnesota -n	Minn.	Legislature	St. Paul	Showy Lady's-slipper
Mississippi -an	Miss.	Legislature	Jackson	Magnolia
Missouri -an	Mo.	General Assembly	Jefferson City	Hawthorn
Montana -n	Mont.	Legislative Assembly	Helena	Bitterroot
Nebraska -n	Nebr.	Legislature⁴	Lincoln	Goldenrod
Nevada -n	Nev.	Legislature¹	Carson City	Sagebrush
New Hampshire -rite	N.H.	General Court	Concord	Purple Lilac
New Jersey -an	N.J.	Legislature³	Trenton	Purple Violet
New Mexico -can	N.Mex.	Legislature	Santa Fe	Yucca
New York -er	N.Y.	Legislature¹	Albany	Rose (any color)
North Carolina -nian	N.C.	General Assembly	Raleigh	Dogwood
North Dakota -n	N.Dak.	Legislative Assembly	Bismarck	Wild Prairie Rose
Ohio -an	Ohio	General Assembly	Columbus	Scarlet Carnation
Oklahoma -n	Okla.	Legislature	Oklahoma City	Mistletoe
Oregon -ian	Oreg.	Legislative Assembly	Salem	Oregon Grape
Pennsylvania‡ -n	Pa.	General Assembly	Harrisburg	Mountain Laurel
Rhode Island -er	R.I.	General Assembly	Providence	Violet
South Carolina -nian	S.C.	General Assembly	Columbia	Carolina Jessamine
South Dakota -n	S.Dak.	Legislature	Pierre	Pasqueflower
Tennessee -ssean	Tenn.	General Assembly	Nashville	Iris
Texas -xan	Tex.	Legislature	Austin	Bluebonnet
Utah -an	Utah	Legislature	Salt Lake City	Sego Lily
Vermont -er	Vt.	General Assembly	Montpelier	Red Clover
Virginia‡ -n	Va.	General Assembly²	Richmond	Flowering Dogwood
Washington -ian	Wash.	Legislature	Olympia	Coast Rhododendron
West Virginia -n	W.Va.	Legislature²	Charleston	Big Rhododendron
Wisconsin -ite	Wis.	Legislature¹	Madison	Violet
Wyoming -ite	Wyo.	Legislature	Cheyenne	Indian Paintbrush

Commonwealth and Territories

Canal Zone (Zonian)	C.Z.	(Canal Zone Govt.)	Balboa Heights	
Guam -anian	Guam	Legislature⁴	Agaña	
Puerto Rico -can	P.R.	Legislative Assembly	San Juan	
American Samoa -n		Legislature	Pago Pago	
Virgin Islands -er	V.I.	Legislature⁴	Charlotte Amalie	Yellow Cedar
Wake & Midway Isls.	(Wake under U.S. Air Force; Midway under Navy)			

* The "official abbreviations" are those in Government usage. Several shorter abbreviations are commonly used, as follows. (For two-letter ZIP Code abbreviations, see p. 338.)

Alas., Ak.	Alaska	Ida., Id.	Idaho	O.	Ohio
Cal.	California	Kan.	Kansas	Ore., Or., Org.	Oregon
Col.	Colorado	Me.	Maine	S.D.	South Dakota
Ct.	Connecticut	N.D.	North Dakota	Ut.	Utah
Hi.	Hawaii	Neb.	Nebraska	Wn.	Washington
Ia.	Iowa	N.M.	New Mexico	Wy.	Wyoming

† Most state legislatures meet in January—some annually, some biennially. The upper house of all is called the "Senate"; the lower house in most states is the "House of Representatives," but is in the states marked ¹ "Assembly," ² "House of Delegates," ³ "General Assembly." ⁴ Legislature is unicameral (one body); all members are "Senators."

‡ Officially called a "commonwealth" rather than a "state."

LARGEST CITIES IN THE UNITED STATES—WITH NAMES OF COUNTIES

Population of 130 Cities of 111,000 or More in 1970   (Final Figures)
Data from the Bureau of the Census; counties from the Directory of U.S. Post Offices
(On the following page, arranged according to rank)

City, County, State	1970	City, County, State	1970
Akron, Summit, Ohio	275,425	Lubbock, Lubbock, Tex	149,101
Albany, Albany, N.Y	114,873	Macon, Bibb, Ga	122,423
Albuquerque, Bernalillo, N.Mex	243,751	Madison, Dane, Wis	173,258
Amarillo, Potter, Tex	127,010	Memphis, Shelby, Tenn	623,530
Anaheim, Orange, Calif	166,701	Miami, Dade, Fla	334,859
Atlanta, Fulton & De Kalb, Ga	496,973	Milwaukee, Milwaukee, Wis	717,099
Austin, Travis, Tex	251,808	Minneapolis, Hennepin, Minn	434,400
Baltimore (Independent City), Md	905,759	Mobile, Mobile, Ala	190,026
Baton Rouge, East Baton Rouge,* La	165,963	Montgomery, Montgomery, Ala	133,386
Beaumont, Jefferson, Tex	115,919	Nashville, Davidson, Tenn	447,877
Berkeley, Alameda, Calif	116,716	Newark, Essex, N.J	382,417
Birmingham, Jefferson, Ala	300,910	New Haven, New Haven, Conn	137,707
Boston, Suffolk, Mass	641,071	New Orleans, Orleans Parish,* La	593,471
Bridgeport, Fairfield, Conn	156,542	Newport News (Independent City), Va	138,177
Buffalo, Erie, N.Y	462,768	New York,† N.Y	7,867,760
Charlotte, Mecklenburg, N.C	241,178	Norfolk (Independent City), Va	307,951
Chattanooga, Hamilton, Tenn	119,082	Oakland, Alameda, Calif	361,561
Chicago, Cook, Ill	3,366,957	Oklahoma City, Oklahoma, Okla	366,481
Cincinnati, Hamilton, Ohio	452,524	Omaha, Douglas, Nebr	347,328
Cleveland, Cuyahoga, Ohio	750,903	Pasadena, Los Angeles, Calif	113,327
Colorado Springs, El Paso, Colo	135,060	Paterson, Passaic, N.J	144,824
Columbia, Richland, S.C	113,542	Peoria, Peoria, Ill	126,963
Columbus, Muscogee, Ga	154,168	Philadelphia, Philadelphia, Pa	1,948,609
Columbus, Franklin, Ohio	539,677	Phoenix, Maricopa, Ariz	581,562
Corpus Christi, Nueces, Tex	204,525	Pittsburgh, Allegheny, Pa	520,117
Dallas, Dallas, Tex	844,401	Portland, Multnomah, Oreg	382,619
Dayton, Montgomery, Ohio	243,601	Providence, Providence, R.I	179,213
Denver, Denver, Colo	514,678	Raleigh, Wake, N.C	121,577
Des Moines, Polk, Iowa	200,587	Richmond (Independent City), Va	249,621
Detroit, Wayne, Mich	1,511,482	Riverside, Riverside, Calif	140,089
Elizabeth, Union, N.J	112,654	Rochester, Monroe, N.Y	296,233
El Paso, El Paso, Tex	322,261	Rockford, Winnebago, Ill	147,370
Erie, Erie, Pa	129,231	Sacramento, Sacramento, Calif	254,413
Evansville, Vanderburgh, Ind	138,764	Salt Lake City, Salt Lake, Utah	175,885
Flint, Genesee, Mich	193,317	San Antonio, Bexar, Tex	654,153
Fort Lauderdale, Broward, Fla	139,590	San Diego, San Diego, Calif	696,769
Fort Wayne, Allen, Ind	177,671	San Francisco, San Francisco, Calif	715,674
Fort Worth, Tarrant, Tex	393,476	San Jose, Santa Clara, Calif	445,779
Fresno, Fresno, Calif	165,972	Santa Ana, Orange, Calif	156,601
Garden Grove, Orange, Calif	122,524	Savannah, Chatham, Ga	118,349
Gary, Lake, Ind	175,415	Seattle, King, Wash	530,831
Glendale, Los Angeles, Calif	132,752	Shreveport, Caddo,* La	182,064
Grand Rapids, Kent, Mich	197,649	South Bend, Saint Joseph, Ind	125,580
Greensboro, Guilford, N.C	147,160	Spokane, Spokane, Wash	170,516
Hampton (Independent City), Va	120,779	Springfield, Hampden, Mass	163,905
Hartford, Hartford, Conn	158,017	Springfield, Greene, Mo	120,096
Honolulu, Honolulu, Hawaii	324,871	St. Louis (Independent City), Mo	622,236
Houston, Harris, Tex	1,232,802	St. Paul, Ramsey, Minn	309,980
Huntington Beach, Orange, Calif	115,960	St. Petersburg, Pinellas, Fla	216,232
Huntsville, Madison, Ala	137,802	Syracuse, Onondaga, N.Y	197,208
Independence, Jackson, Mo	111,662	Tacoma, Pierce, Wash	154,581
Indianapolis, Marion, Ind	744,624	Tampa, Hillsborough, Fla	277,767
Jackson, Hinds, Miss	153,968	Toledo, Lucas, Ohio	383,818
Jacksonville, Duval, Fla	528,865	Topeka, Shawnee, Kans	125,011
Jersey City, Hudson, N.J	260,545	Torrance, Los Angeles, Calif	134,584
Kansas City, Wyandotte, Kans	168,213	Tucson, Pima, Ariz	262,933
Kansas City, Jackson & Clay, Mo	507,087	Tulsa, Tulsa, Okla	331,638
Knoxville, Knox, Tenn	174,587	Virginia Beach (Independent City), Va	172,106
Lansing, Ingham, Mich	131,546	Warren, Macomb, Mich	179,260
Las Vegas, Clark, Nev	125,787	Washington, District of Columbia	756,510
Lincoln, Lancaster, Nebr	149,518	Wichita, Sedgwick, Kans	276,554
Little Rock, Pulaski, Ark	132,483	Winston-Salem, Forsyth, N.C	132,913
Long Beach, Los Angeles, Calif	358,633	Worcester, Worcester, Mass	176,572
Los Angeles, Los Angeles, Calif	2,816,061	Yonkers, Westchester, N.Y	204,370
Louisville, Jefferson, Ky	361,472	Youngstown, Mahoning, Ohio	139,788

* "Parish" is used in Louisiana only, instead of "county."
† New York City ("Greater New York") comprises five boroughs, coextensive with counties: Manhattan (New York County); Brooklyn (Kings County); Bronx; Queens; and Richmond (Staten Is.).
The county in which any city or town in the United States is located may be found in the Directory of U.S. Post Offices under the list of post offices by states.   (See p. 345 for description of Directory.)

POPULATION RANK OF THE LARGEST U.S. CITIES IN 1970

Final figures. (On the preceding page, arranged alphabetically)

1970	City	1970	City	1970	City
7,867,760	New York, N.Y.	322,261	El Paso, Tex.	154,168	Columbus, Ga.
3,366,957	Chicago, Ill.	309,980	St. Paul, Minn.	153,968	Jackson, Miss.
2,816,061	Los Angeles, Calif.	307,951	Norfolk, Va.	149,518	Lincoln, Nebr.
1,948,609	Philadelphia, Pa.	300,910	Birmingham, Ala.	149,101	Lubbock, Tex.
1,511,482	Detroit, Mich.	296,233	Rochester, N.Y.	147,370	Rockford, Ill.
1,232,802	Houston, Tex.	277,767	Tampa, Fla.	147,160	Greensboro, N.C.
905,759	Baltimore, Md.	276,554	Wichita, Kans.	144,824	Paterson, N.J.
844,401	Dallas, Tex.	275,425	Akron, Ohio	140,089	Riverside, Calif.
756,510	Washington, D.C.	262,933	Tucson, Ariz.	139,788	Youngstown, Ohio
750,903	Cleveland, Ohio	260,545	Jersey City, N.J.	139,590	Ft. Lauderdale, Fla.
744,624	Indianapolis, Ind.	254,413	Sacramento, Calif.	138,764	Evansville, Ind.
717,099	Milwaukee, Wis.	251,808	Austin, Tex.	138,177	Newport News, Va.
715,674	San Francisco, Calif.	249,621	Richmond, Va.	137,802	Huntsville, Ala.
696,769	San Diego, Calif.	243,751	Albuquerque, N.Mex.	137,707	New Haven, Conn.
654,153	San Antonio, Tex.	243,601	Dayton, Ohio	135,060	Colorado Spgs., Col.
641,071	Boston, Mass.	241,178	Charlotte, N.C.	134,584	Torrance, Calif.
623,530	Memphis, Tenn.	216,232	St. Petersburg, Fla.	133,386	Montgomery, Ala.
622,236	St. Louis, Mo.	204,525	Corpus Christi, Tex.	132,913	Winston-Salem, N.C.
593,471	New Orleans, La.	204,370	Yonkers, N.Y.	132,752	Glendale, Calif.
581,562	Phoenix, Ariz.	200,587	Des Moines, Iowa	132,483	Little Rock, Ark.
539,677	Columbus, Ohio	197,649	Grand Rapids, Mich.	131,546	Lansing, Mich.
530,831	Seattle, Wash.	197,208	Syracuse, N.Y.	129,231	Erie, Pa.
528,865	Jacksonville, Fla.	193,317	Flint, Mich.	127,010	Amarillo, Tex.
520,117	Pittsburgh, Pa.	190,026	Mobile, Ala.	126,963	Peoria, Ill.
514,678	Denver, Colo.	182,064	Shreveport, La.	125,787	Las Vegas, Nev.
507,087	Kansas City, Mo.	179,260	Warren, Mich.	125,580	South Bend, Ind.
496,973	Atlanta, Ga.	179,213	Providence, R.I.	125,011	Topeka, Kans.
462,768	Buffalo, N.Y.	177,671	Ft. Wayne, Ind.	122,524	Garden Grove, Calif.
452,524	Cincinnati, Ohio	176,572	Worcester, Mass.	122,423	Macon, Ga.
447,877	Nashville-D'n, Tenn.	175,885	Salt Lake City, Utah	121,577	Raleigh, N.C.
445,779	San Jose, Calif.	175,415	Gary, Ind.	120,779	Hampton, Va.
434,400	Minneapolis, Minn.	174,587	Knoxville, Tenn.	120,096	Springfield, Mo.
393,476	Ft. Worth, Tex.	173,258	Madison, Wis.	119,082	Chattanooga, Tenn.
383,818	Toledo, Ohio	172,106	Virginia Beach, Va.	118,349	Savannah, Ga.
382,619	Portland, Oreg.	170,516	Spokane, Wash.	116,716	Berkeley, Calif.
382,417	Newark, N.J.	168,213	Kansas City, Kans.	115,960	Huntington Bch., Cal.
366,481	Oklahoma City, Okla.	166,701	Anaheim, Calif.	115,919	Beaumont, Tex.
361,561	Oakland, Calif.	165,972	Fresno, Calif.	114,873	Albany, N.Y.
361,472	Louisville, Ky.	165,963	Baton Rouge, La.	113,542	Columbia, S.C.
358,633	Long Beach, Calif.	163,905	Springfield, Mass.	113,327	Pasadena, Calif.
347,328	Omaha, Nebr.	158,017	Hartford, Conn.	112,654	Elizabeth, N.J.
334,859	Miami, Fla.	156,601	Santa Ana, Calif.	111,662	Independence, Mo.
331,638	Tulsa, Okla.	156,542	Bridgeport, Conn.		
324,871	Honolulu, Hawaii	154,581	Tacoma, Wash.		

POPULATION OF THE UNITED STATES IN 1970

Final figures. Total for the 50 States and D.C. = 204,765,770

State	1970	State	1970	State	1970
Alabama..........	3,475,885	Kentucky......	3,246,481	North Dakota....	624,181
Alaska............	304,067	Louisiana.......	3,672,008	Ohio.............	10,730,200
Arizona...........	1,787,620	Maine..........	1,006,320	Oklahoma........	2,585,486
Arkansas.........	1,942,303	Maryland......	3,953,698	Oregon..........	2,110,810
California.........	20,098,863	Massachusetts..	5,726,676	Pennsylvania.....	11,884,314
Colorado..........	2,226,771	Michigan.......	8,937,196	Rhode Island......	957,798
Connecticut.......	3,050,693	Minnesota......	3,833,173	South Carolina....	2,617,320
Delaware.........	551,928	Mississippi......	2,233,848	South Dakota.....	673,247
Dist. of Columbia...	762,971*	Missouri.......	4,718,034	Tennessee........	3,961,060
Florida............	6,855,702	Montana.......	701,573	Texas............	11,298,787
Georgia...........	4,627,306	Nebraska.......	1,496,820	Utah.............	1,067,810
Hawaii............	784,901	Nevada........	492,396	Vermont.........	448,327
Idaho.............	719,921	New Hampshire.	746,284	Virginia..........	4,690,742
Illinois............	11,184,320	New Jersey.....	7,208,035	Washington.......	3,443,487
Indiana...........	5,228,156	New Mexico....	1,026,664	West Virginia.....	1,763,331
Iowa.............	2,846,920	New York......	18,287,529	Wisconsin........	4,447,013
Kansas...........	2,265,846	North Carolina.	5,125,230	Wyoming.........	335,719

* Includes 6,461 D.C. inhabitants living abroad.

The **1970 population** of any city or town in the United States (having more than 2500 inhabitants) may be found in the "**United States Summary—Number of Inhabitants**," published by the Bureau of the Census, and for sale by the Superintendent of Documents, Government Printing Office, Washington, D.C. 20402—$2.00.

Reference Books

An office worker is not expected always to have information at his fingertips, but he is expected to know where to turn to find it.

Every office should have:

> An unabridged dictionary
> A good atlas, and a map of the city
> A statistical almanac for the current year.

Dictionaries.   The outstanding American dictionaries are:

> Merriam-Webster's New International Dictionary   (unabridged)
> DESK: Merriam-Webster's New Collegiate Dictionary
> Random House Dictionary (unabridged; and College [desk] Ed.)
> American Heritage Dictionary
> Funk & Wagnalls Standard College Dictionary   (a desk dictionary)
> Webster's New World Dictionary, College Edition   (a desk dictionary)

Every person should own one or all of these desk dictionaries.   Each has some words that the others have not.

A pocket edition of a good dictionary should also be kept near the typewriter as a handy spelling reference.

Buy a new and up-to-date dictionary every five or six years—**it is a most valuable personal investment.**

Technical Dictionaries.   Various technical dictionaries are available, such as chemical, law, medical, and financial dictionaries.

If an office has no technical dictionary, an alphabetic list of words peculiar to the business should be compiled and kept in the front of a small dictionary.   Many technical words recur infrequently enough to present a spelling problem unless they can be verified; and they are often difficult to relocate in the files.   (See also Spelling, p. 138.)

Quotations.   For the verification of quotations, both classical and modern, the following books are authoritative:

> Bartlett's **Familiar Quotations,** arranged according to author.
> The Macmillan (Stevenson's) **Book of Proverbs, Maxims, and Famous Phrases,** arranged according to subject.

WHERE TO FIND INFORMATION

Statistical information on various subjects may be found in standard reference books.   The following are examples:

ADVERTISING RATES

Standard **Rate & Data Service**   (Skokie, Ill.: Standard Rate & Data Service)

> Advertising rates and circulation figures of daily and weekly newspapers in United States and Canada; and of important consumer magazines, farm and business publications, and radio and TV stations.   Transit advertising.

602

ASSOCIATIONS, SOCIETIES, AND FOUNDATIONS

Encyclopedia of American Associations   (Detroit: Gale Research Company)

Detailed information about non-profit American organizations of national scope —listed by fields, key words, locations, and names of executives.

The World Almanac contains lists of prominent associations, societies, and foundations in the United States (alphabetized under the key word in each title).

BANKS

Rand McNally International Bankers Directory (Bankers Blue Book) (Chicago)

Data on banks in United States and its territories, Canada, Mexico, West Indies, Central and South America, Australasia, Europe, Asia, and Africa.
Foreign banks—with head offices—and bankers.
Directors of national and state banks, savings banks, and trust companies.
Bankers associations.   State bank officials and examiners.
Investment Bankers Association officers.   Clearing houses in United States.
400 largest commercial banks in the United States.   Discontinued bank titles.
Federal Reserve System information; and Government banking agencies.
Bank numbering system.   Accessible banking points.   Bank holidays.
Legislatures' regular meeting dates.   Comptroller's calls.
Digest of banking and commercial laws of the United States and Canada.
Uniform Acts—Negotiable Instruments, Fiduciaries, and Trust Receipts.
Legal loan limits to one customer.   Bank Collection Code.
Interest rates; grace on sight drafts; and statutes of limitations.   Maps.

BOOKS

Cumulative Book Index   (New York: The H. W. Wilson Company)

A world list of books in the English language, indexed by author, subject, and title; with the date, edition, number of pages, name of publisher, price, etc.

How and Where to Look It Up, by Murphey (New York: McGraw-Hill Book Co.)

A guide to standard sources of information—arranged by subject.

CHURCHES

Yearbook of American Churches   (New York: National Council of the Churches of Christ in the United States of America)

Directories of religious bodies in the United States and Canada.
Cooperative organizations; local councils; ecumenical and service agencies.
Theological seminaries; colleges and universities.
Religious periodicals; statistical and historical section.

The Official Catholic Directory   (New York: P. J. Kenedy & Sons)

Ecclesiastical statistics of the United States, Puerto Rico, Bermuda, Virgin Islands, Canal Zone, Oceania, Guam, Canada, Ireland, England, Scotland, Wales, Australia, New Zealand, Jamaica, W.I., Cuba, Mexico, Philippines.

The Episcopal Church Annual   (New York: Morehouse–Barlow Co.)

Statistics of the church; names of the clergy; and church schools.
Statistics and officials of each diocese.   Religious orders and institutions.

The annual almanacs, listed on p. 607, give various church statistics, the names of bishops, etc., and the headquarters of the various religious denominations.

CITY OFFICIALS

A **directory** or list of city officials is usually for sale in each city, or may be consulted at the public library.   Names of city officials may also be obtained from the city hall.

Congressional Directory   (Washington, D.C.: Joint Committee on Printing)   (In public libraries; or may be purchased from the Supt. of Documents, Washington, DC   20402—hardback, $8.50; paperback, $6.50.   [Issued annually about March])

> Names, addresses, and brief biographies of all congressmen and chief executives in Washington, D.C.   Senate and House committees and staffs.
> Departments, agencies, and offices of the Government, with executive personnel.   (See also Government, p. 605.)   Judiciary of the United States.
> The Capitol—diagrams; officers of Senate and House.   District of Columbia.
> Diplomatic representatives and consular offices here and abroad.
> International organizations, including the United Nations.
> Press, radio, and television galleries; White House News Photographers' Assn.
> Governors of states.   Maps of congressional districts.

The **American almanacs** listed on p. 607 give the names and terms of the members of Congress.

Dun & Bradstreet Reports and Reference Books   (Local offices or New York: Dun & Bradstreet, Inc.)   (These reports are obtained only through subscription; they are confidential and therefore not in public libraries.)

> Ratings of merchants, manufacturers, and traders throughout the world.

Credit information may be obtained through arrangement with **credit-reporting bureaus or associations,** listed in the classified telephone directory under "Credit."

> Credit information may also be obtained through a company's bank.   A small charge is made therefor if a special investigation is necessary.

Customs Hints for Returning U.S. Residents (with duty rates in a short Tariff List of Most Popular Tourist Items)   (Washington, D.C.: U.S. Customs Service)

> General information about U.S. customs laws and regulations—covering exemptions, time abroad, tourist purchases sent home, gifts, trademarked articles (as perfumes, cameras, watches, musical instruments), automobiles, pets, fruit, plants, food products, liquors, cigars, films, antiques, firearms, etc. (All articles acquired abroad and brought back by the traveler—whether they have been used or worn, or were received as gifts—must be declared.)
> **Customs Hints for Nonresidents** of the U.S. is a separate booklet, published in six languages: English, French, German, Spanish, Italian, and Chinese.
> Copies of these booklets are free and may be obtained in the United States from any customs office, or U.S. Customs Service, Washington, D.C. 20229. Abroad, they may be obtained from the nearest U.S. diplomatic or consular office, or any U.S. Travel Service office; also on ships and planes.

Passport regulations and customs advice are given in The World Almanac.   Information may also be obtained from—and applications made at—many **post offices.**

Customs Regulations of the United States may be obtained from the Superintendent of Documents, Washington, DC   20402—looseleaf; price, $28.50.

Custom House Guide   (New York: Budd Publications, Inc.)

> U.S. tariff schedules; customs ports; customs, shipping, and commerce regulations; internal revenue code; and reciprocal trade agreements.

American Dental Directory   (Chicago: American Dental Association)

> Lists of dentists in the United States and its territories; dental specialists; accredited dental schools; state societies; foreign associations.

ETIQUETTE

Amy Vanderbilt's Complete Book of Etiquette (New York: Doubleday & Co.)
Emily Post's Etiquette (New York: Funk & Wagnalls Company, Inc.)
Service Etiquette (Annapolis, Md.: The United States Naval Institute)

Manners: dining; entertaining; tipping. Invitations; cards; weddings; travel.

FINANCIAL RECORDS

Moody's Surveys and News (New York: Moody's Investors Service)
Standard Corporation Descriptions (New York: Standard & Poor's Corp.)

Financial data, balance sheets, and income accounts of all the large corporations in the United States, Canada, and foreign countries, in which there is a public interest. Information for investors in bonds and stocks, including a brief history of each company, with names of officers and directors.

FRATERNITIES AND SORORITIES

Baird's Manual of American College Fraternities (Menasha, Wisconsin: The Collegiate Press)

Description of all American fraternities, sororities, and honor societies.

The World Almanac contains a list of American college fraternities and sororities; also professional fraternities, and honor and recognition societies.

FREIGHT AND EXPRESS

Bullinger's Postal and Shippers Guide (Westwood, N.J.: Bullinger's Guides)

A shipping guide for the United States and Canada, containing:
Every post office and rural delivery place, railroad station, and steamer landing—with nearest railroad station to every post office; and delivering express company (including air express). Freight stations; steamship lines. Warehouse and storage directory. Piggyback section.
Postal rates; air parcel post; Zip Codes. U.S. counties and county seats.

GOVERNMENT

U.S. Government Manual (Washington, D.C.: Federal Register, National Archives and Records Service [issued annually in July; $6.50, from Supt. of Documents])

Departments and agencies of the Federal Government, with executive personnel; description of functions of each; and sources of information. Quasi-official agencies; selected international organizations; charts; Constitution.

The American almanacs listed on p. 607. (See also Congress, and City Officials, above, and State Officials, below; also Government Departments, p. 503.)

The almanacs give the names, with brief biographies, of the presidents of the United States and their wives. Also a list of their cabinet members.
The names of the following present officials are given in The World Almanac:
President, vice president, and cabinet members.
Executive officers of the departments in Washington, D.C.
Justices of the Supreme Court, Federal court judges and clerks.
Members of Congress, and their terms; standing committees and chairmen.
Heads of the governments of the world. Diplomatic representatives.
Governors, and other government officials, of the states and territories.
Mayors and city managers of principal American cities.

605

HOTELS

Hotel & Motel Red Book (New York: American Hotel & Motel Assn.)

List of hotels and motels, with plan of operation of each, rates, and name of owner or manager. Covers United States, Canada, West Indies, Bermuda, Mexico, Central and South America, Europe, Asia, Africa, and Australia.

Hotels in the various cities will supply the names of reliable hotels in other cities.

LAWS AND LAWYERS

Martindale-Hubbell Law Directory (Summit, N.J.: Martindale-Hubbell, Inc.)

Vols. I, II, III, IV, V—Complete roster of Bar of the United States and its territories, and Canada. Biographical data and ratings. U.S. Government lawyers' roster. American Bar Assn. section.

annual, issued about February

Lawyers registered with U.S. (and Canadian) Patent Office. Foreign lawyers, selected list of; patent lawyers and agents.

Vol. VI—Digests of the laws of every state in the United States and its territories, Puerto Rico, Canada, and other countries. Digests of U.S. copyright, patent, and trademark laws. Court calendars; uniform and model acts; Uniform Commercial Code.

National Laws—Copies of the various national laws, such as the copyright laws, may be purchased for a nominal sum from the Superintendent of Documents, Washington, D.C. 20402. (Ask for Price List 10, Laws, Rules and Regulations.)

Salient points of certain **national laws, such as the Federal income, estate, and gift tax, social security, selective service, immigration, and naturalization laws,** may be found in the current American **almanacs** listed on p. 607.
Public law libraries have copies or synopses of almost all the laws of the land.

The Declaration of Independence ⎫
Constitution of the United States ⎬ may be found in the current American almanacs listed on p. 607.
Charter of the United Nations ⎭

State Laws—Copies of the different state laws are printed in most of the states, and may be purchased for a nominal sum through the Secretary of State, or the State Librarian, at the capital in each state. State laws may also be found in inexpensive law books at stationery and book stores in the cities of the various states; and in law books at public libraries (see Martindale-Hubbell Law Directory, above).

Salient points of state laws on **voting qualifications; inheritance, estate, income, and sales taxes; motor vehicles, labor relations, marriage and divorce, and interest rates,** are in the American almanacs listed on p. 607.

MAPS, MILEAGE, AND STATISTICS

Rand McNally Commercial Atlas and Marketing Guide (Chicago: Rand McNally & Company)

Part I—United States and its Territories and Possessions:
Standard map of the United States. Individual state maps.
Principal U.S. cities, according to population.
Retail trade, trading areas, and principal business centers—analysis by counties and states.
Transportation and communications sections.
U.S. economic maps showing distribution of population, retail sales, and data for manufacturers.
U.S. population map, with analysis of cities and metro areas.
State maps and statistics.
Maps and indexes of U.S. territories and possessions.

606

Airline and railroad maps and distance tables.
Part II—Foreign Countries:
  Maps of continents and foreign countries.
  Principal world cities with populations and physical features.
  Polar region maps.   Altitudes of selected world cities.
  Airline distances between 45 world cities.
  Steamship distances between 25 world ports.
  World time zone chart.   World political information table.
  Principal mountains, oceans, rivers, and islands of world.

Road Atlas of U.S., Canada, and Mexico (annual)—highway color-maps; mileage; driving times.   National parks and monuments; recreation areas. Military and Indian reservations.   Large cities and airports.

MEDICAL DIRECTORY

American Medical Directory   (Chicago: American Medical Association)

A register of legally qualified physicians of the United States and its territories—and U.S. physicians temporarily abroad.
Medical officers within Federal services.
Where to find information about U.S. hospitals, medical schools, libraries; and Canadian and Mexican physicians, hospitals, and medical schools.

MERCHANTS, MANUFACTURERS, AND SHIPPERS

Thomas Register of American Manufacturers   (N.Y.: Thomas Publishing Co.)

Vols. I–VI—Product classifications.
Vol. VII—Leading manufacturers of the United States.
      Leading trademarks and brand names.
      Commercial organizations: boards of trade, chambers of commerce.

Exporters' Encyclopaedia (annual)   ⎱ (New York: Dun &
International Market Guides (semiannual supps.) ⎰   Bradstreet, Inc.)

Encyclopaedia covers shipping information and export regulations for every country in the world: ports, trade centers, routes, carriers, communications, moneys, exchange, licenses, packing hints, weights and measures, holidays, time charts.   Freight forwarders; air cargo.   Foreign trade organizations; political groups.   Law; insurance; export terms; trademarks.
Market Guides cover Latin America and Europe, giving for each company: address, products, trade style, financial strength, and a composite appraisal.

Kelly's Directory of Manufacturers & Merchants   (London: Kelly's Directories)

Names and addresses of companies throughout the world engaged in exporting, importing, and manufacturing.   Classified trades sections.

MISCELLANEOUS INFORMATION

The World Almanac (annual, Jan.)   (New York: Newspaper Enterprise Assn.)
Information Please Almanac (annual, Dec.)   (N.Y.: Information Please Almanac)
Whitaker's Almanack (annual, Jan.)   (London: J. Whitaker and Sons, Ltd.)

NEWSPAPERS AND MAGAZINES

Ayer's Directory of Newspapers and Periodicals   (Philadelphia: N. W. Ayer & Son)

Names of publications printed in the United States, Canada, Puerto Rico, Philippines, Bermuda, and Panama.   Numerous maps.
Description of each publication, telling whether daily, weekly, or monthly, and in what language printed (if foreign); also circulation, and subscription rates; and the salient facts of the state and city where published, including population and airline service.   Classified lists, by issuance and/or fields.

607

Newspaper and Magazine Articles and Stories

The New York Times Index   (New York: The New York Times Company)

All news stories, editorials, articles, and reviews are arranged alphabetically and chronologically under subject, person, and organization name. Following the name or subject, the main point(s) or highlights of the item are given with date, page, and column of publication in The Times.

Other newspapers keep indexes of their own publications in their own libraries, and will assist in locating articles or stories that have appeared in their papers.

Readers' Guide to Periodical Literature   (New York: The H. W. Wilson Co.)

Subject, title, and author index of articles and fiction in a selected list of periodicals, including scientific, technical, and business publications.

RESEARCH

Directory of Information Resources in U.S.: Physical and Biological Sciences, Engineering   (Washington, D.C.: National Referral Center, Library of Congress)

List of libraries, information centers, professional societies, universities, industrial firms, and Government agencies willing to extend their services.

Research Centers Directory   (Detroit: Gale Research Company)
A guide to university-related and other non-profit research organizations.

SCHOOLS AND SCHOLARSHIPS

Education Directory—U.S. Office of Education   (Washington, D.C.: Government Printing Office)   (Issued annually in four parts, from 50¢ to $1.25 each)

Principal U.S. school governing officials: State Governments; Public School Systems; Higher Education; Education Associations.

American Universities and Colleges   Surveys of higher education.
A Guide to Graduate Study: Programs   (Washington, D.C.: American
International Handbook of Universities   Council on Education)

Lovejoy's [U.S.] College Guide (with financial aid information); and
Vocational School Guide (for job training)   (Red Bank, N.J.: Lovejoy's Svc.)

Student Assistance Handbook: Guide to Financial Assistance for Education Beyond High School   (Washington, D.C.: Library of Congress [GPO, 60¢])

Information for each state; selected national private aid; Federal student aid; scholarship testing; college admissions; work-study and training sources.

Patterson's American Education   (Mt. Prospect, Ill.: Educational Directories)

U.S. public, private, endowed, denominational, and special schools, colleges, universities; officers' names.   State and national organizations; officials. County maps to locate schools.   Buying guide for supplies and equipment.

Sargent's Handbook of Private Schools (annual)   (Boston: Porter Sargent)

American private schools.   Tutoring, remedial, boarding, and day schools. Summer academic programs and camps.   Educational organizations and agencies.

New Horizons in Education—abroad   (New York: Pan American World Airways)

Universities and boarding schools: curricula, languages, costs, degrees, credits.

The American almanacs list American colleges and universities: location of each, year founded, governing official, and number of students and teachers.   The World Almanac also gives information on some scholarships, fellowships, and other aids.

SHIPS AND AIRCRAFT

Lloyd's Register of Shipping   (London: Lloyd's Register of Shipping)

Names, classes, and information about all seagoing merchant ships in the world. Refrigerated cargo installations and containers.   Flexible towable containers. Dry, wet, and floating docks.   Marine enginebuilders and boilermakers. List of shipowners, managers, and shipbuilders; marine insurance companies. Telegraphic addresses of, and codes used by, shipping companies.

Lloyd's Register of Yachts, and Lloyd's Register of American Yachts

Names and classification of yachts; builders, and owners; yacht clubs.

Jane's Fighting Ships   } annual editions
Jane's All the World's Aircraft }   (New York: McGraw-Hill, Inc.)

The world's navies—ships afloat and abuilding; types; designs; builders. Civil and military aircraft—designs; engines; performance; manufacturers.

STATE OFFICIALS

Book of the States   (Chicago: Council of State Govts.)   (biennial, even years)

State Directory (Blue Book)—in public libraries in each state—lists state officials and legislators at the capital, and often officials throughout the state.   For a copy, write the Secretary of State, or State Librarian, in the state capital.

STATISTICS

Statistical Abstract of the United States—U.S. Bureau of the Census   (Washington, D.C.: Government Printing Office)   (issued annually about September)

Annual summary statistics on the industrial, social, political, and economic organization of the United States.   Also a guide to other statistical sources.

The Americana Annual—events and statistics   (New York: Americana Corp.)
The New International Year Book   (New York: Funk & Wagnalls Company)
Statesman's Year-Book—by countries   (New York: St. Martin's Press)
The **almanacs** for the current year   (Listed on p. 607)

Annual compendium of the world's progress in scientific, political, business, educational, social, and cultural fields.   Statistics; maps; diagrams.

TRAVEL

Pan Am's World Guide   (New York: Pan American World Airways Inc.)
Fielding's Travel Guide to Europe   (New York: William Morrow & Company)

Travelers' handbooks of the different countries of the world; maps and plans.

(**The World Almanac** gives passport, visa, vaccination, and customs advice.)

Pan Am, New York, NY 10017, also publishes sectionalized travel guides on:

Europe and Mediterranean; Hawaii to Hong Kong; Mexico and South America; Caribbean; Restaurants in Europe; Economy trips to Europe; Trade With China (a businessman's guide).   Also **Tours on Tape** cassettes to help plan trips.

Official Airline Guide—schedules, fares   (Chicago: Official Airline Guide)
Mobil Travel Guides—regional, U.S.A.   (sold at Mobil Oil Stations)
The Real USA—coast-to-coast America   (New York: Pan Am Publications)

Travel Agencies—Thos. Cook & Son, and the American Express Company

These agencies have offices in all the principal cities of the world.

Travel information may also be obtained from airlines, ship lines, bus lines, service stations, the American Automobile Association, and various travel agencies. Most U.S. states have Travel Departments (in state capitals), as do some cities.

609

Certified Professional Secretary

Information regarding the qualifications, study, and examination necessary to become a "Certified Professional Secretary" (CPS) may be obtained from

The National Secretaries Association (Intl.)
Crown Center
2440 Pershing Road, Suite G-10
Kansas City, MO   64108

◇◇◇◇◇◇◇◇◇

Index

(Boldface type indicates words referred to as words. Italics signify incorrect words. An "n." after a page number refers to a note.
(Only the more common words in the Similar Words section are indexed.)

A

a, an, 3
    abbreviations after, 4
    numerals after, 4
    repeated, 112
a, for **of,** 29
Abbot, address to, 334
Abbreviations, 551–72
    capitalization of, 551
    chemical symbols, 552
    Christian (given) names, 311
    compass points, 556
    contractions, 552
    copy for the press, 434
    degree letters, 557
    e.g., viz, and **i.e.,** 230n.
    1st, 2nd or 2d, 3rd or 3d, etc., 553
    French, 554
    Government offices, 502–7
    hyphens in, 556
    legal papers, 476
    letters as descriptive words, 268, 556
    letters as letters, 553
    list of, 558–72
    metric system, 552, 573
    new, how to form, 554
    nicknames, 311
    "percent," 554
    periods, when used, 551–52, 556
    plurals of, 555
    possessives of, 555
    quoting, 556
    radio and television stations, 553
    single words, 557
    slants (diagonal lines) in, 553
    spacing of, 554
    state names, official, 599; Zip Code, 338
    tabulations, 417
    technical work, 553
    titles, 314; military titles, 336
    verbs, used as, 556
    when to use, **551**
abounds in, 66
above, above-mentioned, above-named, 4
"Absolute zero," defined, 582
absolve from, 66
Abstract collectives, 41
Abstract of title, 488
Accent and speech, 462
Accents and markings on words, 272
Acceptance: of draft, 515; of invitation, 308
    banker's, 516; trade, 516
Acceptance corporation, 525
"accessory after the fact," "before the fact," **488**
Accommodation paper, 519
accompanied by, 66
according as, 47
according to, 46
Account sales, 513
Accounting terms, 541–43
accredit, credit, 195
accustomed to use, or **to using,** etc., 91
Acknowledgment, letters of, 302
Acknowledgment, legal, 479; form of, 480
acquiesce in, 66
acquit of, 66
ACTION, including Peace Corps, 508
Actuary, 548
ad, 28
A.D., how written, 280, **558**
adapted to, 66
Address book, 320

Addresses, 309–37 (See also Envelopes, **and**
    Forms of address)
    advertising matter, 348
    block style, 309, 338
    building names, 338
    cable, 392
    foreign: English in, 321
        country and postal district in, 321
        obtaining, 404
    full addresses on envelopes, 340
    Government officials, etc., 322, 502
    hotel names, 339
    indented style, 309, 338
    lines in, number of, 309
    official form of, on envelopes, 338
    personnel, in address book, 320
    post office box, 309
    punctuation of, 309
    radiogram, 396
    return, on envelopes, 340
    state names, 309, 338
    street numbers, 339
    telegram, 380–82
        of senders, 385
    temporary, in address book, 320
    titles in, 310, 313–20
adept at, 66
Adjectives and adverbs, 45–49
Adjuster, 548
Adjutant General, address to, 337
Administrator: address to, 324
    administratrix, of will, 483–84
admit (of), 66
admittance, admission, 187
Adverbs and adjectives, 45–49
    -ed modifiers, 48
    after verbs of the senses, 46
"Advertiser's mail," forwarding, 358
Advertising for position, 473
Advertising matter, mailing, 347–50
Advertising pieces, 446
Advertising rates, where to find, 602
advice, advise, 187
"Advice," letter of, 517
affect, effect, 79
Affidavit, simple form of, 481
A-frame, 268
after, in a subject, 74
after, or **from,** 64
after having, 95
afterward, 24
"Afterword" on pronunciation, 186
again regain, 32
Age: how to write, 282
    legal, 478; marriageable, 479; voting, 479
aged 35, not *age,* 282
Agency, registering at employment, 473
Agenda, for a meeting, 419, 420
ago since, 32
agreeable to, 66; used adverbially, 46
Agreement, simple form of, 480
Agriculture, Department of, 505
ahold, for **hold,** 29
Aide-de-Camp, diplomatic officer, 326
aim to help, aim at helping, 91
ain't, 28, 261
Air cargo, international, 378
Air express, domestic, 377
Air Force: Department of the, 504
    officers, addresses to, 336
    Reserve (AFRes), 337
Air waybills, and airbills, 509
Aircraft, Jane's guidebook, 609

INDEX

INDEX

❖❖❖❖❖❖❖❖